LSAT®
ESSAY
WRITING
STRATEGIES AND TACTICS

BOB VERINI

This publication is designed to provide accurate and authoritative information in regard to the subject matter covered. It is sold with the understanding that the publisher is not engaged in rendering legal, accounting, or other professional service. If legal advice or other expert assistance is required, the services of a competent professional should be sought.

© 2011 Kaplan, Inc.

Published by Kaplan Publishing, a division of Kaplan, Inc.
395 Hudson Street
New York, NY 10014

Printed in the United States of America

10 9 8 7 6 5 4 3 2 1

ISBN-13: 978-1-60978-232-0

Kaplan Publishing books are available at special quantity discounts to use for sales promotions, employee premiums, or educational purposes. For more information or to purchase books, please call the Simon & Schuster special sales department at 866-506-1949.

Table of Contents

About the Experts

Veteran Kaplan teacher and curriculum designer **BOB VERINI** has played a significant role in the design and development of Kaplan's LSAT and other programs for over 30 years. Having taken standardized tests multiple times and to multiple perfect scores, he has turned his first-hand expertise into lessons and question explanations used in live classes, recordings, and retail books (including this one), that arguably have impacted more students' careers in the past quarter century than the work of any other individual. Bob currently serves as the Director of Academic Quality for Kaplan's Digital Media Group, while continuing to enhance applicants' admission chances as an online LSAT teacher and law school admissions consultant.

Kaplan is the #1 Choice for LSAT Prep! With more than 70 years of experience, Kaplan's products and programs are designed with students in mind. Our unique combination of the highest quality study materials, realistic testing experience, and dynamic tutors is unrivaled. We provide the most personalized prep with more options than any competitor—including classroom courses, online programs, small group and one-on-one tutoring, and self-study guides. In fact, Kaplan's prep is so focused and effective, Kaplan guarantees students' scores will improve—or they receive their money back.

How to Use This Booklet

Congratulations! You're well on your way to mastering the LSAT, with your purchase of Kaplan's complete three-book set of *LSAT Logic Games: Strategies and Tactics*, *LSAT Logical Reasoning: Strategies and Tactics*, and *LSAT Reading Comprehension: Strategies and Tactics*.

In this supplemental booklet, you'll find tips and strategies you can use to master the Writing Sample section of the LSAT, from an expert Kaplan instructor. Kaplan has the resources to help you be prepared for anything you encounter on test day, and to help you maximize your LSAT score.

For more information on Kaplan's LSAT products and programs,
please visit us at www.kaptest.com/LSAT.

Good luck!

ABOUT THE LSAT

The LSAT is a standardized test written by the Law School Admission Council (LSAC) and administered four times each year. The test is a required component of your application to all American Bar Association–approved law schools as well as some others.

The LSAT is designed to measure the skills necessary for success in your first year of law school (according to the governing bodies of law schools), such as strategic reading, analyzing arguments, understanding formal logic, and making deductions. Because these skills will serve you well throughout law school and your professional life, consider your LSAT preparation an investment in your career.

You may already possess some level of proficiency with LSAT-tested skills. However, you probably haven't yet mastered how to use those skills to your best advantage in the context of a standardized, skills-based test that requires careful time management.

The LSAT is also a test of endurance—five 35-minute blocks of multiple-choice testing plus a 35-minute writing sample. Add in the administrative tasks at both ends of the test and a 10- to 15-minute break midway through, and you can count on being in the test room for at least four and a half hours. It's a grueling experience, but it's not as bad if you are familiar with the test and ready to handle every section. You want to approach the test with confidence so that you can maintain your focus, limit your stress, and get your highest score on test day. That's why it's so important to take control of the test, just as you will take control of the rest of the application process.

Our material is as up-to-date as possible at the time of this printing, but test specifications may change at any time. Please visit our website at http://kaptest.com/LSAT for the latest news and updates.

How Do I Register for the LSAT?

The LSAT is administered by the Law School Admission Council (LSAC). Be sure to register as soon as possible, as your preferred test site can fill up quickly. You can register for the LSAT in three ways:

- Online: Sign up at http://lsac.org.
- Telephone: Call LSAC at (215) 968-1001.
- Email: Contact LSAC for a registration packet at lsacinfo@lsac.org.

If you have additional questions about registration, contact the LSAC by phone or by email.

ABOUT THE WRITING SAMPLE

On the LSAT, you will be given a prompt consisting of a problem, two criteria or goals that must be met in addressing the problem, and two possible courses of action. You'll have 35 minutes at the end of your LSAT day to make a written case for your position.

Your essay must be confined to the space provided, which is roughly the equivalent of two sheets of standard lined paper. Note that there's really no time or space to change your mind or radically alter your essay once you've begun writing, so *plan your argument carefully before beginning to write*. Make sure to write as legibly as you can.

The Writing Sample is ungraded, but it is sent to law schools along with your LSAT score. In fact, it's the second page admissions committee members see when they open and review your packet. Many law schools use the Writing Sample to help make decisions on borderline cases or to decide between applicants with otherwise comparable credentials. Granted, it may not carry the same weight as the scored sections of the test, but because it can have an impact on your admission chances, your best bet is to take it seriously.

LSAT Writing Sample Strategies and Tactics

by Bob Verini

DO LAW SCHOOLS ACTUALLY READ THE LSAT WRITING SAMPLE?

Yes, of course they do.

Actually, "My goodness, yes, of course" was the response of a law school admissions director from a prestigious East Coast institution. She seemed surprised I would even ask whether LSAC and its members would go to all the trouble and expense of creating, writing, administering, and distributing a writing exercise in which none of them was interested. (Much less do so for the better part of the last 30 years.)

But there may be cynics, and I'll start by addressing them first. **Yes, they read it,** and those who read it take it seriously.

Now, not everyone reads it with the same interest, at the same point in the application review process, or with the same purpose in mind. But saying that some law schools give the Writing Sample a quick look, while others invest it with importance, is very different from the cavalier assumption that as an unscored portion of your LSAT, the Writing Sample is superfluous and deserves no attention.

In this section I will tell you exactly what law schools are looking for, why the Writing Sample serves their purposes, and how to approach the exercise as practically and systematically as these books have (I hope) persuaded you to approach the scored LSAT.

WHAT ARE LAW SCHOOLS LOOKING TO GAUGE, AND WHY?

Three things, but remember, it's mysterious as to which law schools value which of the three. (Some value them all.) If you hit all the bases, you'll have nothing to fear. They want to assess:

Your relationship with the English language. The commerce of the law student is the written word. You will churn out a ton of writing over three years. As such it behooves the admissions committee to judge: Are you and the language on buddy-buddy terms, or are you acquaintances, or have you barely even met? The more easy and fluent your writing under tightly timed, reference-book-free circumstances, the more likely it is that the predominant mode of your law school training won't be a strain for you.

admissions
TIP

Highlight debate background in your application if you have any. It's an excellent "DNA marker" for law school success.

Your affinity for argument. The law is a process whereby two sides attempt to persuade an audience of their reasoning while weakening the arguments on the other side. Alas, the days in which all college students, law school bound or not, were trained in rhetoric and debate are behind us. Because most applicants haven't engaged in formal debate, law schools like to see that you have a sense of how to create a persuasively phrased conclusion, know how to support it with appropriate evidence, and are able to make reasonable assumptions in connecting the two.

admissions
TIP

Make sure your personal statement doesn't sound so polished as to raise doubts. As the substitute for a personal face-to-face interview it's supposed to sound like you anyway, so that shouldn't be a problem.

The degree of help you received in your Personal Statement. Here's another quote from an admissions professional: "We understand that applicants have experts look over the personal statement to proofread and make edits, but we like to know that it's the applicant's own work. And while we don't expect the LSAT essay to be at all polished, it does provide a basis for comparison as to the applicant's writing ability." I take this as code for: "If the word choice, syntax, punctuation and structure are markedly different in the off the cuff writing vs. the personal statement, we might smell a rat."

OKAY, I'M PERSUADED.
SO HOW EXACTLY IS THE EXERCISE STRUCTURED?

The structure of the **prompt** is always the same. A **Decision Maker** (or "D-M"—an individual, married couple, organization, municipality, or other institution) is choosing between two distinct alternatives. Two of the D-M's bulleted **Criteria** are listed. As a rule, one criterion will tend to favor the first alternative or option; the other, the second. Both **Options** have pros and cons in terms of the criteria; neither is a slam dunk.

Your job is to *argue for one of them over the other*—which means you have to come up with as solid an argument as you can for **"The Winner"** (which is what we'll call the one you favor), while attempting to shoot down the appeal of the one you choose as **"The Loser."**

As you'll see, the predetermined prompt structure means that you can pretty much predetermine your Writing Sample structure as well.

WHAT IS MY ROLE OR PERSONA IN ALL OF THIS?

Think of yourself as an outside consultant, one with no personal stake in the outcome. You don't care which nursing home Mrs. Jones goes to, or which location Mr. and Mrs. Smith pick for their new restaurant. You're given criteria and facts, and based on your assumptions as to how the world works, you take a stand and support it. If Jones or the Smiths don't like your choice or reasoning, they're free to reject it. And you'll shrug that off, because you were asked for your opinion and gave it.

Some writers (including me) have written an occasional Writing Sample in which the essential point was, "Both of these alternatives sound fundamentally flawed, and if I were the Smiths I'd keep looking." It's a bold choice, and could be the topic for the final paragraph of your Writing Sample if you truly do believe the alternatives are horrible. Still and all, you have to follow instructions: You have to hold your nose and say in effect, "With a gun to my back I guess I'd tell the Smiths to choose Option X, for these reasons."

TIP
Don't be any more enthusiastic about the choice than your reading of the criteria and your assumptions allow you to be. If you're 100% sure, fine; if you're lukewarm, that's fine too. Just keep the tone of your writing in sync with your feelings.

APPROACHING THE PROMPT: BRAINSTORMING AND PLANNING

First things first: Make sure you have a handle on the overall situation, being sure to accurately paraphrase the key elements. Pore through this prompt from 2007:

A neighborhood association is planning to sponsor a public event on the first day of summer—either a walking tour or a 5 kilometer run. Using the facts below, write an essay in which you argue for one event over the other based on the following two criteria:

- The association wants to encourage more neighborhood residents to become association members.
- In order to conduct other activities during the year, the association wants to minimize the time and resources required by the event.

The first event is a free, self-guided walking tour of some of the neighborhood's private homes and historic buildings. The tour would feature the association's promotional table and exhibits of crafts, music, and cooking. Many neighborhood residents have expressed interest in such a tour. Some of the responsibility for organizing the event would be borne by those who own the homes and buildings; the association would be responsible for the remaining details. The costs of this event would consume most of the association's annual budget. Other neighborhood associations that have conducted similar tours report robust neighborhood participation and accompanying increases in membership.

The second event is a 5 kilometer run through the neighborhood. The association has sponsored this yearly event for almost a decade. In recent years, the association has hired a third-party company to manage the race and would do so again. Registration fees collected from race participants would cover administrative costs. In the past the event has led to modest increases in membership for the association. At its peak, almost 1,000 people participated in the race, most of them from out of town. This year more people are expected to participate because the course has been professionally certified and the race would serve as a qualifying race for a national championship.*

Your **D-M**, the association, will (you hope) sponsor whichever event you choose, "the tour" or "the race." (You don't need to refer to the options any other way.)

Have you read through the two **Options**? Hope so, but don't jump to a conclusion! As a good consultant you want to weigh everything—within time limits—before taking a stand. Reserve judgment until you go through these steps, starting with a serious perusal of the two Criteria.

---

* PrepTest 52, Writing Sample Topic

BRAINSTORMING STEP #1:
Think through and paraphrase the Criteria.

Starting with bullet point #1: How would a neighborhood group encourage new members? Should they emphasize the camaraderie and friendship? Ought they play up the elements of fun? Will they get better results by organizing adult activities or appealing to the entire family? How do you turn nonjoiners into joiners?

Here's where your own personal experiences and assumptions can and should come into play. Whatever you know, or have learned, or believe about people's behavior is fodder for your essay, because all of that is what fundamentally guides your judgment. Here's what one student jotted down:

> <u>Goal</u>: Build members: Emphasize advantages of joining. Make it seem like fun not work,
> make the value of joining clear. Appeal to civic pride / property values. Shld be family oriented.

It doesn't matter whether you agree or disagree, but whether you bring some independent thought to the process. Here's how that same student assessed the second criterion:

> <u>Goal</u>: Minimize time/resources: Keep it cheap. Shldn't need to learn new procedures/logistics.
> As few organizers as possible, pref. unpaid volunteers. Organize fast, and not far in advance.

If phrases other than these came to you, that's great. Notice that the student shows no awareness of having read the descriptions of the tour and the run. That's good! She has endeavored to take the criteria on face value first.

Now you have a deeper understanding of what the D-M wants. You've also come up with some ideas, and even some phrases, likely to end up in your essay.

BRAINSTORMING STEP #2:
Decide whether unmentioned criteria—if any—are, in your judgment, also relevant to consider beyond the ones provided.

You don't *have* to come up with additional factors worth considering, but if you do and can justify your reasoning, why not? Our student made this note on her scratch paper:

> Raising $ is always good for an organization.

In other words, even though the bullet points don't explicitly reference money, it may make sense to factor in how much cash will be required *and* how much cash, if any, an activity is likely to bring in. Just food for thought.

TIP
You can't substitute your own new criterion for the ones offered, but you are certainly permitted to supplement your argument with it.

BRAINSTORMING STEP #3:

Think through how you'd argue for Option A while shooting down Option B.

Your planning should involve thinking through—and jotting down on scrap paper—the points you think you'll want to make, in any order.

Let's consider the facts about Option A and how you could spin them positively. Or better yet, let's listen in on the student's (italicized) inner monologue as she re-reads "Option A"'s paragraph:

TIP

More Writing Samples fail for lack of planning than for any other reason.

WINNER: OPTION A

The first event is a free, self-guided walking tour of some of the neighborhood's private homes and historic buildings.

That will mean plenty of 1:1 conversations between homeowners and tourists—good for recruiting new members. "Free" lowers barriers to participation. And "self-guided" is great, will require fewer volunteer organizers.

The tour would feature the association's promotional table and exhibits of crafts, music, and cooking.

Showing off local skills and talents will make a good impression and involve town artisans. Leave leaflets about the association on the table.

Many neighborhood residents have expressed interest in such a tour.

Already wide awareness of, and demand for, this event means it'll be easier to publicize.

Some of the responsibility for organizing the event would be borne by those who own the homes and buildings; the association would be responsible for the remaining details.

If homeowners live up to their commitments, the duties can be divvied up so as to not strain association resources.

The costs of this event would consume most of the association's annual budget.

You have to spend $ to gain a big result. No plan is without risk.

Other neighborhood associations that have conducted similar tours report robust neighborhood participation and accompanying increases in membership.

That could offset the outflow of dollars. Are there dues? Dues would help. At least it's solid evidence that the idea has merit.

Sounds like the basis for a vigorous argument, but it's "argue for one over the other," so how might one demolish Option B?

LOSER: OPTION B

The second event is a 5 kilometer run through the neighborhood. The association has sponsored this yearly event for almost a decade.

> *Nothing new to get excited about. Those interested are probably already involved. Not much chance for people to meet and greet, get to know each other, talk membership.*

In recent years, the association has hired a third-party company to manage the race and would do so again.

> *Ceding control could mean cost overruns.*

Registration fees collected from race participants would cover administrative costs.

> *Breakeven doesn't sound so great.*

In the past the event has led to modest increases in membership for the association.

> *Just "modest"? That doesn't sound like it'd fit the criterion.*

At its peak, almost 1,000 people participated in the race, most of them from out of town.

> *Oh, great, bring in a lot of out-of-towners, none of whom will end up joining the association.*

This year more people are expected to participate, because the course has been professionally certified and the race would serve as a qualifying race for a national championship.

> *Aha: Even less of a local focus than usual!*

Wow, she's rebutted every one of Option B's points. So it's all set, right? She should start writing, right?

We'd say, *wrong*. We'd say, "Be fair to yourself, and first think through the other side as well." A good advocate always marshals the arguments for the other side, so as to be prepared for all eventualities. And who knows? You might change your mind. So listen in as this very same student thinks through the assignment the other way around. Suppose she supports B, and works to weaken A?

BRAINSTORMING STEP #4:

Switch it up—figure out the arguments you'd make in support of Option B, while shooting down Option A.

WINNER: OPTION B

The second event is a 5 kilometer run through the neighborhood. The association has sponsored this yearly event for almost a decade.

There's already huge awareness about the event with which the association has been "branded." It's "their event" and can get a lot of hoopla. A real all-neighborhood event.

In recent years, the association has hired a third-party company to manage the race and would do so again.

Awesome: This frees up the association's officers and members to work on recruitment and the year's other events.

Registration fees collected from race participants would cover administrative costs.

Even better — the thing will pay for itself.

In the past the event has led to modest increases in membership for the association.

So for years it's gotten more members in, routinely. If they really apply themselves to an all-out membership drive, the results could be amazing! Think of all the 1:1 conversations that can go on before, during, and after the race.

At its peak, almost 1,000 people participated in the race, most of them from out of town.

Out-of-towners become residents when they like the new place they visit. A big push can be made to attract newcomers, who will have the association to thank for bringing the town to their attention.

This year more people are expected to participate, because the course has been professionally certified and the race would serve as a qualifying race for a national championship.

Even more recruitment opportunities this year. And the national qualifying puts the town on the map, gives it visibility and credibility. It's a first-class event that will still leave plenty of money and energy to conduct the rest of the year's activities.

Maybe you find this positive argument for B more effective than the one for A. Maybe not. But for your own sake, you're keeping an open mind, and acknowledging that each side has a good case to make. Moreover, we can poke a lot of holes into Option A if so inclined:

LOSER: OPTION A

The first event is a free, self-guided walking tour of some of the neighborhood's private homes and historic buildings.

"Free" could be perceived as routine; value-less. And self-guided means they're on their own, not thanking the association every step of the way. If the homeowners don't stay home to answer the doors, all you'll have are random people wandering the streets with no sales pitch for membership.

The tour would feature the association's promotional table and exhibits of crafts, music, and cooking.

A table is easy to walk past on a walking tour, and the exhibits would have only a peripheral connection to living there.

Many neighborhood residents have expressed interest in such a tour.

Talk is cheap; are they truly willing to participate? People can guide themselves through town with a brochure. How is that a big "event"?

Some of the responsibility for organizing the event would be borne by those who own the homes and buildings; the association would be responsible for the remaining details.

Could get sticky, deciding who does what, and in the end the association will have to organize and pay for whatever the homeowners balk at.

The costs of this event would consume most of the association's annual budget.

Throws the entire second criterion out the window.

Other neighborhood associations that have conducted similar tours report robust neighborhood participation and accompanying increases in membership.

It's faulty logic to assume that what worked in other communities must be successful in this one. The association would be rolling the dice on one—kind of lame-sounding—event that would wipe out the rest of the year. That's way too big a risk to run!

So which option should I choose?

That's easy: the one you think you'd have an easier time writing. The goal of the essay isn't to build membership in, and manage resources of, a neighborhood association. *It's to get you a step closer to law school.* And you'll have a more impressive piece of writing if you make the strongest possible argument for your case.

Look at it this way. You're going to be an attorney one day. Attorneys by definition have to be able to argue every side of a question. You could do a fine job defending either Option A or B, and the whole situation is fictional anyway, so don't sweat it. Pick the one you *want* to write—the one that'll be more fun, the one that'll show you off better.

At what point should I start writing?

We'd recommend the following rough allocation of time:

> Study and deconstruct prompt—2 mins.
> Brainstorm and plan—6 mins.
> Writing—25 mins.
> Quick last-minute proof—2 mins.

Should I just start writing?

No. Plan the whole essay out first, and pre-write your opening sentence. Once you start writing, you're committed; you can't erase or make changes without making a mess. Have the entire essay's flow in mind before you start to write.

Here's what our student—who has decided to make Option A the Winner—jotted down on her scratch paper as she brainstormed, and how she turned it into a plan:

1 Already wanted; much 1:1	1 Old hat; not too personal
~~Self-guided — little $ outlay~~	5 No excitement here
4 Recruiting leaflets/artisans	4 Cost overruns poss. w/ 3rd party
3 Known to work	3 Breakeven is NSG
2 Divide jobs to our advantage	2 Out-of-towners prob wont join
5 Take risks – charge dues	

Note that having jotted down her thoughts as they occurred to her—positive arguments for A on the left—she doesn't have to write out a formal outline. She simply numbers the points in order, and crosses out anything that doesn't seem to fit into what she has in mind.

All she needs to do now is try out a killer first sentence:

> *All indications are that the walking tour will better ensure reaching the association's goals.*

Well done—especially in terms of using the comparative form "better" rather than "best." Her choice is clear, and people will want to read on to find out what the "indications" are and how she's interpreting them.

Wait a minute, that's "killer"? What about recapping the prompt first? What about an intro?

Naah, you don't need all that stuff. The prompt is right there for the reader to consult as he sees fit. Jump right in to announce your choice.

How should the essay be structured?

In ¶1 you will make the case for The Winner, starting with one of your stronger arguments.

Don't just cite a fact; explain how that fact is desirable, or leads to a desirable outcome, or helps to achieve the criterion.

Link your points with Keywords: "First of all"…"In addition"…"Furthermore"… "Finally."

Before ¶1 is through, acknowledge your Winner's weakness(es) and paper it/them over.

Open ¶2 by acknowledging The Loser's strengths, if any.

Go on to show why the negatives outweigh the positives.

Try to bring the essay back around to The Winner. And end.

That *does* sound pretty programmed. Will every LSAT Writing Sample fit that model?

Yes, because it directly parallels the tasks as defined up front. You're making a case for one (in ¶1) over the other (in ¶2).

May I see an example?

I'll go you one better and show you two. For starters, here's an essay based on the earlier brainstorming of Option A, the walking tour, as "The Winner." The writer would of course not highlight the structural signals as you see below; we did that to make the point that judicious use of Keywords really shapes your essay along classical lines.

As you read, keep an eye on the assessment in the right-hand column.

TIP
Don't waste time recapping the prompt, which is there for the reader's reference if he wants it. Cut to the chase.

TIP
Readers love to see structural Keywords because their use indicates that you are an organized thinker and disciplined writer. Even for someone merely skimming the essay, such Keywords jump out and make a most favorable impression.

TIP
Save a couple of minutes at the end to do some quick proofreading for subject/verb agreement and tense consistency.

TIP
The more of these you write for practice, the easier they'll become.

All indications are that the walking tour will better ensure reaching the association's goals. **For one thing,** the neighborhood has already indicated that it wants such a tour, so demand doesn't seem to be in question. **Moreover,** the neighbors say that they'll handle their share of the organizing burdens, which suggests that it won't eat up either association funds or association volunteers. **Best of all,** the exact same event has been a proven membership builder in other communities. As members chat with nonmember residents, a pitch can be made to join the association. The promotional table will feature local artisans to make an even better impression, and leaflets could be placed there to encourage on-the-spot enrollment. **It's unfortunately true that** the walking tour would eat up much of the association's annual budget. **But** you have to risk some money in this world to gain a potential big return. **In any case,** perhaps the association can levy dues, or raise current dues, to rebuild the treasury so that other activities later in the year might still go on.

The run would certainly be prestigious and attract many participants. But it sounds rather impersonal; over its 10-year history it evidently hasn't had much of an impact on membership. And this year many of the runners will be out-of-towners attracted by the national qualification, unlikely to plant permanent roots in this neighborhood. The fees might cover costs, though "breakeven" isn't an especially dramatic goal to achieve. In any case, ceding control to a third party company might lead to cost overruns. It may not be wise to put the big membership push into someone else's hands. Having been around for 10 years, the run won't get people excited the way a walking tour would, an event we know the neighborhood already craves.

Gets off to a fast start, excellent.

"For one thing...so"; "Moreover... which suggests that" —excellent use of evidence–conclusion. Good qualified language: "doesn't seem"; "suggests that."

"Best of all" clearly indicates the #1 argument.

Acknowledge a weakness — yes!

Immediately brush it aside — yes!!

A clever, plausible possibility you've come up with; shows independent thinking.

Good: Grant the Loser its strengths.

Good solid reasoning based on evidence here.

"Unlikely...might...may not be wise" —all nicely qualified language.

Good conclusion, deftly turning it back to the Winner with no fuss.

In sum, that's a solid piece of work—unambitious, certainly, but you only get 35 minutes; you shouldn't be ambitious in the first place. Believe me, a solid, readable, well-organized essay is an eminently achievable goal in the time provided.

Did you see how little verbatim quoting the writer engages in? She doesn't say "The costs of this event would consume most of the association's annual budget"; she says "the walking tour would eat up much of the association's yearly funds." Not "exhibits of crafts, music, and cooking" but "the promotional table will feature local artisans." Putting some paraphrase spin on the details shows that you've thought things through—you aren't just parroting back words. It also makes the essay more enjoyable to read; that can't hurt.

I thought we were supposed to write a strong argument. How can all that qualified language—"might," "suggests," "unlikely" —lead to strength?

It's precisely *because* the language is qualified that the argument is so effective. Suppose the student wrote this sentence:

> The neighbors will share the organizing burden, which definitely proves that the self-guided event won't eat up funds or take very many volunteers.

No qualification there. But also *no room for exceptions,* and an argument with no room for exceptions is easy to weaken. You read this and say, "That's too strong! She can't be sure that money and volunteers won't be overused." Suddenly you are doubting her logic.

The original sentence is much easier to accept because it allows a modicum of wiggle room. It sounds less sure of itself, meaning it's more reasonable; that in turn actually means that it's *more* acceptable, on its face.

Now, just to prove it can be done, here's an essay raving about Option B and making out Option A to be fallible:

TIP

Bombast and overstatement don't make for a strong argument. Only carefully phrased conclusions, no stronger than the evidence justifies, lead to persuasiveness.

The 5K run is a real "all-neighborhood" event which already boasts the association's brand. It will pay for itself and be managed by a third party company, which will free up the association's officers and members to work on recruitment, as well as the year's other events. In addition, for a decade the run has been a proven membership builder. One can only imagine the amazing results if the association commits itself to a full-out recruitment drive. Think of all the 1:1 conversations about the neighborhood and association that will go on before, during, and after the race. True, the runners hail mostly from elsewhere, but out-of-towners become residents of a new place when they like where they're visiting. A big push can be made to attract this constituency.

The walking tour's success depends on too many variables, especially homeowners' willingness to stay home, answer their doorbells, welcome strangers in, and talk to them about joining the association. Otherwise you have people wandering streets with no recruiting going on. Furthermore, a promotional table is easy to ignore or walk past. Worst of all, this so-called event would eat up the entire annual budget, sticking a knife in any other planned activities for the foreseeable future. By contrast, the financially responsible 5K run is a first class, nationally significant event that will leave plenty of money and energy in place through year's end.

Wastes no time.

Lines up evidence emphatically.

Good structural keywords.

Concede a weakness and paper it over: Excellent.

Good value judgment based on evidence.

"Furthermore..." "Worst of all...": Excellent keywords.

As is "By contrast." Very good to get back to the winner at the very end.

Is one of these samples far superior to the other?

By no means. Either one would bring a smile to admissions officers' faces. Each is unambitious, well planned, well argued, and easy to read.

I notice that neither sample essay has any kind of separate, elaborate conclusion.

That's true. A conclusion paragraph isn't by any means necessary if you follow our "¶1 Winner / ¶2 Loser" format. Each of the samples segues gracefully from the debunking of the Loser back to the Winner and out.

> **TIP**
> Save one point or argument in the Winner's favor, for use in the final sentences.

What about proofreading?

Allot the final two minutes of the 35 for a quick look-see that attends to subject/verb agreement, dangling modifiers, unclear pronoun antecedent— anything that you can quickly and neatly fix with a carat (^) and insertion, or a simple cross-out and overwriting. Law schools understand that you have very little time to plan and write the thing; as long as what you write is legible, and doesn't look like a sea of cross-outs and scribbled insertions, they'll be fine with it.

> **TIP**
> Practice writing one or two of these a week! The more you practice, the easier it'll be to write a fine essay on demand…and the less likely it is that you'll even have to cross out or fix anything more than an odd word here or there.

I'm concerned about my LSAT score, and I don't want to take time away from the test to work on and practice writing because it doesn't affect my score. Why should I take the time to practice?

I am a good writer, and I had to write a few of these essays before I was able to crank out a first-class entry on any prompt, at any time. The LSAT Writing Sample is a very specialized task that requires some trial and error to gain expertise. However, if you need more persuasion to take the Writing Sample seriously, how about these arguments?

- **Students consistently report that planning and writing sample essays helps them with LSAT Logical Reasoning.** That should make sense. In creating a writing sample you are putting an argument together. In LR, you're taking arguments apart. Work on one task ought to inform your command of the other, and so students tell us.

> **TIP**
> The smart move is to do everything you can so that no single aspect of your application is anything less than first-rate.

- **Working on the LSAT writing sample offers a pleasant break from multiple-choice testing.** You can stop juggling (A) (B) (C) (D) (E) for a while without feeling guilty that you're goofing off.

- **Your stiffest competition is probably taking the essay very seriously indeed.** Those with high GPAs, great recommendations, and anticipated excellent LSAT results know that lots and lots of applicants boast the same numerical and qualitative credentials. As such, they look for any opportunity to stand out from the pack, and the LSAT writing sample is certainly one such opportunity.

Using the English language to make a case for one side in an argument should be right in your wheelhouse—if you truly have the mind and soul of an attorney. You should relish this chance to be a skillful debater and make the most of it.

LSAT®
LOGICAL REASONING
STRATEGIES AND TACTICS

Deborah A. Katz, JD, PhD

This publication is designed to provide accurate and authoritative information in regard to the subject matter covered. It is sold with the understanding that the publisher is not engaged in rendering legal, accounting, or other professional service. If legal advice or other expert assistance is required, the services of a competent professional should be sought.

© 2011 Kaplan, Inc.

Published by Kaplan Publishing, a division of Kaplan, Inc.
395 Hudson Street
New York, NY 10014

Printed in the United States of America

10 9 8 7 6 5 4 3 2 1

ISBN-13: 978-1-60978-150-7

Kaplan Publishing books are available at special quantity discounts to use for sales promotions, employee premiums, or educational purposes. For more information or to purchase books, please call the Simon & Schuster special sales department at 866-506-1949.

Contents

About the Author

Deborah A. Katz, JD, PhD, is an elite LSAT instructor and teacher trainer, honored in 2007 as the Columbus Teacher of the Year. Deborah has taught with Kaplan since 2002; in 2007, she was selected to participate in the inaugural Kaplan LSAT Summer Intensive program, and currently serves as Program Director.

Deborah holds both a JD and a PhD from The Ohio State University. She is a consultant for the American NewMedia Educational Foundation, where she consults with the education and athletic communities to evaluate NCAA compliance and develop rules, educational programs, and materials. She also serves as an adjunct professor for the Law of Amateur Sports at Capital University Law School.

Introduction to the LSAT

The Law School Admissions Test (LSAT) is probably unlike any other test you've taken in your academic career. Most tests you've encountered in high school and college have been content based—that is, they have required you to recall facts, formulas, theorems, or other acquired knowledge.

The LSAT, however, is a skills-based test. It doesn't ask you to repeat memorized facts or to apply learned formulas to specific problems. In fact, all you'll be asked to do on the LSAT is think—thoroughly, quickly, and strategically. There's no required content to study.

But the lack of specific content to memorize is one of things that makes preparing for the LSAT so challenging. Before you get the idea that you can skate into the most important test of your life without preparing, remember that learning skills and improving performance take practice. You can't cram for the test.

ABOUT THE LSAT

The LSAT is a standardized test written by the Law School Admissions Council (LSAC) and administered four times each year. The test is a required component of your application to all American Bar Association–approved law schools as well as some others.

The LSAT is designed to measure the skills necessary (according to the governing bodies of law schools) for success in your first year of law school, such as strategic reading, analyzing arguments, understanding formal logic, and making deductions. Because these skills will serve you well throughout law school and your professional life, consider your LSAT preparation an investment in your career.

You may already possess some level of proficiency with LSAT-tested skills. However, you probably haven't yet mastered how to use those skills to your advantage in the context of a standardized, skills-based test that requires careful time management.

The LSAT is also a test of endurance—five 35-minute blocks of multiple-choice testing plus a 35-minute writing sample. Add in the administrative tasks at both ends of the test and a 10- to 15-minute break midway through, and you can count on being in the test room for at least four and a half hours. It's a grueling experience, but it's not as bad if you are familiar with the test and ready to handle every section. You want to approach the test with confidence so that you can maintain your focus, limit your stress, and get your highest score on test day. That's why it's so important to take control of the test, just as you will take control of the rest of the application process.

Our material is as up-to-date as possible at the time of this printing, but test specifications may change at any time. Please visit our website at http://kaptest.com/LSAT for the latest news and updates.

How Do I Register for the LSAT?

The LSAT is administered by the Law School Admissions Council (LSAC). Be sure to register as soon as possible, as your preferred test site can fill up quickly. You can register for the LSAT in three ways:

- Online: Sign up at http://lsac.org.
- Telephone: Call LSAC at (215) 968-1001.
- Email: Contact LSAC for a registration packet at lsacinfo@lsac.org.

If you have additional questions about registration, contact the LSAC by phone or by email.

The LSAT Sections

The LSAT consists of five multiple-choice sections: two Logical Reasoning sections, one Logic Games section, one Reading Comprehension section, and one unscored "experimental" section that looks exactly like one of the other multiple-choice sections. At the end of the test, there is a Writing Sample section during which you'll write a short essay. Here's how the sections break down:

Section	Number of Questions	Minutes
Logical Reasoning	24–26	35
Logical Reasoning	24–26	35
Logic Games	22–24	35
Reading Comprehension	26–28	35
"Experimental"	23–28	35
Writing Sample	n/a	35

The five multiple-choice sections can appear in any order, but the Writing Sample is always last. You will also get a 10- or 15-minute break between the third and fourth sections of the test.

You'll be answering roughly 125 multiple-choice questions (101 of which are scored) over the course of three intense hours. Taking control of the LSAT means increasing your test speed only to the extent that you can do so without sacrificing accuracy.

First, just familiarize yourself with the sections and the kinds of questions asked in each one.

Logical Reasoning

WHAT IT IS: The Logical Reasoning sections consist of 24–26 questions each that reward your ability to analyze a "stimulus" (a paragraph or a dialogue between two speakers) and make judgments accordingly. You will evaluate the logic and structure of arguments and make inferences from the statements as well as find underlying assumptions, strengthen and weaken arguments, determine logical flaws, and identify parallel argument structures.

WHY IT'S ON THE TEST: Law schools want to see whether you can understand, analyze, evaluate, and manipulate arguments, and draw reliable conclusions—as every law student and attorney must. This question type makes up half of your LSAT score, which means this is a valuable skill to master.

Logic Games

WHAT IT IS: In the Logic Games (a.k.a. Analytical Reasoning) section, you'll find four games (aka critical-thinking puzzles) with five to seven questions each for a total of 22–24 questions. They reward your ability to make valid deductions from a set of rules or restrictions in order to determine what can, must, or cannot be true in various circumstances.

WHY IT'S ON THE TEST: In law school, your professors will have you read dozens of cases, extract their rules, and apply them to or distinguish them from hypothetical cases. The Logic Games section rewards the same skill set: attention to detail, rigorous deductive reasoning, an understanding of how rules limit and order behavior (the very definition of law), and the ability to discern the conditions under which those rules do and do not apply.

Reading Comprehension

WHAT IT IS: The Reading Comprehension section consists of three passages, each 450–550 words, and a set of two short passages that total 450–550 words. Each passage is followed by five to eight questions. The topics may range from areas of social science, humanities, natural science, and law. Because content isn't tested, you won't need any outside knowledge.

WHY IT'S ON THE TEST: The Reading Comprehension section tests your ability to quickly understand the gist and structure of long, difficult prose—just as you'll have to do in law school and throughout your career.

The Writing Sample

WHAT IT IS: During the Writing Sample section, you will read a paragraph that presents a problem and lists two possible solutions. Each solution will have strengths and weaknesses; you must argue in favor of one based on the given criteria. There is no right or wrong answer, and the writing sample is unscored. However, law schools will receive a copy of your essay along with your LSAT score.

WHY IT'S ON THE TEST: The Writing Sample shows law schools your ability to argue for a position while attacking an opposing argument under timed conditions. In addition, it may be used to verify that your writing style is similar to that in your personal statement.

How the LSAT Is Scored

You'll receive one score for the LSAT ranging between 120 and 180 (no separate scores for Logical Reasoning, Logic Games, and Reading Comprehension). There are roughly 101 scored multiple-choice questions on each exam:

- About 52 from the two Logical Reasoning sections
- About 22 from the Logic Games section
- About 27 from the Reading Comprehension section

Your **raw score**, the number of questions that you answer correctly, will be multiplied by a complicated scoring formula (different for each test, to accommodate differences in difficulty level) to yield the **scaled score**—the one that will fall somewhere in that 120–180 range—which is reported to the schools.

Because the test is graded on a largely preset curve, the scaled score will always correspond to a certain percentile, also indicated on your score report. A score of 160, for instance, corresponds roughly to the 80th percentile, meaning that 80 percent of test takers scored at or below your level. The percentile figure is important because it allows law schools to see where you fall in the pool of applicants.

All scored questions are worth the same amount—one raw point—and there's no penalty for guessing. That means that you should always fill in an answer for every question, whether you get to that question or not.

What's a "Good" LSAT Score?

What you consider a "good" LSAT score depends on your own expectations and goals, but here are a few interesting statistics.

If you got about half of all of the scored questions right (a raw score of roughly 50), you would earn a scaled score of roughly 147, putting you in about the 30th percentile—not a great performance. But on the LSAT, a little improvement goes a long way. In fact, getting only one

additional question right every 10 minutes would give you a raw score of about 64, pushing you into the 60th percentile—a huge improvement.

Sample Percentiles Approx. Scaled Score		
Percentile	**(Range 120–180)**	**Approx. Raw Score**
99th percentile	174	~94 correct out of 101
95th percentile	168	~88 correct out of 101
90th percentile	164	~82 correct out of 101
80th percentile	160	~76 correct out of 101
75th percentile	157	~71 correct out of 101
50th percentile	152	~61 correct out of 101

Note: Exact percentile-to-scaled-score relationships vary from test to test.

As you can see, you don't have to be perfect to do well. On most LSATs, you can get as many as 28 questions wrong and still remain in the 80th percentile or as many as 20 wrong and still be in the 90th percentile. Most students who score 180 get a handful of questions wrong.

Although many factors play a role in admissions decisions, the LSAT score is usually one of the most important. And—generally speaking—being average won't cut it. The median LSAT score is somewhere around 152. If you're aiming for the top, you've got to do even better.

By using the strategies in this book, you'll learn how to approach—and master—the test in a general way. As you'll see, knowing specific strategies for each type of question is only part of your task. To do your best, you have to approach the entire test with the proactive, take-control kind of thinking it inspires—the LSAT mindset.

For more information on the LSAT experience, see Part IV of this book.

HOW LOGICAL REASONING WORKS

CHAPTER 1

TESTING LOGICAL REASONING

AN INTRODUCTION TO LOGICAL REASONING

Have you ever seen a Logical Reasoning question from the LSAT? Before I talk about methods and skills you will use to achieve your best score on test day, I'll show you what a Logical Reasoning question looks like.

The following two questions appeared on the September 2006 test. Read them over and see whether you can get the correct answer.

1. Typically, people who have diets high in saturated fat have an increased risk of heart disease. Those who replace saturated fat in their diets with unsaturated fat decrease their risk of heart disease. Therefore, people who eat a lot of saturated fat can lower their risk of heart disease by increasing their intake of unsaturated fat.

   Which one of the following, if assumed, most helps to justify the reasoning above?

   (A) People who add unsaturated fat to their diets will eat less food that is high in saturated fat.

   (B) Adding unsaturated fat to a diet brings health benefits other than a reduced risk of heart disease.

   (C) Diet is the most important factor in a person's risk of heart disease.

   (D) Taking steps to prevent heart disease is one of the most effective ways of increasing life expectancy.

   (E) It is difficult to move from a diet that is high in saturated fat to a diet that includes very little fat.

2. Only people who are willing to compromise should undergo mediation to resolve their conflicts. Actual litigation should be pursued only when one is sure that one's position is correct. People whose conflicts are based on ideology are unwilling to compromise.

   If the statements above are true, then which one of the following must be true?

   (A) People who do not undergo mediation to resolve their conflicts should be sure that their positions are correct.

   (B) People whose conflicts are not based on ideology should attempt to resolve their conflicts by means of litigation.

   (C) People whose conflicts are based on ideology are not always sure that their positions are correct.

   (D) People who are sure of the correctness of their positions are not people who should undergo mediation to resolve their conflicts.

   (E) People whose conflicts are based on ideology are not people who should undergo mediation to resolve their conflicts.[2]

Did you select choice (A) as your answer to question 1 and choice (E) for question 2?

If so, congratulations! Maybe you got both wrong or maybe one correct. Frankly, your specific response doesn't matter right now. What is most important is how you answered the questions,

---

[2]PrepTest 50, Sec. 4, Qs 9–10

why you chose the answers you did, and why you did not pick the other answers. If you follow the approach in this book, you'll learn how Logical Reasoning questions are put together and how you can take them apart efficiently, effectively, and routinely. If you practice the methods and strategies introduced here, you will maximize your Logical Reasoning performance and, in turn, your LSAT score.

Logical Reasoning Tests Skills, Not Content

Logical Reasoning, like the other sections on the LSAT, is a skill-based exercise that requires no outside knowledge of the content. Unlike many of your academic endeavors, the test includes no subject matter to memorize and regurgitate. Instead, you use critical-thinking skills to answer the questions.

Starting now, you should think of logical reasoning as a skill, just like playing basketball, strumming the guitar, cooking, or even driving a car. As with any skill, your goal is to perform the activity proficiently at a high level. You may have some innate talent or even some beginner's luck; however, you must develop and practice your skills so you walk in on test day confident in your ability to answer any question put in front of you.

Think about this example: A basketball player first learns the fundamentals of the game by practicing dribbling, passing, and shooting drills. Then she runs through plays that put the skills together, and she adds scrimmages to simulate game situations. In the process, the player works out to improve strength, agility, and endurance. The more comfortable with the skills and the more fit the player becomes, the quicker she can "read" the situation on the floor, make decisions, and respond in a game. Just like the basketball player, you must practice the fundamentals, break down the activities, and put your "game" together for test day.

Part I of this book has three purposes: to familiarize you with the Logical Reasoning sections on the LSAT, to introduce you to the Kaplan Method for tackling any Logical Reasoning question, and to provide you with a chance to practice your fundamental logical reasoning skills.

Later, in Part II, you will apply your skills to the specific question types asked on every LSAT and then put your skills to the test on complete Logical Reasoning sections.

LOGICAL REASONING SKILLS

Logical reasoning refers to the ability to identify, analyze, evaluate, and construct complex reasoning. The LSAT tests your ability to reason logically and critically by asking questions that require you to:

- Distinguish the parts of an argument and understand their relationships
- Recognize unstated assumptions
- Strengthen and weaken an argument

- Determine what must be true based on a set of assertions
- Identify argument flaws
- Identify similarities and differences between patterns of reasoning
- Recognize points of disagreement
- Identify principles and apply them to fact sets
- Detect a method of argument

THE IMPORTANCE OF LOGICAL REASONING ON THE LSAT

Logical reasoning accounts for half your score and assesses critical-thinking skills that are vital to your success in law school and the legal profession. The LSAT is not an end unto itself. Lawyers need critical-thinking skills to meet their professional responsibilities, and a legal education is designed to develop, hone, and refine those skills. Therefore, the LSAT must test your logical reasoning skills. Law schools want to evaluate your ability to think critically, amongst other skills, and use the LSAT, in large part, to determine your fit with their program.

Regardless of the nature of a lawyer's practice, there are some basic analytic, communication, and problem-solving skills that are universal. Lawyers must be able to structure and evaluate arguments for and against propositions to persuade, negotiate, and conduct business. Lawyers must analyze legal issues in light of changing laws and public policy. They must be able to advocate the views of individuals and diverse interest groups within the context of the legal system. They must be able to synthesize and apply material that relates to multifaceted issues. Ultimately, they must give logically reasoned and sound counsel on the law's requirements.

ANATOMY OF A LOGICAL REASONING QUESTION

How does the LSAT present logical reasoning and test the related skills? Every Logical Reasoning question begins with a stimulus: either a single paragraph or a dialogue between two speakers. Each stimulus presents an argument or a set of facts drawn from various sources, such as newspapers and magazines, academic journals, advertisements, and informal discourse. Regardless of whether the topic is art, medicine, or animals, remember that your knowledge of any particular content is not tested.

The stimulus is followed by a question that states your task—for example, to find the assumption, to strengthen the argument, or to identify parallel reasoning. Then, five multiple-choice answers are presented.

Table 1.1 is a breakdown by part of one of the September 2006 logical reasoning questions I showed you earlier:

Table 1.1

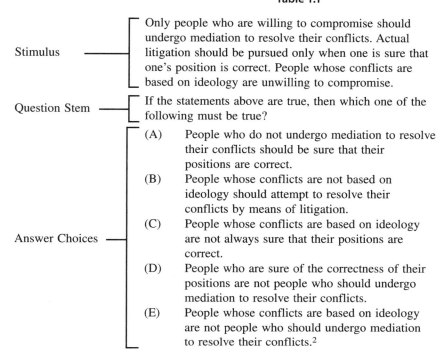

Stimulus — Only people who are willing to compromise should undergo mediation to resolve their conflicts. Actual litigation should be pursued only when one is sure that one's position is correct. People whose conflicts are based on ideology are unwilling to compromise.

Question Stem — If the statements above are true, then which one of the following must be true?

Answer Choices —

(A) People who do not undergo mediation to resolve their conflicts should be sure that their positions are correct.

(B) People whose conflicts are not based on ideology should attempt to resolve their conflicts by means of litigation.

(C) People whose conflicts are based on ideology are not always sure that their positions are correct.

(D) People who are sure of the correctness of their positions are not people who should undergo mediation to resolve their conflicts.

(E) People whose conflicts are based on ideology are not people who should undergo mediation to resolve their conflicts.[2]

Breakdown of Question Types

The 24–26 questions in each Logical Reasoning section are drawn from 12 common question types asked consistently on past LSATs. Kaplan research shows that the number of questions from each category is predictable, although not exact.

Logical Reasoning will comprise two of the four scored sections on your LSAT. You will see a total of approximately 50 scored Logical Reasoning questions out of the 100–101 total scored questions on test day. Half the test! And far more than the 22–24 Logic Games questions.

I will extensively review each question type in Part II of this book. For now, I'll provide you with an introduction to give you some context for the strategies you'll be learning in the meantime. Ultimately, your goal is to integrate this information in your approach to Logical Reasoning and to become more efficient and accurate in completing the sections to increase your score.

In Table 1.2, I've identified the 12 common Logical Reasoning question types, what each question type asks, the number of questions of each type that typically appear, and a sample question for each type.

[2]PrepTest 50, Sec. 4, Q 10

Table 1.2

Question Type	Task	Number of Questions	Sample Question
Assumption	Find the unstated assumption the author makes to go from the evidence provided to the conclusion reached.	8	Which one of the following is an assumption on which the argument depends?
Strengthen	Identify information that can be added to the argument to make it more likely to be so; in other words, to make the assumption of the argument more probable.	8 (Strengthen and Weaken combined)	Which one of the following, if true, most supports the argument?
Weaken	Identify information that can be added to the argument to make it less likely to be so; in other words, to make the assumption of the argument less probable.		Which one of the following, if true, most seriously weakens the argument?
Flaw	Determine the error the author makes in going from the evidence to the conclusion.	8	Which one of the following, if true, identifies a flaw in the plan for the program?
Inference	Find the answer that must be true based on the information provided in the stimulus.	7	If the statements above are true, then which one of the following must be true?
Principle	Identify a general rule that governs or matches a specific situation.	5	The situation described above most closely conforms to which one of the following principles?
Paradox	Provide an alternative explanation or factor to make sense of two facts that seem contradictory.	4	Which of the following would resolve the apparent discrepancy above?
Parallel Reasoning	Identify the choice that contains the same kind of reasoning as the stimulus.	3	The reasoning above is most closely paralleled in which one of the following?
Method of Argument	Explain how an author's argument is put together.	2	Which one of the following describes the author's argumentative strategy?

(continued)

Question Type	Task	Number of Questions	Sample Question
Point at Issue	Identify the issue on which two speakers present differing opinions.	1	Jack and Jeff disagree over whether . . .
Role of a Statement	Determine the function of a given statement in the argument.	2	The assertion that the company must increase production plays which of the following roles in the president's argument?
Main Point	Find the central claim presented in the author's argument.	2	Which one of the following most accurately expresses the main point of the argument?

LOGICAL REASONING SKILLS IN EVERYDAY LIFE

Over the years, most of my students have approached the Logical Reasoning section of the LSAT with some degree of trepidation. After all, the term "logical reasoning" sounds like some lofty endeavor, something practiced in the ivory towers of law schools or in judicial chambers. This couldn't be further from the truth. Logical reasoning is a common practice and something you use in your personal, academic, and professional lives. In fact, you've probably invoked logical reasoning before you had any inkling of what is was. Consider this scenario:

Parent: You can't go to the party tonight. You were out late last night.

Teenager: That's not fair! All my friends are going to the party. Even Andrew's mom is letting him go.

Does this sound familiar? It provides an excellent example of how pervasive logical reasoning is in everyday life. The point at issue between the parent and teenager is whether the teenager should be able to go to the party. Both sides present an argument. The parent concludes the teenager will miss the party and supports it with evidence that he was out late the previous evening. The teenager concludes the decision is not fair because all his friends will be there and he should be able to do what his friends do.

In this situation, the argument may continue in a variety of ways. The parent may come back with a statement like, "I don't care what your friends are doing. If they all shaved their heads, would you shave yours, too?" The teenager might try to negotiate and offer to do extra chores for the week. If a scenario such as this one were presented on the LSAT, you would not be asked to decide whether the parent's decision is fair or whether the teenager should be allowed to attend the party. Instead, you would be asked to analyze the arguments—possibly by identifying the parent's assumption (going to a party means the teenager will be out late), by finding the flaw in the teenager's argument (he shifts scope from staying out late to doing what his friends do, but does not address the argument at hand), or by describing the teenager's method of argument (presenting group behavior and referring to an "expert", i.e., his friend's mom).

Surely you've engaged in logical reasoning in some respect, so the concept is not completely foreign to you. The LSAT and your legal pursuits just require you to take it to a more sophisticated, purposeful level. You must be able to understand the structure of an argument or statement, break it down to its basic elements, and recognize the impact of additional information. To succeed in law school and a law-related profession, you must develop and improve your logical reasoning abilities. And to succeed on the LSAT, you need a plan of action. Fortunately for you, I'll show you the best way to handle anything the Logical Reasoning section can throw at you: the Kaplan Method.

THE IMPORTANCE OF A STRATEGY

The Kaplan Method for Logical Reasoning

Has this ever happened to you on a multiple-choice test? You read the text. You read the question. Then, you go back to reread the text looking for information to answer the question. You read the question again to remind yourself what was asked. Finally, you read each answer choice and check it once more against the paragraph. You rack your brain trying to find the right answer. When you look up at the clock you notice that five minutes have passed and you still have 20 more questions to answer in the final 18 minutes.

Ultimately, that "process" is time consuming and does not necessarily get you to the correct answer. Because you didn't have a plan of action, you probably felt rushed, frustrated, and anxious. I'm not going to let that happen to you again. I'm going to introduce you to the Kaplan Method, which has helped thousands of my students over the years improve their logical reasoning performance.

From now until test day, work through every Logical Reasoning question by taking the following steps:

THE KAPLAN METHOD FOR LOGICAL REASONING

STEP 1 Identify the Question Type
READ the question stem to identify the question type and determine your task.

STEP 2 Untangle the Stimulus
READ the stimulus to find the information you need to answer the question.

STEP 3 Make a Prediction
USE the information to make effective predictions to locate the right answer quickly and efficiently.

STEP 4 Evaluate the Answer Choices
FIND the answer choice that best matches your prediction.

Step 1. Identify the Question Type

Read the question stem to identify the question type. This step may seem counterintuitive because the question stem is presented after the stimulus. However, reading the question stem first lets you identify the question type and determine your task as you read the stimulus. It also allows you to read the stimulus actively by pulling specific information that will help you answer the question.

Step 2. Untangle the Stimulus

Read the stimulus and examine it through the lens of the question type you identified in Step 1. In other words, as you read the stimulus, unpack it for the information you will need to answer the particular question. You will learn skills—analyzing arguments and using formal logic—in chapters 2 and 3 to help you complete this step. In Part II, you will apply your newly learned skills in the context of each Logical Reasoning question type and learn what information to read for based on the question type.

Step 3. Make a Prediction

Now that you've analyzed the information from the question stem and stimulus, it's time to think critically about the answer. You don't need to use complete sentences or formal language. You just need enough to move to the next step and sort through the answers. You also have to be ready for an answer that is similar to, but not an exact replica of, your prediction. This step is very important and is the one you will be most likely to skip. Don't! It will feel awkward in the beginning, but give it a chance. Once you practice it and get better, it will actually improve your speed and efficiency. Without this step, you are more likely to get distracted by wrong answers and waste time analyzing each answer and rechecking it against the stimulus.

Step 4. Evaluate the Answer Choices

Review the answer choices and determine which one best matches your prediction. Most often, one answer will stand out for you. If not, eliminate wrong answers and consider the common wrong answer traps. I'll have more on that later.

THE KAPLAN METHOD IN ACTION

Now I'll walk you through the examples I provided at the beginning of the chapter to demonstrate the Kaplan Method for Logical Reasoning. Again, the Method remains the same regardless of the question type; however, the application may change. I'll continue to break down the steps in the chapters ahead.

1. Typically, people who have diets high in saturated fat have an increased risk of heart disease. Those who replace saturated fat in their diets with unsaturated fat decrease their risk of heart disease. Therefore, people who eat a lot of saturated fat can lower their risk of heart disease by increasing their intake of unsaturated fat.

    Which one of the following, if assumed, most helps to justify the reasoning above?

    (A) People who add unsaturated fat to their diets will eat less food that is high in saturated fat.
    (B) Adding unsaturated fat to a diet brings health benefits other than a reduced risk of heart disease.
    (C) Diet is the most important factor in a person's risk of heart disease.
    (D) Taking steps to prevent heart disease is one of the most effective ways of increasing life expectancy.
    (E) It is difficult to move from a diet that is high in saturated fat to a diet that includes very little fat.[3]

Step 1. Identify the Question Type

Always start with the question stem. As you will learn, the phrase "justify the reasoning" identifies a Strengthen question.

Step 2. Untangle the Stimulus

Because this is a Strengthen question, the stimulus presents an argument. So, read the stimulus to determine the conclusion and evidence. The conclusion is signaled by "Therefore" and

---

[3]PrepTest 50, Sec. 4, Q 9

reads "people who eat a lot of saturated fat can lower their risk of heart disease by increasing their intake of unsaturated fat."

How does the author know that saturated fat eaters can lower their risk of heart disease by eating more unsaturated fat? The author presents evidence saying that replacing saturated fat with unsaturated fat in one's diet decreases the risk of heart disease.

Don't worry if you weren't able to distinguish the conclusion from the evidence at this point. In the next chapter, I'll discuss the skill of analyzing arguments in detail.

Step 3. Make a Prediction

Because a Strengthen question asks you to select an answer that makes the conclusion more likely to be true, you can confirm the assumption; in other words, state the gap that exists between the conclusion and evidence. Notice the subtle shift between the conclusion ("eating *more* unsaturated") and the evidence ("*replacing* saturated"). I can eat more unbuttered popcorn without cutting back on my porkrinds, so the author is making an assumption that eating more good foods with unsaturated fats *replaces* bad foods with saturated fats, rather than just being *more*.

The correct answer should confirm that assumption or make it more likely that the saturated fats really are being *replaced*.

Step 4. Evaluate the Answer Choices

Look over the answer choices to determine whether any match your prediction. Eureka! Choice (A) does perfectly. The more you practice the Logical Reasoning method before test day, the more confident you will be in your ability to spot the correct answer. You will be able to review answer choices quickly and move on when you've found the correct one.

It is also important to consider the wrong answer choices as you learn the Kaplan Method. So, why are the other answers wrong? The other benefits besides a reduced risk of heart disease, presented in choice (B), are outside the scope of the argument. Whether diet is the most important factor in a person's risk of heart disease, as stated in choice (C), is irrelevant to whether replacing saturated fats is one way to reduce the risk of heart disease. Life expectancy, discussed in choice (D), is also outside the scope of the argument. And choice (E)—whether it is difficult to switch from lots of saturated fats to very little fat—is not germane to the point; the argument talks about replacing one kind of fat for another, not cutting overall fat intake.

Now take a look at the second question.

2. Only people who are willing to compromise should undergo mediation to resolve their conflicts. Actual litigation should be pursued only when one is sure that one's position is correct. People whose conflicts are based on ideology are unwilling to compromise.

If the statements above are true, then which one of the following must be true?

(A) People who do not undergo mediation to resolve their conflicts should be sure that their positions are correct.

(B) People whose conflicts are not based on ideology should attempt to resolve their conflicts by means of litigation.

(C) People whose conflicts are based on ideology are not always sure that their positions are correct.

(D) People who are sure of the correctness of their positions are not people who should undergo mediation to resolve their conflicts.

(E) People whose conflicts are based on ideology are not people who should undergo mediation to resolve their conflicts.[4]

Step 1. Identify the Question Type

You will come to learn that the phrase "must be true" indicates an Inference question.

Step 2. Untangle the Stimulus

An Inference question typically presents a series of facts rather than an argument. Read the stimulus to make sure you understand each statement. The information is presented in formal logic, so you will need to translate the sentences and identify the contrapositive of each to best comprehend the statements.

I'll show you all the formal logic you need for the LSAT in chapter 3, but for now accept that the formal logic conversion goes like this:

Table 1.2

Statement	Formal Logic Translation and Contrapositive
Only people who are willing to compromise should undergo mediation to resolve their conflicts.	• If you should undergo mediation → you are willing to compromise • If you are not willing to compromise → you should not undergo mediation
Actual litigation should be pursued only when one is sure that one's position is correct.	• If you pursue litigation → you are sure your position is correct • If you are not sure your position is correct → you will not pursue litigation

(continued)

Statement	Formal Logic Translation and Contrapositive
People whose conflicts are based on ideology are unwilling to compromise.	• If your conflict is ideology-based → you are not willing to compromise • If you are willing to compromise → your conflict is not ideology-based

Step 3. Make a Prediction

Inference questions often require you to combine two statements or make a deduction: formal logic is a ready tool on Inference questions to help you do just that. You can link the third and first statements from question 2 like so: If your conflict is ideology-based → you are not willing to compromise → you should not undergo mediation.

Step 4. Evaluate the Answer Choices

As you review each answer choice, ask yourself whether it *must be true* based on the stimulus. If so, you have found the correct answer.

Choice (E) combines two of the formal logic statements and is the correct answer. If your conflict is ideology-based, then you are not willing to compromise; and if you are not willing to compromise, then you will not undergo mediation. Therefore, if your conflict is ideology-based, then you will not undergo mediation.

For choice (A), check the six formal logic statements you created. You know what happens if someone does undergo mediation, but not if they don't. Don't assume that people who do not undergo mediation must actually litigate, and thereby must be sure their positions are correct.

Choice (B) is wrong because based on the information, people whose conflicts are not based on ideology may be willing to compromise and thus maybe could use mediation.

Choice (C) tries to combine the statements about ideology-based conflict and litigation, but the terms of those statements don't allow us to make any such link.

Finally, in choice (D), even though sureness of belief in the correctness of one's position is necessary for litigation, there is not a statement that precludes people who are sure of their correctness from undergoing mediation, provided they are willing to compromise despite that sureness. You can't assume that people sure of their correctness will not be willing to compromise. Often on the LSAT, you will identify the assumptions of authors, but you must never make your own assumptions.

These steps may seem cumbersome now, but by learning the patterns of the LSAT and predicting what the correct answer should generally indicate, you will become a more efficient, effective, and accurate test taker, and not get distracted by complicated, yet erroneous, answers.

THE IMPORTANCE OF PRACTICE

No one plays a good, complete game when they are handed a basketball for the first time. No one plays a full concert the first day they learn to play the guitar. The same goes with the LSAT. Only after you practice the fundamentals and learn the steps can you become a proficient test taker. Be patient with yourself so you can learn and practice the Kaplan Method and logical reasoning skills and ultimately put together your best score on test day.

CHAPTER 2

ANALYZING ARGUMENTS

ARGUMENTS: THE FOUNDATION OF LEGAL STUDY
Definition of a Legal Argument

Arguments are a fundamental part of the study and practice of law. The ability to analyze arguments is a critical skill for a legal professional to master, so it's no surprise that it's tested on the LSAT. You might think of an argument as a shouting match in which the participants are often more irrational than reasonable. But an argument on the LSAT is simply a process of reasoning; the author makes a point and supports it with relevant evidence. The argument is what the author is trying to convince you of in the form of a supported point of view.

Components of an Argument

The majority of Logical Reasoning stimuli you'll see on test day will contain an argument. An argument consists of two parts: the conclusion—the main point the author is making—and the evidence—the information offered by the author to support the conclusion. Or, put more simply, the conclusion is the "what" of the argument and the first thing you will look for, and the evidence is the "why."

Look at this example from a previous LSAT and find the two parts of the argument:

> Having an efficient, attractive subway system makes
> good economic sense. So, the city needs to purchase new
> subway cars, since the city should always do what makes
> good economic sense.[1]

In the conclusion—signaled by the word "so"—the author declares that the city needs to purchase new subway cars. The author supports this course of action with evidence that answers the question, "Why does the city need to purchase new subway cars?" Here, the word "since" identifies the evidence—the city should always do what makes good economic sense. "Economic sense" is defined in the first sentence as having an efficient, attractive subway system.

Success in answering argument-based question types depends on your ability to break an argument down to its core components. In terms of the Kaplan Method you learned in the last chapter, once you identify the question as argument-based, you will analyze the argument in the second step.

In other words, you will read the stimulus specifically to identify the conclusion and the evidence. Consider the following statement:

Raymond should begin his LSAT preparation with Logical Reasoning.

Is it an argument? If you said no, then you're on the right track. This statement alone is not an argument. It is a recommendation to take a certain action, but no evidence is given to support it. Now, look at the next statement and decide whether it is an argument:

Logical Reasoning accounts for one-half of his LSAT score.

This statement is not an argument either. It could be used to support the previous recommendation, but by itself it does not form an argument. Only when the two statements are combined do you get a complete argument with a conclusion supported by evidence: Raymond should begin his LSAT preparation with Logical Reasoning because it accounts for one-half of his LSAT score.

Keywords Show You the Way

Logical Reasoning questions will ask you to analyze, in some form, the process by which the author moves from the evidence to the conclusion. Therefore, the first step in an argument-based question is to break down the argument into the conclusion and the evidence. There isn't a general rule about where the conclusion and evidence always appear in an argument, so you can't use location to determine the components. The conclusion could be the first sentence, followed by the evidence; it could be the last sentence with the evidence preceding it; or, it could be any sentence in between. Placement of the conclusion and evidence is a stylistic issue and not necessarily indicative of the argument's structure.

---

[1]PrepTest 34, Sec. 2, Q 2

So how can you find the conclusion and evidence in an argument? The test makers commonly use certain words in Logical Reasoning stimuli to signal the conclusion and evidence. Here is a list of some common conclusion Keywords:

- Therefore
- Hence
- Thus
- As a result
- It follows that
- Clearly

Here are some common evidence Keywords:

- Because
- Since
- As
- After all
- For

Also look for structure phrases such as "This is made clear from the fact that . . ." The word "this" indicates that the conclusion is in the preceding sentence and the following fact is the evidence.

Obviously, these lists are not exhaustive, and you will run across other Keywords. A good way to help you keep track of them is to circle them when you see them in the stimulus. This action will draw your attention to them and help you pause to consider their purpose.

No Keywords? No Problem

In a perfect world, you could identify the structure of every argument by using Keywords. However, it's not always that easy. Sometimes you won't have that luxury. If that is the case, don't worry.

There's another way to determine the argument's structure: It's called the one-sentence test. Ask yourself: What does the author want me to walk away thinking? In other words: Which sentence in the stimulus would the author choose to keep if limited to a single sentence? The answer to that question will be the conclusion. You can usually locate it by looking for a statement in which the author presents a recommendation, proposal, thesis, judgment, opinion, or disagreement.

Read the following stimulus and identify the conclusion and evidence:

> Clearly, State University's plan to renovate the football stadium must include additional construction to come into compliance with the Americans with Disabilities Act. After all, the building has no elevator, limiting access to the upper levels. In addition, it has no viewing areas for people in wheelchairs.

The word "clearly" points to the conclusion that the university's stadium renovation plans must include accommodations under the Americans with Disabilities Act (ADA). A piece of evidence is offered to support the conclusion—that the building does not have elevator access and lacks wheelchair viewing areas—and is signaled by "after all." The phrase "in addition" indicates that the sentence is continuing the thought before it and, in this case, is a piece of evidence.

Now suppose this argument appeared on test day without any Keywords.

> State University's plan to renovate the football stadium must include additional construction to come into compliance with the Americans with Disabilities Act. The building has no elevator, limiting access to the upper levels, and it has no viewing areas for people in wheelchairs.

Can you still identify the conclusion and evidence? Of course you can. The first sentence states the author's viewpoint and the following sentence provides reasons to support it. Try it another way. The stadium has no elevator and no viewing area; therefore, construction must include ADA accommodations. If you are still unsure, you can insert Keywords yourself to test your analysis of the argument. Or, try replacing the evidence with the conclusion: The stadium has no elevator and no viewing area because construction must include ADA accommodations. This does not make sense, so you know the first statement cannot be the evidence and the second cannot be the conclusion.

Bracket the Conclusion

Now that you've identified the conclusion and evidence, you'll need an easy way to keep track of them. A simple, effective method is to place brackets around the conclusion. In the argument you just examined, it looks like this:

> <Clearly, State University's plan to renovate the football stadium must include additional construction to come into compliance with the Americans with Disabilities Act.> After all, the building has no elevator, limiting access to the upper levels. In addition, it has no viewing areas for people in wheelchairs.

That one simple step allows you to isolate the conclusion and quickly find it as you go through the questions. From now until test day, do this to every argument you see. It'll soon become a habit that will help improve your speed and efficiency, and—more importantly—add points to your score.

DRILL: IDENTIFYING COMPONENTS OF AN ARGUMENT

Now that you've learned the difference between conclusions and evidence, it's time to practice on your own. Once you develop your argument-analysis skills, you'll be able to take on the questions in Part II.

On test day, you'll be using the Kaplan Method on every Logical Reasoning question you encounter. Here's where you are in the process now:

Step 1. Identify the Question Type

For purposes of this drill, the question is argument-based.

Step 2. Untangle the Stimulus

You are here.

Step 3. Make a Prediction

Step 4. Evaluate the Answer Choices

As you can see, there are two more steps. Step 1 has been done for you, as you'll be working with argument-based questions exclusively in this Drill. You'll learn about all the question types later in the book, but now, you're focusing on Step 2: Untangle the Stimulus.

Argument-based questions require you to read the stimulus and then break down the argument by looking for the conclusion and evidence. For the following LSAT arguments, (1) circle any Keywords, (2) bracket the conclusion, and (3) summarize the evidence. Detailed explanations follow.

1. Psychologist: There are theories that posit completely different causal mechanisms from those posited by Freudian psychological theory and that are more successful at predicting human behavior. Therefore, Freudian theories of behavior, no matter how suggestive or complex they are, ought to be abandoned in favor of these other theories.[2]

Evidence:

_____

_____

_____

2. Skeletal remains of early humans indicate clearly that our ancestors had fewer dental problems than we have. So, most likely, the diet of early humans was very different from ours.[3]

Evidence:

_____

_____

_____

3. Several legislators claim that the public finds many current movies so violent as to be morally offensive. However, these legislators have misrepresented public opinion. In a survey conducted by a movie industry guild, only 17 percent of respondents thought that movies are overly violent, and only 3 percent found any recent movie morally offensive. These low percentages are telling, because the respondents see far more current movies than does the average moviegoer.[4]

Evidence:

_____

_____

_____

4. In countries where government officials are neither selected by free elections nor open to criticism by a free press, the lives of citizens are controlled by policies they have had no role in creating. This is why such countries are prone to civil disorder, in spite of the veneer of calm such countries often present to a visitor. When people do not understand the purpose of the restrictions placed on their behavior they have a greater tendency to engage in civil disorder as an expression of their frustration.[5]

Evidence:

_____

_____

_____

5. Everyone likes repertory theater. Actors like it because playing different roles each night decreases their level of boredom. Stagehands like it because changing sets every night means more overtime and, thus, higher pay. Theater managers like it because, if plays that reflect audience demand are chosen for production, most performances generate large revenues. It is evident, therefore, that more theaters should change to repertory.[6]

Evidence:

_____

_____

_____

6. Investment banker: Democracies require free-market capitalist economies, because a more controlled economy is incompatible with complete democracy. But history shows that repressive measures against certain capitalistic developments are required during the transition from a totalitarian regime to a democracy. Thus, people who bemoan the seemingly anticapitalistic measures certain governments are currently taking are being hasty.[7]

Evidence:

_____

_____

_____

[2]PrepTest 40, Sec. 1, Q 5
[3]PrepTest 40, Sec. 1, Q 6
[4]PrepTest 40, Sec. 1, Q 12

[5]PrepTest 40, Sec. 1, Q 16
[6]PrepTest 40, Sec. 3, Q 8
[7]PrepTest 40, Sec. 3, Q 20

7. The number of applications for admission reported by North American Ph.D. programs in art history has declined in each of the last four years. We can conclude from this that interest among recent North American college and university graduates in choosing art history as a career has declined in the last four years.[8]

Evidence:

_____

_____

_____

8. Air traffic controllers and nuclear power plant operators are not allowed to work exceptionally long hours, because to do so would jeopardize lives. Yet physicians in residency training are typically required to work 80-hour weeks. The aforementioned restrictions on working exceptionally long hours should also be applied to resident physicians, since they too are engaged in work of a life-or-death nature.[9]

Evidence:

_____

_____

_____

9. Studies have shown that specialty sports foods contain exactly the same nutrients in the same quantities as do common foods from the grocery store. Moreover, sports foods cost from two to three times more than regular foods. So very few athletes would buy sports foods were it not for expensive advertising campaigns.[10]

Evidence:

_____

_____

_____

10. Traditionally, students at Kelly University have evaluated professors on the last day of class. But some professors at Kelly either do not distribute the paper evaluation forms or do so selectively, and many students cannot attend the last day of class. Soon, students will be able to use school computers to evaluate their professors at any time during the semester. Therefore, evaluations under the new system will accurately reflect the distribution of student opinion about teaching performance.[11]

Evidence:

_____

_____

_____

Explanations

1. Psychologist: There are theories that posit completely
    different causal mechanisms from those posited by
    Freudian psychological theory and that are more
    successful at predicting human behavior.
    (Therefore,) <Freudian theories of behavior, no
    matter how suggestive or complex they are, ought
    to be abandoned in favor of these other theories.>[12]

The Keyword "therefore" directs you right to the conclusion. To find the evidence, all you need to do is ask yourself why the author recommends abandoning Freud's behavior theory.

Evidence: Some non-Freudian theories are better at predicting human behavior than Freudian theory.

Don't worry if you didn't phrase the evidence exactly like I did. As long as you got the gist of it, you're on the right track.

2. Skeletal remains of early humans indicate clearly that
    our ancestors had fewer dental problems than we have.
    (So,) <most likely, the diet of early humans was very
    different from ours.>[13]

The conclusion Keyword in this argument is "so," which points to the conclusion that early humans ate differently than we do.

Evidence: Our ancestors had fewer dental problems than we do.

3. Several legislators claim that the public finds many
    current movies so violent as to be morally offensive.
    (However,) <these legislators have misrepresented public
    opinion.> In a survey conducted by a movie industry
    guild, only 17 percent of respondents thought that
    movies are overly violent, and only 3 percent found any
    recent movie morally offensive. These low percentages
    are telling, because the respondents see far more current
    movies than does the average moviegoer.[14]

The author presents a claim in the first sentence and then signals his disagreement by using the word "however." He concludes that legislators misrepresented public opinion about current movies and uses a survey to defend his conclusion.

Evidence: A movie industry guild survey found that 17% of respondents found movies overly violent and 3% said any recent movie is morally offensive.

---

[12]PrepTest 40, Sec. 1, Q 5
[13]PrepTest 40, Sec. 1, Q 6
[14]PrepTest 40, Sec. 1, Q 12

4. In countries where government officials are neither selected by free elections nor open to criticism by a free press, the lives of citizens are controlled by policies they have had no role in creating. (This is why) <such countries are prone to civil disorder,> in spite of the veneer of calm such countries often present to a visitor. When people do not understand the purpose of the restrictions placed on their behavior, they have a greater tendency to engage in civil disorder as an expression of their frustration.[15]

Remember, evidence answers why the conclusion is so. When the author says "This is why," she is pointing to the conclusion. In this case, the conclusion splits the evidence. The first sentence states that citizens have no input in governmental policies in despotic countries. The last sentence explains that people who don't understand the policies that control their lives tend to participate in civil disorder.

Evidence: Citizens in these countries have no input in policies that control their lives and they don't understand the purpose of the laws that control them.

5. Everyone likes repertory theater. Actors like it because playing different roles each night decreases their level of boredom. Stagehands like it because changing sets every night means more overtime and, thus, higher pay. Theater managers like it because, if plays that reflect audience demand are chosen for production, most performances generate large revenues. (It is evident) (therefore,) that <more theaters should change to repertory.>[16]

The author recommends that more theaters should change to repertory because everyone likes it. He then lists different groups who like repertory theater and their rationale for enjoying it.

Evidence: Everyone likes repertory theater, although for different reasons.

6. Investment banker: Democracies require free-market capitalist economies, because a more controlled economy is incompatible with complete democracy. But history shows that repressive measures against certain capitalistic developments are required during the transition from a totalitarian regime to a democracy. (Thus,) <people who bemoan the seemingly anticapitalistic measures certain governments are currently taking are being hasty.>[17]

The investment banker concludes that complaints about certain governments' anticapitalistic actions are premature. Why? Check the evidence statement below.

---

[15]PrepTest 40, Sec. 1, Q 16

[16]PrepTest 40, Sec. 3, Q 8

[17]PrepTest 40, Sec. 3, Q 20

Evidence: Anticapitalist measures are necessary during the transition from a totalitarian regime to a democracy.

7. The number of applications for admission reported by North American Ph.D. programs in art history has declined in each of the last four years. (We can conclude from this) that <interest among recent North American college and university graduates in choosing art history as a career has declined in the last four years.>[18]

The author directs you right to the conclusion with the Keywords "We can conclude from this." The author's conclusion is that interest in art history as a career is down among North American graduates. He bases this on the evidence that admission applications for North American doctoral programs in art history are down.

Evidence: Application numbers are down for North American Ph.D. art history programs over the past four years.

8. Air traffic controllers and nuclear power plant operators are not allowed to work exceptionally long hours, because to do so would jeopardize lives. Yet physicians in residency training are typically required to work 80-hour weeks. <The aforementioned restrictions on working exceptionally long hours should also be applied to resident physicians,> (since) they too are engaged in work of a life-or-death nature.[19]

Although the author doesn't use any conclusion Keywords, "since" points to the evidence in the argument that supports the statement preceding it. The author supports the conclusion that long work hours should be limited for resident physicians just like they are air traffic controllers and nuclear power plant operators with the evidence that they all face life-or-death issues at work.

Evidence: The work of residents, like air traffic controllers and nuclear plant operators, involves life-or-death decisions and responsibilities.

9. Studies have shown that specialty sports foods contain exactly the same nutrients in the same quantities as do common foods from the grocery store. Moreover, sports foods cost from two to three times more than regular foods. (So) <very few athletes would buy sports foods were it not for expensive advertising campaigns.>[20]

This argument determines that athletes buy sports foods because of the advertising. The author's rationale is that sports foods have the same nutrition as traditional groceries, but cost more.

---

[18]PrepTest 40, Sec. 3, Q 26
[19]PrepTest 46, Sec. 2, Q 10
[20]PrepTest 46, Sec. 2, Q 25

Evidence: Specialty sports foods have the same nutrients as common food from the grocery, yet they cost two to three times more.

10. Traditionally, students at Kelly University have evaluated professors on the last day of class. But some professors at Kelly either do not distribute the paper evaluation forms or do so selectively, and many students cannot attend the last day of class. Soon, students will be able to use school computers to evaluate their professors at any time during the semester. (Therefore,) <evaluations under the new system will accurately reflect the distribution of student opinion about teaching performance.>[21]

The author predicts that the new evaluation system will be more accurate than the traditional process for a number of reasons. She cites problems with the paper system and notes that the new process will always be accessible.

Evidence: There are problems with the traditional policy of paper teacher evaluations distributed on the last day of class. Students will soon be able to complete teacher evaluations anytime via the computer.

EFFECTIVELY ANALYZING ARGUMENTS EQUALS LSAT SUCCESS

You now have a good idea about what arguments are and how to identify their components. This is very important, because they form the foundation of the entire Kaplan Method for argument-based questions. You may be worried at this point that circling the Keywords and bracketing the conclusions will be too time-consuming to be useful on test day. But with practice, you'll soon find that marking up arguments becomes a natural and automatic part of your approach to Logical Reasoning. And as you'll see throughout the book, being able to quickly and effectively analyze an argument will significantly raise your LSAT score.

---

[21]PrepTest 46, Sec. 3, Q 17

CHAPTER 3

FORMAL LOGIC

If the economy is weak, then prices remain constant
although unemployment rises. But unemployment rises
only if investment decreases. Fortunately, investment is
not decreasing.[1]

Formal logic, like this example, is prevalent on the LSAT, and your ability to identify and interpret formal logic statements is imperative for your success. Over the years, I've seen how a stimulus like this one can intimidate and frustrate students. Such formal logic appears in Logical Reasoning stimuli as well as in Logic Game rules. In this chapter, I will focus on helping you recognize and translate formal logic in the Logical Reasoning section.

Recognizing and translating formal logic is a skill that you use in Step 2 of the Kaplan Method for Logical Reasoning when you untangle the stimulus and extract information from it. You also use it in Step 3 when formulating a prediction for the correct answer. As you hone this skill, you'll be able to take complex statements and transform them into a more manageable format. A strong command of formal logic is critical to improving your accuracy and efficiency on the LSAT, and in this chapter I'll show you how to achieve it.

---

[1]PrepTest 28, Sec. 1, Q 20

Rather than something tested on the LSAT, formal logic is one of the tools you use to help you answer questions on the LSAT. Like a carpenter uses and loves his favorite hammer, use and love your formal logic!

CONDITIONAL STATEMENTS
Necessary vs. Sufficient

Formal logic is all about conditional if-then statements. Every LSAT formal logic statement includes a sufficient condition and a necessary condition. Don't let these terms intimidate you; just use their normal definitions: "Sufficient" means "enough by itself" and "necessary" means "you need it." If a sufficient condition occurs, then the necessary condition will result. If the necessary condition occurs, the sufficient condition could result but is not required. Take a look at a basic example of a formal logic statement:

If you are taking a test, then you turn off your cell phone.

I will discuss the language that signals sufficient and necessary clauses later in this chapter. For now, understand that the sufficient condition is taking a test. What happens when you take a test? You get the necessary condition every time: your cell phone is turned off. Now, what if you turn off your cell phone? Can you identify the necessary result? Does a turned off cell phone mean you are taking a test? No, you could be taking a test but you don't have to be. You could be watching a movie, taking a nap, riding in a car, or doing absolutely nothing. Therefore, turning off your cell phone is not sufficient to know the necessary result.

Now, you may be thinking of a time when you took a test with your cell phone on and want to contradict the formal logic statement. Don't. On the LSAT, the formal logic statement says exactly what it means. The way a statement appears on the test dictates its meaning. The test makers do not want you to supplement the text.

If-then Statements

The most basic form of formal logic is an if-then statement. If X happens, then Y will result. The "if" (or the X) part of the statement is the sufficient condition, and the "then" (or the Y) part of the statement is the necessary condition. In other words, the "if" (X) part of the statement is sufficient for you to know that the "then" (Y) part of the statement will result. Therefore, you must be able to break statements down into their sufficient and necessary elements.

Consider the following example, and see whether you can identify the sufficient and necessary components:

If Riley travels to Europe, then he must have a valid passport.

The "if" identifies the "Riley travels to Europe" as the sufficient phrase, and the "then" identifies the "he must have a valid passport" as the necessary phrase. In other words, a valid passport is *necessary* for Riley's trip to Europe. Also, just knowing that Riley takes a trip to Europe is *sufficient* for you to know that he has a valid passport.

However, if Riley has a valid passport, does he have to take a trip to Europe? Not necessarily. He may or may not. Just knowing he has a valid passport does not tell us whether he takes a trip to Europe or anywhere. The valid passport is necessary, but not sufficient, for Riley to take a trip to Europe. Again, the result is necessary for the condition to occur, but the result is never sufficient by itself to know whether the condition must occur or has already.

Conditional Statements Practice

To help you better understand the idea of sufficient and necessary conditions, consider the following example:

Scott wants to go to a music festival and a ticket costs $100.

Each of the following statements tells you something that is sufficient (but not necessary), necessary (but not sufficient), or both sufficient and necessary in order for Scott to purchase the ticket. Consider each statement and label it accordingly.

Scott has $65.   _____

Scott has $140.   _____

Scott has $100.   _____

Here are the answers:

Scott has $65. *Necessary, but not sufficient.* If Scott doesn't have at least $65, there's no way he can have $100. $65 is not enough for him to buy the ticket, so it's not sufficient.

Scott has $140. *Sufficient, but not necessary.* He could buy the ticket and plenty more. So, it's sufficient for Scott to have $140, but it's not necessary that Scott has so much in order to get the ticket.

Scott has $100. *Sufficient and necessary.* Knowing that Scott has $100 means he has enough to buy a ticket. It's also necessary. If he doesn't have $100, he can't buy the ticket.

RECOGNIZING FORMAL LOGIC

Before you can use formal logic to help you untangle a stimulus, you must be able to recognize it on the test. An if-then statement is the most common form of formal logic, but formal logic can be stated in a variety of ways using different terms. On the Logical Reasoning section of the test, you must be prepared to recognize formal logic whenever it's used and in whatever form it is presented. But don't worry: there are Keywords to help you identify formal logic and determine which part of the statement is sufficient and which part is necessary. The following list of sufficient and necessary terms is by no means comprehensive, but it provides some of the most common indicators.

If this happens . . .	→	Then this is the result
X Sufficient words	→	**Y** Necessary words
If Any All Each Every When(ever) Always No None Never	→	Then Only Only if Unless Not/Never/No . . . unless Not/Never/No . . . without Necessary/Needed/Required Effect Result Must

Please note that the order of the terms in a statement does not indicate whether a term is sufficient or necessary. When evaluating a formal logic statement, always use the Keywords and the language of the terms to determine which clause is sufficient and which is necessary.

For example, "Every Friday night we order pizza for dinner" translates the same way as "We order pizza for dinner every Friday night." The sufficient term, "every Friday night," can appear in the beginning or at the end of the sentence. In either case, "every Friday night" is still the sufficient term.

Also, the chronology in which things happen doesn't determine the sufficient and necessary conditions. For example, consider the following statement: In order for it to rain, there must be clouds.

Even though the clouds appear in the sky before it starts raining, clouds are not the sufficient condition. Because clouds are necessary for rain, knowing that it is raining is sufficient for you to know that there are clouds.

COMMON FORMAL LOGIC TRANSLATIONS

Once you recognize that a statement includes formal logic, your next job is to translate it into a formal logic "equation." There are five basic statement types in which the X is always the sufficient condition and Y is always the necessary result. Although they use different terminology, each of these statement types means the same thing. They are logically equivalent, and you can write them using a shorthand equation to help you quickly identify the X and Y terms.

For example, look at the first statement in the following table: If you apply to law school, then you have to take the LSAT. This is the most straightforward type of formal logic statement, as it is written in "if-then" language. The X term, the sufficient element, is applying to law school. The Y term, the necessary result, is taking the LSAT.

Formal Logic in Text Form	Formal Logic Equation
If you apply to law school, then you have to take the LSAT.	If X, then Y
All students who apply to law school have to take the LSAT.	All X are Y
Only students who have taken the LSAT can apply to law school.	Only Y are X
You can apply to law school *only if* you have taken the LSAT.	X only if Y
No student can apply to law school *unless* he or she has taken the LSAT.	No X unless Y

Now look at the second statement: All students who apply to law school have to take the LSAT. What word tells you this is a formal logic statement? Check the list of indicators for sufficient and necessary words, and you will find "All." Whenever you see "all," translate the statement to the corresponding formal logic equation. Here, it's "All X are Y." The purpose of this step is to specifically identify the X and the Y. What are they in this case? The X is "students who apply to law school," and the Y is "have to take the LSAT."

Now try the next statement: Only students who have taken the LSAT can apply to law school. The "Only" dictates that this is a formal logic statement. Since "only" is a necessary word, what follows "only" is the necessary term. When you see "only," translate the statement to the matching formal logic equation which is "Only Y are X." Again, "taken the LSAT" is the Y and "apply to law school" is the X.

The next statement is a little trickier in that "X only if Y" looks like it combines a sufficient (if) and a necessary (only) indicator. The general rule is easy though. "Only if" combined is always just a necessary term and the related formal logic equation is "X only if Y." Once again, the X is "apply to law school" and the Y is "taken the LSAT." What if you saw the same language on the test but the order was different? Only if you take the LSAT can you apply to law school. Would that change the identity of the terms? Absolutely not. Taking the LSAT still follows "only if" and remains the necessary condition. Just reorder the phrases to return to an "X only if Y" format.

The final statement, the one with "unless," is always the hardest for my students. Start with the basics. "Unless" tells you this is a formal logic statement and what follows "unless" is the necessary term. So the Y is "taken the LSAT." The matching formal logic equation is "No X unless Y." Here is where an "unless" statement differs from the other formal logic translations. To determine the X, you must negate the phrase in the text. In this case, negate the "no" in "no student applies to law school" and you get "student applies to law school." "Student applies to law school" is the X.

Try a few variations of "No student applies to law school unless he or she has taken the LSAT" to cement your understanding. What if the sentence said, "Unless he or she has taken the LSAT, no student applies to law school?" The "unless" identifies it as formal logic, and specifically signals the necessary condition. So change the order of the phrases. Remember, "No X unless Y" is the same as "If X, then Y."

Regardless of the formal logic words and format, each statement yields the same X and Y equations. You must be able to identify formal logic when you see it, and you must be able to translate the text into the corresponding formal logic equation and identify the X and the Y terms.

Creating the "If X, then Y" Statement

Once you know the X and Y terms, your next step is to translate the statement into the basic "If X, then Y" format. When you write in this formal logic shorthand, use an arrow (→) to indicate "then." The phrase to the left of the arrow is the sufficient condition. The phrase to the right of the arrow is the necessary result. You can also drop "if" so you have less to write down.

Here are some examples from the sample formal logic statements you've seen in this chapter. Remember, first you identify formal logic language in the text. Next, you translate the statement into a formal logic equation and identify the X and Y terms. Then you create the basic X → Y statement.

Formal Logic in Text Form	Formal Logic Equation	Formal Logic Shorthand
If you are taking a test, then you must turn off your cell phone.	If X, then Y	Taking test → cell phone off
If Riley travels to Europe, then he must have a valid passport.	If X, then Y	Europe → have passport

(continued)

Formal Logic in Text Form	Formal Logic Equation	Formal Logic Shorthand
If you apply to law school, then you take the LSAT.	If X, then Y	Apply to law school → take LSAT
All students who apply to law school have to take the LSAT.	All X are Y	
Only students who have taken the LSAT are applying to law school.	Only Y are X	
You are applying to law school only if you have taken the LSAT.	X only if Y	
No student applies to law school unless he or she has taken the LSAT.	No X unless Y	

Formal Logic Translation Practice

Here's the stimulus that opened the chapter. Take a minute and try to work through the translation process and determine the X → Y statements.

> If the economy is weak, then prices remain constant although unemployment rises. But unemployment rises only if investment decreases. Fortunately, investment is not decreasing.[2]

1. Identify Formal Logic Language

2. Determine the Matching Equation(s)

3. Translate the Formal Logic

Here are the answers:

1. Identify Formal Logic Language

Note the "if-then" language in the first sentence and "only if" in the second sentence. Move forward with those two sentences.

2. Determine the Matching Equations

"If the economy is weak, then prices remain constant although unemployment rises." The first sentence uses the basic "If X, then Y" format.

---

[2]PrepTest 28, Sec. 1, Q 20

"But unemployment rises *only if* investment decreases." The formal logic equation represented in the second sentence is "X only if Y".

3. Translate the Formal Logic

Now you want to translate the formal logic into a shorthand version of the X → Y statement:

Economy weak → prices constant and unemployment rises

Unemployment rises → investment decreases

I know it seems like a lot of work to untangle a Logical Reasoning stimulus. Keep in mind that the more you practice with formal logic, the faster you will be able to spot and translate the statements.

There's just one more step to complete a formal logic translation: forming the contrapositive.

FORMING THE CONTRAPOSITIVE
Simple If-Then Statements

After you've translated a statement into X → Y form, you will then write its contrapositive, a confusing-sounding aspect of formal logic that's actually quite straightforward.

A contrapositive is the logical equivalent of any conditional formal logic statement with the sufficient and necessary terms reversed and negated. Put simply, the contrapositive is equally valid as the original statement and is nothing more than another way to express the truth of the original statement. The reason you write the contrapositive is to complete your understanding of the formal logic statement. The X → Y statement provides a simpler version of the sentence, and the contrapositive is the only other statement you can know to be true about the statement.

While formal logic language can appear in any Logical Reasoning question type, it is most prevalent in Inference, Parallel Reasoning, and Principle questions. So, for example, an Inference question will ask you to identify the answer that *must be true* based on the information in the stimulus. If the stimulus is presented in formal logic terms, there are only two things that must be true from it, the X → Y statement and its contrapositive. You'll have an opportunity to work with formal logic in the context of different question types in Part II. For now, I'll show you how to form a statement's contrapositive.

Start with the statement in X → Y form

If you apply to law school, then you take the LSAT.

Apply to law school → take the LSAT

Then reverse and negate the sufficient and necessary terms.

Don't take LSAT → can't apply to law school

That's all you have to do in this case to form the contrapositive. One step and you're done. Now you try one. I'll give you a statement and then you reverse and negate it to form the contrapositive.

If you are taking a test, then you turn off your cell phone.

Translation: _____

Contrapositive: _____

Here's the answer:

Translation: Taking test → cell phone off

Contrapositive: Cell phone not off → not taking test

Did you get the right answer? If you did, congratulations! If not, don't worry. You'll have plenty of opportunities to practice. But remember, this is an important fundamental skill to master by test day. Rest assured that the test makers will design wrong answers to catch students who cannot correctly interpret and contrapose formal logic statements.

Before I go on, here's a big caution: Never ever reverse without negating or negate without reversing. Doing so confuses the sufficient and necessary terms in the rule and will lead straight to wrong answers. With that in mind, let me move on to complex "if-then" statements.

Complex If-then Statements: Change "and" to "or"

When either of the clauses in a formal logic rule has more than one term linked with either "and" or "or," you have one more step in making the contrapositive. To see how it works, consider the following example:

If a play is by Shakespeare, then it is by a famous writer *and* it is by an English writer.

You can translate the formal logic statement this way: Play by Shakespeare → famous writer and English writer

Now, imagine you see a play and ask a friend, "Who wrote it?" Your friend answers, "I don't know the writer's name, but I know that he was relatively unknown." What can you infer? Right! The play isn't by Shakespeare.

Try it another way. This time, when you ask your friend who wrote the play, she says, "I don't know the writer's name, but I know he was Italian." Again, you can safely conclude that you're not looking at a work of Shakespeare.

Now put those two inferences together and compare them to the original statement. Here, you form the contrapositives by reversing and negating the terms and by changing "and" to "or." So, the contrapositive would be: Not famous writer or not an English writer → not a Play by Shakespeare

There are different ways to write the negation of a term. You could use words, such as "no", "don't", and "can't". You could also strike through the negative term or use a tilde (~). Use the symbols that are clearest to you, but whatever you choose to do, do it consistently.

That's what you need to know to form the correct contrapositives of any formal logic rule you will encounter on the LSAT. So remember the rules for forming the contrapositive of either a simple or complex formal logic statement.

TO FORM THE CONTRAPOSITIVE

STEP 1   Reverse and negate the sufficient and necessary terms.

STEP 2   If needed, change "and" to "or," or vice versa.

Using Contrapositives to Make Deductions

You must be clear on the deductions you can and can't make based on formal logic statements. Look at this statement:

> Every Friday night we order pizza for dinner.

For this statement, the matching formal logic equation is "Every X is Y." So Friday night is the sufficient term (X) and pizza for dinner is the necessary term (Y). Knowing that it is Friday night is sufficient to know that pizza will be ordered for dinner. Knowing that pizza was ordered for dinner means it could be Friday, but it doesn't have to be. So here is the information I know:

Statement: Every Friday night we order pizza for dinner.

Equation: Every X is Y

Shorthand: Friday night → pizza dinner (X → Y)

Contrapositive: Not pizza dinner → not Friday night (Not Y → Not X)

Given that the previous statements are true, which one of the following statements must also be true?

> If it is not Friday night, then we don't eat pizza for dinner.
> If we eat pizza for dinner, then it is Friday night.
> If we don't have pizza for dinner, then it is not Friday night.

The third statement, the contrapositive, is the only one of the three that you can infer from the original statement. The first statement negates the terms without reversing. The second statement reverses the terms without negating. The terms "not Friday night" and "pizza for dinner" are not sufficient terms, so you can't know the necessary result if they happen.

I'll walk you through one more example. Read the following statement:

> If Jonathan votes, then he must be registered and 18 or older.

The "if" identifies Jonathan voting as the sufficient part of the statement. Jonathan voting is sufficient to know that he must be registered and he must be 18 or older. Being registered and 18 or older is the necessary result of the sufficient clause. Can you reverse the terms and say, "If Jonathan is registered and 18 or older, then he votes?" No. He could vote under those circumstances, but he doesn't have to.

So here's how you would work through this statement on the LSAT:

> If Jonathan votes, he is registered and he is 18 or older.

Step 1. Identify Formal Logic Language

<u>If</u> Jonathan votes, he is registered and he is 18 or older.

Step 2. Determine the Matching Equation

If X, then Y and Z

Step 3. Translate the Formal Logic

Jonathan votes → registered and 18+ (X → Y and Z)

Step 4. Form the Contrapositive

Not registered or not 18+ → Jonathan does not vote (No Y or no Z → no X)

So from the original statement and the contrapositive, you know what happens if Jonathan votes, and you know what the result is if Jonathan is not registered or if he's not 18 or older. That's it. You can't know the result if Jonathan does not vote. You also can't know the result if Jonathan is registered and he's 18 or older. Again, they are not sufficient terms.

FORMAL LOGIC REVIEW

I've introduced a lot of material in this chapter, so here's a summary of the important points to remember regarding formal logic statements.

First, identify formal logic language in the stimulus. Then, determine the matching equation. Translate the statement to identify the X and the Y terms and form the X → Y statement. Finally, form the contrapositive by reversing and negating the sufficient and necessary terms, (and if needed, change "and" to "or," or vice versa).

Once again, return to the stimulus introduced at the beginning of this chapter to see this process in action.

> If the economy is weak, then prices remain constant although unemployment rises. But unemployment rises only if investment decreases. Fortunately, investment is not decreasing.[3]

You'll recall the first three steps of the transformation:

Step 1. Identify Formal Logic Language

The if-then language in sentence one and the "only if" in sentence two signal formal logic.

Step 2. Determine the Matching Equations

"If the economy is weak, then prices remain constant although unemployment rises." The first sentence is presented in the basic "If X, then Y" format.

"But unemployment rises *only* if investment decreases." The formal logic equation represented in the second sentence is "X only if Y."

Step 3. Translate the Formal Logic

Now, translate the formal logic into a shorthand version of the X → Y statement:

Economy weak → prices constant and unemployment rises

Unemployment rises → investment decreases

Step 4. Form the Contrapositive

Prices not constant or unemployment not rise → economy not weak

Investment does not decrease → unemployment does not rise

In the final sentence of the original stimulus, you are told that investment is not decreasing. So you can be assured from sentence two's contrapositive that unemployment does not rise. Therefore, you can use sentence one's contrapositive to determine that the economy is not weak.

Again, you've covered a lot of information here. The following two Drills will help you practice your formal logic skills.

---

[3]PrepTest 28, Sec. 1, Q 20

DRILL: PRACTICING FORMAL LOGIC

Read the following statements, then underline the terms that indicate formal logic, identify the matching equation, write the formal logic translation, and then form the contrapositive. The first one has been done for you.

1. Statement: We have pizza for dinner <u>every</u> Friday night.

   Formal Logic Equation: Every X is Y

   Formal Logic Shorthand: Friday night → pizza for dinner

   Contrapositive: Not pizza for dinner → not Friday night

2. Statement: All employees must wash their hands.

   Formal Logic Equation: _____

   Formal Logic Shorthand: _____

   Contrapositive: _____

3. Statement: Use this product only if the seal is intact.

   Formal Logic Equation: _____

   Formal Logic Shorthand: _____

   Contrapositive: _____

4. Statement: Don't open the test unless the proctor says so.

   Formal Logic Equation: _____

   Formal Logic Shorthand: _____

   Contrapositive: _____

5. Statement: All children under 13 must be accompanied by an adult.

   Formal Logic Equation: _____

   Formal Logic Shorthand: _____

   Contrapositive: _____

6. Statement: Do not eat this product if you are allergic to peanuts.

   Formal Logic Equation: _____

   Formal Logic Shorthand: _____

   Contrapositive: _____

7. Statement: Put your pencil down when the proctor calls time.

   Formal Logic Equation: _____

   Formal Logic Shorthand: _____

   Contrapositive: _____

8. Statement: She drinks hot chocolate only when it is cold outside.

   Formal Logic Equation: _____

   Formal Logic Shorthand: _____

   Contrapositive: _____

9. Statement: If you want to reach the operator or leave a message, press "0."

   Formal Logic Equation: _____

   Formal Logic Shorthand: _____

   Contrapositive: _____

10. Statement: Each graduate must wear a cap and gown.

    Formal Logic Equation: _____

    Formal Logic Shorthand: _____

    Contrapositive: _____

11. Statement: The President cannot go anywhere unless the secret service goes with her.

    Formal Logic Equation: _____

    Formal Logic Shorthand: _____

    Contrapositive: _____

12. Statement: No service without shirt and shoes.

    Formal Logic Equation: _____

    Formal Logic Shorthand: _____

    Contrapositive: _____

13. Statement: Only public libraries lend DVDs for free.

    Formal Logic Equation: _____

    Formal Logic Shorthand: _____

    Contrapositive: _____

14. Statement: Larry has tickets to each home football game.

    Formal Logic Equation: _____

    Formal Logic Shorthand: _____

    Contrapositive: _____

15. Statement: Whenever you're ready, give me a call.

    Formal Logic Equation: _____

    Formal Logic Shorthand: _____

    Contrapositive: _____

16. Statement: No employee took vacation in February.

    Formal Logic Equation: _____

    Formal Logic Shorthand: _____

    Contrapositive: _____

17. Statement: Charlie eats strawberries unless he eats bananas.

    Formal Logic Equation: _____

    Formal Logic Shorthand: _____

    Contrapositive: _____

18. Statement: Charlie does not eat strawberries unless he eats bananas.

    Formal Logic Equation: _____

    Formal Logic Shorthand: _____

    Contrapositive: _____

19. Statement: Scott drinks coffee and reads the newspaper every morning.

    Formal Logic Equation: _____

    Formal Logic Shorthand: _____

    Contrapositive: _____

20. Statement: Airplane travel requires a photo ID.

    Formal Logic Equation: _____

    Formal Logic Shorthand: _____

    Contrapositive: _____

Explanations

1. Statement: We have pizza for dinner every Friday night.

    Formal Logic Equation: Every X is Y

    Formal Logic Shorthand: Friday night → pizza for dinner

    Contrapositive: Not pizza for dinner → not Friday night

2. Statement: <u>All</u> employees <u>must</u> wash their hands.

    Formal Logic Equation: All X must Y

    Formal Logic Shorthand: Employee → wash hands

    Contrapositive: Don't wash hands → not an employee

3. Statement: Use this product <u>only if</u> the seal is intact.

    Formal Logic Equation: X only if Y

    Formal Logic Shorthand: Use product → seal is intact

    Contrapositive: Seal is not intact → don't use product

4. Statement: <u>Don't</u> open the test <u>unless</u> the proctor says so.

    Formal Logic Equation: No X unless Y

    Formal Logic Shorthand: Test open → proctor says to open it

    Contrapositive: Proctor does not say to open the test → the test is not open

5. Statement: <u>All</u> children under 13 <u>must</u> be accompanied by an adult.

    Formal Logic Equation: All X must Y

    Formal Logic Shorthand: Under 13 → with an adult

    Contrapositive: Not with an adult → not under 13

6. Statement: Do not eat this product <u>if</u> you are allergic to peanuts.

    Formal Logic Equation: If X, then not Y

    Formal Logic Shorthand: Allergic to peanuts → do not eat this product

    Contrapositive: Eat this product → not allergic to peanuts

7. Statement: Put your pencil down <u>when</u> the proctor calls time.

    Formal Logic Equation: If X, then Y

    Formal Logic Shorthand: Proctor calls time → put your pencil down

    Contrapositive: Pencil is not down → proctor has not called time

8. Statement: She drinks hot chocolate <u>only when</u> it is cold outside.

    Formal Logic Equation: X only if Y

    Formal Logic Shorthand: Drinking hot chocolate → cold outside

    Contrapositive: Not cold outside → not drinking hot chocolate

9. Statement: <u>If</u> you want to reach the operator or leave a message, press "0."

    Formal Logic Equation: If X or Y, then Z

    Formal Logic Shorthand: Operator or message → press "0"

    Contrapositive: Not press "0" → no operator and no message

10. Statement: <u>Each</u> graduate <u>must</u> wear a cap and gown to walk in the ceremony.

    Formal Logic Equation: Each X must Y and Z

    Formal Logic Shorthand: Graduate → wear cap and gown to walk in the ceremony

    Contrapositive: Don't wear a cap or don't wear a gown → not a graduate

11. Statement: The President cannot go anywhere <u>unless</u> the secret service goes with her.

    Formal Logic Equation: No X unless Y

    Formal Logic Shorthand: President goes anywhere → secret service is with her

    Contrapositive: Secret service is not with her → President cannot go

12. Statement: <u>No</u> service <u>without</u> shirt and shoes.

    Formal Logic Equation: No X unless Y and Z

    Formal Logic Shorthand: Service → shirt and shoes

    Contrapositive: If no shirt or no shoes → no service

13. Statement: <u>Only</u> public libraries lend DVDs for free.

    Formal Logic Equation: Only Y are X

    Formal Logic Shorthand: DVD lent for free → public library

    Contrapositive: Not public library → DVD not lent for free

14. Statement: Larry has tickets to <u>each</u> home football game.

    Formal Logic Equation: If X, then Y

    Formal Logic Shorthand: Home football game → Larry has tickets

    Contrapositive: Larry does not have tickets → not home football game

15. Statement: <u>Whenever</u> you're ready, give me a call.

    Formal Logic Equation: If X, then Y

    Formal Logic Shorthand: Ready → call me

    Contrapositive: Don't call me → not ready

16. Statement: <u>No</u> employee took vacation in February.

     Formal Logic Equation: "No X are Y" becomes "If X, then not Y"

     Formal Logic Shorthand: Employee → no vacation in February

     Contrapositive: Vacation in February → not an employee

17. Statement: Charlie eats strawberries <u>unless</u> he eats bananas.

     Formal Logic Equation: "X unless Y" becomes "If not X, then Y"

     Formal Logic Shorthand: No strawberries → bananas

     Contrapositive: No bananas → strawberries

18. Statement: Charlie does <u>not</u> eat strawberries <u>unless</u> he eats bananas.

     Formal Logic Equation: "No X unless Y" because "if X then Y"

     Formal Logic Shorthand: Strawberries → Bananas

     Contrapositive: no Bananas → no Strawberries

19. Statement: Scott drinks coffee and reads the newspaper <u>every</u> morning.

     Formal Logic Equation: Every X is Y and Z

     Formal Logic Shorthand: Morning → coffee and paper

     Contrapositive: Not coffee or not paper → not morning

20. Statement: Airplane travel <u>requires</u> a photo ID.

     Formal Logic Equation: X only if Y

     Formal Logic Shorthand: Airplane travel → photo ID

     Contrapositive: No photo ID → no airplane travel

DRILL: IDENTIFYING FORMAL LOGIC AND FORMING CONTRAPOSITIVES

The following stimuli appeared on previously released LSATs. Underline the formal logic indicators. Then, write out the formal logic statements and form their contrapositives. Hint: Some stimuli may have more than one formal logic statement.

1. If legislators are to enact laws that benefit constituents, they must be sure to consider what the consequences of enacting a proposed law will actually be. Contemporary legislatures fail to enact laws that benefit constituents. Concerned primarily with advancing their own political careers, legislators present legislation in polemical terms; this arouses in their colleagues either repugnance or enthusiasm for the legislation.[4]

2. All works of art are beautiful and have something to teach us. Thus, since the natural world as a whole is both beautiful and instructive, it is a work of art.[5]

3. Only people who are willing to compromise should undergo mediation to resolve their conflicts. Actual litigation should be pursued only when one is sure that one's position is correct. People whose conflicts are based on ideology are unwilling to compromise.[6]

4. If Juan went to the party, it is highly unlikely that Maria would have enjoyed the party. But in fact it turned out that Maria did enjoy the party; therefore, it is highly unlikely that Juan was at the party.[7]

5. Sonya: Anyone who lives without constant awareness of the fragility and precariousness of human life has a mind clouded by illusion. Yet those people who are perpetually cognizant of the fragility and precariousness of human life surely taint their emotional outlook on existence.[8]

6. Philosopher: An action is morally good if it both achieves the agent's intended goal and benefits someone other than the agent.[9]

7. Only experienced salespeople will be able to meet the company's selling quota. Thus, I must not count as an experienced salesperson, since I will be able to sell only half the quota.[10]

8. Expert: What criteria distinguish addictive substances from nonaddictive ones? Some have suggested that any substance that at least some habitual users can cease to use is nonaddictive. However, if this is taken to be the sole criterion of nonaddictiveness, some substances that most medical experts classify as prime examples of addictive substances would be properly deemed nonaddictive. Any adequate set of criteria for determining a substance's addictiveness must embody the view, held by these medical experts, that a substance is addictive only if withdrawal from its habitual use causes most users extreme psychological and physiological difficulty.[11]

9. Whoever murdered Jansen was undoubtedly in Jansen's office on the day of the murder, and both Samantha and Herbert were in Jansen's office on that day. If Herbert had committed the murder, the police would have found either his fingerprints or his footprints at the scene of the crime. But if Samantha was the murderer, she would have avoided leaving behind footprints or fingerprints. The police found fingerprints but no footprints at the scene of the crime. Since the fingerprints were not Herbert's, he is not the murderer. Thus Samantha must be the killer.[12]

10. Ecologists predict that the incidence of malaria will increase if global warming continues or if the use of pesticides is not expanded. But the use of pesticides is known to contribute to global warming, so it is inevitable that we will see an increase in malaria in the years to come.[13]

[4]PrepTest 50, Sec. 2, Q 14
[5]PrepTest 50, Sec. 4, Q 2
[6]PrepTest 50, Sec. 4, Q 10
[7]PrepTest 50, Sec. 4, Q 14
[8]PrepTest 50, Sec. 4, Q 15
[9]PrepTest 51, Sec. 1, Q 9

[10]PrepTest 51, Sec. 1, Q 20
[11]PrepTest 51, Sec. 3, Q 14
[12]PrepTest 51, Sec. 3, Q 20
[13]PrepTest 51, Sec. 3, Q 24

Explanations

1. If legislators are to enact laws that benefit constituents,
    they <u>must</u> be sure to consider what the consequences of
    enacting a proposed law will actually be. Contemporary
    legislatures fail to enact laws that benefit constituents.
    Concerned primarily with advancing their own political
    careers, legislators present legislation in polemical
    terms; this arouses in their colleagues either repugnance
    or enthusiasm for the legislation.[14]

    Enact laws that benefit constituents → consider consequences of proposed law

    Don't consider consequences of proposed law → don't enact laws that benefit constituents

2. <u>All</u> works of art are beautiful and have something to
    teach us. Thus, since the natural world as a whole is
    both beautiful and instructive, it is a work of art.[15]

    Art → beautiful and teach us

    Not beautiful or not teach us → not art

3. <u>Only</u> people who are willing to compromise should
    undergo mediation to resolve their conflicts. Actual
    litigation should be pursued <u>only when</u> one is sure that
    one's position is correct. <u>People</u> whose conflicts are
    based on ideology are unwilling to compromise.[16]

    Undergo mediation → willing to compromise

    Not willing to compromise → not undergo mediation

    Litigation → position correct

    Position not correct → no litigation

    Conflict based on ideology → unwilling to compromise

    Willing to compromise → conflict not based on ideology

By connecting this string of logic, you can validly deduce the following:

Undergo mediation → willing to compromise → conflict not based on ideology

[14]PrepTest 50, Sec. 2, Q 14
[15]PrepTest 50, Sec. 4, Q 2
[16]PrepTest 50, Sec. 4, Q 10

4. <u>If</u> Juan went to the party, it is highly unlikely that Maria would have enjoyed the party. But in fact it turned out that Maria did enjoy the party; therefore, it is highly unlikely that Juan was at the party.[17]

> Juan to party → Maria likely not enjoy party
> Maria enjoy party → Juan likely not at party

5. Sonya: <u>Anyone</u> who lives without constant awareness of the fragility and precariousness of human life has a mind clouded by illusion. Yet those <u>people</u> who are perpetually cognizant of the fragility and precariousness of human life surely taint their emotional outlook on existence.[18]

> Live without constant awareness → mind clouded by illusion
> Mind not clouded by illusion → live with constant awareness

> Live with constant awareness → taint emotional outlook
> Don't taint emotional outlook → don't live with constant awareness

By connecting this string of logic, you can validly deduce the following:

Don't taint emotional outlook → don't live with constant awareness → mind clouded by illusion

6. Philosopher: An action is morally good <u>if</u> it both achieves the agent's intended goal and benefits someone other than the agent.[19]

> Action achieves intended goal and benefits → action is morally good
> someone else

> Action not morally good → action doesn't achieve intended goal or doesn't benefit someone else

7. <u>Only</u> experienced salespeople will be able to meet the company's selling quota. Thus, I must not count as an experienced salesperson, since I will be able to sell only half the quota.[20]

> Meet sales quota → experienced salespeople
> Not experienced sales people → does not meet sales quota

---

[17]PrepTest 50, Sec. 4, Q 14
[18]PrepTest 50, Sec. 4, Q 15
[19]PrepTest 51, Sec. 1, Q 9
[20]PrepTest 51, Sec. 1, Q 20

8. Expert: What criteria distinguish addictive substances from nonaddictive ones? Some have suggested that any substance that at least some habitual users can cease to use is nonaddictive. However, if this is taken to be the sole criterion of nonaddictiveness, some substances that most medical experts classify as prime examples of addictive substances would be properly deemed nonaddictive. Any adequate set of criteria for determining a substance's addictiveness must embody the view, held by these medical experts, that a substance is addictive <u>only if</u> withdrawal from its habitual use causes most users extreme psychological and physiological difficulty.[21]

Addictive	→	withdrawal causes psychological and physiological difficulty in most users
Withdrawal does not cause psychological or physiological difficulty in most users	→	not addictive

9. Whoever murdered Jansen was undoubtedly in Jansen's office on the day of the murder, and both Samantha and Herbert were in Jansen's office on that day. <u>If</u> Herbert had committed the murder, the police would have found either his fingerprints or his footprints at the scene of the crime. But <u>if</u> Samantha was the murderer, she would have avoided leaving behind footprints or fingerprints. The police found fingerprints but no footprints at the scene of the crime. Since the fingerprints were not Herbert's, he is not the murderer. Thus Samantha must be the killer.[22]

Herbert did it	→	police would find his fingerprints or his footprints at the scene
Police find no fingerprints and no footprints from Herbert	→	Herbert did not do it

Samantha did it	→	she would leave no fingerprints and no footprints
Find fingerprints or footprints from Samantha	→	Samantha did not do it

Note: this is a tricky example with the "and" versus "or" in the second statement. Saying "If Samantha is the murderer then she would avoid leaving footprints or fingerprints" means that she would leave neither fingerprints nor footprints, so, that's why it's written as: Samantha did it ⮕ she would leave no fingerprints *and* no footprints.

---

[21]PrepTest 51, Sec. 3, Q 14
[22]PrepTest 51, Sec. 3, Q 20

10. Ecologists predict that the incidence of malaria will increase _if_ global warming continues or _if_ the use of pesticides is not expanded. But the use of pesticides is known to contribute to global warming, so it is inevitable that we will see an increase in malaria in the years to come.[23]

Global warming continues or use of pesticides not expanded	→	incidence of malaria will increase
Incidence of malaria will not increase	→	global warming does not continue and use of pesticides not expanded

---

PART II

LOGICAL
REASONING
QUESTION TYPES

CHAPTER 4

ASSUMPTION FAMILY OF QUESTIONS

The four question types that make up the Assumption family of questions (Assumption, Strengthen, Weaken, and Flaw) represent half of the points available in the two scored Logical Reasoning sections. So you can expect Assumption, Strengthen, Weaken, and Flaw questions to account for approximately 25 out of 50 scored Logical Reasoning questions, and 25 out of 100 total scored LSAT questions. As you can see, they're a big part of your score, so I'll get started!

Family Members Linked by Arguments

The stimulus of any Assumption, Strengthen, Weaken, or Flaw question will always include an argument. To successfully answer these question types, you need to be able to break their arguments down to their core components: conclusion and evidence. Then, you identify and analyze the author's assumption, an unstated piece of evidence that links the evidence and the conclusion. In the following chapters, you will learn about the Assumption family of questions in greater depth. To provide some context, I'll show you how the questions are related before you begin to learn about each question type.

Consider the following stimulus:

> Companies wishing to boost sales of merchandise should use in-store displays to catch customers' attention. According to a marketing study, today's busy shoppers have less time for coupon-clipping and pay little attention to direct-mail advertising; instead, they make two-thirds of their buying decisions on the spot at the store.[1]

In this stimulus, the author presents an argument. He concludes that companies should use in-store displays to attract shoppers and increase sales because shoppers make their buying decisions in the store and not based on coupons and direct-mail advertising. Notice the mismatched terms: The conclusion talks about in-store displays, while the evidence refers to on-the-spot buying decisions. The assumption must connect these terms, so the author must assume that in-store displays will influence on-the-spot purchases.

I did not include a question because this stimulus presents an argument, while the question could be an Assumption, Strengthen, Weaken, or Flaw question. In fact, you could answer each question type with the information gleaned so far.

If the accompanying question to this stimulus asked for the author's assumption, you could predict that the correct answer will state something along the lines of "in-store displays impact in-store buying."

What if the question asked you to strengthen the argument—to make it more likely to happen? You could confirm the assumption or cite an example of customers buying on-the-spot because of the in-store displays.

How could you weaken the argument—to make it less likely to happen? You could say something like "in-store displays do not influence impulse buying," or you could provide an example of customers ignoring in-store displays.

Flaw questions ask you to identify the logical error the author makes in moving from the evidence to the conclusion. In this case, you could predict a faulty assumption and predict that the author has not made his case because he included no evidence that in-store displays affect impulse buying.

The point that I want you to take away from this is that by practicing these question types, you reinforce your ability to answer the other question types as well. Over the years, I have found that my students typically relate to one of the question types more than the others. If this turns out to be the case for you, start practicing with that question type and then bring your expertise to the other question types. In other words, focus on what you do best, especially in the initial stages of your practice, and then bring that momentum and skill to the rest of the questions.

After you have a chance to learn about the individual question types in the coming chapters, I'll give you an opportunity to review the Assumption family of questions together in one exercise. In the meantime, I'll introduce the first question type in this family: Assumption questions.

---

[1]PrepTest 46, Sec. 2, Q 13

CHAPTER 5

ASSUMPTION QUESTIONS

Assumption questions are the most important question type on the LSAT. You will see 6–8 scored assumption questions—sometimes more—on every test. Assumptions are also a key component of other question types, particularly Strengthen, Weaken, and Flaw. Therefore, your ability to identify the assumptions the authors make is critical for your success on test day.

DEFINITION OF ASSUMPTION QUESTIONS

Assumption questions ask you to identify the unstated premise the author uses to move from the evidence he provides to his conclusion. In other words, you have to identify what the author is taking for granted—the assumption—in the argument.

Take a look at this example:

Desserts are delicious.

Therefore, chocolate cake is delicious.

The author concludes that chocolate cake is delicious based on evidence that desserts are delicious. The author's unstated assumption must logically connect them. So, in this case, the assumption is that chocolate cake is a dessert.

Some LSAT arguments may seem obvious like the previous example, or they may be longer and more complex. Regardless, your task remains the same: Identify the missing piece of the argument to bridge the gap between the evidence and the conclusion. Use the following example as a visual reference:

Figure 5.1

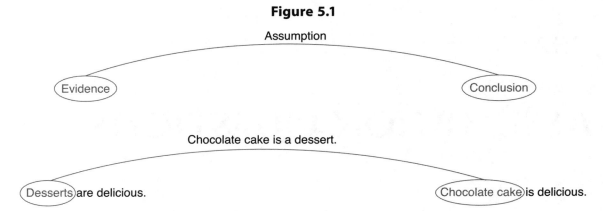

When you look for the author's assumption, it must come from the argument. This is what makes Assumption questions the most difficult Logical Reasoning question type for many students. Your comfort with the assumptions you make in everyday life is based on repetition and context. An LSAT assumption requires you to identify the author's thinking in constructing the argument and determine what is left unsaid.

Can you assume from the previous example that the author eats chocolate cake? No, not on the LSAT. Even though the author says chocolate cake is delicious, it doesn't mean that he eats it. After all, maybe the author is allergic to chocolate or on a diet. Whatever the case, you should never make your own assumptions on the LSAT; only identify the ones the authors must be making. Once you understand and accept that the assumption must remain within the scope of the author's argument, you will find it easier to identify assumptions.

USE THE KAPLAN METHOD TO ANSWER ASSUMPTION QUESTIONS
Identify the Question Type

There are certain words in the question stem that help you to recognize an Assumption question. Some of those include:

- Assumes
- Depends on
- Added to the premise
- Presupposes

The test makers word Assumption questions in a variety of ways, but here are some common Assumption question stems:

- Upon which one of the following assumptions does the author rely?
- Which one of the following, if added to the passage, will make the conclusion follow logically?

- The validity of the argument depends on which one of the following?
- The argument above is based on which one of the following assumptions?
- Her response depends on the presupposition that

As you read the question stem, look for indicator words to identify the question type. After you find Keywords, circle them in your test booklet. This gets you thinking about the question type and serves as a visual reminder of it to keep you from reading the question over and over again.

Untangle the Stimulus

Once you identify a question as an Assumption question, your next step is to strategically read the argument in the stimulus and identify its components. Look for the conclusion by using Keywords or the one-sentence test, and bracket it for easy recall. (Go back to chapter 2 to review conclusion and evidence Keywords and the one-sentence test.) Then, determine and summarize the evidence the author uses to support the conclusion. Remember, don't get distracted by background information.

Make a Prediction

Now, think about the assumption the author makes—the link between the evidence and conclusion. Ask yourself: What does the author take for granted to move from the evidence to the conclusion? What connects them? What words or concepts is the author comparing or treating as similar?

Making the assumption explicit by bridging the gap between the conclusion and evidence will improve your speed and accuracy—and help you score points—on test day. In the next section, I will show you how to use mismatched terms, ignored possibilities, the denial test, and formal logic to predict the author's assumption.

Evaluate the Answer Choices

Finally, take your prediction and compare it to the answer choices. Find the choice that best matches your prediction—that one is your answer. Be sure to avoid comparing the answer choices to each other and picking an answer that is "true" or "sounds good." Those are common mistakes that I've seen my students make over the years, and I don't want you to fall into that trap.

Look again at the example from the beginning of this chapter:

Desserts are delicious.

Therefore, chocolate cake is delicious.

The author's assumption is "chocolate cake is a dessert" because it connects "chocolate cake" in the conclusion to "desserts" in the evidence. But what if you saw the following answer choice: Apple pie is delicious.

It may sound good because the evidence says that desserts are delicious and you know apple pie is a dessert. Apple pie may be your favorite dessert in the whole world, so you know that apple pie is delicious. But choosing this answer would be based on outside knowledge and the truth of the statement—which are not valid LSAT reasons. Apple pie is outside the scope of the argument and cannot be a part of the correct answer.

Like every other question on the LSAT, there is ALWAYS only one right answer. In fact, the test makers write wrong answers to be wrong for a particular reason. Think about why answers are wrong as you move through the practice drills. I will discuss common wrong answers used in Logical Reasoning in a later chapter. Understanding common wrong answers will help you quickly eliminate incorrect answer choices.

THE KAPLAN METHOD IN ACTION

Now, it's time to practice the Kaplan Method by working through a few problems. In the process, I'll show you different techniques to help you identify the assumption in each argument.

Mismatched Terms

The most powerful method to find the author's assumption is to identify the mismatched terms in the conclusion and evidence, and link them together. Consider this example:

Vanwilligan: Some have argued that professional athletes receive unfairly high salaries. But in an unrestricted free market, such as the market these athletes compete in, salaries are determined by what someone else is willing to pay for their services. These athletes make enormous profits for their teams' owners, and that is why owners are willing to pay them extraordinary salaries. Thus the salaries they receive are fair.

Vanwilligan's conclusion follows logically if which one of the following is assumed?

(A)   The fairest economic system for a society is one in which the values of most goods and services are determined by the unrestricted free market.

(B)   If professional athletes were paid less for their services, then the teams for which they play would not make as much money.

(C)   The high level of competition in the marketplace forces the teams' owners to pay professional athletes high salaries.

(D)   Any salary that a team owner is willing to pay for the services of a professional athlete is a fair salary.

(E)   If a professional athlete's salary is fair, then that salary is determined by what an individual is willing to pay for the athlete's services in an unrestricted free market.[1]

Step 1. Identify the Question Type

The word "assumed" tells you that this is an Assumption question.

Step 2. Untangle the Stimulus

Find the components of the argument. The word "thus" reveals the conclusion, which states that salaries received by professional athletes are fair. Why are they fair? Because, Vanwilligan explains, the owners are willing to pay the salaries. Notice the gap between the conclusion and the evidence: The conclusion talks about fairness while the evidence talks about willingness to pay.

Step 3. Make a Prediction

Look for terms that appear in the evidence but not the conclusion, and vice versa; the correct answer will link them together. In this case, the correct answer must connect the owners' willingness to pay high salaries (the evidence) with fairness (the conclusion). The new term that pops up in the conclusion ("fair") without mention in the evidence is usually the focus of the author's assumption.

---

[1]PrepTest 49, Sec. 2, Q 19

Step 4. Evaluate the Answer Choices

Choice (A) focuses on the fairest *economic system*, which is beyond the scope of this argument; this author merely concludes certain *salaries* are fair. Eliminate this choice.

Choice (B) discusses the result of paying athletes less money and does not address the issue of fairness, so this choice is out.

Choice (C) also ignores fairness and instead raises the irrelevant issue of why owners pay high salaries.

Choice (D) matches the prediction: If an owner is willing to pay the salary, then it must be fair. This is the correct answer.

Choice (E) uses a botched contrapositive by reversing the conditional terms without negating them. I hope you didn't fall for it. But if you did, don't worry. You'll have plenty of opportunity to practice and learn from your mistakes.

You can depend on the Kaplan Method to help you answer all Logical Reasoning question types regardless of their difficulty level. The important thing is to use the Method and to apply it consistently. Some students insist on using the Method only when they think they can't get the answer their own way. I can tell you from experience that is a big mistake. By using the Kaplan Method for every question, you will be prepared every time. If it is an easier question for you, you will just be able to work through the problem more quickly. Switching between different methods will only eat up your already short 35 minute time period.

"Ignored" Possibilities

Another way the test makers present assumptions in arguments is the failure to consider—or mention—other possibilities (or other factors, explanations, causes, reasons, options, etc.) to their preferred possibility. Here's an example:

A certain credit-card company awards its customers bonus points for using its credit card. Customers can use accumulated points in the purchase of brand name merchandise by mail at prices lower than the manufacturers' suggested retail prices. At any given time, therefore, customers who purchase merchandise using the bonus points spend less than they would spend if they purchased the same merchandise in retail stores.

Which one of the following is an assumption on which the argument depends?

(A)   The merchandise that can be ordered by mail using the bonus points is not offered at lower prices by other credit-card companies that award bonus points.

(B)   The bonus points cannot be used by the credit-card customers in the purchase of brand name merchandise that is not available for purchase in retail stones.

(C)   The credit-card company does not require its customers to accumulate a large number of bonus points before becoming eligible to order merchandise at prices lower than the manufacturers' suggested retail price.

(D)   The amount credit-card customers pay for shipping the merchandise ordered by mail does not increase the amount customers spend to an amount greater than they would spend if they purchased the same merchandise in retail stores.

(E)   The merchandise available to the company's credit-card customers using the bonus points is frequently sold in retail stores at prices that are higher than the manufacturers' suggested retail prices.[2]

Step 1. Identify the Question Type

The word "assumption" identifies this stem as an Assumption question.

Step 2. Untangle the Stimulus

The word "therefore" signals the author's conclusion that people who buy mail-order merchandise with bonus points spend less money than people who buy merchandise in retail stores. What is his evidence for that? The mail-order merchandise is offered at a lower cost than the store products.

Step 3. Make a Prediction

The author says that mail-order merchandise is less expensive so customers spend less. The author ignores the possibility of other costs. He assumes the mail-order merchandise will

---

present no additional costs to the customer, such as shipping or insurance, which would raise the price above the retail amount. The correct choice should address this assumption.

Step 4. Evaluate the Answer Choices

Choice (A) wanders off point when it raises other credit card companies. The type of merchandise to be purchased using bonus points also strays from the argument. Eliminate this choice.

Choice (B) is outside the scope of the argument; the stimulus says nothing about restricting what customers can and can't buy. Move on to the next choice.

The discussion in choice (C) regarding when a customer can use her bonus points is also beyond the scope of the argument. This choice is out.

Choice (D) takes the general prediction and provides a specific example in which an added cost does not raise the mail-order price above the retail price. This is the correct answer.

Finally, you can eliminate choice (E) because the manufacturer's suggested retail price is irrelevant. This argument is only concerned with the mail-order price versus the retail price.

Denial Test: Necessary Assumptions Only

Assumptions on the LSAT come in two varieties, necessary and sufficient. Necessary assumptions are subject to the denial test, which is one more way to determine if you have found the correct assumption. However, the denial test will not help you if the assumption is sufficient. Let's sort this out.

Necessary Assumption questions—the most common—ask for an unstated piece of evidence needed for the conclusion to be true. Specifically, the question stems ask for the assumption "required by" the author or that the author "depends on" or "relies on." It can also ask for the assumption the author "makes" or for what the "author assumes."

In the case of a necessary assumption, if you negate it, then the argument no longer makes sense.

To illustrate this, go back, again, to the chocolate cake stimulus:

Desserts are delicious.

Therefore, chocolate cake is delicious.

Now imagine that with this argument comes a question stem that asks for the assumption on which the argument depends; in other words, a necessary assumption. You've already identified the assumption as "chocolate cake is a dessert." If you deny the assumption and say "chocolate cake is not a dessert," then the argument makes no sense; "desserts are delicious and chocolate cake is not a dessert" does not lead to a conclusion that chocolate cake is delicious. So, if you deny an assumption that is necessary for the argument to work, the argument will fall apart. You can use this denial test to double-check your answer to a Necessary Assumption question. You don't need to use the denial test on every single answer in every Necessary Assumption question. Other methods may be more direct. However, the denial test is available to review your answer if you are not sure of it.

In contrast to Necessary Assumption questions, Sufficient Assumption questions typically ask for the assumption that "allows the conclusion to follow logically." They are not susceptible to the denial test.

Now I'll walk you through an LSAT example to show you how the denial test works:

> Proponents of organic farming claim that using chemical fertilizers and pesticides in farming is harmful to local wildlife. To produce the same amount of food, however, more land must be under cultivation when organic farming techniques are used than when chemicals are used. Therefore, organic farming leaves less land available as habitat for local wildlife.
>
> Which one of the following is an assumption on which the author's argument depends?
>
> (A)   Chemical fertilizers and pesticides pose no health threat to wildlife.
> (B)   Wildlife living near farms where chemicals are used will not ingest any food or water containing those chemicals.
> (C)   The only disadvantage to using chemicals in farming is their potential effect on wildlife.
> (D)   The same crops are grown on organic farms as on farms where chemicals are used.
> (E)   Land cultivated by organic farming methods no longer constitutes a habitat for wildlife.[3]

Step 1. Identify the Question Type

Because of the phrase "assumption on which the author's argument depends," you know that this is a Necessary Assumption question.

Step 2. Untangle the Stimulus

"Therefore" points out the conclusion to you, that organic farming means there is less land available for wildlife habitat. The reason, according to the author, is that organic farming means that more land must be cultivated. That's your evidence.

Step 3. Make a Prediction

The argument presents mismatched terms in the evidence and conclusion. They both talk about organic farming; however, the evidence relates it to land cultivation and the conclusion connects it to wildlife habitat. The author must assume they are separate—land use is for either one or the other, not both.

---

[3]PrepTest 15, Sec. 3, Q 12

Step 4. Evaluate the Answer Choices

The health threat posed by chemicals is not discussed in the argument, so choice (A) is outside the scope. Just to confirm this, try the denial test. Denying choice (A), chemicals do pose a threat to wildlife, has no effect on the conclusion regarding the impact of organic farming on wildlife habitat. So that answer choice is out.

Choice (B) has a similar problem, as the ingestion of the chemicals is also outside the scope of this problem. If you deny choice (B) and say that wildlife will ingest chemicals in their food and water, it bears no impact on the conclusion. Again, in the conclusion, the author says organic farming uses a wider area and reduces living space for wildlife.

Choice (C) presents another answer that is outside the scope of the argument. The author is not interested in the disadvantages of using chemicals in farming. Denying the answer results in saying the impact on wildlife is not the only disadvantage to using chemicals, and, in this case, other possible disadvantages have no affect on the conclusion.

Whether the same crops are grown is irrelevant to the argument, so you can quickly eliminate choice (D).

The author must assume choice (E), land used for organic farming can no longer be used as a wildlife habitat, which is the correct answer. If you're in doubt, try confirming the answer by using the denial test. Negate the statement and see what effect that has on the conclusion. It becomes "Land cultivated by organic farming can be used as a wildlife habitat." The assumption denied destroys the conclusion and therefore must be the correct answer.

One important lesson to take away from this exercise: While the mismatched terms in this argument lead you directly to answer choice (E), it is important to practice applying the denial test on "easier" questions like this at first. You'll likely find that the denial test is especially helpful on tough assumption questions, and you can count on the test makers giving you at least a couple of those on every test. The ability to answer the harder questions correctly is what sets the high scorers apart from the pack, and by practicing the Kaplan Method, you'll be one of those test takers.

Formal Logic and Sufficient Assumptions

Here's a slightly trickier version of the Assumption question that the test makers can throw at you, but the Kaplan Method has an answer for it, too. If the stimulus includes formal logic, translate the formal logic into if-then statements. Then use the translations to identify the gap between the evidence and the conclusion. You'll find that Sufficient Assumption questions tend to use formal logic. They ask for an assumption that's enough to make an argument acceptable, unlike a necessary assumption required for the argument to make sense.

Marian Anderson, the famous contralto, did not take success for granted. We know this because Anderson had to struggle early in life, and anyone who has to struggle early in life is able to keep a good perspective on the world.

The conclusion of the argument follows logically if which one of the following is assumed?

(A)   Anyone who succeeds takes success for granted.
(B)   Anyone who is able to keep a good perspective on the world does not take success for granted.
(C)   Anyone who is able to keep a good perspective on the world has to struggle early in life.
(D)   Anyone who does not take success for granted has to struggle early in life.
(E)   Anyone who does not take success for granted is able to keep a good perspective on the world.[4]

Step 1. Identify the Question Type

The word "assumed" immediately tells you that this is an Assumption question.

Step 2. Untangle the Stimulus

Although there is no conclusion Keyword, note the evidence phrase at the beginning of the second sentence: "We know this because" indicates that the author is about to provide evidence for a conclusion she just mentioned. Therefore, "Marian Anderson did not take success for granted" is the conclusion. Why didn't she take success for granted? She struggled and, according to the author, anyone who struggles has a good world perspective.

Do you notice anything else about the argument? Look at the language. Do you see "anyone"? You will recall from chapter 3 that "anyone" is an indicator of formal logic, specifically the sufficient term. If you spot formal logic in an assumption argument, translate it to help you find the gap between the conclusion and evidence and identify the assumption.

The basic components of this argument consist of two pieces of evidence and the conclusion. One piece of evidence is a formal logic rule that applies to everybody. There also is a factual piece of evidence specific to Marian Anderson, which is used to support a conclusion specific to Marian Anderson. Map it out as follows:

Formal Logic Evidence:	**Struggle**	→	**good perspective**
Factual Evidence:	**Anderson struggled**	**(thus)**	**Conc: Anderson not take success for granted**

With the common term "struggle" lined up on the left side, the assumption simply is to link the mismatched terms on the right side; link "good perspective" to "not take success for granted." Since this is a Sufficient Assumption question, your goal is to guarantee that the conclusion (Anderson did not take success for granted) is true, so the assumption must go from "good perspective" to "not take success for granted."

[4]PrepTest 35, Sec. 4, Q 14

Step 3. Make a Prediction

In this case, start with the obvious formal logic statement and translate it to the basic X → Y statement. Then, translate the other statements so you can find the gap. Here's what you'll get:

The evidence goes from A (Marian Anderson) → B (struggle) → C (good perspective), and then the conclusion jumps from A (Marian Anderson) → D (don't take success for granted). Let me show it to you in a picture:

Evidence: A → B

                    B → C

Conclusion: A ——————→ D

The gap exists between C and D, which gets you the assumption: If you keep a good perspective, then you don't take success for granted.

Step 4. Evaluate the Answer Choices

What do you notice about all the answer choices? What do they all have in common? They all start with "anyone," which tells you to translate them into formal logic. By test day, your goal is to recognize the formal logic quickly and work through it without a mechanical process. For now, go ahead and translate each answer choice to the basic X → Y form. It's good practice while you are learning the skill:

Choice (A) translates to: Succeed → take success for granted. Succeeding is a new term in the argument and therefore outside the scope. Eliminate this choice.

Choice (B) matches the prediction exactly: Good perspective → not take success for granted. That's your answer.

Choice (C) translates to: Good perspective → struggle. Notice it reverses terms of the evidence without negating, which is a common wrong answer trap.

Choices (D), Not take success for granted → struggle, and (E), Not take success for granted → good perspective, also reverse terms without negating.

ASSUMPTION QUESTIONS NOW YOU TRY IT

Now it's your turn to try a couple Assumption questions on your own. Use the template I've provided after each question to guide you through the four-step Kaplan Method.

(Note: On test day, you won't be writing out all the steps as you are in this exercise. However, as you are learning the Method, it's good practice to help it become second nature.) Remember to bracket the conclusions and circle Keywords.

1. Barnes: The two newest employees at this company have salaries that are too high for the simple tasks normally assigned to new employees and duties that are too complex for inexperienced workers. Hence, the salaries and the complexity of the duties of these two newest employees should be reduced.

    Which one of the following is an assumption on which Barnes's argument depends?

    (A) The duties of the two newest employees are not less complex than any others in the company.
    (B) It is because of the complex duties assigned that the two newest employees are being paid more than is usually paid to newly hired employees.
    (C) The two newest employees are not experienced at their occupations.
    (D) Barnes was not hired at a higher-than-average starting salary.
    (E) The salaries of the two newest employees are no higher than the salaries that other companies pay for workers with a similar level of experience.[5]

Step 1. Identify the Question Type

_____

Step 2. Untangle the Stimulus

_____

Step 3. Make a Prediction

_____

Step 4. Evaluate the Answer Choices

_____

_____

[5]PrepTest 29, Sec. 1, Q 5

2. Human beings can exhibit complex, goal-oriented behavior without conscious awareness of what they are doing. Thus, merely establishing that nonhuman animals are intelligent will not establish that they have consciousness.

Which one of the following is an assumption on which the argument depends?

(A) Complex, goal-oriented behavior requires intelligence.

(B) The possession of consciousness does not imply the possession of intelligence.

(C) All forms of conscious behavior involve the exercise of intelligence.

(D) The possession of intelligence entails the possession of consciousness.

(E) Some intelligent human behavior is neither complex nor goal-oriented.[6]

Step 1. Identify the Question Type

_____

Step 2. Untangle the Stimulus

_____

Step 3. Make a Prediction

_____

Step 4. Evaluate the Answer Choices

_____

---

[6]PrepTest 49, Sec. 2, Q 17

Explanations

1. (C)

Barnes: The two newest employees at this company have salaries that are too high for the simple tasks normally assigned to new employees and duties that are too complex for inexperienced workers. <Hence, the salaries and the complexity of the duties of these two newest employees should be reduced.>

Which one of the following is an assumption on which Barnes's argument depends?

(A) The duties of the two newest employees are not less complex than any others in the company.

(B) It is because of the complex duties assigned that the two newest employees are being paid more than is usually paid to newly hired employees.

(C) The two newest employees are not experienced at their occupations.

(D) Barnes was not hired at a higher-than-average starting salary.

(E) The salaries of the two newest employees are no higher than the salaries that other companies pay for workers with a similar level of experience.[7]

Step 1. Identify the Question Type

The question asks you directly for an assumption, so you will need to link the evidence to the conclusion. "Depends" indicates this is a necessary assumption, so remember you can confirm your answer with the denial test.

Step 2. Untangle the Stimulus

"Hence" points to Barnes' conclusion that the salaries and complexity of the duties of the newest employees should be reduced. What evidence does Barnes give to support this conclusion? He says their salaries are too high for tasks assigned to new employees and their duties are too complex for inexperienced workers. In other words, new employees should have a certain salary based on their duties and inexperienced workers should have a certain level of complexity in their duties.

Step 3. Make a Prediction

This is a classic example of mismatched terms. The conclusion is about the "newest employees," but right before "hence" the author refers to them as "inexperienced workers." So Barnes must assume that the two newest employees are inexperienced. It's certainly possible and sounds reasonable enough to read right over the difference. But couldn't they have experience from prior jobs? Of course! So Barnes is making an assumption. And you've identified it. Now find that assumption in the answer choices.

---

[7]PrepTest 29, Sec. 1, Q 5

Step 4. Evaluate the Answer Choices

Choice (A) broadens the comparison group to all company employees, not just inexperienced workers. Barnes never discusses the complexity of job responsibilities for all company workers, so you cannot make any assumptions about them. This choice is out.

Choice (B) presents the opposite of what Barnes' assumes. It rationalizes the newest employees' higher salary based on the complexity of their job responsibilities. Eliminate this choice.

Choice (C) is correct because it confirms that the two newest employees are inexperienced at their jobs. Deny this choice and it states that the two newest employees have experience; then the argument falls apart, so this must be right.

Choice (D) is outside the scope of the argument. Barnes' salary has no bearing on the salary of the two newest employees.

Choice (E) presents an irrelevant comparison between the newest employees' salaries and salaries of workers outside the company. Pay practices of other companies are also beyond the scope of this argument.

2. **(A)**

Human beings can exhibit complex, goal-oriented behavior without conscious awareness of what they are doing. (Thus,) merely establishing that nonhuman animals are intelligent will not establish that they have consciousness.>

Which one of the following is an (assumption) on which the argument (depends)?

(A) Complex, goal-oriented behavior requires intelligence.
(B) The possession of consciousness does not imply the possession of intelligence.
(C) All forms of conscious behavior involve the exercise of intelligence.
(D) The possession of intelligence entails the possession of consciousness.
(E) Some intelligent human behavior is neither complex nor goal-oriented.[8]

Step 1. Identify the Question Type

Again, the question stem tells you specifically to determine the assumption necessary to the argument.

Step 2. Untangle the Stimulus

"Thus" points you right to the conclusion, where the author maintains that proving nonhumans are intelligent will not prove that they have consciousness. Why not? Because complex, goal-oriented behavior in humans is possible without consciousness. Intelligence, she says, does not demonstrate consciousness because complex, goal-oriented behavior is possible without consciousness.

Step 3. Make a Prediction

Can you spot the mismatched terms? The author must connect intelligence, which only appears in the conclusion, to complex, goal-oriented behavior, found only in the evidence.

Step 4. Evaluate the Answer Choices

Choice (A) is the only answer that links the two unique terms and is therefore the correct answer.

Choice (B) inverts the conclusion and does not connect the mismatched terms. Move on.

Choice (C) says that intelligence is required for conscious behavior. Obviously, this answer does not link the mismatched terms. But, it also doesn't represent the argument which concludes that intelligence does not require consciousness.

Choice (D) contradicts the author's conclusion.

Choice (E) has two problems. First, it distinguishes, rather than ties together, intelligence and complex and goal-oriented behavior. It also separates complex and goal-oriented behavior, which differs from the argument.

DRILL: ANSWERING ASSUMPTION QUESTIONS

Use the Kaplan Method to answer the following Assumption questions. Take this opportunity to practice and apply the steps in the Method so you are comfortable using them on test day. Check your responses against the full explanations provided after the Drill.

1. Braille is a method of producing text by means of raised dots that can be read by touch. A recent development in technology will allow flat computer screens to be made of a material that can be heated in patterns that replicate the patterns used in braille. Since the thermal device will utilize the same symbol system as braille, it follows that anyone who is accustomed to reading braille can easily adapt to the use of this electronic system.

Which one of the following is an assumption on which the conclusion depends?

(A) Braille is the only symbol system that can be readily adapted for use with the new thermal screen.

(B) Only people who currently use braille as their sole medium for reading text will have the capacity to adapt to the use of the thermal screen.

(C) People with the tactile ability to discriminate symbols in braille have an ability to discriminate similar patterns on a flat heated surface.

(D) Some symbol systems encode a piece of text by using dots that replicate the shape of letters of the alphabet.

(E) Eventually it will be possible to train people to read braille by first training them in the use of the thermal screen.[9]

2. Although the charter of Westside School states that the student body must include some students with special educational needs, no students with learning disabilities have yet enrolled in the school. Therefore, the school is currently in violation of its charter.

The conclusion of the argument follows logically if which one of the following is assumed?

(A) All students with learning disabilities have special educational needs.

(B) The school currently has no student with learning disabilities.

(C) The school should enroll students with special educational needs.

(D) The only students with special educational needs are students with learning disabilities.

(E) The school's charter cannot be modified in order to avoid its being violated.[10]

3. Robert: Speed limits on residential streets in Crownsbury are routinely ignored by drivers. People crossing those streets are endangered by speeding drivers, yet the city does not have enough police officers to patrol every street. So the city should install speed bumps and signs warning of their presence on residential streets to slow down traffic.

    Sheila: That is a bad idea. People who are driving too fast can easily lose control of their vehicles when they hit a speed bump.

    Sheila's response depends on the presupposition that

    (A) problems of the kind that Robert describes are worse in Crownsbury than they are in other cities

    (B) Robert's proposal is intended to address a problem that Robert does not in fact intend it to address

    (C) with speed bumps and warning signs in place, there would still be drivers who would not slow down to a safe speed

    (D) most of the people who are affected by the problem Robert describes would be harmed by the installation of speed bumps and warning signs

    (E) problems of the kind that Robert describes do not occur on any nonresidential streets in Crownsbury[11]

4. Physician: Hatha yoga is a powerful tool for helping people quit smoking. In a clinical trial, those who practiced hatha yoga for 75 minutes once a week and received individual counseling reduced their smoking and cravings for tobacco as much as did those who went to traditional self-help groups once a week and had individual counseling.

    Which one of the following is an assumption on which the physician's argument relies?

    (A) The individual counseling received by the smokers in the clinical trial who practiced hatha yoga did not help them quit smoking.

    (B) Most smokers are able to practice hatha yoga more than once a week.

    (C) Traditional self-help groups are powerful tools for helping people quit smoking.

    (D) People who practice hatha yoga for 75 minutes once a week are not damaging themselves physically.

    (E) Other forms of yoga are less effective than hatha yoga in helping people quit smoking.[12]

5. We learn to use most of the machines in our lives through written instructions, without knowledge of the machines' inner workings, because most machines are specifically designed for use by nonexperts. So, in general, attaining technological expertise would prepare students for tomorrow's job market no better than would a more traditional education stressing verbal and quantitative skills.

    The argument depends on assuming which one of the following?

    (A) Fewer people receive a traditional education stressing verbal and quantitative skills now than did 20 years ago.

    (B) Facility in operating machines designed for use by nonexperts is almost never enhanced by expert knowledge of the machines' inner workings.

    (C) Most jobs in tomorrow's job market will not demand the ability to operate many machines that are designed for use only by experts.

    (D) Students cannot attain technological expertise and also receive an education that does not neglect verbal and quantitative skills.

    (E) When learning to use a machine, technological expertise is never more important than verbal and quantitative skills.[13]

6. Ann will either take a leave of absence from Technocomp and return in a year or else she will quit her job there; but she would not do either one unless she were offered a one-year teaching fellowship at a prestigious university. Technocomp will allow her to take a leave of absence if it does not find out that she has been offered the fellowship, but not otherwise. Therefore, Ann will quit her job at Technocomp only if Technocomp finds out she has been offered the fellowship.

Which one of the following, if assumed, allows the conclusion above to be properly drawn?

(A) Technocomp will find out about Ann being offered the fellowship only if someone informs on her.

(B) The reason Ann wants the fellowship is so she can quit her job at Technocomp.

(C) Technocomp does not allow any of its employees to take a leave of absence in order to work for one of its competitors.

(D) Ann will take a leave of absence if Technocomp allows her to take a leave of absence.

(E) Ann would be offered the fellowship only if she quit her job at Technocomp.[14]

7. Vague laws set vague limits on people's freedom, which makes it impossible for them to know for certain whether their actions are legal. Thus, under vague laws people cannot feel secure.

The conclusion follows logically if which one of the following is assumed?

(A) People can feel secure only if they know for certain whether their actions are legal.

(B) If people do not know for certain whether their actions are legal, then they might not feel secure.

(C) If people know for certain whether their actions are legal, they can feel secure.

(D) People can feel secure if they are governed by laws that are not vague.

(E) Only people who feel secure can know for certain whether their actions are legal.[15]

8. Publicity campaigns for endangered species are unlikely to have much impact on the most important environmental problems, for while the ease of attributing feelings to large mammals facilitates evoking sympathy for them, it is more difficult to elicit sympathy for other kinds of organisms, such as the soil microorganisms on which large ecosystems and agriculture depend.

Which one of the following is an assumption on which the argument depends?

(A) The most important environmental problems involve endangered species other than large mammals.

(B) Microorganisms cannot experience pain or have other feelings.

(C) Publicity campaigns for the environment are the most effective when they elicit sympathy for some organism.

(D) People ignore environmental problems unless they believe the problems will affect creatures with which they sympathize.

(E) An organism can be environmentally significant only if it affects large ecosystems or agriculture.[16]

9. Professor: Each government should do all that it can to improve the well-being of all the children in the society it governs. Therefore, governments should help finance high-quality day care since such day care will become available to families of all income levels if and only if it is subsidized.

Which one of the following is an assumption on which the professor's argument depends?

(A) Only governments that subsidize high-quality day care take an interest in the well-being of all the children in the societies they govern.

(B) Government subsidy of high-quality day care would not be so expensive that it would cause a government to eliminate benefits for adults.

(C) High-quality day care should be subsidized only for those who could not otherwise afford it.

(D) At least some children would benefit from high-quality day care.

(E) Government is a more efficient provider of certain services than is private enterprise.[17]

Explanations

1. (C)

Braille is a method of producing text by means of raised dots that can be read by touch. A recent development in technology will allow flat computer screens to be made of a material that can be heated in patterns that replicate the patterns used in braille. (Since) the thermal device will utilize the same symbol system as braille, <it follows that> anyone who is accustomed to reading braille can easily adapt to the use of this electronic system.>

Which one of the following is an (assumption) on which the conclusion (depends)?

(A)   Braille is the only symbol system that can be readily adapted for use with the new thermal screen.

(B)   Only people who currently use braille as their sole medium for reading text will have the capacity to adapt to the use of the thermal screen.

(C)   People with the tactile ability to discriminate symbols in braille have an ability to discriminate similar patterns on a flat heated surface.

(D)   Some symbol systems encode a piece of text by using dots that replicate the shape of letters of the alphabet.

(E)   Eventually it will be possible to train people to read braille by first training them in the use of the thermal screen.[18]

Step 1. Identify the Question Type

The words "assumption and "depends" tell you that this question asks for a necessary assumption.

Step 2. Untangle the Stimulus

The phrase "it follows that" signals the author's conclusion that anyone who can read braille can easily use the electronic system. "Since" identifies the evidence that says the thermal device will use the same symbol system as braille. So the braille symbols are the same, but the delivery system is different.

Step 3. Make a Prediction

Since the symbols are the same, the only shift in the argument is from the raised dots to the thermal screen. The author must assume that anyone who can read braille in a traditional manner can transfer that skill to read the heated computer screen.

---

[18]PrepTest 22, Sec. 2, Q 1

Step 4. Evaluate the Answer Choices

Choice (A) is too extreme, a common "necessary assumption" wrong answer type that can sound attractive, because it's on track, but you can easily eliminate it using the denial test, because it goes too far. Choice (A) indicates that "only" braille can be adapted to the thermal screen. Denied, choice (A) indicates that the thermal screens can be used for other systems besides braille; which in no way destroys the argument that the screen is good for braille users.

Choice (B) is also too extreme; it limits those who can adapt to the new technology to only people who use braille as their sole medium for reading text. Using the denial test, the possibility that additional people could adapt to the new technology in no way destroys the conclusion that current braille readers can.

Choice (C) matches the prediction by linking the evidence and conclusion: People who can read braille can read the same symbols on the heated computer surface. Remember, assumptions will always connect the existing points in an argument and not add new information. If you want additional confirmation that (C) is correct, try the denial test. If people who can read braille don't have an ability to read braille from a heated surface, then the conclusion makes no sense.

Choice (D) discusses symbol systems other than braille, so is out of scope.

Choice (E) talks about training people to read braille in the future, so it is way out of the scope of this argument, which is about what current braille users can do.

2.   **(D)**

Although the charter of Westside School states that the student body must include some students with special educational needs, no students with learning disabilities have yet enrolled in the school. <Therefore, the school is currently in violation of its charter.>

The conclusion of the argument follows logically if which one of the following is assumed?

(A)   All students with learning disabilities have special educational needs.
(B)   The school currently has no student with learning disabilities.
(C)   The school should enroll students with special educational needs.
(D)   The only students with special educational needs are students with learning disabilities.
(E)   The school's charter cannot be modified in order to avoid its being violated.[19]

---

[19]PrepTest 34, Sec. 2, Q 10

Step 1. Identify the Question Type

This question asks you to identify a sufficient assumption.

Step 2. Untangle the Stimulus

"Therefore" in the last sentence points to the conclusion, which states that if we have the current situation at the school, then the charter is violated. When the conclusion refers to a vague term, such a "this policy" or here "the charter," it is helpful to incorporate the definition of the policy or charter into the conclusion. The charter requires that the school must have special-needs students, so the conclusion really indicates that the current situation at the school violates the charter requirement to have special-needs students. So how does the author know the school is in violation of its charter? The Westside School charter requires that special-needs students be included in the student body, yet the school has no students with learning disabilities.

Step 3. Make a Prediction

In this case, the mismatched terms are "learning disabilities" and "special needs." The correct answer should link those terms. If only one answer makes the link, then it will be correct. But if two answers make that connection, you need to determine whether the author assumes that all students with learning disabilities have special needs or conversely all special-needs students have learning disabilities. So the author assumes that if there are no students with learning disabilities then there are no special needs students:

Statement: No learning disabled students → no special-needs students

Contrapositive: Special need students → learning disabled

So the author assumes all special-needs students have learning disabilities.

Step 4. Evaluate the Answer Choices

Choice (A) reverses the logic, so you can eliminate it.

Choice (B) repeats evidence stated in the argument rather than providing an unstated premise, a common wrong answer trap for Assumption questions. Move on to the next choice.

The recommendation in choice (C), that the school enroll special-needs students, is irrelevant to the argument; the charter requires enrollment of special-needs students.

Choice (D) is the only choice that correctly connects the two student groups in the evidence to make the conclusion valid.

Whether the school charter can be modified, as raised in choice (E), has no impact on the argument because the argument already concludes that the school is in violation of its charter.

3. **(C)**

Robert: Speed limits on residential streets in Crownsbury
are routinely ignored by drivers. People crossing those
streets are endangered by speeding drivers, yet the city
does not have enough police officers to patrol every
street. So the city should install speed bumps and signs
warning of their presence on residential streets to slow
down traffic.

Sheila: <That is a bad idea.> People who are driving too fast
can easily lose control of their vehicles when they hit a
speed bump.

Sheila's response depends on the presupposition that

(A)   problems of the kind that Robert describes are
worse in Crownsbury than they are in other
cities

(B)   Robert's proposal is intended to address a
problem that Robert does not in fact intend it to
address

(C)   with speed bumps and warning signs in place,
there would still be drivers who would not slow
down to a safe speed

(D)   most of the people who are affected by the
problem Robert describes would be harmed by
the installation of speed bumps and warning signs

(E)   problems of the kind that Robert describes do not
occur on any nonresidential streets in
Crownsbury[20]

Step 1. Identify the Question Type

"Depends on the presupposition" tells you that this answer requires a necessary assumption.

Step 2. Untangle the Stimulus

Crownsbury has a problem with speeding drivers. Sheila concludes that Robert's recommendation to add speed bumps and warning signs is a bad idea. Her evidence is that speeding drivers will lose control of their cars when they hit a speed bump.

Step 3. Make a Prediction

The purpose of the precautionary measures is to slow drivers down. If Sheila is concerned that drivers will continue to speed and create dangerous situations, she must not think the speed bumps and the warning signs will be effective to slow drivers down.

Step 4. Evaluate the Answer Choices

The comparison of Crownsbury's problems to other cities in choice (A) is irrelevant in this argument.

[20]PrepTest 37, Sec. 4, Q 23

Choices (B) and (E) also raise irrelevant factors; neither Robert's intentions nor nonresidential streets are ever mentioned in the argument.

Choice (C) matches the prediction and is the correct answer.

Choice (D) talks about who would be hurt rather than drivers who continue to speed.

4.   (C)

Physician: <Hatha yoga is a powerful tool for helping people quit smoking.> In a clinical trial, those who practiced hatha yoga for 75 minutes once a week and received individual counseling reduced their smoking and cravings for tobacco as much as did those who went to traditional self-help groups once a week and had individual counseling.

Which one of the following is an assumption on which the physician's argument relies?

(A)   The individual counseling received by the smokers in the clinical trial who practiced hatha yoga did not help them quit smoking.

(B)   Most smokers are able to practice hatha yoga more than once a week.

(C)   Traditional self-help groups are powerful tools for helping people quit smoking.

(D)   People who practice hatha yoga for 75 minutes once a week are not damaging themselves physically.

(E)   Other forms of yoga are less effective than hatha yoga in helping people quit smoking.[21]

Step 1. Identify the Question Type

It doesn't get any easier than this. This question uses "assumption," so you know what to do.

Step 2. Untangle the Stimulus

The physician concludes that Hatha yoga is a powerful tool to help people quit smoking because when combined with individual counseling, it is just as effective as traditional self-help groups and individual counseling.

Step 3. Make a Prediction

Individual counseling is common in both treatments, so to determine that Hatha yoga is powerful, the physician must assume that traditional self-help groups are also powerful.

Step 4. Evaluate the Answer Choices

You can eliminate choice (A) because both groups received individual counseling and you have no way to differentiate the value added by the treatment.

---

[21]PrepTest 37, Sec. 4, Q 19

Choice (B) is outside the scope of the argument since you have no information about how often the smokers could practice yoga.

Choice (C) matches the prediction exactly and is the correct answer.

Choices (D) and (E) also add factors outside the scope of the argument; the physical effect of Hatha yoga and a comparison with other forms of yoga are never discussed.

5.   **(C)**

We learn to use most of the machines in our lives through written instructions, without knowledge of the machines' inner workings, because most machines are specifically designed for use by nonexperts. ⟨So, in general, attaining technological expertise would prepare students for tomorrow's job market no better than would a more traditional education stressing verbal and quantitative skills.⟩

The argument ⟨depends⟩ on ⟨assuming⟩ which one of the following?

(A)   Fewer people receive a traditional education stressing verbal and quantitative skills now than did 20 years ago.

(B)   Facility in operating machines designed for use by nonexperts is almost never enhanced by expert knowledge of the machines' inner workings.

(C)   Most jobs in tomorrow's job market will not demand the ability to operate many machines that are designed for use only by experts.

(D)   Students cannot attain technological expertise and also receive an education that does not neglect verbal and quantitative skills.

(E)   When learning to use a machine, technological expertise is never more important than verbal and quantitative skills.[22]

Step 1. Identify the Question Type

Again, the Assumption question is revealed directly by the language.

Step 2. Untangle the Stimulus

The author concludes that technological training to prepare for the future job market has no value over a traditional education because most machines are designed to be used by non-experts. Notice the scope shift: The conclusion refers to machines in the workplace while the evidence refers to machines in our daily lives.

---

[22]PrepTest 36, Sec. 3, Q 14

Step 3. Make a Prediction

The author assumes that tomorrow's jobs will use those machines designed for nonexperts discussed in the evidence.

Step 4. Evaluate the Answer Choices

The number of students receiving an education is irrelevant in the argument, so choice (A) is out.

Choice (B) strengthens the conclusion that technological expertise won't generally help students, but is too extreme to be a necessary assumption. The denial test is a great way to eliminate answer choices that support the author's conclusion but are too extreme or restrictive to be necessary to the argument. Choice (B) denied indicates that periodically, technological expertise would be an advantage in utilizing those machines designed for nonexperts in the evidence, but that does not preclude the claim that generally students do not gain a significant advantage from a technological education.

Choice (C), the correct answer, does that by saying work-related machines can be operated by nonexperts just like the everyday machines. The other answer choices do not address the scope shift.

The author would disagree with choice (D) because the author denies the need for tech expertise.

Finally, you can eliminate choice (E) because the comparative value of tech expertise and verbal and quantitative skills is never discussed in the argument.

6.   **(D)**

Ann will either take a leave of absence from
Technocomp and return in a year or else she will quit her
job there; but she would not do either one unless she
were offered a one-year teaching fellowship at a
prestigious university. Technocomp will allow her to
take a leave of absence if it does not find out that she has
been offered the fellowship, but not otherwise.
<Therefore, Ann will quit her job at Technocomp only if
Technocomp finds out she has been offered the
fellowship.>

Which one of the following, if assumed, allows the
conclusion above to be properly drawn?

(A)   Technocomp will find out about Ann being
       offered the fellowship only if someone informs
       on her.
(B)   The reason Ann wants the fellowship is so she can
       quit her job at Technocomp.
(C)   Technocomp does not allow any of its employees
       to take a leave of absence in order to work for
       one of its competitors.
(D)   Ann will take a leave of absence if Technocomp
       allows her to take a leave of absence.
(E)   Ann would be offered the fellowship only if she
       quit her job at Technocomp.[23]

Step 1. Identify the Question Type

The question clearly asks for an assumption.

Step 2. Untangle the Stimulus

"Therefore" points to the formal logic conclusion that Ann will quit her job only if Technocomp finds out about the fellowship. The evidence indicates that she will either take a leave or quit her job. Also, the evidence indicates that if Technocomp does not find out about the fellowship, Ann will be able to take a leave of absence.

Step 3. Make a Prediction

You know Ann has two potential options. The contrapositive of the conclusion is helpful to recognize; it states that if Technocomp does not find out about the fellowship, then Ann will not quit her job, indicating that she would opt to take the leave of absence. So the author assumes that if given a choice, Ann prefers the leave of absence. So look for the choice where Ann will take the leave of absence if allowed by Technocomp.

Step 4. Evaluate the Answer Choices

Choice (A) talks about someone informing on Ann which is beyond the scope of the argument.

Similarly, Ann's rationale for her actions are outside the scope of the argument, making choice (B) incorrect.

Choice (C) makes no sense in the context of the argument. Ann is planning to teach at a university, not work for a competitor.

Choice (D) matches the prediction and is the answer.

You can eliminate choice (E) because the circumstances under which she is offered the fellowship are immaterial.

7. **(A)**

Vague laws set vague limits on people's freedom, which makes it impossible for them to know for certain whether their actions are legal. <Thus, under vague laws people cannot feel secure.>

The conclusion follows logically if which one of the following is assumed?

(A) People can feel secure only if they know for certain whether their actions are legal.
(B) If people do not know for certain whether their actions are legal, then they might not feel secure.
(C) If people know for certain whether their actions are legal, they can feel secure.
(D) People can feel secure if they are governed by laws that are not vague.
(E) Only people who feel secure can know for certain whether their actions are legal.[24]

Step 1. Identify the Question Type

The question again asks for an assumption.

Step 2. Untangle the Stimulus

"Thus" introduces the conclusion and the new term "people cannot feel secure" under vague laws. The evidence states that people cannot know the legality of their actions under vague laws.

Step 3. Make a Prediction

People's security must require knowing their actions are legal for the argument to work.

Step 4. Evaluate the Answer Choices

Choice (A) matches the prediction: Certain knowledge of legality is necessary for people to feel secure. This is the correct answer.

---

[24]PrepTest 36, Sec. 3, Q 12

The timid tone of choice (C) represented by "they might not feel secure" takes it out of the running.

Choice (C) reverses the formal logic without negating, so you can eliminate it.

Choice (D) is out because the argument does not refer to laws that are not vague.

Choice (E), like choice (B), reverses the formal logic without negating and therefore mixes up the sufficient and necessary clauses.

8. **(A)**

<Publicity campaigns for endangered species are unlikely to have much impact on the most important environmental problems,> for while the ease of attributing feelings to large mammals facilitates evoking sympathy for them, it is more difficult to elicit sympathy for other kinds of organisms, such as the soil microorganisms on which large ecosystems and agriculture depend.

Which one of the following is an assumption on which the argument depends?

(A)   The most important environmental problems involve endangered species other than large mammals.

(B)   Microorganisms cannot experience pain or have other feelings.

(C)   Publicity campaigns for the environment are the most effective when they elicit sympathy for some organism.

(D)   People ignore environmental problems unless they believe the problems will affect creatures with which they sympathize.

(E)   An organism can be environmentally significant only if it affects large ecosystems or agriculture.[25]

Step 1. Identify the Question Type

The phrase "an assumption on which the argument depends" tells you this is a Necessary Assumption question.

Step 2. Untangle the Stimulus

"For" points to the evidence. Since there is no conclusion Keyword, look at the evidence and determine what it must support. Here, the conclusion is that publicity campaigns aren't likely to work for the most important environmental problems and the evidence is that it is easy to get sympathy only for large mammals, not the smaller, slimy creatures.

---

[25]PrepTest 35, Sec. 4, Q 16

Step 3. Make a Prediction

So, the author is making a couple of assumptions: 1) that eliciting sympathy is the likely way for a publicity campaign to be effective and 2) that most important environmental problems are the small organisms (not the large mammals for which the campaigns do work). Since the author is making a couple of assumptions, you can anticipate that there might be two or more answers that sound good and that you should be ready to use the denial test to confirm which is correct.

Step 4. Evaluate the Answer Choices

Choice (A) makes the connection, and because this is a necessary assumption, you can double-check your answer using the denial test. If choice (A) were false, and most important environmental problems did involve large mammals, then the publicity campaigns for endangered species would have a greater impact. So by denying choice (A), the argument falls apart and you know it is the answer.

Choice (B) does not work because it distorts the idea of feelings. The author does not say the microorganisms cannot feel, but rather people have trouble attributing feelings to them.

Choice (C) is tempting. The author does assume some connection between the ability to elicit sympathy and the likelihood that a publicity campaign will be effective. Your first clue that (C) is incorrect is how absolute it is: "most effective." But use the denial test: Choice (C) denied indicates that some other tactic besides eliciting sympathy could be the most effective. That doesn't prevent the author from properly concluding that sympathy is the way that has the greatest likelihood of being effective. You need to distinguish between probability of being effective and relative level of effectiveness; winning the lottery may be the most effective way of getting really rich, really quick, but the likelihood of that happening is extremely small.

The people ignoring environmental problems in choice (D) are not mentioned in the argument and are therefore outside the scope of the argument.

Choice (E) confuses environmental significance with important problems.

9. **(D)**

Professor: Each government should do all that it can to improve the well-being of all the children in the society it governs. <Therefore, governments should help finance high-quality day care since such day care will become available to families of all income levels if and only if it is subsidized.>

Which one of the following is an assumption on which the professor's argument depends?

(A) Only governments that subsidize high-quality day care take an interest in the well-being of all the children in the societies they govern.
(B) Government subsidy of high-quality day care would not be so expensive that it would cause a government to eliminate benefits for adults.
(C) High-quality day care should be subsidized only for those who could not otherwise afford it.
(D) At least some children would benefit from high-quality day care.
(E) Government is a more efficient provider of certain services than is private enterprise.[26]

Step 1. Identify the Question Type

"Assumption on which the professor's argument depends" signals a Necessary Assumption question.

Step 2. Untangle the Stimulus

"Therefore" identifies the conclusion, which recommends that government help fund high-quality day care. The professor reasons that government subsidization will make day care more widely accessible and that government should do all it can to improve the well-being of children.

Step 3. Make a Prediction

The author must assume that high-quality day care will improve the well-being of children.

Step 4. Evaluate the Answer Choices

Choice (A) talks about government taking an interest in children's well-being, not improving children's well-being. Cross out this choice.

Choice (B) is also out because it talks about benefits for adults, not benefits for children.

The need-based subsidy raised in choice (C) is outside the scope of the argument as is choice (E)'s comparison of government versus private enterprise efficiency.

---

[26]PrepTest 47, Sec. 1, Q 20

Choice (D) matches the prediction and is the correct answer. Notice how modest it is. The author has to believe that at least one child would benefit from day care to recommend that the government finance day care in order to meet its mandate to improve the well-being of children.

ASSUMPTION QUESTION REVIEW

Before you proceed to the next chapter, turn to Appendix A and complete the review exercise for Assumption questions. A completed chart is included in Appendix B.

CHAPTER 6

WEAKEN QUESTIONS

In the legal profession, you need to be able to identify an adversary's argument and weaken it. So it's no surprise that the LSAT includes a question type—Weaken questions—that tests your ability to do just that.

Weaken questions and Strengthen questions will account for approximately eight scored questions on test day, a sizeable chunk of the 50 scored Logical Reasoning questions. You can quickly earn valuable points on test day by mastering Weaken and Strengthen questions now.

DEFINITION OF WEAKEN QUESTIONS

Weaken questions ask you to find the answer choice that makes the conclusion less likely to follow from the evidence. You don't need to prove or disprove the argument. Instead, your task is to loosen the connection between the evidence and conclusion—or, as the chapter title implies, make it a weaker argument. Look at this example:

> A determination by the university that a student-athlete has not taken enough credits to be progressing toward a degree renders that student-athlete academically ineligible to compete. Henry did not play in Saturday's football game. Therefore, he must not have the proper number of credits to be progressing toward a degree.

When the author claims that Henry "must not" have the necessary credits, she is assuming that a lack of credits is the only factor that would make Henry ineligible to compete. To weaken this argument, you don't need to prove that Henry is progressing toward a degree; any new information that makes it less likely that he did not play because he is having trouble progressing toward a degree would weaken the author's claim. Here are some possible statements that could weaken the argument:

- Henry shows up at the game with a cast on his leg.
- The academic advisors for the athletic department follow the student-athletes very closely to ensure they are taking the proper number of credits to meet all eligibility requirements.

Neither statement explicitly or implicitly says that Henry is progressing toward his degree. However, an alternative reason for why he is not in the game (injury) and an attack on the conclusion (close academic monitoring by advisors) reduce the possibility that Henry does not have enough academic credit to progress toward a degree. That's all you need to do to weaken an argument: Find an answer that makes it less likely that the conclusion is true.

USE THE KAPLAN METHOD TO ANSWER WEAKEN QUESTIONS

Identify the Question Type

Obviously, to answer a Weaken question you have to be able to recognize a Weaken question. But don't worry. There are words in the question stem that indicate it's a Weaken question. They include:

- Weaken
- Calls into question
- Casts doubt on
- Undermine
- Counter
- Damages

Here's how these phrases could appear in question stems:

- Which one of the following, if true, most weakens the argument?
- Which one of the following, if true, most seriously undermines the hypothesis?
- Of the following, which one, if true, is the logically strongest counter the legislator can make to the commentator's argument?
- Which one of the following, if true, most calls into question the nutritionist's argument?
- Which one of the following, if true, most weakens the case for the department chair's position?
- The prediction that ends the passage would be most seriously called into question if it were true that in the last few years
- Each of the following, if true, weakens the official's argument EXCEPT:

Don't let the "if true" part fool you. It just tells you to accept the truth of the choice right off the bat, no matter how unlikely it may sound to you. Don't argue with the answer choices.

Untangle the Stimulus

Once you know you have a Weaken question, actively read the stimulus to determine the author's argument by finding the conclusion and the evidence. Just as you did with Assumption questions, circle any Keywords, bracket the conclusion, and then connect the evidence to the conclusion to find the assumption. Remember, to find the assumption, you need to either connect the mismatched terms or use formal logic, if applicable. If this was an Assumption question, you would stop here and compare your prediction to the answer choices. However, with a Weaken question you must use the conclusion, evidence, *and* the assumption to attack the argument and make the conclusion less likely to be true.

Make a Prediction

The key to weakening an argument is by either attacking the conclusion directly or by denying the author's assumption. Both of these viable approaches result in the same prediction; they just take different paths to get there. Look at the following example and I'll demonstrate these two practical ways to weaken the argument.

> Ozzie only read one book in the same week his sister read four books. Obviously, he is a slow reader.

The author concludes that Ozzie reads slowly based on the fact that he read one book while his sister read four books in the same time frame. Notice the mismatched terms: slow reader and one book. The author assumes that the only reason Ozzie read one book is because he is a slow reader. Stated more generally, the author assumes no other explanations exist and considers no other reasons for why Ozzie read just one book.

To weaken the argument, you can:

1. Attack the conclusion: Determine what you can add to the argument to make it more likely that Ozzie is not a slow reader. For example, maybe Ozzie's book was a thousand pages long while his sister read four books under a hundred pages each. Even though Ozzie read just one book, he read more pages than his sister, which casts doubt on whether he really is a slow reader.

2. Deny the assumption: Consider that being a slow reader is not the only explanation for why Ozzie read just one book in the time allotted, and identify other possibilities. For example, maybe Ozzie had a busy week with work deadlines and family obligations to meet. He had little free time to read all week, while his sister was not as busy and could spend much more time reading.

The most common method of weakening an argument is to break down the assumption by considering any alternative possibilities. Regardless of an argument's persuasiveness, you need to think critically and remember that a Weaken question has an inherent problem: an unstated piece of evidence. You need to ask yourself whether the author has ruled out all other possibilities, because when an author ignores alternative explanations in an argument, you can attack that misstep and look for alternative possibilities to reach the same conclusion.

As you read the stimulus of a Weaken question, pay particular attention to argument patterns. You can find two particular patterns in Weaken questions to help you: causal arguments and predictions.

Causality

Causal arguments are arguments in which the author asserts or denies a cause-and-effect relationship between two events or things. Causal arguments are frequently used on the LSAT, especially in Assumption family and Parallel Reasoning questions. Here are some examples:

- The potato chips he ate caused his face to break out.
- The new marketing plan is responsible for the company's rise in sales.
- The devastation in Haiti was brought about by the earthquake.
- Her sense of responsibility started when she got her first apartment.

Notice the explicit causation indicators like "caused," "responsible for," and "brought about by." You will also find more subtle terms, such as "started." Many of my students circle causation indicators to get in the habit of looking for causal arguments and to draw their attention to them. Give it a try as you practice untangling arguments. Here is a list of common of terms you can use to identify a cause-and-effect relationship:

- Caused
- Responsible for
- Brought about by
- Leads to
- Is a result of
- Produces
- Reason for
- Makes happen
- Starts
- Is an effect of
- Set off by

Also note that the causes and effects don't necessarily appear in the same order in every argument. From the previous examples, eating potato chips is the causal factor while breaking out is the result. Or, the marketing plan is identified as the cause of the resulting sales increase. However, the third and fourth examples puts the cause at the end of the sentence: The earthquake caused the devastation, and the first apartment caused the sense of responsibility, respectively. The point to take away is that just because a term comes first in a sentence does not mean it is the cause. You have to read the statement carefully and pay attention to causal indicators.

Recognizing causal arguments is important for Weaken questions because the LSAT offers three classic alternatives to undermine the claim. Take a look at this example:

> Amy got a camera for her birthday and always carries it with her. She wants to take pictures everywhere she goes. So, getting the camera must be the reason for her interest in photography.

Here, the author argues that Amy is interested in photography because she has a new camera. "Reason for" signals a causal relationship between the camera and photography. Notice, however, that the author tells you Amy got a new camera (X) and Amy wants to take pictures everywhere she goes (Y) and then assumes a causal relationship in which the camera is the cause and picture taking is the effect.

To weaken a causal argument, you have three options.

1. Reverse the causality (Y → X)

You know X and Y both happened, but the author assumed the direction of the causality flowed from X to Y. Maybe it's really reversed. Maybe Amy's interest in taking pictures caused her to get a camera.

2. Identify an independent alternative cause (Z → Y)

Maybe an outside factor, Z, caused Y to happen. For example, perhaps Amy wanted to share her travels with family and friends. So it wasn't the camera that sparked her interest in photography, but rather her wanting to show people the places she'd been.

3. Chalk it up to coincidence

The elements of the argument coincidentally happened together in time but there is no causal relationship. Amy got a camera and she took pictures but one did not cause the other.

Predictions

If the conclusion is stated as a prediction—a judgment about what is likely to happen in the future based on what is true in the past or the present—then you can weaken the argument by changing the circumstances on which the prediction is based. You can do this by showing the premise that supports it is inaccurate or irrelevant.

When Pauline opened her pizzeria, she beat her competitors' prices and all my neighbors became loyal customers. I doubt any of us will buy our pizza anywhere besides Pauline's Pizzeria.

In this example, the author predicts that she and her neighbors will always get their pizza from Pauline's Pizzeria because Pauline's sold the pies below her competitors' prices. Well sure, Pauline's prices were the lowest when the restaurant first opened. However, the author assumes the prices will continue to be the lowest and circumstances won't change: Pauline will keep her prices below competitors and the competitors will maintain their prices above Pauline's.

So, to weaken a prediction-based argument like this one, you need to look for an answer choice that changes the circumstances on which the prediction was made. Here, a correct answer choice will make Pauline's prices the same or above her competitors, or it could make a competitor's price the same or lower than Pauline's. For example, The Pizza Slice, a local pizzeria, celebrated its 10th anniversary by charging $10 for any pizza on the menu, the lowest price in town. This statement tells you that The Pizza Slice's prices are now lower than Pauline's. So, it is less likely that diners will stay loyal to Pauline's.

The main point I'm illustrating with these examples is that to make your answer prediction, think about how the author could reach a different conclusion or find an alternative explanation for how the author reached the conclusion.

Evaluate the Answer Choices

Finally, take your prediction and compare it to the answer choices; the selection that most closely matches your prediction is your answer.

It is unlikely you will find an answer that completely negates the conclusion and obliterates the argument. That type of obvious answer seldom occurs on the LSAT. The typical Weaken answer will hurt the conclusion, not destroy it.

Also, pay close attention to any new terminology introduced in the answer choices. Don't let that fool you. The test makers often include new terms in the correct answer to a Weaken question because they are necessary to effectively Weaken the stimulus. (Remember that this is not the case with an Assumption question; the answer to an Assumption question must come from the argument itself).

THE KAPLAN METHOD IN ACTION

Now I'll walk you through a couple examples to show you how the Kaplan Method can help you efficiently solve any Weaken question you'll see on test day.

1. The manager of a nuclear power plant defended the claim that the plant was safe by revealing its rate of injury for current workers: only 3.2 injuries per 200,000 hours of work, a rate less than half the national average for all industrial plants. The manager claimed that, therefore, by the standard of how many injuries occur, the plant was safer than most other plants where the employees could work.

    Which one of the following, if true, most calls into question the manager's claim?

    (A)   Workers at nuclear power plants are required to receive extra training in safety precautions on their own time and at their own expense.
    (B)   Workers at nuclear power plants are required to report to the manager any cases of accidental exposure to radiation.
    (C)   The exposure of the workers to radiation at nuclear power plants was within levels the government considers safe.
    (D)   Workers at nuclear power plants have filed only a few lawsuits against the management concerning unsafe working conditions.
    (E)   Medical problems arising from work at a nuclear power plant are unusual in that they are not likely to appear until after an employee has left employment at the plant.[1]

Step 1. Identify the Question Type

The phrase "calls into question" tells you that this is a Weaken question. The question specifically directs you to find the manager's claim.

Step 2. Untangle the Stimulus

The manager's claim in the last sentence coupled with "therefore" identifies the conclusion. The nuclear power plant was safer than most other plants. The evidence for the claim is the low injury rate compared to all industrial plants.

Step 3. Make a Prediction

The manager is comparing injury rates of a nuclear power plant to all industrial plants. Since this is a Weaken question, look for the questionable assumption. Here, she must assume they are comparable. What if they're not? Look for an answer that affects the injury rate comparison and makes the nuclear plant's rate higher or all plants' rates lower.

Step 4. Evaluate the Answer Choices

It's good to know, as choice (A) tells you, that nuclear-plant workers receive extra training and unfortunately they must train on their own time and at their own expense. However, that has no bearing on the manager's claim of a comparatively low injury rate. Eliminate this choice.

___
[1]PrepTest 25, Sec. 4, Q 3

Choice (B) states that nuclear plant workers must report any radiation exposure not just an actual injury, which implies the injury rate should be higher. Therefore, choice (B) strengthens the argument and is incorrect.

Choices (C) and (D) discuss safe radiation levels and lawsuits filed against the nuclear plant. They don't add any information regarding the rate of injury comparison, and thus, are out of scope.

Choice (E) implies that the lower injury rates at the nuclear plant are artificially low because medical problems are latent and appear after workers leave the plant and those injuries are not included. This is the correct answer.

2. Police commissioner: Last year our city experienced a 15 percent decrease in the rate of violent crime. At the beginning of that year a new mandatory sentencing law was enacted, which requires that all violent criminals serve time in prison. Since no other major policy changes were made last year, the drop in the crime rate must have been due to the new mandatory sentencing law.

Which one of the following, if true, most seriously weakens the police commissioner's argument?

(A)   Studies of many other cities have shown a correlation between improving economic conditions and decreased crime rates.

(B)   Prior to the enactment of the mandatory sentencing law, judges in the city had for many years already imposed unusually harsh penalties for some crimes.

(C)   Last year, the city's overall crime rate decreased by only 5 percent.

(D)   At the beginning of last year, the police department's definition of "violent crime" was broadened to include 2 crimes not previously classified as "violent."

(E)   The city enacted a policy 2 years ago requiring that 100 new police officers be hired in each of the 3 subsequent years.[2]

Step 1. Identify the Question Type

The phrase "most seriously weakens" tells you that this is a Weaken question.

Step 2. Untangle the Stimulus

The police commissioner concludes that the 15 percent drop in the crime rate was due to the new mandatory sentencing law. He supports his statement with evidence that no other major policy change was made last year except for that mandatory sentencing law. Do you see the causal language in the conclusion? That's right, "must have been due to." What is the cause

---

[2]PrepTest 47, Sec. 3, Q 24

and what is the effect? The police commissioner indicates that the sentencing law caused the crime rate reduction.

Step 3. Make a Prediction

To weaken a causal argument, look for the three classic alternatives: reverse the causal relationship, find an alternative cause, or chalk it up to coincidence. Remember, finding an alternative cause is always the most likely of the three alternatives.

In this case, the reversed relationship would mean that the reduced crime rate caused the mandatory sentencing law. But, that doesn't really make sense, so maybe there is another reason for reduction in the crime rate that the commissioner did not consider. Maybe the city added police officers on patrol or expanded neighborhood block watches. It could also be that the occurrence of the crime rate drop and the enactment of the mandatory sentencing laws is a mere coincidence. Keep those options in mind as you look over the answer choices.

Step 4. Evaluate the Answer Choices

Choice (A) alludes to an alternative cause for the drop in crime rate: improved economic conditions. But the study of other cities—not the one in question—identifies a correlation—not a causal relationship—between economic improvement and lower crime rate. Without information about the economic trends in this cities, this answer could weaken *or* strengthen the argument; it is completely ambiguous without knowing what direction the economy is headed in this town. Cross out this choice.

If judges imposed harsh penalties prior to the enactment of the mandatory sentencing law as choice (B) suggests, maybe the law just codified what was already in place. In other words, maybe the law did not do anything new. However, this answer has a problem. It refers to "unusually harsh" punishment applied to "some crimes" (meaning at least one, and not necessarily any violent crimes) rather than all violent crimes, as the new legislation did. Therefore, it is possible the legislation did have a causal relationship with the drop in crime rate. Move on to the next choice.

Choice (C) mentions the city's overall crime rate as opposed to the violent crime rate discussed in the argument. Therefore, it takes you outside the scope. Eliminate this choice.

Choice (D) expands the definition of a violent crime with the addition of a few new crimes but does not indicate any affect on the causality. If the mandatory sentencing law lowered the rate of occurrence of these new violent crimes, then, if anything, it would strengthen the argument.

That leaves one choice, choice (E), which offers an alternative cause for the reduced crime rate. Two years ago, the city decided to hire an additional 100 police officers each year for the next three years. An expanded police force is a viable reason for the drop in crime rate and thus weakens the argument that the reduction is due solely to the mandatory sentencing law. This is the correct answer.

WEAKEN QUESTIONS: NOW YOU TRY IT

Now it's your turn to try a Weaken question. Use the template I've provided after the question to guide you through the four-step Kaplan Method. (Note: On test day, you won't be writing out all the steps as you are in this exercise. However, as you are learning the Method, it's good practice to help it become second nature.) Remember to bracket the conclusion and circle Keywords.

1. Nutritionist: Recently a craze has developed for home juicers, $300 machines that separate the pulp of fruits and vegetables from the juice they contain. Outrageous claims are being made about the benefits of these devices: drinking the juice they produce is said to help one lose weight or acquire a clear complexion, to aid digestion, and even to prevent cancer. But there is no indication that juice separated from the pulp of the fruit or vegetable has any properties that it does not have when unseparated. Save your money. If you want carrot juice, eat a carrot.

   Which one of the following, if true, most calls into question the nutritionist's argument?

   (A) Most people find it much easier to consume a given quantity of nutrients in liquid form than to eat solid foods containing the same quantity of the same nutrients.

   (B) Drinking juice from home juicers is less healthy than is eating fruits and vegetables because such juice does not contain the fiber that is eaten if one consumes the entire fruit or vegetable.

   (C) To most people who would be tempted to buy a home juicer, $300 would not be a major expense.

   (D) The nutritionist was a member of a panel that extensively evaluated early prototypes of home juicers.

   (E) Vitamin pills that supposedly contain nutrients available elsewhere only in fruits and vegetables often contain a form of those compounds that cannot be as easily metabolized as the varieties found in fruits and vegetables.[3]

---

[3]PrepTest 36, Sec. 1, Q 2

Step 1. Identify the Question Type

_____

Step 2. Untangle the Stimulus

_____

Step 3. Make a Prediction

_____

Step 4. Evaluate the Answer Choices

_____

Explanations

1. **(A)**

Nutritionist: Recently a craze has developed for home juicers, $300 machines that separate the pulp of fruits and vegetables from the juice they contain. Outrageous claims are being made about the benefits of these devices: drinking the juice they produce is said to help one lose weight or acquire a clear complexion, to aid digestion, and even to prevent cancer. But there is no indication that juice separated from the pulp of the fruit or vegetable has any properties that it does not have when unseparated. <Save your money.> If you want carrot juice, eat a carrot.

Which one of the following, if true, most calls into question the nutritionist's argument?

(A) Most people find it much easier to consume a given quantity of nutrients in liquid form than to eat solid foods containing the same quantity of the same nutrients.

(B) Drinking juice from home juicers is less healthy than is eating fruits and vegetables because such juice does not contain the fiber that is eaten if one consumes the entire fruit or vegetable.

(C) To most people who would be tempted to buy a home juicer, $300 would not be a major expense.

(D) The nutritionist was a member of a panel that extensively evaluated early prototypes of home juicers.

(E) Vitamin pills that supposedly contain nutrients available elsewhere only in fruits and vegetables often contain a form of those compounds that cannot be as easily metabolized as the varieties found in fruits and vegetables.[4]

Step 1. Identify the Question Type

The phrase "calls into question" is a common weaken indicator; not all Weaken question stems contain the work "weaken." The phrase "nutritionist's argument" directs you specifically to look for what he concluded and why.

Step 2. Untangle the Stimulus

The first two sentences of this stimulus present background information about juicers: they work by separating the pulp of fruits and vegetables from their juice, and they have become quite popular for their health benefits. However, "but" signals that the nutritionist disagrees

---

with these claims. The nutritionist concludes that potential juicer customers should save their $300 and eat the fruits and vegetables in their solid form.

Step 3. Make a Prediction

The nutritionist assumes that there's no reason to drink the juice other than for health reasons. But what if there was? That is, look at the answer choices for alternative reasons to buy the juicer. The correct answer will make the conclusion less likely that customers should not buy the juicer; or, put more clearly, it will provide a reason why customers *should* buy the juicer.

Step 4. Evaluate the Answer Choices

Choice (A) offers a reason to buy a juicer—nutrients in liquid form rather than solid are easier to consume for most people—and therefore is the correct answer.

Choice (B) strengthens the argument, so it is incorrect; the fact that the juice is less healthy supports the choice of not buying the juicer.

Choice (C) is wrong. The cost of the juicer is mentioned in the stimulus but is not a factor in the argument; the juicer's affordability is not the issue, its practical value is. The nutritionist's evaluation of the early juicer prototype, presented in choice (D) is irrelevant.

Choice (E) draws an irrelevant comparison between the nutrition in vitamin pills and fruits and vegetables which is outside the scope of the argument.

DRILL: PRACTICING WEAKEN QUESTIONS

Use the Kaplan Method to answer the following Weaken questions. Take this opportunity to practice and apply the steps in the Method so you are comfortable using them on test day. Be sure to circle conclusion and evidence Keywords and bracket the conclusion. Check your responses against the full explanations provided after the Drill.

1. Opponents of allowing triple-trailer trucks to use the national highway system are wrong in claiming that these trucks are more dangerous than other commercial vehicles. In the western part of the country, in areas where triple-trailers are now permitted on some highways, for these vehicles the rate of road accident fatalities per mile of travel is lower than the national rate for other types of commercial vehicles. Clearly, triple-trailers are safer than other commercial vehicles.

   Which one of the following, if true, most substantially weakens the argument?

   (A) It takes two smaller semitrailers to haul as much weight as a single triple-trailer can.
   (B) Highways in the sparsely populated West are much less heavily traveled and consequently are far safer than highways in the national system as a whole.
   (C) Opponents of the triple-trailers also once opposed the shorter twin-trailers, which are now common on the nation's highways.
   (D) In areas where the triple-trailers are permitted, drivers need a special license to operate them.
   (E) For triple-trailers the rate of road accident fatalities per mile of travel was higher last year than in the two previous years.[5]

2. Compared to us, people who lived a century ago had very few diversions to amuse them. Therefore, they likely read much more than we do today.

   Which one of the following statements, if true, most weakens the argument?

   (A) Many of the books published a century ago were of low literary quality.
   (B) On average, people who lived a century ago had considerably less leisure time than we do today.
   (C) The number of books sold today is larger than it was a century ago.
   (D) On the average, books today cost slightly less in relation to other goods than they did a century ago.
   (E) One of the popular diversions of a century ago was horse racing.[6]

3. The play *Mankind* must have been written between 1431 and 1471. It cannot have been written before 1431, for in that year the rose noble, a coin mentioned in the play, was first circulated. The play cannot have been written after 1471, since in that year King Henry VI died, and he is mentioned as a living monarch in the play's dedication.

   The argument would be most seriously weakened if which one of the following were discovered?

   (A) The Royal Theatre Company includes the play on a list of those performed in 1480.
   (B) Another coin mentioned in the play was first minted in 1422.
   (C) The rose noble was neither minted nor circulated after 1468.
   (D) Although Henry VI was deposed in 1461, he was briefly restored to the throne in 1470.
   (E) In a letter written in early 1428, a merchant told of having seen the design for a much-discussed new coin called the "rose noble."[7]

---

[5]PrepTest 20, Sec. 4, Q 3

[6]PrepTest 37, Sec. 2, Q 4
[7]PrepTest 24, Sec. 3, Q 9

4. It is probably not true that colic in infants is caused by the inability of those infants to tolerate certain antibodies found in cow's milk, since it is often the case that symptoms of colic are shown by infants that are fed breast milk exclusively.

Which one of the following, if true, most seriously weakens the argument?

(A) A study involving 500 sets of twins has found that if one infant has colic, its twin will probably also have colic.

(B) Symptoms of colic generally disappear as infants grow older, whether the infants have been fed breast milk exclusively or have been fed infant formula containing cow's milk.

(C) In a study of 5,000 infants who were fed only infant formula containing cow's milk, over 4,000 of the infants never displayed any symptoms of colic.

(D) When mothers of infants that are fed only breast milk eliminate cow's milk and all products made from cow's milk from their own diets, any colic symptoms that their infants have manifested quickly disappear.

(E) Infants that are fed breast milk develop mature digestive systems at an earlier age than do those that are fed infant formulas, and infants with mature digestive systems are better able to tolerate certain proteins and antibodies found in cow's milk.[8]

5. Parent P: Children will need computer skills to deal with tomorrow's world. Computers should be introduced in kindergarten, and computer languages should be required in high school.

Parent Q: That would be pointless. Technology advances so rapidly that the computers used by today's kindergartners and the computer languages taught in today's high schools would become obsolete by the time these children are adults.

Which one of the following, if true, is the strongest logical counter parent P can make to parent Q's objection?

(A) When technology is advancing rapidly, regular training is necessary to keep one's skills at a level proficient enough to deal with the society in which one lives.

(B) Throughout history people have adapted to change, and there is no reason to believe that today's children are not equally capable of adapting to technology as it advances.

(C) In the process of learning to work with any computer or computer language, children increase their ability to interact with computer technology.

(D) Automotive technology is continually advancing too, but that does not result in one's having to relearn to drive cars as the new advances are incorporated into new automobiles.

(E) Once people have graduated from high school, they have less time to learn about computers and technology than they had during their schooling years.[9]

---

6. Letter to the editor: After Baerton's factory closed, there was a sharp increase in the number of claims filed for job-related injury compensation by the factory's former employees. Hence there is reason to believe that most of those who filed for compensation after the factory closed were just out to gain benefits they did not deserve, and filed only to help them weather their job loss.

Each of the following, if true, weakens the argument above EXCEPT:

(A) Workers cannot file for compensation for many job-related injuries, such as hearing loss from factory noise, until they have left the job.

(B) In the years before the factory closed, the factory's managers dismissed several employees who had filed injury claims.

(C) Most workers who receive an injury on the job file for compensation on the day they suffer the injury.

(D) Workers who incur partial disabilities due to injuries on the job often do not file for compensation because they would have to stop working to receive compensation but cannot afford to live on that compensation alone.

(E) Workers who are aware that they will soon be laid off from a job often become depressed, making them more prone to job-related injuries.[10]

7. Several companies will soon offer personalized electronic news services, delivered via cable or telephone lines and displayed on a television. People using these services can view continually updated stories on those topics for which they subscribe. Since these services will provide people with the information they are looking for more quickly and efficiently than printed newspapers can, newspaper sales will decline drastically if these services become widely available.

Which one of the following, if true, most seriously weakens the argument?

(A) In reading newspapers, most people not only look for stories on specific topics but also like to idly browse through headlines or pictures for amusing stories on unfamiliar or unusual topics.

(B) Companies offering personalized electronic news services will differ greatly in what they charge for access to their services, depending on how wide a range of topics they cover.

(C) Approximately 30 percent of people have never relied on newspapers for information but instead have always relied on news programs broadcast on television and radio.

(D) The average monthly cost of subscribing to several channels on a personalized electronic news service will approximately equal the cost of a month's subscription to a newspaper.

(E) Most people who subscribe to personalized electronic news services will not have to pay extra costs for installation since the services will use connections installed by cable and telephone companies.[11]

Explanations

1. **(B)**

<Opponents of allowing triple-trailer trucks to use the national highway system are wrong in claiming that these trucks are more dangerous than other commercial vehicles.> In the western part of the country, in areas where triple-trailers are now permitted on some highways, for these vehicles the rate of road accident fatalities per mile of travel is lower than the national rate for other types of commercial vehicles. <Clearly, triple-trailers are safer than other commercial vehicles.>

Which one of the following, if true, most substantially (weakens) the argument?

(A)   It takes two smaller semitrailers to haul as much weight as a single triple-trailer can.

(B)   Highways in the sparsely populated West are much less heavily traveled and consequently are far safer than highways in the national system as a whole.

(C)   Opponents of the triple-trailers also once opposed the shorter twin-trailers, which are now common on the nation's highways.

(D)   In areas where the triple-trailers are permitted, drivers need a special license to operate them.

(E)   For triple-trailers the rate of road accident fatalities per mile of travel was higher last year than in the two previous years.[12]

Step 1. Identify the Question Type

The author uses the phrase "most substantially weakens," which is the language of a Weaken question.

Step 2. Untangle the Stimulus

The author states his conclusion twice for emphasis. In the first sentence, he says people are wrong to say triple-trailer trucks (TTTs) are more dangerous than other commercial vehicles. In the last sentence, he adds the word "clearly" to emphasize the conclusive nature of a positive version of a similar statement: TTTs are safer than commercial vehicles. The author offers as evidence of TTT safety the western part of the country where the rate of road incident vehicles per mile of travel is lower than the national rate for other commercial vehicles. Do you see a pattern in the argument? The author says that TTTs are safer than commercial vehicles out West, therefore, TTTs are safer everywhere.

---

[12]PrepTest 20, Sec. 4, Q 3

Step 3. Make a Prediction

The author assumes that TTT safety in the western part of the country is comparable to the whole country. To weaken the argument, you need to reduce the likelihood that western TTT safety would hold in other parts of the country.

Step 4. Evaluate the Answer Choices

Choice (A) is outside the scope as it deals with the hauling capacity of a TTT rather than safety. This choice is out.

Choice (B) provides a rationale for a better safety record for western highways. This matches the prediction and is the correct answer.

The TTT opponents' past opposition to shorter twin-trailers as presented in choice (C) has no bearing on the argument.

Having a special license to drive a TTT as stated in choice (D) has no impact on the argument unless the license carries a requirement for special training that renders the TTTs safer on the road than other trucks. In that case, the special license would strengthen, not weaken, the argument.

The argument compares the TTT safety record to the safety record of other commercial vehicles. Choice (E), which addresses a rise in the TTT accident rate without comparison information about the other commercial vehicles, does not address whether the TTT is safer than other commercial vehicles.

2.   **(B)**

Compared to us, people who lived a century ago had very few diversions to amuse them. <Therefore,> they likely read much more than we do today.>

Which one of the following statements, if true, most (weakens) the argument?

(A)   Many of the books published a century ago were of low literary quality.
(B)   On average, people who lived a century ago had considerably less leisure time than we do today.
(C)   The number of books sold today is larger than it was a century ago.
(D)   On the average, books today cost slightly less in relation to other goods than they did a century ago.
(E)   One of the popular diversions of a century ago was horse racing.[13]

---

[13]PrepTest 37, Sec. 2, Q 4

Step 1. Identify the Question Type

The question uses standard Weaken language.

Step 2. Untangle the Stimulus

The word "Therefore" points you to the conclusion that people who lived a century ago probably read more than we do today. The author supports the claim with evidence that our ancestors had fewer diversions back then.

Step 3. Make a Prediction

According to the author, those who lived a century ago had fewer things to do, so they read more than us. That seems like a big logical jump. For example, the few things they did might have left them no time for reading. Or maybe, they chose a different activity than reading. There are lots of opportunities here to loosen the connection between conclusion and evidence and weaken the argument.

Step 4. Evaluate the Answer Choices

The low level of literary quality discussed in choice (A) does not affect the connection between fewer diversions and more reading. In fact, some might argue that low literary quality may not deter readers with time on their hands looking for anything to read. In that scenario, low literary quality would support the argument that our ancestors read more than us. Eliminate this choice.

Choice (B) matches the prediction. Without much leisure time, people 100 years ago didn't have time to read even if that was their only leisure activity option. This is the correct answer.

Choice (C) states that the number of books sold today is greater than 100 years ago. The implication is that more books sold means more books read. However, you don't know the number of book buyers or the number of books they bought. You also can't use this information to determine whether the buyers actually read the books let alone read more.

Choice (D) offers an irrelevant comparison between the cost of books and other goods. The answer choice insinuates that a lower book cost would influence readers to read. However, this statement does not tell us anything about the actual price, just that it is lower than other goods.

Choice (E) is equally problematic. It identifies horse racing as another diversion for people 100 years ago. However, it does not address the number of readers today compared to a century ago.

3.   **(E)**

<The play *Mankind* must have been written between 1431 and 1471.> It cannot have been written before 1431, (for) in that year the rose noble, a coin mentioned in the play, was first circulated. The play cannot have been written after 1471, (since) in that year King Henry VI died, and he is mentioned as a living monarch in the play's dedication.

The argument would be most seriously (weakened) if which one of the following were discovered?

(A)   The Royal Theatre Company includes the play on a list of those performed in 1480.
(B)   Another coin mentioned in the play was first minted in 1422.
(C)   The rose noble was neither minted nor circulated after 1468.
(D)   Although Henry VI was deposed in 1461, he was briefly restored to the throne in 1470.
(E)   In a letter written in early 1428, a merchant told of having seen the design for a much-discussed new coin called the "rose noble."[14]

Step 1. Identify the Question Type

Again, this question uses standard Weaken language.

Step 2. Untangle the Stimulus

In the first sentence, the author pinpoints the time period in which *Mankind* was written as between 1431 and 1471. The author presents two pieces of evidence to explain why the play must have been written during this span. First, she eliminates the possibility it was written before 1431 because a coin mentioned in the play was not circulated until after 1431. Then, she says 1471 had to be the latest year because the play mentions Henry VI as a living king, and he died in 1471.

Step 3. Make a Prediction

The author assumes that a coin circulated after 1431 and the mention of a living king who died in 1471 absolutely set a boundary for the creation date of the play. The correct answer will attack the assumption and raise the possibility that the play was written before or after the speculated time period. This general prediction is enough to move forward and compare to the given answer choices. However, you may have predicted something more specific, such as "The exact year of King Henry VI's death is in dispute. While some claim he died in 1471, a growing number of historians believe he died in 1476." Whether your prediction is general or specific, it probably won't match the correct answer choice exactly. You must be flexible.

[14]PrepTest 24, Sec. 3, Q 9

Step 4. Evaluate the Answer Choices

Choice (A) states the play was not performed until 1480. However, a 1480 play opening does not mean the play was written after 1471. The performance date is irrelevant in this argument. Cross out this choice.

Choice (B) discusses another coin mentioned in the play that was minted prior to 1431. This earlier-minted coin has no impact on the argument because it has nothing to do with the connection between the rose noble coin and the play's date of origin. Eliminate this choice.

The date of the rose noble coin's disappearance given in choice (C) does nothing to expand the play's time frame. The play could still have been written after 1431. This choice is wrong.

Choice (D) offers information about when King Henry VI was in power. The only important date is the year in which Henry died, 1471. Whether he was on the throne, Henry was a living monarch until he died in 1471. This choice is out, too.

Choice (E) essentially states that a circulation date of 1431 does not eliminate the possibility it was created prior to that year. You don't need to make it absolutely true the coin was created outside of the time frame, but just raise the possibility. That's what (E) does, and so it is the correct answer.

4. **(D)**

<It is probably not true that colic in infants is caused by the inability of those infants to tolerate certain antibodies found in cow's milk,> (since) it is often the case that symptoms of colic are shown by infants that are fed breast milk exclusively.

Which one of the following, if true, most seriously (weakens) the argument?

(A) A study involving 500 sets of twins has found that if one infant has colic, its twin will probably also have colic.

(B) Symptoms of colic generally disappear as infants grow older, whether the infants have been fed breast milk exclusively or have been fed infant formula containing cow's milk.

(C) In a study of 5,000 infants who were fed only infant formula containing cow's milk, over 4,000 of the infants never displayed any symptoms of colic.

(D) When mothers of infants that are fed only breast milk eliminate cow's milk and all products made from cow's milk from their own diets, any colic symptoms that their infants have manifested quickly disappear.

(E) Infants that are fed breast milk develop mature digestive systems at an earlier age than do those that are fed infant formulas, and infants with mature digestive systems are better able to tolerate certain proteins and antibodies found in cow's milk.[15]

Step 1. Identify the Question Type

"Weaken" signals a Weaken question.

Step 2. Untangle the Stimulus

"Since" points to the evidence that infants fed only breast milk can show symptoms of colic. Based on this, the author disagrees with the thought that the inability to tolerate cow's milk causes colic in infants. In other words, the author concludes that cow's milk is not responsible for colic in infants because breast-fed infants also show signs of colic.

Step 3. Make a Prediction

The author assumes that an infant raised exclusively on breast milk has no access to the antibodies in cow's milk. The access to cow's milk is certainly not direct, but is there any way a breast-fed infant could be exposed indirectly to cow's milk? If so, you will weaken the argument. Check the answers for any indication that cow's milk still plays some role in breast-fed infants who have colic.

---

[15]PrepTest 20, Sec. 1, Q 12

Step 4. Evaluate the Answer Choices

Choice (A) does not weaken the argument because it ignores the type of milk the twin infants received. Cross out this choice.

Choice (B) focuses on the disappearance of colic while the argument discusses the cause of colic. So this answer is clearly outside the scope.

Choice (C) has the same problem. The argument is not about infants who don't develop colic, but rather infants who do. If anything, the answer strengthens the author's argument by indicating more than 80% of the infants in the study drank cow's milk and showed no signs of colic.

Choice (D) matches the prediction. When the breast-feeding mothers eliminate all forms of cow's milk from their diets, their infants' colic symptoms disappear. So the mothers may have indirectly exposed their infants to cow's milk. You still don't know if cow's milk definitely causes colic, but the author's conclusion that cow's milk probably does not cause colic is seriously weakened.

Choice (E) sheds no light on the connection between cow's milk and colic and therefore has no effect on the argument.

5. **(C)**

Parent P: Children will need computer skills to deal
with tomorrow's world. Computers should be
introduced in kindergarten, and computer
languages should be required in high school.
Parent Q: <That would be pointless.> Technology
advances so rapidly that the computers used by
today's kindergartners and the computer languages
taught in today's high schools would become
obsolete by the time these children are adults.

Which one of the following, if true, is the strongest
logical (counter) parent P can make to parent Q's
objection?

(A)   When technology is advancing rapidly, regular
       training is necessary to keep one's skills at a
       level proficient enough to deal with the society
       in which one lives.
(B)   Throughout history people have adapted to
       change, and there is no reason to believe that
       today's children are not equally capable of
       adapting to technology as it advances.
(C)   In the process of learning to work with any
       computer or computer language, children
       increase their ability to interact with computer
       technology.
(D)   Automotive technology is continually advancing
       too, but that does not result in one's having to
       relearn to drive cars as the new advances are
       incorporated into new automobiles.
(E)   Once people have graduated from high school,
       they have less time to learn about computers and
       technology than they had during their schooling
       years.[16]

Step 1. Identify the Question Type

"Counter" indicates this is a Weaken question. You are asked to counter, or weaken, parent Q's objection.

Step 2. Untangle the Stimulus

Start with Q's objection "That would be pointless" and determine what "That" is. Q is referring to P's proposal to introduce children to computers and computer language in school, and he concludes the proposal is pointless. His evidence is that the technology the schoolchildren learn will be obsolete by the time they reach adulthood.

Step 3. Make a Prediction

Q assumes that any exposure to technology has no use or relevance in the future. The answer choice indicating that early exposure to technology supports future computer skills will weaken the argument.

---

[16]PrepTest 35, Sec. 1, Q 4

Step 4. Evaluate the Answer Choices

Choice (A) raises the need for ongoing training as technology advances, which reduces the importance of early training. Go on to the next choice.

The ability to adapt to change discussed in choice (B) is outside the scope. Whether today's children can adapt to technology changes like people throughout history have adapted to change has no impact on the argument.

Choice (C) matches the prediction. It says that children who learn to work with computers and computer language are better able to interact with technology. In other words, early computer training benefits the children's future computer work. This is the correct answer.

Choice (D) makes an analogy to automotive technology based on an assumption that automotive technology and computer technology are comparable. Without establishing a direct connection between the two, knowing that early driving training was useful even as the industry instituted advances, does not help establish that the same will happen in the computer industry.

Choice (E) implies that computers and technology should be taught while children are in school because they have more time compared to after high school graduation. It does not address the value of early training, which the correct answer requires.

6. **(C)**

Letter to the editor: After Baerton's factory closed, there was a sharp increase in the number of claims filed for job-related injury compensation by the factory's former employees. <(Hence) there is reason to believe that most of those who filed for compensation after the factory closed were just out to gain benefits they did not deserve, and filed only to help them weather their job loss.>

Each of the following, if true, (weakens) the argument above (EXCEPT:)

(A) Workers cannot file for compensation for many job-related injuries, such as hearing loss from factory noise, until they have left the job.
(B) In the years before the factory closed, the factory's managers dismissed several employees who had filed injury claims.
(C) Most workers who receive an injury on the job file for compensation on the day they suffer the injury.
(D) Workers who incur partial disabilities due to injuries on the job often do not file for compensation because they would have to stop working to receive compensation but cannot afford to live on that compensation alone.
(E) Workers who are aware that they will soon be laid off from a job often become depressed, making them more prone to job-related injuries.[17]

---

[17]PrepTest 24, Sec. 3, Q 22

Step 1. Identify the Question Type

The phrase "weakens the argument above EXCEPT" tells you the answer choices include four answers that weaken the argument and one answer—the correct answer—that either strengthens the argument or has no effect on the argument at all. Circling the word "EXCEPT" will help keep you from marking an answer choice that weakens the argument.

Step 2. Untangle the Stimulus

"Hence" directs you to the conclusion that workers filed job-related injury claims seeking benefits they did not deserve after the factory closed. The letter writer's evidence is that there was a sharp increase in the number of job-related injury claims filed after the factory closed.

Step 3. Make a Prediction

The letter writer jumps from evidence of an increase in claims to a conclusion of fraud and greed. So, he must assume that fraud and greed are the only explanation for the increase in claims after the factory closed. Because this is a Weaken . . . EXCEPT question, the four wrong answers will weaken the argument by presenting an alternative explanation for the increase in claims. As you find those weakeners, cross them out to eliminate them. The correct answer strengthens the argument or is completely irrelevant. Possible strengtheners would eliminate other explanations for the rise in filed claims or confirm that the workers are fraudulent and greedy.

Step 4. Evaluate the Answer Choices

Choice (A) weakens the argument by requiring workers to file for many job-related injury benefits only after they have left the job. So, you would expect the number of filings to rise upon the closing of the factory since the end of the workers' jobs was a necessary condition for filing many injury claims.

Choice (B) provides another explanation for why factory workers would wait and file upon the closing of the factory: They no longer had jobs to lose and did not have to worry about retaliation from the factory managers.

Choice (C) has no weakening impact on the argument and is therefore the correct answer. That most workers file when they suffer an injury does nothing to explain why the workers at this factory would wait until the factory closed. By eliminating a potential alternative explanation for the timing of the claims—that workers typically wait to file a claim—this fact marginally strengthens the argument that greed is the explanation.

Choice (D) offers further incentive for workers to postpone filing injury claims. Filing under the circumstances means they would have to stop work and would receive inadequate compensation.

Choices (A), (B), and (D) all present viable reasons for the workers to file injury claims after the factory closed and thus raise the number of claims filed. In choice (E), workers aren't postponing the filing of a claim, but rather filing for claims that arise legitimately as the factory closes. It's not fraud or greed that causes the rise in filings. It's the injuries that occur as workers anticipate layoffs.

7.   **(A)**

Several companies will soon offer personalized electronic news services, delivered via cable or telephone lines and displayed on a television. People using these services can view continually updated stories on those topics for which they subscribe. (Since) these services will provide people with the information they are looking for more quickly and efficiently than printed newspapers can, <newspaper sales will decline drastically if these services become widely available.>

Which one of the following, if true, most seriously (weakens) the argument?

(A)   In reading newspapers, most people not only look for stories on specific topics but also like to idly browse through headlines or pictures for amusing stories on unfamiliar or unusual topics.

(B)   Companies offering personalized electronic news services will differ greatly in what they charge for access to their services, depending on how wide a range of topics they cover.

(C)   Approximately 30 percent of people have never relied on newspapers for information but instead have always relied on news programs broadcast on television and radio.

(D)   The average monthly cost of subscribing to several channels on a personalized electronic news service will approximately equal the cost of a month's subscription to a newspaper.

(E)   Most people who subscribe to personalized electronic news services will not have to pay extra costs for installation since the services will use connections installed by cable and telephone companies.[18]

Step 1. Identify the Question Type

Again, "weakens" indicates that this a Weaken question.

Step 2. Untangle the Stimulus

In the last half of the final sentence, the author concludes that newspaper sales will experience a drastic decline. The decline is based on evidence that electronic services are more efficient in providing information that people seek.

_____

[18]PrepTest 36, Sec. 3, Q 2

Step 3. Make a Prediction

The author assumes that providing information people want more efficiently is the only factor used to choose a news service and ignores other possibilities. The correct answer will provide an additional factor people use to select their news source.

Step 4. Evaluate the Answer Choices

Choice (A) provides a feature that newspapers offer and that cannot be duplicated by the electronic media, and therefore, gives another reason the newspaper may remain attractive to readers. This is the correct answer.

The different prices of the electronic news services in choice (B) do nothing to make the printed newspaper more attractive or the electronic services less attractive to the reader.

Choice (C) refers to a group of people that don't read the newspapers, which is outside the scope of this argument. Additionally, the group of non-newspaper readers cannot contribute to a decline in newspaper sales.

Choice (D) strengthens the argument. If the subscription prices are the same for the printed and electronic news, cost cannot differentiate the two mediums and circumstances on which the prediction was made remains the same. So, the electronic news service remains more attractive to the reader than the printed service because it is faster and more efficient.

Choice (E) does not give enough information about the electronic compared to the printed news to determine if one service is more enticing to readers than the other. If anything, choice (E) strengthens the argument by making the cost of electronic service installation negligible.

WEAKEN REVIEW

Before you proceed to the next chapter, turn to Appendix A and complete the review exercise for Weaken questions. A completed chart is included in Appendix B.

CHAPTER 7

STRENGTHEN QUESTIONS

Strengthen questions test your ability to identify an argument and add something to it to make it stronger. As a lawyer, you'll need to present your client's best case whether in negotiations or in trial, and so your ability to strengthen an argument is essential to this basic professional responsibility.

Consider the following scenario: A lawyer represents an experienced and highly successful college basketball coach in negotiations to extend his contract with a university. She plans to request a salary increase and additional retirement benefits. She will argue that her client is the best person for the job given his credentials, the job requirements, and the needs of the university. She will strengthen her argument by reminding the university officials of her client's tournament success, recruiting triumphs, and sellout crowds, as well as the difficulty and cost of replacing the coach. Because the lawyer was able to effectively present a strong argument, she increased the chances that the university would grant her client's requests. Now, this may be a simplified example, but I hope it illustrates how essential this skill is in the law profession.

Strengthen questions are similar to Weaken questions—just the opposite side of the coin. The two question types both require you to focus on the argument by identifying the conclusion and evidence and linking them with the assumption. However, they ask you to perform opposite tasks with these elements: Strengthen questions task you to use the elements to build support for an argument, while Weaken questions direct you to use the elements to undermine the argument.

Strengthen and Weaken questions together make up about eight out of 50 scored Logical Reasoning questions on the LSAT. They are also part of the Assumption family of questions, which accounts for half of the scored Logical Reasoning points. So, practicing and mastering Strengthen and Weaken questions can help you earn a substantial number of points on test day.

DEFINITION OF STRENGTHEN QUESTIONS

As I mentioned before, Strengthen questions ask you to provide additional information to an argument to make the conclusion more likely to happen. Strengthening an argument does not mean you must make it true; rather, your job is to add information to bolster the argument so the conclusion is more likely to follow from the evidence.

Look at this example from the Weaken chapter:

> A determination by the university that a student-athlete has not taken enough credits to be progressing toward a degree renders that student-athlete academically ineligible to compete. Henry did not play in Saturday's football game. Therefore, he must not have the proper number of credits to be progressing toward a degree.

To strengthen this argument, you don't have to prove that Henry lacks the requisite number of credits to progress toward his degree, which is why he's not playing. Instead, you need to add something to the argument to make it more likely that Henry is missing credits, can't meet degree standards, and consequently can't compete. Can you think of anything to support the argument? Take a look at the following statements:

- When Henry got sick last semester, he had to drop a few courses in his psychology major.
- Henry is playing injury-free this season.
- Henry's coach reported no disciplinary problems to the pro scouts asking about him last week.
- Henry beat out all his competition for the starting running back position.

None of the statements specifically pinpoint that Henry failed to meet the progress toward degree requirements. However, dropping some courses for his major and eliminating other reasons for Henry to miss a game (injury, disciplinary problems, and competition) support the possibility that Henry missed the game because of academic ineligibility. That's all you need to do to strengthen an argument: Find an answer that makes it more likely that the conclusion is true.

An answer that essentially confirms the conclusion like "Henry, a senior, is five credits shy of the mandatory credits for a fourth year psychology major" would strengthen the argument, but seldom occurs on the LSAT. The typical strengthen answer will support the conclusion, not specifically confirm it. However, just as I discussed in the Weaken chapter, answers to Strengthen questions can include new terms. It's appropriate to look for information outside the argument to make the conclusion more likely to be true from the evidence.

USE THE KAPLAN METHOD TO ANSWER STRENGTHEN QUESTIONS

Identify the Question Type

As was the case with Weaken questions, there are certain words in the question stem that help you to recognize a Strengthen question. Some of those include:

- Strengthen
- Support
- Justify

In addition to those words, there are specific question stems that indicate a Strengthen question. They include:

- Which one of the following, if true, most strengthens the argument above?
- Which one of the following, if true, most strongly supports the claim above?
- Each of the following, if true, strengthens the argument EXCEPT:
- Which one of the following, if true, provides the strongest additional support for the hypotheses above?
- Which one of the following, if true, most helps to justify the company president's criticism of the human resources department's proposal?

Notice that Strengthen question stems typically begin with phrases such as, "Which of the following, if true, most…." Don't get hung up on the words "if true" and "most." Over thinking those terms is a common pitfall for students. "If true" tells you to accept the answer choice as true and not to argue with it. "Most" does not indicate a contest between the five answer choices in which you choose the best from amongst them—so don't approach the answer looking for the choice that best strengthens the argument. Rather, only the correct answer choice—the one you're looking for—will strengthen the argument, while the other four choices will not.

Untangle the Stimulus

Just as you did with Assumption and Weaken questions, read a Strengthen stimulus to find the argument. First, circle any Keywords. Then find the conclusion, bracket it, and look for the evidence the author is using to support the conclusion. Next, connect the evidence to the conclusion to find the author's assumption. Finally, you use the conclusion, evidence, and the assumption to support the argument and make the conclusion more likely to be true.

Make a Prediction

When predicting an answer choice that strengthens an argument, you need to think of ways to bolster the building blocks that make up the argument. You can do this in several different ways:

- Support the conclusion.
- Confirm the assumption.
- Discount objections to the argument.
- Eliminate alternative explanations.

Review the following example to see how this works:

> State University's Athletic Director wants the swimming and diving program to return to its glory days of conference championships and national record holders. Consequently, she committed to building a new, state-of-the-art aquatic facility.

The author concludes that the Athletic Director will build a new aquatic facility. The evidence provided is that she wants to improve the swimming and diving program's record. So, the author must assume that beating the competition requires a new facility.

To strengthen this argument, you can:

1. Support the conclusion: Determine what you can add to the argument to make it more likely that building a new aquatic center will meet the Athletic Director's competitive goal. For instance, the correct answer could cite another university that built a new aquatic facility and improved its competitive success.

2. Confirm the assumption: Determine what you can add to the argument to reinforce that competitive success requires a new aquatic facility. For example, you could indicate that new athletic facilities attract the best student-athletes. The correct answer could cite a study that shows the top collegiate swimming and diving programs in the country all added new facilities in the last five years. The right choice also could state something about how new pools are engineered to reduce waves and promote faster times.

3. Eliminate alternative explanations: Think of alternatives that could explain the argument, and look for an answer that eliminates them. Maybe there are other factors that could possibly contribute to a winning university swim team. If an answer choice disposes of one of those factors, the argument will be stronger. For example, the specific equipment and apparel sponsor of the athletic department is not a big consideration for student-athletes when they choose their schools.

Causality

As I noted in the Weaken chapter, causal arguments—where the author asserts or denies a cause-and-effect relationship between two events or things—are common in the Assumption family of questions. So keep your eye out for causal indicators.

Consider the following example:

> Flo is playing better volleyball this year than in any other season before it. She's spiking harder, jumping higher, and responding quicker on the court. So, her off-season strength and conditioning program is responsible for her improvement.

The author claims that Flo's off-season workout program (X) caused her to be a better player (Y) because her volleyball skills have improved.

To strengthen a causal argument such as this one, you have three options (which are the opposite of those you use to Weaken an argument):

1. Support the causality (X → Y)

Here, you have two options to show that X caused Y—that the off-season workouts caused skill improvement. First, you could give another example of the cause producing the effect. In this example, that could be another player showing skill improvement because of her off-season workouts. Your second option is to support the causality by showing that without the cause the result doesn't happen. In this case, you could add that Flo did not work out last year and she showed no skill improvement.

2. Eliminate an alternative cause for the stated result (Z did not cause Y)

Remember, the author believes that X caused Y. By disposing of an alternative cause, the causal relationship between X and Y is that much closer and it's more likely that X caused Y. So, if you learn that Flo's coach remained the same over the past three years and that the coaching strategy has not changed, then the possibility that coaching was a factor in Flo's improvement is eliminated, and therefore the workout regimen is a stronger choice.

3. Eliminate the possibility of coincidence

The final way to strengthen an argument is to find an answer that proves that the relationship between X and Y was not because of coincidence. In this case, the elements of the argument did not coincidentally happen at the same time—Flo's workout preceded her improvement and the workout led to the improvement.

Evaluate the Answer Choices

Armed with your prediction, review the answer choices and find the one that most closely matches. Remember that the match may not be exact; your prediction may be more specific or more general than the one correct answer, so you need to be open to different presentations.

THE KAPLAN METHOD IN ACTION

Now I'll walk you through a couple examples to show you how the Kaplan Method can help you efficiently solve any Strengthen question you'll see on test day.

1. Poor nutrition is at the root of the violent behavior of many young offenders. Researchers observed that in a certain institution for young offenders, the violent inmates among them consistently chose, from the food available, those items that were low in nutrients. In a subsequent experiment, some of the violent inmates were placed on a diet high in nutrients. There was a steady improvement in their behavior over the four months of the experiment. These results confirm the link between poor nutrition and violent behavior.

   Which one of the following, if true, most strengthens the argument?

   (A) Some of the violent inmates who took part in the experiment had committed a large number of violent crimes.
   (B) Dietary changes are easier and cheaper to implement than any other type of reform program in institutions for young offenders.
   (C) Many young offenders have reported that they had consumed a low-nutrient food sometime in the days before they committed a violent crime.
   (D) A further study investigated young offenders who chose a high-nutrient diet on their own and found that many of them were nonviolent.
   (E) The violent inmates in the institution who were not placed on a high-nutrient diet did not show an improvement in behavior.[1]

Step 1. Identify the Question Type

The word "strengthens" in the question stem indicates that this is a Strengthen question.

Step 2. Untangle the Stimulus

The author makes a causal argument and begins the stimulus with the conclusion, using the words "is at the root of" to tell you that poor nutrition causes violent behavior in young offenders. She bases her conclusion on an experiment in which violent young offenders were given a high-nutrient diet and experienced steady improvement in behavior. So, in other words, poor nutrition causes violent behavior because good nutrition causes improved behavior.

Step 3. Make a Prediction

The author must assume the causal relationship between nutrition and behavior. So to strengthen the argument, you need to find an answer that connects them. Possible correct

---

[1]PrepTest 41, Sec. 1, Q 12

answers may eliminate other explanations for the violent behavior, confirm the assumption, or provide additional research that achieved the same results. Another possibility is to show an absence of one factor is followed by the absence of the other.

Step 4. Evaluate the Answer Choices

The number of violent crimes as discussed in choice (A) does not impact the relationship between nutrition and behavior, and thus it has no impact on the argument.

Likewise, the relative ease and low cost of dietary changes is not related to the effectiveness of the dietary changes, so you can eliminate choice (B).

Do the same with choice (C). Consuming a low-nutrient food sometime prior to a violent crime is too vague. You don't know how much low-nutrient food was consumed and in what proportion to healthy food. You also don't know when in time the low-nutrient food was eaten. So the relationship between food and behavior remains unchanged.

Whether the high-nutrient diet was a voluntary dining choice is also irrelevant and has no effect on the link between food and behavior. Cross out choice (D) as well.

Choice (E) matches the prediction by tying nutrition and behavior closer together. Without the high-nutrition diet, violent inmates showed no behavioral improvement. This is the correct answer.

2. Someone who gets sick from eating a meal will often develop a strong distaste for the one food in the meal that had the most distinctive flavor, whether or not that food caused the sickness. This phenomenon explains why children are especially likely to develop strong aversions to some foods.

   Which one of the following, if true, provides the strongest support for the explanation?

   (A) Children are more likely than adults to be given meals composed of foods lacking especially distinctive flavors.
   (B) Children are less likely than adults to see a connection between their health and the foods they eat.
   (C) Children tend to have more acute taste and to become sick more often than adults do.
   (D) Children typically recover more slowly than adults do from sickness caused by food.
   (E) Children are more likely than are adults to refuse to eat unfamiliar foods.[2]

---

[2]PrepTest 20, Sec. 1, Q 9

Step 1. Identify the Question Type

The word "support" in the question stem indicates you have either a Strengthen or an Inference question. To determine which question type you are dealing with, you need to determine which way the support travels. In this case, the question asks you to find the answer choice that supports the explanation—meaning that the support travels from the answer choice to stimulus. When the correct answer choice supports, or strengthens, the argument, you know you are dealing with a Strengthen question. Besides identifying a Strengthen question, this stem also tells you what to strengthen—the explanation in the argument.

Step 2. Untangle the Stimulus

Once you identify a Strengthen question, read the stimulus to find the conclusion and the evidence. In this example, the stimulus presents a phenomenon in which people tend to dislike the most distinctive-tasting food in a meal from which they got sick, even if that particular food did not cause the illness. Note the phrase "this phenomenon explains why." Since the evidence explains the conclusion, the phenomenon is the evidence, and the conclusion—that children are especially likely to develop strong aversions to some food—must follow.

Step 3. Make a Prediction

To strengthen the argument, you need to identify the assumption and confirm it. In this case, the argument talks about children hating food because some people hate the strongest flavor of a meal from which they get sick. The assumption must connect the children to the factors inherent in the phenomenon, getting sick and picking out a distinctive flavor.

Step 4. Evaluate the Answer Choices

Choices (A) and (B) both weaken the argument by breaking down the assumption: Choice (A) loosens the connection between children and distinctive flavors, while choice (B) loosens the connection between children and linking food to sickness.

Choice (C) states that children have an acute sense of taste and connects that to getting sick. It also compares children to adults, saying children are more likely to pick out distinctive flavors and are more likely to get sick than adults. Therefore, children are more likely to develop a list of foods they dislike. This matches your prediction and makes choice (C) the correct answer.

Choices (D) and (E) are both outside the scope of the argument, which focuses on the development of food aversion at the onset of illness, not the pace of recovery mentioned in choice (D). You can eliminate choice (E) because whether the food is familiar is irrelevant; the argument focuses on the connection between getting sick and distinctive-tasting food.

STRENGTHEN QUESTION: NOW YOU TRY IT

Now it's your turn to try a Strengthen question on your own. Use the template I've provided after the question to guide you through the four-step Kaplan Method. (Note: On test day, you won't be writing out all the steps as you are in this exercise. However, as you are learning the Method, it's good practice to help it become second nature.) Remember to bracket the conclusion and circle Keywords.

1. Ringtail opossums are an Australian wildlife species that is potentially endangered. A number of ringtail opossums that had been orphaned and subsequently raised in captivity were monitored after being returned to the wild. Seventy-five percent of these opossums were killed by foxes, a species not native to Australia. Conservationists concluded that the native ringtail opossum population was endangered not by a scarcity of food, as had been previously thought, but by non-native predator species against which the opossum had not developed natural defenses.

    Which one of the following, if true, most strongly supports the conservationists' argument?

    (A) There are fewer non-native predator species that prey on the ringtail opossum than there are native species that prey on the ringtail opossum.

    (B) Foxes, which were introduced into Australia over 200 years ago, adapted to the Australian climate less successfully than did some other foreign species.

    (C) The ringtail opossums that were raised in captivity were fed a diet similar to that which ringtail opossums typically eat in the wild.

    (D) Few of the species that compete with the ringtail opossum for food sources are native to Australia.

    (E) Ringtail opossums that grow to adulthood in the wild defend themselves against foxes no more successfully than do ringtail opossums raised in captivity.[3]

Step 1. Identify the Question Type

_____

Step 2. Untangle the Stimulus

_____

Step 3. Make a Prediction

_____

Step 4. Evaluate the Answer Choices

_____

_____

[3]PrepTest 34, Sec. 3, Q 24

Explanations

1. (E)

Ringtail opossums are an Australian wildlife species that is potentially endangered. A number of ringtail opossums that had been orphaned and subsequently raised in captivity were monitored after being returned to the wild. Seventy-five percent of these opossums were killed by foxes, a species not native to Australia. <Conservationists concluded that the native ringtail opossum population was endangered not by a scarcity of food, as had been previously thought, but by non-native predator species against which the opossum had not developed natural defenses.>

Which one of the following, if true, most strongly supports the conservationists' argument?

(A) There are fewer non-native predator species that prey on the ringtail opossum than there are native species that prey on the ringtail opossum.

(B) Foxes, which were introduced into Australia over 200 years ago, adapted to the Australian climate less successfully than did some other foreign species.

(C) The ringtail opossums that were raised in captivity were fed a diet similar to that which ringtail opossums typically eat in the wild.

(D) Few of the species that compete with the ringtail opossum for food sources are native to Australia.

(E) Ringtail opossums that grow to adulthood in the wild defend themselves against foxes no more successfully than do ringtail opossums raised in captivity.[4]

Step 1. Identify the Question Type

Since the question stem asks you for an answer that supports the conservationists' argument, this is a Strengthen question.

Step 2. Untangle the Stimulus

You're given the conclusion in direct language: "Conservationists concluded that …" the native ringtail opossum population was endangered by non-native predators. This belief is based on evidence that 75 percent of opossums raised in captivity and returned to the wild were killed by the non-native predators.

Step 3. Make a Prediction

Again, to strengthen the argument you must tighten the connection between the conclusion and the evidence. To identify the assumption, look for the mismatched terms between the

---

[4]PrepTest 34, Sec. 3, Q 24

conclusion and evidence. In this case, the conclusion applies to native opossums generally, while the evidence refers to a subset of the group, those opossums raised in captivity and later returned to the wild. To strengthen the link between the conclusion and evidence, you need an assumption that addresses this scope shift.

Step 4. Evaluate the Answer Choices

Choice (A) talks about the number of non-native vs. native predators, which is out of scope.

In choice (B), foxes serve as an example of a non-native opossum predator. However, it provides only background information about them and does nothing to tie the two opossum groups together and strengthen the argument.

Although choice (C) identifies a shared diet between the two groups of opossums, the connection does not relate to the conclusion about opossums being threatened by non-native predators. Eliminate this choice.

Choice (D) is irrelevant. The origin of the species that compete with the opossum for food sources and the food sources themselves play no role in the argument.

Choice (E) asserts a similarity between the wild and captive opossums. It says the two groups are the same when it comes to their vulnerability to the predatory foxes, which strengthens the argument, and makes choice (E) the correct answer.

DRILL: PRACTICING STRENGTHEN QUESTIONS

Use the Kaplan Method to answer the following Strengthen questions. Take this opportunity to practice and apply the steps in the Method so you are comfortable using them on test day. Check your responses against the full explanations provided after the Drill.

1. One year ago a local government initiated an antismoking advertising campaign in local newspapers, which it financed by imposing a tax on cigarettes of 20 cents per pack. One year later, the number of people in the locality who smoke cigarettes had declined by 3 percent. Clearly, what was said in the advertisements had an effect, although a small one, on the number of people in the locality who smoke cigarettes.

   Which one of the following, if true, most helps to strengthen the argument?

   (A) Residents of the locality have not increased their use of other tobacco products such as snuff and chewing tobacco since the campaign went into effect.
   (B) A substantial number of cigarette smokers in the locality who did not quit smoking during the campaign now smoke less than they did before it began.
   (C) Admissions to the local hospital for chronic respiratory ailments were down by 15 percent one year after the campaign began.
   (D) Merchants in the locality responded to the local tax by reducing the price at which they sold cigarettes by 20 cents per pack.
   (E) Smokers in the locality had incomes that on average were 25 percent lower than those of nonsmokers.[5]

2. Fossil-fuel producers say that it would be prohibitively expensive to reduce levels of carbon dioxide emitted by the use of fossil fuels enough to halt global warming. This claim is probably false. Several years ago, the chemical industry said that finding an economical alternative to the chlorofluorocarbons (CFCs) destroying the ozone layer would be impossible. Yet once the industry was forced, by international agreements, to find substitutes for CFCs, it managed to phase them out completely well before the mandated deadline, in many cases at a profit.

   Which one of the following, if true, most strengthens the argument?

   (A) In the time since the chemical industry phased out CFCs, the destruction of the ozone layer by CFCs has virtually halted, but the levels of carbon dioxide emitted by the use of fossil fuels have continued to increase.
   (B) In some countries, the amount of carbon dioxide emitted by the use of fossil fuels has already been reduced without prohibitive expense, but at some cost in convenience to the users of such fuels.
   (C) The use of CFCs never contributed as greatly to the destruction of the ozone layer as the carbon dioxide emitted by the use of fossil fuels currently contributes to global warming.
   (D) There are ways of reducing carbon dioxide emissions that could halt global warming without hurting profits of fossil-fuel producers significantly more than phasing out CFCs hurt those of the chemical industry.
   (E) If international agreements forced fossil-fuel producers to find ways to reduce carbon dioxide emissions enough to halt global warming, the fossil-fuel producers could find substitutes for fossil fuels.[6]

---

[5]PrepTest 17, Sec. 3, Q 12

[6]PrepTest 50, Sec. 2, Q 13

3. Many scientific studies have suggested that taking melatonin tablets can induce sleep. But this does not mean that melatonin is helpful in treating insomnia. Most of the studies examined only people without insomnia, and in many of the studies, only a few of the subjects given melatonin appeared to be significantly affected by it.

Which one of the following, if true, most strengthens the argument?

(A) A weaker correlation between taking melatonin and the inducement of sleep was found in the studies that included people with insomnia than in the studies that did not.

(B) None of the studies that suggested that taking melatonin tablets can induce sleep examined a fully representative sample of the human population.

(C) In the studies that included subjects with insomnia, only subjects without insomnia were significantly affected by doses of melatonin.

(D) Several people who were in control groups and only given placebos claimed that the tablets induced sleep.

(E) If melatonin were helpful in treating insomnia, then every person with insomnia who took doses of melatonin would appear to be significantly affected by it.[7]

4. The supernova event of 1987 is interesting in that there is still no evidence of the neutron star that current theory says should have remained after a supernova of that size. This is in spite of the fact that many of the most sensitive instruments ever developed have searched for the tell-tale pulse of radiation that neutron stars emit. Thus, current theory is wrong in claiming that supernovas of a certain size always produce neutron stars.

Which one of the following, if true, most strengthens the argument?

(A) Most supernova remnants that astronomers have detected have a neutron star nearby.

(B) Sensitive astronomical instruments have detected neutron stars much farther away than the location of the 1987 supernova.

(C) The supernova of 1987 was the first that scientists were able to observe in progress.

(D) Several important features of the 1987 supernova are correctly predicted by the current theory.

(E) Some neutron stars are known to have come into existence by a cause other than a supernova explosion.[8]

5. Modern navigation systems, which are found in most of today's commercial aircraft, are made with low-power circuitry, which is more susceptible to interference than the vacuum-tube circuitry found in older planes. During landing, navigation systems receive radio signals from the airport to guide the plane to the runway. Recently, one plane with low-power circuitry veered off course during landing, its dials dimming, when a passenger turned on a laptop computer. Clearly, modern aircraft navigation systems are being put at risk by the electronic devices that passengers carry on board, such as cassette players and laptop computers.

Which one of the following, if true, LEAST strengthens the argument above?

(A) After the laptop computer was turned off, the plane regained course and its navigation instruments and dials returned to normal.

(B) When in use, all electronic devices emit electromagnetic radiation, which is known to interfere with circuitry.

(C) No problems with navigational equipment or instrument dials have been reported on flights with no passenger-owned electronic devices on board.

(D) Significant electromagnetic radiation from portable electronic devices can travel up to eight meters, and some passenger seats on modern aircraft are located within four meters of the navigation systems.

(E) Planes were first equipped with low-power circuitry at about the same time portable electronic devices became popular.[9]

Explanations

1. **(D)**

One year ago a local government initiated an antismoking advertising campaign in local newspapers, which it financed by imposing a tax on cigarettes of 20 cents per pack. One year later, the number of people in the locality who smoke cigarettes had declined by 3 percent. <Clearly, what was said in the advertisements had an effect, although a small one, on the number of people in the locality who smoke cigarettes.>

Which one of the following, if true, most helps to strengthen the argument?

(A)   Residents of the locality have not increased their use of other tobacco products such as snuff and chewing tobacco since the campaign went into effect.

(B)   A substantial number of cigarette smokers in the locality who did not quit smoking during the campaign now smoke less than they did before it began.

(C)   Admissions to the local hospital for chronic respiratory ailments were down by 15 percent one year after the campaign began.

(D)   Merchants in the locality responded to the local tax by reducing the price at which they sold cigarettes by 20 cents per pack.

(E)   Smokers in the locality had incomes that on average were 25 percent lower than those of nonsmokers.[10]

Step 1. Identify the Question Type

"Strengthen" indicates this is a Strengthen question. Now, find the argument.

Step 2. Untangle the Stimulus

Identified by the word "clearly," the conclusion states that the antismoking advertising campaign contributed to the decrease in the locality's number of smokers. The author uses the evidence that a local government initiated the advertising campaign and a small decline in the number of smokers followed. In the process of identifying this causal relationship, the author ignores the 20 cent increase in cigarette prices. So, he assumes the cost increase had no effect on the smoking decline.

Step 3. Make a Prediction

Strengthening this argument requires confirmation of or additional support for the assumption. The correct answer will eliminate or reduce the price increase as a factor in the smoking

---

[10]PrepTest 17, Sec. 3, Q 12

decline. It may also provide additional support for the ad campaign as an influential factor in the reduction in smoking.

Step 4. Evaluate the Answer Choices

Choice (A) is outside the scope. The argument is about smoking cigarettes, not the general use of tobacco products.

Choice (B) is also outside the scope. The argument refers to smokers who quit, not smokers who smoke less.

Choice (C) declares that hospital admissions for respiratory ailments are down, but it doesn't tie the information back to an explanation for the reduced number of smokers.

Choice (D) is the correct response. If local merchants responded to the tax by reducing the price of cigarettes by the exact amount of the tax, the price of cigarettes ultimately did not change. So, a tax increase with a consumer cost reduction cannot explain the smoking decline. The author's assumption is validated, and by eliminating a competing explanation for the smoking decline, the author's conclusion is strengthened.

Choice (E) tells you that smokers were generally poorer than nonsmokers. You can't know from that statement whether smokers are poor, just that they have less money than nonsmokers. If they are poor, they may be more sensitive to a cigarette price increase and be more inclined to stop smoking as a result. If that's the case, choice (E) weakens the argument. If it's not the case, choice (E) has no impact on the argument. Either way, it's incorrect.

2.　(D)

Fossil-fuel producers say that it would be prohibitively expensive to reduce levels of carbon dioxide emitted by the use of fossil fuels enough to halt global warming. <This claim is probably false.> Several years ago, the chemical industry said that finding an economical alternative to the chlorofluorocarbons (CFCs) destroying the ozone layer would be impossible. Yet once the industry was forced, by international agreements, to find substitutes for CFCs, it managed to phase them out completely well before the mandated deadline, in many cases at a profit.

Which one of the following, if true, most strengthens the argument?

(A)　In the time since the chemical industry phased out CFCs, the destruction of the ozone layer by CFCs has virtually halted, but the levels of carbon dioxide emitted by the use of fossil fuels have continued to increase.

(B)　In some countries, the amount of carbon dioxide emitted by the use of fossil fuels has already been reduced without prohibitive expense, but at some cost in convenience to the users of such fuels.

(C)　The use of CFCs never contributed as greatly to the destruction of the ozone layer as the carbon dioxide emitted by the use of fossil fuels currently contributes to global warming.

(D)　There are ways of reducing carbon dioxide emissions that could halt global warming without hurting profits of fossil-fuel producers significantly more than phasing out CFCs hurt those of the chemical industry.

(E)　If international agreements forced fossil-fuel producers to find ways to reduce carbon dioxide emissions enough to halt global warming, the fossil-fuel producers could find substitutes for fossil fuels.[11]

Step 1. Identify the Question Type

"Strengthens" tells you this is a Strengthen question. So now, as you should do with all Strengthen questions, look for the argument in the stimulus and find the answer choice that makes the conclusion more likely to be true from the evidence.

Step 2. Untangle the Stimulus

Although there are no conclusion indicator words, any time the author tells you what others think and then says the others are wrong, then that is the conclusion. Here the author tells you

---

[11]PrepTest 50, Sec. 2, Q 13

the fossil fuel producers claim that it would be prohibitively expensive to reduce consumption to slow global warming. The author then says that the fossil fuel producers' claim is probably false. So the author's conclusion is that it is most likely not too expensive to reduce fossil fuel consumption to make a difference—it can be found affordably.

The author supports her conclusion with evidence in the form of an analogy. She says that the chemical industry made a similar claim about finding an alternative to CFCs. Not only was it a quicker process than expected, but the industry managed to make the substitution at a profit. Therefore, she concludes, it will work the same way with the reduction of carbon dioxide. When an author makes a conclusion based on an analogy, she assumes the analogy is sound and a comparison holds.

Notice you don't need to understand the technical information in this stimulus. Whether you know anything about carbon dioxide or fossil fuel is inconsequential to strengthening the argument. You only need to understand the pattern of the argument and how to strengthen it. Here, you are presented with two factors and asked to strengthen their bond.

Step 3. Make a Prediction

To strengthen the argument, you need to look for an answer that supports the author's analogy and provides a strong link between the claims of the fossil-fuel producers and those of the chemical industry regarding CFCs.

Step 4. Evaluate the Answer Choices

While it's nice to know the CFC regulations protected the environment, as mentioned in choice (A), the statement doesn't support the author's CFC analogy to show the reduction process is not expensive.

Choice (B) says a reduction in carbon dioxide emitted by the use of fossil fuels has occurred without great expense. However, the impact on global warming is unclear. Also, choice (B) doesn't connect to the CFC analogy.

Choice (C) is outside the scope, as it talks about the destruction caused by carbon dioxide and CFCs. The argument focuses on reducing these problems and the associated cost. Another problem with this answer choice is that it differentiates the two factors instead of bringing them together.

Choice (D) matches the prediction. It says not only can carbon dioxide emissions be reduced without hurting profits like phasing out CFCs, but it will be better at it. That makes choice (D) the correct answer.

While choice (E) tells you fossil fuels can be substituted, it is silent on whether the substitution would be prohibitively expensive, so you can eliminate it.

3.   **(C)**

Many scientific studies have suggested that taking melatonin tablets can induce sleep. <(But) this does not mean that melatonin is helpful in treating insomnia.> Most of the studies examined only people without insomnia, and in many of the studies, only a few of the subjects given melatonin appeared to be significantly affected by it.

Which one of the following, if true, most (strengthens) the argument?

(A)   A weaker correlation between taking melatonin and the inducement of sleep was found in the studies that included people with insomnia than in the studies that did not.

(B)   None of the studies that suggested that taking melatonin tablets can induce sleep examined a fully representative sample of the human population.

(C)   In the studies that included subjects with insomnia, only subjects without insomnia were significantly affected by doses of melatonin.

(D)   Several people who were in control groups and only given placebos claimed that the tablets induced sleep.

(E)   If melatonin were helpful in treating insomnia, then every person with insomnia who took doses of melatonin would appear to be significantly affected by it.[12]

Step 1. Identify the Question Type

The word "strengthens" identifies this as a Strengthen question. Proceed to the stimulus and locate the conclusion and the evidence.

Step 2. Untangle the Stimulus

"But" in the second sentence indicates a contradiction, which can point to a conclusion. In this case, it points to the conclusion that melatonin can induce sleep, but it won't help people with insomnia. The author says this because most of the studies included people without insomnia. So, the argument is that melatonin helped very few people without insomnia; therefore, it won't help people with insomnia.

Step 3. Make a Prediction

Notice that the author bases her conclusion on "most studies" that didn't look at people with insomnia. The key is to recognize that "most" leaves open the possibility that there were other studies with insomniacs. To bolster the argument, you want to tie insomniacs to the studies and show they were unlikely to be helped by melatonin.

Step 4. Evaluate the Answer Choices

At first glance, choice (A) is tempting because you may think the weaker correlation between melatonin and inducement of sleep in studies with insomniacs argues that melatonin isn't as effective on people with insomnia. However, the source of the weaker correlation is unclear and the relationship between melatonin and inducement of sleep is not the issue here; the effect of melatonin on insomniacs is.

Choice (B) faults the studies for not including a fully representative sample of the human population and thereby weakens the argument. Eliminate this choice.

Choice (C) acknowledges there were some insomniacs included in the studies, and when they were, melatonin had no significant impact on them. Choice (C) matches the prediction and is the correct answer.

Choice (D) discusses the placebo effect and does not shed any light on the effects of melatonin on subjects with insomnia, so you can cross it out.

Choice (E) is an extreme answer because it suggests that if melatonin helps treat insomnia, then it is 100 percent effective with all insomnia sufferers. If anything, this answer weakens the argument. The correct answer connects insomniacs to the studies and makes it more likely they are not affected by melatonin, which this clearly doesn't.

4.   **(B)**

The supernova event of 1987 is interesting in that there is still no evidence of the neutron star that current theory says should have remained after a supernova of that size. This is in spite of the fact that many of the most sensitive instruments ever developed have searched for the tell-tale pulse of radiation that neutron stars emit. <Thus, current theory is wrong in claiming that supernovas of a certain size always produce neutron stars.>

Which one of the following, if true, most (strengthens) the argument?

(A)   Most supernova remnants that astronomers have detected have a neutron star nearby.

(B)   Sensitive astronomical instruments have detected neutron stars much farther away than the location of the 1987 supernova.

(C)   The supernova of 1987 was the first that scientists were able to observe in progress.

(D)   Several important features of the 1987 supernova are correctly predicted by the current theory.

(E)   Some neutron stars are known to have come into existence by a cause other than a supernova explosion.[13]

---

[13]PrepTest 51, Sec. 1, Q 24

Step 1. Identify the Question Type

The word "strengthens" tells you this is a Strengthen question.

Step 2. Untangle the Stimulus

The evidence states that the most sensitive instruments have looked for the neutron star that should have remained after the 1987 supernova event but have found no evidence of it. "Thus", the author concludes in the last sentence, the current theory that supernovas of a certain size always produce neutron stars is wrong.

Step 3. Make a Prediction

To connect the evidence to the conclusion, the author assumes that "no evidence of the supernova" means the supernova does not exist. The correct answer will support this assumption.

Step 4. Evaluate the Answer Choices

Choice (A) repeats current theory already stated in the evidence. Restating evidence never strengthens an argument. Move on to the next choice.

Choice (B) is the correct answer. It makes clear that the instruments were powerful enough to find neutron stars farther away than the 1987 supernova. Consequently, it eliminates an alternative explanation that the instruments were defective or problematic in some way. Remember, you don't need to prove that supernovas don't always produce neutron stars, you just need to make it more likely that they don't.

Choice (C) is irrelevant. Whether the supernova of 1987 was the first that scientists were able to observe in progress has no impact on the correctness of the current theory.

The production of neutron stars, not other features of the 1987 supernova, is your focus. So choice (D) is outside the scope. However, even if you thought (D) was relevant, the fact that the current theory correctly predicted several features of the 1987 supernova makes the theory look better, not worse.

The cause of neutron stars other than a supernova is outside the scope of the argument, so you can eliminate choice (E).

5. (E)

Modern navigation systems, which are found in most of today's commercial aircraft, are made with low-power circuitry, which is more susceptible to interference than the vacuum-tube circuitry found in older planes. During landing, navigation systems receive radio signals from the airport to guide the plane to the runway. Recently, one plane with low-power circuitry veered off course during landing, its dials dimming, when a passenger turned on a laptop computer. <Clearly,> modern aircraft navigation systems are being put at risk by the electronic devices that passengers carry on board,> such as cassette players and laptop computers.

Which one of the following, if true, LEAST strengthens the argument above?

- (A) After the laptop computer was turned off, the plane regained course and its navigation instruments and dials returned to normal.
- (B) When in use, all electronic devices emit electromagnetic radiation, which is known to interfere with circuitry.
- (C) No problems with navigational equipment or instrument dials have been reported on flights with no passenger-owned electronic devices on board.
- (D) Significant electromagnetic radiation from portable electronic devices can travel up to eight meters, and some passenger seats on modern aircraft are located within four meters of the navigation systems.
- (E) Planes were first equipped with low-power circuitry at about the same time portable electronic devices became popular.[14]

Step 1. Identify the Question Type

This question uses the word "strengthens," so you know it is a Strengthen question. However, notice the twist: It asks for the answer that "LEAST" strengthens the argument. An answer that does not strengthen an argument could make it weaker, but it doesn't have to; it could also be outside the scope of the argument. So, for this question, the four wrong answers will strengthen the argument, and the correct answer will not.

Under the pressure of test day, it's easy to skip a word in the question or to misread the question. Be sure to read the question carefully so you answer the question asked.

Step 2. Untangle the Stimulus

"Clearly" in the last sentence indicates the author's conclusion, that electronic devices brought on airplanes by passengers endanger the navigation system. The author provides evidence that

---

[14]PrepTest 28, Sec. 1, Q 26

is full of technical language, but don't let that distract you; you just want to find out why the author thinks the electronic devices put the navigation system at risk. Essentially, the author is basing this sweeping conclusion on a single instance in which a passenger happened to use an electronic device around the same time that a plane malfunctioned.

Step 3. Make a Prediction

The author assumes there is a causal connection between the electronic devices and the plane's malfunctioning. So, any answers that connect electronic devices to plane problems strengthens the argument. The one that weakens the argument or has no effect on the argument is the correct answer.

Step 4. Evaluate the Answer Choices

Choice (A) gives one example of a laptop affecting a navigation system, which strengthens the argument. Eliminate choice (A).

Choice (B) states that all electronic devices interfere with circuitry, which confirms the assumption and strengthens the argument. Move on to the next choice.

To strengthen an argument, an answer need not prove an argument, just make it more likely. Choice (C) is a great example of that concept, indicating that without electronic devices on board, navigational systems did not experience any problems. This strengthens the argument, and is therefore incorrect.

Choice (D) ties electronic devices closer to navigation systems by declaring they have the range and proximity to interfere with navigation systems. This strengthens the argument, so it's incorrect.

Choice (E) indicates that low-power circuitry and electronic devices were both introduced to airplanes around the same time, which raises the possibility of a coincidental relationship between navigation systems and electronic devices. It does nothing to bring the relationship closer or strengthen the argument, so it is the correct answer.

STRENGTHEN REVIEW

Before you proceed to the next chapter, turn to Appendix A and complete the review exercise for Strengthen questions. A completed chart is included in Appendix B.

CHAPTER 8

Flaw Questions

Many arguments presented on the LSAT are flawed—that is the evidence is inadequate to support the conclusion reached by the author. Your ability to spot and describe a defective argument will lead directly to points on test day.

Flaw questions—like the other members of the Assumption family of questions—are prevalent on the LSAT. In fact, you will see approximately eight scored Flaw questions out of the 50 scored Logical Reasoning questions on the LSAT. Because of their frequency, your grasp of Flaw questions is especially important.

DEFINITION OF FLAW QUESTIONS

Flaw questions ask you to recognize a problem with an argument. Usually, you will point out a fallacy in the argument that prevents the evidence from logically establishing the conclusion. Whereas Weaken questions ask you to add something to the argument to damage it, Flaw questions ask you to determine how an argument is already damaged. It's a small distinction, but a very important one.

In this chapter, I will present the classic logical errors that have appeared on LSATs over the years. Knowing the types of flawed reasoning that you will see on test day and being able to quickly and confidently identify them will give you a distinct advantage over your competition.

USE THE KAPLAN METHOD TO ANSWER FLAW QUESTIONS

Identify the Question Type

As is always the case, remember to read the question stem first. After you identify the question as a Flaw question, you can focus on *how* the argument is flawed and not waste any time figuring out *whether* the argument is flawed. The following words and phrases will help you identify a Flaw question:

- Flaw
- Error in reasoning
- Vulnerable to criticism
- Questionable because
- Overlooks the possibility that
- Fails to demonstrate

When you see these phrases in a question, the argument is flawed and your job is to identify the error in reasoning. However, the wording of the question will determine whether your answer will be a general description of a flaw or whether it will point out flawed content. For example, the following question stems ask you to identify the flaw:

- Which one of the following describes a reasoning flaw in the letter's argument?
- The reasoning in the argument is most vulnerable to criticism on the grounds that it
- Which one of the following best describes an error in reasoning in the passage?

However, sometimes the question stem will acknowledge the specific flaw and ask you to point out the flawed content:

- The reasoning in Rebecca's argument is questionable in that she takes for granted that
- Jim's reasoning is questionable in that it fails to consider the possibility that

Untangle the Stimulus

Flaw questions are part of the Assumption family of questions. So, as you would with any other Assumption family question, read the stimulus to locate the argument. As you read, circle any Keywords to help you find the conclusion and evidence. Then, bracket the conclusion.

Make a Prediction

Flaw questions, like Assumption questions, focus on the disconnect between the evidence and conclusion. So, identifying the author's assumption will always lead you to the correct answer in a Flaw question. However, certain logical flaws have repeatedly appeared on the LSAT. Recognizing these recurring flaws can help you identify the author's assumption and, consequently, more efficiently and accurately answer Flaw questions.

Common Flaws

The following is a list of common flaws that appear on the LSAT and an example of each type:

Overlooked Possibilities

Definition: The author assumes only one possible explanation and fails to see that the evidence can lead to multiple possible conclusions. Be on the lookout for forceful, absolute conclusion language that indicates the author is ignoring other possibilities.

Example: If Olivia is in class, she turns her cell phone off. So if her phone is off, she must be in class. (The author errantly assumes Olivia turns off her cell phone only because she is in class, but she may also turn her phone off for other reasons.)

Necessity v. Sufficiency

Definition: The author confuses a sufficient condition for a necessary one. The better you understand the relationship between sufficiency and necessity in formal logic, the easier it will be to spot an error when the author gets the relationship wrong.

The flaws of overlooked possibility and necessity v. sufficiency are similar. In both cases, the author disregards alternative explanations and reverses the formal logic.

Example: If we have dinner at home, then Mike went to the grocery store. I saw Mike picking up groceries today, so we must be having dinner at home. (You can state this formal logic statement in two different ways to highlight the sufficient and necessary terms: Dinner at home necessitates Mike's shopping, and having dinner at home is sufficient to know that Mike went to the grocery store. However, Mike's shopping is sufficient to indicate we could have dinner at home, but it is not necessary. For example, if he shops, we may still go out for dinner.)

Causation v. Correlation

Definition: The author assumes that a correlation (two things happening at the same time) between events means one causes the other to occur. In other words, because two things happen at the same time, the author assumes a causal relationship between them.

Example: In the summer, the Osborn family goes swimming often. They also eat a lot of ice cream in the summer. Therefore, swimming causes the family to eat ice cream. (Swimming and eating ice cream may be related as summer activities, but the argument does not tell us anything about causation.)

Scope Shift

Definition: The author changes the focus of the argument, talking about one thing in the evidence and something else in the conclusion, so the conclusion goes beyond the scope of the evidence.

Certain kinds of scope shifts are quite common on the LSAT: a shift from numbers to percentages (or vice versa), equivocation of a key term or phrase in an argument in two different ways without acknowledging the distinction, a shift from opinion to fact, a shift from possibility to certainty, and a shift from individual factors to generalizing about a group (or vice versa)

Example: Only 15 percent of the school's children have been to Washington DC. Therefore, the school children must not know a lot about our government. (General scope shift: The evidence talks about traveling to our nation's capital, and the conclusion talks about knowledge of government.)

Example: The new vice president for marketing wants to eliminate half of the manager positions and a quarter of the assistant positions. Therefore, she is getting rid of more manager spots than assistant jobs. (Number v. percentage: She could be eliminating 50 percent of ten manager spots and 25 percent of 100 assistant jobs.)

Example: Giving money to charity is the right thing to do. So, charities have the right to our money. (Equivocation: The author changes the meaning of a key term by using "right" to mean appropriate in the first clause and "entitlement" in the second clause.)

Example: The restaurant reviewer said this restaurant has great food. So, it must be great. (Opinion v. fact)

Example: Drugs and alcohol may have been involved in the actor's death. So, he must have overdosed. (Possibility v. certainty)

Example: Maya often wears clothes that have jewel-tone colors like deep red, blue, or green. So, she'll like that scarf with all three colors in it. (Group v. member)

Less-Common Flaws

The following flaws can appear on the LSAT, although they are less common as a correct answer choice and more likely to appear in wrong answers choices.

Analogy

Definition: The author incorrectly assumes that two things are similar enough to draw a valid comparison between them.

Example: Water is a liquid and is good for you. Therefore, soda pop, which is a liquid, is also good for you.

Representativeness

Definition: The author draws a conclusion based on evidence regarding an unrepresentative sample, incorrectly assuming that the one group can represent the other.

Example: When I was your age, mint chocolate chip was my favorite ice cream flavor. So, I'll serve mint chocolate ice cream at your birthday party. (My ice cream preference may not be representative of what you and your friends like.)

Ad hominem

Definition: The author responds to the argument by attacking the arguer rather than focusing on the logic of the argument itself.

Example: Bill is out of work, so you can't believe him when he says the proposed policy would help the economy.

Circular Reasoning

Definition: The author's evidence and conclusion are the same. It is often presented on the LSAT by presupposing what the argument sets out to prove.

Example: The talk show host claims that Taylor's new mystery is the best book of the year because no other book is as well-written.

This list is not exhaustive but it does give you a place to start when thinking about what's gone wrong in an argument. If a question does not fit neatly into a classic flaw category, take a good look at the argument, accept that there is a logical flaw that prevents the evidence from supporting that conclusion, and find what it is.

Evaluate the Answer Choices

Take your prediction and compare it to the answer choices. Be flexible as you review each choice, because the same flaw can be expressed in different ways. If you are unable to match your prediction after initially looking through the answer choices, use your knowledge of common flaws to help you eliminate incorrect answer choices and find the correct answer.

THE KAPLAN METHOD IN ACTION

Now I'll walk you through a couple examples to show you how the Kaplan Method can help you efficiently solve any Flaw question you'll see on test day.

1. Researcher: People with certain personality disorders have more theta brain waves than those without such disorders. But my data show that the amount of one's theta brain waves increases while watching TV. So watching too much TV increases one's risk of developing personality disorders.

   A questionable aspect of the reasoning above is that it

   (A) uses the phrase "personality disorders" ambiguously
   (B) fails to define the phrase "theta brain waves"
   (C) takes correlation to imply a causal connection
   (D) draws a conclusion from an unrepresentative sample of data
   (E) infers that watching TV is a consequence of a personality disorder[1]

Step 1. Identify the Question Type

The phrase "questionable aspect of the reasoning" tells you the researcher made an error in moving from the evidence to the conclusion in this argument, which means this is a Flaw question.

Step 2. Untangle the Stimulus

Once you identify a Flaw question, read the stimulus to identify the conclusion and the evidence. The researcher's conclusion appears in the last sentence identified by the word "so." He states that watching too much TV increases the risk of developing personality disorders. He supports the conclusion with the evidence that people with certain disorders also have a higher number of theta brain waves, which increases when watching TV.

Step 3. Make a Prediction

The researcher presents a correlation between personality disorders and theta brain waves that increase when watching TV. From that correlation, he concludes that watching TV causes an increase in the risk of developing personality disorders. He makes the faulty assumption that correlation between two things means that one caused the other. You are looking for an answer that generally identifies the causation v. correlation flaw.

Step 4. Evaluate the Answer Choices

Look at the answer choices and determine which one most closely resembles your prediction.

Choice (A) is false. A phrase or word is used ambiguously when it has more than one meaning, which is not the case in this argument. Eliminate this choice.

Choice (B) is true, in a way—the researcher does not define theta brain waves. However, the lack of definition does not affect the argument at all and certainly does not point to a flaw. Eliminate this choice as well.

---

[1]PrepTest 41, Sec. 3, Q 13

Answer choice (C) matches the prediction exactly, and so it is the correct answer.

Choice (D) raises the flaw of representativeness but there is no sample data presented in the argument to be unrepresentative.

Finally, choice (E) is the opposite of what the researcher said in the argument.

2. It is widely believed that by age 80, perception and memory are each significantly reduced from their functioning levels at age 30. However, a recent study showed no difference in the abilities of 80-year-olds and 30-year-olds to play a card game devised to test perception and memory. Therefore, the belief that perception and memory are significantly reduced by age 80 is false.

The reasoning above is most vulnerable to criticism on the grounds that it fails to consider the possibility that

(A) the study's card game does not test cognitive abilities other than perception and memory
(B) card games are among the most difficult cognitive tasks one can attempt to perform
(C) perception and memory are interrelated in ways of which we are not currently aware
(D) the belief that 80-year-olds' perception and memory are reduced results from prejudice against senior citizens
(E) playing the study's card game perfectly requires fairly low levels of perception and memory[2]

Step 1. Identify the Question Type

The phrase "reasoning above is most vulnerable to criticism" identifies this as a Flaw question. The phrase "fails to consider the possibility" tells you specifically that the flaw is an overlooked possibility. Since you already know what the flaw is, your task is to look for alternative possibilities as you analyze the argument to predict an answer using content from the stimulus.

Step 2. Untangle the Stimulus

The author concludes that perception and memory are not significantly reduced by age 80 from age 30, as is widely believed. She bases her conclusion on evidence that 30- and 80-year-olds display the same abilities to play a card game designed to test perception and memory. At quick glance, the argument may seem plausible, but it can't be because it's part of a Flaw question that told you specifically the argument fails to consider something. So, you need to determine what the author overlooks in reaching that conclusion from that evidence.

---

[2]PrepTest 35, Sec. 4, Q 8

Step 3. Make a Prediction

You are looking for a possible explanation as to why 30- and 80-year-olds have the same abilities to play a card game designed to test perception and memory. One reason could be that the card game does not demand a high level of perception and memory.

Often when there is technical evidence (e.g., a survey, study, or experiment), there is a built in assumption that the survey, study, test, or in this case card game, is accurate and adequate for the task. So, a problem with the test will weaken the argument and the author's failure to consider that problem is the flaw. Here, the flaw is simply that the test doesn't work as "devised."

Step 4. Evaluate the Answer Choices

You can eliminate choice (A), as other cognitive abilities besides perception and memory are outside the scope of the argument.

If card games are the most difficult cognitive tasks, then choice (B) strengthens the author's argument and does not identify a flaw. Move on to the next choice.

Choice (C) raises an interrelationship between perception and memory that is irrelevant to the argument. This choice is also incorrect.

Choice (D) mentions a prejudice against senior citizens, which is also irrelevant. This choice is incorrect, which leaves only one.

Choice (E) provides the predicted overlooked possibility, and is the correct answer.

FLAW QUESTIONS: NOW YOU TRY IT

It's now your turn to try a Flaw question on your own. Use the template I've provided after the question to guide you through the four-step Kaplan Method. (Note: On test day, you won't be writing out all the steps as you are in this exercise. However, as you are learning the Method, it's good practice to help it become second nature.) Remember to bracket the conclusion and circle Keywords.

1. Consumer advocate: Last year's worldwide alarm about a computer "virus"—a surreptitiously introduced computer program that can destroy other programs and data—was a fraud. Companies selling programs to protect computers against such viruses raised worldwide concern about the possibility that a destructive virus would be activated on a certain date. There was more smoke than fire, however; only about a thousand cases of damage were reported around the world. Multitudes of antivirus programs were sold, so the companies' warning was clearly only an effort to stimulate sales.

   The reasoning in the consumer advocate's argument is flawed because this argument

   (A) restates its conclusion without attempting to offer a reason to accept it

   (B) fails to acknowledge that antivirus programs might protect against viruses other than the particular one described

   (C) asserts that the occurrence of one event after another shows that the earlier event was the cause of the later one

   (D) uses inflammatory language as a substitute for providing any evidence

   (E) overlooks the possibility that the protective steps taken did work and, for many computers, prevented the virus from causing damage[3]

Step 1. Identify the Question Type

_____

Step 2. Untangle the Stimulus

_____

Step 3. Make a Prediction

_____

Step 4. Evaluate the Answer Choices

_____

_____

[3]PrepTest 25, Sec. 2, Q 9

Explanations

1. (E)

Consumer advocate: <Last year's worldwide alarm about a computer "virus"—a surreptitiously introduced computer program that can destroy other programs and data—was a fraud.> Companies selling programs to protect computers against such viruses raised worldwide concern about the possibility that a destructive virus would be activated on a certain date. There was more smoke than fire, however; only about a thousand cases of damage were reported around the world. Multitudes of antivirus programs were sold, so the companies' warning was clearly only an effort to stimulate sales.

The reasoning in the consumer advocate's argument is (flawed) because this argument

(A) restates its conclusion without attempting to offer a reason to accept it

(B) fails to acknowledge that antivirus programs might protect against viruses other than the particular one described

(C) asserts that the occurrence of one event after another shows that the earlier event was the cause of the later one

(D) uses inflammatory language as a substitute for providing any evidence

(E) overlooks the possibility that the protective steps taken did work and, for many computers, prevented the virus from causing damage[4]

Step 1. Identify the Question Type

The question stem tells you specifically that the reasoning is "flawed," so this is a Flaw question.

Step 2. Untangle the Stimulus

The consumer advocate concludes that the worldwide alarm sounded by companies that sold virus protection regarding a destructive virus was a fraud—it was designed only to stimulate antivirus software sales. The author bases this claim on the fact that a relatively small number of cases of damage from the virus were reported.

Step 3. Make a Prediction

This argument assumes only one explanation for the minimal damage reports—that the virus report was a fraud. In making this argument, the author commits the classic flaw of ignoring alternative explanations. So, your job now is to find an answer that presents a possible

[4]PrepTest 25, Sec. 2, Q 9

alternative to explain the low number of reports. You don't need to predict the exact alternative; you just need to be on the lookout for a plausible possibility.

Step 4. Evaluate the Answer Choices

Choice (A) is wrong because the advocate does offer a reason—limited damage caused by the virus—to accept the conclusion of fraud. The problem is that the advocate assumes it is the only explanation and ignores other possibilities.

Choice (B) is irrelevant. Protection against other viruses does not address the issue at hand—that virus protection companies sounded the alarm for fraudulent reasons.

Choice (C) is incorrect because the advocate does not present a causal argument. He does not assert that the sale of antivirus programs is responsible for the limited damage from the virus. Rather, he claims the limited damage means there was no threat for the software to fix at all.

The advocate doesn't really use any inflammatory language as evidence as stated by choice (D). The evidence for fraud is based on the limited amount of damage caused by the virus.

Choice (E) fits the bill. It suggests that computer owners responded to the alarm and bought virus protection that limited the amount of damage.

DRILL: PRACTICING FLAW QUESTIONS

Use the Kaplan Method to answer the following Flaw questions. Take this opportunity to practice and apply the steps in the Method so you are comfortable using them on test day. Be sure to circle conclusion and evidence Keywords and bracket the conclusion. Check your responses against the full explanations provided after the Drill.

1. Formal performance evaluations in the professional world are conducted using realistic situations. Physicians are allowed to consult medical texts freely, attorneys may refer to law books and case records, and physicists and engineers have their manuals at hand for ready reference. Students, then, should likewise have access to their textbooks whenever they take examinations.

The reasoning in the argument is questionable because the argument

(A) cites examples that are insufficient to support the generalization that performance evaluations in the professional world are conducted in realistic situations

(B) fails to consider the possibility that adopting its recommendation will not significantly increase most students' test scores

(C) neglects to take into account the fact that professionals were once students who also did not have access to textbooks during examinations

(D) neglects to take into account the fact that, unlike students, professionals have devoted many years of study to one subject

(E) fails to consider the possibility that the purposes of evaluation in the professional world and in school situations are quite dissimilar[5]

2. In determining the authenticity of a painting, connoisseurs claim to be guided by the emotional impact the work has on them. For example, if a painting purportedly by Rembrandt is expressive and emotionally moving in a certain way, then this is supposedly evidence that the work was created by Rembrandt himself, and not by one of his students. But the degree to which an artwork has an emotional impact differs wildly from person to person. So a connoisseur's assessment cannot be given credence.

The reasoning in the argument is most vulnerable to criticism on the grounds that the argument

(A) ignores the fact that anybody, not just a connoisseur, can give an assessment of the emotional impact of a painting

(B) is based on the consideration of the nature of just one painter's works, even though the conclusion is about paintings in general

(C) neglects the possibility that there may be widespread agreement among connoisseurs about emotional impact even when the public's assessment varies wildly

(D) presumes, without giving justification, that a painting's emotional impact is irrelevant to the determination of that painting's authenticity

(E) presumes, without offering evidence, that Rembrandt was better at conveying emotions in painting than were other painters[6]

3. A group of 1,000 students was randomly selected from three high schools in a medium-sized city and asked the question, "Do you plan to finish your high school education?" More than 89 percent answered "Yes." This shows that the overwhelming majority of students want to finish high school, and that if the national dropout rate among high school students is high, it cannot be due to a lack of desire on the part of the students.

The reasoning of the argument above is questionable because the argument

(A) fails to justify its presumption that 89 percent is an overwhelming majority

(B) attempts to draw two conflicting conclusions from the results of one survey

(C) overlooks the possibility that there may in fact not be a high dropout rate among high school students

(D) contradicts itself by admitting that there may be a high dropout rate among students while claiming that most students want to finish high school

(E) treats high school students from a particular medium-sized city as if they are representative of high school students nationwide[7]

4. The people most likely to watch a televised debate between political candidates are the most committed members of the electorate and thus the most likely to have already made up their minds about whom to support. Furthermore, following a debate, uncommitted viewers are generally undecided about who won the debate. Hence, winning a televised debate does little to bolster one's chances of winning an election.

The reasoning in the argument is most vulnerable to criticism because the argument fails to consider the possibility that

(A) watching an exciting debate makes people more likely to vote in an election

(B) the voting behavior of people who do not watch a televised debate is influenced by reports about the debate

(C) there are differences of opinion about what constitutes winning or losing a debate

(D) people's voting behavior may be influenced in unpredictable ways by comments made by the participants in a televised debate

(E) people who are committed to a particular candidate will vote even if their candidate is perceived as having lost a televised debate[8]

5. The typological theory of species classification, which has few adherents today, distinguishes species solely on the basis of observable physical characteristics, such as plumage color, adult size, or dental structure. However, there are many so-called "sibling species," which are indistinguishable on the basis of their appearance but cannot interbreed and thus, according to the mainstream biological theory of species classification, are separate species. Since the typological theory does not count sibling species as separate species, it is unacceptable.

The reasoning in the argument is most vulnerable to criticism on the grounds that

(A) the argument does not evaluate all aspects of the typological theory

(B) the argument confuses a necessary condition for species distinction with a sufficient condition for species distinction

(C) the argument, in its attempt to refute one theory of species classification, presupposes the truth of an opposing theory

(D) the argument takes a single fact that is incompatible with a theory as enough to show that theory to be false

(E) the argument does not explain why sibling species cannot interbreed[9]

---

[7]PrepTest 34, Sec. 3, Q 4

[8]PrepTest 41, Sec. 1, Q 20

---

[9]PrepTest 51, Sec. 1, Q 15

Explanations

1. **(E)**

Formal performance evaluations in the professional world are conducted using realistic situations. Physicians are allowed to consult medical texts freely, attorneys may refer to law books and case records, and physicists and engineers have their manuals at hand for ready reference. <Students, (then,) should likewise have access to their textbooks whenever they take examinations.>

The reasoning in the argument is (questionable because) the argument

(A)   cites examples that are insufficient to support the generalization that performance evaluations in the professional world are conducted in realistic situations

(B)   fails to consider the possibility that adopting its recommendation will not significantly increase most students' test scores

(C)   neglects to take into account the fact that professionals were once students who also did not have access to textbooks during examinations

(D)   neglects to take into account the fact that, unlike students, professionals have devoted many years of study to one subject

(E)   fails to consider the possibility that the purposes of evaluation in the professional world and in school situations are quite dissimilar[10]

Step 1. Identify the Question Type

The phrase "questionable because" signals a Flaw question.

Step 2. Untangle the Stimulus

The author concludes that students should be able to have open-book tests because physicians, attorneys, and other professionals are allowed to consult their books during performance evaluations.

Step 3. Make a Prediction

The author uses evidence about professionals to form a conclusion about students, so she must assume they are comparable and makes her argument by analogy. The correct answer will point out the flawed comparison between professionals and students.

Step 4. Evaluate the Answer Choices

You can eliminate choice (A) because the argument states specifically that performance evaluations in the professional world are conducted in realistic situations.

---

[10]PrepTest 29, Sec. 4, Q 25

Choice (B) is outside the scope because the argument is about access to books during test evaluation and not about score improvement.

Whether the professionals took closed-book exams when they were students as presented in choice (C) is of no consequence to the argument. The argument focuses on the comparison between professional evaluations and student evaluations, so you need an answer to address that comparison.

Choice (D) has the same problem. Even if it is true that professionals devote many years of study to one subject, choice (D) does not address whether closed-book exams are appropriate for students.

Choice (E) matches the prediction by distinguishing the two groups and raising the possibility that a professional and a student evaluation could serve different purposes. This is the correct answer.

2. **(C)**

In determining the authenticity of a painting, connoisseurs claim to be guided by the emotional impact the work has on them. For example, if a painting purportedly by Rembrandt is expressive and emotionally moving in a certain way, then this is supposedly evidence that the work was created by Rembrandt himself, and not by one of his students. But the degree to which an artwork has an emotional impact differs wildly from person to person. ⟨So⟩ a connoisseur's assessment cannot be given credence.⟩

The reasoning in the argument is most ⟨vulnerable to⟩ ⟨criticism⟩ on the grounds that the argument

(A) ignores the fact that anybody, not just a connoisseur, can give an assessment of the emotional impact of a painting

(B) is based on the consideration of the nature of just one painter's works, even though the conclusion is about paintings in general

(C) neglects the possibility that there may be widespread agreement among connoisseurs about emotional impact even when the public's assessment varies wildly

(D) presumes, without giving justification, that a painting's emotional impact is irrelevant to the determination of that painting's authenticity

(E) presumes, without offering evidence, that Rembrandt was better at conveying emotions in painting than were other painters[11]

---

[11]PrepTest 37, Sec. 4, Q 16

Step 1. Identify the Question Type

The "vulnerable to criticism" language identifies this as a Flaw question.

Step 2. Untangle the Stimulus

The author determines that a connoisseur's assessment of a painting's authenticity is not credible. He reaches this conclusion with evidence that the emotional impact of a painting, which connoisseurs use to determine a painting's authenticity, differs from person to person.

Step 3. Make a Prediction

Notice the author uses evidence about people in general to form a conclusion about connoisseurs, thus committing a scope shift. Although people may have different kinds of emotional reactions, it's possible the connoisseurs agree among each other. If so, then you can trust their authentication.

Step 4. Evaluate the Answer Choices

Choice (A) is not true. The author argues that everyone can have an emotional response to a painting; it's the degree of impact that varies.

Choice (B) confuses the purpose of the Rembrandt example, which the author uses as one example of a painter, not as the basis of his argument.

Choice (C) points out the flaw and is the correct answer.

Choice (D) is incorrect; the author does provide justification that a painting's emotional impact is irrelevant to the determination of that painting's authenticity.

Whether Rembrandt was better at conveying emotions in painting than other painters is irrelevant in the argument. Again, Rembrandt serves as an example of painters, not the point of the argument. Cross out choice (E).

3. **(E)**

A group of 1,000 students was randomly selected from three high schools in a medium-sized city and asked the question, "Do you plan to finish your high school education?" More than 89 percent answered "Yes." <This shows that> the overwhelming majority of students want to finish high school, and that if the national dropout rate among high school students is high, it cannot be due to a lack of desire on the part of the students.>

The reasoning of the argument above is (questionable) (because) the argument

(A) fails to justify its presumption that 89 percent is an overwhelming majority

(B) attempts to draw two conflicting conclusions from the results of one survey

(C) overlooks the possibility that there may in fact not be a high dropout rate among high school students

(D) contradicts itself by admitting that there may be a high dropout rate among students while claiming that most students want to finish high school

(E) treats high school students from a particular medium-sized city as if they are representative of high school students nationwide[12]

Step 1. Identify the Question Type

The phrase "questionable because" signals a Flaw question.

Step 2. Untangle the Stimulus

You can identify the author's conclusion—that the majority of students want to complete high school, and a large number of high school dropouts does not indicate students' lack of interest in finishing school—by the phrase "this shows that." The evidence refers to a study of a thousand students from a medium-sized city, 89 percent of whom said they planned to finish high school.

Step 3. Make a Prediction

The author uses a study about one group of students from one place in the country to form a conclusion about all students nationwide. Whenever an argument is based on research, a study, or an experiment, consider the flaw of representativeness. In this case, the author mistakenly assumes the single group can represent all high school students across the country.

Step 4. Evaluate the Answer Choices

You can rule out choice (A), as the definition of "overwhelming majority" is not at issue in this argument. Even if it was, most people would agree 89 percent could pass for the overwhelming majority.

---

[12]PrepTest 34, Sec. 3, Q 4

The two points made in the conclusion are not contradictory, as choice (B) would have you believe. Rather, it makes sense that students say they want to finish high school, and then if and when they don't, say they had the desire to finish.

The author concedes a high national high school dropout rate, but questions its size. So, choice (C) does not work.

As already mentioned in (B), the notions that the dropout rate can be high and most students want to finish high school can coexist. So, choice (D) doesn't present a contradiction.

Choice (E) correctly identifies the flaw as lack of representativeness, and is your correct answer.

4.   **(B)**

The people most likely to watch a televised debate between political candidates are the most committed members of the electorate and thus the most likely to have already made up their minds about whom to support. Furthermore, following a debate, uncommitted viewers are generally undecided about who won the debate. <Hence, winning a televised debate does little to bolster one's chances of winning an election.>

The reasoning in the argument is most vulnerable to criticism because the argument fails to consider the possibility that

(A)   watching an exciting debate makes people more likely to vote in an election

(B)   the voting behavior of people who do not watch a televised debate is influenced by reports about the debate

(C)   there are differences of opinion about what constitutes winning or losing a debate

(D)   people's voting behavior may be influenced in unpredictable ways by comments made by the participants in a televised debate

(E)   people who are committed to a particular candidate will vote even if their candidate is perceived as having lost a televised debate[13]

Step 1. Identify the Question Type

The phrase "vulnerable to criticism" is a common indicator of a Flaw question. Additionally, the question stem identifies the flaw as something the argument "fails to consider." Your job is to describe what the author overlooked in content-specific terms.

---

[13]PrepTest 41, Sec. 1, Q 20

Step 2. Untangle the Stimulus

"Hence" points you to the conclusion, which states that winning a TV debate does little to improve a candidate's chances of winning an election. The author's evidence is that the people most likely to watch the debate are already committed to a candidate and that voters who are undecided aren't persuaded by the debate to support one candidate or another.

Step 3. Make a Prediction

The author says the people who are either committed to a candidate or undecided will not be affected by the debate. Notice the author presents two extreme groups in the evidence, the fully committed and the uncommitted, and ignores the possibility of a middle ground. The failure to consider there might be some other people to consider is a basic LSAT pattern. Here, the author ignores the potential voters who do not see the debate; can they be influenced by the debate without watching it? The answer is yes. They could be persuaded indirectly by other influences, such as follow-up conversations and media reviews of the debate. The author fails to consider that possibility in reaching her conclusion.

Step 4. Evaluate the Answer Choices

Choice (A) is out; the argument is about who the debate watchers would vote for, not their likelihood of voting.

Choice (B) matches the prediction and is the correct answer.

Choice (C) is outside the scope because the conclusion is about a winning debate candidate.

The determination of what constitutes a winning and losing debate is not relevant. The author's argument—that debate watchers are generally not influenced by the debate—specifically contradicts choice (D). Even if a small number of watchers are affected in an unpredictable way, the argument remains unchanged.

Choice (E) deals with the prospect of voting, not voting behavior. So, like choice (A), you can dismiss this answer.

5. **(C)**

The typological theory of species classification, which has few adherents today, distinguishes species solely on the basis of observable physical characteristics, such as plumage color, adult size, or dental structure. However, there are many so-called "sibling species," which are indistinguishable on the basis of their appearance but cannot interbreed and thus, according to the mainstream biological theory of species classification, are separate species. (Since) the typological theory does not count sibling species as separate species, <it is unacceptable.>

The reasoning in the argument is most (vulnerable to) (criticism) on the grounds that

(A) the argument does not evaluate all aspects of the typological theory

(B) the argument confuses a necessary condition for species distinction with a sufficient condition for species distinction

(C) the argument, in its attempt to refute one theory of species classification, presupposes the truth of an opposing theory

(D) the argument takes a single fact that is incompatible with a theory as enough to show that theory to be false

(E) the argument does not explain why sibling species cannot interbreed[14]

Step 1. Identify the Question Type

The phrase "vulnerable to criticism" identifies this as a Flaw question.

Step 2. Untangle the Stimulus

The author introduces two different theories of species classification—typological theory and mainstream biological theory. The mainstream biological theory considers sibling species to be separate species. In the evidence, identified by the word "since," the author states that the typological theory does not count sibling species as separate species. Therefore, the author concludes, the theory is unacceptable.

Step 3. Make a Prediction

Don't let complicated or unfamiliar language intimidate you. The LSAT does not test content, so you don't need to understand the different theories and how they work. You need only to simplify the text and find any patterns to help you answer the questions.

Look at this argument in simpler terms: The MB (mainstream biological) theory says X, and the T (typological) theory says not X; and so the T theory is wrong. If the T theory is wrong because it doesn't agree with the MB theory, the author must assume that the MB theory is correct.

---

[14]PrepTest 51, Sec. 1, Q 15

Because this is a Flaw question, review the answers to find one that describes a faulty assumption.

Step 4. Evaluate the Answer Choices

Choice (A) is true in that the argument does not evaluate all aspects of the typological theory. But it is not the correct answer. Even a complete evaluation of the typological theory would not address the real problem in the argument, the author's dismissal of typological theory because it doesn't meet a requirement of a different theory.

Eliminate choice (B). The argument does not confuse a necessary or sufficient condition for species distinction.

Choice (C) describes a faulty assumption; it says the argument assumes one theory is true to prove the other theory is false. This is the correct answer.

Cross out choice (D) because the author gives you no information that the ability to interbreed is incompatible with the typological theory.

Again, choice (E) may be true, but it doesn't match the author's faulty assumption. In fact, an explanation for why sibling species cannot interbreed will have no effect on the argument at all.

FLAW REVIEW

Before you proceed to the next chapter, turn to Appendix A and complete the review exercise for Flaw questions. A completed chart is included in Appendix B.

CHAPTER 9

ASSUMPTION FAMILY OF QUESTIONS IN REVIEW

The Assumption family of questions consists of four members: Assumption, Strengthen, Weaken, and Flaw questions. These questions are related through their common components, and they also have a common purpose—to test your ability to analyze an argument.

COMMON ELEMENTS

Every Assumption family argument shares two explicit components: a conclusion and evidence. The conclusion is the author's main point, and identifying it first helps you to determine the evidence used to reach it and evaluate the argument as a whole. The evidence is the information given by the author to support the conclusion. The argument's assumption is the implicit part that bridges the gap between the two and that must be true for the argument to be valid.

Each Assumption family question tests your ability to analyze an argument but in slightly different ways. Some questions directly ask you to identify the assumption while others ask you to weaken or strengthen an argument. This means you have to loosen or tighten the connection between the evidence and conclusion, typically, by undermining or affirming the assumption. Other questions will ask you to determine the flaw committed by the author. Since a flaw is an unwarranted gap in reasoning between the evidence and the conclusion, flaws typically stem from faulty assumptions. Notice that each question type comes back to finding the assumption, a skill that will help you earn a lot of points on test day.

COMMON ARGUMENT STRUCTURES

The common elements of an argument often present themselves in common patterns. While the specifics change from question to question, there are certain argument structures that appear repeatedly on the LSAT. When you recognize them, you'll have a ready-made prediction of the assumption, strengthener, weakener, and flaw.

The following LSAT questions illustrate three of the most prominent argument patterns: recommendation, causal relationship, and prediction. Then I provided a breakdown of the argument elements for each Assumption family question type. Use these examples to revisit Assumption family questions from previous chapters, locate the patterns, and perform the same exercise. Practicing each question type in relation to a single stimulus will improve your argument-analysis skills and ultimately your ability to answer each Assumption family question type.

1. Medical doctor: Sleep deprivation is the cause of many social ills, ranging from irritability to potentially dangerous instances of impaired decision making. Most people today suffer from sleep deprivation to some degree. Therefore, we should restructure the workday to allow people flexibility in scheduling their work hours.[1]

Table 9.1

	Recommendation	
	General	**Specific**
Conclusion	We should/should not adopt the proposal.	Therefore, we should restructure the workday to allow people flexibility in scheduling their work hours.
Evidence	One reason a proposal is good/bad or needed/not needed.	Sleep deprivation causes many problems.
Assumption	There are no other considerations to take into account or the recommendation can/cannot address the problem.	Flexible scheduling can help reduce sleep deprivation and the accompanying effects.
Strengthener	This reason is particularly important/eliminating another possible factor.	• Employees reported two extra hours of sleep when they had greater latitude in scheduling their work hours. • Employees' healthier eating habits have not had any impact on employees' reduced sleep.
Weakener	There is another factor that's relevant.	• Adding fifteen minutes of exercise daily has been shown to reduce sleep deprivation. • The primary cause of sleep deprivation is overwork.
Flaw	Alternative possibilities	The medical doctor ignores the possibility that something else could cause the sleep deprivation.

[1]PrepTest 36, Sec. 3, Q 7

2. Galanin is a protein found in the brain. In an experiment, rats that consistently chose to eat fatty foods when offered a choice between lean and fatty foods were found to have significantly higher concentrations of galanin in their brains than did rats that consistently chose lean over fatty foods. These facts strongly support the conclusion that galanin causes rats to crave fatty foods.[2]

Table 9.2

	Causal Relationship	
	General	**Specific**
Conclusion	One thing (X) caused another (Y).	These facts strongly support the conclusion that galanin causes rats to crave fatty foods.
Evidence	Two things are correlated (X and Y happen to occur together).	Rats who chose fatty foods had a higher concentration of galanin than rats who chose lean foods.
Assumption	Assume the correlation was not a coincidence, not due to a third factor, or not due to reversed causation; or assume a causal relationship from X to Y.	• The relationship is not a coincidence. • A genetic predisposition did not cause the fatty food cravings. • Fatty food cravings do not result in a build-up of galanin. • A causal relationship does exist from galanin to fatty food craving.
Strengthener	Eliminate the possibility of coincidence, third factor, or reversal; or strengthen the likelihood that the first really causes the second.	• Bright lights do not cause fatty food cravings in rats. • The rats that preferred fatty foods had the higher concentrations of galanin in their brains before they were offered fatty foods. • A second study confirmed the findings that galanin does cause rats to crave fatty foods.

(continued)

[2]PrepTest 33, Sec. 3, Q 20

Weakener	Provide evidence that the correlation may really be just a coincidence, due to a third factor, or reversed; or weaken the likelihood that the first really causes the second.	• Sugar causes rats to crave fatty foods. • The rats that preferred fatty foods did not have higher concentrations of galanin in their brains before they were offered fatty foods. • The crucial experiment could not be repeated.
Flaw	Ignore the possibility that the correlation was a coincidence, there was an alternate cause, or causation was reversed.	Ignore the possibility that the correlation was a coincidence, there was an alternate cause, or causation was reversed.

3. Three major laundry detergent manufacturers have concentrated their powdered detergents by reducing the proportion of inactive ingredients in the detergent formulas. The concentrated detergents will be sold in smaller packages. In explaining the change, the manufacturers cited the desire to reduce cardboard packaging and other production costs. Market analysts predict that the decision of these three manufacturers, who control 80 percent of the laundry detergent market, will eventually bring about the virtual disappearance of old-style bulky detergents.[3]

Table 9.3

	Prediction	
	General	**Specific**
Conclusion	Something will/will not occur	Market analysts (predict) that the decision of these three manufacturers, who control 80 percent of the laundry detergent market, (will) eventually bring about the virtual disappearance of old-style bulky detergents.
Evidence	Reasons something will/will not occur	Manufacturers want to reduce cardboard packaging and other production costs.
Assumption	The evidence is relevant to the prediction/no other factor is being ignored.	What the manufacturers want will happen and no other factor influences the prediction.

(continued)

---

[3]PrepTest 17, Sec. 3, Q 6

Strengthener	The basis for the prediction is more relevant.	When available, consumers are increasingly persuaded by environmental concerns to buy concentrated detergents in order to reduce cardboard waste.
Weakener	Some other factor that makes the given basis for the prediction less important/less relevant.	Switching the machines to produce the smaller packages is environmentally hazardous.
Flaw	Overlooks the possibility that the evidence is irrelevant/that another factor does have relevance	• The manufacturers don't always get what they want. • Consumers prefer the larger packaging.

CHAPTER 10

INFERENCE QUESTIONS

If a famous actor is spotted looking at rings in a fancy jewelry store, the tabloids might print pictures that imply he's shopping for an engagement ring for his long-time girlfriend. The tabloid editors and the readers don't know for sure what he was shopping for, but they could make a reasonable inference. While that definition of "inference" is probably the one with which you're most familiar, the LSAT definition is much more specific. For an inference to be valid on the LSAT, it *must be true* based on the information provided in the stimulus.

Try another example. Let's say you offer Jesse a slice of your pepperoni pizza and he says, "No thanks, I'm good." What could you infer about Jesse? He's not hungry? He doesn't like pizza? He is a vegetarian? He's lactose intolerant? He doesn't want to eat with you? There are lots of possible inferences you can make in everyday life, but they would be incorrect on the LSAT.

Inferences in everyday life are essentially educated guesses usually based on experience. LSAT inferences must be 100 percent true based on the information provided.

You will find approximately seven scored Inference questions on the LSAT. Because Inference questions also appear in the Reading Comprehension section, it is especially worthwhile to practice Inference questions to maximize your score on test day.

DEFINITION OF INFERENCE QUESTIONS

Inference questions are different from the question types you've seen so far. Assumption, Strengthen, Weaken, and Flaw questions are all based on an argument and the relationship between the evidence and conclusion. Inference questions don't test the connection between the evidence and the conclusion. In fact, Inference stimuli typically don't contain an argument at all, but rather a set of facts. Your job is to inventory the facts provided and draw a logical conclusion from them. Given the difference between argument-based stimuli and Inference stimuli, you will have to modify your approach to an Inference question, but you will still follow the Kaplan Method.

USE THE KAPLAN METHOD TO ANSWER INFERENCE QUESTIONS

Identify the Question Type

As always, read the question stem first to identify the question type and note any relevant clues. You can identify an Inference question from words and phrases like:

- Must be true
- Logically follows
- Can be inferred
- Supports

You may remember that you already saw "support" as an indicator of a Strengthen question. To differentiate between a Strengthen question and an Inference question, you need to determine the direction of the support. If the stimulus supports the answer, it is an Inference question. If the answer supports the stimulus, it is a Strengthen question.

Here's some typical Inference question stems:

- Which one of the following is most strongly supported by the information above?
- Which one of the following most logically completes the argument?
- If the statements above are true, which one of the following must be true?
- Which one of the following can be properly inferred from the argument above?

Besides recognizing the question type as an Inference, pay close attention to how the answer choices are characterized. Read the stem to determine whether you need an answer that *must be true, must be false, could be true,* or *could be false.* This seems like an obvious step, but you don't get any points for answering the wrong question.

Most Inference questions ask for an answer that *must be true.* In that case, identify what must be true and eliminate any answer choice that *could be false.* If the question asks for what *must be false,* mark the answer that is always false and eliminate the four wrong answers that *could be true.* By taking a moment to characterize the answer choices, you know what you're looking for in a correct answer, which helps you to answer questions quickly and confidently.

Untangle the Stimulus

Inference stimuli differ from the argument-based stimuli you've seen so far in that they don't typically contain a full argument. Instead, they will almost always be a set of facts. So, after you identify an Inference question, don't spend any time looking for a conclusion or identifying an assumption.

As you read the stimulus for an Inference question, you need to accept each statement as true, summarize each new piece of information, and translate any formal logic statements (formal logic shows up in Inference questions more often than any other question type). In other words, you need to get a basic understanding of what the stimulus says. In addition, you should circle qualifying language like "some," "most," and "all," as well as emphasis and opinion Keywords, just as you would on the Reading Comprehension section.

Make a Prediction

This step is where you'll find the biggest difference between Inference questions and all other Logical Reasoning question types. Generally speaking, you won't be able to predict an answer for Inference questions. You'll find that many things *must be true* based on the statements in the stimulus, so it'll be hard to pre-phrase an answer. In that case, move on to step four.

However, if the stimulus includes formal logic or statements that you can combine, the correct answer choice will often be the outcome of the linked statements. In that case, take a moment in this step to combine the statements. For example, if an Inference stimulus states "if A, then B and if B, then C," combining the statements indicates "if A, then C," and that is a prediction you can make.

Evaluate the Answer Choices

As you proceed to the answer choices, remember to characterize them—if the correct answer *must be true*, then the wrong answers *could be false*, and so on. After you know the characteristics of the right and wrong answers, you can assess the answer choices. As you do so, keep the following basic principles in mind:

- The correct answer to an Inference question will not require any information beyond what is provided in the stimulus. So, resist the temptation to add any outside knowledge to the stimulus. The further an answer choice gets from the stimulus and the harder you have to work to prove it is valid, the more likely that it is wrong.
- A valid inference may be a simple summary of the stimulus. Don't eliminate an answer just because you think it's too obvious. Sometimes, it's just that easy.

- The correct answer choice must be indisputable, not just possible or reasonable. So, look out for extreme wording in Inference answers. The correct answer cannot be more extreme than the stimulus. For example, the stimulus states that *some* students got an A in the class, and an answer choice indicates *everyone* got an A—this is extreme and incorrect. On the other hand, if the stimulus states that everybody received an A in the class, and an answer choice indicates a majority of the students (or even just one) got an A, it is within the scope of the stimulus. Look out for words like "never," "always," "some," and "must" so you can make sure the scope of the stimulus matches that of the answer choices.

- The correct inference need not come from the entire stimulus. It may just be a rephrasing of one sentence or a combination of sentences.

THE KAPLAN METHOD IN ACTION

Now I'll walk you through a couple examples to show you how the Kaplan Method can help you efficiently solve any Inference question you see on test day.

1. Having lived through extraordinary childhood circumstances, Robin has no conception of the moral difference between right and wrong, only between what is legally permitted and what is not. When Robin committed an offense, Robin did not recognize the fact that it was a morally wrong act, despite knowing that it was illegal.

   From the statements above, which one of the following can be properly inferred?

   (A) Robin committed no offense that was not legally permissible.
   (B) Robin did something that was morally wrong.
   (C) Moral ignorance is never excusable in the eyes of the law.
   (D) Robin's childhood could have provided more adequate moral training even in the circumstances.
   (E) Robin could now be brought to see the moral difference between right and wrong.[1]

Step 1. Identify the Question Type

The phrase "properly inferred" identifies this as an Inference question. Next, you need to read the stimulus and decide which answer *must be true* based on the information provided.

---

[1]PrepTest 40, Sec. 1, Q 3

Step 2. Untangle the Stimulus

Read the stimulus to get a handle on the basic facts of the statement. Here, you learn that Robin doesn't know the difference between morally right and morally wrong, but she does know the difference between legally right and legally wrong. She committed an offense that she did not know was immoral, but did know it was illegal. Remember, that's all you need to do with an Inference stimulus: You don't need to find the argument or identify the evidence or conclusion.

Step 3. Make a Prediction

Now that you have reviewed the facts of the statement and characterized the correct answer as one that *must be true* (and conversely, the wrong answers *could be false*), move on to the answer choices.

Step 4. Evaluate the Answer Choices

The stimulus says that Robin committed an illegal offense, and choice (A) says the exact opposite, so you can eliminate this answer.

According to the stimulus, Robin did commit an immoral offense, she just didn't know it. So choice (B) must be true and is the correct answer.

Choice (C) raises the topic of moral ignorance as an excuse, which is not discussed in the stimulus. So, choice (C) is outside the scope and you can eliminate it. Also, the word "never" should set off an alarm as an extreme concept that does not fit with the stimulus.

Whether Robin's upbringing could have provided more moral training is not addressed in the stimulus. Therefore, choice (D) is outside the scope of the argument and is incorrect.

Choice (E) is also outside the scope of the stimulus. You can't know Robin's potential to learn the moral difference between right and wrong from the stimulus.

2. Essayist: Every contract negotiator has been lied to by someone or other, and whoever lies to anyone is practicing deception. But, of course, anyone who has been lied to has also lied to someone or other.

    If the essayist's statements are true, which one of the following must also be true?

    (A) Every contract negotiator has practiced deception.
    (B) Not everyone who practices deception is lying to someone.
    (C) Not everyone who lies to someone is practicing deception.
    (D) Whoever lies to a contract negotiator has been lied to by a contract negotiator.
    (E) Whoever lies to anyone is lied to by someone.[2]

---

[2]PrepTest 22, Sec. 4, Q 25

Step 1. Identify the Question Type

The phrase "must also be true" tells you this is an Inference question. Also, note that you are looking for an answer that *must be true*.

Step 2. Untangle the Stimulus

Words such as "every," "whoever," and "anyone" identify formal logic. When formal logic is present in a stimulus, expect the test makers to assess your understanding of what must be true on the basis of these statements. So, as with any formal logic statement, you will need to translate them and form their contrapositives.

The first statement says every contract negotiator has been lied to by someone or other. The matching formal logic equation is "Every X is Y." The translation and contrapositive are:

$$\text{Contract negotiator} \rightarrow \text{lied to}$$
$$\text{Not lied to} \rightarrow \text{not a contract negotiator}$$

The second statement says that whoever lies to anyone is practicing deception. The matching formal logic equation is "Whoever X is Y." The translation and contrapositive are:

$$\text{Liar} \rightarrow \text{deceptive}$$
$$\text{Not deceptive} \rightarrow \text{not liar}$$

The third statement says that anyone who has been lied to has also lied to someone or other. The matching formal logic equation is "Any X is Y." The translation and contrapositive are:

$$\text{Lied to} \rightarrow \text{liar}$$
$$\text{Not liar} \rightarrow \text{not lied to}$$

Step 3. Make a Prediction

You can connect the formal logic statements in the following way: Contract negotiator → lied to → Liar → Deceptive. Proceed to the answer choices to determine which one you can infer from the stimulus.

Step 4. Evaluate the Answer Choices

Each answer is presented in formal logic language. So, be prepared to translate each statement and compare it to the stimulus. When you find a match, you have the correct answer. And remember, you're looking for the correct answer that *must be true* and avoiding the four wrong answers that *could be false*.

Choice (A) says that every contract negotiator practices deception, which in formal logic terms is: Contract negotiator → deceptive. The stimulus does not have a statement that says this directly; however, this formal logic statement is a summary of the connected statements. Every contract negotiator has been lied to, and anyone who has been lied to also has lied to someone. So, every contract negotiator has lied to someone else. Whoever lies to anyone is practicing deception, so every contract negotiator has practiced deception. The equation form looks like this: Contract negotiator → lied to → lies → deceives. In summary, if you are a contract negotiator, then you practice deception. This matches the prediction, so mark choice (A) as the correct answer.

Choice (B) says that not everyone who practices deception is lying to someone. Practicing deception does not trigger a result in this stimulus. You cannot infer anything from practicing deception.

Choice (C) says not everyone who lies to someone is practicing deception. It directly contradicts the stimulus, which states that whoever lies to anyone is practicing deception.

Choice (D) says that whoever lies to a contract negotiator has been lied to by a contract negotiator. The stimulus never mentions what happens if you lie to a contract negotiator, so you can't know it to be true. Eliminate it.

Choice (E) says whoever lies has been lied to. Again, the stimulus never tells you the result of lying. So, it could be true because it's not contradicted by the stimulus, but it also *could be false*, making it a wrong answer.

INFERENCE QUESTIONS: NOW YOU TRY IT

Now it's your turn to try an Inference question on your own. Use the template I've provided after the question to guide you through the four-step Kaplan Method. (Note: On test day, you won't be writing out all the steps as you are in this exercise. However, as you are learning the Method, it's good practice to help it become second nature.)

1.   Professor: The best users of a language are its great authors. However, these authors often use language in ways that are innovative and idiosyncratic, and are therefore less respectful of the strictures of proper usage than most of us are.

   The Professor's statements, if true, most support which one of the following?

   (A)   People who want to become great writers should not imitate great authors' use of language.
   (B)   Writers who do not observe proper language usage risk developing a peculiar or idiosyncratic style.
   (C)   Those most talented at using a language are not as likely as most other people to observe proper language usage.
   (D)   People who use an innovative or idiosyncratic writing style often incur criticism of their language usage.
   (E)   The standard for what constitutes proper language usage should be set by the best users of a language.[3]

Step 1. Identify the Question Type

_____

Step 2. Untangle the Stimulus

_____

Step 3. Make a Prediction

_____

Step 4. Evaluate the Answer Choices

_____

---

[3]PrepTest 40, Sec. 3, Q 3

Explanations

1. **(C)**

Professor: The best users of a language are its great authors. However, these authors often use language in ways that are innovative and idiosyncratic, and are therefore less respectful of the strictures of proper usage than most of us are.

The Professor's statements, if true, (most support) which one of the following?

(A)   People who want to become great writers should not imitate great authors' use of language.

(B)   Writers who do not observe proper language usage risk developing a peculiar or idiosyncratic style.

(C)   Those most talented at using a language are not as likely as most other people to observe proper language usage.

(D)   People who use an innovative or idiosyncratic writing style often incur criticism of their language usage.

(E)   The standard for what constitutes proper language usage should be set by the best users of a language.[4]

Step 1. Identify the Question Type

The phrase "most support" coupled with the downward direction of the support makes this an Inference question. The question stem tells you specifically that the Professor's statements in the stimulus will support the correct answer.

Step 2. Untangle the Stimulus

Paraphrase the stimulus so you have a handle on what it says: Great authors may be the best users of a language, says the Professor, but they have less respect for the proper use of language than the rest of us.

Step 3. Make a Prediction

The summary is straightforward, with no formal logic or statements to connect. Move on to the answer choices and look for the one that *must be true*.

Step 4. Evaluate the Answer Choices

Cross out choice (A), as the Professor gives no career advice in her statement.

Likewise, get rid of choice (B). The Professor does not discuss any negative impact of improperly using language.

---

[4]PrepTest 40, Sec. 3, Q 3

Choice (C) closely matches the summary and is the correct answer. Those most talented or the best users of language are less likely to properly use language.

No mention of criticism is made in the stimulus, so choice (D) won't work.

Choice (E) is out as well because the stimulus does not talk about the origin of proper language use.

DRILL: PRACTICING INFERENCE QUESTIONS

Use the Kaplan Method to answer the following Inference questions. Take this opportunity to practice and apply the steps in the Method so you are comfortable using them on test day. Be sure to circle conclusion and evidence Keywords and bracket the conclusion. Check your responses against the full explanations provided after the Drill.

1. Commentator: Recently, articles criticizing the environmental movement have been appearing regularly in newspapers. According to Winslow, this is due not so much to an antienvironmental bias among the media as to a preference on the part of newspaper editors for articles that seem "daring" in that they seem to challenge prevailing political positions. It is true that editors like to run antienvironmental pieces mainly because they seem to challenge the political orthodoxy. But serious environmentalism is by no means politically orthodox, and antienvironmentalists can hardly claim to be dissidents, however much they may have succeeded in selling themselves as renegades.

    The commentator's statements, if true, most strongly support which one of the following?

    (A) Winslow is correct about the preference of newspaper editors for controversial articles.
    (B) Critics of environmentalism have not successfully promoted themselves as renegades.
    (C) Winslow's explanation is not consonant with the frequency with which critiques of environmentalism are published.
    (D) The position attacked by critics of environmentalism is actually the prevailing political position.
    (E) Serious environmentalism will eventually become a prevailing political position.[5]

2. Among a sample of diverse coins from an unfamiliar country, each face of any coin portrays one of four things: a judge's head, an explorer's head, a building, or a tree. By examining the coins, a collector determines that none of them have heads on both sides and that all coins in the sample with a judge's head on one side have a tree on the other.

    If the statements above are true, which one of the following must be true of the coins in the sample?

    (A) All those with an explorer's head on one side have a building on the other.
    (B) All those with a tree on one side have a judge's head on the other.
    (C) None of those with a tree on one side have an explorer's head on the other.
    (D) None of those with a building on one side have a judge's head on the other.
    (E) None of those with an explorer's head on one side have a building on the other.[6]

---

3. False chicory's taproot is always one half as long as the plant is tall. Furthermore, the more rain false chicory receives, the taller it tends to grow. In fact, false chicory plants that receive greater than twice the average rainfall of the species' usual habitat always reach above-average heights for false chicory.

If the statements above are true, then which one of the following must also be true?

(A) If two false chicory plants differ in height, then it is likely that the one with the shorter taproot has received less than twice the average rainfall of the species' usual habitat.

(B) If a false chicory plant has a longer-than-average taproot, then it is likely to have received more than twice the average rainfall of the species' usual habitat.

(C) It is not possible for a false chicory plant to receive only the average amount of rainfall of the species' usual habitat and be of above-average height.

(D) If the plants in one group of false chicory are not taller than those in another group of false chicory, then the two groups must have received the same amount of rainfall.

(E) If a false chicory plant receives greater than twice the average rainfall of the species' usual habitat, then it will have a longer taproot than that of an average-sized false chicory plant.[7]

4. All highly successful salespersons are both well organized and self-motivated, characteristics absent from many salespersons who are not highly successful. Further, although only those who are highly successful are well known among their peers, no salespersons who are self-motivated regret their career choices.

If all of the statements above are true, which one of the following must be true?

(A) No self-motivated salespersons who are not highly successful are well organized.

(B) All salespersons who are well organized but not highly successful are self-motivated.

(C) No salespersons who are well known among their peers regret their career choices.

(D) All salespersons who are not well organized regret their career choices.

(E) All salespersons who do not regret their career choices are highly successful.[8]

5. Journalist: Recent studies have demonstrated that a regular smoker who has just smoked a cigarette will typically display significantly better short-term memory skills than a nonsmoker, whether or not the nonsmoker has also just smoked a cigarette for the purposes of the study. Moreover, the majority of those smokers who exhibit this superiority in short-term memory skills will do so for at least eight hours after having last smoked.

If the journalist's statements are true, then each of the following could be true EXCEPT:

(A) The short-term memory skills exhibited by a nonsmoker who has just smoked a cigarette are usually substantially worse than the short-term memory skills exhibited by a nonsmoker who has not recently smoked a cigarette.

(B) The short-term memory skills exhibited by a nonsmoker who has just smoked a cigarette are typically superior to those exhibited by a regular smoker who has just smoked a cigarette.

(C) The short-term memory skills exhibited by a nonsmoker who has just smoked a cigarette are typically superior to those exhibited by a regular smoker who has not smoked for more than eight hours.

(D) A regular smoker who, immediately after smoking a cigarette, exhibits short-term memory skills no better than those typically exhibited by a nonsmoker is nevertheless likely to exhibit superior short-term memory skills in the hours following a period of heavy smoking.

(E) The short-term memory skills exhibited by a regular smoker who last smoked a cigarette five hours ago are typically superior to those exhibited by a regular smoker who has just smoked a cigarette.[9]

---

[7]PrepTest 46, Sec. 3, Q 25

[8]PrepTest 40, Sec. 1, Q 22

[9]PrepTest 52, Sec. 1, Q 18

Explanations

1. (A)

Commentator: Recently, articles criticizing the environmental movement have been appearing regularly in newspapers. According to Winslow, this is due not so much to an antienvironmental bias among the media as to a preference on the part of newspaper editors for articles that seem "daring" in that they seem to challenge prevailing political positions. It is true that editors like to run antienvironmental pieces mainly because they seem to challenge the political orthodoxy. But serious environmentalism is by no means politically orthodox, and antienvironmentalists can hardly claim to be dissidents, however much they may have succeeded in selling themselves as renegades.

The commentator's statements, if true, (most strongly) (support) which one of the following?

(A) Winslow is correct about the preference of newspaper editors for controversial articles.

(B) Critics of environmentalism have not successfully promoted themselves as renegades.

(C) Winslow's explanation is not consonant with the frequency with which critiques of environmentalism are published.

(D) The position attacked by critics of environmentalism is actually the prevailing political position.

(E) Serious environmentalism will eventually become a prevailing political position.[10]

Step 1. Identify the Question Type

After you combine the phrase "most strongly support" and the fact that the stimulus supports the correct answer, you know that this stem asks an Inference question.

Step 2. Untangle the Stimulus

Don't let the length of the stimulus bog you down. Get the basics: The commentator reports on recent criticism of the environmental movement in newspapers. Someone named Winslow claims the reason is not antienvironmental bias, but the editors interest in challenging the status quo. The commentator then says that editors may like to challenge the prevailing environmental attitudes as Winslow says, but environmentalism is not the commonly accepted view.

Step 3. Make a Prediction

Don't stop to predict an answer for this Inference question. It includes no formal logic or statements to combine. Go right to the answers and determine which choice *must be true*.

---

[10]PrepTest 51, Sec. 3, Q 12

Step 4. Evaluate the Answer Choices

Choice (A) notes the one point of agreement between Winslow and the commentator, newspaper editors like to challenge the status quo, and thus is correct.

Choice (B) is out because it directly contradicts the last two lines of the stimulus, where the commentator says antienvironmentalists "have succeeded in selling themselves as renegades."

The commentator never mentions the consistency of Winslow's explanation with the frequency of published environmental critiques, so you can't know them to be true from the stimulus. Get rid of choice (C).

Choice (D) won't work either because the stimulus does not identify environmentalism as the prevailing attitude.

The stimulus is set in the present, while choice (E) makes a prediction about environmentalism becoming the mainstream belief. Eliminate it, too.

2. **(D)**

Among a sample of diverse coins from an unfamiliar country, each face of any coin portrays one of four things: a judge's head, an explorer's head, a building, or a tree. By examining the coins, a collector determines that (none) of them have heads on both sides and that (all) coins in the sample with a judge's head on one side have a tree on the other.

If the statements above are true, which one of the following (must be true) of the coins in the sample?

(A) All those with an explorer's head on one side have a building on the other.
(B) All those with a tree on one side have a judge's head on the other.
(C) None of those with a tree on one side have an explorer's head on the other.
(D) None of those with a building on one side have a judge's head on the other.
(E) None of those with an explorer's head on one side have a building on the other.[11]

Step 1. Identify the Question Type

The phrase "must be true" signals an Inference question.

Step 2. Untangle the Stimulus

The stimulus describes a sample of diverse coins in formal logic language signaled by the words "none" and "all." When an Inference question includes formal logic, the correct answer often requires you to translate the statements and form the contrapositives.

---

[11]PrepTest 48, Sec. 1, Q 14

The first statement says that no coins have heads on both sides. The matching formal logic equation is "No Y are X." The translation and contrapositive are:

Coin → no two heads

Two heads → not a coin

You can simplify those statements by specifically applying them to the stimulus with the following:

Judge → not explorer

Explorer → not judge

The second statement says that all coins with a judge's head on one side have a tree on the other side. The matching formal logic equation is "All X are Y." The translation and contrapositive are:

Judge → tree

No tree → no Judge

Step 3. Make a Prediction

Because the stimulus contains formal logic, look for any statements to combine. In this case, the formal logic states that if the judge is on one side of a coin, then a tree is on the other side and not an explorer. Because the tree is necessary when the judge is on the coin, you can also infer that there is no building either.

In all likelihood, the wrong answers will confuse the formal logic statements.

Step 4. Evaluate the Answer Choices

Choice (A) says in formal logic terms that coins with an explorer's head on one side have a building on the other (Explorer → building). This could be true, but you don't know anything from the stimulus about the explorer's head except that another head can't be on the other side. Eliminate it.

Choice (B) commits a classic mistake by reversing a formal logic statement without negating and says: Tree → judge. You can't determine it from the stimulus. Cross it out.

Choice (C) translates to Tree → explorer, and having a tree on one side of the coin does not necessitate anything. This one's out as well.

Choice (D) translates to Building → no judge, and its contrapositive is Judge → no building. This must be true because you know from the stimulus that Judge → tree, and since only one thing can be on each side of coin, there can't be a building on this coin. So, choice (D) is correct.

Choice (E) translates as Explorer → no building, and it is wrong. Nothing in the stimulus contradicts it so it could be true, but nothing in the stimulus confirms it. So, it does not have to be true.

3.   (E)

False chicory's taproot is (always) one half as long as
the plant is tall. Furthermore, the more rain false
chicory receives, the taller it tends to grow. In fact,
false chicory plants that receive greater than twice the
average rainfall of the species' usual habitat (always)
reach above-average heights for false chicory.

If the statements above are true, then which one of
the following (must also be true)?

(A)   If two false chicory plants differ in height, then
       it is likely that the one with the shorter
       taproot has received less than twice the
       average rainfall of the species' usual habitat.

(B)   If a false chicory plant has a longer-than-
       average taproot, then it is likely to have
       received more than twice the average rainfall
       of the species' usual habitat.

(C)   It is not possible for a false chicory plant to
       receive only the average amount of rainfall of
       the species' usual habitat and be of above-
       average height.

(D)   If the plants in one group of false chicory are
       not taller than those in another group of false
       chicory, then the two groups must have
       received the same amount of rainfall.

(E)   If a false chicory plant receives greater than
       twice the average rainfall of the species' usual
       habitat, then it will have a longer taproot than
       that of an average-sized false chicory plant.[12]

Step 1. Identify the Question Type

The phrase "must also be true" tells you this is an Inference question.

Step 2. Untangle the Stimulus

Extreme wording should always get your attention. Here, the word "always" is used in two
different sentences. First, false chicory's taproot is always one half as long as the plant is tall.
Second, if false chicory receives greater than twice the average rainfall, the plant will always
reach above-average height.

Step 3. Make a Prediction

Putting these two statements together, you can infer that when there's greater than twice the
average rainfall, the false chicory taproot must have above-average length. And remember,
the correct answer *must be true*, and so the wrong answers *could be false*.

Step 4. Evaluate the Answer Choices

Choice (A) identifies a difference in rainfall as the reason for the height difference between
two false chicory plants. The stimulus does not. Cross out choice (A).

---

[12]PrepTest 46, Sec. 3, Q 25

Choice (B) refers to rainfall as the likeliest way to get a longer than average taproot, but the stimulus does not address this. Choice (B) is out as well.

The stimulus also does not discuss whether it's possible for a false chicory plant to receive only the average amount of rainfall and be of above-average height. You only know that the more rain false chicory receives, the taller it tends to grow. That eliminates choice (C).

Choice (D) compares groups of false chicory and concludes a specific relationship between the amount of rainfall and plant growth, which is not supported by the stimulus. That only leaves one more choice.

Choice (E) reflects a combination of two statements from the stimulus and is the correct answer. You know that false chicory's taproot is always one half as long as the plant is tall. You also know that when false chicory receives greater than twice the average rainfall the plant will always reach above-average height. Since the plant will be above-average height and the length is always in the same proportion to the height, you can infer the plant will have a longer taproot than that of an average-sized false chicory plant.

4.   **(C)**

(All) highly successful salespersons are both well organized and self-motivated, characteristics absent from many salespersons who are not highly successful. Further, although (only) those who are highly successful are well known among their peers, (no) salespersons who are self-motivated regret their career choices.

If all of the statements above are true, which one of the following (must be true)?

(A)   No self-motivated salespersons who are not highly successful are well organized.

(B)   All salespersons who are well organized but not highly successful are self-motivated.

(C)   No salespersons who are well known among their peers regret their career choices.

(D)   All salespersons who are not well organized regret their career choices.

(E)   All salespersons who do not regret their career choices are highly successful.[13]

Step 1. Identify the Question Type

The question asks for a statement that "must be true" based on the stimulus, signaling that it is an Inference question.

Step 2. Untangle the Stimulus

The words "all," "only," and "no" signal formal logic language throughout the stimulus. Translate each statement and form the contrapositive.

---

[13]PrepTest 40, Sec. 1, Q 22

The first statement says that all highly successful (HS) salespersons are both well-organized (WO) and self-motivated (SM). The matching formal logic equation is "All X are Y." The translation and contrapositive are:

$$HS \rightarrow WO \text{ and } SM$$
$$\text{Not WO or not SM} \rightarrow \text{not HS}$$

The second statement says that only highly successful (HS) salespersons are well-known (WK). The matching formal logic equation is "Only Y are X." The translation and contrapositive are:

$$WK \rightarrow HS$$
$$\text{Not HS} \rightarrow \text{not WK}$$

The third statement says that no salespersons who are self-motivated (SM) regret their career choices (RC). The matching formal logic equation is "No Y are X." The translation and contrapositive are:

$$SM \rightarrow \text{not RC}$$
$$RC \rightarrow \text{not SM}$$

Step 3. Make a Prediction

The three statements connect in the following way: WK → HS → WO and SM → not RC. Armed with the formal logic statements, you are ready to move on to the answer choices.

Step 4. Evaluate the Answer Choices

Notice that each answer is presented in formal logic terms. You will need to translate them and compare them to the formal logic in the stimulus.

Choice (A) says SM and not HS → not WO. While "SM" and "not HS" appear in an "if" or sufficient clause in the stimulus, they do not individually or combined result in "not WO." So according to the stimulus, "SM" and "not HS" both trigger a result. But the result is never "not WO." Cross out this choice.

Choice (B) says WO and not HS → SM. WO is never part of a sufficient clause in the stimulus, so you can eliminate (B).

Choice (C) says WK → not RC. While it does not match an individual translation or contrapositive from the stimulus, it is a summary of the linked statement, and is a valid inference. This is the correct answer.

Choice (D) says not WO → RC. You can find a sufficient clause with "not WO," but there is no way to reach RC as the result. Choice (D) cannot be a valid inference.

Choice (E) says not RC → HS. Once again, check the translations and contrapositives. You will not find "not RC" in the sufficient clause, so you can't know what happens if salespeople don't regret their career choices.

5. **(B)**

Journalist: Recent studies have demonstrated that a regular smoker who has just smoked a cigarette will typically display significantly better short-term memory skills than a nonsmoker, whether or not the nonsmoker has also just smoked a cigarette for the purposes of the study. Moreover, the majority of those smokers who exhibit this superiority in short-term memory skills will do so for at least eight hours after having last smoked.

If the journalist's statements are true, then each of the following could be true EXCEPT:

(A) The short-term memory skills exhibited by a nonsmoker who has just smoked a cigarette are usually substantially worse than the short-term memory skills exhibited by a nonsmoker who has not recently smoked a cigarette.

(B) The short-term memory skills exhibited by a nonsmoker who has just smoked a cigarette are typically superior to those exhibited by a regular smoker who has just smoked a cigarette.

(C) The short-term memory skills exhibited by a nonsmoker who has just smoked a cigarette are typically superior to those exhibited by a regular smoker who has not smoked for more than eight hours.

(D) A regular smoker who, immediately after smoking a cigarette, exhibits short-term memory skills no better than those typically exhibited by a nonsmoker is nevertheless likely to exhibit superior short-term memory skills in the hours following a period of heavy smoking.

(E) The short-term memory skills exhibited by a regular smoker who last smoked a cigarette five hours ago are typically superior to those exhibited by a regular smoker who has just smoked a cigarette.[14]

Step 1. Identify the Question Type

The language "could be true EXCEPT" tells you this is an Inference question with a twist, so it's important to make sure you know what the question is really asking you to find. An Inference... EXCEPT question directs you to identify the one answer choice that *must be false* according

---

[14]PrepTest 52, Sec. 1, Q 18

to the stimulus. That is, it can't be true if the stimulus is true. All four wrong answers *could be true*—they need not be valid inferences from the stimulus; they just can't contradict the stimulus.

Step 2. Untangle the Stimulus

The journalist reports that regular smokers who smoked within the last eight hours typically display better short-term memory skills than a nonsmoker, even if the nonsmoker just smoked a cigarette for the study.

Step 3. Make a Prediction

Pause for a moment to remind yourself that the correct answer *must be false* according to the stimulus and proceed to the answer choices.

Step 4. Evaluate the Answer Choices

Choice (A) compares two groups of nonsmokers who are not addressed in the stimulus. Because you can't know whether the comparison is correct, the statement is possible. So you can eliminate (A). Remember, if the stimulus does not indicate specifically that an answer is false, it remains possible.

Choice (B) says the nonsmoker who just smoked has better short-term memory skills than a regular smoker. The stimulus says the exact opposite, that regular smokers have better short-term memory skills than a nonsmoker even if he just smoked for the study. Choice (B) contradicts the stimulus; therefore it *must be false* and is the correct answer.

Choice (C) makes a comparison between a nonsmoker who has just smoked and a regular smoker who has not smoked for more than eight hours. These two groups are never compared in the stimulus. Therefore, the stimulus does not confirm or contradict it and the answer remains a possibility. Cross it out.

The journalist never discusses the result of heavy smoking so you can't know it to be true or false according to the stimulus. Choice (D) is still a possibility and therefore can be eliminated.

Choice (E) also raises a point that is never made in the stimulus. The journalist never distinguishes the memory skill level at different points in the eight-hour time period. Choice (E) is not dismissed in the stimulus and is therefore still possible. Eliminate it.

INFERENCE REVIEW

Before you proceed to the next chapter, turn to Appendix A and complete the review exercise for Inference questions. A completed chart is included in Appendix B.

CHAPTER 11

PRINCIPLE QUESTIONS

You're probably most familiar with the general definition of "principle"—a moral code of conduct or a foundation of a belief system. The term "principle" on the LSAT, however, specifically refers to a broad standard or rule that guides the decision-maker or actor in the stimulus and that directs her to follow a similar path in other similar situations. Principle questions model how the law actually works.

Principle questions have become increasingly important on the LSAT. Historically, tests have averaged five scored Principle questions; however more recent tests have had as many as seven. Principle questions are also important because they mimic other question types, which means they are amenable to the skills and strategies you've already learned for each question type. So, having a good grasp of the other question types will help you quickly and confidently handle any Principle question you see on test day.

DEFINITION OF PRINCIPLE QUESTIONS

Principle questions ask you to find a general rule and match it to a specific factual situation. The wording of the question determines where the principle appears, either in the stimulus or the answer choices.

USE THE KAPLAN METHOD TO ANSWER PRINCIPLE QUESTIONS

Identify the Question Type

Just as you've done with all other Logical Reasoning question types, read the question stem first to determine the question type. The following terms denote a Principle question:

- Principle (this is used most often)
- Policy
- Proposition
- Generalization

Here's how some of those phrases could appear in a question stem:

- Which one of the following principles, if valid, most helps to justify the reasoning in the argument?
- The passage conforms most closely to which one of the following propositions?
- Which one of the following arguments illustrates a principle most similar to the principle underlying the argument above?
- Which one of the following principles most strongly supports the reasoning above?
- Which one of the following principles underlies the argument above?
- Of the following, which one illustrates a principle that is most similar to the principle illustrated by the passage?
- The situation described above most closely conforms to which one of the following generalizations?

Principle Questions Can Mimic Other Logical Reasoning Question Types

Some Principle questions are just straightforward Principle questions. Others include additional language in the stem that makes them resemble other Logical Reasoning question types.

For example, you may be asked for a principle that justifies (Strengthens) the author's argument, that underlies the argument (Assumption), that comes from the stimulus and is parallel to the principle illustrated by the answer (Parallel Reasoning), or that must be true (Inference). If you recognize the wording of another question type in a Principle question, use that knowledge to help you untangle the stimulus.

Consider the following example:

> Which one of the following principles, if valid, most helps to justify the reasoning in the argument?

The word "principles" signals a Principle question, but "most helps to justify" makes it sound like a Strengthen question.

Try another example:

> Which one of the following principles underlies the argument above?

Again, you see the word "principles" to identify the Principle question. But "underlies" indicates that the Principle question acts like an Assumption question.

Here is a Parallel Reasoning example:

> Which one of the following arguments illustrates a principle most similar to the principle underlying the argument above?

"Principle" tells you this is a Principle question, while "most similar to" tells you the unstated Principle exemplified by the stimulus is parallel to the unstated Principle exemplified by the correct answer choice.

Finally, look at an Inference example:

> Which one of the following must be true based on the policy stated above?

"Policy" identifies a Principle question that asks you to identify what "must be true" or can be inferred from the stimulus.

Find the Principle

After you identify a Principle question and another question type it may mimic, use the language of the question stem to determine the location of the principle. The LSAT asks Principle questions in three different ways. You may be asked to:

- Identify the Principle: Most Principle questions present an argument in the stimulus and ask you to identify the principle in the answer choices that is similar to the stimulus, yet broader in scope. It shifts from narrow reasoning in the stimulus to a broad focus in the answers.

  Example: Which one of the following principles most strongly supports the reasoning above?

- Apply the Principle: Here, you'll find the principle in the stimulus and different scenarios in the answer choices. Your task is to find an example that is covered by the principle but is narrower in scope. Keep your eye out for formal logic in these Principle question types.

  Example: Which one of the following most closely conforms to the principle stated above?

- Identify and Apply the Principle: In this Principle question type, you won't find the principle in the stimulus or in the answer choices. Instead, the stimulus presents a situation and the answer choices each provide a different scenario. Your job is to find a specific situation in the correct answer that falls under the same general rule exemplified by the situation in the stimulus. The principle is unstated, yet both the stimulus and the answer must follow the same principle.

  Example: Of the following, which one illustrates a principle that is most similar to the principle illustrated by the passage?

Untangle the Stimulus

Since Principle questions resemble Strengthen, Assumption, Parallel Reasoning, and Inference questions, you can use those strategies to untangle the stimulus of a Principle question. Simply read a Principle stimulus like the question type it mimics.

For example, if the question resembles a Strengthen question, find the conclusion and evidence, determine the assumption, and make the argument more likely to be so. For an Assumption question, locate the conclusion and evidence and determine what links them together. With a Parallel Reasoning question, look for the same kind of evidence to support the same kind of conclusion in the stimulus and the correct answer choice. And for an Inference question, determine what you can know from the stimulus and evaluate the answer choices, looking for what must be true based on it.

Make a Prediction

Think critically about the answer in the manner you would for the corresponding question type, and phrase the prediction as a broad principle or a narrow situation, depending on what the question calls for.

Evaluate the Answer Choices

Find an answer choice that matches your prediction.

THE KAPLAN METHOD IN ACTION

Now I'll walk you through a couple examples to show you how the Kaplan Method can help you efficiently solve any Principle question you'll see on test day.

1. Philosopher: Some of the most ardent philosophical opponents of democracy have rightly noted that both the inherently best and the inherently worst possible forms of government are those that concentrate political power in the hands of a few. Thus, since democracy is a consistently mediocre form of government, it is a better choice than rule by the few.

   Which one of the following principles, if valid, most helps to justify the philosopher's argument?

   (A) A society should adopt a democratic form of government if and only if most members of the society prefer a democratic form of government.

   (B) In choosing a form of government, it is better for a society to avoid the inherently worst than to seek to attain the best.

   (C) The best form of government is the one that is most likely to produce an outcome that is on the whole good.

   (D) Democratic governments are not truly equitable unless they are designed to prevent interest groups from exerting undue influence on the political process.

   (E) It is better to choose a form of government on the basis of sound philosophical reasons than on the basis of popular preference.[1]

Step 1. Identify the Question Type

There are three important things to note in this question stem. First, the word "principle" identifies it as a Principle question. Second, the "most helps to justify" language tells you the question will behave like a Strengthen question. Third, you're asked about "the following principles," so you know that the principles are in the answer choices.

Step 2. Untangle the Stimulus

Approach this as you would a Strengthen question and look for the conclusion and evidence in the stimulus. The philosopher says that the best and worst governments are those in which power is held by a few. With "Thus," he concludes that democracy is a better form of government than rule by a few because democracy is always mediocre.

Step 3. Make a Prediction

Your task is to find the principle that makes the argument more likely to be so. The philosopher chooses mediocrity over other forms of government that could be the inherently best or the inherently worst. In his eyes, the risk of the worst government does not outweigh the possibility of the best government, so he chooses the safer route: mediocrity. He assumes it's better to be safe than sorry.

---

[1]PrepTest 51, Sec. 3, Q 13

Step 4. Evaluate the Answer Choices

Choice (A) states that societal preference for a democratic government is both sufficient and necessary to adopt a democratic form of government. However, in the stimulus the philosopher never considers the majority preference in determining which form of government to adopt. Eliminate this choice.

Choice (B) matches the prediction and is the correct answer.

Choice (C) raises the likelihood of producing a good outcome, but the stimulus never discusses which form of government is most likely to produce a good outcome.

Choice (D) discusses the components of an equitable democratic government, which is outside the scope of the argument.

Choice (E) compares philosophical reasons to popular preference as a means to choose a form of government. However, the author's argument is concerned with the form of government that is chosen, not how it is chosen, so this choice is out.

2. Any museum that owns the rare stamp that features an airplane printed upside down should not display it. Ultraviolet light causes red ink to fade, and a substantial portion of the stamp is red. If the stamp is displayed, it will be damaged. It should be kept safely locked away, even though this will deny the public the chance to see it.

The reasoning above most closely conforms to which one of the following principles?

(A) The public should judge the quality of a museum by the rarity of the objects in its collection.

(B) Museum display cases should protect their contents from damage caused by ultraviolet light.

(C) Red ink should not be used on items that will not be exposed to ultraviolet light.

(D) A museum piece that would be damaged by display should not be displayed.

(E) The primary purpose of a museum is to educate the public.[2]

Step 1. Identify the Question Type

The phrase "following principles" tells you this is a Principle question and that the principle is in the answer choices. Your job is to make it parallel to (as indicated by "conforms to") the reasoning in the stimulus.

---

[2]PrepTest 52, Sec. 3, Q 1

Step 2. Untangle the Stimulus

The author states that a museum with a rare stamp should not display the stamp because it will become damaged. He concludes with a recommendation to lock up the stamp rather than make it available for public display.

Step 3. Make a Prediction

In broad terms, the author says that preserving museum pieces is more important than allowing the public to see the museum pieces.

Step 4. Evaluate the Answer Choices

Choice (A) discusses how the public should judge the quality of museum objects, a topic never broached in the stimulus and therefore outside the scope. Eliminate this choice.

Choice (B) makes a recommendation to protect the museum objects from damage. However, you're not looking for a solution to the problem; you want a principle that is parallel to the stimulus' argument. So, this answer is out of scope.

Choice (C) has two problems. First, it talks about whether to use red ink, which has no bearing on the predicted principle. Second, the stimulus doesn't mention anything about items that will not be exposed to ultraviolet light. So, you can't know whether red ink would be a problem here. Cross this choice out and move on to the next one.

Choice (D) matches the prediction that if displaying the item would damage it, then it shouldn't be displayed, and thus it is the correct answer.

Choice (E) raises the purpose of a museum, which is irrelevant in the argument, so it is incorrect.

PRINCIPLE QUESTIONS: NOW YOU TRY IT

It's now your turn to try a Principle question on your own. Use the template I've provided after the question to guide you through the four-step Kaplan Method. (Note: On test day, you won't be writing out all the steps as you are in this exercise. However, as you are learning the Method, it's good practice to help it become second nature.) Remember to bracket conclusions and circle Keywords.

1. Consumer advocate: One advertisement that is deceptive, and thus morally wrong, states that "gram for gram, the refined sugar used in our chocolate pies is no more fattening than the sugars found in fruits and vegetables." This is like trying to persuade someone that chocolate pies are not fattening by saying that, calorie for calorie, they are no more fattening than celery. True, but it would take a whole shopping cart full of celery to equal a chocolate pie's worth of calories.

    Advertiser: This advertisement cannot be called deceptive. It is, after all, true.

    Which one of the following principles, if established, would do most to support the consumer advocate's position against the advertiser's response?

    (A) It is morally wrong to seek to persuade by use of deceptive statements.
    (B) A true statement should be regarded as deceptive only if the person making the statement believes it to be false, and thus intends the people reading or hearing it to acquire a false belief.
    (C) To make statements that impart only a small proportion of the information in one's possession should not necessarily be regarded as deceptive.
    (D) It is morally wrong to make a true statement in a manner that will deceive hearers or readers of the statement into believing that it is false.
    (E) A true statement should be regarded as deceptive if it is made with the expectation that people hearing or reading the statement will draw a false conclusion from it.[3]

---
[3]PrepTest 21, Sec. 2, Q 16

Step 1. Identify the Question Type

_____

Step 2. Untangle the Stimulus

_____

Step 3. Make a Prediction

_____

Step 4. Evaluate the Answer Choices

_____

Explanations

1. (E)

Consumer advocate: <One advertisement that is deceptive, and (thus) morally wrong,> states that "gram for gram, the refined sugar used in our chocolate pies is no more fattening than the sugars found in fruits and vegetables." This is like trying to persuade someone that chocolate pies are not fattening by saying that, calorie for calorie, they are no more fattening than celery. True, but it would take a whole shopping cart full of celery to equal a chocolate pie's worth of calories.

Advertiser: <This advertisement cannot be called deceptive.> It is, after all, true.

Which one of the following (principles,) if established, would do most to (support) the consumer advocate's position against the advertiser's response?

(A) It is morally wrong to seek to persuade by use of deceptive statements.

(B) A true statement should be regarded as deceptive only if the person making the statement believes it to be false, and thus intends the people reading or hearing it to acquire a false belief.

(C) To make statements that impart only a small proportion of the information in one's possession should not necessarily be regarded as deceptive.

(D) It is morally wrong to make a true statement in a manner that will deceive hearers or readers of the statement into believing that it is false.

(E) A true statement should be regarded as deceptive if it is made with the expectation that people hearing or reading the statement will draw a false conclusion from it.[4]

Step 1. Identify the Question Type

The phrase "which one of the following principles" indicates that this is a Principle question in which the principle will be in the answer choices. The question also asks you to use the principle answer to "support"—or strengthen—the consumer advocate's position.

Step 2. Untangle the Stimulus

The consumer advocate argues that the advertisement is deceptive even though it is true, and the advertiser argues that the ad is not deceptive because it is true.

Step 3. Make a Prediction

To strengthen the argument, the correct answer choice must define "deception" beyond the truth or falsity of the statement.

---

[4]PrepTest 21, Sec. 2, Q 16

Step 4. Evaluate the Answer Choices

The basis of the dispute between the advocate and the advertiser is the definition of deception. Choice (A) focuses on morality, which the advertiser never mentions. Cross this choice out.

There is no indication the pie manufacturer believes the claim about the pie's sugar content to be false. So, you can discard choice (B).

Choice (C) raises the amount of information revealed, which does not address the advocate's meaning of deception. Eliminate this choice.

Choice (D) provides a definition for morally wrong, not deception. Like choice (A), the focus is on the wrong concept, so you can cross out (D).

By process of elimination you can arrive at choice (E) as the right answer. Choice (E) says a true statement is deceptive if the intent is to mislead. It strengthens the argument that the advertisement is deceptive by dismissing the advertiser's truth standard and by saying that a true statement is still deceptive if it was made with the expectation to mislead.

DRILL: PRACTICING PRINCIPLE QUESTIONS

Use the Kaplan Method to answer the following Principle questions. Take this opportunity to practice and apply the steps in the Method so you are comfortable using them on test day. Be sure to circle conclusion and evidence Keywords and bracket the conclusion. Check your responses against the full explanations provided after the Drill.

1. Jablonski, who owns a car dealership, has donated cars to driver education programs at area schools for over five years. She found the statistics on car accidents to be disturbing, and she wanted to do something to encourage better driving in young drivers. Some members of the community have shown their support for this action by purchasing cars from Jablonski's dealership.

   Which one of the following propositions is best illustrated by the passage?

   (A) The only way to reduce traffic accidents is through driver education programs.
   (B) Altruistic actions sometimes have positive consequences for those who perform them.
   (C) Young drivers are the group most likely to benefit from driver education programs.
   (D) It is usually in one's best interest to perform actions that benefit others.
   (E) An action must have broad community support if it is to be successful.[5]

2. Environmentalists who seek stricter governmental regulations controlling water pollution should be certain to have their facts straight. For if it turns out, for example, that water pollution is a lesser threat than they proclaimed, then there will be a backlash and the public will not listen to them even when dire threats exist.

   Which one of the following best illustrates the principle illustrated by the argument above?

   (A) Middle-level managers who ask their companies to hire additional employees should have strong evidence that doing so will benefit the company; otherwise, higher-level managers will refuse to follow their suggestions to hire additional employees even when doing so really would benefit the company.
   (B) Politicians who defend the rights of unpopular constituencies ought to see to it that they use cool, dispassionate rhetoric in their appeals. Even if they have their facts straight, inflammatory rhetoric can cause a backlash that results in more negative reactions to these constituencies, whether or not they are deserving of more rights.
   (C) People who are trying to convince others to take some sort of action should make every effort to present evidence that is emotionally compelling. Such evidence is invariably more persuasive than dry, technical data, even when the data strongly support their claims.
   (D) Whoever wants to advance a political agenda ought to take the time to convince legislators that their own political careers are at stake in the matter at hand; otherwise, the agenda will simply be ignored.
   (E) Activists who want to prevent excessive globalization of the economy should assign top priority to an appeal to the economic self-interest of those who would be adversely affected by it, for if they fail in such an appeal, extreme economic globalization is inevitable.[6]

3. We have a moral obligation not to destroy books, even if they belong to us. The reason is quite simple: If preserved, books will almost certainly contribute to the intellectual and emotional enrichment of future generations.

    Which one of the following most accurately expresses the principle underlying the argument?

    (A)   It is morally incumbent upon us to devote effort to performing actions that have at least some chance of improving other people's lives.
    (B)   We are morally obligated to preserve anything that past generations had preserved for our intellectual and emotional enrichment.
    (C)   The moral commitments we have to future generations supersede the moral commitments we have to the present generation.
    (D)   We are morally obligated not to destroy anything that will most likely enrich, either intellectually or emotionally, for posterity.
    (E)   Being morally obligated not to destroy something requires that we be reasonably assured that that thing will lead to the betterment of someone we know.[7]

4. If one does not have enough information to make a well-informed decision, one should not make a decision solely on the basis of the information one does possess. Instead, one should continue to seek information until a well-informed decision can be made.

    Of the following, which one most closely conforms to the principle stated above?

    (A)   Economists should not believe the predictions of an economic model simply because it is based on information about the current economy. Many conflicting models are based on such information, and they cannot all be accurate.
    (B)   When deciding which career to pursue, one needs to consider carefully all of the information one has. One should not choose a career solely on the basis of financial compensation; instead, one should consider other factors such as how likely one is to succeed at the career and how much one would enjoy it.
    (C)   Though a researcher may know a great deal about a topic, she or he should not assume that all information relevant to the research is already in her or his possession. A good researcher always looks for further relevant information.
    (D)   When one wants to buy a reliable car, one should not choose which car to buy just on the inadequate basis of one's personal experience with cars. Rather, one should study various models' reliability histories that summarize many owners' experiences.
    (E)   When there is not enough information available to determine the meaning of a line of poetry, one should not form an opinion based on the insufficient information. Instead, one should simply acknowledge that it is impossible to determine what the line means.[8]

Explanations

1. **(B)**

Jablonski, who owns a car dealership, has donated cars to driver education programs at area schools for over five years. She found the statistics on car accidents to be disturbing, and she wanted to do something to encourage better driving in young drivers. Some members of the community have shown their support for this action by purchasing cars from Jablonski's dealership.

Which one of the following (propositions) is (best) (illustrated) by the passage?

(A)   The only way to reduce traffic accidents is through driver education programs.

(B)   Altruistic actions sometimes have positive consequences for those who perform them.

(C)   Young drivers are the group most likely to benefit from driver education programs.

(D)   It is usually in one's best interest to perform actions that benefit others.

(E)   An action must have broad community support if it is to be successful.[9]

Step 1. Identify the Question Type

The phrase "Which of the following propositions" indicates that this is a Principle question and also that the principle is in the answer choices. Your task is to identify the principle that is parallel to the stimulus.

Step 2. Untangle the Stimulus

Note the key points in the stimulus. Jablonski saw a problem with car accidents and donated cars to local driving schools to help address the problem. Community members supported Jablonski's cause by purchasing cars from her dealership.

Step 3. Make a Prediction

The correct answer will be a broad statement of the situation described in the stimulus, probably about good deeds being rewarded.

Step 4. Evaluate the Answer Choices

Don't let the content of choice (A) fool you. Using the same topic in the answer as in the stimulus in a Principle question is often a wrong answer trap. Choice (A) makes no mention of good deeds being rewarded. Cross this choice out and move on to the next one.

Choice (B) is an exact match of the prediction—altruistic actions and positive consequences. This is the correct answer.

Choice (C) presents no good act and no reward. Again, the subject matter is familiar but it certainly doesn't identify the correct answer.

---

[9]PrepTest June 2007, Sec. 3, Q 6

Choice (D) comes close to the answer but is not an exact match. The stimulus provides one example of a good deed being rewarded—that doesn't mean it "usually" works that way as choice (D) states.

Choice (E) asserts that an action must have broad support to be successful, but this falls outside of the scope of the stimulus. It also ignores the good deed–reward principle established in the stimulus. These reasons make this answer incorrect.

2.   **(A)**

<Environmentalists who seek stricter governmental regulations controlling water pollution should be certain to have their facts straight.> For if it turns out, for example, that water pollution is a lesser threat than they proclaimed, then there will be a backlash and the public will not listen to them even when dire threats exist.

Which one of the following best illustrates the principle illustrated by the argument above?

(A)   Middle-level managers who ask their companies to hire additional employees should have strong evidence that doing so will benefit the company; otherwise, higher-level managers will refuse to follow their suggestions to hire additional employees even when doing so really would benefit the company.

(B)   Politicians who defend the rights of unpopular constituencies ought to see to it that they use cool, dispassionate rhetoric in their appeals. Even if they have their facts straight, inflammatory rhetoric can cause a backlash that results in more negative reactions to these constituencies, whether or not they are deserving of more rights.

(C)   People who are trying to convince others to take some sort of action should make every effort to present evidence that is emotionally compelling. Such evidence is invariably more persuasive than dry, technical data, even when the data strongly support their claims.

(D)   Whoever wants to advance a political agenda ought to take the time to convince legislators that their own political careers are at stake in the matter at hand; otherwise, the agenda will simply be ignored.

(E)   Activists who want to prevent excessive globalization of the economy should assign top priority to an appeal to the economic self-interest of those who would be adversely affected by it, for if they fail in such an appeal, extreme economic globalization is inevitable.[10]

---

[10]PrepTest 36, Sec. 3, Q 13

Step 1. Identify the Question Type

The term "principle" tells you that this is a Principle question. Additionally, statements like "following best illustrates" and "illustrated by the argument above" let you know that the principle isn't in the stimulus or the answer choices. Instead, you must identify and apply the principle that is illustrated—not stated—in the stimulus. This Principle/Parallel Reasoning question stem tells you that the correct answer will use the same type of evidence to reach the same kind of conclusion used in the stimulus.

Step 2. Untangle the Stimulus

The author recommends that environmentalists be certain of their claims before they seek tougher regulation of water pollution. Otherwise, their claims will be ignored even in the face of disaster.

Step 3. Make a Prediction

Broadly stated, the author says that people should make sure a claim is solid before they ask for something, or else their claim will be ignored.

Step 4. Evaluate the Answer Choices

Choice (A) recommends that managers have a solid case before asking for additional employees or else they'll be ignored even if their idea is beneficial, which is almost an exact match of the prediction. On the test, you might mark this answer and move on to the next question to save time. Right now, you can take the time to check the other answers.

Choice (B) may seem superficially parallel because it makes a recommendation and then lays out consequences if the recommendation is not followed. However, the recommendation to use specific language and the negative consequences don't match those presented in the stimulus.

Choice (C) makes a recommendation, but it's to present an emotionally compelling case, not necessarily a stronger case. The biggest problem with this answer is that it doesn't list any consequences for not following the recommendation.

Choice (D) also makes a recommendation to those with a political agenda, but it's to take time to make their case, not to make the case stronger, which shifts the scope.

Choice (E) recommends that activists assign top priority to a particular issue, not make a stronger case. The consequences of not following the recommendation are the opposite result of the activists' appeal, not that the activists will be ignored, which makes this answer out of scope.

3. **(D)**

<We have a moral obligation not to destroy books,> even if they belong to us. The (reason) is quite simple:
If preserved, books will almost certainly contribute to the intellectual and emotional enrichment of future generations.

Which one of the following most accurately expresses the (principle underlying) the argument?

(A)   It is morally incumbent upon us to devote effort to performing actions that have at least some chance of improving other people's lives.

(B)   We are morally obligated to preserve anything that past generations had preserved for our intellectual and emotional enrichment.

(C)   The moral commitments we have to future generations supersede the moral commitments we have to the present generation.

(D)   We are morally obligated not to destroy anything that will most likely enrich, either intellectually or emotionally, for posterity.

(E)   Being morally obligated not to destroy something requires that we be reasonably assured that that thing will lead to the betterment of someone we know.[11]

Step 1. Identify the Question Type

The word "principle" tells you that this is a Principle question, and the phrase "which one of the following," directs you to find the principle in the answer choices. Also, the term "underlying" suggests that the question resembles an Assumption question, so untangle the stimulus by identifying the conclusion and evidence.

Step 2. Untangle the Stimulus

The author concludes that we should not destroy books, and he bases this on the evidence that preserved books can contribute to the enrichment of future generations.

Step 3. Make a Prediction

To identify an underlying principle, phrase the gist of this argument in general terms. Essentially, the author is saying that we have a moral obligation not to destroy things that can contribute to the enrichment of future generations.

Step 4. Evaluate the Answer Choices

Choice (A) states we must devote "effort to performing actions" rather than focusing on the need not to destroy things. Also, "have at least some chance" is too weak compared to "will almost certainly contribute to" in the stimulus. Cross this choice out.

Choice (B) confuses the generations, directing us to preserve anything from past generations, while the stimulus directs us to preserve for future generations. This choice is out as well.

---

[11]PrepTest 25, Sec. 4, Q 14

Choice (C) adds a comparison between the commitment owed to future versus present generations and is thus beyond the scope of the stimulus. Move on to the next choice.

Choice (D) matches the prediction and is the correct answer.

Choice (E) requires reasonable assurance that not destroying something will lead to the betterment of someone we know. In the stimulus, the obligation not to destroy books is aimed at the betterment of future generations. So, the target of our moral obligation does not match between choice (E) and the stimulus.

4.   **(D)**

If one does not have enough information to make a well-informed decision, one should not make a decision solely on the basis of the information one does possess. Instead, one should continue to seek information until a well-informed decision can be made.

Of the following, which one (most closely conforms) to the (principle) stated above?

(A)   Economists should not believe the predictions of an economic model simply because it is based on information about the current economy. Many conflicting models are based on such information, and they cannot all be accurate.

(B)   When deciding which career to pursue, one needs to consider carefully all of the information one has. One should not choose a career solely on the basis of financial compensation; instead, one should consider other factors such as how likely one is to succeed at the career and how much one would enjoy it.

(C)   Though a researcher may know a great deal about a topic, she or he should not assume that all information relevant to the research is already in her or his possession. A good researcher always looks for further relevant information.

(D)   When one wants to buy a reliable car, one should not choose which car to buy just on the inadequate basis of one's personal experience with cars. Rather, one should study various models' reliability histories that summarize many owners' experiences.

(E)   When there is not enough information available to determine the meaning of a line of poetry, one should not form an opinion based on the insufficient information. Instead, one should simply acknowledge that it is impossible to determine what the line means.[12]

---

[12]PrepTest 47, Sec. 3, Q 22

Step 1. Identify the Question Type

The word "principle" tells you that this is a Principle question, and "the principle stated above" tells you that the principle is in the stimulus. "Most closely conforms" tells you to find an answer choice with a specific situation that parallels the principle.

Step 2. Untangle the Stimulus

In simplest terms, this stimulus recommends that you should not make a decision unless you have enough information, and you should keep researching until you can make a good decision.

Step 3. Make a Prediction

The correct answer must exemplify the principle given in the stimulus and match up on all parts. In this case, look for an answer that properly illustrates when not to reach a decision and what to do to make an informed decision.

Step 4. Evaluate the Answer Choices

Choice (A) talks about believing information rather than gathering enough information to make a good decision, which is out of scope. Eliminate this choice.

Choice (B) contradicts the stimulus by saying that you should choose a career based on "all of the information one has." The stimulus directs us to look beyond "the information one does possess," so this choice is out as well.

Choice (C) acknowledges there is always more information to learn about a topic. However, choice (C) neglects the issue of when to come to a decision. Move on to the next choice.

Choice (D) tells you to look beyond what you know about cars if you don't know enough and to learn more before you buy one. That matches the prediction and is the correct answer.

Choice (E) starts off on the right track—if you don't have enough information about a line of poetry, don't form an opinion. To be parallel, the next statement would have to be about continuing to collect more information to make an informed decision. Instead, choice (E) says the opposite—don't look for additional information and accept you can't determine the poetry's meaning. Therefore, you can confidently eliminate this answer.

PRINCIPLE REVIEW

Before you proceed to the next chapter, turn to Appendix A and complete the review exercise for Principle questions. A completed chart is included in Appendix B.

CHAPTER 12

PARALLEL REASONING QUESTIONS

At a glance, Parallel Reasoning questions can be daunting. Over the years, I've seen a countless number of my students, as they prepare for the LSAT, try to skip Parallel Reasoning questions altogether. They would look at the length of the stimuli and the length of the answer choices and decide that the questions must be too difficult or too time consuming to handle. I don't want this to happen to you. Don't let the length of Parallel Reasoning questions intimidate you. Parallel Reasoning questions, like every other question type you've examined thus far, are subject to a strategy that allows you to quickly and confidently handle every question you'll see on test day: the Kaplan Method.

You'll see approximately three to four scored Parallel Reasoning questions on the LSAT. While I know that doesn't sound like a lot of points in the big scheme of things, many students will opt not to do these questions at all. As a Kaplan-trained student, however, you will have the opportunity to start a few points ahead of your peers.

DEFINITION OF PARALLEL REASONING QUESTIONS

Parallel Reasoning questions ask you to identify the answer that has the same argument structure as the stimulus. That is, your task is to find the answer that uses the same kind of evidence to reach the same kind of conclusion as the stimulus.

The correct answer of a Parallel Reasoning question is not based on argument content or placement of the conclusion and evidence. The stimulus may talk about international relations with China, and the correct answer may discuss the price of vegetables at the grocery store. That's okay because the subject matter is irrelevant. The stimulus may have its conclusion in the beginning and the correct answer may have its conclusion at that end. The arrangement is irrelevant. Keep your focus on the underlying structure of the argument.

USE THE KAPLAN METHOD TO ANSWER PARALLEL REASONING QUESTIONS

Identify the Question Type

Just as you've done with all other Logical Reasoning question types, read the question stem first to determine the question type. The following terms denote a Parallel Reasoning question:

- Parallel to
- Similar to
- Pattern of reasoning

Here's how some of those phrases could appear in a question stem:

- The reasoning above is most closely paralleled in which one of the following?
- Which one of the following arguments is most similar in its reasoning to the argument above?
- Which one of the following arguments has a pattern of reasoning most like the one in the argument above?
- The pattern of flawed reasoning in which one of the following is most similar to that in the argument above?
- Which one of the following most closely parallels the questionable reasoning cited above?

Untangle the Stimulus

Every Parallel Reasoning stimulus contains an argument. As you would with the Assumption family of questions, read the stimulus to identify the author's conclusion. For some Parallel Reasoning questions, that's all you'll need from the argument to hone in on the correct answer.

Types of Conclusions

Next, characterize the conclusion and then compare it to the conclusion types presented in the answer choices. Cross out the answer choices that have a different kind of conclusion. If you find only one answer choice with the same conclusion type, you have the correct answer and can move on to the next question. If the process of comparing conclusion types eliminates only some of the wrong answer choices, you then have to compare the type of evidence used to support the conclusion in the stimulus to the type of evidence used in the remaining answer choices.

You will see six basic types of conclusions on the LSAT, which are listed in Table 12.1. You can use the pneumonic "CAPRI V" or CAPRI Five to remember them.

Table 12.1

Conclusion Types	Definition	Example
Comparison	Weighs one thing against another	In conclusion, Haley's LSAT practice went better today than it did yesterday.
Assertion of fact	States what the author believes is or isn't so	Therefore, Haley benefited from practicing for the LSAT in the building she will take the actual test.
Prediction	Makes a claim about the future (often identified by "will" or "will not")	We can conclude that Haley will improve her LSAT score by practicing more questions.
Recommendation	Advocates or discourages a course of action (often identified by "should" or "should not")	So, Haley should practice more to improve her LSAT score.
If-then	Forms a conditional statement in any formal logic format	Thus, Haley won't improve her LSAT score unless she practices more Logical Reasoning questions.
Value Judgment	Presents the author's subjective evaluation of the argument subject	Hence, making sure you get enough uninterrupted sleep during the week of the LSAT is good test-taking strategy.

Most of the time, these broad conclusion types won't be enough to identify the matching conclusion in the correct answer choice, and you'll have to consider other factors such as:

Table 12.2

Additional Conclusion Factors	Description
Positive or negative status	Pay attention to the positive or negative status of the conclusion. A recommendation to do something is different from a recommendation not to do something.
	But don't just rely on the wording and dismiss an answer because a conclusion in the stimulus is positive and the conclusion in the answer choice is negative. For example, a conclusion might say, "The LSAT taker must have picture identification to register at the test site." The conclusion also could have been stated as "The LSAT taker must not forget to bring picture identification to register at the test site."
	Remember to think about what the conclusion means, regardless of whether it is stated in positive or negative terms.
Level of certainty	An argument qualified by words such as "possibly," "likely," and "probably" is weaker than a claim about something that is "definitely" true or "impossible," and therefore, is different. For example, a claim that Haley will *definitely* achieve her goal LSAT score is different from a claim that Haley will *probably* get her goal LSAT score.
	So, be sure to find an answer choice that matches the level of certainty presented in the argument's conclusion.
Mix of conclusion types	A conclusion may include a combination of types. For example, "So, if you follow the Kaplan Method, you will become more efficient and accurate in answering LSAT questions." This conclusion is both an if-then statement and a prediction. The correct answer will have to follow suit.

The more precisely you characterize the stimulus conclusion, the easier it will be to match in the answer.

Check the Evidence

If more than one answer's conclusion matches the argument structure of the stimulus' conclusion type, you'll need to characterize the evidence as well. Ask yourself, "Does the author provide evidence in the form of an opinion, causation, necessary condition, numbers, examples, etc.?" If so, you'll need to find evidence in the answer choice that matches that structure.

Characterize the Stimulus

If you've characterized and compared the conclusion and the evidence and you still haven't found the correct answer choice, then you will need to characterize the whole stimulus and analyze its form of reasoning. For example, it could present a formal logic statement and its contrapositive, or it could use an analogy or make a causal argument. The correct answer must also follow the same form of reasoning. So, check the answer choices to determine and compare their form of reasoning with the stimulus'.

Look for Flaws

Sometimes the test makers will ask you not for an answer with Parallel Reasoning but rather a Parallel Flaw. In that case, the stimulus contains a flawed argument, and your job is to find an argument in the answer that is not only flawed, but flawed in the same manner as the argument in the stimulus. Use your knowledge of common flaw types to quickly characterize the flaws you find, and keep in mind that some of the wrong answers may not contain a flaw at all.

Make a Prediction

Take the information you've learned about the stimulus and compare it to the answer choices. Make the first comparison between the stimulus and the answer choices after you characterize the conclusion to hopefully eliminate some answers. If necessary, check the evidence, flaw, and/or entire stimulus.

Evaluate the Answer Choices

Match the correct answer to your summary of the argument's structure. First, find the conclusion of each answer to determine whether it is a match. If not, eliminate it—there is no need to check the rest of that answer. If you have more than one answer left after checking the conclusions, go back to those and compare the evidence structure.

THE KAPLAN METHOD IN ACTION

Now I'll walk you through a couple examples to show you how the Kaplan Method can help you efficiently solve any Parallel Reasoning question you'll see on test day.

1. Often, a product popularly believed to be the best of its type is no better than any other; rather, the product's reputation, which may be independent of its quality, provides its owner with status. Thus, although there is no harm in paying for status if that is what one wants, one should know that one is paying for prestige, not quality.

Which one of the following arguments is most similar in its reasoning to the argument above?

(A) Often, choosing the best job offer is a matter of comparing the undesirable features of the different jobs. Thus, those who choose a job because it has a desirable location should know that they might be unhappy with its hours.

(B) Most people have little tolerance for boastfulness. Thus, although one's friends may react positively when hearing the details of one's accomplishments, it is unlikely that their reactions are entirely honest.

(C) Those beginning a new hobby sometimes quit it because of the frustrations involved in learning a new skill. Thus, although it is fine to try to learn a skill quickly, one is more likely to learn a skill if one first learns to enjoy the process of acquiring it.

(D) Personal charm is often confused with virtue. Thus, while there is nothing wrong with befriending a charming person, anyone who does so should realize that a charming friend is not necessarily a good and loyal friend.

(E) Many theatrical actors cannot enjoy watching a play because when they watch others, they yearn to be on stage themselves. Thus, although there is no harm in yearning to perform, such performers should, for their own sakes, learn to suppress that yearning.[1]

Step 1. Identify the Question Type

The phrase "most similar in its reasoning" is typical of a Parallel Reasoning question.

Step 2. Untangle the Stimulus

Read the stimulus to determine the argument's structure. Start by identifying the conclusion, which is signaled by the Keyword "Thus." Next, characterize the conclusion. The word "should" tells you that it's a recommendation. Notice the exact formation of the recommendation: It's OK to pay for status (X), but you should know you're paying for status (X) and not quality (not Y).

[1]PrepTest 47, Sec. 1, Q 15

Step 3. Make a Prediction

A parallel answer will have a conclusion in the form of a positive recommendation that matches the conclusion structure. So, start by evaluating the conclusion in each answer choice.

Step 4. Evaluate the Answer Choices

Choice (A)'s conclusion, identified by "Thus," is a recommendation because of "should." But the recommendation pattern does not match the stimulus. Choice (A) recommends awareness of a possible negative aspect of something you choose, but the stimulus recommends awareness that you're doing X and not Y.

Choice (B)'s conclusion is not a recommendation, it's a qualified assertion of fact—the fact that friends' reactions to boasting probably aren't all that honest. Eliminate this choice.

Choice (C)'s conclusion is an if-then statement about the likelihood of learning a skill. Choice (C) is not a match. Cross it out.

Choice (D)'s conclusion—signaled by "Thus"—is a recommendation that it's OK to be friends with a charming person (X) as long as you know the friend is charming (X) and not good and loyal (not Y). Choice (D) seems promising; it's a recommendation with the same pattern as the stimulus' conclusion. But you need to check the last answer choice before you can say it's the right answer. If any others match the conclusion, you'll have to compare the evidence as well.

Choice (E)'s conclusion, noted by "Thus," is also a recommendation. But it's a recommendation to take action, to learn to suppress that yearning. The stimulus recommends awareness, not action.

Choice (D) is the only answer with a matching conclusion. So you don't need to review and compare any other part of the stimulus. Mark choice (D) and move on.

2. People who are good at playing the game Drackedary are invariably skilled with their hands. Mary is a very competent watchmaker. Therefore, Mary would make a good Drackedary player.

The flawed pattern of reasoning in the argument above is most similar to that in which one of the following?

(A) People with long legs make good runners. Everyone in Daryl's family has long legs. Therefore, Daryl would make a good runner.

(B) People who write for a living invariably enjoy reading. Julie has been a published novelist for many years. Therefore, Julie enjoys reading.

(C) All race car drivers have good reflexes. Chris is a champion table tennis player. Therefore, Chris would make a good race car driver.

(D) The role of Santa Claus in a shopping mall is often played by an experienced actor. Erwin has played Santa Claus in shopping malls for years. Therefore, Erwin must be an experienced actor.

(E) Any good skier can learn to ice-skate eventually. Erica is a world-class skier. Therefore, Erica could learn to ice-skate in a day or two.[2]

Step 1. Identify the Question Type

The phrases "flawed pattern of reasoning" and "most similar to" identify this as a Parallel Flaw question.

Step 2. Untangle the Stimulus

The complete argument in the stimulus must match the complete argument in the correct answer choice. Before you determine the flaw in the argument, you need to evaluate the conclusion. The word "Therefore" leads you right to the conclusion of the argument; in this case, the author makes a value judgment. The author subjectively evaluates Mary and says that she would make a good Drackedary player.

Step 3. Make a Prediction

Move to the answer choices to determine whether any of them have a similar conclusion. If more than one answer choice does, return to the stimulus to determine the flaw and look for a parallel flaw in the remaining answer choices.

Step 4. Evaluate the Answer Choices

Quickly scan the answer choices. All five of them have the word "Therefore" in the statement, so you can go right to the conclusions and compare them to the stimulus conclusion.

Choice (A)'s conclusion is an exact structural match with the stimulus. It's a value judgment that states Daryl would make a good runner. Because you haven't checked the complete argument

---

[2]PrepTest 33, Sec. 1, Q 15

yet, you can't mark this as the right answer. Check the other conclusions to see whether you find any more matches. If so, you'll come back to this answer and analyze the flaw in the argument.

Choice (B)'s conclusion is an assertion of fact. "Julie enjoys reading" is a statement of what the author believes to be true. It doesn't match the stimulus' conclusion, so you can cross it out.

Choice (C)'s conclusion also makes a value judgment that Chris would make a good race car driver. It's a parallel conclusion, so keep it and check choices (D) and (E) for any other matches.

Choice (D)'s conclusion is a strong assertion of fact, not a value judgment. Eliminate this choice.

Choice (E)'s conclusion is a weak prediction. The author doesn't state what will happen; instead she states what could happen, that Erica could learn to ice-skate in a day or two. This choice is out.

You are now down to choices (A) and (C). In addition to having the same conclusion structure as the stimulus, they both have the same positive tone. You can't use the conclusion to identify the correct answer, so go back to the stimulus to determine the flaw in the argument.

Repeat Step 2. Untangle the Stimulus

In the stimulus, the author claims Mary would make a good Drackedary player because people who are good at Drackedary are skilled with their hands, and Mary is a competent watchmaker. In formal logic terms, the argument looks like this:

Conclusion:		Mary $\rightarrow$	good Drackedary player (X)
Evidence:	Good Drackedary player (X) $\rightarrow$		skilled with hands (Y)
Evidence:		Mary $\rightarrow$	competent watchmaker (Z)
Assumption:	Competent watchmaker (Z) $\rightarrow$		good Drackedary player (X)

The author must be connecting the evidence in the following way to reach the given conclusion.

Mary $\rightarrow$ Z $\rightarrow$ X $\rightarrow$ Y and assuming Z $\rightarrow$ Y. Because this is a Parallel Flaw question, the assumption must be considered unwarranted.

Repeat Step 3. Make a Prediction

Go back to choices (A) and (C) to look for similar formal logic and a similar flaw.

Repeat Step 4. Evaluate the Answer Choices

In choice (A), the author states that Daryl would make a good runner (Y) because people with long legs (X) make good runners (Y). Everyone in Daryl's family has long legs (X). The argument's formal logic shows a valid argument, and thus does not match the stimulus' format.

Conclusion:		Daryl $\rightarrow$	Y
Evidence:		X $\rightarrow$	Y
Evidence:	Daryl and family $\rightarrow$		X

Eliminate this choice.

You are safe to mark choice (C) and move on to the next question. Choice (C) presents the same structure and makes the same unwarranted assumption as the stimulus:

All race car drivers (X) have good reflexes (Y). Chris is a champion table tennis player (Z). Therefore, Chris would make a good race car driver (X).

Conclusion:	Chris	→	Y
Evidence:	X	→	Y
Evidence:	Chris	→	Z
Assumption:	Z	→	X

PARALLEL REASONING QUESTIONS: NOW YOU TRY IT

It's now your turn to try a Parallel Reasoning question on your own. Use the template I've provided after the question to guide you through the four-step Kaplan Method. (Note: On test day, you won't be writing out all the steps as you are in this exercise. However, as you are learning the Method, it's good practice to help it become second nature.) Remember to bracket the conclusions and circle Keywords.

1. It is inaccurate to say that a diet high in refined sugar cannot cause adult-onset diabetes, since a diet high in refined sugar can make a person overweight, and being overweight can predispose a person to adult-onset diabetes.

   The argument is most parallel, in its logical structure, to which one of the following?

   (A) It is inaccurate to say that being in cold air can cause a person to catch a cold, since colds are caused by viruses, and viruses flourish in warm, crowded places.

   (B) It is accurate to say that no airline flies from Halifax to Washington. No airline offers a direct flight, although some airlines have flights from Halifax to Boston and others have flights from Boston to Washington.

   (C) It is correct to say that overfertilization is the primary cause of lawn disease, since fertilizer causes lawn grass to grow rapidly and rapidly growing grass has little resistance to disease.

   (D) It is incorrect to say that inferior motor oil cannot cause a car to get poorer gasoline mileage, since inferior motor oil can cause engine valve deterioration, and engine valve deterioration can lead to poorer gasoline mileage.

   (E) It is inaccurate to say that Alexander the Great was a student of Plato; Alexander was a student of Aristotle and Aristotle was a student of Plato.[3]

Step 1. Identify the Question Type

_____

Step 2. Untangle the Stimulus

_____

Step 3. Make a Prediction

_____

Step 4. Evaluate the Answer Choices

_____

---

[3]PrepTest 30, Sec. 2, Q 14

Explanations

1. **(D)**

<It is inaccurate to say that a diet high in refined sugar cannot cause adult-onset diabetes,> (since) a diet high in refined sugar can make a person overweight, and being overweight can predispose a person to adult-onset diabetes.

The argument is (most parallel) in its logical structure, (to) which one of the following?

(A)   It is inaccurate to say that being in cold air can cause a person to catch a cold, since colds are caused by viruses, and viruses flourish in warm, crowded places.

(B)   It is accurate to say that no airline flies from Halifax to Washington. No airline offers a direct flight, although some airlines have flights from Halifax to Boston and others have flights from Boston to Washington.

(C)   It is correct to say that overfertilization is the primary cause of lawn disease, since fertilizer causes lawn grass to grow rapidly and rapidly growing grass has little resistance to disease.

(D)   It is incorrect to say that inferior motor oil cannot cause a car to get poorer gasoline mileage, since inferior motor oil can cause engine valve deterioration, and engine valve deterioration can lead to poorer gasoline mileage.

(E)   It is inaccurate to say that Alexander the Great was a student of Plato; Alexander was a student of Aristotle and Aristotle was a student of Plato.[4]

Step 1. Identify the Question Type

The language "most parallel...to" signals a Parallel Reasoning question. Your job is to find an answer that has a logical structure parallel to that of the stimulus.

Step 2. Untangle the Stimulus

The author concludes that it is not accurate to claim that a diet high in refined sugar can't cause diabetes. Or, in other words, that refined sugar CAN cause diabetes. The author's assertion of fact is based on evidence, identified by "since," that a diet high in refined sugar can make a person overweight, which leads to diabetes. You can symbolize the argument as: It's wrong to say that X can't cause Y, because X can lead to Z, which in turn can lead to Y.

Step 3. Make a Prediction

The correct answer must present an assertion of fact with a parallel argument structure. Start by analyzing the conclusions of the answer choices.

---

[4]PrepTest 30, Sec. 2, Q 14

Step 4. Evaluate the Answer Choices

Choice (A)'s conclusion is an assertion of fact, but it's not parallel to the stimulus. Choice (A) asserts a statement of no causation: that it's wrong to say that cold air can lead to colds. In the stimulus, the author asserts a statement of causation, once you eliminate the negative phrasing.

Choice (B)'s conclusion is also an assertion of fact, but it's problematic because it lacks a causal relationship in the conclusion. Keep moving.

Choice (C)'s conclusion goes wrong by making an assertion of fact referring to the "primary" cause of an effect. Eliminate choice (C).

In choice (D), you find an assertion of fact conclusion of what is not correct. So far so good. Specifically, what's incorrect is to say inferior motor oil (X) can't cause poorer gas mileage (Y), because inferior motor oil (X) can cause engine valve deterioration (Z) and lead to poorer gas mileage (Y). This answer looks pretty good, but you have to check choice (E).

Choice (E) starts out okay, stating that it's inaccurate to say Alexander the Great was a student of Plato, but there isn't a causal statement in the conclusion. Eliminate this choice and mark choice (D) as the correct answer.

DRILL: PRACTICING PARALLEL REASONING QUESTIONS

Use the Kaplan Method to answer the following Parallel Reasoning questions. Take this opportunity to practice and apply the steps in the Method so you are comfortable using them on test day. Be sure to circle conclusion and evidence Keywords and bracket the conclusion. Check your responses against the full explanations provided after the Drill.

1. K, a research scientist, was accused of having falsified laboratory data. Although the original data in question have disappeared, data from K's more recent experiments have been examined and clearly none of them were falsified. Therefore, the accusation should be dismissed.

   Which one of the following contains questionable reasoning that is most similar to that in the argument above?

   (A) L, an accountant, was charged with having embezzled funds from a client. The charge should be ignored, however, because although the records that might reveal this embezzlement have been destroyed, records of L's current clients show clearly that there has never been any embezzlement from them.

   (B) M, a factory supervisor, was accused of failing to enforce safety standards. This accusation should be discussed, because although the identity of the accuser was not revealed, a survey of factory personnel revealed that some violations of the standards have occurred.

   (C) N, a social scientist, was charged with plagiarism. The charge is without foundation because although strong similarities between N's book and the work of another scholar have been discovered, the other scholar's work was written after N's work was published.

   (D) O, an auto mechanic, has been accused of selling stolen auto parts. The accusation seems to be justified since although no evidence links O directly to these sales, the pattern of distribution of the auto parts points of O as the source.

   (E) P, a politician, has been accused of failing to protect the public interest. From at least some points of view, however, the accusation will undoubtedly be considered false, because there is clearly disagreement about where the public interest lies.[5]

2. A worker for a power company trims the branches of trees that overhang power lines as a prevention against damage to the lines anticipated because of the impending stormy season. The worker reasons that there will be no need for her to trim the overhanging branches of a certain tree because the owners of the tree have indicated that they might cut it down anyway.

   Which one of the following decisions is based on flawed reasoning that is most similar to the worker's flawed reasoning?

   (A) A well inspector has a limited amount of time to inspect the wells of a town. The inspector reasons that the wells should be inspected in the order of most used to least used, because there might not be enough time to inspect them all.

   (B) All sewage and incoming water pipes in a house must be replaced. The plumber reasons that the cheaper polyvinyl chloride pipes should be used for sewage rather than copper pipes, since the money saved might be used to replace worn fixtures.

   (C) A mechanic must replace the worn brakes on a company's vans that are used each weekday. The mechanic reasons that since one of the vans is tentatively scheduled to be junked, he will not have to replace its brakes.

   (D) A candidate decides to campaign in the areas of the city where the most new votes are concentrated. The candidate reasons that campaigning in other areas is unnecessary because in those areas the candidate's message is actually liable to alienate voters.

   (E) None of the children in a certain kindergarten class will take responsibility for the crayon drawing on the classroom wall. The teacher reasons that it is best to keep all the kindergarten children in during recess in order to be certain to punish the one who did the drawing on the wall.[6]

---

[5]PrepTest 24, Sec. 3, Q 16

[6]PrepTest 22, Sec. 4, Q 6

3. The fact that politicians in a certain country are trying to reduce government spending does not by itself explain why they have voted to eliminate all government-supported scholarship programs. Government spending could have been reduced even more if instead they had cut back on military spending.

Which one of the following arguments is most similar in its reasoning to the argument above?

(A) The fact that Phyllis does not make much money at her new job does not by itself explain why she refuses to buy expensive clothing. Phyllis has always bought only inexpensive clothing even though she used to make a lot of money.

(B) The fact that Brooks has a part-time job does not by itself explain why he is doing poorly in school. Many students with part-time jobs are able to set aside enough time for study and thus maintain high grades.

(C) The fact that Sallie and Jim have different work styles does not by itself explain why they could not work together. Sallie and Jim could have resolved their differences if they had communicated more with one another when they began to work together.

(D) The fact that Roger wanted more companionship does not by itself explain why he adopted ten cats last year. He would not have adopted them all if anyone else had been willing to adopt some of them.

(E) The fact that Thelma's goal is to become famous does not by itself explain why she took up theatrical acting. It is easier to become famous through writing or directing plays than through theatrical acting.[7]

4. From the fact that people who studied music as children frequently are quite proficient at mathematics, it cannot be concluded that the skills required for mathematics are acquired by studying music: it is equally likely that proficiency in mathematics and studying music are both the result of growing up in a family that encourages its children to excel at all intellectual and artistic endeavors.

The pattern of reasoning in which one of the following arguments is most parallel to that in the argument above?

(A) Although children who fail to pay attention tend to perform poorly in school, it should not necessarily be thought that their poor performance is caused by their failure to pay attention, for it is always possible that their failure to pay attention is due to undiagnosed hearing problems that can also lead to poor performance in school.

(B) People who attend a university in a foreign country are usually among the top students from their native country. It would therefore be wrong to conclude from the fact that many foreign students perform better academically than others in this country that secondary schools in other countries are superior to those in this country; it may be that evaluation standards are different.

(C) People whose diet includes relatively large quantities of certain fruits and vegetables have a slightly lower than average incidence of heart disease. But it would be premature to conclude that consuming these fruits and vegetables prevents heart disease, for this correlation may be merely coincidental.

(D) Those who apply to medical school are required to study biology and chemistry. It would be a mistake, however, to conclude that those who have mastered chemistry and biology will succeed as physicians, for the practical application of knowledge is different from its acquisition.

(E) Those who engage in vigorous exercise tend to be very healthy. But it would be silly to conclude that vigorous exercise is healthful simply because people who are healthy exercise vigorously, since it is possible that exercise that is less vigorous also has beneficial results.[8]

[7]PrepTest 37, Sec. 4, Q 14

[8]PrepTest 49, Sec. 4, Q 17

5. Opposition leader: Our country has the least fair
    court system of any country on the continent
    and ought not to be the model for others.
    Thus, our highest court is the least fair of any
    on the continent and ought not to be emulated
    by other countries.

The flawed reasoning in which one of the following
arguments is most similar to that in the opposition
leader's argument?

(A) The residents of medium-sized towns are, on
     average, more highly educated than people
     who do not live in such towns. Therefore,
     Maureen, who was born in a medium-sized
     town, is more highly educated than Monica,
     who has just moved to such a town.

(B) At a certain college, either philosophy or
     engineering is the most demanding major.
     Therefore, either the introductory course in
     philosophy or the introductory course in
     engineering is the most demanding
     introductory-level course at that college.

(C) For many years its superior engineering has
     enabled the Lawson Automobile Company to
     make the best racing cars. Therefore, its
     passenger cars, which use many of the same parts,
     are unmatched by those of any other
     company.

(D) Domestic cats are closely related to tigers.
     Therefore, even though they are far smaller
     than tigers, their eating habits are almost the
     same as those of tigers.

(E) If a suit of questionable merit is brought in the
     first district rather than the second district, its
     chances of being immediately thrown out are
     greater. Therefore, to have the best chance of
     winning the case, the lawyers will bring the
     suit in the second district.[9]

---

[9]PrepTest 47, Sec. 1, Q 21

Explanations

1. (A)

K, a research scientist, was accused of having falsified laboratory data. Although the original data in question have disappeared, data from K's more recent experiments have been examined and clearly none of them were falsified. <Therefore, the accusation should be dismissed.>

Which one of the following contains questionable reasoning that is most similar to that in the argument above?

(A) L, an accountant, was charged with having embezzled funds from a client. The charge should be ignored, however, because although the records that might reveal this embezzlement have been destroyed, records of L's current clients show clearly that there has never been any embezzlement from them.

(B) M, a factory supervisor, was accused of failing to enforce safety standards. This accusation should be discussed, because although the identity of the accuser was not revealed, a survey of factory personnel revealed that some violations of the standards have occurred.

(C) N, a social scientist, was charged with plagiarism. The charge is without foundation because although strong similarities between N's book and the work of another scholar have been discovered, the other scholar's work was written after N's work was published.

(D) O, an auto mechanic, has been accused of selling stolen auto parts. The accusation seems to be justified since although no evidence links O directly to these sales, the pattern of distribution of the auto parts points of O as the source.

(E) P, a politician, has been accused of failing to protect the public interest. From at least some points of view, however, the accusation will undoubtedly be considered false, because there is clearly disagreement about where the public interest lies.[10]

Step 1. Identify the Question Type

The question is asking for an argument with "questionable reasoning" that is "most similar to" the stimulus, making this a Parallel Flaw question. The correct answer will have the same argument structure and the flaw that the stimulus has.

---

[10]PrepTest 24, Sec. 3, Q 16

Step 2. Untangle the Stimulus

The word "Therefore" in the last sentence identifies the conclusion, that the accusation should be dismissed. The "should" tells you it's a recommendation, specifically, to throw something out.

Step 3. Make a Prediction

First, find and characterize the conclusions in the answer choices to determine whether they are recommendations to throw something out as in the stimulus. If not, you can discard those choices right away. If you get more than one match, you will take the next step and compare the evidence.

Step 4. Evaluate the Answer Choices

In choice (A), the conclusion recommends that "the charge should be ignored." That sounds like a match, so keep it as a possibility and check the other choices for any other recommendations to do something.

The conclusion in choice (B) is also a recommendation to do something, to discuss the accusation. Put it aside as well and keep checking the other choices.

Choice (C)'s conclusion, "the charge is without foundation," is an assertion of fact, so you can discard this choice.

Choice (D)'s conclusion presents a weak assertion of fact that "the accusation seems to be justified." Dismiss this choice as well.

The conclusion of choice (E), that the accusation will undoubtedly be considered false, is a prediction with strong conviction. This is another unparalleled conclusion, so you can cross it out. If the conclusion is not similar to the stimulus, there is no point to analyze the rest of the argument.

Repeat Step 2. Untangle the Stimulus

With just (A) and (B) remaining, go back to the stimulus and quickly assess the evidence. The author recommends dismissal of data falsification charges because current records show no data falsification. The records in question are missing, but current records are clean. So, the author, in error, uses current, unrelated data as evidence and assumes they indicate the truth of past records.

Repeat Step 3. Make a Prediction

Return to choices (A) and (B) to see which one matches the pattern of evidence and flaw.

Repeat Step 4. Evaluate the Answer Choices

Choice (A) also recommends dismissal of charges, this time for embezzlement. Current records show no indication of embezzlement and should be used in place of the missing, relevant records. Again, the author, in error, uses current, unrelated data as evidence and assumes they indicate the truth of past records. It's like saying someone's not guilty for one crime because he didn't commit another one.

Check choice (B) quickly, but you can feel confident that choice (A) is the correct answer. Choice (B) fails on the evidence. The relevant evidence is available.

2. **(C)**

A worker for a power company trims the branches of trees that overhang power lines as a prevention against damage to the lines anticipated because of the impending stormy season. <The worker reasons that there will be no need for her to trim the overhanging branches of a certain tree> because the owners of the tree have indicated that they might cut it down anyway.

Which one of the following decisions is based on flawed reasoning that is most similar to the worker's flawed reasoning?

(A)   A well inspector has a limited amount of time to inspect the wells of a town. The inspector reasons that the wells should be inspected in the order of most used to least used, because there might not be enough time to inspect them all.

(B)   All sewage and incoming water pipes in a house must be replaced. The plumber reasons that the cheaper polyvinyl chloride pipes should be used for sewage rather than copper pipes, since the money saved might be used to replace worn fixtures.

(C)   A mechanic must replace the worn brakes on a company's vans that are used each weekday. The mechanic reasons that since one of the vans is tentatively scheduled to be junked, he will not have to replace its brakes.

(D)   A candidate decides to campaign in the areas of the city where the most new votes are concentrated. The candidate reasons that campaigning in other areas is unnecessary because in those areas the candidate's message is actually liable to alienate voters.

(E)   None of the children in a certain kindergarten class will take responsibility for the crayon drawing on the classroom wall. The teacher reasons that it is best to keep all the kindergarten children in during recess in order to be certain to punish the one who did the drawing on the wall.[11]

Step 1. Identify the Question Type

The question asks for "flawed reasoning" in the answer that is "most similar to" the stimulus. Therefore, it is a Parallel Flaw question.

---

[11]PrepTest 22, Sec. 4, Q 6

Step 2. Untangle the Stimulus

The worker predicts there will be no need to trim the branches because the owners might take the tree down anyway. So, generally speaking, someone decides that taking a specific action is not necessary because something that would preclude the need to perform the action might happen.

Step 3. Make a Prediction

Check the answer choices for an argument with a structure similar to that of the stimulus.

Step 4. Evaluate the Answer Choices

Choice (A) recommends a course of action (to inspect wells) to serve a particular purpose (optimize available time). This is not a match, so you can dismiss choice (A).

Choice (B) also recommends a course of action (to use cheaper pipe instead of copper) to achieve a goal (save money and use it elsewhere). Eliminate this choice.

Choice (C) predicts that an action will not need to be taken (that tires won't need to be changed) because another action might happen (the van might be junked). This sounds promising, so hold on to choice (C) and check the other answers.

Choice (D) asserts that an action is not necessary (that campaigning in other areas is unnecessary) because it is counterproductive, not because of something that might happen. No match here, so cross this choice out.

Quickly eliminate choice (E). Like choices (A) and (B), it recommends a course of action (to keep all the kindergarten children in during recess) to achieve a particular goal (punish). Go with choice (C), the correct answer.

3.   **(E)**

The fact that politicians in a certain country are trying to reduce government spending does not by itself explain why they have voted to eliminate all government-supported scholarship programs. Government spending could have been reduced even more if instead they had cut back on military spending.

Which one of the following arguments is (most similar) in its reasoning (to) the argument above?

(A)   The fact that Phyllis does not make much money at her new job does not by itself explain why she refuses to buy expensive clothing. Phyllis has always bought only inexpensive clothing even though she used to make a lot of money.

(B)   The fact that Brooks has a part-time job does not by itself explain why he is doing poorly in school. Many students with part-time jobs are able to set aside enough time for study and thus maintain high grades.

(C)   The fact that Sallie and Jim have different work styles does not by itself explain why they could not work together. Sallie and Jim could have resolved their differences if they had communicated more with one another when they began to work together.

(D)   The fact that Roger wanted more companionship does not by itself explain why he adopted ten cats last year. He would not have adopted them all if anyone else had been willing to adopt some of them.

(E)   The fact that Thelma's goal is to become famous does not by itself explain why she took up theatrical acting. It is easier to become famous through writing or directing plays than through theatrical acting.[12]

Step 1. Identify the Question Type

The phrase "most similar...to" identifies this as a Parallel Reasoning question.

Step 2. Untangle the Stimulus

The stimulus does not present a clear argument with a conclusion and evidence, so the best course of action is to paraphrase the stimulus in general terms and compare the summary to the answer choices.

The author states that politicians are trying to achieve a goal (to reduce government spending), but that does not explain why they took a particular action (voted to eliminate all government-

---

[12]PrepTest 37, Sec. 4, Q 14

supported scholarship programs). The author then states that politicians could have achieved the goal with better results if they would have taken another action (cut back on military spending).

Step 3. Make a Prediction

Look for the choice that matches the general summary of the stimulus.

Step 4. Evaluate the Answer Choices

Choice (A) doesn't work. It doesn't even present a goal. Instead, it ponders the motive behind the refusal to do something (buy expensive clothes) and doesn't offer a better alternative.

Choices (B) and (C) aren't parallel either. Like choice (A), they don't present a goal. Go on to the next choice.

Choice (D) starts out promising. It presents Roger's goal (more companionship) and says the goal does not explain why Roger took a particular action (adopted ten cats). However, this is where choice (D) goes wrong. Instead of offering a better way to achieve the goal (like get a roommate) to make the rest of the answer parallel with the stimulus, choice (D) explains why the action taken would not have been taken under other circumstances. That leaves only one choice.

By process of elimination, it looks like choice (E) is the correct answer. Let's find out why. Like the stimulus, choice (E) presents Thelma's goal (to become famous), which does not explain why she took a particular action (took up acting). The goal could have been achieved with better results if Thelma did something different (wrote or directed). We have a winner.

4. **(A)**

From the fact that people who studied music as children frequently are quite proficient at mathematics, <it cannot be concluded that the skills required for mathematics are acquired by studying music>: it is equally likely that proficiency in mathematics and studying music are both the result of growing up in a family that encourages its children to excel at all intellectual and artistic endeavors.

The (pattern of reasoning) in which one of the following arguments is (most parallel to) that in the argument above?

(A)   Although children who fail to pay attention tend to perform poorly in school, it should not necessarily be thought that their poor performance is caused by their failure to pay attention, for it is always possible that their failure to pay attention is due to undiagnosed hearing problems that can also lead to poor performance in school.

(B)   People who attend a university in a foreign country are usually among the top students from their native country. It would therefore be wrong to conclude from the fact that many foreign students perform better academically than others in this country that secondary schools in other countries are superior to those in this country; it may be that evaluation standards are different.

(C)   People whose diet includes relatively large quantities of certain fruits and vegetables have a slightly lower than average incidence of heart disease. But it would be premature to conclude that consuming these fruits and vegetables prevents heart disease, for this correlation may be merely coincidental.

(D)   Those who apply to medical school are required to study biology and chemistry. It would be a mistake, however, to conclude that those who have mastered chemistry and biology will succeed as physicians, for the practical application of knowledge is different from its acquisition.

(E)   Those who engage in vigorous exercise tend to be very healthy. But it would be silly to conclude that vigorous exercise is healthful simply because people who are healthy exercise vigorously, since it is possible that exercise that is less vigorous also has beneficial results.[13]

---

[13]PrepTest 49, Sec. 4, Q 17

Step 1. Identify the Question Type

The phrases "pattern of reasoning" and "most parallel to" tell you that this is a Parallel Reasoning question.

Step 2. Untangle the Stimulus

The author concludes it can't be said that studying music (X) causes better math skills (Y). He also states that it's possible that growing up in a family that encourages intellectual and artistic endeavors (Z) causes proficiency in music and math (X and Y). In other words, X did not necessarily cause Y because Z could have caused X and Y.

Step 3. Make a Prediction

Check the answer choices for that pattern.

Step 4. Evaluate the Answer Choices

Choice (A) concludes that children's failure to pay attention in school (X) does not necessarily cause their poor performance (Y), because undiagnosed hearing problems (Z) may be the cause of their failure to pay attention (X) and their poor performance (Y). Choice (A) looks like a match. Let's check the other answers.

Choice (B) starts strong, with evidence of a correlation between people who attend a university in a foreign country and their status as a top student from their native country. However, choice (B) veers off course with a discussion of the superiority of secondary schools that is not part of the causal relationship. Eliminate this choice.

Choice (C) is problematic from the beginning. It says it's too early to tell whether consuming fruits and vegetables prevents heart disease and that the relationship may just be coincidence. This is not parallel to the structure of the stimulus, so dismiss this choice and keep going.

Choice (D) also misses the pattern. While it says you can't conclude that mastering biology and chemistry (X) will lead to success as a physician (Y), it doesn't present another possible factor (Z) that could cause X and Y.

Choice (E) reaches a conclusion against a causal relationship between vigorous exercise and good health by suggesting that maybe less-vigorous exercise may be as effective as vigorous exercise. Cross this choice out and stick with choice (A).

5. **(B)**

Opposition leader: Our country has the least fair court system of any country on the continent and ought not to be the model for others. <Thus, our highest court is the least fair of any on the continent and ought not to be emulated by other countries.>

The flawed reasoning in which one of the following arguments is most similar to that in the opposition leader's argument?

(A)   The residents of medium-sized towns are, on average, more highly educated than people who do not live in such towns. Therefore, Maureen, who was born in a medium-sized town, is more highly educated than Monica, who has just moved to such a town.

(B)   At a certain college, either philosophy or engineering is the most demanding major. Therefore, either the introductory course in philosophy or the introductory course in engineering is the most demanding introductory-level course at that college.

(C)   For many years its superior engineering has enabled the Lawson Automobile Company to make the best racing cars. Therefore, its passenger cars, which use many of the same parts, are unmatched by those of any other company.

(D)   Domestic cats are closely related to tigers. Therefore, even though they are far smaller than tigers, their eating habits are almost the same as those of tigers.

(E)   If a suit of questionable merit is brought in the first district rather than the second district, its chances of being immediately thrown out are greater. Therefore, to have the best chance of winning the case, the lawyers will bring the suit in the second district.[14]

Step 1. Identify the Question Type

The phrases "flawed reasoning" and "most similar to" identify this as a Parallel Flaw question.

Step 2. Untangle the Stimulus

The opposition leader concludes that his country's highest court is the least fair on the continent because his country has the least fair court system of any country on the continent. In other words, a single member of a group (the country's highest court) has X characteristic

---

[14]PrepTest 47, Sec. 1, Q 21

because the large group (country's court system) has X characteristic. The opposition commits a classic scope-shift flaw.

Step 3. Make a Prediction

Check the answer choices for a scope shift between a group and an individual.

Step 4. Evaluate the Answer Choices

Choice (A) does have a scope shift, but not the same kind as that in the stimulus. While the argument looks at a group (residents of medium-sized towns) and Maureen and Monica (two group members), the conclusion adds another scope shift of whether someone was born in or moved to a small town. Eliminate this choice.

Choice (B) reaches a conclusion about the difficulty of individual classes based on the difficulty of the related major. Don't let the "either…or" language confuse you. Choice (B) takes a group characteristic and says the characteristic applies to individual members of the group. You have the correct answer here. Keep going to find out why the last three choices are wrong.

Choice (C) commits a scope shift, but the wrong kind. The shift occurs between two different groups: Racing cars and passenger cars.

Choice (D) differs from the stimulus in that the individual member and group have the same characteristic. Here, the conclusion qualifies the similar eating habits of cats and tigers with "almost."

Choice (E) presents a scope shift but again, it's different from the stimulus. It shifts scope between a case getting thrown out and winning a case, which is not the same as shifting between a member and a group.

PARALLEL REASONING REVIEW

Before you proceed to the next chapter, turn to Appendix A and complete the review exercise for Parallel Reasoning questions. A completed chart is included in Appendix B.

CHAPTER 13

METHOD OF ARGUMENT QUESTIONS

You learned in previous chapters that LSAT arguments consist of a conclusion and evidence, and they are connected by an unstated assumption. While every argument has the same building blocks, they can be structured in a variety of different ways. For example, they may present expert testimony or the results of a study, or they may question the motives behind a recommendation or propose alternative explanations. On the LSAT, Method of Argument questions test your ability to analyze how an argument is put together.

You can expect to see approximately two scored Method of Argument questions on an LSAT. Although this question type doesn't account for a large number of points, you'll still need to effectively handle them on test day to maximize your score. Fortunately for you, the Kaplan Method can help you do this.

DEFINITION OF METHOD OF ARGUMENT QUESTIONS

Method of Argument questions ask you to identify the approach used to make an argument. You will not be asked for the facts of the argument, but rather for a general description of the argument's organization or for the type of evidence the author relies upon.

USE THE KAPLAN METHOD TO ANSWER METHOD OF ARGUMENT QUESTIONS

Identify the Question Type

Just as you've done with all other Logical Reasoning question types, read the question stem first to determine the question type. The following terms denote a Method of Argument question:

- Argumentative technique
- Method
- Process
- Argumentative strategy
- Responds to . . . by

Here's how some of those phrases could appear in a question stem:

- The argument proceeds by presenting evidence that
- Which one of the following most accurately describes the method of reasoning used in the argument?
- The economist's argument employs which one of the following techniques?
- The argument does which one of the following?
- Which one of the following describes the author's argumentative strategy?
- Ralph responds to Laura by pointing out that

Untangle the Stimulus

A Method of Argument stimulus will be presented either as a paragraph or as a conversation between two people. As you read the stimulus, look for the conclusion and evidence, and look for how they are connected.

Make a Prediction

Summarize the argument in general terms and characterize the type of evidentiary support the author uses (e.g., expert testimony or a research study).

Evaluate the Answer Choices

Review the answer choices and select the one that matches your prediction. The correct answer to a Method of Argument question will have a 1:1 matchup with the stimulus. As you read each answer choice, ask yourself: Does the author do this? Then, match up the action in the answer choice with the components of the stimulus, especially the type of evidence upon which the author relies.

THE KAPLAN METHOD IN ACTION

Now I'll walk you through a couple examples to show you how the Kaplan Method can help you efficiently solve any Method of Argument question you'll see on test day.

1. Lahar: We must now settle on a procedure for deciding on meeting agendas. Our club's constitution allows three options: unanimous consent, majority vote, or assigning the task to a committee. Unanimous consent is unlikely. Forming a committee has usually led to factionalism and secret deals. <Clearly, we should subject meeting agendas to majority vote.>

    Lahar's argument does which one of the following?

    (A) rejects suggested procedures on constitutional grounds
    (B) claims that one procedure is the appropriate method for reaching every decision in the club
    (C) suggests a change to a constitution on the basis of practical considerations
    (D) recommends a choice based on the elimination of alternative options
    (E) supports one preference by arguing against those who have advocated alternatives[1]

Step 1. Identify the Question Type

The phrase "does which one of the following" indicates that this is a Method of Argument question. You want to determine how the author uses her evidence to build up to the conclusion.

Step 2. Untangle the Stimulus

Lahar says there are three possible ways to determine the club's meeting agenda. He then eliminates two options and concludes that the third option should be used.

Step 3. Make a Prediction

Here, Lahar reaches a conclusion by eliminating two other possibilities. So, the correct answer will do this as well. As you read the answer choices, ask yourself: Does the author do this?

Step 4. Evaluate the Answer Choices

Choice (A) is wrong according to the stimulus, as Lahar doesn't reject any option based on constitutional grounds. In fact, all three options are allowed under the club's constitution.

Choice (B) starts off on the right track but takes a wrong turn. Lahar does recommend one procedure, just not as a way to reach every club decision. The recommendation is narrowly directed at developing the club's meeting agenda. Cross this choice out.

[1]PrepTest 52, Sec. 3, Q 5

You can also eliminate choice (C). Lahar doesn't mention anything about changing the club's constitution. Again, he says all three options are allowed by the constitution.

Choice (D) matches the prediction and is the correct answer.

Choice (E) adds information that's not included in the stimulus. Lahar doesn't argue against those who advocate alternatives; he argues against the alternatives.

2. According to the proposed Factory Safety Act, a company may operate an automobile factory only if that factory is registered as a class B factory. In addressing whether a factory may postpone its safety inspections, this Act also stipulates that no factory can be class B without punctual inspections. <Thus> under the Factory Safety Act, a factory that manufactures automobiles would not be able to postpone its safety inspections.>

The argument proceeds by

(A)   pointing out how two provisions of the proposed Factory Safety Act jointly entail the unacceptability of a certain state of affairs

(B)   considering two possible interpretations of a proposed legal regulation and eliminating the less plausible one

(C)   showing that the terms of the proposed Factory Safety Act are incompatible with existing legislation

(D)   showing that two different provisions of the proposed Factory Safety Act conflict and thus cannot apply to a particular situation

(E)   pointing out that if a provision applies in a specific situation, it must apply in any analogous situation[2]

Step 1. Identify the Question Type

The phrase "proceeds by" tells you that this is a Method of Argument question. As was the case in the previous example, your task is to untangle the structure of the argument.

Step 2. Untangle the Stimulus

This argument concludes in the last sentence that a factory that manufactures automobiles would not be able to postpone its safety inspections under the Factory Safety Act. The evidence used to support it is presented in formal logic language signaled by "only if" and "no . . . without."

Translate the formal logic to determine the argument's structure.

---

[2]PrepTest 49, Sec. 4, Q 15

The first sentence says that if a company operates an auto factory, it must register that facility as a class B factory. The second statement says that if a factory is class B, then it must have punctual inspections. The argument concludes that under the Factory Safety Act, auto factories could not postpone inspections. Combine the negatives and the result is that auto factories must have punctual inspections. Note the classic formal logic statements and the more general equations depicted in the stimulus.

Auto factory → class B	Class B → punctual inspections	Auto factory → punctual inspections
A → B	B → C	A → C

Step 3. Make a Prediction

The correct answer will describe the argument in structural terms. In this case, you have two statements from a piece of legislation that combine to indicate that something must happen.

Step 4. Evaluate the Answer Choices

Choice (A) matches the prediction by pointing out two provisions of the Factory Safety Act that combine to produce a certain result. This is the correct answer.

Choice (B) is incorrect because the argument does not consider two interpretations of the Factory Safety Act. There is only one interpretation of the Act given in the stimulus, and it's reached by combining two provisions.

Choice (C) brings in existing legislation that is never mentioned in the stimulus or compared to the proposed Factory Safety Act.

Choice (D) is also wrong because the two provisions of the proposed Factory Safety Act don't conflict at all. Actually, they combine to produce a certain result.

Choice (E) discusses an analogy that does not exist in the stimulus. The provisions of the Factory Safety Act are only applied to a single situation.

METHOD OF ARGUMENT QUESTIONS: NOW YOU TRY IT

It's now your turn to try a Method of Argument question on your own. Use the template I've provided after the question to guide you through the four-step Kaplan Method. (Note: On test day, you won't be writing out all the steps as you are in this exercise. However, as you are learning the Method, it's good practice to help it become second nature.) Remember to bracket conclusions and circle Keywords.

1. Xavier: Demand by tourists in Nepal for inexpensive thangka paintings has resulted in the proliferation of inferior thangkas containing symbolic inaccuracies—a sure sign of a dying art form. Nepal should prohibit sales of thangkas to tourists, for such a prohibition will induce artists to create thangkas that meet traditional standards.

    Yvette: An art form without dedicated young artists will decay and die. If tourists were forbidden to buy thangkas, young artists would cease making thangkas and concentrate instead on an art form tourists can buy.

    Yvette responds to Xavier by

    (A) denying the existence of the problem that Xavier's proposal is designed to ameliorate
    (B) challenging the integrity of Xavier's sources of information
    (C) arguing that Xavier's proposal, if implemented, would result in the very consequences it is meant to prevent
    (D) using an analogy to draw a conclusion that is inconsistent with the conclusion drawn by Xavier
    (E) showing that the evidence presented by Xavier has no bearing on the point at issue[3]

Step 1. Identify the Question Type

_____

Step 2. Untangle the Stimulus

_____

Step 3. Make a Prediction

_____

Step 4. Evaluate the Answer Choices

_____

_____

[3] PrepTest 41, Sec. 1, Q 3

Answer Explanations follow on the next page.

Explanations

1. (C)

Xavier: Demand by tourists in Nepal for inexpensive thangka paintings has resulted in the proliferation of inferior thangkas containing symbolic inaccuracies—a sure sign of a dying art form. <Nepal should prohibit sales of thangkas to tourists,> for such a prohibition will induce artists to create thangkas that meet traditional standards.

Yvette: An art form without dedicated young artists will decay and die. <If tourists were forbidden to buy thangkas, young artists would cease making thangkas and concentrate instead on an art form tourists can buy.>

Yvette (responds to) Xavier (by)

(A)   denying the existence of the problem that Xavier's proposal is designed to ameliorate

(B)   challenging the integrity of Xavier's sources of information

(C)   arguing that Xavier's proposal, if implemented, would result in the very consequences it is meant to prevent

(D)   using an analogy to draw a conclusion that is inconsistent with the conclusion drawn by Xavier

(E)   showing that the evidence presented by Xavier has no bearing on the point at issue[4]

Step 1. Identify the Question Type

The phrase "responds to . . . by" is a common indicator of a Method of Argument question in which there is a dialogue between two people and you are asked to describe how the second speaker responds to the first speaker. In this case, you're asked to describe the structure of Yvette's response to Xavier.

Step 2. Untangle the Stimulus

While it is tempting to go right to Yvette's response, never skip the first speaker's argument in a Method of Argument stimulus presented as a dialogue. You must summarize both speakers' arguments to know whether Yvette agrees or disagrees with Xavier and on what grounds.

Xavier recommends that Nepal prohibit tourist sales of thangkas to encourage young artists to create the traditional ones rather than inferior versions. Yvette says that young people are necessary to prevent the disappearance of an art form and raises her concern that if Nepal does prohibit tourist sales of thangkas, young people won't make them at all.

---

[4]PrepTest 41, Sec. 1, Q 3

Step 3. Make a Prediction

Xavier wants to solve a problem (artists have stopped making traditional thangkas; they make inferior thangkas for tourists) and proposes a solution (prohibit thangka sales to tourists). Yvette points out that Xavier's solution will achieve the result he wants to avoid (artists will stop making thangkas; they will make something else for the tourists).

Step 4. Evaluate the Answer Choices

Choice (A) is an inaccurate description because Yvette does not deny the existence of a problem. In fact, she shows concern for the same problem raised by Xavier, the decay and death of the traditional thangka as an art form. Cross out this answer.

Choice (B) is simply not something that Yvette says anywhere in her statement. Xavier's sources of information are never raised in the stimulus, and the integrity of these sources is never challenged. Move on to the next choice.

Choice (C) matches the prediction and is the correct answer.

Choice (D) is outside the scope in that Yvette never presents any kind of analogy. She identifies a necessary condition for an art form to thrive and then speculates on an unwanted result of Xavier's plan.

Choice (E) is outside the scope as well. Yvette does not argue with Xavier's evidence. She points out that the proposed solution will not achieve the desired results and ultimately contribute to the problem.

DRILL: PRACTICING METHOD OF ARGUMENT QUESTIONS

Use the Kaplan Method to answer the following Method of Argument questions. Take this opportunity to practice and apply the steps in the Method so you are comfortable using them on test day. Be sure to circle conclusion and evidence Keywords and bracket the conclusion. Check your responses against the full explanations provided after the Drill.

1. Yang: Yeast has long been known to be a leaven, that is, a substance used in baking to make breads rise. Since biblical evidence ties the use of leavens to events dating back to 1,200 B.C., we can infer that yeast was already known to be a leaven at that time.

   Campisi: I find your inference unconvincing; several leavens other than yeast could have been known in 1,200 B.C.

   Campisi counters Yang's argument by

   (A) suggesting that an alternative set of evidence better supports Yang's conclusion
   (B) questioning the truth of a presumption underlying Yang's argument
   (C) denying the truth of Yang's conclusion without considering the reason given for that conclusion
   (D) pointing out that the premises of Yang's argument more strongly support a contrary conclusion
   (E) calling into question the truth of the evidence presented in Yang's argument[5]

2. Zachary: The term "fresco" refers to paint that has been applied to wet plaster. Once dried, a fresco indelibly preserves the paint that a painter has applied in this way. Unfortunately, additions known to have been made by later painters have obscured the original fresco work done by Michelangelo in the Sistine Chapel. Therefore, in order to restore Michelangelo's Sistine Chapel paintings to the appearance that Michelangelo intended them to have, everything except the original fresco work must be stripped away.

   Stephen: But it was extremely common for painters of Michelangelo's era to add painted details to their own fresco work after the frescos had dried.

   Stephen's response to Zachary proceeds by

   (A) calling into question an assumption on which Zachary's conclusion depends
   (B) challenging the definition of a key term in Zachary's argument
   (C) drawing a conclusion other than the one that Zachary reaches
   (D) denying the truth of one of the stated premises of Zachary's argument
   (E) demonstrating that Zachary's conclusion is not consistent with the premises he uses to support it[6]

3. Gamba: Muñoz claims that the Southwest Hopeville Neighbors Association overwhelmingly opposes the new water system, citing this as evidence of citywide opposition. The association did pass a resolution opposing the new water system, but only 25 of 350 members voted, with 10 in favor of the system. Furthermore, the 15 opposing votes represent far less than 1 percent of Hopeville's population. One should not assume that so few votes represent the view of the majority of Hopeville's residents.

Of the following, which one most accurately describes Gamba's strategy of argumentation?

(A)   questioning a conclusion based on the results of a vote, on the grounds that people with certain views are more likely to vote

(B)   questioning a claim supported by statistical data by arguing that statistical data can be manipulated to support whatever view the interpreter wants to support

(C)   attempting to refute an argument by showing that, contrary to what has been claimed, the truth of the premises does not guarantee the truth of the conclusion

(D)   criticizing a view on the grounds that the view is based on evidence that is in principle impossible to disconfirm

(E)   attempting to cast doubt on a conclusion by claiming that the statistical sample on which the conclusion is based is too small to be dependable[7]

---

[7]PrepTest June 2007, Sec. 2, Q 20

Explanations

1. **(B)**

Yang: Yeast has long been known to be a leaven, that is, a substance used in baking to make breads rise. Since biblical evidence ties the use of leavens to events dating back to 1,200 B.C., <we can infer that yeast was already known to be a leaven at that time.>

Campisi: <I find your inference unconvincing;> several leavens other than yeast could have been known in 1,200 B.C.

Campisi (counters) Yang's argument (by)

(A) suggesting that an alternative set of evidence better supports Yang's conclusion

(B) questioning the truth of a presumption underlying Yang's argument

(C) denying the truth of Yang's conclusion without considering the reason given for that conclusion

(D) pointing out that the premises of Yang's argument more strongly support a contrary conclusion

(E) calling into question the truth of the evidence presented in Yang's argument[8]

Step 1. Identify the Question Type

Typically, the term "counter" indicates a Weaken question. However, in this case, the phrase "counters . . . by" identifies a Method of Argument question asking how Campisi attempted to weaken Yang's argument. So, rather than adding a new fact that would weaken the argument, the correct answer will describe what Campisi does to attack Yang's argument.

Step 2. Untangle the Stimulus

Yang concludes that because leavens were used at that time, yeast was a known leavening agent in the year 1,200 B.C. Notice the scope shift in Yang's argument from "leavens" generally to "yeast" specifically. Campisi recognizes that assumption and goes right at it: Yang assumes that the leaven was yeast, but other types of leavens could have existed at the time.

Step 3. Make a Prediction

Campisi challenges an assumption that Yang makes, so the correct answer should reflect this approach.

Step 4. Evaluate the Answer Choices

Choice (A) brings in an alternative set of evidence that is outside the scope of the argument. Campisi doesn't add anything to the argument or support Yang's conclusion. Rather, he questions Yang's argument and offers no support for Yang's conclusion. Eliminate this answer

---

[8]PrepTest 41, Sec. 3, Q 12

Choice (B), the correct answer, identifies the problem Campisi raised regarding Yang's assumption.

Choice (C) uses extreme language and is outside the scope. Campisi doesn't deny the truth of Yang's conclusion; he merely finds Yang's assumption unconvincing. In addition, Campisi does consider the reason given and argues that it fails to prove Yang's point.

Choice (D) is outside the scope because Campisi never discusses a contrary conclusion nor does he mention Yang's evidence supporting a contrary conclusion.

Choice (E) contradicts Campisi's response. He challenges Yang's assumption, not his evidence.

2. **(A)**

Zachary: The term "fresco" refers to paint that has been applied to wet plaster. Once dried, a fresco indelibly preserves the paint that a painter has applied in this way. Unfortunately, additions known to have been made by later painters have obscured the original fresco work done by Michelangelo in the Sistine Chapel. ⟨Therefore⟩ in order to restore Michelangelo's Sistine Chapel paintings to the appearance that Michelangelo intended them to have, everything except the original fresco work must be stripped away.⟩

Stephen: ⟨But⟩ it was extremely common for painters of Michelangelo's era to add painted details to their own fresco work after the frescos had dried.

Stephen's ⟨response⟩ to Zachary ⟨proceeds by⟩

(A) calling into question an assumption on which Zachary's conclusion depends
(B) challenging the definition of a key term in Zachary's argument
(C) drawing a conclusion other than the one that Zachary reaches
(D) denying the truth of one of the stated premises of Zachary's argument
(E) demonstrating that Zachary's conclusion is not consistent with the premises he uses to support it[9]

Step 1. Identify the Question Type

The phrase "response . . . proceeds by" tells you that this is a Method of Argument question.

Step 2. Untangle the Stimulus

Zachary concludes in his last sentence that to restore the Sistine Chapel paintings to what Michelangelo intended, everything except the original fresco work must be stripped away. He supports his conclusion with evidence that later painters made additions to the paintings.

---

[9]PrepTest 35, Sec. 4, Q 25

Zachary must assume that Michelangelo did not himself make any additions to his original work to fulfill his intentions.

Notice the "but" in Stephen's response, which indicates Stephen's disagreement with Zachary. Stephen points out a gap between the evidence and conclusion and questions it. He raises the possibility that Michelangelo added paint to his own original work, so stripping away everything except the original work would not achieve Michelangelo's intentions at all.

Step 3. Make a Prediction

In general terms, Stephen casts doubt on Zachary's assumption.

Step 4. Evaluate the Answer Choices

Correct choice (A) matches the prediction that Stephen would question Zachary's assumption.

Choice (B) is wrong because Stephen never challenges Zachary's terminology.

Choice (C) incorrectly indicates that Stephen reached a conclusion of his own. He did question Zachary's assumption, which could ultimately endanger Zachary's conclusion. However, he never reached a conclusion of his own.

Choice (D) is also wrong because Stephen never attacks the premises of Zachary's argument. Instead, he questions the unstated assumption.

Choice (E) is out. Stephen never demonstrates an inconsistency between Zachary's evidence and conclusion. He adds information that raises doubt about Zachary's assumption.

3. **(E)**

Gamba: Muñoz claims that the Southwest Hopeville Neighbors Association overwhelmingly opposes the new water system, citing this as evidence of citywide opposition. The association did pass a resolution opposing the new water system, but only 25 of 350 members voted, with 10 in favor of the system. Furthermore, the 15 opposing votes represent far less than 1 percent of Hopeville's population. <One should not assume that so few votes represent the view of the majority of Hopeville's residents.>

Of the following, which one most accurately describes Gamba's strategy of argumentation?

(A) questioning a conclusion based on the results of a vote, on the grounds that people with certain views are more likely to vote

(B) questioning a claim supported by statistical data by arguing that statistical data can be manipulated to support whatever view the interpreter wants to support

(C) attempting to refute an argument by showing that, contrary to what has been claimed, the truth of the premises does not guarantee the truth of the conclusion

(D) criticizing a view on the grounds that the view is based on evidence that is in principle impossible to disconfirm

(E) attempting to cast doubt on a conclusion by claiming that the statistical sample on which the conclusion is based is too small to be dependable[10]

Step 1. Identify the Question Type

The phrase "strategy of argumentation" tells you that this is a Method of Argument question.

Step 2. Untangle the Stimulus

Gamba begins by noting Muñoz's claim, that the Southwest Hopeville Neighbors Association opposes the new water system, so the opposition is citywide. Typically, when an author mentions someone else' claim, you can expect the author to disagree with that claim. That's exactly what happens here. Gamba proceeds to discredit Muñoz's claim by pointing out the small size of the sample, which he says doesn't accurately represent the Association, let alone the whole city. Gamba concludes by noting that the small number of votes doesn't necessarily represent the views of the city's residents. Notice the word "represent" in the conclusion; it points out where Gamba identifies the flaw of representativeness in Muñoz's argument.

---

[10]PrepTest June 2007, Sec. 2, Q 20

Step 3. Make a Prediction

Gamba questions Muñoz's claim by pointing out that the study sample is not representative of the larger population.

Step 4. Evaluate the Answer Choices

All the answer choices begin by noting in some form that Gamba does not believe Muñoz's claim, but the answers differ based on the reason for Gamba's concern. You are looking for the answer choice that questions the sample size, as predicted.

Choice (A) raises an issue that is not addressed in the stimulus, as Gamba doesn't question whether people with certain views were more likely to vote.

Choice (B) also brings up a point that Gamba never mentions; he does not talk about the possibility of statistical manipulation.

Choice (C) adds another contention not discussed in the stimulus. Gamba is not concerned with whether the truth of the premises guarantees the truth of the conclusion. He questions the representativeness of the evidence altogether.

Choice (D) also falls outside the scope. Gamba says the evidence is not representative. He never claims the evidence is impossible to disconfirm.

Finally, you get to choice (E), which matches the prediction by questioning the sample size. This is the correct answer.

METHOD OF ARGUMENT REVIEW

Before you proceed to the next chapter, turn to Appendix A and complete the review exercise for Method of Argument questions. A completed chart is included in Appendix B.

CHAPTER 14

PARADOX QUESTIONS

Paradox questions ask you to make something that does not appear to make sense into something that does. A Paradox question presents you with two statements that contradict each other, but are nonetheless both true. While a real-life paradox may not have a simple resolution, an LSAT paradox can always be resolved with the correct answer. You will see about four scored Paradox questions on test day.

DEFINITION OF PARADOX QUESTIONS

On the LSAT, a paradox exists when a stimulus contains two inconsistent ideas or situations. The correct answer will reconcile the seemingly incompatible statements while allowing them both to remain true. Essentially, each question asks you to fix a problem.

USE THE KAPLAN METHOD TO ANSWER PARADOX QUESTIONS

Identify the Question Type

As always, read the question stem first to identify the question type and note any relevant clues. You can identify a Paradox question from words and phrases like:

- Solve the apparent paradox
- Resolve the discrepancy
- Explain
- Solve the mystery

Here's how some of those phrases could appear in a question stem:

- Which one of the following, if true, most helps to resolve the apparent paradox described above?
- Which one of the following, if true, most helps to account for the apparent discrepancy in the students' preferences?
- Which one of the following, if true, most helps to explain the facts cited above?
- Which one of the following solves the mystery presented above?

Untangle the Stimulus

A Paradox stimulus does not present an argument. Instead, you're given information that sets up a contradiction, so read the stimulus looking for that paradox. Ask yourself: What doesn't make sense? Your task is to identify the statements that are at odds with each other.

Make a Prediction

Think about how to reconcile the paradox. You need to provide an explanation or an alternative factor that accounts for the contradictory elements and makes them consistent.

Evaluate the Answer Choices

Compare your prediction to the answer choices and choose the match.

THE KAPLAN METHOD IN ACTION

Now I'll walk you through a couple examples to show you how the Kaplan Method can help you efficiently solve any Paradox question you'll see on test day.

1. In a study, shoppers who shopped in a grocery store without a shopping list and bought only items that were on sale for half price or less spent far more money on a comparable number of items than did shoppers in the same store who used a list and bought no sale items.

    Which one of the following, if true, most helps to explain the apparent paradox in the study's results?

    (A)   Only the shoppers who used a list used a shopping cart.
    (B)   The shoppers who did not use lists bought many unnecessary items.
    (C)   Usually, only the most expensive items go on sale in grocery stores.
    (D)   The grocery store in the study carries many expensive items that few other grocery stores carry.
    (E)   The grocery store in the study places relatively few items on sale.[1]

---

[1]PrepTest 50, Sec. 4, Q 16

Step 1. Identify the Question Type

Because the question asks you for an answer that "most helps to explain the apparent paradox," this is a Paradox question. Look for the paradox in the study's results.

Step 2. Untangle the Stimulus

The stimulus presents two groups of shoppers who purchased the same number of items at the same grocery store. One group had no list and bought only sale items (half price or less), while the other group used a list and bought no sale items at all. The latter group spent less money than the former.

Step 3. Make a Prediction

You would have expected the sale items to be less expensive than the full-price items; therein lies the paradox. To resolve it, the answer must explain why sale items cost more than the full-price items. Let that principle guide you as you evaluate the answer choices.

Step 4. Evaluate the Answer Choices

Choice (A) is out of scope; shopping carts don't have any apparent impact on the amount of money spent, so they can't help resolve the paradox. Eliminate this choice.

Choice (B) has the same problem. Whether items were necessary does not address the amount of money spent. At first glance, you might think unnecessary means the shoppers splurged, but the answer doesn't tie price to it. You still don't know how the sale shoppers spent more money. Move on to the next choice.

Choice (C) explains the paradox. If the sale items were originally the most expensive items in the store, they could still cost more on sale than other items at full price. This is the correct answer.

Choice (D) mentions cost but doesn't identify which group buys the expensive items. So, choice (D) doesn't add anything to help explain why the sale items cost more than the full price items.

Choice (E) doesn't address the cost issue either. The number of items on sale does not explain the higher grocery bill of those who only bought sale items.

2. After replacing his old gas water heater with a new, pilotless, gas water heater that is rated as highly efficient, Jimmy's gas bills increased.

Each of the following, if true, contributes to an explanation of the increase mentioned above EXCEPT:

(A) The new water heater uses a smaller percentage of the gas used by Jimmy's household than did the old one.

(B) Shortly after the new water heater was installed, Jimmy's uncle came to live with him, doubling the size of the household.

(C) After having done his laundry at a laundromat, Jimmy bought and started using a gas dryer when he replaced his water heater.

(D) Jimmy's utility company raised the rates for gas consumption following installation of the new water heater.

(E) Unusually cold weather following installation of the new water heater resulted in heavy gas usage.[2]

Step 1. Identify the Question Type

The phrase "contributes to an explanation" signals a Paradox question. Be careful with this question; make sure you know what kind of answer you're looking for. The "EXCEPT" in this stem means that four answers will reconcile the paradox, while the one right answer—the one you're looking for—will not. It will have no effect at all, or it will contribute to the paradox. Now that you know what you're looking for, read the stimulus.

Step 2. Untangle the Stimulus

Jimmy's gas bills went up after he installed a new, highly efficient gas water heater.

Step 3. Make a Prediction

You would expect the bill to go down with a new, efficient heater. So, either the new water heater is less efficient than the old one, or some other factor is driving up his gas bills. Remember: The four wrong answers will explain why the gas bills rose. The correct answer will not.

Step 4. Evaluate the Answer Choices

Choice (A) says the new heater really does use less gas. Rather than explain why the gas bill went up, it leaves you wondering why the gas bill did not go down. This answer doesn't solve the paradox, and is therefore the correct answer.

Choice (B) adds Jimmy's uncle as a user of the new heater. Additional usage could explain an increase in the gas bill.

---

[2]PrepTest June 2007, Sec. 3, Q 2

Choice (C) also shows increased use of the new heater and supports an explanation for an increase in the gas bill.

Choice (D) raises the gas rates. So, even if Jimmy used less gas, his gas bill could increase.

Choice (E) gives another reason for increased use of the new heater and thereby contributes to an explanation for the higher gas bill.

PARADOX QUESTIONS: NOW YOU TRY IT

It's now your turn to try a Paradox question on your own. Use the template I've provided after the question to guide you through the four-step Kaplan Method. (Note: On test day, you won't be writing out all the steps as you are in this exercise. However, as you are learning the Method, it's good practice to help it become second nature.) Remember to circle Keywords.

1. Recent investigations of earthquakes have turned up a previously unknown type of seismic shock, known as a displacement pulse, which is believed to be present in all earthquakes. Alarmingly, high-rise buildings are especially vulnerable to displacement pulses, according to computer models. Yet examination of high-rises within cities damaged by recent powerful earthquakes indicates little significant damage to these structures.

    Which one of the following, if true, contributes to a resolution of the apparent paradox?

    (A) Displacement pulses travel longer distances than other types of seismic shock.
    (B) Scientific predictions based on computer models often fail when tested in the field.
    (C) While displacement pulses have only recently been discovered, they have accompanied all earthquakes that have ever occurred.
    (D) The displacement pulses made by low- and medium-intensity earthquakes are much less powerful than those made by the strongest earthquakes.
    (E) Computer models have been very successful in predicting the effects of other types of seismic shock.[3]

Step 1. Identify the Question Type

_____

Step 2. Untangle the Stimulus

_____

Step 3. Make a Prediction

_____

Step 4. Evaluate the Answer Choices

_____

_____

[3] PrepTest 47, Sec. 1, Q 6

Answer Explanations follow on the next page.

Explanations

1. (B)

Recent investigations of earthquakes have turned up a previously unknown type of seismic shock, known as a displacement pulse, which is believed to be present in all earthquakes. Alarmingly, high-rise buildings are especially vulnerable to displacement pulses, according to computer models. Yet examination of high-rises within cities damaged by recent powerful earthquakes indicates little significant damage to these structures.

Which one of the following, if true, contributes to a resolution of the apparent paradox?

(A) Displacement pulses travel longer distances than other types of seismic shock.

(B) Scientific predictions based on computer models often fail when tested in the field.

(C) While displacement pulses have only recently been discovered, they have accompanied all earthquakes that have ever occurred.

(D) The displacement pulses made by low- and medium-intensity earthquakes are much less powerful than those made by the strongest earthquakes.

(E) Computer models have been very successful in predicting the effects of other types of seismic shock.[4]

Step 1. Identify the Question Type

The phrase "contributes to a resolution of the apparent paradox" indicates that this is a Paradox question.

Step 2. Untangle the Stimulus

Displacement pulses occur in all earthquakes and are especially dangerous to high-rise buildings, according to computer simulations. However, high-rises located in cities recently hit by earthquakes show little damage. The paradox is the discrepancy between the computer model and actual results.

Step 3. Make a Prediction

The correct answer will explain why in reality there was only minor damage from earthquakes despite computer models predicting major damage.

[4] PrepTest 47, Sec. 1, Q 6

Step 4. Evaluate the Answer Choices

Choice (A) provides information that would make the displacement pulses more dangerous to high-rises and thus deepens the discrepancy between the computer model and reality. Cross this choice out.

Choice (B) helps explain the discrepancy and is the correct answer. If computer models often fail in the field, it's possible the displacement pulse models are not accurate.

Choice (C) doesn't help resolve the paradox. Knowing that the recently discovered displacement pulses have always accompanied earthquakes doesn't explain the discrepancy between the computer model and the actual earthquake results.

Choice (D) also doesn't explain why the high-rises weren't damaged. They were hit by "powerful" earthquakes, which supposedly would have stronger displacement pulses.

Choice (E) extends the paradox by saying computer models are accurate in predicting the effects of seismic shock. In other words, it would make less sense that successful computer models show earthquake damage to high-rises when in reality the high-rises show little damage.

DRILL: PRACTICING PARADOX QUESTIONS

Use the Kaplan Method to answer the following Paradox questions. Take this opportunity to practice and apply the steps in the Method so you are comfortable using them on test day. Be sure to circle conclusion and evidence Keywords and bracket the conclusion. Check your responses against the full explanations provided after the Drill.

1. Most economists believe that reducing the price of any product generally stimulates demand for it. However, most wine merchants have found that reducing the price of domestic wines to make them more competitive with imported wines with which they were previously comparably priced is frequently followed by an increase in sales of those imported wines.

   Which one of the following, if true, most helps to reconcile the belief of most economists with the consequences observed by most wine merchants?

   (A) Economists' studies of the prices of grocery items and their rates of sales rarely cover alcoholic beverages.
   (B) Few merchants of any kind have detailed knowledge of economic theories about the relationship between item prices and sales rates.
   (C) Consumers are generally willing to forgo purchasing other items they desire in order to purchase a superior wine.
   (D) Imported wines in all price ranges are comparable in quality to domestic wines that cost less.
   (E) An increase in the demand for a consumer product is compatible with an increase in demand for a competing product.[5]

2. A recent study revealed that the percentage of people treated at large, urban hospitals who recover from their illnesses is lower than the percentage for people treated at smaller, rural hospitals.

   Each of the following, if true, contributes to an explanation of the difference in recovery rates EXCEPT:

   (A) Because there are fewer patients to feed, nutritionists at small hospitals are better able to tailor meals to the dietary needs of each patient.
   (B) The less friendly, more impersonal atmosphere of large hospitals can be a source of stress for patients at those hospitals.
   (C) Although large hospitals tend to draw doctors trained at the more prestigious schools, no correlation has been found between the prestige of a doctor's school and patients' recovery rate.
   (D) Because space is relatively scarce in large hospitals, doctors are encouraged to minimize the length of time that patients are held for observation following a medical procedure.
   (E) Doctors at large hospitals tend to have a greater number of patients and consequently less time to explain to staff and to patients how medications are to be administered.[6]

3. When companies' profits would otherwise be reduced by an increase in the minimum wage (a wage rate set by the government as the lowest that companies are allowed to pay), the companies often reduce the number of workers they employ. Yet a recent increase in the minimum wage did not result in job cutbacks in the fast-food industry, where most workers are paid the minimum wage.

Which one of the following, if true, most helps to explain why the increase in the minimum wage did not affect the number of jobs in the fast-food industry?

(A) After the recent increase in the minimum wage, decreased job turnover in the fast-food industry allowed employers of fast-food workers to save enough on recruiting costs to cover the cost of the wage increase.

(B) If, in any industry, an increase in the minimum wage leads to the elimination of many jobs that pay the minimum wage, then higher-paying supervisory positions will also be eliminated in that industry.

(C) With respect to its response to increases in the minimum wage, the fast-food industry does not differ significantly from other industries that employ many workers at the minimum wage.

(D) A few employees in the fast-food industry were already earning more than the new, higher minimum wage before the new minimum wage was established.

(E) Sales of fast food to workers who are paid the minimum wage did not increase following the recent change in the minimum wage.[7]

[7]PrepTest 50, Sec. 2, Q 8

Explanations

1. **(E)**

Most economists believe that reducing the price of any product generally stimulates demand for it. However, most wine merchants have found that reducing the price of domestic wines to make them more competitive with imported wines with which they were previously comparably priced is frequently followed by an increase in sales of those imported wines.

Which one of the following, if true, (most helps to) (reconcile) the belief of most economists with the consequences observed by most wine merchants?

(A) Economists' studies of the prices of grocery items and their rates of sales rarely cover alcoholic beverages.

(B) Few merchants of any kind have detailed knowledge of economic theories about the relationship between item prices and sales rates.

(C) Consumers are generally willing to forgo purchasing other items they desire in order to purchase a superior wine.

(D) Imported wines in all price ranges are comparable in quality to domestic wines that cost less.

(E) An increase in the demand for a consumer product is compatible with an increase in demand for a competing product.[8]

Step 1. Identify the Question Type

Because the question asks for something that "most helps to reconcile," this is a Paradox question. The stem also directs you to the paradox: Something will not make sense between "the belief of most economists with the consequences observed by most wine merchants."

Step 2. Untangle the Stimulus

Most economists believe that reducing the price of an item increases demand. Yet, most wine sellers find that reducing the price of domestic wines increases sales of similarly priced imported wines. So what's the paradox? You'd expect domestic wine sales to rise. But the stimulus doesn't say what happened to demand for domestic wine, just that imported wine sales went up. How can sales increase for a competing imported product when the price of a domestic product decreases?

Step 3. Make a Prediction

You need to reconcile the belief of economists with the experience of wine sellers. The correct answer will explain how a price reduction of a domestic wine followed by increased demand

---

[8]PrepTest 52, Sec. 3, Q 22

for a competing imported wine remains consistent with the belief that price reductions increase demand for a product. In this case, maybe lowering the price of domestic wine increases demand for wine in general.

Step 4. Evaluate the Answer Choices

Choice (A) doesn't reconcile the wine sellers' experience with the economists' belief, but rather explains why the wine sellers' experience doesn't fit the theory. Cross this choice out.

Choice (B) is irrelevant. The merchants' knowledge of economics has no bearing on the occurrence of economic forces. Move on to the next choice.

Choice (C) explains why domestic wine sales might decrease if you assume imported items are superior to domestic. However, it doesn't explain a sales increase. This choice is out.

Choice (D) is also incorrect, because it furthers the paradox. An increase in imported wine sales doesn't make sense if domestic wines are similar in quality and less expensive.

Choice (E) is the winner by explaining that demand for a competing product, in this case imported wine, does not indicate a demand reduction for a consumer product, the domestic wine. Consequently, the wine sellers' experience is not incompatible with the economists' theory.

2. **(C)**

A recent study revealed that the percentage of people treated at large, urban hospitals who recover from their illnesses is lower than the percentage for people treated at smaller, rural hospitals.

Each of the following, if true, contributes to an explanation of the difference in recovery rates EXCEPT:

(A) Because there are fewer patients to feed, nutritionists at small hospitals are better able to tailor meals to the dietary needs of each patient.

(B) The less friendly, more impersonal atmosphere of large hospitals can be a source of stress for patients at those hospitals.

(C) Although large hospitals tend to draw doctors trained at the more prestigious schools, no correlation has been found between the prestige of a doctor's school and patients' recovery rate.

(D) Because space is relatively scarce in large hospitals, doctors are encouraged to minimize the length of time that patients are held for observation following a medical procedure.

(E) Doctors at large hospitals tend to have a greater number of patients and consequently less time to explain to staff and to patients how medications are to be administered.[9]

---

[9]PrepTest 52, Sec. 1, Q 11

Step 1. Identify the Question Type

The phrase "contributes to an explanation," indicates a Paradox question. This is an "EXCEPT" question, so be careful. The four wrong answers will resolve the paradox. The correct answer will have no effect on the paradox or will deepen the mystery.

Step 2. Untangle the Stimulus

The stimulus says that people treated at large, urban hospitals are less likely to recover from their illnesses than people treated at smaller, rural hospitals. The four wrong answer choices will explain why that might be.

Step 3. Make a Prediction

Generally, it is assumed that a bigger hospital with more resources will be better for recovery. To resolve this paradox, the four wrong answer choices will provide another factor that is good about small, rural hospitals or bad about large, urban hospitals.

Step 4. Evaluate the Answer Choices

Choice (A) discusses the ability of patients at small hospitals to get nutrition better tailored to their needs. Such individualized attention from the nutritionist could certainly explain better recovery at a small hospital. This is a positive factor about small hospitals that helps to resolve the mystery, so this choice is incorrect.

Choice (B) says that large hospitals put stress on patients which could also explain why they are less likely to recover there. This is a negative factor about large hospitals, which also helps resolve the paradox. Eliminate this choice.

Choice (C) does not address the different recovery rates between large hospital and small hospital patients, and therefore doesn't resolve the paradox. So, in this "EXCEPT" question, it is the correct answer.

Choice (D) indicates that patients in large hospitals tend to have shorter hospital stays which could certainly hurt their recovery. Again, this is a negative factor about large hospitals and helps resolve the mystery.

Choice (E) tells you that doctors at large hospitals have less time to explain to staff and patients how to best administer medication. Consequently, patients at large hospitals may not receive their medication under the best circumstances, which is another reason why patients are less likely to recover at large hospitals. This is yet another negative factor about large hospitals that helps to resolve the paradox.

3.   **(A)**

When companies' profits would otherwise be reduced by
an increase in the minimum wage (a wage rate set by the
government as the lowest that companies are allowed to
pay), the companies often reduce the number of workers
they employ. Yet a recent increase in the minimum wage
did not result in job cutbacks in the fast-food industry,
where most workers are paid the minimum wage.

Which one of the following, if true, (most helps to)
(explain) why the increase in the minimum wage did not
affect the number of jobs in the fast-food industry?

(A)   After the recent increase in the minimum wage,
      decreased job turnover in the fast-food industry
      allowed employers of fast-food workers to save
      enough on recruiting costs to cover the cost of
      the wage increase.

(B)   If, in any industry, an increase in the minimum
      wage leads to the elimination of many jobs that
      pay the minimum wage, then higher-paying
      supervisory positions will also be eliminated in
      that industry.

(C)   With respect to its response to increases in the
      minimum wage, the fast-food industry does not
      differ significantly from other industries that
      employ many workers at the minimum wage.

(D)   A few employees in the fast-food industry were
      already earning more than the new, higher
      minimum wage before the new minimum wage
      was established.

(E)   Sales of fast food to workers who are paid the
      minimum wage did not increase following the
      recent change in the minimum wage.[10]

Step 1. Identify the Question Type

The phrase "most helps to explain" is a classic Paradox indicator. The question stem also identifies the paradox in the stimulus—that an "increase in the minimum wage did not affect the
number of jobs in the fast-food industry."

Step 2. Untangle the Stimulus

Companies often cut the number of employees when an increase in minimum wage would
reduce their profits. However, a recent increase in the minimum wage did not result in employee
downsizing in the fast-food industry, an industry that employs a lot of minimum-wage workers.
As noted in the question stem, the paradox is that despite an increase in the minimum wage,
the number of jobs in the fast-food industry did not change.

---

[10]PrepTest 50, Sec. 2, Q 8

Step 3. Make a Prediction

It's not just an increase in minimum wage that results in a staff cut. It's an increase in minimum wage that reduces profits that results in a staff cut. Because the fast-food industry did not cut their staff, the minimum-wage increase must not have reduced the industry's profit. Look for an answer that provides a way for the fast-food industry to save money in spite of a minimum-wage increase.

Step 4. Evaluate the Answer Choices

Choice (A) tells you that reduced recruiting costs covered the wage increase. So, profits were not affected by the minimum-wage increase, which explains why jobs were not cut. The paradox is resolved and you have the correct answer.

Choice (B) says supervisory positions are cut when a minimum wage increase leads to a reduction of minimum wage paying jobs. This doesn't explain why the fast-food industry didn't cut any jobs at all.

Choice (C) adds to the paradox. If the fast-food industry is like other industries, you would expect it to cut jobs like those other industries.

Choice (D) discusses a few fast-food employees who earn more than the higher minimum wage. However, according to the stimulus, most fast-food workers are paid minimum wage, so you have no reason to believe that these few higher-paid workers will affect the industry's bottom line.

Choice (E) presents a situation in which sales of fast food did not increase. So, choice (E) eliminates one way to maintain profits in the face of a minimum wage increase, which is the opposite of the answer you want.

PARADOX REVIEW

Before you proceed to the next chapter, turn to Appendix A and complete the review exercise for Paradox questions. A completed chart is included in Appendix B.

CHAPTER 15

POINT AT ISSUE QUESTIONS

Point at Issue questions present a conversation between two speakers and ask you to identify the issue on which they disagree. These questions reflect the common task of law students and lawyers who read cases to identify the point at issue between the two parties. Before you can analyze a case, you must know what the parties are at odds about and what the issue is before the court.

Typically, the LSAT will include one scored Point at Issue question. While not a big point pay-off, Point at Issue questions tend to be straightforward, so practicing this question type is a relatively easy way to get a quick point on test day.

DEFINITION OF POINT AT ISSUE QUESTIONS

Point at Issue questions ask you to determine the point of disagreement between two speakers. So essentially, your job is to identify what the speakers are arguing about. In a very rare instance, you may be asked to identify the point of agreement, so be sure to read the question stem carefully.

USE THE KAPLAN METHOD TO ANSWER POINT AT ISSUE QUESTIONS

Identify the Question Type

Read the question stem first to identify the question type and note any relevant clues. Phrases that indicate a Point at Issue question include:

- Disagree over whether
- Point at issue between them is
- Disagree about which one of the following

Here's how some of those phrases could appear in a question stem:

- On the basis of their statements, Price and Albrecht are committed to disagreeing about whether
- The dialogue most strongly supports the claim that Pat and Amar disagree with each other about whether
- Antonio and Marla disagree over

Again, a Point at Issue question rarely asks what the two speakers agree on. In this case, the stem would look like:

- Their dialogue provides the most support for the claim that Denise and Reshmi agree that

Untangle the Stimulus

A Point at Issue stimulus is always presented in the form of a dialogue. Keep in mind, though, that a dialogue does not always indicate a Point at Issue question; it could be a Method of Argument question, for example. Use the wording of the question to direct you. Read each speaker's argument and briefly summarize it as you go along. As always, bracket the conclusion and identify any indicator words to help you understand the speakers' arguments.

Make a Prediction

You may be able to predict the point at issue as you read the stimulus. For example, one speaker may say something like "The key to increasing sales is good customer service." The second speaker may respond with "I disagree. Offering products that meet customer needs is the most important factor in raising sales." The speakers are telling you directly that they disagree about the key factor to raise product sales.

Evaluate the Answer Choices

If you were able to form a prediction, compare it to the answer choices and find the match. If not, find the answer that describes a point addressed by **both** speakers and about which the speakers hold conflicting views. The trick is to stay within the scope of both speakers' arguments; the point at issue can't be something that one speaker raises, but the other doesn't address at all.

Watch out for common wrong answer choices for Point at Issue questions, which include statements on which only one speaker comments or statements on which the speakers agree.

THE KAPLAN METHOD IN ACTION

Now I'll walk you through a couple examples to show you how the Kaplan Method can help you efficiently solve any Point at Issue question you'll see on test day.

1. Aaron: A prominent judge, criticizing "famous lawyers who come before courts ill-prepared to argue their cases," recently said, "This sort of cavalier attitude offends the court and can do nothing but harm to the client's cause." <I find the judge's remarks irresponsible.>

    Belinda: I find it natural and an admirable display of candor. <Letting people know of the damage their negligence causes is responsible behavior.>

    The point at issue between Aaron and Belinda is whether

    (A) ill-prepared lawyers damage their clients' causes
    (B) the judge's criticism of lawyers is irresponsible
    (C) a lawyer's being ill-prepared to argue a client's case constitutes negligence
    (D) famous lawyers have a greater responsibility to be well prepared than do lawyers who are not famous
    (E) it is to be expected that ill-prepared lawyers would offend the court in which they appear[1]

Step 1. Identify the Question Type

The phrase "the point at issue" tells you directly that this is a Point at Issue question.

Step 2. Untangle the Stimulus

Aaron calls a judge's criticism of famous, ill-prepared lawyers "irresponsible." Belinda supports the judge's remarks and calls them "responsible."

Step 3. Make a Prediction

The speakers disagree over whether the judge's disapproval of certain lawyers was responsible or not.

---

[1]PrepTest 47, Sec. 1, Q 4

Step 4. Evaluate the Answer Choices

Choice (A) gets Belinda's support. She indicates that negligent lawyers damage their clients, which is her reason for concluding the judge was responsible. Aaron, however, directs his opinion to the judge who commented on ill-prepared lawyers without revealing his own opinion about ill-prepared lawyers damaging their clients' cases. Move on to the next choice.

Choice (B) matches the prediction exactly. Both speakers address the judge's criticism of lawyers and disagree on whether the action is irresponsible. This is the correct answer.

Choice (C) might get Belinda's support but Aaron does not discuss whether being unprepared for a client's case constitutes negligence.

Choice (D) gets no attention from either speaker. The level of responsibility owed to clients by famous versus little-known attorneys is outside the scope.

Choice (E) may get Belinda's agreement, but Aaron does not give any indication of whether ill-prepared lawyers would offend the court in which they appear.

2. Mark: To convey an understanding of past events, <a historian should try to capture what it was like to experience those events.> For instance, a foot soldier in the Battle of Waterloo knew through direct experience what the battle was like, and it is this kind of knowledge that the historian must capture.

    Carla: But how do you go about choosing whose perspective is the valid one? Is the foot soldier's perspective more valid than that of a general? Should it be a French or an English soldier? Your approach would generate a biased version of history, and to avoid that, <historians must stick to general and objective characterizations of the past.>

    Mark's and Carla's positions indicate that they disagree about the truth of which one of the following?

    (A) The purpose of writing history is to convey an understanding of past events.
    (B) The participants in a battle are capable of having an objective understanding of the ramifications of the events in which they are participating.
    (C) Historians can succeed in conveying a sense of the way events in the distant past seemed to someone who lived in a past time.
    (D) Historians should aim to convey past events from the perspective of participants in those events.
    (E) Historians should use fictional episodes to supplement their accounts of past events if the documented record of those events is incomplete.[2]

---

[2]PrepTest 37, Sec. 2, Q 11

Step 1. Identify the Question Type

This stem asks for what Mark and Carla "disagree about" so it's a Point at Issue question.

Step 2. Untangle the Stimulus

Mark concludes that historians should convey history through the perspective of those who lived it. Carla voices her concern that such an approach would result in a biased version of history and concludes that historians should present history through a general and objective perspective.

Step 3. Make a Prediction

Mark and Carla's conclusions tell you they are talking about how best to present history. Mark supports a personalized viewpoint, while Carla endorses a more general approach.

Step 4. Evaluate the Answer Choices

Choice (A) presents a point of agreement for Mark and Carla, so this choice is out.

Choice (B) is about whether participants can have an objective understanding of the events they live through. This is not discussed by either speaker. Mark offers a participant in battle as an example of someone who could best convey history through personal experience. While you may infer that Mark considers the participant's account to be subjective, he doesn't directly address whether the participant can be objective. Carla raises the difficulty of deciding whose perspective is the most appropriate to use in conveying history and the bias of whoever is chosen. She wants history to be presented objectively, but does not address who can be objective.

Choice (C) says that it's possible for historians to convey history through someone who lived it. While this may be a tempting answer choice, the speakers don't address this possibility; their arguments are focused on whether it's a good idea to take that approach. Eliminate this choice.

Choice (D) identifies the point at issue: Mark thinks historians should convey past events from the participants' perspectives, while Carla disagrees because the approach would generate a biased version of history. This is the correct answer.

Choice (E) is outside the scope. Neither speaker addresses the possibility of using fictional episodes to supplement incomplete historical accounts.

POINT AT ISSUE QUESTIONS: NOW YOU TRY IT

It's now your turn to try a Point at Issue question on your own. Use the template I've provided after the question to guide you through the four-step Kaplan Method. (Note: On test day, you won't be writing out all the steps as you are in this exercise. However, as you are learning the Method, it's good practice to help it become second nature.) Remember to bracket conclusions and circle Keywords.

1. Davis: The only relevant factor in determining appropriate compensation for property damage or theft is the value the property loses due to damage or the value of the property stolen; the harm to the victim is directly proportional to the pertinent value.

    Higuchi: I disagree. More than one factor must be considered: A victim who recovers the use of personal property after two years is owed more than a victim who recovers its use after only one year.

    Davis's and Higuchi's statements most strongly support the view that they would disagree with each other about which one of the following?

    (A) It is possible to consistently and reliably determine the amount of compensation owed to someone whose property was damaged or stolen.
    (B) Some victims are owed increased compensation because of the greater dollar value of the damage done to their property.
    (C) Victims who are deprived of their property are owed compensation in proportion to the harm they have suffered.
    (D) Some victims are owed increased compensation because of the greater amount of time they are deprived of the use of their property.
    (E) The compensation owed to victims should be determined on a case-by-case basis rather than by some general rule.[3]

---

[3]PrepTest 43, Sec. 2, Q 13

Step 1. Identify the Question Type

_____

Step 2. Untangle the Stimulus

_____

Step 3. Make a Prediction

_____

Step 4. Evaluate the Answer Choices

_____

Explanations

1. **(D)**

Davis: <The only relevant factor in determining appropriate compensation for property damage or theft is the value the property loses due to damage or the value of the property stolen;> the harm to the victim is directly proportional to the pertinent value.

Higuchi: <I disagree. More than one factor must be considered:> A victim who recovers the use of personal property after two years is owed more than a victim who recovers its use after only one year.

Davis's and Higuchi's statements most strongly support the view that they would (disagree with each other) about which one of the following?

(A)   It is possible to consistently and reliably determine the amount of compensation owed to someone whose property was damaged or stolen.

(B)   Some victims are owed increased compensation because of the greater dollar value of the damage done to their property.

(C)   Victims who are deprived of their property are owed compensation in proportion to the harm they have suffered.

(D)   Some victims are owed increased compensation because of the greater amount of time they are deprived of the use of their property.

(E)   The compensation owed to victims should be determined on a case-by-case basis rather than by some general rule.[4]

Step 1. Identify the Question Type

The phrase "disagree with each other" tells you directly this is a Point at Issue question.

Step 2. Untangle the Stimulus

When it comes to assessing compensation for property damage or theft, Davis argues there is only one factor to consider: the property value lost due to damage or the value of the property stolen. Higuchi argues for more than one factor, such as the length of time the victim is left without his property.

Step 3. Make a Prediction

The speakers are talking about how to determine compensation for property damage or theft. Davis identifies one factor to consider and Higuchi thinks more than one factor must be considered.

---

[4]PrepTest 43, Sec. 2, Q 13

Step 4. Evaluate the Answer Choices

Choice (A) is outside the scope. Neither speaker addresses the possibility of a consistent and reliable determination of compensation. Eliminate this choice.

Choice (B) reflects Davis's view, but Higuchi doesn't voice an opinion on this specific consideration for compensation. You just know that she thinks more than one factor must be considered. So, this choice is out.

Choice (C) has the same problem as choice (B): It echoes Davis's viewpoint, but Higuchi doesn't address it. Move on to the next choice.

Choice (D) is the correct answer. Davis limits determination of compensation to one factor, the value of the property lost. Higuchi says consider other factors and gives one such factor, the length of time the victim is deprived of the property.

Choice (E) presents a point of agreement, not disagreement, between Davis and Higuchi. Rather than specify one rule, both speakers identify a factor or factors to consider for compensation. Thus, they both imply that determination must be made on a case-by-case basis.

DRILL: PRACTICING POINT AT ISSUE QUESTIONS

Use the Kaplan Method to answer the following Point at Issue questions. Take this opportunity to practice and apply the steps in the Method so you are comfortable using them on test day. Be sure to circle conclusion and evidence Keywords and bracket the conclusion. Check your responses against the full explanations provided after the Drill.

1. Constance: The traditional definition of full employment as a 5 percent unemployment rate is correct, because at levels below 5 percent, inflation rises.

    Brigita: That traditional definition of full employment was developed before the rise of temporary and part-time work and the fall in benefit levels. When people are juggling several part-time jobs with no benefits, or working in a series of temporary assignments, as is now the case, 5 percent unemployment is not full employment.

    The dialogue most strongly supports the claim that Constance and Brigita disagree with each other about which one of the following?

    (A) what definition of full employment is applicable under contemporary economic conditions

    (B) whether it is a good idea, all things considered, to allow the unemployment level to drop below 5 percent

    (C) whether a person with a part-time job should count as fully employed

    (D) whether the number of part-time and temporary workers has increased since the traditional definition of full employment was developed

    (E) whether unemployment levels above 5 percent can cause inflation levels to rise[5]

2. Samuel: Because communication via computer is usually conducted privately and anonymously between people who would otherwise interact in person, it contributes to the dissolution, not the creation, of lasting communal bonds.

    Tova: You assume that communication via computer replaces more intimate forms of communication and interaction, when more often it replaces asocial or even antisocial behavior.

    On the basis of their statements, Samuel and Tova are committed to disagreeing about which one of the following?

    (A) A general trend of modern life is to dissolve the social bonds that formerly connected people.

    (B) All purely private behavior contributes to the dissolution of social bonds.

    (C) Face-to-face communication is more likely to contribute to the creation of social bonds than is anonymous communication.

    (D) It is desirable that new social bonds be created to replace the ones that have dissolved.

    (E) If people were not communicating via computer, they would most likely be engaged in activities that create stronger social bonds.[6]

3. Antonio: One can live a life of moderation by never deviating from the middle course. But then one loses the joy of spontaneity and misses the opportunities that come to those who are occasionally willing to take great chances, or to go too far.

Marla: But one who, in the interests of moderation, never risks going too far is actually failing to live a life of moderation: one must be moderate even in one's moderation.

Antonio and Marla disagree over

(A) whether it is desirable for people occasionally to take great chances in life

(B) what a life of moderation requires of a person

(C) whether it is possible for a person to embrace other virtues along with moderation

(D) how often a person ought to deviate from the middle course in life

(E) whether it is desirable for people to be moderately spontaneous[7]

---

[7]PrepTest June 2007, Sec. 3, Q 7

Explanations

1.   **(A)**

Constance: <The traditional definition of full employment as a 5 percent unemployment rate is correct,> (because) at levels below 5 percent, inflation rises.

Brigita: That traditional definition of full employment was developed before the rise of temporary and part-time work and the fall in benefit levels. When people are juggling several part-time jobs with no benefits, or working in a series of temporary assignments, as is now the case, <5 percent unemployment is not full employment.>

The dialogue most strongly supports the claim that Constance and Brigita (disagree with each other about) which one of the following?

(A)   what definition of full employment is applicable under contemporary economic conditions
(B)   whether it is a good idea, all things considered, to allow the unemployment level to drop below 5 percent
(C)   whether a person with a part-time job should count as fully employed
(D)   whether the number of part-time and temporary workers has increased since the traditional definition of full employment was developed
(E)   whether unemployment levels above 5 percent can cause inflation levels to rise[8]

Step 1. Identify the Question Type

The phrase "disagree with each other about" tells you this is a Point at Issue question.

Step 2. Untangle the Stimulus

Constance concludes that the traditional definition of full employment (5 percent unemployment rate) is correct. Brigita disagrees and argues the traditional definition is not correct because it doesn't consider additional factors.

Step 3. Make a Prediction

Constance and Brigita disagree over the definition of full employment.

Step 4. Evaluate the Answer Choices

Choice (A) is a match, and is the correct answer. Both speakers address the definition of full employment and disagree about whether to apply contemporary economic conditions.

---

[8]PrepTest 51, Sec. 1, Q 23

Choice (B) is outside the scope. Neither speaker discusses the consequences of allowing the unemployment level to drop below 5 percent or whether it's a good idea.

Choice (C) presents information addressed by Brigita but never discussed by Constance.

Choice (D) is wrong for the same reason as choice (D).

Choice (E) is wrong because neither speaker talks about what happens above 5 percent unemployment.

2. **(E)**

Samuel: (Because) communication via computer is usually conducted privately and anonymously between people who would otherwise interact in person, <it contributes to the dissolution, not the creation, of lasting communal bonds.>

Tova: You assume that communication via computer replaces more intimate forms of communication and interaction, when <more often it replaces asocial or even antisocial behavior.>

On the basis of their statements, Samuel and Tova are (committed to disagreeing about) which one of the following?

(A) A general trend of modern life is to dissolve the social bonds that formerly connected people.
(B) All purely private behavior contributes to the dissolution of social bonds.
(C) Face-to-face communication is more likely to contribute to the creation of social bonds than is anonymous communication.
(D) It is desirable that new social bonds be created to replace the ones that have dissolved.
(E) If people were not communicating via computer, they would most likely be engaged in activities that create stronger social bonds.[9]

Step 1. Identify the Question Type

The question stem asks for what Samuel and Tova are "committed to disagreeing about," so this is a Point at Issue question.

Step 2. Untangle the Stimulus

Samuel argues that communication by computer helps dissolve, rather than develop, lasting communal bonds. He bases his conclusion on the evidence that the private, anonymous communication takes the place of in-person interaction. Tova claims that communication via computer replaces asocial or even antisocial behavior.

[9]PrepTest 52, Sec. 3, Q 10

Step 3. Make a Prediction

Both speakers discuss the impact of communication by computer on interpersonal relationships. Samuel says that form of communication is destructive to positive relations while Tova says it replaces negative relations.

Step 4. Evaluate the Answer Choices

Choice (A) discusses a general trend of modern life, something neither speaker addresses. Actually, they talk about one phenomenon, communication via computer. So, you can cross this choice out.

Choice (B) is too extreme. The speakers talk about one type of behavior, not all private behavior. This choice is also out.

Choice (C) is something Samuel agrees with, but it's hard to get an exact read on Tova's thinking on it. If anything, she might agree with choice (C) based on her "more intimate forms of communication" statement that implies in-person communication provides better bonding opportunities. You can eliminate this choice.

Choice (D) is incorrect for two reasons. Neither speaker discusses the creation of new bonds nor do they talk about the desirability of one condition over another.

Choice (E) is weighed in on by both speakers and their positions conflict. Samuel thinks computer interaction keeps people from other interaction that develops bonds. Tova thinks it replaces nonbonding interaction. Choice (E) is the correct answer.

3. **(B)**

Antonio: <One can live a life of moderation by never deviating from the middle course.> But then one loses the joy of spontaneity and misses the opportunities that come to those who are occasionally willing to take great chances, or to go too far.

Marla: But one who, in the interests of moderation, never risks going too far is actually failing to live a life of moderation: <one must be moderate even in one's moderation.>

Antonio and Marla (disagree over)

(A) whether it is desirable for people occasionally to take great chances in life
(B) what a life of moderation requires of a person
(C) whether it is possible for a person to embrace other virtues along with moderation
(D) how often a person ought to deviate from the middle course in life
(E) whether it is desirable for people to be moderately spontaneous[10]

[10]PrepTest June 2007, Sec. 3, Q 7

Step 1. Identify the Question Type

The phrase "disagree over" is a common Point at Issue indicator.

Step 2. Untangle the Stimulus

Antonio defines a life of moderation as "never deviating from the middle course." Marla says never taking risks is really not a life of moderation.

Step 3. Make a Prediction

Antonio and Marla disagree about the nature of a life of moderation.

Step 4. Evaluate the Answer Choices

Choice (A) is discussed by Antonio when he says people miss the joy of spontaneity when they don't take chances. But Marla limits her discussion to the definition of a moderate life and takes no position on desirability. So, cross this choice out.

Choice (B) is the correct answer. Both speakers define a life of moderation, but they differ on its meaning.

Choice (C) is outside the scope of both speakers. Neither one mentions embracing other virtues.

Choice (D) presents the same problem. Neither speaker talks about how often a person should deviate from the middle of the road.

Choice (E) adds a new topic to the speakers' conversation. Neither speaker brings up moderate spontaneity, so they can't take a position on its desirability.

POINT AT ISSUE REVIEW

Before you proceed to the next chapter, turn to Appendix A and complete the review exercise for Point at Issue questions. A completed chart is included in Appendix B.

CHAPTER 16

ROLE OF A STATEMENT QUESTIONS

Role of a Statement questions ask you to identify the function served by a specific assertion in a stimulus. This question type is yet another way in which the LSAT tests your ability to analyze an argument and identify its parts.

You will see about two scored Role of a Statement questions on an LSAT. Take advantage of the straightforward nature of these questions and earn these points quickly and confidently.

DEFINITION OF ROLE OF A STATEMENT QUESTIONS

Role of a Statement question stems include a statement from the stimulus (usually verbatim) and ask you to determine the role it plays in the argument.

USE THE KAPLAN METHOD TO ANSWER ROLE OF A STATEMENT QUESTIONS

Identify the Question Type

Read the question stem first to identify the question type and note any relevant clues. You can identify a Role of a Statement question from words and phrases like:

- Plays which one of the following roles
- Figures in the argument
- Plays which part

Here's how some of those phrases could appear in a question stem:

- Which one of the following most accurately expresses the role played in the argument by the observation that attending a live musical performance is a richer experience than is listening to recorded music?
- The statement that human food-producing capacity has increased more rapidly than human population plays which one of the following roles in the argument?
- The statement that the educational use of computers enables schools to teach far more courses with far fewer teachers figures in the argument in which one of the following ways?

Untangle the Stimulus

To untangle the stimulus of a Role of a Statement question, you need to find the phrase that appears in both the question stem and the stimulus, and then determine the role it plays in the argument. (I also recommend that you underline the statement so you can quickly refer to it if you need to.) Then, locate the components of the argument: Find and bracket the conclusion, and then find and summarize the evidence.

Make a Prediction

Your prediction is the part of the argument in which you locate the statement in question. Additionally, think about what the author is trying to do with the statement (e.g., support a particular claim, rebut a certain hypothesis, or reach a specific conclusion). This consideration is also helpful if you can't classify the repeated statement as part of the arguments' conclusion or as part of the evidence

Evaluate the Answer Choices

Determine an answer that matches your prediction. Remember, the answer may not be as explicit as "conclusion" or "evidence." Instead, it may be presented as a definition of those terms.

THE KAPLAN METHOD IN ACTION

Now I'll walk you through an example to show you how the Kaplan Method can help you efficiently solve any Role of a Statement question you'll see on test day.

1. Teacher: Participating in organized competitive athletics may increase a child's strength and coordination. As critics point out, however, it also instills in those children who are not already well developed in these respects a feeling of inferiority that never really disappears. Yet, since research has shown that adults with feelings of inferiority become more successful than those free of such anxieties, funding for children's athletic programs should not be eliminated.

   Which one of the following most accurately describes the role played in the teacher's argument by the assertion that participating in organized competitive athletics may increase a child's strength and coordination?

   (A) It is mentioned as one possible reason for adopting a policy for which the teacher suggests an additional reason.
   (B) It is a claim that the teacher attempts to refute with counterarguments.
   (C) It is a hypothesis for which the teacher offers additional evidence.
   (D) It is cited as an insufficient reason for eliminating funding for children's athletic programs.
   (E) It is cited as an objection that has been raised to the position that the teacher is supporting.[1]

Step 1. Identify the Question Type

The question asks you to describe the "role played" by an assertion made in the teacher's argument. This is standard language for a Role of a Statement question. The statement, the role of which you must identify, is, "participating in organized competitive athletics may increase a child's strength and coordination." Underline this statement in the question stem (you will also underline it in the stimulus in the next step).

Step 2. Untangle the Stimulus

Read the stimulus and look for the conclusion, evidence, and the specific assertion in the question. The statement you underlined in the question stem—in which the teacher asserts a benefit of organized athletics—appears right away in the first sentence. Underline it. Then, note that the teacher also points to a criticism of organized athletics, but rebuts it providing an additional benefit. The teacher then concludes with a recommendation to keep funding for children's athletics.

---

[1]PrepTest 42, Sec. 4, Q 3

Step 3. Make a Prediction

The assertion is one piece of evidence provided to support the teacher's recommendation.

Step 4. Evaluate the Answer Choices

Choice (A) matches the prediction and is the correct answer. The assertion is one of two reasons the teacher mentions for the recommendation.

Choice (B) is wrong because the teacher doesn't attack the notion that organized athletics makes children stronger and more coordinated. In fact, she provides it in support of her conclusion.

Choice (C) is wrong. It suggests that the teacher returns to the assertion to offer additional evidence for it as if it was the conclusion; however, the teacher never goes back to the assertion. She adds another piece of evidence in support of the conclusion in the final sentence.

Choice (D) is also wrong. The assertion is presented as a sufficient reason to continue funding for children's athletics.

Choice (E) is wrong as well. The critics' objection is in the second sentence. The assertion is offered in support of the teacher's position.

ROLE OF A STATEMENT QUESTIONS: NOW YOU TRY IT

It's now your turn to try a Role of a Statement question on your own. Use the template I've provided after the question to guide you through the four-step Kaplan Method. (Note: On test day, you won't be writing out all the steps as you are in this exercise. However, as you are learning the Method, it's good practice to help it become second nature.) Remember to bracket conclusions and circle Keywords.

1. It would not be surprising to discover that the trade routes between China and the West were opened many centuries, even millennia, earlier than 200 B.C., contrary to what is currently believed. After all, what made the Great Silk Road so attractive as a trade route linking China and the West—level terrain, easily traversable mountain passes, and desert oases—would also have made it an attractive route for the original emigrants to China from Africa and the Middle East, and this early migration began at least one million years ago.

    That a migration from Africa and the Middle East to China occurred at least one million years ago figures in the above reasoning in which one of the following ways?

    (A) It is cited as conclusive evidence for the claim that trade links between China and the Middle East were established long before 200 B.C.

    (B) It is an intermediate conclusion made plausible by the description of the terrain along which the migration supposedly took place.

    (C) It is offered as evidence in support of the claim that trade routes between China and the West could easily have been established much earlier than is currently believed.

    (D) It is offered as evidence against the claim that trade routes between China and Africa preceded those eventually established between China and the Middle East.

    (E) It is the main conclusion that the argument attempts to establish about intercourse between China and the West.[2]

---

[2]PrepTest 51, Sec. 1, Q 14

Step 1. Identify the Question Type

_____

Step 2. Untangle the Stimulus

_____

Step 3. Make a Prediction

_____

Step 4. Evaluate the Answer Choices

_____

Explanations

1. (C)

<It would not be surprising to discover that the trade routes between China and the West were opened many centuries, even millennia, earlier than 200 B.C., contrary to what is currently believed.> (After all) what made the Great Silk Road so attractive as a trade route linking China and the West—level terrain, easily traversable mountain passes, and desert oases—would also have made it an attractive route for the original emigrants to China from Africa and the Middle East, and this early migration began at least one million years ago.

That a migration from Africa and the Middle East to China occurred at least one million years ago figures in the above reasoning in which one of the following ways?

(A) It is cited as conclusive evidence for the claim that trade links between China and the Middle East were established long before 200 B.C.

(B) It is an intermediate conclusion made plausible by the description of the terrain along which the migration supposedly took place.

(C) It is offered as evidence in support of the claim that trade routes between China and the West could easily have been established much earlier than is currently believed.

(D) It is offered as evidence against the claim that trade routes between China and Africa preceded those eventually established between China and the Middle East.

(E) It is the main conclusion that the argument attempts to establish about intercourse between China and the West.[3]

Step 1. Identify the Question Type

This stem includes a statement taken from the stimulus along with the phrase "figures in the above reasoning," which indicates that this a Role of the Statement question.

Step 2. Untangle the Stimulus

The conclusion—that it would not be a surprise to learn that trade routes between China and the West were much older than currently believed—appears in the first sentence in the form of the author's opinion. The words "After all" point to the evidence that backs up her thinking, which states that the trade route is probably much older because the features that made it an attractive trade route would have also been attractive to emigrants from a much earlier time period.

---

[3]PrepTest 51, Sec. 1, Q 14

Step 3. Make a Prediction

The information in question is the evidence in the last sentence of the argument, which provides support for the conclusion that the China-West trade route opened earlier than is currently believed.

Step 4. Evaluate the Answer Choices

Choice (A) is extreme. The author does not present the information as conclusive evidence but rather as a possibility in support of an alternative theory. Eliminate this choice.

Choice (B) is wrong. The information is not an intermediary conclusion, it's part of the evidence.

Choice (C) is the correct answer. It is evidence that supports the possibility that trade routes between China and the West were in place much earlier than is now thought. Notice that to identify choice (C) as the correct answer, you needed to identify the statement as a piece of evidence and also to be clear as to the conclusion it supported. Often, every answer choice will correctly identify the statement as a piece of evidence, and you will need to select the one that correctly describes the conclusion it supports.

Choice (D) has it backward. The information in question is evidence, but it is offered in support of the author's conclusion, not against it.

Choice (E) misidentifies the statement in question. The statement is evidence located at the end of the stimulus, not the conclusion, which is in the first sentence.

DRILL: PRACTICING ROLE OF A STATEMENT QUESTIONS

Use the Kaplan Method to answer the following Role of a Statement questions. Take this opportunity to practice and apply the steps in the Method so you are comfortable using them on test day. Be sure to circle conclusion and evidence Keywords, bracket the conclusion, and underline the statement. Check your responses against the full explanations provided after the Drill.

1. When a major record label signs a contract with a band, the label assumes considerable financial risk. It pays for videos, album art, management, and promotions. Hence, the band does not need to assume nearly as much risk as it would if it produced its own records independently. For this reason, it is only fair for a major label to take a large portion of the profits from the record sales of any band signed with it.

   Which one of the following most accurately describes the role played in the argument by the claim that a band signed with a major label does not need to assume nearly as much risk as it would if it produced its own records independently?

   (A) It is the only conclusion that the argument attempts to establish.

   (B) It is one of two unrelated conclusions, each of which the same premises are used to support.

   (C) It is a general principle from which the argument's conclusion follows as a specific instance.

   (D) It describes a phenomenon for which the rest of the argument offers an explanation.

   (E) Premises are used to support it, and it is used to support the main conclusion.[4]

2. It is primarily by raising interest rates that central bankers curb inflation, but an increase in interest rates takes up to two years to affect inflation. Accordingly, central bankers usually try to raise interest rates before inflation becomes excessive, at which time inflation is not yet readily apparent either. But unless inflation is readily apparent, interest rate hikes generally will be perceived as needlessly restraining a growing economy. Thus, central bankers' success in temporarily restraining inflation may make it harder for them to ward off future inflation without incurring the public's wrath.

   Which one of the following most accurately describes the role played in the argument by the claim that it is primarily by raising interest rates that central bankers curb inflation?

   (A) It is presented as a complete explanation of the fact that central bankers' success in temporarily restraining inflation may make it harder for them to ward off future inflation without incurring the public's wrath.

   (B) It is a description of a phenomenon for which the claim that an increase in interest rates takes up to two years to affect inflation is offered as an explanation.

   (C) It is a premise offered in support of the conclusion that central bankers' success in temporarily restraining inflation may make it harder for them to ward off future inflation without incurring the public's wrath.

   (D) It is a conclusion for which the statement that an increase in interest rates takes up to two years to affect inflation is offered as support.

   (E) It is a premise offered in support of the conclusion that unless inflation is readily apparent, interest rate hikes generally will be perceived as needlessly restraining a growing economy.[5]

3. Philosopher: Graham argues that since a person is truly
    happy only when doing something, the best life is
    a life that is full of activity. But we should not be
    persuaded by Graham's argument. People sleep,
    and at least sometimes when sleeping, they are
    truly happy, even though they are not doing
    anything.

    Which one of the following most accurately describes
    the role played in the philosopher's argument by the
    claim that at least sometimes when sleeping, people are
    truly happy, even though they are not doing anything?

    (A) It is a premise of Graham's argument.
    (B) It is an example intended to show that a premise
         of Graham's argument is false.
    (C) It is an analogy appealed to by Graham but that
         the philosopher rejects.
    (D) It is an example intended to disprove the
         conclusion of Graham's argument.
    (E) It is the main conclusion of the philosopher's
         argument.[6]

---

[6]PrepTest 52, Sec. 3, Q 17

Explanations

1. **(E)**

When a major record label signs a contract with a band, the label assumes considerable financial risk. It pays for videos, album art, management, and promotions. (Hence,) the band does not need to assume nearly as much risk as it would if it produced its own records independently. <(For this reason,) it is only fair for a major label to take a large portion of the profits from the record sales of any band signed with it.>

Which one of the following most accurately describes the (role played) in the argument by the claim that a band signed with a major label does not need to assume nearly as much risk as it would if it produced its own records independently?

(A) It is the only conclusion that the argument attempts to establish.

(B) It is one of two unrelated conclusions, each of which the same premises are used to support.

(C) It is a general principle from which the argument's conclusion follows as a specific instance.

(D) It describes a phenomenon for which the rest of the argument offers an explanation.

(E) Premises are used to support it, and it is used to support the main conclusion.[7]

Step 1. Identify the Question Type

The question mentions a claim from the argument and asks what role it played, which indicates a Role of a Statement question.

Step 2. Untangle the Stimulus

At first glance, the claim in the question stem—that bands signed by major record labels don't assume as much risk as they would by producing their own records independently—appears to be the conclusion of the argument because it follows the word "hence." If you stopped your analysis here and went right to the answer choices, you would lose a point. While the claim is a conclusion, it is not the primary conclusion of the argument.

The stimulus begins with evidence that the record label assumes great risk when it signs a band and therefore a band need not assume as much risk. The words "For this reason" indicate the conclusion—that the record labels are justified in taking a big portion of the proceeds.

Step 3. Make a Prediction

The claim identified in the question stem is a subsidiary conclusion that serves as evidence and supports the main conclusion.

---

[7]PrepTest 51, Sec. 3, Q 11

Step 4. Evaluate the Answer Choices

Choice (A) is wrong. The claim is not the only conclusion in the argument.

Choice (B) is also wrong. The claim is related to the other conclusion and, in fact, supports it.

Choice (C) is wrong for two reasons: The claim is not a general principle, and the conclusion is not a specific example of the claim.

Choice (D) suggests that the claim is the primary conclusion and the rest of the argument is evidence in support of it, which is not the case. This choice is also wrong.

Choice (E) is the correct answer. Evidence supports the claim as a subsidiary conclusion and it provides support for the primary conclusion.

2. **(C)**

It is primarily by raising interest rates that central bankers curb inflation, but an increase in interest rates takes up to two years to affect inflation. Accordingly, central bankers usually try to raise interest rates before inflation becomes excessive, at which time inflation is not yet readily apparent either. But unless inflation is readily apparent, interest rate hikes generally will be perceived as needlessly restraining a growing economy. ⟨Thus,⟩ central bankers' success in temporarily restraining inflation may make it harder for them to ward off future inflation without incurring the public's wrath.⟩

Which one of the following most accurately describes the (role played) in the argument by the claim that it is primarily by raising interest rates that central bankers curb inflation?

(A) It is presented as a complete explanation of the fact that central bankers' success in temporarily restraining inflation may make it harder for them to ward off future inflation without incurring the public's wrath.
(B) It is a description of a phenomenon for which the claim that an increase in interest rates takes up to two years to affect inflation is offered as an explanation.
(C) It is a premise offered in support of the conclusion that central bankers' success in temporarily restraining inflation may make it harder for them to ward off future inflation without incurring the public's wrath.
(D) It is a conclusion for which the statement that an increase in interest rates takes up to two years to affect inflation is offered as support.
(E) It is a premise offered in support of the conclusion that unless inflation is readily apparent, interest rate hikes generally will be perceived as needlessly restraining a growing economy.[8]

Step 1. Identify the Question Type

The question asks for the role played by a claim in the stimulus, signaling a Role of a Statement question.

Step 2. Untangle the Stimulus

The stimulus starts with the claim identified in the question stem that explains raising interest rates is the primary tool central bankers use to curb inflation. It continues with a discussion of

---

[8]PrepTest 49, Sec. 2, Q 12

the impact of its implementation. The stimulus ends with the argument's conclusion identified by "Thus." Restraining inflation in the short term makes it harder to ward off in the long run.

Step 3. Make a Prediction

The claim is part of the chain of evidence that results in the conclusion.

Step 4. Evaluate the Answer Choices

Choice (A) is too extreme in calling the initial clause a complete explanation when it is just an introduction of the mechanism used by bankers to curb inflation. It does not address the other issues of short-term versus long-term success or the public's reaction.

Choice (B) is wrong; the "But" says the phenomenon and the claim contrast each other, not support each other.

Choice (C) correctly identifies the initial claim as supporting evidence for the conclusion regarding the short-term versus long-term impact of curbing inflation.

Choice (D) misidentifies the claim as a conclusion supported by the second clause in the sentence. Just as in choice (B), the contrast word "But" puts the two clauses in opposition to each other.

Choice (E) incorrectly identifies the third sentence as the conclusion.

3. **(B)**

Philosopher: Graham argues that (since) a person is truly happy only when doing something, the best life is a life that is full of activity. <(But) we should not be persuaded by Graham's argument.> People sleep, and <u>at least sometimes when sleeping, they are truly happy, even though they are not doing anything</u>.

Which one of the following most accurately describes the (role played) in the philosopher's argument by the claim that <u>at least sometimes when sleeping, people are truly happy, even though they are not doing anything</u>?

(A) It is a premise of Graham's argument.
(B) It is an example intended to show that a premise of Graham's argument is false.
(C) It is an analogy appealed to by Graham but that the philosopher rejects.
(D) It is an example intended to disprove the conclusion of Graham's argument.
(E) It is the main conclusion of the philosopher's argument.[9]

---

[9]PrepTest 52, Sec. 3, Q 17

Step 1. Identify the Question Type

The phrase "role played," along with a claim from the stimulus, both indicate a Role of a Statement question. Note that you are looking for the role of the claim in the philosopher's argument, an important point because the stimulus presents two arguments: one from the philosopher and one from Graham.

Step 2. Untangle the Stimulus

The philosopher starts with Graham's argument that the best life is one full of activity because people are only happy when they do something. He follows it with "But," which signals that he is about to disagree. The philosopher concludes you shouldn't be swayed by Graham's assertion because people can be happy when they're sleeping and not doing anything. This evidence is the claim referred to in the question stem.

Step 3. Make a Prediction

The philosopher's evidence obviously supports his conclusion, but it also rebuts Graham's evidence.

Step 4. Evaluate the Answer Choices

Choice (A) credits the evidence to the wrong person. This choice is out.

Choice (B) correctly identifies the evidence as an example intended to attack Graham's evidence. This is the correct answer.

Choice (C) incorrectly identifies the evidence as an analogy and attributes it to the wrong person.

Choice (D) is directed at the wrong part of Graham's argument.

Choice (E) mislabels the philosopher's evidence as his conclusion.

ROLE OF A STATEMENT REVIEW

Before you proceed to the next chapter, turn to Appendix A and complete the review exercise for Role of a Statement questions. A completed chart is included in Appendix B.

CHAPTER 17

Main Point Questions

Of all the question types on the LSAT, Main Point questions will probably seem the most familiar to you. They are exactly what they sound like: They ask you to find the central claim in the argument. You will see about two scored Main Point questions on test day. Go after them.

DEFINITION OF MAIN POINT QUESTIONS

Simply enough, Main Point questions ask you to identify the conclusion of the the author's argument.

USE THE KAPLAN METHOD TO ANSWER MAIN POINT QUESTIONS

Identify the Question Type

Read the question stem first to identify the question type and note any relevant clues. You can identify a Main Point question from words and phrases like:

- Conclusion
- Main idea
- Main point

Here's how some of those phrases could appear in a question stem:

- Which one of the following most accurately expresses the main conclusion drawn in the above argument?
- The main point of the argument is

Untangle the Stimulus

All stimuli for Main Point questions present an argument. Your task is to identify the conclusion, so read the argument to break it down to it components: the evidence and the conclusion.

Main Point questions rarely include clear conclusion indicator words, making it a bit more difficult to find the conclusion. However, the test makers will often still give you evidence keywords, and identifying the evidence will help you to identify the conclusion it supports.

There are other ways you can find the conclusion. One way is to look for a disagreement in the stimulus; LSAT arguments often present a claim by one person or group followed by the author's conclusion that refutes the other view. So, if you find the author refuting a claim, there's a good chance that it's part of the conclusion.

You can also try using the "one-sentence test." Eliminate all extra information and keep the one sentence the author would need to keep to express her point. Hone in on emphatic statements and remember the conclusion types you learned about in the chapter on Parallel Reasoning questions. Recommendations, value judgments, and predictions will trump mundane assertions of fact and generally point to the author's big idea.

Another tool to find the conclusion is to determine whether the statement answers the question "why," making it evidence, or if the statement is supported by other information that answers the question "why," making it the conclusion.

Make a Prediction

Paraphrase the main idea without getting bogged down in the details of the argument. Remember, the author's conclusion is the part of the stimuli that you bracket, as you have now done for dozens of arguments; the conclusion is NOT a summary of everything going on in the argument.

Evaluate the Answer Choices

Find the answer choice that matches your summary of the author's conclusion.

THE KAPLAN METHOD IN ACTION

Now I'll walk you through an example to show you how the Kaplan Method can help you efficiently solve any Main Point question you'll see on test day.

1. Industrial engineer: Some people have suggested that the problem of global warming should be addressed by pumping some of the carbon dioxide produced by the burning of fossil fuels into the deep ocean. Many environmentalists worry that this strategy would simply exchange one form of pollution for an equally destructive form. This worry is unfounded, however; much of the carbon dioxide now released into the atmosphere eventually ends up in the ocean anyway, where it does not cause environmental disturbances as destructive as global warming.

    Which one of the following most accurately expresses the conclusion of the industrial engineer's argument as a whole?

    (A) Global warming from the emission of carbon dioxide into the atmosphere could be reduced by pumping some of that carbon dioxide into the deep ocean.
    (B) Environmentalists worry that the strategy of pumping carbon dioxide into the deep ocean to reduce global warming would simply exchange one form of pollution for another, equally destructive one.
    (C) Worrying that pumping carbon dioxide into the deep ocean to reduce global warming would simply exchange one form of pollution for another, equally destructive, form is unfounded.
    (D) Much of the carbon dioxide now released into the atmosphere ends up in the ocean where it does not cause environmental disturbances as destructive as global warming.
    (E) To reduce global warming, the strategy of pumping into the deep ocean at least some of the carbon dioxide now released into the atmosphere should be considered.[1]

Step 1. Identify the Question Type

The term "conclusion" tells you this is a Main Point question.

Step 2. Untangle the Stimulus

The industrial engineer first tells you what some people think about how to address global warming, and then adds that many environmentalists object to the strategy. When an author

---

[1]PrepTest 50, Sec. 2, Q 20

describes what "some people" think, be on the lookout for the author to rebut that statement, which is exactly what happens here. The engineer gives his opinion, set off by the contrast word "however." The author believes that the worry is unfounded because much of the carbon dioxide now released into the atmosphere eventually ends up in the ocean anyway. Bracket "This worry is unfounded." Those four words are the conclusion.

Step 3. Make a Prediction

The correct answer will match the statement that you should bracket as the conclusion. However, note that the word "this" in the conclusion refers back to the prior sentence; the author's conclusion is that the worry about exchanging one form of pollution for another is unfounded.

Step 4. Evaluate the Answer Choices

Choice (A) supports the suggestion that "some people" make in the first sentence. However, the engineer never endorses the strategy; he just says the environmentalists shouldn't worry about it. Eliminate this choice.

Choice (B) reiterates the environmentalists' concerns, not the engineer's conclusion. Cross this choice out.

Choice (C) correctly paraphrases the engineer's conclusion and is the correct answer.

Choice (D) comes from the evidence cited by the engineer at the end of the last sentence, not from the conclusion.

Choice (E) has the same problem as choice (A). The engineer never backs a strategy to address global warming. He says that one particular objection is unfounded.

MAIN POINT QUESTIONS: NOW YOU TRY IT

It's now your turn to try a Main Point question on your own. Use the template I've provided after the question to guide you through the four-step Kaplan Method. (Note: On test day, you won't be writing out all the steps as you are in this exercise. However, as you are learning the Method, it's good practice to help it become second nature.) Remember to bracket conclusions and circle Keywords.

1. Tallulah: The columnist attributes the decline of interest in novels to consumerism, technology, and the laziness of people who prefer watching television to reading a novel. However, in reaching this conclusion, the columnist has overlooked important evidence. It is surely relevant that contemporary fiction is frequently of poor quality—indeed, much of it is meaningless and depressing—whereas many good newspapers, magazines, professional journals, and books of other types are currently available.

   Which one of the following most accurately expresses the main conclusion of Tallulah's argument?

   (A) Contemporary fiction is unpopular because it is meaningless, depressing, and of poor overall quality.

   (B) The columnist's claim that novels are being displaced by consumerism, technology, and television is false.

   (C) The view expressed by the columnist was formed without considering all of the pertinent evidence.

   (D) People read as much as they used to, but most of the works they now read are not novels.

   (E) A large number of high-quality newspapers, magazines, professional journals, and nonfiction books are currently published.[2]

Step 1. Identify the Question Type

Step 2. Untangle the Stimulus

Step 3. Make a Prediction

Step 4. Evaluate the Answer Choices

---

[2]PrepTest 41, Sec. 3, Q 18

Explanations

1. (C)

Tallulah: The columnist attributes the decline of interest in novels to consumerism, technology, and the laziness of people who prefer watching television to reading a novel. ⟨However,⟩ in reaching this conclusion, the columnist has overlooked important evidence.> It is surely relevant that contemporary fiction is frequently of poor quality—indeed, much of it is meaningless and depressing—whereas many good newspapers, magazines, professional journals, and books of other types are currently available.

Which one of the following most accurately expresses the (main conclusion) of Tallulah's argument?

(A) Contemporary fiction is unpopular because it is meaningless, depressing, and of poor overall quality.

(B) The columnist's claim that novels are being displaced by consumerism, technology, and television is false.

(C) The view expressed by the columnist was formed without considering all of the pertinent evidence.

(D) People read as much as they used to, but most of the works they now read are not novels.

(E) A large number of high-quality newspapers, magazines, professional journals, and nonfiction books are currently published.[3]

Step 1. Identify the Question Type

The question asks for the "main conclusion," which indicates a Main Point question.

Step 2. Untangle the Stimulus

The author begins with a statement of someone else's thinking. Here, Tallulah states the columnist's explanation for the decline of interest in novels. She concludes—set off by the contrast Keyword "However"—that the columnist overlooked important information in reaching his conclusion. Tallulah then supports her conclusion with the evidence she thinks the columnist overlooked.

Step 3. Make a Prediction

The correct answer choice will summarize Tallulah's belief that the columnist overlooked evidence in reaching his conclusion about the decline of interest in novels.

---

[3]PrepTest 41, Sec. 3, Q 18

Step 4. Evaluate the Answer Choices

Choice (A) points out Tallulah's evidence that the columnist's appraisal is deficient, and doesn't mention the conclusion. Cross this choice out.

Choice (B) is extreme. Tallulah never says the columnist is wrong, she just says that the columnist's assessment is incomplete. Eliminate this choice as well.

Choice (C) properly captures Tallulah's conclusion, so it is the correct answer.

Choice (D) is incorrect for two reasons. First, Tallulah does not address whether people read as much as they did before. Second, it's an issue taken up by the columnist—not Tallulah—and he limits his discussion to reading novels—not other reading.

Choice (E) presents Tallulah's evidence, not her conclusion.

DRILL: PRACTICING MAIN POINT QUESTIONS

Use the Kaplan Method to answer the following Main Point questions. Take this opportunity to practice and apply the steps in the Method so you are comfortable using them on test day. Be sure to circle conclusion and evidence Keywords and bracket the conclusion. Check your responses against the full explanations provided after the Drill.

1. Double-blind techniques should be used whenever possible in scientific experiments. They help prevent the misinterpretations that often arise due to expectations and opinions that scientists already hold, and clearly scientists should be extremely diligent in trying to avoid such misinterpretations.

   Which one of the following most accurately expresses the main conclusion of the argument?

   (A) Scientists' objectivity may be impeded by interpreting experimental evidence on the basis of expectations and opinions that they already hold.
   (B) It is advisable for scientists to use double-blind techniques in as high a proportion of their experiments as they can.
   (C) Scientists sometimes neglect to adequately consider the risk of misinterpreting evidence on the basis of prior expectations and opinions.
   (D) Whenever possible, scientists should refrain from interpreting evidence on the basis of previously formed expectations and convictions.
   (E) Double-blind experimental techniques are often an effective way of ensuring scientific objectivity.[4]

2. A strong correlation exists between what people value and the way they act. For example, those who value wealth tend to choose higher-paying jobs in undesirable locations over lower-paying jobs in desirable locations. Thus, knowing what people value can help one predict their actions.

   Which one of the following most accurately expresses the conclusion of the argument?

   (A) Knowing how people behave allows one to infer what they value.
   (B) People's claims concerning what they value are symptomatic of their actions.
   (C) No two people who value different things act the same way in identical circumstances.
   (D) People who value wealth tend to allow their desire for it to outweigh other concerns.
   (E) What people value can be a reliable indicator of how they will act.[5]

3. Publisher: The new year is approaching, and with it the seasonal demand for books on exercise and fitness. We must do whatever it takes to ship books in that category on time; our competitors have demonstrated a high level of organization, and we cannot afford to be outsold.

   Which one of the following most accurately expresses the main conclusion drawn in the publisher's argument?

   (A) The company should make shipping books its highest priority.
   (B) By increasing its efficiency, the company can maintain its competitive edge.
   (C) The company will be outsold if it does not maintain its competitors' high level of organization.
   (D) It is imperative that the company ship fitness and exercise books on time.
   (E) The company should do whatever is required in order to adopt its competitors' shipping practices.[6]

---

[4]PrepTest June 2007, Sec. 2, Q 10

[5]PrepTest 50, Sec. 2, Q 4
[6]PrepTest 51, Sec. 3, Q 16

Answer Explanations follow on the next page.

Explanations

1. **(B)**

<Double-blind techniques should be used whenever possible in scientific experiments.> They help prevent the misinterpretations that often arise due to expectations and opinions that scientists already hold, and clearly scientists should be extremely diligent in trying to avoid such misinterpretations.

Which one of the following most accurately expresses the (main conclusion) of the argument?

(A)   Scientists' objectivity may be impeded by interpreting experimental evidence on the basis of expectations and opinions that they already hold.

(B)   It is advisable for scientists to use double-blind techniques in as high a proportion of their experiments as they can.

(C)   Scientists sometimes neglect to adequately consider the risk of misinterpreting evidence on the basis of prior expectations and opinions.

(D)   Whenever possible, scientists should refrain from interpreting evidence on the basis of previously formed expectations and convictions.

(E)   Double-blind experimental techniques are often an effective way of ensuring scientific objectivity.[7]

Step 1. Identify the Question Type

The question asks for the "main conclusion," which indicates a Main Point question.

Step 2. Untangle the Stimulus

Because this is a Main Point question, it's unlikely that the stimulus will include a conclusion Keyword. However, this stimulus includes the word "clearly." Don't let it fool you, though. In this case, "clearly" is part of the evidence, not the conclusion.

The argument starts with a recommendation to use double-blind techniques in scientific experiments. The next sentence tells you why—because they help prevent misinterpretations and avoiding misinterpretations is important.

Remember that recommendations are important LSAT conclusion types, and the word "should" indicates a recommendation. If you are unsure whether the recommendation in the first sentence of the stimulus is the conclusion or the recommendation at the end is the conclusion, you can test which one supports the other by sticking the word "because" between them. For example, read the following two sentences. Which one makes sense?

---

[7]PrepTest June 2007, Sec. 2, Q 10

Double-blind techniques should be used whenever possible in scientific experiments BECAUSE scientists should be extremely diligent in trying to avoid such misinterpretations.

Scientists should be extremely diligent in trying to avoid such misinterpretations BECAUSE double-blind techniques should be used whenever possible in scientific experiments.

The first sentence puts the two statements in their proper claim and support format. Claim: Use Double-blind techniques. Why use them? Reason: want to avoid misinterpretations. It doesn't work the other way around.

Step 3. Make a Prediction

Scientists should use double-blind techniques wherever possible. The rest of the argument is evidence for that conclusion.

Step 4. Evaluate the Answer Choices

Choice (A) restates the evidence, so it is wrong. Cross it out.

Choice (B) reiterates the conclusion, so it is the correct answer.

Choice (C) is not mentioned in the argument, but adds evidence to institute double-blind techniques.

Choice (D), like choice (A), repeats the evidence.

Choice (E) may be true, but the conclusion goes beyond *recognizing* the effectiveness of double-blind procedures. It *recommends* them.

2. **(E)**

A strong correlation exists between what people value and the way they act. For example, those who value wealth tend to choose higher-paying jobs in undesirable locations over lower-paying jobs in desirable locations. <Thus, knowing what people value can help one predict their actions.>

Which one of the following most accurately expresses the conclusion of the argument?

(A) Knowing how people behave allows one to infer what they value.

(B) People's claims concerning what they value are symptomatic of their actions.

(C) No two people who value different things act the same way in identical circumstances.

(D) People who value wealth tend to allow their desire for it to outweigh other concerns.

(E) What people value can be a reliable indicator of how they will act.[8]

---

[8]PrepTest 50, Sec. 2, Q 4

Step 1. Identify the Question Type

The word "conclusion" tells you that this is a Main Point question.

Step 2. Untangle the Stimulus

Unlike most Main Point questions, this argument does include a conclusion Keyword—"Thus," in the last sentence. The author states that knowing what people value helps predict what they'll do. The author points out a correlation between what people value and the way they act and gives an example to support the conclusion.

Step 3. Make a Prediction

The correct answer will summarize the last sentence of the stimulus.

Step 4. Evaluate the Answer Choices

Choice (A) get the terms backward. The conclusion says people's values predict their behavior. Because you were given a clear conclusion Keyword, expect the wrong answer choices to closely mimic—but be slightly off—the correct match to your bracketed statement. This answer has all the right words, but it takes the logic in the wrong direction. Cross this choice out.

Choice (B) also misses the mark. The conclusion talks about what people value, not what they claim they value. Move on to the next choice.

Choice (C) is extreme as well as outside the scope of the argument. The author claims that values predict behavior, not that values tell you exactly how someone or a group of people will act in any particular situation. Eliminate this choice.

Choice (D) is outside the scope. The conclusion refers to values generally and not to any specific value. With this choice out, that leaves only one.

Choice (E) presents a correct summary of the conclusion and is the correct answer.

3. **(D)**

Publisher: The new year is approaching, and with it the seasonal demand for books on exercise and fitness. <We must do whatever it takes to ship books in that category on time;> our competitors have demonstrated a high level of organization, and we cannot afford to be outsold.

Which one of the following most accurately expresses the (main conclusion) drawn in the publisher's argument?

(A) The company should make shipping books its highest priority.
(B) By increasing its efficiency, the company can maintain its competitive edge.
(C) The company will be outsold if it does not maintain its competitors' high level of organization.
(D) It is imperative that the company ship fitness and exercise books on time.
(E) The company should do whatever is required in order to adopt its competitors' shipping practices.[9]

Step 1. Identify the Question Type

The phrase "main conclusion" indicates that this is a Main Point question.

Step 2. Untangle the Stimulus

The publisher recognizes a demand for certain books. She knows the competitors are ready and organized, and she cannot let them outsell her. These facts support the publisher's conclusion that her team must do whatever it takes to ship the books on time.

You can also use the "one-sentence test" to find the conclusion. In this case, the only sentence that can stand on its own as the main point is, "We must do whatever it takes to ship books in that category on time."

Step 3. Make a Prediction

Find the answer choice that best matches the conclusion you bracketed.

Step 4. Evaluate the Answer Choices

Choice (A) is too broad. The argument doesn't advise making book shipping the highest priority. Rather, the publisher insists that exercise and fitness books be shipped by whatever means necessary and on time. Eliminate this choice.

Choice (B) is outside the scope of the argument. The publisher doesn't discuss efficiency. This choice is out.

[9]PrepTest 51, Sec. 3, Q 16

Choice (C) is extreme. You know the publisher can't afford to be outsold, but you don't know she will be outsold if her team doesn't maintain its competitors' high level of organization. Go on to the next choice.

Choice (D) correctly rephrases the publisher's main point. This is the correct answer.

Choice (E) is outside the scope of the argument. The publisher concludes the exercise and fitness books must be shipped on time. She doesn't talk about how to accomplish that directive.

MAIN POINT REVIEW

Before you proceed to the next chapter, turn to Appendix A and complete the review exercise for Main Point questions. A completed chart is included in Appendix B.

CHAPTER 18

RECENT TRENDS

With all the effort you're putting into your test preparation, it makes sense that you keep up to date on the most recent trends appearing in the Logical Reasoning sections. While the exact distribution of question types isn't set in stone, there are patterns that contribute to the predictability of the LSAT. In this brief chapter, I'll review the structural trends on the most recent LSATs with you.

LOGICAL REASONING ON RECENT LSATS: BREAKDOWN BY QUESTION TYPE

Table 18.1 shows the question breakdown of the four most recent tests at the time of this writing, along with the average number of questions per question type.

Please note that no February tests are included because the LSAC does not regularly release them.

Table 18.1

Question Types	PrepTests			
	61 Oct. '10	60 June '10	59 Dec. '09	58 Oct. '09
Assumption	6	7	7	12
Weaken/Strengthen	10	9	9	6
Flaw	6	7	10	7
Inference	7	6	7	7
Principle	5	5	4	7
Method of Argument	1	2	2	3
Parallel Reasoning	3	4	3	2
Paradox	5	3	4	5
Point at Issue	2	1	1	0
Role of a Statement	3	3	2	0
Main Point	3	2	2	2
Total Logical Reasoning Questions	51	49*	51	51

*One question was removed from scoring by LSAC

PREDICTABILITY IS THE TREND

The good news about the Logical Reasoning sections is they've remained consistent over the last few years. Generally speaking, the two scored Logical Reasoning sections per test represent 50 to 51 questions on the LSAT, with each section having 24 to 26 questions.

Assumption, Weaken, Strengthen, and Flaw questions make up half the Logical Reasoning questions and thus demand most of your attention. While an individual question type may have a few more or a few less questions in the mix, the Logical Reasoning section has not been a surprise for test takers. In addition to consistent numbers, the question types have remained the same.

Since this is the LSAT, you know you can't infer what is not provided to you. So, predictability doesn't guarantee that the test won't change at all. However, predictability, combined with the slow rate of changes made to the LSAT, indicate that Logical Reasoning is unlikely to present big surprises on test day.

THE IMPORTANCE OF THE KAPLAN METHOD

In this book, you have learned the Kaplan Method, a proven approach to efficiently and accurately navigate the Logical Reasoning sections on the LSAT. And you know the LSAT and each section are predictable. Use that to your advantage on test day and in your preparation.

PART III

FULL-SECTION PRACTICE

CHAPTER 19

TIMING AND SECTION MANAGEMENT IN A NUTSHELL

In Parts I and II, you learned the Kaplan Method for Logical Reasoning and applied it to the twelve question types. While familiarity with the questions and mastery of the logical reasoning skills will help you score points on test day, your preparation is incomplete without training in section timing and management. In Part III, I'll introduce you to some basic concepts to help you manage the section most efficiently and maximize your score. Then, you'll have a chance to take two complete Logical Reasoning sections.

I want to offer one bit of caution before you proceed. Don't take a timed section until you've completed Parts I and II in this book. Remember we talked in the beginning about treating LSAT preparation like learning a skill. Timed training without adequate preparation doesn't make sense. You wouldn't run a race without practicing the fundamentals and conditioning. Don't do it on the LSAT either.

EFFICIENCY, NOT SPEED

Every LSAT student I've ever taught wished they had more time on each section or wished they had no time restriction at all. However, every section is strictly timed at 35 minutes, so you need to learn to work within that time frame and use every minute to get as much out of every section as you can. Your goal is not to finish a section but rather to get as many right answers as you can in the time allotted. So, you must strategically decide how you can get the most points in your limited time.

As I tell my students, I don't care how fast you got it wrong because the LSAT only gives points for correct answers. As you become more proficient at the Kaplan Method, practice more questions, and make strategic section decisions, you will become more efficient and accurate in your work. You can measure your progress by an increase in the number of questions you get to in 35 minutes and in the number you get correct—not by your speed.

OPTIMAL TIMING

Ideally, you will process and answer each of the approximately 25 Logical Reasoning questions in a section in 75 to 90 seconds to stay within the 35-minute time limit. A practiced strategy is essential to achieve this pace and maintain the necessary focus. While finishing the section with efficiency and accuracy is the goal, I also know that you may not complete every section. To maximize your score, approach that situation with control and strategic thinking.

Strategic Guessing

The last thing you want to do is run out of time on a section with blank answers on your test grid. Unlike the SAT, the LSAT has no penalty for wrong answers. So, be sure to enter an answer for every question. If you know you will not get to every question, set aside time at the end of the 35 minutes to fill in the blanks with your guess. I recommend picking a letter and using that same letter as your fall back. Using a consistent letter to guess actually takes less time than if you try to think about it. You're also more likely to get something right than if you switch it up. No letter is more likely to be the answer than any other so pick your own lucky letter and stick with it.

Just remember, this is a competition and you need to maximize the value of every second of the test. If you are running out of time, fill in those other bubbles with a guess, but continue working until the very second that the proctor calls "pencils down." Then, immediately put your pencil down.

What can you do in very limited time at the end of sections? Well, Parallel Reasoning questions are often a time drain, but if you save them for last, remember that you can make a lot of progress toward honing in on the right answer just by comparing conclusion types between the stimulus and the answer choices. An educated guess from one of three remaining choices is much better odds than a blind one of five.

If you don't have enough time to work a problem, but have 15 seconds to scan the choices, then generally you are better off with a more modest-sounding answer and should eliminate the extreme sounding answers, especially on an Inference or a Necessary Assumption question. Of course, you have seen plenty of exceptions to this rule, so don't think you can just skip reading the problem when you have the time to do so!

If you only have 30 seconds to work on a Strengthen or Weaken question, then try to immediately hone in on the conclusion. It's the most important component of the argument. Scan the choices for the one that is either most in line with the conclusion (Strengthen) or opposed to the conclusion (Weaken).

The main point is that there is always something that you can do to try to improve your score in every second of those limited 35 minutes of a Logical Reasoning section, even if you don't have the normal minute and a half to work the problem fully. The LSAT tests your competitive drive and efficiency, as well as your logic skills.

SECTION MANAGEMENT: YOU'RE IN CONTROL
Basic Anatomy of a Logical Reasoning Section

By understanding the basic anatomy of a Logical Reasoning section, you can take more control of it and spend your time more efficiently.

Take a look at Kaplan's Logical Reasoning: Typical Question Difficulties Chart.

The Logical Reasoning Section: The Inside Story

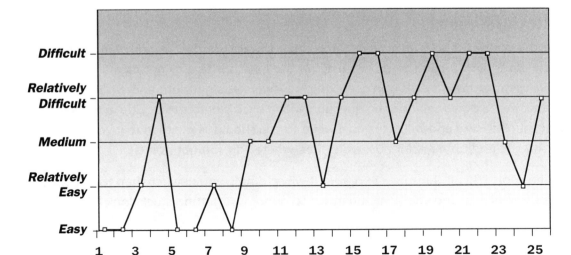

Questions 1–25

Notice the questions generally go from less difficult to more difficult as you proceed through a section. Of course, you'll find a difficult question or two early in the section. Such placement rewards test takers who answer skillfully or skip a tough question and punishes test takers who insist on sticking with a question regardless of the amount of time they've wasted on it. You'll also find easier questions toward the end of the section, rewarding those who get there and penalizing those who get bogged down and never get to the end.

One more point about the typical layout of a Logical Reasoning section: The difficulty level tends to spike from around questions 14 to 22, in what we at Kaplan call the "danger zone." Practice working up to question 13, 14, or 15 (wherever there is a natural page break) and then turn to the end of the section and work back from there. For example, you can work through the first four pages then turn to the last page and the last question of the section and begin working from the last question in to the middle. Be sure you stay within the section and do not accidentally turn to the following section—that could result in a penalty. Taking the questions in the manner described will get you to the "danger zone" at the end of your 35 minutes. If you are running out of time, you want to run out of time where the questions are harder and you might do just as well to guess anyway.

Understanding the anatomy of a Logical Reasoning section helps you set a pace for yourself. Although you need to be aware of where you are in the 35 minutes, it's a waste of time and energy to track your time on individual questions. Set a goal of 15 minutes for the first fifteen questions. The difficulty level generally builds through the section so you want to set a brisker pace in the beginning and bank some time for the more difficult questions in the danger zone. If you find that a question is bogging you down, skip it and come back to it at the end. Use the next 15 minutes to work from the last question back toward question 15. Use the final five minutes to make a guess with your lucky letter on all the questions you skipped and to revisit any answers you are not confident about.

Strategic Skipping

Because each question is worth the same value toward your score, you want to manage the Logical Reasoning section to put yourself in the best position to get as many points as you can. Remember, law schools don't see which answers you get right and wrong. They just get a final score, so don't belabor one question. Move on. It's better to decide in ten seconds that the question is hard and will take you a while so you should skip it than to invest three minutes in it and still end up guessing. Use your time where you can get points.

You can spot difficult questions in different ways to help you decide when to skip a question. Aside from recognizing your location in the layout or just getting stuck, look for the following characteristics.

- Longer stimulus and/or answers: The more text there is, the longer it can take to get through the material. Principle and Parallel Reasoning questions typically fall in this category. The Kaplan Method will help you work through the text more efficiently. However, longer text is one way to make a question objectively more difficult.

- General language: Language that is not specific to the content of the stimulus but describes it in general terms can also be difficult to wade through.
- Similar answer choices: Each choice may use similar wording from the stimulus making it more difficult to distinguish between them.
- Formal logic: While formal logic is a useful tool to simplify a stimulus and you want to embrace it as such, it does add a layer of work until you're comfortable with it.
- Difficult topic: The LSAT does not require any outside knowledge, but some topics like science and economics can be difficult for some students. If you find yourself confused by the text because of the topic and you're on your second read yet no closer to untangling the stimulus, move on.
- Unknown question type: If you can't determine the question type, you can't know your task. Working through the stimulus without that direction will just slow you down and waste your time.
- Historically tough question type: Certainly, you can't skip every Assumption question, for example, if that's your toughest type. However, use that knowledge when you run in to your toughest type in the danger zone or when you're down to minimal time and you can only get to one more question.

The important lesson is that you recognize questions that are more challenging for you and use that knowledge to decide whether to skip a question or not. You're not admitting defeat, just making a strategic choice to keep moving and return to it if you have time. Remember to circle a question you skip so you can refer to it later. Also, make sure you bubble your answers properly on the grid sheet. If you skip a question in your test booklet, be sure to skip it on the bubble sheet.

COMMON WRONG ANSWER TYPES

The most direct route to finding the correct answer to a Logical Reasoning question is to predict the answer and find a match in the answer choices. Sometimes, however, your prediction is wrong, you can't find a match, or you get down to two or three answers and can't decide between them. Being familiar with the common wrong answer types will help you sort through the remaining answers. If nothing else, you can eliminate answers that fall into these categories to improve your chance of picking the right answer.

Extreme Answers

Extreme answers include words like "always," "must," "will," "never," "all," "none," and "every."

Extreme language is not problematic if the language in the stimulus matches the extreme nature of the answer choice. However, extreme language often indicates a wrong answer.

The correct answer for most question types can never be more extreme than the stimulus. In general, more modest is better, especially for Necessary Assumption and Inference questions.

Here's an example:

Braille is a method of producing text by means of raised dots that can be read by touch. A recent development in technology will allow flat computer screens to be made of a material that can be heated in patterns that replicate the patterns used in braille. (Since) the thermal device will utilize the same symbol system as braille, <it follows that> anyone who is accustomed to reading braille can easily adapt to the use of this electronic system.>

Which one of the following is an (assumption) on which the conclusion (depends)?

(A)   Braille is the only symbol system that can be readily adapted for use with the new thermal screen. (*Extreme answer*)

(C)   People with the tactile ability to discriminate symbols in braille have an ability to discriminate similar patterns on a flat heated surface.[1] (*Correct assumption*)

Out of Scope Answers

Out of scope answers bring in new information that is immaterial or irrelevant to the stimulus.

Don't be fooled by new information not included in the stimulus; it may or may not be outside the scope of the argument depending on the question type. For example, Strengthen and Weaken answers often present new information to the argument to make the argument more or less likely to be true. Here's an example:

The people most likely to watch a televised debate between political candidates are the most committed members of the electorate and thus the most likely to have already made up their minds about whom to support. Furthermore, following a debate, uncommitted viewers are generally undecided about who won the debate. <(Hence,) winning a televised debate does little to bolster one's chances of winning an election.>

The reasoning in the argument is most (vulnerable to) (criticism) because the argument (fails to consider) the possibility that

(B)   the voting behavior of people who do not watch a televised debate is influenced by reports about the debate (*Correct answer that describes the flaw in the argument*)

(C)   there are differences of opinion about what constitutes winning or losing a debate[2] (*Out of scope answer*)

---

[1]PrepTest 22, Sec. 2, Q 1
[2]PrepTest 41, Sec. 1, Q 20

180 Answers

A 180 answer is the opposite answer to the correct choice. It can appear in all question types, but is especially prevalent in Strengthen and Weaken questions.

For example, a 180 answer to a Strengthen question will weaken the argument, and vice versa. What makes 180s so tricky is that they typically include terms or ideas that are similar to the correct answer, but take the argument in the wrong direction.

Here's an example:

Several companies will soon offer personalized electronic news services, delivered via cable or telephone lines and displayed on a television. People using these services can view continually updated stories on those topics for which they subscribe. (Since) these services will provide people with the information they are looking for more quickly and efficiently than printed newspapers can, <newspaper sales will decline drastically if these services become widely available.>

Which one of the following, if true, most seriously (weakens) the argument?

(A)   In reading newspapers, most people not only look for stories on specific topics but also like to idly browse through headlines or pictures for amusing stories on unfamiliar or unusual topics. (*Correct answer weakens the argument*)

(D)   The average monthly cost of subscribing to several channels on a personalized electronic news service will approximately equal the cost of a month's subscription to a newspaper.[3] (*180 answer strengthens the argument*)

---

[3]PrepTest 36, Sec. 3, Q 2

Distorted Answers

A distorted answer will use language or concepts from the stimulus but misapply them in some way.

Here's an example:

<Publicity campaigns for endangered species are unlikely to have much impact on the most important environmental problems,> (for) while the ease of attributing feelings to large mammals facilitates evoking sympathy for them, it is more difficult to elicit sympathy for other kinds of organisms, such as the soil microorganisms on which large ecosystems and agriculture depend.

Which one of the following is an (assumption) on which the argument (depends)?

(A)   The most important environmental problems involve endangered species other than large mammals. (*Correct assumption*)

(B)   Microorganisms cannot experience pain or have other feelings.[4] (*Distorted answer*)

Irrelevant Comparisons

Irrelevant comparisons will compare two things that are unrelated or don't affect the argument. If the argument is comparative, however, it's likely that the correct answer will be comparative in nature as well.

Here's an example:

Barnes: The two newest employees at this company have salaries that are too high for the simple tasks normally assigned to new employees and duties that are too complex for inexperienced workers. (Hence,) <the salaries and the complexity of the duties of these two newest employees should be reduced.>

Which one of the following is an (assumption) on which Barnes's argument (depends)?

(C)   The two newest employees are not experienced at their occupations. (*Correct assumption*)

(E)   The salaries of the two newest employees are no higher than the salaries that other companies pay for workers with a similar level of experience.[5] (*Irrelevant comparison*)

---

[4]PrepTest 35, Sec. 4, Q 16
[5]PrepTest 29, Sec. 1, Q 5

TAKE CONTROL WITH THE KAPLAN METHOD

Of course, the best approach is to improve your logical reasoning skills and practice the Kaplan Method. But it's inevitable that everyone runs into questions they need to let go of, so practice it.

The best test takers take control of the Logical Reasoning sections and strategically use the time available to make accurate choices and get the most points possible. If you follow the Kaplan Method, you can be one of them.

CHAPTER 20

How to Use the Practice Section

The following two chapters include the two full-length Logical Reasoning sections as they appeared on the December 2007 LSAT (now called PrepTest 53). Set aside 35 minutes for each section and take them in a place where you won't be interrupted. If you can access the building in which you'll take your actual test, consider going there for practice. You'll want to time yourself strictly and follow the test instructions to the letter, just as you'll have to on test day.

TAKE THE PRACTICE SECTIONS

As I cautioned earlier, don't take a full-length section before you've completed the first two parts of this book. Full-length section practice is about "putting it all together" and pacing. It's not for learning the fundamentals of question types and methods, but rather for improving your ability to quickly and efficiently apply best practices to each question. Of course, you'll conduct a review of your performance using the explanations that follow each section and use that information to hone your skills.

With timed, section-length practice, your goal is to get as many points as possible. Skip and guess as needed to maximize your efficiency and increase the overall number of correct answers you can produce. Use the tools you will use on test day—a number 2 pencil and an analog watch. Also, clear your desk of all prohibited test day items including food, drinks, and cell phones.

Remember that there is no "guessing penalty," so fill in an answer for every question. Don't leave an answer blank because you want to see what you would get without guessing. You should guess on test day, so it's unrealistic not to do it in practice. If you can eliminate two or three of the wrong answers, guess from the remaining choices. When you review the section, you can look to see how you would be able to answer the question quickly and effectively, but don't let that deter you from guessing and skipping when it's in your interest to do so.

On test day, you will get credit only for the answers on your bubble sheet. No one will look in your test booklet to see what you've circled or the work you've done. So, practice now by scoring your section based only on what you bubbled into the grid.

CALCULATE YOUR SCORE

Use the answer key that follows each section to determine your score. Mark each of the answers you got right or wrong. There's no way to determine your overall LSAT score from any single section. Test scores are produced based on the overall number of correct answers you produced.

Here are a couple of score conversion tables from recently-released LSATs. There are almost always 101 scored questions per LSAT, of which 24–26 come from the Logical Reasoning section.

SCORING WORKSHEET

1. Enter the number of questions you answered correctly in each section

   NUMBER
   CORRECT

   SECTION I . . . . _____

   SECTION II . . . . _____

   SECTION III. . . . . _____

   SECTION IV . . . . _____

2. Enter the sum here: _____ THIS IS YOUR
   RAW SCORE.

Conversion Chart

For converting Raw Score to the 120–180 LSAT Scaled Score
LSAT Prep Test 47

Reported Score	Lowest Raw Score	Highest Raw Score
180	99	100
179	98	98
178	97	97
177	96	96
176	--*	--*
175	95	95
174	94	94
173	93	93
172	92	92
171	91	91
170	90	90
169	89	89
168	88	88
167	87	87
166	85	86
165	84	84
164	83	83
163	81	82
162	80	80
161	78	79
160	77	77
159	75	76
158	73	74
157	72	72
156	70	71
155	68	69
154	66	67
153	65	65
152	63	64
151	61	63
150	59	60
149	57	58
148	55	56
147	54	54
146	52	53
145	50	51
144	48	49
143	46	47
142	45	45
141	43	44
140	41	42
139	40	40
138	38	39
137	36	37
136	35	35
135	33	34
134	32	32
133	30	31
132	29	29
131	27	28
130	26	26
129	25	25
128	24	24
127	22	23
126	21	21
125	20	20
124	19	19
123	18	18
122	17	17
121	16	16
120	0	15

*There is no raw score that will produce this scaled score for the test.

Conversion Chart

For converting Raw Score to the 120–180 LSAT Scaled Score
LSAT Prep Test 50

Reported Score	Lowest Raw Score	Highest Raw Score
180	98	100
179	97	97
178	--*	--*
177	96	96
176	95	95
175	94	94
174	--*	--*
173	93	93
172	92	92
171	91	91
170	90	90
169	89	89
168	88	88
167	86	87
166	85	85
165	84	84
164	83	83
163	81	82
162	80	80
161	78	79
160	77	77
159	75	76
158	73	74
157	72	72
156	70	71
155	68	69
154	66	67
153	64	65
152	63	63
151	61	62
150	59	60
149	57	58
148	55	56
147	53	54
146	52	52
145	50	51
144	48	49
143	46	47
142	45	45
141	43	44
140	41	42
139	40	40
138	38	39
137	36	37
136	35	35
135	33	34
134	32	32
133	30	31
132	29	29
131	27	28
130	26	26
129	25	25
128	23	24
127	22	22
126	21	21
125	20	20
124	18	19
123	17	17
122	16	16
121	15	15
120	0	14

*There is no raw score that will produce this scaled score for the test.

By estimating the number of correct responses you'd generate from the remaining sections of the test, you can gain an idea of the impact that your Logical Reasoning performance will have on your score.

To improve your performance on the other sections of the test, study this book's companion volumes, *LSAT Reading Comprehension: Strategies and Tactics* and *LSAT Logic Games: Strategies and Tactics*.

If you haven't done so already, register for the Kaplan LSAT Experience test for additional section practice at www.kaptest.com/LSAT.

The Kaplan LSAT Experience provides you with the chance to take the most recently released, full-length LSAT under all of the proctoring conditions and rules that will apply on test day. You'll receive your score and a detailed performance analysis, answers and explanations for all of the questions, and access to an On Demand review of the test's most difficult questions (as determined by aggregate test-taker performance) delivered by some of Kaplan's most experienced LSAT instructors. Register at www.kaplanlsat.com/lsatexperience.

I recommend that you get as much full-length test practice and additional Logical Reasoning section practice as you can. The more questions you see, and the more familiar and proficient you become with the Kaplan Method, the better prepared you'll be on test day.

LEARN FROM YOUR PERFORMANCE

Most importantly, put time aside to review your performance. You need to go back to each question whether you got it right or wrong and review the Kaplan Method as well as the reason why the right answer is right and why the other four are wrong. You don't have to do it all in one sitting. What's important is that you do it. Think of this exercise like a project debriefing or watching game film to review your performance. What do you see that you want to make sure you do again or change? What do you need to practice?

Proceed with calm, focus, confidence, and patience. You need to find your LSAT zone and practice what you've learned. Good luck!

CHAPTER 21

FULL-LENGTH SECTION I[1]

Section I
Time—35 minutes
25 Questions

<u>Directions:</u> The questions in this section are based on the reasoning contained in brief statements or passages. For some questions, more than one of the choices could conceivably answer the question. However, you are to choose the <u>best</u> answer; that is, the response that most accurately and completely answers the question. You should not make assumptions that are by commonsense standards implausible, superfluous, or incompatible with the passage. After you have chosen the best answer, blacken the corresponding space on your answer sheet.

_____
[1]PrepTest 53, Sec. 1

1. Consumer advocate: Businesses are typically motivated primarily by the desire to make as great a profit as possible, and advertising helps businesses to achieve this goal. But it is clear that the motive of maximizing profits does not impel businesses to present accurate information in their advertisements. It follows that consumers should be skeptical of the claims made in advertisements.

   Each of the following, if true, would strengthen the consumer advocate's argument EXCEPT:

   (A) Businesses know that they can usually maximize their profits by using inaccurate information in their advertisements.
   (B) Businesses have often included inaccurate information in their advertisements.
   (C) Many consumers have a cynical attitude toward advertising.
   (D) Those who create advertisements are less concerned with the accuracy than with the creativity of advertisements.
   (E) The laws regulating truth in advertising are not applicable to many of the most common forms of inaccurate advertising.

2. Elaine: The purpose of art museums is to preserve artworks and make them available to the public. Museums, therefore, should seek to acquire and display the best examples of artworks from each artistic period and genre, even if some of these works are not recognized by experts as masterpieces.

   Frederick: Art museums ought to devote their limited resources to acquiring the works of recognized masters in order to ensure the preservation of the greatest artworks.

   Elaine's and Frederick's statements provide the most support for the claim that they would disagree about whether

   (A) many artistic masterpieces are not recognized as such by art experts
   (B) museums should seek to represent all genres of art in their collections
   (C) art museums should seek to preserve works of art
   (D) an art museum ought to acquire an unusual example of a period or genre if more characteristic examples are prohibitively expensive
   (E) all of the artworks that experts identify as masterpieces are actually masterpieces

3. Science columnist: It is clear why humans have so many diseases in common with cats. Many human diseases are genetically based, and cats are genetically closer to humans than are any other mammals except nonhuman primates. Each of the genes identified so far in cats has an exact counterpart in humans.

   Which one of the following, if true, most weakens the science columnist's explanation for the claim that humans have so many diseases in common with cats?

   (A) Cats have built up resistance to many of the diseases they have in common with humans.
   (B) Most diseases that humans have in common with cats have no genetic basis.
   (C) Cats have more diseases in common with nonhuman primates than with humans.
   (D) Many of the diseases humans have in common with cats are mild and are rarely diagnosed.
   (E) Humans have more genes in common with nonhuman primates than with cats.

4. This region must find new ways to help business grow. After all, shoe manufacturing used to be a major local industry, but recently has experienced severe setbacks due to overseas competition, so there is a need for expansion into new manufacturing areas. Moreover, our outdated public policy generally inhibits business growth.

   Which one of the following most accurately expresses the main conclusion drawn in the argument?

   (A) The region needs to find new ways to enhance business growth.
   (B) Shoe manufacturing is no longer a major source of income in the region.
   (C) Shoe manufacturing in the region has dramatically declined due to overseas competition.
   (D) Business in the region must expand into new areas of manufacturing.
   (E) Outdated public policy inhibits business growth in the region.

5. As a result of modern medicine, more people have been able to enjoy long and pain-free lives. But the resulting increase in life expectancy has contributed to a steady increase in the proportion of the population that is of advanced age. This population shift is creating potentially devastating financial problems for some social welfare programs.

   Which one of the following propositions is most precisely exemplified by the situation presented above?

   (A) Technical or scientific innovation cannot be the solution to all problems.
   (B) Implementing technological innovations should be delayed until the resulting social changes can be managed.
   (C) Every enhancement of the quality of life has unavoidable negative consequences.
   (D) All social institutions are affected by a preoccupation with prolonging life.
   (E) Solving one set of problems can create a different set of problems.

6. Since Jackie is such a big fan of Moral Vacuum's music, she will probably like The Cruel Herd's new album. Like Moral Vacuum, The Cruel Herd on this album plays complex rock music that employs the acoustic instrumentation and harmonic sophistication of early sixties jazz. The Cruel Herd also has very witty lyrics, full of puns and sardonic humor, like some of Moral Vacuum's best lyrics.

   Which one of the following, if true, most strengthens the argument?

   (A) Jackie has not previously cared for The Cruel Herd, but on the new album The Cruel Herd's previous musical arranger has been replaced by Moral Vacuum's musical arranger.
   (B) Though The Cruel Herd's previous albums' production quality was not great, the new album is produced by one of the most widely employed producers in the music industry.
   (C) Like Moral Vacuum, The Cruel Herd regularly performs in clubs popular with many students at the university that Jackie attends.
   (D) All of the music that Jackie prefers to listen to on a regular basis is rock music.
   (E) Jackie's favorite Moral Vacuum songs have lyrics that are somber and marked by a strong political awareness.

7. Superconductors are substances that conduct electricity without resistance at low temperatures. Their use, however, will never be economically feasible, unless there is a substance that superconducts at a temperature above minus 148 degrees Celsius. If there is such a substance, that substance must be an alloy of niobium and germanium. Unfortunately, such alloys superconduct at temperatures no higher than minus 160 degrees Celsius.

   If the statements above are true, which one of the following must also be true?

   (A) The use of superconductors will never be economically feasible.
   (B) If the alloys of niobium and germanium do not superconduct at temperatures above minus 148 degrees Celsius, then there are other substances that will do so.
   (C) The use of superconductors could be economically feasible if there is a substance that superconducts at temperatures below minus 148 degrees Celsius.
   (D) Alloys of niobium and germanium do not superconduct at temperatures below minus 160 degrees Celsius.
   (E) No use of alloys of niobium and germanium will ever be economically feasible.

8. Doctor: In three separate studies, researchers compared children who had slept with night-lights in their rooms as infants to children who had not. In the first study, the children who had slept with night-lights proved more likely to be nearsighted, but the later studies found no correlation between night-lights and nearsightedness. However, the children in the first study were younger than those in the later studies. This suggests that if night-lights cause nearsightedness, the effect disappears with age.

Which one of the following, if true, would most weaken the doctor's argument?

(A) A fourth study comparing infants who were currently sleeping with night-lights to infants who were not did not find any correlation between night-lights and nearsightedness.

(B) On average, young children who are already very nearsighted are no more likely to sleep with night-lights than young children who are not already nearsighted.

(C) In a study involving children who had not slept with night-lights as infants but had slept with night-lights when they were older, most of the children studied were not nearsighted.

(D) The two studies in which no correlation was found did not examine enough children to provide significant support for any conclusion regarding a causal relationship between night-lights and nearsightedness.

(E) In a fourth study involving 100 children who were older than those in any of the first three studies, several of the children who had slept with night-lights as infants were nearsighted.

9. Global surveys estimate the earth's population of nesting female leatherback turtles has fallen by more than two-thirds in the past 15 years. Any species whose population declines by more than two-thirds in 15 years is in grave danger of extinction, so the leatherback turtle is clearly in danger of extinction.

Which one of the following is an assumption that the argument requires?

(A) The decline in the population of nesting female leatherback turtles is proportional to the decline in the leatherback turtle population as a whole.

(B) If the global population of leatherback turtles falls by more than two-thirds over the next 15 years, the species will eventually become extinct.

(C) The global population of leatherback turtles consists in roughly equal numbers of females and males.

(D) Very few leatherback turtles exist in captivity.

(E) The only way to ensure the continued survival of leatherback turtles in the wild is to breed them in captivity.

10. Public health experts have waged a long-standing educational campaign to get people to eat more vegetables, which are known to help prevent cancer. Unfortunately, the campaign has had little impact on people's diets. The reason is probably that many people simply dislike the taste of most vegetables. Thus, the campaign would probably be more effective if it included information on ways to make vegetables more appetizing.

Which one of the following, if true, most strengthens the argument?

(A) The campaign to get people to eat more vegetables has had little impact on the diets of most people who love the taste of vegetables.

(B) Some ways of making vegetables more appetizing diminish vegetables' ability to help prevent cancer.

(C) People who find a few vegetables appetizing typically do not eat substantially more vegetables than do people who dislike the taste of most vegetables.

(D) People who dislike the taste of most vegetables would eat many more vegetables if they knew how to make them more appetizing.

(E) The only way to make the campaign to get people to eat more vegetables more effective would be to ensure that anyone who at present dislikes the taste of certain vegetables learns to find those vegetables appetizing.

11. Pure science—research with no immediate commercial or technological application—is a public good. Such research requires a great amount of financial support and does not yield profits in the short term. Since private corporations will not undertake to support activities that do not yield short-term profits, a society that wants to reap the benefits of pure science ought to use public funds to support such research.

The claim about private corporations serves which one of the following functions in the argument?

(A) It expresses the conclusion of the argument.
(B) It explains what is meant by the expression "pure research" in the context of the argument.
(C) It distracts attention from the point at issue by introducing a different but related goal.
(D) It supports the conclusion by ruling out an alternative way of achieving the benefits mentioned.
(E) It illustrates a case where unfortunate consequences result from a failure to accept the recommendation offered.

12. Melinda: Hazard insurance decreases an individual's risk by judiciously spreading the risk among many policyholders.

Jack: I disagree. It makes sense for me to buy fire insurance for my house, but I don't see how doing so lessens the chances that my house will burn down.

Jack's response most clearly trades on an ambiguity in which one of the following expressions used by Melinda?

(A) judiciously spreading
(B) many policyholders
(C) risk
(D) decreases
(E) hazard insurance

13. Some doctors believe that a certain drug reduces the duration of episodes of vertigo, claiming that the average duration of vertigo for people who suffer from it has decreased since the drug was introduced. However, during a recent three-month shortage of the drug, there was no significant change in the average duration of vertigo. Thus, we can conclude that the drug has no effect on the duration of vertigo.

Which one of the following is an assumption required by the argument?

(A) If a drug made a difference in the duration of vertigo, a three-month shortage of that drug would have caused a significant change in the average duration of vertigo.
(B) If there were any change in the average duration of vertigo since the introduction of the drug, it would have demonstrated that the drug has an effect on the duration of vertigo.
(C) A period of time greater than three months would not have been better to use in judging whether the drug has an effect on the duration of vertigo.
(D) Changes in diet and smoking habits are not responsible for any change in the average duration of vertigo since the introduction of the drug.
(E) There are various significant factors other than drugs that decrease the duration of vertigo for many people who suffer from it.

14. It has been suggested that a television set should be thought of as nothing more than "a toaster with pictures" and that since we let market forces determine the design of kitchen appliances we can let them determine what is seen on television. But that approach is too simple. Some governmental control is needed, since television is so important politically and culturally. It is a major source of commercial entertainment. It plays an important political role because it is the primary medium through which many voters obtain information about current affairs. It is a significant cultural force in that in the average home it is on for more than five hours a day.

Which one of the following most accurately expresses the role played in the argument by the claim that television is so important politically and culturally?

(A) It states a view that the argument as a whole is designed to discredit.

(B) It is an intermediate conclusion that is offered in support of the claim that a television set should be thought of as nothing more than "a toaster with pictures" and for which the claim that we can let market forces determine what is seen on television is offered as support.

(C) It is a premise that is offered in support of the claim that we let market forces determine the design of kitchen appliances.

(D) It is an intermediate conclusion that is offered in support of the claim that some governmental control of television is needed and for which the claim that the television is on for more than five hours a day in the average home is offered as partial support.

(E) It is a premise that is offered in support of the claim that television is the primary medium through which many voters obtain information about current affairs.

15. Earthworms, vital to the health of soil, prefer soil that is approximately neutral on the acid-to-alkaline scale. Since decomposition of dead plants makes the top layer of soil highly acidic, application of crushed limestone, which is highly alkaline, to the soil's surface should make the soil more attractive to earthworms.

Which one of the following is an assumption on which the argument depends?

(A) As far as soil health is concerned, aiding the decomposition of dead plants is the most important function performed by earthworms.

(B) After its application to the soil's surface, crushed limestone stays in the soil's top layer long enough to neutralize some of the top layer's acidity.

(C) Crushed limestone contains available calcium and magnesium, both of which are just as vital as earthworms to healthy soil.

(D) By itself, acidity of soil does nothing to hasten decomposition of dead plants.

(E) Alkaline soil is significantly more likely to benefit from an increased earthworm population than is highly acidic soil.

16. Jurist: A nation's laws must be viewed as expressions of a moral code that transcends those laws and serves as a measure of their adequacy. Otherwise, a society can have no sound basis for preferring any given set of laws to all others. Thus, any moral prohibition against the violation of statutes must leave room for exceptions.

Which one of the following can be properly inferred from the jurist's statements?

(A) Those who formulate statutes are not primarily concerned with morality when they do so.

(B) Sometimes criteria other than the criteria derived from a moral code should be used in choosing one set of laws over another.

(C) Unless it is legally forbidden ever to violate some moral rules, moral behavior and compliance with laws are indistinguishable.

(D) There is no statute that a nation's citizens have a moral obligation to obey.

(E) A nation's laws can sometimes come into conflict with the moral code they express.

17. An association between two types of conditions does not establish that conditions of one type cause conditions of the other type. Even persistent and inviolable association is inconclusive; such association is often due to conditions of both types being effects of the same kind of cause.

Which one of the following judgments most closely conforms to the principle stated above?

(A) Some people claim that rapid growth of the money supply is what causes inflation. But this is a naive view. What these people do not realize is that growth in the money supply and inflation are actually one and the same phenomenon.

(B) People who have high blood pressure tend to be overweight. But before we draw any inferences, we should consider that an unhealthy lifestyle can cause high blood pressure, and weight gain can result from living unhealthily.

(C) In some areas, there is a high correlation between ice cream consumption and the crime rate. Some researchers have proposed related third factors, but we cannot rule out that the correlation is purely coincidental.

(D) People's moods seem to vary with the color of the clothes they wear. Dark colors are associated with gloomy moods, and bright colors are associated with cheerful moods. This correlation resolves nothing, however. We cannot say whether it is the colors that cause the moods or the converse.

(E) Linguists propose that the similarities between Greek and Latin are due to their common descent from an earlier language. But how are we to know that the similarities are not actually due to the two languages having borrowed structures from one another, as with the languages Marathi and Telegu?

18. Salesperson: When a salesperson is successful, it is certain that that person has been in sales for at least three years. This is because to succeed as a salesperson, one must first establish a strong client base, and studies have shown that anyone who spends at least three years developing a client base can eventually make a comfortable living in sales.

The reasoning in the salesperson's argument is vulnerable to criticism on the grounds that it fails to consider the possibility that

(A) salespeople who have spent three years developing a client base might not yet be successful in sales

(B) some salespeople require fewer than three years in which to develop a strong client base

(C) a salesperson who has not spent three years developing a client base may not succeed in sales

(D) it takes longer than three years for a salesperson to develop a strong client base

(E) few salespeople can afford to spend three years building a client base

19. People who have habitually slept less than six hours a night and then begin sleeping eight or more hours a night typically begin to feel much less anxious. Therefore, most people who sleep less than six hours a night can probably cause their anxiety levels to fall by beginning to sleep at least eight hours a night.

The reasoning in which one of the following arguments is most similar to that in the argument above?

(A) When a small company first begins to advertise on the Internet, its financial situation generally improves. This shows that most small companies that have never advertised on the Internet can probably improve their financial situation by doing so.

(B) Certain small companies that had never previously advertised on the Internet have found that their financial situations began to improve after they started to do so. So, most small companies can probably improve their financial situations by starting to advertise on the Internet.

(C) It must be true that any small company that increases its Internet advertising will improve its financial situation, since most small companies that advertise on the Internet improved their financial situations soon after they first began to do so.

(D) Usually, the financial situation of a small company that has never advertised on the Internet will improve only if that company starts to advertise on the Internet. Therefore, a typical small company that has never advertised on the Internet can probably improve its financial situation by doing so.

(E) A small company's financial situation usually improves soon after that company first begins to advertise on the Internet. Thus, most small companies that have never advertised on the Internet could probably become financially strong.

20. Biologist: Lions and tigers are so similar to each other anatomically that their skeletons are virtually indistinguishable. But their behaviors are known to be quite different: tigers hunt only as solitary individuals, whereas lions hunt in packs. Thus, paleontologists cannot reasonably infer solely on the basis of skeletal anatomy that extinct predatory animals, such as certain dinosaurs, hunted in packs.

The conclusion is properly drawn if which one of the following is assumed?

(A) The skeletons of lions and tigers are at least somewhat similar in structure in certain key respects to the skeletons of at least some extinct predatory animals.

(B) There have existed at least two species of extinct predatory dinosaurs that were so similar to each other that their skeletal anatomy is virtually indistinguishable.

(C) If skeletal anatomy alone is ever an inadequate basis for inferring a particular species' hunting behavior, then it is never reasonable to infer, based on skeletal anatomy alone, that a species of animals hunted in packs.

(D) If any two animal species with virtually indistinguishable skeletal anatomy exhibit quite different hunting behaviors, then it is never reasonable to infer, based solely on the hunting behavior of those species, that the two species have the same skeletal anatomy.

(E) If it is unreasonable to infer, solely on the basis of differences in skeletal anatomy, that extinct animals of two distinct species differed in their hunting behavior, then the skeletal remains of those two species are virtually indistinguishable.

21. The trees always blossom in May if April rainfall exceeds 5 centimeters. If April rainfall exceeds 5 centimeters, then the reservoirs are always full on May 1. The reservoirs were not full this May 1 and thus the trees will not blossom this May.

Which one of the following exhibits a flawed pattern of reasoning most similar to the flawed pattern of reasoning in the argument above?

(A) If the garlic is in the pantry, then it is still fresh. And the potatoes are on the basement stairs if the garlic is in the pantry. The potatoes are not on the basement stairs, so the garlic is not still fresh.

(B) The jar reaches optimal temperature if it is held over the burner for 2 minutes. The contents of the jar liquefy immediately if the jar is at optimal temperature. The jar was held over the burner for 2 minutes, so the contents of the jar must have liquefied immediately.

(C) A book is classified "special" if it is more than 200 years old. If a book was set with wooden type, then it is more than 200 years old. This book is not classified "special," so it is not printed with wooden type.

(D) The mower will operate only if the engine is not flooded. The engine is flooded if the foot pedal is depressed. The foot pedal is not depressed, so the mower will operate.

(E) If the kiln is too hot, then the plates will crack. If the plates crack, then the artisan must redo the order. The artisan need not redo the order. Thus, the kiln was not too hot.

22. Doctor: Being overweight has long been linked with a variety of health problems, such as high blood pressure and heart disease. But recent research conclusively shows that people who are slightly overweight are healthier than those who are considerably underweight. Therefore, to be healthy, it suffices to be slightly overweight.

The argument's reasoning is flawed because the argument

(A) ignores medical opinions that tend to lead to a conclusion contrary to the one drawn

(B) never adequately defines what is meant by "healthy"

(C) does not take into account the fact that appropriate weight varies greatly from person to person

(D) holds that if a person lacks a property that would suffice to make the person unhealthy, then that person must be healthy

(E) mistakes a merely relative property for one that is absolute

23. Robust crops not only withstand insect attacks more successfully than other crops, they are also less likely to be attacked in the first place, since insects tend to feed on weaker plants. Killing insects with pesticides does not address the underlying problem of inherent vulnerability to damage caused by insect attacks. Thus, a better way to reduce the vulnerability of agricultural crops to insect pest damage is to grow those crops in good soil—soil with adequate nutrients, organic matter, and microbial activity.

Which one of the following is an assumption on which the argument depends?

(A) The application of nutrients and organic matter to farmland improves the soil's microbial activity.

(B) Insects never attack crops grown in soil containing adequate nutrients, organic matter, and microbial activity.

(C) The application of pesticides to weak crops fails to reduce the extent to which they are damaged by insect pests.

(D) Crops that are grown in good soil tend to be more robust than other crops.

(E) Growing crops without the use of pesticides generally produces less robust plants than when pesticides are used.

24. People perceive color by means of certain photopigments in the retina that are sensitive to certain wavelengths of light. People who are color-blind are unable to distinguish between red and green, for example, due to an absence of certain photopigments. What is difficult to explain, however, is that in a study of people who easily distinguish red from green, 10 to 20 percent failed to report distinctions between many shades of red that the majority of the subjects were able to distinguish.

Each of the following, if true, helps to explain the result of the study cited above EXCEPT:

(A) People with abnormally low concentrations of the photopigments for perceiving red can perceive fewer shades of red than people with normal concentrations.

(B) Questions that ask subjects to distinguish between different shades of the same color are difficult to phrase with complete clarity.

(C) Some people are uninterested in fine gradations of color and fail to notice or report differences they do not care about.

(D) Some people are unable to distinguish red from green due to an absence in the retina of the photopigment sensitive to green.

(E) Some people fail to report distinctions between certain shades of red because they lack the names for those shades.

25. Occultist: The issue of whether astrology is a science is easily settled: it is both an art and a science. The scientific components are the complicated mathematics and the astronomical knowledge needed to create an astrological chart. The art is in the synthesis of a multitude of factors and symbols into a coherent statement of their relevance to an individual.

The reasoning in the occultist's argument is most vulnerable to criticism on the grounds that the argument

(A) presumes, without providing justification, that any science must involve complicated mathematics

(B) incorrectly infers that a practice is a science merely from the fact that the practice has some scientific components

(C) denies the possibility that astrology involves components that are neither artistic nor scientific

(D) incorrectly infers that astronomical knowledge is scientific merely from the fact that such knowledge is needed to create an astrological chart

(E) presumes, without providing justification, that any art must involve the synthesis of a multitude of factors and symbols

Answer Explanations follow on the next page.

ANSWER KEY

1. C	14. D
2. B	15. B
3. B	16. E
4. A	17. B
5. E	18. B
6. A	19. A
7. A	20. C
8. D	21. A
9. A	22. E
10. D	23. D
11. D	24. D
12. C	25. B
13. A	

SECTION TRIAGE

Section management means taking control of the test. You want to answer the easier questions with efficiency so you bank some time for the more difficult questions at the end. If you do run out of time on a section, you want to run out on the most difficult questions on which you might have had to guess anyway.

Remember that you don't have to answer each question in the order in which it is presented. However, ordering each question individually as you would with Reading Comprehension passages and Logic Games is time consuming. So, you'll use your knowledge of the general flow of difficulty across the section to guide your section-management decisions.

The following table lists the difficulty level (as reported by Kaplan students) of each question from the first Logical Reasoning section in PrepTest 53. One star indicates the lowest difficulty and four stars represent the highest difficulty. Of course, the actual difficulty level for you can be higher or lower; however, it's important for you to be aware of the general trends.

The level of difficulty generally progresses from beginning to end with some tougher questions scattered in the beginning and some moderate questions tucked in the back. Note what I call the "danger zone"—a stretch of tough questions that shows up in every Logical Reasoning section and, in this case, from question 16 to 22. Based on this consistent pattern, I recommend that you work through about four pages of the section and then turn to the end of the section and answer questions from the end, working your way backward toward the middle.

Pay attention to the factors that make a question difficult for you. For example, question 16 is an Inference question with a relatively short stimulus and answer choices. However, the abstract nature of the text might have caused you some difficulty. Sometimes just the question type is enough to make a question difficult. Knowing that a question is difficult for you allows you to make a quick decision on whether to skip it or attack it immediately.

But always remember the bulk of the easier questions, regardless of question type, are in the first dozen or so questions. You need those points. So while there is great strategic advantage in skipping a question that you recognize quickly as highly difficult and moving on through the section, just attack in order most of the early questions. Also, pick up any easy to moderate points tucked into the back. And, finally, be selective and strategic in the danger zone, based on objective difficulty and also your question type preferences. The ultimate, and only, goal is maximizing the number of correct answers.

Use this table as a guide to review your own section management, to assess the questions that were difficult for you, and to recognize there are other questions up ahead with points. Keep moving through the section!

Table 21.1

PrepTest 53: Section 1		
Question	Question Type	Difficulty Level
1	Strengthen	*
2	Point at Issue	***
3	Weaken	*
4	Main Point	*
5	Principle	*
6	Strengthen	*
7	Inference	**
8	Weaken	**
9	Assumption	**
10	Strengthen	*
11	Role of a Statement	*
12	Flaw	*
13	Assumption	**
14	Role of a Statement	**
15	Assumption	**
16	Inference	****
17	Principle	***
18	Flaw	****
19	Parallel Reasoning	****
20	Assumption	***
21	Parallel Reasoning	****
22	Flaw	***
23	Assumption	**
24	Paradox	**
25	Flaw	**

Explanations

1. **(C)**

> Consumer advocate: Businesses are typically motivated
> primarily by the desire to make as great a profit as
> possible, and advertising helps businesses to
> achieve this goal. But it is clear that the motive of
> maximizing profits does not impel businesses to
> present accurate information in their advertisements.
> <It follows that consumers should be skeptical of
> the claims made in advertisements.>
>
> Each of the following, if true, would strengthen the
> consumer advocate's argument EXCEPT:

> (A) Businesses know that they can usually maximize
> their profits by using inaccurate information in
> their advertisements.
> (B) Businesses have often included inaccurate
> information in their advertisements.
> (C) Many consumers have a cynical attitude toward
> advertising.
> (D) Those who create advertisements are less
> concerned with the accuracy than with the
> creativity of advertisements.
> (E) The laws regulating truth in advertising are not
> applicable to many of the most common forms
> of inaccurate advertising.

Step 1. Identify the Question Type

The word "strengthen" tells you directly this is a Strengthen question. Because this is an "EXCEPT" question, be sure to characterize the answer choices: the four wrong answers will strengthen the argument, while the one correct answer will either weaken the argument or have no effect on it.

Step 2. Untangle the Stimulus

The consumer advocate generalizes that businesses are motivated by profit, and profit, not accuracy, drives their advertising. Using "It follows that" to signal the conclusion, the advocate warns consumers to be wary of advertising claims. In other words, be careful because they might lie.

Step 3. Make a Prediction

The advocate assumes that because businesses could lie, they will. Anything that validates this assumption will strengthen the argument. Find them and cross them out. Remember, you're looking for the answer that weakens the argument or makes no impact.

Step 4. Evaluate the Answer Choices

Choice (A) states that inaccurate ads can increase profits and thus provide incentive to businesses to use inaccurate ads. Choice (A) supports the assumption that businesses will cheat and consumers should be skeptical. Therefore, cross it out.

Choice (B) provides specific evidence of the advocate's claim and makes it more convincing. The message is if they've done it before, they'll do it again. Eliminate this choice.

Choice (C) raises the notion that many consumers are already cynical toward advertising. While this is in line with the author's recommendation, this answer choice, unlike the other four, doesn't provide any concrete reason or evidence supporting the claim against the businesses' integrity. The consumers' attitude has no impact on the advocate's assumption that those with a motive to lie will or can act on it. So, choice (C) does not strengthen the argument and is therefore the right answer.

Choice (D) indicates that accuracy is not a priority in advertising, strengthening the argument that ads should be questioned.

Choice (E) suggests that businesses are more likely to present inaccurate advertising because there is little regulation of it, thus strengthening the argument.

2. **(B)**

Elaine: The purpose of art museums is to preserve artworks and make them available to the public. <Museums, (therefore,) should seek to acquire and display the best examples of artworks from each artistic period and genre,> even if some of these works are not recognized by experts as masterpieces.

Frederick: <Art museums ought to devote their limited resources to acquiring the works of recognized masters in order to ensure the preservation of the greatest artworks.>

Elaine's and Frederick's statements provide the most support for the claim that they would (disagree about) whether

(A) many artistic masterpieces are not recognized as such by art experts

(B) museums should seek to represent all genres of art in their collections

(C) art museums should seek to preserve works of art

(D) an art museum ought to acquire an unusual example of a period or genre if more characteristic examples are prohibitively expensive

(E) all of the artworks that experts identify as masterpieces are actually masterpieces

Step 1. Identify the Question Type

This question asks for what the two speakers "disagree about" and is therefore a Point at Issue question.

Step 2. Untangle the Stimulus

Elaine concludes that museums should acquire and display art from every artistic period and genre to preserve art and expose the public to a broad range of artwork. Frederick recommends that museums acquire masterpieces to preserve the greatest artwork.

Step 3. Make a Prediction

The speakers obviously agree that museums should acquire and preserve art. They differ on the reason for it and the type of art to be collected: Elaine seeks to preserve examples of all the different genres, while Frederick believes that preservation efforts should be restricted to the greatest artwork.

Step 4. Evaluate the Answer Choices

Choice (A) is outside the scope of both speakers' arguments. Neither suggests any failure to recognize masterpieces by experts. Although Frederick does suggest that museums should focus their collections on "recognized masters," he doesn't discuss whether masterpieces are overlooked by art experts. Elaine's recommendation to preserve other works of art is based on a goal of preserving genres, not necessarily any implied failure to recognize the greatness of them.

Choice (B) correctly identifies the point at issue. It focuses on the type of art museums should acquire. Elaine would agree that collections should broadly represent all genres of art. Frederick would disagree and focus collections on masterpieces regardless of genre.

Choice (C) presents a point of agreement for Elaine and Frederick. While they agree on preservation, they disagree on the type of art to preserve.

Choice (D), like (A) is outside the score of both speakers' arguments. While Frederick does raise the issue of limited resources, neither speaker advocates this course of action of preserving "unusual" examples. Frederick does not believe in preserving all periods and genres, while Elaine explicitly advocates preserving the best examples of all genres.

Choice (E), like choice (A), raises the issue of whether you can trust an expert to identify a masterpiece. Again, neither speaker suggests any failure by experts to recognize masterpieces.

3. **(B)**

> Science columnist: (It is clear why) humans have so
> many diseases in common with cats. <Many human
> diseases are genetically based>, and cats are
> genetically closer to humans than are any other
> mammals except nonhuman primates. Each of the
> genes identified so far in cats has an exact
> counterpart in humans.

Which one of the following, if true, most (weakens) the
science columnist's explanation for the claim that
humans have so many diseases in common with cats?

(A)   Cats have built up resistance to many of the
        diseases they have in common with humans.
(B)   Most diseases that humans have in common with
        cats have no genetic basis.
(C)   Cats have more diseases in common with
        nonhuman primates than with humans.
(D)   Many of the diseases humans have in common
        with cats are mild and are rarely diagnosed.
(E)   Humans have more genes in common with
        nonhuman primates than with cats.

Step 1. Identify the Question Type

The question stem specifically identifies this as a Weaken question with the term "weaken."
As with many Strengthen and Weaken questions, the question stem tells you what you need
to use as the conclusion. In this case, you are tasked with weakening the science columnist's
explanation.

Step 2. Untangle the Stimulus

The author's "explanation" for the number of diseases shared by humans and cats is that many
human diseases are genetically based. The author supports this explanation by documenting
the genetic closeness of humans and cats.

Step 3. Make a Prediction

On the LSAT, words like "some," "many," "few," and "often" simply mean "at least one." So
when the author puts forward "many" human genetic based diseases as the explanation for
the shared disease between cats and humans, it should strike you as a potentially limited
explanation. The scope shift here is from an undefined number of genetic-based diseases in
humans to the better defined genetic commonalities. The science columnist assumes lots of
shared genes indicate lots of shared genetic diseases. Weaken this argument with an answer
that indicates that shared genes do not necessarily mean shared genetic diseases or that provides an alternative explanation for why cats and humans share diseases.

The other important pattern to recognize here is that this is a causal argument. The way to
weaken a causal argument is to break the connection between the science columnist's proposed cause (genetic diseases) and the effect (shared diseased among humans and cats), or
to provide an alternative cause for the shared diseases.

Step 4. Evaluate the Answer Choices

Choice (A) has no effect on the argument because it does not address the issue of why cats and humans share diseases in common. The question stem clearly identifies the central issue as explaining why cats and humans share diseases. Any answer that does not attack the science columnist's explanation of genetics or provide an alternative explanation (cause) is wrong.

Choice (B) negates the assumption and therefore weakens the argument. This is the correct answer.

Choice (C) makes an irrelevant comparison and, like choice (A), has no bearing on the central issue of explaining "why" cats and humans share a certain number of diseases.

Choice (D) exposes the mild nature and low diagnosis rate of the diseases shared by humans and cats. While it identifies common characteristics, it does nothing to explain the commonalities or weaken the argument.

Choice (E), like choice (C), makes an irrelevant comparison and provides no explanation for why cats and humans share diseases in common.

4.   **(A)**

> <This region must find new ways to help business grow.>
> (After all,) shoe manufacturing used to be a major local industry, but recently has experienced severe setbacks due to overseas competition, so there is a need for expansion into new manufacturing areas. (Moreover,) our outdated public policy generally inhibits business growth.
>
> Which one of the following most accurately expresses the (main conclusion) drawn in the argument?

(A)   The region needs to find new ways to enhance business growth.
(B)   Shoe manufacturing is no longer a major source of income in the region.
(C)   Shoe manufacturing in the region has dramatically declined due to overseas competition.
(D)   Business in the region must expand into new areas of manufacturing.
(E)   Outdated public policy inhibits business growth in the region.

Step 1. Identify the Question Type

The question stem asks for the "main conclusion" making this a Main Point question.

Step 2. Untangle the Stimulus

The conclusion is stated right away: This region must find new ways to support the growth of businesses. She presents her evidence using Keywords: She starts her second sentence with "after all" and her third sentence with "moreover" indicating the information will support her conclusion. While you will usually not be given clear conclusion Keywords on a Main Point question, you may well be provided with evidence Keywords.

Step 3. Make a Prediction

The correct answer will paraphrase the conclusion, the sentence you bracketed.

Step 4. Evaluate the Answer Choices

Choice (A) is the correct answer as it repeats the first sentence almost word for word.

Choice (B) might be implied in the evidence, but it's definitely not the argument conclusion.

Choices (C), (D), and (E) repeat evidence provided to support the conclusion. They don't state the conclusion itself.

5. **(E)**

As a result of modern medicine, more people have been able to enjoy long and pain-free lives. But the resulting increase in life expectancy has contributed to a steady increase in the proportion of the population that is of advanced age. <This population shift is creating potentially devastating financial problems for some social welfare programs.>

Which one of the <u>following</u> (propositions) is most precisely exemplified by the situation presented above?

(A)   Technical or scientific innovation cannot be the
        solution to all problems.
(B)   Implementing technological innovations should
        be delayed until the resulting social changes
        can be managed.
(C)   Every enhancement of the quality of life has
        unavoidable negative consequences.
(D)   All social institutions are affected by a
        preoccupation with prolonging life.
(E)   Solving one set of problems can create a
        different set of problems.

Step 1. Identify the Question Type

The term "propositions" signals a Principle question, and the word "following" tells you the principle is in the answer choice. Your task is to find the broad rule that is exemplified by the specific example in the stimulus.

Step 2. Untangle the Stimulus

People are living longer, pain-free lives because of modern medicine creating a larger proportion of older people in the population. Consequently, some social welfare programs are facing major financial problems.

Step 3. Make a Prediction

Take the narrow situation and generalize it. Solving one problem (shorter, more painful lives) can contribute to another problem (financial crisis for some social welfare programs).

Step 4. Evaluate the Answer Choices

Choice (A) is not a good match. The technical innovations in the stimulus solved some problems, but an important contrast is that they created other problems rather than simply failing to solve all problems.

Choice (B) recommends delaying innovation to avoid resulting social problems. But the stimulus doesn't include a recommendation to manage problems. In fact, it says dealing with one issue creates another. This is a common type of out-of-scope answer that takes the logic of the argument another step forward to what may seem like an entirely reasonable next step. Recognize that the author is simply saying what has happened and is not recommending what to do in response to this information. Resist the urge to take that next step.

Choice (C) is extreme. The stimulus does not address every enhancement of the quality of life and does not suggest whether or not the problems created are avoidable.

Choice (D) is extreme on the other end. The stimulus specifically says that some social institutions are affected, not all.

Choice (E) matches the prediction and is the correct answer.

6. **(A)**

Since Jackie is such a big fan of Moral Vacuum's music, <she will probably like The Cruel Herd's new album.> Like Moral Vacuum, The Cruel Herd on this album plays complex rock music that employs the acoustic instrumentation and harmonic sophistication of early sixties jazz. The Cruel Herd also has very witty lyrics, full of puns and sardonic humor, like some of Moral Vacuum's best lyrics.

Which one of the following, if true, most strengthens the argument?

(A) Jackie has not previously cared for The Cruel Herd, but on the new album The Cruel Herd's previous musical arranger has been replaced by Moral Vacuum's musical arranger.

(B) Though The Cruel Herd's previous albums' production quality was not great, the new album is produced by one of the most widely employed producers in the music industry.

(C) Like Moral Vacuum, The Cruel Herd regularly performs in clubs popular with many students at the university that Jackie attends.

(D) All of the music that Jackie prefers to listen to on a regular basis is rock music.

(E) Jackie's favorite Moral Vacuum songs have lyrics that are somber and marked by a strong political awareness.

Step 1. Identify the Question Type

Since the question asks for something that "most strengthens" the argument, this is a Strengthen question.

Step 2. Untangle the Stimulus

Presented in the first sentence, the conclusion states that Jackie will probably like The Cruel Herd's new album. This qualified prediction ("will probably") is based on evidence, signaled by "since," that Jackie likes Moral Vacuum's music. The argument then details characteristics shared by the bands: complex rock music, acoustic instrumentation, harmonic sophistication, and witty lyrics.

Step 3. Make a Prediction

The author provides some similarities between The Cruel Herd and Moral Vacuum and assumes that such similarities indicate she will like both bands. The correct answer will confirm the assumption, provide another reason why the two bands are similar, or eliminate some potential difference between the bands that might have prevented Jackie from liking The Cruel Herd despite the similarities to Moral Vacuum.

Step 4. Evaluate the Answer Choices

Choice (A) supports the assumption indicating that The Cruel Herd's music will likely further resemble Moral Vacuum's now that The Cruel Herd has enlisted Moral Vacuum's musical arranger. Therefore, this is the correct answer. Most importantly, notice that only choices (A) and (B) focus on The Cruel Herd's new album, which is the real subject of the author's conclusion. The author does not claim that Jackie will like the band generally, just the new album. Staying on topic with the conclusion is one of the most important things you can do on the Logical Reasoning section of the LSAT.

Choice (B) tells you that The Cruel Herd's production quality will probably improve, but there is no indication that Jackie favors production quality. More importantly, this argument is based on an analogy or comparison between the two bands. To strengthen an analogy or comparison, you need either another similarity or to eliminate a potential difference.

Choice (C) fails to directly connect the music of the two bands, especially The Cruel Herd's new album. The fact that both bands play in clubs popular with university students doesn't address similarity of musical elements, nor the music on the new album.

Choice (D) adds nothing to the argument by indicating a general preference for rock music, since the stimulus provides far more detailed information on the types of rock music that Jackie likes. Just because she only likes rock would not dictate that she likes all rock music; in fact, the stimulus indicates she has specific tastes in rock music.

Choice (E) may weaken the argument. By identifying things that Jackie likes about Moral Vacuum songs and not connecting them back to The Cruel Herd, (E) suggests why Jackie would like Moral Vacuum and not The Cruel Herd. Since, there is no connection to The Cruel Herd's new album, this answer cannot strengthen the author's argument.

7. **(A)**

> Superconductors are substances that conduct electricity without resistance at low temperatures. Their use, however, will (never) be economically feasible, (unless) there is a substance that superconducts at a temperature above minus 148 degrees Celsius. If there is such a substance, that substance must be an alloy of niobium and germanium. Unfortunately, such alloys superconduct at temperatures no higher than minus 160 degrees Celsius.
>
> If the statements above are true, which one of the following (must also be true)?

(A) The use of superconductors will never be economically feasible.

(B) If the alloys of niobium and germanium do not superconduct at temperatures above minus 148 degrees Celsius, then there are other substances that will do so.

(C) The use of superconductors could be economically feasible if there is a substance that superconducts at temperatures below minus 148 degrees Celsius.

(D) Alloys of niobium and germanium do not superconduct at temperatures below minus 160 degrees Celsius.

(E) No use of alloys of niobium and germanium will ever be economically feasible.

Step 1. Identify the Question Type

The phrase "must also be true" identifies this is an Inference question. The correct answer must be true based on the information in the stimulus.

Step 2. Untangle the Stimulus

The LSAT does not test your knowledge of content, so don't let the technical science language throw you off. Instead, use the formal logic language in the stimulus to help you get a handle on the material so you can spot an answer that must be true based on it. Remember, the correct answer to an Inference question that includes formal logic often comes from the statement's contrapositive.

The stimulus starts with a definition of superconductors and then doubts their economic feasibility unless there's a substance that superconducts above –148 degrees Celsius. "Never … unless" signals formal logic, so you can translate this sentence using the "No X unless Y" equation, then into an "If X, then Y," and then form the contrapositive. Here is what the progression looks like:

Table 21.2

Never economically feasible unless superconducts above –148 degrees Celsius If economically feasible then superconducts above –148 degrees Celsius	On test day, you will not want to take the time to write out this part of the formal logic. As you practice, though, it's important to think it through and write it out to improve your accuracy and efficiency.
Econ feas → sc above –148 Not sc above –148 → not econ feasible	On test day, consider jotting down the basic X → Y statement and its contrapositive so you don't have to reread any information and you have something to compare to the answer choices.

The stimulus then says that the only substances that superconduct above –148 Celsius are alloys of niobium and germanium. Finally, you learn that the alloys can't superconduct at temperatures above –160 Celsius. Notice you can combine the last two statements. If niobium and germanium alloys can't superconduct above –160, they can't superconduct above –148, and that triggers the contrapositive. Therefore, superconductors can't be economically feasible.

Step 3. Make a Prediction

Once you have a handle on an Inference stimulus, go right to the answer choices. In this case, you've translated the formal logic and combined statements where possible. You're ready to move to the answers with the understanding that there is a necessary condition for economic feasibility; that condition can't be met; so, superconductors are not economically feasible.

Step 4. Evaluate the Answer Choices

Choice (A) *must be true.* The first formal logic statement told you that economic feasibility required conduction at certain temperatures. Later, you were told that such conduction was not possible. Thus, without the necessary prerequisite, economic feasibility is not possible.

Choice (B) contradicts the stimulus. The stimulus specifically states that the only substances that can superconduct above –148 degrees must be an alloy of niobium and germanium. Therefore, if they don't superconduct above –148 degrees, then there are no other substances that will do so.

Choice (C) confuses necessity and sufficiency. You know that economic feasibility requires conductivity at such temperatures, but that does not mean that conductivity at such temperatures will allow for economic feasibility. This answer changes the direction of the arrow in your formal logic, making it an incomplete contrapositive.

Choice (D) also contradicts the stimulus that says the alloys of niobium and germanium do not superconduct at temperatures higher than –160, which means that they must superconduct below –160.

Choice (E) is tempting, but you only know that these elements will not be economically feasible as superconductors, not that they will never have any other economically viable uses.

8. **(D)**

> Doctor: In three separate studies, researchers compared children who had slept with night-lights in their rooms as infants to children who had not. In the first study, the children who had slept with night-lights proved more likely to be nearsighted, but the later studies found no correlation between night-lights and nearsightedness. However, the children in the first study were younger than those in the later studies. <(This suggests that) if night-lights cause nearsightedness, the effect disappears with age.>

Which one of the following, if true, would most (weaken) the doctor's argument?

(A) A fourth study comparing infants who were currently sleeping with night-lights to infants who were not did not find any correlation between night-lights and nearsightedness.

(B) On average, young children who are already very nearsighted are no more likely to sleep with night-lights than young children who are not already nearsighted.

(C) In a study involving children who had not slept with night-lights as infants but had slept with night-lights when they were older, most of the children studied were not nearsighted.

(D) The two studies in which no correlation was found did not examine enough children to provide significant support for any conclusion regarding a causal relationship between night-lights and nearsightedness.

(E) In a fourth study involving 100 children who were older than those in any of the first three studies, several of the children who had slept with night-lights as infants were nearsighted.

Step 1. Identify the Question Type

The term "weaken" tells you directly that this is a Weaken question.

Step 2. Untangle the Stimulus

The doctor's conclusion appears at the end of the stimulus, signaled by the phrase "This suggests that." It says that if night-lights cause nearsightedness, the effect disappears with age. It's based on the results of three different studies. The first study reported that children who slept with night-lights were more likely to be nearsighted. The two later studies found no correlation between sleeping with night-lights and nearsightedness. Because the children were older in the last two studies than in the first study, the doctor determines that nearsightedness must go away with age.

Step 3. Make a Prediction

Any argument based on a study assumes the study is valid. To weaken such an argument, you need to attack the assumption and identify a problem with the research. Not every Weaken question involving a study will have a correct answer that identifies a problem with the study itself, but it is a common pattern on LSAT Weaken questions to watch out for.

Step 4. Evaluate the Answer Choices

Choice (A) introduces a study group that is not representative of the original research population. The doctor is only interested in testing children who slept or didn't sleep with night-lights when they were infants. The fourth study deals with infants who currently sleep with night-lights. Therefore, this sample can't be used to weaken (or strengthen for that matter) a study to determine if night-light sleepers outgrow nearsightedness. Eliminate this choice.

Choice (B) does not attack the argument either. It deals with children who are already nearsighted, so knowing whether they sleep with night-lights will not be helpful.

Choice (C) also reaches outside the scope of the argument by introducing an unrepresentative study group. This group of children did not sleep with night-lights until they were older.

Choice (D) attacks the validity of the two later studies saying the sample size was too small to support the doctor's conclusion. Choice (D) weakens the argument and is the correct answer.

Choice (E) indicates a correlation between night-lights and nearsightedness but doesn't address the doctor's conclusion that if night-lights cause nearsightedness, the effect disappears with age.

9.   **(A)**

Global surveys estimate the earth's population of <u>nesting female leatherback turtles</u> has fallen by more than two-thirds in the past 15 years. Any species whose population declines by more than two-thirds in 15 years is in grave danger of extinction, <so the <u>leatherback turtle</u> is clearly in danger of extinction.>

Which one of the following is an (assumption) that the argument requires?

(A)   The decline in the population of nesting female leatherback turtles is proportional to the decline in the leatherback turtle population as a whole.

(B)   If the global population of leatherback turtles falls by more than two-thirds over the next 15 years, the species will eventually become extinct.

(C)   The global population of leatherback turtles consists in roughly equal numbers of females and males.

(D)   Very few leatherback turtles exist in captivity.

(E)   The only way to ensure the continued survival of leatherback turtles in the wild is to breed them in captivity.

Step 1. Identify the Question Type

The term "assumption" makes this an Assumption question.

Step 2. Untangle the Stimulus

The author draws a conclusion in the last sentence, set off by "so," that the leatherback turtle is in danger of extinction. Her evidence is that the nesting female leatherback turtle population has dropped by more than two-thirds in the past fifteen years, a sure indicator the group is in danger of extinction.

Step 3. Make a Prediction

The author uses evidence about the nesting female leatherbacks to reach a conclusion about all leatherbacks. To make that jump, the author must assume the nesting female population is representative of the whole group.

Step 4. Evaluate the Answer Choices

Choice (A) correctly indicates that the decline of the nesting female leatherback turtle population is proportional to and therefore representative of the leatherback turtle population decline.

Choice (B) is an extreme distortion of the evidence in saying that the species will become extinct. The argument says a species is in grave danger of extinction. The result is not certain. Also, even if this answer more accurately restated that evidence, the correct assumption answer choice cannot simply restate a piece of evidence. Watch out for this type of wrong answer trap specific to Assumption questions.

Choice (C) does not make any connection between the population decline of nesting female leatherbacks and the whole leatherback population. Instead it adds another factor, the general female leatherback population.

Choice (D) strengthens the author's claim of imminent extinction, but is not a necessary assumption of the author's argument that a decline in nesting females indicates a danger of extinction of the species. Use the denial test: denied, this choice indicates that more than a few turtles exist in captivity. The existence of more than a few turtles in captivity does not prevent the author from being right that the species is in danger of extinction. A Necessary Assumption answer cannot bring in out of scope information or concepts, even if it seems to support the conclusion.

Choice (E) is also outside the scope by discussing captive breeding. It is extreme in indicating that it is the only way to prevent extinction. Again, use the denial test. Denied, this answer indicates that captive breeding is not the only possible way to prevent extinction. Just because there are more than one possible way, even multiple ways, to potentially prevent extinction does not mean that any will be implemented or will ultimately work. Denying this choice does not destroy the author's claim that the turtles are in danger of extinction.

10. **(D)**

Public health experts have waged a long-standing educational campaign to get people to eat more vegetables, which are known to help prevent cancer. Unfortunately, the campaign has had little impact on people's diets. The reason is probably that many people simply dislike the taste of most vegetables. ⟨Thus,⟩ the campaign would probably be more effective if it included information on ways to make vegetables more appetizing.⟩

Which one of the following, if true, most ⟨strengthens⟩ the argument?

(A) The campaign to get people to eat more vegetables has had little impact on the diets of most people who love the taste of vegetables.

(B) Some ways of making vegetables more appetizing diminish vegetables' ability to help prevent cancer.

(C) People who find a few vegetables appetizing typically do not eat substantially more vegetables than do people who dislike the taste of most vegetables.

(D) People who dislike the taste of most vegetables would eat many more vegetables if they knew how to make them more appetizing.

(E) The only way to make the campaign to get people to eat more vegetables more effective would be to ensure that anyone who at present dislikes the taste of certain vegetables learns to find those vegetables appetizing.

Step 1. Identify the Question Type

The word "strengthens" in the stem tells you this is a Strengthen question.

Step 2. Untangle the Stimulus

A public health campaign to encourage people to eat more vegetables is not working. The author surmises that people just don't like the taste of vegetables. "Thus," the author concludes, the campaign should tell people how to make their vegetables more appetizing so they're more likely to eat them.

Step 3. Make a Prediction

To reach that conclusion, the author must assume that people don't know how to prepare their vegetables so that they like the taste. A strengthener will confirm that assumption.

Step 4. Evaluate the Answer Choices

Choice (A) talks about people who love the taste of vegetables, while the stimulus deals with people who don't like the taste of vegetables. Choice (A) goes beyond the scope of the argument, so it's out.

Choice (B) creates a conundrum. The whole purpose of the campaign to eat more vegetables is to prevent cancer. Choice (B) would threaten the value of the campaign, so you can cross it out.

Choice (C) makes an irrelevant comparison between people who like a few vegetables and those who don't like most vegetables. The author focuses the argument on people who don't like the taste of vegetables. Move on to the next choice.

Choice (D) confirms the assumption by making the argument more likely. Once people who don't like vegetables learn how to make them more tasty, they'll eat them. This is the correct answer.

Choice (E) reverses the logic, so it's incorrect.

11. **(D)**

> Pure science—research with no immediate commercial or technological application—is a public good. Such research requires a great amount of financial support and does not yield profits in the short term. (Since) private corporations will not undertake to support activities that do not yield short-term profits, <a society that wants to reap the benefits of pure science ought to use public funds to support such research.>

The claim about private corporations (serves which one) (of the following functions) in the argument?

(A) It expresses the conclusion of the argument.
(B) It explains what is meant by the expression "pure research" in the context of the argument.
(C) It distracts attention from the point at issue by introducing a different but related goal.
(D) It supports the conclusion by ruling out an alternative way of achieving the benefits mentioned.
(E) It illustrates a case where unfortunate consequences result from a failure to accept the recommendation offered.

Step 1. Identify the Question Type

The phrases "claim about private corporations" and "serves which one of the following functions" indicate that this is a Role of the Statement question.

Step 2. Untangle the Stimulus

The stimulus begins with some background information that defines "pure science" as research with no prospects for short-term profits. It's followed by the claim in question: that private corporations won't support activities that don't have short-term profitability. The word "Since" indicates that the claim is evidence. It supports the final clause, the conclusion.

Step 3. Make a Prediction

The correct answer will identify the claim as evidence in the argument.

Step 4. Evaluate the Answer Choices

Choice (A) is wrong. The claim is the evidence, not the conclusion.

Choice (B) misattributes the definition of pure research to the claim in question. The term is explained in the background information immediately preceding the claim.

Choice (C) also gets it wrong. The claim in question is relevant to the point at issue and does not introduce any other goals.

Choice (D) correctly identifies the claim as evidence by defining evidence as support for the conclusion and more specifically defining its purpose.

Choice (E) misdirects attention to the recommendation made in the conclusion to use public funds to support pure science and adds information about consequences for ignoring the recommendation not in the argument at all.

12. **(C)**

> Melinda: Hazard insurance decreases an individual's risk by judiciously spreading the risk among many policyholders.
>
> Jack: I disagree. It makes sense for me to buy fire insurance for my house, but I don't see how doing so lessens the chances that my house will burn down.
>
> Jack's response most clearly trades on an ambiguity in which one of the following expressions used by Melinda?
> (A) judiciously spreading
> (B) many policyholders
> (C) risk
> (D) decreases
> (E) hazard insurance

Step 1. Identify the Question Type

This question has no clear Keywords to help you identify the question type. But stop and think what it's really asking. You are tasked with identifying how Jack responds to Melinda, specifically to an ambiguity in one of Melinda's expressions. So, this is a Method of Argument question with a twist. You need to identify the expression that is used by Melinda with two different meanings or connotations.

Step 2. Untangle the Stimulus

Read both speakers' statements looking for the ambiguous term. Melinda says that hazard insurance decreases individual risk by spreading risk among lots of policyholders. Jack disagrees and claims that insurance doesn't reduce the risk his house will burn down.

Step 3. Make a Prediction

Jack and Melinda are both talking about risk, but the term is not specifically defined. Melinda talks about spreading the risk of disaster among insurance policyholders, which indicates concern for financial loss, while Jack's response focuses on the chances of something bad happening. Melinda never asserts that buying insurance reduces the risk of her house burning down. So, Jack's method of argument is to play word games with the term "risk."

Step 4. Evaluate the Answer Choices

Choice (A) does not have ambiguity. Jack may disagree that hazard insurance judiciously spreads risk, but Melinda's use of the phrase is clear.

Choice (B) is overlooked by Jack. He's not focused on others, just his own insurance and his own risk. So, he can't trade on an ambiguity of a term he ignores.

Choice (C) matches the prediction and is the correct answer.

Choice (D) is used by both speakers in the same way.

Choice (E) is also consistently understood by Jack and Melinda as a type of insurance policy.

13. **(A)**

Some doctors believe that a certain drug reduces the duration of episodes of vertigo, claiming that the average duration of vertigo for people who suffer from it has decreased since the drug was introduced. (However,) during a recent three-month shortage of the drug, there was no significant change in the average duration of vertigo. <(Thus,) we can (conclude) that the drug has no effect on the duration of vertigo.>

Which one of the following is an (assumption) required by the argument?

(A)   If a drug made a difference in the duration of vertigo, a three-month shortage of that drug would have caused a significant change in the average duration of vertigo.

(B)   If there were any change in the average duration of vertigo since the introduction of the drug, it would have demonstrated that the drug has an effect on the duration of vertigo.

(C)   A period of time greater than three months would not have been better to use in judging whether the drug has an effect on the duration of vertigo.

(D)   Changes in diet and smoking habits are not responsible for any change in the average duration of vertigo since the introduction of the drug.

(E)   There are various significant factors other than drugs that decrease the duration of vertigo for many people who suffer from it.

Step 1. Identify the Question Type

This question specifically asks for the argument's assumption, so it's an Assumption question.

Step 2. Untangle the Stimulus

The stimulus begins with some background information about what some doctors believe—that a certain drug cuts the length of time of vertigo episodes. The contrast Keyword "However" tells you that the author is about to disagree. He offers evidence that limited availability of the drug over a three-month period did not result in a significant change in the duration of a vertigo episode. The conclusion appears in the last sentence, signaled by "Thus" and "conclude." In it, the author determines that the drug has no effect on the length of time of a vertigo episode. In other words, the author argues that since there is no increase in the duration of a vertigo episode after a three-month absence of the drug, the drug has no effect.

Step 3. Make a Prediction

Because the drug was not used for three months, the author determines that the drug has no effect. The author must assume then that three months without the drug is enough time for the duration of the vertigo episodes to increase again. Maybe the episodes increase after a longer period.

Generally speaking, if an author relies on a certain duration of time in the evidence, she must assume it was enough time to prove her conclusion.

Step 4. Evaluate the Answer Choices

Choice (A) is phrased as a conditional statement, but don't let that throw you off. It's just another way of saying that three months should have been enough time for a change to occur. In making an argument, the author assumes that "If I have this evidence, then I can reach this conclusion." Here the evidence is: no change in three months, and the conclusion is: the drug has no effect. So the author assumes:

No change in 3 months → no effect

And the contrapositive is:

Effect → change within 3 months

Choice (A) is the contrapositive form of: If evidence, then conclusion. So, choice (A) is the correct answer.

Choice (B) is also in conditional statement form, but it commits a classic formal logic flaw. This choice takes the conditional, if evidence, then conclusion, and negates both sides without reversing the sides.

This choice in short says:

Change → effect rather than no change → no effect

Choice (C) is tempting. The author must assume that three months is a sufficient amount of time in which to make a judgment whether the drug has any effect on vertigo. So, it is not a great leap to think that the author assumes that a longer test would not be any better judge of the effect, or lack thereof, of the drug. This choice certainly strengthens the argument. But it is not necessary to the author's argument that three months is the ideal length of study, that no longer length would be a better test. All that is necessary to the author's argument is that three months is a sufficient length of time for the study. Again, the denial test can help you eliminate Assumption answer choices that support the conclusion but are not essential to the argument. Here, denying this choice indicates that a longer time period would be a better judge of the effects of the drug on vertigo, but that in no way tells you that a longer test would reach a different conclusion than the three-month test or contradict the author's claim.

Choice (D) eliminates another cause for any changes in the duration of vertigo. The elimination of other possibilities is a common Assumption answer pattern. This would be an attractive answer if the author had, in fact, concluded that the drugs DID cause a change in the duration of vertigo. With such a causal conclusion, the author would have assumed there were no other causes. Here the author does the opposite and concludes that the drug does NOT cause a change in the duration of vertigo. So, you are not looking for an answer that eliminates other potential causes.

Choice (E) brings in out of scope factors. It adds "various significant factors" not included in the argument. The answer to an assumption will never reach beyond the scope of the argument.

14. **(D)**

It has been suggested that a television set should be thought of as nothing more than "a toaster with pictures" and that since we let market forces determine the design of kitchen appliances we can let them determine what is seen on television. But that approach is too simple. <Some governmental control is needed, > (since) television is so important politically and culturally. It is a major source of commercial entertainment. It plays an important political role because it is the primary medium through which many voters obtain information about current affairs. It is a significant cultural force in that in the average home it is on for more than five hours a day.

Which one of the following most accurately expresses the (role played) in the argument by the claim that television is so important politically and culturally?

(A) It states a view that the argument as a whole is designed to discredit.

(B) It is an intermediate conclusion that is offered in support of the claim that a television set should be thought of as nothing more than "a toaster with pictures" and for which the claim that we can let market forces determine what is seen on television is offered as support.

(C) It is a premise that is offered in support of the claim that we let market forces determine the design of kitchen appliances.

(D) It is an intermediate conclusion that is offered in support of the claim that some governmental control of television is needed and for which the claim that the television is on for more than five hours a day in the average home is offered as partial support.

(E) It is a premise that is offered in support of the claim that television is the primary medium through which many voters obtain information about current affairs.

Step 1. Identify the Question Type

The question identifies a specific claim in the stimulus and asks for the "role played" by it. This is a Role of a Statement question.

Step 2. Untangle the Stimulus

The stimulus begins with one school of thought that television programming should be determined by market forces. Just like other LSAT arguments, you can expect the author's disagreement when an argument introduces how some people think. The author concludes that some government control is needed and goes on to explain why in the evidence signaled by "since." And that's where you'll find the claim in question.

If you stop your stimulus review here and proceed to the answer choices, you'll be looking for an answer that identifies the claim as evidence that supports the conclusion. While it is, you won't find that answer as one of the choices. You need to untangle the whole stimulus.

The rest of the argument explains why television is so important politically and culturally—because it entertains us, informs us about current affairs, and provides a cultural presence in our homes. The last few sentences are evidence of the claim of television's political and cultural importance.

Step 3. Make a Prediction

The claim in question is support for the conclusion, but also has its own evidentiary support. Thus, it is a subsidiary conclusion.

Step 4. Evaluate the Answer Choices

Choice (A) is a 180. You know the argument is not intended to discredit the claim because the author spends the last half of the argument supporting it.

Choice (B) should get your attention, but it falls short. The claim is an intermediate conclusion, but it does not support the thought that television is a toaster with pictures. The author disagrees with that thought and uses the claim in question to discredit that idea.

Choice (C) is convoluted and wrong. The claim is a premise, but it's certainly not offered to support the notion that market forces determine the design of kitchen appliances. That idea is part of the school of thought with which the author disagrees.

Choice (D) correctly defines the role of the claim in question.

Choice (E) gets it backward. The claim that television is the primary medium through which many voters obtain information about current affairs supports the claim that television is politically and culturally important, not the other way around.

15. **(B)**

Earthworms, vital to the health of soil, prefer soil that is approximately neutral on the acid-to-alkaline scale. (Since) decomposition of dead plants makes the top layer of soil highly acidic, <application of crushed limestone, which is highly alkaline, to the soil's surface should make the soil more attractive to earthworms.>

Which one of the following is an (assumption) on which the argument depends?

(A)   As far as soil health is concerned, aiding the decomposition of dead plants is the most important function performed by earthworms.

(B)   After its application to the soil's surface, crushed limestone stays in the soil's top layer long enough to neutralize some of the top layer's acidity.

(C)   Crushed limestone contains available calcium and magnesium, both of which are just as vital as earthworms to healthy soil.

(D)   By itself, acidity of soil does nothing to hasten decomposition of dead plants.

(E)   Alkaline soil is significantly more likely to benefit from an increased earthworm population than is highly acidic soil.

Step 1. Identify the Question Type

The word "assumption" tells you that this is an Assumption question.

Step 2. Untangle the Stimulus

The author concludes in the last sentence that crushed limestone should be added to soil to attract earthworms. The evidence says that decomposing plants make soil acidic and earthworms prefer soil that is acid-to-alkaline neutral.

Step 3. Make a Prediction

Limestone is discussed in the conclusion, but not in the evidence. There must be something about the limestone that the author assumes will solve the problem of the high acid content of the soil and attract earthworms.

Step 4. Evaluate the Answer Choices

Choice (A) is stuck on the background information that earthworms are vital to soil health, which has nothing to do with whether adding limestone will make soil more attractive to earthworms, as the author concludes. Knowing that earthworms' most important function is to aid decomposing plants does nothing to tie together the evidence and conclusion. Also, be wary of extreme answers like this one, which says something is the "most" important factor.

Choice (B) works because it explains that limestone neutralizes some of the soil's acidity which makes the soil more attractive to the earthworms. This is the correct answer. If you are unsure, use the denial test and it should become clear that this answer is necessary to the author's recommendation. If the limestone does not stay in the soil long enough to reduce the acidity, then the recommendation to add it to attract earthworms holds no merit.

Choice (C) does not address the high acidity level of the soil. So, even if limestone offers vital nutrients to earthworms, the acid in the soil will keep them away.

Choice (D) doesn't address limestone, which is what you want to connect the evidence and conclusion. Whether soil acidity does anything to hasten plant decomposition has no impact on the argument.

Choice (E) misses the point. The author doesn't care about the type of soil that will benefit from a larger earthworm population but rather how crushed limestone will make the soil more attractive to earthworms.

16. **(E)**

> Jurist: A nation's laws must be viewed as expressions of
> a moral code that transcends those laws and
> serves as a measure of their adequacy. Otherwise,
> a society can have no sound basis for preferring
> any given set of laws to all others. Thus, any
> moral prohibition against the violation of statutes
> must leave room for exceptions.
>
> Which one of the following can be properly (inferred)
> from the jurist's statements?
>
> (A)   Those who formulate statutes are not primarily
>   concerned with morality when they do so.
> (B)   Sometimes criteria other than the criteria derived
>   from a moral code should be used in choosing
>   one set of laws over another.
> (C)   Unless it is legally forbidden ever to violate
>   some moral rules, moral behavior and
>   compliance with laws are indistinguishable.
> (D)   There is no statute that a nation's citizens have a
>   moral obligation to obey.
> (E)   A nation's laws can sometimes come into conflict
>   with the moral code they express.

Step 1. Identify the Question Type

Because the stem asks for something that can be "inferred" from the jurist's statement, this is an Inference question.

Step 2. Untangle the Stimulus

This atypical Inference stimulus presents an argument. The evidence states that a nation's laws are based on a moral code, supporting the conclusion that any moral ban on breaking the law must allow for exceptions.

Step 3. Make a Prediction

The argument deals with two things: law and morality. The jurist largely equates the two, but by saying that there must be room for exceptions, there must be some differences. Also remember that even though the statements in the stimulus are largely absolute and forceful, a modest-sounding answer is usually the one that must be true. Scan the answers for the choice that generally indicates that morality and law are not exactly in sync.

Step 4. Evaluate the Answer Choices

Choice (A) is nowhere to be found in the stimulus, which is concerned with what the jurist believes should be the case in formulating law. It never describes the concerns lawmakers have or don't have.

Choice (B) distorts the stimulus by adding additional criteria to the moral code that is necessary to choose a set of laws.

Choice (C) contradicts the stimulus by saying moral behavior and legal compliance are the same thing. The last sentence of the stimulus suggests otherwise.

Choice (D) conflicts with the jurist's statements. If laws are expressions of a moral code, there are many statutes that citizens have a moral obligation to obey.

Choice (E) can be inferred from the last sentence of the stimulus. If a moral ban on lawbreaking must have exceptions, there must be times when the law and the moral code don't agree. This is the correct answer.

17. **(B)**

An association between two types of conditions does not establish that conditions of one type cause conditions of the other type. Even persistent and inviolable association is inconclusive; such association is often due to conditions of both types being effects of the same kind of cause.

Which one of the following judgments most closely conforms to the principle stated above?

(A)   Some people claim that rapid growth of the money supply is what causes inflation. But this is a naive view. What these people do not realize is that growth in the money supply and inflation are actually one and the same phenomenon.

(B)   People who have high blood pressure tend to be overweight. But before we draw any inferences, we should consider that an unhealthy lifestyle can cause high blood pressure, and weight gain can result from living unhealthily.

(C)   In some areas, there is a high correlation between ice cream consumption and the crime rate. Some researchers have proposed related third factors, but we cannot rule out that the correlation is purely coincidental.

(D)   People's moods seem to vary with the color of the clothes they wear. Dark colors are associated with gloomy moods, and bright colors are associated with cheerful moods. This correlation resolves nothing, however. We cannot say whether it is the colors that cause the moods or the converse.

(E)   Linguists propose that the similarities between Greek and Latin are due to their common descent from an earlier language. But how are we to know that the similarities are not actually due to the two languages having borrowed structures from one another, as with the languages Marathi and Telegu?

Step 1. Identify the Question Type

The word "principle" identifies the stem as a Principle question. The stem also tells you the principle is "stated above" in the stimulus and your task is to apply it to a parallel situation in the answer.

Step 2. Untangle the Stimulus

This is a classic LSAT pattern. A correlation between two conditions does not necessarily mean that one condition caused the other. Even a long-standing correlation can be due to both conditions having a common cause.

372 | Part III: Full-Section Practice
Chapter 21

Step 3. Make a Prediction

Look for an answer that presents a strong correlation and no causation between two conditions and shows they have the same cause.

Step 4. Evaluate the Answer Choices

Choice (A) denies causation between growth of the money supply and inflation by saying they are the same thing. This is not a match.

Choice (B) conforms to the principle. It acknowledges a correlation between having high blood pressure and being overweight, and warns against drawing an inference about whether one caused the other. Instead, it says both conditions are probably the result of a common cause, unhealthy living. This is the correct answer.

Choice (C) considers whether the correlation between ice cream consumption and the crime rate is coincidental. Coincidental correlation is not part of the principle.

Choice (D) identifies a correlation between clothing color and mood and says one causes the other, but it's not clear which one is the cause and which one is the effect. Eliminate this choice.

Choice (E) looks promising by proposing a common cause of Greek and Latin similarities (common descent from an earlier language). But choice (E) dismisses the common cause theory by wondering whether the two languages are similar because they borrowed structures from each other.

18. **(B)**

Salesperson: <When> a salesperson is successful, it is certain that person has been in sales for at least three years.> This is because to succeed as a salesperson, one must first establish a strong client base, and studies have shown that anyone who spends at least three years developing a client base can eventually make a comfortable living in sales.

The reasoning in the salesperson's argument is vulnerable to criticism on the grounds that it fails to consider the possibility that

(A) salespeople who have spent three years developing a client base might not yet be successful in sales
(B) some salespeople require fewer than three years in which to develop a strong client base
(C) a salesperson who has not spent three years developing a client base may not succeed in sales
(D) it takes longer than three years for a salesperson to develop a strong client base
(E) few salespeople can afford to spend three years building a client base

Step 1. Identify the Question Type

The phrase "vulnerable to criticism" makes this a Flaw question, and "fails to consider the possibility that" identifies the flaw as an overlooked possibility. Your task is to describe what the salesperson overlooks in his argument.

Step 2. Untangle the Stimulus

The second sentence begins with "This is because," which indicates that the conclusion preceded the statement and the evidence will follow. Note the formal logic language in the stimulus, and use it to translate the statements. The conclusion says that if a salesperson is successful, he's been in sales for at least three years. The evidence tells you that if a salesperson is successful, he has a strong customer base and that if he spends at least three years developing that customer base, he'll make a comfortable living.

Step 3. Make a Prediction

The evidence says that three years in sales is *sufficient* to be successful in sales. The conclusion says that three years in sales is *necessary* to be successful in sales. The salesperson confuses a sufficient condition with a necessary condition, which can always be expressed as an ignored possibility flaw. The salesperson does not consider other ways to be successful in sales, besides three years at the job. When the salesperson concludes that it is absolutely necessary to have three years at the job, then he ignores the possibility that a salesperson might not need those three years to be successful.

Step 4. Evaluate the Answer Choices

Choice (A) talks about salespeople who are not successful in sales, which is beyond the scope of the argument.

Choice (B) is correct. It presents an overlooked way for a salesperson to be successful (in two years instead of three).

Choice (C) is not overlooked by the salesperson. He argues three years is necessary for success.

Choice (D) is not overlooked either. The salesperson says it takes at least three years to develop a client base which leaves room for the possibility that salespeople may need longer than three years to develop that client base.

Choice (E) is irrelevant to the argument. Whether salespeople can afford to spend three years developing a client base, the salesperson deems it necessary.

19. **(A)**

People who have habitually slept less than six hours a night and then begin sleeping eight or more hours a night typically begin to feel much less anxious. <Therefore,> most people who sleep less than six hours a night can probably cause their anxiety levels to fall by beginning to sleep at least eight hours a night.>

The reasoning in which one of the following arguments is most similar to that in the argument above?

(A) When a small company first begins to advertise on the Internet, its financial situation generally improves. This shows that most small companies that have never advertised on the Internet can probably improve their financial situation by doing so.

(B) Certain small companies that had never previously advertised on the Internet have found that their financial situations began to improve after they started to do so. So, most small companies can probably improve their financial situations by starting to advertise on the Internet.

(C) It must be true that any small company that increases its Internet advertising will improve its financial situation, since most small companies that advertise on the Internet improved their financial situations soon after they first began to do so.

(D) Usually, the financial situation of a small company that has never advertised on the Internet will improve only if that company starts to advertise on the Internet. Therefore, a typical small company that has never advertised on the Internet can probably improve its financial situation by doing so.

(E) A small company's financial situation usually improves soon after that company first begins to advertise on the Internet. Thus, most small companies that have never advertised on the Internet could probably become financially strong.

Step 1. Identify the Question Type

The phrase "most similar to" tells you that this is a Parallel Reasoning question.

Step 2. Untangle the Stimulus

The conclusion appears in the second sentence, indicated by "Therefore." It's a prediction that most people who sleep less than six hours a night can probably reduce their anxiety levels by sleeping at least eight hours a night. What else can help you focus the description before you check the answers? It covers a majority of the subjects ("most people"), the prediction is qualified ("can probably"), and it's based on behaving in a new way ("sleeping at least eight hours a night"). The evidence appears in the first sentence and says that sleeping eight hours instead of six (the new behavior) reduces anxiety (is typically successful).

Step 3. Make a Prediction

The correct answer will account for all features of the conclusion: a qualified prediction that a majority will improve from behaving in a new way. If more than one answer has a similar conclusion to the stimulus, compare the evidence.

Step 4. Evaluate the Answer Choices

Choice (A) correctly parallels the stimulus. It predicts that most small companies that don't advertise on the Internet can probably help their financial situations by doing so. The evidence provides that the new behavior of advertising on the Internet does work.

Choice (B) is close, but leaves out one important distinction. The conclusion talks about most small companies, not most small companies that have not used Internet advertising. The course of action the companies take must be new.

Choice (C) uses extreme language ("It must be true") that differentiates if from the stimulus. Another problem with choice (C) is that it refers to companies that increase their Internet advertising, rather than companies that have never advertised on the Internet before. The majority must be trying new behavior to match the stimulus.

Choice (D), like choice (A), has a conclusion similar to the stimulus'. It predicts that a typical small company that has never advertised on the Internet can probably improve its financial situation by doing so. However, the difference arises in the evidence. The stimulus' evidence states that new behavior typically produces improvement. Choice (D) distorts this by saying that improvement comes "only if" the new behavior is followed.

Choice (E) is missing an important feature from the stimulus' conclusion. Choice (E)'s conclusion predicts that most small companies that have never advertised on the Internet could probably become financially strong. The problem is the conclusion doesn't attribute the improvement to the new behavior.

20. **(C)**

> Biologist: Lions and tigers are so similar to each other anatomically that their skeletons are virtually indistinguishable. But their behaviors are known to be quite different: tigers hunt only as solitary individuals, whereas lions hunt in packs. <Thus,> paleontologists cannot reasonably infer solely on the basis of skeletal anatomy that extinct predatory animals, such as certain dinosaurs, hunted in packs.>

The conclusion is properly drawn if which one of the following is (assumed)?

(A)   The skeletons of lions and tigers are at least somewhat similar in structure in certain key respects to the skeletons of at least some extinct predatory animals.

(B)   There have existed at least two species of extinct predatory dinosaurs that were so similar to each other that their skeletal anatomy is virtually indistinguishable.

(C)   If skeletal anatomy alone is ever an inadequate basis for inferring a particular species' hunting behavior, then it is never reasonable to infer, based on skeletal anatomy alone, that a species of animals hunted in packs.

(D)   If any two animal species with virtually indistinguishable skeletal anatomy exhibit quite different hunting behaviors, then it is never reasonable to infer, based solely on the hunting behavior of those species, that the two species have the same skeletal anatomy.

(E)   If it is unreasonable to infer, solely on the basis of differences in skeletal anatomy, that extinct animals of two distinct species differed in their hunting behavior, then the skeletal remains of those two species are virtually indistinguishable.

Step 1. Identify the Question Type

Because the question asks "which one of the following is assumed," it is an Assumption question. Moreover, it is a Sufficient Assumption question, so the correct answer choice *must be true*. The correct answer to a Sufficient Assumption question is likely to be very forceful and absolute, as opposed to Necessary Assumption correct answers, which tend to be more modest.

Step 2. Untangle the Stimulus

The biologist explains that lions and tigers are almost anatomically identical and can't be distinguished by their skeletons. Yet their hunting behaviors are quite different. "Thus," she concludes, paleontologists can't just use the skeletal anatomy of extinct predatory animals, such as certain dinosaurs, to determine they hunted in packs.

Step 3. Make a Prediction

The biologist makes quite a scope shift. The evidence is based on lions and tigers and the conclusion refers to extinct predatory animals. The assumption will need to bridge the gap between the two. Here, the biologist assumes that if skeletal anatomy can't be used to determine the hunting behavior of lions and tigers, then it can't be used to determine the hunting behavior of any set of animals, past or present.

Step 4. Evaluate the Answer Choices

Choice (A) makes an irrelevant comparison between the skeletons of lions and tigers to some extinct predatory animals. The similarities between them does nothing to connect the skeleton of one group to its hunting behavior. Eliminate this choice.

Choice (B) compares the skeletons of two species of dinosaurs, but does not tie the experience of lions and tigers to the extinct predatory animals. Cross out this choice.

When (C) is added to the biologist's argument, it becomes ironclad. Choice (C) confirms the biologist's assumption: that an inability to infer hunting behavior from skeletal anatomy in just one case makes it impossible to do so in any other case. This is the correct answer.

Choice (D) is wrong because it uses the hunting behavior to infer something about the skeletal anatomy. Actually, the biologist uses the skeletal anatomy to infer something about the hunting behavior.

Choice (E) goes off track in two ways. First, it focuses on differences in skeletal anatomy rather than similarities. Second, it uses hunting behavior to determine skeletal anatomy rather than the other way around.

21. **(A)**

The trees always blossom in May if April rainfall exceeds 5 centimeters. If April rainfall exceeds 5 centimeters, then the reservoirs are always full on May 1. The reservoirs were not full this May 1 and ⟨thus⟩ the trees will not blossom this May.⟩

Which one of the following exhibits a ⟨flawed pattern of⟩ ⟨reasoning most similar to the flawed pattern of⟩ ⟨reasoning⟩ in the argument above?

(A) If the garlic is in the pantry, then it is still fresh. And the potatoes are on the basement stairs if the garlic is in the pantry. The potatoes are not on the basement stairs, so the garlic is not still fresh.

(B) The jar reaches optimal temperature if it is held over the burner for 2 minutes. The contents of the jar liquefy immediately if the jar is at optimal temperature. The jar was held over the burner for 2 minutes, so the contents of the jar must have liquefied immediately.

(C) A book is classified "special" if it is more than 200 years old. If a book was set with wooden type, then it is more than 200 years old. This book is not classified "special," so it is not printed with wooden type.

(D) The mower will operate only if the engine is not flooded. The engine is flooded if the foot pedal is depressed. The foot pedal is not depressed, so the mower will operate.

(E) If the kiln is too hot, then the plates will crack. If the plates crack, then the artisan must redo the order. The artisan need not redo the order. Thus, the kiln was not too hot.

Step 1. Identify the Question Type

The question asks for the "flawed pattern of reasoning most similar to the flawed pattern of reasoning" in the stimulus, making this a Parallel Flaw question.

Step 2. Untangle the Stimulus

Translate the formal logic language in Parallel Reasoning arguments to make it easier to compare the stimulus with the answer choices.

Table 21.3

	Statement	Translation
Evidence	If April rainfall exceeds 5 centimeters, then the trees always blossom in May.	X → Y
	If April rainfall exceeds 5 centimeters, then the reservoirs are always full on May 1.	X → Z
Conclusion	The reservoirs were not full this May 1 and thus the trees will not blossom this May.	not Z → not Y

The flaw in the argument comes from the formal logic. The absence of one result (Z) does not guarantee the absence of the other (Y), as stated in the conclusion.

Step 3. Make a Prediction

The correct answer will follow the same flawed formal logic.

Step 4. Evaluate the Answer Choices

Once you find a discrepancy in the formal logic, move on to the next answer. For purposes of explanation, the full translations are provided.

Table 21.4

Choice (A)	Statement	Translation
Evidence	If the garlic is in the pantry, then it is still fresh.	X → Y
	If the garlic is in the pantry, then the potatoes are on the basement stairs.	X → Z
Conclusion	The potatoes are not on the basement stairs, so the garlic is not still fresh.	not Z → not Y

Choice (A) is the correct answer, matching the stimulus point by point.

For the record:

Table 21.5

Choice (B)	Statement	Translation
Evidence	If it is held over the burner for 2 minutes, then the jar reaches optimal temperature.	X → Y
	If the jar is at optimal temperature, then the contents of the jar liquefy immediately.	Y → Z
Conclusion	The jar was held over the burner for 2 minutes, so the contents of the jar must have liquefied immediately.	X → Z

Choice (B) does not match the logic of the stimulus nor does it contain a flaw in the reasoning.

Table 21.6

Choice (C)	Statement	Translation
Evidence	If it is more than 200 years old, then a book is classified "special."	X → Y
	If a book was set with wooden type, then it is more than 200 years old.	Z → X
Conclusion	This book is not classified "special," so it is not printed with wooden type.	not Y → not Z

Choice (C) does not match the logic of the stimulus either nor does it contain a flaw in the reasoning.

Table 21.7

Choice (D)	Statement	Translation
Evidence	If the mower operates, then the engine is not flooded.	X → not Y
	If the foot pedal is depressed, the engine is flooded.	Z → Y
Conclusion	The foot pedal is not depressed, so the mower will operate.	Not Z → X

Choice (D) does not match the formal logic of the stimulus. It is flawed, but not in the same way as the stimulus. From the evidence, you have no way to know what happens if the foot pedal is not depressed.

Table 21.8

Choice (E)	Statement	Translation
Evidence	If the kiln is too hot, then the plates will crack.	X → Y
	If the plates crack, then the artisan must redo the order.	Y → Z
Conclusion	The artisan need not redo the order. Thus, the kiln was not too hot.	Not Z → not X

Choice (E) does not match the logic of the stimulus, and like (C), does not have a flaw.

22. **(E)**

> Doctor: Being overweight has long been linked with a variety of health problems, such as high blood pressure and heart disease. But recent research conclusively shows that people who are slightly overweight are healthier than those who are considerably underweight. <Therefore, to be healthy, it suffices to be slightly overweight.>

The argument's reasoning is (flawed) because the argument

(A) ignores medical opinions that tend to lead to a conclusion contrary to the one drawn

(B) never adequately defines what is meant by "healthy"

(C) does not take into account the fact that appropriate weight varies greatly from person to person

(D) holds that if a person lacks a property that would suffice to make the person unhealthy, then that person must be healthy

(E) mistakes a merely relative property for one that is absolute

Step 1. Identify the Question Type

The term "flawed" tells you this is a Flaw question.

Step 2. Untangle the Stimulus

Signaled by "Therefore," the doctor concludes in the last sentence that you can be slightly overweight and be healthy. She bases her statement on recent research that showed slightly overweight people were healthier than considerably underweight people.

Step 3. Make a Prediction

The argument says that slightly overweight people are healthier than considerably underweight people, so slightly overweight people are healthy. The scope shift here is from evidence that discusses becoming "healthier" to a conclusion about what it takes to be "healthy." The doctor jumps from a relative condition (healthier) to a discrete condition (healthy). Comparative healthiness does not establish health. The correct answer will make that point.

Step 4. Evaluate the Answer Choices

Choice (A) contradicts the stimulus. The doctor does pay attention to the medical research and cites it in her argument.

Choice (B) is irrelevant. The flaw in the argument is the doctor's faulty assumption that being healthier than someone else means being healthy, not the absent definition of healthy.

Choice (C) adds information not raised in the stimulus. You don't know whether the doctor accounted for weight variations or not.

Choice (D) goes beyond the scope of the argument. The doctor doesn't argue that lacking weight suffices to make someone unhealthy. She argues that having a few extra pounds suffices to make someone healthy.

Choice (E) may not jump out to you as the correct answer because it's presented in abstract terms, but it is. The doctor argues that relative health (slightly overweight is healthier than considerably underweight) establishes the health of the slightly overweight.

23. **(D)**

> Robust crops not only withstand insect attacks more successfully than other crops, they are also less likely to be attacked in the first place, since insects tend to feed on weaker plants. Killing insects with pesticides does not address the underlying problem of inherent vulnerability to damage caused by insect attacks. <Thus,> a better way to reduce the vulnerability of agricultural crops to insect pest damage is to grow those crops in good soil—soil with adequate nutrients, organic matter, and microbial activity.>

Which one of the following is an (assumption) on which the argument depends?

(A)   The application of nutrients and organic matter to farmland improves the soil's microbial activity.

(B)   Insects never attack crops grown in soil containing adequate nutrients, organic matter, and microbial activity.

(C)   The application of pesticides to weak crops fails to reduce the extent to which they are damaged by insect pests.

(D)   Crops that are grown in good soil tend to be more robust than other crops.

(E)   Growing crops without the use of pesticides generally produces less robust plants than when pesticides are used.

Step 1. Identify the Question Type

The word "assumption" identifies this as an Assumption question.

Step 2. Untangle the Stimulus

"Thus" points to the conclusion: grow crops in good soil to reduce the crops' vulnerability to insect damage. The author backs up the recommendation with evidence that robust crops are more resistant to insect attacks and less likely to be attacked at all.

Step 3. Make a Prediction

The evidence refers to robust crops and the conclusion talks about crops grown in good soil. The author must assume a connection between the two unmatched terms—that crops grown in good soil are more robust.

Step 4. Evaluate the Answer Choices

Choice (A) explains what makes good soil, but doesn't link good soil to robustness. This choice is out.

Choice (B) is extreme in saying insects never attack crops grown in good soil. Move on to the next choice.

Choice (C) refers to a side point in the evidence, not a connection between the evidence and the conclusion. Eliminate this choice.

Choice (D) is a perfect match of the prediction.

Choice (E) conflicts with the argument. If crops are less robust without pesticides, then pesticides should make them more robust.

24. **(D)**

> People perceive color by means of certain photopigments in the retina that are sensitive to certain wavelengths of light. People who are color-blind are unable to distinguish between red and green, for example, due an absence of certain photopigments. What is difficult to explain, however, is that in a study of people who easily distinguish red from green, 10 to 20 percent failed to report distinctions between many shades of red that the majority of the subjects were able to distinguish.
>
> Each of the following, if true, (helps to explain) the result of the study cited above (EXCEPT):
>
> (A) People with abnormally low concentrations of the photopigments for perceiving red can perceive fewer shades of red than people with normal concentrations.
> (B) Questions that ask subjects to distinguish between different shades of the same color are difficult to phrase with complete clarity.
> (C) Some people are uninterested in fine gradations of color and fail to notice or report differences they do not care about.
> (D) Some people are unable to distinguish red from green due to an absence in the retina of the photopigment sensitive to green.
> (E) Some people fail to report distinctions between certain shades of red because they lack the names for those shades.

Step 1. Identify the Question Type

"Helps to explain" identifies a Paradox question. The "EXCEPT" tells you that the correct answer will not resolve the paradox and that the four wrong answers will.

Step 2. Untangle the Stimulus

Color-blind people can't distinguish between red and green due to the lack of certain photopigments. Yet in a study of people who easily distinguish red from green (and therefore not color-blind), 10–20% of the subjects failed to report distinctions between shades of red.

Step 3. Make a Prediction

The paradox is that some people who are not color-blind don't report distinction between shades of red, and therefore appear to show signs of colorblindness. Four answers will help explain this paradox. The correct answer will not.

Step 4. Evaluate the Answer Choices

Choice (A) explains that some people, color-blind or not, have trouble perceiving different shades of red. They just have abnormally low concentrations of the photopigments that would typically allow them to differentiate reds. They may be able to distinguish red from green due to the presence of photopigments for green, but lack the pigments for reds. Eliminate this choice.

Choice (B) explains that subjects might have been able to distinguish between different shades of red, but may not have been able to articulate the differences.

Choice (C) explains that some people just aren't interested in fine color distinctions. So, even if they see them, they don't report them. This choice is out.

Choice (D) takes the discussion outside the scope and is therefore the right answer. It gives an explanation for why some color-blind people can't tell the difference between red and green. You are looking for an explanation of why some people who are not color-blind can't distinguish some shades of red.

Choice (E) provides one more reason why some of the subjects didn't report distinctions. Without names for certain shades of red, they could not accurately report their differences.

25. **(B)**

> Occultist: The issue of whether astrology is a science is easily settled: <it is both an art and a science.> The scientific components are the complicated mathematics and the astronomical knowledge needed to create an astrological chart. The art is in the synthesis of a multitude of factors and symbols into a coherent statement of their relevance to an individual.

The reasoning in the occultist's argument is (most) (vulnerable to criticism) on the grounds that the argument

(A)   presumes, without providing justification, that any science must involve complicated mathematics

(B)   incorrectly infers that a practice is a science merely from the fact that the practice has some scientific components

(C)   denies the possibility that astrology involves components that are neither artistic nor scientific

(D)   incorrectly infers that astronomical knowledge is scientific merely from the fact that such knowledge is needed to create an astrological chart

(E)   presumes, without providing justification, that any art must involve the synthesis of a multitude of factors and symbols

Step 1. Identify the Question Type

The "most vulnerable to criticism" language indicates a Flaw question.

Step 2. Untangle the Stimulus

The occultist concludes that astrology is both science and an art. The reason, the occultist says, is because astrology has both scientific and artistic components.

Step 3. Make a Prediction

Notice the shift in terms between the evidence (scientific components and artistic components) and conclusion (a science and an art). The faulty assumption is that because astrology has features of science and art, it actually *is* a science and an art.

Step 4. Evaluate the Answer Choices

Choice (A) is too broad. The occultist doesn't presume anything about all science. He merely states that complicated math is one of the scientific components of astrology. Move on to the next choice.

Choice (B) correctly identifies the faulty assumption made by the occultist.

Choice (C) is never addressed in the argument. The occultist says that astrology is a science and an art. He doesn't reject the possibility that astrology includes non-scientific and non-artistic components.

Choice (D) reverses the occultist's reasoning. He doesn't say that astronomy is scientific because it's used in astrology. Rather, astrology is scientific because it uses astronomy.

Choice (E), like choice (A), is too broad. The occultist doesn't presume anything about all art. He simply states that the synthesis of multiple factors and symbols is one of the artistic elements of astrology.

CHAPTER 22

FULL-LENGTH SECTION II[1]

Section II

Time—35 minutes

25 Questions

<u>Directions:</u> The questions in this section are based on the reasoning contained in brief statements or passages. For some questions, more than one of the choices could conceivably answer the question. However, you are to choose the <u>best</u> answer; that is, the response that most accurately and completely answers the question. You should not make assumptions that are by commonsense standards implausible, superfluous, or incompatible with the passage. After you have chosen the best answer, blacken the corresponding space on your answer sheet.

---

[1]PrepTest 53, Sec. 3

1. At many electronics retail stores, the consumer has the option of purchasing product warranties that extend beyond the manufacturer's warranty. However, consumers are generally better off not buying extended warranties. Most problems with electronic goods occur within the period covered by the manufacturer's warranty.

   Which one of the following, if true, most strengthens the argument?

   (A) Problems with electronic goods that occur after the manufacturer's warranty expires are generally inexpensive to fix in comparison with the cost of an extended warranty.

   (B) Because problems are so infrequent after the manufacturer's warranty expires, extended warranties on electronic goods are generally inexpensive.

   (C) Most of those who buy extended warranties on electronic goods do so because special circumstances make their item more likely to break than is usually the case.

   (D) Some extended warranties on electronic goods cover the product for the period covered by the manufacturer's warranty as well as subsequent years.

   (E) Retail stores sell extended warranties in part because consumers who purchase them are likely to purchase other products from the same store.

2. Since the 1970s, environmentalists have largely succeeded in convincing legislators to enact extensive environmental regulations. Yet, as environmentalists themselves not only admit but insist, the condition of the environment is worsening, not improving. Clearly, more environmental regulations are not the solution to the environment's problems.

   The argument's reasoning is flawed because the argument

   (A) attacks the environmentalists themselves instead of their positions

   (B) presumes, without providing warrant, that only an absence of environmental regulations could prevent environmental degradation

   (C) fails to consider the possibility that the condition of the environment would have worsened even more without environmental regulations

   (D) fails to justify its presumption that reducing excessive regulations is more important than preserving the environment

   (E) fails to consider the views of the environmentalists' opponents

3. Although it is unwise to take a developmental view of an art like music—as if Beethoven were an advance over Josquin, or Miles Davis an advance over Louis Armstrong—there are ways in which it makes sense to talk about musical knowledge growing over time. We certainly know more about certain sounds than was known five centuries ago; that is, we understand how sounds that earlier composers avoided can be used effectively in musical compositions. For example, we now know how the interval of the third, which is considered dissonant, can be used in compositions to create consonant musical phrases.

   Which one of the following most accurately expresses the main conclusion of the argument?

   (A) Sounds that were never used in past musical compositions are used today.

   (B) Sounds that were once considered dissonant are more pleasing to modern listeners.

   (C) It is inappropriate to take a developmental view of music.

   (D) It is unwise to say that one composer is better than another.

   (E) Our understanding of music can improve over the course of time.

4. A recent test of an electric insect control device discovered that, of the more than 300 insects killed during one 24-hour period, only 12 were mosquitoes. Thus this type of device may kill many insects, but will not significantly aid in controlling the potentially dangerous mosquito population.

   Which one of the following, if true, most seriously weakens the argument?

   (A) A careful search discovered no live mosquitoes in the vicinity of the device after the test.

   (B) A very large proportion of the insects that were attracted to the device were not mosquitoes.

   (C) The device is more likely to kill beneficial insects than it is to kill harmful insects.

   (D) Many of the insects that were killed by the device are mosquito-eating insects.

   (E) The device does not succeed in killing all of the insects that it attracts.

5. Brain-scanning technology provides information about processes occurring in the brain. For this information to help researchers understand how the brain enables us to think, however, researchers must be able to rely on the accuracy of the verbal reports given by subjects while their brains are being scanned. Otherwise brain-scan data gathered at a given moment might not contain information about what the subject reports thinking about at that moment, but instead about some different set of thoughts.

Which one of the following most accurately expresses the main conclusion of the argument?

(A)   It is unlikely that brain-scanning technology will ever enable researchers to understand how the brain enables us to think.

(B)   There is no way that researchers can know for certain that subjects whose brains are being scanned are accurately reporting what they are thinking.

(C)   Because subjects whose brains are being scanned may not accurately report what they are thinking, the results of brain-scanning research should be regarded with great skepticism.

(D)   Brain scans can provide information about the accuracy of the verbal reports of subjects whose brains are being scanned.

(E)   Information from brain scans can help researchers understand how the brain enables us to think only if the verbal reports of those whose brains are being scanned are accurate.

6. Ornithologist: This bird species is widely thought to subsist primarily on vegetation, but my research shows that this belief is erroneous. While concealed in a well-camouflaged blind, I have observed hundreds of these birds every morning over a period of months, and I estimate that over half of what they ate consisted of insects and other animal food sources.

The reasoning in the ornithologist's argument is most vulnerable to criticism on the grounds that the argument

(A)   assumes, without providing justification, that the feeding behavior of the birds observed was not affected by the ornithologist's act of observation

(B)   fails to specify the nature of the animal food sources, other than insects, that were consumed by the birds

(C)   adopts a widespread belief about the birds' feeding habits without considering the evidence that led to the belief

(D)   neglects the possibility that the birds have different patterns of food consumption during different parts of the day and night

(E)   fails to consider the possibility that the birds' diet has changed since the earlier belief about their diet was formed

7. Educator: Only those students who are genuinely curious about a topic can successfully learn about that topic. They find the satisfaction of their curiosity intrinsically gratifying, and appreciate the inherent rewards of the learning process itself. However, almost no child enters the classroom with sufficient curiosity to learn successfully all that the teacher must instill. A teacher's job, therefore, _____.

Which one of the following most logically completes the educator's argument?

(A)   requires for the fulfillment of its goals the stimulation as well as the satisfaction of curiosity

(B)   necessitates the creative use of rewards that are not inherent in the learning process itself

(C)   is to focus primarily on those topics that do not initially interest the students

(D)   is facilitated by students' taking responsibility for their own learning

(E)   becomes easier if students realize that some learning is not necessarily enjoyable

8. Environmentalist: When bacteria degrade household cleaning products, vapors that are toxic to humans are produced. Unfortunately, household cleaning products are often found in landfills. Thus, the common practice of converting landfills into public parks is damaging human health.

Which one of the following is an assumption the environmentalist's argument requires?

(A) In at least some landfills that have been converted into public parks there are bacteria that degrade household cleaning products.

(B) Converting a landfill into a public park will cause no damage to human health unless toxic vapors are produced in that landfill and humans are exposed to them.

(C) If a practice involves the exposure of humans to vapors from household cleaning products, then it causes at least some damage to human health.

(D) When landfills are converted to public parks, measures could be taken that would prevent people using the parks from being exposed to toxic vapors.

(E) If vapors toxic to humans are produced by the degradation of household cleaning products by bacteria in any landfill, then the health of at least some humans will suffer.

9. Tea made from camellia leaves is a popular beverage. However, studies show that regular drinkers of camellia tea usually suffer withdrawal symptoms if they discontinue drinking the tea. Furthermore, regular drinkers of camellia tea are more likely than people in general to develop kidney damage. Regular consumption of this tea, therefore, can result in a heightened risk of kidney damage.

Which one of the following, if true, most seriously weakens the argument?

(A) Several other popular beverages contain the same addictive chemical that is found in camellia tea.

(B) Addictive chemicals are unlikely to cause kidney damage solely by virtue of their addictive qualities.

(C) Some people claim that regular consumption of camellia tea helps alleviate their stress.

(D) Most people who regularly drink camellia tea do not develop kidney damage.

(E) Many people who regularly consume camellia tea also regularly consume other beverages suspected of causing kidney damage.

10. Artist: Avant-garde artists intend their work to challenge a society's mainstream beliefs and initiate change. And some art collectors claim that an avant-garde work that becomes popular in its own time is successful. However, a society's mainstream beliefs do not generally show any significant changes over a short period of time. Therefore, when an avant-garde work becomes popular it is a sign that the work is not successful, since it does not fulfill the intentions of its creator.

The reference to the claim of certain art collectors plays which one of the following roles in the artist's argument?

(A) It serves to bolster the argument's main conclusion.

(B) It identifies a view that is ultimately disputed by the argument.

(C) It identifies a position supported by the initial premise in the argument.

(D) It provides support for the initial premise in the argument.

(E) It provides support for a counterargument to the initial premise.

11. A recent epidemiological study found that businesspeople who travel internationally on business are much more likely to suffer from chronic insomnia than are businesspeople who do not travel on business. International travelers experience the stresses of dramatic changes in climate, frequent disruption of daily routines, and immersion in cultures other than their own, stresses not commonly felt by those who do not travel. Thus, it is likely that these stresses cause the insomnia.

Which one of the following would, if true, most strengthen the reasoning above?

(A) Most international travel for the sake of business occurs between countries with contiguous borders.

(B) Some businesspeople who travel internationally greatly enjoy the changes in climate and immersion in another culture.

(C) Businesspeople who already suffer from chronic insomnia are no more likely than businesspeople who do not to accept assignments from their employers that require international travel.

(D) Experiencing dramatic changes in climate and disruption of daily routines through international travel can be beneficial to some people who suffer from chronic insomnia.

(E) Some businesspeople who once traveled internationally but no longer do so complain of various sleep-related ailments.

12. Many mountain climbers regard climbing Mount Everest as the ultimate achievement. But climbers should not attempt this climb since the risk of death or serious injury in an Everest expedition is very high. Moreover, the romantic notion of gaining "spiritual discovery" atop Everest is dispelled by climbers' reports that the only profound experiences they had at the top were of exhaustion and fear.

Which one of the following principles, if valid, most helps to justify the reasoning above?

(A) Projects undertaken primarily for spiritual reasons ought to be abandoned if the risks are great.

(B) Dangerous activities that are unlikely to result in significant spiritual benefits for those undertaking them should be avoided.

(C) Activities that are extremely dangerous ought to be legally prohibited unless they are necessary to produce spiritual enlightenment.

(D) Profound spiritual experiences can be achieved without undergoing the serious danger involved in mountain climbing.

(E) Mountain climbers and other athletes should carefully examine the underlying reasons they have for participating in their sports.

13. Each of the smallest particles in the universe has an elegantly simple structure. Since these particles compose the universe, we can conclude that the universe itself has an elegantly simple structure.

Each of the following arguments exhibits flawed reasoning similar to that in the argument above EXCEPT:

(A) Each part of this car is nearly perfectly engineered. Therefore this car is nearly perfect, from an engineering point of view.

(B) Each part of this desk is made of metal. Therefore this desk is made of metal.

(C) Each brick in this wall is rectangular. Therefore this wall is rectangular.

(D) Each piece of wood in this chair is sturdy. Therefore this chair is sturdy.

(E) Each sentence in this novel is well constructed. Therefore this is a well-constructed novel.

14. Criminologist: A judicial system that tries and punishes criminals without delay is an effective deterrent to violent crime. Long, drawn-out trials and successful legal maneuvering may add to criminals' feelings of invulnerability. But if potential violent criminals know that being caught means prompt punishment, they will hesitate to break the law.

Which one of the following, if true, would most seriously weaken the criminologist's argument?

(A) It is in the nature of violent crime that it is not premeditated.

(B) About one-fourth of all suspects first arrested for a crime are actually innocent.

(C) Many violent crimes are committed by first-time offenders.

(D) Everyone accused of a crime has the right to a trial.

(E) Countries that promptly punish suspected lawbreakers have lower crime rates than countries that allow long trials.

15. Journalist: Many people object to mandatory retirement at age 65 as being arbitrary, arguing that people over 65 make useful contributions. However, if those who reach 65 are permitted to continue working indefinitely, we will face unacceptable outcomes. First, young people entering the job market will not be able to obtain decent jobs in the professions for which they were trained, resulting in widespread dissatisfaction among the young. Second, it is not fair for those who have worked 40 or more years to deprive others of opportunities. Therefore, mandatory retirement should be retained.

The journalist's argument depends on assuming which one of the following?

(A) Anyone who has worked 40 years is at least 65 years old.

(B) All young people entering the job market are highly trained professionals.

(C) It is unfair for a person not to get a job in the profession for which that person was trained.

(D) If people are forced to retire at age 65, there will be much dissatisfaction among at least some older people.

(E) If retirement ceases to be mandatory at age 65, at least some people will choose to work past age 65.

16. Editorial: Contrary to popular belief, teaching preschoolers is not especially difficult, for they develop strict systems (e.g., for sorting toys by shape), which help them to learn, and they are always intensely curious about something new in their world.

    Which one of the following, if true, most seriously weakens the editorial's argument?

    (A) Preschoolers have a tendency to imitate adults, and most adults follow strict routines.
    (B) Children intensely curious about new things have very short attention spans.
    (C) Some older children also develop strict systems that help them learn.
    (D) Preschoolers ask as many creative questions as do older children.
    (E) Preschool teachers generally report lower levels of stress than do other teachers.

17. Lawyer: A body of circumstantial evidence is like a rope, and each item of evidence is like a strand of that rope. Just as additional pieces of circumstantial evidence strengthen the body of evidence, adding strands to the rope strengthens the rope. And if one strand breaks, the rope is not broken nor is its strength much diminished. Thus, even if a few items of a body of circumstantial evidence are discredited, the overall body of evidence retains its basic strength.

    The reasoning in the lawyer's argument is most vulnerable to criticism on the grounds that the argument

    (A) takes for granted that no items in a body of circumstantial evidence are significantly more critical to the strength of the evidence than other items in that body
    (B) presumes, without providing justification, that the strength of a body of evidence is less than the sum of the strengths of the parts of that body
    (C) fails to consider the possibility that if many items in a body of circumstantial evidence were discredited, the overall body of evidence would be discredited
    (D) offers an analogy in support of a conclusion without indicating whether the two types of things compared share any similarities
    (E) draws a conclusion that simply restates a claim presented in support of that conclusion

18. Ethicist: Many environmentalists hold that the natural environment is morally valuable for its own sake, regardless of any benefits it provides us. However, even if nature has no moral value, nature can be regarded as worth preserving simply on the grounds that people find it beautiful. Moreover, because it is philosophically disputable whether nature is morally valuable but undeniable that it is beautiful, an argument for preserving nature that emphasizes nature's beauty will be less vulnerable to logical objections than one that emphasizes its moral value.

    The ethicist's reasoning most closely conforms to which one of the following principles?

    (A) An argument in favor of preserving nature will be less open to logical objections if it avoids the issue of what makes nature worth preserving.
    (B) If an argument for preserving nature emphasizes a specific characteristic of nature and is vulnerable to logical objections, then that characteristic does not provide a sufficient reason for preserving nature.
    (C) If it is philosophically disputable whether nature has a certain characteristic, then nature would be more clearly worth preserving if it did not have that characteristic.
    (D) Anything that has moral value is worth preserving regardless of whether people consider it to be beautiful.
    (E) An argument for preserving nature will be less open to logical objections if it appeals to a characteristic that can be regarded as a basis for preserving nature and that philosophically indisputably belongs to nature.

19. An editor is compiling a textbook containing essays by several different authors. The book will contain essays by Lind, Knight, or Jones, but it will not contain essays by all three. If the textbook contains an essay by Knight, then it will also contain an essay by Jones.

    If the statements above are true, which one of the following must be true?

    (A) If the textbook contains an essay by Lind, then it will not contain an essay by Knight.
    (B) The textbook will contain an essay by only one of Lind, Knight, and Jones.
    (C) The textbook will not contain an essay by Knight.
    (D) If the textbook contains an essay by Lind, then it will also contain an essay by Jones.
    (E) The textbook will contain an essay by Lind.

20. The ability of mammals to control their internal body temperatures is a factor in the development of their brains and intelligence. This can be seen from the following facts: the brain is a chemical machine, all chemical reactions are temperature dependent, and any organism that can control its body temperature can assure that these reactions occur at the proper temperatures.

    Which one of the following is an assumption on which the argument depends?

    (A) Organisms unable to control their body temperatures do not have the capacity to generate internal body heat without relying on external factors.
    (B) Mammals are the only animals that have the ability to control their internal body temperatures.
    (C) The brain cannot support intelligence if the chemical reactions within it are subject to uncontrolled temperatures.
    (D) The development of intelligence in mammals is not independent of the chemical reactions in their brains taking place at the proper temperatures.
    (E) Organisms incapable of controlling their internal body temperatures are subject to unpredictable chemical processes.

21. People who object to the proposed hazardous waste storage site by appealing to extremely implausible scenarios in which the site fails to contain the waste safely are overlooking the significant risks associated with delays in moving the waste from its present unsafe location. If we wait to remove the waste until we find a site certain to contain it safely, the waste will remain in its current location for many years, since it is currently impossible to guarantee that any site can meet that criterion. Yet keeping the waste at the current location for that long clearly poses unacceptable risks.

    The statements above, if true, most strongly support which one of the following?

    (A) The waste should never have been stored in its current location.
    (B) The waste should be placed in the most secure location that can ever be found.
    (C) Moving the waste to the proposed site would reduce the threat posed by the waste.
    (D) Whenever waste must be moved, one should limit the amount of time allotted to locating alternative waste storage sites.
    (E) Any site to which the waste could be moved will be safer than its present site.

22. A recent survey indicates that the average number of books read annually per capita has declined in each of the last three years. However, it also found that most bookstores reported increased profits during the same period.

    Each of the following, if true, helps to resolve the survey's apparently paradoxical results EXCEPT:

    (A) Recent cutbacks in government spending have forced public libraries to purchase fewer popular contemporary novels.
    (B) Due to the installation of sophisticated new antitheft equipment, the recent increase in shoplifting that has hit most retail businesses has left bookstores largely unaffected.
    (C) Over the past few years many bookstores have capitalized on the lucrative coffee industry by installing coffee bars.
    (D) Bookstore owners reported a general shift away from the sale of inexpensive paperback novels and toward the sale of lucrative hardback books.
    (E) Citing a lack of free time, many survey respondents indicated that they had canceled magazine subscriptions in favor of purchasing individual issues at bookstores when time permits.

23. Naturalist: A species can survive a change in
environment, as long as the change is not too
rapid. Therefore, the threats we are creating to
woodland species arise not from the fact that we
are cutting down trees, but rather from the rate at
which we are doing so.

The reasoning in which one of the following is most
similar to that in the naturalist's argument?

(A) The problem with burning fossil fuels is that the
supply is limited; so, the faster we expend
these resources, the sooner we will be left
without an energy source.
(B) Many people gain more satisfaction from
performing a job well—regardless of whether
they like the job—than from doing merely
adequately a job they like; thus, people who
want to be happy should choose jobs they can
do well.
(C) Some students who study thoroughly do well in
school. Thus, what is most important for
success in school is not how much time a
student puts into studying, but rather how
thoroughly the student studies.
(D) People do not fear change if they know what
the change will bring; so, our employees' fear
stems not from our company's undergoing
change, but from our failing to inform them of
what the changes entail.
(E) Until ten years ago, we had good soil and our
agriculture flourished. Therefore, the recent
decline of our agriculture is a result of our soil
rapidly eroding and there being nothing that
can replace the good soil we lost.

24. Professor: A person who can select a beverage from
among 50 varieties of cola is less free than one
who has only these 5 choices: wine, coffee, apple
juice, milk, and water. It is clear, then, that
meaningful freedom cannot be measured simply
by the number of alternatives available; the
extent of the differences among the alternatives is
also a relevant factor.

The professor's argument proceeds by

(A) supporting a general principle by means of an
example
(B) drawing a conclusion about a particular case on
the basis of a general principle
(C) supporting its conclusion by means of an
analogy
(D) claiming that whatever holds for each member
of a group must hold for the whole group
(E) inferring one general principle from another,
more general, principle

25. Principle: Meetings should be kept short, addressing
only those issues relevant to a majority of those
attending. A person should not be required to
attend a meeting if none of the issues to be
addressed at the meeting are relevant to that
person.

Application: Terry should not be required to attend
today's two o'clock meeting.

Which one of the following, if true, most justifies the
stated application of the principle?

(A) The only issues on which Terry could make a
presentation at the meeting are issues irrelevant
to at least a majority of those who could
attend.
(B) If Terry makes a presentation at the meeting,
the meeting will not be kept short.
(C) No issue relevant to Terry could be relevant to a
majority of those attending the meeting.
(D) If Terry attends the meeting a different set of
issues will be relevant to a majority of those
attending than if Terry does not attend.
(E) The majority of the issues to be addressed at the
meeting are not relevant to Terry.

Answer Explanations follow on the next page.

ANSWER KEY

1. A	14. A
2. C	15. E
3. E	16. B
4. A	17. A
5. E	18. E
6. D	19. A
7. A	20. D
8. A	21. C
9. E	22. B
10. B	23. D
11. C	24. A
12. B	25. C
13. B	

SECTION TRIAGE

Be sure to evaluate the section-management decisions you made just as you did on the previous full-length section. Using the table below, review the difficulty levels of the questions. (One star indicates the lowest difficulty and four stars represent the highest difficulty.) Remember that the actual difficulty level for you can be higher or lower, but you should be aware of the general trends in the section.

This section started with an easier set of questions and a tough assumption question thrown in the mix, became more difficult in an expanded "danger zone" from question 13 to 22, and ended with a lower difficulty question set. Again, I recommend that you work through about four pages of the section and then turn to the end of the section and answer questions from the end, working your way backward toward the middle. It's imperative that you use your knowledge of the Logical Reasoning section anatomy to help guide you through the questions so you don't get bogged down by individual questions or leave easier questions behind.

Table 22.1

	PrepTest 53: Section 3	
Question	Question Type	Difficulty Level
1	Strengthen	*
2	Flaw	*
3	Main Point	*
4	Weaken	**
5	Main Point	**
6	Flaw	*
7	Inference	**
8	Assumption	***
9	Weaken	**
10	Role of a Statement	*
11	Strengthen	**
12	Principle	***
13	Parallel Reasoning	****
14	Weaken	**
15	Assumption	**
16	Weaken	**
17	Flaw	****
18	Principle	****
19	Inference	***
20	Assumption	**
21	Inference	***

(continued)

Question	Question Type	Difficulty Level
22	Paradox	***
23	Parallel Reasoning	**
24	Method of Argument	**
25	Principle	**

Explanations

1. **(A)**

    At many electronics retail stores, the consumer has the option of purchasing product warranties that extend beyond the manufacturer's warranty. <However, consumers are generally better off not buying extended warranties.> Most problems with electronic goods occur within the period covered by the manufacturer's warranty.

    Which one of the following, if true, most strengthens the argument?

    (A)   Problems with electronic goods that occur after the manufacturer's warranty expires are generally inexpensive to fix in comparison with the cost of an extended warranty.

    (B)   Because problems are so infrequent after the manufacturer's warranty expires, extended warranties on electronic goods are generally inexpensive.

    (C)   Most of those who buy extended warranties on electronic goods do so because special circumstances make their item more likely to break than is usually the case.

    (D)   Some extended warranties on electronic goods cover the product for the period covered by the manufacturer's warranty as well as subsequent years.

    (E)   Retail stores sell extended warranties in part because consumers who purchase them are likely to purchase other products from the same store.

Step 1. Identify the Question Type

The word "strengthens" identifies this as a Strengthen question.

Step 2. Untangle the Stimulus

The author's main point, noted by the contrast Keyword "However," is that consumers are generally better off not buying extended warranties. The evidence follows in the last sentence and explains that most problems with electronics happen in the period covered by the manufacturer's warranty.

Step 3. Make a Prediction

Focus on the qualifying language in the evidence: "Most." Most problems occur during the covered time period. What about the ones that don't? The author must assume that the few problems that happen after the warranty expires aren't bad enough to justify purchasing the extended warranty. A valid strengthener will confirm the assumption and thereby make the conclusion more likely to follow from the evidence.

Step 4. Evaluate the Answer Choices

Choice (A) strengthens the argument by supporting the assumption. If post-warranty problems are inexpensive compared to the cost of an extended warranty, the author's conclusion makes even more sense. This is the correct answer.

Choice (B) is an ambivalent answer choice that you should watch out for on Strengthen and Weaken questions. Sure, emphasizing the infrequency of post-warranty problems strengthens the argument, but mentioning the low cost of extended warranties could support purchasing the extension. While a Strengthen answer choice need not prove the conclusion true, it does have to unequivocally make the conclusion at least a little more likely to be true. Choice (A) does that, while it is debatable whether choice (B) makes the conclusion more or less likely.

Choice (C) is compatible with the author's recommendation to generally not buy the extension by explaining that people who do buy extended warranties have special circumstances under which they make that purchase. But, though compatible with the author's reasoning, this information does nothing to bolster an argument against buying an extension.

Choice (D) misses the point. The overlap of coverage does nothing to make the extension more, or less, valuable to the buyer. Therefore, it does not weaken, nor strengthen the argument against purchasing extensions.

Choice (E) presents a rationale for stores to sell the extended warranties but it doesn't address whether consumers should buy them.

2. **(C)**

Since the 1970s, environmentalists have largely
succeeded in convincing legislators to enact extensive
environmental regulations. Yet, as environmentalists
themselves not only admit but insist, the condition of
the environment is worsening, not improving. <Clearly,
more environmental regulations are not the solution to
the environment's problems.>

The argument's reasoning is flawed because the
argument

(A) attacks the environmentalists themselves instead
of their positions
(B) presumes, without providing warrant, that only
an absence of environmental regulations could
prevent environmental degradation
(C) fails to consider the possibility that the
condition of the environment would have
worsened even more without environmental
regulations
(D) fails to justify its presumption that reducing
excessive regulations is more important than
preserving the environment
(E) fails to consider the views of the
environmentalists' opponents

Step 1. Identify the Question Type

The term "flawed" clearly tells you that this is a Flaw question.

Step 2. Untangle the Stimulus

"Clearly" points to the conclusion in the last sentence, which says more regulation will not
solve environmental problems. The evidence provided states that environmental problems
keep getting worse despite the enactment of extensive regulations.

Step 3. Make a Prediction

The author must assume that environmental regulation does not work, at least not well, since
there have been environmental regulations yet the situation has still deteriorated. However,
maybe the environment would have more problems without the regulations. That's the possibility the author fails to consider and the classic flaw he commits.

Step 4. Evaluate the Answer Choices

Choice (A) describes an ad hominem, which is a type of flaw, but not the flaw in this argument.
The author never makes a personal attack on the environmentalists. Cross out this choice.

Choice (B) is extreme. The author says more regulation is not the answer to environmental
problems, not that eliminating all regulation is the only way to prevent further problems. Move
on to the next choice.

Choice (C) correctly identifies the flaw in the argument and is the correct answer.

Choice (D) raises an irrelevant comparison between the importance of reducing excessive regulations and preserving the environment. The author doesn't assume anything about this comparison, only that reducing regulation will not preserve the environment.

Choice (E) is a 180 answer. Does the author really ignore environmental opponents? No way, the author is an opponent of environmental regulations.

3. **(E)**

> (Although) it is unwise to take a developmental view of an art like music—as if Beethoven were an advance over Josquin, or Miles Davis an advance over Louis Armstrong—<there are ways in which it makes sense to talk about musical knowledge growing over time.> We certainly know more about certain sounds than was known five centuries ago; that is, we understand how sounds that earlier composers avoided can be used effectively in musical compositions. (For example,) we now know how the interval of the third, which is considered dissonant, can be used in compositions to create consonant musical phrases.

> Which one of the following most accurately expresses the (main conclusion) of the argument?
>
> (A) Sounds that were never used in past musical compositions are used today.
> (B) Sounds that were once considered dissonant are more pleasing to modern listeners.
> (C) It is inappropriate to take a developmental view of music.
> (D) It is unwise to say that one composer is better than another.
> (E) Our understanding of music can improve over the course of time.

Step 1. Identify the Question Type

"Main conclusion" signals that this is a Main Point question.

Step 2. Untangle the Stimulus

The argument begins with "Although" signaling a concession by the author. He acknowledges it's not a good idea to think of music in developmental terms, but, he says, it does make sense to talk about musical knowledge expanding over time. The rest of the argument supports this statement with information and examples of how we know more about sound today than we did five centuries ago.

Step 3. Make a Prediction

Like most Main Point questions, the stimulus offers no conclusion Keywords to direct you to the conclusion. Instead use the evidence Keywords and the author's opinion. Here, the correct answer will identify the main point as the notion that musical knowledge can expand over time.

Step 4. Evaluate the Answer Choices

Choice (A) is an example of our expanding musical knowledge, and as so, is part of the evidence not the conclusion. Eliminate this choice.

Choice (B) offers a statement that is part of the sentence that begins with "For example," an indication of evidence not the conclusion. Move on to the next choice.

Choice (C) presents the information conceded by the author as part of the "Although" phrase at the beginning of the argument. This choice is out.

Choice (D) is another point of concession for the author.

Choice (E), the remaining choice, captures the first sentence and is the correct answer.

4. **(A)**

    A recent test of an electric insect control device discovered that, of the more than 300 insects killed during one 24-hour period, only 12 were mosquitoes. ⟨Thus⟩ this type of device may kill many insects, but will not significantly aid in controlling the potentially dangerous mosquito population.⟩

    Which one of the following, if true, most seriously ⟨weakens⟩ the argument?

    (A)   A careful search discovered no live mosquitoes in the vicinity of the device after the test.
    (B)   A very large proportion of the insects that were attracted to the device were not mosquitoes.
    (C)   The device is more likely to kill beneficial insects than it is to kill harmful insects.
    (D)   Many of the insects that were killed by the device are mosquito-eating insects.
    (E)   The device does not succeed in killing all of the insects that it attracts.

Step 1. Identify the Question Type

The term "weaken" is classic language for a Weaken question

Step 2. Untangle the Stimulus

The author concludes (note the indicator "Thus") that the electric insect control device kills insects but won't really help control the mosquito population. The author supports this conclusion with test results that found only 12 mosquitoes were killed out of more than 300 insects in a 24-hour period.

Step 3. Make a Prediction

The author determines that the device doesn't work well enough to control the mosquito population based on the number of mosquitoes killed. He assumes the 12 killed is a low number in relation to the mosquito population. So, to weaken the argument and make it less likely that the device won't control the mosquito population, find an answer that attacks the assumption.

Step 4. Evaluate the Answer Choices

Choice (A) challenges the assumption and weakens the argument by suggesting the device got rid of all the mosquitoes in the vicinity and therefore controlled the mosquito population. In this case, 12 mosquitoes is the whole population. This is the correct answer.

Choice (B) does not address the proportion of mosquitoes killed by the device, so it cannot weaken the argument. In fact, choice (B) may strengthen the argument that the device doesn't control the mosquito population if a large portion of the mosquito population is not attracted to it.

Choice (C), far from weakening the argument, is in line with the author's claim that at least one harmful insect, the mosquito, will not be controlled by the device.

Choice (D) strengthens the argument that the device will not control mosquitoes by indicating that in addition to the apparent anemic effect on mosquitoes, it also eliminates mosquito predators.

Choice (E) is too broad in referencing all insects attracted to the device but also provides a deficiency in its killing power. So, choice (E) also marginally strengthens, not weakens the argument.

5. **(E)**

Brain-scanning technology provides information about processes occurring in the brain. <For this information to help researchers understand how the brain enables us to think, (however,) researchers must be able to rely on the accuracy of the verbal reports given by subjects while their brains are being scanned.> Otherwise brain-scan data gathered at a given moment might not contain information about what the subject reports thinking about at that moment, but instead about some different set of thoughts.

Which one of the following most accurately expresses the (main conclusion) of the argument?

(A) It is unlikely that brain-scanning technology will ever enable researchers to understand how the brain enables us to think.

(B) There is no way that researchers can know for certain that subjects whose brains are being scanned are accurately reporting what they are thinking.

(C) Because subjects whose brains are being scanned may not accurately report what they are thinking, the results of brain-scanning research should be regarded with great skepticism.

(D) Brain scans can provide information about the accuracy of the verbal reports of subjects whose brains are being scanned.

(E) Information from brain scans can help researchers understand how the brain enables us to think only if the verbal reports of those whose brains are being scanned are accurate.

Step 1. Identify the Question Type

The phrase "main conclusion" tells you that this is a Main Point question.

Step 2. Untangle the Stimulus

The stimulus begins with a statement of the information provided by a brain scan. As background information, it sets the stage for the author's strong opinion highlighted by "however" in the next sentence. It says that for brain scans to be helpful, researchers must rely on the reports of the subjects as they are scanned. The next sentence, starting with "Otherwise," tells you the result if they don't.

Step 3. Make a Prediction

Without conclusion Keywords, look for opinion and other Keywords to help you determine the author's main point. Here, the second sentence gives the author's point and receives support from the statements around it. The correct answer will paraphrase that sentence.

Step 4. Evaluate the Answer Choices

Choice (A) distorts information in the stimulus. The author identifies a necessary condition for the scans to be helpful. He doesn't conclude that brain scans are unlikely to be helpful.

Choice (B) is not mentioned in the stimulus. The author says that researchers must be able to trust the subjects' reports. He never questions whether researchers can know for sure that subjects can accurately report their thinking during a scan.

Choice (C) isn't discussed in the stimulus either. The author doesn't mention the possibility of inaccurate reports from subjects nor does he conclude that brain-scan research should be regarded with skepticism.

Choice (D) reverses the information. Brain scans don't shed light on the verbal reports of subjects being scanned. It's the other way around. The verbal reports are necessary for the researchers to use brain scans to help them understand how we think.

Choice (E) correctly states the author's main point. Remember, the phrase "only if" indicates a necessary condition, just like the word "must" in the sentence of the stimulus bracketed as the conclusion. So, this answer choice matches perfectly. Fluency in the language of necessity and sufficiency is invaluable on the Logical Reasoning section.

6. **(D)**

Ornithologist: This bird species is widely thought to subsist primarily on vegetation, <but my research shows that this belief is erroneous.> While concealed in a well-camouflaged blind, I have observed hundreds of these birds every morning over a period of months, and I estimate that over half of what they ate consisted of insects and other animal food sources.

The reasoning in the ornithologist's argument is most vulnerable to criticism on the grounds that the argument

(A) assumes, without providing justification, that the feeding behavior of the birds observed was not affected by the ornithologist's act of observation

(B) fails to specify the nature of the animal food sources, other than insects, that were consumed by the birds

(C) adopts a widespread belief about the birds' feeding habits without considering the evidence that led to the belief

(D) neglects the possibility that the birds have different patterns of food consumption during different parts of the day and night

(E) fails to consider the possibility that the birds' diet has changed since the earlier belief about their diet was formed

Step 1. Identify the Question Type

The phrase "most vulnerable to criticism" indicates that this is a Flaw question.

Step 2. Untangle the Stimulus

When a stimulus begins with a widely held belief, expect the author to disagree. Here, the ornithologist presents a common belief that certain bird species primarily eat vegetation. In her disagreement, signaled by "but," she states the belief is false and tells you specifically she bases her conclusion on her research. She observed hundreds of the birds each morning over a period of months and estimates that over half their diet consisted of insects and other animals.

Step 3. Make a Prediction

When a Flaw question includes research or a study, consider the common flaw of representativeness. While the number of birds observed sounds like it might be a large enough sample, notice the ornithologist observed the birds in the morning only, which may not represent their day-long eating habits. She overlooks the possibility that they eat differently—specifically different vegetation—during the rest of the day.

Step 4. Evaluate the Answer Choices

Choice (A) accuses the ornithologist of not providing justification for the assumption, which she does make—she claims she was well-concealed. Do not try to argue, especially from outside knowledge, whether such camouflage would work. The only relevant question is "does the ornithologist really do this?" Does the ornithologist really not provide justification? No.

Choice (B) is irrelevant. What's important is that the non-insect animal food sources were not vegetation.

Choice (C) contradicts the stimulus. Remember on Flaw questions your task is to describe the author's logic, particularly its flawed logic. Your task is not to weaken the argument or dispute the author's claims. The ornithologist disagrees with the widespread belief, so this choice doesn't describe her argument at all.

Choice (D) correctly points out that the birds' morning eating habits may not represent their general eating habits and the ornithologist failed to consider that possibility.

Choice (E) is not at issue in the stimulus. Whether the birds changed their diet is of no consequence in the ornithologist's quest to disprove the widely held belief that the birds currently eat mostly vegetation. The ornithologist does not assert what was or was not the case in the past.

7. **(A)**

Educator: (Only) those students who are genuinely curious about a topic can successfully learn about that topic. They find the satisfaction of their curiosity intrinsically gratifying, and appreciate the inherent rewards of the learning process itself. However, almost no child enters the classroom with sufficient curiosity to learn successfully all that the teacher must instill. A teacher's job, therefore, _____.

Which one of the following (most logically completes) the educator's argument?

(A) requires for the fulfillment of its goals the stimulation as well as the satisfaction of curiosity

(B) necessitates the creative use of rewards that are not inherent in the learning process itself

(C) is to focus primarily on those topics that do not initially interest the students

(D) is facilitated by students' taking responsibility for their own learning

(E) becomes easier if students realize that some learning is not necessarily enjoyable

Step 1. Identify the Question Type

Because this question asks for a statement that "most logically completes" the argument, it is an Inference question. Recognizing this as an Inference question should be a reminder to not get creative in tagging on a "conclusion" to this argument that goes beyond what *must be true* based on the information already provided.

Step 2. Untangle the Stimulus

When an inference stimulus includes formal logic, translate the statement to help you understand the argument. "Only" signals formal logic in this case, so translate the statement from its "Only Y are X" form to "X → Y." "Only curious students can learn" becomes "Learn → curious." Then you find out that being curious means students are gratified by curiosity and appreciate the rewards of the learning process. The stimulus ends with a problem: Most students enter the classroom without enough curiosity to sustain learning. So, what's a teacher to do to instill learning?

Step 3. Make a Prediction

Some Inference questions are not susceptible to prediction. In this case, however, you are asked for the logical conclusion to a formal logic chain of reasoning, so a prediction is possible. And here is what you know: Curiosity is necessary for learning and most students don't have enough curiosity. Therefore, a teacher's job must be to stimulate curiosity.

Step 4. Evaluate the Answer Choices

Choice (A) correctly defines a teacher's responsibility to arouse curiosity.

Choice (B) distorts the stimulus. It says that a curious student will appreciate the inherent rewards of the learning process, not that a teacher must use rewards that are not inherent in the learning process.

Choice (C) is a reasonable potential course of action based on the information provided, but such speculation, no matter how reasonable, must be resisted. This is precisely the type of answer that requires thinking of this as an Inference question, whose answer *must be true* based on the information in the stimulus, rather than feeling free to tag on a reasonable conclusion that *could be true* from this information.

Choice (D) must not be true based on the stimulus. Student responsibility is never discussed. Besides, how can students take responsibility for their own learning if they lack the curiosity needed to learn?

Choice (E) also reaches beyond the stimulus and therefore cannot be true based on it. The stimulus never says that a teacher's job will be easier if students understand that learning is not always enjoyable.

8.   **(A)**

Environmentalist: When bacteria degrade household cleaning products, vapors that are toxic to humans are produced. Unfortunately, household cleaning products are often found in landfills. <Thus, the common practice of converting landfills into public parks is damaging human health.>

Which one of the following is an assumption the environmentalist's argument requires?

(A)   In at least some landfills that have been converted into public parks there are bacteria that degrade household cleaning products.

(B)   Converting a landfill into a public park will cause no damage to human health unless toxic vapors are produced in that landfill and humans are exposed to them.

(C)   If a practice involves the exposure of humans to vapors from household cleaning products, then it causes at least some damage to human health.

(D)   When landfills are converted to public parks, measures could be taken that would prevent people using the parks from being exposed to toxic vapors.

(E)   If vapors toxic to humans are produced by the degradation of household cleaning products by bacteria in any landfill, then the health of at least some humans will suffer.

Step 1. Identify the Question Type

Because the stem specifically asks for an "assumption," this is an Assumption question.

Step 2. Untangle the Stimulus

"Thus" in the last sentence identifies the conclusion: The common practice of turning landfills into public parks damages human health. To support his conclusion, the environmentalist offers evidence that toxic vapors are produced when bacteria degrade household cleaning products which are often found in landfills.

Step 3. Make a Prediction

With an Assumption question, you know a gap exists between the conclusion and the evidence. Your task is to bridge that gap. Here, you have mismatched terms in the conclusion and evidence. The conclusion mentions converting landfills to public parks, while the evidence says that toxic vapors are released when bacteria degrade household cleaning products. Connect these terms and you will have a prediction for the assumption: The environmentalist must assume that converting landfills into parks must result in bacterial degradation of household cleaning products.

Step 4. Evaluate the Answer Choices

Choice (A) matches the prediction and is the correct answer.

Choice (B) distorts the stimulus by saying toxic vapors are the only way to harm human health in the conversion of a landfill to a public park.

Choice (C) connects vapor exposure to damaged health, but never makes the connection back to the conversion of landfills to parks in the conclusion.

Choice (D) attempts to solve the problem of exposure to toxic vapors, which goes beyond the scope of the argument.

Choice (E) has the same problem as choice (C) by not linking to the conclusion.

9.   **(E)**

Tea made from camellia leaves is a popular beverage.
However, studies show that regular drinkers of camellia
tea usually suffer withdrawal symptoms if they
discontinue drinking the tea. Furthermore, regular
drinkers of camellia tea are more likely than people in
general to develop kidney damage. <Regular
consumption of this tea, (therefore,) can result in a
heightened risk of kidney damage.>

Which one of the following, if true, most seriously
(weakens) the argument?

(A)   Several other popular beverages contain the
same addictive chemical that is found in
camellia tea.

(B)   Addictive chemicals are unlikely to cause
kidney damage solely by virtue of their
addictive qualities.

(C)   Some people claim that regular consumption of
camellia tea helps alleviate their stress.

(D)   Most people who regularly drink camellia tea do
not develop kidney damage.

(E)   Many people who regularly consume camellia
tea also regularly consume other beverages
suspected of causing kidney damage.

Step 1. Identify the Question Type

The term "weaken" makes this a Weaken question.

Step 2. Untangle the Stimulus

The stimulus indicates that regular drinkers of camellia tea are more likely than people in
general to develop kidney damage. Based on that, the author concludes with "therefore" that
regular consumption of this tea can result in a heightened risk of kidney damage. The phrase
"can result in" indicates a causal relationship between tea and kidney damage. The problem
is that it's based on evidence of a correlation.

Step 3. Make a Prediction

There are three possibilities to weaken a causal argument: reverse the causation (maybe kidney
damage caused people to drink the tea), offer an alternative cause (maybe the tea drinkers
consume or do something else that causes kidney damage), or write it off as coincidence.

Step 4. Evaluate the Answer Choices

Choice (A) doesn't weaken the argument by any of the three stated methods. Even if camellia
tea contains the same addictive chemical as other popular beverages, that doesn't make the
tea less likely to cause kidney damage. Eliminate this choice.

Choice (B) focuses on addictive chemicals, not on weakening the causal connection between camellia tea and kidney damage. Move on to the next choice.

Choice (C) says camellia tea may relieve stress. But, it could do that and still cause kidney damage. Choice (C) does nothing to weaken the relationship between the tea and kidney damage.

Choice (D) may be tempting, but remember to check the three standard methods for weakening a causal argument. Choice (D) doesn't fit. The author simply claims some causal connection between the tea and a heightened risk of kidney damage. An answer that indicates a majority, meaning at least 51%, of tea drinkers do NOT get kidney damage, does not undermine the author's modest conclusion of some causal connection. This answer allows for up to 49% of tea drinkers having kidney damage, which could very well be considered a heightened risk.

Choice (E) correctly offers an alternative cause: other beverages that could increase the risk of kidney damage.

10. **(B)**

> Artist: Avant-garde artists intend their work to challenge a society's mainstream beliefs and initiate change. And <u>some art collectors claim that an avant-garde work that becomes popular in its own time is successful.</u> (However,) a society's mainstream beliefs do not generally show any significant changes over a short period of time. <(Therefore,) when an avant-garde work becomes popular it is a sign that the work is not successful, > (since) it does not fulfill the intentions of its creator.

The reference to the <u>claim of certain art collectors</u> (plays which one of the following roles) in the artist's argument?

(A) It serves to bolster the argument's main conclusion.
(B) It identifies a view that is ultimately disputed by the argument.
(C) It identifies a position supported by the initial premise in the argument.
(D) It provides support for the initial premise in the argument.
(E) It provides support for a counterargument to the initial premise.

Step 1. Identify the Question Type

The question refers to a claim in the stimulus and asks for the role the claim plays. Therefore, this stem is a Role of a Statement question.

Step 2. Untangle the Stimulus

The claim in question is in the second sentence; it says that avant-garde art that becomes popular in its own time is successful. The next sentence, which starts with "However," signals a contrast ahead. The artist presents her shift in the conclusion marked by "Therefore" and says that the popularity of avant-garde work is not a sign of success. Her evidence follows in the clause that starts with "since."

Step 3. Make a Prediction

The claim is not part of the argument's conclusion or evidence. It's the target of the artist's disagreement.

Step 4. Evaluate the Answer Choices

Choice (A) has it backward; the claim contrasts the conclusion, it doesn't support it.

Choice (B) is a perfect match and is the correct answer.

Choice (C) doesn't work. The initial premise that avant-garde artists intend their work to challenge society has no clear connection to the claim made by some art collectors that an avant-garde work that becomes popular in its own time is successful.

Choice (D) has the same problem. The initial premise doesn't support or isn't supported by the claim in question.

Choice (E) references a counterargument not included in the stimulus.

11. **(C)**

A recent epidemiological study found that businesspeople who travel internationally on business are much more likely to suffer from chronic insomnia than are businesspeople who do not travel on business. International travelers experience the stresses of dramatic changes in climate, frequent disruption of daily routines, and immersion in cultures other than their own, stresses not commonly felt by those who do not travel. <Thus, it is likely that these stresses <u>cause</u> the insomnia.>

Which one of the following would, if true, most (strengthen) the reasoning above?

(A)   Most international travel for the sake of business occurs between countries with contiguous borders.

(B)   Some businesspeople who travel internationally greatly enjoy the changes in climate and immersion in another culture.

(C)   Businesspeople who already suffer from chronic insomnia are no more likely than businesspeople who do not to accept assignments from their employers that require international travel.

(D)   Experiencing dramatic changes in climate and disruption of daily routines through international travel can be beneficial to some people who suffer from chronic insomnia.

(E)   Some businesspeople who once traveled internationally but no longer do so complain of various sleep-related ailments.

Step 1. Identify the Question Type

This is a Strengthen question, signaled by "strengthen" in the question stem.

Step 2. Untangle the Stimulus

The author concludes at the end of the stimulus that the stresses associated with international business travel cause travelers to suffer from insomnia. This claim of causation is based on a correlation found in a study that said international business travelers are more likely to be chronic insomniacs than those businesspeople who do not travel on business.

Step 3. Make a Prediction

Causal arguments can be strengthened in three different ways: by confirming the causality, by eliminating an alternative cause for the stated result (or eliminating the possibility of reverse causation), or by reducing the possibility of coincidence. Look for an answer that fits into one of these categories.

Step 4. Evaluate the Answer Choices

Choice (A) has no impact on the argument. The specific destination of international business travel doesn't affect a relationship between international business travel and insomnia.

Choice (B) contradicts the stimulus by calling some factors of international business travel enjoyable, while the author considers them stressors.

Choice (C) strengthens the argument by making it less likely that causation is reversed. In other words, choice (C) confirms the causal relationship from the stress of international travel to insomnia by pointing out that it's unlikely that the reverse is true, that insomnia causes the stress of international business travel. Choice (C) is the correct answer.

Choice (D) weakens the causal link between the stresses of international travel and insomnia by suggesting the so-called stresses may be beneficial to insomnia sufferers.

Choice (E) broadens the argument beyond insomnia to include various sleep-related ailments.

12. **(B)**

> Many mountain climbers regard climbing Mount Everest as the ultimate achievement. But <climbers should not attempt this climb> since the risk of death or serious injury in an Everest expedition is very high. Moreover, the romantic notion of gaining "spiritual discovery" atop Everest is dispelled by climbers' reports that the only profound experiences they had at the top were of exhaustion and fear.
>
> Which one of the following principles, if valid, most helps to justify the reasoning above?
>
> (A) Projects undertaken primarily for spiritual reasons ought to be abandoned if the risks are great.
> (B) Dangerous activities that are unlikely to result in significant spiritual benefits for those undertaking them should be avoided.
> (C) Activities that are extremely dangerous ought to be legally prohibited unless they are necessary to produce spiritual enlightenment.
> (D) Profound spiritual experiences can be achieved without undergoing the serious danger involved in mountain climbing.
> (E) Mountain climbers and other athletes should carefully examine the underlying reasons they have for participating in their sports.

Step 1. Identify the Question Type

The term "principles" tells you that this is a Principle question, and "following" tells you to find the principle in the answer choices. Because of the phrase "most helps to justify," you also know that the principle will act like a strengthener for the specific situation in the stimulus.

Step 2. Untangle the Stimulus

The author warns against climbing Mount Everest because it's very dangerous and dismisses any notion of spiritual discovery with reports of exhaustion and fear at the peak.

Step 3. Make a Prediction

The correct answer will take this specific situation and broaden it to a general rule, such as: Don't bother with dangerous activities that hold no spiritual reward.

Step 4. Evaluate the Answer Choices

Choice (A) distorts the argument by contorting it into a balance of risk versus spiritual reward and coming down on the side of safety. However, the author's recommendation is limited to endeavors that are both risky and do not provide the spiritual reward anticipated.

Choice (B) matches the prediction and is the correct answer.

Choice (C) is extreme in recommending legal prohibition for extremely dangerous activities. The stimulus never mentions what the law should or should not permit.

Choice (D) is out because the author never discusses achieving profound spiritual experiences. Rather, he talks about one activity in which spiritual discovery is unlikely.

Choice (E) does not match up with the author's recommendation to avoid the activity, not just think about it first.

13. **(B)**

Each of the smallest particles in the universe has an elegantly simple structure. (Since) these particles compose the universe, <we can (conclude that) the universe itself has an elegantly simple structure.>

Each of the following arguments exhibits (flawed) (reasoning similar to) that in the argument above (EXCEPT:)

(A) Each part of this car is nearly perfectly engineered. Therefore this car is nearly perfect, from an engineering point of view.
(B) Each part of this desk is made of metal. Therefore this desk is made of metal.
(C) Each brick in this wall is rectangular. Therefore this wall is rectangular.
(D) Each piece of wood in this chair is sturdy. Therefore this chair is sturdy.
(E) Each sentence in this novel is well constructed. Therefore this is a well-constructed novel.

Step 1. Identify the Question Type

The phrase "flawed reasoning similar to" denotes a Parallel Flaw question. "EXCEPT" means that the four wrong answers will share a similar type of argument with a similar flaw with the stimulus, while the correct answer will not.

Step 2. Untangle the Stimulus

The conclusion at the end of the stimulus asserts that the universe has a simple structure. The evidence, noted by "since," explains that the particles that make up the universe have the same structure.

Step 3. Make a Prediction

A quick check of the answer choices shows that the conclusions are all assertions of fact like the stimulus. So, move on and compare the flaws. The argument commits a classic flaw by assuming that what is true of the parts is true of the whole. The four wrong answers will have the same flaw. The one right answer will have a different flaw or will not have a flaw at all.

Step 4. Evaluate the Answer Choices

Choice (A) has a parallel flaw because it claims that perfect engineering of each car part means a perfectly engineered car. The flaw arises in the process of putting the parts together. The car is not just the sum of its parts, but also the process of putting the parts together. The argument does not account for that. Eliminate this choice.

Choice (B) has a superficially similar structure as the stimulus, but it is not flawed. Consequently, (B) is the correct answer. If every part of a desk is metal, the whole desk really is metal. On Parallel Flaw questions, it is common for one or more answers to not contain a logic flaw. On a Parallel Flaw EXCEPT question, there can be only one, and it will be the correct answer.

Choice (C) commits the same flaw as the stimulus and can therefore be eliminated. Each brick in the wall may be rectangular, but the bricks can be arranged to form different shapes. The wall does not necessarily have to be rectangular.

Choice (D) runs into the same flaw as the stimulus. With poor construction, you can create a not-so-sturdy chair with sturdy individual pieces.

You can eliminate choice (E) as well because it has a parallel flaw. Well-constructed sentences don't guarantee a well-constructed novel, especially if the sentences have no logical relationship to each other.

14. **(A)**

> Criminologist: <A judicial system that tries and punishes criminals without delay is an effective deterrent to violent crime.> Long, drawn-out trials and successful legal maneuvering may add to criminals' feelings of invulnerability. But if potential violent criminals know that being caught means prompt punishment, they will hesitate to break the law.

> Which one of the following, if true, would most seriously (weaken) the criminologist's argument?

> (A)   It is in the nature of violent crime that it is not premeditated.
> (B)   About one-fourth of all suspects first arrested for a crime are actually innocent.
> (C)   Many violent crimes are committed by first-time offenders.
> (D)   Everyone accused of a crime has the right to a trial.
> (E)   Countries that promptly punish suspected lawbreakers have lower crime rates than countries that allow long trials.

Step 1. Identify the Question Type

The question asks you to "weaken" the criminologist's argument, so it's a Weaken question.

Step 2. Untangle the Stimulus

The criminologist concludes that prompt punishment helps prevent violent crime. He bases this on the evidence that lengthy trials and legal maneuvering make criminals feel like they can work the system to their own benefit. But, people thinking of committing a crime will hesitate if they know punishment will be swift.

Step 3. Make a Prediction

If knowledge of swift punishment will deter crime, the criminologist must assume that would-be criminals can consider the consequences. If they can't do that, the argument is weaker. In other words, attack the assumption to weaken the argument.

Step 4. Evaluate the Answer Choices

Choice (A) weakens the argument. If violent crime is not premeditated, then criminals don't stop to consider the consequences. This is the correct answer.

Choice (B) does not impact the argument, which is about whether speedy trials deter violent crime, not the guilt or innocence of suspects when they're first arrested.

Choice (C) brings in the history of violent criminals and does not address whether someone can think about the consequences of his crime before he commits it.

Choice (D) doesn't work either. The criminologist isn't talking about a right to trial, but rather a quick trial as a deterrent.

Choice (E) strengthens the argument by suggesting that speedy trials do reduce the crime rate.

15. **(E)**

> Journalist: Many people object to mandatory retirement at age 65 as being arbitrary, arguing that people over 65 make useful contributions. However, if those who reach 65 are permitted to continue working indefinitely, we will face unacceptable outcomes. First, young people entering the job market will not be able to obtain decent jobs in the professions for which they were trained, resulting in widespread dissatisfaction among the young. Second, it is not fair for those who have worked 40 or more years to deprive others of opportunities. <̲T̲h̲e̲r̲e̲f̲o̲r̲e̲,̲ mandatory retirement should be retained.>

The journalist's argument (depends) on (assuming) which one of the following?

(A) Anyone who has worked 40 years is at least 65 years old.

(B) All young people entering the job market are highly trained professionals.

(C) It is unfair for a person not to get a job in the profession for which that person was trained.

(D) If people are forced to retire at age 65, there will be much dissatisfaction among at least some older people.

(E) If retirement ceases to be mandatory at age 65, at least some people will choose to work past age 65.

Step 1. Identify the Question Type

The word "assuming" identifies the stem as an Assumption question. "Depends" indicates a necessary assumption.

Step 2. Untangle the Stimulus

The journalist concludes that the mandatory retirement age should be preserved because allowing people to work past the age of 65 will produce unacceptable outcomes.

Step 3. Make a Prediction

The journalist is assuming that the downside of older people continuing to work is outweighed by the rights of older people or benefits of them continuing to work.

Step 4. Evaluate the Answer Choices

Choice (A) refers to details in the argument and just confuses them. Eliminate this choice.

Choice (B) is too extreme in referring to all young people entering the job market and is not mentioned in the stimulus. Cross out this choice.

Choice (C) distorts the details of the unacceptable outcomes outlined in the stimulus. Move on.

Choice (D) doesn't make sense in light of the fact the journalist wants to maintain mandatory retirement for people over 65. So, she wouldn't assume that older people will be dissatisfied with it.

Choice (E) was a tough one to predict in advance because it is so basic and not at all profound. But anytime the journalist makes a recommendation, the journalist inherently assumes that the proposal is not impossible and that there is some point to the proposal. Use the denial test, and see how if nobody will continue working, then the author's claim that mandatory retirement provisions should be retained is pointless.

16. **(B)**

Editorial: Contrary to popular belief, <teaching preschoolers is not especially difficult,> (for) they develop strict systems (e.g., for sorting toys by shape), which help them to learn, and they are always intensely curious about something new in their world.

Which one of the following, if true, most seriously (weakens) the editorial's argument?

(A) Preschoolers have a tendency to imitate adults, and most adults follow strict routines.
(B) Children intensely curious about new things have very short attention spans.
(C) Some older children also develop strict systems that help them learn.
(D) Preschoolers ask as many creative questions as do older children.
(E) Preschool teachers generally report lower levels of stress than do other teachers.

Step 1. Identify the Question Type

The term "weakens" in the stem tells you that this is a Weaken question.

Step 2. Untangle the Stimulus

According to the editorial, a common belief holds that preschoolers are hard to teach. However, the editorial disagrees and says preschoolers are actually easier to teach because they have strict systems to help them learn and because they are very curious.

Step 3. Make a Prediction

To jump from learning systems and curiosity to easy to teach, the editorial must assume that students who learn with strict systems and are curious are easier to teach. The correct answer will invalidate the assumption, suggesting that these qualities make the preschoolers less easy to teach.

Step 4. Evaluate the Answer Choices

Choice (A) connects preschoolers to adults, but does not address whether they are easier to teach. Move on to the next choice.

Choice (B) weakens the argument by suggesting that children who are curious might not be easy to teach. This is the correct answer.

Choice (C) veers outside the scope of the argument introducing older children. The argument is only concerned with preschoolers.

Choice (D) provides an irrelevant comparison between preschoolers and older children. While choice (D) might suggest that preschoolers are curious, it doesn't break the connection between curiosity and preschoolers being easy to teach.

Choice (E) focuses on the teachers and doesn't address the relationship between preschoolers' learning characteristics and the ease of teaching them.

17. **(A)**

Lawyer: A body of circumstantial evidence is like a rope, and each item of evidence is like a strand of that rope. Just as additional pieces of circumstantial evidence strengthen the body of evidence, adding strands to the rope strengthens the rope. And if one strand breaks, the rope is not broken nor is its strength much diminished. ⟨Thus,⟩ even if a few items of a body of circumstantial evidence are discredited, the overall body of evidence retains its basic strength.⟩

The reasoning in the lawyer's argument is ⟨most⟩ ⟨vulnerable to criticism⟩ on the grounds that the argument

   (A) takes for granted that no items in a body of circumstantial evidence are significantly more critical to the strength of the evidence than other items in that body
   (B) presumes, without providing justification, that the strength of a body of evidence is less than the sum of the strengths of the parts of that body
   (C) fails to consider the possibility that if many items in a body of circumstantial evidence were discredited, the overall body of evidence would be discredited
   (D) offers an analogy in support of a conclusion without indicating whether the two types of things compared share any similarities
   (E) draws a conclusion that simply restates a claim presented in support of that conclusion

Step 1. Identify the Question Type

The phrase "most vulnerable to criticism" signals a Flaw question.

Step 2. Untangle the Stimulus

Be on the lookout for classic flaws when you read a Flaw stimulus. Here, the lawyer makes an analogy between a body of circumstantial evidence and a rope. The lawyer concludes that a body of evidence remains strong even if a few pieces are discredited because a rope remains strong even if a few strands break.

Step 3. Make a Prediction

An analogy is based on the assumption that what's being analogized is comparable. In a Flaw question, that assumption is faulty. So, the correct answer will draw a distinction between rope and circumstantial evidence.

Step 4. Evaluate the Answer Choices

Choice (A) correctly points out that individual pieces of circumstantial evidence may have different levels of importance to the body of evidence, unlike strands of rope that are equally important.

Choice (B) gets it backward. The lawyer says the strength of a body of evidence is more than the sum of the parts because you can sacrifice some of the parts without compromising the strength of the whole.

Choice (C) need not be considered because the lawyer's conclusion concerns discrediting a few items of circumstantial evidence, not many.

Choice (D) ignores the lawyer's attempts to describe similarities between rope and a body of evidence. While, the lawyer does offer an analogy in support of the conclusion, she then attempts to support a comparison between a rope and a body of evidence by describing how adding each new piece of circumstantial evidence strengthens the whole, just like adding a strand strengthens the rope.

Choice (E) defines the flaw as circular reasoning, but the evidence and conclusion are not the same in this argument.

18. **(E)**

> Ethicist: Many environmentalists hold that the natural environment is morally valuable for its own sake, regardless of any benefits it provides us. (However,) even if nature has no moral value, nature can be regarded as worth preserving simply on the grounds that people find it beautiful. (Moreover,) (because) it is philosophically disputable whether nature is morally valuable but undeniable that it is beautiful, <an argument for preserving nature that emphasizes nature's beauty will be less vulnerable to logical objections than one that emphasizes its moral value.>

The ethicist's (reasoning) most closely conforms to which one of the following (principles)?

(A) An argument in favor of preserving nature will be less open to logical objections if it avoids the issue of what makes nature worth preserving.

(B) If an argument for preserving nature emphasizes a specific characteristic of nature and is vulnerable to logical objections, then that characteristic does not provide a sufficient reason for preserving nature.

(C) If it is philosophically disputable whether nature has a certain characteristic, then nature would be more clearly worth preserving if it did not have that characteristic.

(D) Anything that has moral value is worth preserving regardless of whether people consider it to be beautiful.

(E) An argument for preserving nature will be less open to logical objections if it appeals to a characteristic that can be regarded as a basis for preserving nature and that philosophically indisputably belongs to nature.

Step 1. Identify the Question Type

The stem specifically asks you to pick a principle, so this is a Principle question. Your task is to identify the broad rule in the answers that conforms to the specific situation, or in this case the argument, laid out in the stimulus. The reference to "reasoning" in the question stem, indicates that the stimulus is an argument with evidence and a conclusion, rather than just a factual situation.

Step 2. Untangle the Stimulus

The stimulus is dense and abstract, so slow down if you need to and take it one sentence at a time:

It is widely held amongst environmentalists that the natural world is morally valuable. Even if it's not, some believe nature should be preserved because it's beautiful. Nature's moral value is disputable, but its beauty is not. Therefore, a preservation argument based on beauty will face fewer objections than an argument based on moral value.

Step 3. Make a Prediction

The ethicist is saying that an argument is less objectionable if it is based on an indisputable trait.

Step 4. Evaluate the Answer Choices

Choice (A) is wrong because it talks about avoiding the issue. Actually, the ethicist supports emphasizing what makes nature worth preserving.

Choice (B) distorts the ethicist's reasoning. The ethicist reasons that an argument in favor of preserving nature that emphasizes nature's moral value may be more logically vulnerable than one emphasizing nature's beauty, but that's different from saying that moral value is not a sufficient reason for preserving nature.

Choice (C) ignores the ethicist's principle about what makes an argument more or less defensible.

Choice (D) goes too far. The ethicist says that beauty, not moral value, is sufficient grounds for arguing for the preservation of nature. The ethicist never says that anything morally valuable is worth preserving.

Choice (E) matches the prediction and is the correct answer.

19. **(A)**

An editor is compiling a textbook containing essays by several different authors. The book will contain essays by Lind, Knight, or Jones, but it will not contain essays by all three. If the textbook contains an essay by Knight, then it will also contain an essay by Jones.

If the statements above are true, which one of the following must be true?

(A)   If the textbook contains an essay by Lind, then it will not contain an essay by Knight.
(B)   The textbook will contain an essay by only one of Lind, Knight, and Jones.
(C)   The textbook will not contain an essay by Knight.
(D)   If the textbook contains an essay by Lind, then it will also contain an essay by Jones.
(E)   The textbook will contain an essay by Lind.

Step 1. Identify the Question Type

The question asks what "must be true," so it is an Inference question.

Step 2. Untangle the Stimulus

The issue is which authors will be included in the textbook. Lind, Knight, and Jones are three authors who may be included in the book, but the book will never contain all three. Also, if Knight's included, then Jones is included.

Write out the formal logic statement to help you know what must be true in the stimulus. You already know that K → J, so you also know the contrapositive, Not J → not K.

Step 3. Make a Prediction

When you have formal logic in an Inference stimulus, be on the lookout for a contrapositive or a combined statement in the correct answer choice. Here you have additional information to combine with the formal logic statements you already have. You know all three authors will never be together in a book. So if K is in the book and then J is in the book, then L must not be included. In other words, K → no L. The contrapositive is L → no K. Since you do have a prediction, scan the answer choices for your prediction before you analyze the answer choices in more detail.

Step 4. Evaluate the Answer Choices

Notice the answer choices are all presented in formal logic language. Translate them quickly if necessary and compare them to what you know from the stimulus.

Choice (A) gives the correct answer (L → no K). Notice it matches the contrapositive of the combined statement from the stimulus.

Choice (B) doesn't have to be true because according to the stimulus, one textbook could include essays from Knight and Jones or Jones and Lind.

Choice (C) also contradicts the stimulus. Knight could have an essay in the textbook as long as Jones did too.

Choice (D) translates to L → J, which cannot be inferred from the stimulus. If Lind has an essay in the textbook, you know from the contraposed statement that Knight will not. The stimulus gives no indication of whether or not Jones will have an essay in the book.

Choice (E) incorrectly states that the textbook must always include an essay by Lind. The stimulus indicates otherwise. The textbook can contain an essay by Knight and one by Jones, or just Jones.

20. **(D)**

<The ability of mammals to control their internal body temperatures is a factor in the development of their brains and intelligence.> This can be seen from the following facts: the brain is a chemical machine, all chemical reactions are temperature dependent, and any organism that can control its body temperature can assure that these reactions occur at the proper temperatures.

Which one of the following is an assumption on which the argument depends?

(A) Organisms unable to control their body temperatures do not have the capacity to generate internal body heat without relying on external factors.

(B) Mammals are the only animals that have the ability to control their internal body temperatures.

(C) The brain cannot support intelligence if the chemical reactions within it are subject to uncontrolled temperatures.

(D) The development of intelligence in mammals is not independent of the chemical reactions in their brains taking place at the proper temperatures.

(E) Organisms incapable of controlling their internal body temperatures are subject to unpredictable chemical processes.

Step 1. Identify the Question Type

The stem asks for an "assumption," so it's an Assumption question.

Step 2. Untangle the Stimulus

In the first sentence, the conclusion says that mammals' ability to control their internal body temperatures influences the development of their brains and intelligence. The evidence, clearly identified by "this can be seen from," says the brain is a chemical machine and chemical reactions must occur at proper temperatures. The ability to control body temperature ensures that the chemical reactions occur at the proper temperatures.

Step 3. Make a Prediction

The development of brains and intelligence is nowhere to be found in the evidence, and the conclusion ignores chemical reactions. The assumption will make the connection and provide that development of brains and intelligence is influenced by chemical reactions in the brain occurring at the right temperatures.

Step 4. Evaluate the Answer Choices

Choice (A) talks about organisms that can't control their internal body temperature, which are not discussed in this stimulus and are therefore outside the scope of the argument.

Choice (B) is extreme because the argument says that mammals have the ability to control their body temperatures. It doesn't say they are the only animals that can do so. So, this choice is out.

Choice (C) is also extreme. The author indicates that the regulation of chemical reaction temperatures is a factor in the development of intelligence, but doesn't say that intelligence can't develop without such regulation.

Choice (D) presents the correct assumption, just with negative wording. The notion that the development of intelligence is not independent of the temperature of chemical reactions means that it *is* influenced by the temperature of chemical reactions.

Choice (E) has the same problem as choice (A). Organisms incapable of controlling their internal body temperatures are outside the scope.

21. **(C)**

People who object to the proposed hazardous waste storage site by appealing to extremely implausible scenarios in which the site fails to contain the waste safely are overlooking the significant risks associated with delays in moving the waste from its present unsafe location. If we wait to remove the waste until we find a site certain to contain it safely, the waste will remain in its current location for many years, since it is currently impossible to guarantee that any site can meet that criterion. Yet keeping the waste at the current location for that long clearly poses unacceptable risks.

The statements above, if true, most strongly support which one of the following?

(A) The waste should never have been stored in its current location.
(B) The waste should be placed in the most secure location that can ever be found.
(C) Moving the waste to the proposed site would reduce the threat posed by the waste.
(D) Whenever waste must be moved, one should limit the amount of time allotted to locating alternative waste storage sites.
(E) Any site to which the waste could be moved will be safer than its present site.

Step 1. Identify the Question Type

Since the statements in the stimulus "most strongly support" a certain answer choice, the stem is an Inference question.

Step 2. Untangle the Stimulus

The author says that objecting to a proposed hazardous waste site poses risks by delaying movement of the waste. Waiting for a location certain to contain all the waste ensures the waste will remain in its current site for many years, a situation that the author says poses "unacceptable risks."

Step 3. Make a Prediction

The stimulus offers no formal logic or statements to combine, so there is no prediction to be made. Proceed to the answer choices with an understanding of what the stimulus says. The correct answer to an Inference question *must be true* based on the stimulus.

Step 4. Evaluate the Answer Choices

Choice (A) is extreme and is not addressed in the stimulus. The current location may have been the best option at the time, but the stimulus provides no background information.

Choice (B) is wrong because the author says we can't afford to wait to find the most secure location that can ever be found.

Choice (C) *must be true* based on the stimulus because the author eliminates the possibility of keeping the waste where it is. Notice that this answer choice is the most modest of the choices, as the correct Inference answer choice often is. This choice simply indicates that moving the waste reduces the risk, not that it is the best solution or the only solution or that it will completely eliminate the risk.

Choice (D) is extreme in saying that time used to locate alternative waste sites should be limited whenever waste must be moved. The author might agree in this specific instance, but you don't know about every other situation.

Choice (E) is problematic because you don't know whether the author believes every single alternative site would be safer than the current site, just the site to which the author advocates moving the waste.

22. **(B)**

A recent survey indicates that the average number of books read annually per capita has declined in each of the last three years. However, it also found that most bookstores reported increased profits during the same period.

Each of the following, if true, helps to (resolve the) (survey's apparently paradoxical results EXCEPT:)

(A)   Recent cutbacks in government spending have forced public libraries to purchase fewer popular contemporary novels.

(B)   Due to the installation of sophisticated new antitheft equipment, the recent increase in shoplifting that has hit most retail businesses has left bookstores largely unaffected.

(C)   Over the past few years many bookstores have capitalized on the lucrative coffee industry by installing coffee bars.

(D)   Bookstore owners reported a general shift away from the sale of inexpensive paperback novels and toward the sale of lucrative hardback books.

(E)   Citing a lack of free time, many survey respondents indicated that they had canceled magazine subscriptions in favor of purchasing individual issues at bookstores when time permits.

Step 1. Identify the Question Type

The phrase "resolve the survey's apparently paradoxical results" identifies a Paradox question, and "EXCEPT" indicates that the four wrong answers will resolve the paradox and that the one right answer will not.

Step 2. Untangle the Stimulus

Reading is declining yet bookstore profits are up. That doesn't seem to make sense.

Step 3. Make a Prediction

The correct answer will not explain this conundrum. Maybe the fewer books sold are more expensive or something other than books accounts for the higher profits. Check the answers and eliminate the four that resolve the paradox.

Step 4. Evaluate the Answer Choices

Choice (A) suggests that libraries have less-popular books, so readers may have to buy them at the bookstore. However, purchasing the books, and thus raising bookstore profits, doesn't necessarily mean the customers are reading them. Choice (A) gives one explanation for how bookstore profits could go up while reading declines. Therefore, it resolves the paradox and is not the correct answer choice.

Choice (B) explains why bookstores may have seen higher profits relative to other retail businesses, but that's not the paradox in question. Because choice (B) doesn't explain how bookstores are making more money while people read less, it is the correct answer.

Choice (C) accounts for the higher profits with higher sales of coffee not books.

Choice (D) explains the higher profits with the sale of higher priced books. A higher price point makes up for lower sales.

Choice (E) offers another income source in the form of magazine sales.

23. **(D)**

> Naturalist: A species can survive a change in environment, as long as the change is not too rapid. ⟨Therefore,⟩ the threats we are creating to woodland species arise not from the fact that we are cutting down trees, but rather from the rate at which we are doing so.⟩

The reasoning in which one of the following is ⟨most⟩ ⟨similar to⟩ that in the naturalist's argument?

(A) The problem with burning fossil fuels is that the supply is limited; <so, the faster we expend these resources, the sooner we will be left without an energy source.>

(B) Many people gain more satisfaction from performing a job well—regardless of whether they like the job—than from doing merely adequately a job they like; <thus, people who want to be happy should choose jobs they can do well.>

(C) Some students who study thoroughly do well in school. <Thus, what is most important for success in school is not how much time a student puts into studying, but rather how thoroughly the student studies.>

(D) People do not fear change if they know what the change will bring; <so, our employees' fear stems not from our company's undergoing change, but from our failing to inform them of what the changes entail.>

(E) Until ten years ago, we had good soil and our agriculture flourished. <Therefore, the recent decline of our agriculture is a result of our soil rapidly eroding and there being nothing that can replace the good soil we lost.>

Step 1. Identify the Question Type

The phrase "most similar to" tells you that this is a Parallel Reasoning question.

Step 2. Untangle the Stimulus

The naturalist states a basic principle that a species can survive a change of environment if the change is not too quick. Then, he applies the principle to a specific species and concludes that the woodland species isn't in danger because its environment is changing, but because its environment is changing too quickly.

Step 3. Make a Prediction

The naturalist claims with an assertion of fact that it's not the cutting down of trees in general, but the rate of cutting down trees that is harming the species. Generally, the naturalist is asserting that it's not the thing *itself* that is causing the problem, but something about *how that thing is done* that is causing the problem. Look for a similar conclusion in the answer choices, and if necessary, compare the evidence to find a parallel argument.

Step 4. Evaluate the Answer Choices

Choice (A)'s conclusion is a prediction, not an assertion of fact. Eliminate this choice.

Choice (B) is wrong because the conclusion is a recommendation, not an assertion of fact.

Choice (C) weighs the importance of two factors (time and thoroughness of studying) to achieve success in school. Move on to the next choice.

Choice (D) correctly matches the stimulus because it is not the change itself that is causing the problem but how the change is undertaken (without informing the employees).

Choice (E) is not similar. It asserts two causes for a negative result and doesn't dismiss one in favor of the other.

24. **(A)**

> Professor: A person who can select a beverage from among 50 varieties of cola is less free than one who has only these 5 choices: wine, coffee, apple juice, milk, and water. It is clear, then, that meaningful freedom cannot be measured simply by the number of alternatives available;> the extent of the differences among the alternatives is also a relevant factor.

The professor's argument proceeds by

(A) supporting a general principle by means of an example

(B) drawing a conclusion about a particular case on the basis of a general principle

(C) supporting its conclusion by means of an analogy

(D) claiming that whatever holds for each member of a group must hold for the whole group

(E) inferring one general principle from another, more general, principle

Step 1. Identify the Question Type

The phrase "argument proceeds by" means this is a Method of Argument question.

Step 2. Untangle the Stimulus

The phrase "It is clear, then" at the start of the second sentence points to the professor's conclusion that freedom can't be measured by the number of alternatives available. The professor supports her conclusion with an example about the freedom of a person selecting among beverages.

Step 3. Make a Prediction

The professor makes a broad statement in the conclusion and backs it up with an example of that principle. The correct answer will match this prediction.

Step 4. Evaluate the Answer Choices

Choice (A) correctly restates the prediction and is the correct answer.

Choice (B) is backward. The professor's conclusion is general, and she supports it with a specific example, not the other way around.

Choice (C) adds an analogy to the answer not mentioned in the stimulus. The professor uses an example, not an analogy, to support the conclusion.

Choice (D) is wrong because the professor doesn't claim any properties are true for "each member of a group."

Choice (E) adds a second principle which is not mentioned in the stimulus. The professor's conclusion is a principle, but the professor never claims it's derived from another principle.

25. **(C)**

> Principle: Meetings should be kept short, addressing only those issues relevant to a majority of those attending. A person should not be required to attend a meeting if none of the issues to be addressed at the meeting are relevant to that person.
>
> Application: <Terry should not be required to attend today's two o'clock meeting.>

Which one of the following, if true, most <u>justifies</u> the stated application of the (principle)?

(A)   The only issues on which Terry could make a presentation at the meeting are issues irrelevant to at least a majority of those who could attend.

(B)   If Terry makes a presentation at the meeting, the meeting will not be kept short.

(C)   No issue relevant to Terry could be relevant to a majority of those attending the meeting.

(D)   If Terry attends the meeting a different set of issues will be relevant to a majority of those attending than if Terry does not attend.

(E)   The majority of the issues to be addressed at the meeting are not relevant to Terry.

Step 1. Identify the Question Type

This is a Principle question, signaled by "principle." In this case, the principle is in the stimulus and you're asked to justify, or strengthen, its application. So, the principle is the evidence, and the application is the conclusion.

Step 2. Untangle the Stimulus

The principle says that meetings should cover issues relevant to a majority of attendees and if the issues are not relevant to a person, that person shouldn't have to attend. The application of the principle concludes that Terry shouldn't have to attend today's meeting.

Step 3. Make a Prediction

So if the issues are not relevant, you don't have to attend the meeting. And if you're Terry, you don't have to attend the meeting. Therefore, the argument assumes that the issues are not relevant to Terry. The correct answer will confirm the assumption.

Step 4. Evaluate the Answer Choices

Choice (A) contradicts the stimulus. According to the principle, if the issues are irrelevant, the person shouldn't have to attend the meeting.

Choice (B) doesn't work. The principle says meetings should be kept short, but it doesn't connect back to Terry and let him out of the meeting.

Choice (C) is the correct answer. If an issue is relevant to Terry, then it is not relevant to the meeting majority. Contrapose the statement and you learn that if meeting issues are relevant to the meeting majority, they are not relevant to Terry. Therefore, he is not required to attend.

Choice (D) suggests Terry may decide to attend the meeting even though he's not required to be in attendance. However, his voluntary attendance would not have any impact on the meeting agenda.

Choice (E) requires a close read. The principle allows a person to skip a meeting if none of the issues are relevant to him. It doesn't allow a person to skip the meeting if a majority of the issues are not relevant to him. "Majority" in the stimulus refers to the attendees, not the issues.

PART IV

THE TEST DAY EXPERIENCE

CHAPTER 23

GET READY FOR TEST DAY

Congratulations. Your work with the Kaplan Method and strategies gives you the knowledge and practice you need for LSAT success. Now, it's time for you to schedule a test date, register for the exam (if you haven't done so already), and put yourself in the right frame of mind to take the next step on the road to law school.

The details of registering for the test are covered in "An Introduction to the LSAT" at the beginning of the book. Follow the steps and recommendations mentioned there to ensure that you have a spot at the next test administration or on the test date that's best for you. In the remainder of this chapter, I'll cover what you need to do to have yourself mentally and emotionally ready for the rigors and rewards of test day.

YOU ARE PREPARED

First, remember (and remind yourself) that you are prepared. By learning the lessons and doing the work from this book, you can know, with confidence, that there is nothing else you need to *know* about LSAT Logical Reasoning. The Kaplan Method, the specific strategies, and their application to specific question types that I've presented in this book are the result not only of my own 9-year tenure as an LSAT instructor; they're the summation of five decades of Kaplan expertise and research. Hundreds of great LSAT minds—including those of perfect scorers, legal scholars, and psychometricians—have contributed to the development, testing, and refinement of Kaplan's LSAT pedagogy. If we know it, you now know it. So strike from your mind any concern that there's one more secret to uncover or a mysterious LSAT Rosetta Stone to search for. You have the most complete, proven system for LSAT Logical Reasoning success available. If you've already studied and practiced from this book's companion volumes—*Kaplan LSAT Reading Comprehension: Strategies and Tactics* and *Kaplan LSAT Logic Games: Strategies and Tactics*—you can say the same thing about the entire exam.

Now, saying that you *know* everything you need to about the Logical Reasoning section doesn't mean you're ready to *do* everything you need to do to achieve your goal score. You need to continue to practice and review. Indeed, I'll cover that in the next section of this chapter. But first, I want to make sure you're translating your comprehensive knowledge of logical reasoning into confidence on test day. From now until the day you sit for your official administration of the LSAT, you need to exhibit the confidence your preparation has earned you.

There are some very practical steps you can take to reinforce your test day confidence. Once you're registered for the test, visit your test site. You may even want to take some logical reasoning questions to practice in the very room where you'll be sitting for the real test. At a minimum, know where you're going to be, how you'll get there, and where you'll park or where public transportation will drop you off. You want no surprises on the morning of your official LSAT.

The day before your test, relax. There's no way to cram for a skills-based exam. While your competition is scrambling and fretting, go to the gym, watch your favorite movie, or have a nice dinner. Gather what you need for the next day, and keep yourself one step ahead of everything you need to do. It sounds a little corny, but acting confident will actually make you feel more confident. Get to bed relatively early, have a good night's sleep, and wake ready to have the best day of your (test-taking) life.

The following is a list of what you'll need to have with you on test day:

LSAT SURVIVAL KIT

You MUST have the following:
- Admissions ticket
- Photo ID
- Several sharpened #2 pencils
- 1-gallon transparent zip-top bag

You SHOULD also have:
- Pencil sharpener
- Eraser
- Analog wristwatch
- Aspirin
- Snack and drink for the break

You CANNOT have:
- Cell phone
- MP3 player
- Computer or electronic reader
- Electronic or digital timers
- Weapons
- Papers other than your admission ticket

That list conforms to the rules for the test site as they stand at the time of this writing. You should check www.lsac.org periodically before your test date to make sure there haven't been any changes or amendments to the Law School Administration Council's (LSAC) policies.

Of course, the "MUSTs" are non-negotiable. You need those to be allowed entry to the testing room. Some of the "SHOULDs," on the other hand, you may not need at all. But if you begin to feel a little headache coming on, or if you find your stomach grumbling midway through Section 3 of the test, you'll be awfully glad you took along those "just in case" items. As for the "CANNOTs," do yourself a favor and avoid any conflict with the proctors or test administrators. Just leave your phone or electronics in the car or at home.

One other very practical thing you can do is to dress in layers. The LSAT is usually administered during the weekend and almost always in a large, institutional building. It's really tough to predict whether the room will be too hot or too cold or whether it will fluctuate throughout the day. Take the Goldilocks approach and make sure the temperature is always "just right" for you by wearing or taking the kind of sweater or light jacket that's easy (and quiet) to slip on or off.

The stress levels of test takers around you will be high. But if you demonstrate nothing but preparation and confidence on the morning of the test, you'll feel calmer, more clear-headed, and ready for the real challenges of the test itself.

CHAMPIONS PRACTICE. VIRTUOSOS PRACTICE. YOU PRACTICE.

To put my earlier point about practice into formal logic terms, knowledge of the test is necessary, but not sufficient, for test day success. Mistaking this relationship is something that leads a lot of test takers off track. They haven't achieved the score they want, so they say, "There must be something I don't know yet," or, "What am I missing?" The fact is that many of these test takers know all about the test, but they haven't practiced taking the test. Ask almost any great performer, musician, public speaker, or athlete and they'll tell you that the key to their success is practice. A great violinist may study a composer's compositional theory, historical context, or even personal life in order to better understand a piece before performing it. But all of that will mean little if the performer hasn't practiced. The audience would be pretty disappointed if the violinist showed up to give a lecture about the composer instead of playing a concert. It's the same with the LSAT. Your audience, law school admissions officers, won't care what you know about the exam, just how well you perform on it.

So how can you best practice? First, lay out a study and practice schedule for yourself that runs from now until test day—one that's ambitious but practical. Fill in as much as you can about which sections or question types you'll be practicing each day or week. If you're working on different parts of the test, vary the sections you're practicing and the materials you're using.

If you haven't completed and reviewed the full-section practice in this book, make sure you do so. Leave time for review of your work. Remember that you're not just checking to see whether you produced the correct answer, you're asking whether you did so as efficiently and effectively as you could have. That means that you should always be reviewing the questions you got right as well as those you got wrong. Look for what features and patterns in a question you're likely to see again on test day. You won't see the questions from this book on your test, but every question on your test will have similarities to those you've practiced here.

If you're looking for additional practice, consider the following additional resources:

OTHER KAPLAN LSAT RESOURCES

Logic Games On Demand
Logical Reasoning On Demand
Reading Comprehension On Demand
Comprehensive, section-specific courses for in-depth instruction and targeted practice.

LSAT Advantage—On Site, Anywhere or On Demand
Our most popular option—complete, targeted, and focused prep designed for busy students.

LSAT Advanced—On Site or Anywhere
Fast-paced for high-scorers focusing on the most advanced content. (158+ required to enroll.)

LSAT Extreme—On Site or Anywhere
Maximum in-class instruction plus tutoring for students who want extra time, review, and more practice.

LSAT One on One—On Site or Anywhere
An expert tutor designs a one-on-one, custom program around your individual needs, goals, and schedule.

LSAT Summer Intensive
Six weeks of total LSAT immersion in a residential academic program at Boston University

Check out *www.kaplanlsat.com* for courses and free events in live, online and in your area.

All of those additional resources will provide the outstanding instruction, coaching, and practice you expect from Kaplan test prep. Consider which ones work best for your schedule, learning style, and admissions timeline. Kaplan is committed to helping you achieve your educational and career goals.

THE PSYCHOLOGICAL DIMENSIONS OF TEST DAY

There's no doubt that taking your official LSAT is one of the most important steps (maybe *the* most important) you'll take on the road to law school. That's a lot of pressure. It's natural to have a little excitement and some extra adrenaline for such a big event. Those are actually healthy things to feel, provided that you channel your emotions into energy and concentration, rather than anxiety and confusion. I'd be pretty disappointed if, after weeks or months of practice and preparation, one of my students said, "Eh, I don't really care what happens on the test." Of course you care. That's why you're reading this book and working so hard. So embrace the big day.

I've already talked about how you can begin to foster an attitude of confidence and act in ways that support and sustain it. Here are a couple of practical steps you can take to carry your confidence right into the testing room.

Know What to Expect

It is easy to lay out the order of events on test day. Here's a chart that shows you what will happen from the time you arrive at the test site.

Event	What Happens	Time
Check-In	Show admissions ticket, ID, fingerprints, room and seat assignment	10–30 minutes
Rules and Procedures	Test booklets distributed, proctor reads the rules, test takers fill out grid information	30 minutes
LSAT Administration		
Section 1	Logic Games, Logical Reasoning, or Reading Comprehension Section	35 minutes
Section 2	Logic Games, Logical Reasoning, or Reading Comprehension Section	35 minutes
Section 3	Logic Games, Logical Reasoning, or Reading Comprehension Section	35 minutes

Break	Test booklets and grids collected, test takers have break, return to seats, booklets and grids redistributed	12–20 minutes (10 minute break with additional time for administrative tasks)
Section 4	Logic Games, Logical Reasoning, or Reading Comprehension Section	35 minutes
Section 5	Logic Games, Logical Reasoning, or Reading Comprehension Section	35 minutes
Prepare for Writing Sample	Test booklets and grids collected, test takers given a chance to cancel scores, Writing Sample booklets distributed	5–10 minutes
Writing Sample	Test takers produce Writing Samples	35 minutes

You can see that even if everything goes as smoothly as possible, you're in for around five hours from start to finish. This is another reason that it's so important to be rested, comfortable, and nourished. Students who are too groggy to be at their best in Section 1 or too exhausted and hungry to keep up their performance in Section 5 will have trouble competing with someone like you, who's prepared for the entire testing day, from start to finish.

One thing that star performers do—I don't care if you're thinking of singers, actors, athletes, or even great trial lawyers—is to warm up before they "go on." You can do the same on the morning of your test by reviewing a Logic Game, Logical Reasoning question, or Reading Comprehension passage that you've done before. As you revisit the game or question, go over the steps in the Kaplan Method that allowed you to be successful with the item before. This will get your brain warmed up just as a quarterback would loosen his arm or a singer would warm up her vocal cords. Don't try new material, and certainly don't try a full section. Just start reading and thinking—calmly and confidently—in the LSAT way. You'll be miles ahead of the unprepared test taker who looks shell-shocked for most of Section 1.

In order to maintain a high level of performance, it's important to stay hydrated and nourished. Mental work makes most people hungry. So drink water at the break and have a small, healthy snack. Don't, however, eat a sleep-inducing turkey sandwich or gobble sugar that will have you crashing out during Section 5.

Knowing what to expect also helps you manage your mental preparation for test day in other small, but important, ways. A lot of test takers don't know that the proctors will ask whether

anyone in the room wants to cancel his or her score right after Section 5 is completed and the test booklets are collected. If you're not expecting that question, it can throw you into a moment of self-doubt. It's human nature to underestimate your performance on the test. You will remember the handful of questions that gave you trouble while ignoring the dozens of questions you answered routinely with no problem. I've personally known students who canceled their scores when they shouldn't have. The LSAC allows you a number of days after the test to cancel your score, so don't worry about it during the exam. Complete the Writing Sample to the best of your ability. You can always consider things that might have caused you to underperform—illness, a personal crisis—after you've completed the test.

You Will Panic, but Don't Panic

Over the course of four to five hours of rigorous, detailed, strictly timed test taking, you're going to reach a point at which you lose focus, feel overwhelmed, or just downright panic for a moment. It's normal. So first thing, don't feed the panic by blaming yourself or saying, "Oh, I knew this would happen." There's nothing wrong with you for having those feelings. In fact, panic is a physical response to high-pressure situations. It's related to the autonomic nervous system, the "flight or fight" response we've adapted to survive danger. Your heart beats faster; blood leaves your brain to go to your extremities; your breathing gets rapid and shallow. That's all very important when the danger you face is a predator or enemy. It's just not very helpful when you're facing a standardized test.

If—when—you face a point of doubt, confusion, or panic on test day, take a moment. Collect yourself physically first. Take a deep breath; sit up in a straight, comfortable posture; put both feet flat on the floor and lower your shoulders; even close your eyes for a second while you breathe. Then open your eyes and remind yourself that whatever you're looking at, it's just an LSAT question. The fact is that you've seen one like it and done one like it before. You know that's the case because of your preparation. Get your concentration back by reciting the Kaplan Method as you work through the problem. You know that will provide a strategic, purposeful approach every time.

Worry Only about What's in Your Control

When I have students in LSAT prep courses, they often ask a lot of questions about what to do if things go wrong on test day. "What if the proctor doesn't give us a verbal five minute warning?" "What if someone is being noisy right behind me?" "What if the school marching band is rehearsing in the courtyard under the window?" All of those and a few weirder, more distracting things have happened to test takers. But my students' concern about such occurrences before test day is misplaced. They should be taking care of the things that are within their control—learning the Kaplan Method, practicing logical reasoning questions—not worrying about the things that aren't. The vast majority of LSAT administrations go off without more than a minor hitch. Your job is to be ready to have a peak performance on a routine test day.

When the unexpected happens, stay calm. If there is something that you notice before the test begins—a window is open, letting in cold air or street noise; the lights in the back of the room aren't turned on, making it dark where you're sitting—just let the proctor know (politely) and ask if it can be remedied. If something happens during a section—another test taker is unconsciously tapping his pencil; the proctor forgets the five-minute announcement—keep working. Raise your hand and get a proctor's attention. When they come to your seat, quickly and quietly explain the situation. Most of the time, they'll take action to remedy the situation. But don't let those things throw you off your game. If something truly bizarre happens that seriously impedes your performance—a fire alarm goes off, a wrecking crew starts to jackhammer the building—follow the proctor's instructions, keep a record of what happened, and follow up with the LSAC by telephone or in writing after the test concludes. You are welcome to contact 1-800-KAPTEST and ask for advice from one of our LSAT experts, too. A word to the wise: The LSAC will not add points to a score as a remedy for a distracting test administration, but they have found other ways to accommodate test takers who, through no fault of their own, have been unable to complete the test or who encountered unmanageable distractions.

GET READY FOR TEST DAY

This chapter really boils down to one message: Prepare yourself for the perfect test day. Display confidence and preparation in all that you do. Get ready for a consistent, focused performance from start to finish. When that's the attitude you take into the test, you're more likely to outperform your competition and have your best day regardless of what else does or doesn't happen.

CHAPTER 24

SECRETS OF THE LSAT

The "secrets" of the LSAT aren't really secrets at all. They're well-known facts that many test takers fail to take full advantage of. The best test takers use the structure and format of the test to their advantage. Just as a great football or basketball coach adjusts the team's strategy when time is running out on the clock, or just as a great conductor rearranges an orchestra to take advantage of the acoustics in a new venue, you can learn to adjust your approach to the test you're taking. We might well laud the insightful coach or conductor by saying, "Wow, he really knows the 'secrets' of this game (or stadium or theater)." But in fact, he's simply taking account of all the circumstances and making the right strategic decisions for that time and place. Consider a handful of facts that make the LSAT a unique testing experience, and see how you can use them to your advantage.

EVERY QUESTION IS WORTH THE SAME AMOUNT TO YOUR SCORE

Many tests you've taken (even some standardized tests) rewarded you more for certain questions or sections than for others. In school, it's common for a professor to say, "The essay counts for half of your score," or to make a section of harder questions worth five points each while easier ones are worth less. With such exams, you may simply be unable to get a top score without performing well on a given question or topic. It makes sense, then, to target the areas the professor will reward most highly.

As you well know, that's not the case on the LSAT. Every question—easy or hard, short or long, common or rare—is worth exactly the same amount as every other question. That means that you should seek out the questions, games, and passages that are the easiest for you to handle. Far too many test takers get their teeth into a tough question and won't let go. That hurts them

in two ways. First, they spend too much time—sometimes three or four minutes—on such a question, sacrificing their chances with other, easier questions. Second, since questions like these are tough or confusing, they're less likely to produce a right answer no matter how much time you spend. Learn to skip questions when it's in your interest to do so. Mark questions that you skip by circling the entire question in your test booklet. That way, those questions will be easy to spot if you have time left after you complete the other questions in the section. If you've eliminated one or two obviously incorrect answer choicess, strike them through completely so that you don't spend time rethinking them when you come back to the question.

When schools receive your score report, the only thing they see is your score. They don't know—and they don't care—whether you've answered the easiest or the toughest questions on the LSAT. They only care that you answered more questions correctly than the other applicants. Becoming a good manager of the test sections is invaluable. You'll do that, in part, by triaging the games or passages and choosing to put off the toughest for last. Even more often, you'll manage the section by skipping and guessing strategically. Don't slug it out with a tough question for minutes and then grudgingly move on. Boldly seek out questions on which you can exert your strengths, and be clearheaded and decisive in your decisions to move past questions you know are targeted at your weaknesses. Take the test; don't let it take you.

ONE RIGHT, FOUR ROTTEN

I'm sure you've had the experience, on a multiple-choice test in school, of having a teacher tell you, "More than one answer may be correct, but pick the best answer for each question." Given that you're a future law student, I wouldn't be surprised to learn that you may even have debated with your instructor, making a case for why a certain answer should receive credit. As a result, you're used to comparing answer choices to one another. On the LSAT, however, that's a recipe for wasted time and effort. The test makers design the correct answer to be unequivocally correct; it will respond to the call of the question stem precisely. Likewise, the four wrong answers are demonstrably wrong, not just "less good."

For the well-trained test taker—for you, that is—this leads to an important, practical adjustment in strategy. Throughout the test, you should seek to predict the correct answer before assessing the answer choices. In Logical Reasoning, you will, on most questions, be able to anticipate the content of the correct answer, sometimes almost word for word. In Reading Comprehension and Logic Games, you should spend the time up front to have a clear passage road map or game sketch. At a minimum, you must characterize the correct and incorrect answers (if the correct answer *must be true*, for example, each of the wrong answers *could be false*). Then seek out the one answer that matches your prediction or characterization.

The bottom line is that, on the LSAT, you are always comparing the answers against what you know must be correct, not against one another. When locating the correct choice is difficult or time-consuming, you can always turn the tables on the test maker and eliminate the wrong ones with your knowledge of common wrong answer traps. Because you know that there will always be one correct choice and that you can always identify the characteristics that make wrong answers wrong, you can always take the most direct route to the LSAT point.

THERE'S NO WRONG-ANSWER PENALTY

This point is easy to understand, but sometimes hard to remember when you're working quickly through an LSAT section. The LSAT is scored only by counting the number of correct responses you bubble in. Unlike some standardized tests—the SAT is the most notorious example—you're not penalized for marking incorrect responses. Simply put, there's nothing to lose, so mark a response, even if it's a blind guess, for every answer.

Of course, strategic guessing is better than just taking a wild stab at the correct answer. Even if a question gives you a lot of trouble, see if you can eliminate one or more answer choices as clearly wrong. When you can, take your guess from the remaining choices. Removing even one clearly incorrect choice improves your chances of hitting on the right one from 20 percent to 25 percent; getting rid of two wrong answers, of course, gives you a one-in-three chance of guessing correctly. Provided that you do it quickly (not taking time away from questions you can handle with little trouble), strategic guessing can improve your score.

Students ask another question related to this point about the answer choices. They want to know if a particular answer choice—(A), (B), (C), (D), or (E)—shows up more often than others, or whether it's better, when guessing, to pick a particular choice for all guesses. The answer to both questions is no. Over the course of a full LSAT, all five answer choices show up just about equally. There's no pattern associated with particular question types. You're no more likely to see any particular answer early or late in a section. Thus, when you're blind guessing, you have a one-in-five chance of hitting the correct answer whatever you choose. And there's no benefit from guessing choice (C) or choice (D) over and over. It's far more valuable to spend your limited time trying to eliminate one or more wrong answers than it is to fret over any illusory patterns within the choices.

THE LSAT IS A MARATHON . . . MADE UP OF SPRINTS

At this point in your academic career, you've had long tests and you've had tests that put time pressure on you. But chances are, you've never encountered as intense a combination of the two as you will on the LSAT. In the last chapter, I already talked about the importance of stamina. Including the administrative tasks at the beginning, the breaks, and the collection and distribution of your testing materials, you're in for around a five-hour test day. It's important to remember that, over the course of that marathon, the first and fifth sections are just as valuable as those in the middle. Unsurprisingly, Kaplan's research has shown that, for the untrained test taker, those sections are likely to produce the poorest performance. You can counteract the inherent difficulties in the schedule by doing a little warm-up so that you're ready to hit the ground running at the start of Section 1, and by staying relaxed and having a healthy snack at the break so that you're still going strong at the end of Section 5. Just taking these simple steps could add several points to your score.

At the same time that you're striving to maintain focus and sustain your performance, you're trying to manage a very fast 35 minutes in each section. I've talked already about how you can triage a section to maximize your opportunity to attack the easiest questions up front and save the danger zone for the end. Combine that with confident, strategic guessing and you'll be outperforming many test takers who succumb to the "ego battle" with tough or time-consuming questions. But there's one more thing that you have to add to your repertoire of test day tactics: You have to learn to not look back. Over the years, I've talked to many students who could tell me how they thought they performed on each of the test's sections. To be honest with you, I find that a little disappointing. Sure, you may remember that the game with the Cowboys and Horses or the passage on Nanotechnology was really challenging, but it's a waste of time and mental capacity to try and assess your performance as you're taking the test. Once you've answered a question, leave it behind. Give your full concentration to what you're working on. This is even more important when it comes to sections. Once time is called, you may no longer work on the section, not even to bubble in the answers to questions you completed in your test booklet. If a proctor sees you continuing to work on a section for which the time has expired, he or she can issue you a misconduct slip, and the violation will be reported to all of the schools to which you apply. More importantly, you're harming your work on the current section.

There's no rearview mirror on the LSAT. Work diligently, mark the correct answers, and move on to the next question. Keep this in mind: Even if you could accurately assess your performance as you worked (you can't, but imagine it for a moment), it wouldn't change anything. You'd still need to get the remaining questions right. So learn this lesson—and the other "secrets" of the LSAT—now. Be like those seemingly brilliant coaches and performers. By knowing how the LSAT test day works, you can gain an edge over test takers who treat this just as they have every other exam in their academic careers.

CHAPTER 25

LSAT STRATEGIES AND TACTICS

At last, I'll bring you full circle back to the premise at the start of this book. The LSAT may be unlike any other test you've studied or prepared for, but it need not be mysterious or overwhelming. The underlying principle that has informed this book is that **every question has an answer**. The twist is that you're not expected to know the answers. How could you? This is a test that rewards what you can do, not what you've learned. In that sense, you can't *study* for the test. And you certainly can't cram for it. What you can do, indeed what you've been doing throughout this book, is to *practice* for the test. Instead of thinking of the LSAT as a test, think of it as your law school audition or tryout. A play's director or a team's coach doesn't ask you what you know; she wants to see what you can do. And just as the director or coach will give you everything you need to demonstrate your skill, the test makers always give you everything you need to produce the correct answers on the LSAT.

THE LSAT REWARDS THE CORE 4 SKILLS

Law schools don't expect incoming students to know the law. Indeed, much as the LSAT does, your professors may try to use your outside knowledge and assumptions against you. What the schools are looking for is incoming students who have the skills they'll need to succeed through the coming three years of rigorous legal training. That, at least in part, is what they're looking for your LSAT score to indicate. That's why the LSAT is a skills-based, rather than a knowledge-based, exam. Back near the beginning of this book, you learned the central skills rewarded on the test.

THE CORE 4 LSAT SKILLS

1. **Strategic Reading**
2. **Analyzing Arguments**
3. **Understanding Formal Logic**
4. **Making Deductions**

USE WHAT YOU'VE LEARNED THROUGHOUT THE TEST

One nice thing to realize is that much of the work you've done here, preparing for the Logical Reasoning sections specifically, will translate to exceptional performance throughout the test. Your understanding of the sufficient-necessary relationship highlighted by formal logic rules will be rewarded in the Logic Games sections. Your ability to analyze arguments and draw valid inferences will support your strategic reading skills. And, of course, to be successful on the Reading Comprehension section, you will use your reasoning strategy and skill to answer specific logical reasoning questions.

So let me leave you with this: The LSAT is designed to reward the skills that will make you a successful law student. You know that you have those skills. You are, after all, seeking this path with passion and focus. The work you've done in this book is all about honing your skills and preparing you for a successful test day. Take the insights you've gathered about LSAT logical reasoning and apply them throughout the exam. Take what you've learned about yourself as a test taker, and use it not only for a stronger, more confident performance on test day, but also throughout your law school endeavor, during your bar exam, and into your legal career. Best of luck to you. Now, go out and accomplish great things.

PART V

APPENDICES

KAPLAN METHOD FOR LOGICAL REASONING: REVIEW SHEET EXERCISE

Directions: At the end of every chapter in Part II of this book, review the Kaplan Method for Logical Reasoning by answering the questions in the first column and entering your responses under the designated question type. Consider this sheet your "playbook" and use it to answer other practice questions as you learn the Kaplan Method.

Table Appendix A.1

Question Types

Method	Assumption	Strengthen	Weaken	Flaw	Inference	Principle	Method of Argument	Parallel Reasoning	Paradox	Point at Issue	Role of a Statement	Main Point
Step 1. Identify the Question Type What words and phrases tell you the question type?												
Step 2. Untangle the Stimulus How do you unpack the stimulus for the particular question type?												

(continued)

Step 3. Make a Prediction What do you do with the information gathered in Step 2?	Step 4. Evaluate the Answer Choices How do you compare your prediction with the answer choices?

KAPLAN METHOD FOR LOGICAL REASONING: REVIEW SHEET

Directions: Do NOT read this chart until you refer to the review exercise in Appendix A and complete the blank Review Sheet on your own. Use this sheet to check your work and supplement it as appropriate. Keep your sheet in front of you as you practice questions so you can learn and apply the Kaplan Method correctly. The more you can refer to it in the beginning of your practice, the more comfortable and efficient you can become in implementing it.

Table Appendix B.1

Method	Question Types											
	Assumption	Strengthen	Weaken	Flaw	Inference	Principle	Method of Argument	Parallel Reasoning	Paradox	Point at Issue	Role of a Statement	Main Point
Step 1. Identify the Question Type What words and phrases tell you the question type?	Assumes Assumption Presupposes Added to the premise Depends on If assumed ... conclusion follows logically	Strengthen Support (answer supports stimulus) Justify	Weaken Calls into question Casts doubt on Undermine Counter Damages	Flaw Vulnerable to criticism Questionable because Error in reasoning Overlooks the possibility Fails to demonstrate	Must be true Logically follows from Can be inferred Support (stimulus supports answer) Logically completes the passage	Principle Policy Proposition Generalization	Argumentative technique Method Process Argumentative strategy Responds to... by	Parallel to Similar to Pattern of reasoning	Solve the apparent paradox Resolve the discrepancy Explain Solve the mystery	Disagree over whether Point at issue between them is Disagree about which one of the following	Plays which one of the following roles Figures in the argument Plays which part	Conclusion Main idea Main point
Step 2. Untangle the Stimulus How do you unpack the stimulus for the particular question type?	Identify the conclusion and summarize the evidence in the argument.	Identify the conclusion and summarize the evidence in the argument.	Identify the conclusion and summarize the evidence in the argument.	Identify the conclusion and summarize the evidence in the argument.	Get the gist of each statement and accept as true.	Identify the conclusion and evidence or untangle the stimulus as you would for the question type it mimics.	Identify the conclusion and the evidence.	Identify the conclusion and its type, check the evidence, characterize the stimulus, and look for flaws.	Identify the discrepancy.	Summarize each speaker's argument.	Find the phrase noted in the question, conclusion, and evidence.	Identify the conclusion using Keywords, disagreement, or the one-sentence test.

(continued)

	Step 3. Make a Prediction. What do you do with the information gathered in Step 2?	Step 4. Evaluate the Answer Choices. How do you compare your prediction with the answer choices?
	Confirm the assumption, affirm the conclusion, or eliminate a plausible alternative to make the argument more likely. Necessary assumption will be core and basic to the argument, usually modestly phrased. Sufficient assumption will be forceful and guarantee that conclusion is true.	Find the answer that matches your prediction. Beware of "EXCEPT" questions and common wrong answers. Answer can be modest or forceful, making the conclusion a little more likely or absolutely proving the conclusion.
	Reject the assumption, contradict the conclusion, or propose a plausible alternative to make the argument less likely.	Find the answer that matches your prediction. Beware of "EXCEPT" questions and common wrong answers. Answer can be modest or forceful, making the conclusion a little less likely or absolutely disproving conclusion.
	Describe the disconnect between the conclusion and evidence, consider the classic flaws, or identify the possibility overlooked by the author.	Find the answer that matches your prediction. Beware of "EXCEPT" questions and common wrong answers.
	Translate any formal logic statements and combine statements with shared terms. Otherwise, do not predict.	Find the answer that must be true based on the stimulus. Be especially wary of extreme and out of scope answers. Correct answer must be as extreme or less extreme than stimulus. Usually more modest is better.
	Predict the answer as you would for the question type it mimics in terms of a broad principle or a specific situation depending on what is asked for in the question.	Find the answer that matches your prediction. Beware of "EXCEPT" questions and common wrong answers.
	Describe the argument in abstract terms and characterize the evidence.	Find the answer that matches your prediction. Beware of "EXCEPT" questions and common wrong answers.
	Compare conclusions, and if necessary, evidence, flaw or entire stimulus.	Find the answer that matches your prediction. Beware of "EXCEPT" questions and common wrong answers.
	Determine an explanation that reconciles the discrepancy and makes the statements consistent.	Find the answer that matches your prediction. Beware of "EXCEPT" questions and common wrong answers.
	Determine the issue both speakers address and on which they disagree.	Find the answer that matches your prediction. Beware of "EXCEPT" questions and common wrong answers.
	Characterize the function of the identified statement in the argument.	Find the answer that matches your prediction. Beware of "EXCEPT" questions and common wrong answers.
	Paraphrase the conclusion.	Find the answer that matches your prediction. Beware of "EXCEPT" questions and common wrong answers.

APPENDIX C

DRILL: IDENTIFY THE QUESTION TYPE

The first step in the Kaplan Method for Logical Reasoning is to identify the question type. You must be able to instantly recognize each question type so you can move quickly to the next step of untangling the stimulus—and know what to do when you get there.

Directions: In the following question stems, circle the words and phrases that indicate a particular question type and write the question type on the line provided. For additional practice, you can make flashcards with question stems on them and test yourself. Once you've mastered the question stems, create another set of flashcards with the question types on the front and strategy tips for that question type on the back.

Table Appendix C.1

	Question Stem	Question Type
1.	The reasoning in the argument is in error because	_____
2.	The conclusion drawn above would be most undermined if it were true that	_____
3.	Henry responds to Anne by	_____

4.   Which one of the following, if true, most strongly supports Eleanor's argument?

_____

5.   Which one of the following logically follows from the statement above?

_____

6.   Which one of the following principles most helps to justify Patrick's argument?

_____

7.   Which one of the following states an assumption on which the argument depends?

_____

8.   Which one of the following most accurately expresses the main conclusion of the historian's argument?

_____

9.   Mia and Clint disagree with each other over whether

_____

10   Each of the following, if true, most strengthens the argument EXCEPT:

_____

11.   The reasoning in which one of the following is most similar to the reasoning in the argument above?

_____

12.   If all the statements above are true, which one of the following must also be true?

_____

13.   Derek's reasoning is most vulnerable to criticism that he

_____

14.   The conclusion can be properly drawn if which one of the following is assumed?

_____

15.   Which one of the following, if true, helps to explain the trend in weather patterns?

_____

16.   Which one of the following, if true, would most damage the argument above?

_____

17. The passage provides the most support for which one of the following? _____

18. The argument depends on which one of the following? _____

19. Upon which one of the following does the author rely in the passage? _____

20. The announcement that a new income stream for the university comes as state lawmakers begin to debate a budget bill that would impose deep cuts on higher education funding figures in the argument in which one of the following ways? _____

21. Shannon's reasoning is questionable in that it fails to consider the possibility that _____

22. The pattern of flawed reasoning in which one of the following arguments is most similar to that in the advertiser's argument? _____

23. The argumentative strategy used by Kate is to _____

24. Which one of the following arguments illustrates a principle most similar to the principle underlying the argument above? _____

25. Which one of the following, if true, most helps to resolve the apparent discrepancy described above? _____

26. Which one of the following most seriously calls into question the argument above? _____

IDENTIFY THE QUESTION TYPE ANSWERS

Table Appendix C.2

Question Stem	Question Type
1. The reasoning in the argument is in error because	Flaw
2. The conclusion drawn above would be most undermined if it were true that	Weaken
3. Henry responds to Anne by	Method of Argument
4. Which one of the following, if true, most strongly supports Eleanor's argument?	Strengthen (answer supports stimulus)
5. Which one of the following logically follows from the statement above?	Inference
6. Which one of the following principles most helps to justify Patrick's argument?	Principle
7. Which one of the following states an assumption on which the argument depends?	Assumption (necessary)
8. Which one of the following most accurately expresses the main conclusion of the historian's argument?	Main Point
9. Mia and Clint disagree with each other over whether	Point at Issue
10 Each of the following, if true, most strengthens the argument EXCEPT:	Strengthen (EXCEPT)
11. The reasoning in which one of the following is most similar to the reasoning in the argument above?	Parallel Reasoning
12. If all the statements above are true, which one of the following must also be true?	Inference

13. Derek's reasoning is most (vulnerable to criticism) that he

Flaw

14. The (conclusion) can be properly drawn if which one of the following is (assumed?)

Assumption (sufficient)

15. Which one of the following, if true, helps to (explain) the trend in weather patterns?

Paradox

16. Which one of the following, if true, would most (damage) the argument above?

Weaken

17. The passage provides the most (support) for (which one of the following?)

Inference (stimulus supports answer)

18. The argument (depends on) which one of the following?

Assumption (necessary)

19. Upon which one of the following does the author (rely) in the passage?

Assumption (necessary)

20. The announcement that a new income stream for the university comes as state lawmakers begin to debate a budget bill that would impose deep cuts on higher education funding (figures in the argument) in which one of the following ways?

Role of a Statement

21. Shannon's reasoning is (questionable) in that it (fails to) (consider the possibility that)

Flaw

22. The (pattern of flawed reasoning) in which one of the following arguments is (most similar to) that in the advertiser's argument?

Parallel Reasoning (Parallel Flaw)

23. The (argumentative strategy) used by Kate is to

Method of Argument

24.   Which one of the following arguments illustrates a   **Principle**
        (principle) most similar to the principle underlying the
        argument above?

25.   Which one of the following, if true, most helps to   **Paradox**
        (resolve the apparent discrepancy) described above?

26.   Which one of the following most seriously (calls into)   **Weaken**
        (question) the argument above?

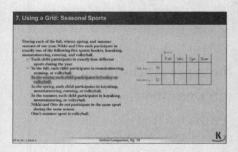
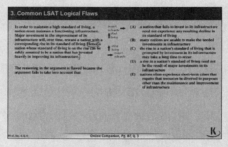
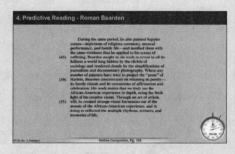

NOTES

NOTES

NOTES

LSAT®

READING COMPREHENSION

STRATEGIES AND TACTICS

100% OFFICIAL LSAT PREPTEST® QUESTIONS

Scott Emerson

LSAT® is a registered trademark of the Law School Admissions Council, which neither sponsors nor endorses this product.

This publication is designed to provide accurate and authoritative information in regard to the subject matter covered. It is sold with the understanding that the publisher is not engaged in rendering legal, accounting, or other professional service. If legal advice or other expert assistance is required, the services of a competent professional should be sought.

© 2011 Kaplan, Inc.

Published by Kaplan Publishing, a division of Kaplan, Inc.
395 Hudson Street
New York, NY 10014

Printed in the United States of America

10 9 8 7 6 5 4 3 2 1

ISBN-13: 978-1-60978-152-1

Kaplan Publishing books are available at special quantity discounts to use for sales promotions, employee premiums, or educational purposes. For more information or to purchase books, please call the Simon & Schuster special sales department at 866-506-1949.

Contents

About the Author

Scott Emerson, began his work with Kaplan in 2004 after achieving a 99th percentile LSAT score. He is a veteran classroom instructor, an experienced and highly demanded private tutor, and a trainer of excellent Kaplan instructors. In his seven years with Kaplan he has helped over 2,000 students achieve LSAT success, with nearly 200 of those students reporting scores above the 90th percentile. He has been actively involved in the evolution of Kaplan's proven approach to the LSAT, bringing his expertise to the research and development of a cutting-edge curriculum that has made Reading Comprehension approachable to students around the world. He currently teaches and resides in the Los Angeles area.

Introduction to the LSAT

The Law School Admissions Test (LSAT) is probably unlike any other test you've taken in your academic career. Most tests you've encountered in high school and college have been content based—that is, they have required you to recall facts, formulas, theorems, or other acquired knowledge.

The LSAT, however, is a skills-based test. It doesn't ask you to repeat memorized facts or to apply learned formulas to specific problems. In fact, all you'll be asked to do on the LSAT is think—thoroughly, quickly, and strategically. There's no required content to study.

But the lack of specific content to memorize is one of things that makes preparing for the LSAT so challenging. Before you get the idea that you can skate into the most important test of your life without preparing, remember that learning skills and improving performance take practice. You can't cram for the test.

ABOUT THE LSAT

The LSAT is a standardized test written by the Law School Admissions Council (LSAC) and administered four times each year. The test is a required component of your application to all American Bar Association–approved law schools as well as some others.

The LSAT is designed to measure the skills necessary (according to the governing bodies of law schools) for success in your first year of law school, such as strategic reading, analyzing arguments, understanding formal logic, and making deductions. Because these skills will serve you well throughout law school and your professional life, consider your LSAT preparation an investment in your career.

You may already possess some level of proficiency with LSAT-tested skills. However, you probably haven't yet mastered how to use those skills to your best advantage in the context of a standardized, skills-based test that requires careful time management.

The LSAT is also a test of endurance—five 35-minute blocks of multiple-choice testing plus a 35-minute writing sample. Add in the administrative tasks at both ends of the test and a 10- to 15-minute break midway through, and you can count on being in the test room for at least four and a half hours. It's a grueling experience, but it's not as bad if you are familiar with the test and ready to handle every section. You want to approach the test with confidence so that you can maintain your focus, limit your stress, and get your highest score on test day. That's why it's so important to take control of the test, just as you will take control of the rest of the application process.

Our material is as up-to-date as possible at the time of this printing, but test specifications may change at any time. Please visit our website at http://kaptest.com/LSAT for the latest news and updates.

How Do I Register for the LSAT?

The LSAT is administered by the Law School Admissions Council (LSAC). Be sure to register as soon as possible, as your preferred test site can fill up quickly. You can register for the LSAT in three ways:

- Online: Sign up at http://lsac.org.
- Telephone: Call LSAC at (215) 968-1001.
- Email: Contact LSAC for a registration packet at lsacinfo@lsac.org.

If you have additional questions about registration, contact the LSAC by phone or by email.

The LSAT Sections

The LSAT consists of five multiple-choice sections: two Logical Reasoning sections, one Logic Games section, one Reading Comprehension section, and one unscored "experimental" section that looks exactly like one of the other multiple-choice sections. At the end of the test, there is a Writing Sample section during which you'll write a short essay. Here's how the sections break down:

Section	Number of Questions	Minutes
Logical Reasoning	24–26	35
Logical Reasoning	24–26	35
Logic Games	22–24	35
Reading Comprehension	26–28	35
"Experimental"	23–28	35
Writing Sample	n/a	35

The five multiple-choice sections can appear in any order, but the Writing Sample is always last. You will also get a 10- or 15-minute break between the third and fourth sections of the test.

You'll be answering roughly 125 multiple-choice questions (101 of which are scored) over the course of three intense hours. Taking control of the LSAT means increasing your test speed only to the extent that you can do so without sacrificing accuracy.

First, just familiarize yourself with the sections and the kinds of questions asked in each one.

Logical Reasoning

WHAT IT IS: The Logical Reasoning sections consist of 24–26 questions each that reward your ability to analyze a "stimulus" (a paragraph or a dialogue between two speakers) and make judgments accordingly. You will evaluate the logic and structure of arguments and make inferences from the statements as well as find underlying assumptions, strengthen and weaken arguments, determine logical flaws, and identify parallel argument structures.

WHY IT'S ON THE TEST: Law schools want to see whether you can understand, analyze, evaluate, and manipulate arguments, and draw reliable conclusions—as every law student and attorney must. This question type makes up half of your LSAT score, which means this is a valuable skill to master.

Logic Games

WHAT IT IS: In the Logic Games (aka Analytical Reasoning) section, you'll find four games (aka critical-thinking puzzles) with five to seven questions each for a total of 22–24 questions. They reward your ability to make valid deductions from a set of rules or restrictions in order to determine what can, must, or cannot be true in various circumstances.

WHY IT'S ON THE TEST: In law school, your professors will have you read dozens of cases, extract their rules, and apply them to or distinguish them from hypothetical cases. The Logic Games section rewards the same skill set: attention to detail, rigorous deductive reasoning, an understanding of how rules limit and order behavior (the very definition of law), and the ability to discern the conditions under which those rules do and do not apply.

Reading Comprehension

WHAT IT IS: The Reading Comprehension section consists of three passages, each 450–550 words, and a set of two short passages that total 450–550 words. Each passage is followed by five to eight questions. The topics may range from areas of social science, humanities, natural science, and law. Because content isn't tested, you won't need any outside knowledge.

WHY IT'S ON THE TEST: The Reading Comprehension section tests your ability to quickly understand the gist and structure of long, difficult prose—just as you'll have to do in law school and throughout your career.

The Writing Sample

WHAT IT IS: During the Writing Sample section, you will read a paragraph that presents a problem and lists two possible solutions. Each solution will have strengths and weaknesses; you must argue in favor of one based on the given criteria. There is no right or wrong answer, and the writing sample is unscored. However, law schools will receive a copy of your essay along with your LSAT score.

WHY IT'S ON THE TEST: The Writing Sample shows law schools your ability to argue for a position while attacking an opposing argument under timed conditions. In addition, it may be used to verify that your writing style is similar to that in your personal statement.

How the LSAT Is Scored

You'll receive one score for the LSAT ranging between 120 and 180 (no separate scores for Logical Reasoning, Logic Games, and Reading Comprehension). There are roughly 101 scored multiple-choice questions on each exam:

- About 52 from the two Logical Reasoning sections
- About 22 from the Logic Games section
- About 27 from the Reading Comprehension section

Your **raw score**, the number of questions that you answer correctly, will be multiplied by a complicated scoring formula (different for each test, to accommodate differences in difficulty level) to yield the **scaled score**—the one that will fall somewhere in that 120–180 range—which is reported to the schools.

Because the test is graded on a largely preset curve, the scaled score will always correspond to a certain percentile, also indicated on your score report. A score of 160, for instance, corresponds roughly to the 80th percentile, meaning that 80 percent of test takers scored at or below your level. The percentile figure is important because it allows law schools to see where you fall in the pool of applicants.

All scored questions are worth the same amount—one raw point—and there's no penalty for guessing. That means that you should always fill in an answer for every question, whether you get to that question or not.

What's a "Good" LSAT Score?

What you consider a "good" LSAT score depends on your own expectations and goals, but here are a few interesting statistics.

If you got about half of all of the scored questions right (a raw score of roughly 50), you would earn a scaled score of roughly 147, putting you in about the 30th percentile—not a great performance. But on the LSAT, a little improvement goes a long way. In fact, getting only one

additional question right every 10 minutes would give you a raw score of about 64, pushing you into the 60th percentile—a huge improvement.

Sample Percentiles Approx. Scaled Score		
Percentile	(Range 120–180)	Approx. Raw Score
99th percentile	174	~94 correct out of 101
95th percentile	168	~88 correct out of 101
90th percentile	164	~82 correct out of 101
80th percentile	160	~76 correct out of 101
75th percentile	157	~71 correct out of 101
50th percentile	152	~61 correct out of 101

Note: Exact percentile-to-scaled-score relationships vary from test to test.

As you can see, you don't have to be perfect to do well. On most LSATs, you can get as many as 28 questions wrong and still remain in the 80th percentile or as many as 20 wrong and still be in the 90th percentile. Most students who score 180 get a handful of questions wrong.

Although many factors play a role in admissions decisions, the LSAT score is usually one of the most important. And—generally speaking—being average won't cut it. The median LSAT score is somewhere around 152. If you're aiming for the top, you've got to do even better.

By using the strategies in this book, you'll learn how to approach—and master—the test in a general way. As you'll see, knowing specific strategies for each type of question is only part of your task. To do your best, you have to approach the entire test with the proactive, take-control kind of thinking it inspires—the LSAT mindset.

For more information on the LSAT experience, see Part IV of this book.

Good luck!

PART I

HOW READING COMPREHENSION WORKS

CHAPTER 1

LSAT READING IS CRITICAL READING

Many of the students I've worked with over the years have been surprised by the difficulties they've encountered when trying to complete the Reading Comprehension section of the LSAT. Perhaps you feel the same way. After all, this is a job you've faced before: You are given a brief passage and tasked with reading it, understanding it, and then answering a series of questions. You've been doing this in one form or another throughout your scholastic career, and now that you're preparing to go to law school you're undoubtedly expecting to do more of the same. So why does such a familiar task suddenly seem so daunting? Once you understand the answer to this question, you'll be ready to learn the correct approach to LSAT Reading Comprehension and ultimately raise your LSAT score.

YOU CAN MASTER LSAT READING COMPREHENSION

Although the challenges of LSAT Reading Comprehension haven't changed much over the years, different test takers approach the section with their own specific problems and concerns. I'll walk you through a few of the more common ones.

"I've Always Been a Slow Reader."

Perhaps you're concerned about the speed at which you read. How can you be expected to read so much information in so little time? If this is one of your worries, I have great news for you: The LSAT rewards test takers who read for the right information, not those who dwell on every sentence. Read the following excerpt from a previously released LSAT passage and do your best to understand precisely what it is saying:

> Although philanthropy—the volunteering of
> private resources for humanitarian purposes—reached
> its apex in England in the late nineteenth century,
> modern commentators have articulated two major
> (5)   criticisms of the philanthropy that was a mainstay of
> England's middle-class Victorian society.[1]

Now, without looking back at the excerpt, can you remember when philanthropy reached its apex in England? On the LSAT, it actually doesn't matter whether you can or not, because this information probably won't be useful in answering any of the questions. In fact, the test makers rarely expect you to take notice of the minor details in the passage and instead reward you for staying focused on the big ideas. I'll discuss these concepts in greater detail very soon, but for now, remember that the LSAT isn't designed to reward fast reading, but rather strategic reading—a Kaplan skill that anyone can learn.

"I'm Intimidated by Complicated Language and Topics."

Every LSAT Reading Comprehension section will contain four passages, one from each of four broad subject areas: Humanities, Natural Sciences, Social Sciences, and Law. When I teach in the classroom, I always ask my students if they have one subject in particular that makes them nervous. Invariably their hands fly up as they confess their fears of arcane-seeming scientific jargon or dense, abstract legal theory. Usually at the root of this fear is a lack of familiarity with the subject. How can you be expected to answer questions about Victorian philanthropy if you haven't studied it? Here's an example:

23.   Which one of the following best describes the
      attitude of the author of the passage toward the
      "Whig" interpretation of Victorian philanthropy?

      (A)   strong disagreement
      (B)   mild skepticism
      (C)   cynical amusement
      (D)   bland indifference
      (E)   unqualified support[2]

---

[1]PrepTest 41, Sec 4, Passage 4
[2]PrepTest 41, Sec 4, Q 23

How familiar is the average reader with the Whig interpretation of Victorian philanthropy? At a glance this question might seem intimidating or unfair. But look a little more carefully:

23. Which one of the following best describes the attitude of the author of the passage toward the "Whig" interpretation of Victorian philanthropy?

    (A) strong disagreement
    (B) mild skepticism
    (C) cynical amusement
    (D) bland indifference
    (E) unqualified support[3]

The question isn't really asking about the Whig interpretation at all, but rather the author's opinion of it. Read the LSAT passage excerpt below and try to find the information that provides the correct answer.

(35)　　Modern critics of Victorian philanthropy often use the words "amateurish" or "inadequate" to describe Victorian philanthropy, as though Victorian charity can only be understood as an antecedent to the era of state-sponsored, professionally administered charity. This
(40)　assumption is typical of the "Whig fallacy": the tendency to read the past as an inferior prelude to an enlightened present.[4]

The author of the passage clearly refers to the Whig interpretation as a fallacy, explaining that she regards it as incorrect. The only answer that states this correctly is choice (A).

I hope you have already realized what this example reveals about LSAT Reading Comprehension: The LSAT is not designed to test content, and it requires absolutely no outside knowledge of the topics addressed in the passages. Every question has only one correct answer, and all the information you need to find that correct answer is right there in the passage. Once again, you can see that the test makers reward those who stay focused on important information and use it to score points.

"There Just Isn't Enough Time. I Can Never Finish all Four Passages!"

This is the most common problem that my students have. You've probably encountered this problem as well. Maybe you can confidently tackle the first two passages, but you begin to feel rushed as you begin the third, and you just don't have time to read the fourth. I know how discouraging it can feel to desperately read and re-read the text of the passage in the hopes of scoring a needed point, all the while knowing that time is ticking away. Consider a very common type of question:

---

[3]PrepTest 41, Sec 4, Q 23
[4]PrepTest 41, Sec 4, Passage 4

21. Which one of the following best summarizes the main idea of the passage?

   (A) While the motives of individual practitioners have been questioned by modern commentators, Victorian philanthropy successfully dealt with the social ills of nineteenth-century England.

   (B) Philanthropy, inadequate to deal with the massive social and economic problems of the twentieth century, has slowly been replaced by state-sponsored charity.

   (C) The practice of reading the past as a prelude to an enlightened present has fostered revisionist views of many institutions, among them Victorian philanthropy.

   (D) Although modern commentators have perceived Victorian philanthropy as either inadequate or self-serving, the theoretical bias behind these criticisms leads to an incorrect interpretation of history.

   (E) Victorian philanthropists, aware of public resentment of their self-congratulatory attitude, used devious methods to camouflage their self-serving motives.[5]

The question asks you to identify the main idea of the passage, but the author presented many different ideas. How are you supposed to find the correct answer among these five long, dense choices? The answer is simple: If you employ the Kaplan Method as you read the passage, by the time you come to this question, you've already predicted the correct response. You won't need to re-read the passage, and you'll score this point in less than 30 seconds! There are only five commonly occurring question types within the LSAT Reading Comprehension section, and the Kaplan Method will help you identify and answer them accurately and efficiently.

I'll come back to question 21 in a short while. Before I move on, I want to revisit what I've covered so far. You don't have to be a fast reader to master LSAT Reading Comprehension. You don't need a background in law or science. Once you've mastered the Kaplan Method, on test day you'll never have to ask yourself, "What do I do next?" It will take time, patience, practice, and careful study, but if you dedicate yourself to learning the proper approach, you can master LSAT Reading Comprehension.

LSAT READING IS NOT CASUAL READING
Active Reading vs. Passive Reading

Take a moment to imagine yourself in your first year of law school. Think about what academic challenges are sure to await you. Regardless of what other images come to your mind, reading

---

[5]PrepTest 41, Sec 4, Q 21

should certainly be one of them. You are likely to find yourself reading and briefing hundreds of cases in preparation for in-depth discussion in your classes. That's a lot of reading, and it can easily amount to 300 pages per week.

Now think about the way you read a magazine or a novel. When you read for leisure, you probably read casually. You're not in any particular hurry, you linger over interesting details, and you follow along wherever the author leads you. If you become distracted or feel that you didn't understand something completely, you may go back and re-read a paragraph or two.

It's probably obvious at this point that leisure reading and law school reading are very, very different. When you read for pleasure or to pass the time, you're reading passively. To succeed in law school, you must prepare to read actively.

As an active reader you will engage with the passage and seek out the most important ideas in each paragraph. Details are of less importance, so you'll read them quickly to keep from getting bogged down in them. With time and practice, you'll even be able to predict the direction that a passage is likely to take as you read it, using clues the test makers provide for you. Unsurprisingly, the LSAT is designed to reward those who have mastered this crucial skill, so your first step toward a great LSAT score is to learn how to read actively.

Using the Clues

Take a look at the first paragraph of another LSAT Reading Comprehension passage. Read it as quickly as you can:

> Countee Cullen (Countee Leroy Porter, 1903–1946) was one of the foremost poets of the Harlem Renaissance, the movement of African American writers, musicians, and artists centered in the
> (5) Harlem section of New York City during the 1920s. Beginning with his university years, Cullen strove to establish himself as an author of romantic poetry on abstract, universal topics such as love and death. Believing poetry should consist of "lofty thoughts
> (10) beautifully expressed," Cullen preferred controlled poetic forms. He used European forms such as sonnets and devices such as quatrains, couplets, and conventional rhyme, and he frequently employed classical allusions and Christian religious imagery,
> (15) which were most likely the product both of his university education and of his upbringing as the adopted son of a Methodist Episcopal reverend.[6]

This paragraph is a good example of the kind of writing you will see on test day. After introducing Countee Cullen, the author describes several defining aspects of Cullen's poetry. Chances

---

[6]PrepTest 41, Sec 4, Passage 2

are good that you remember a few details, but you've probably already forgotten a lot of what you just read. Don't worry! This doesn't mean that you're a poor reader. It simply means that you read the paragraph passively. Take another look at the first few sentences, and be sure to pay close attention to the circled words:

> Countee Cullen (Countee Leroy Porter,
> 1903–1946) was one of the (foremost) poets of the
> Harlem Renaissance, the movement of African
> American writers, musicians, and artists centered in the
> (5) Harlem section of New York City during the 1920s.
> (Beginning with) his university years, Cullen (strove) to
> establish himself as an author of romantic poetry on
> abstract, universal topics such as love and death.
> (Believing) poetry should consist of "lofty thoughts
> (10) beautifully expressed," Cullen (preferred) controlled
> poetic forms.[7]

Why are these particular words so important? Examine each one and think about what it tells you:

- "Foremost" emphasizes that Cullen was a notable figure in American literature.
- "Beginning with" identifies the start of a sequence of potentially important ideas.
- "Strove" points to a key element of Cullen's poetic style.
- "Believing" indicates that you're about to get more insight into Cullen's ideas about poetry.
- "Preferred" points to another element of Cullen's style.

Notice that none of these words contain much information by themselves, but every one of them indicates that an important fact is to follow. Not only do they help you to better understand the structure of the author's ideas, but they also help you to find the information that is likely to be tested when you get to the questions. And the test makers place these kinds of clues in *every single passage*. From now on I will refer to them as Keywords.

Take a look at this LSAT question:

10. The passage suggests which one of the following about Cullen's use of controlled poetic forms?[8]

Don't worry about the lack of answer choices; I'll present them momentarily. For now, refer back to the circled Keywords and see whether you can find information you can use to answer this question:

---

[7]PrepTest 41, Sec 4, Passage 2
[8]PrepTest 41, Sec 4, Q 10

Countee Cullen (Countee Leroy Porter,
1903–1946) was one of the (foremost) poets of the
Harlem Renaissance, the movement of African
American writers, musicians, and artists centered in the
(5)   Harlem section of New York City during the 1920s.
(Beginning with) his university years, Cullen (strove) to
establish himself as an author of romantic poetry on
abstract, universal topics such as love and death.
(Believing) poetry should consist of "lofty thoughts
(10)   beautifully expressed," Cullen (preferred) controlled
poetic forms.[9]

You probably went directly to the final sentence. By referring to the Keywords, you can easily see that this is where Cullen's preference for "controlled poetic forms" is mentioned. Why did Cullen express this preference? The answer immediately follows the Keyword "believing." Try to summarize that part of the text in your mind before reading on.

Whether you realize it or not, you have just made an extremely important step toward Reading Comprehension mastery. By coming up with your summary, you have effectively predicted what the answer to question 10 is likely to be. Now all you have to do is look at the answer choices and pick the one that resembles your summary. Try it:

(A)   Cullen used controlled poetic forms because
        he believed they provided the best means to
        beautiful poetic expression.
(B)   Cullen's interest in religious themes naturally
        led him to use controlled poetic forms.
(C)   Only the most controlled poetic forms allowed
        Cullen to address racial issues in his poems.
(D)   Cullen had rejected the less controlled poetic
        forms he was exposed to prior to his
        university years.
(E)   Less controlled poetic forms are better suited
        to poetry that addresses racial or political issues.[10]

Hopefully you spotted choice (A) as the correct answer and scored the point. Most test takers waste a lot of time on test day reading the answer choices over and over again, letting the choices guide their thinking. As you'll learn, this is a very poor approach to the LSAT; it wastes precious time, and it is likely to lead you to an incorrect answer. You, on the other hand, just took a very active approach to this question. You paid attention to the Keywords in the passage that pointed to important information, you predicted what the correct answer would look like, and you selected it with confidence.

At this point you may be wondering how to find Keywords on your own. You'll learn about this in great detail in chapter 2. For now, take a brief look at how you can use Keywords to make an entire passage easier to understand.

---

[9]PrepTest 41, Sec 4, Passage 2
[10]PrepTest 41, Sec 4, Q 10

ANATOMY OF AN LSAT PASSAGE
Reading the Kaplan Way

Earlier in this chapter you saw selected fragments of an LSAT passage about Victorian-era philanthropy. Now take a look at the passage in its entirety:

Although philanthropy—the volunteering of private resources for humanitarian purposes—reached its apex in England in the late nineteenth century, modern commentators have articulated two major
(5) criticisms of the philanthropy that was a mainstay of England's middle-class Victorian society. The earlier criticism is that such philanthropy was even by the later nineteenth century obsolete, since industrialism had already created social problems that were beyond the
(10) scope of small, private voluntary efforts. Indeed, these problems required substantial legislative action by the state. Unemployment, for example, was not the result of a failure of diligence on the part of workers or a failure of compassion on the part of employers, nor
(15) could it be solved by well-wishing philanthropists.

The more recent charge holds that Victorian philanthropy was by its very nature a self-serving exercise carried out by philanthropists at the expense of those whom they were ostensibly serving. In this view,
(20) philanthropy was a means of flaunting one's power and position in a society that placed great emphasis on status, or even a means of cultivating social connections that could lead to economic rewards. Further, if philanthropy is seen as serving the interests
(25) of individual philanthropists, so it may be seen as serving the interests of their class. According to this "social control" thesis, philanthropists, in professing to help the poor, were encouraging in them such values as prudence, thrift, and temperance, values perhaps

(30) worthy in themselves but also designed to create more productive members of the labor force. Philanthropy, in short, was a means of controlling the labor force and ensuring the continued dominance of the management class.
(35) Modern critics of Victorian philanthropy often use the words "amateurish" or "inadequate" to describe Victorian philanthropy, as though Victorian charity can only be understood as an antecedent to the era of state-sponsored, professionally administered charity. This
(40) assumption is typical of the "Whig fallacy": the tendency to read the past as an inferior prelude to an enlightened present. If most Victorians resisted state control and expended their resources on private, voluntary philanthropies, it could only be, the argument
(45) goes, because of their commitment to a vested interest, or because the administrative apparatus of the state was incapable of coping with the economic and social needs of the time.

This version of history patronizes the Victorians,
(50) who were in fact well aware of their vulnerability to charges of condescension and complacency, but were equally well aware of the potential dangers of state-managed charity. They were perhaps condescending to the poor, but—to use an un-Victorian metaphor—they
(55) put their money where their mouths were, and gave of their careers and lives as well.[11]

---

[11]PrepTest 41, Sec 4, Passage 4

This lengthy, dense passage poses a formidable challenge to passive readers. It deals with an unfamiliar subject, it is rife with jargon, and it explores abstract concepts while providing very few concrete examples to illustrate them. Perhaps you felt a little overwhelmed while you were reading it. If so, you probably don't feel ready to answer the six questions that follow it.

Fortunately, this won't happen to you on test day, because you will know how to read actively. Figure 1.1 shows the same passage after I've applied the Kaplan Method to it.

Vict. philanthropy def.

(Although) philanthropy—the volunteering of private resources for humanitarian purposes—reached its apex in England in the late nineteenth century, (modern commentators) have articulated two major

(5) (criticisms) of the philanthropy that was a mainstay of England's middle-class Victorian society. The (earlier) criticism is that such philanthropy was even by the later nineteenth century obsolete, (since) industrialism had already created social problems that were beyond the

Early crit.

Philanthropy obsolete

(10) scope of small, private voluntary efforts. (Indeed,) these problems required substantial legislative action by the state. Unemployment, (for example,) was not the result of a failure of diligence on the part of workers (or) a failure of compassion on the part of employers, (nor)

(15) could it be solved by well-wishing philanthropists.

Modern crit.

The (more recent) charge holds that Victorian philanthropy was by its very nature a self-serving exercise carried out by philanthropists at the expense of those whom they were ostensibly serving. (In) this view,

(20) philanthropy was a means of flaunting one's power and position in a society that placed (great emphasis) on status, or (even) a means of cultivating social connections that could (lead to) economic rewards. (Further,) if philanthropy is seen as serving the interests

Philanthropy self serving

(25) of individual philanthropists, (so) it may be seen as serving the interest of their class. (According to) this "social control" thesis, philanthropists, in professing to help the poor, were encouraging in them such values as prudence, thrift, and temperance, values perhaps

(30) worthy in themselves (but also) designed to create more productive members of the labor force. Philanthropy, in short, was a means of controlling the labor force and ensuring the continued dominance of the management class.

Author:
Modern crit.
wrong

(35)   (Modern critics) of Victorian philanthropy often use
         the words "amateurish" or "inadequate" to describe
         Victorian philanthropy, (as though) Victorian charity can
         only be understood as an antecedent to the era of state-
         sponsored, professionally administered charity. This
(40)   (assumption) is typical of the "Whig fallacy": the
         tendency to read the past as an (inferior) prelude to an
         enlightened present. If most Victorians resisted state
         control and expended their resources on private,
         voluntary philanthropies, it could (only) be, the argument
(45)   goes, (because) of their commitment to a vested interest,
         (or because) the administrative apparatus of the status was
         incapable of coping with the economic and social
         needs of the time.

Critics
incorrect

         This version of history (patronizes) the Victorians,
(50)   who were in fact well aware of their vulnerability to
         charges of condescension and complacency, (but) were
         equally well aware of the potential dangers of state-
         managed charity. They were perhaps condescending to
         the poor, (but)—to use an un-Victorian metaphor—they
(55)   put their money where their mouths were, (and) gave of
         their careers and lives as well.[12]

Quite a difference! First, notice that I circled important Keywords throughout the passage. Just as in the Countee Cullen passage, Keywords are vital to your ability to make sense of what you're reading. I'll explain a couple of specific ones.

The phrase "For example" in line 12 helps you to return to this bit of illustrative text easily if you need to answer a question about it. When you read an LSAT passage using the Kaplan Method, you won't dwell on examples and details. You *do* read them, and you always circle the Keywords surrounding them, but you don't make any effort to memorize or completely understand them. This idea might make you a bit nervous at first, but there are two very good reasons why you must do it. First, while specific details are often necessary to answer questions, there's no guarantee that this particular example will show up in the question set. If you dwell on details that aren't tested, you waste your time. Second, if it turns out that you do need this detail in order to answer a question, you're going to have to come back to the passage to look it up anyway. The test makers reward those who research the right information at the right time, and they set out answer traps for those who try to rely on memorization. In any case, if you need this example later, you'll be able to find it very easily, thanks to your attention to Keywords.

Now look at a particularly important set of Keywords at the beginning of the third paragraph. I circled "Modern critics" in line 35 because the ideas that follow are those of the critics, and *not* necessarily the author's. On test day, on every passage, you will encounter questions that relate to the author's viewpoint. It is therefore very important that you differentiate between

[12]PrepTest 41, Sec 4, Passage 4

the author's opinions and those of other parties mentioned in the passage. Most passages contain multiple points of view, and the test makers will write questions that reward you for knowing which is which.

Scan over the other Keywords and think about why they are important. It's good practice for chapter 2.

The Roadmap

The Keywords I circled in the previous example probably looked familiar to you, but what about the notes written in the margins beside each paragraph? Read them carefully. They're brief, but they're extremely important. Each one of those notes is a summary of all the major ideas present in the associated paragraph. Look at the notes next to the first paragraph shown in Figure 1.2.

Vict.
philanthropy
def.

Early crit.

Philanthropy
obsolete

(Although) philanthropy—the volunteering of private resources for humanitarian purposes—reached its apex in England in the late nineteenth century, (modern commentators) have articulated two major
(5) (criticisms) of the philanthropy that was a mainstay of England's middle-class Victorian society. The (earlier) criticism is that such philanthropy was even by the later nineteenth century obsolete, (since) industrialism had already created social problems that were beyond the
(10) scope of small, private voluntary efforts. (Indeed,) these problems required substantial legislative action by the state. Unemployment, (for example,) was not the result of a failure of diligence on the part of workers (or) a failure of compassion on the part of employers, (nor)
(15) could it be solved by well-wishing philanthropists.[13]

The first note simply says, "Vict. philanthropy def." This shorthand tells you that the first paragraph began by defining Victorian philanthropy. The second note, "Early crit," reminds you that a criticism is being leveled against the philanthropists, and that it's the earlier of the two presented. Take a moment to read over the rest of the margin notes and get a sense for how each one summarizes the key information in each paragraph.

I call this series of notes a Roadmap. I'd like you to take particular note of two very important aspects of the Roadmap: It's succinct, and yet it spells out every major idea the author presents in this passage. In other words, all of this dense text can be summarized in a few simple lines of shorthand, and as you will learn, every single LSAT passage can be summarized in this way, no matter how complicated it may appear at first glance.

As you become proficient in the Kaplan Method, you will learn to create Roadmaps of your own. The Roadmap serves a number of important purposes. It helps you to keep track of the

[13]PrepTest 41, Sec 4, Passage 4

author's primary ideas and the structure of the passage as a whole, both of which will be the subject of test questions. It also gives you a handy index to use when you scan the passage for information. Even the act of writing down the Roadmap is useful, as it helps you to clarify your thoughts. I'll come back to Roadmaps in greater detail in chapter 3. For now, I'd like to present one more element of the Kaplan Method to you before you tackle a couple of questions.

The Big Picture

So far, I've explained how you can use Keywords and the Roadmap to avoid dwelling on details and to keep your focus where it belongs: on the larger themes of the text. In order to make sure you've really captured the essence of the author's big ideas, there are four attributes of the passage that you should think about before you move on. You won't see them written down anywhere in Figure 1.1, and that's because on test day you shouldn't write them down either. Instead, you will develop the habit of working them out in your mind. I'll define each one of them for you in brief:

- Topic: A very general description of its subject matter
- Scope: The narrower area of interest within the Topic that the author explores
- Purpose: A description of *why* the author wrote the passage
- Main Idea: A summary of the author's primary point

I'll walk you through the topic, scope, purpose, and main idea of the Victorian philanthropy passage. Actually, I've already named the topic: Victorian philanthropy. So what about philanthropy is the author interested in exploring? She spends most of the passage examining the merits of the two criticisms that have been leveled against it. That's the scope: criticisms of Victorian philanthropy.

In order to decide on the purpose, refer to the Roadmap for guidance. Going paragraph by paragraph, you can see that the author wrote this passage in order to describe two specific criticisms of Victorian philanthropy and then to refute those criticisms; that's the purpose. Finally, articulate the main idea. If you could summarize the entire passage in a sentence or two, what would you say? Think about it before reading on.

You probably came up with something like this: "Various critics have described the Victorian philanthropists as inadequate and self-serving, but these critics are incorrect." Your version of the main idea may have been a bit briefer or more detailed than mine, but as long as you came up with something similar you're on the right track. I'll discuss topic, scope, purpose, and main idea more thoroughly in chapter 4, but for now you might be asking, "Why do I need to bother thinking about this?" The answer is simple: It helps you earn points on the LSAT.

Pulling It All Together

Now use your new skills to answer a couple of questions. Begin by returning to question 21:

21. Which one of the following best summarizes the main idea of the passage?

   (A) While the motives of individual practitioners have been questioned by modern commentators, Victorian philanthropy successfully dealt with the social ills of nineteenth-century England.

   (B) Philanthropy, inadequate to deal with the massive social and economic problems of the twentieth century, has slowly been replaced by state-sponsored charity.

   (C) The practice of reading the past as a prelude to an enlightened present has fostered revisionist views of many institutions, among them Victorian philanthropy.

   (D) Although modern commentators have perceived Victorian philanthropy as either inadequate or self-serving, the theoretical bias behind these criticisms leads to an incorrect interpretation of history.

   (E) Victorian philanthropists, aware of public resentment of their self-congratulatory attitude, used devious methods to camouflage their self-serving motives.[14]

The question is asking for the main idea of the passage, and you've already worked out what it is. Which answer choice matches the prediction you just made? Perhaps choice (A) looks tempting at first, but if you compare it to your prediction, you can see that it's incorrect; at no point did the author claim that the Victorian philanthropists successfully dealt with the ills of their time. (When you see a clever wrong answer trap like this one, it's very important that you stick to your prediction.) Of the remaining choices, choice (D) matches your prediction note for note. It's a bit wordier than what you may have come up with, but that will almost always be the case. You don't need to look for the same words, but rather the same concept.

Look at another question:

24. Which one of the following best describes the primary purpose of the passage?

   (A) providing an extended definition of a key term

   (B) defending the work of an influential group of theorists

   (C) narrating the chronological development of a widespread practice

   (D) examining modern evaluations of a historical phenomenon

   (E) analyzing a specific dilemma faced by workers of the past[15]

---

[14]PrepTest 41, Sec 4, Q 21
[15]PrepTest 41, Sec 4, Q 24

This question asks for the primary purpose, and once again you've already made a prediction. Only choice (D) matches your prediction, and it's the correct answer. If you had encountered this passage on test day, you would have already scored two quick points simply by understanding and identifying the author's purpose and main idea. Try one more:

26. Which one of the following best describes the organization of the passage?

   (A)   Two related positions are discussed, then both are subjected to the same criticism.

   (B)   Two opposing theories are outlined, then a synthesis between the two is proposed.

   (C)   A position is stated, and two differing evaluations of it are given.

   (D)   Three examples of the same logical inconsistency are given.

   (E)   A theory is outlined, and two supporting examples are given.[16]

Questions that ask for passage structure can appear baffling, but you've got exactly what you need to answer this question quickly and correctly: your Roadmap. Look back over the structure of the passage as described in the Roadmap and you'll see that the only answer choice that matches is choice (A). The other choices may tempt you if you haven't analyzed the passage structure carefully, but with the aid of the Kaplan Method, they won't fool you. All three of these questions demonstrate something very important about LSAT Reading Comprehension as a whole. The test makers reward those who think about the big issues and don't allow themselves to get mired in the details.

Congratulations are in order! You've made it this far and have already learned many important LSAT concepts. I've also introduced you to the basics of the Kaplan Method. To conclude chapter 1, I'll explain the Kaplan Method in more detail.

THE KAPLAN METHOD

As you know, LSAT Reading Comprehension is timed, and 35 minutes may not seem like a generous amount of time to work with. In order to master Reading Comprehension you must not only be accurate, but efficient as well. One of the biggest fears my students have on their first day of class is imagining opening their booklets on test day, looking at the page, and having no idea what to do next as time slips away. Perhaps you have the same fear. Fortunately, there is a solution: If you follow a methodical approach, you'll always know what to do next. Here is the Kaplan Method:

---

[16]PrepTest 41, Sec 4, Q 26

KAPLAN'S METHOD FOR READING COMPREHENSION

STEP 1 **Read the Passage Strategically.**
Read for Topic, Scope, Purpose, and Main Idea and build your Roadmap.

STEP 2 **Identify the Question Type.**
Look for clues to identify the question and help you find the answer in the passage.

STEP 3 **Research the Relevant Text.**
Use your Roadmap to guide your research.

STEP 4 **Make a Prediction.**
Make effective predictions to help you get the right answer quickly and efficiently.

STEP 5 **Evaluate the Answer Choices.**
Evaluate each choice and eliminate those that don't match your prediction, keeping your eye out for common wrong answer traps.

You've already executed each step of the Kaplan Method at various stages. For now, I'll discuss each step briefly and then expand on them in subsequent chapters.

Step 1: Read the Passage Strategically

I've already introduced you to all of the important aspects of Step 1. I've discussed Keywords, building a Roadmap, and the importance of determining Topic, Scope, Purpose, and Main Idea. I'll explore all of these ideas in greater detail moving forward, but for now I want to emphasize the importance of practicing this new way of reading. It may not be easy at first and will certainly require a good deal of practice to master, but the benefit of mastery is a higher LSAT score. Part I of this book will primarily focus on strategic reading.

Step 2: Identify the Question Type

There are only five common question types in LSAT Reading Comprehension, and the Kaplan Method will allow you to master each one of them. In Part II of this book, I'll teach you how to identify each type and introduce you to those strategies. I'll also show you how to use clues in the question stem to quickly determine where in the passage you should look to find the answer.

Step 3: Research the Relevant Text

Most Reading Comprehension questions require you to reference specific information from the passage. This step is crucial in answering those questions correctly. One of the biggest mistakes I see students make is to over-rely on memory. This is a terrible habit, one that I want to prevent you from forming. As you begin to apply the Kaplan Method to every question, you'll soon learn to use your Roadmap to correctly identify which text is relevant to a given question. That way you can answer the question quickly without sacrificing accuracy.

Step 4: Make a Prediction

You've already seen the power of making predictions before you look at the answer choices. Nevertheless, this approach may seem counterintuitive to you initially, and you might fear that it's too time-consuming to apply. With practice, you will make predictions quickly and accurately, saving time and allowing you to eliminate wrong answer traps with ease. Once you've made it a habit, you will enjoy a boost to your confidence and, in turn, your score. The answer to most Reading Comprehension questions can be predicted, making this a particularly vital skill to master.

Step 5: Evaluate the Answer Choices

Most of the time, this means seeking out a choice that matches the prediction you made in Step 4. For questions less amenable to prediction, you will learn to apply alternative ways of evaluating the choices. You will also become familiar with the most common types of wrong answer that appear on the LSAT so that you are less likely to be enticed by them.

When you follow the steps of the Kaplan Method, you will always know what to do on test day, and you can be sure that you're always approaching the test the right way. That brings me right back to the main point of chapter 1.

YOU CAN MASTER LSAT READING COMPREHENSION

LSAT Reading Comprehension can be challenging, intimidating, and confusing. It can also be a fantastic opportunity to improve your score and take a big step forward on the road to law school. Keep this in mind as you learn more about the Kaplan Method and begin to practice. I know from experience that while it's sometimes difficult to keep a positive outlook when taking on a big challenge, it's also absolutely essential. You won't master the methods overnight, and you'll make some mistakes along the way. I'll do my best to help you see those mistakes for what they are: opportunities to learn. And as you start to attain mastery, you'll begin to wonder why you were ever intimidated by Reading Comprehension at all. For now, let's continue with a more thorough discussion of Keywords in chapter 2.

CHAPTER 2

ALL ABOUT KEYWORDS

WHY KEYWORDS MATTER

In the last chapter I introduced you to Keywords, and I hope I convinced you that learning to make use of them is vital to your LSAT success. But just to be certain, I'll begin with a brief discussion of why Keywords are so important.

Keywords Make Reading Easier

LSAT Reading Comprehension is designed to be challenging to all readers. The test makers purposefully choose subjects that are diverse, nuanced, and sometimes complex. They gravitate toward formal, scholarly language that can be dense, dull, and laden with complex details or abstract ideas. Such language can be difficult to comprehend even when you have plenty of time to read it; the LSAT rachets up the difficulty level by adding the pressure of the clock.

Fortunately, Keywords are there to help. They provide structure to the passage, allowing you to discern one idea from another and to organize important information as you read. Let me show you what I mean. Read the following:

Charlie sat down. He took a pencil out of his pocket. He wanted to work through some sample questions. His pencil wasn't sharpened. He had a spare pencil. It was sharpened. He was ready to get to work.

If that seemed confusing or odd, that's because it was completely lacking in useful Keywords. No one ever writes like this, at least not in formal writing. You would instead expect to see something more like this:

(First) Charlie sat down, (and then) he took a pencil out of his pocket. He wanted to work through some sample questions, (but) his pencil wasn't sharpened. (Fortunately,) he had a spare pencil, (and) (since) it was sharpened, he was ready to get to work.

It still isn't Shakespeare, but it's certainly much easier to follow. Notice that the highlighted Keywords provide bits of information that assist us in linking the various ideas together. The guidance that Keywords provide is helpful in a simple example, and they become absolutley crucial in a more challenging passage:

Drilling a well
creates a conduit connecting all the formations that it
(30) has penetrated. (Consequently,) without appropriate
safeguards, wells that penetrate both groundwater and
oil or saline water formations (inevitably) contaminate
the groundwater. (Initial) attempts to prevent this
contamination (consisted of) sealing off the
(35) groundwater formations with some form of protective
barrier to prevent the oil flowing up the well from
entering or mixing with the natural groundwater
reservoir. This method, which is still in use today,
(initially) involved using hollow trees to seal off the
(40) groundwater formations; (now,) (however,) large metal
pipe casings, set in place with cement, are used.[1]

In this LSAT passage excerpt, you are bombarded with information. The provided Keywords help you to understand the logic of what the author is saying. Words like "initially," "consequently," and "however" provide the sequence of events and their relationship to one another. Hopefully it has occurred to you that everything you've ever read that was written in formal English contained dozens of Keywords. Because they're so ubiquitous, you may tend to take them for granted, rarely noticing them at all. As part of your Kaplan training, I will teach you to re-acquaint yourself with these useful words and to use them to become a more confident and efficient reader.

Keywords Denote Emphasis

There are different kinds of Keywords that guide us in a variety of ways, and I'll explain all of them in this chapter. LSAT passages invariably contain Keywords that denote emphasis, and any emphasized idea is likely to be important when you proceed to the questions. Sometimes emphatic Keywords are quite obvious, but they can be subtle as well. See whether you can spot the emphasis Keywords in this sentence:

---

[1]PrepTest 43, Sec 1, Passage 1

Because the well was drilled in a channel
accessing the ocean, not only was the area's
(60) groundwater completely contaminated, but widespread
coastal contamination also occurred, prompting
international concern over oil exploration and
initiating further attempts to refine regulations.[2]

Hopefully you recognized a number of Keywords, but here are the ones I want you to pay particular attention to:

Because the well was drilled in a channel
(60) accessing the ocean, (not only) was the area's
groundwater completely contaminated, (but) widespread
coastal contamination (also) occurred, prompting
international concern over oil exploration and
initiating further attempts to refine regulations.[3]

In this sentence, the author describes two consequences of the drilling of a well. The Keyword pairing "not only . . . but also" helps you keep track of them. It also implies that the second consequence, the coastal contamination, is the one that the author is most interested in. If you're not sure why, think about the way these Keywords are used in everyday life:

The senator was contrite in his remarks, not only apologizing for his mistakes, but also announcing his resignation to his constituents.

The senator did two things, and one of them was more important or more surprising than the other. If he gave a contrite speech, you would expect him to issue apologies. You wouldn't necessarily expect him to abandon his post. You can see that with this particular Keyword pairing, whatever follows the "not only" is generally less emphatic, and what follows the "but also" is usually more emphatic.

Understanding which ideas the author emphasizes is extremely important, because the majority of the questions you see when you take your LSAT will reference those ideas. Put simply: Knowing what has been emphasized will earn you points. If it's important to the author, it's important to you as well.

Keywords Are Always There

To conclude this overview of Keywords, I want to restate something I mentioned in the first chapter of this book: *Every single LSAT passage is loaded with Keywords.* This, above all, is the reason that they are so important. The test makers deliberately provide you with all the Keywords you need because they want to reward you for noticing them and using them correctly. The ability to navigate dense language quickly and understand its structure and core ideas is

---

[2]PrepTest 43, Sec 1, Passage 1
[3]PrepTest 43, Sec 1, Passage 1

an imperative for law school students. That's why Reading Comprehension is on the LSAT, and that's why the Keywords are always there.

In order to read strategically, you must learn to identify Keywords. Now I'll introduce the most common Keywords you should expect to see on test day, broken down into six categories.

Contrast Keywords

Contrast Keywords indicate that the passage is about to move in a different direction. Here's an example:

> Most of what has been written about Thurgood
> Marshall, a former United States Supreme Court justice
> who served from 1967 to 1991, has just focused on his
> judicial record and on the ideological content of his
> (5)   earlier achievements as a lawyer pursuing civil rights
> issues in the courts. But when Marshall's career is
> viewed from a technical perspective, his work with the
> NAACP (National Association for the Advancement of
> Colored People) reveals a strategic and methodological
> (10) legacy to the field of public interest law.[4]

The author begins this passage with a description of what has generally been written about Marshall's work. But she's actually more interested in examining aspects of his work with the NAACP. In order to alert the reader to this change, she uses the Keyword "but." Here's another example from an excerpt you examined previously:

> This method, which is still in use today,
> initially involved using hollow trees to seal off the
> (40) groundwater formations; now, however, large metal
> pipe casings, set in place with cement, are used.[5]

In this case, the author uses contrast Keywords to indicate a shift from what was previously true to what is true now.

Contrast Keywords are important because LSAT passages tend to involve conflict. Science passages frequently pit one theory or model against another, and Law passages will often feature debates between legal scholars or schools of thought. You will almost certainly encounter

[4]PrepTest 42, Sec 3, Passage 1
[5]PrepTest 43, Sec 1, Passage 1

passages on test day that introduce multiple points of view and then demonstrate how and why they differ. Any time a conflict is present in a passage, you should take heed; it will probably be the subject of at least one question. To illustrate:

(In addition,) Marshall used sociological (and) psychological statistics—presented in expert testimony, (for example,) about the psychological impact of enforced segregation—(as a means) of transforming constitutional law by persuading the courts that certain discriminatory laws produced public harms in violation
(40) of constitutional principles. This tactic, (while) often effective, has been (criticized) by (some legal scholars) as a pragmatic attempt to give judges nonlegal material with which to fill gaps in their justifications for decisions where the purely legal principles appear
(45) inconclusive.[6]

In the first sentence, the author describes one of Marshall's tactics. The Keyword "while" in the second sentence points to a contrast. Even though the tactic is effective, certain scholars have criticized it.

Here is the final question from this passage:

7. According to the passage, some legal scholars have criticized which one of the following?

   (A) the ideology Marshall used to support his goals
   (B) recent public interest campaigns
   (C) the use of Marshall's techniques by politically conservative lawyers
   (D) the use of psychological statistics in court cases
   (E) the set of criteria for selecting public interest litigants[7]

You can find support for correct answer (D) in the text immediately following the Keywords "in addition" at the paragraph's beginning. It's worth noting that these critics are not mentioned anywhere else in the passage; the test makers regarded this sole bit of critique to be important enough to warrant a question. Careful attention to Keywords makes this an easy point to earn. Among the most common contrast Keywords are "not," "although," "while," "even though," "despite," and "however." Be on the lookout for them, but know that you don't need to memorize long lists of Keywords to improve your LSAT score. Most of them you will recognize instinctively, and with practice you'll soon identify them by habit.

---

[6]PrepTest 42, Sec 3, Passage 1
[7]PrepTest 42, Sec 3, Q 7

Continuation Keywords

Continuation Keywords are the opposites of contrast Keywords. They indicate that the author is continuing ahead in the same vein:

> The effects of groundwater bacteria, traffic
> vibrations, and changing groundwater chemistry are
> (50) likewise unassessed. (Further,) there is no guarantee that
> wells drilled in compliance with existing regulations will
> not expose a need for research in additional areas: on the
> west coast of North America, a major disaster recently
> occurred because a well's location was based on a poor
> (55) understanding of the area's subsurface geology.[8]

Here's one more:

> (In addition,) Marshall used sociological
> and psychological statistics—presented in expert
> testimony, for example, about the psychological
> impact of enforced segregation—as a means of
> (40) transforming constitutional law by persuading the
> courts that certain discriminatory laws produced
> public harms in violation of constitutional
> principles.[9]

Continuation Keywords are useful for breaking up long chains of ideas and for anticipating the structure of a passage quickly. In the first example above, the word "Further" helps us quickly see where one concept ends and where another related concept begins. Taking note of this now will help immensely if you need to re-examine these examples quickly while answering a question. The sentence in the second example is the first of a new paragraph. LSAT passages frequently begin paragraphs with Keywords; pay special heed to them, because they provide invaluable information about the structure of the passage.

Conclusion Keywords and Evidence Keywords

The Logical Reasoning section of the LSAT requires that you become very skillful at identifying an argument's conclusion and its evidence. That same skill is also useful in Reading Comprehension. For the purposes of Reading Comprehension, a conclusion Keyword indicates an important

---

[8]PrepTest 43, Sec 1, Passage 1
[9]PrepTest 42, Sec 3, Passage 1

opinion being expressed, and an evidence Keyword denotes any type of supporting information, including examples. Since these types of Keywords often work in pairs, I'll examine them together. Begin with a passage excerpt:

> ⟨Because⟩ the market system enables entrepreneurs
> and investors who develop new technology to reap
> financial rewards from their risk of capital, it may seem
> that the primary ⟨result⟩ of this activity is that some
> (5)   people who have spare capital accumulate more.[10]

The conclusion Keyword "result" points directly to a conclusion that the author wishes to discuss. The evidence Keyword "because" at the beginning of the sentence indicates the evidence provided for this conclusion.

Evidence and conclusion Keywords don't always have to be directly paired with one another. For instance:

> When commercial drilling for oil began in North
> America in the mid-nineteenth century, regulations
> reflected the industry's concern for the purity of the
> wells' oil. In 1893, for example, ⟨regulations⟩ were
> (15)   enacted specifying well construction requirements to
> protect oil and gas reserves from contamination by
> fresh water.[11]

Here is a very common evidence Keyword: "for example." The author uses the example to illustrate the industry concerns mentioned in the first sentence. There aren't any obvious conclusion Keywords, but the presence of the example informs you that a conclusion is nearby. This is important to remember: The examples in a passage exist primarily to substantiate conclusions, so any time you see examples, you should also be on the lookout for a key idea.

Common evidence Keywords include "since," "because," and "for example." There is an abundance of conclusion Keywords, but some of the most common are "thus," "therefore," "as a result," and "in conclusion." Note that conclusions may also be identified by field-specific Keywords such as "hypothesis," "theory," and "interpretation." These are particularly common in natural science and law passages.

POV Keywords

POV (point of view) Keywords indicate that a point of view is about to be expressed, and they help you to differentiate one opinion from another in the passage. Since most passages contain

---

[10] PrepTest 42, Sec 3, Passage 3
[11] PrepTest 43, Sec 1, Passage 1

multiple viewpoints (including the author's), you must be careful not to confuse them. Here's an example that should look familiar:

(40) This tactic, while often
effective, has been criticized by some legal scholars as
a pragmatic attempt to give judges nonlegal material
with which to fill gaps in their justifications for
decisions where the purely legal principles appear
(45) inconclusive.[12]

It is very common for the author to present a criticism from a third party. Because this is the case, take care to note which opinions are the author's and which are not. In the above example, note that the author is stating that the tactic is effective, while the legal scholars are providing the criticism. Does the author agree with the critics? I hope your answer was, "I don't know." The author has neither disputed nor endorsed the critics' stance. Perhaps she will render an opinion at a later time, but for now, you should not make any assumptions beyond what is presented to us in the text of the passage.

POV Keywords generally appear as short phrases such as "according to," "the critics claim," "scholars agree," and "scientists hypothesize." Note that these phrases not only indicate that a claim is being made, but also who is making the claim.

Emphasis Keywords

At the beginning of this chapter I told you that one of the most important functions that Keywords serve is to denote emphasis. Look at one more example of an emphasis Keyword:

An essential element in the success of this tactic was
the explicit recognition that in a public interest legal
campaign, choosing the right plaintiff can mean the
(30) difference between success and failure.[13]

Emphasis Keywords are extremely varied, and it would be almost impossible to list them all. This doesn't mean they're difficult to identify; they're simply words or phrases that indicate that a given concept is important or interesting. Common examples include "crucial," "essential," "vital," "of course," "interesting," and "important." The author may also use qualifying words and phrases to denote emphasis, such as "the most influential" or "the greatest reason." These are all just different ways the author might indicate the importance of an idea. And as I said before, anything that's important to the author is likely to be the subject of questions.

[12]PrepTest 42, Sec 3, Passage 1
[13]PrepTest 42, Sec 3, Passage 1

A slight variation on the emphasis Keyword is the opinion Keyword:

> This version of history (patronizes) the Victorians,
> (50) who were (in fact) well aware of their vulnerability to
> charges of condescension and complacency, but were
> equally well aware of the potential dangers of state-
> managed charity.[14]

In this example, the author uses the opinion Keyword "patronizes" to express disapproval of a particular historical viewpoint. He then introduces his contrary opinion with the phrase "in fact." Opinion Keywords usually indicate that the author is taking sides in a debate.

Please remember that these categories don't perfectly encapsulate every possible Keyword that you might encounter on the LSAT, and there are some Keywords that may seem to fit into multiple categories. But that's fine; on test day, you don't identify Keywords to categorize them. You identify them to break down the passage more efficiently and to answer the questions more easily.

---

[14]PrepTest 41, Sec 4, Passage 4

DRILL: IDENTIFYING KEYWORDS

Now try the following exercise. In each of the five excerpts below, identify and circle every Keyword you can find. Take your time; right now your goal is accuracy, not speed. Complete answers and explanations follow the drill. Be sure to read them carefully before you move on.

1.

        Most Internet communication
(5)   consists of sending electronic mail or exchanging ideas
        on electronic bulletin boards; however, a growing
        number of transmissions are of copyrighted works—
        books, photographs, videos and films, and sound
        recordings.[15]

2.

        But while many muralist works express populist or
        nationalist ideas, it is a mistake to attempt to reduce
        Mexican mural painting to formulaic, official
        government art.[16]

3.

        Moreover, while they shared a common interest in
        rediscovering their Mexican national identity, they
(35)   developed their own distinct styles. Rivera, for
        example, incorporated elements from pre-Columbian
        sculpture and the Italian Renaissance fresco into his
        murals and used a strange combination of mechanical
        shapes to depict the faces and bodies of people.[17]

4.

        Some experts propose simply adding unauthorized
        digitalization to the list of activities proscribed under
        current law, to make it clear that copyright holders own
(35)   electronic reproduction rights just as they own rights to
        other types of reproduction. But criminalizing
        digitalization raises a host of questions.[18]

5.

        One fundamental assumption of wave
        theory was that as the length of a wave of radiation
        shortens, its energy increases smoothly—like a volume
(10)   dial on a radio that adjusts smoothly to any setting—
        and that any conceivable energy value could thus occur
        in nature.[19]

---

[15] PrepTest 39, Sec 3, Passage 4

[16] PrepTest 39, Sec 3, Passage 1

[17] PrepTest 39, Sec 3, Passage 1

[18] PrepTest 39, Sec 3, Passage 4

[19] PrepTest 39, Sec 3, Passage 3

Answer Explanations follow on the next page.

Explanations

Now compare your work to the explanations. Don't worry if you didn't find every Keyword, or if you identified Keywords that aren't listed here. Detecting Keywords isn't an exact science. Your goal is simply to understand which Keywords are the most important ones.

1.

(Most) Internet communication
(5)   consists of sending electronic mail or exchanging ideas
on electronic bulletin boards; (however,) a growing
number of transmissions are of copyrighted works—
books, photographs, videos and films, and sound
recordings.[20]

The Keyword "most" suggests that a contrast is coming up, and sure enough, you soon see "however." This pair of Keywords allows you to quickly see that the author is pointing out an exception to the rule that will probably be discussed in greater detail.

2.

(But) while many muralist works express populist or
nationalist ideas, it is (a mistake) to attempt to reduce
Mexican mural painting to formulaic, official
government art.[21]

The sentence begins with a common contrast Keyword, "but," which tells you that this part of the passage is in opposition to what came before it. "A mistake" conveys the author's disapproval of the opinion that follows.

3.

(Moreover,) (while) they shared a common interest in
rediscovering their Mexican national identity, they
(35)   developed their own (distinct) styles. Rivera, (for)
(example,) incorporated elements from pre-Columbian
sculpture and the Italian Renaissance fresco into his
murals and used a strange combination of mechanical
shapes to depict the faces and bodies of people.[22]

"Moreover" is a continuation Keyword and tells you that the author is extending whatever ideas were presented immediately before the excerpt. "While" sets up a potentially important contrast, leading to the emphasis that the author places on "distinct" styles; this is a great example

---

[20] PrepTest 39, Sec 3, Passage 4

[21] PrepTest 39, Sec 3, Passage 1

[22] PrepTest 39, Sec 3, Passage 1

of how Keywords work together to bracket an important idea. Finally, "for example" tells you that the author is mentioning Rivera in order to illustrate the distinct styles already mentioned.

4.

> (Some experts) propose simply adding unauthorized
> digitalization to the list of activities proscribed under
> current law, to make it clear that copyright holders own
> (35) electronic reproduction rights just as they own rights to
> other types of reproduction. (But) criminalizing
> digitalization raises a host of questions.[23]

Here is an excellent illustration of a common LSAT passage structure. The author introduces the opinion of "some experts" in the first sentence and then quickly raises doubts about their ideas by starting the next sentence with the contrast/opinion indicator "but."

5.

> One (fundamental) assumption of wave
> theory was that as the length of a wave of radiation
> shortens, its energy increases smoothly—(like) a volume
> (10) dial on a radio that adjusts smoothly to any setting—
> and that any conceivable energy value could (thus) occur
> in nature.[24]

Keywords are especially helpful in passages that feature technical language or abstract ideas. In this excerpt from a natural science passage, "fundamental" gives emphasis to the assumption described by the author. "Like" points to a useful illustration, and "thus" leads you to the assumption's conclusion.

WHAT KEYWORDS TELL YOU
Keywords Establish Context

So far I've shown you how to identify Keywords and encouraged you to circle them when you see them. This is an important habit to learn, so be sure to circle every Keyword you find in every passage you read, from now until test day. But merely identifying Keywords isn't enough.

When I first began to teach for Kaplan, I counseled a student who was experiencing a lot of frustration with strategic reading. I asked him to execute the first step of the Kaplan Method on a passage and I observed him while he worked, trying to pinpoint the problem. Within a few minutes he had read the passage and dutifully circled every Keyword. When he had finished, I asked him if he could tell me the Topic, Scope, Purpose, and Main Idea of the passage. He

---

[23] PrepTest 39, Sec 3, Passage 4
[24] PrepTest 39, Sec 3, Passage 3

replied, "No. I'm sorry, but I have no idea what I just read." I realized at that instant what his problem was: He was identifying the Keywords, but he wasn't thinking about what they were telling him. I was able to help him correct the problem, but I'd like you to avoid it altogether by thinking about the context of Keywords from day one.

Fortunately, you've already made good progress toward understanding this important concept. In the first half of this chapter, you learned that Keywords come in a variety of types. Now I'll show you how to use the Keywords to guide your reading.

The Two-Part Process

The process is very simple: First, every time you spot a Keyword, circle or underline it. Second, think about what the Keyword is telling you before reading on. By doing this, you keep focused on the most important information in the passage.

I want you to take a moment to think about what this really means. You can actually use the clues provided by the test maker to predict what is coming next in the passage, sentence by sentence and paragraph by paragraph. You can instantly separate crucial information from details likely to be untested. And you'll never become bogged down in a dense, difficult passage, because all of the clues you need are there to guide you. Does this sound too good to be true? Let me show you what I mean. Examine the first paragraph of a previously released passage and put this strategy to work.

> The (myth) persists that in 1492 the Western
> Hemisphere was an untamed wilderness and that it was
> European settlers who harnessed and transformed its
> ecosystems.[25]

This passage starts off with a great Keyword. "Myth" indicates that the author disagrees with the notion that an untamed wilderness existed prior to European settlement. So you know that the author holds a contrary opinion, and that he thinks the wilderness was already being transformed.

---

[25]PrepTest 38, Sec 3, Passage 1

(But) scholarship shows that forests, (in)
(5) (particular,) had been altered to varying degrees well
before the arrival of Europeans. Native populations had
converted much of the forests to successfully cultivated
stands, (especially) by means of burning. (Nevertheless,)
(some researchers) have maintained that the extent,
(10) frequency, and impact of such burning was minimal.
(One geographer claims) that climatic change could have
accounted for some of the changes in forest
composition; (another) (argues) that burning by native
populations was done only sporadically, to augment the
(15) effects of natural fires.[26]

Unsurprisingly, the next sentence begins with a contrast Keyword. The author reveals that, contrary to the myth, native populations had been altering the environment. Also note the emphasis Keyword "especially." The passage will probably go into greater detail about the burning of forests as it proceeds.

"Nevertheless" immediately signals that a contrary opinion is about to be presented. You can even predict what it will be: Since the author believes that the native population *did* frequently burn forests, the opposing opinion must suggest that it did not. And that's exactly what you are told: Some researchers believe burning was minimal.

Next you reach the geographer's claim. Since there are no Keywords of contrast, you should expect this claim to support the "minimal burning" theory. Sure enough, that's what happens. The same goes for the other geographer. The geographers aren't really presenting any important new ideas; their claims are simply evidence in support of the broader claim that was made at the beginning of the first sentence.

Let me take a moment to summarize what a few well-placed Keywords told you about this paragraph. You were presented with a myth that the author disagreed with. Then several supporters of the original myth were cited. In all of the text of the first paragraph, *that's all that really happened!* This is the true power of strategic reading. You just broke an entire paragraph down into two simple sentences, a skill that you will further hone in chapter 3. But first, try out your Keyword skills with a brief exercise:

---

[26]PrepTest 38, Sec 3, Passage 1

DRILL: WORKING WITH KEYWORDS

In this exercise, I'll present you with excerpts from two Reading Comprehension passages. Read each one, circle any Keywords you identify, and answer the questions in your own words. The questions will help you think about what the Keywords are telling you and what you should expect as a consequence. Take your time with this exercise and make sure you understand each example. I've provided explanations after the drill.

1.

> Because the memoirs were written so long after the
> events they describe, some historians question their
> reliability. Certainly,[27]

Whose point of view is presented here?

_____

What is the author likely to describe next?

_____

2.

> Certainly, memory is subject to the loss or
> confusion of facts and, more to the point in these
> (20) partisan accounts, to the distortions of a mind intent on
> preserving its particular picture of the past. But[28]

On which idea does the author place the most emphasis?

_____

What will happen next?

_____

3.

> But other
> scholars have shown that close inspection of these
> documents resolves such doubts on two scores.[29]

What Keywords should we expect immediately after this sentence?

_____

_____

[27]PrepTest 35, Sec 2, Passage 1
[28]PrepTest 35, Sec 2, Passage 1
[29]PrepTest 35, Sec 2, Passage 1

The following three exercises are from a tougher passage, one that deals with abstract natural science concepts. But don't worry; you can apply the same thinking to simplify complex ideas!

4.
(15) Philosophers of science have not been alone in
      claiming that science must consist of universal laws.[30]

Whose point of view does the author describe?

_____

What point of view will be described next?

_____

5.
      Some evolutionary biologists have also acceded to the
      general intellectual disdain for the merely particular
      and tried to emulate physicists, constructing their
(20) science as a set of universal laws. In formulating the
      notion of a universal "struggle for existence" that is the
      engine of biological history or in asserting that
      virtually all DNA evolves at a constant clocklike rate,
      they have attempted to find their own versions of the
(25) law of gravity. Recently, however,[31]

Use the context of what you've read so far to write a simplified version of the first sentence.

_____

What purpose does the second sentence serve?

_____

What will the author describe next?

_____

6.
(25) Recently, however, some biologists
      have questioned whether biological history is really the
      necessary unfolding of universal laws of life, and they
      have raised the possibility that historical contingency is
      an integral factor in biology.[32]

What does the phrase "historical contingency" mean in the context of this sentence?

_____

_____

[30]PrepTest 35, Sec 2, Passage 3
[31]PrepTest 35, Sec 2, Passage 3
[32]PrepTest 35, Sec 2, Passage 3

Explanations

1.

> Because the memoirs were written so long after the events they describe, some historians question their reliability. Certainly,[33]

Whose point of view is presented here?

The point of view of "some historians" is being described in this sentence. Be sure to note that you can't yet ascertain whether the author agrees with the historians.

What is the author likely to describe next?

In order to know what's coming next, think about the Keyword, "certainly." What idea did the author present immediately prior to this Keyword? It was the opinion of the historians, that the memoirs may not be reliable. Since "certainly" is a Keyword of continuation, you should expect the author to provide some details concerning this lack of reliability. You should similarly expect that the author will agree to some extent with the historians.

2.

> Certainly, memory is subject to the loss or confusion of facts and, more to the point in these
> (20) partisan accounts, to the distortions of a mind intent on preserving its particular picture of the past. But[34]

On which idea does the author place the most emphasis?

As predicted, the author is now describing ways in which a memoir might be unreliable. He describes two main reasons: faulty memory and deliberate distortion. Of these two, the second is more central to the author's argument. Why? Because it is signaled by the Keywords "more to the point," which indicate clear emphasis. When several similar ideas are presented to you in a passage, look for any clues that may tell you which are most important.

What will happen next?

Once again, you've got an excellent Keyword to help you stay one step ahead of the author. The contrast word "but" tells you that the author is going to change course. Here's an important question to consider: In the context of what you've read so far, do you think the author will disagree with the details you just read (reasons for unreliability) or with the historians' conclusion presented in exercise 1 (the memoirs may be unreliable)? Since the details are only there to support the conclusion, the conclusion is more important. Hence, the author will probably argue that the memoirs are reliable after all.

---

[33]PrepTest 35, Sec 2, Passage 1
[34]PrepTest 35, Sec 2, Passage 1

3.

(But)(other)
(scholars) have shown that close inspection of these
documents resolves such doubts on (two scores).[35]

What Keywords should we expect immediately after this sentence?

When a sentence ends with a clear indicator of structure like "two scores," you should be on the alert for Keywords that will help you easily find each one of the arguments that the author is preparing to introduce. Incidentally, here is the text that follows, with two expected Keywords identified:

(First,)
for major public happenings, there are often multiple
(25)   accounts, allowing for cross-verification. (Second,)
regarding the truth of personal events known only to
the author, more subjective guidelines must be used:[36]

Once again, you can see that Keywords work together in order to help you easily break down the structure of a passage.

4.

(15) (Philosophers of science) have not been alone in
(claiming) that science must consist of universal laws.[37]

Whose point of view does the author describe?

The author describes a central claim of the "philosophers of science" in this sentence. Even though this passage contains potentially intimidating subject matter, the same common Keywords are there to help guide you through the text.

What point of view will be described next?

Hopefully you clued in on the words "have not been alone." They indicate that another party is about to be introduced to the conversation, one that will express agreement with the philosophers. In an abstract passage like this one, it's a good idea to make sure you're comfortable with the primary point of agreement before you move on. In this case, the philosophers claim that science consists of universal laws. If you don't yet understand what that means, don't worry. You'll probably get a more detailed description when the author introduces the next point of view.

---

[35] PrepTest 35, Sec 2, Passage 1
[36] PrepTest 35, Sec 2, Passage 1
[37] PrepTest 35, Sec 2, Passage 3

5.

> (Some) evolutionary biologists have (also) acceded to the
> general intellectual disdain for the (merely) particular
> and tried to emulate physicists, constructing their
> (20) science as a set of universal laws. (In formulating) the
> notion of a universal "struggle for existence" that is the
> engine of biological history or in asserting that
> virtually all DNA evolves at a constant clocklike rate,
> they have (attempted) to find their own versions of the
> (25) law of gravity. (Recently,) (however,)[38]

Use the context of what you've read so far to write a simplified version of the first sentence. This might have been a little tricky. Take a look at the clues you have to work with. The author is now describing the views of the evolutionary biologists. You know that their views are in accordance with the philosophers from the previous sentence. Both groups seem to be interested in describing science as "universal" in some way. Whenever you see a term like this one repeated in a passage, it's sure to be important. So you could simplify this sentence like so: "The biologists want their science to be universal." Your answer may have included some other details, and that's fine. The main thing I'm pointing out in this example is that LSAT passages will frequently bury simple ideas in piles of complex text. As you master the Kaplan Method, you'll become better and better at looking beyond the jargon.

What purpose does the second sentence serve?

The second sentence is long and complex and deals with abstract ideas. But why is it really here? The Keywords "in formulating" probably indicate continuation, so this entire sentence is likely to be a long example that backs up what you already know: The biologists want their science to be universal. Since you never want to get bogged down in the details of a passage, you should read through this example quickly without trying to understand it in depth. It's more important to know *why* the evidence is here than to know exactly what it's saying. Thinking this way will keep you focused on the big picture as you read and save you time as you proceed toward the question set.

What will the author describe next?

"However" at the end of the excerpt tells you that dissenting opinions are about to appear. What are they likely to say? That science *doesn't* have to be universal. This prediction will help you understand the next sentence.

---

[38]PrepTest 35, Sec 2, Passage 3

6.

> Recently, however, some biologists
> have questioned whether biological history is really the
> necessary unfolding of universal laws of life, and they
> (30) have raised the possibility that historical contingency is
> an integral factor in biology.[39]

What does the phrase "historical contingency" mean in the context of this sentence?

Here's your opportunity to pull it all together and clear up this dense passage. The prediction was correct: The author introduces some new biologists who question the ideas of the other biologists. What idea do they challenge? As you know, they must be against the idea of universal laws in their science. So when you see an unfamiliar phrase like "historical contingency," you can use what you've already learned to make sense of it. It must be the opposite of universal laws. From the clues in the previous sentences, you've probably deduced that universal laws refer to laws that are true all the time. Historical contingency must therefore relate somehow to laws that *aren't* always true. Once again, strategic reading helps you simplify the structure and meaning of complex ideas.

KEYWORDS RAISE YOUR SCORE

You now have a good idea about what Keywords are, how to identify them, and what they tell you about the structure and meaning of a passage. This is very important, because they form the foundation of strategic reading. You may be worried at this point that circling the Keywords and thinking about the structure they provide will be too time consuming to be useful on test day. As with any other new skill that you learn, this one may not be easy at first. But with practice, you'll soon find that working with Keywords becomes a natural and automatic part of your approach to Reading Comprehension. And since Keywords clue you in to the most important ideas in the passage, mastery of Keywords will raise your LSAT score. I'll show you how in chapter 3.

---

[39]PrepTest 35, Sec 2, Passage 3

CHAPTER 3

BUILDING A ROADMAP

THE ROADMAP DEFINED
How Do You Get Where You're Going?

Imagine that you're in Dallas and you need to drive to Chicago. You're on a very tight schedule, and you need to get there as quickly as possible . . . and as luck would have it, you've never even been to Chicago before. How do you ensure a successful trip?

You probably know that Chicago is somewhere northeast of Dallas, so perhaps you could just start driving north, getting hints from whatever signs you happen to see on your way, and work out your route as you go. But this is clearly a flawed plan. You may or may not actually end up at your destination, and even if you do, you're not likely to make very good time. Imagine the anxiety you would feel if your were actually in this situation. You would never do this in real life, except as a last resort.

An alternative would be to get a detailed map of North America and consult it as you drive. This is a better approach, but it still has some problems. Certainly it may help you stay on course city by city as you make your way to Chicago, but it's also likely to contain a lot of distracting information that isn't directly relevant to your goal. It will likely present you with a number of different possible routes you could take, while providing little or no information about which route is the fastest. If you choose this solution you're probably going to reach your destination, but not as efficiently as you might like.

Now imagine what you almost certainly *would* do in this situation. You would probably use a GPS or an online navigation service that would show you precisely which route to take. You could specify that you want to take the fastest route available and be sure that the information you receive is accurate and up to date. In addition to detailed directions, you'll also get a roadmap displaying the specific route you wish to take. This is definitely the way to travel; you'll reach your destination, and you'll get there at top speed.

So the answer to the original question should be clear: To ensure a successful trip, you don't set off at random, and you don't consult useless information. You use a Roadmap.

Reading Without Direction

I'm sure you've already realized that the above example is illustrative of the way you should approach Reading Comprehension on the LSAT, but I'd like to break down the analogy a little before moving on.

The first approach I asked you to consider in the Chicago scenario was that of driving off in the general direction of your destination with no guidance except for a vague notion of where you think you should go. This is obviously a bad idea, and yet it is the approach that most of my students initially employ when faced with Reading Comprehension. I had one student in particular who, before starting her class, was absolutely convinced that it was impossible to complete all four passages in the alotted 35 minutes. It didn't take me long to discover why.

I observed her as she attempted to read a passage and answer its questions. She skimmed the passage, taking no notes, and then began to grapple with the questions. Each time she came to a new question she would go back to the passage and carefully re-read entire paragraphs from beginning to end. She often repeated this exercise for each answer choice. By the time she answered all of the questions nearly fifteen minutes had elapsed. Even if she answered every question correctly she would almost certainly have to guess at an equal number as time began to run out. It's no wonder she was frustrated.

When my students get into time trouble, it's usually because they aren't reading with any direction, and therefore are constantly lost. They're lost when they read the passage, they're lost when they read a question, and they're lost when they try to evaluate the answer choices. And since we know that the LSAT awards efficiency, being lost is big trouble. If this sounds like you, don't worry. In this chapter I'm going to show you how to take control of the passage and provide yourself with the guidance you need.

Reading Without a Goal

Think back to the second solution to the Chicago travel problem, referring to a detailed map of North America. In the context of the example, you can easily see why that's not the ideal solution. But once again, this is exactly the type of approach that unprepared test takers often use.

My students are very aware that after they read a passage, they're going to have to answer a series of questions based on its content. With that awareness comes a very strong desire to thoroughly understand everything in the passage. So their initial inclination is to read each sentence with great care, absorbing every example, parsing each jargon-laden sentence, struggling with all the concepts. If they don't understand something, they read it again and again until it makes sense. This is a time-consuming process, but it makes them feel prepared for anything the question set may happen to throw at them.

But a strange thing happens. Despite all that careful reading, they find they still don't really have a clear understanding of what the passage was all about. Questions about the author's opinions are challenging because those opinions got lost in the barrage of ideas they encountered. Most frustrating of all, when they try to answer questions about the very details they spent so much time reading, they find that they have to go right back to the passage and read them all over again. If they try to rely on memory, they lose points because their recollection of the material isn't as complete as they think it is. In short, test takers who try to read for total comprehension become mired in unimportant details, and as a result they waste time and they score fewer points.

If this sounds like you, take heart. You've already learned about the importance of Keywords, and you're using them to help you read more actively. Now you're ready to take your mastery of strategic reading to the next level.

Reading the Kaplan Way

Returning one final time to our Chicago trip, it's easy to see that the third solution, the one that you almost certainly came up with on your own, is clearly superior to the others. A specific, guided roadmap keeps you from wandering aimlessly. At the same time, it helps you stay focused on the goal and avoid wasteful digressions.

Most LSAT Reading Comprehension questions test your understanding of the major themes contained in the passage, but some simply ask for specific details. You therefore must read the passage in a very focused way. You've got to understand the big ideas, while at the same time knowing where crucial details can be found if you need them. Let me emphasize this extremely important concept: You absolutely do not have time to dwell on the details of the passage the first time you read, because when questions ask for them, you're going to have to revisit the passage and examine the relevant text anyway.

This brings me to the solution, which I introduced you to briefly in chapter 1. The test makers don't provide you with a Roadmap to guide you through the passage. So in this chapter, I'll show you how to create one yourself, and how it will help you score more points in less time.

BUILDING A ROADMAP

I'll begin with an experiment. Try reading this LSAT passage without taking any notes. Read as quickly as you are able.

Wherever the crime novels of P. D. James are discussed by critics, there is a tendency on the one hand to exaggerate her merits and on the other to castigate her as a genre writer who is getting above
(5) herself. Perhaps underlying the debate is that familiar, false opposition set up between different kinds of fiction, according to which enjoyable novels are held to be somehow slightly lowbrow, and a novel is not considered true literature unless it is a tiny bit dull.

(10) Those commentators who would elevate James's books to the status of high literature point to her painstakingly constructed characters, her elaborate settings, her sense of place, and her love of abstractions: notions about morality, duty, pain, and
(15) pleasure are never far from the lips of her police officers and murderers. Others find her pretentious and tiresome; an inverted snobbery accuses her of abandoning the time-honored conventions of the detective genre in favor of a highbrow literary style.
(20) The critic Harriet Waugh wants P. D. James to get on with "the more taxing business of laying a tricky trail and then fooling the reader"; Philip Oakes in *The Literary Review* groans, "Could we please proceed with the business of clapping the handcuffs on the
(25) killer?"

James is certainly capable of strikingly good writing. She takes immense trouble to provide her characters with convincing histories and passions. Her descriptive digressions are part of the pleasure of her
(30) books and give them dignity and weight. But it is equally true that they frequently interfere with the story; the patinas and aromas of a country kitchen receive more loving attention than does the plot itself. Her devices to advance the story can be shameless and
(35) thin, and it is often impossible to see how her detective arrives at the truth; one is left to conclude that the detective solves crimes through intuition. At this stage in her career P. D. James seems to be less interested in the specifics of detection than in her characters'
(40) vulnerabilities and perplexities.

However, once the rules of a chosen genre cramp creative thought, there is no reason why an able and interesting writer should accept them. In her latest book, there are signs that James is beginning to feel
(45) constrained by the crime-novel genre. Here her determination to leave areas of ambiguity in the solution of the crime and to distribute guilt among the murderer, victim, and bystanders points to a conscious rebellion against the traditional neatness of detective
(50) fiction. It is fashionable, though reprehensible, for one writer to prescribe to another. But perhaps the time has come for P. D. James to slide out of her handcuffs and stride into the territory of the mainstream novel.[1]

_____
[1]PrepTest 19, Sec 3, Passage 1

Now think about what you just read. Test your memory of the passage with a few questions. Can you describe the primary complaint leveled against James by her critics? Did the author agree or disagree with the critics? What was the primary purpose of the second paragraph of the passage?

Some of these questions may be easier to answer than others, but taken together, they present a daunting challenge. Your first instinct is probably to review the text of the passage to find the answers, but where do you start? The confusion that you experience when you read a passage quickly rather than efficiently is a liability to your LSAT score. Fortunately, there's a better way. It's time to build your first Roadmap. Building a good Roadmap is a natural extension of the thinking you apply when you seek out Keywords As you identify important ideas, jot down a couple of brief notes in the margins of the paragraph summarizing them. Your notes should include authorial opinion, key conclusions, and alternating points of view. I'm going to guide you through the process paragraph by paragraph.

Read the following excerpt, noting the circled Keywords and thinking about what they mean. The author begins by describing critics' different views of P.D. James's works. It's not unusual for the first paragraph of a passage to introduce conflicting ideas; they tend to form the basis for what is to follow. Since this is structurally important, jot down some brief notes in the margin of the paragraph summarizing the dichotomy:

Critics: Praise James or attack her

(Wherever) the crime novels of P. D. James are discussed by (critics,) there is a tendency (on the one) hand to exaggerate her merits and (on the other) to castigate her as a genre writer who is getting above
(5) herself. Perhaps (underlying) the debate is that familiar, (false) opposition set up (between) different kinds of fiction, (according to) which enjoyable novels are held to be somehow slightly lowbrow, (and) a novel is not considered true literature unless it is a tiny bit dull.[2]

Notice that the notes do not restate in detail information that is already in the passage; they simply point the way to it. You should follow this principle when building your own Roadmaps. In general, keep your annotations as concise as possible. Abbreviations and other forms of shorthand are useful, as long as you can clearly understand what you've written. Note also that I've indicated that it is the critics who are attacking or praising James as opposed to the author.

As you move on through the paragraph, you should pay particular attention to the opinion/emphasis keyword "false." The author tells you that the debate is based on a false opposition. This is *extremely* important, as it's your first clue about the author's attitude. You should annotate this as well.

---

[2]PrepTest 19, Sec 3, Passage 1

Critics: Praise
James or
attack her

Auth: False
opp.

(Wherever) the crime novels of P. D. James are discussed by (critics,) there is a tendency (on the one) hand to exaggerate her merits and (on the other) to castigate her as a genre writer who is getting above (5) herself. Perhaps (underlying) the debate is that familiar (false) opposition set up (between) different kinds of fiction, (according to) which enjoyable novels are held to be somehow slightly lowbrow, (and) a novel is not considered true literature unless it is a tiny bit dull.[3]

And with that, you've successfully Roadmapped paragraph 1. Take a moment to appreciate this accomplishment: When you write a Roadmap, you pare down an entire paragraph into a few words, and you give yourself exactly the guidance you need if a question directs you back to these concepts. On test day, this kind of guidance will improve both your timing and your accuracy.

Now read the next paragraph. Again, take note of the Keywords, but this time try to summarize the main ideas yourself before reading on.

(10) Those (commentators) who would (elevate) James's books to the status of high literature (point to) her painstakingly constructed characters, her elaborate settings, her sense of place, and her love of (abstractions:) notions about morality, duty, pain, and (15) pleasure are never far from the lips of her police officers and murderers. (Others) find her pretentious and tiresome; an inverted snobbery (accuses) her of abandoning the time-honored conventions of the detective genre (in favor of) a highbrow literary style. (20) The (critic) Harriet Waugh wants P. D. James to get on with "the more taxing business of laying a tricky trail and then fooling the reader"; Philip Oakes in *The Literary Review* (groans,) "Could we please proceed with the business of clapping the handcuffs on the (25) killer?"[4]

A good question to stay in the habit of asking yourself when you read is, "Why is the author telling me this?" You recall from the first paragraph that various critics are at odds with one another regarding James's work. All this paragraph does is flesh out that idea by giving examples. Should you attempt to memorize all of these examples? Absolutely not! Just note that if a question requires in-depth knowledge of the critics' opinions, this is the paragraph you should come to.

---

[3]PrepTest 19, Sec 3, Passage 1
[4]PrepTest 19, Sec 3, Passage 1

Critics:
opinions about
James

(10)   Those ⬭commentators⬭ who would ⬭elevate⬭ James's
books to the status of high literature ⬭point to⬭ her
painstakingly constructed characters, her elaborate
settings, her sense of place, and her love of
⬭abstractions:⬭ notions about morality, duty, pain, and
(15)   pleasure are never far from the lips of her police
officers and murderers. ⬭Others⬭ find her pretentious and
tiresome; an inverted snobbery ⬭accuses⬭ her of
abandoning the time-honored conventions of the
detective genre ⬭in favor⬭ of a highbrow literary style.
(20)   The ⬭critic⬭ Harriet Waugh wants P. D. James to get on
with "the more taxing business of laying a tricky trail
and then fooling the reader"; Philip Oakes in *The
Literary Review* ⬭groans,⬭ "Could we please proceed
with the business of clapping the handcuffs on the
(25)   killer?"[5]

You might be thinking, "Is that really all I should be writing down?" The answer: probably. All of my students have their own Roadmapping styles, and while there are good principles to follow, there are few definitive rules. For instance, perhaps you would rather write your Roadmap for paragraph two more like this:

Critics: who
like James

(10)   Those ⬭commentators⬭ who would ⬭elevate⬭ James's
books to the status of high literature ⬭point to⬭ her
painstakingly constructed characters, her elaborate
settings, her sense of place, and her love of
⬭abstractions:⬭ notions about morality, duty, pain, and
(15)   pleasure are never far from the lips of her police

Critics: who
dislike James

officers and murderers. ⬭Others⬭ find her pretentious and
tiresome; an inverted snobbery ⬭accuses⬭ her of
abandoning the time-honored conventions of the
detective genre ⬭in favor⬭ of a highbrow literary style.
(20)   The ⬭critic⬭ Harriet Waugh wants P. D. James to get on
with "the more taxing business of laying a tricky trail
and then fooling the reader"; Philip Oakes in *The
Literary Review* ⬭groans,⬭ "Could we please proceed
with the business of clapping the handcuffs on the
(25)   killer?"[6]

Is one way better than the other? Not really. As long as your Roadmap is clear, concise, accurate, and useful, you're doing it correctly.

---

[5]PrepTest 19, Sec 3, Passage 1
[6]PrepTest 19, Sec 3, Passage 1

Ready for paragraph three? As before, try to come up with your own notes as you read:

> James is certainly capable of (strikingly) good
> writing. She takes (immense) trouble to provide her
> characters with convincing histories and passions. Her
> descriptive digressions are part of the pleasure of her
> (30) books (and) give them dignity and weight. (But) it is
> equally true that they frequently interfere with the
> story; the patinas and aromas of a country kitchen
> receive more loving attention (than) does the plot itself.
> Her devices to advance the story can be (shameless) and
> (35) thin, (and) it is often impossible to see how her detective
> arrives at the truth; one is left to (conclude) that the
> detective solves crimes through intuition. At (this stage)
> in her career P. D. James seems to be (less) interested in
> the specifics of detection (than) in her characters'
> (40) vulnerabilities and perplexities.[7]

I hope you noticed right away whose opinion is presented in this paragraph. When the author speaks, it's time to pay attention. Has the author sided with one group of critics over the other? To the contrary, she's in agreement to some extent with both camps, noting toward the end of the paragraph that James's most recent work shows a preference for character development over plot.

> *Auth: James is*
> *striking writer*
>
> James is certainly capable of (strikingly) good
> writing. She takes (immense) trouble to provide her
> characters with convincing histories and passions. Her
> descriptive digressions are part of the pleasure of her
> (30) books (and) give them dignity and weight. (But) it is
> equally true that they frequently interfere with the
> story; the patinas and aromas of a country kitchen
> receive more loving attention (than) does the plot itself.
>
> *Sometimes bad*
> *for plot*
>
> Her devices to advance the story can be (shameless) and
> (35) thin, (and) it is often impossible to see how her detective
> arrives at the truth; one is left to conclude that the
> detective solves crimes through intuition. At (this stage)
> in her career P. D. James seems to be (less) interested in
> the specifics of detection (than) in her characters'
> (40) vulnerabilities and perplexities.[8]

Now you have a nice summary of the author's attitudes, and you know exactly where to do your research if you need to examine them in detail.

One more paragraph to go. Another common pattern you should expect to encounter in LSAT passages is a final paragraph that summarizes the author's primary viewpoint, sometimes going in directions you didn't necessarily see coming. The author ultimately supports James's

---

[7]PrepTest 19, Sec 3, Passage 1
[8]PrepTest 19, Sec 3, Passage 1

"rebellion" against the norms of the crime novel and even suggests that she should consider leaving it behind:

Auth: James
not limited by
genre

(However,) once the rules of a chosen genre cramp creative thought, there is (no reason) why an able and interesting writer should accept them. In her (latest)
(45) book, there are signs that James is beginning to (feel) constrained by the crime-novel genre. Here her (determination) to leave areas of ambiguity in the solution of the crime (and) to distribute guilt among the murderer, victim, and bystanders (points to) a conscious (rebellion) against the (traditional) neatness of detective
(50) fiction. It is fashionable, (though reprehensible,) for one writer to prescribe to another. (But) perhaps the time has come for P. D. James to slide out of her handcuffs (and) stride into the territory of the mainstream novel.[9]

Auth: James
maybe go mainstr.

Well done. You've just completed your first Roadmap. By thinking through the core ideas of every paragraph, you accomplish a number of goals: You give yourself points of reference, you elucidate the structure of the passage, and you solidify your own understanding of what the passage is saying. With careful practice, creating Roadmaps will become second nature to you, and in a moment I'll give you a drill to get some practice. But first, take a look at how a good Roadmap helps you to answer questions quickly and correctly:

3. The second paragraph serves primarily to

    (A) propose an alternative to two extreme opinions
         described earlier
    (B) present previously mentioned positions in greater
         detail
    (C) contradict an assertion cited previously
    (D) introduce a controversial interpretation
    (E) analyze a dilemma in greater depth[10]

This question type requires you to quickly summarize the purpose of the second paragraph. You need look no further than your Roadmap to predict the correct answer:

Critics: Praise
James or
attack her

Auth: False
opp.

(Wherever) the crime novels of P. D. James are discussed by (critics,) there is a tendency (on the one) hand to exaggerate her merits and (on the other) to castigate her as a genre writer who is getting above
(5) herself. Perhaps (underlying) the debate is that familiar, (false) opposition set up (between) different kinds of fiction, (according to) which enjoyable novels are held to be somehow slightly lowbrow, (and) a novel is not considered true literature unless it is a tiny bit dull.

---

[9]PrepTest 19, Sec 3, Passage 1
[10]PrepTest 19, Sec 3, Q 3

(10) Those commentators who would elevate James's
Critics: who
like James books to the status of high literature point to her
painstakingly constructed characters, her elaborate
settings, her sense of place, and her love of
abstractions; notions about morality, duty, pain, and
(15) pleasure are never far from the lips of her police
Critics: who officers and murderers. Others find her pretentious and
dislike James tiresome; an inverted snobbery accuses her of
abandoning the time-honored conventions of the
detective genre in favor of a highbrow literary style.
(20) The critic Harriet Waugh wants P. D. James to get on
with "the more taxing business of laying a tricky trail
and then fooling the reader"; Philip Oakes in *The
Literary Review* groans, "Could we please proceed
with the business of clapping the handcuffs on the
(25) killer?"

Auth: James James is certainly capable of strikingly good
very descriptive writing. She takes immense trouble to provide her
characters with convincing histories and passions. Her
descriptive digressions are part of the pleasure of her
(30) books and give them dignity and weight. But it is
equally true that they frequently interfere with the
story; the patinas and aromas of a country kitchen
receive more loving attention than does the plot itself.
Auth: Sometimes Her devices to advance the story can be shameless and
bad for plot (35) thin, and it is often impossible to see how her detective
arrives at the truth; one is left to conclude that the
detective solves crimes through intuition. At this stage
in her career P. D. James seems to be less interested in
the specifics of detection than in her characters'
(40) vulnerabilities and perplexities.

However, once the rules of a chosen genre cramp
Auth: James not creative thought, there is no reason why an able and
limited by genre interesting writer should accept them. In her latest
book, there are signs that James is beginning to feel
(45) constrained by the crime-novel genre. Here her
determination to leave areas of ambiguity in the
solution of the crime and to distribute guilt among the
murderer victim, and bystanders points to a conscious
rebellion against the traditional neatness of detective
(50) fiction. It is fashionable, though reprehensible, for one
Auth: James writer to prescribe to another. But perhaps the time has
maybe go mainstr. come for P. D. James to slide out of her handcuffs and
stride into the territory of the mainstream novel.[11]

---

[11]PrepTest 19, Sec 3, Passage 1

The Roadmap reminds you that this paragraph supplies examples of the critics mentioned in the first paragraph. Armed with this prediction, the correct answer must be choice (B). The Roadmap allows you to score this point in a matter of seconds. Try one more question:

2. The author refers to the "patinas and aromas of a country kitchen" (line 32) most probably in order to

   (A) illustrate James's gift for innovative phrasing
   (B) highlight James's interest in rural society
   (C) allow the reader to experience the pleasure of James's books
   (D) explain how James typically constructs her plots
   (E) exemplify James's preoccupation with descriptive writing[12]

At first you might think that the Roadmap isn't particularly useful in answering this question. After all, you've already got a specific line reference. But be careful: The test maker is asking you to explain *why* the author used this example, and this requires you to read for context. The Roadmap is exceptionally useful for providing such context:

Auth: James is
striking writer

James is certainly capable of strikingly good writing. She takes immense trouble to provide her characters with convincing histories and passions. Her descriptive digressions are part of the pleasure of her
(30) books and give them dignity and weight. But it is equally true that they frequently interfere with the story; the patinas and aromas of a country kitchen receive more loving attention than does the plot itself.

Auth:
Sometimes
bad for plot

Her devices to advance the story can be shameless and
(35) thin, and it is often impossible to see how her detective arrives at the truth; one is left to conclude that the detective solves crimes through intuition. At this stage in her career P. D. James seems to be less interested in the specifics of detection than in her characters'
(40) vulnerabilities and perplexities.[13]

At the point in which the quote from the question appears, you noted that the author was agreeing with the critics who find James overly expressive. A quick glance at the surrounding text confirms this prediction, and you should confidently choose choice (E), the correct answer.

Now that you understand how to construct a Roadmap and how to put it to good use, it's time for some practice.

---

[12]PrepTest 19, Sec 3, Q 2
[13]PrepTest 19, Sec 3, Passage 1

DRILL: CONSTRUCTING A ROADMAP

Part 1: Read the following passage, circling Keywords as you go. As you discover major ideas and key examples, note them in your Roadmap. When you've finished, carefully compare your Roadmap to the one I provide in the explanations. Take your time, and don't worry if this first Roadmap is a little tough to build. You'll have plenty of opportunities to practice as you continue to prepare for the LSAT.

Even in the midst of its resurgence as a vital tradition, many sociologists have viewed the current form of the powwow, a ceremonial gathering of native Americans, as a sign that tribal culture is in decline.
(5) Focusing on the dances and rituals that have recently come to be shared by most tribes, they suggest that an intertribal movement is now in ascension and claim the inevitable outcome of this tendency is the eventual dissolution of tribes and the complete assimilation of
(10) native Americans into Euroamerican society. Proponents of this "Pan-Indian" theory point to the greater frequency of travel and communication between reservations, the greater urbanization of native Americans, and, most recently, their increasing
(15) politicization in response to common grievances as the chief causes of the shift toward intertribalism.

Indeed, the rapid diffusion of dance styles, outfits, and songs from one reservation to another offers compelling evidence that intertribalism has been
(20) increasing. However, these sociologists have failed to note the concurrent revitalization of many traditions unique to individual tribes. Among the Lakota, for instance, the Sun Dance was revived, after a forty-year hiatus, during the 1950's. Similarly, the Black Legging
(25) Society of the Kiowa and the Hethuska Society of the Ponca—both traditional groups within their respective tribes—have gained new popularity. Obviously, a more complex societal shift is taking place than the theory of Pan-Indianism can account for.

(30) An examination of the theory's underpinnings may be critical at this point, especially given that native Americans themselves chafe most against the Pan-Indian classification. Like other assimilationist theories with which it is associated, the Pan-Indian view is
(35) predicated upon an a priori assumption about the nature of cultural contact: that upon contact minority societies immediately begin to succumb in every respect—biologically, linguistically, and culturally—to the majority society. However, there is no evidence
(40) that this is happening to native American groups.

Yet the fact remains that intertribal activities are a major facet of native American culture today. Certain dances at powwows, for instance, are announced as intertribal, others as traditional. Likewise, speeches
(45) given at the beginnings of powwows are often delivered in English, while the prayer that follows is usually spoken in a native language. Cultural borrowing is, of course, old news. What is important to note is the conscious distinction native Americans
(50) make between tribal and intertribal tendencies.

Tribalism, although greatly altered by modern history, remains a potent force among native Americans: It forms a basis for tribal identity, and aligns music and dance with other social and cultural
(55) activities important to individual tribes. Intertribal activities, on the other hand, reinforce native American identity along a broader front, where this identity is directly threatened by outside influences.[14]

---

[14]PrepTest 25, Sec 1, Passage 3

Answer Explanations follow on the next page.

Explanations

Compare your Roadmap to mine, paragraph by paragraph:

Soc: gatherings mean tribal decline

(Even) in the midst of its (resurgence) as a vital tradition, many (sociologists) have viewed the current form of the powwow, a ceremonial gathering of native Americans, (as a sign) that tribal culture is in decline.
(5) (Focusing) on the dances and rituals that have (recently) come to be shared by most tribes, they (suggest) that an intertribal movement is now in ascension and (claim) the (inevitable) outcome of this tendency is the eventual dissolution of tribes and the complete assimilation of
(10) native Americans into Euroamerican society.

Pan-Indian theory, evidence

(Proponents) of this "Pan-Indian" theory (point to) the greater frequency of travel and communication between reservations, the greater urbanization of native Americans, (and,) most (recently,) their increasing
(15) politicization in (response) to common grievances as the chief causes of the shift toward intertribalism.[15]

This first paragraph is a little wordy, but there were plenty of Keywords to guide you. The author is describing the proponents of a "Pan-Indian" theory that suggests tribal culture is in decline. Notice that the author is using several different terms to describe the same idea: "Pan-Indian" theory and "intertribalism" in particular. I hope you noted that the last sentence of this paragraph gives a list of reasons why the proponets support this theory; such key evidence may be the subject of questions.

Auth: Intertribalism on rise

(Indeed,) the rapid diffusion of dance styles, outfits, and songs from one reservation to another offers (compelling evidence) that intertribalism has been
(20) increasing. (However,) these (sociologists) have (failed) to note the concurrent revitalization of many traditions

Unique traditions rising too

unique to individual tribes. (Among) the Lakota, for (instance,) the Sun Dance was revived, after a forty-year hiatus, during the 1950's. (Similarly,) the Black Legging
(25) Society of the Kiowa and the Hethuska Society of the Ponca—(both) traditional groups within their respective

Auth: P.I.T doesn't explain

tribes—have gained (new popularity.) (Obviously,) a more complex societal shift is taking place (than) the theory of Pan-Indianism can account for.[16]

The Keyword "Indeed" at the beginning of this paragraph signals continuation, but you should really focus on the text following "However" in the second sentence. This contrast alerts you to the author's true intent: To indicate that individual tribes have revitalized their own traditions, a fact that the sociologists from paragraph 1 have overlooked. (I've used the abbreviation P.I.T. to refer to the sociologists' Pan-Indian Theory. Remember, shorthand can streamline the

---

[15]PrepTest 25, Sec 1, Passage 3
[16]PrepTest 25, Sec 1, Passage 3

Roadmapping process as long as it doesn't interfere with clarity.) This idea is reinforced in the final sentence, introduced by the emphasis Keyword "Obviously."

Auth: must
examine theory

(30)   An examination of the theory's underpinnings may
be critical at this point, especially given that native
Americans themselves chafe most against the Pan-
Indian classification. Like other assimilationist theories
with which it is associated, the Pan-Indian view is
(35) predicated upon an a priori assumption about the nature
of cultural contact: that upon contact minority

Theory based on   societies immediately begin to succumb in every
wrong assump.   respect—biologically, linguistically, and culturally—to
the majority society. However, there is no evidence
(40) that this is happening to native American groups.[17]

Look at the profusion of emphasis Keywords that begin this sentence: A look at the theory is "critical," "especially" because native Americans aren't fans of it. When the author is this clear about the intent of the paragraph you should start Roadmapping right away. Don't worry about potentially unfamiliar terms like "assimilationist" and "a priori." Remember, you're not reading for total comprehension, just the central ideas. When you encounter complex language like this, sift though it for ideas that are more plainly stated. Following the emphasis Keyword "immediately" you get a nice, simple summary of what the author is really getting at: The sociologists think that all minority cultures immediately succumb to majority cultures. And the author is quick to point out that this isn't happening in the case of the native Americans discussed in the passage. Your passage map should clearly point out these conflicting opinions.

Auth: Intertribal
act. still
important

Yet the fact remains that intertribal activities are a
major facet of native American culture today. Certain
dances at powwows, for instance, are announced as
intertribal, others as traditional. Likewise, speeches
(45) given at the beginnings of powwows are often
delivered in English, while the prayer that follows is
usually spoken in a native language. Cultural

Tribal and   borrowing is, of course, old news. What is important to
Intertribal   note is the conscious distinction native Americans
distinct   (50) make between tribal and intertribal tendencies.[18]

The author immediately prepares us for a shift with "Yet" at the beginning. Most of what follows are examples of intertribal practices. Once again, the author provides emphasis words to highlight the main point: "What is important to note" couldn't be any clearer. Take the author's advice and note this important information, the distinction between tribal and intertribal activites.

---

[17]PrepTest 25, Sec 1, Passage 3
[18]PrepTest 25, Sec 1, Passage 3

Auth: Both are
important

Tribalism, (although greatly altered) by modern
history, (remains) a (potent) force among native
Americans: It forms a (basis) for tribal identity, (and)
aligns music and dance with other social and cultural
(55)   activities (important) to individual tribes. Intertribal
activities, on the (other hand,) (reinforce) native American
identity along a broader front, (where) this identity is
directly threatened by outside influences.[19]

The passage wraps up nicely with a summary of the dichotomy that the author has been examining. While tribalism remains a "potent" force in native American communities, "on the other hand" intertribal communities serve an important role as well. If you found this to be a predictable ending for the passage, congratulations! You'll find as you develop your strategic reading skills that most LSAT passages *are* very predictable in structure. I'll elaborate on this idea more in chapter 6.

Part 2: You've completed your first Roadmap, and that's an important accomplishment. Now it's time to put it to use. Answer the following selected questions, using your Roadmap to guide you back to the passage as necessary. *Do not rely on your memory of the text.* This is a bad habit and will rob you of crucial points if you adopt it. Read each question carefully, determine what it is asking, and do your research. As always, complete explanations follow.

---

[19]PrepTest 25, Sec 1, Passage 3

17. The primary function of the third paragraph is to
   (A) search for evidence to corroborate the basic assumption of the theory of Pan-Indianism
   (B) demonstrate the incorrectness of the theory of Pan-Indianism by pointing out that native American groups themselves disagree with the theory
   (C) explain the origin of the theory of Pan-Indianism by showing how it evolved from other assimilationist theories
   (D) examine several assimilationist theories in order to demonstrate that they rest on a common assumption
   (E) criticize the theory of Pan-Indianism by pointing out that it rests upon an assumption for which there is no supporting evidence[20]

18. Which one of the following most accurately describes the author's attitude toward the theory of Pan-Indianism?
   (A) critical of its tendency to attribute political motives to cultural practices
   (B) discomfort at its negative characterization of cultural borrowing by native Americans
   (C) hopeful about its chances for preserving tribal culture
   (D) offended by its claim that assimilation is a desirable consequence of cultural contact
   (E) skeptical that it is a complete explanation of recent changes in native American society[21]

20. Which one of the following situations most clearly illustrates the phenomenon of intertribalism, as that phenomenon is described in the passage?
   (A) a native American tribe in which a number of powerful societies attempt to prevent the revival of a traditional dance
   (B) a native American tribe whose members attempt to learn the native languages of several other tribes
   (C) a native American tribe whose members attempt to form a political organization in order to redress several grievances important to that tribe
   (D) a native American tribe in which a significant percentage of the members have forsaken their tribal identity and become assimilated into Euroamerican society
   (E) a native American tribe whose members often travel to other parts of the reservation in order to visit friends and relatives[22]

---

[20]PrepTest 25, Sec 1, Q 17

[21]PrepTest 25, Sec 1, Q 18

[22]PrepTest 25, Sec 1, Q 20

Explanations

17. **(E)**

The primary function of the third paragraph is to
(A) search for evidence to corroborate the basic assumption of the theory of Pan-Indianism
(B) demonstrate the incorrectness of the theory of Pan-Indianism by pointing out that native American groups themselves disagree with the theory
(C) explain the origin of the theory of Pan-Indianism by showing how it evolved from other assimilationist theories
(D) examine several assimilationist theories in order to demonstrate that they rest on a common assumption
(E) criticize the theory of Pan-Indianism by pointing out that it rests upon an assumption for which there is no supporting evidence[23]

When a question asks you to provide the primary purpose of a paragraph, the answer always lies right in the Roadmap. A review of your notes should give you a good prediction for the correct answer: The author critiqued the sociologists' theory and demonstrated that it didn't really apply to Native Americans. That prediction matches the correct answer, choice (E), spot-on. Choices (A) and (C) are both out of scope; your Roadmap reminds you that this paragraph is written to critique, not to explain or provide evidence, and in any case choice (A) says that the author gives support to the Pan-Indian theory, which never happens. Choice (B) wrongly states that the author demonstrates the incorrectness of Pan-Indianism, which does not occur in the third paragraph. Finally, choice (D) also wanders out of scope. The author's goal is to critique Pan-Indianism, not to examine numerous theories.

18. **(E)**

Which one of the following most accurately describes the author's attitude toward the theory of Pan-Indianism?
(A) critical of its tendency to attribute political motives to cultural practices
(B) discomfort at its negative characterization of cultural borrowing by native Americans
(C) hopeful about its chances for preserving tribal culture
(D) offended by its claim that assimilation is a desirable consequence of cultural contact
(E) skeptical that it is a complete explanation of recent changes in native American society[24]

Where does your Roadmap tell you to look for the author's attitude toward Pan-Indianism? The second paragraph introduced authorial point of view. Keywords should guide you right back

---

[23]PrepTest 25, Sec 1, Q 17
[24]PrepTest 25, Sec 1, Q 18

to lines 27–29 in order to find a good summary: Something more complex is happening than the Pan-Indian theory can account for. Going to the choices, notice that (A), (B), (C), and (D) all bring outside ideas into the passage; they are all out of scope. Only correct choice (E) remains, and it matches your prediction perfectly by pointing out that Pan-Indianism is incomplete.

20. **(B)**

Which one of the following situations most clearly illustrates the phenomenon of intertribalism, as that phenomenon is described in the passage?

(A) a native American tribe in which a number of powerful societies attempt to prevent the revival of a traditional dance

(B) a native American tribe whose members attempt to learn the native languages of several other tribes

(C) a native American tribe whose members attempt to form a political organization in order to redress several grievances important to that tribe

(D) a native American tribe in which a significant percentage of the members have forsaken their tribal identity and become assimilated into Euroamerican society

(E) a native American tribe whose members often travel to other parts of the reservation in order to visit friends and relatives[25]

This question asks you to provide an illustration of intertribalism *as it is described in the passage.* Your Roadmap may have guided you either to paragraph one or two, and you can find similar definitions in either location: Intertribalism involves the sharing of cultural traditions among different tribes. Which answer choice describes this? Only the correct answer, choice (B). Choice (A) introduces the completely unsupported notion of the suppression of cultural revival. Choice (C) is a distortion of what the passage is truly saying; while political action is mentioned at the end of the first paragraph, it is presented as evidence that the Pan-Indian theory may be true, not as a definition of intertribalism. Choices (D) and (E) are incorrect for the same reason, presenting the sociologists' evidence for their theory.

Even if you struggled with these questions, be sure to notice that each correct answer was supported by text from the passage and that your Roadmap provided you with an efficient way to sort through the information.

ROADMAPPING RULES OF THUMB

Earlier in this chapter I mentioned that all of my students Roadmap their passages a little bit differently. It will almost certainly take a little experimentation to learn exactly what

---

[25]PrepTest 25, Sec 1, Q 20

information to put in your Roadmap and how to write it. That said, there are a few good general principles you should follow.

Keep It Simple

Your Roadmap will only be useful insofar as it makes the passage easier to navigate. If you include too many details, you begin to defeat the purpose of having a Roadmap at all, and you'll find yourself in one of the bad situations I presented to you at the beginning of this chapter. As an illustration, take another look at this paragraph:

Auth: James is striking writer

James is certainly capable of (strikingly) good writing. She takes (immense) trouble to provide her characters with convincing histories and passions. Her descriptive digressions are part of the pleasure of her (30) books (and) give them dignity and weight. (But) it is equally true that they frequently interfere with the story; the patinas and aromas of a country kitchen receive more loving attention (than) does the plot itself.

Auth: Sometimes bad for plot (35)

Her devices to advance the story can be (shameless) and thin, (and) it is often impossible to see how her detective arrives at the truth; one is left to conclude that the detective solves crimes through intuition. At (this stage) in her career P. D. James seems to be (less) interested in the specifics of detection (than) in her characters' (40) vulnerabilities and perplexities.[26]

Remember that this paragraph is composed mostly of details. You were able to sum up its purpose in just a few words. But what if your Roadmap looked more like this?

James writes strikingly

James is certainly capable of (strikingly) good writing. She takes (immense) trouble to provide her characters with convincing histories and passions. Her

characters w/ stories give (30) *dignity*

descriptive digressions are part of the pleasure of her books (and) give them dignity and weight. (But) it is equally true that they frequently interfere with the story; the patinas and aromas of a country kitchen

Kitchen vs. plot/ story too thin

receive more loving attention (than) does the plot itself. Her devices to advance the story can be (shameless) and (35) thin, (and) it is often impossible to see how her detective arrives at the truth; one is left to conclude that the

crimes solved by intuition / char. more than plot

detective solves crimes through intuition. At (this stage) in her career P. D. James seems to be (less) interested in the specifics of detection (than) in her characters' (40) vulnerabilities and perplexities.[27]

This Roadmap restates practically everything that the passage already says. Your goal isn't to rewrite the passage, a time-consuming and wasteful approach. Trust in a simple Roadmap, and remember that you've still got all those Keywords to help you narrow down your search

---

[26]PrepTest 19, Sec 3, Passage 1
[27]PrepTest 19, Sec 3, Passage 1

to a specific detail should you need it. Keywords are the foundation of your Roadmap, and you should use both tools together when answering the questions.

Note Important Examples

The Roadmap's primary goal is to allow you to see, at a glance, each paragraph's main ideas. But if the paragraph contains emphasized supporting examples you can call attention to them with a couple of simple annotations, like this:

```
                           H. L. A. Hart's The Concept of Law is still the
Hart's theory of      clearest and most persuasive statement of both the
hard cases    (10)    standard theory of hard cases and the standard
                      theory of law on which it rests. For Hart, the law
                      consists of legal rules formulated in general terms;
Core and              these terms he calls "open textured," which means
penumbra →            that they contain a "core" of settled meaning and a
              (15)    "penumbra" or "periphery" where their meaning is
                      not determinate. For example, suppose an
                      ordinance prohibits the use of vehicles in a park.
Ex: Vehicle →         "Vehicle" has a core of meaning which includes
                      cars and motorcycles. But, Hart claims, other
              (20)    vehicles, such as bicycles, fall within the peripheral
                      meaning of "vehicle," so that law does not
                      establish whether they are prohibited. There will
                      always be cases not covered by the core meaning of
Ex is legally         legal terms within existing laws; Hart considers
indeterm.     (25)    these cases to be legally indeterminate. Since courts
                      cannot decide such cases on legal grounds, they
                      must consider nonlegal (for example, moral and
                      political) grounds, and thereby exercise judicial
                      discretion to make, rather than apply, law.[28]
```

The Roadmap doesn't actually restate the key example or attempt to break it down. It simply provides you with a simple way to find this part of the text in case you need it. If it doesn't always seem clear to you which examples are most likely to show up in the questions, never fear; with practice and close attention to Keywords of emphasis the distinction will become clearer, and this is a subject that I'll revisit in future chapters.

Denote Differing Points of View

You know that the author's voice is of paramount importance in any LSAT passage, but other viewpoints are likely to be tested as well. You've already learned to circle Keywords that indicate shifting points of view. Now you should get into the habit of denoting point of view in your Roadmap as well:

---

[28]PrepTest 17, Sec 4, Passage 2

Diff. between
groups

(30)   To illustrate the difference between biologists
favoring universal, deterministic laws of evolutionary
development and those leaving room for historical
contingency, consider two favorite statements of
philosophers (both of which appear, at first sight, to be

Ex of universal
law

(35)   universal assertions): "All planets move in ellipses"
and "All swans are white." The former is truly
universal because it applies not only to those planets
that actually do exist, but also to those that could
exist—for the shape of planetary orbits is a necessary

Bio Determ:
swans =
universal

(40)   consequence of the laws governing the motion of
objects in a gravitational field.
        Biological determinists would say that "All swans
are white" is universal in the same way, since, if all
swans were white, it would be because the laws of

(45)   natural selection make it impossible for swans to be
otherwise: natural selection favors those

Bio non-determ:
swans = historical

characteristics that increase the average rate of
offspring production, and so traits that maximize
flexibility and the ability to manipulate nature will

(50)   eventually appear. Nondeterminist biologists would
deny this, saying that "swans" is merely the name of a
finite collection of historical objects that may happen

Auth: undecided

all to be white but not of necessity. The history of
evolutionary theory has been the history of the struggle

(55)   between these two views of swans.[29]

In these two paragraphs, we have three separate voices. The determinist biologists are discussed in the first paragraph, nondeterminist biologists take the floor in the second, and the author summarizes the debate in the final sentence. The test makers will reward you for recognizing and differentiating the different opinions present in the passage; one of the easiest ways to keep track of them is to clearly mark them in your Roadmap.

Strategic Reading Requires a Roadmap

I'll close this chapter by encouraging you to Roadmap every single passage you read in your practice from now until test day. Creating Roadmaps may feel awkward and time-consuming at first, and this is to be expected. As you become more proficient with this skill, it will become second nature to you. Since everyone maps a little differently, don't be alarmed if the Roadmaps you create aren't exactly like the ones you see in Kaplan's answers and explanations. Getting the major ideas down on paper is the most important thing.

When you're ready, proceed to chapter 4, where your Roadmapping skills will come in handy once again.

---

[29]PrepTest 35, Sec 2, Passage 3

CHAPTER 4

TOPIC, SCOPE, PURPOSE, AND MAIN IDEA

Now that you understand the importance of Keywords and have learned how to Roadmap passages, you are almost fully conversant with Step 1 of Kaplan's Method for Reading Comprehension. I'd like to congratulate you for making it this far. It isn't necessarily easy to change the way you read, but strategic reading isn't just useful on the LSAT—it's indispensable.

In this chapter, I'm going to reintroduce you to your final task when reading a passage strategically. After you've created your Roadmap, you should think through four key attributes that you will use to describe the passage: Topic, Scope, Purpose, and Main Idea. Put simply, every passage can be defined in terms of these four ideas, and knowing them will lead you directly to correct answers—and a higher score—while helping you steer clear of wrong answer traps.

TOPIC AND SCOPE

I'll start by introducing the two more general ideas, Topic and Scope. These are two fairly generalized descriptions of the passage, and over the years I've seen far too many students fail to grasp their importance. Because I don't want you to make that mistake, I'm going to define each of these important concepts and explain why understanding them will improve your LSAT score.

Topic: Broad Subject Area

Every passage you read addresses a generally defined Topic. The Topic of a passage is simply the broad, general subject that the passage describes. The author's Topic is usually very easy to determine, and it is generally obvious by the time you've finished reading the first paragraph. Take another look at the first paragraph from the P. D. James passage:

Critics: Praise James or attack her

Auth: False opp.

Wherever the crime novels of P. D. James are discussed by critics, there is a tendency on the one hand to exaggerate her merits and on the other to castigate her as a genre writer who is getting above
(5) herself. Perhaps underlying the debate is that familiar false opposition set up between different kinds of fiction, according to which enjoyable novels are held to be somehow slightly lowbrow, and a novel is not considered true literature unless it is a tiny bit dull.[1]

Once you've read this paragraph strategically, there's little doubt that the passage is going to explore some aspect of James's work. That's as far as you need to go in determining the Topic; the only real rule to follow is to keep it very general. For this passage the Topic is simply the works of P. D. James.

Look at another opening paragraph from the previous chapter and try to determine the Topic of the passage:

Soc: gatherings mean tribal decline

Pan-Indian theory, evidence

Even in the midst of its resurgence as a vital tradition, many sociologists have viewed the current form of the powwow, a ceremonial gathering of native Americans, as a sign that tribal culture is in decline.
(5) Focusing on the dances and rituals that have recently come to be shared by most tribes, they suggest that an intertribal movement is now in ascension and claim the inevitable outcome of this tendency is the eventual dissolution of tribes and the complete assimilation of
(10) native Americans into Euroamerican society. Proponents of this "Pan-Indian" theory point to the greater frequency of travel and communication between reservations, the greater urbanization of native Americans, and, most recently, their increasing
(15) politicization in response to common grievances as the chief causes of the shift toward intertribalism.[2]

In this paragraph, many ideas are presented to you: the powwow, the "Pan-Indian" theory, and intertribalism. Fortunately, with a good Roadmap you've cut through some of the jargon. Just as with the last exercise, keep the Topic very broad. Hopefully you came up with something along the lines of "Native American culture" or "theories about tribal life." These two topics

---

[1]PrepTest 19, Sec 3, Passage 1
[2]PrepTest 25, Sec 1, Passage 3

may seem very different, but they're both perfectly good descriptions of the broad subject that the author will go on to address in the passage.

Given the very general nature of the Topic, you may already be wondering why you should bother thinking about it at all. The primary reason is that the Topic guides you naturally to the Scope, and as I will show you, knowing the Scope of the passage is crucial to understanding the passage.

Scope: The Author's Focus

The Scope of the passage can be defined in a couple of ways, and I'll describe them both in this section. Put plainly, the Scope of the passage is the narrower area of specific interest within the Topic that the author wishes to explore. Returning to the P. D. James passage:

Critics: Praise James or attack her

Auth: False opp.

Critics who like James

Critics who dislike James

(1) Wherever the crime novels of P. D. James are discussed by critics, there is a tendency on the one hand to exaggerate her merits and on the other to castigate her as a genre writer who is getting above
(5) herself. Perhaps underlying the debate is that familiar false opposition set up between different kinds of fiction, according to which enjoyable novels are held to be somehow slightly lowbrow, and a novel is not considered true literature unless it is a tiny bit dull.
(10) Those commentators who would elevate James's books to the status of high literature point to her painstakingly constructed characters, her elaborate settings, her sense of place, and her love of abstractions: notions about morality, duty, pain, and
(15) pleasure are never far from the lips of her police officers and murderers. Others find her pretentious and tiresome; an inverted snobbery accuses her of abandoning the time-honored conventions of the detective genre in favor of a highbrow literary style.
(20) The critic Harriet Waugh wants P. D. James to get on with "the more taxing business of laying a tricky trail and then fooling the reader"; Philip Oakes in *The Literary Review* groans, "Could we please proceed with the business of clapping the handcuffs on the
(25) killer?"[3]

I've presented the first two paragraphs this time because, while the Scope can often be gleaned from the first paragraph alone, you'll sometimes need to read a bit further before it becomes clear. Earlier I identified the Topic of this passage as the works of P. D. James. As you dig a little deeper into the passage, it becomes clear that the author's focus is not on the works in general, but on the various criticisms that have been leveled against them. That's the Scope: criticisms of James's work.

---

[3]PrepTest 19, Sec 3, Passage 1

Another way to think about the Scope is to ask yourself, "What question about the Topic is the author interested in answering?" If you think about it this way, you might define the Scope as "What are some common criticisms of James's work?" or "Are James's critics correct in their views?" The second of these two questions is a bit more specific than the first, but by the end of the passage you definitely know that the author evaluates the critics' position. This raises an important point: You may make a prediction about the author's Scope toward the beginning of the passage only to revise it as you learn more about the author's primary motives. This is perfectly fine. The further you read into a passage, the more clearly defined the Scope will become.

As I hinted at above, knowing the Scope of the passage is of immediate pragmatic value to you on test day. The reason is simple: Many of the incorrect answers you encounter on the LSAT will be wrong because they fall *outside the author's Scope*. As a demonstration, look carefully at the following answer choices removed from their associated question:

(A) Critics of literature must acknowledge that they are less talented than creators of literature.

(B) Critics should hesitate to disparage popular authors.

(C) P. D. James's novels should focus less on characters from the English landed gentry.

(D) Detective fiction should be content to remain an unambitious literary genre.

(E) P. D. James should be less fastidious about portraying violence.[4]

Examine each answer choice and try to determine whether it falls within the author's Scope. Choice (A) does mention critics, but it isn't discussing their individual criticisms, but rather their own talent or lack thereof. It is likely to be out of scope. Choice (B) doesn't really address the critics' views either, instead suggesting that they shouldn't be critics at all. Choice (C) does mention a specific criticism of James, but take a moment to tighten the Scope by reviewing the actual claims made by the critics: That James is either too highbrow as a writer or too lowbrow. Choice (C) therefore is out of Scope. Skipping ahead to choice (E): Once again, this is not one of the criticisms that the author explores, placing choice (E) out of Scope, too.

What's left? Only choice (D) is within the author's Scope. It addresses a specific criticism mentioned in the passage, and it matches the passage's established dichotomy of highbrow literature vs. popular genre writing. Choice (D) must therefore be the right answer.

---

[4]PrepTest 19, Sec 3, Q 7

Just for context, take a look at the entire question:

7. The author characterizes the position of some critics as "inverted snobbery" (line 17) because they hold which one of the following views?

    (A) Critics of literature must acknowledge that they are less talented than creators of literature.
    (B) Critics should hesitate to disparage popular authors.
    (C) P. D. James's novels should focus less on characters from the English landed gentry.
    (D) Detective fiction should be content to remain an unambitious literary genre.
    (E) P. D. James should be less fastidious about portraying violence.[5]

I want to be very clear about something: This exercise is in no way meant to suggest that on test day you should answer the questions using this process of elimination. To the contrary, as you advance through this book and learn more about Steps 2–5 of the Kaplan Method, you will find that it is generally possible to know exactly what the right answer will look like before you evaluate the choices, which is a much more efficient approach to the questions. Regardless, adherence to the author's Scope remains a powerful method of discerning which choices are possible candidates for selection and which should be eliminated immediately. It also gives you a focused approach to the passage, making you less likely to misunderstand the author's Purpose.

Purpose: Why Is the Author Writing This?

As you reach the end of a passage, your careful attention to structure should give you a clear understanding of the author's motivations. When defining the Purpose of the passage, your task is to summarize each of the author's goals as they relate to the structure of the passage as a whole. A demonstration will probably make this concept easier to understand. Take a moment to review the full James passage:

Critics: Praise James or attack her

(Wherever) the crime novels of P. D. James are discussed by (critics,) there is a tendency (on the one) hand to exaggerate her merits and (on the other) to castigate her as a genre writer who is getting above

(5)   herself. Perhaps (underlying) the debate is that familiar,

Auth: False opp.

(false) opposition set up (between) different kinds of fiction, (according to) which enjoyable novels are held to be somehow slightly lowbrow, (and) a novel is not considered true literature unless it is a tiny bit dull.

---

[5]PrepTest 19, Sec 3, Q 7

Critics who
like James

(10)   Those commentators who would elevate James's
books to the status of high literature point to her
painstakingly constructed characters, her elaborate
settings, her sense of place, and her love of
abstractions; notions about morality, duty, pain, and
(15) pleasure are never far from the lips of her police

Critics who
dislike James

officers and murderers. Others find her pretentious and
tiresome; an inverted snobbery accuses her of
abandoning the time-honored conventions of the
detective genre in favor of a highbrow literary style.
(20)   The critic Harriet Waugh wants P. D. James to get on
with "the more taxing business of laying a tricky trail
and then fooling the reader"; Philip Oakes in *The
Literary Review* groans, "Could we please proceed
with the business of clapping the handcuffs on the
(25) killer?"

Auth: James
very descriptive

James is certainly capable of strikingly good
writing. She takes immense trouble to provide her
characters with convincing histories and passions. Her
descriptive digressions are part of the pleasure of her
(30) books and give them dignity and weight. But it is
equally true that they frequently interfere with the
story; the patinas and aromas of a country kitchen
receive more loving attention than does the plot itself.

Auth: Sometimes
bad for plot

Her devices to advance the story can be shameless and
(35) thin, and it is often impossible to see how her detective
arrives at the truth; one is left to conclude that the
detective solves crimes through intuition. At this stage
in her career P. D. James seems to be less interested in
the specifics of detection than in her characters'
(40) vulnerabilities and perplexities.

Auth: James not
limited by genre

However, once the rules of a chosen genre cramp
creative thought, there is no reason why an able and
interesting writer should accept them. In her latest
book, there are signs that James is beginning to feel
(45) constrained by the crime-novel genre. Here her
determination to leave areas of ambiguity in the
solution of the crime and to distribute guilt among the
murderer victim, and bystanders points to a conscious
rebellion against the traditional neatness of detective

Auth: James
maybe go mainstr.

(50) fiction. It is fashionable, though reprehensible, for one
writer to prescribe to another. But perhaps the time has
come for P. D. James to slide out of her handcuffs and
stride into the territory of the mainstream novel.[6]

To define the Purpose of this passage, review your Roadmap carefully and ask of each paragraph, "Why did the author write this? What was the intended goal?" Then summarize your thoughts in a brief sentence. You should work through it like this:

Paragraph 1: The author begins by describing a debate that surrounds the works of P. D. James.
Paragraph 2: She then describes several specific criticisms of James's work.

---

[6]PrepTest 19, Sec 3, Passage 1

Paragraph 3: She acknowledges that there is some legitimacy in the critics' claims.

Paragraph 4: She suggests that James's writing surpasses the restrictions of her chosen genre.

Summarizing the entire passage structure is very easy to do once you've become proficient at Roadmapping , which is another reason why you should continue to practice and perfect that vital skill. Now all you need to do is combine those statements to come up with the author's Purpose: to examine several criticisms of a writer and to suggest that the writer rise above those criticisms.

Notice that I've used simple, general language as well as specific action verbs in describing the Purpose of the passage: The author wrote to examine, to describe, to suggest. These are the kinds of words you should use as well. In fact, you'll find that certain common actions will show up again and again as you continue to practice. LSAT passages are very predictable and the range of possible motivations for their authors isn't terribly wide. Here are some common examples. The author may write to:

- Describe a theory or idea
- Explain a phenomenon
- Compare one explanation to another
- Support a given theory
- Refute a claim made about an artist's work
- Defend an assumption against critics

Again, because the passages are limited in Scope, there are only so many Purposes that an author can pursue. This is great news because it demonstrates that no passage will ever be too complex to summarize in a sentence or two. For practice, take another look at the Intertribalism passage and try to define its primary Purpose using the process I just described.

Soc: gatherings mean tribal decline

(Even) in the midst of its (resurgence) as a vital tradition, many (sociologists) have viewed the current form of the powwow, a ceremonial gathering of native Americans, (as a sign) that tribal culture is in decline.
(5) (Focusing) on the dances and rituals that have (recently) come to be shared by most tribes, they (suggest) that an intertribal movement is now in ascension and (claim) the (inevitable) outcome of this tendency is the eventual dissolution of tribes and the complete assimilation of
(10) native Americans into Euroamerican society.

Pan-Indian theory, evidence

(Proponents) of this "Pan-Indian" theory (point to) the greater frequency of travel and communication between reservations, the greater urbanization of native Americans, (and,) most (recently,) their increasing
(15) politicization in (response) to common grievances as the chief causes of the shift toward intertribalism.

Auth: Intertribalism on rise

(20)

Unique traditions rising too

(25)

P.I.T doesn't explain

(30)

Auth: must examine theory

(35)

Theory based on wrong assump.

(40)

Auth: Intertribal act. still important

(45)

Tribal and Intertribal distinct

(50)

Auth: Both are important

(55)

(Indeed,) the rapid diffusion of dance styles, outfits, and songs from one reservation to another offers (compelling evidence) that intertribalism has been increasing. (However,) these (sociologists) have (failed) to note the concurrent revitalization of many traditions unique to individual tribes. (Among) the Lakota, for (instance,) the Sun Dance was revived, after a forty-year hiatus, during the 1950's. (Similarly,) the Black Legging Society of the Kiowa and the Hethuska Society of the Ponca—(both) traditional groups within their respective tribes—have gained (new popularity.) (Obviously) a more complex societal shift is taking place (than) the theory of Pan-Indianism can account for.

An (examination) of the theory's underpinnings may be (critical) at this point, (especially) given that native Americans themselves (chafe most) against the Pan-Indian classification. (Like) other assimilationist theories with which it is associated, the Pan-Indian view is (predicated upon) an a priori assumption about the nature of cultural contact: that (upon) contact minority societies (immediately) begin to succumb in every respect—biologically, linguistically, and culturally—to the majority society. (However,) there is (no evidence) that this is happening to native American groups.

(Yet) the fact remains that intertribal activities are a (major facet) of native American culture today. Certain dances at powwows, (for instance,) are announced as intertribal, (others) as traditional. (Likewise,) speeches given at the beginnings of powwows are (often) delivered in English, (while) the prayer that follows is (usually) spoken in a native language. Cultural borrowing is, (of course,) old news. What is (important) to note is the conscious (distinction) native Americans make (between) tribal and intertribal tendencies.

Tribalism, (although greatly altered) by modern history, (remains) a (potent) force among native Americans: It forms a (basis) for tribal identity, (and) aligns music and dance with other social and cultural activities (important) to individual tribes. Intertribal activities, on the (other hand,) (reinforce) native American identity along a broader front, (where) this identity is directly threatened by outside influences.[7]

Hopefully you thought about the passage like this:

Paragraph 1: The author explains the views of sociologists who believe that intertribalism is on the rise and that tribal culture is fading.

Paragraph 2: He points out that these sociologists overlook the revitalization of specific cultural traditions.

---

[7]PrepTest 25, Sec 1, Passage 3

Paragraph 3: He demonstrates possible weaknesses in the Pan-Indian theory.

Paragraph 4: He shows that Native Americans distinguish between tribal and intertribal activities.

Paragraph 5: He suggests that tribal culture is actually strengthened by intertribal activities.

Purpose: The author wrote this passage to examine claims made by sociologists about declining tribal life and to demonstrate that the opposite is true.

Understanding and articulating the author's primary Purpose will lead to immediate rewards on test day, since many of the questions will directly test your knowledge of it. In fact, take a look at this question:

21. In the passage, the author is primarily concerned with doing which one of the following?[8]

Before I reveal the answer choices, I want you to recognize that this is a "Global" question type, one that is specifically asking for the Purpose we just summarized. (I'll discuss the different Reading Comprehension question types in greater detail in Part 2 of this book). Recall the Purpose you just defined. Now look at the answer choices and find the one that matches your prediction:

(A) identifying an assumption common to various assimilationist theories and then criticizing these theories by showing this assumption to be false

(B) arguing that the recent revival of a number of tribal practices shows sociologists are mistaken in believing intertribalism to be a potent force among native American societies

(C) questioning the belief that native American societies will eventually be assimilated into Euroamerican society by arguing that intertribalism helps strengthen native American identity

(D) showing how the recent resurgence of tribal activities is a deliberate attempt to counteract the growing influence of intertribalism

(E) proposing an explanation of why the ascension of intertribalism could result in the eventual dissolution of tribes and complete assimilation of native Americans into Euroamerican society[9]

You can quickly see that the correct answer is choice (C), which restates the primary Purpose.

There is a clever wrong answer trap here that is worth taking a moment to examine. Perhaps you thought at first that choice (B) was the proper match for your prediction. But recall from your analysis of the passage that while the author does claim that the sociologists are mistaken,

---

[8]PrepTest 25, Sec 1, Q 21
[9]PrepTest 25, Sec 1, Q 21

he doesn't say that intertribalism fails to be a potent force in Native American society. To the contrary, he claims that intertribalism is alive and well, and that it points to a strengthening of tribal culture rather than a weakening of it. Don't be disheartened if you picked choice (B) over choice (C). This is a one of the most common traps that occur regularly on the LSAT, and I'll discuss them all in greater detail later in this book.

You are very likely to encounter a question or two on test day that will be exactly like the one you just examined. For this reason alone, determining the author's Purpose is extremely important. As you continue to practice, you'll learn that some questions that don't directly ask you to identify the Purpose will still rely upon your understanding of it to find the credited answer among the traps. Bottom line: To be successful on Reading Comprehension, you must determine the Purpose of every passage you read from now until test day.

Main Idea: What's It All About?

Once you've determined the author's Topic, Scope, and Purpose, the Main Idea isn't far behind. In essence, it's the simplest, most direct summary of the author's primary conclusion that you can come up with. When trying to articulate the Main Idea of a passage, ask yourself, "If the author wanted me to come away from this text believing only *one* thing, what would it be?" The answer to this question is the Main Idea.

You'll find that as you become adept at defining the Purpose of the passage, the Main Idea is usually a natural extension of it. For example, you determined that the primary Purpose of the James passage was to examine several criticisms of a writer and to suggest that the writer rises above those criticisms. To get the Main Idea, you simply go from this general description of the passage's goals to a more specific and declarative one. The Main Idea of the passage is: James's work surpasses the limits of the crime-novel genre in spite of the claims of her critics. Again, notice that the difference is primarily one of specificity. Instead of referring to a writer who "rises above . . . criticisms" as I did in the Purpose, in the Main Idea I provide the specifics: James is the writer, and she breaks the conventions of a particular genre.

The difference may seem minor, but it's extremely important:

1. Which one of the following best states the author's main conclusion?[10]

---

[10]PrepTest 19, Sec 3, Q 1

This question is not asking for structure. It's asking for the Main Idea. Think over your prediction, then look at the choices:

(A) Because P. D. James's potential as a writer is stifled by her chosen genre, she should turn her talents toward writing mainstream novels.

(B) Because the requirements of the popular novel are incompatible with true creative expression, P. D. James's promise as a serious author has been diminished.

(C) The dichotomy between popular and sophisticated literature is well illustrated in the crime novels of P. D. James.

(D) The critics who have condemned P. D. James's lack of attention to the specifics of detection fail to take into account her carefully constructed plots.

(E) Although her plots are not always neatly resolved, the beauty of her descriptive passages justifies P. D. James's decision to write in the crime-novel genre.[11]

Hopefully this time you found the match with no difficulty: Choice (A) matches the author's ultimate recommendation perfectly and is a good match for our prediction as well.

The majority of LSAT passages will immediately be followed by a question that asks for the Main Idea. And as with Purpose, even those questions that don't ask for the Main Idea directly will often require that you demonstrate a clear understanding of it. Because Main Idea is so important, I'd like you to try one more exercise. Take a moment to review the primary Purpose of the Intertribalism Passage: to examine claims made by sociologists about declining tribal life, and to demonstrate that the opposite is true.

---

[11]PrepTest 19, Sec 3, Q 1

Now take a minute to articulate the Main Idea. Then try to answer this question:

14. Which one of the following best summarizes the main
     idea of the passage?

   (A) Despite the fact that sociologists have only
        recently begun to understand its importance,
        intertribalism has always been an influential
        factor in native American culture.
   (B) Native Americans are currently struggling with an
        identity crisis caused primarily by the two
        competing forces of tribalism and intertribalism.
   (C) The recent growth of intertribalism is unlikely to
        eliminate tribalism because the two forces do not
        oppose one another but instead reinforce distinct
        elements of native American identity.
   (D) The tendency toward intertribalism, although
        prevalent within native American culture, has
        had a minimal effect on the way native
        Americans interact with the broader community
        around them.
   (E) Despite the recent revival of many native
        American tribal traditions, the recent trend
        toward intertribalism is likely to erode cultural
        differences among the various native American
        tribes.[12]

The Main Idea of this passage could be stated as: Intertribalism isn't causing a decline in tribal life, but rather strengthening it. As always, don't worry if your prediction didn't exactly match mine; little differences are to be expected. Armed with this prediction, there's no doubt that the correct answer to this question is choice (C).

Topic, Scope, Purpose, Main Idea: A Summary

Although Topic, Scope, Purpose, and Main Idea may appear to be four very different concepts, I hope you can see that there's a binding relationship among them. Topic gives you a sense of general context, and helps lead you to the Scope. Purpose allows you to summarize passage structure, and the Main Idea is the central theme that ties everything together. Understanding these four attributes of every Reading Comprehension passage is the final stage of strategic reading and will allow you to approach the question set with confidence. I can't stress this enough: The majority of the questions that you will encounter on test day will require you to understand these ideas, either directly or indirectly, and the test makers will reward you for doing so. For this reason, you should *always* make sure you understand the Topic, Scope, Purpose, and Main Idea of every LSAT passage. Don't write them down (this can take more time than it's worth), but do clearly identify them in your mind before attempting any of the questions. With this in mind, it's time for some practice.

[12]PrepTest 25, Sec 1, Q 14

DRILL: IDENTIFYING TOPIC, SCOPE, PURPOSE, AND MAIN IDEA

Part 1: This will be your first attempt at applying Step 1 of the Kaplan Method in its entirety. As in the previous chapter, this Drill will be split into two separate tasks. First, read the passage strategically, noting Keywords, creating your Roadmap, and noting the Topic, Scope, Purpose, and Main Idea of the passage. (As I mentioned earlier, you won't write the Topic, Scope, Purpose, and Main Idea down on test day, but it's a good idea to do so now, as it gets you in the habit of thinking about them.) This passage is full of intricate details, but don't let them distract you. Also, remember that your Roadmap will be particularly helpful as you formulate the Purpose and Main Idea of the passage, so refer to it as needed. Explanations will follow. Read them carefully and double-check your work before you move on to Part 2 of the Drill.

In England before 1660, a husband controlled his wife's property. In the late seventeenth and eighteenth centuries, with the shift from land-based to commercial wealth, marriage began to incorporate certain features
(5) of a contract. Historians have traditionally argued that this trend represented a gain for women, one that reflects changing views about democracy and property following the English Restoration in 1660. Susan Staves contests this view; she argues that whatever
(10) gains marriage contracts may briefly have represented for women were undermined by judicial decisions about women's contractual rights.

Shifting through the tangled details of court cases, Staves demonstrates that, despite surface changes, a
(15) rhetoric of equality, and occasional decisions supporting women's financial power, definitions of men's and women's property remained inconsistent—generally to women's detriment. For example, dower lands (property inherited by wives after their husbands'
(20) deaths) could not be sold, but "curtesy" property (inherited by husbands from their wives) could be sold. Furthermore, comparatively new concepts that developed in conjunction with the marriage contract, such as jointure, pin money, and separate maintenance,
(25) were compromised by peculiar rules. For instance, if a woman spent her pin money (money paid by the husband according to the marriage contract for the wife's personal items) on possessions other than clothes she could not sell them; in effect they belonged
(30) to her husband. In addition, a wife could sue for pin money only up to a year in arrears—which rendered a suit impractical. Similarly, separate maintenance allowances (stated sums of money for the wife's support if husband and wife agreed to live apart) were

(35) complicated by the fact that if a couple tried to agree in a marriage contract on an amount, they were admitting that a supposedly indissoluble bond could be dissolved, an assumption courts could not recognize. Eighteenth-century historians underplayed these inconsistencies,
(40) calling them "little contrarieties" that would soon vanish. Staves shows, however, that as judges gained power over decisions on marriage contracts, they tended to fall back on pre-1660 assumptions about property.

(45) Staves' work on women's property has general implications for other studies about women in eighteenth-century England. Staves revises her previous claim that separate maintenance allowances proved the weakening of patriarchy; she now finds that
(50) an oversimplification. She also challenges the contention by historians Jeanne and Lawrence Stone that in the late eighteenth century wealthy men married widows less often than before because couples began marrying for love rather than for financial reasons.
(55) Staves does not completely undermine their contention, but she does counter their assumption that widows had more money than never-married women. She points out that jointure property (a widow's lifetime use of an amount of money specified in the marriage contract)
(60) was often lost on remarriage.[13]

Topic:_____

Scope:_____

Purpose:_____

Main Idea:_____

---

[13]PrepTest 26, Sec 4, Passage 4

Explanations

Marriage =
Contract

Hist: gain for
women

Staves: no
gain

In England (before) 1660, a husband controlled his wife's property. (In) the late seventeenth and eighteenth centuries, (with) the shift from land-based to commercial wealth, marriage (began) to incorporate certain features

(5) of a contract. (Historians) have (traditionally argued) that this trend (represented) a gain for women, one that reflects (changing views) about democracy and property (following) the English Restoration in 1660. Susan Staves (contests) this view; (she argues) that whatever

(10) gains marriage contracts may briefly have represented for women were (undermined) by judicial decisions about women's contractual rights.

Staves: legal
definitions
didn't help
women

Examples →

(Shifting) through the tangled details of court cases, Staves (demonstrates) that, (despite) surface changes, a

(15) rhetoric of equality, and occasional decisions supporting women's financial power, (definitions) of men's and women's property (remained) inconsistent— (generally) to women's detriment. For (example,) dower lands (property inherited by wives after their husbands'

(20) deaths) could not be sold, (but) "curtesy" property (inherited by husbands from their wives) could be sold. (Furthermore,) comparatively (new concepts) that developed in conjunction with the marriage contract, (such as) jointure, pin money, and separate maintenance,

(25) were compromised by (peculiar) rules. (For instance,) if a woman spent her pin money (money paid by the husband according to the marriage contract for the wife's personal items) on possessions (other than) clothes she could not sell them; (in effect) they belonged

(30) to her husband. (In addition,) a wife could sue for pin money (only) up to a year in arrears—(which) rendered a suit impractical. (Similarly,) separate maintenance allowances (stated sums of money for the wife's support if husband and wife agreed to live apart) were

(35) (complicated) by the fact that if a couple tried to agree in a marriage contract on an amount, they were (admitting) that a supposedly indissoluble bond could be dissolved, an (assumption) courts could not recognize. Eighteenth-century historians (underplayed) these inconsistencies,

(40) calling them "little contrarieties" that would soon vanish. Staves (shows, however,) that as judges gained power over decisions on marriage contracts, they (tended) to fall back on pre-1660 assumptions about property.

Implications of
Staves' work

(45)   Staves' work on women's property has general
implications for other studies about women in
eighteenth-century England. Staves revises her
previous claim that separate maintenance allowances
proved the weakening of patriarchy; she now finds that
(50)   an oversimplification. She also challenges the
contention by historians Jeanne and Lawrence Stone
that in the late eighteenth century wealthy men married
widows less often than before because couples began
marrying for love rather than for financial reasons.
(55)   Staves does not completely undermine their contention,
but she does counter their assumption that widows had
more money than never-married women. She points
out that jointure property (a widow's lifetime use of an
amount of money specified in the marriage contract)
(60)   was often lost on remarriage.[14]

Paragraph Structure: **Paragraph 1** gives you a brief introduction to the subject matter (and some excellent clues to guide you toward the Topic and Scope). The author describes a traditional view held by historians: that womens' rights were generally improved in the seventeenth and eighteenth centuries by the shift toward contract-based marriages. This view is challenged by Susan Staves, who asserts the opposite. Your Roadmap should reflect this conflict.

Paragraph 2 unsurprisingly provides evidence for Staves's claim; it's always a plus when you see a Keyword like "demonstrates" right away. This paragraph is comparatively long, and it is packed with detailed examples of how marriage contracts and legal definitions often worked to the detriment of women's property rights. Such a paragraph gives you an excellent opportunity to do the right thing and refuse to dwell on these examples in depth. The terminology and definitions in this paragraph can easily become confusing, but never forget that active reading means recognizing the difference between main points and supporting evidence (and giving the latter less of your attention). By judiciously circling Keywords, you can research any of this evidence if a question requires you to. For now, take note of the primary reason why all of that information is provided: to shore up Staves's assertion that the legal definitions of the time worked against the interests of women.

Paragraph 3 starts with a clue right off the bat: When you see a Keyword like "implications" in line 46, pay close attention. The author widens the Scope of the passage somewhat by describing how Staves' work affects the studies of others. What follows are, of course, examples that illustrate how this is so. Please note the presence of several important tone Keywords in this paragraph. In line 55, the author states that Staves doesn't "completely undermine" the work of Jeanne and Lawrence Stone, but that she does counter one of their assumptions. This is very different from asserting that Staves *disproves* others' work, and the test makers always reward those who recognize the difference.

---

[14]PrepTest 26, Sec 4, Passage 4

Topic: The opening paragraph introduces us to the Topic right away: the rights of English women after 1660. As always, keep the Topic very general.

Scope: What about women's rights did the author explore? From the beginning, he seems more interested in the work of Susan Staves and her assertion that the laws of the time did not contribute to the betterment of women, than in the traditional views mentioned in lines 5–8. There are many ways you might have phrased this, such as, "The failure of contract law to protect women's property rights," or "Why didn't marriage contracts advance women's rights?" As long as you stayed close to these concepts you're on the right track.

Purpose: Stay in the habit of using simple active verbs to define the Purpose. In this passage, the author wrote to *describe* how Susan Staves undermines a commonly held view of history and what some of the implications of her work are. Note that the author doesn't directly agree or disagree with Staves, but is content to simply describe her point of view.

Main Idea: Your Main Idea should always be simple, declarative, and very tightly focused, so boil it all down to one simple sentence: Susan Staves challenges the assumption that changes in marriage law after 1660 worked to the benefit of English women.

Part 2: Now that you've executed Step 1 of the Kaplan Method, try three practice questions. Use your Roadmap and your knowledge of the passage's Topic, Scope, Purpose, and Main Idea to predict the answer to each question before you select your answer choice.

1. Which one of the following best expresses the main idea of the passage?
   (A) As notions of property and democracy changed in late seventeenth- and eighteenth-century England, marriage settlements began to incorporate contractual features designed to protect women's property rights.
   (B) Traditional historians have incorrectly identified the contractual features that were incorporated into marriage contracts in late seventeenth- and eighteenth-century England.
   (C) The incorporation of contractual features into marriage settlements in late seventeenth- and eighteenth-century England did not represent a significant gain for women.
   (D) An examination of late seventeenth- and eighteenth-century English court cases indicates that most marriage settlements did not incorporate contractual features designed to protect women's property rights.
   (E) Before marriage settlements incorporated contractual features protecting women's property rights, women were unable to gain any financial power in England.[15]

---

[15]PrepTest 26, Sec 4, Q 22

2. Which one of the following best describes the function of the last paragraph in the context of the passage as a whole?
   (A) It suggests that Staves' recent work has caused significant revision of theories about the rights of women in eighteenth-century England.
   (B) It discusses research that may qualify Staves' work on women's property in eighteenth-century England.
   (C) It provides further support for Staves' argument by describing more recent research on women's property in eighteenth-century England.
   (D) It asserts that Staves' recent work has provided support for two other hypotheses developed by historians of eighteenth-century England.
   (E) It suggests the implications Staves' recent research has for other theories about women in eighteenth-century England.[16]

3. The primary purpose of the passage is to
   (A) compare two explanations for the same phenomenon
   (B) summarize research that refutes an argument
   (C) resolve a long-standing controversy
   (D) suggest that a recent hypothesis should be reevaluated
   (E) provide support for a traditional theory[17]

---

[16]PrepTest 26, Sec 4, Q 23
[17]PrepTest 26, Sec 4, Q 24

Explanations

1. **(C)**

    Which one of the following best expresses the main idea of the passage?
    (A) As notions of property and democracy changed in late seventeenth- and eighteenth-century England, marriage settlements began to incorporate contractual features designed to protect women's property rights.
    (B) Traditional historians have incorrectly identified the contractual features that were incorporated into marriage contracts in late seventeenth- and eighteenth-century England.
    (C) The incorporation of contractual features into marriage settlements in late seventeenth- and eighteenth-century England did not represent a significant gain for women.
    (D) An examination of late seventeenth- and eighteenth-century English court cases indicates that most marriage settlements did not incorporate contractual features designed to protect women's property rights.
    (E) Before marriage settlements incorporated contractual features protecting women's property rights, women were unable to gain any financial power in England.[18]

    You've seen this type of question before, and you have just the tool with which to answer it. The only choice that matches the Main Idea of the passage is the correct answer, choice (C). Choice (A) focuses far too narrowly on details presented in the first paragraph. Choices (B) and (D) are both too narrow and they also distort the passage; the author never asserted that historians incorrectly identified contractual features or that settlements failed to incorporate them. Finally, choice (E) is far too extreme and very much out of scope. The passage provides very little specific information about women's property rights prior to the incorporation of contractual features.

2. **(E)**

    Which one of the following best describes the function of the last paragraph in the context of the passage as a whole?
    (A) It suggests that Staves' recent work has caused significant revision of theories about the rights of women in eighteenth-century England.
    (B) It discusses research that may qualify Staves' work on women's property in eighteenth-century England.
    (C) It provides further support for Staves' argument by describing more recent research on women's property in eighteenth-century England.

---

[18]PrepTest 26, Sec 4, Q 22

(D)   It asserts that Staves' recent work has provided support for two other hypotheses developed by historians of eighteenth-century England.

(E)   It suggests the implications Staves' recent research has for other theories about women in eighteenth-century England.

Here's a great example of good preparation yielding results. Because the correct answer must mention the implications of Staves's research, a quick glance at your Roadmap should give you exactly what you need to earn this point. On the basis of this prediction, you can eliminate choices (B) and (C) immediately. Choice (D) mentions the relationship between Staves's work and the work of others, but describes this relationship incorrectly—Staves did not support the historians' hypotheses. Choice (A) is also incorrect; it makes claims that are extreme. Staves may have revised one of her own claims, and she has challenged the work of others, but that isn't the same as asserting that her work caused the "significant revision" of other theories as well. This kind of wrong answer trap is designed to ensnare those who fail to take tone into account, a bad habit that you've learned to avoid. The correct answer, choice (E), is a direct match of your prediction.

3.   **(B)**

The primary purpose of the passage is to
(A)   compare two explanations for the same phenomenon
(B)   summarize research that refutes an argument
(C)   resolve a long-standing controversy
(D)   suggest that a recent hypothesis should be reevaluated
(E)   provide support for a traditional theory

Which answer choice matches the Purpose? Choice (A) distorts the Purpose; the author isn't comparing two theories, but rather describing the implications of one for the other. Choice (C) is out because nothing is resolved, only described. The author never makes the suggestion described by choice (D), and choice (E) is the opposite of our prediction. That leaves choice (B), the correct answer, and the only choice that mentions Staves's challenge to a commonly held assumption.

THE FINAL PIECE OF THE BIG PICTURE

You now have a basic understanding of every component of Step 1 of the Kaplan Method. You've learned how to use Keywords to create a sense of context. You've begun to break down passage structure into a succinct and useful Roadmap. And now you've learned how to identify Topic, Scope, Purpose, and Main Idea, and how to use them to improve your LSAT score. You might be thinking that Purpose and Main Idea are primarily useful for answering questions that directly ask for them, but as you will soon learn, these ideas are so powerful and far-ranging that you will find yourself referring back to them again and again as you work through test questions. You should get into the habit of identifying them every time you read an LSAT passage. Mastery of these concepts will come only with practice, but with patience and diligence Kaplan's Method will become an instinctive part of your approach to the LSAT.

Because the skills I've taught you so far are vitally important, I'll encourage you to take a cue from the last couple of drills you completed and practice in the following way: Whenever you read a passage, start by executing Step 1 of the Kaplan Method, and then go immediately to the Explanations and check your work *before* you begin answering questions. Be certain you've understood the big picture before you proceed, and make sure your Roadmap is solid and that your understanding of the Main Idea is accurate. If you struggled with the passage, or if you find significant discrepancies between your reading and ours, take the time to reexamine your work. After you're confident that you've read the passage correctly, *then* attempt the question set. You'll find that this compartmentalized approach will allow you to master these core skills much more quickly than if you try to do everything at once. You shouldn't practice this way forever, but try it on your next few practice passages, and return to it whenever you need to.

CHAPTER 5

THE AUTHOR'S VOICE

UNDERSTANDING THE AUTHOR'S VOICE: A COMMON PROBLEM

A very specific problem crops up in every LSAT class I teach. It doesn't always happen during the same lesson or while the class is examining a particular passage. But it always comes up.

For the purposes of demonstration, read the following passage excerpt passively without applying the Kaplan Method:

> One of the greatest challenges facing medical
> students today, apart from absorbing volumes of
> technical information and learning habits of scientific
> thought, is that of remaining empathetic to the needs of
> (5) patients in the face of all this rigorous training.
> Requiring students to immerse themselves completely
> in medical coursework risks disconnecting them from
> the personal and ethical aspects of doctoring, and such
> strictly scientific thinking is insufficient for grappling
> (10) with modern ethical dilemmas. For these reasons,
> aspiring physicians need to develop new ways of
> thinking about and interacting with patients. Training
> in ethics that takes narrative literature as its primary
> subject is one method of accomplishing this.[1]

The author describes what he considers to be a great challenge facing medical students, the ability to remain empathetic toward patients. The strictly scientific nature of medical course-

---

[1]PrepTest 38, Sec 3, Passage 4

work is insufficient to prepare students to deal with ethical problems. The author then proposes that one method of dealing with this problem is the study of narrative literature. So far the author's intent seems fairly clear. The second paragraph goes on to explore the problem in greater detail:

(15)   Although training in ethics is currently provided by medical schools, this training relies heavily on an abstract, philosophical view of ethics. Although the conceptual clarity provided by a traditional ethics course can be valuable, theorizing about ethics
(20)   contributes little to the understanding of everyday human experience or to preparing medical students for the multifarious ethical dilemmas they will face as physicians. A true foundation in ethics must be predicated on an understanding of human behavior that
(25)   reflects a wide array of relationships and readily adapts to various perspectives, for this is what is required to develop empathy. Ethics courses drawing on narrative literature can better help students prepare for ethical dilemmas precisely because such literature attaches its
(30)   readers so forcefully to the concrete and varied world of human events.[2]

The author describes some of the deficiencies in the ethical training provided by medical schools, suggesting that the theoretical nature of such training is inadequate to prepare students for the real-life situations they will eventually face. Unsurprisingly, he once again suggests that the study of narrative literature may help remedy these shortcomings. The passage presents a clear dichotomy between these two approaches: if you encountered this passage on test day, you probably wouldn't be too surprised to see the following question:

27.   The author's attitude regarding the traditional method of teaching ethics in medical school can most accurately be described as

You know from a quick examination of the first two paragraphs that the author considers traditional ethics training to be inadequate. With this in mind, examine the answer choices.

(A)   unqualified disapproval of the method and disapproval of all of its effects
(B)   reserved judgment regarding the method and disapproval of all of its effects
(C)   partial disapproval of the method and clinical indifference toward its effects
(D)   partial approval of the method and disapproval of all of its effects
(E)   partial disapproval of the method and approval of some of its effects[3]

---

[2]PrepTest 38, Sec 3, Passage 4
[3]PrepTest 38, Sec 3, Passage 4, Q 27

Do any of these choices stand out as clearly correct? Each of them mentions some degree of disapproval, so how do you know which one accurately reflects the author's attitude? The challenge presented by this question exemplifies the common problem I referred to earlier. When you read passively, you run the risk of developing an incorrect or incomplete understanding of the author's point of view. This is a costly mistake to make on the LSAT, because you will invariably be tested on your knowledge of the author's opinions.

THREE COMMON TRAPS TO AVOID

I began by saying that the problem of misunderstanding authorial intent is one that nearly all of my students encounter. Furthermore, it's the kind of mistake that any student can make, regardless of skill and experience. Since you are now on the path to LSAT mastery, I would very much like to see you avoid this mistake. In this chapter I will help you do so with a brief discussion of three common errors to watch out for: structural misunderstanding, distortion of tone, and multiple points of view.

Structural Misunderstanding

I already alluded to this common error with the example at the beginning of this chapter. Structural misunderstanding most often occurs when you either fail to take notice of a vital Keyword or neglect to think about what it tells you in the context of what you've already learned. Examine the opening of the second paragraph once more, this time with the Keywords identified:

> Although training in ethics is currently provided by medical schools, this training relies heavily on an abstract, philosophical view of ethics. Although the conceptual clarity provided by a traditional ethics course can be valuable, theorizing about ethics contributes little to the understanding of everyday human experience or to preparing medical students for the multifarious ethical dilemmas they will face as physicians.[4]

The contrast Keyword "although" at the beginning of the paragraph prepares you for the critique that follows it: Even though ethics training is provided, it relies too much on abstraction. Now, pay very close attention to the second "although" in line 17. The author makes a concession, then contrasts this with another criticism. This structural nuance is extremely important, because it reveals the full extent of the author's opinion—while there is some benefit in traditional ethics courses, there are also problematic gaps.

---

[4]PrepTest 38, Sec 3, Passage 4

Bearing this in mind, revisit question 27:

27. The author's attitude regarding the traditional method of teaching ethics in medical school can most accurately be described as

   (A) unqualified disapproval of the method and
         disapproval of all of its effects
   (B) reserved judgment regarding the method and
         disapproval of all of its effects
   (C) partial disapproval of the method and clinical
         indifference toward its effects
   (D) partial approval of the method and disapproval
         of all of its effects
   (E) partial disapproval of the method and approval of
         some of its effects[5]

Choices (A), (B), and (D) each indicate that the author disapproves of *all* the effects of traditional ethics training. This is in direct opposition to the text, in which the author declares that such training "can be valuable" (line 19). Choice (C) is similarly flawed, since the author's concession can't be interpreted as indifference. Only correct Choice (E) properly characterizes both the author's reservations and partial approval.

This question can be confusing and time-consuming if you don't pay close attention to the structural clues in the passage. A passive reader is likely to overlook the contrast Keywords that inform the strategic reader of the author's intent, and even a test taker who is familiar with the Kaplan Method might notice the two occurrences of "although" at the paragraph's onset but fail to take note of the opinions they highlight.

You might be nodding your head at this point, thinking, "That sounds exactly like something I would do." Or perhaps you're wondering how anyone could make such a mistake. The fact is, no matter how skilled you become at strategic reading, this is an easy error to make, and it usually occurs when you rely on Keywords to do the thinking for you. Remember that in chapter 2, I pointed out that working with Keywords is a two-part process: You must identify the Keyword, but you must also understand what it is telling you in relation to the surrounding text.

Another contributor to structural misunderstanding is a shortage of Keywords pointing to the author's voice. You know from previous lessons that the author doesn't always present strong opinions in a passage. You also know that any opinions the author *does* present are usually tested, and you have learned to watch out for them. Try a little experiment: Read the following excerpt from an LSAT social science passage as quickly as you can, and see whether you can spot any authorial opinion:

---

[5]PrepTest 38, Sec 3, Passage 4, Q 27

Bettelheim interprets all fairy tales as driven by children's fantasies of desire and revenge, and in doing so suppresses the true nature of parental behavior ranging from abuse to indulgence. Fortunately, these
(50) characterizations of selfish children and innocent adults have been discredited to some extent by recent psychoanalytic literature. The need to deny adult evil has been a pervasive feature of our society, leading us to position children not only as the sole agents of evil
(55) but also as the objects of unending moral instruction, hence the idea that a literature targeted for them must stand in the service of pragmatic instrumentality rather than foster an unproductive form of playful pleasure.[6]

The paragraph primarily discusses the view of Bettelheim and those who agree with him, but did you spot the one crucial keyword that gives the author's opinion? Here it is:

Fortunately, these
(55) characterizations of selfish children and innocent adults have been discredited to some extent by recent psychoanalytic literature.[7]

This lone, vital Keyword is the means by which you know that the author finds it "fortunate" that Bettelheim's views have been partially discredited. Without it, the author's attitude would remain neutral; he would simply tell you that Bettelheim's ideas are under attack, and then go on to further explore the significance of those ideas in society as a whole.

How important is this one word and its implications?

11. Which one of the following is the most accurate description of the author's attitude toward Bettelheim's view of fairy tales?

(A)   concern that the view will undermine the ability of fairy tales to provide moral instruction

(B)   scorn toward the view's supposition that moral tenets can be universally valid

(C)   disapproval of the view's depiction of children as selfish and adults as innocent

(D)   anger toward the view's claim that children often improve as a result of deserved punishment

(E)   disappointment with the view's emphasis on the manifest content of a tale[8]

---

[6]PrepTest 39, Sec 3, Passage 2

[7]PrepTest 39, Sec 3, Passage 2

[8]PrepTest 39, Sec 3, Passage 2, Q 11

All of the answer choices are to some degree negatively connotated, but only one matches point for point the author's opinion and the reasons he provides in the quoted paragraph: choice (C), the correct answer.

The LSAT is full of examples like that. In order to avoid a structural misunderstanding, you must always note Keywords of opinion, and you must always think about them in the context of the passage as a whole.

Distortion of Tone

Another common error is to misunderstand the author's tone. This is a problem I've presented to you before, but it's important enough to warrant a brief review. As a quick illustration, think for a moment about the incorrect answer choices in the question you just examined:

11. Which one of the following is the most accurate
    description of the author's attitude toward Bettelheim's
    view of fairy tales?

    (A)   concern that the view will undermine the ability
          of fairy tales to provide moral instruction
    (B)   scorn toward the view's supposition that moral
          tenets can be universally valid
    (C)   disapproval of the view's depiction of children as
          selfish and adults as innocent
    (D)   anger toward the view's claim that children often
          improve as a result of deserved punishment
    (E)   disappointment with the view's emphasis on the
          manifest content of a tale[9]

Choice (A) is contrary to the author's opinion, and choice (B) is out of the scope of this question. Pay particular attention to the verbs used in choices (D) and (E). In the paragraph you read, did the author ever use language that indicated he was angry or disappointed with Bettelheim's hypothesis? Not at all. He did clearly state the disapproval mentioned in correct choice (C), but to confuse disapproval with anger or disappointment is to distort the author's tone.

Since the test makers will reward you for understanding the author's tone, they will provide correct answer choices that fall perfectly in line with it, but they will also list incorrect answer choices that vary from it in ways that can be quite nuanced.

Here's another example that often catches my students off guard. This time you'll read a short excerpt from a passage detailing a specific criticism and the author's response to it. Read strategically, paying attention to Keywords, and note the author's opinion (don't worry if the context of the excerpt isn't totally clear; for now all you really need to understand is the author's point of view):

---

[9]PrepTest 39, Sec 3, Passage 2, Q 11

This brand of criticism has
met opposition from the formalists, who study the
text alone and argue that reader-response theory can
(15)   encourage and even validate fragmented views of a
work, rather than the unified view acquired by
examining only the content of the text. However,
since no theory has a monopoly on divining meaning
from a text, the formalists' view appears
(20)   unnecessarily narrow.[10]

Now, take a moment to articulate in your mind the author's attitude toward the formalists, then answer the following question:

14.   Which one of the following most accurately describes
the author's attitude toward formalism as expressed in
the passage?

(A)   scholarly neutrality
(B)   grudging respect
(C)   thoughtless disregard
(D)   cautious ambivalence
(E)   reasoned dismissal[11]

The author declares the formalists' view to be "unnecessarily narrow" (line 20). An opinion has been provided, specifically a negative one. This makes it simple to rule out choices (A), (B), and (D), since the author is neither neutral nor respectful. This leaves (C) and (E) to choose from. Was the author's disapproval of formalism "thoughtless" or "reasoned"?

Many students choose incorrect choice (C) because they're uncomfortable with the word "dismissal" in correct choice (E). In the excerpt above, the author does indeed *dismiss* the formalists' claim, and does so "since" (line 18) no theory can completely describe the meaning of a text. This *must* be described as reasoned "dismissal", since a specific reason was provided.

Even at this relatively early stage of your LSAT training you've probably learned to be wary of language in the answer choices that seems too extreme, and rightfully so—many wrong answer traps do contain such language. When in doubt, research the relevant text and let the passage be your guide; the answer is always there.

Multiple Points of View

The final common trap I want to point out occurs when numerous viewpoints are presented in the passage. In such a situation, the pressure of the clock may cause you to rush through the passage and mistake one viewpoint for another or to confuse a third-party viewpoint with the

---

[10]PrepTest 43, Sec 1, Passage 3
[11]PrepTest 43, Sec 1, Passage 3, Q 14

author's. The best response to this situation is, as always, strategic reading. When numerous viewpoints are presented to you, take note of them right away in your Roadmap.

Read the following opening paragraph and based on your analysis of it, predict how many viewpoints at a minimum will be presented in the passage:

> Two impressive studies have reexamined Eric
> Williams' conclusion that Britain's abolition of the
> slave trade in 1807 and its emancipation of slaves in
> its colonies in 1834 were driven primarily by economic
> (5)   rather than humanitarian motives. Blighted by depleted
> soil, indebtedness, and the inefficiency of coerced labor,
> these colonies, according to Williams, had by 1807
> become an impediment to British economic progress.[12]

I hope you were keeping count. This paragraph tells you to expect no fewer than four different opinions in the passage. You have Eric Williams' conclusion, you're told about "two impressive studies" that comment on his opinions, and you should always be on the lookout for the author's point of view as well.

I'm going to come back to this passage and discuss various ways of staying ahead of multiple viewpoints in general in the next chapter. But for now, I want you to remember one important tip: When a passage clues you in to the presence of multiple opinions, actively prepare to seek them out and add them to your Roadmap; they will undoubtedly be crucial to scoring points in the question set. As a preview, take a look at a few of the questions:

23.   Which one of the following best states Williams' view of the primary reason for Britain's abolition of the slave trade and the emancipation of slaves in its colonies?

24.   According to Eltis, low wages and Draconian vagrancy laws in Britain in the seventeenth and eighteenth centuries were intended to

25.   It can be inferred that the author of the passage views Drescher's presentation of British traditions concerning liberty as

26.   The information in the passage suggests that Eltis and Drescher agree that[13]

A quick glance at these questions confirms that there are, indeed, at least four opinions to keep track of: Williams, Eltis, Drescher, and the author. Note how questions 23 and 24 each ask for some specific aspect of a single viewpoint, while question 25 asks for the author's opinion of Drescher's ideas, and question 26 asks you to find common ground between Eltis and Drescher. Not only must you understand each viewpoint separately, but you must be prepared to compare and contrast them as well in order to score these points.

---

[12]PrepTest 19, Sec 3, Passage 4
[13]PrepTest 19, Sec 3, Qs 23–26

Here's the good news. While a passage like this may appear intimidating, there is one thing you can be absolutely certain of: With so many opinions present, there will be a wealth of Keywords to help you keep track of them. And remember, your goal isn't to completely understand or memorize them, but only to summarize them, add them to your Roadmap, and be prepared to research them as necessary. Incidentally, most of my students find that passages containing definite opinions, even if there are several of them, tend to seem less abstract, and therefore less difficult, than passages that do not.

In any case, my purpose here is to remind you that you must always be aware, not just of what opinions are present in a passage, but to whom they belong as well.

DRILL: UNDERSTANDING THE AUTHOR

Now for some practice. Read and Roadmap the following passage, and then answer the questions that follow. I've chosen a passage that illustrates some of the traps I've described in this chapter, so watch for them as you work. When you've finished, carefully read the explanations that follow.

It has recently been discovered that many attributions of paintings to the seventeenth-century Dutch artist Rembrandt may be false. The contested paintings are not minor works, whose removal from the
(5) Rembrandt corpus would leave it relatively unaffected: they are at its very center. In her recent book, Svetlana Alpers uses these cases of disputed attribution as a point of departure for her provocative discussion of the radical distinctiveness of Rembrandt's approach to
(10) painting.

Alpers argues that Rembrandt exercised an unprecedentedly firm control over his art, his students, and the distribution of his works. Despite Gary Schwartz's brilliant documentation of Rembrandt's
(15) complicated relations with a wide circle of patrons, Alpers takes the view that Rembrandt refused to submit to the prevailing patronage system. He preferred, she claims, to sell his works on the open market and to play the entrepreneur. At a time when Dutch artists were
(20) organizing into professional brotherhoods and academies, Rembrandt stood apart. In fact, Alpers' portrait of Rembrandt shows virtually every aspect of his art pervaded by economic motives. Indeed, so complete was Rembrandt's involvement with the
(25) market, she argues, that he even presented himself as a commodity, viewing his studio's products as extensions of himself, sent out into the world to earn money. Alpers asserts that Rembrandt's enterprise is found not just in his paintings, but in his refusal to limit
(30) his enterprise to those paintings he actually painted. He marketed Rembrandt.

Although there may be some truth in the view that Rembrandt was an entrepreneur who made some aesthetic decisions on the basis of what he knew the
(35) market wanted, Alpers' emphasis on economic factors sacrifices discussion of the aesthetic qualities that make Rembrandt's work unique. For example, Alpers asserts that Rembrandt deliberately left his works unfinished so as to get more money for their revision and
(40) completion. She implies that Rembrandt actually wished the Council of Amsterdam to refuse the great *Claudius Civilis*, which they had commissioned for

their new town hall, and she argues that "he must have calculated that he would be able to get more money by
(45) retouching [the] painting." Certainly the picture is painted with very broad strokes but there is no evidence that it was deliberately left unfinished. The fact is that the look of a work like *Claudius Civilis* must also be understood as the consequence of
(50) Rembrandt's powerful and profound meditations on painting itself. Alpers makes no mention of the pictorial dialectic that can be discerned between, say, the lessons Rembrandt absorbed from the Haarlem school of painters and the styles of his native Leiden.
(55) The trouble is that while Rembrandt's artistic enterprise may indeed not be reducible to the works he himself painted, it is not reducible to marketing practices either.

1. Which one of the following best summarizes the main conclusion of the author of the passage?

(A) Rembrandt differed from other artists of his time both in his aesthetic techniques and in his desire to meet the demands of the marketplace.

(B) The aesthetic qualities of Rembrandt's work cannot be understood without consideration of how economic motives pervaded decisions he made about his art.

(C) Rembrandt was one of the first artists to develop the notion of a work of art as a commodity that could be sold in an open marketplace.

(D) Rembrandt's artistic achievement cannot be understood solely in terms of decisions he made on the basis of what would sell in the marketplace.

(E) Rembrandt was an entrepreneur whose artistic enterprise was not limited to the paintings he actually painted himself.

2. According to the passage, Alpers and Schwartz disagree about which one of the following?

    (A)   the degree of control Rembrandt exercised over the production of his art
    (B)   the role that Rembrandt played in organizing professional brotherhoods and academies
    (C)   the kinds of relationships Rembrandt had with his students
    (D)   the degree of Rembrandt's involvement in the patronage system
    (E)   the role of the patronage system in seventeenth-century Holland

3. It can be inferred that the author of the passage and Alpers would be most likely to agree on which one of the following?

    (A)   Rembrandt made certain aesthetic decisions on the basis of what he understood about the demands of the marketplace.
    (B)   The Rembrandt corpus will not be affected if attributions of paintings to Rembrandt are found to be false.
    (C)   Stylistic aspects of Rembrandt's painting can be better explained in economic terms than in historical or aesthetic terms.
    (D)   Certain aesthetic aspects of Rembrandt's art are the result of his experimentation with different painting techniques.
    (E)   Most of Rembrandt's best-known works were painted by his students, but were sold under Rembrandt's name.[14]

Explanations

Paragraph Structure:

Paragraph 1 begins with a brief discussion of potential forgeries in Rembrandt's body of work. You must be careful, however, as the author quickly takes the passage in a very different direction. In lines 6–10, the true scope of the passage is revealed: Susan Alpers uses the questionable paintings as a "point of departure" for her discussion of Rembrandt's approach to painting.

Paragraph 2 describes Aplers' view, that Rembrandt was driven primarily by economic motives. Note the abundance of Keywords of emphasis and tone in this paragraph. In line 22 Alpers claims that "virtually every aspect" of Rembrandt's work was influenced by these motives, and line 24 begins with, "Indeed, so complete was Rembrandt's involvement with the market" before going on to further describe Alpers' claim. I hope you also noticed the brief (but important) mention of a conflicting point of view beginning in line 13. Alpers claims that Rembrandt did not submit to the prevailing patronage system of his time "despite" Schwatz's "brilliant" claim to the contrary.

Paragraph 3 signals the author's opinion immediately, beginning with the contrast Keyword "although." Note that the author's tone is very clear: There may be "some truth" in Alpers' claim, but her work sacrifices a discussion of Rembrandt's aesthetic concerns. There follows a lengthy discussion of *Claudius Civilis*, an easy place to get bogged down in details, but "for example" in line 37 forewarns you that the following text is evidence for the conclusion already stated. The author returns to the main point at the end of the paragraph, identifying the "trouble" with Alpers' analysis in lines 55–58: Rembrandt can't be understood solely as an entrepreneur.

Topic: The work of Rembrandt

Scope: Alpers' view of Rembrandt as an entrepreneur

Purpose: To describe a study about Rembrandt's approach to art and to refute its central assumption

Main Idea: Rembrandt cannot be understood simply as an entrepreneur as Alpers claims.

1. **(D)**

   Which one of the following best summarizes the
   main conclusion of the author of the passage?
   (A) Rembrandt differed from other artists of his
       time both in his aesthetic techniques and in
       his desire to meet the demands of the
       marketplace.
   (B) The aesthetic qualities of Rembrandt's work
       cannot be understood without consideration
       of how economic motives pervaded decisions
       he made about his art.
   (C) Rembrandt was one of the first artists to
       develop the notion of a work of art as a
       commodity that could be sold in an open
       marketplace.
   (D) Rembrandt's artistic achievement cannot be
       understood solely in terms of decisions he
       made on the basis of what would sell in the
       marketplace.
   (E) Rembrandt was an entrepreneur whose artistic
       enterprise was not limited to the paintings he
       actually painted himself.[15]

This type of question should be very familiar to you by now, and correct choice (D) perfectly
matches the author's Main Idea. Choice (B) contains a common wrong answer trap; it describes
Alpers' central assertion rather than the author's. Choices (A) and (C) distort the facts by claiming that Rembrandt's techniques were exclusive to his work, something the passage never
claims. Choice (E) focuses on a single aspect of Alpers' thesis without ever addressing the
author's central claim.

2. **(D)**

   According to the passage, Alpers and Schwartz
   disagree about which one of the following?
   (A) the degree of control Rembrandt exercised
       over the production of his art
   (B) the role that Rembrandt played in organizing
       professional brotherhoods and academies
   (C) the kinds of relationships Rembrandt had with
       his students
   (D) the degree of Rembrandt's involvement in the
       patronage system
   (E) the role of the patronage system in
       seventeenth-century Holland[16]

Question 2 reminds you that conflicting points of view are usually tested. The only opinion
attributed to Schwartz appears in lines 13–15. Schwartz claims that Rembrandt worked within
the patronage system, and Alpers disagrees. Only choice (D) falls within this scope.

---

[15]PrepTest 23, Sec 4, Passage 1, Q 1
[16]PrepTest 23, Sec 4, Passage 1, Q 2

3. **(A)**

    It can be inferred that the author of the passage and Alpers would be most likely to agree on which one of the following?
    (A)   Rembrandt made certain aesthetic decisions on the basis of what he understood about the demands of the marketplace.
    (B)   The Rembrandt corpus will not be affected if attributions of paintings to Rembrandt are found to be false.
    (C)   Stylistic aspects of Rembrandt's painting can be better explained in economic terms than in historical or aesthetic terms.
    (D)   Certain aesthetic aspects of Rembrandt's art are the result of his experimentation with different painting techniques.
    (E)   Most of Rembrandt's best-known works were painted by his students, but were sold under Rembrandt's name.[17]

Approach a question like this one with the author's tone in mind. Remember that the author didn't completely reject Alpers' claim, but instead insisted that it was inappropriately one-sided. Since both Alpers and the author did agree that Rembrandt made decisions that were to some extent influenced by the marketplace, choice (A) must be correct. Choice (C) describes a view that Alpers would probably agree with but that is contrary to the author's Main Idea. Choices (B), (D), and (E) are all out of scope.

LISTEN CAREFULLY TO THE AUTHOR

I can't say it often enough: The test makers reward those who understand the author's main ideas. This is a concept that you're very familiar with by now, but common pitfalls do exist. In summary, please remember the following:

- Don't just read and circle opinion Keywords; think about what they tell you, and pay close attention to the context in which they appear.
- Take note of *every* opinion Keyword, especially when they are scarce.
- Keep an eye out for qualifiers that help you understand the nuances of the author's opinions.
- Trust the text. The language you need to understand the author's voice is always there.
- When the passage contains multiple viewpoints, be sure to take note of who is saying what. Don't confuse the author's opinion with the opinions of others.

I've watched a lot of students learn these lessons the hard way, and you've probably made some of these mistakes yourself at one time or another. That's fine; in fact, it's an important part of the learning process. Keep these concepts in mind as you become more confident in your mastery of the Kaplan Method.

---

[17]PrepTest 23, Sec 4, Passage 1, Q 5

CHAPTER 6

READING PREDICTIVELY

THE PASSAGES ARE PREDICTABLE
Why Does LSAT Reading Seem Difficult?

I'd like you to think about a question that I haven't raised prior to this chapter, but that you may have already considered yourself: Why are certain LSAT Reading Comprehension passages so much harder to read than anything else you've read in your life? You might have thought of several answers right away, and I'll mention a few of the more common ones that I hear from my students.

Most of my students say that the Reading Comprehension passages are difficult because they contain difficult terminology and dense linguistic construction, especially law and science passages. They mention their own discomfort and lack of familiarity with these subjects as a further complication. Sometimes they complain that the passages don't follow any discernible logic, seeming to randomly jump from idea to idea without warning. Finally, what they all mention without fail is that if it weren't for the ticking of the clock (combined with the impending questions), LSAT reading wouldn't be any more challenging than any other reading they've already done.

You most likely agreed with some, possibly all, of these points. But if you take a moment to think about each one in the context of what you've learned so far, you'll make an important discovery.

The Real Challenge

The final point, that it's really the ticking clock that makes Reading Comprehension challenging, by its very definition weakens all the other points. Here's what I mean. The first complaint is that the text is dense and unfamiliar. That's a fair point, and very few test takers will get through a Reading Comprehension section without running into some unfamiliar words or concepts. But haven't you run into the same problem when reading in school, at work, or in your leisure time? Do you have to reach for a dictionary every time you encounter a new word? Most likely not; you can use the context of what you're reading to work out what the word means, or the author provides a definition a short while later. In any case, encountering one difficult word doesn't sabotage your ability to understand what you're reading.

The second point is only marginally different. Certainly, LSAT passages may wander into territory that you don't personally find familiar. But once again, think back to your prior reading experiences and you'll realize that you've been reading about unfamiliar topics your entire life. After all, there isn't much to be gained from reading the same thing over and over again. Clearly, then, you know how to grapple with unfamiliar ideas and learn what they mean.

The third problem—that the passages don't follow a logical path—should seem instinctively wrong to you now that you've learned the Kaplan Method. After all, every passage you've read thus far has been peppered with Keywords that spelled out the author's intent every step of the way. You know that the passages occasionally go in a direction that is surprising, but such a move will always be within the author's scope. Ultimately, you've learned that very little of what you encounter in the Reading Comprehension section will be surprising, because you've learned to read actively by predicting where the author is going to go next.

So that leaves the final point, and it bears repeating: It is the time limit, combined with the pressure of the question set, that makes LSAT reading challenging. This is, for the vast majority of test takers, unequivocally true. You've already demonstrated in various contexts your ability to deal with tough language, new subjects, and unusual structure. It's being forced to do these things under time constraints that makes the LSAT challenging. And the one thing you can't do is add minutes to the clock.

Staying One Step Ahead of the Author

The solution, as always, is to become a more skillful reader. Not merely faster, but more efficient. The next step is for you to begin reading predictively.

Reading predictively is a simple process, one that derives directly from ideas I've already introduced in earlier chapters. In fact, you've already begun to form the habit of reading predictively by learning to identify and analyze the Keywords in passages. Now you must simply take the process a step further: As you read a passage, you must actively predict the main ideas that are likely to occur next.

To illustrate this concept, I'll present you with an LSAT passage and walk you through the process of predictive reading. As you read, you should stop periodically and ask yourself: What is the author likely to do next?

> The debate over the environmental crisis is not new; anxiety about industry's impact on the environment has existed for over a century.[1]

The author begins by introducing the Topic, the environmental crisis. He asserts that the debate has been going on for over a century. Since passages usually focus on recent developments rather than well-established facts, you should immediately ask: **Are there any recent developments?**

> What is new is the extreme polarization of views.[2]

Perfect. The Scope of the passage is the polarization of views on the subject. You've probably already guessed what question you should ask next: **What are these polarized views?**

> (5) Mounting evidence of humanity's capacity to damage the environment irreversibly coupled with suspicions that government, industry, and even science might be impotent to prevent environmental destruction have provoked accusatory polemics on the part of
> (10) environmentalists. In turn, these polemics have elicited a corresponding backlash from industry. The sad effect of this polarization is that it is now even more difficult for industry than it was a hundred years ago to respond appropriately to impact analyses that demand action.[3]

As predicted, the author presents the polarized views. Notice the emphasis Keywords that help you spot them easily; words like "accusatory," "polemics," and "backlash" all indicate that there is a debate between environmentalists and industry. Your Roadmap should look something like this:

Auth: Env. debate is now polarized

> The (debate) over the environmental crisis is not new; anxiety about industry's impact on the environment has existed for over a century. What is (new) is the (extreme) polarization of views. Mounting
> (5) (evidence) of humanity's capacity to damage the environment irreversibly (coupled with) suspicions that government, industry, and even science might be impotent to prevent environmental destruction have (provoked) accusatory (polemics) on the part of
> (10) environmentalists. In turn, these (polemics) have elicited a corresponding (backlash) from industry. The (sad effect) of this polarization is that it is now even (more difficult) for industry than it was a hundred years ago to respond appropriately to impact analyses that demand action.[4]

[1]PrepTest 23, Sec 4, Passage 3
[2]PrepTest 23, Sec 4, Passage 3
[3]PrepTest 23, Sec 4, Passage 3
[4]PrepTest 23, Sec 4, Passage 3

You may be wondering why it's helpful to go through the trouble of asking these questions. The answer: If you can predict what is likely to come next, then you always have context for what you are reading. No matter how dense the language may become, you stay one step ahead of the author, and when she makes her main point you're already prepared to see it and understand it.

What is likely to happen in the next paragraph? Since the debate is between polarized points of view, the author will likely elaborate on those viewpoints.

(15)   Unlike today's adversaries, earlier ecological
reformers shared with advocates of industrial growth a
confidence in timely corrective action.[5]

The author presents the viewpoint of a group of "earlier" ecological reformers. This Keyword-laden sentence is extremely important, because it allows you to predict a slight twist in this passage that might otherwise catch you by surprise. **What is the author likely to discuss next?** Undoubtedly she will describe the earlier reformers, but the Keyword "unlike" tells you that soon after she will almost certainly contrast them with a more recent group.

This insight is extremely valuable; the first paragraph may have led you to believe that the author would primarily discuss the differences between ecological reformers and their industrial foes. That might still be true, but now you are prepared to see a different conflict, in this case between two separate groups of reformers. Being prepared for what comes next gives you an *enormous* advantage on test day. Less-alert readers may become confused when the author begins to discuss this secondary debate, thinking that the passage has thrown them a curveball. You, on the other hand, know it is going to happen.

To continue with paragraph two:

       George P.
Marsh's pioneering conservation tract *Man and Nature*
(1864) elicited wide acclaim without embittered
(20)   denials. *Man and Nature* castigated Earth's despoilers
for heedless greed, declaring that humanity "has
brought the face of the Earth to a desolation almost as
complete as that of the Moon." But no entrepreneur or
industrialist sought to refute Marsh's accusation, to
(25)   defend the gutting of forests or the slaughter of wildlife
as economically essential, or to dismiss his ecological
warnings as hysterical. To the contrary, they generally
agreed with him.[6]

The author elaborates on one particular early reformer, then points out that industrialists tended to agree with him. This may seem surprising in light of your earlier predictions. Didn't the first paragraph indicate that the views of reformers and industry were polarized? Don't

---

[5]PrepTest 23, Sec 4, Passage 3
[6]PrepTest 23, Sec 4, Passage 3

worry; if you continue to read strategically the author's purpose will become clear. For now, review the Roadmap for the first two paragraphs, then predict what is likely to come next:

Auth: Env.
debate is now
polarized

The (debate) over the environmental crisis is not new; anxiety about industry's impact on the environment has existed for over a century. What is (new) is the (extreme) polarization of views. Mounting (5) (evidence) of humanity's capacity to damage the environment irreversibly (coupled with) suspicions that government, industry, and even science might be impotent to prevent environmental destruction have (provoked) accusatory (polemics) on the part of (10) environmentalists. In turn, these (polemics) have elicited a corresponding (backlash) from industry. The (sad effect) of this polarization is that it is now even (more difficult) for industry than it was a hundred years ago to respond appropriately to impact analyses that demand action.

Earlier
reformers

(15)   (Unlike) today's adversaries, (earlier) ecological reformers (shared) with advocates of industrial growth a confidence in timely corrective action. George P. Marsh's pioneering conservation tract *Man and Nature* (1864) (elicited) wide acclaim (without) embittered (20) denials. *Man and Nature* (castigated) Earth's despoilers for heedless greed, (declaring) that humanity "has brought the face of the Earth to a desolation almost as complete as that of the Moon." (But) no entrepreneur or industrialist sought to (refute) Marsh's accusation, to

Industry
agreed

(25) defend the gutting of forests or the slaughter of wildlife as economically essential, (or) to dismiss his ecological warnings as hysterical. To the (contrary,) they generally agreed with him.[7]

What will happen next? The author is likely to explain why industry tended to agree with the earlier reformers. It is also likely that the author will soon discuss the more modern reformers. Either could occur in the next paragraph. Read on with these predictions in mind:

Why? Marsh and his followers took environmental (30) improvement and economic progress as givens; they disputed not the desirability of conquering nature but the bungling way in which the conquest was carried out. Blame was not personalized; Marsh denounced general greed rather than particular entrepreneurs, and (35) the media did not hound malefactors. Further, corrective measures seemed to entail no sacrifice, to demand no draconian remedies. Self-interest underwrote most prescribed reforms. Marsh's emphasis on future stewardship was then a widely accepted ideal (40) (if not practice). His ecological admonitions were in keeping with the Enlightenment premise that humanity's mission was to subdue and transform nature.[8]

---

[7]PrepTest 23, Sec 4, Passage 3

[8]PrepTest 23, Sec 4, Passage 3

The third paragraph explains why Marsh and the industrialists weren't in conflict; they shared many common views. The Roadmap should look something like this:

Why ind. didn't dispute Marsh

(Why?) Marsh and his followers took environmental
(30)   improvement and economic progress as givens; they
        (disputed) not the desirability of conquering nature (but)
        the bungling way in which the conquest was carried
        out. Blame was not personalized; (Marsh denounced)
        general greed rather than particular entrepreneurs, (and)
(35)   the media did not hound malefactors. (Further,)
        corrective measures seemed to entail no sacrifice, to
        demand no draconian remedies. Self-interest
        underwrote most prescribed reforms. (Marsh's emphasis)
        on future stewardship was then a widely accepted ideal
(40)   (if not practice). His ecological admonitions were in
        (keeping with) the Enlightenment premise that
        humanity's mission was to subdue and transform
        nature.[9]

What will happen next? Using the context of what you've read so far, you can be fairly certain you'll soon encounter the modern ecological reformers. You can take this prediction a step further. **How do the new reformers differ from the old ones?** Since the earlier reformers were at least partially in agreement with industry, it must be that the modern reformers are in conflict with industry. You can make this prediction confidently; the author has been preparing you for it since the first paragraph. Reading on:

        Not until the 1960s did a gloomier perspective gain
(45)   popular ground. Frederic Clements' equilibrium model
        of ecology, developed in the 1930s, seemed consistent
        with mounting environmental disasters. In this view,
        nature was most fruitful when least altered. Left
        undisturbed, flora and fauna gradually attained
(50)   maximum diversity and stability. Despoliation
        thwarted the culmination or shortened the duration of
        this beneficent climax; technology did not improve
        nature but destroyed it.[10]

Notice how your predictions allow you to cut through the jargon of this paragraph and easily place it within the overall context of the passage. The author describes the "gloomier" perspective of the modern reformers. These reformers believe that nature should remain untouched and are in opposition to technology. This is precisely what you expected to read.

---

[9]PrepTest 23, Sec 4, Passage 3
[10]PrepTest 23, Sec 4, Passage 3

New view:
industry
bad for
environ.

(45) (Not until) the 1960s did a (gloomier) perspective gain
popular ground. Frederic Clements' equilibrium model
of ecology, developed in the 1930s, seemed (consistent)
with mounting environmental disasters. In (this view,)
nature was most fruitful when least altered. Left
undisturbed, flora and fauna gradually attained
(50) maximum diversity and stability. Despoliation
thwarted the culmination (or) shortened the duration of
this beneficent climax; technology did not improve
nature (but) destroyed it.[11]

What will the author conclude with? A better way to think about this might be, "What is the only major point introduced by the author that has yet to be discussed?" Since the author still hasn't explicitly discussed the debate between industry and environmentalists, you can confidently predict that the final paragraph will elaborate on this debate.

With this prediction in mind, read the final paragraph:

The equilibrium model became an ecological
(55) mystique: environmental interference was now taboo,
wilderness adored. Nature as unfinished fabric
perfected by human ingenuity gave way to the image of
nature debased and endangered by technology. In
contrast to the Enlightenment vision of nature,
(60) according to which rational managers construct an ever
more improved environment, twentieth-century
reformers' vision of nature calls for a reduction of
human interference in order to restore environmental
stability.[12]

Without a good sense of context, a paragraph like this one can be alarming. It shifts back and forth between two viewpoints, providing a healthy dose of jargon along the way. Terminology like "ecological mystique" and the "Enlightenment vision of nature" may not be helpful. Still, predictive reading provides clarity: The author is elaborating on the ways in which the modern reformers differ from their predecessors. You've already become acquainted with these two views, and this paragraph merely confirms what you already know; the modern reformers consider human encroachment on nature "taboo," and instead desire a "reduction of human interference." Your Roadmap should reflect this difference:

---

[11]PrepTest 23, Sec 4, Passage 3
[12]PrepTest 23, Sec 4, Passage 3

The equilibrium model (became) an ecological

(55) mystique: environmental interference was now taboo,
wilderness adored. Nature as unfinished fabric
perfected by human ingenuity (gave way) to the image of
nature debased and endangered by technology. In
(contrast) to the Enlightenment vision of nature,

(60) (according to) which rational managers construct an ever
more improved environment, twentieth-century
reformers' vision of nature (calls for) a reduction of
human interference in order to restore environmental
stability.[13]

New view:
no human
interference
w/ nature

With the Roadmap complete, take a moment to identify the author's Purpose and Main Idea before reading on.

Since the author didn't provide much strong opinion language, the Purpose of this passage could best be termed descriptive: The author describes polarized viewpoints. The Main Idea was laid out in the opening paragraph: A new group of environmental reformers who clash with both past reformers and modern industry have emerged.

This is the essence of predictive reading. Each time you reach a key idea or a new paragraph, take a moment to predict what is likely to happen next. Ask specific questions that help you understand the author's intent. Use the context of your predictions and your Roadmap as a guide when you encounter difficult paragraphs, and don't worry if the passage takes a turn that you didn't expect; simply adjust your Roadmap and proceed.

Predictive reading is a skill that takes some time to build, but with a strong foundation in strategic reading it will quickly become second nature to you. The advantages of this nuanced form of reading are tremendous: By staying one step ahead of the author at all times, you will read more efficiently and with greater confidence, and you will avoid becoming bogged down in challenging details. Predictive reading translates directly into saved time, an indispensable part of LSAT success.

PREDICTIVE READING IN CHALLENGING PASSAGES

In the last example, you used predictive reading to help you keep track of assorted viewpoints and make sense of a "twisty" science passage. While the passage certainly presented some challenges, its content and structure were probably familiar to you. Now I'll show you another passage, this one with a more challenging structure.

---

[13]PrepTest 23, Sec 4, Passage 3

In recent years, a growing belief that the way
society decides what to treat as true is controlled
through largely unrecognized discursive practices has
led legal reformers to examine the complex
(5)   interconnections between narrative and law.[14]

Don't let phrases like "unrecognized discursive practices" intimidate you. Read strategically and stay focused on the Keywords. The phrase "has led" points you to the author's main concern, a growing interest in the relationship between narrative and law. **What is coming next?** Most likely some detail describing this relationship. Keep this in mind as you read on.

In many
legal systems, legal judgments are based on competing
stories about events. Without having witnessed these
events, judges and juries must validate some stories as
true and reject others as false. This procedure is rooted
(10)   in objectivism, a philosophical approach that has
supported most Western legal and intellectual systems
for centuries.[15]

Simplified, the author is discussing the stories upon which judgments are made. It isn't important for you to understand exactly what the author is saying here; notice instead that the author *is* providing details about narratives and law, matching the prediction, and has yet to divulge his main point. **Are there any Keywords here that help you predict what's coming next?** "Rooted in" emphasizes the idea of objectivism. The author is likely to describe objectivism in greater detail.

Objectivism holds that there is a single
neutral description of each event that is unskewed by
any particular point of view and that has a privileged
(15)   position over all other accounts. The law's quest for
truth, therefore, consists of locating this objective
description, the one that tells what really happened, as
opposed to what those involved thought happened. The
serious flaw in objectivism is that there is no such thing
(20)   as the neutral, objective observer.[16]

Spot on. The author provided a wordy description of objectivism. Hopefully you stayed strategic and focused on that last sentence, wherein the author provided some excellent opinion and emphasis Keywords: he sees a "serious flaw" in objectivism. **What will the author discuss next?** Since objectivism is so problematic, he will likely present a more viable alternative. Read strategically, and keep an eye out for the alternative if it occurs.

---

[14]PrepTest 22, Sec 1, Passage 2
[15]PrepTest 22, Sec 1, Passage 2
[16]PrepTest 22, Sec 1, Passage 2

As psychologists
have demonstrated, all observers bring to a situation a
set of expectations, values, and beliefs that determine
what the observers are able to see and hear. Two
individuals listening to the same story will hear
(25)   different things, because they emphasize those aspects
that accord with their learned experiences and ignore
those aspects that are dissonant with their view of the
world. Hence there is never any escape in life or in law
from selective perception, or from subjective
(30)   judgments based on prior experiences, values, and
beliefs.[17]

Did the author present an alternative to objectivism here? No. The expected contrast Keywords never arrived, and this text simply gave a more thorough description of the flaw in objectivism. Be prepared for this to happen occasionally as you read passages on test day. This doesn't mean that your prediction was incorrect or badly made, but it does remind you not to let your prediction take precedence over what the author is actually saying. You're only one paragraph into the passage and there's still plenty of time for the alternative to make an appearance. Before moving on, examine the Roadmap so far:

In recent years, a growing belief that the way
society decides what to treat as true is controlled
through largely unrecognized discursive practices has
led legal reformers to examine the complex
(5)   interconnections between narrative and law. In many
legal systems, legal judgments are based on competing
stories about events. Without having witnessed these
events, judges and juries must validate some stories as
true and reject others as false. This procedure is rooted

Objectivism: (10)   in objectivism, a philosophical approach that has
one version of   supported most Western legal and intellectual systems
truth   for centuries. Objectivism holds that there is a single
                        neutral description of each event that is unskewed by
                        any particular point of view and that has a privileged
(15)   position over all other accounts. The law's quest for
                        truth, therefore, consists of locating this objective
                        description, the one that tells what really happened, as
                        opposed to what those involved thought happened. The

Flaw: there   serious flaw in objectivism is that there is no such thing
isn't a   (20)   as the neutral, objective observer. As psychologists
neutral   have demonstrated, all observers bring to a situation a
POV   set of expectations, values, and beliefs that determine
                        what the observers are able to see and hear. Two
                        individuals listening to the same story will hear
(25)   different things, because they emphasize those aspects
                        that accord with their learned experiences and ignore

---

[17]PrepTest 22, Sec 1, Passage 2

those aspects that are dissonant with their view of the
world. (Hence) there is never any escape in life or in law
from selective perception, or from subjective
(30)   judgments based on prior experiences, values, and
beliefs.[18]

What is likely to occur next? Possibly the alternative, or possibly a continued discussion of objectivism. You should be prepared for either so you won't be taken by surprise.

Auth: Harm
caused by
objectivism

      The societal harm (caused by) the assumption of
objectivist principles in traditional legal discourse is
that, historically, the stories judged to be objectively
(35)   true are those told by people who are trained in legal
discourse, (while) the stories of those who are not fluent
in the language of the law are rejected as false.[19]

The author discussed the harm caused by objectivism. There's nothing surprising about that. Before moving on to the final paragraph, think about what you already know and revise your prediction:

What is likely to occur next? You still haven't heard from the reformers that the author mentioned at the beginning of the passage. The most logical next step for the author is to finally present an alternative to objectivism.

      Legal scholars such as Patricia Williams, Derrick
Bell, and Mari Matsuda have sought empowerment for
(40)   the latter group of people through the construction of
alternative legal narratives. Objectivist legal discourse
systematically disallows the language of emotion and
experience by focusing on cognition in its narrowest
sense. These legal reformers propose replacing such
(45)   abstract discourse with powerful personal stories. They
argue that the absorbing, nonthreatening structure and
tone of personal stories may convince legal insiders for
the first time to listen to those not fluent in legal
language. The compelling force of personal narrative
(50)   can create a sense of empathy between legal insiders
and people traditionally excluded from legal discourse
and, hence, from power. Such alternative narratives can
shatter the complacency of the legal establishment and
disturb its tranquility. Thus, the engaging power of
(55)   narrative might play a crucial, positive role in the
process of legal reconstruction by overcoming
differences in background and training and forming a
new collectivity based on emotional empathy.[20]

---

[18]PrepTest 22, Sec 1, Passage 2

[19]PrepTest 22, Sec 1, Passage 2

[20]PrepTest 22, Sec 1, Passage 2

At last! The author introduces the reformers and provides an alternative to objectivism, which he refers to as "alternative legal narratives." He then goes on to provide evidence for the superiority of the alternative, contrasting it with objectivism every step of the way. This long, detail-laden paragraph becomes much easier to understand when you know exactly what it's going to say before you ever see it.

Alternative: personal stories

(40) (Legal scholars) such as Patricia Williams, Derrick Bell, and Mari Matsuda have (sought) empowerment for the latter group of people (through) the construction of alternative legal narratives. Objectivist legal discourse systematically disallows the language of emotion and experience (by focusing) on cognition in its narrowest sense. These legal reformers (propose) replacing such

(45) abstract discourse with (powerful) personal stories. They argue that the absorbing, nonthreatening structure and tone of personal stories may (convince) legal insiders for the first time to listen to those not fluent in legal language. The (compelling) force of personal narrative

Auth: Possible benefits

(50) can create a sense of empathy (between) legal insiders (and) people traditionally excluded from legal discourse and, (hence,) from power. Such alternative narratives can shatter the complacency of the legal establishment and disturb its tranquility. (Thus,) the engaging power of

(55) narrative might play a (crucial,) positive role in the process of legal reconstruction (by) overcoming differences in background and training (and) forming a new collectivity based on emotional empathy.[21]

In order to truly appreciate the true scope of predictive reading, I'd like you to take a quick look at the passage presented as a whole. Don't read it in detail. Just take a moment to examine its appearance on the page:

In recent years, a growing belief that the way society decides what to treat as true is controlled through largely unrecognized discursive practices has led legal reformers to examine the complex

(5) interconnections between narrative and law. In many legal systems, legal judgments are based on competing stories about events. Without having witnessed these events, judges and juries must validate some stories as true and reject others as false. This procedure is rooted

(10) in objectivism, a philosophical approach that has supported most Western legal and intellectual systems for centuries. Objectivism holds that there is a single neutral description of each event that is unskewed by any particular point of view and that has a privileged

(15) position over all other accounts. The law's quest for truth, therefore, consists of locating this objective

---

[21]PrepTest 22, Sec 1, Passage 2

description, the one that tells what really happened, as opposed to what those involved thought happened. The serious flaw in objectivism is that there is no such thing

(20) as the neutral, objective observer. As psychologists have demonstrated, all observers bring to a situation a set of expectations, values, and beliefs that determine what the observers are able to see and hear. Two individuals listening to the same story will hear

(25) different things, because they emphasize those aspects that accord with their learned experiences and ignore those aspects that are dissonant with their view of the world. Hence there is never any escape in life or in law from selective perception, or from subjective

(30) judgments based on prior experiences, values, and beliefs.

The societal harm caused by the assumption of objectivist principles in traditional legal discourse is that, historically, the stories judged to be objectively

(35) true are those told by people who are trained in legal discourse, while the stories of those who are not fluent in the language of the law are rejected as false.

Legal scholars such as Patricia Williams, Derrick Bell, and Mari Matsuda have sought empowerment for

(40) the latter group of people through the construction of alternative legal narratives. Objectivist legal discourse systematically disallows the language of emotion and experience by focusing on cognition in its narrowest sense. These legal reformers propose replacing such

(45) abstract discourse with powerful personal stories. They argue that the absorbing, nonthreatening structure and tone of personal stories may convince legal insiders for the first time to listen to those not fluent in legal language. The compelling force of personal narrative

(50) can create a sense of empathy between legal insiders and people traditionally excluded from legal discourse and, hence, from power. Such alternative narratives can shatter the complacency of the legal establishment and disturb its tranquility. Thus, the engaging power of

(55) narrative might play a crucial, positive role in the process of legal reconstruction by overcoming differences in background and training and forming a new collectivity based on emotional empathy.[22]

---

[22]PrepTest 22, Sec 1, Passage 2

This passage presents an intimidating appearance. Three paragraphs, two of them very long, and plenty of jargon throughout. Compare this with the summary provided by a solid Roadmap:

In recent years, a growing belief that the way
society decides what to treat as true is controlled
through largely unrecognized discursive practices has
led legal reformers to examine the complex
(5) interconnections between narrative and law. In many
legal systems, legal judgments are based on competing
stories about events. Without having witnessed these
events, judges and juries must validate some stories as
true and reject others as false. This procedure is rooted

Objectivism: one version of truth

(10) in objectivism, a philosophical approach that has
supported most Western legal and intellectual systems
for centuries. Objectivism holds that there is a single
neutral description of each event that is unskewed by
any particular point of view and that has a privileged
(15) position over all other accounts. The law's quest for
truth, therefore, consists of locating this objective
description, the one that tells what really happened, as
opposed to what those involved thought happened. The
serious flaw in objectivism is that there is no such thing

Flaw: there isn't a neutral POV

(20) as the neutral, objective observer. As psychologists
have demonstrated, all observers bring to a situation a
set of expectations, values, and beliefs that determine
what the observers are able to see and hear. Two
individuals listening to the same story will hear
(25) different things, because they emphasize those aspects
that accord with their learned experiences and ignore
those aspects that are dissonant with their view of the
world. Hence there is never any escape in life or in law
from selective perception, or from subjective
(30) judgments based on prior experiences, values, and
beliefs.[23]

Auth: Harm caused by objectivism

The societal harm caused by the assumption of
objectivist principles in traditional legal discourse is
that, historically, the stories judged to be objectively
(35) true are those told by people who are trained in legal
discourse, while the stories of those who are not fluent
in the language of the law are rejected as false.

Alternative: personal stories

Legal scholars such as Patricia Williams, Derrick
Bell, and Mari Matsuda have sought empowerment for
(40) the latter group of people through the construction of
alternative legal narratives. Objectivist legal discourse
systematically disallows the language of emotion and
experience by focusing on cognition in its narrowest
sense. These legal reformers propose replacing such
(45) abstract discourse with powerful personal stories. They
argue that the absorbing, nonthreatening structure and
tone of personal stories may convince legal insiders for

[23]PrepTest 22, Sec 1, Passage 2

Auth: possible
benefits

the first time to listen to those not fluent in legal
language. The (compelling) force of personal narrative
(50) can create a sense of empathy (between) legal insiders
(and) people traditionally excluded from legal discourse
and, (hence,) from power. Such alternative narratives can
shatter the complacency of the legal establishment and
disturb its tranquility. (Thus,) the engaging power of
(55) narrative might play a (crucial) positive role in the
process of legal reconstruction (by) overcoming
differences in background and training (and) forming a
new collectivity based on emotional empathy.

Notice how few ideas there actually were in this passage. By reading strategically, and by actively predicting the nature of the author's main points, you can reduce this dense, difficult passage to the following Main Idea: Objectivism is flawed, but personal narrative is a good alternative. Use this simple prediction to answer the following LSAT question:

9.   Which one of the following best states the main idea of
     the passage?

     (A)   Some legal scholars have sought to empower
           people historically excluded from traditional
           legal discourse by instructing them in the forms
           of discourse favored by legal insiders.
     (B)   Some legal scholars have begun to realize the
           social harm caused by the adversarial
           atmosphere that has pervaded many legal
           systems for centuries.
     (C)   Some legal scholars have proposed alleviating the
           harm caused by the prominence of objectivist
           principles within legal discourse by replacing
           that discourse with alternative forms of legal
           narrative.
     (D)   Some legal scholars have contended that those
           who feel excluded from objectivist legal systems
           would be empowered by the construction of a
           new legal language that better reflected
           objectivist principles.
     (E)   Some legal scholars have argued that the basic
           flaw inherent in objectivist theory can be
           remedied by recognizing that it is not possible to
           obtain a single neutral description of a particular
           event.[24]

The only choice that matches your prediction is choice (C).

This is how predictive reading translates into points on test day; it keeps you focused on the big picture, helps you sift through the details, and saves you crucial time that you can spend on the question set. Furthermore, while predictive reading is very helpful on a simple passage, it is absolutely indispensable on a tougher example like this one.

---

[24]PrepTest 22, Sec 1, Passage 2, Q 9

DRILL: READING PREDICTIVELY

Now it's time for you to practice predictive reading. I'd like to return to a passage that you examined partially in the last chapter. This passage contains multiple viewpoints and a dense paragraph structure, but, like all LSAT passages, it contains the clues you need to map out its structure. I've broken down the passage into small portions, each followed by predictive-reading questions. As always, circle Keywords as you spot them, and answer each question as you reach it. Be sure to keep your predictions in mind as you continue to read; the insight they provide will help you untangle the author's main ideas more quickly and easily.

Paragraph 1

Two impressive studies have reexamined Eric Williams' conclusion that Britain's abolition of the slave trade in 1807 and its emancipation of slaves in its colonies in 1834 were driven primarily by economic

(5) rather than humanitarian motives. Blighted by depleted soil, indebtedness, and the inefficiency of coerced labor, these colonies, according to Williams, had by 1807 become an impediment to British economic progress.[25]

1.   Whose opinions are likely to be presented in the coming paragraphs?

_____

2.   How might they differ from Williams' conclusion?

_____

Paragraph 2

(10)   Seymour Drescher provides a more balanced view. Rejecting interpretations based either on economic interest or the moral vision of abolitionists, Drescher has reconstructed the populist characteristics of British abolitionism, which appears to have cut across lines of class, party, and religion.[26]

3.   What is likely to follow the presentation of Drescher's idea?

_____

---

[25]PrepTest 19, Sec 3, Passage 4
[26]PrepTest 19, Sec 3, Passage 4

Noting that between 1780
(15)   and 1830 antislavery petitions outnumbered those on
any other issue, including parliamentary reform,
Drescher concludes that such support cannot be
explained by economic interest alone, especially when
much of it came from the unenfranchised masses. Yet,
(20)   aside from demonstrating that such support must have
resulted at least in part from widespread literacy and a
tradition of political activism, Drescher does not finally
explain how England, a nation deeply divided by class
struggles, could mobilize popular support for
(25)   antislavery measures proposed by otherwise
conservative politicians in the House of Lords and
approved there with little dissent.[27]

4.   What is the author's opinion of Drescher's work?

_____

5.   Based on the author's opinion of Drescher, combined with what you know so far, what is
likely to come next?

_____

Paragraph 3

David Eltis' answer to that question actually
supports some of Williams' insights.[28]

6.   What was Williams' main idea?

_____

7.   What ideas will likely appear in Eltis' answer?

_____

Eschewing
Drescher's idealization of British traditions of liberty,
(30)   Eltis points to continuing use of low wages and
Draconian vagrancy laws in the seventeenth and
eighteenth centuries to ensure the industriousness of
British workers. Indeed, certain notables even called
for the enslavement of unemployed laborers who
(35)   roamed the British countryside—an acceptance of
coerced labor that Eltis attributes to a preindustrial
desire to keep labor costs low and exports competitive.[29]

---

[27]PrepTest 19, Sec 3, Passage 4

[28]PrepTest 19, Sec 3, Passage 4

[29]PrepTest 19, Sec 3, Passage 4

8. What is likely to happen next?

_____

By the late eighteenth century, however, a growing
home market began to alert capitalists to the
(40) importance of "want creation" and to incentives such
as higher wages as a means of increasing both worker
productivity and the number of consumers.
Significantly, it was products grown by slaves, such as
sugar, coffee, and tobacco, that stimulated new wants
(45) at all levels of British society and were the forerunners
of products intended in modern capitalist societies to
satisfy what Eltis describes as "nonsubsistence or
psychological needs." Eltis concludes that in an
economy that had begun to rely on voluntary labor to
satisfy such needs, forced labor necessarily began to
(50) appear both inappropriate and counterproductive to
employers.[30]

9. Whose point of view is the author discussing?

_____

10. What is likely to follow?

_____

Eltis thus concludes that, while Williams
(55) may well have underestimated the economic viability
of the British colonies employing forced labor in the
early 1800s, his insight into the economic motives for
abolition was partly accurate. British leaders became
committed to colonial labor reform only when they
became convinced, for reasons other than those cited
by Williams, that free labor was more beneficial to the
imperial economy.[31]

11. What is the main difference between the viewpoints of Eltis and Williams?

_____

[30]PrepTest 19, Sec 3, Passage 4
[31]PrepTest 19, Sec 3, Passage 4

Explanations

Paragraph 1

(5) Two impressive studies have reexamined Eric Williams' conclusion that Britain's abolition of the slave trade in 1807 and its emancipation of slaves in its colonies in 1834 were driven primarily by economic rather than humanitarian motives. Blighted by depleted soil, indebtedness, and the inefficiency of coerced labor, these colonies, according to Williams, had by 1807 become an impediment to British economic progress.[32]

1. Whose opinions are likely to be presented in the coming paragraphs?

The first paragraph begins with excellent Keywords you can use to make an immediate prediction: Since "two impressive studies" have reexamined Williams's work, you should expect to see those studies appear in subsequent paragraphs, and you should be prepared to pick out the thesis of each one. This prediction may seem rather obvious, but remember that one of the key advantages of predictive reading is focus: You know what important ideas are coming next and you will be prepared for them when you see them.

2. How might they differ from Williams's conclusion?

I hope you were careful to note the gist of Williams' conclusion, that the abolition of British slavery was primarily motivated by economics. Since the two upcoming studies "reexamine" his work, you should expect them to contrast in some way with Williams's conclusion.

Paragraph 2

(10) Seymour Drescher provides a more balanced view. Rejecting interpretations based either on economic interest or the moral vision of abolitionists, Drescher has reconstructed the populist characteristics of British abolitionism, which appears to have cut across lines of class, party, and religion.[33]

3. What is likely to follow the presentation of Drescher's idea?

According to the author, Drescher's view is more "balanced," and involves an examination of the British population at large. You should expect to see support for this idea in the following sentences. Be prepared to read these ideas quickly, without getting lost in them.

---

[32]PrepTest 19, Sec 3, Passage 4

[33]PrepTest 19, Sec 3, Passage 4

(15)   Noting that between 1780
and 1830 antislavery petitions outnumbered those on
any other issue, including parliamentary reform,
Drescher concludes that such support cannot be
explained by economic interest alone, especially when
much of it came from the unenfranchised masses. Yet,
(20) aside from demonstrating that such support must have
resulted at least in part from widespread literacy and a
tradition of political activism, Drescher does not finally
explain how England, a nation deeply divided by class
struggles, could mobilize popular support for
(25) antislavery measures proposed by otherwise
conservative politicians in the House of Lords and
approved there with little dissent.[34]

4. What is the author's opinion of Drescher's work?

True to the prediction, the next two sentences expand upon Drescher's main point. But the contrast Keyword "yet" signals a contrast, and in line 23 the author indicates that Drescher does not adequately make clear how his explanation could have been possible.

5. Based on the author's opinion of Drescher, combined with what you know so far, what is likely to come next?

Here you can make a more sophisticated predication, one that can provide needed context for the final paragraph. You know that the author intends to present *two* examinations of Williams's work, and so far you've only seen one. You also know that the author believes that Drescher's ideas were inadequate to explain abolition. It's therefore extremely plausible that the author is preparing not only to introduce a second review of Williams, but also to indicate whether it provides a better explanation than Drescher's. Taking a few seconds to prepare yourself in this way for the detail-rich third paragraph begins to pay off almost immediately.

Paragraph 3
    David Eltis' answer to that question actually
(30) supports some of Williams' insights.[35]

6. What was Williams's main idea?

As predicted, the second review of Williams appears, and the author states that it answers the question that Drescher didn't address. The author also points out that Eltis supports some of Williams's original ideas. You should take a moment to review what those ideas were before proceeding, and it doesn't take long: The crux of Williams's conclusion was that abolition was primarily the result of economic pressures.

---

[34]PrepTest 19, Sec 3, Passage 4
[35]PrepTest 19, Sec 3, Passage 4

7. What ideas will likely appear in Eltis's answer?

Since Eltis must partially support Williams, you can therefore expect Eltis's explanation to involve economic issues as well.

(30)　　　Eschewing
　　　Drescher's idealization of British traditions of liberty,
　　　Eltis points to continuing use of low wages and
　　　Draconian vagrancy laws in the seventeenth and
　　　eighteenth centuries to ensure the industriousness of
(35)　British workers. Indeed, certain notables even called
　　　for the enslavement of unemployed laborers who
　　　roamed the British countryside—an acceptance of
　　　coerced labor that Eltis attributes to a preindustrial
　　　desire to keep labor costs low and exports competitive.[36]

8. What is likely to happen next?

Predictably, the author is now explaining Eltis' view in earnest, and it centers on issues related to the British economy, specifically the problems of low wages and unemployment. Don't get bogged down in these details. At this point, since there are no Keywords to indicate a change in direction, you should expect the explanation to continue.

(40)　　　By the late eighteenth century, however, a growing
　　　home market began to alert capitalists to the
　　　importance of "want creation" and to incentives such
　　　as higher wages as a means of increasing both worker
　　　productivity and the number of consumers.
(45)　Significantly, it was products grown by slaves, such as
　　　sugar, coffee, and tobacco, that stimulated new wants
　　　at all levels of British society and were the forerunners
　　　of products intended in modern capitalist societies to
　　　satisfy what Eltis describes as "nonsubsistence or
(50)　psychological needs." Eltis concludes that in an
　　　economy that had begun to rely on voluntary labor to
　　　satisfy such needs, forced labor necessarily began to
　　　appear both inappropriate and counterproductive to
　　　employers.[37]

9. Whose point of view is the author discussing?

The author is still discussing Eltis and continues to do so right through to his conclusion. Don't be thrown by the presence of the Keyword "however." While you should certainly circle it and note that the author is demonstrating a contrast, it is a contrast within his continuing description of Eltis's ideas.

---

[36]PrepTest 19, Sec 3, Passage 4
[37]PrepTest 19, Sec 3, Passage 4

10. What is likely to follow?

Now that Eltis's conclusion has been revealed, the author is likely to reveal his final evaluation.

(55) Eltis thus concludes that, while Williams may well have underestimated the economic viability of the British colonies employing forced labor in the early 1800s, his insight into the economic motives for abolition was partly accurate. British leaders became committed to colonial labor reform only when they
(60) became convinced, for reasons other than those cited by Williams, that free labor was more beneficial to the imperial economy.[38]

11. What is the main difference between the viewpoints of Eltis and Williams?

Eltis is in partial agreement with Williams, acknowledging that economic forces did play an important role in the abolition of slavery, but he disagrees with the reasons that Williams provides.

---

[38]PrepTest 19, Sec 3, Passage 4

DRILL: ANSWERING THE QUESTIONS

Now use your understanding of the passage to answer a few questions. I'll provide a sample Roadmap to assist your research. Be sure to write down the Topic, Scope, Purpose, and Main Idea in the blanks provided before attempting to answer the questions. When you're finished, review the explanations carefully.

Williams: abolition for economic reasons.

Two impressive studies have reexamined Eric Williams' conclusion that Britain's abolition of the slave trade in 1807 and its emancipation of slaves in its colonies in 1834 were driven primarily by economic
(5)   rather than humanitarian motives. Blighted by depleted soil, indebtedness, and the inefficiency of coerced labor, these colonies, according to Williams, had by 1807 become an impediment to British economic progress.

Drescher: more balanced

(10)   Seymour Drescher provides a more balanced view. Rejecting interpretations based either on economic interest or the moral vision of abolitionists, Drescher has reconstructed the populist characteristics of British abolitionism, which appears to have cut across lines of
(15)   class, party, and religion. Noting that between 1780 and 1830 antislavery petitions outnumbered those on any other issue, including parliamentary reform,

Not just economics.

Drescher concludes that such support cannot be explained by economic interest alone, especially when
(20)   much of it came from the unenfranchised masses. Yet, aside from demonstrating that such support must have resulted at least in part from widespread literacy and a tradition of political activism, Drescher does not finally

Auth: Drescher doesn't fully explain

explain how England, a nation deeply divided by class
(25)   struggles, could mobilize popular support for antislavery measures proposed by otherwise conservative politicians in the House of Lords and approved there with little dissent.

Eltis: partly agrees w/ Williams

David Eltis' answer to that question actually
(30)   supports some of Williams' insights. Eschewing Drescher's idealization of British traditions of liberty, Eltis points to continuing use of low wages and Draconian vagrancy laws in the seventeenth and eighteenth centuries to ensure the industriousness of
(35)   British workers. Indeed, certain notables even called for the enslavement of unemployed laborers who roamed the British countryside—an acceptance of coerced labor that Eltis attributes to a preindustrial desire to keep labor costs low and exports competitive.
(40)   By the late eighteenth century, however, a growing home market began to alert capitalists to the importance of "want creation" and to incentives such as higher wages as a means of increasing both worker productivity and the number of consumers.

(45) (Significantly,) it was products grown by slaves, such as
sugar, coffee, and tobacco, that stimulated new wants
at all levels of British society (and) were the forerunners
of products intended in modern capitalist societies to
satisfy what (Eltis describes) as "nonsubsistence or

voluntary (50) psychological needs." (Eltis concludes) that in an
labor leads to economy that had begun to rely on voluntary labor to
abolition satisfy such needs, forced labor (necessarily) began to
appear (both) inappropriate (and) counterproductive to
employers. Eltis (thus concludes) that, (while) Williams

Eltis on (55) may well have underestimated the economic viability
Williams of the British colonies employing forced labor in the
early 1800s, his insight into the economic motives for
abolition was (partly accurate.) British leaders became
committed to colonial labor reform (only when) they

(60) became (convinced,) for reasons (other than) those cited
by Williams, that free labor was more beneficial to the
imperial economy.[39]

Topic: _____

Scope: _____

Purpose: _____

Main Idea: _____

1. Which one of the following best describes the main idea
   of the passage?

   (A)   Although they disagree about the degree to which
         economic motives influenced Britain's abolition
         of slavery, Drescher and Eltis both concede that
         moral persuasion by abolitionists was a
         significant factor.

   (B)   Although both Drescher and Eltis have
         questioned Williams' analysis of the motivation
         behind Britain's abolition of slavery, there is
         support for part of Williams' conclusion.

   (C)   Because he has taken into account the populist
         characteristics of British abolitionism,
         Drescher's explanation of what motivated
         Britain's abolition of slavery is finally more
         persuasive than that of Eltis.

   (D)   Neither Eltis nor Drescher has succeeded in
         explaining why support for Britain's abolition of
         slavery appears to have cut across lines of party,
         class, and religion.

   (E)   Although flawed in certain respects, Williams'
         conclusions regarding the economic condition of
         British slave colonies early in the nineteenth
         century have been largely vindicated.[40]

---

[39]PrepTest 19, Sec 3, Passage 4
[40]PrepTest 19, Sec 3, Passage 4, Q 21

2. Which one of the following best states Williams' view of the primary reason for Britain's abolition of the slave trade and the emancipation of slaves in its colonies?

    (A)   British populism appealed to people of varied classes, parties, and religions.
    (B)   Both capitalists and workers in Britain accepted the moral precepts of abolitionists.
    (C)   Forced labor in the colonies could not produce enough goods to satisfy British consumers.
    (D)   The operation of colonies based on forced labor was no longer economically advantageous.
    (E)   British workers became convinced that forced labor in the colonies prevented paid workers from receiving higher wages.[41]

3. It can be inferred that the author of the passage views Drescher's presentation of British traditions concerning liberty as

    (A)   accurately stated
    (B)   somewhat unrealistic
    (C)   carefully researched
    (D)   unnecessarily tentative
    (E)   superficially convincing[42]

---

[41]PrepTest 19, Sec 3, Passage 4, Q 23
[42]PrepTest 19, Sec 3, Passage 4, Q 25

Explanations

Topic: The abolition of the slave trade in Britain, as introduced in the first paragraph

Scope: Various explanations for British abolition

Purpose: To examine an explanation of abolition, and to evaluate two responses to the original explanation

Main Idea: Williams' ideas are partially vindicated by Eltis' conclusions.

1. **(B)**

    Which one of the following best describes the main idea of the passage?
    (A) Although they disagree about the degree to which economic motives influenced Britain's abolition of slavery, Drescher and Eltis both concede that moral persuasion by abolitionists was a significant factor.
    (B) Although both Drescher and Eltis have questioned Williams' analysis of the motivation behind Britain's abolition of slavery, there is support for part of Williams' conclusion.
    (C) Because he has taken into account the populist characteristics of British abolitionism, Drescher's explanation of what motivated Britain's abolition of slavery is finally more persuasive than that of Eltis.
    (D) Neither Eltis nor Drescher has succeeded in explaining why support for Britain's abolition of slavery appears to have cut across lines of party, class, and religion.
    (E) Although flawed in certain respects, Williams' conclusions regarding the economic condition of British slave colonies early in the nineteenth century have been largely vindicated.[43]

Recall that when you read the passage predictively you were careful to actively anticipate differing viewpoints. When the author presented (and favorably evaluated) Eltis's conclusion at the beginning of paragraph 3, he was careful to point out that Eltis was in partial agreement with Williams. Only choice (B) matches the author's opinion.

---

[43]PrepTest 19, Sec 3, Passage 4, Q 21

2. **(D)**

> Which one of the following best states Williams' view of
> the primary reason for Britain's abolition of the slave
> trade and the emancipation of slaves in its colonies?
> (A)   British populism appealed to people of varied
>   classes, parties, and religions.
> (B)   Both capitalists and workers in Britain accepted
>   the moral precepts of abolitionists.
> (C)   Forced labor in the colonies could not produce
>   enough goods to satisfy British consumers.
> (D)   The operation of colonies based on forced labor
>   was no longer economically advantageous.
> (E)   British workers became convinced that forced
>   labor in the colonies prevented paid workers
>   from receiving higher wages.[44]

The Roadmap reminds you that Williams' central assertion appears in the first paragraph, and as you read the passage predictively you consistently came back to Williams in order to provide context for Eltis and Drescher. What was Williams' main idea? That abolition ultimately came about as a result of economic considerations. Choice (D) is correct.

3. **(B)**

> It can be inferred that the author of the passage views
> Drescher's presentation of British traditions concerning
> liberty as
> (A)   accurately stated
> (B)   somewhat unrealistic
> (C)   carefully researched
> (D)   unnecessarily tentative
> (E)   superficially convincing[45]

The author states that Drescher's viewpoint is not sufficiently explanatory in lines 23–28. You used this information to provide context for the third paragraph and, hence, for the Main Idea of the passage. As it happens, this question rewards you for being alert to the author's voice. The only two choices that disparage Drescher's scholarship are (B) and (D). Choice (D) is out of scope, while correct choice (B) matches the author's evaluation perfectly.

PREDICTIVE READING IN REVIEW

I want to close this chapter by reinforcing the major concepts presented in this chapter. Since the LSAT demands efficiency from you as a reader, you absolutely must stay a step ahead of the author whenever you can. The presence of Keywords and predictable passage structures provide you with the tools you need to do so.

---

[44]PrepTest 19, Sec 3 Passage 4, Q 23
[45]PrepTest 19, Sec 3 Passage 4, Q 25

As you practice, get into the habit of pausing after each major idea and paragraph break to predict what is likely to occur next in the passage. Use the context of what you've already read to help you make accurate predictions, and don't be afraid to review earlier portions of your Roadmap if necessary. Remember that predictive reading is a fluid process; if you encounter something unexpected in the passage, continue reading strategically and adjust your predictions accordingly. Be confident in your ability to stay ahead of the author, but don't let your expectations blind you to what the author is really saying. Finally, remember that predictive reading is a tool to help you focus on the right things. You're likelier to spot and incorporate the author's primary ideas into your Roadmap more quickly and accurately if you already have a good idea about what those ideas will be.

This skill can be challenging to develop at first. As always, practice slowly and methodically until you feel the process begin to feel more natural. With dedication, you'll find that you're soon asking anticipatory questions of every passage by reflex. This level of mastery will come with repetition. It will also come with familiarity; LSAT passages tend to follow a small number of predictable structural patterns, and once you learn to recognize them, the art of predictive reading becomes even easier. I'll explain this idea further in the next chapter.

CHAPTER 7

COMMON PASSAGE STRUCTURES

PATTERNS IN THE PASSAGES

By this point you should feel fairly comfortable with Kaplan's Method for strategic reading. You've read and Roadmapped a number of passages and you've gotten into the habit of identifying the Topic, Scope, Purpose, and Main Idea. In the last chapter I illustrated the predictable nature of LSAT Reading Comprehension passages and showed you how to read predictively.

Through practice and repetition you may have begun to notice that there are only a limited number of passage structures that tend to occur regularly, and that sometimes the Purpose of one passage is very much like the Purpose of another. Of course, you've been exposed to many different Topics in your practice—so far you've read passages about Victorian philanthropy, objectivist legal discourse, and environmentalist doctrines, just to mention a few. But now that you're reading strategically and focusing on structure, you've learned that these passages aren't really as diverse as they seem.

Take a moment to think through the last passage you read. Try to remember the author's Purpose and what you wrote in your Roadmap. The passage probably presented several points of view, some of which were in conflict. Perhaps the author supported one viewpoint over another, or perhaps she presented an original argument. Even if you can't remember precisely what the passage was about, you can probably recall the presence of these broader ideas in the passage structure because you used them to formulate the author's Purpose.

I've already demonstrated that the skill of prediction is one of your greatest advantages in Reading Comprehension. Knowing that the passages are predictable will boost your confidence as well as your score. To supplement the skills you've already learned, I'll now illustrate the most common Purposes in the passages.

THREE COMMON PURPOSES

Although the passages will vary widely in their content, there are three common Purposes that the author will pursue:

- To support or refute an opinion other than his own
- To argue in favor of his own opinion
- To describe a series of ideas without taking sides

As I describe each Purpose in greater detail, please keep in mind that they are not inflexible categories that must exclude one another in every passage. For example, authors will frequently refute others' opinions before presenting their own opinions. But as you determine the author's primary Purpose, you'll often find that it primarily follows one of these three basic patterns, and knowing which one will make all the difference as you answer the questions.

Support or Refute an Opinion

You know from previous chapters that when the author presents outside viewpoints in a passage, you should seek the author's evaluations of them. Because LSAT passages tend to be argumentative in tone (the LSAT is designed for law schools, after all), the authors usually voice strong opinions. Review the following passage and its Roadmap:

Soc: gatherings
mean tribal
decline

(Even) in the midst of its (resurgence) as a vital tradition, many (sociologists) have viewed the current form of the powwow, a ceremonial gathering of native Americans (as a sign) that tribal culture is in decline.
(5) (Focusing) on the dances and rituals that have (recently) come to be shared by most tribes, they (suggest) that an intertribal movement is now in ascension and (claim) the (inevitable) outcome of this tendency is the eventual dissolution of tribes (and) the complete assimilation of
(10) native Americans into Euroamerican society.

Pan-Indian
theory,
evidence

(Proponents) of this "Pan-Indian" theory (point to) the greater frequency of travel and communication between reservations, the greater urbanization of native Americans, (and,) most (recently,) their increasing
(15) politicization in (response) to common grievances as the chief causes of the shift toward intertribalism.

Intertribalism
on rise

(Indeed) the rapid diffusion of dance styles, outfits, and songs from one reservation to another offers (compelling evidence) that intertribalism has been

Unique traditions rising too

(20) increasing. However, these sociologists have failed to note the concurrent revitalization of many traditions unique to individual tribes. Among the Lakota, for instance, the Sun Dance was revived, after a forty-year hiatus, during the 1950's. Similarly the Black Legging

(25) Society of the Kiowa and the Hethuska Society of the Ponca—both traditional groups within their respective

P.I.T doesn't explain

tribes—have gained new popularity. Obviously, a more complex societal shift is taking place than the theory of Pan-Indianism can account for.

(30) An examination of the theory's underpinnings may

Auth: must examine theory

be critical at this point, especially given that native Americans themselves chafe most against the Pan-Indian classification. Like other assimilationist theories with which it is associated, the Pan-Indian view is

(35) predicated upon an a priori assumption about the nature

Theory based on wrong assump.

of cultural contact: that upon contact minority societies immediately begin to succumb in every respect—biologically, linguistically, and culturally—to the majority society. However, there is no evidence

(40) that this is happening to native American groups.

Intertribal act. Still important

Yet the fact remains that intertribal activities are a major facet of native American culture today. Certain dances at powwows for instance are announced as intertribal, other as traditional. Likewise, speeches

(45) given at the beginnings of powwows are often delivered in English, while the prayer that follows is usually spoken in a native language. Cultural borrowing is of course, old news. What is important to note is the conscious distinction native Americans

Tribal and Intertribal distinct

(50) make between tribal and intertribal tendencies.

Tribalism, although greatly altered by modern history, remains a potent force among native

Auth: Both are important

Americans: It forms a basis for tribal identity, and aligns music and dance with other social and cultural

(55) activities important to individual tribes. Intertribal activities, on the other hand reinforce native American identity along a broader front, where this identity is directly threatened by outside influences.[1]

Think about the structure of the passage and try to define the author's Purpose. In the first paragraph, the author introduces the proponents of the "Pan-Indian" theory, who state that tribalism is in decline. Does the author agree with them?

No. In the final three paragraphs, the author demonstrates that the theory's predictions have failed to come true, and concludes in line 52 that tribalism "remains a potent force among native Americans." Does the author provide an alternative theory? Again, no. The author's primary Purpose is to refute the theory that tribalism is in decline. It's true that in doing so

---

[1]PrepTest 25, Sec 1, Passage 3

the author provides evidence that intertribal activities strengthen tribal communities rather than weaken them, but the discussion is still centered around the theory put forward by the sociologists in the first paragraph.

This may seem like a minor distinction, but it can be a very important concept to be aware of before answering the questions. Take a look at this one:

21. In the passage, the author is primarily concerned with doing which one of the following?

(A) identifying an assumption common to various assimilationist theories and then criticizing these theories by showing this assumption to be false

(B) arguing that the recent revival of a number of tribal practices shows sociologists are mistaken in believing intertribalism to be a potent force among native American societies

(C) questioning the belief that native American societies will eventually be assimilated into Euroamerican society by arguing that intertribalism helps strengthen native American identity

(D) showing how the recent resurgence of tribal activities is a deliberate attempt to counteract the growing influence of intertribalism

(E) proposing an explanation of why the ascension of intertribalism could result in the eventual dissolution of tribes and complete assimilation of native American into Euroamerican society[2]

Choices (D) and (E) fail to mention the author's core disagreement with the sociologists. Choice (A) might look tempting at first, but its scope is far too broad—the author is primarily concerned with refuting a single theory. Choice (B) distorts the author's viewpoint—she clearly believes that intertribalism *is* a potent force in tribal life. That leaves choice (C), the correct choice. As in your prediction, the author's Purpose is to question a given belief by presenting counter evidence. Your understanding of the author's goal guides you past the traps to score the point.

Try another question:

---

[2]PrepTest 25, Sec 1, Q 21

16. The author of the passage would most likely agree with which one of the following assertions?

    (A) Though some believe the current form of the powwow signals the decline of tribal culture, the powwow contains elements that indicate the continuing strength of tribalism.

    (B) The logical outcome of the recent increase in intertribal activity is the eventual disappearance of tribal culture.

    (C) Native Americans who participate in both tribal and intertribal activities usually base their identities on intertribal rather than tribal affiliations.

    (D) The conclusions of some sociologists about the health of native American cultures show that these sociologists are in fact biased against such cultures.

    (E) Until it is balanced by revitalization of tribal customs, intertribalism will continue to weaken the native American sense of identity.[3]

The correct answer, choice (A), explicitly references the author's Purpose by asserting that her conclusion is true despite the fact that "some believe" that tribal culture is in decline. Note that even though this question didn't explicitly ask for the author's Purpose, understanding it was instrumental in scoring the point.

The LSAT is riddled with passages in which the author's primary goal is to support or refute a given theory. Here's another variation. Review this passage and Roadmap from the previous chapter:

> In (recent) years, a growing (belief) that the way society decides what to treat as true is controlled through largely unrecognized discursive practices has (led) legal (reformers) to examine the complex
> (5) interconnections between narrative and law. In many legal systems, legal judgments are (based on) competing stories about events. (Without) having witnessed these events, judges and juries (must) validate some stories as true (and) reject others as false. This procedure is (rooted)
>
> *Objectivism: one version of truth*
> (10) in objectivism, a philosophical approach that has (supported) most Western legal and intellectual systems for centuries. Objectivism (holds) that there is a single neutral description of each event that is unskewed by any particular point of view (and) that has a privileged
> (15) position over all other accounts. The law's quest for truth, (therefore,) consists of locating this objective description, the one that tells what really happened, as (opposed to) what those involved thought happened. The (serious flaw) in objectivism is that there is no such thing

---

Flaw—
there isn't
a neutral
POV

(20)　as the neutral, objective observer. (As) psychologists
have demonstrated, all observers bring to a situation a
set of expectations, values, and beliefs that determine
what the observers are able to see and hear. Two
individuals listening to the same story will hear
(25)　different things, (because) they emphasize those aspects
that accord with their learned experiences (and) ignore
those aspects that are dissonant with their view of the
world. (Hence) there is never any escape in life or in law
from selective perception, or from subjective
(30)　judgments based on prior experiences, values, and
beliefs.

Harm
caused by
objectivism

　　The societal harm (caused by) the assumption of
objectivist principles in traditional legal discourse is
that, historically, the stories judged to be objectively
(35)　true are those told by people who are trained in legal
discourse, (while) the stories of those who are not fluent
in the language of the law are rejected as false.

Alternative:
personal
stories

　　(Legal scholars) such as Patricia Williams, Derrick
Bell, and Mari Matsuda have (sought) empowerment for
(40)　the latter group of people (through) the construction of
alternative legal narratives. Objectivist legal discourse
systematically disallows the language of emotion and
experience (by focusing) on cognition in its narrowest
sense. These legal reformers (propose) replacing such
(45)　abstract discourse with (powerful) personal stories. They
(argue) that the absorbing, nonthreatening structure and
tone of personal stories may (convince) legal insiders for
the first time to listen to those not fluent in legal
language. The (compelling) force of personal narrative
(50)　can create a sense of empathy (between) legal insiders
(and) people traditionally excluded from legal discourse
and, (hence,) from power. Such alternative narratives can
shatter the complacency of the legal establishment and
disturb its tranquility. (Thus,) the engaging power of
(55)　narrative might play a (crucial) positive role in the
process of legal reconstruction (by) overcoming
differences in background and training (and) forming a
new collectivity based on emotional empathy.[4]

In this passage, the author begins by describing the principles of objectivism and then refutes them. Next, she introduces the alternative theory of the legal scholars listed in lines 38–39 and supports it, noting in line 55 that it "might play a crucial, positive role" in our legal system.

Notice how similar the structure of this passage is to the prior example. The only real difference is that this author endorses the specific alternative provided by the legal scholars, whereas the author of the previous passage simply demonstrated that the sociologists were wrong.

Once again, an example from the question set shows why the difference matters:

---

[4]PrepTest 22, Sec 1, Passage 2

9. Which one of the following best states the main idea of the passage?[5]

   (A) Some legal scholars have sought to empower people historically excluded from traditional legal discourse by instructing them in the forms of discourse favored by legal insiders.

   (B) Some legal scholars have begun to realize the social harm caused by the adversarial atmosphere that has pervaded many legal systems for centuries.

   (C) Some legal scholars have proposed alleviating the harm caused by the prominence of objectivist principles within legal discourse by replacing that discourse with alternative forms of legal narrative.

   (D) Some legal scholars have contended that those who feel excluded from objectivist legal systems would be empowered by the construction of a new legal language that better reflected objectivist principles.

   (E) Some legal scholars have argued that the basic flaw inherent in objectivist theory can be remedied by recognizing that it is not possible to obtain a single neutral description of a particular event.[5]

All of the answer choices focus on the opinions of the legal scholars with whom the author sided. Your prediction should take this into account. The correct answer should indicate that the scholars reject objectivism and seek to replace it with personal stories. Only correct choice (C) matches this prediction.

These examples reinforce the importance of the author's point of view. When the author of an LSAT passage mentions outside opinions, be on the lookout for her reaction.

Provide a New Opinion

By now, you're very familiar with the author's tendency to support and refute third party opinions. Sometimes the author goes a step further and provides an entirely new opinion that doesn't necessarily flow directly from prior viewpoints. To illustrate, review the passage about the fiction of P. D. James, along with its Roadmap:

Critics: Praise James or attack her   Wherever the crime novels of P. D. James are discussed by critics, there is a tendency on the one hand to exaggerate her merits and on the other to castigate her as a genre writer who is getting above
(5) herself. Perhaps underlying the debate is that familiar, false opposition set up between different kinds of fiction, according to which enjoyable novels are held to

be somehow slightly lowbrow, and a novel is not
considered true literature unless it is a tiny bit dull.

(10)   Those commentators who would elevate James's
books to the status of high literature point to her
painstakingly constructed characters, her elaborate
settings, her sense of place, and her love of
abstractions: notions about morality, duty, pain, and
(15) pleasure are never far from the lips of her police
officers and murderers. Others find her pretentious and
tiresome; an inverted snobbery accuses her of
abandoning the time-honored conventions of the
detective genre in favor of a highbrow literary style.
(20) The critic Harriet Waugh wants P.D. James to get on
with "the more taxing business of laying a tricky trail
and then fooling the reader"; Philip Oakes in *The
Literary Review* groans, "Could we please proceed
with the business of clapping the handcuffs on the
(25) killer?"

James is certainly capable of strikingly good
writing. She takes immense trouble to provide her
characters with convincing histories and passions. Her
descriptive digressions are part of the pleasure of her
(30) books and give them dignity and weight. But it is
equally true that they frequently interfere with the
story; the patinas and aromas of a country kitchen
receive more loving attention than does the plot itself.
Her devices to advance the story can be shameless and
(35) thin, and it is often impossible to see how her detective
arrives at the truth; one is left to conclude that the
detective solves crimes through intuition. At this stage
in her career P. D. James seems to be less interested in
the specifics of detection than in her characters'
(40) vulnerabilities and perplexities.

However, once the rules of a chosen genre cramp
creative thought, there is no reason why an able and
interesting writer should accept them. In her latest
book, there are signs that James is beginning to feel
(45) constrained by the crime-novel genre. Here her
determination to leave areas of ambiguity in the
solution of the crime and to distribute guilt among the
murderer, victim, and bystanders points to a conscious
rebellion against the traditional neatness of detective
(50) fiction. It is fashionable, though reprehensible, for one
writer to prescribe to another. But perhaps the time has
come for P. D. James to slide out of her handcuffs and
stride into the territory of the mainstream novel.[6]

Margin notes:

Critics: who like James

Critics: who dislike James

Auth: James very descriptive

Sometimes bad for plot

James not limited by genre

James maybe go mainstr.

The author presents and agrees to some extent with two separate groups of critics as described in the first paragraph—those who "exaggerate her merits" and those consider her a genre writer "getting above herself." But pay close attention to lines 5–9, in which the author describes these conflicting opinions as a "false opposition."

---

[6]PrepTest 19, Sec 3, Passage 1

The author's true Purpose is revealed in the final paragraph, in which the author suggests that James should consider becoming a mainstream novelist. This time, the author isn't content to simply refute one side of an argument or agree with another. She ultimately defies both groups of critics and produces her own interpretation of James's work. In formulating the Purpose, you also know the Main Idea should reflect this new interpretation: P. D. James should consider moving beyond the detective novel genre. With this in mind, take another look at this question:

1. Which one of the following best states the author's main conclusion?

   (A) Because P. D. James's potential as a writer is stifled by her chosen genre, she should turn her talents toward writing mainstream novels.
   (B) Because the requirements of the popular novel are incompatible with true creative expression, P. D. James's promise as a serious author has been diminished.
   (C) The dichotomy between popular and sophisticated literature is well illustrated in the crime novels of P. D. James.
   (D) The critics who have condemned P. D. James's lack of attention to the specifics of detection fail to take into account her carefully constructed plots.
   (E) Although her plots are not always neatly resolved, the beauty of her descriptive passages justifies P. D. James's decision to write in the crime-novel genre.[7]

Correct choice (A) restates the author's opinion just as predicted. The other choices offer confused distortions of the various themes presented in the passage. Once again, a clear understanding of the author's Purpose guides you directly to the correct answer.

To reiterate, the key difference between this passage and the two previous examples is that the author of the James passage doesn't ultimately agree with the critics, but neither does she simply disagree with them and assume a clear opposite opinion. Instead she breaks away from the critics' arguments, using them as a launching point for her own separate Purpose.

Here's another example:

Star system of 20's

As one of the most pervasive and influential popular arts, the movies feed into and off of the rest of the culture in various ways. In the United States, the star system of the mid-1920s—in which actors were
(5) placed under exclusive contract to particular Hollywood film studios—was a consequence of studios' discovery that the public was interested in actors' private lives, and that information about actors could be used to promote their films. Public relations

---
[7]PrepTest 19, Sec 3, Q 1

Press benefits
from film

(10) agents fed the information to gossip columnists,
      whetting the public's appetite for the films—which,
      audiences usually discovered, had the additional virtue
      of being created by talented writers, directors, and
      producers devoted to the art of storytelling. The
(15) important feature of this relationship was not the
      benefit to Hollywood, but rather to the press; in what
      amounted to a form of cultural cross-fertilization, the
      press saw that they could profit from studios'
      promotion of new films.

(20)   Today this arrangement has mushroomed into an
      intricately interdependent mass-media entertainment
      industry. The faith by which this industry sustains itself
      is the belief that there is always something worth
      promoting. A vast portion of the mass media—

Media
promotes
movies

(25) television and radio interviews, magazine articles, even
      product advertisements—now does most of the work
      for Hollywood studios attempting to promote their
      movies. It does so not out of altruism but because it
      makes for good business: If you produce a talk show
(30) or edit a newspaper, and other media are generating
      public curiosity about a studio's forthcoming film, it
      would be unwise for you not to broadcast or publish
      something about the film, too, because the audience for
      your story is already guaranteed.

Problem:
affects films

(35)   The problem with this industry is that it has begun
      to affect the creation of films as well as their
      promotion. Choices of subject matter and actors are
      made more and more frequently by studio executives
      rather than by producers, writers, or directors. This
(40) problem is often referred to simply as an obsession
      with turning a profit, but Hollywood movies have
      almost always been produced to appeal to the largest
      possible audience. The new danger is that,

Films are not
satisfying

      increasingly, profit comes only from exciting an
(45) audience's curiosity about a movie instead of satisfying
      its desire to have an engaging experience watching the
      film. When movies can pull people into theaters
      instantly on the strength of media publicity rather than
      relying on the more gradual process of word of mouth
(50) among satisfied moviegoers, then the intimate
      relationship with the audience—on which the vitality
      of all popular art depends—is lost. But studios are
      making more money than ever by using this formula,
      and for this reason it appears that films whose appeal is
(55) due not merely to their publicity value but to their
      ability to affect audiences emotionally will become
      increasingly rare in the U.S. film industry.[8]

What is the author's Purpose? The author describes the developing relationship between film
and the media in paragraphs 1 and 2. Then, in the final paragraph, the author describes the

---

[8]PrepTest 28, Sec 4, Passage 4

danger this relationship creates for the film industry. With this in mind, try to answer the following question:

25. Which one of the following most accurately describes the organization of the passage?

   (A)   description of the origins of a particular aspect of a popular art; discussion of the present state of this aspect; analysis of a problem associated with this aspect; introduction of a possible solution to the problem

   (B)   description of the origins of a particular aspect of a popular art; discussion of the present state of this aspect; analysis of a problem associated with this aspect; suggestion of a likely consequence of the problem

   (C)   description of the origins of a particular aspect of a popular art; analysis of a problem associated with this aspect; introduction of a possible solution to the problem; suggestion of a likely consequence of the solution

   (D)   summary of the history of a particular aspect of a popular art; discussion of a problem that accompanied the growth of this aspect; suggestion of a likely consequence of the problem; appraisal of the importance of avoiding this consequence

   (E)   summary of the history of a particular aspect of a popular art; analysis of factors that contributed to the growth of this aspect; discussion of a problem that accompanied the growth of this aspect; appeal for assistance in solving the problem[9]

The answer choices may seem abstract, and they're certainly repetitive, but don't worry. Apply the Kaplan Method and compare them to the author's Purpose. The only match is choice (B). The others all mention extraneous ideas; the author did mention a problem, but he never mentioned a solution to the problem or any way to avoid it.

How does the structure of this passage differ from that of the P. D. James passage? The author of the film industry passage never presents any opinion other than his own. The first two paragraphs are purely informational, and there isn't anyone for the author to agree or disagree with. But in spite of this difference, the two passages essentially follow the same pattern: In both cases, the author uses the bulk of the passage to provide context for the primary opinion delivered in the final paragraph.

That last LSAT question demonstrates why knowledge of these common patterns is worth points on test day. The test makers will often complicate a familiar question type by making

---

[9]PrepTest 28, Sec 4, Q 25

the answer choices wordy, abstract, and similar to one another. You absolutely must have a solid prediction to score the point efficiently, and that's much easier to do when you're able to identify a commonly recurring Purpose.

Remain Neutral

The final common passage pattern occurs when the author provides no opinion at all. Other opinions may be present, but the author simply describes them without evaluating them. Here's an example:

Phil. of Science like physics/certainty

Philosophers of science have long been uneasy with biology, preferring instead to focus on physics. At the heart of this preference is a misstrust of uncertainty. Science is supposed to be the study of what is true
(5) everywhere and for all times, and the phenomena of science are supposed to be repeatable, arising from universal laws, rather than historically contingent. After all if something pops up only on occasional Tuesdays or Thursdays, it is not classified as science
(10) but as history. Philosophers of science have thus been fascinated with the fact that elephants and mice would fall at the same rate if dropped from the Tower of Pisa, but not much interested in how elephants and mice got to be such different sizes in the first place.

(15)   Philosophers of science have not been alone in claiming that science must consist of universal laws.

Biologists: bio is universal

Some evolutionary biologists have also acceded to the general intellectual disdain for the merely particular and tried to emulate physicists, constructing their
(20) science as a set of universal laws. In formulating the notion of a universal "struggle for existence that is the engine of biological history" or in asserting that virtually all DNA evolves at a constant clocklike rate, they have attempted to find their own versions of the

Other biologists: bio based on history

(25) law of gravity. Recently, however, some biologists have questioned whether biological history is really the necessary unfolding of universal laws of life, and they have raised the possibility that historical contingency is an integral factor in biology.

(30)   To illustrate the difference between biologists favoring universal, deterministic laws of evolutionary development and those leaving room for historical contingency, consider two favorite statements of philosophers (both of which appear, at first sight, to be
(35) universal assertions): "All planets move in ellipses" and "All swans are white." The former is truly universal because it applies not only to those planets

Ex: planets are universal

that actually do exist, but also to those that could exist—for the shape of planetary orbits is a necessary
(40) consequence of the laws governing the motion of objects in a gravitational field.

Bio determ.
say swans =
universal

      Biological determinists would say that "All swans
are white" is universal in the same way, since, if all
swans were white, it would be because the laws of
(45) natural selection make it impossible for swans to be
otherwise; natural selection favors those
characteristics that increase the average rate of
offspring production, and so traits that maximize
flexibility and the ability to manipulate nature will
(50) eventually appear. Nondeterminist biologists would

Nondeterm.
say swans not
universal

deny this, saying that "swans" is merely the name of a
finite collection of historical object that may happen
all to be white, but not of necessity. The history of
evolutionary theory has been the history of the struggle
(55) between these two views of swans.[10]

Take a moment to review the various commentators in this passage: philosophers of science
and physicists in the first paragraph, determinist biologists and nondeterminist biologists
further in. Notably absent is the author of the passage. Does the author side with one group
of biologists over the other? It's never stated. The author's primary Purpose should reflect this
neutral tone: The author wrote to describe conflicting views of science. As always, the Main
Idea follows from the Purpose, and it is similarly neutral: Biologists disagree about how certain
their science is.

15. Which one of the following best summarizes the main
     idea of the passage?

    (A) Just as philosophers of science have traditionally
         been reluctant to deal with scientific phenomena
         that are not capable of being explained by
         known physical laws, biologists have tended to
         shy away from confronting philosophical
         questions.

    (B) While science is often considered to be concerned
         with universal laws, the degree to which certain
         biological phenomena can be understood as
         arising from such laws is currently in dispute.

    (C) Although biologists have long believed that the
         nature of their field called for a theoretical
         approach different from that taken by physicists,
         some biologists have recently begun to emulate
         the methods of physicists.

    (D) Whereas physicists have achieved a far greater
         degree of experimental precision than has been
         possible in the field of biology, the two fields
         employ similar theoretical approaches.

    (E) Since many biologists are uncomfortable with the
         emphasis placed by philosophers of science on
         the need to construct universal laws, there has
         been little interaction between the two
         disciplines.[11]

---

[10]PrepTest 35, Sec 2, Passage 3

[11]PrepTest 35, Sec 2, Q 15

Choice (B) describes the unresolved nature of the dispute as predicted.

My students often express anxiety when working with a passage that, like this one, lacks a strong authorial viewpoint. Such passages tend to be somewhat abstract. They're also less common than passages with opinionated authors, and you may reach the end thinking to yourself, "Why didn't the author take sides? They *always* take sides!"

Let this exercise be a reminder: While the author usually is opinionated, there are exceptions. If the author remains neutral, don't be tempted to ascribe to her an opinion that she doesn't express. As always, read strategically and be sure to note any other viewpoints the passage provides. If the author was primarily concerned with describing the opinions of others, then those opinions are sure to show up in the questions:

17. Which one of the following statements about biology is most consistent with the view held by determinist biologists, as that view is presented in the passage?

18. It can be inferred from the passage that philosophers of science view the laws of physics as

19. It can be inferred from the passage that determinist biologists have tried to emulate physicists because these biologists believe that[12]

As long as you've applied the Kaplan Method, your Roadmap will guide you directly to the information you need to score these points.

---

[12]PrepTest 35, Sec 2, Qs 17–19

DRILL: RECOGNIZING THE PATTERNS

This Drill contains three LSAT passages, each with a question that requires knowledge of the author's Purpose. Remember, the author's primary Purpose is usually to support or refute an opinion, to provide an alternative opinion, or to remain neutral. Read each passage strategically, create a Roadmap, and answer its accompanying question. This is a longer exercise, so take your time. Explanations are provided after the Drill.

Three kinds of study have been performed on Byron. There is the biographical study—the very valuable examination of Byron's psychology and the events in his life; Escarpit's 1958 work is an example
(5) of this kind of study, and biographers to this day continue to speculate about Byron's life. Equally valuable is the study of Byron as a figure important in the history of ideas; Russell and Praz have written studies of this kind. Finally, there are
(10) studies that primarily consider Byron's poetry. Such literary studies are valuable, however, only when they avoid concentrating solely on analyzing the verbal shadings of Byron's poetry to the exclusion of any discussion of biographical considerations. A
(15) study with such a concentration would be of questionable value because Byron's poetry, for the most part, is simply not a poetry of subtle verbal meanings. Rather, on the whole, Byron's poems record the emotional pressure of certain moments
(20) in his life. I believe we cannot often read a poem of Byron's, as we often can one of Shakespeare's, without wondering what events or circumstances in his life prompted him to write it.

No doubt the fact that most of Byron's poems
(25) cannot be convincingly read as subtle verbal creations indicates that Byron is not a "great" poet. It must be admitted too that Byron's literary craftsmanship is irregular and often his temperament disrupts even his lax literary method
(30) (although the result, an absence of method, has a significant purpose: it functions as a rebuke to a cosmos that Byron feels he cannot understand). If Byron is not a "great" poet, his poetry is nonetheless of extraordinary interest to us because
(35) of the pleasure it gives us. Our main pleasure in reading Byron's poetry is the contact with a singular

personality. Reading his work gives us illumination—self-understanding—after we have seen our weaknesses and aspirations mirrored in
(40) the personality we usually find in the poems. Anyone who thinks that this kind of illumination is not a genuine reason for reading a poet should think carefully about why we read Donne's sonnets.

It is Byron and Byron's idea of himself that hold
(45) his work together (and that enthralled early-nineteenth-century Europe). Different characters speak in his poems, but finally it is usually he himself who is speaking: a far cry from the impersonal poet Keats. Byron's poetry alludes to
(50) Greek and Roman myth in the context of contemporary affairs, but his work remains generally of a piece because of his close presence in the poetry. In sum, the poetry is a shrewd personal performance, and to shut out Byron the man is to fabricate a work of pseudocriticism.

1. Which one of the following titles best expresses the main idea of the passage?

   (A) An Absence of Method: Why Byron Is Not a "Great" Poet
   (B) Byron: The Recurring Presence in Byron's Poetry
   (C) Personality and Poetry: The Biographical Dimension of Nineteenth-Century Poetry
   (D) Byron's Poetry: Its Influence on the Imagination of Early-Nineteenth-Century Europe
   (E) Verbal Shadings: The Fatal Flaw of Twentieth-Century Literary Criticism[13]

---

[13]PrepTest 16, Sec 4, Q 1

The United States Supreme Court has not always resolved legal issues of concern to Native Americans in a manner that has pleased the Indian nations. Many of the Court's decisions have been
(5) products of political compromise that looked more to the temper of the times than to enduring principles of law. But accommodation is part of the judicial system in the United States, and judicial decisions must be assessed with this fact in mind.

(10) Despite the "accommodating" nature of the judicial system, it is worth noting that the power of the Supreme Court has been exercised in a manner that has usually been beneficial to Native Americans, at least on minor issues, and has not
(15) been wholly detrimental on the larger, more important issues. Certainly there have been decisions that cast doubt on the validity of this assertion. Some critics point to the patronizing tone of many Court opinions and the apparent rejection
(20) of Native American values as important points to consider when reviewing a case. However, the validity of the assertion can be illustrated by reference to two important contributions that have resulted from the exercise of judicial power.

(25) First, the Court has created rules of judicial construction that, in general, favor the rights of Native American litigants. The Court's attitude has been conditioned by recognition of the distinct disadvantages Native Americans faced when
(30) dealing with settlers in the past. Treaties were inevitably written in English for the benefit of their authors, whereas tribal leaders were accustomed to making treaties without any written account, on the strength of mutual promises sealed by religious
(35) commitment and individual integrity. The written treaties were often broken, and Native Americans were confronted with fraud and political and

military aggression. The Court recognizes that past unfairness to Native Americans cannot be
(40) sanctioned by the force of law. Therefore, ambiguities in treaties are to be interpreted in favor of the Native American claimants, treaties are to be interpreted as the Native Americans would have understood them, and, under the reserved rights
(45) doctrine, treaties reserve to Native Americans all rights that have not been specifically granted away in other treaties.

A second achievement of the judicial system is the protection that has been provided against
(50) encroachment by the states into tribal affairs. Federal judges are not inclined to view favorably efforts to extend states' powers and jurisdictions because of the direct threat that such expansion poses to the exercise of federal powers. In the
(55) absence of a federal statute directly and clearly allocating a function to the states, federal judges are inclined to reserve for the federal government—and the tribal governments under its charge—all those powers and rights they can be said to have
(60) possessed historically.[14]

2. The author's attitude toward the United States Supreme Court's resolution of legal issues of concern to Native Americans can best be described as one of

   (A) wholehearted endorsement
   (B) restrained appreciation
   (C) detached objectivity
   (D) cautious opposition
   (E) suppressed exasperation[15]

---

[14]PrepTest 16, Sec 4, Passage 2
[15]PrepTest 16, Sec 4, Q 12

When catastrophe strikes, analysts typically blame some combination of powerful mechanisms. An earthquake is traced to an immense instability along a fault line; a stock market crash is blamed on
(5) the destabilizing effect of computer trading. These explanations may well be correct. But systems as large and complicated as the Earth's crust or the stock market can break down not only under the force of a mighty blow but also at the drop of a pin.
(10) In a large interactive system, a minor event can start a chain reaction that leads to a catastrophe.

Traditionally, investigators have analyzed large interactive systems in the same way they analyze small orderly systems, mainly because the methods
(15) developed for small systems have proved so successful. They believed they could predict the behavior of a large interactive system by studying its elements separately and by analyzing its component mechanisms individually. For lack of a better
(20) theory, they assumed that in large interactive systems the response to a disturbance is proportional to that disturbance.

During the past few decades, however, it has become increasingly apparent that many large
(25) complicated systems do not yield to traditional analysis. Consequently, theorists have proposed a "theory of self-organized criticality": many large interactive systems evolve naturally to a critical state in which a minor event starts a chain reaction
(30) that can affect any number of elements in the system. Although such systems produce more minor events than catastrophes, the mechanism that leads to minor events is the same one that leads to major events.

(35) A deceptively simple system serves as a paradigm for self-organized criticality: a pile of sand. As sand is poured one grain at a time onto a flat disk, the grains at first stay close to the position where they land. Soon they rest on top of one
(40) another, creating a pile that has a gentle slope. Now and then, when the slope becomes too steep, the grains slide down, causing a small avalanche. The system reaches its critical state when the amount of sand added is balanced, on average, by the amount
(45) falling off the edge of the disk.

Now when a grain of sand is added, it can start an avalanche of any size, including a "catastrophic" event. Most of the time the grain will fall so that no avalanche occurs. By studying a specific area of the
(50) pile, one can even predict whether avalanches will occur there in the near future. To such a local observer, however, large avalanches would remain unpredictable because they are a consequence of the total history of the entire pile. No matter what
(55) the local dynamics are, catastrophic avalanches would persist at a relative frequency that cannot be altered. Criticality is a global property of the sandpile.[16]

3. In the passage, the author is primarily concerned with

(A) arguing against the abandonment of a traditional approach
(B) describing the evolution of a radical theory
(C) reconciling conflicting points of view
(D) illustrating the superiority of a new theoretical approach
(E) advocating the reconsideration of an unfashionable explanation[17]

---

[16]PrepTest 16, Sec 4, Passage 3
[17]PrepTest 16, Sec 4, Q 21

Explanations

1. **(B)**

Three studies on Byron

Three kinds of study have been performed on Byron. There is the biographical study—the very valuable examination of Byron's psychology and the events in his life; Escarpit's 1958 work is an example
(5) of this kind of study, and biographers to this day continue to speculate about Byron's life. Equally valuable is the study of Byron as a figure important in the history of ideas; Russell and Praz have written studies of this kind. Finally, there are
(10) studies that primarily consider Byron's poetry. Such literary studies are valuable, however, only when they avoid concentrating solely on analyzing the verbal shadings of Byron's poetry to the exclusion of any discussion of biographical considerations. A

Auth: must examine Byron's life

(15) study with such a concentration would be of questionable value because Byron's poetry, for the most part, is simply not a poetry of subtle verbal meaning. Rather, on the whole, Byron's poems record the emotional pressure of certain moments
(20) in his life. I believe we cannot often read a poem of Byron's, as we often can one of Shakespeare's, without wondering what events or circumstances in his life prompted him to write it.

No doubt the fact that most of Byron's poems
(25) cannot be convincingly read as subtle verbal creations indicates that Byron is not a "great" poet.

Byron not great poet

It must be admitted too that Byron's literary craftsmanship is irregular and often his temperament disrupts even his lax literary method
(30) (although the result, an absence of method, has a significant purpose: it functions as a rebuke to a cosmos that Byron feels he cannot understand). If Byron is not a "great" poet, his poetry is nonetheless of extraordinary interest to us because
(35) of the pleasure it gives us. Our main pleasure in reading Byron's poetry is the contact with a singular personality. Reading his work gives us

Gives personal insights

illumination—self-understanding—after we have seen our weaknesses and aspirations mirrored in
(40) the personality we usually find in the poems. Anyone who thinks that this kind of illumination is not a genuine reason for reading a poet should think carefully about why we read Donne's sonnets.

It is Byron and Byron's idea of himself (that hold)
(45) his work together (and that enthralled early-
nineteenth-century Europe). Different characters
speak in his poems, (but finally) it is usually he
himself who is speaking: a (far cry from) the
impersonal poet Keats. Byron's poetry alludes to
(50) Greek and Roman myth in the context of
contemporary affairs, (but) his work remains
generally of a piece because of his close presence in
the poetry. (In sum,) the poetry is a shrewd personal
performance, (and) to shut out Byron the man is to
(55) fabricate a work of pseudocriticism.[18]

Byron is in his poetry

1. Which one of the following titles best expresses the main idea of the passage?

   (A) An Absence of Method: Why Byron Is Not a "Great" Poet

   (B) Byron: The Recurring Presence in Byron's Poetry

   (C) Personality and Poetry: The Biographical Dimension of Nineteenth-Century Poetry

   (D) Byron's Poetry: Its Influence on the Imagination of Early-Nineteenth-Century Europe

   (E) Verbal Shadings: The Fatal Flaw of Twentieth-Century Literary Criticism[19]

This passage is an excellent illustration of the second common pattern I discussed in this chapter. The author describes three kinds of studies of Byron in the first paragraph and then promptly discards them in favor of her own interpretation in the subsequent paragraphs. The beginning of paragraph 3 provides a major clue—the author states that "Byron and Byron's idea of himself" constitute his work, going on to call his work a "shrewd personal performance" in lines 53–55. Don't worry about the odd wording of the question: You should look for an answer that refers to Byron's insertion of himself into his poetry. Choice (B) is the match.

2. **(B)**

The United States Supreme Court (has not)
always resolved legal issues of concern to Native
Americans in a manner that has (pleased) the Indian
nations. (Many) of the Court's decisions have been
(5) (products of) political compromise that looked more
to the temper of the times (than to) enduring
principles of law. (But) accommodation is part of the
judicial system in the United States, (and) judicial
decisions must be assessed with this fact in mind.

Courts not always good for Native Americans

Auth: always accommodation

---

[18]PrepTest 16, Sec 4, Passage 1

[19]PrepTest 16, Sec 4, Q 1

(10)   Despite the "accommodating" nature of the
judicial system, it is worth noting that the power of
the Supreme Court has been exercised in a manner
that has usually been beneficial to Native

Courts usually Americans, at least on minor issues, and has not

beneficial (15) been wholly detrimental on the larger, more
important issues. Certainly there have been
decisions that cast doubt on the validity of this
assertion. Some critics point to the patronizing tone
of many Court opinions and the apparent rejection

(20) of Native American values as important points to

Counterexamples consider when reviewing a case. However, the
validity of the assertion can be illustrated by

Auth: two reference to two important contributions that have

contributions resulted from the exercise of judicial power.

(25)   First, the Court has created rules of judicial
construction that, in general, favor the rights of

Laws favor Native American litigants. The court's attitude has

Native been conditioned by recognition of the distinct

Americans disadvantages Native Americans faced when

(30) dealing with settlers in the past. Treaties were
inevitably written in English for the benefit of their
authors, whereas tribal leaders were accustomed to
making treaties without any written account, on the
strength of mutual promises sealed by religious

(35) commitment and individual integrity. The written
treaties were often broken, and Native Americans
were confronted with fraud and political and
military aggression. The Court recognizes that past
unfairness to Native Americans cannot be

(40) sanctioned by the force of law. Therefore,
ambiguities in treaties are to be interpreted in favor
of the Native American claimants, treaties are to be
interpreted as the Native Americans would have
understood them, and under the reserved rights

(45) doctrine, treaties reserve to Native Americans all
rights that have not been specifically granted away
in other treaties.

     A second achievement of the judicial system is

Native the protection that has been provided against

Americans (50) encroachment by the states into tribal affairs.

protected from Federal judges are not inclined to view favorably

states efforts to extend states' powers and jurisdictions
because of the direct threat that such expansion
poses to the exercise of federal powers. In the

(55) absence of a federal statute directly and clearly
allocating a function to the states, federal judges are
inclined to reserve for the federal government—and
the tribal governments under its charge—all those
powers and rights they can be said to have

(60) possessed historically.[20]

---

[20]PrepTest 16, Sec 4, Passage 2

2. The author's attitude toward the United States
    Supreme Court's resolution of legal issues of concern
    to Native Americans can best be described as one of

    (A) wholehearted endorsement
    (B) restrained appreciation
    (C) detached objectivity
    (D) cautious opposition
    (E) suppressed exasperation[21]

This passage exemplifies the first of the three common patterns. The author's primary Purpose in this passage is to rebut the Supreme Court's critics, primarily those mentioned in paragraph 2. In fact, paragraph 2 is where the author makes his primary assertions—that the Supreme Court's decisions have usually been beneficial and other times "not . . . wholly detrimental." Attention to tone is crucial when pinpointing the author's attitude, so be sure to note the qualifying language here. Words like "usually" in line 13 indicate the author may not *always* agree with the Supreme Court, but believes their judgments are generally sound. You should accordingly look for a choice that is positive but with some reservations. This should lead you to choice (B). Note the wrong answer trap, choice (A), which is too extreme and ignores the author's carefully qualified tone.

3.   **(D)**

Catastrophes usually blamed on major causes

(When) catastrophe strikes, analysts (typically) (blame) some combination of powerful mechanisms. An earthquake is traced to an immense instability along a fault line; a stock market crash is blamed on
(5) the destabilizing effect of computer trading. These (explanations) may well be correct. (But) systems as large and complicated as the Earth's crust or the stock market can break down (not only) under the force of a mighty blow (but also) at the drop of a pin.

Causes can be minor too

(10) In a large interactive system, a (minor event) can start a chain reaction that leads to a catastrophe.

(Traditionally,) investigators have analyzed large interactive systems in the (same way) they analyze small orderly systems, mainly (because) the methods

Trad. treat big systems like small systems

(15) developed for small systems have proved so (successful.) They (believed) they could predict the behavior of a large interactive system (by studying) its elements separately (and by) analyzing its component mechanisms individually. (For lack) of a better
(20) theory, they (assumed) that in large interactive systems the response to a disturbance is proportional to that disturbance.

---

[21]PrepTest 16, Sec 4, Q 12

Now big systems
different/new (25)
theory

(During) the past few decades, (however,) it has become increasingly (apparent) that many large complicated systems (do not yield) to traditional analysis. (Consequently,) theorists have (proposed) a "theory of self-organized criticality": many large interactive systems evolve naturally to a (critical) state in which a minor event (starts) a chain reaction

(30)   that (can affect) any number of elements in the system. (Although) such systems produce more minor events than catastrophes, the mechanism that leads to minor events (is the same) one that leads to major events.

Ex: sandpile

(35)   A (deceptively simple) system serves as a paradigm for self-organized criticality: a pile of sand. (As) sand is poured one grain at a time onto a flat disk, the grains (at first) stay close to the position where they land. (Soon) they rest on top of one

(40)   another, (creating) a pile that has a gentle slope. Now and then, when the slope becomes too steep, the grains slide down, (causing) a small avalanche. The system reaches its (critical state) when the amount of sand added is balanced, on average, by the amount

(45)   falling off the edge of the disk.

Ex. continued

(Now) when a grain of sand is added, it (can start) an avalanche of any size, (including) a "catastrophic" event. (Most of the time) the grain will fall so that no avalanche occurs. (By studying) a specific area of the

(50)   pile, one can even (predict) whether avalanches will occur there in the near future. To such a local observer, (however,) large avalanches would remain unpredictable (because) they are a consequence of the total history of the entire pile. (No matter) what

(55)   the local dynamics are, catastrophic avalanches would (persist) at a relative frequency that cannot be altered. Criticality is a (global property) of the sandpile.[22]

3. In the passage, the author is primarily concerned with

(A)   arguing against the abandonment of a traditional approach

(B)   describing the evolution of a radical theory

(C)   reconciling conflicting points of view

(D)   illustrating the superiority of a new theoretical approach

(E)   advocating the reconsideration of an unfashionable explanation[23]

This passage is neutral in tone. In the first two paragraphs, the author describes a traditional view of the causes of catastrophes. She then shifts gears, describing a new theory that has

---

[22]PrepTest 16, Sec 4, Passage 3

[23]PrepTest 16, Sec 4, Q 21

been proposed to address the flaws in the older one. She never explicitly favors one theory over another, sticking to passive description. For example, she notes that complicated systems "do not yield" to traditional analysis in lines 23–26, but instead of critiquing the old theory, she simply goes on to state how investigators have compensated for this problem. This passage is purely descriptive, and while the author does acknowledge that the new theory is more robust, the balance of the passage is spent in detail-laden explanation. The author's Purpose is descriptive, which is noted in correct choice (D). Notice that choices (A), (C), and (E) all suggest a more vigorous tone than the author displays in this passage; she's doesn't argue, reconcile, or advocate anything. Choice (B) contains the properly neutral verb "describing," but then distorts the author's intent. She doesn't describe the evolution of a theory, but rather its replacement.

THE PURPOSE IS PREDICTABLE

I hope that in working through this chapter you've gained some further insight into the predictable nature of the LSAT. It's a subject that I'll return to often in this book. You may recall that in chapter 6 I mentioned that my students consistently cite the pressure of the clock as the primary reason that Reading Comprehension seems difficult. In order to lessen that pressure and increase your efficiency and confidence, you must gain a master's familiarity with the contents of the test. Learning to recognize common passage structures and the authorial Purposes that derive from them is part of that process. On test day, every passage should look familiar to you, not because you've actually seen them before (the test makers never reuse a passage) but because you've already applied the Kaplan Method to other passages that were structurally similar.

This same kind of thinking applies to questions as well, and I'll introduce that subject soon. But first, because it forms the foundation of Reading Comprehension success, a review of strategic reading as a whole is in order. That's coming up in chapter 8.

CHAPTER 8

STRATEGIC READING REVIEW

SUCCESS THROUGH STRATEGIC READING

When you began preparing for the LSAT, you might have thought it was impossible to read all four passages in a single Reading Comprehension section and complete every question in the allotted time period. I hope you can now see that, far from being a mysterious test of random knowledge, the LSAT is designed to reward skilled, confident test takers who understand how to read each passage efficiently and focus on the right information. Through the proper application of the Kaplan Method, you have learned to read passages not just quickly, but correctly, focusing on the information that will increase your score by noting the clues that the test makers provide. And remember, the clues are there in *every* LSAT passage, no matter how intimidating it may appear to a casual reader.

You still have plenty to learn about Reading Comprehension, and in Part II of this book I'll teach you about the different question types you'll see on test day and the most common types of wrong answers you're likely to see. But first I want you to review strategic reading as a whole, then put your understanding of the Kaplan Method to the test.

Locating and Understanding Keywords

When I first introduced strategic reading, I showed you how to stay focused on the big picture behind every passage, and how to avoid wasting time pondering details. I also pointed out that the test makers provide you with clues to aid you in this task: the Keywords located throughout the text. Because strategic reading depends so heavily upon the proper identification and usage of Keywords, I'll review the three core ideas you should remember on test day.

Keywords separate main ideas from supporting evidence.

The majority of the questions you'll see on test day will examine your knowledge of the author's primary opinions. It is therefore crucial that you always read with an eye for Keywords that indicate conclusion and emphasis. Review the following excerpt, keeping an eye out for Keywords:

> Although philanthropy—the volunteering of
> private resources for humanitarian purposes—reached
> its apex in England in the late nineteenth century,
> modern commentators have articulated two major
> (5)   criticisms of the philanthropy that was a mainstay of
> England's middle-class Victorian society.[1]

What was the author most interested in communicating here? The Keyword "although" at the beginning of the excerpt prepares you for a potentially important contrast to follow, and soon you learn that commentators have voiced two "major criticisms" of Victorian philanthropy. These Keywords separate less important background information (the definition of philanthropy and the century during which it reached its peak) from the line of inquiry the author plans to pursue further, the validity of the criticisms. This leads to another core idea:

When you find Keywords in a passage, circle them and think about what they mean.

It's never enough to simply acknowledge that Keywords are there; you must always take the second step of using them to guide your thinking about the passage. In the previous example, the Keyword "although" was the author's way of signaling that a contrasting idea was approaching, and that this idea was likely to be important. Hopefully this thought process is becoming second nature to you by now, but it doesn't hurt to remember just how important this two-step process is: Circle each Keyword you find, and then determine what it tells you about the structure of the passage.

---

[1]PrepTest 41, Sec 4, Passage 4

Keywords help you answer the questions.

It can't be overstated: No matter how difficult the passage may appear, Keywords always point the way to the answers you need. Review the following excerpt, again circling Keywords along the way:

> In addition, Marshall used sociological and
> (35) psychological statistics—presented in expert testimony,
> for example, about the psychological impact of
> enforced segregation—as a means of transforming
> constitutional law by persuading the courts that certain
> discriminatory laws produced public harms in violation
> (40) of constitutional principles. This tactic, while often
> effective, has been criticized by some legal scholars as
> a pragmatic attempt to give judges nonlegal material
> with which to fill gaps in their justifications for
> decisions where the purely legal principles appear
> (45) inconclusive.[2]

Now, consider the following question:

7. According to the passage, some legal scholars have criticized which one of the following?

   (A) the ideology Marshall used to support his goals
   (B) recent public interest campaigns
   (C) the use of Marshall's techniques by politically
        conservative lawyers
   (D) the use of psychological statistics in court cases
   (E) the set of criteria for selecting public interest
        litigants[3]

The critics have disparaged one of Marshall's tactics. How can you quickly summarize what it was? The description of Marshall's tactic is denoted by the Keywords "in addition" and "for example" in the first sentence. A re-examination of the text shows you that it was the use of social and psychological statistics in the courtroom that irked the critics. With this summary in mind, choice (D) is the clear winner.

It is important to remember that, while most questions deal with the author's main ideas, sometimes you will need to reference supporting evidence, and important evidence is *always* surrounded by Keywords.

Creating and Using a Roadmap

Hopefully, you've reached the point in your practice at which you've become comfortable with Roadmapping passages. You may still be in the process of developing your own particular

---

[2]PrepTest 42, Sec 3, Passage 1
[3]PrepTest 42, Sec 3, Q 7

style of Roadmap, determining which information you should include, how to use shorthand effectively, and how much to write. That's perfectly fine. The most important thing is that you continue to practice and deepen your level of comfort on every passage you complete. Keep in mind the following points each time you construct a Roadmap.

Your Roadmap should be concise.

Perhaps you remember this example of a poorly Roadmapped paragraph from chapter 3:

James writes strikingly

characters w/ stories give (30) dignity

Kitchen vs. plot/story too thin (35)

crimes solved by intuition / char, more than plot (40)

> James is certainly capable of ⟨strikingly⟩ good writing. She takes ⟨immense⟩ trouble to provide her characters with convincing histories and passions. Her descriptive digressions are part of the pleasure of her (30) books ⟨and⟩ give them dignity and weight. ⟨But⟩ it is equally true that they frequently interfere with the story; the patinas and aromas of a country kitchen receive more loving attention ⟨than⟩ does the plot itself. Her devices to advance the story can be ⟨shameless⟩ and (35) thin, ⟨and⟩ it is often impossible to see how her detective arrives at the truth; one is left to conclude that the detective solves crimes through intuition. At ⟨this stage⟩ in her career P. D. James seems to be ⟨less⟩ interested in the specifics of detection ⟨than⟩ in her characters' (40) vulnerabilities and perplexities.[4]

The margin notes are very thorough—so thorough that they no longer provide a quick and simple way to access information in the passage, which defeats the purpose of making notes. Once you've pinpointed that James writes "strikingly" according to the author, there's no need to reiterate all the evidence supplied. Remember that the information you need to answer the questions correctly is already in the passage, and sometimes you will have to return to the passage to find the text you need. The goal of the Roadmap is to help you do this quickly, not to restate everything the author says:

Auth: James is striking writer

(30)

Sometimes bad for plot (35)

(40)

> James is certainly capable of ⟨strikingly⟩ good writing. She takes ⟨immense⟩ trouble to provide her characters with convincing histories and passions. Her descriptive digressions are part of the pleasure of her (30) books ⟨and⟩ give them dignity and weight. ⟨But⟩ it is equally true that they frequently interfere with the story; the patinas and aromas of a country kitchen receive more loving attention ⟨than⟩ does the plot itself. Her devices to advance the story can be ⟨shameless⟩ and (35) thin, ⟨and⟩ it is often impossible to see how her detective arrives at the truth; one is left to conclude that the detective solves crimes through intuition. At ⟨this stage⟩ in her career P. D. James seems to be ⟨less⟩ interested in the specifics of detection ⟨than⟩ in her characters' (40) vulnerabilities and perplexities.[5]

---

[4]PrepTest 19, Sec 3, Passage 1
[5]PrepTest 19, Sec 3, Passage 1

This Roadmap simply reflects what the paragraph is about and provides you with a good point of reference. Your Roadmap should contain just as much information as is necessary to be useful and no more. My students usually require a fair amount of practice before they feel that they've struck the correct balance. Keep practicing, and always compare your own Roadmap to the answers and explanations in this book to help you refine your margin notes.

Your Roadmap makes passage structure easy to understand.

Students frequently tell me that, while they are diligently Roadmapping every passage they read, they don't often consult the notes that they've written once they actually get to the question set. So if they're not actually referencing it, why should they bother to create it?

It's true that different test takers will rely on the Roadmap as a reference tool to varying degrees. It's also true that some passages require more extensive research than others. But what some fail to realize is that, in constructing their Roadmaps, they're actively clarifying and committing to memory vital structural information about the passage. If they hadn't Roadmapped the passage, they wouldn't understand the passage as well as they do.

The implication of this is extremely important: No matter how often you reference your Roadmap, the very act of creating it helps you to clarify the structure of the passage. For this reason alone, you must stay in the habit of creating a Roadmap every time you practice LSAT Reading Comprehension, and you must Roadmap every passage you read on test day.

Your Roadmap helps you score points.

To reinforce the importance of understanding passage structure, revisit this passage and question from the previous chapter:

Star system of 20's

⟨As⟩ one of the most pervasive and influential popular arts, the movies feed into and off of the rest of the culture in various ways. ⟨In⟩ the United States, the star system of the mid-1920s—⟨in which⟩ actors were
(5) placed under exclusive contract to particular Hollywood film studios—was a ⟨consequence⟩ of studios' discovery that the public was interested in actors' private lives, ⟨and⟩ that information about actors could be used to promote their films. Public relations
(10) agents fed the information to gossip columnists, whetting the public's appetite for the films—⟨which,⟩ audiences usually discovered, had the ⟨additional⟩ virtue of being created by talented writers, directors, and producers devoted to the art of storytelling. The

Press benefits from film

(15) ⟨important⟩ feature of this relationship was ⟨not⟩ the benefit to Hollywood, ⟨but rather⟩ to the press; in what amounted to a form of cultural cross-fertilization, the press ⟨saw⟩ that they could profit from studios' promotion of new films.

(20)   Today this arrangement has mushroomed into an
intricately interdependent mass-media entertainment
industry. The faith by which this industry sustains itself
is the belief that there is always something worth
promoting. A vast portion of the mass media—

Media
promotes
movies

(25)   television and radio interviews, magazine articles, even
product advertisements—now does most of the work
for Hollywood studios attempting to promote their
movies. It does so not out of altruism but because it
makes for good business: If you produce a talk show

(30)   or edit a newspaper, and other media are generating
public curiosity about a studio's forthcoming film, it
would be unwise for you not to broadcast or publish
something about the film, too, because the audience for
your story is already guaranteed.

Problem:
affects films

(35)   The problem with this industry is that it has begun
to affect the creation of films as well as their
promotion. Choices of subject matter and actors are
made more and more frequently by studio executives
rather than by producers, writers, or directors. This

(40)   problem is often referred to simply as an obsession
with turning a profit, but Hollywood movies have
almost always been produced to appeal to the largest
possible audience. The new danger is that,

Films are not
satisfying

increasingly, profit comes only from exciting an
(45)   audience's curiosity about a movie instead of satisfying
its desire to have an engaging experience watching the
film. When movies can pull people into theaters
instantly on the strength of media publicity rather than
relying on the more gradual process of word of mouth

(50)   among satisfied moviegoers, then the intimate
relationship with the audience—on which the vitality
of all popular art depends—is lost. But studios are
making more money than ever by using this formula,
and for this reason it appears that films whose appeal is

(55)   due not merely to their publicity value but to their
ability to affect audiences emotionally will become
increasingly rare in the U.S. film industry.[6]

---

[6]PrepTest 28, Sec 4, Passage 4

25. Which one of the following most accurately describes
     the organization of the passage?

    (A) description of the origins of a particular aspect of
     a popular art; discussion of the present state of
     this aspect; analysis of a problem associated
     with this aspect; introduction of a possible
     solution to the problem

    (B) description of the origins of a particular aspect of
     a popular art; discussion of the present state of
     this aspect; analysis of a problem associated
     with this aspect; suggestion of a likely
     consequence of the problem

    (C) description of the origins of a particular aspect of
     a popular art; analysis of a problem associated
     with this aspect; introduction of a possible
     solution to the problem; suggestion of a likely
     consequence of the solution

    (D) summary of the history of a particular aspect of a
     popular art; discussion of a problem that
     accompanied the growth of this aspect;
     suggestion of a likely consequence of the
     problem; appraisal of the importance of avoiding
     this consequence

    (E) summary of the history of a particular aspect of a
     popular art; analysis of factors that contributed
     to the growth of this aspect; discussion of a
     problem that accompanied the growth of this
     aspect; appeal for assistance in solving the
     problem[7]

A question like this one is virtually impossible to answer quickly and accurately without a strong sense of passage structure. Note once more how correct choice (B) follows directly from the Roadmap, piece by piece. There's no denying that your ability to read for structure will be vital to your success in your first year of law school; that's why the test makers reward this skill so consistently. The more you practice thinking about the big picture of every passage, the easier it will become.

Identifying Topic, Scope, Purpose, and Main Idea

The good habits you form in identifying Keywords and creating solid Roadmaps will help you to identify Topic, Scope, Purpose, and Main Idea. To briefly review:

The Topic provides you with a broad sense of context.

Even though the Topic of the passage will not be directly tested, it's important that you establish a good sense of context from the moment you begin reading. At least some of the passages you encounter on test day will contain subject matter with which you are not familiar. Becoming acquainted with the Topic of the passage right away removes some of the mystery and abstraction from the passage and helps keeps you focused on the passage's content.

---

[7]PrepTest 28, Sec 4, Q 25

The Scope gives you insight into the author's goals.

Since the Scope specifies what narrower area within the Topic the author will address, you should pay close attention to it. If you know the author is writing on the Topic of dinosaurs, for example, it's to your advantage to determine what specifically about dinosaurs the author is interested in discussing so that you can deepen your sense of context. Staying focused on the Scope helps you avoid wrong answer choices, which are frequently outside the author's Scope.

The Purpose summarizes the structure of the passage.

Remember that a good Roadmap will allow you to describe the author's Purpose with ease. The number of Purposes that LSAT passages pursue is very limited; authors generally write to support or refute arguments, to explain phenomena, or to describe varying ideas. Questions that directly ask for the author's Purpose are common on the LSAT.

The Main Idea summarizes the author's opinions.

You've seen many examples of test questions that ask for the author's opinion. Having a solid description of the Main Idea makes these questions much easier to answer correctly and can significantly reduce the amount of time it takes you to conduct your research. As with Purpose, questions that directly ask for the author's Main Idea are common on the test.

Patterns and Predictions

Before you give your strategic reading skills some further practice, don't forget that predictive reading is one of the most powerful tools at your disposal. No matter how convoluted the passage may seem at first, if you stay in the habit of anticipating the author's direction as you read, you'll become a more confident and efficient reader. Far from being a totally distinct skill from those already discussed, prediction follows naturally from the habits you've already begun to form. Identifying and thinking about Keywords helps you anticipate where in the passage important ideas are likely to occur, and each time you Roadmap a paragraph, you've given yourself a sense of context with which to predict what is coming next.

Finally, if your practice thus far has shown you anything about LSAT Reading Comprehension, it should be that the passages just aren't terribly varied. The subjects change but the structures become familiar with practice. Even the types of questions that the test makers write are easily predictable and follow identifiable patterns. I'm not suggesting that Reading Comprehension is easy—if it was, you wouldn't have to practice—but it's good to reflect on the limited nature of the passages. They're predictable, and since they're predictable, you can prepare for them.

DRILL: COMPLETING A PASSAGE

Now it's time to apply everything that you've learned so far. In this Drill, your task is straight-forward: Read and Roadmap the passage, circling Keywords as you go; identify Topic, Scope, Purpose, and Main Idea; and then answer each of the five questions that follow. Don't let the abstract nature of the passage disrupt the good habits you've established. Take your time, be patient, and stick to the Kaplan Method. Full answers and explanations follow, and, as always, review them carefully.

Scientists typically advocate the analytic method of studying complex systems: systems are divided into component parts that are investigated separately. But nineteenth-century critics of this method claimed that
(5) when a system's parts are isolated its complexity tends to be lost. To address the perceived weaknesses of the analytic method these critics put forward a concept called organicism, which posited that the whole determines the nature of its parts and that the parts of a
(10) whole are interdependent.

Organicism depended upon the theory of internal relations, which states that relations between entities are possible only within some whole that embraces them, and that entities are altered by the relationships
(15) into which they enter. If an entity stands in a relationship with another entity, it has some property as a consequence. Without this relationship, and hence without the property, the entity would be different— and so would be another entity. Thus, the property is
(20) one of the entity's defining characteristics. Each of an entity's relationships likewise determines a defining characteristic of the entity.

One problem with the theory of internal relations is that not all properties of an entity are defining
(25) characteristics: numerous properties are accompanying characteristics—even if they are always present, their presence does not influence the entity's identity. Thus, even if it is admitted that every relationship into which an entity enters determines some characteristic of the
(30) entity, it is not necessarily true that such characteristics will define the entity; it is possible for the entity to enter into a relationship yet remain essentially unchanged.

The ultimate difficulty with the theory of internal
(35) relations is that it renders the acquisition of knowledge impossible. To truly know an entity, we must know all of its relationships; but because the entity is related to everything in each whole of which it is a part, these wholes must be known completely before the entity
(40) can be known. This seems to be a prerequisite impossible to satisfy.

Organicists' criticism of the analytic method arose from their failure to fully comprehend the method. In rejecting the analytic method, organicists overlooked
(45) the fact that before the proponents of the method analyzed the component parts of a system, they first determined both the laws applicable to the whole system and the initial conditions of the system; proponents of the method thus did not study parts of a
(50) system in full isolation from the system as a whole. Since organicists failed to recognize this, they never advanced any argument to show that laws and initial conditions of complex systems cannot be discovered. Hence, organicists offered no valid reason for rejecting
(55) the analytic method or for adopting organicism as a replacement for it.[8]

1. Which one of the following most completely and accurately summarizes the argument of the passage?

   (A) By calling into question the possibility that complex systems can be studied in their entirety, organicists offered an alternative to the analytic method favored by nineteenth-century scientists.

   (B) Organicists did not offer a useful method of studying complex systems because they did not acknowledge that there are relationships into which an entity may enter that do not alter the entity's identity.

   (C) Organicism is flawed because it relies on a theory that both ignores the fact that not all characteristics of entities are defining and ultimately makes the acquisition of knowledge impossible.

   (D) Organicism does not offer a valid challenge to the analytic method both because it relies on faulty theory and because it is based on a misrepresentation of the analytic method.

   (E) In criticizing the analytic method, organicists neglected to disprove that scientists who employ the method are able to discover the laws and initial conditions of the systems they study.

---

[8]PrepTest 25, Sec 1, Passage 4

2. According to the passage, organicists' chief objection to the analytic method was that the method

   (A) oversimplified systems by isolating their components
   (B) assumed that a system can be divided into component parts
   (C) ignored the laws applicable to the system as a whole
   (D) claimed that the parts of a system are more important than the system as a whole
   (E) denied the claim that entities enter into relationships

3. The passage offers information to help answer each of the following questions EXCEPT:

   (A) Why does the theory of internal relations appear to make the acquisition of knowledge impossible?
   (B) Why did the organicists propose replacing the analytic method?
   (C) What is the difference between a defining characteristic and an accompanying characteristic?
   (D) What did organicists claim are the effects of an entity's entering into a relationship with another entity?
   (E) What are some of the advantages of separating out the parts of a system for study?

4. The passage most strongly supports the ascription of which one of the following views to scientists who use the analytic method?

   (A) A complex system is best understood by studying its component parts in full isolation from the system as a whole.
   (B) The parts of a system should be studied with an awareness of the laws and initial conditions that govern the system.
   (C) It is not possible to determine the laws governing a system until the system's parts are separated from one another.
   (D) Because the parts of a system are interdependent, they cannot be studied separately without destroying the system's complexity.
   (E) Studying the parts of a system individually eliminates the need to determine which characteristics of the parts are defining characteristics.

5. Which one of the following is a principle upon which the author bases an argument against the theory of internal relations?

   (A) An adequate theory of complex systems must define the entities of which the system is composed.
   (B) An acceptable theory cannot have consequences that contradict its basic purpose.
   (C) An adequate method of study of complex systems should reveal the actual complexity of the systems it studies.
   (D) An acceptable theory must describe the laws and initial conditions of a complex system.
   (E) An acceptable method of studying complex systems should not study parts of the system in isolation from the system as a whole.[9]

Answer Explanations follow on the next page.

Explanations

Organicism
vs. analytic
method

Scientist (typically) advocate the analytic method of studying complex systems: systems are divided into component parts that are investigated separately. (But) nineteenth-century (critics) of this method (claimed) that
(5)   when a system's parts are isolated its complexity tends to be lost. (To address) the perceived (weaknesses) of the analytic method these (critics) put forward a concept called organicism, which (posited) that the whole determines the nature of its parts (and) that the parts of a
(10) whole are interdependent.

Organicism:
depends on
relations

Organicism (depended) upon the theory of internal relations, which (states) that relations between entities are possible (only) within some whole that embraces them, (and) that entities are altered by the relationships
(15) into which they enter. (If) an entity stands in a relationship with another entity, it has some property as a (consequence.) Without this relationship, (and hence) without the property, the entity would be different— (and so) would be another entity. (Thus,) the property is
(20) one of the entity's defining characteristics. Each of an entity's relationships (likewise) determines a defining characteristic of the entity.

Problem: not
all relations
define

(One problem) with the theory of internal relations is that (not all) properties of an entity are defining
(25) characteristics: numerous properties are accompanying characteristics—(even if) they are always present, their presence does not influence the entity's identity. (Thus,) (even if) it is admitted that every relationship into which an entity enters determines some characteristic of the
(30) entity, it is (not necessarily) true that such characteristics will define the entity; it is possible for the entity to enter into a relationship yet remain essentially unchanged.

Big
problem:
impossible

The (ultimate difficulty) with the theory of internal
(35) relations is that it renders the acquisition of knowledge impossible. To truly know an entity, we must know all of its relationships, (but because) the entity is related to everything in each whole of which it is part, these wholes must be known completely (before) the entity
(40) can be known. This seems to be a prerequisite (impossible) to satisfy.

Critics don't
understand
analytic
method

(Organicists' criticism) of the analytic method arose (from) their (failure) to fully comprehend the method. In (rejecting) the analytic method, organicists overlooked
(45) the fact that (before) the proponents of the method analyzed the component parts of a system, they (first) determined both the laws applicable to the whole system (and) the initial conditions of the system;

(50) proponents of the method thus did not study parts of a
system in full isolation from the system as a whole.
Since organicists failed to recognize this, they never
advanced any argument to show that laws and initial
conditions of complex systems cannot be discovered.
Hence, organicists offered no valid reason for rejecting
(55) the analytic method or for adopting organicism as a
replacement for it.[10]

Paragraph Structure: Paragraph 1 sets up the central conflict that the author explores in the passage: The analytic method, currently in use by most scientists, and the theory of organicism proposed by 19th-century critics.

Paragraph 2 goes into more detail about the claims of the organicists. The author mentions the theory of internal relations, which underlies the organicists central ideas. This paragraph contains a lot of redundancy, which is typical of tougher LSAT science passages. Notice how keywords like "consequence," "thus," and "likewise" give some order to all this jargon.

Paragraphs 3 and 4 are very similar to one another structurally—both introduce an objection the author levels against the organicists. Paragraph three deals with the notion that relationships aren't always defining characteristics. Paragraph four begins with some very emphatic language, positing that the "ultimate difficulty" with the theory of internal relations is that it makes knowledge impossible to acquire (quite a handicap for any scientific theory).

Paragraph 5 closes the argument against the organicists and vindicates the analytic method. In lines 42–43 the author states that the organicists failed to comprehend the analytic method, thus leading to their objections to it. The author reinforces the importance of this idea in line 54 beginning with the keyword "hence."

Topic: competing scientific theories

Scope: organicism vs. analytic method

Purpose: to describe why organicism failed to successfully challenge the analytic method

Main Idea: The organicists failed to replace the analytic method because they misunderstood it, and because their own methods were fatally flawed.

---

[10]PrepTest 25, Sec 1, Passage 4

1. **(D)**

    Which one of the following most completely and
    accurately summarizes the argument of the passage?

    (A)   By calling into question the possibility that
           complex systems can be studied in their entirety,
           organicists offered an alternative to the analytic
           method favored by nineteenth-century scientists.

    (B)   Organicists did not offer a useful method of
           studying complex systems because they did not
           acknowledge that there are relationships into
           which an entity may enter that do not alter the
           entity's identity.

    (C)   Organicism is flawed because it relies on a theory
           that both ignores the fact that not all
           characteristics of entities are defining and
           ultimately makes the acquisition of knowledge
           impossible.

    (D)   Organicism does not offer a valid challenge to the
           analytic method both because it relies on faulty
           theory and because it is based on a
           misrepresentation of the analytic method.

    (E)   In criticizing the analytic method, organicists
           neglected to disprove that scientists who employ
           the method are able to discover the laws and
           initial conditions of the systems they study.[11]

The Main Idea question should be a familiar sight to you. Correct choice (D) perfectly matches
the author's thesis; it states that organicism failed, and it gives the author's primary reasons
for why it failed. Choices (A) and (E) both fail to explicitly state that organicism failed to successfully challenge the analytic method. Choice (B) is too narrowly focused; there were other
more important ideas given for the failure of organicism. Choice (C) may look good at first, as
it presents some of the author's objections to organicism, but it ultimately fails to capture the
author's biggest complaint, that the organicists misunderstood the method they were attacking.

2. **(A)**

    According to the passage, organicists' chief objection to
    the analytic method was that the method

    (A)   oversimplified systems by isolating their
           components

    (B)   assumed that a system can be divided into
           component parts

    (C)   ignored the laws applicable to the system as a
           whole

    (D)   claimed that the parts of a system are more
           important than the system as a whole

    (E)   denied the claim that entities enter into
           relationships[12]

---

[11]PrepTest 25, Sec 1, Q 22
[12]PrepTest 25, Sec 1, Q 23

Your Roadmap should have guided you directly to the first paragraph to research the answer to this question—this is the only place where the organicists' objections are explained. Beginning in line 4, the "claim" of the critics is spelled out: that complexity is lost when the pieces of a system are isolated. Correct choice (A) states this nearly word for word. Choice (B) doesn't describe a criticism made by the organicists, and choices (C) and (D) have no textual support, and are thus out of scope. Choice (E) is also out of scope—the practitioners of the analytic method never respond to the organicists' claims anywhere in the passage. When approaching this type of question, don't rely on your memory—use your Roadmap to research the correct answer.

3.   **(E)**

The passage offers information to help answer each of the following questions EXCEPT:

(A)   Why does the theory of internal relations appear to make the acquisition of knowledge impossible?

(B)   Why did the organicists propose replacing the analytic method?

(C)   What is the difference between a defining characteristic and an accompanying characteristic?

(D)   What did organicists claim are the effects of an entity's entering into a relationship with another entity?

(E)   What are some of the advantages of separating out the parts of a system for study?[13]

This kind of question can be a frustrating waste of time; the correct answer must be the only one that gets no support from the passage. Your Roadmap is essential in helping you eliminate wrong choices quickly. Choice (A) gets support in paragraph four; choice (B) in paragraph one (in fact, you just researched this very information); choice (C) is discussed in paragraph three; and choice (D) is covered in paragraph two. That leaves correct choice (E), which is not addressed in the passage.

---

[13]PrepTest 25, Sec 1, Q 24

4. **(B)**

The passage most strongly supports the ascription of which one of the following views to scientists who use the analytic method?

(A) A complex system is best understood by studying its component parts in full isolation from the system as a whole.

(B) The parts of a system should be studied with an awareness of the laws and initial conditions that govern the system.

(C) It is not possible to determine the laws governing a system until the system's parts are separated from one another.

(D) Because the parts of a system are interdependent, they cannot be studied separately without destroying the system's complexity.

(E) Studying the parts of a system individually eliminates the need to determine which characteristics of the parts are defining characteristics.[14]

Take your time when reading an oddly worded question like this one. Which view is held by scientists who adhere to the analytic method? Since most of the passage is devoted to the view of the organicists, your Roadmap should draw you to the final paragraph, in which the author vindicates the analytic method. Lines 45–50 provide the Keywords you need: "First" practitioners of the analytic method examine the entirety of the system, and "thus" do not examine parts in isolation. Correct choice (B) describes this kind of thinking perfectly. Choices (A), (C), and (D) are more in line with the organicists' view of the analytic method, not the author's. Choice (E) is out of Scope, referencing ideas from paragraph three that are not applicable to this question (and distorting them as well).

5. **(B)**

Which one of the following is a principle upon which the author bases an argument against the theory of internal relations?

(A) An adequate theory of complex systems must define the entities of which the system is composed.

(B) An acceptable theory cannot have consequences that contradict its basic purpose.

(C) An adequate method of study of complex systems should reveal the actual complexity of the systems it studies.

(D) An acceptable theory must describe the laws and initial conditions of a complex system.

(E) An acceptable method of studying complex systems should not study parts of the system in isolation from the system as a whole.[15]

---

[14]PrepTest 25, Sec 1, Q 25
[15]PrepTest 25, Sec 1, Q 26

This question requires you to recall the author's reasons for rejecting organicism. The emphatic Keywords "ultimate difficulty" in line 34 give you a good place to start; organicism seeks to explain systems, but it makes explanations impossible to achieve. Correct choice (B) echoes this sentiment, albeit using more general language. Choices (A), (C), and (E) are out of Scope, and choice (D) describes a principle underlying the author's acceptance of the analytic method, not his refutation of organicism.

PRACTICE, CONSISTENCY, AND CONFIDENCE

You undoubtedly still have many questions about LSAT Reading Comprehension at this point, and rest assured that I'll address them. But before you move on to Part II, I want you to take a moment to recommit yourself to strategic reading. It's not easy to change the way you've probably been reading all your life, which is why it is so very important to remain consistent when applying the Kaplan Method. Each time you work on a practice passage, remind yourself to read strategically, and review the core concepts laid out in this chapter. It is especially important for you to do this when you time yourself; I know from experience that many students revert to bad habits when the clock starts running. Stay focused and consistent, and be confident in your abilities.

It's worth stating one last time: *Anyone* can master LSAT Reading Comprehension, because the clues are *always* there. Now it's up to you to continue to take advantage of them!

PART II

PASSAGE AND QUESTION TYPES

CHAPTER 9

COMPARATIVE READING

COMPARATIVE READING BASICS

In the first section of this book you learned how, through dedicated practice and application of the Kaplan Method, you can increase your LSAT score. One of the primary reasons that the LSAT is so vulnerable to preparation is its predictability. Any LSAT administered in the last several years will be similar in all respects to the LSAT that you're preparing to take. Since the tests themselves are predictable, it follows that strategies that are effective on one test will be effective on all of them. In Part II of the book I'm going to introduce you to the common question types, challenging passages, trends the test has followed in recent years, and the Kaplan strategies that you need to prepare for them.

First, however, you should become familiar with one of the few major changes the test makers have made to the LSAT in recent years. Prior to this change, Reading Comprehension always consisted of four passages covering four broad subject areas: law, natural science, social science, and humanities. Each passage was accompanied by five to eight questions.

In the June 2007 administration of the LSAT, the test makers introduced a new exercise, called comparative reading. In comparative reading, instead of a single passage, you are presented with two separate, shorter passages, and a set of five to eight questions. It is important to note that the test makers announced this change months before they implemented it, and they provided examples and explanations on their website, www.lsac.org. I mention this because I don't want you to fear that the test makers will make sudden and unpredictable changes to the LSAT before you take it; they have historically announced when major changes were made and provided plenty of information well in advance.

Since its introduction in 2007, comparative reading has remained a consistent and predictable component of the Reading Comprehension section. In this chapter, I'll show you exactly what to expect from comparative reading and teach you the appropriate strategies to apply to it.

Comparative Passages vs. Single Passages

To begin, take a look at the first comparative reading passage set to appear on the LSAT. Don't read the passages carefully yet; just take a quick glance for now.

Passage A

Readers, like writers, need to search for answers. Part of the joy of reading is in being surprised, but academic historians leave little to the imagination. The perniciousness of the historiographic approach became
(5) fully evident to me when I started teaching. Historians require undergraduates to read scholarly monographs that sap the vitality of history; they visit on students what was visited on them in graduate school. They assign books with formulaic arguments that transform
(10) history into an abstract debate that would have been unfathomable to those who lived in the past. Aimed so squarely at the head, such books cannot stimulate students who yearn to connect to history emotionally as well as intellectually.

(15) In an effort to address this problem, some historians have begun to rediscover stories. It has even become something of a fad within the profession. This year, the American Historical Association chose as the theme for its annual conference some putative connection to
(20) storytelling: "Practices of Historical Narrative." Predictably, historians responded by adding the word "narrative" to their titles and presenting papers at sessions on "Oral History and the Narrative of Class Identity," and "Meaning and Time: The Problem of
(25) Historical Narrative." But it was still historiography, intended only for other academics. At meetings of historians, we still encounter very few historians telling stories or moving audiences to smiles, chills, or tears.

Passage B

Writing is at the heart of the lawyer's craft, and so,
(30) like it or not, we who teach the law inevitably teach aspiring lawyers how lawyers write. We do this in a few stand-alone courses and, to a greater extent, through the constraints that we impose on their writing throughout the curriculum. Legal writing, because of the purposes
(35) it serves, is necessarily ruled by linear logic, creating a path without diversions, surprises, or reversals. Conformity is a virtue, creativity suspect, humor forbidden, and voice mute.

Lawyers write as they see other lawyers write, and,
(40) influenced by education, profession, economic constraints, and perceived self-interest, they too often write badly. Perhaps the currently fashionable call for attention to narrative in legal education could have an effect on this. It is not yet exactly clear what role
(45) narrative should play in the law, but it is nonetheless true that every case has at its heart a story—of real events and people, of concerns, misfortunes, conflicts, feelings. But because legal analysis strips the human narrative content from the abstract, canonical legal
(50) form of the case, law students learn to act as if there is no such story.

It may well turn out that some of the terminology and public rhetoric of this potentially subversive movement toward attention to narrative will find its
(55) way into the law curriculum, but without producing corresponding changes in how legal writing is actually taught or in how our future colleagues will write. Still, even mere awareness of the value of narrative could perhaps serve as an important corrective.[1]

---

[1]PrepTest 52, Sec 4, Passage 2

This set is representative of what the comparative reading format always looks like: two passages written by two different authors, labeled "Passage A" and "Passage B." The combined length of the two passages amounts to the average length of a single, noncomparative passage. Comparative passages fall within the same general subject categories as other passages, and they are structurally similar as well. Every reading comprehension section contains exactly one set of comparative reading passages.

The comparative passages always share the same broad Topic and are similar in Scope, although their authors can vary markedly in tone. Be sure to note that, while the two passages will always represent two different viewpoints on a similar Topic, their authors never directly address one another—that is, the author of Passage B will not directly reference any part of Passage A, either in agreement or refutation. Instead, the authors will take approaches to the Topic that are similar in some ways and different in others.

The purpose of comparative reading is to test your ability to understand the nuances between different points of view, a skill you have developed throughout your study of strategic reading. Ultimately, comparative reading is not very different from the sort of reading you've already become familiar with, and you'll be able to apply the same Kaplan Method strategies you've been learning thus far.

READ PAIRED PASSAGES STRATEGICALLY

To maximize your score on comparative reading passages, stay methodical and read strategically. Apply the Kaplan Method to comparative reading just as you do to any other Reading Comprehension passage—identify and circle Keywords, construct a Roadmap, and identify the Topic, Scope, Purpose, and Main Idea. The only real difference is that you will have to perform this process twice before moving on to the questions.

Now, take a closer look at passage A from the previous example. Read and Roadmap it on your own before moving on.

Passage A

Readers, like writers, need to search for answers. Part of the joy of reading is in being surprised, but academic historians leave little to the imagination. The perniciousness of the historiographic approach became
(5) fully evident to me when I started teaching. Historians require undergraduates to read scholarly monographs that sap the vitality of history; they visit on students what was visited on them in graduate school. They assign books with formulaic arguments that transform
(10) history into an abstract debate that would have been unfathomable to those who lived in the past. Aimed so squarely at the head, such books cannot stimulate students who yearn to connect to history emotionally as well as intellectually.

(15)   In an effort to address this problem, some historians have begun to rediscover stories. It has even become something of a fad within the profession. This year, the American Historical Association chose as the theme for its annual conference some putative connection to
(20)   storytelling: "Practices of Historical Narrative." Predictably, historians responded by adding the word "narrative" to their titles and presenting papers at sessions on "Oral History and the Narrative of Class Identity," and "Meaning and Time: The Problem of
(25)   Historical Narrative." But it was still historiography, intended only for other academics. At meetings of historians, we still encounter very few historians telling stories or moving audiences to smiles, chills, or tears.[2]

Paragraph Structure: This passage is not different in any way from the examples you've already seen in this book. The author begins by introducing the historiographic approach to scholarship, of which he seems to disapprove (in line 4, he describes the "perniciousness" of this approach). In the second paragraph, he describes the efforts of some historians to make their scholarship less dry, noting that narrative has become "something of a fad" (line 17) among them. Ultimately, however, the author notes that historical scholarship is still largely lacking in compelling stories.

Compare your reading of this passage to this sample Roadmap:

Passage A

                     Readers, like writers, need to search for answers. Part of the joy of reading is in being surprised, but academic historians leave little to the imagination. The

History
teaching
too dry
                (5)   perniciousness of the historiographic approach became fully evident to me when I started teaching. Historians require undergraduates to read scholarly monographs that sap the vitality of history; they visit on students what was visited on them in graduate school. They assign books with formulaic arguments that transform
(10)   history into an abstract debate that would have been unfathomable to those who lived in the past. Aimed so squarely at the head, such books cannot stimulate students who yearn to connect to history emotionally as well as intellectually.
(15)   In an effort to address this problem, some historians have begun to rediscover stories. It has even become something of a fad within the profession. This year, the

Some efforts,
but historians
still not
interested in
stories
                     American Historical Association chose as the theme for its annual conference some putative connection to
(20)   storytelling: "Practices of Historical Narrative." Predictably, historians responded by adding the word "narrative" to their titles and presenting papers at

---

[2]PrepTest 52, Sec 4, Passage 2

sessions on "Oral History and the Narrative of Class
Identity," and "Meaning and Time: The Problem of
(25) Historical Narrative." (But) it was still historiography,
intended (only) for other academics. At meetings of
historians, we still encounter (very few) historians telling
stories or moving audiences to smiles, chills, or tears.[3]

I'll stress once more just how similar this passage is to others you've already completed. Before moving on to Passage B, be sure to identify the Topic, Scope, Purpose, and Main Idea of this passage:

Topic: Historiography

Scope: Lack of narrative in historical scholarship

Purpose: To describe a problem with historiography

Main Idea: Although some efforts have been made to enliven history with compelling narrative, most historians prefer a drier form of scholarship

This is precisely how you should approach comparative reading on test day: Be sure not to begin reading Passage B until you've finished applying the Kaplan Method to Passage A.

Now move on to Passage B. Remember that, although there will be some similarities, this is a different passage with a different author, so be sure to read it as such. Try reading and Road-mapping this passage on your own.

Passage B

Writing is at the heart of the lawyer's craft, and so,
(30) like it or not, we who teach the law inevitably teach
aspiring lawyers how lawyers write. We do this in a few
stand-alone courses and, to a greater extent, through the
constraints that we impose on their writing throughout
the curriculum. Legal writing, because of the purposes
(35) it serves, is necessarily ruled by linear logic, creating a
path without diversions, surprises, or reversals.
Conformity is a virtue, creativity suspect, humor
forbidden, and voice mute.
Lawyers write as they see other lawyers write, and,
(40) influenced by education, profession, economic
constraints, and perceived self-interest, they too often
write badly. Perhaps the currently fashionable call for
attention to narrative in legal education could have an
effect on this. It is not yet exactly clear what role
(45) narrative should play in the law, but it is nonetheless
true that every case has at its heart a story—of real
events and people, of concerns, misfortunes, conflicts,

---

[3]PrepTest 52, Sec 4, Passage 2

feelings. But because legal analysis strips the human
narrative content from the abstract, canonical legal
(50) form of the case, law students learn to act as if there is
no such story.
   It may well turn out that some of the terminology
and public rhetoric of this potentially subversive
movement toward attention to narrative will find its
(55) way into the law curriculum, but without producing
corresponding changes in how legal writing is actually
taught or in how our future colleagues will write. Still,
even mere awareness of the value of narrative could
perhaps serve as an important corrective.[4]

Paragraph Structure: In the first paragraph, the author introduces the Topic of legal writing, describing it as "necessarily ruled by linear logic" (line 35) and, consequently, humorless and unsurprising. In the second paragraph, he introduces the possibility of narrative playing a role in legal writing, but suggests that the role such narrative would play is "not yet exactly clear" (line 44). The author concludes in the final paragraph that, although it may not make any major changes to legal writing, the awareness of narrative might still form some sort of "corrective" (line 59) to current forms of discourse.

Once again, compare your Roadmap to this sample:

Passage B

Legal
writing =
dry,
logical

Narrative
left out
of legal
writing

   Writing is at the heart of the lawyer's craft, and so,
(30) like it or not, we who teach the law inevitably teach
aspiring lawyers how lawyers write. We do this in a few
stand-alone courses and, to a greater extent, through the
constraints that we impose on their writing throughout
the curriculum. Legal writing, because of the purposes
(35) it serves, is necessarily ruled by linear logic, creating a
path without diversions, surprises, or reversals.
Conformity is a virtue, creativity suspect, humor
forbidden, and voice mute.
   Lawyers write as they see other lawyers write, and,
(40) influenced by education, profession, economic
constraints, and perceived self-interest, they too often
write badly. Perhaps the currently fashionable call for
attention to narrative in legal education could have an
effect on this. It is not yet exactly clear what role
(45) narrative should play in the law, but it is nonetheless
true that every case has at its heart a story—of real
events and people, of concerns, misfortunes, conflicts,
feelings. But because legal analysis strips the human
narrative content from the abstract, canonical legal
(50) form of the case, law students learn to act as if there is
no such story.

4PrepTest 52, Sec 4, Passage 2

Awareness
of narrative
may help

It may well (turn out) that some of the terminology and public rhetoric of this potentially subversive movement toward attention to narrative will find its (55) way into the law curriculum, (but) without producing corresponding changes in how legal writing is actually taught (or) in how our future colleagues will write. (Still,) even (mere awareness) of the value of narrative could perhaps serve as an (important) corrective.[5]

Now think about the Topic, Scope, Purpose, and Main Idea of this passage:

Topic: Legal writing

Scope: The role of narrative in legal writing

Purpose: To describe a problem with legal writing and consider a possible partial solution

Main Idea: Although current interest in narrative is unlikely to greatly change the way legal writing is taught, it might have some beneficial effects.

Now that you've applied the Kaplan Method to both passages, take a few seconds to identify the key similarities and differences between them. Both authors express dissatisfaction with a specific field of scholarship: history in Passage A and legal writing in Passage B. Notice also that both authors seem personally invested in the problems they describe—the first author initially noticed them "when I started teaching" (line 5) and the second lays the issue at the feet of "we who teach the law" (line 30). Finally, you should definitely note that both authors describe a lack of compelling narrative as problematic in their respective fields.

Both authors reach similar conclusions, but there is an important and nuanced difference. The author of Passage A finishes rather pessimistically, noting that very few historians bother with interesting stories. The author of Passage B, in contrast, is slightly more hopeful that narrative may improve the dry discourse of legal writing.

Look for Similarities and Differences in Comparative Passages

The kind of similarities and differences you'll see in comparative reading will vary from example to example. In this exercise, the two authors observe similar problems in two different fields, and both think that more storytelling would help. But the relationship between the two passages won't always follow this template. Here are just a few of the possible ways in which the two authors might relate to one another:

- They examine similar evidence and reach contrary conclusions.
- One author describes a problem, and the other proposes a solution to that problem.
- Both authors agree that a policy is appropriate, but disagree on how it should be implemented.

---

[5]PrepTest 52, Sec 4, Passage 2

- One author takes a detached view of a subject, and the other a more partisan approach.
- The authors describe a phenomenon and propose different causes for it.

Regardless of exactly how the authors differ or coincide in their ideas, there are two things you can be certain of: There will always be similarities and differences, and you can always use the Kaplan Method to identify them. Thinking through the relationship between these passages is important to your LSAT score, because questions will directly test your understanding of it.

COMPARATIVE READING QUESTIONS

Since comparative reading is largely about comparison (hence the name), the time you spend thinking about the relationship between the two passages will be worth points in the question set:

7. Which one of the following does each of the passages display?[6]

Try to predict what the correct answer should say. Both authors were dissatisfied with bad writing within a given academic area, and both suggested that a lack of compelling narrative is the culprit.

Now identify the answer choice that matches this prediction:

7. Which one of the following does each of the passages display?

(A)   a concern with the question of what teaching methods are most effective in developing writing skills

(B)   a concern with how a particular discipline tends to represent points of view it does not typically deal with

(C)   a conviction that writing in specialized professional disciplines cannot be creatively crafted

(D)   a belief that the writing in a particular profession could benefit from more attention to storytelling

(E)   a desire to see writing in a particular field purged of elements from other disciplines

Choice (D) is the perfect match, since both authors advocate storytelling as a cure for dry writing. Neither of the passages support any of the other choices.

---

[6]PrepTest 52, Sec 4, Q 7

This is exactly the kind of question you should expect to see on test day, and it's a question that you can answer quickly and confidently if you've already thought through the primary similarities and differences between the two passages.

The following question shouldn't look very surprising:

10. In which one of the following ways are the passages NOT parallel?

   (A) Passage A presents and rejects arguments for an opposing position, whereas passage B does not.
   (B) Passage A makes evaluative claims, whereas passage B does not.
   (C) Passage A describes specific examples of a phenomenon it criticizes, whereas passage B does not.
   (D) Passage B offers criticism, whereas passage A does not.
   (E) Passage B outlines a theory, whereas passage A does not.[7]

This time you are asked to identify a key difference between the two passages. Since the passages were, overall, more similar than dissimilar, the correct answer may be tougher to predict. Note also that the answer choices employ structural language, suggesting that the Roadmap and Keywords of each passage are likely to be helpful.

Think about each choice in turn. Choice (A) is completely out of scope, since Passage A never presents and rejects any particular argument. Choice (B) is only partially correct, as both passages make evaluative claims (they both claim that scholarly writing is too dry, for example). Choice (C) is supported by the text, and is therefore the correct answer. Passage A does indeed cite specific examples of historians making use of the word "narrative" in a faddish way. Following the Keyword "predictably" in line 21 you'll find the names of specific presentations, such as "Oral History and the Narrative of Class Identity." In contrast, Passage B describes legal writing only in general terms. Choice (D) is wrong for the same reason as choice (B), since both passages offer criticism. Choice (E) is also completely out of scope. The authors describe problems, but neither outlines a theory.

Comparative reading questions are often designed to reward you for recognizing tone. Take a look at this example:

---

[7]PrepTest 52, Sec 4, Q 10

8. The passages most strongly support which one of the
    following inferences regarding the authors' relationships
    to the professions they discuss?

    (A)   Neither author is an active member of the
          profession that he or she discusses.
    (B)   Each author is an active member of the profession
          he or she discusses.
    (C)   The author of passage A is a member of the
          profession discussed in that passage, but the
          author of passage B is not a member of either of
          the professions discussed in the passages.
    (D)   Both authors are active members of the profession
          discussed in passage B.
    (E)   The author of passage B, but not the author of
          passage A, is an active member of both of the
          professions discussed in the passages.[8]

Recall that you identified language in the passage that denotes each author's personal investment; each author self-identifies as a teacher. This prediction matches correct choice (B). Choice
(A) is the exact opposite of the correct choice, a common wrong answer trap that I'll refer to as
a 180. Choice (C) is wrong on both counts—the first author may or may not be a historian, and
the second author is definitely a legal scholar. Choice (D) incorrectly assumes that the author of
Passage A is a legal scholar, and choice (E) presumes without warrant that the second author
is a historian. Please notice how often the incorrect answer choices in comparative reading
describe a distorted view of the relationship between the passages—a trap you'll avoid with
ease as long as you keep reading strategically.

Take a look at one more example:

11. The phrase "scholarly monographs that sap the vitality of
     history" in passage A (lines 6–7) plays a role in that
     passage's overall argument that is most analogous to the
     role played in passage B by which one of the following
     phrases?

    (A)   "Writing is at the heart of the lawyer's craft"
          (line 29)
    (B)   "Conformity is a virtue, creativity suspect, humor
          forbidden, and voice mute" (lines 37–38)
    (C)   "Lawyers write as they see other lawyers write"
          (line 39)
    (D)   "every case has at its heart a story" (line 46)
    (E)   "Still, even mere awareness of the value of
          narrative could perhaps serve as an important
          corrective" (lines 57–59)[9]

---

[8]PrepTest 52, Sec 4, Q 8
[9]PrepTest 52, Sec 4, Q 11

Don't be intimidated by the wordiness of the question stem—your firm grasp of the intentions of both authors will allow you to work through it. The question asks about the role played by the quoted text in lines 6–7. What is the author of Passage A talking about when he reaches this example? He's describing the dryness of historiography, claiming that its writing leaves "little to the imagination" (line 3). The reference to scholarly monographs mentioned in the question is an example of this sort of dryness. With this in mind, you must now find the answer choice that similarly describes ("is most analogous to") dull writing, but this time in Passage B.

Choice (A) does no such thing; it emphasizes the importance of writing, not its dullness. Choice (B), on the other hand, is a perfect match, describing the blandness of legal writing in great detail. Choices (C), (D), and (E) are just as far off as choice (A)—none of these quotes are used by the author to emphasize the dryness of legal writing.

Not every question in comparative reading will focus on the relationships between the passages, and you're likely to see a question or two on test day that focuses strictly on one passage or the other. You should approach these questions as you would any other, using the specific strategies I'll describe to you in the next few chapters. You should, however, expect most of the questions to test your ability to compare one passage to another as in each of the above examples.

DRILL: WORKING WITH COMPARATIVE PASSAGES

It's time to try a comparative passage on your own. Begin by reading each passage strategically, and don't forget to completely Roadmap Passage A and determine its Topic, Scope, Purpose, and Main Idea before proceeding to Passage B. When you've finished reading, take 10–20 seconds to think through the key similarities and differences between the two passages, then try to answer each question. Detailed explanations follow the Drill.

The passages discuss relationships between business interests and university research.

Passage A

As university researchers working in a "gift economy" dedicated to collegial sharing of ideas, we have long been insulated from market pressures. The recent tendency to treat research findings as
(5) commodities, tradable for cash, threatens this tradition and the role of research as a public good.

The nurseries for new ideas are traditionally universities, which provide an environment uniquely suited to the painstaking testing and revision of
(10) theories. Unfortunately, the market process and values governing commodity exchange are ill suited to the cultivation and management of new ideas. With their shareholders impatient for quick returns, businesses are averse to wide-ranging experimentation. And, what
(15) is even more important, few commercial enterprises contain the range of expertise needed to handle the replacement of shattered theoretical frameworks.

Further, since entrepreneurs usually have little affinity for adventure of the intellectual sort, they can
(20) buy research and bury its products, hiding knowledge useful to society or to their competitors. The growth of industrial biotechnology, for example, has been accompanied by a reduction in the free sharing of research methods and results—a high price to pay for
(25) the undoubted benefits of new drugs and therapies.

Important new experimental results once led university scientists to rush down the hall and share their excitement with colleagues. When instead the rush is to patent lawyers and venture capitalists, I
(30) worry about the long-term future of scientific discovery.

Passage B

The fruits of pure science were once considered primarily a public good, available for society as a whole. The argument for this view was that most of
(35) these benefits were produced through government support of universities, and thus no individual was entitled to restrict access to them.

Today, however, the critical role of science in the modern "information economy" means that what was
(40) previously seen as a public good is being transformed into a market commodity. For example, by exploiting the information that basic research has accumulated about the detailed structures of cells and genes, the biotechnology industry can derive profitable
(45) pharmaceuticals or medical screening technologies. In this context, assertion of legal claims to "intellectual property"—not just in commercial products but in the underlying scientific knowledge—becomes crucial.

Previously, the distinction between a scientific
(50) "discovery" (which could not be patented) and a technical "invention" (which could) defined the limits of industry's ability to patent something. Today, however, the speed with which scientific discoveries can be turned into products and the large profits
(55) resulting from this transformation have led to a blurring of both the legal distinction between discovery and invention and the moral distinction between what should and should not be patented.

Industry argues that if it has supported—either in
(60) its own laboratories or in a university—the makers of a scientific discovery, then it is entitled to seek a return on its investment, either by charging others for using the discovery or by keeping it for its own exclusive use.[10]

---

[10]PrepTest 53, Sec 4, Passage 3

1. Which one of the following is discussed in passage B but not in passage A?

    (A)   the blurring of the legal distinction between discovery and invention
    (B)   the general effects of the market on the exchange of scientific knowledge
    (C)   the role of scientific research in supplying public goods
    (D)   new pharmaceuticals that result from industrial research
    (E)   industry's practice of restricting access to research findings

2. Both passages place in opposition the members of which one of the following pairs?

    (A)   commercially successful research and commercially unsuccessful research
    (B)   research methods and research results
    (C)   a marketable commodity and a public good
    (D)   a discovery and an invention
    (E)   scientific research and other types of inquiry

3. Both passages refer to which one of the following?

    (A)   theoretical frameworks
    (B)   venture capitalists
    (C)   physics and chemistry
    (D)   industrial biotechnology
    (E)   shareholders[11]

---

[11] PrepTest 53, Sec 4, Qs 15–17

Explanations

The passages discuss relationships between business interests and university research.

Passage A

Commercial
research is bad

   As university researchers working in a "gift economy" (dedicated to) collegial sharing of ideas, we have (long been) insulated from market pressures. The (recent tendency) to treat research findings as
(5) commodities, tradable for cash, (threatens) this tradition and the role of research as a public good.

University
vs.
marketplace

   The nurseries for new ideas are (traditionally) universities, which provide an environment (uniquely) suited to the painstaking testing and revision of
(10) theories. (Unfortunately,) the market process and values governing commodity exchange are (ill suited) to the cultivation and management of new ideas. With their shareholders impatient for quick returns, businesses are (averse) to wide-ranging experimentation. And, what
(15) is even (more important,) few commercial enterprises contain the range of expertise needed to handle the replacement of shattered theoretical frameworks.

Market bad
for new
ideas

   (Further, since) entrepreneurs usually have little affinity for adventure of the intellectual sort, (they can)
(20) buy research and bury its products, hiding knowledge useful to society or to their competitors. The growth of industrial biotechnology, (for example) has been (accompanied by) a reduction in the free sharing of research methods and results—a high price to pay for
(25) the undoubted benefits of new drugs and therapies.

Market bad
for future

   (Important) new experimental results once led university scientists to rush down the hall and share their excitement with colleagues. When (instead) the rush is to patent lawyers and venture capitalists, I
(30) (worry) about the long-term future of scientific discovery.

Passage B

Science used
to be
a public good

   The fruits of pure science were (once considered) primarily a public good, available for society as a whole. The (argument) for this view was that most of
(35) these benefits were produced (through) government support of universities, and (thus) no individual was entitled to restrict access to them.

Science
is now a
commodity

   (Today, however,) the critical role of science in the modern "information economy" means that what was
(40) (previously) seen as a public good is being (transformed) into a market commodity. (For example,) by exploiting the information that basic research has accumulated about the detailed structures of cells and genes, the biotechnology industry (can derive) profitable
(45) pharmaceuticals or medical screening technologies. In this context, (assertion) of legal claims to "intellectual

property"—not just in commercial products but in the
underlying scientific knowledge—become crucial.
Previously, the distinction between a scientific

(50)   "discovery" (which could not be patented) and a
technical "invention" (which could) defined the limits
of industry's ability to patent something. Today,
however, the speed with which scientific discoveries
can be turned into products and the large profits

Patent rules   (55)   resulting from this transformation have led to a
less clear   blurring of both the legal distinction between
discovery and invention and the moral distinction
between what should and should not be patented.
              Industry argues that if it has supported—either in

Industry   (60)   its own laboratories or in a university—the makers of
argues for   a scientific discovery, then it is entitled to seek a return
profit earned   on its investment either by charging others for using
the discovery or by keeping it for its own exclusive
use.[12]

Paragraph Structure:

Passage A

The author begins by identifying a problem that "threatens" (line 5) the safety of collegiate research as a common good, namely the "recent tendency" (line 4) of some to view research as a commodity. The second paragraph expands on this idea, describing marketplace ideals as "ill suited" (line 11) to the goals of pure research. "Further" (line 18) at the beginning of the third paragraph signals more evidence from the author, this time describing the quashing of beneficial research by market pressures. In the final paragraph, the author summarizes a final "worry" (line 30) that commercial interests will be detrimental to research in the long run.

Topic: Academic research

Scope: The effect of the marketplace on research

Purpose: To give evidence for the detrimental effect of enterprise on research

Main Idea: The goals of the marketplace are incompatible with the goals of pure research, and the intrusion of commercial interests is detrimental to science.

Passage B

The author sets up a past/present dichotomy in the opening two paragraphs. Research was "once considered" (line 32) a public good, principally because of government support for universities. "Today, however" (line 38) the author indicates that science is being "transformed" (line 40) into a part of the marketplace. The third paragraph introduces a second, related dichotomy. "Previously" (line 49) there was a clear distinction between what was patentable and what

---

[12]PrepTest 53, Sec 4, Passage 3

wasn't, but "today" (line 52) the rapid pace of new discoveries has confused the issue. In the final paragraph, "industry argues" (line 59) that if it has contributed resources to institutions that conduct research, it has the right to expect a return on that investment.

Topic: Research

Scope: The role of industry in research

Purpose: To describe changes in industry's relationship to science over time

Main Idea: Through the privatization of research funding, scientific research is no longer seen as a public good, but as a commodity that industry supports and profits from.

Passage Comparison: Both authors address the intertwining of the marketplace with scientific research, and both agree that science has come to be seen less as a public good and more as a commodity. The author of Passage A is disheartened by this change, and worries that it will be damaging to science, providing evidence that this is the case. The author of Passage B doesn't render any such opinion, instead presenting the facts dispassionately and providing industry's point of view without necessarily endorsing it.

1. **(A)**

    Which one of the following is discussed in passage B but not in passage A?
    (A)   the blurring of the legal distinction between discovery and invention
    (B)   the general effects of the market on the exchange of scientific knowledge
    (C)   the role of scientific research in supplying public goods
    (D)   new pharmaceuticals that result from industrial research
    (E)   industry's practice of restricting access to research findings[13]

Passage B explored the change from science as a public good to science as a commodity in greater detail than Passage A, and in doing so provided several examples of these changes. The Roadmap shows that the third paragraph of Passage B discusses an idea that is never raised in Passage A, that "previously" (line 49) the rules about what could and couldn't be patented (based on what was classified as a "discovery" or an "invention") were very clear but are now less so. This prediction leads to correct choice (A). Choices (B), (C), (D), and (E) are all touched on by both passages.

---

[13]PrepTest 53, Sec 4, Q 15

2. **(C)**

Both passages place in opposition the members
of which one of the following pairs?
(A)   commercially successful research and
         commercially unsuccessful research
(B)   research methods and research results
(C)   a marketable commodity and a
         public good
(D)   a discovery and an invention
(E)   scientific research and other types
         of inquiry[14]

If you take the time to think through the key relationships between the passages, you can answer this question quickly and easily. Both passages center on the opposition between science as a public good and science as a commodity. This prediction should lead directly to correct choice (C). Neither passage explores the relationship expressed in choices (A) and (B), placing them completely out of scope. The opposition between discovery and invention in choice (D) is only mentioned in Passage B, and the difference between scientific inquiry and market forces described in choice (E) is explored in Passage A but not in Passage B.

3. **(D)**

Both passages refer to which one of
the following?
(A)   theoretical frameworks
(B)   venture capitalists
(C)   physics and chemistry
(D)   industrial biotechnology
(E)   shareholders[15]

This question simply asks for an example common to both passages. Keywords help you answer this question swiftly, as biotechnology is highlighted by "for example" in line 22 of Passage A and line 41 of Passage B. This should lead you straight to correct choice (D), the only idea mentioned in both passages. Remember that while you shouldn't dwell on examples during your initial strategic reading, you should always take note of the Keywords that identify them in case you run into a question like this one.

THE KAPLAN METHOD STILL APPLIES

Although I began this chapter by introducing comparative reading as a major recent change to the LSAT, by now you've seen that you should approach these passages with the same strategies you've been perfecting since the beginning of your studies. Be certain to read each passage strategically, note the Topic, Scope, Purpose, and Main Idea of both, and identify their key points of similarity and difference. If you follow this approach carefully you'll be just as

---

[14]PrepTest 53, Sec 4, Q 16
[15]PrepTest 53, Sec 4, Q 17

prepared for comparative reading as the more familiar single passages you've worked with thus far. As with everything else in the LSAT, comparative reading is predictable and amenable to the Kaplan Method.

In the next five chapters, I'll show you how the same predictability applies to the questions as well as the passages.

CHAPTER 10

GLOBAL QUESTIONS

READING COMPREHENSION QUESTION TYPES

You've learned a lot about strategic reading, and you've had plenty of opportunities to practice. At this point you may still feel that you need a lot *more* practice, and that's no problem. The more proficient you become with the Kaplan Method, the more points you'll score on test day.

That said, it's now time to change focus. Reading the passages strategically is very important, but you score points by answering the questions correctly. You've seen plenty of questions in this book so far, and you've surely noticed that the same types of questions keep appearing repeatedly throughout. You may not have found a way to categorize the different types of questions, and I haven't been referring to them by specific names in the explanations. It might surprise you to discover that there are only five types of questions that commonly appear in the Reading Comprehension section. It's now time for you to learn what the five question types are, how to identify them, and, most importantly, what strategies you should apply to them to maximize your score.

Review of the Kaplan Method

Before I introduce Global questions, take a moment to review the Kaplan Method for Reading Comprehension in its entirety:

THE KAPLAN METHOD FOR READING COMPREHENSION

Step 1 Read the Passage Strategically

Step 2 Identify the Question Type

Step 3 Research the Relevant Text

Step 4 Make a Prediction

Step 5 Evaluate the Answer Choices

Up until now, you've primarily focused on mastering the first step of the Method—identifying Keywords, creating a Roadmap, and identifying the Topic, Scope, Purpose, and Main Idea of every passage. Now I want you to pay particular attention to the remaining steps; this is the process you'll follow each time you encounter a question. I haven't presented this information to you since the first chapter, so take this opportunity to review these steps before moving on:

Step 1: Read the Passage Strategically

As always, begin by reading the passage strategically, circling Keywords, creating a Roadmap, and identifying the Topic, Scope, Purpose, and Main Idea.

Step 2: Identify the Question Type

To identify the question type, you simply need to read the question stem. Although it may seem obvious to begin by reading the question stem, remember that you're not reading it passively. Your goal in Step 2 is to actively identify the question type you're working on. Since there are only five types, it won't take you long to become familiar with them. It's very important to always identify the question type—that's how you know which Kaplan strategy to apply.

Step 3: Research the Relevant Text

Once you know the question type, you'll probably need to return to the passage to review relevant information. The clues that help you find the right text will come from several sources: the question stem, your Roadmap, and Keywords you've circled. Of the five question types, only Global questions don't require you to look up specific text in the passage. *All of the others do.* This is extremely important. One of the most common mistakes I see students make is to over-rely on memory and intuition, selecting an answer choice that seems to match something they remember reading. But as you've seen in previous chapters, the wrong answer choices are frequently written to look similar to information in the passage, but with subtle distortions built in. Fortunately it's very easy to avoid this mistake—research the text and then move on to Step 4.

STEP 4: Make a Prediction

After you've done your research, but before you look at the answer choices, you should always try to predict what the correct answer will say. In the vast majority of Reading Comprehension questions, you will be able to predict the correct choice, and I will be sure to point out the rare exceptions as they come. Making a solid prediction serves two important purposes: It allows you to zero in on the correct answer quickly, and it makes it easier for you to avoid clever answer traps that might otherwise snare you. Remember that the top-scoring LSAT test takers are those who take the most control of the test day experience. It's much better to look at a choice and ask, "Does this match my prediction?" than to ask, "Does this seem right?" The former approach is confident and methodical, the latter uncertain and prone to error.

STEP 5: Evaluate the Answer Choices

As I just noted, most of the time Step 5 simply involves finding the choice that matches your prediction and selecting it. It's important to remember that you're looking for the choice that correctly matches the *concept* embodied in your prediction, not necessarily the specific wording of your prediction. Occasionally you may need to employ the process of elimination, either because you weren't able to make a prediction or because you aren't sure about the right match. In any case, remember that for every LSAT question there is precisely one—and only one—correct answer. The other four answers are completely incorrect. Further, the wrong answer choices also follow predictable patterns, and I'll explain those patterns as we go.

When taken in total, the Kaplan Method for Reading Comprehension provides you with a specific strategy to use in every situation the test makers present to you. You don't have time to spend on test day wondering what to do next; with diligent practice, you'll soon internalize the Method, and applying it will come naturally to you.

Now, with the Kaplan Method in mind, it's time to look at the five question types, beginning with one that will look very familiar to you: Global questions.

GLOBAL QUESTIONS
What Are Global Questions?

Global questions, as the name implies, ask about the big ideas of the passage. Any question that asks about the author's main point, the primary purpose of the passage, or the structure of the passage as a whole is classified as a Global question. Most passages come with one or more Global questions as part of their question set, and they're typically located at the beginning or the end of the set.

How Do You Identify Global Questions?

There aren't many variations on Global questions, and you've seen most of them already. Here are a few examples:

22. Which one of the following most completely and accurately summarizes the argument of the passage?[1]

21. Which one of the following best summarizes the main idea of the passage?[2]

26. Which one of the following best describes the organization of the passage?[3]

The highlighted words in each question provide you with clues that identify them as Global questions. Notice that in each case the question is asking for big-picture ideas. Presented in terms of the Kaplan Method, your thinking should go like this:

STEP 2: Identify the Question Type: When the question asks for the Purpose, Main Idea, or organization of the passage as a whole, you know it's a Global question.

Global Question Strategy

Global questions require you to be fluent with the author's overarching themes and the passage structure. Fortunately, you've already gotten into the habit of identifying Topic, Scope, Purpose, and Main Idea—exactly what you need to answer this type of question correctly. For clarity, I'll present the strategy you should employ in each of Steps 3–5 of the Kaplan Method.

STEP 3: Research the Relevant Text: Since you've already identified the author's big ideas by reading strategically, this is the one question type that doesn't require you to review specific text in the passage. Move on to Step 4 instead.

STEP 4: Make a Prediction: In order to make a prediction, recall what the question is asking for, and then paraphrase the idea in your mind before going to the answer choices. Most Global questions will ask for either the Purpose or the Main Idea, and since you've already discovered them in Step 1, making a prediction won't take more than a few seconds. If the question asks for the organization of the passage, use your Roadmap to form your prediction—the notes you made next to each paragraph will give you structure at a glance.

STEP 5: Evaluate the Answer Choices: Find the answer choice that matches your prediction.

Global Question Practice

To illustrate, try applying the Kaplan Method to a set of questions initially introduced in chapter 1. Don't worry if they look familiar to you—your goal is to get used to approaching each

[1]PrepTest 25, Sec 1, Q 22
[2]PrepTest 41, Sec 4, Q 21
[3]PrepTest 41, Sec 4, Q 26

question methodically, something you weren't thinking about the first time you saw them. Begin by rereading the passage, taking note of the sample Roadmap. Think about the Topic, Scope, Purpose, and Main Idea of the passage as you discover them.

Step 1:

Vict.
philanthropy
def.

Early crit.

Philanthropy
obsolete

(Although) philanthropy—the volunteering of private resources for humanitarian purposes—reached its apex in England in the late nineteenth century, (modern commentators) have articulated two major
(5) (criticisms) of the philanthropy that was a mainstay of England's middle-class Victorian society. The (earlier) criticism is that such philanthropy was even by the later nineteenth century obsolete, (since) industrialism had already created social problems that were beyond the
(10) scope of small, private voluntary efforts. (Indeed,) these problems required substantial legislative action by the state. Unemployment, (for example,) was not the result of a failure of diligence on the part of workers (or) a failure of compassion on the part of employers, (nor)
(15) could it be solved by well-wishing philanthropists.

Modern
crit.

Philanthropy
self serving

The (more recent) charge holds that Victorian philanthropy was by its very nature a self-serving exercise carried out by philanthropists at the expense of those whom they were ostensibly serving. (In) this view,
(20) philanthropy was a means of flaunting one's power and position in a society that placed (great emphasis) on status, (or) even a means of cultivating social connections that could (lead to) economic rewards.

(Further,) if philanthropy is seen as serving the interests
(25) of individual philanthropists, (so) it may be seen as serving the interests of their class. (According to) this "social control" thesis, philanthropists, in professing to help the poor, were encouraging in them such values as prudence, thrift, and temperance, values perhaps
(30) worthy in themselves (but also) designed to create more productive members of the labor force. Philanthropy, in short, was a means of controlling the labor force and ensuring the continued dominance of the management class.

Author:
Modern
crit. Wrong

(35) (Modern critics) of Victorian philanthropy often use the word's "amateurish" or "inadequate" to describe Victorian philanthropy, (as though) Victorian charity can only be understood as an antecedent to the era of state-sponsored, professionally administered charity. This
(40) (assumption) is typical of the "Whig fallacy": the tendency to read the past as an (inferior) prelude to an enlightened present. If most Victorians resisted state control and expended their resources on private, voluntary philanthropies, it could (only) be, the argument
(45) goes, (because) of their commitment to a vested interest, (or because) the administrative apparatus of the state was incapable of coping with the economic and social needs of the time.

Critics
incorrect

      This version of history (patronizes) the Victorians,
(50) who were in fact well aware of their vulnerability to
charges of condescension and complacency, (but) were
equally well aware of the potential dangers of state-
managed charity. They were perhaps condescending to
the poor, (but)—to use an un-Victorian metaphor—they
(55) put their money where their mouths were, (and) gave of
their careers and lives as well.[4]

Paragraph Structure: The first paragraph introduces the Topic—Victorian philanthropy—and then introduces two criticisms beginning at line 4. The "earlier criticism" (line 6) is that Victorian philanthropy was obsolete even by the standards of its own time.

The second paragraph introduces a "more recent" criticism (line 16), something you were certainly prepared to see if you were reading predictively. This new criticism is that the Victorian philanthropists were ultimately self-serving, promoting values that may have helped the poor but that were also intended to create a more productive workforce.

The author responds to the critics in the final two paragraphs. He critiques the "assumption" (line 40) that underlies the two criticisms, that the behavior of the Victorians can "only be understood" (line 38) in the context of modern charity. He ultimately concludes that this assumption "patronizes" (line 49) the Victorians.

Topic: Victorian philanthropy

Scope: criticisms of Victorian philanthropists

Purpose: to examine criticisms of the Victorian philanthropists and refute them

Main Idea: Criticisms of Victorian philanthropy fail because they are based on flawed reasoning.

Now read the following question:

21.   Which one of the following best summarizes the
main idea of the passage?[5]

Work through this question using the Kaplan Method.

Step 2: The question asks you to summarize the main idea. This is definitely a Global question.

Step 3: Global questions don't require you to reference specific text, so move on to the next step.

Step 4: Base your prediction on your knowledge of the passage's Main Idea. The author's main point was that the critics of Victorian Philanthropy were incorrect because their arguments were based on bad logic.

---

[4]PrepTest 41, Sec 4, Passage 4
[5]PrepTest 41, Sec 4, Q 21

Step 5: Now examine the answer choices and identify the one that matches the prediction:

21. Which one of the following best summarizes the main idea of the passage?

    (A) While the motives of individual practitioners have been questioned by modern commentators, Victorian philanthropy successfully dealt with the social ills of nineteenth-century England.

    (B) Philanthropy, inadequate to deal with the massive social and economic problems of the twentieth century, has slowly been replaced by state-sponsored charity.

    (C) The practice of reading the past as a prelude to an enlightened present has fostered revisionist views of many institutions, among them Victorian philanthropy.

    (D) Although modern commentators have perceived Victorian philanthropy as either inadequate or self-serving, the theoretical bias behind these criticisms leads to an incorrect interpretation of history.

    (E) Victorian philanthropists, aware of public resentment of their self-congratulatory attitude, used devious methods to camouflage their self-serving motives.[6]

Now evaluate each answer choice. Choice (A) mentions that the philanthropists were the subject of criticism but it then goes astray by claiming that they successfully solved social problems. Eliminate it. Choice (B) has nothing to do with the author's refutation of the critics, so it's out as well. While choice (C) mentions an argument that the author made, it doesn't capture the author's central argument as you predicted in Step 4. Move on to the next one. Choice (D) is a perfect match: It nicely summarizes both the arguments of the critics and the author's reason for rejecting them. This is the correct answer. For the record, choice (E), like choice (B), fails to address the author's response to the critics, and likewise fails to match your prediction. Using the Kaplan Method, you quickly spot correct choice (D), score this point, and go on to the next question.

Try another question from the same passage. This time, execute Steps 2–5 on your own before moving on to the explanation that follows.

---

24. Which one of the following best describes the primary purpose of the passage?

   (A) providing an extended definition of a key term
   (B) defending the work of an influential group of theorists
   (C) narrating the chronological development of a widespread practice
   (D) examining modern evaluations of a historical phenomenon
   (E) analyzing a specific dilemma faced by workers of the past[7]

Now compare your reasoning to this step-by-step explanation.

Step 2: The identifying phrase "primary purpose" tells you that this is a Global question.

Step 3: Once again, no specific research is necessary.

Step 4: Because you already identified it in Step 1, you know that the author's Purpose in this passage was to refute the critics of Victorian philanthropy.

Step 5: Finding a match for your prediction might have been a little more difficult in this case, but remember, you're looking for a *concept* that matches, not necessarily the exact wording of your prediction. Correct choice (D) is slightly more general than the wording of the prediction above, but it still perfectly describes the author's Purpose: to take on the critics' ideas (described in the choice as "modern evaluations"). None of the other choices refer to this central conflict of ideas at all and therefore are out of scope.

Try one more question from the same passage, once again applying the Kaplan Method:

26. Which one of the following best describes the organization of the passage?

   (A) Two related positions are discussed, then both are subjected to the same criticism.
   (B) Two opposing theories are outlined, then a synthesis between the two is proposed.
   (C) A position is stated, and two differing evaluations of it are given.
   (D) Three examples of the same logical inconsistency are given.
   (E) A theory is outlined, and two supporting examples are given.[8]

Now compare your reasoning with mine:

Step 2: This time the phrase "organization of the passage" is the clue that identifies this as a Global question. Questions that ask for the overall structure of a passage are considered Global.

---

[7]PrepTest 41, Sec 4, Q 24
[8]PrepTest 41, Sec 4, Q 26

Step 3: As with all Global questions, you don't need to do any specific textual research.

Step 4: Your best tool when tackling a question like this one is your Roadmap. The correct answer should indicate that criticisms were leveled at the philanthropists, and that the author then refuted them.

Step 5: With the strong prediction provided by a good Roadmap, correct choice (A) should be easy to spot. Notice how most of the incorrect answers use similar language but in a distorted way. Choice (B) mentions two theories, but suggests that they were opposed and ultimately synthesized, which never occurred in this passage. Choice (C) mentions the evaluation of a position, but there weren't two differing evaluations, just the one that the author provided. The three examples mentioned in choice (D) and the supporting examples in choice (E) are nowhere to be found in your prediction, making these choices incorrect.

This question illustrates just why prediction is such an important part of the Kaplan Method. If you attempt to answer this question without a review of the passage structure, you risk selecting a choice that contains familiar-looking language but that ultimately misses the mark.

I'd also like to remind you that all three of the practice questions you just examined came from the same LSAT passage. Since there are only six questions total, that means you scored half of the points available from this passage simply by understanding the big picture. Most passages will feature at least one global question, reinforcing the necessity of Strategic Reading—it pays off in points earned and time saved.

DRILL: ANSWERING GLOBAL QUESTIONS

Now practice applying the Kaplan Method to a new passage, beginning with Step 1. After you've read the passage strategically, answer each of the questions that follow by applying Steps 2–5 of the Method each time. Execute each step with care and focus on becoming comfortable with them. Explanations follow the Drill.

Most authoritarian rulers who undertake democratic reforms do so not out of any intrinsic commitment or conversion to democratic ideals, but rather because they foresee or recognize that certain changes and
(5) mobilizations in civil society make it impossible for them to hold on indefinitely to absolute power.

Three major types of changes can contribute to a society's no longer condoning the continuation of
(10) authoritarian rule. First, the values and norms in the society alter over time, reducing citizens' tolerance for repression and concentration of power and thus stimulating their demands for freedom. In some Latin American countries during the 1970s and 1980s, for
(15) example, this change in values came about partly as a result of the experience of repression, which brought in its wake a resurgence of democratic values. As people come to place more value on political freedom and civil liberties they also become more inclined to speak
(20) out, protest, and organize for democracy, frequently beginning with the denunciation of human rights abuses.

In addition to changing norms and values, the alignment of economic interests in a society can shift.
(25) As one scholar notes, an important turning point in the transition to democracy comes when privileged people in society—landowners, industrialists, merchants, bankers—who had been part of a regime's support base come to the conclusion that the authoritarian regime is
(30) dispensable and that its continuation might damage their long-term interests. Such a large-scale shift in the economic interests of these elites was crucial in bringing about the transition to democracy in the Philippines and has also begun occurring incrementally
(35) in other authoritarian nations.

A third change derives from the expanding resources, autonomy, and self-confidence of various segments of society and of newly formed organizations both formal and informal. Students march in the streets
(40) demanding change; workers paralyze key industries; lawyers refuse to cooperate any longer in legal charades; alternative sources of information pierce and then shatter the veil of secrecy and disinformation; informal networks of production and exchange emerge
(45) that circumvent the state's resources and control. This profound development can radically alter the balance of power in a country, as an authoritarian regime that could once easily dominate and control its citizens is placed on the defensive.

(50) Authoritarian rule tends in the long run to generate all three types of changes. Ironically, all three types can be accelerated by the authoritarian regime's initial success at producing economic growth and maintaining social order—success that, by creating a period of
(55) stability, gives citizens the opportunity to reflect on the circumstances in which they live. The more astute or calculating of authoritarian rulers will recognize this and realize that their only hope of retaining some power in the future is to match these democratic social
(60) changes with democratic political changes.[9]

---

[9]PrepTest 34, Sec 1, Passage 1

1. Which one of the following most accurately expresses the main point of the passage?

   (A) Authoritarian rulers tend to undertake democratic reforms only after it becomes clear that the nation's economic and social power bases will slow economic growth and disrupt social order until such reforms are instituted.

   (B) Authoritarian regimes tend to ensure their own destruction by allowing opposition groups to build support among the wealthy whose economic interests are easily led away from support for the regime.

   (C) Authoritarian policies tend in the long run to alienate the economic power base in a nation once it becomes clear that the regime's initial success at generating economic growth and stability will be short lived.

   (D) Authoritarian principles tend in the long run to be untenable because they demand from the nation a degree of economic and social stability that is impossible to maintain in the absence of democratic institutions.

   (E) Authoritarian rulers who institute democratic reforms are compelled to do so because authoritarian rule tends to bring about various changes in society that eventually necessitate corresponding political changes.

2. Which one of the following titles most completely summarizes the content of the passage?

   (A) "Avenues for Change: The Case for Dissent in Authoritarian Regimes"

   (B) "Human Rights Abuses under Authoritarian Regimes: A Case Study"

   (C) "Democratic Coalitions under Authoritarian Regimes: Strategies and Solutions"

   (D) "Why Authoritarian Regimes Compromise: An Examination of Societal Forces"

   (E) "Growing Pains: Economic Instability in Countries on the Brink of Democracy"

3. Which one of the following most accurately describes the organization of the passage?

   (A) A political phenomenon is linked to a general set of causes; this set is divided into categories and the relative importance of each category is assessed; the possibility of alternate causes is considered and rejected.

   (B) A political phenomenon is linked to a general set of causes; this set is divided into categories and an explication of each category is presented; the causal relationship is elaborated upon and reaffirmed.

   (C) A political phenomenon is identified; the possible causes of the phenomenon are described and placed into categories; one possible cause is preferred over the others and reasons are given for the preference.

   (D) A political phenomenon is identified; similarities between this phenomenon and three similar phenomena are presented; the similarities among the phenomena are restated in general terms and argued for.

   (E) A political phenomenon is identified; differences between this phenomenon and three similar phenomena are presented; the differences among the phenomena are restated in general terms and argued for.[10]

Explanations

Step 1:

Authoritarians change b/c they have to

　　　　Most authoritarian rulers who undertake democratic reforms do so (not) out of any intrinsic commitment or conversion to democratic ideals, but (rather because) they foresee or recognize that certain

(5)　changes and mobilizations in civil society make it impossible for them to hold on indefinitely to absolute power.

First change: values

　　　　(Three major types of) changes can contribute to a society's no longer condoning the continuation of

(10)　authoritarian rule. (First,) the values and norms in the society alter over time, reducing citizens' tolerance for repression and concentration of power and (thus) stimulating their demands for freedom. In some Latin American countries during the 1970s and 1980s, for

(15)　(example,) this change in values came about partly as a (result) of the experience of repression, which brought in its wake a resurgence of democratic values. As people come to place more value on political freedom and civil liberties they (also) become more inclined to speak

(20)　out, protest, and organize for democracy, frequently beginning with the denunciation of human rights abuses.

Second change: economy

　　　　(In addition) to changing norms and values, the alignment of economic interests in a society can shift.

(25)　As one (scholar notes,) an (important) turning point in the transition to democracy comes when privileged people in society—landowners, industrialists, merchants, bankers—who had been part of a regime's support base come to the (conclusion) that the authoritarian regime is

(30)　dispensable (and) that its continuation might damage their long-term interests. Such a large-scale shift in the economic interests of these elites was (crucial) in bringing about the transition to democracy in the Philippines and has (also) begun occurring incrementally

(35)　in other authoritarian nations.

Third change: people more confident

　　　　A (third) change derives from the expanding resources, autonomy, and self-confidence of various segments of society (and) of newly formed organizations both formal and informal. Students march in the streets

(40)　demanding change; workers paralyze key industries; lawyers refuse to cooperate any longer in legal charades; alternative sources of information pierce and then shatter the veil of secrecy and disinformation; informal networks of production and exchange emerge

(45)　that circumvent the state's resources and control. This (profound) development can (radically) alter the balance of power in a country, as an authoritarian regime that could (once) easily dominate and control its citizens is placed on the defensive.

Auth. regimes cause own problems

(50)　Authoritarian rule (tends) in the long run to generate all three types of changes. (Ironically,) all three types can

be accelerated by the authoritarian regime's initial
success at producing economic growth and maintaining
social order—success that, by creating a period of
(55) stability, gives citizens the opportunity to reflect on the
circumstances in which they live. The more astute or
calculating of authoritarian rulers will recognize this
Change to
retain power
and realize that their only hope of retaining some
power in the future is to match these democratic social
(60) changes with democratic political changes.[11]

Paragraph Structure: The first paragraph contains a single sentence and sets the stage for the author's primary argument. Contrast Keywords "but rather because" in lines 3–4 point you toward the author's chief theme: authoritarian rulers generally adopt democratic principles because they require such principles to stay in power.

The next paragraph begins with an excellent group of Keywords: "Three major types of change" lead to trouble for authoritarian rulers. Unsurprisingly, paragraphs two through four go on to describe each of these changes. The author first mentions the alteration of values in a society, and then prepares to illustrate this idea with the keywords "for example" in lines 14–15. The second change, introduced in the third paragraph, is a shift in economic interests. Once again, the author illustrates this idea throughout the rest of the paragraph, citing evidence provided by the scholar mentioned in line 25. In the fourth paragraph, the author mentions the third change: the growing wealth and autonomy of society. As with the prior two paragraphs, the author goes on to describe this change in greater detail.

Hopefully you were prepared for the author to deliver some kind of final verdict about these changes in the final paragraph. She points out that, "ironically" (line 51), these changes typically come about by the regime's initial successes, and suggests that an authoritarian leader's "only hope" (line 58) of retaining power is to introduce democratic changes to society.

Topic: authoritarian regimes

Scope: why authoritarian leaders sometimes adopt democratic policies

Purpose: to illustrate the kinds of social changes that force authoritarian states to shift toward democratic policies

Main Idea: Authoritarian leaders who institute democratic changes in their regimes typically do so as a result of social changes that force them to.

---

[11]PrepTest 34, Sec 1, Passage 1

1. **(E)**

    Which one of the following most accurately expresses
    the main point of the passage?
    (A) Authoritarian rulers tend to undertake democratic
         reforms only after it becomes clear that the
         nation's economic and social power bases will
         slow economic growth and disrupt social order
         until such reforms are instituted.
    (B) Authoritarian regimes tend to ensure their own
         destruction by allowing opposition groups to
         build support among the wealthy whose
         economic interests are easily led away from
         support for the regime.
    (C) Authoritarian policies tend in the long run to
         alienate the economic power base in a nation
         once it becomes clear that the regime's initial
         success at generating economic growth and
         stability will be short lived.
    (D) Authoritarian principles tend in the long run to be
         untenable because they demand from the nation
         a degree of economic and social stability that is
         impossible to maintain in the absence of
         democratic institutions.
    (E) Authoritarian rulers who institute democratic
         reforms are compelled to do so because
         authoritarian rule tends to bring about various
         changes in society that eventually necessitate
         corresponding political changes.[12]

Step 2: Any question that asks for the "main point" of the passage is a Global question.

Step 3: No research is necessary.

Step 4: Reflecting on the Main Idea of the passage, you should predict that the correct answer
will mention that authoritarian regimes tend to become more democratic when changes in
society make it necessary.

Step 5: Correct choice (E) is the match—it describes the causal relationship between social
changes and democratic political changes. Choice (A) focuses too narrowly on two of the three
changes mentioned by the author, and the remaining choices all fail to address the reasons
why authoritarian rulers move toward democracy, placing them out of scope.

---

[12]PrepTest 34, Sec 1, Q 1

2. **(D)**

    Which one of the following titles most completely
    summarizes the content of the passage?
    (A)   "Avenues for Change: The Case for Dissent in
           Authoritarian Regimes"
    (B)   "Human Rights Abuses under Authoritarian
           Regimes: A Case Study"
    (C)   "Democratic Coalitions under Authoritarian
           Regimes: Strategies and Solutions"
    (D)   "Why Authoritarian Regimes Compromise: An
           Examination of Societal Forces"
    (E)   "Growing Pains: Economic Instability in
           Countries on the Brink of Democracy"[13]

Step 2: This is an unusual variant on the Global question stem that shows up on the LSAT from time to time. When the question asks you to provide the proper title for the piece, it's really asking you to summarize the author's thesis; once again, you're being asked for the big picture.

Step 3: No textual research is necessary.

Step 4: An exact prediction might be tricky to come up with on this question, but you should still remind yourself what the essential content of the correct answer will be: The correct title will reflect the idea that societal changes cause authoritarian regimes to become more democratic.

Step 5: Correct choice (D) matches the prediction: It encapsulates the author's Purpose by describing why authoritarian regimes change politically. The author never makes a case for dissent as described in choice (A), and choice (B) is far too narrowly focused. The strategies and solutions proposed in choice (C) never appeared in the passage, and choice (E) overly focuses on economic issues. It's also extreme—the author is talking about regimes that make democratic changes, not "countries on the brink of democracy."

---

[13]PrepTest 34, Sec 1, Q 3

3.   **(B)**

Which one of the following most accurately describes
the organization of the passage?

(A)   A political phenomenon is linked to a general set
of causes; this set is divided into categories and
the relative importance of each category is
assessed; the possibility of alternate causes is
considered and rejected.

(B)   A political phenomenon is linked to a general set
of causes; this set is divided into categories and
an explication of each category is presented; the
causal relationship is elaborated upon and reaffirmed.

(C)   A political phenomenon is identified; the possible
causes of the phenomenon are described and
placed into categories; one possible cause is
preferred over the others and reasons are given
for the preference.

(D)   A political phenomenon is identified; similarities
between this phenomenon and three similar
phenomena are presented; the similarities among
the phenomena are restated in general terms and
argued for.

(E)   A political phenomenon is identified; differences
between this phenomenon and three similar
phenomena are presented; the differences among
the phenomena are restated in general terms and
argued for.[14]

Step 2: Since the stem asks for the "organization of the passage," you know you're dealing
with a Global question.

Step 3: No research is necessary.

Step 4: A review of the Roadmap gives you an excellent prediction about the organization of
the passage: The author explains why authoritarian regimes move toward democracy, gives
three examples, and finally restates her original assertion.

Step 5: The passage structure is described by correct choice (B). Choice (A) begins correctly,
using the very same opening text as the correct answer but then veers off course by mentioning
the "relative importance" of the various causes. Choice (C) makes a similar error in suggesting
that the author prefers one explanation over another. Choice (D) gets the author's approach
entirely wrong; she didn't present "similar phenomena" to the original but suggested causes
for it. Choice (E) makes essentially the same mistake, this time suggesting that the author was
concerned with the differences in phenomena.

---

[14]PrepTest 34, Sec 1, Q 4

COMMON WRONG ANSWER TYPES

Before moving on to the next Reading Comprehension question type, I'll point out some of the most common types of wrong answers you're likely to see when answering Global questions. Most of them appeared in the exercise above, so be on the lookout for them in your practice.

Overly Narrow Focus

Remember that the correct answer to a global question must stay high level—that is, it has to encapsulate the author's primary goals or conclusions. Beware of answer choices that dwell on a specific example presented in the passage.

> Which one of the following most accurately expresses the main point of the passage?
>
> (A) Authoritarian rulers tend to undertake democratic reforms only after it becomes clear that the nation's economic and social power bases will slow economic growth and disrupt social order until such reforms are instituted.
>
> (B) Authoritarian regimes tend to ensure their own destruction by allowing opposition groups to build support among the wealthy whose economic interests are easily led away from support for the regime.
>
> (C) Authoritarian policies tend in the long run to alienate the economic power base in a nation once it becomes clear that the regime's initial success at generating economic growth and stability will be short lived.
>
> (D) Authoritarian principles tend in the long run to be untenable because they demand from the nation a degree of economic and social stability that is impossible to maintain in the absence of democratic institutions.
>
> (E) Authoritarian rulers who institute democratic reforms are compelled to do so because authoritarian rule tends to bring about various changes in society that eventually necessitate corresponding political changes.[15]

Recall that the passage *did* mention the specific type of reform mentioned in choice (A), but this wasn't the author's main point. The author only mentioned this idea in service of the larger goal expressed in correct choice (E). This type of wrong answer can be tempting because it does identify concepts that the author mentioned, but don't confuse the Main Idea with supporting evidence.

---

[15]PrepTest 34, Sec 1, Q 1

Extreme

This answer trap is common on almost every type of Reading Comprehension question.

Which one of the following titles most completely summarizes the content of the passage?

(A) "Avenues for Change: The Case for Dissent in Authoritarian Regimes"

(B) "Human Rights Abuses under Authoritarian Regimes: A Case Study"

(C) "Democratic Coalitions under Authoritarian Regimes: Strategies and Solutions"

(D) "Why Authoritarian Regimes Compromise: An Examination of Societal Forces"

(E) "Growing Pains: Economic Instability in Countries on the Brink of Democracy"[16]

The author of the passage discussed reasons why authoritarian regimes sometimes make democratic changes, but at no point does he mention regimes that are actually becoming democracies, as choice (E) implies. Because this wrong answer type is so prevalent, you need to note the difference, and the test makers will reward you for taking notice of it.

Half Right/Half Wrong

This can be a dangerous wrong answer trap, particularly if you aren't carefully checking the answer choices against a strong prediction.

---

[16]PrepTest 34, Sec 1, Q 3

Which one of the following most accurately describes the organization of the passage?

(A)   A political phenomenon is linked to a general set of causes; this set is divided into categories and the relative importance of each category is assessed; the possibility of alternate causes is considered and rejected.

(B)   A political phenomenon is linked to a general set of causes; this set is divided into categories and an explication of each category is presented; the causal relationship is elaborated upon and reaffirmed.

(C)   A political phenomenon is identified; the possible causes of the phenomenon are described and placed into categories; one possible cause is preferred over the others and reasons are given for the preference.

(D)   A political phenomenon is identified; similarities between this phenomenon and three similar phenomena are presented; the similarities among the phenomena are restated in general terms and argued for.

(E)   A political phenomenon is identified; differences between this phenomenon and three similar phenomena are presented; the differences among the phenomena are restated in general terms and argued for.[17]

Note how choice (A) begins exactly like correct choice (B), but then goes out of scope by implying that the author evaluates the relative importance of his examples and posits alternative explanations. None of these things occur in the passage. You are likely to select this type of choice if you fail to identify the Purpose and Main Idea of the passage or if you read the choices carelessly; don't let the pressure of the clock lead you into this error.

TRUST IN THE KAPLAN METHOD

These aren't the only types of wrong answer that you'll see in Global questions, but they are among the most common. The best way to avoid them is to follow the Kaplan Method carefully and consistently so that you approach every question with a solid prediction. This holds true for other question types as well, as you'll see in the coming chapters.

---

[17]PrepTest 34, Sec 1, Q 4

CHAPTER 11

Detail Questions

ALL ABOUT DETAIL QUESTIONS

Now that you've reviewed the Kaplan Method and learned how to apply it to Global questions, it's time to examine another Reading Comprehension question type: Detail questions.

What Are Detail Questions?

Detail questions are, in a way, the direct opposites of Global questions. While Global questions ask about the overarching themes of a passage, Detail questions require you to review the text and identify specific information that the author cited in the passage, usually in the form of evidence provided to support central conclusions. This may seem like a pretty simple task—after all, the information you need is right there in the passage. Nevertheless, there are a couple of considerations I want you to keep in mind as you familiarize yourself with this common question type.

First, do not let the presence of Detail questions on the LSAT interfere with your commitment to strategic reading. You may find yourself thinking, "If some of the questions are going to ask me about particular examples in the text, shouldn't I read the examples more carefully?" This line of reasoning is understandable, but it isn't the best way to approach the test. Remember that no matter how carefully you dive into the details when you read, two things are certain to be true: Not all of the examples will be tested, and you won't be able to memorize the ones that *are* tested—there's simply too much information in the passage.

This brings me to the second point. Do *not* try to rely on your memory when answering Detail questions. As you will see in the examples in this chapter, the test makers are very good at distorting answer choices in subtle ways so that they resemble information in the passage while still being categorically wrong. Unlike the approach to Global questions you worked with in chapter 10, you absolutely must stay in the habit of researching the relevant text before predicting the correct answer to a Detail question.

You might be concerned about the time this takes, and I've certainly worked with many students who succumbed to the pressure of the clock and tried to answer these questions from memory. The results were predictable: They would become very good at getting the questions wrong in a short amount of time.

To avoid this problem, remember that by rigorously applying Step 1 of the Kaplan Method (Read the Passage Strategically) to every passage, you will save time that you can later spend researching the correct answers to the questions. Additionally, your careful attention to Keywords and a solid Roadmap will allow you to quickly and accurately find the information you need.

How Do You Identify Detail Questions?

Detail questions will always ask unambiguously for information specifically cited in the passage. Common identifying phrases include "the passage mentions which of the following" and "which of the following is an example cited by the author." Here are a few examples drawn from previous tests:

2. The author indicates that all politicians agree about the[1]

16. Which one of the following does the passage identify as being a result of a technological development?[2]

10. According to the passage, the term "legal principles" as used by Dworkin refers to[3]

Notice that there is no qualifying language in any of these examples. Detail questions don't ask what the passage "suggests" or what the author is "likely" to agree with (this kind of qualification indicates an Inference question, which I will introduce in the next chapter). They simply ask for what's explicitly stated. Detail questions often begin with the phrase "according to" as demonstrated in question 10 above, but other question types may feature this phrase as well. In terms of the Kaplan Method:

Step 2: Identify the Question Type

When the stem asks you to identify information that is explicitly stated in the passage, you know you're working with a Detail question.

---

[1]PrepTest 26, Sec 4, Q 2
[2]PrepTest 42, Sec 3, Q 16
[3]PrepTest 17, Sec 4, Q 10

Detail Question Strategy

There aren't many variations on Detail questions, and they all require the same essential strategy; use whatever clues the question provides in order to conduct your research as quickly as you can. In most cases your task is to simply paraphrase what you read in the passage and then identify the answer choice that expresses the same concept. In terms of the Kaplan Method:

Step 3: Research the Relevant Text

Find the relevant text in the passage. Use your Roadmap and circled Keywords in the passage to direct you to the information you need. Since Detail questions tend to ask about examples that you moved through quickly when first reading the passage, be prepared to take some time to understand what the example is saying now that you know it's worth points.

Step 4: Make a Prediction

Simplify the information you researched, and paraphrase it in your mind. The correct answer choice must embody the idea conveyed by the text, but it may not use the same words. Putting the example in your own words will help you stay flexible as you work through the answer choices.

Step 5: Evaluate the Answer Choices

Select the choice that best matches the information you paraphrased.

Detail Question Practice

Now for some examples. Read the following passage, noting the circled Keywords and the provided Roadmap. Determine the Topic, Scope, Purpose, and Main Idea of the passage before moving on to the questions.

Step 1:

	The (myth) persists that in 1492 the Western Hemisphere was an untamed wilderness (and) that it was European settlers who harnessed and transformed its ecosystems. (But) scholarship shows that forests, in
	(5) particular, had been altered to varying degrees well
Myth:	before the arrival of Europeans. Native populations had
Native	converted much of the forests to successfully cultivated
pop's	stands, (especially) by means of burning. (Nevertheless,)
didn't	some (researchers) have (maintained) that the extent,
burn	(10) frequency, and impact of such burning was minimal.
forests	One (geographer claims) that climatic change could have
	accounted for some of the changes in forest
	composition; (another argues) that burning by native
	populations was done only sporadically, to augment the
	(15) effects of natural fires.

Ev. for
burning
in U.S.

(However,) a large body of (evidence) for the routine
practice of burning exists in the geographical record.
One group of researchers found, (for example,) that
sedimentary charcoal accumulations in what is now the
(20)   northeastern United States are greatest where known
native American settlements were greatest. Other
(evidence) shows that, (while) the characteristics and
impact of fires set by native populations varied
regionally according to population size, extent of
(25)   resource management techniques, and environment, all
such fires had (markedly different) effects on vegetation
patterns than did natural fires. Controlled burning
created grassy openings such as meadows and glades.
Burning (also) promoted a mosaic quality to North and
(30)   South American ecosystems, creating forests in many
different stages of ecological development. Much of
the mature forestland was characterized by open,
herbaceous undergrowth, (another result) of the clearing
brought about by burning.

Ev. in
North
America

(35)   In North America, controlled burning created
conditions favorable to berries and other fire-tolerant
and sun-loving foods. Burning (also) converted mixed
stands of trees to homogeneous forest, (for example) the
longleaf, slash pine, and scrub oak forests of the
(40)   southeastern U.S. Natural fires do account for some of
this vegetation, (but) regular burning clearly extended
and maintained it. Burning (also) influenced forest
composition in the tropics, where natural fires are rare.
(An example) is the pine-dominant forests of Nicaragua,

Ev. in
tropics

(45)   where warm temperatures and heavy rainfall naturally
favor mixed tropical or rain forests. (While) there are
extensive pine forests in Guatemala and Mexico, these
(primarily) grow in cooler, drier, higher elevations,
regions where such vegetation is in large part natural
(50)   and even prehuman. (Today) the Nicaraguan pines
occur where there has been clearing (followed by)
regular burning (and) the same is likely to have occurred
in the past: such forests were present when Europeans
arrived and were found (only in) areas where native
(55)   settlements were substantial; when these settlements
were abandoned, the land returned to mixed
hardwoods. This succession is (also evident) elsewhere
in similar low tropical elevations in the Caribbean and
Mexico.[4]

Paragraph Structure: Structurally, this passage is quite simple. The author introduces the "myth" (line 1) of untamed wilderness in the Western Hemisphere prior to the arrival of European settlers, "but" (line 4) notes that scholarship indicates that native populations had been practicing controlled burning of forests. "Nevertheless" (line 8) some researchers still believe

---

[4]PrepTest 38, Sec 3, Passage 1

the myth. The remainder of the paragraph presents the views of these researchers—"one geographer" in line 11 and "another" in line 13.

Given that the author identified the researchers' view as a myth in the first sentence, you hopefully weren't surprised when the second paragraph began with "however" (line 16), introducing the author's claim that there's an abundance of evidence for the burning of forests. The remainder of the passage consists entirely of examples to back up the author's claim. As always, you should resist the temptation to read these examples carefully, since you already understand their purpose (to bolster the author's claim). Instead, take careful note of Keywords that will help you locate them easily later, such as "for example" (line 18), "other evidence" (lines 21–22), "another result" (line 33), and "also" (line 42). Your Roadmap should reflect the general kind of evidence that each paragraph contains, perhaps noting that paragraph two shows evidence of burning in the United States and paragraph three describes examples in both North and South America. But note that the author doesn't state any opinions in these paragraphs—the author's sole claim, and the Main Idea of the passage, was stated in lines 16–17.

Topic: Controlled burning of forests

Scope: Burning by non-European natives in North and South America

Purpose: To demonstrate that a myth about the Western Hemisphere is untrue

Main Idea: Despite claims to the contrary, there is much evidence that the native people of North and South America cultivated forests by controlled burning.

3. Which one of the following is a type of forest identified
    by the author as a product of controlled burning in recent
    times?[5]

Before looking at the answer choices, apply the Kaplan Method.

Step 2: The stem asks for a type of forest "identified by the author." Since you're being asked to find a specific example, you know this is a Detail question.

Step 3: What clues appeared in the question stem to guide you to the proper text? The question asked about the product of burning in "recent times." Skim the Roadmap and circled Keywords to locate the proper place to research the answer.

Hopefully you clued in on the Keyword "today" (line 50) which shows where you'll find information about "recent times." The text indicates that Nicaraguan pines are found in places where burning has been applied, noting that the forests tend to return to "mixed hardwoods" when the burning stops. The author also mentions that this phenomenon occurs in other low tropical elevations. Since this is the only part of the text in which the author specifically mentions burning in recent times, this must be the information you're looking for.

---

[5]PrepTest 38, Sec 3, Q 3

Step 4: Before moving on to the choices, take a moment to paraphrase what you've just read, and make a prediction. The correct answer should mention pine trees growing in tropical areas of low elevation, as opposed to the mixed forests one would ordinarily expect to see.

Step 5: Now go to the choices and find the answer that matches your prediction.

3. Which one of the following is a type of forest identified by the author as a product of controlled burning in recent times?

   (A) scrub oak forests in the southeastern U.S.
   (B) slash pine forests in the southeastern U.S.
   (C) pine forests in Guatemala at high elevations
   (D) pine forests in Mexico at high elevations
   (E) pine forests in Nicaragua at low elevations[6]

The only answer choice that references the Nicaraguan pines of your prediction is correct choice (E). As expected, the correct answer is simply a paraphrase of information found in the passage.

I want to stress once more how very important it is to follow Steps 3 and 4 carefully. The incorrect answer choices represent a jumble of concepts that appeared in various places throughout the passage. Answering a question like this correctly from memory *might* be possible, but for most test takers it's highly unlikely. Do your research and make a prediction, and the right answer will clearly stand out from the others, allowing you to score the point with confidence.

Try the next question on your own, applying the Kaplan Method as always. When you have selected an answer choice, read on to the explanation.

4. Which one of the following is presented by the author as evidence of controlled burning in the tropics before the arrival of Europeans?

   (A) extensive homogeneous forests at high elevation
   (B) extensive homogeneous forests at low elevation
   (C) extensive heterogeneous forests at high elevation
   (D) extensive heterogeneous forests at low elevation
   (E) extensive sedimentary charcoal accumulations at
         high elevation[7]

Step 2: You are looking for information "presented by the author as evidence" for burning in the tropics. Such information will come directly from the passage, so you know this is a Detail question.

Step 3: The best clue offered by the question stem is the phrase "in the tropics." Your Road-map directs you back to the third paragraph, and more specifically, to the example that begins

---

[6]PrepTest 38, Sec 3, Q 3
[7]PrepTest 38, Sec 3, Q 4

in line 44. This text should look very familiar; it's the same part of the passage you used to answer question 3.

Step 4: Take a moment to review the paraphrase you used in the previous question. As evidence of controlled burning in the tropics the author mentioned pine forests growing at low elevations, rather than mixed hardwoods that spring up when burning is absent. The correct answer will reflect this evidence.

Step 5: The terminology in the answer choices might be confusing, but you've got a strong prediction to aid you. Begin by determining which choices are potential matches and which can be eliminated. Choices (A) and (C) mention forests growing at high elevations rather than low, so they can be eliminated right away. Choice (E) is completely outside of the scope of your prediction and can also be discarded. That leaves choices (B) and (D). Are the pine forests of your prediction homogeneous or heterogeneous? If you aren't sure, try scanning the text prior to line 44 to see if these key terms are mentioned in context. Near the Keyword "also" in line 37 you'll see that burning was responsible for creating homogenous forests of various kinds, including pine. That's the final clue you need. Answer choice (B) is correct.

Detail EXCEPT Questions: A Slight Variation

I'll come back to the idea of researching for context again soon; it's a skill that has broad application in the Reading Comprehension section. Right now I want to introduce you to a common variant on the standard Detail question:

6. As evidence for the routine practice of forest burning by native populations before the arrival of Europeans, the author cites all of the following EXCEPT:[8]

Step 2: This is a Detail EXCEPT question. In this case, you are trying to find the one answer choice that *wasn't* explicitly stated in the passage as evidence of controlled burning.

This type of question will require a modified strategy, since it will be nearly impossible for you to predict something that didn't appear in the passage. This doesn't mean that you can't apply predictive thinking—it simply means you have to apply it in a slightly different way.

Step 3: This question stem isn't as generous with clues as the previous two. Evidence for controlled burning by native populations was provided throughout the entirety of the second and third paragraphs. The proper approach in this case is to use the answer choices to help guide your research and prediction.

---

[8]PrepTest 38, Sec 3, Q 6

(A)   the similar characteristics of fires in different
      regions
(B)   the simultaneous presence of forests at varying
      stages of maturity
(C)   the existence of herbaceous undergrowth in
      certain forests
(D)   the heavy accumulation of charcoal near populous
      settlements
(E)   the presence of meadows and glades in certain
      forests[9]

Based on the research you've performed so far, you know that the author's evidence has centered around the characteristics of forests in the Western hemisphere as they appear today. A glance at the choices confirms that most of them mention such evidence, specifically choices (B), (C), and (E). That leaves choices (A) and (D) as most likely to be correct.

Your Roadmap indicates that the evidence for controlled burning was first introduced in the second paragraph, so you should return there to look for evidence that will help you eliminate answer choices. Use the Keywords to navigate the text efficiently. "For example" (line 18) leads you to evidence for charcoal accumulation, allowing you to eliminate choice (D). The "other evidence" presented in lines 21–27 refers to the differences in fires set across North America, which is the exact opposite of choice (A). Since you're trying to find an exception, choice (A) is almost certainly the correct answer.

Step 4: At this point you have a couple of options. You can either predict that choice (A) is correct and move on to Step 5, or you can continue to use the process of elimination to whittle down the choices until you're left with one. Since you've found a direct counterexample to choice (A) in the passage, you can be sure that it is correct.

Step 5: Based on your prediction, you should select correct choice (A) and move on. For the record, the examples cited in choices (B), (C), and (E) are from lines 27–34.

When working with a Detail EXCEPT question, remember that you won't always locate a specific counterexample as you did here; often the correct answer will simply contain information never mentioned in the passage. In such a situation, continue to use the process of elimination to get rid of wrong choices until you are left with the correct one. Don't forget that the choices themselves often contain clues that help you conduct your research. Just because this type of question doesn't lend itself to a straightforward prediction doesn't mean that you should simply reread the entire passage. Use all the clues that are available to you to make your research as efficient as possible. Above all, remember to stick to the Kaplan Method even in unusual situations. Although Detail EXCEPT questions are relatively rare, you'll probably see one or two of them on test day. Stay methodical and you'll score the point.

---

[9]PrepTest 38, Sec 3, Q 6

DRILL: ANSWERING DETAIL QUESTIONS

Now for some practice. Read the following passage strategically, applying Step 1 of the Kaplan Method. Then answer the three questions that follow, applying Steps 2–5 each time. Explanations follow the Drill.

Until recently, few historians were interested in analyzing the similarities and differences between serfdom in Russia and slavery in the United States. Even Alexis de Tocqueville, who recognized the
(5) significant comparability of the two nations, never compared their systems of servitude, despite his interest in United States slavery. Moreover, the almost simultaneous abolition of Russian serfdom and United States slavery in the 1860s—a riveting
(10) coincidence that should have drawn more modern scholars to a comparative study of the two systems of servitude—has failed to arouse the interest of scholars. Though some historians may have been put off by the forbidding political differences
(15) between nineteenth-century Russia and the United States—one an imperial monarchy, the other a federal democracy—a recent study by Peter Kolchin identifies differences that are illuminating, especially with regard to the different kinds of
(20) rebellion exhibited by slaves and serfs.

Kolchin points out that nobles owning serfs in Russia constituted only a tiny proportion of the population, while in the southern United States, about a quarter of all White people were members
(25) of slave-owning families. And although in the southern United States only 2 percent of slaves worked on plantations where more than a hundred slaves worked, in Russia almost 80 percent of the serfs worked for nobles who owned more than a
(30) hundred serfs. In Russia most serfs rarely saw their owners, who tended to rely on intermediaries to manage their estates, while most southern planters lived on their land and interacted with slaves on a regular basis.

(35) These differences in demographics partly explain differences in the kinds of resistance that slaves and serfs practiced in their respective countries. Both serfs and slaves engaged in a wide variety of rebellious activity, from silent sabotage, much of
(40) which has escaped the historical record, to organized armed rebellions, which were more common in Russia. The practice of absentee ownership, combined with the large numbers in which serfs were owned, probably contributed

(45) significantly to the four great rebellions that swept across Russia at roughly fifty-year intervals in the seventeenth and eighteenth centuries. The last of these, occurring between 1773 and 1774, enlisted more than a million serfs in a futile attempt to
(50) overthrow the Russian nobility. Russian serfs also participated in smaller acts of collective defiance called the *volnenie*, which typically started with a group of serfs who complained of grievances by petition and went out on strike. Confrontations
(55) between slaves and plantation authorities were also common, but they tended to be much less collective in nature than those that occurred in Russia, probably in part because the number of workers on each estate was smaller in the United States than
(60) was the case in Russia.[10]

1. According to the author, de Tocqueville was similar to many modern historians in his

    (A) interest in the demographic differences between Russia and the United States during the nineteenth century
    (B) failure to undertake a comparison of Russian serfdom and United States slavery
    (C) inability to explain why United States slavery and Russian serfdom were abolished during the same decade
    (D) overestimation of the significance of the political differences between Russia and the United States
    (E) recognition of the essential comparability of Russia and the United States

---

[10]PrepTest 14, Sec 3, Passage 4

2. The author cites which one of the following as a
    factor that might have discouraged historians from
    undertaking a comparative study of Russian serfdom
    and United States slavery?

    (A)   major differences in the political systems of the
          two counties
    (B)   major differences in the demographics of the
          two counties
    (C)   the failure of de Tocqueville to address the
          subject
    (D)   differences in the size of the estates on which
          slaves and serfs labored
    (E)   the comprehensiveness of Kolchin's own work

3. According to the passage, Kolchin's study asserts
    that which one of the following was true of Russian
    nobles during the nineteenth century?

    (A)   They agreed to the abolition of serfdom in the
          1860s largely as a result of their having been
          influenced by the abolition of slavery in the
          United States.
    (B)   They became more directly involved in the
          management of their estates as a result of the
          rebellions that occurred in the previous
          century.
    (C)   They commonly agreed to at least some of the
          demands that arose out of the *volnenie*.
    (D)   They had relatively little direct contact with the
          serfs who worked on their estates.
    (E)   They hastened the abolition of serfdom by
          failing to devise an effective response to the
          collective nature of the serfs' rebellious
          activity.[11]

[11]PrepTest 14, Sec 3, Qs 22, 25, 26

Answer Explanations follow on the next page.

Explanations

Step 1:

*Not many
studies
of
slave /
serf*

(Until recently) few historians were interested in analyzing the similarities and differences (between) serfdom in Russia (and) slavery in the United States. (Even) Alexis de Tocqueville, who recognized the
(5) significant comparability of the two nations, never compared their systems of servitude, (despite) his interest in United States slavery. (Moreover,) the almost simultaneous abolition of Russian serfdom and United States slavery in the 1860s—a (riveting)
(10) coincidence that should have drawn more modern scholars to a comparative study of the two systems of servitude—has (failed) to arouse the interest of scholars. (Though) some historians may have been put off by the forbidding political differences
(15) between nineteenth-century Russia and the United States—one an imperial monarchy, the other a federal democracy—a (recent study) by Peter
*Kolchin's
study-
differences*
Kolchin identifies differences that are illuminating, (especially) with regard to the different kinds of
(20) rebellion exhibited by slaves and serfs.

(Kolchin points out) that nobles owning serfs in Russia constituted only a tiny proportion of the population, (while) in the southern United States, about a quarter of all White people were members
(25) of slave-owning families. And (although) in the
*Diff's
between
slaves
and
serfs*
southern United States only 2 percent of slaves worked on plantations where more than a hundred slaves worked, in Russia almost 80 percent of the serfs worked for nobles who owned more than a
(30) hundred serfs. In Russia most serfs rarely saw their owners, who tended to rely on intermediaries to manage their estates (while) most southern planters lived on their land and interacted with slaves on a regular basis.

(35) These differences in demographics (partly explain) differences in the kinds of resistance that slaves and serfs practiced in their respective countries. (Both) serfs (and) slaves engaged in a wide variety of rebellious activity, from silent sabotage, much of
(40) which has escaped the historical record, to organized armed rebellions, which were more common in Russia. The practice of absentee ownership, combined with the large numbers in
*Diff.
types
of
rebellion*
which serfs were owned, probably (contributed)
(45) (significantly) to the four great rebellions that swept across Russia at roughly fifty-year intervals in the seventeenth and eighteenth centuries. The last of these, occurring between 1773 and 1774, enlisted more than a million serfs in a futile attempt to
(50) overthrow the Russian nobility. Russian serfs (also)

participated in smaller acts of collective defiance
called the *volnenie*, which typically (started) with a
group of serfs who complained of grievances by
petition (and) went out on strike. Confrontations
(55) between slaves and plantation authorities were (also)
common, (but) they tended to be much less collective
in nature than those that occurred in Russia,
probably in part (because) the number of workers on
each estate was smaller in the United States than
(60) was the case in Russia.[12]

Paragraph Structure: The opening paragraph starts by asserting that "until recently" historians weren't interested in comparing serfdom in Russia to slavery in the United States. Although most of the paragraph describes these uninterested historians, the expected turnabout comes in line 16, when the author introduces Peter Kolchin, who was interested in exploring important differences between the two, with a particular focus on different forms of rebellion.

In the second paragraph, Kolchin points out several differences between serf-owning nobles in Russia and slave-owning families in the United States. The author stays focused on this comparison throughout the paragraph, using contrast Keywords like "although" (line 24) and "while" (line 30) to clearly illustrate these differences.

The third paragraph returns to rebellion as hinted at in the first paragraph. The author explains how the differences described in the second paragraph caused the varying forms of rebellion referenced in the third. Language of causality located throughout the paragraph (such as "contributed significantly" in line 42 and "in part because" in line 54) guides you through this relationship.

Topic: Serfdom and slavery

Scope: Differences between Russian serfdom and United States slavery

Purpose: To demonstrate important differences between two systems of bondage

Main Idea: Peter Kolchin points out that, because of key differences in demographics, the forms of rebellion enacted by Russian serfs were very different from those enacted by slaves in the United States.

---

[12]PrepTest 14, Sec 3, Passage 4

1. **(B)**

   According to the author, de Tocqueville was similar to many modern historians in his
   - (A) interest in the demographic differences between Russia and the United States during the nineteenth century
   - (B) failure to undertake a comparison of Russian serfdom and United States slavery
   - (C) inability to explain why United States slavery and Russian serfdom were abolished during the same decade
   - (D) overestimation of the significance of the political differences between Russia and the United States
   - (E) recognition of the essential comparability of Russia and the United States[13]

Step 2: The phrase "according to the author" combined with a lack of qualified language identifies this as a Detail question.

Step 3: How was de Tocqueville similar to modern historians? The only place he was referenced was in the first paragraph. Lines 5–6 indicate that "despite" his interest in slavery in the United States, he never compared slavery to serfdom. This lack of interest is shared with other historians, as indicated in the first sentence.

Step 4: To summarize: de Tocqueville was similar to other historians in that he wasn't interested in comparing serfdom to slavery.

Step 5: Correct choice (B) is an exact match. Choices (A), (C), and (D) are completely outside the scope of what little the passage says about de Tocqueville's views. Choice (E) does mention something that de Tocqueville was interested in, but not an interest he shared with the other historians in the passage.

2. **(A)**

   The author cites which one of the following as a factor that might have discouraged historians from undertaking a comparative study of Russian serfdom and United States slavery?
   - (A) major differences in the political systems of the two counties
   - (B) major differences in the demographics of the two counties
   - (C) the failure of de Tocqueville to address the subject
   - (D) differences in the size of the estates on which slaves and serfs labored
   - (E) the comprehensiveness of Kolchin's own work[14]

---

[13]PrepTest 14, Sec 3, Q 22
[14]PrepTest 14, Sec 3, Q 25

Step 2: The stem asks for a factor cited by the author. This is a Detail question.

Step 3: Why didn't historians compare serfdom to slavery? Your Roadmap should remind you that these historians are discussed in the first paragraph. Scanning for Keywords, you should quickly spot "though" in line 12, which introduces the contrast you're looking for. Historians were "put off" by political differences between the two countries.

Step 4: There isn't much to paraphrase here, since no other reasons are given for the historians' lack of enthusiasm, but stay in the habit. The correct answer should mention the political differences cited in the text.

Step 5: The only choice that mentions political differences is correct choice (A). The others are all completely outside the scope of this question.

3. **(D)**

    According to the passage, Kolchin's study asserts
    that which one of the following was true of Russian
    nobles during the nineteenth century?
    (A) They agreed to the abolition of serfdom in the
         1860s largely as a result of their having been
         influenced by the abolition of slavery in the
         United States.
    (B) They became more directly involved in the
         management of their estates as a result of the
         rebellions that occurred in the previous
         century.
    (C) They commonly agreed to at least some of the
         demands that arose out of the *volnenie*.
    (D) They had relatively little direct contact with the
         serfs who worked on their estates.
    (E) They hastened the abolition of serfdom by
         failing to devise an effective response to the
         collective nature of the serfs' rebellious
         activity.[15]

Step 2: The phrase "according to the passage" combined with the word "asserts" helps you identify this as a Detail question.

Step 3: The stem references Russian nobles, who were mentioned in their relationships to their serfs. Your Roadmap should indicate that the second paragraph is the likeliest place to find this information, since it explores the essential differences between serfdom and slavery. The author reveals that serf-owning nobles were a tiny proportion of the population in lines 20–22, and that they rarely came into direct contact with their serfs in lines 28–30.

Step 4: To summarize, the correct answer should state that serf-owning nobles were a small part of the overall Russian population, or that they didn't directly deal with their serfs.

[15]PrepTest 14, Sec 3, Q 26

Step 5: Correct choice (D) is an exact match for the second part of your prediction. Choice (A) is completely out of scope; the author never reveals how nobles were connected to the abolition of serfdom. Choices (B), (C), and (E) all refer to possible responses of nobles to rebellion, another subject that the author never addresses.

COMMON WRONG ANSWER TYPES

Like Global questions, Detail questions are common and predictable. It follows that their wrong answer patterns are also predictable. Here are a few wrong answer types to look for:

Out of Scope

As you probably noticed, choices that are outside the scope of the question, or in some cases the passage as a whole, are very common in Detail questions. A strong prediction combined with a good sense of the Scope of the passage will allow you to dispose of these choices with confidence.

1. According to the author, de Tocqueville was similar many modern historians in his

   (A) interest in the demographic differences between Russia and the United States during the nineteenth century
   (B) failure to undertake a comparison of Russian serfdom and United States slavery
   (C) inability to explain why United States slavery and Russian serfdom were abolished during the same decade
   (D) overestimation of the significance of the political differences between Russia and the United States
   (E) recognition of the essential comparability of Russia and the United State[16]

In this question, three of the five answer choices refer to ideas that have no significance to the question at all, since the passage never relates them to de Tocqueville.

180

Occasionally, an answer choice will state the precise opposite of what you've predicted. I'll refer to this type of wrong answer as a 180. A 180 can be among the most dangerous wrong answer traps because it will often contain language very similar to what you would expect to see in the correct answer.

[16]PrepTest 14, Sec 3, Q 22

3. Which one of the following is a type of forest identified
    by the author as a product of controlled burning in recent
    times?

    (A)   scrub oak forests in the southeastern U.S.
    (B)   slash pine forests in the southeastern U.S.
    (C)   pine forests in Guatemala at high elevations
    (D)   pine forests in Mexico at high elevations
    (E)   pine forests in Nicaragua at low elevations[17]

Choice (E) is the correct answer, but notice how similar it looks to wrong answer traps (C) and
(D), despite the fact that they describe opposing elevations. The easiest way to dodge this
trap is to read the choices carefully when executing Step 5; don't become careless once you've
made your prediction. You still have to find the right match.

Distortion

Similar to the 180, answer choices that refer to ideas mentioned in the passage while slightly
skewing them are also quite common.

1. According to the author, de Tocqueville was similar
    to many modern historians in his

    (A)   interest in the demographic differences between
          Russia and the United States during the
          nineteenth century
    (B)   failure to undertake a comparison of Russian
          serfdom and United States slavery
    (C)   inability to explain why United States slavery
          and Russian serfdom were abolished during
          the same decade
    (D)   overestimation of the significance of the
          political differences between Russia and the
          United States
    (E)   recognition of the essential comparability of
          Russia and the United States[18]

Returning to this question, recall that the passage did refer to de Tocqueville's interest in the
"significant comparability" of Russia to the United States. However, this was not something
that he shared with other historians. If you attempt to rely on your memory when answering
Detail questions you will become vulnerable to distortions in the answer choices. To avoid this
trap, follow the Kaplan Method and always research the text as necessary.

I hope you're starting to feel very comfortable with the process of research and prediction.
These skills will serve you well as you learn about Inference questions in the next chapter.

---

[17]PrepTest 38, Sec 3, Q 3
[18]PrepTest 14, Sec 3, Q 22

CHAPTER 12

INFERENCE QUESTIONS

ALL ABOUT INFERENCE QUESTIONS

I've shown you how to systematically employ the Kaplan Method when dealing with Global and Detail questions. Now I'll introduce you to Inference questions, which appear in both the Reading Comprehension and the Logical Reasoning sections. Similar to other question types, Inference questions are extremely predictable and appear in a limited number of variations. The skills you put into practice in chapter 11 will come in handy here—especially your growing mastery of research and prediction.

What Are Inference Questions?

Take a moment to think about the word "inference." What does it mean to you? How do you use it in everyday speech?

Now suppose I tell you that I'm a concert pianist. Assuming I'm telling you the truth, what might you infer from this statement? There are several conclusions that are very likely to come to your mind immediately. You'll probably infer that I've spent many hours practicing piano music, that I most likely received some kind of formal training in music, and that I'm familiar with the works of many composers. In real life, these would be reasonable inferences to make. They are all things that are very likely to be true of someone who is a concert pianist.

On the LSAT, *none* of the above inferences would be considered valid, and that's because the LSAT follows a very specific definition of the word "inference" that is quite different from the one you probably use in daily life. The definition is very simple: On the LSAT, an inference is something that *must be true*, using only those facts that are available to you in the passage.

In the above scenario I presented you with conclusions that are very likely to be true . . . but none of them *must be true*. It's certainly possible, though perhaps very unlikely, that you'll meet a concert pianist who rarely ever practiced, didn't receive any kind of training, and is familiar only with the works of a single composer.

In other words, if an LSAT passage informs you that Emily is a concert pianist, there isn't much you can infer about her other than that she plays the piano at concerts.

A few important principles follow from this extremely limited definition. First, when a question asks you to make an inference, it's simply asking you to take information from the passage and use it to draw a new conclusion that *must be true*. Second, an LSAT inference will never be a large leap of logic, but rather a small step from one fact to another. Third, inferences never require information outside of the passage, and you must be careful not to bring your own knowledge or ideas into an Inference question—use only what you read in the passage.

I'll illustrate all of these principles in a moment. In keeping with the Kaplan Method, however, I'll first show you how to identify the question type.

How Do You Identify Inference Questions?

Inference question stems tend to be a little more varied than Global or Detail stems. In general, any question that asks you to take the information from the passage and draw unstated conclusions from it is considered an Inference question. Here are a few common examples.

13. It can be inferred that the author of the passage regards Hart's theory of hard cases and the theory of standard law as[1]

11. Which one of the following expresses a view that the author of the passage would most probably hold concerning legal principles and legal rules?[2]

5. Based on the information in the passage, which one of the following would most likely be found objectionable by those who oppose compulsory national service?[3]

1. Which one of the following most accurately describes the author's attitude toward the relationship between citizenship and individual rights in a democracy?[4]

The first example is pretty straightforward, as it directly asks for an inference. But look closely at the second and third examples. The key language "most probably" and "most likely" is what

---

[1]PrepTest 17, Sec 4, Q 13
[2]PrepTest 17, Sec 4, Q 11
[3]PrepTest 26, Sec 4, Q 5
[4]PrepTest 26, Sec 4, Q 1

identifies both as Inference questions. In fact, qualified language is the most common identifying feature you should look for—unlike Detail questions, which ask for what is directly cited in the passage, Inference questions ask for what is *probably* true or what views the author (or any other speaker) is *likely* to agree or disagree with.

This might seem confusing at first. An Inference is something that *must be true*, and yet the question stem asks for something that is likely to be true. Don't let this contradiction throw you off; regardless of how the question is worded, the correct answer choice will be the only one that absolutely must follow from the text.

The final example above asks for the author's attitude about a particular idea. This is a somewhat less-common variety of Inference question, but one that you've seen before in this book. In order to pinpoint the author's attitude, you must research the text for Keywords indicating tone and opinion, then use this information to create a general description that isn't explicitly expressed at any point in the passage. Putting it all together:

Step 2: Identify the Question Type

When the stem asks you to draw a new conclusion from the passage, to identify the author's attitude, or to indicate what is likely to be true, you know you're working with an Inference question.

Inference Question Strategy

The proper strategic approach to Inference questions is very similar to that used in Detail questions. Here it is, step by step.

Step 3: Research the Relevant Text

Find the relevant text in the passage. The question stem contains clues that help you determine what you need to know and where you can find it, although some Inference questions provide more clues than others. Use your Roadmap and circled Keywords in the passage to find the information you need.

Step 4: Make a Prediction

Think about what facts *must be true*, remembering that the correct answer can't stray very far from the text.

Step 5: Evaluate the Answer Choices

Find the answer choice that best matches your prediction. If there is no obvious match, use your research to determine which answer choice must be true.

Inference Question Practice

It's time to look at some examples. First, read the following passage and its sample Roadmap. Then try to identify the Topic, Scope, Purpose, and Main Idea of the passage before reading on.

Step 1:

Chinese cult. rev. affected art

The Cultural Revolution of 1966 to 1976, initiated by Communist Party Chairman Mao Zedong in an attempt to reduce the influence of China's intellectual elite on the country's institutions, has had
(5) lasting repercussions on Chinese art. It intensified the absolutist mind-set of Maoist Revolutionary Realism, which had dictated the content and style of Chinese art even before 1966 by requiring that artists "truthfully" depict the realities of socialist life in

Art had to be political, approved by party

(10) China. Interest in nonsocial, nonpolitical subjects was strictly forbidden and, during the Cultural Revolution, what constituted truth was entirely for revolutionary forces to decide—the only reality artists could portray was one that had been thoroughly
(15) colored and distorted by political ideology.

Led to opposite kinds of art

Ironically the same set of requirments that constricted artistic expression during the Cultural Revolution has had the opposite effect since; many artistic movements have flourished in reaction to the
(20) monotony of Revolutionary Realism. One of these, the Scar Art movement of the 1980s, was spearheaded by a group of intellectual painters who had been trained in Maoist art schools and then exiled to rural areas during the Cultural Revolution.

Scar art: exposed rural poverty

(25) In exile, these painters were for perhaps the first time confronted with the harsh realities of rural poverty and misery—aspects of life in China that their Maoist mentors would probably have preferred they ignore, As a result of these experiences, they developed a
(30) radically new approach to realism. Instead of depicting the version of reality sanctioned by the government, the Scar Art painters chose to represent the "scarred reality" they had seen during their exile. Their version of realist painting emphasized the day-

Scar art opposed to Rev. Realism

(35) to-day hardship or rural life. While the principles of Revolutionary Realism had insisted that artists choose public, monumental, and universal subjects, the Scar artists chose instead to focus on the private, the mundane, and the particular; where the principles of
(40) Revolutionary Realism had demanded that they depict contemporary Chines society as outstanding or perfect, the Scar artists chose instead to portray the bleak realities of modernization.

Gov co-opted
scar art

Native Soil:
focused on rural
settings

Trivialized
by subject
matter

(45) As the 1980s progressed, the Scar artists' radical approach to realism became (increasingly) co-opted for political purposes, and as this political cast became stronger and more obvious, many artists abandoned the movement. (Yet) a preoccupation with rural life persisted, (giving rise) to a related development known
(50) as the Native Soil movement, which (focused on) the native landscape and embodied a growing nostalgia for the charms of peasant society in the face of modernization. (Where) the Scar artists had reacted to the ideological rigidity of the Cultural Revolution by
(55) emphasizing the damage inflicted by modernization, the Native Soil painters reacted (instead) by idealizing traditional peasant life. (Unfortunately) in the end Native Soil painting was (trivialized) by a tendency to romanticize certain qualities of rural Chinese society
(60) in order to appeal Western galleries and collectors.[5]

Paragraph Structure: The author begins by providing historical context for the Topic, explaining that the Cultural Revolution has had "lasting repercussions" (line 5) on Chinese art. Artists were required by the government to "truthfully" (line 9) depict life in socialist china. I hope you noticed the quotation marks around the word "truthfully," a clue that the author believes that these artists were *not* truthful in their work. In fact, the "only reality" (line 13) that artists could portray was one described by politicians.

The second, lengthier paragraph makes the author's Scope clearer – beginning with "ironically" in line 16, the author describes the unintended effect the government's policies had on subsequent artistic movements. She then focuses specifically on the Scar Art movement, describing its creators as exiled intellectuals who became aware of the "harsh realities" (line 26) of rural life. "As a result" (line 29), the Scar Artists depicted reality as they observed it rather than as described by politicians. The author highlights this dichotomy with Keywords of contrast throughout the remainder of the paragraph, specifically "while (line 35), and "instead" in lines 38 and 42. This kind of repetition simplifies the paragraph considerably.

In the third paragraph the author notes that Scar Art became "increasingly co-opted" (line 45) by the government, leading to a weakening of the movement. "Yet" (line 48) there remained an interest in rural life, which was subsequently explored by the Native Soil movement. But "where" (line 53) the Scar Artists portrayed the misery of impoverishment, the Native Soil artists "instead" (line 56) idealized rural life, and "unfortunately" (line 57) this led to the trivialization of the movement.

Topic: Chinese art

Scope: Effects of the Cultural Revolution on Chinese art

[5]PrepTest 47, Sec 2, Passage 2

Purpose: To describe artistic movements that came into being as a result of the Cultural Revolution

Main Idea: Artistic movements such as Scar Art and Native Soil came about as an unintended consequence of the state-sanctioned art of the Cultural Revolution.

The strong grasp of authorial opinion that strategic reading provides you gives you a great advantage when you encounter Inference questions. Look at this example:

> 8. Which one of the following statements about realism in Chinese art can most reasonably be inferred from the passage?[6]

Step 2: The stem provides you with very clear identifying language. "Most reasonably inferred" indicates that this is an Inference question. You need to determine what must be true about realism in Chinese art.

Step 3: Where in the passage should you go for information about realism? Because the question mentioned Chinese art in general, not a specific artistic movement, you should prepare to look in several places. Using your Roadmap as a guide, you'll see that the first paragraph described Revolutionary Realist art as "colored and distorted" (line 15) by the government. Scar Art, as described in paragraph 2, opposed Revolutionary Realism, instead describing a harsher reality. By paying close attention to these contrasts in the passage you can clearly see that realism in Chinese art has changed from movement to movement, and that the reality depicted hasn't always been accurate.

Step 4: Make your prediction, remembering that the correct answer must be true. The author has demonstrated that realism in Chinese art has changed from movement to movement, and hasn't always reflected the truth of Chinese life. The correct answer should describe this ambivalence.

Step 5: Now examine the choices and find the one that matches your prediction:

---

[6]PrepTest 47, Sec 2, Passage 2, Q 8

8. Which one of the following statements about realism in Chinese art can most reasonably be inferred from the passage?

   (A) The artists who became leaders of the Native Soil movement practiced a modified form of realism in reaction against the styles and techniques of Scar Art.

   (B) Chinese art has encompassed conflicting conceptions of realism derived from contrasting political and artistic purposes.

   (C) The goals of realism in Chinese art have been effectively furthered by both the Scar Art movement and the Native Soil movement.

   (D) Until the development of the Scar Art movement, interest in rural life had been absent from the types of art that prevailed among Chinese realist painters.

   (E) Unlike the art that was predominant during the Cultural Revolution, Scar Art was not a type of realist art.[7]

The correct answer, choice (B), matches your prediction and must be true. Choice (A) brings in ideas that are out of Scope, since the author never described Native Soil as a reaction against Scar Art. Choice (C) describes the goals of realism, something that was never clarified in the passage, so you can't know whether or not particular movements advanced those goals. Similarly, choice (D) is incorrect because there is no way to know whether or not an interest in rural life was or wasn't absent from Chinese art prior to the Scar Art movement. Choice (E) is in opposition to the passage, which says that the Scar Artists developed a new approach to realism, not that they didn't produce realist art.

I'd like to emphasize once more that LSAT inferences are small leaps of logic. In the last example, the correct answer was simply a broad restatement of ideas that the passage presented explicitly. Most of the other choices described ideas that were possible, but not definitely true.

With this in mind, try the following question on your own before reading the explanations that follow.

---

[7]PrepTest 47, Sec 2, Passage 2, Q 8

11. It can be inferred from the passage that the author
would be most likely to agree with which one of the
following views of the Native Soil movement?

(A) Its development was the inevitable
consequence of the Scar Art movement's
increasing politicization.

(B) It failed to earn the wide recognition that Scar
Art had achieved.

(C) The rural scenes it depicted were appealing to
most people in China.

(D) Ironically, it had several key elements in
common with Revolutionary Realism, in
opposition to which it originally developed.

(E) Its nostalgic representation of rural life was the
means by which it stood in opposition to
Revolutionary Realism.[8]

Step 2: Once again, the word "inferred" identifies this as an Inference question. You must determine what the author believes must be true about the Native Soil movement.

Step 3: The Roadmap indicates that the Native Soil movement was discussed in the final paragraph. The author contrasts this movement with its predecessor, Scar Art, explaining that the Native Soil painters reacted to the Cultural Revolution by idealizing rural life, and that this eventually led to their art becoming trivialized.

Step 4: The relatively brief discussion of the Native Soil painters means that a good prediction should be easy to formulate. Since the correct answer must be true, it must conform to one of the handful of ideas you found in your research. It will likely focus on the primary contrast between Native Soil and Scar Art, so you should expect an answer that describes a tendency to romanticize rural life.

Step 5: Correct choice (E) must be true. It essentially paraphrases the description of the Native Soil movement found in lines 53–57. Choice (A) goes too far in describing Native Soil as an inevitable consequence of Scar Art. Choice (C) is similarly extreme. The passage does describe a preoccupation with rural life, but never suggests that rural scenes appealed to most people in China. Choice (B) describes a comparison that is never made in the passage, and choice (D) distorts the author's ideas—Native Soil was a reaction to the Cultural Revolution, but the passage never says it was developed in opposition to Revolutionary Realism.

These examples are typical of the kinds of Inference questions you should expect to see on test day. Now take a look at a slight variation:

9. It can be inferred from the passage that the author
would be LEAST likely to agree with which one of
the following statements regarding the Cultural
Revolution?[9]

---

[8]PrepTest 47, Sec 2, Passage 2, Q 11

[9]PrepTest 47, Sec 2, Passage 2, Q 9

You've seen EXCEPT questions in previous chapters, so this example shouldn't look too unusual. As always, apply the Kaplan Method, but be prepared to think carefully about how to characterize the right and wrong answer choices. Here's how:

Step 2: The stem asks which idea regarding the Cultural Revolution the author would be LEAST likely to agree with. This is an Inference question, but this time, the correct answer will be something that *isn't* a proper inference. There are a couple of possibilities—the right answer might contradict the author's opinion, or it might simply be out-of-scope (an out-of-scope choice can't be proved or disproved by the text, so by definition it doesn't have to be true.) By contrast, the four wrong answer choices will all be proper inferences.

If you encounter this type of question on test day, make sure you take a moment to think about what characteristics the right and wrong choices will display. Because out-of-scope choices are usually incorrect, you're probably in the habit of discarding them on sight, and in this case you would miss the question as a result. You can't afford to lose points to a careless reading of the question stem, so always apply Step 2 carefully!

Step 3: The stem refers to the Cultural Revolution. Since the scope of the question is somewhat broad, let your Roadmap be your guide. According to the first paragraph, the Cultural Revolution led to a type of art that was strictly controlled by the government, required to reflect dominating political ideas. The second paragraph begins the author's discussion of artistic movements that "ironically" (line 16) came into being later, and which contrasted in many ways with Revolutionary Realism.

Step 4: Since the right answer can be anything that the author doesn't explicitly agree with, trying to make a specific prediction is a waste of time. Instead, keep the author's broad ideas in mind and prepare to use the process of elimination to get rid of incorrect choices.

Step 5:

9. It can be inferred from the passage that the author would be LEAST likely to agree with which one of the following statements regarding the Cultural Revolution?

   (A) It had the ironic effect of catalyzing art movements at odds with its policies.
   (B) The art that was endorsed by its policies was less varied and interesting than Chinese art since the Cultural Revolution.
   (C) Much of the art that it endorsed did not accurately depict the realities of life in China but rather a politically motivated idealization.
   (D) Its effects demonstrate that restrictive policies generally foster artistic growth more than liberal policies do.
   (E) Its impact has continued to be felt in the Chinese art world years after it ended.[10]

---

[10]PrepTest 47, Sec 2, Passage 2, Q 9

Choice (A) is definitely true, summarizing much of the content of the second and third paragraphs, so you should eliminate it. Choice (B) can also be inferred—the author describes later artistic movements as a contrast to the "monotony" (line 20) of Revolutionary Realism. Choice (C) paraphrases the latter half of the first paragraph and can likewise be eliminated. But correct choice (D) must be *false*. The author goes to great lengths to contrast the flourishing of artistic movements after the Revolution with the restrictive political art it fostered. Finally, the truth of choice (E) is confirmed by the very first sentence of the passage, so it too must be incorrect.

Questions like this one can be intimidating, and can potentially be time-consuming, so it's especially important that you approach them with care. Read the question stem carefully and make sure you don't confuse a *true* answer with the *correct* one. Also note that, because the stem didn't provide highly specific research clues, the Roadmap became indispensable in allowing you to find useful information in the text quickly. Inference EXCEPT questions are much less common on the LSAT than straightforward Inference, but you should still expect to see one or two questions of this type on test day. As I've demonstrated, they're just as vulnerable to the Kaplan Method as any other.

I'll come back to the subject of challenging Inference questions later in this book. For now, it's time to put your Inference skills to the test.

DRILL: TACKLING INFERENCE QUESTIONS

Read the following passage strategically, applying Step 1 of the Kaplan Method. Then answer the three questions, applying Steps 2–5 each time. Explanations follow the Drill.

Faced with the problems of insufficient evidence, of conflicting evidence, and of evidence relayed through the flawed perceptual, retentive, and narrative abilities of witnesses, a jury is forced to
(5) draw inferences in its attempt to ascertain the truth. By applying the same cognitive tools they have developed and used over a lifetime, jurors engage in the inferential exercise that lawyers call fact-finding. In certain decision-making contexts that are
(10) relevant to the trial of lawsuits, however, these normally reliable cognitive tools may cause jurors to commit inferential errors that distort rather than reveal the truth.

Although juries can make a variety of inferential
(15) errors, most of these mistakes in judgment involve the drawing of an unwarranted conclusion from the evidence, that is, deciding that the evidence proves something that, in reality, it does not prove. For example, evidence that the defendant in a criminal
(20) prosecution has a prior conviction may encourage jurors to presume the defendant's guilt, because of their preconception that a person previously convicted of a crime must be inclined toward repeated criminal behavior. That commonly held
(25) belief is at least a partial distortion of reality; not all former convicts engage in repeated criminal behavior. Also, a jury may give more probative weight than objective analysis would allow to vivid photographic evidence depicting a shooting victim's
(30) wounds, or may underestimate the weight of defense testimony that is not delivered in a sufficiently forceful or persuasive manner. Finally, complex or voluminous evidence might be so confusing to a jury that its members would draw
(35) totally unwarranted conclusions or even ignore the evidence entirely.

Recent empirical research in cognitive psychology suggests that people tend to commit inferential errors like these under certain
(40) predictable circumstances. By examining the available information, the situation, and the type of decision being made, cognitive psychologists can describe the kinds of inferential errors a person or group is likely to make. These patterns of human
(45) decision-making may provide the courts with a guide to evaluating the effect of evidence on the reliability of the jury's inferential processes in certain situations.

The notion that juries can commit inferential
(50) errors that jeopardize the accuracy of the fact-finding process is not unknown to the courts. In fact, one of a presiding judge's duties is to minimize jury inferential error through explanation and clarification. Nonetheless, most judges now employ
(55) only a limited and primitive concept of jury inferential error: limited because it fails to recognize the potential for error outside certain traditional situations, primitive because it ignores the research and conclusions of psychologists in
(60) favor of notions about human cognition held by lawyers."[11]

1. Which one of the following best describes the author's attitude toward the majority of judges today?

   (A) apprehensive about whether they are consistent in their instruction of juries
   (B) doubtful of their ability to draw consistently correct conclusions based on the evidence
   (C) critical of their failure to take into account potentially helpful research
   (D) pessimistic about their willingness to make significant changes in trial procedure
   (E) concerned about their allowing the presentation of complex and voluminous evidence in the courtroom

[11]PrepTest 13, Sec 3, Passage 4

2. It can be inferred from the passage that the author
    would be most likely to agree with which one of the
    following generalizations about lawyers?

    (A)   They have a less sophisticated understanding
          of human cognition than do psychologists.
    (B)   They often present complex or voluminous
          information merely in order to confuse a jury.
    (C)   They are no better at making logical inferences
          from the testimony at a trial than are most
          judges.
    (D)   They have worked to help judges minimize jury
          inferential error.
    (E)   They are unrealistic about the ability of jurors to
          ascertain the truth.

3. The author would be most likely to agree with which
    one of the following generalizations about a jury's
    decision-making process?

    (A)   The more evidence that a jury has, the more
          likely it is that the jury will reach a reliable
          verdict.
    (B)   Juries usually overestimate the value of visual
          evidence such as photographs.
    (C)   Jurors have preconceptions about the behavior of
          defendants that prevent them from making an
          objective analysis of the evidence in a criminal
          trial.
    (D)   Most of the jurors who make inferential errors
          during a trial do so because they are
          unaccustomed to having to make difficult
          decisions based on inferences.
    (E)   The manner in which evidence is presented to
          a jury may influence the jury either to
          overestimate or to underestimate the value of
          that evidence.[12]

[12]PrepTest 13, Sec 3, Qs 24, 26, 27

Answer Explanations follow on the next page.

Explanations

Step 1:

Juries make inferences

Faced with the (problems) of insufficient evidence, of conflicting evidence, and of evidence relayed through the flawed perceptual, retentive, and narrative abilities of witnesses, a jury (is forced) to

(5) draw inferences in its attempt to ascertain the truth. By applying the same cognitive tools they have developed and used over a lifetime, jurors (engage in) the inferential exercise that lawyers call fact-finding. In certain decision-making contexts that are

They can be mistaken

(10) relevant to the trial of lawsuits, (however,) these (normally) reliable cognitive tools may (cause) jurors to commit inferential errors that distort (rather than) reveal the truth.

(Although) juries can make a variety of inferential

(15) errors, most of these mistakes in judgment (involve)

Juries draw bad conclusions

the drawing of an unwarranted conclusion from the evidence, (that is,) deciding that the evidence proves something that, in reality, it does not prove. For (example,) evidence that the defendant in a criminal

(20) prosecution has a prior conviction may encourage jurors to (presume) the defendant's guilt (because) of their preconception that a person previously convicted of a crime must be inclined toward repeated criminal behavior. That commonly held

(25) belief is at least a partial (distortion) of reality; not all former convicts engage in repeated criminal behavior. (Also) a jury may give more probative weight than objective analysis would allow to vivid photographic evidence depicting a shooting victim's

(30) wounds, (or) may underestimate the weight of defense testimony that is not delivered in a sufficiently forceful or persuasive manner. (Finally,) complex or voluminous evidence might be (so) (confusing) to a jury that its members would draw

(35) totally unwarranted conclusions (or even) ignore the evidence entirely.

(Recent) empirical research in cognitive psychology (suggests) that people tend to commit inferential errors like these under certain

Research: how errors are made

(40) predictable circumstances. (By examining) the available information, the situation, and the type of decision being made, cognitive psychologists can (describe) the kinds of inferential errors a person or group is likely to make. These patterns of human

(45) decision-making (may provide) the courts with a guide to evaluating the effect of evidence on the reliability of the jury's inferential processes in certain situations.

The notion that juries can commit inferential
(50) errors that jeopardize the accuracy of the fact-
finding process is not unknown to the courts. (In
fact,) one of a presiding judge's duties is to minimize
jury inferential error (through) explanation and
clarification. (Nonetheless,) most judges now employ
(55) only a limited primitive concept of jury
inferential error: limited (because) it fails to
recognize the potential for error outside certain
traditional situations, primitive (because) it ignores
the research and conclusions of psychologists in
(60) (favor of) notions about human cognition held by
lawyers.[13]

Judges don't fully understand problem

Paragraph Structure: The author opens the passage by discussing the methods by which jurors reach conclusions. His true scope is signaled by the Keyword "however" in line 10; he thinks these methods are flawed and can cause jurors to distort the truth.

The second paragraph is somewhat longer, but it is mostly composed of details. The author states that "although" (line 14) juries can make many different errors, most of the time they draw unwarranted conclusions. This is immediately followed by "for example" (lines 18–19), signaling the first of many supporting ideas. The chain of evidence continues with "also" in line 27 and concludes with "finally" in line 32. Be sure to circle these important Keywords, but don't get lost in the details; they'll still be there if you need to research them later.

The third paragraph is somewhat technical, but "suggests" in line 38 points to the gist of the research. Psychologists believe that the circumstances under which people are likely to make errors are predictable. The author believes this research "may provide" (line 45) courts with a means of determining how reliable juries really are in certain situations. Again, be careful not to get bogged down in a dense paragraph like this one; read for the basic idea behind the research and move on.

The final paragraph reveals that judges are aware of the cognitive problems that jurors exhibit, but opines that they "nonetheless" (line 54) employ a "limited and primitive" understanding of them. Take heed when the author voices strong opinions; they're likely to be tested.

Topic: Fact-finding in juries

Scope: Inferential errors

Purpose: To describe the errors jurors are likely to make as well as judges' current understanding of research into such errors

Main Idea: Although cognitive science has revealed how jurors might make inferential errors, judges currently rely on a more primitive view of the problem.

---

[13]PrepTest 13, Sec 3, Passage 4

1. **(C)**

    Which one of the following best describes the
    author's attitude toward the majority of judges
    today?
    (A) apprehensive about whether they are
         consistent in their instruction of juries
    (B) doubtful of their ability to draw consistently
         correct conclusions based on the evidence
    (C) critical of their failure to take into account
         potentially helpful research
    (D) pessimistic about their willingness to make
         significant changes in trial procedure
    (E) concerned about their allowing the
         presentation of complex and voluminous
         evidence in the courtroom[14]

Step 2: This is an Inference question—it asks for the author's attitude.

Step 3: Specifically, the question stem asks for the author's attitude about judges. Your Roadmap should lead you straight to the final paragraph, and to the opinionated language therein.
The author describes the judges' understanding of inferential error as "limited and primitive"
because it ignores recent advances in cognitive psychology.

Step 4: The correct answer must reflect disapproval of the judges' failure to understand current science.

Step 5: The match for your prediction is correct choice (C). The only other choice that comes
near the concepts described in the final paragraph is choice (A), but the author never expresses
any apprehension about judges' ability to instruct juries. The remaining choices are completely
out of scope.

2. **(A)**

    It can be inferred from the passage that the author
    would be most likely to agree with which one of the
    following generalizations about lawyers?
    (A) They have a less sophisticated understanding
         of human cognition than do psychologists.
    (B) They often present complex or voluminous
         information merely in order to confuse a jury.
    (C) They are no better at making logical inferences
         from the testimony at a trial than are most
         judges.
    (D) They have worked to help judges minimize jury
         inferential error.
    (E) They are unrealistic about the ability of jurors
         to ascertain the truth.[15]

---

[14]PrepTest 13, Sec 3, Q 24
[15]PrepTest 13, Sec 3, Q 26

Step 2: The identifying phrase in this stem is "most likely to agree." This is an Inference question.

Step 3: You need to research the author's opinion about lawyers. Since most of this passage is concerned with the inferential errors of jurors, lawyers are only mentioned in a couple of places specifically. The only time the author offers any strong opinion language is, once again, at the end of the final paragraph. The author considers judges' understanding of inferential error to be primitive because they ignore current science in "favor of" (line 60) views held by lawyers.

Step 4: Based on this research, you can make a solid prediction. If judges are wrong to favor the views of lawyers over the views of scientists, that must mean the author considers the lawyers' views to be inferior.

Step 5: Choice (A) is correct, matching your prediction. Choice (B) is a distortion of information in the second paragraph. The author does state that information is sometimes overwhelming and confusing to a jury, but never claims that lawyers do this intentionally. The comparison made in choice (C) is irrelevant and never appears in the passage. Choices (D) and (E) are also completely out of scope.

3. **(E)**

    The author would be most likely to agree with which one of the following generalizations about a jury's decision-making process?
    (A)   The more evidence that a jury has, the more likely it is that the jury will reach a reliable verdict.
    (B)   Juries usually overestimate the value of visual evidence such as photographs.
    (C)   Jurors have preconceptions about the behavior of defendants that prevent them from making an objective analysis of the evidence in a criminal trial.
    (D)   Most of the jurors who make inferential errors during a trial do so because they are unaccustomed to having to make difficult decisions based on inferences.
    (E)   The manner in which evidence is presented to a jury may influence the jury either to overestimate or to underestimate the value of that evidence.[16]

Step 2: The phrase "most likely to agree" in the stem tells you that this is an Inference question.

Step 3: Your only real clue in the stem is the reference to a jury's decision-making process. Since most of the text in the passage describes this process (and the errors in it) it may not immediately be clear where you should begin to conduct your research. It's likely that you can find the information you need somewhere in the second paragraph; recall the extensive list of examples demarcated by Keywords in lines 19 (because), 27 (also), and 32 (finally). Rather than attempting to summarize the entire paragraph, you should proceed to Step 4 and think about the big picture.

[16]PrepTest 13, Sec 3, Q 27

Step 4: Review your Roadmap and the author's Main Idea, recalling the author's principal ideas regarding how juries make decisions. His primary focus was on the flaws inherent in the process, and the fact that juries are likely to follow the evidence presented to false conclusions. With this general prediction in mind, move on to the choices and prepare to employ the process of elimination.

Step 5: Choice (A) is in direct conflict with lines 32–36, wherein the author says that too much evidence can actually overwhelm and confuse a jury. Choices (B) and (C) are both too extreme. Remember to keep the author's tone in mind at all times—he never claims that juries "usually" overestimate the value of photographs or that they definitely have preconceptions that prevent them from staying objective. He does say that these things *can* happen in certain circumstances, an important difference. Choice (D) is false; the author states in the first paragraph that jurors use cognitive skills that have been developed "over a lifetime" (lines 6–8). The only choice remaining is (E), the correct answer. Unlike choices (B) and (C), this one gets the author's tone just right: the way in which evidence is presented "may influence" the jury to make inferential errors.

Don't be discouraged if you found this question to be tricky; careful research will always get you to the correct answer, and the information you require is always in the passage. With practice, you'll be able to research efficiently and accurately on test day.

COMMON WRONG ANSWER TYPES

Inference questions share many common wrong answer types with Global and Detail questions. In addition, there are two types you should be especially wary of.

Distorted POV

Since LSAT passages frequently describe multiple viewpoints, sometimes the test makers will ask for one party's opinion and present an opposing opinion in the answer choices. Other times distortion of viewpoint may be more subtle.

8. Which one of the following statements about realism in Chinese art can most reasonably be inferred from the passage?

   (A) The artists who became leaders of the Native Soil movement practiced a modified form of realism in reaction against the styles and techniques of Scar Art.

   (B) Chinese art has encompassed conflicting conceptions of realism derived from contrasting political and artistic purposes.

   (C) The goals of realism in Chinese art have been effectively furthered by both the Scar Art movement and the Native Soil movement.

   (D) Until the development of the Scar Art movement, interest in rural life had been absent from the types of art that prevailed among Chinese realist painters.

   (E) Unlike the art that was predominant during the Cultural Revolution, Scar Art was not a type of realist art.[17]

Recall that the author did say that the Scar Artists were realists, but they defined realism differently than the state-controlled art that preceded them. Choice (E) therefore sounds more like an opinion that the Revolutionary Realists in the first paragraph of the passage might have endorsed. As always, be mindful of the different opinions presented in the text, and use your Roadmap to avoid confusing one for another.

Extreme

Answer choices that take the opinions expressed in the passage too far are among the most common wrong answers you'll encounter when tackling Inference questions.

27. The author would be most likely to agree with which one of the following generalizations about a jury's decision-making process?

    (A) The more evidence that a jury has, the more likely it is that the jury will reach a reliable verdict.

    (B) Juries usually overestimate the value of visual evidence such as photographs.

    (C) Jurors have preconceptions about the behavior of defendants that prevent them from making an objective analysis of the evidence in a criminal trial.

    (D) Most of the jurors who make inferential errors during a trial do so because they are unaccustomed to having to make difficult decisions based on inferences.

    (E) The manner in which evidence is presented to a jury may influence the jury either to overestimate or to underestimate the value of that evidence.[18]

---

[17]PrepTest 47, Sec 2, Passage 2, Q 8

[18] PrepTest 13, Sec 3, Q 27

Be very careful to note any qualifying language you come across in the passage; if the author says that certain evidence "may encourage" a juror to reach a certain conclusion, don't mistake this for the claim that the jurors will *usually* be compelled by that evidence. The test makers reward those who pay attention to these vitally important distinctions, so be on the lookout for them in your practice.

Inference questions are among the most common to appear on the LSAT, and they can sometimes be among the most nuanced. As always, practice and adherence to the Kaplan Method are the keys to scoring these points. In the next two chapters, I'll walk you through the final two Reading Comprehension question types.

CHAPTER 13

LOGIC QUESTIONS: REASONING

ALL ABOUT LOGIC: REASONING QUESTIONS

The final two question types left to examine—Logical Reasoning and Logic Function—are two variations of the same general category, called Logic questions. I'll begin by introducing you to questions of Logical Reasoning (which I'll hereafter refer to as "Reasoning questions").

What Are Reasoning Questions?

While the focus of this book has been exclusively on the Reading Comprehension section of the LSAT, you are no doubt also preparing for the Logical Reasoning section of the test as well. Reasoning questions in Reading Comprehension simply mimic similar questions in the Logical Reasoning section of the test. Fortunately, there are only a small number of commonly occurring Reasoning questions, and the strategies you'll use to tackle each of them are similar. Before moving on, I'll describe each of these common types in a little more detail.

Strengthen/Weaken

One common Reasoning question is called Strengthen/Weaken. As the name suggests, these questions ask you to examine an argument made in the passage and select the answer choice that either strengthens or weakens it. It's important to remember that on the LSAT, you don't have to *prove* an argument in order to strengthen it, and you don't have to *disprove* it to weaken it. Strengthening and weakening simply means to make an argument more or less likely to be true.

Principle

A second common reasoning question is the Principle question. Principle questions usually ask you to identify a general principle, policy or guiding rule that governs the thinking in the passage. Here's an example:

> Most of what has been written about Thurgood Marshall, a former United States Supreme Court justice who served from 1967 to 1991, has just focused on his judicial record and on the ideological content of his
> (5) earlier achievements as a lawyer pursuing civil rights issues in the courts. But when Marshall's career is viewed from a technical perspective, his work with the NAACP (National Association for the Advancement of Colored People) reveals a strategic and methodological
> (10) legacy to the field of public interest law.[1]

In the excerpt above, a specific claim is being made about the body of scholarship on Thurgood Marshall. In LSAT terms, a principle is a more general rule that can be drawn from such a claim. In this case, you might say that a principle that guides the author's thinking is that "some scholarship on Supreme Court justices excludes important aspects of their work." Note that this principle doesn't stray far from what the text already says, but merely expands the scope of the claim from Thurgood Marshall in particular to justices in general. I'll come back to this concept a little later, but for now just think of a principle as a general rule that can be extrapolated from specific examples.

Parallel Reasoning

A third reasoning question you might encounter is called Parallel Reasoning, a question that cites a situation or example in the passage and asks you to identify an analogous example in the answer choices. Parallel Reasoning questions are slightly more rare than Strengthen/ Weaken and Principle questions, but they are susceptible to the same strategies.

If you already have some experience with these types of questions from your work with the Logical Reasoning section of the LSAT, that's great. If not, don't worry—the Kaplan Method provides a solution in each case, and you'll soon become as familiar with this question type as with all the others.

How Do You Identify Reasoning Questions?

There are a variety of Reasoning question types, so it's important that you learn to differentiate them. As with all other question types, the question stem will always contain the clues you need.

---

[1]PrepTest 42, Sec 3, Passage 1

3. Which one of the following pairs of tactics used by an environmental-advocacy public interest law firm is most closely analogous to the strategies that Marshall utilized during his work with the NAACP?[2]

13. Which one of the following principles most likely underlies the author's characterization of literary interpretation?[3]

20. Which one of the following, if true, would most weaken Papi's theory regarding homing pigeons' homing ability?[4]

All of the above are Reasoning questions, but each is a different type. In the first example, the key phrase "analogous to" identifies the question as Parallel Reasoning. In the second, you are asked to find an underlying principle in the author's argument, making this a Principle question. The third question requires you to weaken an argument. These examples are typical of Reasoning questions in general; their identifying language is usually easy to spot. As always, I'll summarize in terms of Step 2 of the Kaplan Method:

Step 2: Identify the Question Type

When the question stem asks you to perform a task similar to one in the Logical Reasoning section, such as strengthening an argument or identifying a principle, you know you are working with a Reasoning question.

Reasoning Question Strategy

The strategies you should employ when working with Reasoning questions vary from type to type, but they all fit within the structure of the Kaplan Method.

Step 3: Research the Relevant Text

As always, you'll find clues in the question stem that will guide you to the relevant portion of the text. Reasoning questions tend to focus on a single specific argument or example from the passage, such as a hypothesis. They may provide you with line references, but if not, your Roadmap will help you locate the required information.

Step 4: Make a Prediction

Reasoning questions are almost always amenable to prediction. Your prediction will sometimes have to be a relatively general one (as you'll see in Parallel Reasoning questions) but even a broad prediction will help you accurately locate the correct answer.

---

[2]PrepTest 42, Sec 3, Q 3
[3]PrepTest 39, Sec 3, Q 13
[4]PrepTest 27, Sec 3, Q 20

Step 5: Evaluate the Answer Choices

Locate a match for your prediction. In rare cases you may need to proceed by elimination, but overall a strong prediction is the best approach.

Reasoning Question Practice

Now for some examples. Read the following passage, noting the circled Keywords in the provided Roadmap. Determine the Topic, Scope, Purpose, and Main Idea of the passage before moving on to the questions.

Step 1:

Trad. communities decline

Traditionally, members of a community such as a town or neighborhood share a common location and a sense of necessary interdependence that includes, for
(5) example, mutual respect and emotional support. But as modern societies grow more technological and sometimes more alienating, people tend to spend less time in the kinds of interactions that their communities, require in order to thrive. Meanwhile technology has made it possible for individuals to interact via personal
(10) computer with others who are geographically distant.

comp. conf. become communities

Advocates claim that these computer conferences, in which large numbers of participants communicate by typing comments that are immediately read by other participants and responding immediately to those
(15) comments they read, function as communities that can substitute for traditional interactions with neighbors.

Char. of comp conf. communities

What are the characteristics that advocates claim allow computer conferences to function as communities? For one participants often share
(20) common interests or concerns; conferences are frequently organized around specific topics such as music or parenting. Second, because these conferences are conversations, participants have adopted certain conventions in recognition of the importance of
(25) respecting each others' sensibilities. Abbreviations are used to convey commonly expressed sentiments of

Conventions show respect

courtesy such as "pardon me for cutting in" ("pmfci") or "in my humble opinion" ("imho"). Because a humorous tone can be difficult to communicate in
(30) writing, participants will often end an intentionally humorous comment with a set of characters that, when looked at sideways, resembles a smiling or winking face. Typing messages entirely in capital letters is avoided, because its tendency to demand the attention
(35) of a reader's eye is considered the computer equivalent of shouting. These conventions, advocates claim,

Form genuine relationships

constitute a form of etiquette, and with this etiquette as a foundation, people often form genuine, trusting relationships, even offering advice and support during
(40) personal crises such as illness or the loss of a loved one.

But while it is true that conferences can be both respectful and supportive, they nonetheless fall short of communities. For example, conferences discriminate
(45) along educational and economic lines because participation requires a basic knowledge of computers and the ability to afford access to conferences. Further, while advocates claim that a shared interest makes computer conferences similar to traditional
(50) communities—insofar as the shared interest is analogous to a traditional community's shared location—this analogy simply does not work. Conference participants are a self-selecting group; they are drawn together by their shared interest in the topic
(55) of the conference. Actual communities, on the other hand, are "nonintentional": the people who inhabit towns or neighborhoods are thus more likely to exhibit genuine diversity—of age, career, or personal interests—than are conference participants. It might be
(60) easier to find common ground in a computer conference than in today's communities, but in so doing it would be unfortunate if conference participants cut themselves off further from valuable interactions in their own towns or neighborhoods.[5]

Auth: Comp. conf. not community

Actual communities nonintentional

---

[5]PrepTest 36, Sec 2, Passage 1

Paragraph Structure: This passage follows a fairly straightforward progression as indicated by its abundant keywords. In the opening paragraph, the author describes what "traditionally" (line 1) defines a community, specifically an interdependent group of individuals in a single location. "But" (line 4) modernization has weakened the traditional community. "Meanwhile" (line 8) technology has led to the development of computer conferences, which "advocates claim" (line 11) can function as substitute communities.

The second paragraph begins with a rhetorical question: "What are the characteristics that allow computer conferences to function as communities?" The answers are indicated by Keywords of sequence. "For one" (line 19) conferences tend to center around common interests. "Second" (line 22) the members demonstrate respect for one another through conventions of communication. The "advocates claim" (line 36) that such conventions form the basis of genuinely caring relationships.

"But" (line 42) in spite of these claims, the author declares, computer conferences aren't actually communities. "For example" (line 44) they cater only to certain groups of individuals, and "further" (line 47) their members self-select on the basis of shared interests, unlike "actual communities" (line 55) which are comprised of more diverse groups of individuals. Because of this, the author would consider it "unfortunate" (line 62) if participants in computer conferences neglect their own neighborhoods.

Topic: The characteristics of communities

Scope: Computer conferences as substitute communities

Purpose: To argue against the advocates' claim that computer conferences can function as surrogate communites

Main Idea: Computer conferences aren't truly communities because they are self-selecting and therefore lack the diversity of traditional communities.

Now apply the Kaplan Method to the following question:

6. Which one of the following, if true, would most weaken one of the author's arguments in the last paragraph?

   (A) Participants in computer conferences are generally more accepting of diversity than is the population at large.

   (B) Computer technology is rapidly becoming more affordable and accessible to people from a variety of backgrounds.

   (C) Participants in computer conferences often apply the same degree of respect and support they receive from one another to interactions in their own actual communities.

   (D) Participants in computer conferences often feel more comfortable interacting on the computer because they are free to interact without revealing their identities.

   (E) The conventions used to facilitate communication in computer conferences are generally more successful than those used in actual communities.[6]

Step 2: The Reasoning question language is fairly clear: you're being asked to weaken an argument made by the author.

Step 3: The question stem specifically guides you to arguments presented by the author in the final paragraph. Keywords highlight the author's primary claims, all of which describe reasons why computer conferences shouldn't be considered true communities. "For example" in line 44 introduces the idea that conferences discriminate against those who lack the money or education to use a home computer, and "further" in line 47 leads to the author's complaint about their self-selecting nature.

Step 4: The correct answer will provide data that runs contrary to one or both of these arguments. A highly specific prediction might be difficult to make, but that doesn't mean you should read the choices idly. Actively search for the answer suggesting that computer conferences aren't discriminatory, or that they don't self-select.

Step 5: The match for your prediction is choice (B). If computers are becoming more available to those who traditionally can't afford them, the author's claim of discrimination is weakened considerably. Choice (A) contains a distortion: the author's argument wasn't that computer conferences fail to accept diversity, but that they lack diversity. Choices (C), (D), and (E) fail to address either of the author's arguments, and are therefore out of Scope.

Sometimes Logic Reasoning questions combine elements of more than one common question type. Here's an example from the same passage:

------

[6]PrepTest 36, Sec 2, Passage 1, Q 6

4. Given the information in the passage, the author can most reasonably be said to use which one of the following principles to refute the advocates' claim that computer conferences can function as communities (line 15)?

(A) A group is a community only if its members are mutually respectful and supportive of one another.

(B) A group is a community only if its members adopt conventions intended to help them respect each other's sensibilities.

(C) A group is a community only if its members inhabit the same geographic location.

(D) A group is a community only if its members come from the same educational or economic background.

(E) A group is a community only if its members feel a sense of interdependence despite different economic and educational backgrounds.[7]

Step 2: This question stem is somewhat more complex. You are being asked to identify a principle that refutes the claim that computer conferences can be considered communities. This is a Reasoning question of Principle, but it also requires you to weaken an argument.

Step 3: The stem provides a specific line reference, so begin your research there. The claim referenced actually begins at line 11, and describes the position of the advocates: computer conferences are communities. This doesn't provide any useful new information, so use your Roadmap to determine where the author's primary arguments against this claim are located. This should take you right back to the third paragraph and the objections of discrimination and self-selection that the author raises there.

Step 4: Recall the definition of a Principle on the LSAT. You need to determine a general rule that the author follows in declaring that computer conferences aren't communities. The author describes such a rule when he defines "actual communities" (line 55) as groups of individuals who are interdependent despite the fact that they're grouped together by chance rather than intention. The correct answer should describe this relationship.

Step 5: The correct answer, choice (E), encapsulates the author's argument against the advocates perfectly. You might have been drawn to choice (C), but the author never claims that geographic closeness is in and of itself a requirement for community, but rather the diversity that tends to spring from such closeness. Choices (A) and (B) both describe characteristics that computer conferences display, and therefore strengthen the advocates' claim. Choice (D) states the complete opposite of what the author claims: a group whose members come from similar backgrounds are likely *not* to be a community.

---

[7]PrepTest 36, Sec 2, Passage 1, Q 4

Notice that while questions 4 and 6 both required you to weaken an argument, they asked you to weaken different, opposing arguments—the author's in one case, the advocates' in the other. This should remind you just how important it is to execute Step 2 of the Kaplan Method with care. Be sure you understand whose point of view the question is asking for!

Before moving on, I'll present one more example. First read the following passage excerpt, noting the sample Roadmap provided:

The blues =
not just sadness

Blues similar
to spirituals

Blues + spirituals
from same
experience

     The term "blues" is conventionally used to refer to a state of sadness or melancholy, but to conclude from this that the musical genre of the same name is merely an expression of unrelieved sorrow is to miss its deeper
(5) meaning. Despite its frequent focus on such themes as suffering and self-pity, and despite the censure that it has sometimes received from church communities, the blues, understood more fully, actually has much in common with the traditional religious music known as
(10) spirituals. Each genre, in its own way, aims to bring about what could be called a spiritual transformation: spirituals produce a religious experience and the blues elicits an analogous response. In fact the blues has even been characterized as a form of "secular spiritual." The
(15) implication of this apparently contradictory terminology is clear: the blues shares an essential aspect of spirituals. Indeed the blues and spirituals may well arise from a common reservoir of experience, tapping into an aesthetic that underlies many aspects of
(20) African American culture.

Afr. Amer.
folk traditions

Similar to
blues + spirituals

Rooted in
W. Afr.
religion

     Critics have noted that African American folk tradition, in its earliest manifestations, does not sharply differentiate reality into sacred and secular strains or into irreconcilable dichotomies between good and evil,
(25) misery and joy. This is consistent with the apparently dual aspect of the blues and spirituals. Spirituals, like the blues, often express longing or sorrow, but these plaintive tones are indicative of neither genre's full scope: both aim at transforming their participants'
(30) spirits to elation and exaltation. In this regard, both musical forms may be linked to traditional African American culture in North America and to its ancestral cultures in West Africa, in whose traditional religions worshippers play an active role in invoking the
(35) divine—in creating the psychological conditions that are conducive to religious experience. These conditions are often referred to as "ecstasy," which is to be understood here with its etymological connotation of standing out from oneself, or rather from one's
(40) background psychological state and from one's centered concept of self.[8]

---

[8]PrepTest 34, Sec 1, Passage 2

Now take a look at this question:

12. Which one of the following is most closely analogous to the author's account of the connections among the blues, spirituals, and certain West African religious practices?

(A) Two species of cacti, which are largely dissimilar, have very similar flowers; this has been proven to be due to the one's evolution from a third species, whose flowers are nonetheless quite different from theirs.

(B) Two species of ferns, which are closely similar in most respects, have a subtly different arrangement of stem structures; nevertheless, they may well be related to a third, older species, which has yet a different arrangement of stem structures.

(C) Two types of trees, which botanists have long believed to be unrelated, should be reclassified in light of the essential similarities of their flower structures and their recently discovered relationship to another species, from which they both evolved.

(D) Two species of grass, which may have some subtle similarities, are both very similar to a third species, and thus it can be inferred that the third species evolved from one of the two species.

(E) Two species of shrubs, which seem superficially unalike, have a significantly similar leaf structure; this may be due to their relation to a third, older species, which is similar to both of them.[9]

Step 2: The stem asks for something that is analogous to the relationships among the blues, spirituals, and certain religious practices. Since you must describe a new situation that follows the same pattern as one described in the text, this is a Parallel Reasoning question.

Step 3: The scope of this question is quite wide, since the connections referenced in the stem are described throughout two paragraphs. For this reason, the Roadmap will be indispensable in helping you make a prediction quickly. Review it carefully. The first paragraph describes an essential similarity between spirituals and the blues. The second paragraph suggests that both art forms can be linked to West African religious practices, with which they share some characteristics.

Step 4: Remember that the answer choices in Parallel Reasoning questions can encompass virtually any subject matter, and may therefore appear unrelated to the question at hand. It's therefore especially important that you approach them with a strong prediction. Stay focused on a general description of the passage content. Two types of music were described as similar

---

[9]PrepTest 34, Sec 1, Passage 2, Q 12

to one another, and then both were shown to be similar to a third, related set of practices. Keep this pattern in mind as you examine the answer choices.

Step 5: Examine each choice and compare it to your prediction. Choice (A) describes two species that are largely dissimilar. That's the opposite of what you predicted. Choice (B) also focuses on differences among different items, so eliminate it as well. Choice (C) is a little trickier, but is goes wrong in suggesting that two types of trees should be reclassified. No such reclassification is part of your prediction. Choice (D) distorts the relationship described in your prediction, as the similarities between music and religious practices weren't used to infer that one evolved from the other. That only leaves correct choice (E), which matches your prediction note for note. It describes two things that are alike in specific way, and then traces their connection to a predecessor.

I want to stress again just how vitally important a strong prediction is to answering a question like this one correctly and efficiently. The similarities in the answer choices can easily lead to error and frustration. Before you begin to work with them, determine what you're looking for and be prepared to stick with it. Parallel Reasoning questions are traditionally among the toughest the LSAT will throw at you, so you must approach them methodically and with confidence.

Now that you've seen a few of the most common types of Logic Reasoning questions, it's time for some practice.

DRILL: ANSWERING REASONING QUESTIONS

Read the following passage strategically, applying Step 1 of the Kaplan Method. Then answer the two questions, applying Steps 2–5 each time. Explanations follow the Drill.

In a recent court case, a copy-shop owner was accused of violating copyright law when, in the preparation of "course packs"—materials photocopied from books and journals and packaged as readings for
(5) particular university courses—he copied materials without obtaining permission from or paying sufficient fees to the publishers. As the owner of five small copy shops serving several educational institutions in the area, he argued, as have others in the photocopy
(10) business, that the current process for obtaining permissions is time-consuming, cumbersome, and expensive. He also maintained that course packs, which are ubiquitous in higher education, allow professors to assign important readings in books and journals too
(15) costly for students to be expected to purchase individually. While the use of copyrighted material for teaching purposes is typically protected by certain provisions of copyright law, this case was unique in that the copying of course packs was done by a copy
(20) shop and at a profit.

Copyright law outlines several factors involved in determining whether the use of copyrighted material is protected, including: whether it is for commercial or nonprofit purposes; the nature of the copyrighted work;
(25) the length and importance of the excerpt used in relation to the entire work; and the effect of its use on the work's potential market value. In bringing suit, the publishers held that other copy-shop owners would cease paying permission fees, causing the potential
(30) value of the copyrighted works of scholarship to diminish. Nonetheless, the court decided that this reasoning did not demonstrate that course packs would have a sufficiently adverse effect on the current or potential market of the copyrighted works or on the
(35) value of the copyrighted works themselves. The court instead ruled that since the copies were for educational purposes, the fact that the copy-shop owner had profited from making the course packs did not prevent him from receiving protection under the law.
(40) According to the court, the owner had not exploited copyrighted material because his fee was not based on the content of the works he copied; he charged by the page, regardless of whether the content was copyrighted.
(45) In the court's view, the business of producing and selling course packs is more properly seen as the exploitation of professional copying technologies and a result of the inability of academic parties to reproduce printed materials efficiently, not the exploitation of

(50) these copyrighted materials themselves. The court held that copyright laws do not prohibit professors and students, who may make copies for themselves, from using the photo reproduction services of a third party in order to obtain those same copies at lesser cost.

1. Which one of the following describes a role most similar to that of professors in the passage who use copy shops to produce course packs?

   (A) An artisan generates a legible copy of an old headstone engraving by using charcoal on newsprint and frames and sells high-quality photocopies of it at a crafts market.

   (B) A choir director tapes a selection of another well-known choir's best pieces and sends it to a recording studio to be reproduced in a sellable package for use by members of her choir.

   (C) A grocer makes several kinds of sandwiches that sell for less than similar sandwiches from a nearby upscale café.

   (D) A professional graphic artist prints reproductions of several well-known paintings at an exhibit to sell at the museum's gift shop.

   (E) A souvenir store in the center of a city sells miniature bronze renditions of a famous bronze sculpture that the city is noted for displaying.

2. Which one of the following, if true, would have most strengthened the publishers' position in this case?

(A)   Course packs for courses that usually have large enrollments had produced a larger profit for the copy-shop owner.

(B)   The copy-shop owner had actively solicited professors' orders for course packs.

(C)   The revenue generated by the copy shop's sale of course packs had risen significantly within the past few years.

(D)   Many area bookstores had reported a marked decrease in the sales of books used for producing course packs.

(E)   The publishers had enlisted the support of the authors to verify their claims that the copy-shop owner had not obtained permission.[10]

---

[10]PrepTest 41, Sec 4, Qs 5–6

Explanations

Step 1:

In a recent court case, a copy-shop owner was accused of violating copyright law when, in the

Suit over
course packs

preparation of "course packs"—materials photocopied from books and journals and packaged as readings for
(5) particular university courses—he copied materials without obtaining permission from or paying sufficient fees to the publishers. As the owner of five small copy shops serving several educational institutions in the area, he argued, as have others in the photocopy
(10) business, that the current process for obtaining permissions is time-consuming, cumbersome, and expensive. He also maintained that course packs, which are ubiquitous in higher education, allow professors to assign important readings in books and journals too
(15) costly for students to be expected to purchase individually. While the use of copyrighted material for teaching purposes is typically protected by certain

Unique:
profit

provisions of copyright law, this case was unique in that the copying of course packs was done by a copy
(20) shop and at a profit.

Copyright law outlines several factors involved in determining whether the use of copyrighted material is protected, including; whether it is for commercial or nonprofit purposes; the nature of the copyrighted work;
(25) the length and importance of the excerpt used in relation to the entire work; and the effect of its use on the work's potential market value. In bringing suit, the publishers held that other copy-shop owners would

Court: copies
didn't hurt
copyright

cease paying permission fees, causing the potential
(30) value of the copyrighted works of scholarship to diminish. Nonetheless, the court decided that this reasoning did not demonstrate that course packs would have a sufficiently adverse effect on the current or potential market of the copyrighted works or on the
(35) value of the copyrighted works themselves. The court instead ruled that since the copies were for educational purposes, the fact that the copy-shop owner had profited from making the course packs did not prevent him from receiving protection under the law.
(40) According to the court, the owner had not exploited copyrighted material because his fee was not based on the content of the works he copied; he charged by the page, regardless of whether the content was copyrighted.

Court:

packs not

exploitative

(45)   In the court's view, the business of producing and
selling course packs is more properly seen as the
exploitation of professional copying technologies and a
result of the inability of academic parties to reproduce
printed materials efficiently, not the exploitation of

(50)   these copyrighted materials themselves. The court held
that copyright laws do not prohibit professors and
students, who may make copies for themselves, from
using the photoreproduction services of a third party in
order to obtain those same copies at lesser cost.[11]

Paragraph Structure: The opening paragraph introduces a court case. A copy-shop owner was accused of copyright violations by reproducing course packs for students. The author spends most of this paragraph describing the owner's arguments, but the contrast word "while" in line 16 points to what made this particular case noteworthy (or "unique" as the author puts it in line 18): There was profit involved.

The second paragraph moves on to the arguments made by the copyright holders, who "held" (line 28) that the shop owner was setting a bad precedent. "Nonetheless" (line 31), the court ruled that the owner was not in violation of copyright since the course packs were for educational purposes and were priced without reference to content.

"In the court's view" (line 45), the reproduction of course packs is not exploitative of copyright holders.

Topic: Copyright law

Scope: A case involving course packs

Purpose: To explain the reasoning behind the verdict in a specific court case

Main Idea: The court ruled that, since the copy-shop owner didn't charge for content, he didn't violate copyright laws in reproducing course packs.

---

[11]PrepTest 41, Sec 4, Passage 1

1. **(B)**

   Which one of the following describes a role most similar to that of professors in the passage who use copy shops to produce course packs?

   (A) An artisan generates a legible copy of an old headstone engraving by using charcoal on newsprint and frames and sells high-quality photocopies of it at a crafts market.

   (B) A choir director tapes a selection of another well-known choir's best pieces and sends it to a recording studio to be reproduced in a sellable package for use by members of her choir.

   (C) A grocer makes several kinds of sandwiches that sell for less than similar sandwiches from a nearby upscale café.

   (D) A professional graphic artist prints reproductions of several well-known paintings at an exhibit to sell at the museum's gift shop.

   (E) A souvenir store in the center of a city sells miniature bronze renditions of a famous bronze sculpture that the city is noted for displaying.[12]

Step 2: The phrase "a role most similar" is your main clue here. When the stem asks you to find a situation that is analogous to one mentioned in the passage, you know it's a Parallel Reasoning question.

Step 3: The description of professors formed part of the copy-shop owner's defense, which was given in the first paragraph. Course packs "allow" (line 13) professors to provide students with vital reading that they wouldn't otherwise be able to afford.

Step 4: A specific prediction would be impossible to make in this case; the analogous situation could be almost anything. Instead, you should take the specific situation described in the passage and think about it in general terms (much like with questions of principle): The professors hired a vendor to make copies of protected material for the purposes of education. The correct answer will follow this same general structure, regardless of subject matter.

Step 5: Choice (A) goes wrong in several directions, as the artisan is both making copies himself and then turning his own profit. Choice (B), however, is spot-on. The choir director, like the professors, hires a vendor to provide copies for educational purposes. It matches the structure of the prediction and is the correct answer. Choice (C) has nothing to do with reproduction, choice (D) focuses incorrectly on profit, and choice (E) doesn't necessarily have anything to do with copyrighted material. Remember that, while a *specific* prediction is hard to make on

---

a Parallel Reasoning question, a general prediction based on structure makes a question like this very manageable.

2. **(D)**

Which one of the following, if true, would have most strengthened the publishers' position in this case?

(A)   Course packs for courses that usually have large enrollments had produced a larger profit for the copy-shop owner.

(B)   The copy-shop owner had actively solicited professors' orders for course packs.

(C)   The revenue generated by the copy shop's sale of course packs had risen significantly within the past few years.

(D)   Many area bookstores had reported a marked decrease in the sales of books used for producing course packs.

(E)   The publishers had enlisted the support of the authors to verify their claims that the copy-shop owner had not obtained permission.[13]

Step 2: This Reasoning question asks you to strengthen an argument.

Step 3: The publishers' side of the story was located in the second paragraph. In lines 27–31, the publishers "held" that the copy-shop owner's sale of course packs diminished the value of their intellectual property, a claim that the court says they "did not demonstrate" (line 32).

Step 4: If the publishers failed to demonstrate a loss of value, then new evidence showing that the creation of course packs *does* diminish the worth of the publishers' property would strengthen their claim. The correct answer should reflect this loss of value.

Step 5: Correct choice (D) describes just the sort of scenario predicted. A decrease in sales of books certainly represents a loss of value. Choice (A) introduces the irrelevant idea of large enrollments, and choice (B) has nothing to do with the value of the published material. Choices (C) and (E) similarly fall totally out of scope; they have nothing to do with the claim of purported loss of value, and hence cannot strengthen the publishers' argument.

COMMON WRONG ANSWER TYPES

Hopefully you noticed two wrong answer traps in particular that are common to all kinds of reasoning questions:

Out of Scope

This type of wrong answer should be very familiar to you by now.

---

[13]PrepTest 41, Sec 4, Q 6

6. Which one of the following, if true, would most weaken one of the author's arguments in the last paragraph?

(A) Participants in computer conferences are generally more accepting of diversity than is the population at large.

(B) Computer technology is rapidly becoming more affordable and accessible to people from a variety of backgrounds.

(C) Participants in computer conferences often apply the same degree of respect and support they receive from one another to interactions in their own actual communities.

(D) Participants in computer conferences often feel more comfortable interacting on the computer because they are free to interact without revealing their identities.

(E) The conventions used to facilitate communication in computer conferences are generally more successful than those used in actual communities.[14]

Recall that this question asked you to argue against the author's claim that computer conferences shouldn't be considered true communities because they are self-selecting. The ideas referenced in choices (D) and (E) have nothing to do with this argument and therefore fall outside the Scope of the question. If you stay in the habit of making strong predictions you'll have little trouble avoiding answers like these.

180

Prediction is equally vital in avoiding answer choices that reflect the opposite of the correct answer.

4. Given the information in the passage, the author can most reasonably be said to use which one of the following principles to refute the advocates' claim that computer conferences can function as communities (line 15)?

(A) A group is a community only if its members are mutually respectful and supportive of one another.

(B) A group is a community only if its members adopt conventions intended to help them respect each other's sensibilities.

(C) A group is a community only if its members inhabit the same geographic location.

(D) A group is a community only if its members come from the same educational or economic background.

(E) A group is a community only if its members feel a sense of interdependence despite different economic and educational backgrounds.[15]

---

[14]PrepTest 36, Sec 2, Passage 1, Q 6
[15]PrepTest 36, Sec 2, Passage 1, Q 4

In this case, choice (D) reverses the author's claim that groups of individuals that gather on the basis of a shared background are not likely to be a true community. This type of wrong answer trap is most dangerous to the test taker who becomes careless and reads the choices too quickly. Stay methodical on test day and keep focused on your prediction to avoid 180s.

There are a few rarer variations on Reasoning questions that I'll address in chapter 16. For now, it's time to move on to the final common Reading Comprehension question type: Logic Function.

CHAPTER 14

LOGIC QUESTIONS: FUNCTION

ALL ABOUT LOGIC: FUNCTION QUESTIONS

Now that you've learned about Reasoning questions, it's time to turn to the final Reading Comprehension question type: Function questions. Function questions are less varied than Reasoning questions, and they all provide you with the same essential task in slightly differing formats. Since they've been appearing with increased frequency on more recent tests, it's imperative that you become comfortable with them in order to maximize your LSAT score.

What Are Function Questions?

In general, Function questions ask about structure. Specifically, they ask why the author used a specific word, phrase, or example. The typical Function question will point you directly to a relevant portion of the text, often with an accompanying line number, and ask you to explain what the author's purpose was in presenting the example cited.

Students are sometimes initially confused about the difference between Detail questions and Function questions, since both make reference to specific details in the passage and may use similar language. The difference is simple. Detail questions ask you to simply identify the example and paraphrase it. Function questions ask *why* the example was there to begin with.

For this reason, Function questions demand a thorough understanding of overall passage structure, and reward you for respecting the importance of context in a passage. I'll explain this concept in greater detail a little later on, but for the moment, it's important that you know how to spot a function question so that you can apply the appropriate strategy.

How Do You Identify Function Questions?

You can identify the most common function questions by one of two key phrases: "in order to" and "for which of the following reasons." Examine a few sample Function question stems:

12. In the passage, the author uses the example of the word "vehicle" to[1]

2. The author refers to the "patinas and aromas of a country kitchen" (line 32) most probably in order to[2]

17. The primary function of the third paragraph is to[3]

17. As used in the passage, the word "democratizing" (line 9) most nearly means equalizing which one of the following?[4]

The first stem asks you to identify why the author chose to use a particular example. The second stem is very similar, asking for the author's purpose in mentioning the quoted phrase. The third stem asks you to identify the purpose of an entire paragraph in the context of the passage as a whole, while the fourth asks for the approximate meaning of a specific word as used by the author. I'll refer to this final type of Function question as a Vocab-in-Context question.

Though the examples may seem varied at first, notice that they all center around the question *why*. Why did the author mention the example, or write a particular paragraph, or choose a particular word or phrase? To summarize in terms of Step 2 of the Kaplan Method:

Step 2: Identify the Question Type
When the stem asks you to identify the reason why a particular word, phrase, or example was used in the passage, you know you are working with a Function question.

Function Question Strategy

The proper strategy for dealing with Function questions always comes down to understanding context, either of a specific part of the passage or the passage as a whole. I'll show you what I mean. Read the following question stem and think about how you might answer it:

---

[1]PrepTest 17, Sec 4, Q 12
[2]PrepTest 19, Sec 3, Q 2
[3]PrepTest 25, Sec 1, Q 17
[4]PrepTest 42, Sec 3, Q 17

15.   The author most likely states that "cultural borrowing is, of course, old news" (lines 47–48) primarily to[5]

How would you determine why the author made this statement? You might start by going back to the line references, but what do you expect to see there? Probably the text that's already been quoted in the stem. That isn't likely to be very helpful. Without understanding how the phrase fits contextually into the author's larger argument, there's no way to determine why it's there.

Instead we should approach this question the Kaplan way. You've seen this passage before, but re-read it carefully, thinking about its Topic, Scope, Purpose, and Main Idea.

Soc: gatherings mean tribal decline

(5)

(Even) in the midst of its (resurgence) as a vital tradition, many (sociologists) have viewed the current form of the powwow, a ceremonial gathering of native Americans, (as a sign) that tribal culture is in decline. (Focusing) on the dances and rituals that have (recently) come to be shared by most tribes, they (suggest) that an intertribal movement is now in ascension and (claim) the (inevitable) outcome of this tendency is the eventual dissolution of tribes (and) the complete assimilation of native Americans into Euroamerican society.

(10)

Pan-Indian theory, evidence

(15)

(Proponents) of this "Pan-Indian" theory (point to) the greater frequency of travel and communication between reservations, the greater urbanization of native Americans, (and,) most (recently,) their increasing politicization in (response) to common grievances as the chief causes of the shift toward intertribalism.

Intertribalism on rise

Unique traditions rising too

(20)

(Indeed) the rapid diffusion of dance styles, outfits, and songs from one reservation to another offers (compelling evidence) that intertribalism has been increasing. (However,) these (sociologists) have (failed) to note the concurrent revitalization of many traditions unique to individual tribes. (Among) the Lakota, for (instance,) the Sun Dance was revived, after a forty-year hiatus, during the 1950's. (Similarly,) the Black Legging Society of the Kiowa and the Hethuska Society of the Ponca—(both) traditional groups within their respective tribes—have gained (new popularity.) (Obviously,) a more complex societal shift is taking place (than) the theory of Pan-Indianism can account for.

(25)

P.I.T doesn't explain

(30)

Auth: must examine theory

(35)

An (examination) of the theory's underpinnings may be (critical) at this point, (especially) given that native Americans themselves (chafe most) against the Pan-Indian classification. (Like) other assimilationist theories with which it is associated, the Pan-Indian view is (predicated upon) an a priori assumption about the nature or cultural contact: that (upon) contact minority societies (immediately) begin to succumb in every respect—biologically, linguistically, and culturally—to the majority society. (However,) there is (no evidence) that this is happening to native American groups.

Theory based on wrong assump.

(40)

Intertribal act.
still important

> Yet the fact remains that intertribal activities are a major facet of native American culture today. Certain dances at powwows, for instance, are announced as intertribal, others as traditional. Likewise, speeches (45) given at the beginnings of powwows are often delivered in English, while the prayer that follows is usually spoken in a native language. Cultural

Tribal and
intertribal
distinct

> borrowing is, of course, old news. What is important to note is the conscious distinction native Americans (50) make between tribal and intertribal tendencies.

Auth: Both
are important

> Tribalism, although greatly altered by modern history, remains a potent force among native Americans: It forms a basis for tribal identity, and aligns music and dance with other social and cultural (55) activities important to individual tribes. Intertribal activities, on the other hand, reinforce native American identity along a broader front, where this identity is directly threatened by outside influences.[6]

Topic: Native American culture

Scope: The effects of intertribalism

Purpose: To argue against the proponents of the Pan-Indian theory

Main Idea: Despite the claims of proponents of the Pan-Indian theory, intertribalism indicates a strengthening of tribal life rather than a decline.

15.   The author most likely states that "cultural borrowing is, of course, old news" (lines 47–48) primarily to[7]

Step 2: Identify the Question Type

The author mentioned a specific idea "primarily to" do what? The stem asks why the specified text was mentioned, and is therefore a Function question.

Step 3: Research the Relevant Text

It's time to read for context. Instead of going directly to the text quoted in the stem, examine the Roadmap and recall the purpose of the paragraph as a whole. The author is demonstrating the distinctiveness of tribal and intertribal activities. Now scan the text surrounding lines 47–48, looking for helpful Keywords. Line 48 says that what "is important" is that Native Americans view different activities in different ways.

Step 4: Make a Prediction

Now to put it all together. If the author's goal in the latter half of this paragraph is to emphasize the distinction Native Americans make between certain activities, why did he mention that

---

[6]PrepTest 25, Sec 1, Passage 3
[7]PrepTest 25, Sec 1, Q 15

cultural borrowing is "old news?" The Keywords indicate that cultural borrowing isn't really all that important to the author, so that must be the reason he mentioned it: To indicate what is *less* important before moving on to discuss what is *more* important.

Step 5: Evaluate the Answer Choices

15. The author most likely states that "cultural borrowing is, of course, old news" (lines 47–48) primarily to

    (A) acknowledge that in itself the existence of intertribal tendencies at powwows is unsurprising
    (B) suggest that native Americans' use of English in powwows should be accepted as unavoidable
    (C) argue that the deliberate distinction of intertribal and traditional dances is not a recent development
    (D) suggest that the recent increase in intertribal activity is the result of native Americans borrowing from non-native American cultures
    (E) indicate that the powwow itself could have originated by combining practices drawn from both native and non-native American cultures[8]

The only choice that matches the contextual reading is (A), the correct answer. Choices (B), (D), and (E) are all completely out of scope for this question. Choice (C) contains a distortion—the text quoted in the stem demonstrates that cultural borrowing is old news, not the distinction between tribal and intertribal dances. This answer choice might look good if you hadn't conducted your research and paid careful attention to context, but because you did, you avoided it and earned the point.

Function Question Practice

I'll say it again: Context is key. Function questions reward your ability to understand the role of a specific bit of text when set against the purpose of the whole paragraph or passage. To hone your skills further, read the following passage. Note the sample Roadmap, and identify the Topic, Scope, Purpose, and Main Idea.

Step 1:

Women's participation in the revolutionary events in France between 1789 and 1795 has (only recently) been given nuanced treatment. (Early) twentieth-century historians of the French Revolution are
(5) (typified) by Jaures, who, (though) sympathetic to the woman's movement of his own time, (never even) mentions its antecedents in revolutionary France.

New
research:

women in
rev. France

3 phases
of partic.

Studies
look
at
end of
movement

Studies
differ but
all are
good

(Even today) most general histories treat only cursorily
a few individual women, like Marie Antoinette. The
(10) (recent studies) by Landes, Badinter, Godineau, and
Roudinesco, (however,) should signal a (much-needed)
reassessment of women's participation.

Godineau and Roudinesco (point to) three
significant phases in that participation. (The first,) up
(15) to mid-1792, involved those women who wrote
political tracts. (Typical of) their orientation to
theoretical issues—in Godineau's view, without
practical effect—is Marie Gouze's *Declaration of the
Rights of Women*. The emergence of vocal middle-
(20) class women's political clubs marks the (second phase.)
Formed in 1791 as adjuncts of middle-class male
political clubs, and (originally) philanthropic in
function, (by) late 1792 independent clubs of women
began to (advocate) military participation for women.
(25) In the (final phase,) the famine of 1795 (occasioned) a
mass women's movement: women seized food
supplies, held officials hostage, and argued for the
implementation of democratic politics. This phase
(ended) in May of 1795 with the military suppression
(30) of this multiclass movement. (In all three) phases
women's participation in politics (contrasted)
markedly with their participation before 1789.
(Before) that date some noblewomen participated
indirectly in elections, (but) such participation by more
(35) than a narrow range of the population—women or
men—came only with the Revolution.

What makes the (recent) studies particularly
compelling, (however,) is (not) so much their
organization of chronology (as) their unflinching
(40) willingness to confront the reasons for the collapse of
the woman's movement. For Landes and Badinter,
the (necessity) of women's having to speak in the
established vocabularies of certain intellectual and
political traditions diminished the ability of the
(45) women's movement to resist suppression. Many
women, and many men, (they argue,) located their
vision within the confining tradition of Jean-Jacques
Rousseau, who linked male and female roles with
public and private spheres respectively. (But) when
(50) women went on to make political alliances with
radical Jacobin men, Badinter (asserts,) they adopted a
vocabulary and a violently extremist viewpoint that
(unfortunately) was even more damaging to their
political interests.

(55) Each of these scholars has a (different) political
agenda and takes a different approach—Godineau,
(for example), works with police archives (while)
Roudinesco uses explanatory schema from modern
psychology. (Yet,) (admirably,) each gives center stage
(60) to a group that previously has been marginalized, or

at best undifferentiated by historians. And (in the) (case) of Landes and Badinter, the reader is left with a sobering awareness of the cost to the women of the Revolution of speaking in borrowed voices.[9]

Paragraph Structure: The author begins by emphasizing that "only recently" (line 2) have historians closely examined the role of women in the French Revolution. He substantiates this assertion by contrasting the new scholarship with that of "early" (line 3) historians, noting that one prominent scholar "never even mentions" (line 6–7) the subject. The recent studies, "however" (line 11), supply a "much needed' (line 11) analysis.

As you probably predicted, the second paragraph goes on to examine the recent scholarship in detail. The author notes that scholars "point to three significant phases" (lines 13–14) in the participation of women in the revolution. Each phase is described, marked by the Keywords "first" (line 14), "second" (line 20), and "final" (line 25). The author ties the three phases together by noting that they "contrasted" (line 30) with the role women played in earlier years.

The third and fourth paragraphs provide the author's opinions of these studies in greater detail. What makes the studies compelling is "not" (line 38) their chronology "so much . . . as" (lines 38–39) their treatment of the end of the women's movement. Some of the scholars trace this collapse back to the "necessity" (line 42) of women's use of a particular vocabulary. The author describes this phenomenon in greater detail, then presents a final conclusion in the fourth paragraph. Each scholar has a "different" (line 55) political agenda, "yet admirably" (line 59) they all provided necessary examination of a neglected area of history—something the author approves of.

Topic: Women in the French Revolution

Scope: Recent studies of the participation of women in rebellion

Purpose: To describe several recent studies of a historical phenomenon

Main Idea: Though they emerge from different political and social agendas, all of the recent studies are valuable.

17. The primary function of the first paragraph of the passage is to[10]

Step 2: The key phrase "primary function" tells you that this is a Function question.

Step 3: The question stem asks for the function of the first paragraph, and you have just the tool to help you identify it—your Roadmap. The first paragraph describes the lack of scholarship regarding the revolutionary activities of French women. The author mentions "recent

---

[9]PrepTest 4, Sec 2, Passage 3
[10]PrepTest 4, Sec 2, Q 17

studies" (line 10) that mark the turning point, signaling a "much needed" reexamination of history. The importance of this new scholarship appears in the Roadmap as the central idea of the paragraph.

Step 4: To summarize: The first paragraph introduced the new scholarship, contrasting it with the lack of scholarship that preceded it. The correct answer should reflect this idea.

Step 5:

17. The primary function of the first paragraph of the passage is to

   (A)   outline the author's argument about women's roles in France between 1789 and 1795
   (B)   anticipate possible challenges to the findings of the recent studies of women in France between 1789 and 1795
   (C)   summarize some long-standing explanations of the role of individual women in France between 1789 and 1795
   (D)   present a context for the discussion of recent studies of women in France between 1789 and 1795
   (E)   characterize various eighteenth-century studies of women in France[11]

Choice (A) is completely off track; the author doesn't outline any arguments in the first paragraph. Choices (B) and (C) are similarly out of scope. Choice (D) is the match you're looking for. The first paragraph creates context for the discussion to follow by pointing out why the new scholarship is relevant. Choice (E) represents a faulty use of detail; the passage does mention (briefly) studies from the 20th century, but nothing from the 18th century. In any case, the purpose of the paragraph wasn't to mention individual studies, but to demonstrate why the new ones are important.

19. In the context of the passage, the word "cost" in line 63 refers to the[12]

Step 2: The stem asks you to define a key term in the context in which it was used. This is a Function question, specifically a Vocabulary-in-Context question.

Step 3: The word "cost" refers to the penalty paid by women who spoke in "borrowed voices." This information alone doesn't really define what that cost was, so you'll need to conduct additional research. Back up a bit and look for context earlier in the passage. A scan of Keywords should bring you to line 42, wherein the author describes the necessity of women having to use established vocabularies when speaking out. This paragraph is ultimately about the col-

---

[11]PrepTest 4, Sec 2, Q 17
[12]PrepTest 4, Sec 2, Q 19

lapse of the women's movement, as indicated by the Roadmap, and if you scan further through the text, the author asserts that the language used by the women "diminished" (line 44) their ability to resist suppression.

Remember that, when searching for the context that will allow you to answer the question, you may need to conduct research outside of the paragraph in which the text cited in the question stem appears. When the need arises, use Keywords and the Roadmap to guide you.

Step 4: It's time to make a prediction. According to the third paragraph, the ultimate result of the rhetorical devices used by women led to the demise of their movement. This is the "cost" referred to in the final paragraph.

Step 5:

19. In the context of the passage, the word "cost" in line 63 refers to the

    (A) dichotomy of private roles for women and public roles for men
    (B) almost nonexistent political participation of women before 1789
    (C) historians' lack of differentiation among various groups of women
    (D) political alliances women made with radical Jacobin men
    (E) collapse of the women's movement in the 1790s[13]

The proper match is choice (E), which unequivocally refers to the end of the movement. Note that, with a good prediction in hand, none of the other answer choices even remotely reflect what your research revealed. These choices make reference to various small details found in the latter paragraphs of the passage but none of them define the "cost" paid by the women mentioned in the stem.

You've now seen the three most common varieties of function questions—those that ask for the function of an example, the function of a paragraph, or the definition of a key term. All of them rely on your ability to read for context. To solve Function questions efficiently, you should be prepared to use your Roadmap to understand that context.

---

[13]PrepTest 4, Sec 2, Q 19

DRILL: ANSWERING FUNCTION QUESTIONS

Now for some additional practice. Read the following passage strategically, applying Step 1 of the Kaplan Method. Then answer the two questions, applying Steps 2–5 each time. Explanations follow the Drill.

Social scientists have traditionally defined multipolar international systems as consisting of three or more nations, each of roughly equal military and economic strength. Theoretically, the members of such
(5) systems create shifting, temporary alliances in response to changing circumstances in the international environment. Such systems are, thus, fluid and flexible. Frequent, small confrontations are one attribute of multipolar systems and are usually the result of less
(10) powerful members grouping together to counter threats from larger, more aggressive members seeking hegemony. Yet the constant and inevitable counterbalancing typical of such systems usually results in stability. The best-known example of a
(15) multipolar system is the Concert of Europe, which coincided with general peace on that continent lasting roughly 100 years beginning around 1815.

Bipolar systems, on the other hand, involve two major members of roughly equal military and
(20) economic strength vying for power and advantage. Other members of lesser strength tend to coalesce around one or the other pole. Such systems tend to be rigid and fixed, in part due to the existence of only one axis of power. Zero-sum political and military
(25) maneuverings, in which a gain for one side results in an equivalent loss for the other, are a salient feature of bipolar systems. Overall superiority is sought by both major members, which can lead to frequent confrontations, debilitating armed conflict, and,
(30) eventually, to the capitulation of one or the other side. Athens and Sparta of ancient Greece had a bipolar relationship, as did the United States and the USSR during the Cold War.

However, the shift in the geopolitical landscape
(35) following the end of the Cold War calls for a reassessment of the assumptions underlying these two theoretical concepts. The emerging but still vague multipolar system in Europe today brings with it the unsettling prospect of new conflicts and shifting

(40) alliances that may lead to a diminution, rather than an enhancement, of security. The frequent, small confrontations that are thought to have kept the Concert of Europe in a state of equilibrium would today, as nations arm themselves with modern
(45) weapons, create instability that could destroy the system. And the larger number of members and shifting alliance patterns peculiar to multipolar systems would create a bewildering tangle of conflicts.

This reassessment may also lead us to look at the
(50) Cold War in a new light. In 1914 smaller members of the multipolar system in Europe brought the larger members into a war that engulfed the continent. The aftermath—a crippled system in which certain members were dismantled, punished, or voluntarily
(55) withdrew—created the conditions that led to World War II. In contrast, the principal attributes of bipolar systems—two major members with only one possible axis of conflict locked in a rigid yet usually stable struggle for power—may have created the necessary
(60) parameters for general peace in the second half of the twentieth century.[14]

1. Which one of the following statements most accurately describes the function of the final paragraph?

   (A) The weaknesses of both types of systems are discussed in the context of twentieth-century European history.
   (B) A prediction is made regarding European security based on the attributes of both types of systems.
   (C) A new argument is introduced in favor of European countries embracing a new bipolar system.
   (D) Twentieth-century European history is used to expand on the argument in the previous paragraph.
   (E) The typical characteristics of the major members of a bipolar system are reviewed.

---

[14]PrepTest 40, Sec 4, Passage 1

2. The author's reference to the possibility that
    confrontations may lead to capitulation (lines 27–30)
    serves primarily to

    (A)   indicate that bipolar systems can have certain
            unstable characteristics
    (B)   illustrate how multipolar systems can transform
            themselves into bipolar systems
    (C)   contrast the aggressive nature of bipolar members
            with the more rational behavior of their
            multipolar counterparts
    (D)   indicate the anarchic nature of international
            relations
    (E)   suggest that military and economic strength shifts
            in bipolar as frequently as in multipolar systems[15]

---

[15]PrepTest 40, Sec 4, Qs 2–3

Explanations

Step 1:

Multipolar systems

Social scientists have (traditionally) defined multipolar international systems as (consisting of) three or more nations, each of roughly equal military and economic strength. (Theoretically,) the members of such
(5) systems create shifting, temporary alliances (in response) to changing circumstances in the international environment. Such systems are, (thus,) fluid and flexible. Frequent, small confrontations are one (attribute) of multipolar systems and are usually the (result) of less
(10) powerful members grouping together to (counter) threats from larger, more aggressive members seeking hegemony. (Yet) the constant and (inevitable) counterbalancing typical of such systems usually (results) in stability. The best-known (example) of a
(15) multipolar system is the Concert of Europe, which coincided with general peace on that continent lasting roughly 100 years beginning around 1815.

Bipolar systems

Bipolar systems, (on the other hand,) involve two major members of roughly equal military and
(20) economic strength vying for power and advantage. (Other) members of lesser strength (tend to) coalesce around one or the other pole. Such systems (tend to) be rigid and fixed, in part (due to) the existence of only one axis of power. Zero-sum political and military
(25) maneuverings, (in which) a gain for one side results in an equivalent loss for the other, are a (salient feature) of bipolar systems. (Overall) superiority is sought by (both) major members, which can (lead to) frequent confrontations, debilitating armed conflict, and,
(30) (eventually,) to the capitulation of one or the other side. Athens and Sparta of ancient Greece had a bipolar relationship, (as did) the United States and the USSR during the Cold war.

New landscape= changes in systems

(However,) the shift in the geopolitical landscape
(35) (following) the end of the Cold War calls for a reassessment of the (assumptions) underlying these two theoretical concepts. The emerging (but still) vague multipolar system in Europe (today) brings with it the unsettling prospect of new conflicts and shifting
(40) alliances that may (lead to) a diminution, rather (than an) enhancement, of security. The frequent, small confrontations that are thought to have kept the Concert of Europe in a state of equilibrium would (today,) as nations arm themselves with modern
(45) weapons, create instability that could destroy the system. (And) the larger number of members and shifting alliance patterns peculiar to multipolar systems would create a bewildering tangle of conflicts.

This reassessment may (also lead) us to look at the
(50) Cold War in a new light. In 1914 smaller members of
the multipolar system in Europe (brought) the larger
members into a war that engulfed the continent. The
(aftermath)—a crippled system in which certain
members were dismantled, punished, or voluntarily
(55) withdrew—created the conditions that (led to) World
War II. In (contrast,) the principal attributes of bipolar
systems—two major members with only one possible
axis of conflict locked in a rigid yet usually stable
struggle for power—may have (created) the necessary
(60) parameters for general peace in the second half of the
twentieth century.[16]

Review of past systems

Paragraph Structure: The author sets the stage by describing multipolar systems in the first paragraph and bipolar systems in the second. Note that these two paragraphs have very similar structures; the first begins by describing how multipolar systems are "traditionally" defined, goes on to describe their essential flexibility, and then gives the "best-known" example of such a system in lines 14–17. The second paragraph follows the same pattern: bipolar systems, "on the other hand" (line 18), tend to be more stable. The author gives examples at the conclusion of the paragraph.

"However," as the author begins the third paragraph, a reexamination of these ideas is in order. Changes in politics and technology may "lead to" (line 40) a lessening of security in multipolar systems. In the final paragraph, the author suggests that we "may also" (line 49) need to rethink current assumptions about the Cold War, suggesting that the existence of a bipolar system, "in contrast" (line 56) to the conflicts brought about by multipolar systems in previous years, may have led to a stable peace.

Topic: International relations

Scope: Bipolar and multipolar systems

Purpose: To describe how geopolitical changes may affect the functioning of certain international systems

Main Idea: Major geopolitical changes in the 20th century should lead us to reassess the functions of multipolar and bipolar systems in the past and present.

---

[16]PrepTest 40, Sec 4, Passage 1

1. **(D)**

    Which one of the following statements most accurately
    describes the function of the final paragraph?
    (A)   The weaknesses of both types of systems are
          discussed in the context of twentieth-century
          European history.
    (B)   A prediction is made regarding European security
          based on the attributes of both types of systems.
    (C)   A new argument is introduced in favor of
          European countries embracing a new bipolar
          system.
    (D)   Twentieth-century European history is used to
          expand on the argument in the previous
          paragraph.
    (E)   The typical characteristics of the major members
          of a bipolar system are reviewed.[17]

Step 2: Because the stem asks for the function of a paragraph, this is a Function question.

Step 3: The final paragraph begins by saying the reasoning described previously "may also lead" us to reexamine the Cold War. The rest of the paragraph goes on to describe this new interpretation of history.

Step 4: The continuation language that begins the final paragraph is an excellent clue. The purpose of this paragraph is to further the logic of the previous one, providing examples from recent history.

Step 5: Choice (D) describes the continuation perfectly and is the correct answer. Choice (A) distorts the facts, since the weaknesses of one system are discussed, not both. Choices (B) and (C) are out of scope; the author makes no predictions or arguments for political change. Choice (E) misuses detail. The final paragraph does mention an important bipolar system, but that isn't its primary purpose. The example is only there as part of a larger confirmation of the author's argument.

2. **(A)**

    The author's reference to the possibility that
    confrontations may lead to capitulation (lines 27–30)
    serves primarily to
    (A)   indicate that bipolar systems can have certain
          unstable characteristics
    (B)   illustrate how multipolar systems can transform
          themselves into bipolar systems
    (C)   contrast the aggressive nature of bipolar members
          with the more rational behavior of their
          multipolar counterparts
    (D)   indicate the anarchic nature of international
          relations
    (E)   suggest that military and economic strength shifts
          in bipolar as frequently as in multipolar systems[18]

---

[17]PrepTest 40, Sec 4, Q 2
[18]PrepTest 40, Sec 4, Q 3

Step 2: The key phrase "serves primarily to" alerts you that this is a Function question.

Step 3: According to the Roadmap, this paragraph is descriptive of bipolar systems. Indeed, Keywords spread throughout ("tend to" in line 22, "salient feature" in line 26) point to the various attributes that define such a system.

Step 4: Since the author uses this paragraph to describe bipolar systems, the reference to catastrophic conflicts must be considered a part of that description.

Step 5: Choice (A), the correct answer, fulfills the prediction right away. The reference did indeed describe bipolar systems, specifically describing one of their unstable attributes. Choices (B) and (C) veer out of scope, as the author never mentions the transformation of one system to another, nor does he use this paragraph to make a direct comparison between the two. Choice (D), a gross generalization, is also well out of scope. Choice (E) once again introduces a comparison that doesn't apply to the reference in question.

COMMON WRONG ANSWER TYPES

Most of the wrong answer traps you've seen in previous question types will show up in Function questions as well. I'll point out two of note from the previous exercise.

Distortion

Always be on the lookout for answer choices that are similar to your prediction but not quite right.

1. Which one of the following statements most accurately describes the function of the final paragraph?

    (A) The weaknesses of both types of systems are discussed in the context of twentieth-century European history.
    (B) A prediction is made regarding European security based on the attributes of both types of systems.
    (C) A new argument is introduced in favor of European countries embracing a new bipolar system.
    (D) Twentieth-century European history is used to expand on the argument in the previous paragraph.
    (E) The typical characteristics of the major members of a bipolar system are reviewed.[19]

The final paragraph did mention the major members of a bipolar system (the US and the USSR), but the purpose of the paragraph was not to "review" their characteristics, but rather to mention them as support of a standing argument. When thinking about the function of a paragraph, stick to your Roadmap and keep the big picture in mind.

---

[19]PrepTest 40, Sec 4, Q 2

Irrelevant comparison

The test makers will occasionally write answer choices that take advantage of the tendency to focus on comparisons and contrasts in the passage.

2. The author's reference to the possibility that confrontations may lead to capitulation (lines 27–30) serves primarily to

    (A) indicate that bipolar systems can have certain unstable characteristics
    (B) illustrate how multipolar systems can transform themselves into bipolar systems
    (C) contrast the aggressive nature of bipolar members with the more rational behavior of their multipolar counterparts
    (D) indicate the anarchic nature of international relations
    (E) suggest that military and economic strength shifts in bipolar as frequently as in multipolar systems[20]

The second paragraph of the passage was solely focused on describing bipolar systems, and this question asked about a detail in service of that goal. It's not uncommon in Function questions for wrong answer traps to leave the context of the stem behind and focus instead on larger issues that are out of scope. This passage *does* eventually comment on the interrelations between bipolar and multipolar systems, but not in the paragraph that's relevant to this question. Remember not to lose sight of what the question is asking for.

YOU KNOW THE QUESTION TYPES

Take a deep breath, then congratulate yourself on reaching an important milestone: You've now learned how to identify and apply the proper strategies to every type of question that appears in LSAT Reading Comprehension. I'll revisit rare variations on these question types a little later, but first it's time to challenge yourself. In the next chapter you'll bring everything you've learned to bear as you learn how to score the toughest points on the test.

---

[20]PrepTest 40, Sec 4, Q 3

CHAPTER 15

CHALLENGING PASSAGES

SOME PASSAGES ARE HARDER THAN OTHERS

Now that you've had time to practice and apply the Kaplan Method, I hope you're feeling an increased confidence with every Reading Comprehension passage you take on. You've learned that the passages and questions follow predictable patterns, and you're well on your way to mastering the strategies that will help you to maximize your score. For the most part, each time you practice, the passages should become a little more familiar, the questions a little easier, and the correct answers simpler to spot.

Nonetheless, you'll still encounter the occasional bump in the road. Perhaps you've read a natural science passage that you just couldn't wrap your head around, and found the questions consequently bewildering. Maybe you've come across law passages that seemed too abstract to understand, or passages so steeped in jargon that it seemed only an expert in the field could possibly understand them. Perhaps you've encountered questions that seem impossible to answer quickly.

If you're like most of my students, you've had all of these experiences at one time or another, and I understand the frustration these situations cause. The fact is that some passages are designed by the test makers to be more challenging than others, and on average every LSAT Reading Comprehension section contains one such passage. Certainly there is some subjectivity here—what's challenging for one test taker might seem quite straightforward for another—but like everything else on the LSAT, the attributes of challenging passages are pattern-oriented and predictable. Here are some of the ways in which the test makers craft a high-difficulty passage.

Abstraction

The passage may deal with concepts that aren't easily imagined, such as philosophical ideas or schools of legal thought. Abstract passages are often made more challenging by a lack of concrete examples to illustrate its ideas.

> Organicism depended upon the theory of internal relations, which states that relations between entities are possible only within some whole that embraces them, and that entities are altered by the relationships
> (15) into which they enter. If an entity stands in a relationship with another entity, it has some property as a consequence. Without this relationship, and hence without the property, the entity would be different— and so would be another entity. Thus, the property is
> (20) one of the entity's defining characteristics. Each of an entity's relationships likewise determines a defining characteristic of the entity.[1]

This paragraph is a perfect illustration of abstraction in a passage. The theory of internal relations is described in some detail, but the language is vague throughout. The highlighted sentence, describing the relationship of "entities" to one another and acquiring "some property" as a result isn't by itself easy to imagine. It is vital that, when reading such a passage, you adhere scrupulously to Step 1 of the Kaplan Method and read strategically, using Keywords to help you navigate the vague language.

Organicism: depends on relations

> Organicism (depended) upon the theory of internal relations, which (states) that relations between entities are possible (only) within some whole that embraces them, (and) that entities are altered by the relationships
> (15) into which they enter. (If) an entity stands in a relationship with another entity, it has some property as a (consequence.) Without this relationship, (and hence) without the property, the entity would be different— (and so) would be another entity. (Thus,) the property is
> (20) one of the entity's defining characteristics. Each of an entity's relationships (likewise) determines a defining characteristic of the entity.[2]

Recall from the sample Roadmap what really matters—the main point that the author is trying to convey. The Keywords "depended upon" tell you that, regardless of what else the paragraph may say, there is an important relationship between organicism and the theory of internal relations. Once you understand that much and get it into your Roadmap, the esoteric ideas can wait until it's time to research them for a question.

---

[1]PrepTest 25, Sec 1, Passage 4
[2]PrepTest 25, Sec 1, Passage 4

Jargon

If you've been working through this book carefully, you're very familiar with passages that rely on field-specific jargon to communicate their ideas. Unfamiliar language can make a passage seem intimidating and may give you the false impression that it cannot be understood without specialized knowledge of the subject matter.

> H. L. A. Hart's *The Concept of Law* is still the clearest and most persuasive statement of both the
> (10) standard theory of hard cases and the standard theory of law on which it rests. For Hart, the law consists of legal rules formulated in general terms; these terms he calls "open textured," which means that they contain a "core" of settled meaning and a "penumbra" or "periphery" where their meaning is not determinate.[3]

This excerpt is full of jargon. Many of its key terms are in quotes, and while they are all defined, it still might not be entirely clear what the core, penumbra, and periphery of legal rules really are.

> For example, suppose an ordinance prohibits the use of vehicles in a park.
> (15) "Vehicle" has a core of meaning which includes cars and motorcycles. But, Hart claims, other vehicles, such as bicycles, fall within the peripheral meaning of "vehicle," so that the law does not establish whether they are prohibited.[4]

As the paragraph continues, an example is provided that clarifies the jargon somewhat. Keep in mind that while you should generally skim through examples, in a more challenging passage they can provide the context you need to decipher key ideas. As always, Keywords will help you parse this information efficiently. In this case, the Keyword "but" allows you to quickly identify the key distinction—peripheral meanings are unclear, so it must follow that core meanings are well-established.

It is important to remember that *every* passage, no matter how difficult its language, will contain sufficient Keywords and other context clues to allow you to understand its main ideas. Law schools don't expect you to begin your first year already understanding the law; similarly, the LSAT test makers don't expect you to approach Reading Comprehension with full knowledge of the passages' content (in fact, they're counting on the opposite).

Structure

Sometimes the structure of a passage can make it more difficult to comprehend. Don't reread the following passage in depth, but rather glance quickly at the beginning of each paragraph.

---

[3]PrepTest 17, Sec 4, Passage 2
[4]PrepTest 17, Sec 4, Passage 2

Traditionally, members of a community such as a town or neighborhood share a common location and a sense of necessary interdependence that includes, for example, mutual respect and emotional support. But as
(5) modern societies grow more technological and sometimes more alienating, people tend to spend less time in the kinds of interactions that their communities require in order to thrive. Meanwhile, technology has made it possible for individuals to interact via personal
(10) computer with others who are geographically distant. Advocates claim that these computer conferences, in which large numbers of participants communicate by typing comments that are immediately read by other participants and responding immediately to those
(15) comments they read, function as communities that can substitute for traditional interactions with neighbors.

What are the characteristics that advocates claim allow computer conferences to function as communities? For one, participants often share
(20) common interests or concerns; conferences are frequently organized around specific topics such as music or parenting. Second, because these conferences are conversations, participants have adopted certain conventions in recognition of the importance of
(25) respecting each others' sensibilities. Abbreviations are used to convey commonly expressed sentiments of courtesy such as "pardon me for cutting in" ("pmfci") or "in my humble opinion" ("imho"). Because a humorous tone can be difficult to communicate in
(30) writing, participants will often end an intentionally humorous comment with a set of characters that, when looked at sideways, resembles a smiling or winking face. Typing messages entirely in capital letters is avoided, because its tendency to demand the attention
(35) of a reader's eye is considered the computer equivalent of shouting. These conventions, advocates claim, constitute a form of etiquette, and with this etiquette as a foundation, people often form genuine, trusting relationships, even offering advice and support during
(40) personal crises such as illness or the loss of a loved one.

But while it is true that conferences can be both respectful and supportive, they nonetheless fall short of communities. For example, conferences discriminate
(45) along educational and economic lines because participation requires a basic knowledge of computers and the ability to afford access to conferences. Further, while advocates claim that a shared interest makes computer conferences similar to traditional
(50) communities—insofar as the shared interest is analogous to a traditional community's shared location—this analogy simply does not work. Conference participants are a self-selecting group; they are drawn together by their shared interest in the topic
(55) of the conference. Actual communities, on the other hand, are "nonintentional": the people who inhabit towns or neighborhoods are thus more likely to exhibit genuine diversity—of age, career, or personal interests—than are conference participants. It might be
(60) easier to find common ground in a computer conference than in today's communities, but in so doing it would be unfortunate if conference participants cut themselves off further from valuable interactions in their own towns or neighborhoods.[5]

---

[5]PrepTest 36, Sec 2, Passage 1

Even if you hadn't already worked with this passage, the simplicity of its structure should be obvious. It is neatly divided into several paragraphs, each of which signals its primary purpose immediately with familiar Keywords. You get a good approximation of the author's goals without even reading the rest of the text.

Compare it with this passage. Again, skim the text, paying attention primarily to the highlighted text at the beginning of each paragraph.

Because the market system enables entrepreneurs and investors who develop new technology to reap financial rewards from their risk of capital, it may seem that the primary result of this activity is that some
(5) people who have spare capital accumulate more. But in spite of the fact that the profits derived from various technological developments have accrued to relatively few people, the developments themselves have served overall as a remarkable democratizing force. In fact,
(10) under the regime of the market, the gap in benefits accruing to different groups of people has been narrowed in the long term.

This tendency can be seen in various well-known technological developments. For example, before the
(15) printing press was introduced centuries ago, few people had access to written materials, much less to scribes and private secretaries to produce and transcribe documents. Since printed materials have become widely available, however, people without special
(20) position or resources—and in numbers once thought impossible—can take literacy and the use of printed texts for granted. With the distribution of books and periodicals in public libraries, this process has been extended to the point where people in general can have
(25) essentially equal access to a vast range of texts that would once have been available only to a very few. A more recent technological development extends this process beyond printed documents. A child in school with access to a personal computer and modem—
(30) which is becoming fairly common in technologically

advanced societies—has computing power and database access equal to that of the best-connected scientists and engineers at top-level labs of just fifteen years ago, a time when relatively few people had
(35) personal access to any computing power. Or consider the uses of technology for leisure. In previous centuries only a few people with abundant resources had the ability and time to hire professional entertainment, and to have contact through travel and written
(40) communication—both of which were prohibitively expensive—with distant people. But now broadcast technology is widely available, and so almost anyone can have an entertainment cornucopia unimagined in earlier times. Similarly, the development of
(45) inexpensive mail distribution and telephone connections and, more recently, the establishment of the even more efficient medium of electronic mail have greatly extended the power of distant communication.

This kind of gradual diffusion of benefits across
(50) society is not an accident of these particular technological developments, but rather the result of a general tendency of the market system. Entrepreneurs and investors often are unable to maximize financial success without expanding their market, and this
(55) involves structuring their prices to the consumers so as to make their technologies genuinely accessible to an ever-larger share of the population. In other words, because market competition drives prices down, it tends to diffuse access to new technology across
(60) society as a result.[6]

The structure of this passage is less simple than in the previous example. There are longer paragraphs, making the author's Purpose more challenging to map out. The second paragraph is particularly long and laden with details. The paragraphs begin with longer sentences containing more complex ideas. You're not likely to skim this passage and come away with a firm grasp of its ideas.

But once again, I'll remind you that the Keywords are still there. No matter how complex the passage structure may seem, you still have all the clues you need to make sense of it.

> Because the market system enables entrepreneurs and investors who develop new technology to reap financial rewards from their risk of capital, it may seem that the primary result of this activity is that some
> (5) people who have spare capital accumulate more. But in spite of the fact that the profits derived from various technological developments have accrued to relatively few people, the developments themselves have served overall as a remarkable democratizing force. In fact,
> (10) under the regime of the market, the gap in benefits accruing to different groups of people has been narrowed in the long term.[7]

"Because" of certain features of the market system, you might expect the "primary" result to be that people with spare cash earn more.

Predictive reading allows you to guess what comes next: "But" market forces have "overall" been democratizing. If this term is unfamiliar to you, use the Keywords to help you approximate its meaning. Since the author is describing a contrast to the expected result (those with extra money make even more), a democratizing force must be one that *doesn't* simply allow the rich to become richer. "In fact," the gap between different groups has narrowed.

Strategic reading always allows you to take an unwieldy block of text and reduce it to a handful of simpler ideas, no matter how challenging the structure may look initially.

YOU CAN NAVIGATE ANY PASSAGE

Challenging passages are a reality of the LSAT, but the test makers aren't in the business of crafting impossible tasks; the test will always be fair, if not always simple. In all of the above cases, I demonstrated ways in which you can navigate difficult text by properly applying the Kaplan Method. The solutions should have looked very familiar to you: reliance on context, Keywords, and predictive reading, tools you've been using throughout this book.

Perhaps most importantly, you must approach challenging passages with confidence and a dedication to methodical thinking. It's very easy to become intimidated by a tough passage when

---

[7]PrepTest 42, Sec 3, Passage 3

the clock is ticking, and it's just as easy to let method fall by the wayside. Don't let this happen. Remember that you always have control over the way you approach the passage—maintain this control and you can handle any challenge the Reading Comprehension section throws at you.

Challenging Passage Practice

Put these ideas to the test on a tough passage, one paragraph at a time.

> Many legal theorists have argued that the only
> morally legitimate goal in imposing criminal penalties
> against certain behaviors is to prevent people from
> harming others. Clearly, such theorists would oppose
> (5) laws that force people to act purely for their own
> good or to refrain from certain harmless acts purely
> to ensure conformity to some social norm. But the
> goal of preventing harm to others would also justify
> legal sanctions against some forms of nonconforming
> (10) behavior to which this goal might at first seem not to
> apply.[8]

The first paragraph indicates an abstract topic, so careful attention to Keywords will be vital as you apply Step 1 of the Kaplan Method. The theorists in line 1 "have argued" that the only good reason to impose criminal penalties is to prevent people from harming each other. So far so good; keep this definition in mind as you proceed.

"Clearly" (line 4) you would expect theorists to oppose laws that prevent harmless acts. Predictive reading should prepare you for what comes next, since LSAT passages rarely focus on the expected. The author will likely introduce a contrary opinion soon. "But" (line 7) it turns out there are some forms of behavior that should be illegal even though they might at first seem harmless.

> Only reason for
> law = prevent
> harm
>
> Many (legal theorists) have (argued) that the only
> morally legitimate goal in imposing criminal penalties
> against certain behaviors is to prevent people from
> harming others. (Clearly,) such theorists would (oppose)
> (5) laws that force people to act purely for their own
> good (or to) refrain from certain harmless acts purely
> to ensure conformity to some social norm. (But) the
> goal of preventing harm to others would also justify
>
> Unexpected
> cases
>
> legal sanctions against some forms of nonconforming
> (10) behavior to which this goal might at first seem not to
> apply.[9]

When faced with an abstract passage, it's especially important that you remember to read predictively. The author has asserted that there are certain kinds of "nonconforming behavior" that cause harm even though they appear not to. The following paragraphs are likely to

---

[8]PrepTest 46, Sec 1, Passage 4
[9]PrepTest 46, Sec 1, Passage 4

provide examples of these behaviors. Keep this in mind as you read the next paragraph. This time, circle Keywords as you come to them and create a Roadmap as you go.

> In many situations it is in the interest of each
> member of a group to agree to behave in a certain
> way on the condition that the others similarly agree.
> (15) In the simplest cases, a mere coordination of
> activities is itself the good that results. For example,
> it is in no one's interest to lack a convention about
> which side of the road to drive on, and each person
> can agree to drive on one side assuming the others do
> (20) too. Any fair rule, then, would be better than no rule
> at all. On the assumption that all people would
> voluntarily agree to be subject to a coordination rule
> backed by criminal sanctions, if people could be
> assured that others would also agree, it is argued to
> (25) be legitimate for a legislature to impose such a rule.
> This is because prevention of harm underlies the
> rationale for the rule, though it applies to the problem
> of coordination less directly than to other problems,
> for the act that is forbidden (driving on the other side
> (30) of the road) is not inherently harm-producing, as are
> burglary and assault; instead, it is the lack of a
> coordinating rule that would be harmful.[10]

This lengthy, detail-filled paragraph is much easier to work with if you keep the context of the first paragraph in mind as you read it. There are "many situations" (line 12) in which people should agree to behave the same way. This is presumably because doing so will prevent harm. "For example" in line 16 marks the beginning of a dense example—one that is very easy to get lost in. Remember your sense of context, and stay active as you read; think about why the author would use the example. According to your prediction, it should describe a situation where conformity serves to prevent harm. The example makes perfect sense in this context; people should agree to drive on the same side of the road, because failing to do so would be dangerous. The paragraph makes this simple idea seem more complex than it really is, but take note of the repetitive nature of the language. It is ultimately "argued" (line 24) that a rule requiring people to drive on the same side of the road is legitimate, "because" (line 26) it is designed to prevent harm. The paragraph becomes rather long-winded toward line 27, but don't fall into the trap of trying to parse every word of this detailed language—stay focused on useful Keywords. The author's gist is signaled by a contrast in line 31: The text following "instead" ties the paragraph up by centering once again on the idea that it would be harmful not to have a conformity rule for drivers.

At this point, you may be nervous about what appears to be a cursory treatment of the text. Wouldn't it be better to dive into this paragraph and really understand everything that it's saying? By now I hope your answer to this question is a resounding "No!" On test day, you absolutely do not have time to work through the minutiae of this paragraph. Trust the clues, and use the repetitious ideas to your advantage. All this paragraph really does is point out that

---

[10]PrepTest 46, Sec 1, Passage 4

a rule requiring conformity (such as making everyone drive on the same side of the road) can achieve the goal of preventing harm. Your Roadmap should reflect this.

Ex: coordination: can be good

In (many situations) it is in the interest of each member of a group to agree to behave in a certain way on the condition that the others similarly agree.
(15) In the simplest (cases,) a mere coordination of activities is itself the good that results. (For example,) it is in no one's interest to lack a convention about which side of the road to drive on, and each person can agree to drive on one side (assuming) the others do
(20) too. Any fair rule, (then,) would be better than no rule at all. On the (assumption) that all people would voluntarily agree to be subject to a coordination rule backed by criminal sanctions, (if) people could be assured that others would also agree, it (is argued) to
(25) be legitimate for a legislature to impose such a rule. This is (because) prevention of harm underlies the rationale for the rule, (though) it applies to the problem of coordination less directly than to other problems, (for) the act that is forbidden (driving on the other side
(30) of the road) is not inherently harm-producing, (as are) burglary and assault; (instead,) it is the lack of a coordinating rule that would be harmful.[11]

Take a moment to predict what is likely to come next. Then read the final paragraph strategically, circling Keywords and creating a Roadmap. Use the Keywords to stay focused on the main idea.

In some other situations involving a need for legally enforced coordination, the harm to be averted
(35) goes beyond the simple lack of coordination itself. This can be illustrated by an example of a coordination rule—instituted by a private athletic organization—which has analogies in criminal law. At issue is whether the use of anabolic steroids, which
(40) build muscular strength but have serious negative side effects, should be prohibited. Each athlete has at stake both an interest in having a fair opportunity to win and an interest in good health. If some competitors use steroids, others have the option of either
(45) endangering their health or losing their fair opportunity to win. Thus they would be harmed either way. A compulsory rule could prevent that harm and thus would be in the interest of all competitors. If they understand its function and trust the techniques
(50) for its enforcement, they will gladly consent to it. So while it might appear that such a rule merely forces people to act for their own good, the deeper rationale for coercion here—as in the above example—is a somewhat complex appeal to the legitimacy of
(55) enforcing a rule with the goal of preventing harm.[12]

[11] PrepTest 46, Sec 1, Passage 4
[12] PrepTest 46, Sec 1, Passage 4

You probably predicted that the author would continue to provide examples of conformity rules that can be legally justified. This prediction is important, since the opening of the paragraph doesn't clearly spell out what it's going to describe; it merely asserts that sometimes the need to prevent harm goes beyond a "simple lack of coordination" (line 35). If this doesn't make sense, read on for more concrete text. The example of anabolic steroids given in lines 38–50 provides the clarity you need.

The problem described once again comes down to harm. "If" (line 43) some athletes use steroids, others have to choose between taking harmful drugs themselves or becoming less competitive. Either way, harm is done (line 46). Lines 50–55 simply summarize the author's logic. "While" (line 51) it might seem as though the steroid rule doesn't prevent people from harming others, it contains a "deeper rationale" (line 52) that causes it to do so.

Ex: beyond coordination	This can be illustrated by an example of a coordination rule—instituted by a private athletic organization—which has analogies in criminal law. At issue is whether the use of anabolic steroids, which
	(40) build muscular strength but have serious negative side effects, should be prohibited. Each athlete has at stake both an interest in having a fair opportunity to win and an interest in good health. If some competitors use steroids, others have the option of either
	(45) endangering their health or losing their fair opportunity to win. Thus they would be harmed either way. A compulsory rule could prevent that harm and thus would be in the interest of all competitors. If they understand its function and trust the techniques
	(50) for its enforcement, they will gladly consent to it. So while it might appear that such a rule merely forces
Rule = not causing harm	people to act for their own good, the deeper rationale for coercion here—as in the above example—is a somewhat complex appeal to the legitimacy of
	(55) enforcing a rule with the goal of preventing harm.[13]

In summary, this abstract passage really only proposes a single idea in the first paragraph and then provides two very detailed examples of that idea.

	Many legal theorists have argued that the only
Only reason for law = prevent harm	morally legitimate goal in imposing criminal penalties against certain behaviors is to prevent people from harming others. Clearly, such theorists would oppose
	(5) laws that force people to act purely for their own good or to refrain from certain harmless acts purely to ensure conformity to some social norm. But the goal of preventing harm to others would also justify
Unexpected cases	legal sanctions against some forms of nonconforming
	(10) behavior to which this goal might at first seem not to apply.

---

[13]PrepTest 46, Sec 1, Passage 4

Ex:
coordination
can be
good

(15)

(20)

(25)

(30)

In (many situations) it is in the interest of each member of a group to agree to behave in a certain way on the condition that the others similarly agree. In the simplest (cases,) a mere coordination of activities is itself the good that results. (For example,) it is in no one's interest to lack a convention about which side of the road to drive on, and each person can agree to drive on one side (assuming) the others do too. Any fair rule, (then,) would be better than no rule at all. On the (assumption) that all people would voluntarily agree to be subject to a coordination rule backed by criminal sanction, (if) people could be assured that others would also agree, it (is argued) to be legitimate for a legislature to impose such rule. This is (because) prevention of harm underlies the rationale for the rule, (though) it applies to the problem of coordination less directly than to other problems, (for) the act that is forbidden (driving on the other side of the road) is not inherently harm-producing, (as are) burglary and assault; (instead,) it is the lack of a coordinating rule that would be harmful.

Ex: beyond
coordination

(35)

(40)

(45)

(50)

Rule =
not causing
harm

(55)

In some (other situations) involving a need for legally enforced coordination, the harm to be averted goes beyond the simple lack of coordination itself. This can be (illustrated by) an example of a coordination rule—instituted by a private athletic organization—which has analogies in criminal law. At (issue) is whether the use of anabolic steroids, which build muscular strength but have serious negative side effects, should be prohibited. Each athlete has at stake (both) an interest in having a fair opportunity to win (and) an interest in good health. (If) some competitors use steroids, others have the option of either endangering their health or losing their fair opportunity to win. (Thus) they would be harmed either way. A compulsory rule could prevent that harm and (thus) would be in the interest of all competitors. (If) they understand its function and trust the techniques for its enforcement, they will gladly consent to it. (So) while it might appear that such a rule merely forces people to act for their own good, the (deeper rationale) for coercion here—as in the above example—is a somewhat complex appeal to the legitimacy of enforcing a rule with the goal of preventing harm.[14]

Topic: Legal rules

Scope: Rules that prevent harm

Purpose: To provide examples of a particular legal principle

Main Idea: Although certain coordinating rules might not at first seem to prevent people from harming each other, they actually do.

---

[14] PrepTest 46, Sec 1, Passage 4

Take a moment to appreciate how basic the Main Idea of this passage is, and just how much text the author used to communicate it. Abstract passages put your understanding of Strategic Reading to the test; over-thinking this passage is a dangerous waste of time. You understand the big picture, and that's all you need to confidently approach the questions.

22. Which one of the following most accurately states the main point of the passage?

    (A)   In order to be morally justifiable, laws prohibiting activities that are not inherently harm-producing must apply equitably to everyone.
    (B)   It is justifiable to require social conformity where noncompliance would be harmful to either the nonconforming individual or the larger group.
    (C)   Achieving coordination can be argued to be a morally legitimate justification for rules that prevent directly harmful actions and others that prevent indirectly harmful actions.
    (D)   It is reasonable to hold that restricting individual liberty is always justified on the basis of mutually agreed-upon community standards.
    (E)   The principle of preventing harm to others can be used to justify laws that do not at first glance appear to be designed to prevent such harm.[15]

Approach this question using the Kaplan Method.

Step 2: Identify the Question Type
Stems that ask for the "main point" indicate Global questions.

Step 3: Research the Relevant Text
You've already identified the Main Idea, so you can proceed directly to Step 4.

Step 4: Make a Prediction
To summarize: Rules that prevent people from harming one another may not always appear to do so at first.

Step 5: : Evaluate the Answer Choices
Choices (A) and (B) are too narrow in their focus, focusing on specific evidence rather than the author's larger argument. Choice (C) brings in the out-of-scope idea of indirectly harmful actions, and choice (D) is both too narrow and too extreme (the author never claims that restricting individual liberties is "always" justified in cases if community agreement). Choice (E), however, matches the prediction and is the correct answer.

---

[15]PrepTest 46, Sec 1, Passage 4, Q 22

Try the next question:

23. It can be most reasonably inferred from the passage that the author considers which one of the following factors to be generally necessary for the justification of rules compelling coordination of people's activities?

(A) evidence that such rules do not force individuals to act for their own good

(B) enactment of such rules by a duly elected or appointed government lawmaking organization

(C) the assurance that criminal penalties are provided as a means of securing compliance with such rules

(D) some form of consent on the part of rational people who are subject to such rules

(E) a sense of community and cultural uniformity among those who are required to abide by such rules[16]

Step 2: The key phrase "most reasonably inferred" marks this as an Inference question.

Step 3: The stem asks what the author considers "generally necessary" for the justification of coordinating rules. Since the second and third paragraphs lay out the author's reasoning for the acceptance of rules, either one might contain the information you need. A glance through the Keywords reveals that a rule is "argued" to be legitimate (lines 24–25) on the assumption (line 21) that people agree to follow the rule. Similar reasoning can be found in the second paragraph, lines 48–50, where the author notes that "if" people understand the rule "they will gladly consent to it."

Step 4: The author's primary concern regarding the legitimacy of rules seems to center around the agreement of people to follow those rules. The correct answer should reflect this idea.

Step 5: Choice (A) is a distortion; the author never specifically decries rules that prevent self-harm. Choice (B) is completely out of scope. Choice (C) mentions criminal penalties, which the author does cite in paragraph two, but not as a required feature of a coordination rule. Choice (D), consent of the governed, matches your prediction and is the correct answer. For the record, choice (E) brings in the out-of-scope concept of cultural uniformity.

As you can see, the questions that accompany a tough passage are just as amenable to the Kaplan Method as those that follow a simpler one. It's also worth noting that, just because the passage may be challenging, it doesn't mean that all of the questions will be as well. Most tough passages come with a mix of simpler and harder questions, and I'll discuss the importance of managing questions of differing difficulty a bit later.

---

[16]PrepTest 46, Sec 1, Passage 4, Q 23

DRILL: WORKING WITH CHALLENGING PASSAGES

Now I want you to attempt a challenging passage on your own. Read the passage strategically, applying Step 1 of the Kaplan Method. Circle Keywords, create a Roadmap, and identify the Topic, Scope, Purpose, and Main Idea. This passage is among the toughest to have ever appeared on the LSAT, so be sure to apply the strategies covered in this chapter. Then try the four questions that follow. Be sure to review the explanations carefully when you've finished.

In explaining the foundations of the discipline known as historical sociology—the examination of history using the methods of sociology—historical sociologist Philip Abrams argues that, while people are
(5) made by society as much as society is made by people, sociologists' approach to the subject is usually to focus on only one of these forms of influence to the exclusion of the other. Abrams insists on the necessity for sociologists to move beyond these one-sided
(10) approaches to understand society as an entity constructed by individuals who are at the same time constructed by their society. Abrams refers to this continuous process as "structuring."

Abrams also sees history as the result of
(15) structuring. People, both individually and as members of collectives, make history. But our making of history is itself formed and informed not only by the historical conditions we inherit from the past, but also by the prior formation of our own identities and capacities,
(20) which are shaped by what Abrams calls "contingencies"—social phenomena over which we have varying degrees of control. Contingencies include such things as the social conditions under which we come of age, the condition of our household's
(25) economy, the ideologies available to help us make sense of our situation, and accidental circumstances. The ways in which contingencies affect our individual or group identities create a structure of forces within which we are able to act, and that partially determines
(30) the sorts of actions we are able to perform.

In Abrams's analysis, historical structuring, like social structuring, is manifold and unremitting. To understand it, historical sociologists must extract from it certain significant episodes, or events, that their
(35) methodology can then analyze and interpret. According to Abrams, these events are points at which action and contingency meet, points that represent a cross section of the specific social and individual forces in play at a given time. At such moments, individuals stand forth
(40) as agents of history not simply because they possess a

unique ability to act, but also because in them we see the force of the specific social conditions that allowed their actions to come forth. Individuals can "make their mark" on history, yet in individuals one also finds the
(45) convergence of wider social forces. In order to capture the various facets of this mutual interaction, Abrams recommends a fourfold structure to which he believes the investigations of historical sociologists should conform: first, description of the event itself; second,
(50) discussion of the social context that helped bring the event about and gave it significance; third, summary of the life history of the individual agent in the event; and fourth, analysis of the consequences of the event both for history and for the individual.

1. Which one of the following most accurately states the central idea of the passage?

    (A)   Abrams argues that historical sociology rejects the claims of sociologists who assert that the sociological concept of structuring cannot be applied to the interactions between individuals and history.

    (B)   Abrams argues that historical sociology assumes that, despite the views of sociologists to the contrary, history influences the social contingencies that affect individuals.

    (C)   Abrams argues that historical sociology demonstrates that, despite the views of sociologists to the contrary, social structures both influence and are influenced by the events of history.

    (D)   Abrams describes historical sociology as a discipline that unites two approaches taken by sociologists to studying the formation of societies and applies the resulting combined approach to the study of history.

    (E)   Abrams describes historical sociology as an attempt to compensate for the shortcomings of traditional historical methods by applying the methods established in sociology.

2. Given the passage's argument, which one of the following sentences most logically completes the last paragraph?

    (A)   Only if they adhere to this structure, Abrams believes, can historical sociologists conclude with any certainty that the events that constitute the historical record are influenced by the actions of individuals.

    (B)   Only if they adhere to this structure, Abrams believes, will historical sociologists be able to counter the standard sociological assumption that there is very little connection between history and individual agency.

    (C)   Unless they can agree to adhere to this structure, Abrams believes, historical sociologists risk having their discipline treated as little more than an interesting but ultimately indefensible adjunct to history and sociology.

    (D)   By adhering to this structure, Abrams believes, historical sociologists can shed light on issues that traditional sociologists have chosen to ignore in their one-sided approaches to the formation of societies.

    (E)   By adhering to this structure, Abrams believes, historical sociologists will be able to better portray the complex connections between human agency and history.

3. The passage states that a contingency could be each of the following EXCEPT:

    (A)   a social phenomenon
    (B)   a form of historical structuring
    (C)   an accidental circumstance
    (D)   a condition controllable to some extent by an individual
    (E)   a partial determinant of an individual's actions

4. Which one of the following is most analogous to the ideal work of a historical sociologist as outlined by Abrams?

    (A)   In a report on the enactment of a bill into law, a journalist explains why the need for the bill arose, sketches the biography of the principal legislator who wrote the bill, and ponders the effect that the bill's enactment will have both on society and on the legislator's career.

    (B)   In a consultation with a patient, a doctor reviews the patient's medical history, suggests possible reasons for the patient's current condition, and recommends steps that the patient should take in the future to ensure that the condition improves or at least does not get any worse.

    (C)   In an analysis of a historical novel, a critic provides information to support the claim that details of the work's setting are accurate, explains why the subject of the novel was of particular interest to the author, and compares the novel with some of the author's other books set in the same period.

    (D)   In a presentation to stockholders, a corporation's chief executive officer describes the corporation's most profitable activities during the past year, introduces the vice president largely responsible for those activities, and discusses new projects the vice president will initiate in the coming year.

    (E)   In developing a film based on a historical event, a filmmaker conducts interviews with participants in the event, bases part of the film's screenplay on the interviews, and concludes the screenplay with a sequence of scenes speculating on the outcome of the event had certain details been different.[17]

[17]PrepTest 38, Sec 3, Passage 3, Qs 15–18

Explanations

Step 1:

Soc: focus
on people or
society only

In explaining the foundations of the discipline known as historical sociology—the examination of history using the methods of sociology—historical sociologist Philip Abrams argues that, while people are
(5) made by society as much as society is made by people, sociologists' approach to the subject is usually to focus on only one of these forms of influence to the exclusion of the other. Abrams insists on the necessity

Abrams: people
and society
affect one
another

for sociologists to move beyond these one-sided
(10) approaches to understand society as an entity constructed by individuals who are at the same time constructed by their society. Abrams refers to this continuous process as "structuring."

History =
structuring

Abram also sees history as the result of
(15) structuring. People, both individually and as members of collectives, make history. But our making of history is itself formed and informed not only by the historical conditions we inherit from the past, but also by the prior formation of our own identities and capacities,
(20) which are shaped by what Abrams calls

Contingencies

"contingencies"—social phenomena over which we have varying degrees of control. Contingencies include such things as the social conditions under which we come of age, the condition of our household's
(25) economy, the ideologies available to help us make sense of our situation, and accidental circumstances. The ways in which contingencies affect our individual or group identities create a structure of forces within which we are able to act, and that partially determines
(30) the sorts of actions we are able to perform.

Need to
examine
specific events

In Abrams's analysis, historical structuring, like social structuring, is manifold and unremitting. To understand it, historical sociologists must extract from it certain significant episodes, or events, that their
(35) methodology can then analyze and interpret. According to Abrams, these events are points at which action and contingency meet, points at represent a cross section of the specific social and individual forces in play at a given time. At such moments, individuals stand forth
(40) as agents of history not simply because they possess a unique ability to act, but also because in them we see the force of the specific social conditions that allowed their actions to come forth. Individuals can "make their mark" on history, yet in individuals one also finds the
(45) convergence of wider social forces. In order to capture

Structure for
examination

the various facets of this mutual interaction, Abrams
(recommends) a fourfold structure to which he believes
the investigations of historical sociologists should
conform: (first,) description of the event itself; (second,)

(50) discussion of the social context that helped bring the
event about and gave it significance; (third,) summary of
the life history of the individual agent in the event; and
(fourth,) analysis of the consequences of the event both
for history and for the individual.[18]

Paragraph Structure: The opening paragraph introduces historical sociology and, more importantly, the views of Philip Abrams. He "argues" (line 4) that society is made by people and vice versa. This view contrasts with the view held by sociologists, who "usually" (line 6) focus only on one influence or the other. Note the emphatic language in line 8: Abrams "insists" that sociologists embrace a model that is less one-sided, coming again to the notion of society affecting people as people affect society. This is the second time in one short paragraph that this two-way influence has been mentioned, so it definitely belongs in your Roadmap.

The second paragraph describes Abrams's views in greater detail. The long, jargon-filled sentence beginning at line 16 is easier to understand by putting it into context. Abrams believes that people affect history, and history affects people; the author is now restating that idea in slightly different terms, saying that our making of history is informed "not only" (line 17) by our own history, "but also" (line 18) by our identities as shaped by "contingencies." The rest of the paragraph describes what contingencies are and how they affect us. While you shouldn't delve too deeply into these details now, be sure to take note of their location; they'll almost certainly be the focus of at least one question.

The third paragraph delves more deeply into historical structuring, describing it as "manifold and unremitting" in line 32. If this is confusing, move on and look for Keywords that will help clear things up. "According to Abrams" in lines 35 to 45, the passage returns to a familiar dichotomy: Individuals can make history at crucial moments "not simply" (line 40) because they can act, "but also" (line 41) because specific social conditions have made their actions possible. Abrams concludes by providing a specific structure in which to understand these relationships beginning in line 45. Like the contingencies of the second paragraph, be ready to return to this information when the questions call for it, but don't waste your time memorizing it now.

This abrupt ending to the passage may seem surprising, but ultimately all the author seemed interested in was explaining Abrams's views on historical sociology. As always, stay focused on the big picture in a passage like this; don't succumb to the details, and be on the lookout for repetitious ideas.

---

[18]PrepTest 38, Sec 3, Passage 3

Topic: Historical sociology

Scope: Abrams's approach to historical sociology

Purpose: To describe Abrams's views on historical sociology

Main Idea: Abrams suggests that history is best understood by examining the relationships between individuals that make history and the history that affects those individuals.

1. **(D)**

    Which one of the following most accurately states the central idea of the passage?

    (A)   Abrams argues that historical sociology rejects the claims of sociologists who assert that the sociological concept of structuring cannot be applied to the interactions between individuals and history.

    (B)   Abrams argues that historical sociology assumes that, despite the views of sociologists to the contrary, history influences the social contingencies that affect individuals.

    (C)   Abrams argues that historical sociology demonstrates that, despite the views of sociologists to the contrary, social structures both influence and are influenced by the events of history.

    (D)   Abrams describes historical sociology as a discipline that unites two approaches taken by sociologists to studying the formation of societies and applies the resulting combined approach to the study of history.

    (E)   Abrams describes historical sociology as an attempt to compensate for the shortcomings of traditional historical methods by applying the methods established in sociology.[19]

Step 2: This is a Global question, as identified by the stem's request for a "central idea."

Step 3: No research is necessary.

Step 4: In summary: Abrams's view of historical sociology was that we should study the influence of people on history as well as history on people.

Step 5: Correct choice (D) describes Abrams's approach accurately. He does seek to unite the two approaches taken by sociologists (people make history, history makes people). Choice (A) contains a major distortion; the sociologists in the passage never make any claims about the

---

applicability of structuring. Choice (B) again gives a view to the sociologists that they don't express and distorts Abrams views to boot. Choice (C) is a bit more tricky, but it too distorts the views of the sociologists, who make no claims about "social structures" in this passage. Choice (E) is out of scope; Abrams is never described as compensating for history.

2. **(E)**

    Given the passage's argument, which one of the following sentences most logically completes the last paragraph?

    (A)   Only if they adhere to this structure, Abrams believes, can historical sociologists conclude with any certainty that the events that constitute the historical record are influenced by the actions of individuals.

    (B)   Only if they adhere to this structure, Abrams believes, will historical sociologists be able to counter the standard sociological assumption that there is very little connection between history and individual agency.

    (C)   Unless they can agree to adhere to this structure, Abrams believes, historical sociologists risk having their discipline treated as little more than an interesting but ultimately indefensible adjunct to history and sociology.

    (D)   By adhering to this structure, Abrams believes, historical sociologists can shed light on issues that traditional sociologists have chosen to ignore in their one-sided approaches to the formation of societies.

    (E)   By adhering to this structure, Abrams believes, historical sociologists will be able to better portray the complex connections between human agency and history.[20]

Step 2: This odd question type is a rare variety of Inference, since you are being asked to suggest a new idea that the author must agree with in order to complete the passage.

Step 3: Research this question on a Global-question scale; take notice that the author's primary goal was to describe Abrams's approach to his field, and the fourth paragraph begins by describing the relationships between human action and history before moving on to the fourfold approach Abrams offers to help sociologists understand these "mutual interactions" (line 46).

---

[20]PrepTest 38, Sec 3, Q 16

Step 4: The correct answer should provide a logical addendum to Abrams's thoughts. It is likely to mention the mutual interactions described in line 46, reaffirming that Abrams's approach to historical sociology will help sociologists understand them.

Step 5: Choice (E) correctly completes the author's thoughts, just as predicted. Choices (A), (B), and (C) are extreme; the author never portrays Abrams's approach as mandatory, and Abrams himself "recommends" (line 47) his approach rather than demanding it. Choice (D) distorts the views of the sociologists, suggesting that they've "chosen" to ignore issues. Once again, this harshness of tone does not fit with the author's neutral voice.

3. **(B)**

    The passage states that a contingency could be each of
    the following EXCEPT:
    (A)   a social phenomenon
    (B)   a form of historical structuring
    (C)   an accidental circumstance
    (D)   a condition controllable to some extent by an
           individual
    (E)   a partial determinant of an individual's actions[21]

Step 2: The question asks about what the passage "states." Such unequivocal language indicates a Detail question, or in this case, a Detail EXCEPT question.

Step 3: The stem asks which choice would not be considered a contingency. This leads you straight to the end of the third paragraph, starting at line 21, wherein the author defines a "contingency" as a social phenomenon over which we have varying degrees of control, then goes on to give a number of examples.

Step 4: Since the correct answer will not conform to the definition you just researched, you should proceed by process of elimination, expecting a correct answer choice that is out of scope.

Step 5: Choice (B) is the correct answer; contingencies are not defined as a form of historical structuring, a concept that was discussed earlier in the paragraph. All of the other choices are supported by the text; contingencies are defined as social phenomena that are both controlling and controlled by a person's actions and may include accidental circumstances.

---

[21]PrepTest 38, Sec 3, Passage 3, Q 17

4. **(A)**

Which one of the following is most analogous to the ideal work of a historical sociologist as outlined by Abrams?

(A)   In a report on the enactment of a bill into law, a journalist explains why the need for the bill arose, sketches the biography of the principal legislator who wrote the bill, and ponders the effect that the bill's enactment will have both on society and on the legislator's career.

(B)   In a consultation with a patient, a doctor reviews the patient's medical history, suggests possible reasons for the patient's current condition, and recommends steps that the patient should take in the future to ensure that the condition improves or at least does not get any worse.

(C)   In an analysis of a historical novel, a critic provides information to support the claim that details of the work's setting are accurate, explains why the subject of the novel was of particular interest to the author, and compares the novel with some of the author's other books set in the same period.

(D)   In a presentation to stockholders, a corporation's chief executive officer describes the corporation's most profitable activities during the past year, introduces the vice president largely responsible for those activities, and discusses new projects the vice president will initiate in the coming year.

(E)   In developing a film based on a historical event, a filmmaker conducts interviews with participants in the event, bases part of the film's screenplay on the interviews, and concludes the screenplay with a sequence of scenes speculating on the outcome of the event had certain details been different.[22]

Step 2: The word "analogous" is your clue; this is a Parallel Reasoning question.

Step 3: The "ideal work" most likely refers to Abrams's recommended four-step approach at the end of the passage. Abrams believes, starting at line 49 with the Keyword "first," that a historical sociologist should describe an event, discuss its context in history, summarize the historical figure involved, and finally examine consequences for the individual and history.

---

[22]PrepTest 38, Sec 3, Passage 3, Q 18

Step 4: The correct answer will adhere to the general format of Abrams's approach without referencing the same specific subject matter. Evaluate the choices with this in mind.

Step 5: Choice (A) is a perfect match. In it, the journalist describes events that prompted the bill, the author of the bill, and the bill's likely effect on both history and the author. Choice (B) doesn't reflect this two-way relationship, describing the strictly one-way dictates of the doctor to the patient. Choice (C) brings in an out-of-scope comparison between the author's novel and other books. Choices (D) and (E) are similarly out of scope, failing to describe events that fall within the context of an event and the human agent that affects and is affected by the event.

CHALLENGING PASSAGES ARE VULNERABLE TO STRATEGY

Take a deep breath. You've just worked through a couple of very challenging examples, and you should be proud of your diligence. A lot of ideas were presented in this chapter; most of them were review, but I want to summarize the main points so that you have them at hand as you practice.

Read Predictively

Challenging passages often present excellent contextual information in the first paragraph. Read predictively, building a sense of structure as you go. This will help you understand the more abstract ideas in the passage.

> Many legal theorists have argued that the only
> morally legitimate goal in imposing criminal penalties
> against certain behaviors is to prevent people from
> harming others. Clearly, such theorists would oppose
> (5) laws that force people to act purely for their own
> good or to refrain from certain harmless acts purely
> to ensure conformity to some social norm. But the
> goal of preventing harm to others would also justify
> legal sanctions against some forms of nonconforming
> (10) behavior to which this goal might at first seem not to
> apply.[23]

Recall that the two complicated paragraphs following this one served no other purpose than to illustrate the concept described in the highlighted sentence. It's much easier to understand the author's potentially confusing examples if you know that they *must* provide support for this much more simply stated idea.

---

[23]PrepTest 46, Sec 1, Passage 4

Look for Repetition

Many tough passages are extremely repetitive. Learn to recognize when the author is using different terms to repeat the same idea.

In many situations it is in the interest of each
member of a group to agree to behave in a certain
way on the condition that the others similarly agree.
(15) In the simplest cases, a mere coordination of
activities is itself the good that results. For example,
it is in no one's interest to lack a convention about
which side of the road to drive on, and each person
can agree to drive on one side assuming the others do
(20) too. Any fair rule, then, would be better than no rule
at all. On the assumption that all people would
voluntarily agree to be subject to a coordination rule
backed by criminal sanctions, if people could be
assured that others would also agree, it is argued to
(25) be legitimate for a legislature to impose such a rule.
This is because prevention of harm underlies the
rationale for the rule, though it applies to the problem
of coordination less directly than to other problems,
for the act that is forbidden (driving on the other side
(30) of the road) is not inherently harm-producing, as are
burglary and assault; instead, it is the lack of a
coordinating rule that would be harmful.[24]

While each of these sentences serves a slightly different purpose in the paragraph, they all center around the same idea: Sometimes it's a good idea to make everyone do the same thing.

Use Examples to Clarify

Resist the urge to pore over every detail, but at the same time, recognize that an abstractly worded idea may be clarified by more concrete examples provided by the author. Be prepared to use such examples to help you understand the author's Main Idea if necessary.

In some other situations involving a need for
legally enforced coordination, the harm to be averted
(35) goes beyond the simple lack of coordination itself.
This can be illustrated by an example of a
coordination rule—instituted by a private athletic
organization—which has analogies in criminal law. At
issue is whether the use of anabolic steroids, which
(40) build muscular strength but have serious negative side
effects, should be prohibited.[25]

---

[24]PrepTest 46, Sec 1, Passage 4
[25]PrepTest 46, Sec 1, Passage 4

Even the most well-prepared test taker could be forgiven for finding the first sentence of this paragraph confusing. But if it "can be illustrated by an example," and the example is a straightforward one (most readers will be familiar with the steroid ban in sports), use the example to help you clarify the issue.

Keep Moving

The most common mistake that my students make when faced with a difficult passage is to slow to a crawl and attempt to understand every word, when the author's principle conclusion can be summed up in a short sentence. If the text you're reading is hopelessly unclear, review your Roadmap and move forward to find a better sense of context.

In some other situations involving a need for legally enforced coordination, the harm to be averted
(35)   goes beyond the simple lack of coordination itself. This can be illustrated by an example of a coordination rule—instituted by a private athletic organization—which has analogies in criminal law. At issue is whether the use of anabolic steroids, which
(40)   build muscular strength but have serious negative side effects, should be prohibited. Each athlete has at stake both an interest in having a fair opportunity to win and an interest in good health. If some competitors use steroids, others have the option of either
(45)   endangering their health or losing their fair opportunity to win. Thus they would be harmed either way. A compulsory rule could prevent that harm and thus would be in the interest of all competitors. If they understand its function and trust the techniques
(50)   for its enforcement, they will gladly consent to it. So while it might appear that such a rule merely forces people to act for their own good, the deeper rationale for coercion here—as in the above example—is a somewhat complex appeal to the legitimacy of
(55)   enforcing a rule with the goal of preventing harm.[26]

Note how the final sentence neatly sums up the entire paragraph. If the steroid-ban example didn't clarify the author's goals for you, this brief conclusion certainly will, particularly because it references the concept of "preventing harm." This idea should look familiar—it's part of the author's Main Idea and should already be in your Roadmap by the time you reach this paragraph.

---

[26]PrepTest 46, Sec 1, Passage 4

Stay Confident

Finally, and most importantly, don't let the pressure of a challenging passage lead you to abandon the Kaplan Method. Stay in control of the passage and approach it the right way; remember that confidence leads to a higher score.

REVIEW, REVIEW, REVIEW

I would strongly encourage you to review all of the examples in this chapter. Dealing with tough passages efficiently takes practice and often will require you to more thoroughly review your work. When you're ready, move on to the next chapter, where I'll be leading you through some examples of odd variations on familiar question types.

CHAPTER 16

UNUSUAL QUESTIONS

RARE VARIATIONS ON COMMON QUESTIONS

Now that you've become familiar with the common Reading Comprehension question types that you'll see on test day, I hope their predictability has boosted your confidence. With only five common question types and proven Kaplan strategies to counter each one, Reading Comprehension is revealed to be very limited, and therefore very manageable.

That said, the test makers will occasionally write questions that at first glance don't appear to fit neatly into a single category or that present a common task in an unusual way. These unusual questions can be worrisome. My students frequently ask me about such questions in a state of near-panic, concerned that the predictability of the test has become suspect, and fearful that their LSAT will be full of strange tasks they've never seen before and that they are completely unprepared to deal with.

I tell them the same thing I'll tell you—that unusual questions are nothing to fear. First of all, by definition they don't appear often on the test (otherwise they wouldn't be unusual questions). Second, while these questions may look bizarre initially, they can always be reduced to variations on common types with which you're already familiar. And this means that, like all LSAT questions, they are amenable to the Kaplan Method.

My students eventually learn to stay calm and methodical when they encounter strange-looking questions, once they understand that such questions aren't very different from questions they've already mastered. That's the primary lesson I want you to take away from this chapter: Although the occasional odd question will appear on the test, if you confidently apply the

Kaplan Method, you will score the point. Every question has an answer, and all the information you need is *always* in the passage.

Before I present some specific examples, I want to point out that in this chapter I'll be focusing more on specific question variations than on strategic reading. For this reason, you'll see shorter excerpts from passages rather than complete Roadmaps. Please remember that in your practice you should *always* create a Roadmap for every passage you read just as you will on test day.

Common Questions in Disguise

An exhaustive list of every unusual question to appear on the LSAT would be very hard to compile, and rather subjective as well. A better way to prepare for such questions is to learn how to properly apply the Kaplan Method to any unusual situation. In fact, you've already seen examples of such questions in previous chapters of this book.

3. Which one of the following titles most completely summarizes the content of the passage?

   (A) "Avenues for Change: The Case for Dissent in Authoritarian Regimes"
   (B) "Human Rights Abuses under Authoritarian Regimes: A Case Study"
   (C) "Democratic Coalitions under Authoritarian Regimes: Strategies and Solutions"
   (D) "Why Authoritarian Regimes Compromise: An Examination of Societal Forces"
   (E) "Growing Pains: Economic Instability in Countries on the Brink of Democracy"[1]

The question stem asks you to select an appropriate title for the passage. What function does the title of a work serve? Ideally, it should briefly encapsulate the author's thesis. In LSAT terms, it should reflect the author's Main Idea. So, this question is just a Global question in disguise, which you may recall first seeing in chapter 10.

You might have been surprised by the wording of this question when you initially encountered it, but it probably didn't take you very long to understand what it was really asking for. Here's another example, this time from chapter 15:

16. Given the passage's argument, which one of the following sentences most logically completes the last paragraph?[2]

---

[1]PrepTest 34, Sec 1, Q 3
[2]PrepTest 38, Sec 3, Q 16

The stem asks you to select an appropriate ending for the final paragraph of a passage. Once again, take a moment to think through the task. The last sentence should logically complete the author's thoughts, bringing the paragraph to a tidy conclusion. Since the stem asks you to infer what new information could appropriately be added to the passage, this is simply a rare form of Inference question.

In order to determine what would logically follow, you should go back to the text and think about what the author's goals were in the final paragraph. Review the paragraph and note any Keywords, as always:

> In Abrams's analysis, historical structuring, like social structuring, is manifold and unremitting. To understand it, historical sociologists must extract from it certain significant episodes, or events, that their
> (35) methodology can then analyze and interpret. According to Abrams, these events are points at which action and contingency meet, points that represent a cross section of the specific social and individual forces in play at a given time. At such moments, individuals stand forth
> (40) as agents of history not simply because they possess a unique ability to act, but also because in them we see the force of the specific social conditions that allowed their actions to come forth. Individuals can "make their mark" on history, yet in individuals one also finds the
> (45) convergence of wider social forces. In order to capture the various facets of this mutual interaction, Abrams recommends a fourfold structure to which he believes the investigations of historical sociologists should conform: first, description of the event itself; second,
> (50) discussion of the social context that helped bring the event about and gave it significance; third, summary of the life history of the individual agent in the event; and fourth, analysis of the consequences of the event both for history and for the individual.[3]

Abrams emphatically states that historical sociologists "must extract" significant episodes from history and then elaborates on why this is the case, focusing on the importance of the relationship between events and individuals. He then "recommends a fourfold structure" that he believes others should adhere to. This paragraph is all about Abrams's recommendations. The correct answer should reflect this, reemphasizing the importance of the structured approach Abrams lays out.

---

[3]PrepTest 38, Sec 3, Passage 3

16. Given the passage's argument, which one of the following sentences most logically completes the last paragraph?

   (A)   Only if they adhere to this structure, Abrams believes, can historical sociologists conclude with any certainty that the events that constitute the historical record are influenced by the actions of individuals.

   (B)   Only if they adhere to this structure, Abrams believes, will historical sociologists be able to counter the standard sociological assumption that there is very little connection between history and individual agency.

   (C)   Unless they can agree to adhere to this structure, Abrams believes, historical sociologists risk having their discipline treated as little more than an interesting but ultimately indefensible adjunct to history and sociology.

   (D)   By adhering to this structure, Abrams believes, historical sociologists can shed light on issues that traditional sociologists have chosen to ignore in their one-sided approaches to the formation of societies.

   (E)   By adhering to this structure, Abrams believes, historical sociologists will be able to better portray the complex connections between human agency and history.[4]

The only answer choice that connects Abrams's recommendations back to a better understanding of history is correct choice (E).

The examples you've seen so far may be somewhat unusual, but you could ultimately identify each one as belonging to one of the five common question types. However, other questions might seem to defy such simple categorization. In any case, every question you see on the LSAT will present tasks that you've seen before. As long as you read each question carefully and think about what clues will lead you to the correct answer, the familiar process of research and prediction will allow you to score the point.

Here's another example, this time in terms of the Kaplan Method:

15. Which one of the following persons displays an approach that most strongly suggests sympathy with the principles of reader-response theory?[5]

Step 2: Identify the Question Type

You're asked to identify a person who behaves in accordance with the principles of reader-response theory. Hopefully you recognized this as a variant of Parallel Reasoning, since the correct answer should be in some way analogous to the theory as it's presented in the passage.

---

[4]PrepTest 38, Sec 3Q16
[5]PrepTest 43, Sec 1, Passage 3

Step 3: Research the Relevant Text

Review the following text:

> Reader-response theory, a type of literary theory
> that arose in reaction to formalist literary criticism,
> has endeavored to shift the emphasis in the
> interpretation of literature from the text itself to the
> (5) contributions of readers to the meaning of a text.
> According to literary critics who endorse reader-
> response theory, the literary text alone renders no
> meaning; it acquires meaning only when encountered
> by individual readers, who always bring varying
> (10) presuppositions and ways of reading to bear on the
> text, giving rise to the possibility—even probability—
> of varying interpretations.[6]

Reader-response theory suggests that the meaning of a text is derived not from the author, but from the reader. In fact, it claims that the text alone "renders no meaning" (lines 7–8) and that a work will likely give rise to varying interpretations based on the assumptions supplied by readers.

Step 4: Make a Prediction

What kind of person would sympathize with reader response theory? Simply put, someone who believes that his or her interpretation of a work is valuable, possible more valuable than the original work itself. The correct answer should reflect this idea in some way.

Step 5: Evaluate the Answer Choices

15. Which one of the following persons displays an approach that most strongly suggests sympathy with the principles of reader-response theory?

    (A) a translator who translates a poem from Spanish to English word for word so that its original meaning is not distorted

    (B) a music critic who insists that early music can be truly appreciated only when it is played on original instruments of the period

    (C) a reviewer who finds in the works of a novelist certain unifying themes that reveal the novelist's personal concerns and preoccupations

    (D) a folk artist who uses conventional cultural symbols and motifs as a way of conveying commonly understood meanings

    (E) a director who sets a play by Shakespeare in nineteenth-century Japan to give a new perspective on the work[7]

---

[6]PrepTest 43, Sec 1, Passage 3
[7]PrepTest 43, Sec 1, Passage 3, Q 15

Correct choice (E) is the match. The director takes the work of another author and reinterprets it, which is very much in line with reader-response theory. Choices (A) and (B) run contrary to your prediction—they insist on conformity to aspects of an original work. Choice (C) is similarly off the mark, as it is concerned with divining the ideas of a work's author. Choice (D) goes out of Scope in describing a process of writing rather than a method of interpretation.

Once again, an unusual question proves to be vulnerable to critical thinking and the Kaplan Method.

Convoluted Question Stems

Sometimes a question stem may seem too complicated or wordy to deal with efficiently. Here is an example:

23. Suppose that pesticide X drastically slows the reproductive rate of cyclamen mites and has no other direct effect on cyclamen mites or *Typhlodromus*. Based on the information in the passage, which one of the following would most likely have occurred if, in the experiments mentioned in the passage, pesticide X had been used instead of parathion, with all other conditions affecting the experiments remaining the same?[8]

I want to stress once more how important it is not to be intimidated by a question like this one. Read the stem carefully, think about what you're being asked, and proceed through the Kaplan Method.

Step 2: This is an Inference question, since the stem asks what "would most likely have occurred" in a given situation. You are given some additional hypothetical information to consider: A pesticide slows the reproduction of cyclamen mites. What would have to be true if, in an experiment, this new pesticide had been used instead of parathion?

Step 3: Read the following excerpt from the passage, which details the experiment referenced in the question:

Greenhouse experiments have verified the importance of *Typhlodromus* predation for keeping
(40) cyclamen mites in check. One group of strawberry plants was stocked with both predator and prey mites; a second group was kept predator-free by regular application of parathion, an insecticide that kills the predatory species but does not affect the cyclamen
(45) mite. Throughout the study, populations of cyclamen mites remained low in plots shared with *Typhlodromus*, but their infestation attained significantly damaging proportions on predator-free plants.[9]

---

[8]PrepTest 53, Sec 4, Q 23
[9]PrepTest 53, Sec 4, Passage 4

The experiment demonstrates that a certain kind of predator mite, *Typhlodromus*, is useful in controlling the population of cyclamen mites. When parathion was used to control the predators, cyclamen mites reproduced to damaging levels.

Step 4: Now think through the hypothetical provided by the question stem and make a prediction. What if the experimenters used pesticide X, which slows the reproductive rate of cyclamen mites, instead of parathion? You would expect to see a drop in the number of cyclamen mites on the plants treated with pesticide X. There is evidence that the cyclamen mites will also be subject to control by predation, since the new pesticide doesn't negatively affect the *Typhlodromus* mites. In sum, you should predict that the use of pesticide X would result in control of the cyclamen mite population.

Step 5:

23. Suppose that pesticide X drastically slows the reproductive rate of cyclamen mites and has no other direct effect on cyclamen mites or *Typhlodromus*. Based on the information in the passage, which one of the following would most likely have occurred if, in the experiments mentioned in the passage, pesticide X had been used instead of parathion, with all other conditions affecting the experiments remaining the same?

    (A) In both treated and untreated plots inhabited by both *Typhlodromus* and cyclamen mites, the latter would have been effectively controlled.

    (B) Cyclamen mite populations in all treated plots from which *Typhlodromus* was absent would have been substantially lower than in untreated plots inhabited by both kinds of mites.

    (C) In the treated plots, slowed reproduction in cyclamen mites would have led to a loss of reproductive synchrony between *Typhlodromus* and cyclamen mites.

    (D) In the treated plots, *Typhlodromus* populations would have decreased temporarily and would have eventually increased.

    (E) In the treated plots, cyclamen mite populations would have reached significantly damaging levels more slowly, but would have remained at those levels longer, than in untreated plots.[10]

The prediction should lead you directly to correct choice (A). Since the new pesticide controls cyclamen mites while leaving its predators unharmed, cyclamen mites should be controlled in all cases. Choice (B) is extreme, suggesting without warrant that the new pesticide would be more effective in controlling cyclamen mites than natural predation—which might be true, but doesn't necessarily have to be. Choices (D) and (E) similarly cannot be inferred with available information, and choice (C) is completely out of scope.

No matter how complicated the question stem may seem at first glance, the task is always there for you to discover, provided that you approach every question methodically. Here's one more example of a complicated-looking question:

> 20. Suppose a study is conducted that measures the amount of airtime allotted to imported television programming in the daily broadcasting schedules of several developing nations. Given the information in the passage, the results of that study would be most directly relevant to answering which one of the following questions?[11]

Step 2: A hypothetical study is presented, and you are asked to determine what question this study might best help to answer. The question type may seem unclear, but the correct answer must be the one that falls within the scope of the proposed study; you're looking for what the study would be "most directly relevant" in answering. Since the answer choices will present a series of hypothetical questions that were never mentioned in the passage, you're essentially being asked to identify new information that is compatible with the text. You can therefore think of this as an Inference question. Use these clues to guide you as you apply Step 3 of the Kaplan Method.

Step 3: The first paragraph is helpful in finding the answer to this question:

> Specialists in international communications almost unanimously assert that the broadcasting in developing nations of television programs produced by industrialized countries amounts to cultural
> (5) imperialism: the phenomenon of one culture's productions overwhelming another's, to the detriment of the flourishing of the latter. This assertion assumes the automatic dominance of the imported productions and their negative effect on the domestic culture. But
> (10) the assertion is polemical and abstract, based on little or no research into the place held by imported programs in the economies of importing countries or in the lives of viewers.[12]

Whether the author agrees with these specialists, the passage presents the view that the broadcasting of foreign programs into developing nations presents that nation with new cultural productions (which may or may not be a form of cultural imperialism).

---

[11]PrepTest 51, Sec 2, Q 20
[12]PrepTest 51, Sec 2, Passage 3

Step 4: Since all you know for sure is that the nations in question are receiving new cultural products, a study that examines how much outside broadcasting is allowed in a particular nation would be useful in determining, in part, how much exposure that nation gets to such cultural products.

Step 5:

20. Suppose a study is conducted that measures the amount of airtime allotted to imported television programming in the daily broadcasting schedules of several developing nations. Given the information in the passage, the results of that study would be most directly relevant to answering which one of the following questions?

    (A) How does the access to imported cultural productions differ among these nations?
    (B) What are the individual viewing habits of citizens in these nations?
    (C) How influential are the domestic television industries in these nations?
    (D) Do imported programs attract larger audiences than domestic ones in these nations?
    (E) What model best describes the relationship between imported cultural influences and domestic culture in these nations?[13]

The correct answer, choice (A), matches the prediction. Choices (B) and (C) fall out of scope by introducing individual viewing habits and domestic television industries, neither of which are relevant to the experiment described in the question stem. Choices (D) and (E) present irrelevant comparisons—the information in the passage doesn't provide the sort of detailed information about imported vs. domestic culture that would be required to make either of these choices correct.

When faced with a wordy question stem, particularly one that presents you with hypothetical information, it is crucial that you take your time when executing Step 2 of the Kaplan Method. As always, all the information you need to answer the question is provided, but the more complex the stem, the more opportunities there are to misunderstand what the question is asking or to overlook a key piece of information. Don't let the pressure of the clock interfere with your thinking when you approach this type of question—be sure you've understood what the question asks you, and carefully follow each step of the method.

---

[13]PrepTest 51, Sec 2, Q 20

Challenging Research

You know that some questions provide more precise research clues than others. Compare these questions:

4. Which one of the following is presented by the author as evidence of controlled burning in the tropics before the arrival of Europeans?[14]

6. As evidence for the routine practice of forest burning by native populations before the arrival of Europeans, the author cites all of the following EXCEPT:[15]

These two Detail questions give you the same essential task, but question 6 presents a potentially greater research challenge—since detail EXCEPT questions require you to identify the single piece of information that *doesn't* appear in the passage, you may have to reexamine several portions of the text to eliminate incorrect answers. Because EXCEPT questions are not as amenable to simple prediction, they can also be time-consuming.

The challenge of complex research can also present itself in other types of questions. Here's one example:

22. The logical relationship of lines 8–13 of the passage to lines 23–25 and 49–53 of the passage is most accurately described as[16]

By itself, this question may look so abstract as to defy solution. As always, you'll find the solution by applying the Kaplan Method.

Step 2: The question asks for a "logical relationship" between various sections of the passage. This question is likely asking about structure, and it resembles a Logic Function question since it requires you to identify what role specific parts of the text play.

Step 3: Take a look at the quoted portions of the text. Start with lines 8–13:

> But the
> (10) practical benefits of such automated reasoning
> systems have fallen short of optimistic early
> predictions and have not resulted in computer systems
> that can independently provide expert advice about
> substantive law.[17]

---

[14]PrepTest 38, Sec 3, Q 4

[15]PrepTest 38, Sec 3, Q 6

[16]PrepTest 51, Sec 2, Q 22

[17]PrepTest 51, Sec 2, Passage 4

This portion of the text describes the shortcomings of certain kinds of computer systems despite predictions to the contrary. Now examine lines 23–25:

> Such systems underestimated the
> problems of interpretation that can arise at every
> (25) stage of a legal argument.[18]

This appears to be supporting evidence for the shortcomings described earlier. Similar evidence appears in lines 49–53:

> Unfortunately, in the case-based systems
> (50) currently in development, the criteria for similarity
> among cases are system dependent and fixed by the
> designer, so that similarity is found only by testing
> for the presence or absence of predefined factors.[19]

Even if you don't understand all the jargon, the Keyword "unfortunately" at the beginning would indicate that the case-based systems are disappointing in some respect.

Step 4: Although a fair amount of research was required, you're now in a good place to make a prediction. The first quoted sentence described a problem with certain computer systems, and the following two quotes provided illustrations of the problem.

Step 5:

22. The logical relationship of lines 8–13 of the passage to lines 23–25 and 49–53 of the passage is most accurately described as

    (A) a general assertion supported by two specific observations
    (B) a general assertion followed by two arguments, one of which supports and one of which refutes the general assertion
    (C) a general assertion that entails two more specific assertions
    (D) a theoretical assumption refuted by two specific observations
    (E) a specific observation that suggests two incompatible generalizations[20]

Choice (A), the correct answer, gives an excellent general description that matches the prediction. Choice (B) incorrectly identifies the supporting evidence as arguments, and choice (C) suggests that that the two pieces of evidence follow from the assertion—a 180, since the evidence supports the claim, not vice versa. The refutation mentioned in choice (D) never occurred, and neither do the two incompatible generalizations mentioned in choice (E).

---

[18]PrepTest 51, Sec 2, Passage 4
[19]PrepTest 51, Sec 2, Passage 4
[20]PrepTest 51, Sec 2, Q 22

Take a moment to appreciate how quickly the Kaplan Method allowed you to transform this very abstract-looking question into a simple, familiar task. Once you identified the language of a Logic Function question in Step 2 and conducted proper research in Step 3, a prediction was not far behind.

Now for one final example. In the previous example, your research was spread out over the passage, but specific line references made the task much easier. Sometimes the question won't provide such straightforward clues:

> 6. Which one of the following aspects of Mphahlele's work does the author of the passage appear to value most highly?[21]

Step 2: This is an Inference question, albeit an oddly worded one. The stem asks for the author's attitude, specifically the aspect of Mphahlele's work that the author is most interested in.

Step 3: A scan for Keywords of emphasis across the passage will tell you where the author's primary interest lies. Examine the following excerpts:

> Critics have variously
> decried the former as too fictionalized and the latter
> as too autobiographical, but those who focus on
> (15) traditional labels inevitably miss the fact that
> Mphahlele manipulates different prose forms purely
> in the service of the social message he
> advances.

> But his greater concern is the social vision
> that pervades his work, though it too is prone to
> (35) misunderstandings and underappreciation.

> As
> he claims, the whole point of the exercise of writing
> has nothing to do with classification; in all forms
> writing is the transmission of ideas, and important
> (55) ideas at that: "Whenever you write prose or poetry or
> drama you are writing a social criticism of one kind
> or another. If you don't, you are completely
> irrelevant—you don't count."[22]

Step 4: In each of the above quotes, the author emphasizes Mphahlele's devotion to social commentary in his work.

---

[21]PrepTest 51, Sec 2, Q 6
[22]PrepTest 51, Sec 2, Passage 1

Step 5:

6. Which one of the following aspects of Mphahlele's work does the author of the passage appear to value most highly?

    (A) his commitment to communicating social messages

    (B) his blending of the categories of fiction and autobiography

    (C) his ability to redefine established literary categories

    (D) his emphasis on the importance of details

    (E) his plan for bringing about the future he envisions[23]

Only correct choice (A) mentions the importance of social commentary. Choice (B) is a distortion; the author does mention Mphahlele's blending of categories, but only because they don't impede his ability to communicate social messages. Choice (C) also distorts the author's ideas, since the redefining of categories is not mentioned. Choice (D) presents the out of Scope idea of the importance of details, and choice (E) is extreme—Mphahlele is described as having a "social vision," but there is no mention of any plan to fulfill such a vision.

This question represents only a slight variation on author's-attitude questions you've seen before. As always, the author's primary concerns will be identified by plenty of Keywords. Methodical attention to these Keywords will make short work of what might at first appear to be a time-consuming research task.

THE KAPLAN METHOD ALWAYS APPLIES

It isn't within anyone's power to predict exactly how the test makers will phrase the questions on the LSAT. You should expect the majority of the Reading Comprehension questions you see on your test to look very familiar to the ones you most commonly see in your practice. Nonetheless, you must also be prepared for the occasional oddly worded stem. As you've learned, most of these questions are variations of familiar types, and all of them—without exception—are amenable to the Kaplan Method. If you encounter an unfamiliar-looking question on test day, don't panic—read the stem carefully, use the clues the test makers provide you, and apply the Kaplan Method with care. Every question has a correct answer, and the information you need is *always* there.

[23]PrepTest 51, Sec 2, Q 6

CHAPTER 17

RECENT TRENDS

READING COMPREHENSION REMAINS PREDICTABLE

You've now learned everything you need to know about Kaplan's Method for Reading Comprehension, and you've applied what you've learned to a variety of LSAT passages and questions. A major theme throughout this book has been the predictability of the LSAT in general and the Reading Comprehension section in particular. Before you move on to Part III, I'd like to share a little information with you about the composition of recent tests and what this means for your test day experience.

The great news is that very little has changed in LSAT Reading Comprehension over the last few years, and a passage randomly selected from a test administered ten years ago is very much like a passage from the last few years. The essential composition of the section—that is, four exercises representing humanities, social sciences, natural sciences, and law—has remained the same. There have been a few observable changes of note, and the most obvious one is the recent addition of comparative reading.

Comparative Reading

As you learned in chapter 9, comparative reading was first introduced in the June 2007 administration of the LSAT. Since then, exactly one set of paired passages has appeared in each Reading Comprehension section. This came as no surprise, as the LSAC formally announced this change months in advance of its occurrence, providing a sample passage and question set on their official website immediately following the February 2007 test.

No strong trends have emerged regarding the placement of the comparative reading section. Among the released LSATs as of the time of this writing there are examples of the comparative passages appearing first, second, third, and fourth within the section. Given the small number of paired passages that have been released (twelve disclosed pairs at the end of 2010) it's difficult to say how the distribution of the paired passages will trend in the coming years.

A slightly stronger trend has emerged regarding the subject area of comparative reading. Of the eleven passage pairs available at the time of writing, six have been written about the natural sciences, two about the social sciences, two about humanities, and one about law. This makes natural science comparative passages representative of just over half of the disclosed pairs through the October 2010 administration of the LSAT. While this by no means guarantees that the comparative reading on your LSAT will deal with the natural sciences, it may indicate a preference on the part of the test makers. What is most important for you to note is that there have been passage pairs representing each of the four subject areas, so you should be prepared to see any one of them on test day.

It's also worth noting that comparative passages tend to feature relatively high numbers of Logic Function, Logic Reasoning, and Inference questions. Because these question types are generally considered more challenging than Global and Detail questions, comparative passages are usually considered to be more difficult than an average single passage. This is useful to know when you consider how to best manage an entire Reading Comprehension section. I'll go into greater detail about section management in the next chapter.

Section Difficulty

As Kaplan continues to collect data from students taking practice sections and previously released LSATs, trends also emerge regarding the difficulty (both real and perceived) of the Reading Comprehension section as a whole.

It is interesting (and hopefully reassuring) to note that our students have generally reported that they considered the Reading Comprehension sections of their tests to be of lower difficulty in the last three years than in the years immediately preceding. In 2010, of Kaplan students taking the December, September, and June tests, a range of 22% to 37% reported that they considered Reading Comprehension to be the most challenging section. These percentages have declined significantly since 2007, during which there was a significant spike in the perceived difficulty of Reading Comprehension which peaked at 47% of students—nearly half of those reporting—identifying this section as the most challenging of their exam in December of 2007.

There are two interesting facts that, once again, suggest that Reading Comprehension hasn't actually changed very much in difficulty over the years. One is that as our students take previously released LSATs under timed conditions, the overall difficulty level of Reading Comprehension sections as a whole (as determined by percentage of questions answered correctly vs. incorrectly) has remained very consistent over the last five years. The other thing to note is that the spike in perceived difficulty of the test began with the June 2007 administration of the LSAT—the first time that comparative reading appeared. By December of 2008 a significantly smaller percentage of our students (only 30% for the December 2008 test) reported that they considered Reading Comprehension to be the most difficult LSAT section. It's therefore a definite possibility that students perceived the section to be more difficult in 2007–2008 because of the relative newness of comparative reading.

Taken all together, this data suggests a disparity between how our students *perceive* the difficulty of the section and how difficult it actually is. This should serve to remind you just how important confidence is to your LSAT score. No matter how challenging a section or passage may seem to you, it isn't likely to deviate in a significant way from what you've already seen in your practice. The familiarity you gain through practice is one of your most powerful advantages on test day—remember to trust in what you've learned.

Question Trends

Once again, the composition of question types from test to test is extremely predictable, and there haven't been many notable shifts in either the overall difficulty of the questions or the types of questions appearing. At the time of this writing, every released practice test in the last three years has contained 27 Reading Comprehension questions. Averaged out, each passage will come with about seven questions (although the actual range will always be between five to eight questions).

From 2008 to the present, an average Reading Comprehension section comprised approximately four Global questions, five Detail questions, five Logic Function questions, five Logic Reasoning questions, and eight Inference questions. These numbers are fairly representative of older LSATs as well, although there has been a very slight increase in the number of Inference and Reasoning questions over the last ten years. More than anything, this should remind you that the test makers seek to reward your ability to think critically about the information in the passage much more than your ability to repeat details. This makes strategic reading that much more crucial to the overall health of your LSAT score.

It's also important to note that, of the questions most often missed by our students in their reported practice on recent tests, the majority are Inference questions. This is probably partially due to the larger number of such questions appearing on a given test, and because they tend to be more challenging than Global and Detail questions; in any case, a thorough review of Inference questions is advisable for any LSAT student. Keep this in mind as you review the full-length practice sections coming up a bit later in this book.

Stick to the Kaplan Method

There have been a few other smaller trends—Parallel Reasoning questions have made a bit of a comeback in the last five years, for example—but on the whole the Reading Comprehension section of 2010 is very, very similar to the section of 2005, with the exception of comparative reading. The Kaplan Method has been an effective approach to the Reading Comprehension regardless of small changes in the composition of the section, and careful research has allowed us to adapt it to fit the larger ones. The questions and passages that you've seen in this book are representative of the ones you'll see on test day, and the full-length practice sections you'll complete in Part III of this book are from recently administered tests. Reading Comprehension is not likely to hold any big surprises for you when you take your LSAT. Keep this in mind as you continue to practice, and let it motivate you to stick to the strategies that have proven to be effective.

PART III

FULL-LENGTH SECTION PRACTICE

CHAPTER 18

TIMING AND SECTION MANAGEMENT IN A NUTSHELL

TAKE CONTROL OF THE SECTION

If you've made it this far, you've learned everything you need to know about Reading Comprehension passages, the kinds of questions you'll encounter on test day, and how to apply the Kaplan Method to all of them. You've learned a whole new way of reading and you've internalized the strategies you require to score the points. This is a fantastic accomplishment, and I congratulate you for your perseverance and dedication.

Now it's time to start thinking about the bigger picture and learn how to effectively approach an entire Reading Comprehension section. Just as you might think about the LSAT as a series of five individual mini-tests (six if you include the Writing Sample), you can also think of a single Reading Comprehension section as a set of four distinct challenges. In this chapter, I'll give you some general guidelines to follow as you take on these challenges.

When you first began to learn the Kaplan Method, you may have thought it impossible to read the passages in the time allotted. As you became more familiar with the predictable nature of the passages, you learned that by reading in an active, purposeful way, you can efficiently focus on the right information. You learned how to take control of the passages.

Similarly, you might have found the questions confusing and the answer choices abstract and difficult to deal with. If you're like the majority of my students, you were almost certainly answering most questions by a laborious process of elimination, evaluating the answer choices without a clear idea of what you were looking for. Now you understand the tasks that the questions present you, and you know how to approach them actively, answering the questions efficiently and accurately. In this way, you take control of the questions.

Now you must take everything you've learned and use it to take control of the entire section. Without this sense of control, the pressure of the clock will always work against you in unpredictable ways. To help you begin countering this problem, I'll introduce you to some basic principles, then move on to specific strategies that deal with passage and question selection.

GENERAL TIMING PRINCIPLES
Efficiency vs. Speed

I've been very careful throughout this book to use the word "efficient" when describing the merits of a time-saving strategy, and I've used this word for a very specific reason. To score your best on the LSAT, you must accomplish the tasks it presents you with efficiently, but this is very different from simply doing things quickly.

Efficiency is all about saving time while still doing everything you need to do in order to score points. For example, Step 1 of the Kaplan Method is focused on efficiency. By staying focused on the big picture as you read and by focusing on the author's main ideas (and refusing to dwell on details), you ultimately read more efficiently. At the same time, you circle and think about Keywords, write a solid Roadmap, and ask predictive questions of the passage as you move from paragraph to paragraph.

You might think that you can save even more time by skipping the Roadmap or making a mental note of Keywords instead of actually circling them, but this is a classic example of favoring speed over efficiency. If you ignore the crucial elements of the Kaplan Method, it is certainly possible that you'll spend less time reading the passage, but the consequences would outweigh any time gained. You're much less likely to have a sound understanding of the author's Purpose and Main Idea, making Global questions cumbersome and difficult to answer. Without a Roadmap to guide you, you'll find it harder to research relevant text, and may be tempted to rely on your memory too much when answering questions (a very risky thing to do). Not only will you have sacrificed accuracy in the question set, but any time you gained by careless reading will likely be lost as you struggle to answer the questions without a solid grasp of the passage.

The same principles apply to individual questions. Taking the time to correctly identify the question type allows you to instantly recall the proper strategy to use, rather than wasting time trying to figure out how to proceed. Skillful research (aided by Keywords and your Roadmap) allows you to predict and match your answer with confidence rather than fumbling with each answer choice (and thereby letting the test guide your thinking rather than you taking control of the test . . . another risky practice). Any time you gain by cutting corners is likely to be lost again when you struggle with the questions, and if you rely upon your intuition rather than a proven, methodical approach, your accuracy will suffer.

This is what I mean when I tell you to be efficient. Be patient, adhere to the Kaplan Method, and save time by doing the right things, not by skipping steps.

Divide and Conquer

On any given passage (or set of paired passages) there are optimal timing guidelines you should follow. Since you have four passages to complete in 35 minutes, you have an average of eight minutes and 45 seconds for each one. Since you will begin every timed section with a brief overview of the section (discussed later in this chapter), that average is actually closer to eight minutes and 30 seconds. With patience and practice, your goal should be to strategically read any given passage in 3–4 minutes, leaving the remaining time (about five minutes) to work with the questions.

If at first you struggle to hit these timing guidelines, take a look at your work and try to get a sense for where you're investing too much time. Be sure that you're not merely circling Keywords, but actively using them to guide your thinking. If you circle the words "for example" but then go right on to pore over the example in exacting detail, you're not using the Keywords to your maximum advantage. Remember to always read predictively; anticipate where the author is going from paragraph to paragraph, and use the understanding of structure this provides you to find the author's key ideas more easily. Look critically at your Roadmap and be sure you're not over-annotating. While the Roadmap must be thorough enough to guide your research, it shouldn't amount to a summary of every detail presented in the text.

Be similarly critical of your approach to individual questions. Are you able to easily identify the five common question types? Can you confidently recall the strategies that are associated with each one? If not, some review is in order. One of the big advantages of the Kaplan Method is the time you save by never having to wonder what to do next. Make sure you're reaping the full benefits of this advantage.

If in the last section I encouraged you to be patient in your practice, I'm now urging you to be confident. Far too many of my students begin their LSAT journeys with the entirely mistaken notion that scoring more points will lead to a feeling of confidence, when the relationship is actually the complete opposite. Approach every passage and every question with a confident knowledge of the strategies that work, and your timing will improve, as well as your score. Build that confidence by continuing to improve your application of the Kaplan Method.

Know When to Guess Strategically

One of the most useful things to know about great timing is that there is no penalty for guessing on the LSAT. That means that, unlike the SAT, you aren't penalized for bubbling in an incorrect answer. You should therefore answer every question and be prepared to guess when time is tight. If you must guess on multiple questions in a section, you are statistically more likely to score additional points if you guess a consistent choice each time (that is, fill in every unanswered question with (A), (B), or whichever choice you prefer, rather than choosing a different choice each time).

Another crucial lesson, one that my students sometimes find difficult to learn, is that you absolutely must be prepared to skip a time-consuming question if it's in your best interest to do so. This is innately challenging for most students—you probably don't want to feel like you're giving up, and you certainly don't want to let go of a valuable point. Nevertheless, the best test takers also understand that your only goal on the LSAT is to score as many points as possible in every section. If you read a question stem and realize you aren't sure how to proceed with your research, or that the research required is likely to take a lot of time, skip the question and move on to others that you can answer more quickly. In your test booklet, circle each question you skip (and be sure to circle the entire question, not just the question number—this will make it much easier to find if you return to it later). A skipped question will still be there for you to come back to once you've scored the easier points in the section. And if you have to guess, it's much better to guess on a difficult question than an easy one. Remember, each question is worth a single point, regardless of difficulty. If you have to sacrifice one tough question in order to answer two or three easier ones, the trade is worth it.

Remember also that a question that seems difficult when you first approach it may become easier after you've completed other questions in the section, usually because of the research you've conducted. Take a look at three questions, presented in their original order from an actual LSAT passage, and think about the order in which you should answer them:

21. The passage provides information that answers each of
     the following questions EXCEPT:[1]

22. The primary function of the first two paragraphs of the
     passage is to[2]

23. The passage is primarily concerned with[3]

Question 21 will almost certainly require some careful research to answer accurately and is not amenable to easy prediction. If you're savvy, you'll skip this question and move on to question 23, a straightforward Global question, and then proceed to question 22, which you

---

[1] PrepTest 39, Sec 3, Q 21
[2] PrepTest 39, Sec 3, Q 22
[3] PrepTest 39, Sec 3, Q 23

can answer in seconds with a glance at your Roadmap. Return to question 21 if you can, but don't waste valuable time on tough questions when there are still easy ones left in the section.

PASSAGE TRIAGE

Another important timing fundamental to remember is that you don't have to complete the passages in the order in which they're presented. An average LSAT Reading Comprehension section will consist of one easy passage, two of medium difficulty, and one that is more difficult than the others. Always begin a section by taking one minute to look over the passages and scan them for clues that help you determine which are easier and which are more challenging.

To demonstrate, try an experiment. Read the following paragraphs. Each is the opening paragraph of a different LSAT passage from the same 35-minute section. Take no more than 30 seconds to glance at these two paragraphs and try to determine which passage is likely to be more challenging.

> With the approach of the twentieth century, the classical wave theory of radiation—a widely accepted theory in physics—began to encounter obstacles. This theory held that all electromagnetic radiation—the
> (5) entire spectrum from gamma and X rays to radio frequencies, including heat and light—exists in the form of waves. One fundamental assumption of wave theory was that as the length of a wave of radiation shortens, its energy increases smoothly—like a volume
> (10) dial on a radio that adjusts smoothly to any setting— and that any conceivable energy value could thus occur in nature.[4]

> Users of the Internet—the worldwide network of interconnected computer systems—envision it as a way for people to have free access to information via their personal computers. Most Internet communication
> (5) consists of sending electronic mail or exchanging ideas on electronic bulletin boards; however, a growing number of transmissions are of copyrighted works— books, photographs, videos and films, and sound recordings. In Canada, as elsewhere, the goals of
> (10) Internet users have begun to conflict with reality as copyright holders look for ways to protect their material from unauthorized and uncompensated distribution.[5]

Both paragraphs are roughly the same length. At a glance, you probably noticed that the first paragraph is somewhat abstract and filled with scientific jargon, whereas the second deals with the familiar topic of the Internet and is written in simpler language. I want you to note

---

[4]PrepTest 39, Sec 3, Passage 3
[5]PrepTest 39, Sec 3, Passage 4

that these examples are presented in order, excerpted from the third and fourth passages, respectively, from the same section.

Since you have the option of completing the passages in any order, you'd be wiser to start with the second passage and then move back to the first. This isn't to say that tougher passages always come with tougher questions, but more challenging passages usually take longer to read and Roadmap, and therefore present added time pressure when you reach the question set. The general rule is that you should always score easy points before going after hard ones. If you are having a difficult time choosing between two passages that seem to be of equivalent difficulty, start with the passage that has more questions—this way you get a larger return on the reading you invest. If both passages have an equivalent number of questions, simply take them in order.

Passage triage is a skill and takes practice to develop. (It might be helpful to review chapter 15, in which you worked with abstract passages.) I would also encourage you to take note of which content areas you feel most comfortable with. Your LSAT will include one comparative reading exercise and three single passages. Because comparative passages tend to feature challenging question types, it's generally a good idea to tackle them after you've finished one or two simpler passages, or to save them for the end. Ultimately, passage order is not an exact science, since what is challenging is subjective to a degree. Take note of what *you* find challenging in the passages, and when you practice a 35-minute section, complete those more challenging passages after you've finished the ones that are more comfortable.

QUESTION TRIAGE

I've already mentioned how important it is to know when to skip a question. To help you do this, there are some guidelines to follow when deciding whether to answer a question immediately or leave it for later. Generally speaking, here is how you should prioritize the different question types:

- Global Questions: You should always answer Global questions first, since they require little or no research and are based on Purpose and Main Idea, concepts you've already thought through. Global questions are usually located at the very beginning and very end of question sets, so look for them in these locations and complete them immediately. Even if you are running out of time on a passage, you can still score Global points if you've read the passage strategically.

- Detail Questions: Tackle these next, remembering that they can often be identified by the opening phrase "according to the passage/author." Most Detail questions will provide you with enough information to conduct research easily in conjunction with your Roadmap, and since they ask you to paraphrase information that is already present in the passage, they're usually easy to predict.

- Logic Questions: Function and Reasoning questions should typically come next. Logic Function stems often provide you with specific line or paragraph references, making research more efficient. Reasoning questions are somewhat more varied, but you've become familiar with the most common types.

- Inference Questions: Inference questions tend to be more challenging than other types of questions. This is because they usually require thorough research and often force you to make a more general prediction than other types, which may lead to more time spent working with the answer choices. Be particularly alert for Inference questions that provide few clues in the stem to help guide your research. These tend to be among the most time-consuming on the test, so work with them after you've scored the easier points.

- EXCEPT Questions: Regardless of type, be wary of questions that contain the word EXCEPT. Sometimes these questions have answers that are hard to predict, and so they may force you to proceed by process of elimination. This doesn't necessarily mean that they're harder to answer correctly, but they can be more time consuming, and therefore should be given lower priority.

- Unusual Questions: As you saw in chapter 16, you may occasionally run into questions that are oddly worded and challenging to understand. If you can't immediately work out what the question stem is asking you to do, consider skipping it and coming back to it after you've completed questions that are more familiar.

I want to stress that these guidelines, while useful, are by no means mandatory. In your practice, you may find that a different priority works better for you. In any case, as with passages, your ultimate goal is to complete easier, less time-consuming questions first, leaving tougher questions for later. If you have to guess, make sure you're guessing on a question that might have taken three minutes to complete instead of thirty seconds.

As a final note, try to avoid random guessing, as an educated guess is always preferable. Keep track in your test booklet of which answer choices you've eliminated, and remember that your knowledge of the author's Scope can make it easier for you to get rid of wrong answer choices at a quick glance (but to be clear, this is the kind of strategy you should use *only* when you're short of time; in general, you should read answer choices carefully to avoid careless mistakes). In other words, if you have to guess, guess as strategically as possible.

KEEP MOVING, STAY METHODICAL

There is a common theme running through all of the advice that I've given you in this chapter, and I'll summarize it here: When you take on a 35-minute section, you must not get bogged down. You can only score points if you keep moving forward. If a question is holding you up, don't be afraid to skip it and come back to it. If a passage looks challenging during your initial overview of the section, save it for the end. Just as you shouldn't let yourself become mired in the details of any one passage, you must never get caught up in a time-wasting battle with a single question.

Remember that time management is always your responsibility. Keep track of time as you work on each passage; if you're nearing the 8.5-minute mark, you must prepare to move on to the next passage. This may require you to leave a point or two behind, but that's better than having to leave an entire *passage* behind.

Similarly, use your knowledge of the test to make good timing decisions, but never simply speed up and neglect the proper application of the Kaplan Method. All of the strategies you've worked so hard to master are designed to make you efficient without sacrificing accuracy, and it won't do your LSAT score any favors if you complete the Reading Comprehension section in 30 minutes but miss all the questions. Your goal is to score as many points as possible. Stay focused on the strategies that will allow you to be successful, and remember that you *can* take control of the section. Keep this in mind as you work with the 35-minute sections coming up in the next two chapters.

CHAPTER 19

FULL-LENGTH SECTION PRACTICE

In the following two chapters, you'll have the opportunity to take two full Reading Comprehension sections, just as they appeared on the original exams. When you take them, make sure that you'll have 35 uninterrupted minutes in a quiet place. Time yourself carefully using an analog watch (the only kind of timepiece you'll be allowed to bring to your LSAT), and be sure to complete an entire section before referring to its answers and explanations.

WHEN AND HOW TO USE SECTION PRACTICE

First and foremost, do *not* complete either timed section before you have completed all of the preceding chapters in this book. You may be eager to apply the strategies you've learned to a whole section, and I certainly understand if you're curious to tabulate how many questions you're getting correct or incorrect on average. This kind of information is certainly important, but if you rush into full sections before you've gained a thorough understanding of the Kaplan Method, you're likely to find the experience frustrating rather than enlightening.

Before you begin working on a timed section, please take a few minutes to review Kaplan's Method for Reading Comprehension and remind yourself to stay methodical. A phenomenon I've observed in my students is that, no matter how well they've understood the proper approach to individual passages and questions, they sometimes throw everything they've learned out the window as soon as they begin doing timed work, completing the section by intuition instead (and losing points that they would have otherwise scored). The remarkable thing is that these students are rarely aware that they're doing this. The pressure of the clock can easily cause even a well-prepared student to revert to bad habits. I want you to avoid this problem, so review the method before you begin working, and you'll be sure to apply it properly.

When your 35 minutes have expired, stop working immediately. You won't be able to sneak in a few extra answers on your actual LSAT, so don't do so in your practice either. After you've completed the first section, be sure to review the provided answers and explanations thoroughly before completing the second one. This is *very* important; the only way to get maximum benefit from both sections is to learn everything you can from the first, then apply what you've learned to the second. Remember that there is no guess penalty on the LSAT, so try to answer every question before your time runs out. Don't be afraid to make the best guess you can when necessary. Any guess—whether it's based on partial elimination of wrong choices or it's completely random—is better than leaving a question blank.

Finally, don't forget what you've learned about section management. Review the ideas I presented to you in chapter 18 carefully before moving on, and don't forget to triage passages and questions. The test makers reward those who make good decisions, so stay alert and don't be afraid to skip a time-consuming question if it makes sense to do so. Remember that your goal is to score as many points as possible, not to complete every question in a given passage.

HOW TO CALCULATE YOUR SCORE

Once you've completed the section, score your responses against the provided answer key. Mark each of the answers you got right or wrong, but review every passage and question using the Explanations following the section. There's no way to determine your overall LSAT score from any single section. Test scores are produced based on the overall number of correct answers. Figure 19.1 shows a couple of score conversion tables from recently-released LSATs. There are almost always 101 scored questions per LSAT, of which 26–28 come from the Reading Comprehension section.

CONVERSION CHART

For converting Raw Score to the 120–180 LSAT Scaled Score
LSAT Prep Test 47

REPORTED SCORE	LOWEST RAW SCORE	HIGHEST RAW SCORE
180	99	100
179	98	98
178	97	97
177	96	96
176	--*	--*
175	95	95
174	94	94
173	93	93
172	92	92
171	91	91
170	90	90
169	89	89
168	88	88
167	87	87
166	85	86
165	84	84
164	83	83
163	81	82
162	80	80
161	78	79
160	77	77
159	75	76
158	73	74
157	72	72
156	70	71
155	68	69
154	66	67
153	65	65
152	63	64
151	61	63
150	59	60
149	57	58
148	55	56
147	54	54
146	52	53
145	50	51
144	48	49
143	46	47
142	45	45
141	43	44
140	41	42
139	40	40
138	38	39
137	36	37
136	35	35
135	33	34
134	32	32
133	30	31
132	29	29
131	27	28
130	26	26
129	25	25
128	24	24
127	22	23
126	21	21
125	20	20
124	19	19
123	18	18
122	17	17
121	16	16
120	0	15

*There is no raw score that will produce this scaled score for the test.

CONVERSION CHART

For converting Raw Score to the 120–180 LSAT Scaled Score
LSAT Prep Test 50

REPORTED SCORE	LOWEST RAW SCORE	HIGHEST RAW SCORE
180	98	100
179	97	97
178	--*	--*
177	96	96
176	95	95
175	94	94
174	--*	--*
173	93	93
172	92	92
171	91	91
170	90	90
169	89	89
168	88	88
167	86	87
166	85	85
165	84	84
164	83	83
163	81	82
162	80	80
161	78	79
160	77	77
159	75	76
158	73	74
157	72	72
156	70	71
155	68	69
154	66	67
153	64	65
152	63	63
151	61	62
150	59	60
149	57	58
148	55	56
147	53	54
146	52	52
145	50	51
144	48	49
143	46	47
142	45	45
141	43	44
140	41	42
139	40	40
138	38	39
137	36	37
136	35	35
135	33	34
134	32	32
133	30	31
132	29	29
131	27	28
130	26	26
129	25	25
128	23	24
127	22	22
126	21	21
125	20	20
124	18	19
123	17	17
122	16	16
121	15	15
120	0	14

*There is no raw score that will produce this scaled score for the test.

Figure 19.1   Score Conversion Tables

SCORING WORKSHEET

1. Enter the number of questions you answered
    correctly in each section

                                NUMBER
                                CORRECT

    SECTION I . . . . _____

    SECTION II . . . . _____

    SECTION III. . . . . _____

    SECTION IV . . . . _____

2. Enter the sum here: _____   THIS IS YOUR
                                     RAW SCORE.

Figure 19.2

By estimating the number of points you'd score from the remaining sections of the test, you can gain an idea of the impact that your Reading Comprehension performance will have on your score. To improve your performance on the other sections of the test, study this book's companion volumes, *LSAT Logic Games: Strategies and Tactics* and *LSAT Logical Reasoning: Strategies and Tactics*.

If you haven't done so already, register for the Kaplan LSAT Experience test. This provides you with the chance to take the most recently released, full-length LSAT under all of the proctoring conditions and rules that will apply on test day. You'll receive your score, explanations for all of the questions, and a video review of test delivered by some of Kaplan's most experienced LSAT teachers along with your admission to the LSAT Experience exam.

One final thought: No matter how important section practice is, remember that it's still practice, and still an opportunity to learn and improve. Approach each section with confidence and do the best you can.

CHAPTER 20

FULL-LENGTH SECTION 1[1]

Time—35 minutes

27 Questions

<u>Directions:</u> Each set of questions in this section is based on a single passage or a pair of passages. The questions are to be answered on the basis of what is <u>stated</u> or <u>implied</u> in the passage or pair of passages. For some of the questions, more than one of the choices could conceivably answer the question. However, you are to choose the <u>best</u> answer, that is, the response that most accurately and completely answers the question, and blacken the corresponding space on your answer sheet.

---

[1]PrepTest 54, Section 1

This passage was adapted from an article published in 1996.

The Internet is a system of computer networks that allows individuals and organizations to communicate freely with other Internet users throughout the world. As a result, an astonishing
(5) variety of information is able to flow unimpeded across national and other political borders, presenting serious difficulties for traditional approaches to legislation and law enforcement, to which such borders are crucial.

(10) Control over physical space and the objects located in it is a defining attribute of sovereignty. Lawmaking presupposes some mechanism for enforcement, i.e., the ability to control violations. But jurisdictions cannot control the information and
(15) transactions flowing across their borders via the Internet. For example, a government might seek to intercept transmissions that propagate the kinds of consumer fraud that it regulates within its jurisdiction. But the volume of electronic communications
(20) crossing its territorial boundaries is too great to allow for effective control over individual transmissions. In order to deny its citizens access to specific materials, a government would thus have to prevent them from using the Internet altogether. Such a draconian
(25) measure would almost certainly be extremely unpopular, since most affected citizens would probably feel that the benefits of using the Internet decidedly outweigh the risks.

One legal domain that is especially sensitive to
(30) geographical considerations is that governing trademarks. There is no global registration of trademarks; international protection requires registration in each country. Moreover, within a country, the same name can sometimes be used
(35) proprietarily by businesses of different kinds in the same locality, or by businesses of the same kind in different localities, on the grounds that use of the trademark by one such business does not affect the others. But with the advent of the Internet, a business
(40) name can be displayed in such a way as to be accessible from any computer connected to the Internet anywhere in the world. Should such a display advertising a restaurant in Norway be deemed to infringe a trademark in Brazil just because it can be
(45) accessed freely from Brazil? It is not clear that any particular country's trademark authorities possess, or

should possess, jurisdiction over such displays. Otherwise, any use of a trademark on the Internet could be subject to the jurisdiction of every country
(50) simultaneously.

The Internet also gives rise to situations in which regulation is needed but cannot be provided within the existing framework. For example, electronic communications, which may pass through many
(55) different territorial jurisdictions, pose perplexing new questions about the nature and adequacy of privacy protections. Should French officials have lawful access to messages traveling via the Internet from Canada to Japan? This is just one among many
(60) questions that collectively challenge the notion that the Internet can be effectively controlled by the existing system of territorial jurisdictions.

1. Which one of the following most accurately expresses the main point of the passage?

(A) The high-volume, global nature of activity on the Internet undermines the feasibility of controlling it through legal frameworks that presuppose geographic boundaries.

(B) The system of Internet communications simultaneously promotes and weakens the power of national governments to control their citizens' speech and financial transactions.

(C) People value the benefits of their participation on the Internet so highly that they would strongly oppose any government efforts to regulate their Internet activity.

(D) Internet communications are responsible for a substantial increase in the volume and severity of global crime.

(E) Current Internet usage and its future expansion pose a clear threat to the internal political stability of many nations.

2. The author mentions French officials in connection with messages traveling between Canada and Japan (lines 57–59) primarily to

    (A) emphasize that the Internet allows data to be made available to users worldwide
    (B) illustrate the range of languages that might be used on the Internet
    (C) provide an example of a regulatory problem arising when an electronic communication intended for a particular destination passes through intermediate jurisdictions
    (D) show why any use of a trademark on the Internet could be subject to the jurisdiction of every country simultaneously
    (E) highlight the kind of international cooperation that made the Internet possible

3. According to the passage, which one of the following is an essential property of political sovereignty?

    (A) control over business enterprises operating across territorial boundaries
    (B) authority over communicative exchanges occurring within a specified jurisdiction
    (C) power to regulate trademarks throughout a circumscribed geographic region
    (D) control over the entities included within a designated physical space
    (E) authority over all commercial transactions involving any of its citizens

4. Which one of the following words employed by the author in the second paragraph is most indicative of the author's attitude toward any hypothetical measure a government might enact to deny its citizens access to the Internet?

    (A) benefits
    (B) decidedly
    (C) unpopular
    (D) draconian
    (E) risks

5. What is the main purpose of the fourth paragraph?

    (A) to call into question the relevance of the argument provided in the second paragraph
    (B) to provide a practical illustration that questions the general claim made in the first paragraph
    (C) to summarize the arguments provided in the second and third paragraphs
    (D) to continue the argument that begins in the third paragraph
    (E) to provide an additional argument in support of the general claim made in the first paragraph

Passage A

Drilling fluids, including the various mixtures known as drilling muds, play essential roles in oil-well drilling. As they are circulated down through the drill pipe and back up the well itself, they lubricate the
(5) drill bit, bearings, and drill pipe; clean and cool the drill bit as it cuts into the rock; lift rock chips (cuttings) to the surface; provide information about what is happening downhole, allowing the drillers to monitor the behavior, flow rate, pressure, and
(10) composition of the drilling fluid; and maintain well pressure to control cave-ins.

Drilling muds are made of bentonite and other clays and polymers, mixed with a fluid to the desired viscosity. By far the largest ingredient of drilling
(15) muds, by weight, is barite, a very heavy mineral of density 4.3 to 4.6. It is also used as an inert filler in some foods and is more familiar in its medical use as the "barium meal" administered before X-raying the digestive tract.
(20) Over the years individual drilling companies and their expert drillers have devised proprietary formulations, or mud "recipes," to deal with specific types of drilling jobs. One problem in studying the effects of drilling waste discharges is that the drilling
(25) fluids are made from a range of over 1,000, sometimes toxic, ingredients—many of them known, confusingly, by different trade names, generic descriptions, chemical formulae, and regional or industry slang words, and many of them kept secret by companies or individual
(30) formulators.

Passage B

Drilling mud, cuttings, and associated chemicals are normally released only during the drilling phase of a well's existence. These discharges are the main environmental concern in offshore oil production, and
(35) their use is tightly regulated. The discharges are closely monitored by the offshore operator, and releases are controlled as a condition of the operating permit.

One type of mud—water-based mud (WBM)—is a mixture of water, bentonite clay, and chemical
(40) additives, and is used to drill shallow parts of wells. It is not particularly toxic to marine organisms and disperses readily. Under current regulations, it can be dumped directly overboard. Companies typically recycle WBMs until their properties are no longer
(45) suitable and then, over a period of hours, dump the entire batch into the sea.

For drilling deeper wells, oil-based mud (OBM) is normally used. The typical difference from WBM is the high content of mineral oil (typically 30 percent).
(50) OBMs also contain greater concentrations of barite, a powdered heavy mineral, and a number of additives. OBMs have a greater potential for negative environmental impact, partly because they do not disperse as readily. Barite may impact some
(55) organisms, particularly scallops, and the mineral oil may have toxic effects. Currently only the residues of OBMs adhering to cuttings that remain after the cuttings are sieved from the drilling fluids may be discharged overboard, and then only mixtures up to a
(60) specified maximum oil content.

6. A primary purpose of each of the passages is to

(A) provide causal explanations for a type of environmental pollution
(B) describe the general composition and properties of drilling muds
(C) point out possible environmental impacts associated with oil drilling
(D) explain why oil-well drilling requires the use of drilling muds
(E) identify difficulties inherent in the regulation of oil-well drilling operations

7. Which one of the following is a characteristic of barite that is mentioned in both of the passages?

(A) It does not disperse readily in seawater.
(B) It is not found in drilling muds containing bentonite.
(C) Its use in drilling muds is tightly regulated.
(D) It is the most commonly used ingredient in drilling muds.
(E) It is a heavy mineral.

8. Each of the following is supported by one or both of the passages EXCEPT:

(A) Clay is an important constituent of many, if not all, drilling muds.
(B) At least one type of drilling mud is not significantly toxic to marine life.
(C) There has been some study of the environmental effects of drilling-mud discharges.
(D) Government regulations allow drilling muds to contain 30 percent mineral oil.
(E) During the drilling of an oil well, drilling mud is continuously discharged into the sea.

9. Which one of the following can be most reasonably inferred from the two passages taken together, but not from either one individually?

    (A) Barite is the largest ingredient of drilling muds, by weight, and also the most environmentally damaging.

    (B) Although barite can be harmful to marine organisms, it can be consumed safely by humans.

    (C) Offshore drilling is more damaging to the environment than is land-based drilling.

    (D) The use of drilling muds needs to be more tightly controlled by government.

    (E) If offshore drilling did not generate cuttings, it would be less harmful to the environment.

10. Each of the following is supported by one or both of the passages EXCEPT:

    (A) Drillers monitor the suitability of the mud they are using.

    (B) The government requires drilling companies to disclose all ingredients used in their drilling muds.

    (C) In certain quantities, barite is not toxic to humans.

    (D) Oil reserves can be found within or beneath layers of rock.

    (E) Drilling deep oil wells requires the use of different mud recipes than does drilling shallow oil wells.

11. Based on information in the passages, which one of the following, if true, provides the strongest support for a prediction that the proportion of oil-well drilling using OBMs will increase in the future?

    (A) The cost of certain ingredients in WBMs is expected to increase steadily over the next several decades.

    (B) The deeper an offshore oil well, the greater the concentration of barite that must be used in the drilling mud.

    (C) Oil reserves at shallow depths have mostly been tapped, leaving primarily much deeper reserves for future drilling.

    (D) It is unlikely that oil drillers will develop more efficient ways of removing OBM residues from cuttings that remain after being sieved from drilling fluids.

    (E) Barite is a common mineral, the availability of which is virtually limitless.

12. According to passage B, one reason OBMs are potentially more environmentally damaging than WBMs is that OBMs

    (A) are slower to disperse

    (B) contain greater concentrations of bentonite

    (C) contain a greater number of additives

    (D) are used for drilling deeper wells

    (E) cannot be recycled

Aida Overton Walker (1880–1914), one of the most widely acclaimed African American performers of the early twentieth century, was known largely for popularizing a dance form known as the cakewalk
(5) through her choreographing, performance, and teaching of the dance. The cakewalk was originally developed prior to the United States Civil War by African Americans, for whom dance was a means of maintaining cultural links within a slave society. It
(10) was based on traditional West African ceremonial dances, and like many other African American dances, it retained features characteristic of African dance forms, such as gliding steps and an emphasis on improvisation.
(15) To this African-derived foundation, the cakewalk added certain elements from European dances: where African dances feature flexible body postures, large groups and separate-sex dancing, the cakewalk developed into a high-kicking walk performed by a
(20) procession of couples. Ironically, while these modifications later enabled the cakewalk to appeal to European Americans and become one of the first cultural forms to cross the racial divide in North America, they were originally introduced with satiric
(25) intent. Slaves performed the grandiloquent walks in order to parody the processional dances performed at slave owners' balls and, in general, the self-important manners of slave owners. To add a further irony, by the end of the nineteenth century, the cakewalk was
(30) itself being parodied by European American stage performers, and these parodies in turn helped shape subsequent versions of the cakewalk.
While this complex evolution meant that the cakewalk was not a simple cultural phenomenon—
(35) one scholar has characterized this layering of parody upon parody with the phrase "mimetic vertigo"—it is in fact what enabled the dance to attract its wide audience. In the cultural and socioeconomic flux of the turn-of-the-century United States, where
(40) industrialization, urbanization, mass immigration, and rapid social mobility all reshaped the cultural landscape, an art form had to be capable of being many things to many people in order to appeal to a large audience.
(45) Walker's remarkable success at popularizing the cakewalk across otherwise relatively rigid racial boundaries rested on her ability to address within her interpretation of it the varying and sometimes conflicting demands placed on the dance. Middle-
(50) class African Americans, for example, often denounced the cakewalk as disreputable, a complaint reinforced by the parodies circulating at the time. Walker won over this audience by refining the cakewalk and emphasizing its fundamental grace.
(55) Meanwhile, because middle- and upper-class European Americans often felt threatened by the tremendous cultural flux around them, they prized what they regarded as authentic art forms as bastions of stability; much of Walker's success with this

audience derived from her distillation of what was widely acclaimed as the most authentic cakewalk. Finally, Walker was able to gain the admiration of many newly rich industrialists and financiers, who found in the grand flourishes of her version of the
(65) cakewalk a fitting vehicle for celebrating their newfound social rank.

13. Which one of the following most accurately expresses the main point of the passage?

(A) Walker, who was especially well known for her success in choreographing, performing, and teaching the cakewalk, was one of the most widely recognized African American performers of the early twentieth century.

(B) In spite of the disparate influences that shaped the cakewalk, Walker was able to give the dance broad appeal because she distilled what was regarded as the most authentic version in an era that valued authenticity highly.

(C) Walker popularized the cakewalk by capitalizing on the complex cultural mix that had developed from the dance's original blend of satire and cultural preservation, together with the effects of later parodies.

(D) Whereas other versions of the cakewalk circulating at the beginning of the twentieth century were primarily parodic in nature, the version popularized by Walker combined both satire and cultural preservation.

(E) Because Walker was able to recognize and preserve the characteristics of the cakewalk as African Americans originally performed it, it became the first popular art form to cross the racial divide in the United States.

14. The author describes the socioeconomic flux of the turn-of-the-century United States in the third paragraph primarily in order to

(A) argue that the cakewalk could have become popular only in such complex social circumstances

(B) detail the social context that prompted performers of the cakewalk to fuse African and European dance forms

(C) identify the target of the overlapping parodic layers that characterized the cakewalk

(D) indicate why a particular cultural environment was especially favorable for the success of the cakewalk

(E) explain why European American parodies of the cakewalk were able to reach wide audiences

15. Which one of the following is most analogous to the author's account in the second paragraph of how the cakewalk came to appeal to European Americans?

    (A) Satirical versions of popular music songs are frequently more popular than the songs they parody.
    (B) A style of popular music grows in popularity among young listeners because it parodies the musical styles admired by older listeners.
    (C) A style of music becomes admired among popular music's audience in part because of elements that were introduced in order to parody popular music.
    (D) A once popular style of music wins back its audience by incorporating elements of the style of music that is currently most popular.
    (E) After popular music begins to appropriate elements of a traditional style of music, interest in that traditional music increases.

16. The passage asserts which one of the following about the cakewalk?

    (A) It was largely unknown outside African American culture until Walker popularized it.
    (B) It was mainly a folk dance, and Walker became one of only a handful of people to perform it professionally.
    (C) Its performance as parody became uncommon as a result of Walker's popularization of its authentic form.
    (D) Its West African origins became commonly known as a result of Walker's work.
    (E) It was one of the first cultural forms to cross racial lines in the United States.

17. It can be inferred from the passage that the author would be most likely to agree with which one of the following statements?

    (A) Because of the broad appeal of humor, satiric art forms are often among the first to cross racial or cultural divisions.
    (B) The interactions between African American and European American cultural forms often result in what is appropriately characterized as "mimetic vertigo."
    (C) Middle-class European Americans who valued the cakewalk's authenticity subsequently came to admire other African American dances for the same reason.
    (D) Because of the influence of African dance forms, some popular dances that later emerged in the United States featured separate-sex dancing.
    (E) Some of Walker's admirers were attracted to her version of the cakewalk as a means for bolstering their social identities.

18. The passage most strongly suggests that the author would be likely to agree with which one of the following statements about Walker's significance in the history of the cakewalk?

    (A) Walker broadened the cakewalk's appeal by highlighting elements that were already present in the dance.
    (B) Walker's version of the cakewalk appealed to larger audiences than previous versions did because she accentuated its satiric dimension.
    (C) Walker popularized the cakewalk by choreographing various alternative interpretations of it, each tailored to the interests of a different cultural group.
    (D) Walker added a "mimetic vertigo" to the cakewalk by inserting imitations of other performers' cakewalking into her dance routines.
    (E) Walker revitalized the cakewalk by disentangling its complex admixture of African and European elements.

19. The passage provides sufficient information to answer which one of the following questions?

    (A) What were some of the attributes of African dance forms that were preserved in the cakewalk?
    (B) Who was the first performer to dance the cakewalk professionally?
    (C) What is an aspect of the cakewalk that was preserved in other North American dance forms?
    (D) What features were added to the original cakewalk by the stage parodies circulating at the end of the nineteenth century?
    (E) For about how many years into the twentieth century did the cakewalk remain widely popular?

In principle, a cohesive group—one whose members generally agree with one another and support one another's judgments—can do a much better job at decision making than it could if it were
(5) noncohesive. When cohesiveness is low or lacking entirely, compliance out of fear of recrimination is likely to be strongest. To overcome this fear, participants in the group's deliberations need to be confident that they are members in good standing and
(10) that the others will continue to value their role in the group, whether or not they agree about a particular issue under discussion. As members of a group feel more accepted by the others, they acquire greater freedom to say what they really think, becoming less
(15) likely to use deceitful arguments or to play it safe by dancing around the issues with vapid or conventional comments. Typically, then, the more cohesive a group becomes, the less its members will deliberately censor what they say out of fear of being punished socially
(20) for antagonizing their fellow members.

But group cohesiveness can have pitfalls as well: while the members of a highly cohesive group can feel much freer to deviate from the majority, their desire for genuine concurrence on every important
(25) issue often inclines them not to use this freedom. In a highly cohesive group of decision makers, the danger is not that individuals will conceal objections they harbor regarding a proposal favored by the majority, but that they will think the proposal is a good one
(30) without attempting to carry out a critical scrutiny that could reveal grounds for strong objections. Members may then decide that any misgivings they feel are not worth pursuing—that the benefit of any doubt should be given to the group consensus. In this way, they
(35) may fall victim to a syndrome known as "groupthink," which one psychologist concerned with collective decision making has defined as "a deterioration of mental efficiency, reality testing, and moral judgment that results from in-group pressures."
(40) Based on analyses of major fiascoes of international diplomacy and military decision making, researchers have identified groupthink behavior as a recurring pattern that involves several factors: overestimation of the group's power and morality,
(45) manifested, for example, in an illusion of invulnerability, which creates excessive optimism;

closed-mindedness to warnings of problems and to alternative viewpoints; and unwarranted pressures toward uniformity, including self-censorship with
50 respect to doubts about the group's reasoning and a concomitant shared illusion of unanimity concerning group decisions. Cohesiveness of the decision-making group is an essential antecedent condition for this syndrome but not a sufficient one, so it is important
(55) to work toward identifying the additional factors that determine whether group cohesiveness will deteriorate into groupthink or allow for effective decision making.

20.   Which one of the following most accurately expresses the main point of the passage?

(A)   Despite its value in encouraging frank discussion, high cohesion can lead to a debilitating type of group decision making called groupthink.

(B)   Group members can guard against groupthink if they have a good understanding of the critical role played by cohesion.

(C)   Groupthink is a dysfunctional collective decision-making pattern that can occur in diplomacy and military affairs.

(D)   Low cohesion in groups is sometimes desirable when higher cohesion involves a risk of groupthink behavior.

(E)   Future efforts to guard against groupthink will depend on the results of ongoing research into the psychology of collective decision making.

21. A group of closely associated colleagues has made a disastrous diplomatic decision after a series of meetings marked by disagreement over conflicting alternatives. It can be inferred from the passage that the author would be most likely to say that this scenario

    (A) provides evidence of chronic indecision, thus indicating a weak level of cohesion in general
    (B) indicates that the group's cohesiveness was coupled with some other factor to produce a groupthink fiasco
    (C) provides no evidence that groupthink played a role in the group's decision
    (D) provides evidence that groupthink can develop even in some groups that do not demonstrate an "illusion of unanimity"
    (E) indicates that the group probably could have made its decision-making procedure more efficient by studying the information more thoroughly

22. Which one of the following, if true, would most support the author's contentions concerning the conditions under which groupthink takes place?

    (A) A study of several groups, each made up of members of various professions, found that most fell victim to groupthink.
    (B) There is strong evidence that respectful dissent is more likely to occur in cohesive groups than in groups in which there is little internal support.
    (C) Extensive analyses of decisions made by a large number of groups found no cases of groupthink in groups whose members generally distrust one another's judgments.
    (D) There is substantial evidence that groupthink is especially likely to take place when members of a group develop factions whose intransigence prolongs the group's deliberations.
    (E) Ample research demonstrates that voluntary deference to group opinion is not a necessary factor for the formation of groupthink behavior.

23. The passage mentions which one of the following as a component of groupthink?

    (A) unjustified suspicions among group members regarding an adversary's intentions
    (B) strong belief that the group's decisions are right
    (C) group members working under unusually high stress, leading to illusions of invulnerability
    (D) the deliberate use of vapid, clichéd arguments
    (E) careful consideration of objections to majority positions

24. It can be inferred from the passage that both the author of the passage and the researchers mentioned in the passage would be most likely to agree with which one of the following statements about groupthink?

    (A) Groupthink occurs in all strongly cohesive groups, but its contribution to collective decision making is not fully understood.
    (B) The causal factors that transform group cohesion into groupthink are unique to each case.
    (C) The continued study of cohesiveness of groups is probably fruitless for determining what factors elicit groupthink.
    (D) Outside information cannot influence group decisions once they have become determined by groupthink.
    (E) On balance, groupthink cannot be expected to have a beneficial effect in a group's decision making.

25. In the passage, the author says which one of the following about conformity in decision-making groups?

    (A) Enforced conformity may be appropriate in some group decision situations.
    (B) A high degree of conformity is often expected of military decision-making group members.
    (C) Inappropriate group conformity can result from inadequate information.
    (D) Voluntary conformity occurs much less frequently than enforced conformity.
    (E) Members of noncohesive groups may experience psychological pressure to conform.

26. In line 5, the author mentions low group cohesiveness primarily in order to

    (A) contribute to a claim that cohesiveness can be conducive to a freer exchange of views in groups
    (B) establish a comparison between groupthink symptoms and the attributes of low-cohesion groups
    (C) suggest that there may be ways to make both cohesive and noncohesive groups more open to dissent
    (D) indicate that both cohesive and noncohesive groups may be susceptible to groupthink dynamics
    (E) lay the groundwork for a subsequent proposal for overcoming the debilitating effects of low cohesion

27. Based on the passage, it can be inferred that the author would be most likely to agree with which one of the following?

    (A) Highly cohesive groups are more likely to engage in confrontational negotiating styles with adversaries than are those with low cohesion.
    (B) It is difficult for a group to examine all relevant options critically in reaching decisions unless it has a fairly high degree of cohesiveness.
    (C) A group with varied viewpoints on a given issue is less likely to reach a sound decision regarding that issue than is a group whose members are unified in their outlook.
    (D) Intense stress and high expectations are the key factors in the formation of groupthink.
    (E) Noncohesive groups can, under certain circumstances, develop all of the symptoms of groupthink.

Answer Explanations follow on the next page.

ANSWER KEY

1.	A	15.	C
2.	C	16.	E
3.	D	17.	E
4.	D	18.	A
5.	E	19.	A
6.	B	20.	A
7.	E	21.	C
8.	E	22.	C
9.	B	23.	B
10.	B	24.	E
11.	C	25.	E
12.	A	26.	A
13.	C	27.	B
14.	D		

TRIAGE REVIEW

The first passage is probably the best place to begin this section. The Topic deals with the Internet, a subject you're probably familiar with to some degree, and the four medium-length paragraphs present few obvious structural challenges. You might be dismayed by the lack of questions—only five—but remember that your goal is to grab the easiest points right away, and these questions are short and straightforward.

The third passage should also take high priority. Five brief paragraphs suggest a simple structure, and the language is nontechnical. Because this passage is worth seven points, you might prefer to tackle it first. Either order is fine; as long as you identify the simpler passages and score their points before moving on to the more challenging passages, you've made the right decision.

You would be wise to complete passages two and four later in the section. Passage two is comparative reading and appears to address a more technical subject. Additionally, you may have noticed two EXCEPT questions (these are easy to spot out during your question triage because the word EXCEPT will always be in all caps) and a large number of Inference questions. All of these clues suggest that this passage is likely to be more time-consuming.

Passage four appears abstract even at a quick glance (although it clearly has something to do with "cohesiveness"), and the three long, dense paragraphs will require some time to work through. Although there are eight questions, the stems and choices are lengthy, and a glance at the beginning and end of the question set will confirm that there's only one global question—most of the remaining questions are Logic and Inference. You should tackle this one either third or fourth, depending on whether you prefer to complete it before or after the comparative passages.

Explanations

Passage One: "Internet Regulations"
Step 1:

This passage was adapted from an article published in 1996.

The Internet is a system of computer networks that (allows) individuals and organizations to communicate freely with other Internet users throughout the world. (As a result,) an (astonishing)

Internet raises internat. legal problems

(5) variety of information is able to flow unimpeded across national and other political borders, presenting (serious difficulties) for (traditional) approaches to legislation and law enforcement, to which such borders are (crucial.)

(10) Control over physical space and the objects located in it is a (defining) attribute of sovereignty.

Net info can't be controlled

Lawmaking (presupposes) some mechanism for enforcement, i.e., the ability to control violations. (But) jurisdictions (cannot control) the information and

(15) transactions flowing across their borders via the Internet. (For example,) a government might seek to intercept transmissions that propagate the kinds of consumer fraud that it regulates within its jurisdiction. (But) the volume of electronic communications

(20) crossing its territorial boundaries is too great to allow for effective control over individual transmissions. (In order) to deny its citizens access to specific materials, a government would (thus) have to prevent them from using the Internet altogether. Such a (draconian)

Tough laws would be unpopular

(25) measure would almost certainly be extremely unpopular, (since) most affected citizens would probably feel that the benefits of using the Internet decidedly (outweigh) the risks.

One legal domain that is (especially) sensitive to

(30) geographical considerations is that governing

TMs

trademarks. There is no global registration of trademarks; international protection (requires) registration in each country. (Moreover,) within a country, the same name can sometimes be used

(35) proprietarily by businesses of different kinds in the same locality, (or by) businesses of the same kind in different localities, (on the grounds) that use of the trademark by one such business does not affect the others. (But) with the advent of the Internet, a business

Net makes TM law difficult

(40) name can be displayed in such a way as to be accessible from any computer connected to the Internet anywhere in the world. (Should) such a display advertising a restaurant in Norway be deemed to infringe a trademark in Brazil just (because) it can be

(45)   accessed freely from Brazil? It is (not clear) that any
       particular country's trademark authorities possess, or
       should possess, jurisdiction over such displays.
       (Otherwise,) any use of a trademark on the Internet
       (could be) subject to the jurisdiction of every country
(50)   simultaneously.
           The Internet (also) gives rise to situations in which
       regulation is needed (but) cannot be provided within
Needed   the existing framework. (For example,) electronic
regulations communications, which may pass through many
can't be (55)   different territorial jurisdictions, pose (perplexing) new
provided questions about the nature and adequacy of privacy
       protections. (Should) French officials have lawful
       access to messages traveling via the Internet from
       Canada to Japan? This is just one among many
(60)   questions that collectively (challenge) the notion that
       the Internet can be effectively controlled by the
       existing system of territorial jurisdictions.

Paragraph Structure: This explanatory passage follows a straightforward structure that likely didn't provide any unusual challenges to your strategic reading skills. The first paragraph introduces the **Topic** of the passage immediately: Internet regulations. The author's **Scope** involves the "serious difficulties" (line 7) that arise when attempting to regulate the Internet across international borders.

The second paragraph explores this problem in a bit more detail. Since physical space is a "defining" (line 11) characteristic of state sovereignty, the Internet necessarily introduces unforeseen problems since nations cannot control the flow of information across their borders. This is complicated by the fact that any "draconian" (line 24) measures such as banning Internet access altogether would likely be unpopular.

The final two paragraphs consist primarily of supporting details—the enforcement of trademarks is complicated by the Internet, and certain regulations that might be necessary to control the flow of information can't be provided within the "existing framework" (line 53), primarily because of issues of privacy.

Taken all together, you should note the author's neutral tone as you consider the **Purpose** of the passage: to describe legal problems associated with the Internet. Note that the author doesn't propose solutions to these problems, but merely explains them. The **Main Idea** of the passage, then, is that the Internet has introduced new legal challenges to the international community that defy easy solution.

Question Triage: Look for the Global questions first, as always. Question 1 should be a quick point, so score it right away. Questions 3 and 5 are good ones to consider next—a Detail question and a Function question that can be answered with a quick glance at your Roadmap. That leaves question 2, a Function question, and question 4, an author's attitude Inference question, which you should take in order.

1. **(A)**

   Which one of the following most accurately expresses the main point of the passage?
   (A) The high-volume, global nature of activity on the Internet undermines the feasibility of controlling it through legal frameworks that presuppose geographic boundaries.
   (B) The system of Internet communications simultaneously promotes and weakens the power of national governments to control their citizens' speech and financial transactions.
   (C) People value the benefits of their participation on the Internet so highly that they would strongly oppose any government efforts to regulate their Internet activity.
   (D) Internet communications are responsible for a substantial increase in the volume and severity of global crime.
   (E) Current Internet usage and its future expansion pose a clear threat to the internal political stability of many nations.[2]

Step 2: The clue "main point" identifies this as a Global question.

Step 3: Instead of researching the text, think about the Main Idea of the passage.

Step 4: The Main Idea was that the Internet has raised legal challenges that aren't easily solved.

Step 5: Correct choice (A) properly reflects the prediction. Choice (B) addresses issues that are completely out of scope of the Main Idea, choice (C) focuses too narrowly on a specific detail, and choices (D) and (E) propose ideas that were never mentioned in the passage and are therefore outside the scope.

2. **(C)**

   The author mentions French officials in connection with messages traveling between Canada and Japan (lines 57–59) primarily to
   (A) emphasize that the Internet allows data to be made available to users worldwide
   (B) illustrate the range of languages that might be used on the Internet
   (C) provide an example of a regulatory problem arising when an electronic communication intended for a particular destination passes through intermediate jurisdictions
   (D) show why any use of a trademark on the Internet could be subject to the jurisdiction of every country simultaneously
   (E) highlight the kind of international cooperation that made the Internet possible[3]

---

[2]PrepTest 54, Sec 1, Q 1

[3]PrepTest 54, Sec 1, Q 2

Step 2: The question asks for the primary reason why the passage mentions an example, making this a Logic Function question.

Step 3: Although you are provided with a specific line reference, you should start reading at the beginning of the paragraph to get a good sense of context. The paragraph describes "perplexing" (line 55) questions that arise when communications pass through several jurisdictions; this seems to be what the author is chiefly interested in describing here.

Step 4: So why did the author mention the French officials? The Keywords "for example" (line 53) tell you that this is an illustration of the point the author just made: That communications crossing jurisdictions are problematic for lawmakers.

Step 5: The match for your prediction is choice (C). Note that none of the wrong answer choices even come close to mentioning the context you researched in Step 3. It's true that choice (D) mentions the term "jurisdiction" (line 62), but then goes out of scope by bringing up the issue of trademarks, which was dealt with in an earlier paragraph (line 32). Be careful not to fall for the half right/half wrong answer trap. This is why application of the Kaplan Method and careful attention to context is so important when dealing with a Logic Function question.

3. **(D)**

    According to the passage, which one of the following is an essential property of political sovereignty?
    (A) control over business enterprises operating across territorial boundaries
    (B) authority over communicative exchanges occurring within a specified jurisdiction
    (C) power to regulate trademarks throughout a circumscribed geographic region
    (D) control over the entities included within a designated physical space
    (E) authority over all commercial transactions involving any of its citizens[4]

Step 2: When the question asks for a specific fact, or "property" in this case, you know you're working with a Detail question. Also note "according to the passage," another common Detail question identifier.

Step 3: The Keywords in the second paragraph help you discover the "defining" (line 11) attributes of sovereignty.

Step 4: The passage simply describes "control over physical space" (line 10) as defining sovereignty. The correct answer must reflect this.

Step 5: A quick scan of the choices should bring you to correct choice (D). None of the other choices mentions the idea of physical space, making them all out of scope.

---

[4]PrepTest 54, Sec 1, Q 3

4. **(D)**

Which one of the following words employed by the author in the second paragraph is most indicative of the author's attitude toward any hypothetical measure a government might enact to deny its citizens access to the Internet?
(A) benefits
(B) decidedly
(C) unpopular
(D) draconian
(E) risks[5]

Step 2: Questions that ask for the "author's attitude" are Inference questions. Research the text carefully to determine what must be true.

Step 3: The question stem directs you to the second paragraph, where you discover that the author refers to Internet bans as "draconian" (line 24) and certain to be "unpopular" (line 26) with citizens.

Step 4: The research you've already conducted gives you the prediction you need: The author used the word "draconian" to describe these hypothetical laws. Even if you're not sure about the meaning of this word, it forms the basis of a strong prediction.

Step 5: Correct choice (D) contains the term you were looking for. Choice (B) isn't quoted in the relevant portion of the second paragraph. The remaining choices refer to words that the author used to describe *citizens'* views of such laws, but not necessarily the author's. Always pay close attention to whose point of view a question is asking for.

5. **(E)**

What is the main purpose of the fourth paragraph?
(A) to call into question the relevance of the argument provided in the second paragraph
(B) to provide a practical illustration that questions the general claim made in the first paragraph
(C) to summarize the arguments provided in the second and third paragraphs
(D) to continue the argument that begins in the third paragraph
(E) to provide an additional argument in support of the general claim made in the first paragraph[6]

Step 2: The phrase "main purpose" might suggest a Global question at first glance, but since the stem focuses on a single paragraph, you're instead working with a Logic Function question. You must determine why the author included the fourth paragraph in the overall structure.

---

[5]PrepTest 54, Sec 1, Q 4
[6]PrepTest 54, Sec 1, Q 5

Step 3: You can't ask for a better research source than your Roadmap. Use it to review the passage structure as a whole.

Step 4: The author's Main Idea was laid out in the first paragraph: The Internet has created new legal challenges. Each of the remaining paragraphs supports this idea; according to the Roadmap, the final paragraph specifically mentions that needed regulations become hard to provide across multiple jurisdictions.

Step 5: The correct answer, choice (E), identifies the final paragraph as evidence for the author's Main Idea. Choice (A) describes a relationship that doesn't exist—paragraph four in no way refutes paragraph two. Choice (B) is a classic 180—paragraph four *supports* the first paragraph. It doesn't question it. Choice (C) is irrelevant, as there is no summary of paragraphs two and three here. Choice (D) suggests that paragraph four is a continuation of paragraph three, also incorrect. Strategic Reading is *crucial* when you face this type of question. Trust in your Roadmap and your understanding of the big picture in order to score this point easily and efficiently.

Passage Two: "Comparative Passages on Drilling Muds"
Step 1:

Passage A

Drilling muds defined

Drilling fluids, including the various mixtures known as drilling muds, play essential roles in oil-well drilling. As they are circulated down through the drill pipe and back up the well itself, they lubricate the
(5) drill bit, bearings, and drill pipe; clean and cool the drill bit as it cuts into the rock; lift rock chips (cuttings) to the surface; provide information about what is happening downhole, allowing the drillers to monitor the behavior, flow rate, pressure, and
(10) composition of the drilling fluid; and maintain well pressure to control cave-ins.

How they're made

Drilling muds are made of bentonite and other clays and polymers, mixed with a fluid to the desired viscosity. By far the largest ingredient of drilling
(15) muds, by weight, is barite, a very heavy mineral of density 4.3 to 4.6. It is also used as an inert filler in some foods and is more familiar in its medical use as the "barium meal" administered before X-raying the digestive tract.
(20) Over the years individual drilling companies and their expert drillers have devised proprietary formulations, or mud "recipes," to deal with specific types of drilling jobs. One problem in studying the effects of drilling waste discharges is that the drilling

Prob. with studies: too many fluids

(25) fluids are made from a range of over 1,000, sometimes toxic, ingredients—many of them known, confusingly, by different trade names, generic descriptions, chemical formulae, and regional or industry slang words, and many of them kept secret by companies or individual
(30) formulators.

Passage B

Drilling
discharges
carefully
controlled

Drilling mud, cuttings, and associated chemicals are (normally) released (only during) the drilling phase of a well's existence. These discharges are the (main) environmental (concern) in offshore oil production, (and) (35) their use is tightly regulated. The discharges are closely monitored by the offshore operator, (and) releases are controlled as a condition of the operating permit.

(One type) of mud—water-based mud (WBM)—is a mixture of water, bentonite clay, and chemical (40) additives, and (is used) to drill shallow parts of wells. It

WBM not as
bad

is not particularly toxic to marine organisms (and) disperses readily. Under (current regulations,) it can be dumped directly overboard. Companies (typically) recycle WBM (until) their properties are no longer (45) suitable and (then,) over a period of hours, dump the entire batch into the sea.

OBM more
dangerous

For drilling deeper wells, oil-based mud (OBM) is (normally) used. The typical (difference) from WBM is the high content of mineral oil (typically 30 percent). (50) OBMs (also) contain greater concentrations of barite, a powdered heavy mineral (and) a number of additives. OBMs have a (greater potential) for negative environmental impact, partly (because) they do not disperse as readily. Barite may (impact) some (55) organisms, particularly scallops, (and) the mineral oil may have toxic effects. (Currently) only the residues of OBMs adhering to cuttings that remain after the cuttings are sieved from the drilling fluids (may be) discharged overboard, and (then only) mixtures up to a (60) specified maximum oil content.

Paragraph Structure: As always, with comparative reading passages you should read and Roadmap each passage independently. Be sure to determine the **Topic, Scope, Purpose,** and **Main Idea** for Passage A before moving on to Passage B.

Passage A: The opening paragraph is purely descriptive, presenting the author's **Topic** (drilling muds) and the "essential roles" (line 2) they play in offshore oil production (the author's **Scope**). The second paragraph is similarly concerned with detail, describing the creation and composition of drilling muds. The author does note that barite is "by far" (line 14) the largest ingredient in most muds, an emphasis that you should definitely take note of. The final paragraph switches direction slightly, describing "one problem" (line 23) with the study of the environmental effects of the discharge of drilling muds and other fluids from drilling operations—there is a large profusion of different fluids currently in use, and their varying compositions and trade names make them difficult to examine closely. The **Purpose** of this passage is to describe drilling muds and some problems associated with them, and the **Main Idea** encapsulates all of this: Drilling muds have many uses, they are composed largely of barite, and their environmental ramifications are hard to study.

Passage B: This passage begins by addressing the "main environmental concern" (lines 33–34) with offshore drilling (the **Topic**), the discharge of muds and other fluids. The author's **Scope** becomes clear in the second and third paragraphs: a discussion of WBMs as compared to OBMs. The primary difference lies in the threat to the environment and resultant levels of regulation. The second paragraph describes WBMs as less environmentally dangerous, and therefore subject to fewer regulations. The "difference" (line 48) with OBMs, as described in the third paragraph, is that the composition of OBMs makes them more dangerous to the environment, and thus more tightly regulated. Once again, the author's **Purpose** was descriptive: to explain differences between different types of drilling muds. The **Main Idea** should define this difference: Drilling muds can pose environmental threats, although OBMs are more hazardous on the whole than WBMs.

By quickly comparing and contrasting the passages, you can see many similarities. Both passages discuss drilling muds, and both touch on some of the environmental problems associated with their use. Passage A is more concerned with the manufacture and composition of muds generally, only raising environmental issues in the final paragraph, while Passage B leads with environmental concerns and centers the discussion around them, although it too addresses drilling mud composition. Both authors maintain a neutral, scholarly tone throughout their respective passages, preferring to remain descriptive without offering suggestions or judgments.

Question Triage: There's a single Global point to be scored—question 6—so grab it right away. Avoiding the EXCEPT questions for now, questions 7 and 12 ask for specific details in the passages, so tackle them next. Question 11, a Strengthen question with plenty of clues in the stem, is a better choice than question 9, a vaguely worded Inference question. Questions 8 and 10 are identically worded and will probably require more challenging research. Save them for last, and skip one or both of them for now if necessary.

6. **(B)**

    A primary purpose of each of the passages is to

    (A)   provide causal explanations for a type of environmental pollution

    (B)   describe the general composition and properties of drilling muds

    (C)   point out possible environmental impacts associated with oil drilling

    (D)   explain why oil-well drilling requires the use of drilling muds

    (E)   identify difficulties inherent in the regulation of oil-well drilling operations[7]

Step 2: "Primary purpose" in the stem identifies this as a Global question.

---

[7]PrepTest 54, Sec 1, Q 6

Step 3: Recall the Main Ideas of both passages and prepare to base your prediction in the next step on them

Step 4: Passage A was primarily concerned with describing drilling muds generally. In distinguishing between the threat to the environment posed by two different types of muds, Passage B also described some of their chemical properties. This is the similarity you're looking for in the choices.

Step 5: Correct choice (B) is a direct match for the prediction. Choice (A) is completely out of the scope of Passage A, which mentions pollution only in passing, as is choice (C). (Passage A never mentions specific environmental impacts.) Passage B never addresses why muds are required, eliminating choice (D), and choice (E) is touched upon briefly in Passage A but not in Passage B.

7. **(E)**

    Which one of the following is a characteristic of
    barite that is mentioned in both of the passages?
    (A)   It does not disperse readily in seawater.
    (B)   It is not found in drilling muds containing
          bentonite.
    (C)   Its use in drilling muds is tightly regulated.
    (D)   It is the most commonly used ingredient in
          drilling muds.
    (E)   It is a heavy mineral.[8]

Step 2: The question asks for a specific characteristic mentioned in both passages. This is a Detail question.

Step 3: Your Roadmap should lead you back to the second paragraph of Passage A, which describes the composition of muds. In Passage B, barite is only specifically mentioned in the third paragraph dealing with OBMs.

Step 4: What do both passages explicitly mention about barite? Only that it is a heavy mineral. The correct answer must reflect this.

Step 5: With a strong prediction, correct choice (E) is the clear winner. Choice (A) is only referenced in Passage B, and choice (B) isn't mentioned in either passage. Choice (C) contains a distortion—the discharge of certain muds is regulated, not necessarily their barite content. Choice (D) is only mentioned in Passage A.

---

[8]PrepTest 54, Sec 1, Q 7

8. **(E)**

Each of the following is supported by one or both of the passages EXCEPT:

(A)   Clay is an important constituent of many, if not all, drilling muds.

(B)   At least one type of drilling mud is not significantly toxic to marine life.

(C)   There has been some study of the environmental effects of drilling-mud discharges.

(D)   Government regulations allow drilling muds to contain 30 percent mineral oil.

(E)   During the drilling of an oil well, drilling mud is continuously discharged into the sea.[9]

Step 2: This Inference EXCEPT question might be a bit tricky—you are looking for something that is *not* supported in either passage.

Step 3: The stem doesn't give you any concrete clues to guide your research, so process of elimination is likely to be the appropriate strategy. First, think through the Main Idea of each passage in order to make elimination easier.

Step 4: Passage A describes the composition and usage of muds, and Passage B compares two specific types. Keep this in mind as you work through the choices to maximize your research efficiency.

Step 5: You can eliminate choice (A) with a quick glance back at Passage A, paragraph two. Choice (B) is supported by paragraph two of Passage B. Both passages support choice (C). You can find the specific information in choice (D) in Passage B, paragraph two, which mentions specific regulations. The only remaining choice, (E), is never mentioned in either passage and is therefore the correct answer.

A question like this one can be time consuming, but you can eliminate choices more easily by skillfully using your Roadmap. When dealing with an EXCEPT question, read the question stem carefully and make sure you've completely understood the task at hand. Finally, remember that Inference EXCEPT questions are definitely low-priority, so don't be afraid to skip this one and come back to it if time permits.

---

[9]PrepTest 54, Sec 1, Q 8

9. **(B)**

Which one of the following can be most reasonably inferred from the two passages taken together, but not from either one individually?

(A)   Barite is the largest ingredient of drilling muds, by weight, and also the most environmentally damaging.

(B)   Although barite can be harmful to marine organisms, it can be consumed safely by humans.

(C)   Offshore drilling is more damaging to the environment than is land-based drilling.

(D)   The use of drilling muds needs to be more tightly controlled by government.

(E)   If offshore drilling did not generate cuttings, it would be less harmful to the environment.[10]

Step 2: The obvious clue in the stem is the word "inferred." This is an Inference question. It is, however, an unusual type of Inference question—you must find the choice that can only be inferred by combining information from both passages.

Step 3: Once again, this stem doesn't provide specific research clues. You should think about the big picture instead.

Step 4: What concepts did both passages mention? Both described properties of drilling muds and their composition (you may recall thinking through this when you tackled question 6). The correct answer is likely to fall within this general scope, but a more specific prediction might be hard to make. Use your general prediction to make the answer choices easier to evaluate.

Step 5: Choice (A) describes barite, which does appear in both passages, but includes a fatal distortion—neither passage describes barite as the "most damaging" component of drilling muds (note the extreme language). Choice (B), by contrast, *is* supported by both passages and is the correct answer. Passage A indicates that barite can be safely ingested by humans, and Passage B describes some of barite's harmful effects on sea life. Choices (C), (D), and (E) are not supported by either passage.

10. **(B)**

Each of the following is supported by one or both of the passages EXCEPT:

(A)   Drillers monitor the suitability of the mud they are using.

(B)   The government requires drilling companies to disclose all ingredients used in their drilling muds.

(C)   In certain quantities, barite is not toxic to humans.

(D)   Oil reserves can be found within or beneath layers of rock.

(E)   Drilling deep oil wells requires the use of different mud recipes than does drilling shallow oil wells.[11]

---

[10]PrepTest 54, Sec 1, Q 9
[11]PrepTest 54, Sec 1, Q 10

Step 2: This question is identical to question 8. Once again, you must find the Inference that *can't* be made from either passage.

Step 3: Little is provided in the way of specific research clues. Not to worry—all the information you need is in the passage.

Step 4: As with the previous two questions, stay focused on the big picture and prepare to employ the process of elimination.

Step 5: You're likely to find support for choice (A) in Passage A, which discussed muds in a more general sense. The third paragraph mentions that drillers devise better muds to suit their purposes; this allows you to eliminate choice (A). The same paragraph mentions that many mud formulae are kept secret, which directly contradicts answer choice (B). Since choice (B) is false, it must be the correct answer. Choices (C) and (D) can be inferred from Passage A, and choice (E) is mentioned in Passage B.

11. **(C)**

Based on information in the passages, which one of the following, if true, provides the strongest support for a prediction that the proportion of oil-well drilling using OBMs will increase in the future?

(A) The cost of certain ingredients in WBMs is expected to increase steadily over the next several decades.

(B) The deeper an offshore oil well, the greater the concentration of barite that must be used in the drilling mud.

(C) Oil reserves at shallow depths have mostly been tapped, leaving primarily much deeper reserves for future drilling.

(D) It is unlikely that oil drillers will develop more efficient ways of removing OBM residues from cuttings that remain after being sieved from drilling fluids.

(E) Barite is a common mineral, the availability of which is virtually limitless.[12]

Step 2: The question asks you which choice provides "support" for the prediction that OBM use will increase. This is a Logic Reasoning question, one that requires you to strengthen a prediction.

Step 3: A glance at your Roadmap should direct you straight to Passage B, paragraph three.

Step 4: What might cause an increase in the use of OBMs? The information you need is at the very beginning of the paragraph. OBMs are typically used in deeper wells. The correct answer choice should indicate an increased proportion of deep wells—this would require a greater proportion of OBMs.

Step 5: The correct choice is (C)—if most future wells will be much deeper, you should expect to see a resultant increase in the use of OBMs. Choice (A) may have looked tempting, but even if the cost of WBM ingredients goes up, this doesn't necessarily imply that more OBMs will be used as a consequence (recall that the passages specify different usages for the different types of muds). Choices (B), (D), and (E) are irrelevant to the issue at hand; none of them gives a compelling reason why the proportion of OBMs would rise in the future.

12. **(A)**
    According to passage B, one reason OBMs are
    potentially more environmentally damaging than
    WBMs is that OBMs
    - (A) are slower to disperse
    - (B) contain greater concentrations of bentonite
    - (C) contain a greater number of additives
    - (D) are used for drilling deeper wells
    - (E) cannot be recycled[13]

Step 2: The stem asks for an explicitly stated reason why OBMs may be more damaging than WBMs. This is a Detail question.

Step 3: The stem directs you to Passage B, and your Roadmap indicates that the dangers of OBMs are discussed in paragraph three.

Step 4: The passage indicates that there is a "greater potential" (line 52) for harm because the hazardous components of OBMs do not disperse as quickly as those in WBMs.

Step 5: With so many excellent clues available, choice (A) is the clear match. Choice (B) contains a distortion—OBMs contain a greater concentration of barite, not necessarily bentonite. Choice (C) is not cited as a specific reason for the increased danger of OBMs, and neither is choice (E). While choice (D) does describe a property of OBMs, it's not a property that is tied to environmental damage.

Passage Three: "Overton Walker's 'Cakewalk'"

Step 1:

Aida Overton Walker (1880–1914), one of the
most widely acclaimed African American performers
of the early twentieth century, was known largely for
popularizing a dance form known as the cakewalk
(5) through her choreographing, performance, and
teaching of the dance. The cakewalk was originally
developed prior to the United States Civil War by
African Americans, for whom dance was a means of
maintaining cultural links within a slave society. It
(10) was based on traditional West African ceremonial
dances, and like many other African American
dances, it retained features characteristic of African
dance forms, such as gliding steps and an emphasis
on improvisation.

*Walker
popularized
cakewalk*

---

[13]PrepTest 54, Sec 1, Q 12

(15)   To this African-derived foundation, the cakewalk
        added certain elements from European dances: where

Cakewalk mix African dances feature flexible body postures, large

of African and groups and separate-sex dancing, the cakewalk

European developed into a high-kicking walk performed by a

(20)   procession of couples. Ironically, while these
        modifications later enabled the cakewalk to appeal to
        European Americans and become one of the first
        cultural forms to cross the racial divide in North
        America, they were originally introduced with satiric

(25)   intent. Slaves performed the grandiloquent walks in

Different levels order to parody the processional dances performed at

of parody slave owners' balls and, in general, the self-important
        manners of slave owners. To add a further irony, by
        the end of the nineteenth century, the cakewalk was

(30)   itself being parodied by European American stage
        performers, and these parodies in turn helped shape
        subsequent versions of the cakewalk
            While this complex evolution meant that the
        cakewalk was not a simple cultural phenomenon—

(35)   one scholar has characterized this layering of parody
        upon parody with the phrase "mimetic vertigo"—it is
        in fact what enabled the dance to attract its wide

Complex audience. In the cultural and socioeconomic flux of

roots led to the turn-of-the-century United States, where

popularity (40)   industrialization, urbanization, mass immigration, and
        rapid social mobility all reshaped the cultural
        landscape, an art form had to be capable of being
        many things to many people in order to appeal to a
        large audience.

(45)   Walker's remarkable success at popularizing the
        cakewalk across otherwise relatively rigid racial

Walker's boundaries rested on her ability to address within her

interpr. was interpretation of it the varying and sometimes

diversify conflicting demands placed on the dance. Middle-

(50)   class African Americans, for example, often
        denounced the cakewalk as disreputable, a complaint
        reinforced by the parodies circulating at the time.

Won over Walker won over this audience by refining the

different social cakewalk and emphasizing its fundamental grace.

groups (55)   Meanwhile, because middle- and upper-class
        European American often felt threatened by the
        tremendous cultural flux around them, they prized
        what they regarded as authentic art forms as bastions
        of stability; much of Walker's success with this

(60)   audience derived from her distillation of what was
        widely acclaimed as the most authentic cakewalk.
        Finally, Walker was able to gain the admiration of
        many newly rich industrialists and financiers, who
        found in the grand flourishes of her version of the

(65)   cakewalk a fitting vehicle for celebrating their
        newfound social rank.

Paragraph Structure: The passage introduces the **Topic** right out of the gate (the cakewalk) and the **Scope**, specifically Walker's popularization of it. The first paragraph establishes that Walker was known "largely" (line 3) for her performance of the cakewalk, then goes on to describe some defining features of the dance itself, noting that it was "based on" (line 10) traditional West African styles of dance.

The second paragraph expands on the cakewalk's background. It "added" (line 16) to its West African roots influences derived from European dances. These led to an interesting number of ironies (lines 20 & 28); "originally" (line 24) the dance was crafted as a parody of the self-important mannerisms of slave holders, but a "further irony" (line 28) was introduced later when European Americans began to parody the cakewalk, adding to its evolution. These layers of irony have the potential to be confusing, but don't get bogged down in them. As you read strategically, get the general gist of what the author is saying and move on. You can always return to this third paragraph and dig into it if a question requires it.

The lengthy fourth paragraph explains that Walker's success in popularizing this complex dance "rested on" (line 47) her ability to make it accessible to different audiences. This idea is followed by specific descriptions of exactly how she brought about acceptance of the cakewalk among different groups of Americans. This passage is descriptive rather than argumentative, so the author's **Purpose** was to describe the origins of the cakewalk and explain how Walker was able to popularize it. The **Main Idea:** The cakewalk evolved into a complex mix of different dance styles and ironic elements, and Walker's understanding of its complexities allowed her to make it accessible to different groups of Americans.

Question Triage: Begin with question 13, a Global question, and then look for straightforward Detail questions. The only one is question 16, so tackle it next. There are two Logic questions here—question 14 (Function) and question 15 (Parallel Reasoning). Since they both provide plenty of research clues it makes sense to complete them before the remaining Inference questions. Of the two Inference questions, 18 provides a slightly more specific reference in its stem than 17, so consider completing them in that order.

13. **(C)**

Which one of the following most accurately expresses the main point of the passage?

(A)   Walker, who was especially well known for her success in choreographing, performing, and teaching the cakewalk, was one of the most widely recognized African American performers of the early twentieth century.

(B)   In spite of the disparate influences that shaped the cakewalk, Walker was able to give the dance broad appeal because she distilled what was regarded as the most authentic version in an era that valued authenticity highly.

(C)   Walker popularized the cakewalk by capitalizing on the complex cultural mix that had developed from the dance's original blend of satire and cultural preservation, together with the effects of later parodies.

(D)   Whereas other versions of the cakewalk circulating at the beginning of the twentieth century were primarily parodic in nature, the version popularized by Walker combined both satire and cultural preservation.

(E)   Because Walker was able to recognize and preserve the characteristics of the cakewalk as African Americans originally performed it, it became the first popular art form to cross the racial divide in the United States.[14]

Step 2: This Global question asks for the "main point" of the passage.

Step 3: Consult the Main Idea of the passage in order to make your prediction.

Step 4: The correct answer should mention Walker's success in popularizing the cakewalk through her understanding of its complex history.

Step 5: The prediction matches correct choice (C) beautifully. Choice (A) focuses too narrowly on a single detail of the passage. Choice (B) distorts the reason why Walker's approach to the dance was popular, and choice (D) incorrectly suggests that Walker's version of the dance was the only one that contained cultural preservation. Choice (E) also contains a distortion—the cakewalk was identified as "one of the first" (lines 22–23) art forms to cross the racial divide.

[14]PrepTest 54, Sec 1, Q 13

14. **(D)**

The author describes the socioeconomic flux of the turn-of-the-century United States in the third paragraph primarily in order to

(A) argue that the cakewalk could have become popular only in such complex social circumstances

(B) detail the social context that prompted performers of the cakewalk to fuse African and European dance forms

(C) identify the target of the overlapping parodic layers that characterized the cakewalk

(D) indicate why a particular cultural environment was especially favorable for the success of the cakewalk

(E) explain why European American parodies of the cakewalk were able to reach wide audiences[15]

Step 2: The words "primarily in order to" identify this as a Logic Function question.

Step 3: The stem directs you to the third paragraph, so glance at your Roadmap in order to get the sense of context that Logic Function questions require. The paragraph as a whole explains that the cakewalk's complex roots are what allowed it to gain the level of popularity it eventually reached.

Step 4: The author mentions the state of flux quoted in the stem while explaining that an art form had to be "many things to many people" (line 43) in order to be popular. The author was providing an example of the kind of environment that led to this requirement, and that in turn allowed the cakewalk to become popular.

Step 5: Correct choice (D) describes the illustration predicted. Choice (A) is extreme; the author never suggests that the cakewalk could *only* have been popular in such times. Choices (B) and (C) are totally out of scope, and choice (E) distorts the author's intent. The third paragraph explained why Walker's version of the cakewalk flourished, not European American parodies.

15. **(C)**

> Which one of the following is most analogous to the author's account in the second paragraph of how the cakewalk came to appeal to European Americans?
> (A) Satirical versions of popular music songs are frequently more popular than the songs they parody.
> (B) A style of popular music grows in popularity among young listeners because it parodies the musical styles admired by older listeners.
> (C) A style of music becomes admired among popular music's audience in part because of elements that were introduced in order to parody popular music.
> (D) A once popular style of music wins back its audience by incorporating elements of the style of music that is currently most popular.
> (E) After popular music begins to appropriate elements of a traditional style of music, interest in that traditional music increases.[16]

Step 2: The question asks for an analogous situation to something mentioned in the passage, identifying this as a Parallel Reasoning question.

Step 3: Returning to the second paragraph, you discover that "ironically" (line 20) it was the element of parody (specifically parody of the formal dances held by slave owners) in the cakewalk that led to its popularization among European Americans.

Step 4: The correct answer will describe a situation that follows the general form that you discovered in your research—an art form that, in parodying a cultural group, adopts elements that make it popular among that group.

Step 5: Answer choice (C) is a match of the predicted relationship. It applies this relationship to classical music, but logically it is equivalent, and that's all that counts in a Parallel Reasoning question. Choice (A) misses the point by suggesting a satire that is more popular than the original—such a comparison was absent from the passage. Choice (B) brings in the irrelevant idea of younger vs. older listeners, and choice (D) describes a comeback, not a spreading of popularity. Choice (E) fails to mention the element of parody that was crucial to the prediction.

16. **(E)**

The passage asserts which one of the following about the cakewalk?

(A)   It was largely unknown outside African American culture until Walker popularized it.

(B)   It was mainly a folk dance, and Walker became one of only a handful of people to perform it professionally.

(C)   Its performance as parody became uncommon as a result of Walker's popularization of its authentic form.

(D)   Its West African origins became commonly known as a result of Walker's work.

(E)   It was one of the first cultural forms to cross racial lines in the United States.[17]

Step 2: "The passage asserts" a particular idea, which tells you that this is a Detail question.

Step 3: While the stem doesn't point to a specific area of the text in which to conduct your research, your Roadmap should remind you that, in general, descriptions of the cakewalk were primarily discussed in the first two paragraphs, with paragraphs three and four focused more heavily on Walker's popularization of the dance. So, you can probably find the correct answer in the first half of the passage.

Step 4: With so much text to research, don't waste your time trying to summarize the whole of paragraphs one and two—a brief glance at some key points will suffice. The cakewalk was originally based on West African ceremonial dances, and later went through a series of transformations as its popularity spread among different groups and was subsequently parodied and refined.

Step 5: With such a broad prediction, it may be necessary to go choice by choice. Choice (A) is refuted in the passage (the first paragraph describes the dance's roots in African American culture). Choice (B) also contradicts the passage, which describes the cakewalk as widely popular. Choice (C) distorts the role that parody played in the cakewalk's development, and choice (D) is out of scope. That leaves choice (E), the correct answer, which is directly supported by text in the second paragraph.

Note that, even without highly specific research clues in the stem, a solid knowledge of the author's main ideas can still help you eliminate wrong answer choices quickly and confidently.

---

[17]PrepTest 54, Sec 1, Q 16

17. **(E)**

It can be inferred from the passage that the author would be most likely to agree with which one of the following statements?

(A) Because of the broad appeal of humor, satiric art forms are often among the first to cross racial or cultural divisions.

(B) The interactions between African American and European American cultural forms often result in what is appropriately characterized as "mimetic vertigo."

(C) Middle-class European Americans who valued the cakewalk's authenticity subsequently came to admire other African American dances for the same reason.

(D) Because of the influence of African dance forms, some popular dances that later emerged in the United States featured separate-sex dancing.

(E) Some of Walker's admirers were attracted to her version of the cakewalk as a means for bolstering their social identities.[18]

Step 2: This is an Inference question, so you should be on the lookout for something that *must be true.*

Step 3: The only clue the stem gives you is a reference to the author. By reviewing the author's primary goals in writing the passage, you can make this question easier to work with.

Step 4: The author was most concerned with describing the reasons for Walker's ability to popularize the cakewalk—reasons described in paragraphs three and four. The dance appealed to a disparate audience because Walker was able to present its many layers to people with different cultural expectations. Keep the big picture in mind when evaluating the answer choices.

Step 5: Choice (A) is far too extreme. Just because the cakewalk contained elements of parody doesn't imply that it was a satiric art form, or that such art forms generally cross racial divisions. Choice (B) is also extreme; the author only mentions "mimetic vertigo" (line 36) as a specific description of the cakewalk's layers of parody. Choices (C) and (D) are out of scope and are not supported by the passage. Choice (E), the correct answer, is in line with the author's description of the cakewalk's popularity and is directly supported by examples at the end of the final paragraph.

---

[18]PrepTest 54, Sec 1, Q 17

18. **(A)**

The passage most strongly suggests that the author
would be likely to agree with which one of the
following statements about Walker's significance in
the history of the cakewalk?

(A)   Walker broadened the cakewalk's appeal by
        highlighting elements that were already
        present in the dance.

(B)   Walker's version of the cakewalk appealed to
        larger audiences than previous versions did
        because she accentuated its satiric dimension.

(C)   Walker popularized the cakewalk by
        choreographing various alternative
        interpretations of it, each tailored to the
        interests of a different cultural group.

(D)   Walker added a "mimetic vertigo" to the
        cakewalk by inserting imitations of other
        performers' cakewalking into her dance
        routines.

(E)   Walker revitalized the cakewalk by
        disentangling its complex admixture of
        African and European elements.[19]

Step 2: "Most strongly suggests" identifies this as another Inference question.

Step 3: There are some good clues in the stem—you need to find information in the passage reflecting the author's assessment of Walker's significance in the history of the cakewalk. Your Roadmap will indicate that the fourth paragraph contains the text you need.

Step 4: The author emphasizes that Walker's success "rested on" (line 47) her ability to interpret the dance's different demands in such a way that they appealed to diverse audiences. The correct answer should be supported by this central idea.

Step 5: Correct answer choice (A) is true—Walker did popularize the dance by emphasizing diverse elements that were already a part of its evolution. The comparison described in choice (B) is not supported by the passage. Choice (C) is in opposition to the author's Main Idea (and is therefore a 180); Walker didn't recreate the dance for different cultural groups, but rather interpreted the dance as a whole in such a way as to appeal to a large audience. Choice (D) misuses the concept of "mimetic vertigo" (line 36), and choice (E) is never suggested in the passage.

---

[19]PrepTest 54, Sec 1, Q 18

19. **(A)**

The passage provides sufficient information to answer which one of the following questions?

(A)   What were some of the attributes of African dance forms that were preserved in the cakewalk?

(B)   Who was the first performer to dance the cakewalk professionally?

(C)   What is an aspect of the cakewalk that was preserved in other North American dance forms?

(D)   What features were added to the original cakewalk by the stage parodies circulating at the end of the nineteenth century?

(E)   For about how many years into the twentieth century did the cakewalk remain widely popular?[20]

Step 2: This oddly worded question doesn't easily fall into a single category. Since you're trying to derive new information from the passage, think of it as an Inference question.

Step 3: The stem provides no clues to help you conduct your research.

Step 4: As with other vague questions, keep the author's Main Idea in mind as you work through the choices.

Step 5: The question in choice (A) asks about the attributes of African dance that were present in the cakewalk, which is addressed in the first paragraph. So, choice (A) is the correct answer. Choice (B) is unanswerable from the passage; the author describes Walker as a very popular performer, but not necessarily the first. The cakewalk's influence on other dances was not addressed in the passage, eliminating choice (C). The specific details asked about in choices (D) and (E) aren't mentioned, so both of these choices can be eliminated as well.

Passage Four: "Group Decision Making"

Step 1:

Cohesive groups are better

In principle a cohesive group—one whose members generally agree with one another and support one another's judgments—can do a much better job at decision making than it could if it were
(5)   noncohesive. When cohesiveness is low or lacking entirely, compliance out of fear of recrimination is likely to be strongest. To overcome this fear, participants in the group's deliberations need to be confident that they are members in good standing and
(10)   that the others will continue to value their role in the group, whether or not they agree about a particular issue under discussion. As members of a group feel more accepted by the others, they acquire greater

---

Members become more vocal/honest

(15) freedom to say what they really think, becoming less likely to use deceitful arguments or to play it safe by dancing around the issues with vapid or conventional comments. Typically, then, the more cohesive a group becomes, the less its members will deliberately censor what they say out of fear of being punished socially

(20) for antagonizing their fellow members.

Problem: members won't deviate

But group cohesiveness can have pitfalls as well: while the members of a highly cohesive group can feel much freer to deviate from the majority, their desire for genuine concurrence on every important

(25) issue often inclines them not to use this freedom. In a highly cohesive group of decision makers, the danger is not that individuals will conceal objections they harbor regarding a proposal favored by the majority, but that they will think the proposal is a good one

(30) without attempting to carry out a critical scrutiny that could reveal grounds for strong objections. Members may then decide that any misgivings they feel are not worth pursuing—that the benefit of any doubt should be given to the group consensus. In this way, they

Groupthink leads to bad decisions

(35) may fall victim to a syndrome known as "groupthink," which one psychologist concerned with collective decision making has defined as "a deterioration of mental efficiency, reality testing, and moral judgment that results from in-group pressures."

(40) Based on analyses of major fiascoes of international diplomacy and military decision making, researchers have identified groupthink behavior as a recurring pattern that involves several factors: overestimation of the group's power and morality,

Groupthink patterns

(45) manifested, for example, in an illusion of invulnerability, which creates excessive optimism; closed-mindedness to warnings of problems and to alternative viewpoints; and unwarranted pressures toward uniformity, including self-censorship with

(50) respect to doubts about the group's reasoning and a concomitant shared illusion of unanimity concerning group decisions. Cohesiveness of the decision-making group is an essential antecedent condition for this

Other factors besides cohesiveness lead to groupthink

syndrome but not a sufficient one, so it is important

(55) to work toward identifying the additional factors that determine whether group cohesiveness will deteriorate into groupthink or allow for effective decision making.

Passage Structure: This passage discusses decision making in groups (the **Topic**) and asserts that more cohesive groups make better decisions. The author investigates this phenomenon further—in order to "overcome" (line 7) the fear of speaking out, members of a group "need to be" (line 8) confident that they're valued, and "typically" (line 17) they will speak more honestly as a consequence.

The Keyword "but" (line 21) at the onset of paragraph two draws you nearer to the author's primary intentions: There are problems associated with high levels of cohesion as members become more concerned with agreement than with critical thinking. In this way, they may fall "victim" (line 35) to the phenomenon of "groupthink" (line 36), the author's **Scope**. Groupthink is "defined" (line 37) by a psychologist as leading to the deterioration of a group's ability to make sound decisions.

The author begins the third paragraph with some emphatic Keywords, connecting groupthink to a number of "major fiascoes" (line 40) throughout history. The author notes that group cohesiveness is "essential" (line 53) to groupthink, but "not . . . sufficient" (line 54), also stressing the need to understand other factors that may lead to this unfortunate condition.

The author's **Purpose** is to describe the phenomenon of groupthink and examine some of its implications for decision making in groups. The **Main Idea:** Groupthink is a dangerous phenomenon that can sometimes follow from cohesiveness in groups, but other factors may be responsible as well.

Question Triage: Your only Global point is question 20, so score it first. Questions 23 and 25 are natural follow-ups—they're relatively brief Detail questions. Question 26 is also fairly straightforward—a Function question with a specific line reference. Your next stop should probably be question 22, a Strengthen question, because the remaining Inference questions don't look as inviting. Question 24 is Inference, but the stem is fairly specific (asking what the author and certain researchers would agree on), making it a better choice than both 21, which is somewhat convoluted, and 27, which provides less information. Depending on time constraints, you can finish up 21 and 27 in either order, but be ready to guess strategically if you're running low on time.

20. **(A)**

Which one of the following most accurately expresses the main point of the passage?

(A)   Despite its value in encouraging frank discussion, high cohesion can lead to a debilitating type of group decision making called groupthink.

(B)   Group members can guard against groupthink if they have a good understanding of the critical role played by cohesion.

(C)   Groupthink is a dysfunctional collective decision-making pattern that can occur in diplomacy and military affairs.

(D)   Low cohesion in groups is sometimes desirable when higher cohesion involves a risk of groupthink behavior.

(E)   Future efforts to guard against groupthink will depend on the results of ongoing research into the psychology of collective decision making.[21]

Step 2: The phrase "main point" alerts you that this is a Global question.

Step 3: Think about the author's Main Idea rather than researching specific text.

Step 4: The author's primary goal is to describe groupthink, a negative consequence that can sometimes follow from high cohesiveness in groups.

Step 5: The correct match is choice (A). Choice (B) is too specific and unsupported by the passage. Choice (C) correctly defines groupthink, but it is too narrow in scope, failing to capture the author's connection of groupthink to cohesiveness. Choice (D) distorts the author's intent, as it's never suggested that low cohesion is desirable. Choice (E) wanders out of scope, since the author never makes any predictions about future analysis of groupthink.

---

[21]PrepTest 54, Sec 1, Q 20

21. **(C)**

A group of closely associated colleagues has made a disastrous diplomatic decision after a series of meetings marked by disagreement over conflicting alternatives. It can be inferred from the passage that the author would be most likely to say that this scenario

(A)   provides evidence of chronic indecision, thus indicating a weak level of cohesion in general

(B)   indicates that the group's cohesiveness was coupled with some other factor to produce a groupthink fiasco

(C)   provides no evidence that groupthink played a role in the group's decision

(D)   provides evidence that groupthink can develop even in some groups that do not demonstrate an "illusion of unanimity"

(E)   indicates that the group probably could have made its decision-making procedure more efficient by studying the information more thoroughly[22]

Step 2: The words "it can be inferred" tell you that this is an Inference question.

Step 3: Read the question carefully for clues. The stem describes a group making a disastrous decision following a lot of disagreement. This doesn't necessarily guide you directly to a specific part of the text in which to conduct research, but it does relate to the author's definition of "groupthink" and its causes. Recall that the author describes a close relationship between groupthink and cohesiveness—in fact, he states that cohesion is "essential" (line 53) to groupthink.

Step 4: In the hypothetical situation, the group making the decision is argumentative. The author of this passage is not primarily concerned with such groups; they lack the cohesiveness that can lead to groupthink. This may not seem like much to go on, but it does give you enough information to state with certainty that groupthink was probably not a factor in the disastrous decisions made by this group.

Step 5: Choice (C) is a perfect match of the prediction. The hypothetical situation doesn't supply enough information for the deduction described in choice (A), since there's no way to assess whether this group displays "chronic indecision." Choices (B) and (D) suggest that groupthink was at work, in direct opposition to the passage. Choice (E) is completely out of scope; there's no way to know whether more information would have helped this group.

---

[22]PrepTest 54, Sec 1, Q 21

22. **(C)**

Which one of the following, if true, would most support the author's contentions concerning the conditions under which groupthink takes place?

(A)   A study of several groups, each made up of members of various professions, found that most fell victim to groupthink.

(B)   There is strong evidence that respectful dissent is more likely to occur in cohesive groups than in groups in which there is little internal support.

(C)   Extensive analyses of decisions made by a large number of groups found no cases of groupthink in groups whose members generally distrust one another's judgments.

(D)   There is substantial evidence that groupthink is especially likely to take place when members of a group develop factions whose intransigence prolongs the group's deliberations.

(E)   Ample research demonstrates that voluntary deference to group opinion is not a necessary factor for the formation of groupthink behavior.[23]

Step 2: The stem asks you to "support" one of the author's arguments. This is a Logical Reasoning question, and your task is to strengthen the argument.

Step 3: According to the Roadmap, you can find the conditions under which groupthink occurs in the second paragraph. The primary cause that the author is concerned with is a high degree of cohesiveness within a group, which leads to the uncritical acceptance of ideas.

Step 4: How can you best support the author's idea? If it's true that high cohesion leads to groupthink, evidence that groupthink fails to occur in the absence of such cohesiveness would bolster the author's causal assertion. The correct answer will probably reflect this idea.

Step 5: Correct choice (C) is a perfect match, indicating a lack of groupthink where cohesiveness is low. Choices (A) and (B) are totally irrelevant to the comparison of highly cohesive groups to more argumentative groups. Choice (D) suggests that groupthink is likely to occur in fractious groups, but if this were true it would weaken the author's argument. Choice (E) similarly works against the author's hypothesis by suggesting that uncritical acceptance of group ideas doesn't lead to groupthink.

---

[23]PrepTest 54, Sec 1, Q 22

23. **(B)**

The passage mentions which one of the following as a component of groupthink?

(A)   unjustified suspicions among group members regarding an adversary's intentions

(B)   strong belief that the group's decisions are right

(C)   group members working under unusually high stress, leading to illusions of invulnerability

(D)   the deliberate use of vapid, clichéd arguments

(E)   careful consideration of objections to majority positions[24]

Step 2: Since the stem asks for something explicitly mentioned in the passage, this is a Detail question.

Step 3: Your Roadmap should lead you to the final paragraph, as this is where the author describes specific patterns of groupthink, including excessive optimism, closed-mindedness toward opposing viewpoints, and the suppression of any doubts that the group is right.

Step 4: The correct answer will paraphrase one or more of the ideas you uncovered in your research. If you read them carefully you'll find the match.

Step 5: Choice (B) is the correct answer, paraphrasing the convictions described in the final paragraph. Choices (A) and (D) are out of scope. Choice (C) distorts the language of the passage, describing a definition of the term "stress" that doesn't comply with author's use of it. Choice (E) is a 180.

24. **(E)**

It can be inferred from the passage that both the author of the passage and the researchers mentioned in the passage would be most likely to agree with which one of the following statements about groupthink?

(A)   Groupthink occurs in all strongly cohesive groups, but its contribution to collective decision making is not fully understood.

(B)   The causal factors that transform group cohesion into groupthink are unique to each case.

(C)   The continued study of cohesiveness of groups is probably fruitless for determining what factors elicit groupthink.

(D)   Outside information cannot influence group decisions once they have become determined by groupthink.

(E)   On balance, groupthink cannot be expected to have a beneficial effect in a group's decision making.[25]

24PrepTest 54, Sec 1, Q 23
25PrepTest 54, Sec 1, Q 24

Step 2: Since the stem asks for what can be inferred, this is an Inference question.

Step 3: There are good clues in the question stem. You need to compare the author's point of view with that of the researchers. A scan of the passage leads to paragraph three, where researchers examining "fiascoes" (line 40) have identified specific patterns of behavior in groupthink.

Step 4: How does the author's opinion coincide with that of the researchers? In the second paragraph, the author says that cohesive groups may "fall victim" (line 35) to groupthink. What the researchers and the author seem to agree on is that groupthink is undesirable and leads to poor decision making. The correct answer should reflect this idea.

Step 5: The match is correct answer choice (E). Choice (A) is extreme and voices an idea that neither the author nor the researchers express. Choice (D) is similarly extreme; the researchers suggest that groupthink leads to closed mindedness, but stop short of saying that no outside information can get in. Choice (B) is not supported by any specific text, and the prediction described in choice (C) is never mentioned by the author or the researchers.

25. **(E)**

   In the passage, the author says which one of the
   following about conformity in decision-making
   groups?
   (A)   Enforced conformity may be appropriate in
         some group decision situations.
   (B)   A high degree of conformity is often expected
         of military decision-making group members.
   (C)   Inappropriate group conformity can result
         from inadequate information.
   (D)   Voluntary conformity occurs much less
         frequently than enforced conformity.
   (E)   Members of noncohesive groups may
         experience psychological pressure to conform.[26]

Step 2: The stem asks for something the author mentions about conformity. This is a Detail question.

Step 3: The first paragraph describes the author's general pronouncements about conformity in groups. How conformity is achieved is, according to the author, dependent on the level of cohesiveness in the group; if the group lacks cohesiveness, conformity is established through fear. In order to "overcome this fear" (line 7), members of the group need to feel valued.

Step 4: As with other Detail questions, you should expect the correct answer to paraphrase information you've reviewed in your research.

---

[26]PrepTest 54, Sec 1, Q 25

Step 5: Correct choice (E) accurately describes the fear described in the first paragraph. The author never opines whether such conformity is "appropriate," eliminating choice (A). Choices (B) and (C) are entirely outside the scope of this question, and choice (D) is irrelevant, as the author never compares the frequency of voluntary vs. enforced conformity.

26. **(A)**

In line 5, the author mentions low group cohesiveness primarily in order to

(A)   contribute to a claim that cohesiveness can be conducive to a freer exchange of views in groups

(B)   establish a comparison between groupthink symptoms and the attributes of low-cohesion groups

(C)   suggest that there may be ways to make both cohesive and noncohesive groups more open to dissent

(D)   indicate that both cohesive and noncohesive groups may be susceptible to groupthink dynamics

(E)   lay the groundwork for a subsequent proposal for overcoming the debilitating effects of low cohesion[27]

Step 2: The key phrase "in order to" identifies this as a Logic Function question.

Step 3: Remember that Logic Function questions rely on your understanding of context. Use your Roadmap to review the main point of the first paragraph as a whole before considering the role that low group cohesiveness plays within it.

Step 4: The author was primarily concerned in the first paragraph with describing the advantages of cohesiveness in group decision making. The brief reference to low cohesion allowed the author to demonstrate how, by contrast, high cohesion is preferable. This context will lead you to the correct answer choice.

Step 5: Choice (A) is the match—the cited text served author's overall claim about cohesive groups. Choices (B) and (D) erroneously refer to groupthink, which is not addressed until paragraph two. Choice (C) is completely out of scope, and choice (E) refers to a proposal that never appears in the passage.

---

[27]PrepTest 54, Sec 1, Q 26

27. **(B)**

Based on the passage, it can be inferred that the author would be most likely to agree with which one of the following?

(A)   Highly cohesive groups are more likely to engage in confrontational negotiating styles with adversaries than are those with low cohesion.

(B)   It is difficult for a group to examine all relevant options critically in reaching decisions unless it has a fairly high degree of cohesiveness.

(C)   A group with varied viewpoints on a given issue is less likely to reach a sound decision regarding that issue than is a group whose members are unified in their outlook.

(D)   Intense stress and high expectations are the key factors in the formation of groupthink.

(E)   Noncohesive groups can, under certain circumstances, develop all of the symptoms of groupthink.[28]

Step 2: The word "inferred" makes this stem easy to identify as an Inference question.

Step 3: As with other Inference questions that provide little direction for your research, think about the author's main ideas before moving on to the choices.

Step 4: The author opined that groups with a high level of cohesiveness were more apt to make good decisions than groups with low cohesion, although such groups are vulnerable to the debilitating effects of groupthink. Keep these ideas in mind and proceed to the answer choices.

Step 5: The comparison in choice (A) has no support in the passage. Choice (B), the correct answer, is supported by the author's contention that in cohesive groups, members feel freer to express dissenting views—a definite requirement for the examination of all relevant options. Choice (C) might be true in some cases, but overlooks the possibility that a unified group may fall prey to groupthink. Choice (D) confuses the results of groupthink with its causes, and choice (E) has no support in the text of the passage.

---

[28]PrepTest 54, Sec 1, Q 27

CHAPTER 21

FULL-LENGTH SECTION 2[1]

Time—35 minutes

27 Questions

<u>Directions:</u> Each set of questions in this section is based on a single passage or a pair of passages. The questions are to be answered on the basis of what is <u>stated</u> or <u>implied</u> in the passage or pair of passages. For some of the questions, more than one of the choices could conceivably answer the question. However, you are to choose the <u>best</u> answer, that is, the response that most accurately and completely answers the question, and blacken the corresponding space on your answer sheet.

---

[1]PrepTest 55, Sec 2

Often when a highly skilled and experienced employee leaves one company to work for another, there is the potential for a transfer of sensitive information between competitors. Two basic principles
(5) in such cases appear irreconcilable: the right of the company to its intellectual property—its proprietary data and trade secrets—and the right of individuals to seek gainful employment and to make free use of their abilities. Nevertheless, the courts have often tried to
(10) preserve both parties' legal rights by refusing to prohibit the employee from working for the competitor, but at the same time providing an injunction against disclosure of any of the former employer's secrets. It has been argued that because such measures help
(15) generate suspicions and similar psychological barriers to full and free utilization of abilities in the employee's new situation, they are hardly effective in upholding the individual's rights to free employment decisions. But it is also doubtful that they are effective in
(20) preserving trade secrets.

It is obviously impossible to divest oneself of that part of one's expertise that one has acquired from former employers and coworkers. Nor, in general, can one selectively refrain from its use, given that it has
(25) become an integral part of one's total intellectual capacity. Nevertheless, almost any such information that is not public knowledge may legitimately be claimed as corporate property: normal employment agreements provide for corporate ownership of all
(30) relevant data, including inventions, generated by the employee in connection with the company's business.

Once an employee takes a position with a competitor, the trade secrets that have been acquired by that employee may manifest themselves clearly and
(35) consciously. This is what court injunctions seek to prohibit. But they are far more likely to manifest themselves subconsciously and inconspicuously—for example, in one's daily decisions at the new post, or in the many small contributions one might make to a large
(40) team effort—often in the form of an intuitive sense of what to do or to avoid. Theoretically, an injunction also prohibits such inadvertent "leakage." However, the former employer faces the practical problem of securing evidence of such leakage, for little will
(45) usually be apparent from the public activities of the new employer. And even if the new employee's activities appear suspicious, there is the further problem of distinguishing trade secrets from what may be legitimately asserted as technological skills
(50) developed independently by the employee or already possessed by the new employer. This is a major stumbling block in the attempt to protect trade secrets, since the proprietor has no recourse against others who independently generate the same information. It is
(55) therefore unlikely that an injunction against disclosure of trade secrets to future employers actually prevents any transfer of information except for the passage of documents and other concrete embodiments of the secrets.

1. Which one of the following most accurately expresses the main point of the passage?

(A) There are more effective ways than court injunctions to preserve both a company's right to protect its intellectual property and individuals' rights to make free use of their abilities.

(B) Court injunctions must be strengthened if they are to remain a relevant means of protecting corporations' trade secrets.

(C) Enforcement of court injunctions designed to protect proprietary information is impossible when employees reveal such information to new employers.

(D) Court injunctions prohibiting employees from disclosing former employers' trade secrets to new employers probably do not achieve all of their intended objectives.

(E) The rights of employees to make full use of their talents and previous training are being seriously eroded by the prohibitions placed on them by court injunctions designed to prevent the transfer of trade secrets.

2. Given the passage's content and tone, which one of the following statements would most likely be found elsewhere in a work from which this passage is an excerpt?

   (A)   Given the law as it stands, corporations concerned about preserving trade secrets might be best served by giving their employees strong incentives to stay in their current jobs.

   (B)   While difficult to enforce and interpret, injunctions are probably the most effective means of halting the inadvertent transfer of trade secrets while simultaneously protecting the rights of employees.

   (C)   Means of redress must be made available to companies that suspect, but cannot prove, that former employees are revealing protected information to competitors.

   (D)   Even concrete materials such as computer disks are so easy to copy and conceal that it will be a waste of time for courts to try to prevent the spread of information through physical theft.

   (E)   The psychological barriers that an injunction can place on an employee in a new workplace are inevitably so subtle that they have no effect on the employee.

3. The author's primary purpose in the passage is to

   (A)   suggest that injunctions against the disclosure of trade secrets not only create problems for employees in the workplace, but also are unable to halt the illicit spread of proprietary information

   (B)   suggest that the information contained in "documents and other concrete embodiments" is usually so trivial that injunctions do little good in protecting intellectual property

   (C)   argue that new methods must be found to address the delicate balance between corporate and individual rights

   (D)   support the position that the concept of protecting trade secrets is no longer viable in an age of increasing access to information

   (E)   argue that injunctions are not necessary for the protection of trade secrets

4. The passage provides the most support for which one of the following assertions?

   (A)   Injunctions should be imposed by the courts only when there is strong reason to believe that an employee will reveal proprietary information.

   (B)   There is apparently no reliable way to protect both the rights of companies to protect trade secrets and the rights of employees to seek new employment.

   (C)   Employees should not be allowed to take jobs with their former employer's competitors when their new job could compromise trade secrets of their former employers.

   (D)   The multiplicity of means for transferring information in the workplace only increases the need for injunctions.

   (E)   Some companies seek injunctions as a means of punishing employees who take jobs with their competitors.

5. With which one of the following statements regarding documents and other concrete embodiments mentioned in line 58 would the author be most likely to agree?

   (A)   While the transfer of such materials would be damaging, even the seemingly innocuous contributions of an employee to a competitor can do more harm in the long run.

   (B)   Such materials are usually less informative than what the employee may recollect about a previous job.

   (C)   Injunctions against the disclosure of trade secrets should carefully specify which materials are included in order to focus on the most damaging ones.

   (D)   Large-scale transfer of documents and other materials cannot be controlled by injunctions.

   (E)   Such concrete materials lend themselves to control and identification more readily than do subtler means of transferring information.

6. In the passage, the author makes which one of the following claims?

   (A) Injunctions against the disclosure of trade secrets limit an employee's chances of being hired by a competitor.

   (B) Measures against the disclosure of trade secrets are unnecessary except in the case of documents and other concrete embodiments of the secrets.

   (C) Employees who switch jobs to work for a competitor usually unintentionally violate the law by doing so.

   (D) Employers are not restricted in the tactics they can use when seeking to secure protected information from new employees.

   (E) What may seem like intellectual theft may in fact be an example of independent innovation.

The following passages concern a plant called purple loosestrife. Passage A is excerpted from a report issued by a prairie research council; passage B from a journal of sociology.

Passage A

Purple loosestrife (*Lythrum salicaria*), an aggressive and invasive perennial of Eurasian origin, arrived with settlers in eastern North America in the early 1800s and has spread across the continent's
(5) midlatitude wetlands. The impact of purple loosestrife on native vegetation has been disastrous, with more than 50 percent of the biomass of some wetland communities displaced. Monospecific blocks of this weed have maintained themselves for at least 20 years.
(10) Impacts on wildlife have not been well studied, but serious reductions in waterfowl and aquatic furbearer productivity have been observed. In addition, several endangered species of vertebrates are threatened with further degradation of their
(15) breeding habitats. Although purple loosestrife can invade relatively undisturbed habitats, the spread and dominance of this weed have been greatly accelerated in disturbed habitats. While digging out the plants can temporarily halt their spread, there has been little
(20) research on long-term purple loosestrife control. Glyphosate has been used successfully, but no measure of the impact of this herbicide on native plant communities has been made.

With the spread of purple loosestrife growing
(25) exponentially, some form of integrated control is needed. At present, coping with purple loosestrife hinges on early detection of the weed's arrival in areas, which allows local eradication to be carried out with minimum damage to the native plant community.

Passage B

(30) The war on purple loosestrife is apparently conducted on behalf of nature, an attempt to liberate the biotic community from the tyrannical influence of a life-destroying invasive weed. Indeed, purple loosestrife control is portrayed by its practitioners as
(35) an environmental initiative intended to save nature rather than control it. Accordingly, the purple loosestrife literature, scientific and otherwise, dutifully discusses the impacts of the weed on endangered species—and on threatened biodiversity
(40) more generally. Purple loosestrife is a pollution, according to the scientific community, and all of nature suffers under its pervasive influence.

Regardless of the perceived and actual ecological effects of the purple invader, it is apparent that
(45) popular pollution ideologies have been extended into the wetlands of North America. Consequently, the scientific effort to liberate nature from purple loosestrife has failed to decouple itself from its philosophical origin as an instrument to control nature
(50) to the satisfaction of human desires. Birds, particularly game birds and waterfowl, provide the bulk of the justification for loosestrife management. However, no bird species other than the canvasback has been identified in the literature as endangered by
(55) purple loosestrife. The impact of purple loosestrife on furbearing mammals is discussed at great length, though none of the species highlighted (muskrat, mink) can be considered threatened in North America. What is threatened by purple loosestrife is the
(60) economics of exploiting such preferred species and the millions of dollars that will be lost to the economies of the United States and Canada from reduced hunting, trapping, and recreation revenues due to a decline in the production of the wetland
(65) resource.

7. Both passages explicitly mention which one of the following?

(A) furbearing animals
(B) glyphosate
(C) the threat purple loosestrife poses to economies
(D) popular pollution ideologies
(E) literature on purple loosestrife control

8. Each of the passages contains information sufficient to answer which one of the following questions?

(A) Approximately how long ago did purple loosestrife arrive in North America?
(B) Is there much literature discussing the potential benefit that hunters might derive from purple loosestrife management?
(C) What is an issue regarding purple loosestrife management on which both hunters and farmers agree?
(D) Is the canvasback threatened with extinction due to the spread of purple loosestrife?
(E) What is a type of terrain that is affected in at least some parts of North America by the presence of purple loosestrife?

9. It can be inferred that the authors would be most likely to disagree about which one of the following?

    (A) Purple loosestrife spreads more quickly in disturbed habitats than in undisturbed habitats.
    (B) The threat posed by purple loosestrife to local aquatic furbearer populations is serious.
    (C) Most people who advocate that eradication measures be taken to control purple loosestrife are not genuine in their concern for the environment.
    (D) The size of the biomass that has been displaced by purple loosestrife is larger than is generally thought.
    (E) Measures should be taken to prevent other non-native plant species from invading North America.

10. Which one of the following most accurately describes the attitude expressed by the author of passage B toward the overall argument represented by passage A?

    (A) enthusiastic agreement
    (B) cautious agreement
    (C) pure neutrality
    (D) general ambivalence
    (E) pointed skepticism

11. It can be inferred that both authors would be most likely to agree with which one of the following statements regarding purple loosestrife?

    (A) As it increases in North America, some wildlife populations tend to decrease.
    (B) Its establishment in North America has had a disastrous effect on native North American wetland vegetation in certain regions.
    (C) It is very difficult to control effectively with herbicides.
    (D) Its introduction into North America was a great ecological blunder.
    (E) When it is eliminated from a given area, it tends to return to that area fairly quickly.

12. Which one of the following is true about the relationship between the two passages?

    (A) Passage A presents evidence that directly counters claims made in passage B.
    (B) Passage B assumes what passage A explicitly argues for.
    (C) Passage B displays an awareness of the arguments touched on in passage A, but not vice versa.
    (D) Passage B advocates a policy that passage A rejects.
    (E) Passage A downplays the seriousness of claims made in passage B.

13. Which one of the following, if true, would cast doubt on the argument in passage B but bolster the argument in passage A?

    (A) Localized population reduction is often a precursor to widespread endangerment of a species.
    (B) Purple loosestrife was barely noticed in North America before the advent of suburban sprawl in the 1950s.
    (C) The amount by which overall hunting, trapping, and recreation revenues would be reduced as a result of the extinction of one or more species threatened by purple loosestrife represents a significant portion of those revenues.
    (D) Some environmentalists who advocate taking measures to eradicate purple loosestrife view such measures as a means of controlling nature.
    (E) Purple loosestrife has never become a problem in its native habitat, even though no effort has been made to eradicate it there.

With their recognition of Maxine Hong Kingston as a major literary figure, some critics have suggested that her works have been produced almost *ex nihilo*, saying that they lack a large traceable body of direct (5) literary antecedents especially within the Chinese American heritage in which her work is embedded. But these critics, who have examined only the development of written texts, the most visible signs of a culture's narrative production, have overlooked Kingston's (10) connection to the long Chinese tradition of a highly developed genre of song and spoken narrative known as "talk-story" (*gong gu tsai*).

Traditionally performed in the dialects of various ethnic enclaves, talk-story has been maintained within (15) the confines of the family and has rarely surfaced into print. The tradition dates back to Sung dynasty (A.D. 970–1279) storytellers in China, and in the United States it is continually revitalized by an overlapping sequence of immigration from China. (20) Thus, Chinese immigrants to the U.S. had a fully established, sophisticated oral culture, already ancient and capable of producing masterpieces, by the time they began arriving in the early nineteenth century. This transplanted oral heritage simply embraced new (25) subject matter or new forms of Western discourse, as in the case of Kingston's adaptations written in English.

Kingston herself believes that as a literary artist she is one in a long line of performers shaping a recalcitrant history into talk-story form. She (30) distinguishes her "thematic" storytelling memory processes, which sift and reconstruct the essential elements of personally remembered stories, from the memory processes of a print-oriented culture that emphasizes the retention of precise sequences of (35) words. Nor does the entry of print into the storytelling process substantially change her notion of the character of oral tradition. For Kingston, "writer" is synonymous with "singer" or "performer" in the ancient sense of privileged keeper, transmitter, and creator of stories (40) whose current stage of development can be frozen in print, but which continue to grow both around and from that frozen text.

Kingston's participation in the tradition of talk-story is evidenced in her book *China Men*, which (45) utilizes forms typical of that genre and common to most oral cultures including: a fixed "grammar" of repetitive themes; a spectrum of stock characters; symmetrical structures, including balanced oppositions (verbal or physical contests, antithetical characters, (50) dialectical discourse such as question-answer forms and riddles); and repetition. In *China Men*, Kingston also succeeds in investing idiomatic English with the allusive texture and oral-aural qualities of the Chinese language, a language rich in aural and visual puns, (55) making her work a written form of talk-story.

14. Which one of the following most accurately states the main point of the passage?

   (A) Despite some critics' comments, Kingston's writings have significant Chinese American antecedents, which can be found in the traditional oral narrative form known as talk-story.

   (B) Analysis of Kingston's writings, especially *China Men*, supports her belief that literary artists can be performers who continue to reconstruct their stories even after they have been frozen in print.

   (C) An understanding of Kingston's work and of Chinese American writers in general reveals that critics of ethnic literatures in the United States have been mistaken in examining only written texts.

   (D) Throughout her writings Kingston uses techniques typical of the talk-story genre, especially the retention of certain aspects of Chinese speech in the written English text.

   (E) The writings of Kingston have rekindled an interest in talk-story, which dates back to the Sung dynasty, and was extended to the United States with the arrival of Chinese immigrants in the nineteenth century.

15. Which one of the following can be most reasonably inferred from the passage?

   (A) In the last few years, written forms of talk-story have appeared in Chinese as often as they have in English.

   (B) Until very recently, scholars have held that oral storytelling in Chinese ethnic enclaves was a unique oral tradition.

   (C) Talk-story has developed in the United States through a process of combining Chinese, Chinese American, and other oral storytelling forms.

   (D) Chinese American talk-story relies upon memory processes that do not emphasize the retention of precise sequences of words.

   (E) The connection between certain aspects of Kingston's work and talk-story is argued by some critics to be rather tenuous and questionable.

16. It can be inferred from the passage that the author uses the phrase "personally remembered stories" (line 32) primarily to refer to

    (A) a literary genre of first-person storytelling
    (B) a thematically organized personal narrative of one's own past
    (C) partially idiosyncratic memories of narratives
    (D) the retention in memory of precise sequences of words
    (E) easily identifiable thematic issues in literature

17. In which one of the following is the use of cotton fibers or cotton cloth most analogous to Kingston's use of the English language as described in lines 51–55?

    (A) Scraps of plain cotton cloth are used to create a multicolored quilt.
    (B) The surface texture of woolen cloth is simulated in a piece of cotton cloth by a special process of weaving.
    (C) Because of its texture, cotton cloth is used for a certain type of clothes for which linen is inappropriate.
    (D) In making a piece of cloth, cotton fiber is substituted for linen because of the roughly similar texture of the two materials.
    (E) Because of their somewhat similar textures, cotton and linen fibers are woven together in a piece of cloth to achieve a savings in price over a pure linen cloth.

18. The passage most clearly suggests that Kingston believes which one of the following about at least some of the stories contained in her writings?

    (A) Since they are intimately tied to the nature of the Chinese language, they can be approximated, but not adequately expressed, in English.
    (B) They should be thought of primarily as ethnic literature and evaluated accordingly by critics.
    (C) They will likely be retold and altered to some extent in the process.
    (D) Chinese American history is best chronicled by traditional talk-story.
    (E) Their significance and beauty cannot be captured at all in written texts.

19. The author's argument in the passage would be most weakened if which one of the following were true?

    (A) Numerous writers in the United States have been influenced by oral traditions.
    (B) Most Chinese American writers' work is very different from Kingston's.
    (C) Native American storytellers use narrative devices similar to those used in talk-story.
    (D) *China Men* is for the most part atypical of Kingston's literary works.
    (E) Literary critics generally appreciate the authenticity of Kingston's work.

20. The author's specific purpose in detailing typical talk-story forms (lines 43–51) is to

    (A) show why Kingston's book *China Men* establishes her as a major literary figure
    (B) support the claim that Kingston's use of typically oral techniques makes her work a part of the talk-story tradition
    (C) dispute the critics' view that Chinese American literature lacks literary antecedents
    (D) argue for Kingston's view that the literary artist is at best a "privileged keeper" of stories
    (E) provide an alternative to certain critics' view that Kingston's work should be judged primarily as literature

21. Which one of the following most accurately identifies the attitude shown by the author in the passage toward talk-story?

    (A) scholarly appreciation for its longstanding artistic sophistication
    (B) mild disappointment that it has not distinguished itself from other oral traditions
    (C) tentative approval of its resistance to critical evaluations
    (D) clear respect for the diversity of its ancient sources and cultural derivations
    (E) open admiration for the way it uses song to express narrative

In economics, the term "speculative bubble" refers to a large upward move in an asset's price driven not by the asset's fundamentals—that is, by the earnings derivable from the asset—but rather by
(5) mere speculation that someone else will be willing to pay a higher price for it. The price increase is then followed by a dramatic decline in price, due to a loss in confidence that the price will continue to rise, and the "bubble" is said to have burst. According to
(10) Charles Mackay's classic nineteenth-century account, the seventeenth-century Dutch tulip market provides an example of a speculative bubble. But the economist Peter Garber challenges Mackay's view, arguing that there is no evidence that the Dutch tulip
(15) market really involved a speculative bubble.

By the seventeenth century, the Netherlands had become a center of cultivation and development of new tulip varieties, and a market had developed in which rare varieties of bulbs sold at high prices. For
(20) example, a Semper Augustus bulb sold in 1625 for an amount of gold worth about U.S.$11,000 in 1999. Common bulb varieties, on the other hand, sold for very low prices. According to Mackay, by 1636 rapid price rises attracted speculators, and prices of many
(25) varieties surged upward from November 1636 through January 1637. Mackay further states that in February 1637 prices suddenly collapsed; bulbs could not be sold at 10 percent of their peak values. By 1739, the prices of all the most prized kinds of bulbs had fallen
(30) to no more than one two-hundredth of 1 percent of Semper Augustus's peak price.

Garber acknowledges that bulb prices increased dramatically from 1636 to 1637 and eventually reached very low levels. But he argues that this
(35) episode should not be described as a speculative bubble, for the increase and eventual decline in bulb prices can be explained in terms of the fundamentals. Garber argues that a standard pricing pattern occurs for new varieties of flowers. When a particularly
(40) prized variety is developed, its original bulb sells for a high price. Thus, the dramatic rise in the price of some original tulip bulbs could have resulted as tulips in general, and certain varieties in particular, became fashionable. However, as the prized bulbs become
(45) more readily available through reproduction from the original bulb, their price falls rapidly; after less than 30 years, bulbs sell at reproduction cost. But this does not mean that the high prices of original bulbs are irrational, for earnings derivable from the millions
(50) of bulbs descendent from the original bulbs can be

very high, even if each individual descendent bulb commands a very low price. Given that an original bulb can generate a reasonable return on investment even if the price of descendent bulbs decreases
(55) dramatically, a rapid rise and eventual fall of tulip bulb prices need not indicate a speculative bubble.

22. Which one of the following most accurately expresses the main point of the passage?

(A) The seventeenth-century Dutch tulip market is widely but mistakenly believed by economists to provide an example of a speculative bubble.
(B) Mackay did not accurately assess the earnings that could be derived from rare and expensive seventeenth-century Dutch tulip bulbs.
(C) A speculative bubble occurs whenever the price of an asset increases substantially followed by a rapid and dramatic decline.
(D) Garber argues that Mackay's classic account of the seventeenth-century Dutch tulip market as a speculative bubble is not supported by the evidence.
(E) A tulip bulb can generate a reasonable return on investment even if the price starts very high and decreases dramatically.

23. Given Garber's account of the seventeenth-century Dutch tulip market, which one of the following is most analogous to someone who bought a tulip bulb of a certain variety in that market at a very high price, only to sell a bulb of that variety at a much lower price?

(A) someone who, after learning that many others had withdrawn their applications for a particular job, applied for the job in the belief that there would be less competition for it
(B) an art dealer who, after paying a very high price for a new painting, sells it at a very low price because it is now considered to be an inferior work
(C) someone who, after buying a box of rare motorcycle parts at a very high price, is forced to sell them at a much lower price because of the sudden availability of cheap substitute parts
(D) a publisher who pays an extremely high price for a new novel only to sell copies at a price affordable to nearly everyone
(E) an airline that, after selling most of the tickets for seats on a plane at a very high price, must sell the remaining tickets at a very low price

24. The passage most strongly supports the inference that Garber would agree with which one of the following statements?

    (A) If speculative bubbles occur at all, they occur very rarely.
    (B) Many of the owners of high-priced original tulip bulbs could have expected to at least recoup their original investments from sales of the many bulbs propagated from the original bulbs.
    (C) If there is not a speculative bubble in a market, then the level of prices in that market is not irrational.
    (D) Most people who invested in Dutch tulip bulbs in the seventeenth century were generally rational in all their investments.
    (E) Mackay mistakenly infers from the fact that tulip prices dropped rapidly that the very low prices that the bulbs eventually sold for were irrational.

25. The passage states that Mackay claimed which one of the following?

    (A) The rapid rise in price of Dutch tulip bulbs was not due to the fashionability of the flowers they produced.
    (B) The prices of certain varieties of Dutch tulip bulbs during the seventeenth century were, at least for a time, determined by speculation.
    (C) The Netherlands was the only center of cultivation and development of new tulip varieties in the seventeenth century.
    (D) The very high prices of bulbs in the seventeenth-century Dutch tulip market were not irrational.
    (E) Buyers of rare and very expensive Dutch tulip bulbs were ultimately able to derive earnings from bulbs descendent from the original bulbs.

26. The main purpose of the second paragraph is to

    (A) present the facts that are accepted by all experts in the field
    (B) identify the mistake that one scholar alleges another scholar made
    (C) explain the basis on which one scholar makes an inference with which another scholar disagrees
    (D) undermine the case that one scholar makes for the claim with which another scholar disagrees
    (E) outline the factual errors that led one scholar to draw the inference that he drew

27. The phrase "standard pricing pattern" as used in line 38 most nearly means a pricing pattern

    (A) against which other pricing patterns are to be measured
    (B) that conforms to a commonly agreed-upon criterion
    (C) that is merely acceptable
    (D) that regularly recurs in certain types of cases
    (E) that serves as an exemplar

Answer Explanations follow on the next page.

ANSWER KEY

1. D	10. E	19. D
2. A	11. A	20. B
3. A	12. C	21. A
4. B	13. A	22. D
5. E	14. A	23. D
6. E	15. D	24. B
7. A	16. C	25. B
8. E	17. B	26. C
9. B	18. C	27. D

TRIAGE REVIEW

This section provides a number of excellent clues to help you distinguish the simpler passages from the more challenging ones. The first passage is a good place to start your work. Structurally it's very inviting—note that each paragraph contains solid Keyword clues ("often" in line 1, "obviously impossible" in line 21, "therefore unlikely" in line 55) that you can spot with a quick glance at the beginning and end of each paragraph. The language of the passage is comparatively basic, and a glance at the question set reveals two Global questions: 1 and 3.

The fourth passage would be a good place to continue. While the Topic may seem rather esoteric, the opening paragraph begins with a clear definition of the key term "speculative bubble" (line 1) and the third paragraph contains strong opinion language ("Garber acknowledges" in line 32). While question 23 may look a little odd, the others are relatively short and familiar looking.

This leaves the second and third passages as the more formidable challenges. The second passage is the comparative reading pair, and it deals with the natural sciences. While the language of the passages may not look particularly challenging, the majority of the questions are Logic and Inference. Kudos if you noticed that there are no Global questions here, meaning you'll likely need to research every question to earn the points.

The third passage also presents some challenges. Structurally it's not too intimidating, consisting of four short paragraphs and plenty of opinion Keywords. (Pay particular attention to "Kingston herself believes" in line 27 and "Kingston's participation" in line 43, which is enough to tell you that the author is very interested in this Kingston person, whoever she may turn out to be.) That said, most of the questions are Logic and Inference, and therefore likely to be somewhat more challenging.

Ideally, you should complete passages one and four in either order, followed by two and three in either order. This way you're guaranteed to earn the easiest points in the section as quickly as possible, banking time to work with the more challenging passages toward the end. Most of your clues in this section come from the question sets, so don't neglect them when you triage the section; passages that are primarily accompanied by Logic and Inference questions will generally be tougher than those dominated by simpler question types.

Explanations

Passage One: "Nondisclosure Injunctions"

Step 1:

Intell. prop.
rights vs.
individual
rights

Some say
laws fail to
protect either

Knowledge
impossible to
lose = corp.
property

Knowledge leaks
happen in small
ways

Hard for
employer to
prove

(Often) when a highly skilled and experienced employee leaves one company to work for another, (there is) the potential for a transfer of sensitive information between competitors. Two (basic principles)
(5) in such cases appear (irreconcilable:) the right of the company to its intellectual property—its proprietary data and trade secrets—(and) the right of individuals to seek gainful employment and to make free use of their abilities. (Nevertheless,) the courts have (often tried) to
(10) preserve both parties' legal rights by (refusing) to prohibit the employee from working for the competitor, (but) at the same time providing an injunction against disclosure of any of the former employer's secrets. It has been (argued) that (because) such measures help
(15) generate suspicions and similar psychological barriers to full and free utilization of abilities in the employee's new situation, they are (hardly effective) in upholding the individual's rights to free employment decisions. (But) it is also (doubtful) that they are effective in
(20) preserving trade secrets.

It is (obviously impossible) to divest oneself of that part of one's expertise that one has acquired from former employers and coworkers. (Nor,) in general, can one selectively refrain from its use, given that it has
(25) become an integral part of one's total intellectual capacity. (Nevertheless,) almost any such information that is not public knowledge may (legitimately) be claimed as corporate property: normal employment agreements (provide for) corporate ownership of all
(30) relevant data, (including) inventions, generated by the employee in connection with the company's business.

Once (an employee) takes a position with a competitor, the trade secrets that have been acquired by that employee (may manifest) themselves clearly and
(35) consciously. This is what court injunctions seek to prohibit. (But) they are far (more likely) to manifest themselves subconsciously and inconspicuously—for (example) in one's daily decisions at the new post, (or) in the many small contributions one might make to a large
(40) team effort—(often) in the form the of an intuitive sense of what to do or to avoid. (Theoretically,) an injunction also prohibits such inadvertent "leakage." (However,) the former employer faces the practical problem of securing evidence of such leakage, (for) little will
(45) usually be apparent from the public activities of the new employer. (And even) if the new employee's activities appear suspicious, there is the (further) (problem) of distinguishing trade secrets (from) what may be legitimately asserted as technological skills

(50) developed independently by the employee (or) already possessed by the new employer. This is a (major) stumbling block in the attempt to protect trade secrets, (since) the proprietor has no recourse against others who independently generate the same information. It is
(55) (therefore unlikely) that an injunction against disclosure of trade secrets to future employers (actually) prevents any transfer of information (except) for the passage of documents and other concrete embodiments of the secrets.

Laws can only stop concrete exchanges

Paragraph Structure: The author introduces the **Topic** of nondisclosure injunctions in law and then describes two "basic principles" (line 4) that appear to be irreconcilable: the rights of employers to retain their intellectual property, and the rights of individuals to seek employment. This clash of interests forms the author's **Scope**. Despite the problem, courts "nevertheless" (line 9) try to solve the problem through legislation. The author notes that it "has been argued" (line 14) that this legislation fails to protect the rights of either group.

The author expands on this problem in the second paragraph, noting that it's "obviously impossible" (line 21) for an individual to forget learned skills, but that "nevertheless" (line 26) such skills may be considered corporate property.

This leads to the author's notion in the third paragraph that individuals are "more likely" (line 36) to divulge trade secrets in small, unintentional ways rather than ways that are blatantly obvious. While even this kind of violation is "theoretically" (line 41) prohibited by nondisclosure injunctions, it is very difficult for companies to provide evidence that it happens. The author concludes that it is "therefore unlikely" (line 55) that current injunctions will prevent the disclosure of trade secrets except in very obvious cases. The author's **Purpose** was to describe the problems associated with nondisclosure injunctions and the protection of trade secrets. The **Main Idea** of the passage was summarized at the end of the final paragraph: current injunctions are unlikely to prohibit the revealing of trade secrets in many circumstances.

Question Triage: With six relatively simple questions, priorities shouldn't be too tough to determine. Begin with questions 1 and 3, both Global questions, and score these points quickly. Question 6 is a Detail question, but its stem doesn't provide many research clues. Question 5 gives you a specific line reference, so it's better to tackle that one and then move on to question 6. Of the two remaining questions, 4 probably looks more familiar, so answer it next, and finish with question 2, which is oddly worded and may take a little more time to work with.

1. **(D)**

    Which one of the following most accurately expresses the main point of the passage?

    (A)   There are more effective ways than court injunctions to preserve both a company's right to protect its intellectual property and individuals' rights to make free use of their abilities.

    (B)   Court injunctions must be strengthened if they are to remain a relevant means of protecting corporations' trade secrets.

    (C)   Enforcement of court injunctions designed to protect proprietary information is impossible when employees reveal such information to new employers.

    (D)   Court injunctions prohibiting employees from disclosing former employers' trade secrets to new employers probably do not achieve all of their intended objectives.

    (E)   The rights of employees to make full use of their talents and previous training are being seriously eroded by the prohibitions placed on them by court injunctions designed to prevent the transfer of trade secrets.[2]

Step 2: Since this questions asks you to describe the author's main point, it is a Global question.

Step 3: As is always the case with Global questions, eschew specific passage research and instead think about the author's big ideas to form your prediction. In this case, focus on the author's Main Idea.

Step 4: The author uses a neutral and descriptive tone to express the Main Idea that current injunctions against the revealing of trade secrets aren't likely to be very effective in many cases.

Step 5: Correct choice (D) is the perfect match for your prediction. The "more effective ways" mentioned in choice (A) are never mentioned in the passage. Choice (B) describes a recommendation the author doesn't make, and choice (C) is extreme; the author never suggests that injunctions can never be enforced. Choice (E) is also extreme and too narrow in its focus. The author mentions some difficulties for employees, but they're not the primary focus of the passage.

---

[2]PrepTest 55, Sec 2, Q 1

2.   **(A)**

Given the passage's content and tone, which one of the following statements would most likely be found elsewhere in a work from which this passage is an excerpt?

(A)   Given the law as it stands, corporations concerned about preserving trade secrets might be best served by giving their employees strong incentives to stay in their current jobs.

(B)   While difficult to enforce and interpret, injunctions are probably the most effective means of halting the inadvertent transfer of trade secrets while simultaneously protecting the rights of employees.

(C)   Means of redress must be made available to companies that suspect, but cannot prove, that former employees are revealing protected information to competitors.

(D)   Even concrete materials such as computer disks are so easy to copy and conceal that it will be a waste of time for courts to try to prevent the spread of information through physical theft.

(E)   The psychological barriers that an injunction can place on an employee in a new workplace are inevitably so subtle that they have no effect on the employee.[3]

Step 2: The wording of this stem is less straightforward, but the qualified language "would be most likely to be found" helps you identify this as an Inference question.

Step 3: This stem doesn't provide any specific clues to guide your research; you are simply told to keep the content and tone of the passage in mind.

Step 4: A specific prediction is difficult to come up with here. Think about the content and tone before moving on to evaluate the choices. The author ultimately concludes that current laws designed to protect employees and trade secrets fall short of their goals. The correct answer *must be true* on the basis of these ideas.

Step 5: Choice (A), the correct answer, *must be true*. Its qualified tone (corporations "might best be served") fits in with the tone of the passage, and its suggestion follows from the idea that injunctions against the revelation of trade secrets aren't generally effective. The author never states that injunctions are probably the most effective way of protecting secrets, eliminating choice (B). The author never makes demands such as those in choice (C). Choices (D) and (E) are both too extreme.

---

[3]PrepTest 55, Sec 2, Q 2

3. **(A)**

The author's primary purpose in the passage is to

(A) suggest that injunctions against the disclosure of trade secrets not only create problems for employees in the workplace, but also are unable to halt the illicit spread of proprietary information

(B) suggest that the information contained in "documents and other concrete embodiments" is usually so trivial that injunctions do little good in protecting intellectual property

(C) argue that new methods must be found to address the delicate balance between corporate and individual rights

(D) support the position that the concept of protecting trade secrets is no longer viable in an age of increasing access to information

(E) argue that injunctions are not necessary for the protection of trade secrets[4]

Step 2: The key phrase "primary purpose" tells you that this is a Global question.

Step 3: Think back to the author's Purpose to find the correct answer.

Step 4: The author wrote this passage to describe the shortcomings of current injunctions against the revelation of trade secrets. So, find the answer choice that matches this prediction.

Step 5: Correct choice (A) is a perfect match. Choice (B) distorts the author's ideas and is too narrowly focused. Choices (C), (D), and (E) all fail to match the author's tone; this passage wasn't written to support or argue any particular point, but only to suggest that a certain state of affairs is the case. If you find yourself pressed for time on a primary Purpose question, you can use this quick approach to determine which answer choices are likeliest to be correct and focus your attention on them. Scan the beginning of each answer choice, looking for verbs that conform to your prediction, and focus on those choices before looking at any others. This technique can help you hone in on the correct answer quickly without wasting time reading answer traps in their entirety.

[4]PrepTest 55, Sec 2, Q 3

4. **(B)**

The passage provides the most support for which one of the following assertions?

(A)   Injunctions should be imposed by the courts only when there is strong reason to believe that an employee will reveal proprietary information.

(B)   There is apparently no reliable way to protect both the rights of companies to protect trade secrets and the rights of employees to seek new employment.

(C)   Employees should not be allowed to take jobs with their former employers' competitors when their new job could compromise trade secrets of their former employers.

(D)   The multiplicity of means for transferring information in the workplace only increases the need for injunctions.

(E)   Some companies seek injunctions as a means of punishing employees who take jobs with their competitors.[5]

Step 2: When you're asked to identify an assertion supported by the text, you know you're working with an Inference question.

Step 3: The stem doesn't provide many clues. Think about the author's major goals and prepare to use process of elimination.

Step 4: A concrete prediction isn't easy to make in this case, so bear in mind the author's conviction that current injunctions are ineffective before moving on to the choices.

Step 5: The author never suggests that injunctions should only be imposed in specific situations, but only that they're often hard to enforce. This eliminates choice (A). Correct choice (B), on the other hand, falls directly in line with the author's Main Idea. Choice (C) opposes the author's point of view (recall that the rights of employees are asserted in the first paragraph). The author never calls for more injunctions, eliminating choice (D), and choice (E) is never suggested in the passage.

---

[5]PrepTest 55, Sec 2, Q 4

5. **(E)**

    With which one of the following statements regarding documents and other concrete embodiments mentioned in line 58 would the author be most likely to agree?

    (A)   While the transfer of such materials would be damaging, even the seemingly innocuous contributions of an employee to a competitor can do more harm in the long run.

    (B)   Such materials are usually less informative than what the employee may recollect about a previous job.

    (C)   Injunctions against the disclosure of trade secrets should carefully specify which materials are included in order to focus on the most damaging ones.

    (D)   Large-scale transfer of documents and other materials cannot be controlled by injunctions.

    (E)   Such concrete materials lend themselves to control and identification more readily than do subtler means of transferring information.[6]

Step 2: The stem asks you to find the choice that the author would likely agree with, so this is an Inference question.

Step 3: If you go back to line 54 for proper context, you discover that the author mentions concrete embodiments of information as possible exceptions to the general rule that injunctions are not effective in protecting trade secrets.

Step 4: Based on your research, you should expect the correct answer to refer to the fact that trade secrets passed in the form of concrete media are easier to detect, and therefore more vulnerable to injunction.

Step 5: Correct answer choice (E) is a good paraphrase of the prediction and is the correct answer. Choice (A) presents a comparison of harm never mentioned in the passage. Similarly, the passage never mentions how informative such materials are, eliminating choice (B). The recommendation in choice (C) is not supported by the passage, and choice (D) is out of scope; the author doesn't mention the large-scale transfer of materials.

---

[6]PrepTest 55, Sec 2, Q 5

6. **(E)**

In the passage, the author makes which one of the
following claims?

(A)   Injunctions against the disclosure of trade
       secrets limit an employee's chances of being
       hired by a competitor.
(B)   Measures against the disclosure of trade
       secrets are unnecessary except in the case of
       documents and other concrete embodiments
       of the secrets.
(C)   Employees who switch jobs to work for a
       competitor usually unintentionally violate the
       law by doing so.
(D)   Employers are not restricted in the tactics they
       can use when seeking to secure protected
       information from new employees.
(E)   What may seem like intellectual theft may in fact
       be an example of independent innovation.[7]

Step 2: Since the question asks for a specific claim, it is a Detail question.

Step 3: The only clue you have is that the author is making the claim. That doesn't help much,
so a specific prediction will be hard to make.

Step 4: Think through the author's Main Idea and prepare to apply the process of elimination.

Step 5: Be careful with choice (A); it may look tempting at first, but recall that the passage says
"it has been argued" (line 14) that injunctions may prohibit an employee from making full use
of his or her abilities. Choice (A) claims that injunctions limit an employee's chances of getting
a job, so this is a distortion. Choice (B) is also a distortion. The author claims that concrete
embodiments are easier to detect and prohibit, not that they represent the only situations in
which injunctions are necessary. Choice (C) misses the author's point. Merely switching jobs
doesn't violate an injunction. Choice (D) is contradicted by the passage, since injunctions do
seek to protect the rights of employees. Only correct choice (E) remains, which is supported
in the third paragraph.

Passage Two: "Comparative Passages on Purple Loosestrife"
Step 1:

*The following passages concern a plant called purple loosestrife. Passage A is excerpted from a
report issued by a prairie research council; passage B from a journal of sociology.*

---

[7]PrepTest 55, Sec 2, Q 6

Passage A

Purple loosestrife (Lythrum salicaria), an aggressive and invasive perennial of Eurasian origin, arrived with settlers in eastern North America in the early 1800s and has spread across the continent's

(5) midlatitude wetlands. The impact of purple loosestrife on native vegetation has been disastrous, with more than 50 percent of the biomass of some wetland communities displaced. Monospecific blocks of this weed have maintained themselves for at least 20 years.

(10) Impacts on wildlife have not been well studied, but serious reductions in waterfowl and aquatic

furbearer productivity have been observed. In addition, several endangered species of vertebrates are threatened with further degradation of their

(15) breeding habitats. Although purple loosestrife can invade relatively undisturbed habitats, the spread and dominance of this weed have been greatly accelerated in disturbed habitats. While digging out the plants can temporarily halt their spread, there has been little

(20) research on long-term purple loosestrife control. Glyphosate has been used successfully, but no measure of the impact of this herbicide on native plant communities has been made.

With the spread of purple loosestrife growing

(25) exponentially, some form of integrated control is needed. At present, coping with purple loosestrife

hinges on early detection of the weed's arrival in areas, which allows local eradication to be carried out with minimum damage to the native plant community.

Passage B

(30)   The war on purple loosestrife is apparently conducted on behalf of nature, an attempt to liberate the biotic community from the tyrannical influence of a life-destroying invasive weed. Indeed, purple

loosestrife control is portrayed by its practitioners as

(35) an environmental initiative intended to save nature rather than control it. Accordingly, the purple loosestrife literature, scientific and otherwise, dutifully discusses the impacts of the weed on endangered species—and on threatened biodiversity

(40) more generally. Purple loosestrife is a pollution, according to the scientific community, and all of nature suffers under its pervasive influence.

Regardless of the perceived and actual ecological effects of the purple invader, it is apparent that

(45) popular pollution ideologies have been extended into the wetlands of North America. Consequently, the scientific effort to liberate nature from purple

loosestrife (has failed) to decouple itself from its
philosophical (origin) as an instrument to control nature
(50) to the satisfaction of human desires. Birds,
(particularly) game birds and waterfowl, (provide) the
bulk of the (justification) for loosestrife management.
(However,) no bird species (other than) the canvasback
has been identified in the literature as endangered by
(55) purple loosestrife. (The impact) of purple loosestrife on
furbearing mammals is discussed at great length,
(though) none of the species highlighted (muskrat,
mink) can be considered threatened in North America.
(What is threatened) by purple loosestrife is the
(60) economics of exploiting such preferred species (and)
the millions of dollars that will be lost to the
economies of the United States and Canada (from)
reduced hunting, trapping, and recreation revenues
(due to) a decline in the production of the wetland
(65) resource.

Impact exaggerated

Real threat is to economy

Paragraph Structure: As always, read and Roadmap each comparative reading passage independently. Be sure to determine the **Topic, Scope, Purpose**, and **Main Idea** for Passage A before moving on to Passage B.

Passage A: You can determine the author's **Topic** (purple loosestrife) and **Scope** (the danger it poses to the environment) from the first paragraph, and you can also find supporting examples of this danger. The author notes that "while" (line 18) certain measures can temporarily halt the advance of purple loosestrife, little research has been conducted on its long-term effects on ecosystems. The brief second paragraph indicates that "at present" (line 26) the best known way to combat the infestation is to detect it early and take quick action. The author's **Purpose** in this passage was to describe the dangers posed by loosestrife and current prevention measures. The **Main Idea** is that loosestrife poses a clear threat to wetland ecosystems, and integrated control is necessary to combat the threat.

Passage B: This author also writes on the **Topic** of purple loosestrife, but with a decidedly different tone. The **Scope** of Passage B is the motivations of those who seek to control loosestrife. This becomes evident with the author's use of subtle opinion Keywords. Proponents of waging "war" (line 30) on purple loosestrife do so "apparently" (line 30) to defend nature, and their efforts are "portrayed" (line 34) as an attempt to save nature "rather than" (line 36) control it. All of this qualification implies that the author holds an opposing viewpoint, a prediction that is borne out in the second paragraph. The author indicates that loosestrife-control proponents have failed to separate themselves from "popular…ideologies" (line 45) and are "consequently" (line 46) seeking to control nature, not to defend it. Their "justification[s]" (line 52) aren't supported by evidence. The author finally concludes that "what is threatened" (line 59) by the purple loosestrife is the economic benefit provided by the wetlands that are being invaded. Taken in total, the author's **Purpose** is to question the motives of the proponents of loosestrife control, and the **Main Idea** is that these proponents are not truly interested in defending nature, but in controlling it for their own economic benefit.

Both of these authors are concerned with the invasion of purple loosestrife into certain eco-systems, but their goals are very different. Passage A presents evidence for the highly destructive nature of loosestrife and urges its control, whereas Passage B suggests that the damage loosestrife causes has been exaggerated and questions the motives underlying its control. Being aware of these differences will certainly help you answer the questions accurately.

Question Triage: As I noted in the section overview, this comparative passage set contains no Global questions, so you should begin by looking for straightforward Detail questions. The first two questions, 7 and 8, are good starting candidates. The remaining questions are a mix of Logical Reasoning and Inference. While it's generally a good idea to bypass Inference questions in favor of simpler points, questions 9 and 10 are both amenable to your understanding of the authors' Main Ideas; question 9 asks for a central point of disagreement, and question 10 asks for an author's attitude. These are concepts you should already have a good understanding of by the time you've finish reading strategically. Question 11 asks for a point of agreement between the two authors and is therefore similarly amenable to the comparison strategy you've learned to apply to these passages. That leaves questions 12 and 13, both Logical Reasoning questions, which you can tackle in any order as time allows.

7. **(A)**

    Both passages explicitly mention which one of the following?
    (A) furbearing animals
    (B) glyphosate
    (C) the threat purple loosestrife poses to economies
    (D) popular pollution ideologies
    (E) literature on purple loosestrife control[8]

Step 2: The stem asks for explicit information, a clear indication of a Detail question.

Step 3: Although the stem doesn't provide any specific research cues, you can still think about the general ideas mentioned in both passages in order to make the choices easier to evaluate.

Step 4: Both passages deal with evidence that purple loosestrife is invasive to local ecosystems, though they disagree about the legitimacy of such evidence. The correct answer is likely to refer to this kind of evidence.

Step 5: Choice (A) is correct—both passages mentioned the claim that purple loosestrife negatively affects populations of furbearing animals. Choice (B) is only mentioned in Passage A, and choices (C), (D), and (E) are specific to Passage B.

---

[8]PrepTest 55, Sec 2, Q 7

8. **(E)**

   Each of the passages contains information sufficient
   to answer which one of the following questions?
   (A)   Approximately how long ago did purple
         loosestrife arrive in North America?
   (B)   Is there much literature discussing the
         potential benefit that hunters might derive
         from purple loosestrife management?
   (C)   What is an issue regarding purple loosestrife
         management on which both hunters and
         farmers agree?
   (D)   Is the canvasback threatened with extinction
         due to the spread of purple loosestrife?
   (E)   What is a type of terrain that is affected in at
         least some parts of North America by the
         presence of purple loosestrife?[9]

Step 2: The question is asking for a specific Detail that can be found in either source.

Step 3: Since there aren't any specific clues to help your research, think about your comparison of the two passages before moving on to the choices.

Step 4: Much like question 7, you must seek information common to both passages. Since both passages considered much of the same evidence, focus your attention there while employing the process of elimination.

Step 5: Choice (A) is mentioned in Passage A but not in Passage B. References to game hunting are particular to Passage B, eliminating choices (B) and (C). The canvasback was also specific to Passage B, so choice (D) is out. Since both passages refer to the loosestrife's invasion of the wetlands of North America, choice (E) must be correct.

9. **(B)**

   It can be inferred that the authors would be most
   likely to disagree about which one of the following?
   (A)   Purple loosestrife spreads more quickly in
         disturbed habitats than in undisturbed
         habitats.
   (B)   The threat posed by purple loosestrife to local
         aquatic furbearer populations is serious.
   (C)   Most people who advocate that eradication
         measures be taken to control purple
         loosestrife are not genuine in their concern
         for the environment.
   (D)   The size of the biomass that has been displaced
         by purple loosestrife is larger than is generally
         thought.
   (E)   Measures should be taken to prevent other
         non-native plant species from invading North
         America.[10]

---

[9]PrepTest 55, Sec 2, Q 8
[10]PrepTest 55, Sec 2, Q 9

Step 2: The question stem asks for an Inference, in this case one that the authors would disagree about.

Step 3: The question stem doesn't give many specific research clues, but you can still make a solid prediction based on your understanding of the big ideas.

Step 4: Think about each author's Main Idea and the tonal differences in the passages. The author of Passage A asserted that local ecosystems are gravely threatened by loosestrife, while the author of Passage B downplays the threat, suggesting that few endangered species are threatened. The correct answer is likely to reflect this core disagreement.

Step 5: The match for your prediction is correct choice (B). Choice (A) is specific to Passage A, choice (C) is specific to Passage B, and choices (D) and (E) are not supported by either author. Only an idea that is mentioned in *both* passages can be a source of disagreement, so you can eliminate all of the choices that refer to ideas specific to one passage.

10. **(E)**

Which one of the following most accurately describes
the attitude expressed by the author of passage B
toward the overall argument represented by passage A?
(A) enthusiastic agreement
(B) cautious agreement
(C) pure neutrality
(D) general ambivalence
(E) pointed skepticism[11]

Step 2: The phrase "most accurately describes" tells you that this is an Inference question. You need to infer the attitude of author B toward the argument made in Passage A.

Step 3: Once again, this question focuses on the larger ideas of both passages rather than specific details. Think about contrasts between the passages to make your prediction.

Step 4: All the clues you need for a solid prediction are right there in the passages. From the beginning of Passage B, the author expresses disagreement with the views presented in Passage A, using terms like "apparently" (line 30) and "dutifully" (line 38) to cast doubt on them. In the final sentences of Passage B, the author explicitly denies the motivations stated by those who seek to control purple loosestrife. The correct answer must demonstrate this clear disagreement.

Step 5: This should be an easy match if you've made a good prediction, since the only answer choice that expresses disagreement is correct choice (E). The remaining choices describe either agreement or neutrality, making them wrong.

---

[11]PrepTest 55, Sec 2, Q 10

11. **(A)**

It can be inferred that both authors would be most
likely to agree with which one of the following
statements regarding purple loosestrife?
(A)   As it increases in North America, some wildlife
       populations tend to decrease.
(B)   Its establishment in North America has had a
       disastrous effect on native North American
       wetland vegetation in certain regions.
(C)   It is very difficult to control effectively with
       herbicides.
(D)   Its introduction into North America was a
       great ecological blunder.
(E)   When it is eliminated from a given area, it
       tends to return to that area fairly quickly.[12]

Step 2: This Inference question asks you to identify something that the two authors would
agree on.

Step 3: As with question 10, compare the authors' Main Ideas to reach a solid prediction.

Step 4: While the authors disagree about the big issues, there is some agreement on the
smaller details. Both authors agree that loosestrife is invasive in certain ecosystems, and that
it negatively affects some wildlife. The authors clearly disagree on the degree of this effect,
but they both acknowledge that it exists. Expect the correct choice to reflect one of these
points of agreement.

Step 5: Choice (A) is a direct match for the prediction. As is commonly the case in comparative-
reading wrong-answer choices, choices (B), (C), and (E) all refer to ideas present in only one of
the passages (Passage A), and choice (C) is also extreme. Choice (D) is never explicitly stated
in either passage, and though the author of Passage A probably would agree with it, there's
no agreement from the author of Passage B.

12. **(C)**

Which one of the following is true about the
relationship between the two passages?
(A)   Passage A presents evidence that directly
       counters claims made in passage B.
(B)   Passage B assumes what passage A explicitly
       argues for.
(C)   Passage B displays an awareness of the
       arguments touched on in passage A, but not
       vice versa.
(D)   Passage B advocates a policy that passage A
       rejects.
(E)   Passage A downplays the seriousness of claims
       made in passage B.[13]

---

[12]PrepTest 55, Sec 2, Q 11
[13]PrepTest 55, Sec 2, Q 12

Step 2: This is a rare form of Logical Reasoning question, known as Method of Argument. The stem asks you to provide a structural analysis of how one passage relates to the other.

Step 3: This is another big picture question. Instead of conducting specific research, compare the primary Purpose of Passage A to that of Passage B.

Step 4: Passage A presents a specific argument for the control of purple loosestrife, and Passage B calls the conclusions and motivations of this argument into question. The correct answer will reflect some aspect of this relationship.

Step 5: Correct choice (C) may not have jumped out at you at first. It doesn't explicitly describe the adversarial relationship between the passages, but it *does* remark on the fact that Passage B responds to the arguments made in Passage A, demonstrating that the author of Passage B is aware of those arguments. (Note that this is different than asserting that the author of Passage B is aware of the specific *author* of Passage A; the authors of paired passages never refer to one another directly, though they may refer to the same ideas.) It is equally true that the author of Passage A demonstrates no awareness of the arguments made in Passage B. Choice (A) is off base, since Passage A doesn't respond in any way to the claims made in Passage B. Choice (B) implies an agreement that doesn't exist. Choices (D) and (E) reverse the relationships between the two passages—wrong answer traps you'll avoid as long as you read the choices carefully.

13. **(A)**

Which one of the following, if true, would cast doubt on the argument in passage B but bolster the argument in passage A?

(A)   Localized population reduction is often a precursor to widespread endangerment of a species.

(B)   Purple loosestrife was barely noticed in North America before the advent of suburban sprawl in the 1950s.

(C)   The amount by which overall hunting, trapping, and recreation revenues would be reduced as a result of the extinction of one or more species threatened by purple loosestrife represents a significant portion of those revenues.

(D)   Some environmentalists who advocate taking measures to eradicate purple loosestrife view such measures as a means of controlling nature.

(E)   Purple loosestrife has never become a problem in its native habitat, even though no effort has been made to eradicate it there.[14]

Step 2: The words "cast doubt" and "bolster" tell you that this is a Logical Reasoning question. You must strengthen the argument made by one passage and weaken the argument of the other.

---

[14]PrepTest 55, Sec 2, Q 13

Step 3: Once more, rather than conducting specific passage research, think about the big ideas. The argument of Passage A (the one you need to strengthen) is that purple loosestrife is ecologically dangerous and should be controlled. Passage B claims that the danger is exaggerated and that calls for such control are motivated by economic concerns rather than a true desire to protect the environment.

Step 4: Since Passage B calls the evidence presented by Passage A into question, you should seek to bolster A's evidence. The author of Passage B downplays the threat posed to wetland wildlife, so a good prediction would suggest that the threat is more serious than Passage B acknowledges. This would make the author of Passage A more likely to be correct while casting doubt on the central argument of Passage B.

Step 5: Correct choice (A) fulfills the prediction. If population reduction can lead to species endangerment, then the evidence of such reduction present in Passage B becomes support for Passage A's central assertion that wildlife is endangered. Choices (B) and (C) are outside the scope of the argument, and therefore can neither strengthen nor weaken it. Choice (D) is a 180; it supports Passage B over Passage A. Choice (E) introduces irrelevant information, since the behavior of purple loosestrife in its own environment has no bearing on how it affects the wetlands of North America.

Passage Three: "Kingston and 'Talk-Story'"
Step 1:

Critics: Kingston's work not influenced by previous work

(With) their recognition of Maxine Hong Kingston as a (major) literary figure, (some critics) have (suggested) that her works have been (produced) almost *ex nihilo*, (saying that) they lack a large traceable body of direct
(5) literary antecedent (especially) within the Chinese American heritage in which her work is embedded. (But) these critics, who have examined (only) the development of written texts, the (most visible) signs of a culture's narrative production, have (overlooked) Kingston's
(10) (connection) to the long Chinese tradition of a highly developed genre of song and spoken narrative (known) as "talk-story" (*gong gu tsai*).

Auth: Kingston connected to talk-story

History of talk-story

(Traditionally) performed in the dialects of various ethnic enclaves, talk-story has been (maintained) within
(15) the confines of the family (and) has (rarely) surfaced into print. The tradition (dates back) to Sung dynasty (A.D. 970–1279) storytellers in China, (and) in the United States it is continually (revitalized) by an overlapping sequence of immigration from China.
(20) (Thus) Chinese immigrants to the U.S. had a fully established, sophisticated oral culture, (already) ancient and (capable) of producing masterpieces, (by the time) they began arriving in the early nineteenth century. This transplanted oral heritage simply (embraced) new
(25) subject matter or new forms of Western discourse, (as in) the case of Kingston's adaptations written in English.

(Kingston) herself (believes) that as a literary artist she
is one in a long line of performers shaping a
recalcitrant history into talk-story form. She
(30) (distinguishes) her "thematic" storytelling memory

How Kingston processes, (which) sift and reconstruct the essential
adapts talk- elements of personally remembered stories (from) the
story memory processes of a print-oriented culture that
(emphasizes) the retention of precise sequences of
(35) words. (Nor) does the entry of print into the storytelling
process (substantially) change her notion of the character
of oral tradition. (For Kingston,) "writer" is (synonymous)
with "singer" or "performer" in the ancient sense of
privileged keeper, transmitter, and creator of stories
(40) (whose current) stage of development can be frozen in
print, (but) which continue to grow both around and
from that frozen text.

Kingston's (participation) in the tradition of
talk-story is (evidenced) in her book *China Men*, which
Example: (45) (utilizes) forms typical of that genre and common to
China Men most oral cultures (including:) a fixed "grammar" of
repetitive themes; a spectrum of stock characters;
symmetrical structures, (including) balanced oppositions
(verbal or physical contests, antithetical characters,
(50) dialectical discourse such as question-answer forms
and riddles); (and) repetition. In *China Men*, Kingston
(also succeeds) in investing idiomatic English with the
allusive texture and oral-aural qualities of the Chinese
language, a language rich in aural and visual puns,
(55) (making) her work a written form of talk-story.

Paragraph Structure: The author's **Topic** (the work of Kingston) and **Scope** (her use of talk-story) are presented in the first paragraph by way of a dichotomy between how "some critics" (line 2) view Kingston's work and how the author interprets it. The critics suggest that Kingston's work is not essentially influenced by previous literary works or by her own cultural background, "but" (line 6) they've "overlooked" (line 9) her connection to the tradition of the talk-story.

The second paragraph provides some background on the talk-story, describing both its history and how it has been "maintained" (line 14) within families and from generation to generation, finally producing an established and "already ancient" (line 21) art form in the Chinese American community. This new form of talk-story "embraced" (line 24) forms of western storytelling, and the author uses this connection as a way to bring Kingston back into the conversation.

The third paragraph presents Kingston's own point of view: She "believes" (line 27) that she's employing the talk-story form in her own work and has "distinguished" (line 30) the elements of talk-story in her work from those of the "print-oriented" (line 33) culture in which she lives. This idea is summarized in her view that a writer is "synonymous" (line 37) with a "singer" (line 38) or "poet" (line 38).

The author completes the passage with a specific example, "China Men" (line 44), demonstrating how this work "utilizes" (line 45) elements of oral culture. As always, note the presence of this lengthy example without wasting time trying to memorize it; it will probably show up in the questions, but proper research will allow you to come back to this paragraph when necessary.

The author's ultimate **Purpose** was to describe the influence of talk-story in Kingston's work, and the **Main Idea** follows suit: Despite the opinions of some critics, Kingston's work is rooted in the tradition of the talk-story.

Question Triage: Begin by grabbing the sole Global point: question 14. The remaining seven questions are a mix of Inference and Logic, so it's best to approach them one at a time and skip the ones that are likely to be time-consuming. Questions 15 and 16 are both Inference questions, but 16 provides a specific line reference, so tackle it next. Question 17, a Parallel Reasoning question, also directs you to a specific portion of the passage, so it shouldn't be too tough to make a prediction and score the point. Question 18 asks you to consider Kingston's opinions, which were primarily located in a single paragraph, so consider answering it next. Questions 19 and 20 both contain enough contextual information in their stems to be worth a look at this point—since question 19 asks you to weaken the author's argument, you should be able to work with this one easily if you've understood the Main Idea (which embodies the author's argument), and 20 is a Function question with specific line references. Question 21 asks for the author's attitude toward a particular concept, so depending on time constraints, consider tackling it before returning to question 15, an Inference question that provides you with no clues to guide your research (and is therefore likely to be challenging).

14. **(A)**

Which one of the following most accurately states the main point of the passage?

(A) Despite some critics' comments, Kingston's writings have significant Chinese American antecedents, which can be found in the traditional oral narrative form known as talk-story.

(B) Analysis of Kingston's writings, especially *China Men*, supports her belief that literary artists can be performers who continue to reconstruct their stories even after they have been frozen in print.

(C) An understanding of Kingston's work and of Chinese American writers in general reveals that critics of ethnic literatures in the United States have been mistaken in examining only written texts.

(D) Throughout her writings Kingston uses techniques typical of the talk-story genre, especially the retention of certain aspects of Chinese speech in the written English text.

(E) The writings of Kingston have rekindled an interest in talk-story, which dates back to the Sung dynasty, and was extended to the United States with the arrival of Chinese immigrants in the nineteenth century.[15]

Step 2: The phrase "Main point" signals a Global question in which you will identify the Main Idea of the passage.

Step 3: No specific research is necessary.

Step 4: Recall and paraphrase the Main Point: Kingston's work is rooted in the tradition of the talk-story, despite what some critics have suggested.

Step 5: Choice (A) is a perfect match. Choices (B) and (D) focus to specifically on details to capture the author's Main Idea, and choices (C) and (E) produce ideas that are out of scope.

---

[15]PrepTest 55, Sec 2, Q 14

15. **(D)**

Which one of the following can be most reasonably inferred from the passage?

(A) In the last few years, written forms of talk-story have appeared in Chinese as often as they have in English.

(B) Until very recently, scholars have held that oral storytelling in Chinese ethnic enclaves was a unique oral tradition.

(C) Talk-story has developed in the United States through a process of combining Chinese, Chinese American, and other oral storytelling forms.

(D) Chinese American talk-story relies upon memory processes that do not emphasize the retention of precise sequences of words.

(E) The connection between certain aspects of Kingston's work and talk-story is argued by some critics to be rather tenuous and questionable.[16]

Step 2: The key language "inferred" identifies this as an Inference question.

Step 3: There aren't any specific clues to guide your research, so think about the author's main concerns and be prepared to proceed by process of elimination.

Step 4: The author is most concerned with describing the deep connection between Kingston's work and the tradition of the talk-story. Use this knowledge to guide your assessment of the answer choices.

Step 5: Choice (A) generalizes far beyond the scope of the passage, which only concerns the work of one author. Choice (B) is not supported by the passage. Choice (C) distorts information from the second paragraph, incorrectly suggesting that talk-story combined with storytelling forms outside of the Chinese and Chinese American communities. Choice (D), the correct answer, is referenced in lines 30–35, in which Kingston describes key differences between Western and talk-story traditions. Choice (E) presents another distortion; the critics mentioned in the beginning of the passage don't argue that Kingston's connection to talk-story is tenuous, they completely ignore its existence.

[16]PrepTest 55, Sec 2, Q 15

16. **(C)**

It can be inferred from the passage that the author
uses the phrase "personally remembered stories"
(line 32) primarily to refer to
(A) a literary genre of first-person storytelling
(B) a thematically organized personal narrative of
one's own past
(C) partially idiosyncratic memories of narratives
(D) the retention in memory of precise sequences
of words
(E) easily identifiable thematic issues in literature[17]

Step 2: The question asks what a specific phrase refers to, telling you that it is a Logic Function question.

Step 3: As with any Logic Function question, be sure to research for context. In the third paragraph, the author presents Kingston's description of the way she merges talk-story with Western forms of writing. This paragraph describes important contrasts, specifically a contrast between the personally remembered stories mentioned in the stem and the "memory processes of a print-oriented culture" (line 33) that emphasizes precise sequences of words.

Step 4: The correct answer must take the dichotomy described by the contrast Keywords in the third paragraph into account. Since the personally remembered stories serve as a contrast to specific retention, the correct answer should describe these stories as a looser form of memory.

Step 5: Although it uses language that is perhaps surprising, the only choice that matches the prediction is correct choice (C)—"partially idiosyncratic memories" is another way of describing the looser form of narrative predicted. Always remember that the correct answer must match the *concept* of your prediction, even though it may not use the same words. None of the other choices describe the less-precise form of narrative that the structure of the paragraph led you to expect.

---

[17]PrepTest 55, Sec 2, Q 16

17. **(B)**

In which one of the following is the use of cotton fibers or cotton cloth most analogous to Kingston's use of the English language as described in lines 51–55?
(A)   Scraps of plain cotton cloth are used to create a multicolored quilt.
(B)   The surface texture of woolen cloth is simulated in a piece of cotton cloth by a special process of weaving.
(C)   Because of its texture, cotton cloth is used for a certain type of clothes for which linen is inappropriate.
(D)   In making a piece of cloth, cotton fiber is substituted for linen because of the roughly similar texture of the two materials.
(E)   Because of their somewhat similar textures, cotton and linen fibers are woven together in a piece of cloth to achieve a savings in price over a pure linen cloth.[18]

Step 2: The stem asks you to identify an analogous situation based on the text, so this is a Logical Reasoning question, specifically Parallel Reasoning.

Step 3: Reviewing the lines referenced in the question stem tells you that Kingston's use of English in *China Men* was primarily important because she infused it with qualities of the Chinese language.

Step 4: The correct answer must reflect the relationship described in the text; specifically, one type of language taking on the attributes of another very different language. Since the stem refers to cotton cloth, you should expect the correct answer to describe cotton cloth taking on the properties of some other, different kind of cloth.

Step 5: Choice (B) perfectly matches the prediction—cotton cloth takes on the properties of woolen cloth. Choice (A) fails to refer to two different types of cloth and is therefore not properly analogous. Choice (C) refers to a substitution, which doesn't match the relationship described in the passage. Choice (D) refers to types of cloth that are similar rather than dissimilar, as does choice (E).

It is worth noting that, even in a rather abstract question like this one, a strong prediction always helps you score the point.

---

[18]PrepTest 55, Sec 2, Q 17

18. **(C)**

The passage most clearly suggests that Kingston believes which one of the following about at least some of the stories contained in her writings?
(A)   Since they are intimately tied to the nature of the Chinese language, they can be approximated, but not adequately expressed, in English.
(B)   They should be thought of primarily as ethnic literature and evaluated accordingly by critics.
(C)   They will likely be retold and altered to some extent in the process.
(D)   Chinese American history is best chronicled by traditional talk-story.
(E)   Their significance and beauty cannot be captured at all in written texts.[19]

Step 2: You are asked to identify what the passage "suggests" that Kingston believes. The qualified language is indicative of an Inference question.

Step 3: Your Roadmap should lead you back to paragraph three to research Kingston's description of her own work. Toward the end of the paragraph, signaled by "for Kingston" in line 37, she states that the stories she tells can be "frozen in print" (lines 40–41) but continue to grow outside of the text.

Step 4: Based on your research, you should expect the correct answer to refer to the process of change beyond the printed page described in the text.

Step 5: Correct choice (C) does indeed describe the process of change predicted. Choice (A) distorts Kingston's view, as she never suggests that the stories are "[in]adequately expressed" in English. Choice (B) is never mentioned and is therefore out of scope. Choice (D) runs counter to Kingston's attempts to express elements of talk-story in English, as does the extreme view of choice (E).

19. **(D)**

The author's argument in the passage would be most weakened if which one of the following were true?
(A)   Numerous writers in the United States have been influenced by oral traditions.
(B)   Most Chinese American writers' work is very different from Kingston's.
(C)   Native American storytellers use narrative devices similar to those used in talk-story.
(D)   *China Men* is for the most part atypical of Kingston's literary works.
(E)   Literary critics generally appreciate the authenticity of Kingston's work.[20]

[19]PrepTest 55, Sec 2, Q 18
[20]PrepTest 55, Sec 2, Q 19

Step 2: The stem asks you to weaken the author's argument, so this is a Logical Reasoning question.

Step 3: The author argues that Kingston's work is rooted in the tradition of talk-story. To weaken this argument, you can undermine the evidence the author provides. Where in the passage is this evidence provided? According to your Roadmap, the author's primary example was the novel *China Men* as described in the final paragraph. A quick review of this paragraph shows that the author indicates that *China Men* contains a number of elements specific to oral culture generally.

Step 4: Now that you've identified the chief evidence for the author's case, the hard work is over. The correct answer should show that *China Men* is not representative of Kingston's work, thus casting doubt on her argument.

Step 5: Choice (D), the correct answer, is the clear match. Choice (A) is out of scope; other authors are irrelevant to this argument. The same goes for choice (B). Choice (C) isn't any better, since the practices of Native American storytellers have no bearing on Kingston's work. Choice (E) is also irrelevant. Whatever the critics may think, the author's argument isn't about Kingston's authenticity.

20. **(B)**
    The author's specific purpose in detailing typical talk-story forms (lines 43–51) is to
    (A)   show why Kingston's book *China Men* establishes her as a major literary figure
    (B)   support the claim that Kingston's use of typically oral techniques makes her work a part of the talk-story tradition
    (C)   dispute the critics' view that Chinese American literature lacks literary antecedents
    (D)   argue for Kingston's view that the literary artist is at best a "privileged keeper" of stories
    (E)   provide an alternative to certain critics' view that Kingston's work should be judged primarily as literature[21]

Step 2: The word "purpose" helps you identify this as a Logic Function question.

Step 3: Lines 43–51 encompass most of the final paragraph. A glance at your Roadmap should remind you of the function of this paragraph as a whole—to provide a supporting example of the author's argument that Kingston's work is rooted in the tradition of talk-story.

Step 4: You've already got the prediction in hand; the lines quoted were in support of the author's Main Idea.

Step 5: Choice (A) misunderstands the reason why *China Men* was discussed. However, choice (B) matches the prediction exactly and is the correct answer. Choice (C) is a little trickier; the author does argue against the critics' claim that Kingston in particular lacks literary antecedents, but the critics never claim that Chinese American literature as a whole lacks such antecedents. Choice (D) is too narrow in focus, and choice (E) misinterprets both the function of the quoted text and the viewpoint of the critics.

21. **(A)**

Which one of the following most accurately identifies the attitude shown by the author in the passage toward talk-story?

(A) scholarly appreciation for its longstanding artistic sophistication

(B) mild disappointment that it has not distinguished itself from other oral traditions

(C) tentative approval of its resistance to critical evaluations

(D) clear respect for the diversity of its ancient sources and cultural derivations

(E) open admiration for the way it uses song to express narrative[22]

Step 2: This is an Inference question, as identified by a request for the author's attitude.

Step 3: The stem asks for the author's attitude regarding talk-story. According to the Roadmap, this was most generally discussed in the second paragraph, in which the author describes the history of talk-story and then discusses its evolution in the Chinese American community. Be sure to note Keywords of emphasis in this paragraph; the author describes talk-story as a "sophisticated oral culture" (line 21) that is "capable of producing masterpieces" (line 22).

Step 4: Based on the author's language, the correct answer should reflect a respect for talk-story's history and artistry.

Step 5: Your prediction should lead you straight to correct choice (A). Choices (B) and (C) describe disappointment and tentative approval, neither of which match the author's tone. Choice (D) starts off well with "clear respect" for talk-story but gets the details wrong, since the author doesn't show particular interest in the "diversity of its ancient sources." Choice (E) introduces the out of scope notion of song.

Passage Four: "Speculative Bubbles"
Step 1:

Def. of bubble

(In economics,) the term "speculative bubble" (refers to) a large upward move in an asset's price driven (not by) the asset's fundamentals—(that is,) by the earnings derivable from the asset—(but rather by)

(5) mere speculation that someone else will be willing to pay a higher price for it. The price increase is (then) (followed) by a dramatic decline in price (due to) a loss in confidence that the price will continue to rise, (and) the "bubble" is said to have burst. (According to)

Mackay: tulip market= bubble

(10) Charles Mackay's classic nineteenth-century account, the seventeenth-century Dutch tulip market (provides) (an example) of a speculative bubble. (But) the economist Peter Garber (challenges) Mackay's view, (arguing) that there is (no evidence) that the Dutch tulip

Garber: no bubble

(15) market really involved a speculative bubble.

Dutch tulip sales

(By) the seventeenth century, the Netherlands had (become) a center of cultivation and development of new tulip varieties, and a market (had developed) in which rare varieties of bulbs sold at high prices. For

(20) (example,) a Semper Augustus bulb sold in 1625 for an amount of gold worth about U.S.$11,000 in 1999. Common bulb varieties, (on the other hand,) sold for very low prices. (According to Mackay,) by 1636 rapid price rises attracted speculator (and) prices of many

(25) varieties surged upward from November 1636 (through) January 1637. (Mackay further) states that in February

Mackay's argument

1637 prices suddenly (collapsed;) bulbs could not be sold at 10 percent of their peak values. (By) 1739, the prices of all the (most prized) kinds of bulbs had (fallen)

(30) to no more than one two-hundredth of 1 percent of Semper Augustus's peak price.

(Garber acknowledges) that bulb prices increased dramatically from 1636 to 1637 and eventually reached very low levels. (But he argues) that this

(35) episode (should not) be described as a speculative

Garber's argument

bubble, (for) the increase and eventual decline in bulb prices (can be explained) in terms of the fundamentals. (Garber argues) that a standard pricing pattern occurs for new varieties of flowers. (When) a particularly

(40) prized variety is developed, its original bulb sells for a high price. (Thus,) the (dramatic rise) in the price of some original tulip bulbs could have (resulted) as tulips in general, (and) certain varieties in particular, (became) fashionable. (However,) as the prized bulbs (become)

(45) more readily available through reproduction from the original bulb, their price (falls) rapidly; (after) less than 30 years, bulbs sell at reproduction cost. (But) this does (not mean) that the high prices of original bulbs are irrational, (for) earnings derivable from the millions

(50) of bulbs descendent from the original bulbs (can be) very high, (even) if each individual descendent bulb

commands a very low price. (Given) that an original
bulbs can generate a reasonable return on investment
(even if) the price of descendent bulbs decreases
(55)   dramatically, a rapid rise and eventual fall of tulip
bulb prices (need not indicate) a speculative bubble.

Paragraph Structure: The author introduces the **Topic** right away by defining the concept of speculative bubbles: The price of a commodity is driven up not by its actual value, "but rather by" (line 4) what speculators guess that others are willing to pay for it. When this speculation reaches its peak, the bubble "burst[s]" (line 9) and prices fall precipitously. The **Scope** becomes apparent in the second half of the paragraph as the author introduces two opposed views of the Dutch tulip market: Mackay believes the tulip market "provides an example" (lines 11–12) of such a bubble, whereas Garber argues that there is "no evidence" (line 14) that such a bubble existed. The author is most concerned with exploring these conflicting views.

The second and third paragraphs describe Mackay's and Garber's theses respectively. Mackay points out that a Semper Augustus bulb sold for an astonishing amount of money. Common bulbs, "on the other hand" (line 22), were not nearly so expensive. "According to Mackay" (line 23) speculators inflated the price of new tulip varieties, and he "further states" (line 26) that soon thereafter prices collapsed.

In the third paragraph, Garber "argues" (line 34) the price fluctuations described by Mackay can be described in rational terms. He suggests that the sudden rise in price of certain bulbs "could have resulted" (line 42) from their fashionable status at the time. "However" (line 44), he notes, as a rare bulb becomes more common, their prices fall rapidly. "But" (line 47) this price decrease "does not mean" (line 48) that the original prices were based on speculation, given that the total sales of a particular type of tulip represent a significant return on investment. He concludes that the price fluctuations "need not indicate a speculative bubble" (line 56).

Don't lose sight of the author's Purpose and **Main Idea** amidst all these details; the author's tone was neutral, and the **Purpose** of the passage was to describe two different interpretations of a particular phenomenon (the price fluctuations in the Dutch tulip market). The **Main Idea**, similarly, is that while Mackay believes the tulip market is evidence of a speculative bubble, Garber argues that no such bubble was present and that the price changes were based on rational principles.

Question Triage: With only six questions of common types, this group of questions isn't terribly challenging to triage. Answer Global question 22 immediately, then move on to Detail question 25. From here, questions 26 and 27 are both good options: question 26 is a paragraph Function question, amenable to a quick glance at your Roadmap, and 27 is a Vocab-in-Context complete with a line reference. With only two questions left, 24 is the better choice. It's an Inference question, but it refers to a specific point of view, simplifying your research. Save 23, the oddly worded Parallel Reasoning question, for last.

22. **(D)**

Which one of the following most accurately expresses the main point of the passage?

(A) The seventeenth-century Dutch tulip market is widely but mistakenly believed by economists to provide an example of a speculative bubble.

(B) Mackay did not accurately assess the earnings that could be derived from rare and expensive seventeenth-century Dutch tulip bulbs.

(C) A speculative bubble occurs whenever the price of an asset increases substantially followed by a rapid and dramatic decline.

(D) Garber argues that Mackay's classic account of the seventeenth-century Dutch tulip market as a speculative bubble is not supported by the evidence.

(E) A tulip bulb can generate a reasonable return on investment even if the price starts very high and decreases dramatically.[23]

Step 2: This Global question asks you to identify the main point of the passage.

Step 3: As always, paraphrase the author's Main Idea before scanning the choices.

Step 4: The author's Main Idea was purely descriptive: Mackay believes a bubble occurred in the Dutch tulip market, and Garber doesn't.

Step 5: Choice (D) correctly describes the point of contention between Mackay and Garber. Choice (A) wrongly describes Mackay's ideas as widely believed and also refers to them as mistaken, something the author never does. Choice (B) is similarly flawed, as it focuses too much on detail and assumes that Mackay is wrong. Choice (C) misses the larger issues at work in the passage by only mentioning the definition of a speculative bubble, and choice (E) is similarly focused on a single detail. Wrong answer choices in Global questions frequently obsess over small details to the exclusion of major ideas—watch for this trap on test day.

---

23. **(D)**

Given Garber's account of the seventeenth-century
Dutch tulip market, which one of the following is
most analogous to someone who bought a tulip bulb
of a certain variety in that market at a very high
price, only to sell a bulb of that variety at a much
lower price?

(A) someone who, after learning that many others
had withdrawn their applications for a
particular job, applied for the job in the belief
that there would be less competition for it

(B) an art dealer who, after paying a very high
price for a new painting, sells it at a very low
price because it is now considered to be an
inferior work

(C) someone who, after buying a box of rare
motorcycle parts at a very high price, is forced
to sell them at a much lower price because of
the sudden availability of cheap substitute parts

(D) a publisher who pays an extremely high price
for a new novel only to sell copies at a price
affordable to nearly everyone

(E) an airline that, after selling most of the tickets
for seats on a plane at a very high price, must
sell the remaining tickets at a very low price[24]

Step 2: The stem asks for a situation analogous to a specific situation. This is a Logical Reasoning question, specifically Parallel Reasoning.

Step 3: There's plenty of information in this stem, so be sure to read it carefully. You must review Garber's account of a person buying at a high price and selling low. According to the Roadmap, this information is in the third paragraph. Garber describes the devaluation of the tulip bulb in terms of market fundamentals; a buyer might invest in a rare bulb on the expectation that the sale of millions of bulbs descendent from the original would provide a return on the original investment.

Step 4: Although you can't predict the specific subject matter of the correct answer, the logic will match Garber's as described in the third paragraph. You should look for an example of someone investing in a rare item in order to profit on reproductions sold at a lower price.

Step 5: Correct choice (D) describes the same kind of logic that Garber describes in the passage. None of the other choices reference the sale of reproductions from an original, and they all can be eliminated for that reason. Once again, a strong prediction makes the correct choice much easier to find.

---

[24]PrepTest 55, Sec 2, Q 23

24. **(B)**

The passage most strongly supports the inference that Garber would agree with which one of the following statements?

(A)   If speculative bubbles occur at all, they occur very rarely.

(B)   Many of the owners of high-priced original tulip bulbs could have expected to at least recoup their original investments from sales of the many bulbs propagated from the original bulbs.

(C)   If there is not a speculative bubble in a market, then the level of prices in that market is not irrational.

(D)   Most people who invested in Dutch tulip bulbs in the seventeenth century were generally rational in all their investments.

(E)   Mackay mistakenly infers from the fact that tulip prices dropped rapidly that the very low prices that the bulbs eventually sold for were irrational.[25]

Step 2: This time you're looking for an Inference that Garber would agree with.

Step 3: As with question 23, a review of Garber's description of the Dutch tulip market is in order. Garber bases his views on market fundamentals—the price fluctuations he observes are rational, because a person who purchases a rare bulb at a high price can expect to sell reproductions at lower prices in order to make a profit.

Step 4: The correct answer should reflect Garber's assessment of the tulip market, so look for a choice that conforms to his description of market fundamentals.

Step 5: Choice (B) is an almost exact paraphrase of Garber's viewpoint and is therefore the correct answer. Choice (A) is extreme. Just because Garber doesn't believe a bubble occurred in this case you can't assert that he believes bubbles are generally rare. Choice (C) sets up a false dichotomy, as Garber never claims that the absence of a bubble implies a rational market. Choice (D) is also extreme; there's not enough information to make an inference about the investments of "most people." Finally, choice (E) misrepresents Garber's disagreement with Mackay.

---

[25]PrepTest 55, Sec 2, Q 24

25. **(B)**

The passage states that Mackay claimed which one of the following?

(A)   The rapid rise in price of Dutch tulip bulbs was not due to the fashionability of the flowers they produced.

(B)   The prices of certain varieties of Dutch tulip bulbs during the seventeenth century were, at least for a time, determined by speculation.

(C)   The Netherlands was the only center of cultivation and development of new tulip varieties in the seventeenth century.

(D)   The very high prices of bulbs in the seventeenth-century Dutch tulip market were not irrational.

(E)   Buyers of rare and very expensive Dutch tulip bulbs were ultimately able to derive earnings from bulbs descendent from the original bulbs.[26]

Step 2: The phrase "the passage states" identifies this as a straightforward Detail question.

Step 3: Mackay's claims are detailed in the second paragraph in which he suggests that the price fluctuations in the Dutch tulip market were based on speculation and were therefore indicative of a bubble.

Step 4: The correct answer should paraphrase the details you've already researched.

Step 5: Correct choice (B) reflects Mackay's belief that the tulip market was affected by speculation. Mackay never denies the effect of fashionability on price as suggested in choice (A), and choice (C) has no support in the passage. Choice (D) is a 180; Mackay believes that the price increases *were* irrational, at least in part. This sounds more like something Garber would have said, as does choice (E). Beware of wrong answer traps that confuse one point of view for another. Careful research will help you avoid losing points to this common error.

26. **(C)**

The main purpose of the second paragraph is to
(A)   present the facts that are accepted by all
       experts in the field
(B)   identify the mistake that one scholar alleges
       another scholar made
(C)   explain the basis on which one scholar makes
       an inference with which another scholar
       disagrees
(D)   undermine the case that one scholar makes for
       the claim with which another scholar
       disagrees
(E)   outline the factual errors that led one scholar
       to draw the inference that he drew[27]

Step 2: This is a Logic Function question. You must describe how the second paragraph functions within the passage as a whole.

Step 3: Refer to your Roadmap to get the context you need.

Step 4: Paragraph two describes the price fluctuations in that occurred in the Dutch tulip market as well as Mackay's interpretation of them. The correct answer should assert that this paragraph demonstrates evidence for one of two conflicting viewpoints present in the passage.

Step 5: Correct choice (C) is the match. Choice (A) is extreme (how can we know how all experts in the field feel about this?) and choice (B) misinterprets the function of the paragraph. It was intended to describe Mackay's position, not identify his mistakes. No undermining occurs in the second paragraph, eliminating choice (D), and choice (E) makes a completely out of scope reference to factual errors.

27. **(D)**

The phrase "standard pricing pattern" as used in
line 38 most nearly means a pricing pattern
(A)   against which other pricing patterns are to be
       measured
(B)   that conforms to a commonly agreed-upon
       criterion
(C)   that is merely acceptable
(D)   that regularly recurs in certain types of cases
(E)   that serves as an exemplar[28]

Step 2: This is another Logic Function question, this time asking you to define a phrase in context.

Step 3: Start your research at the beginning of paragraph three in order to establish the context you need. Garber's position is that the price fluctuations are based on market fundamentals, leading to his assertion that a standard pricing pattern occurs for new types of flowers.

[27]PrepTest 55, Sec 2, Q 26
[28]PrepTest 55, Sec 2, Q 27

Step 4: In context, Garber's reference to a standard pricing pattern is quoted as support for his central idea, that the price fluctuations described in the passage are representative of ordinary changes in the market and not indicative of a bubble. The correct answer should show that a standard pricing pattern is one that is expected.

Step 5: Correct choice (D) describes a predictable pattern. The remaining choices all describe varying everyday usages of the word "standard," none of which make sense in the context of this passage. As always, Logic Function questions rely completely on your sense of context within the passage. Be sure to research this context carefully before examining the answer choices.

PART IV

THE TEST DAY
EXPERIENCE

CHAPTER 22

GET READY FOR TEST DAY

Congratulations. Your work with the Kaplan Method and strategies gives you the knowledge and practice you need for LSAT success. Now, it's time for you to schedule a test date, register for the exam (if you haven't done so already), and put yourself in the right frame of mind to take the next step on the road to law school.

The details of registering for the test are covered in "An Introduction to the LSAT" at the beginning of the book. Follow the steps and recommendations mentioned there to ensure that you have a spot at the next test administration or on the test date that's best for you. In the remainder of this chapter, I'll cover what you need to do to have yourself mentally and emotionally ready for the rigors and rewards of test day.

YOU ARE PREPARED

First, remember (and remind yourself) that you are prepared. By learning the lessons and doing the work from this book, you can know, with confidence, that there is nothing else you need to *know* about LSAT reading comprehension. The Kaplan Method, the specific strategies, and the analysis that I've presented in this book are the result not only of my own tenure as an LSAT instructor; they're the summation of five decades of Kaplan expertise and research. Hundreds of great LSAT minds—including those of perfect scorers, legal scholars, and psychometricians—have contributed to the development, testing, and refinement of Kaplan's LSAT pedagogy. If we know it, you now know it. So strike from your mind any concern that there's one more secret to uncover or a mysterious LSAT Rosetta Stone to search for. You have the most complete, proven system for LSAT Reading Comprehension success available. If you've already studied and practiced from this book's companion volumes—*Kaplan LSAT Logic Games: Strategies and Tactics* and *Kaplan LSAT Logical Reasoning: Strategies and Tactics*—you can say the same thing about the entire exam.

Now, saying that you *know* everything you need to about the Reading Comprehension section doesn't mean you're ready to *do* everything you need to do to achieve your goal score. You need to continue to practice and review. Indeed, I'll cover that in the next section of this chapter. But first, I want to make sure you're translating your comprehensive knowledge of reading comprehension into confidence on test day. From now until the day you sit for your official administration of the LSAT, you need to exhibit the confidence your preparation has earned you.

There are some very practical steps you can take to reinforce your test day confidence. Once you're registered for the test, visit your test site. You may even want to take a reading comprehension passage to practice in the very room where you'll be sitting for the real test. At a minimum, know where you're going to be, how you'll get there, and where you'll park or where public transportation will drop you off. You want no surprises on the morning of your official LSAT.

The day before your test, relax. There's no way to cram for a skills-based exam. While your competition is scrambling and fretting, go to the gym, watch your favorite movie, or have a nice dinner. Gather what you need for the next day, and keep yourself one step ahead of everything you need to do. It sounds a little corny, but acting confident will actually make you feel more confident. Get to bed relatively early, have a good night's sleep, and wake ready to have the best day of your (test-taking) life.

The following is a list of what you'll need to have with you on test day:

LSAT SURVIVAL KIT

You MUST have the following:
- Admissions ticket
- Photo ID
- Several sharpened #2 pencils
- 1-gallon transparent zip-top bag

You SHOULD also have:
- Pencil sharpener
- Eraser
- Analog wristwatch
- Aspirin
- Snack and drink for the break

You CANNOT have:
- Cell phone
- MP3 player
- Computer or electronic reader
- Electronic or digital timers
- Weapons
- Papers other than your admission ticket

That list conforms to the rules for the test site as they stand at the time of this writing. You should check www.lsac.org periodically before your test date to make sure there haven't been any changes or amendments to the Law School Administration Council's (LSAC) policies.

Of course, the "MUSTs" are non-negotiable. You need those to be allowed entry to the testing room. Some of the "SHOULDs," on the other hand, you may not need at all. But if you begin to feel a little headache coming on, or if you find your stomach grumbling midway through Section 3 of the test, you'll be awfully glad you took along those "just in case" items. As for the "CANNOTs," do yourself a favor and avoid any conflict with the proctors or test administrators. Just leave your phone or electronics in the car or at home.

One other very practical thing you can do is to dress in layers. The LSAT is usually administered during the weekend and almost always in a large, institutional building. It's really tough to predict whether the room will be too hot or too cold or whether it will fluctuate throughout the day. Take the Goldilocks approach and make sure the temperature is always "just right" for you by wearing or taking the kind of sweater or light jacket that's easy (and quiet) to slip on or off.

The stress levels of test takers around you will be high. But if you demonstrate nothing but preparation and confidence on the morning of the test, you'll feel calmer, more clear-headed, and ready for the real challenges of the test itself.

CHAMPIONS PRACTICE. VIRTUOSOS PRACTICE. YOU PRACTICE.

To put my earlier point about practice into formal logic terms, knowledge of the test is necessary, but not sufficient, for test day success. Mistaking this relationship is something that leads a lot of test takers off track. They haven't achieved the score they want, so they say, "There must be something I don't know yet," or, "What am I missing?" The fact is that many of these test takers know all about the test, but they haven't practiced taking the test. Ask almost any great performer, musician, public speaker, or athlete and they'll tell you that the key to their success is practice. A great violinist may study a composer's compositional theory, historical context, or even personal life in order to better understand a piece before performing it. But all of that will mean little if the performer hasn't practiced. The audience would be pretty disappointed if the violinist showed up to give a lecture about the composer instead of playing a concert. It's the same with the LSAT. Your audience, law school admissions officers, won't care what you know about the exam, just how well you perform on it.

So how can you best practice? First, lay out a study and practice schedule for yourself that runs from now until test day—one that's ambitious but practical. Fill in as much as you can about which sections or question types you'll be practicing each day or week. If you're working on different parts of the test, vary the sections you're practicing and the materials you're using.

If you haven't completed and reviewed the full-section practice in this book, make sure you do so. Leave time for review of your work. Remember that you're not just checking to see whether you produced the correct answer, you're asking whether you did so as efficiently and effectively as you could have. That means that you should always be reviewing the questions you got right as well as those you got wrong. Look for what features and patterns in a question or passage you're likely to see again on test day. You won't see the passages from this book on your test, but every question on your test will have similarities to those you've practiced here.

If you're looking for additional practice, consider the following additional resources:

OTHER KAPLAN LSAT RESOURCES

Logic Games On Demand
Logical Reasoning On Demand
Reading Comprehension On Demand
Comprehensive, section-specific courses for in-depth instruction and targeted practice.

LSAT Advantage—On Site, Anywhere or On Demand
Our most popular option—complete, targeted, and focused prep designed for busy students.

LSAT Advanced—On Site or Anywhere
Fast-paced for high-scorers focusing on the most advanced content. (158+ required to enroll.)

LSAT Extreme—On Site or Anywhere
Maximum in-class instruction plus tutoring for students who want extra time, review, and more practice.

LSAT One on One—On Site or Anywhere
An expert tutor designs a one-on-one, custom program around your individual needs, goals, and schedule.

LSAT Summer Intensive
Six weeks of total LSAT immersion in a residential academic program at Boston University

Check out *www.kaplanlsat.com* for courses and free events in live, online and in your area.

All of those additional resources will provide the outstanding instruction, coaching, and practice you expect from Kaplan test prep. Consider which ones work best for your schedule, learning style, and admissions timeline. Kaplan is committed to helping you achieve your educational and career goals.

THE PSYCHOLOGICAL DIMENSIONS OF TEST DAY

There's no doubt that taking your official LSAT is one of the most important steps (maybe *the* most important) you'll take on the road to law school. That's a lot of pressure. It's natural to have a little excitement and some extra adrenaline for such a big event. Those are actually healthy things to feel, provided that you channel your emotions into energy and concentration, rather than anxiety and confusion. I'd be pretty disappointed if, after weeks or months of practice and preparation, one of my students said, "Eh, I don't really care what happens on the test." Of course you care. That's why you're reading this book and working so hard. So embrace the big day.

I've already talked about how you can begin to foster an attitude of confidence and act in ways that support and sustain it. Here are a couple of practical steps you can take to carry your confidence right into the testing room.

Know What to Expect

It is easy to lay out the order of events on test day. Here's a chart that shows you what will happen from the time you arrive at the test site.

Event	What Happens	Time
Check-In	Show admissions ticket, ID, fingerprints, room and seat assignment	10–30 minutes
Rules and Procedures	Test booklets distributed, proctor reads the rules, test takers fill out grid information	30 minutes
LSAT Administration		
Section 1	Logic Games, Logical Reasoning, or Reading Comprehension Section	35 minutes
Section 2	Logic Games, Logical Reasoning, or Reading Comprehension Section	35 minutes
Section 3	Logic Games, Logical Reasoning, or Reading Comprehension Section	35 minutes

Break	Test booklets and grids collected, test takers have break, return to seats, booklets and grids redistributed	12–20 minutes (10 minute break with additional time for administrative tasks)
Section 4	Logic Games, Logical Reasoning, or Reading Comprehension Section	35 minutes
Section 5	Logic Games, Logical Reasoning, or Reading Comprehension Section	35 minutes
Prepare for Writing Sample	Test booklets and grids collected, test takers given a chance to cancel scores, Writing Sample booklets distributed	5–10 minutes
Writing Sample	Test takers produce Writing Samples	35 minutes

You can see that even if everything goes as smoothly as possible, you're in for around five hours from start to finish. This is another reason that it's so important to be rested, comfortable, and nourished. Students who are too groggy to be at their best in Section 1 or too exhausted and hungry to keep up their performance in Section 5 will have trouble competing with someone like you, who's prepared for the entire testing day, from start to finish.

One thing that star performers do—I don't care if you're thinking of singers, actors, athletes, or even great trial lawyers—is to warm up before they "go on." You can do the same on the morning of your test by reviewing a Logic Game, Logical Reasoning question, or Reading Comprehension passage that you've done before. As you revisit the game or question, go over the steps in the Kaplan Method that allowed you to be successful with the item before. This will get your brain warmed up just as a quarterback would loosen his arm or a singer would warm up her vocal cords. Don't try new material, and certainly don't try a full section. Just start reading and thinking—calmly and confidently—in the LSAT way. You'll be miles ahead of the unprepared test taker who looks shell-shocked for most of Section 1.

In order to maintain a high level of performance, it's important to stay hydrated and nourished. Mental work makes most people hungry. So drink water at the break and have a small, healthy snack. Don't, however, eat a sleep-inducing turkey sandwich or gobble sugar that will have you crashing out during Section 5.

Knowing what to expect also helps you manage your mental preparation for test day in other small, but important, ways. A lot of test takers don't know that the proctors will ask whether

anyone in the room wants to cancel his or her score right after Section 5 is completed and the test booklets are collected. If you're not expecting that question, it can throw you into a moment of self-doubt. It's human nature to underestimate your performance on the test. You will remember the handful of questions that gave you trouble while ignoring the dozens of questions you answered routinely with no problem. I've personally known students who canceled their scores when they shouldn't have. The LSAC allows you a number of days after the test to cancel your score, so don't worry about it during the exam. Complete the Writing Sample to the best of your ability. You can always consider things that might have caused you to underperform—illness, a personal crisis—after you've completed the test.

You Will Panic, but Don't Panic

Over the course of four to five hours of rigorous, detailed, strictly timed test taking, you're going to reach a point at which you lose focus, feel overwhelmed, or just downright panic for a moment. It's normal. So first thing, don't feed the panic by blaming yourself or saying, "Oh, I knew this would happen." There's nothing wrong with you for having those feelings. In fact, panic is a physical response to high-pressure situations. It's related to the autonomic nervous system, the "flight or fight" response we've adapted to survive danger. Your heart beats faster; blood leaves your brain to go to your extremities; your breathing gets rapid and shallow. That's all very important when the danger you face is a predator or enemy. It's just not very helpful when you're facing a standardized test.

If—when—you face a point of doubt, confusion, or panic on test day, take a moment. Collect yourself physically first. Take a deep breath; sit up in a straight, comfortable posture; put both feet flat on the floor and lower your shoulders; even close your eyes for a second while you breathe. Then open your eyes and remind yourself that whatever you're looking at, it's just an LSAT question. The fact is that you've seen one like it and done one like it before. You know that's the case because of your preparation. Get your concentration back by reciting the Kaplan Method as you work through the problem. You know that will provide a strategic, purposeful approach every time.

Worry Only about What's in Your Control

When I have students in LSAT prep courses, they often ask a lot of questions about what to do if things go wrong on test day. "What if the proctor doesn't give us a verbal five minute warning?" "What if someone is being noisy right behind me?" "What if the school marching band is rehearsing in the courtyard under the window?" All of those and a few weirder, more distracting things have happened to test takers. But my students' concern about such occurrences before test day is misplaced. They should be taking care of the things that are within their control—learning the Kaplan Method, practicing reading comprehension passages—not worrying about the things that aren't. The vast majority of LSAT administrations go off without more than a minor hitch. Your job is to be ready to have a peak performance on a routine test day.

When the unexpected happens, stay calm. If there is something that you notice before the test begins—a window is open, letting in cold air or street noise; the lights in the back of the room aren't turned on, making it dark where you're sitting—just let the proctor know (politely) and ask if it can be remedied. If something happens during a section—another test taker is unconsciously tapping his pencil; the proctor forgets the five-minute announcement—keep working. Raise your hand and get a proctor's attention. When they come to your seat, quickly and quietly explain the situation. Most of the time, they'll take action to remedy the situation. But don't let those things throw you off your game. If something truly bizarre happens that seriously impedes your performance—a fire alarm goes off, a wrecking crew starts to jack-hammer the building—follow the proctor's instructions, keep a record of what happened, and follow up with the LSAC by telephone or in writing after the test concludes. You are welcome to contact 1-800-KAPTEST and ask for advice from one of our LSAT experts, too. A word to the wise: The LSAC will not add points to a score as a remedy for a distracting test administration, but they have found other ways to accommodate test takers who, through no fault of their own, have been unable to complete the test or who encountered unmanageable distractions.

GET READY FOR TEST DAY

This chapter really boils down to one message: Prepare yourself for the perfect test day. Display confidence and preparation in all that you do. Get ready for a consistent, focused performance from start to finish. When that's the attitude you take into the test, you're more likely to outperform your competition and have your best day regardless of what else does or doesn't happen.

CHAPTER 23

SECRETS OF THE LSAT

The "secrets" of the LSAT aren't really secrets at all. They're well-known facts that many test takers fail to take full advantage of. The best test takers use the structure and format of the test to their advantage. Just as a great football or basketball coach adjusts the team's strategy when time is running out on the clock, or just as a great conductor rearranges an orchestra to take advantage of the acoustics in a new venue, you can learn to adjust your approach to the test you're taking. We might well laud the insightful coach or conductor by saying, "Wow, he really knows the 'secrets' of this game (or stadium or theater)." But in fact, he's simply taking account of all the circumstances and making the right strategic decisions for that time and place. Consider a handful of facts that make the LSAT a unique testing experience, and see how you can use them to your advantage.

EVERY QUESTION IS WORTH THE SAME AMOUNT TO YOUR SCORE

Many tests you've taken (even some standardized tests) rewarded you more for certain questions or sections than for others. In school, it's common for a professor to say, "The essay counts for half of your score," or to make a section of harder questions worth five points each while easier ones are worth less. With such exams, you may simply be unable to get a top score without performing well on a given question or topic. It makes sense, then, to target the areas the professor will reward most highly.

As you well know, that's not the case on the LSAT. Every question—easy or hard, short or long, common or rare—is worth exactly the same amount as every other question. That means that you should seek out the questions, games, and passages that are the easiest for you to handle. Far too many test takers get their teeth into a tough question and won't let go. That hurts them

in two ways. First, they spend too much time—sometimes three or four minutes—on such a question, sacrificing their chances with other, easier questions. Second, since questions like these are tough or confusing, they're less likely to produce a right answer no matter how much time you spend. Learn to skip questions when it's in your interest to do so. Mark questions that you skip by circling the entire question in your test booklet. That way, those questions will be easy to spot if you have time left after you complete the other questions in the section. If you've eliminated one or two obviously incorrect answer choicess, strike them through completely so that you don't spend time rethinking them when you come back to the question.

When schools receive your score report, the only thing they see is your score. They don't know—and they don't care—whether you've answered the easiest or the toughest questions on the LSAT. They only care that you answered more questions correctly than the other applicants. Becoming a good manager of the test sections is invaluable. You'll do that, in part, by triaging the games or passages and choosing to put off the toughest for last. Even more often, you'll manage the section by skipping and guessing strategically. Don't slug it out with a tough question for minutes and then grudgingly move on. Boldly seek out questions on which you can exert your strengths, and be clearheaded and decisive in your decisions to move past questions you know are targeted at your weaknesses. Take the test; don't let it take you.

ONE RIGHT, FOUR ROTTEN

I'm sure you've had the experience, on a multiple-choice test in school, of having a teacher tell you, "More than one answer may be correct, but pick the best answer for each question." Given that you're a future law student, I wouldn't be surprised to learn that you may even have debated with your instructor, making a case for why a certain answer should receive credit. As a result, you're used to comparing answer choices to one another. On the LSAT, however, that's a recipe for wasted time and effort. The test makers design the correct answer to be unequivocally correct; it will respond to the call of the question stem precisely. Likewise, the four wrong answers are demonstrably wrong, not just "less good."

For the well-trained test taker—for you, that is—this leads to an important, practical adjustment in strategy. Throughout the test, you should seek to predict the correct answer before assessing the answer choices. In Logical Reasoning, you will, on most questions, be able to anticipate the content of the correct answer, sometimes almost word for word. In Reading Comprehension and Logic Games, you should spend the time up front to have a clear passage road map or game sketch. At a minimum, you must characterize the correct and incorrect answers (if the correct answer *must be true*, for example, each of the wrong answers *could be false*). Then seek out the one answer that matches your prediction or characterization.

The bottom line is that, on the LSAT, you are always comparing the answers against what you know must be correct, not against one another. When locating the correct choice is difficult or time-consuming, you can always turn the tables on the test maker and eliminate the wrong ones.

Because you know that there will always be one correct choice and that you can always identify the characteristics that make wrong answers wrong, you can always take the most direct route to the LSAT point.

THERE'S NO WRONG-ANSWER PENALTY

This point is easy to understand, but sometimes hard to remember when you're working quickly through an LSAT section. The LSAT is scored only by counting the number of correct responses you bubble in. Unlike some standardized tests—the SAT is the most notorious example—you're not penalized for marking incorrect responses. Simply put, there's nothing to lose, so mark a response, even if it's a blind guess, for every answer.

Of course, strategic guessing is better than just taking a wild stab at the correct answer. Even if a question gives you a lot of trouble, see if you can eliminate one or more answer choices as clearly wrong. When you can, take your guess from the remaining choices. Removing even one clearly incorrect choice improves your chances of hitting on the right one from 20 percent to 25 percent; getting rid of two wrong answers, of course, gives you a one-in-three chance of guessing correctly. Provided that you do it quickly (not taking time away from questions you can handle with little trouble), strategic guessing can improve your score.

Students ask another question related to this point about the answer choices. They want to know if a particular answer choice—(A), (B), (C), (D), or (E)—shows up more often than others, or whether it's better, when guessing, to pick a particular choice for all guesses. The answer to both questions is no. Over the course of a full LSAT, all five answer choices show up just about equally. There's no pattern associated with particular question types. You're no more likely to see any particular answer early or late in a section. Thus, when you're blind guessing, you have a one-in-five chance of hitting the correct answer whatever you choose. And there's no benefit from guessing choice (C) or choice (D) over and over. It's far more valuable to spend your limited time trying to eliminate one or more wrong answers than it is to fret over any illusory patterns within the choices.

THE LSAT IS A MARATHON . . . MADE UP OF SPRINTS

At this point in your academic career, you've had long tests and you've had tests that put time pressure on you. But chances are, you've never encountered as intense a combination of the two as you will on the LSAT. In the last chapter, I already talked about the importance of stamina. Including the administrative tasks at the beginning, the breaks, and the collection and distribution of your testing materials, you're in for around a five-hour test day. It's important to remember that, over the course of that marathon, the first and fifth sections are just as valuable as those in the middle. Unsurprisingly, Kaplan's research has shown that, for the untrained test taker, those sections are likely to produce the poorest performance. You can counteract the inherent difficulties in the schedule by doing a little warm-up so that you're ready to hit the ground running at the start of Section 1, and by staying relaxed and having a healthy snack at the break so that you're still going strong at the end of Section 5. Just taking these simple steps could add several points to your score.

At the same time that you're striving to maintain focus and sustain your performance, you're trying to manage a very fast 35 minutes in each section. Attack each section with confident, strategic guessing and you'll be outperforming many test takers who succumb to the "ego battle" with tough or time-consuming questions. But there's one more thing that you have to add to your repertoire of test day tactics: You have to learn to not look back. Over the years, I've talked to many students who could tell me how they thought they performed on each of the test's sections. To be honest with you, I find that a little disappointing. Sure, you may remember that the game with the Cowboys and Horses or the passage on Nanotechnology was really challenging, but it's a waste of time and mental capacity to try and assess your performance as you're taking the test. Once you've answered a question, leave it behind. Give your full concentration to what you're working on. This is even more important when it comes to sections. Once time is called, you may no longer work on the section, not even to bubble in the answers to questions you completed in your test booklet. If a proctor sees you continuing to work on a section for which the time has expired, he or she can issue you a misconduct slip, and the violation will be reported to all of the schools to which you apply. More importantly, you're harming your work on the current section.

There's no rearview mirror on the LSAT. Work diligently, mark the correct answers, and move on to the next question. Keep this in mind: Even if you could accurately assess your performance as you worked (you can't, but imagine it for a moment), it wouldn't change anything. You'd still need to get the remaining questions right. So learn this lesson—and the other "secrets" of the LSAT—now. Be like those seemingly brilliant coaches and performers. By knowing how the LSAT test day works, you can gain an edge over test takers who treat this just as they have every other exam in their academic careers.

CHAPTER 24

LSAT Strategies and Tactics

At last, I'll bring you full circle back to the premise at the start of this book. The LSAT may be unlike any other test you've studied or prepared for, but it need not be mysterious or overwhelming. The underlying principle that has informed this book is that **every question has an answer**. The twist is that you're not expected to know the answers. How could you? This is a test that rewards what you can do, not what you've learned. In that sense, you can't *study* for the test. And you certainly can't cram for it. What you can do, indeed what you've been doing throughout this book, is to *practice* for the test. Instead of thinking of the LSAT as a test, think of it as your law school audition or tryout. A play's director or a team's coach doesn't ask you what you know; she wants to see what you can do. And just as the director or coach will give you everything you need to demonstrate your skill, the test makers always give you everything you need to produce the correct answers on the LSAT.

THE LSAT REWARDS THE CORE 4 SKILLS

Law schools don't expect incoming students to know the law. Indeed, much as the LSAT does, your professors may try to use your outside knowledge and assumptions against you. What the schools are looking for is incoming students who have the skills they'll need to succeed through the coming three years of rigorous legal training. That, at least in part, is what they're looking for your LSAT score to indicate. That's why the LSAT is a skills-based, rather than a knowledge-based, exam. Back near the beginning of this book, you learned the central skills rewarded on the test.

THE CORE 4 LSAT SKILLS
1. **Strategic Reading**
2. **Analyzing Arguments**
3. **Understanding Formal Logic**
4. **Making Deductions**

USE WHAT YOU'VE LEARNED THROUGHOUT THE TEST

One nice thing to realize is that much of the work you've done here, preparing for the Reading Comprehension section specifically, will translate to exceptional performance throughout the test. To be successful on the LSAT, you must make deductions and draw valid inferences from related rules and statements dozens of times in every scored section.

So let me leave you with this: The LSAT is designed to reward the skills that will make you a successful law student. You know that you have those skills. You are, after all, seeking this path with passion and focus. The work you've done in this book is all about honing your skills and preparing you for a successful test day. Take the insights you've gathered about LSAT reading comprehension and apply them throughout the exam. Take what you've learned about yourself as a test taker, and use it not only for a stronger, more confident performance on test day, but also throughout your law school endeavor, during your bar exam, and into your legal career. Best of luck to you. Now, go out and accomplish great things.

Test Drive Test Day **For Less** at:

The LSAT* Experience

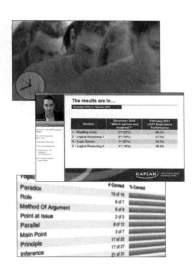

First, you'll take the most-recently released LSAT either:

- in a fully-simulated Test Day environment; or
- at home using our self-proctoring tool

Then, watch a comprehensive review class featuring:

- national performance analysis
- the most missed and representative questions

Plus, get study tools to aid you the week before Test Day:

- Smart Reports™ personal performance analysis
- complete answers and explanations to every question

Register at KaplanLSAT.com/lsatexperience

1-800-KAP-TEST
KaplanLSAT.com

*LSAT is a registered trademark of the Law School Admission Council, Inc. 11-LSAT-0233

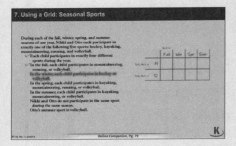
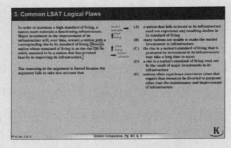
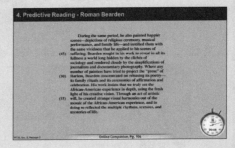

NOTES

NOTES

NOTES

NOTES

NOTES

NOTES

LSAT®
LOGIC
GAMES
STRATEGIES AND TACTICS

100% OFFICIAL LSAT PrepTest® Questions

GLEN STOHR, JD

© 2011 Kaplan, Inc.

Published by Kaplan Publishing, a division of Kaplan, Inc.
395 Hudson Street
New York, NY 10014

Printed in the United States of America

10 9 8 7 6 5 4 3 2 1

ISBN-13: 978-1-60978-151-4

Kaplan Publishing books are available at special quantity discounts to use for sales promotions, employee premiums, or educational purposes. For more information or to purchase books, please call the Simon & Schuster special sales department at 866-506-1949.

Contents

About the Author

GLEN STOHR, JD, is a 15-year veteran LSAT instructor who has helped thousands of students improve their LSAT scores and present winning applications to their law schools of choice. Glen's students have gone on to matriculate at Yale, Duke, UC Berkeley, Georgetown, and many other top schools. Others have parlayed their LSAT score improvements into full-ride scholarships that made their law school goals a reality. Glen's direct, no-nonsense approach to the LSAT as a test that rewards specific, relevant, and coachable skills has made him one of Kaplan's most sought-after instructors by students at all skill levels. His students' dramatic score improvements and positive feedback made him Kaplan's national Teacher of the Year in 2005. In addition to teaching and tutoring more than 1,500 test takers, Glen's work on Kaplan's courses and curriculum has touched tens of thousands of others. Glen's strategic innovations are found throughout Kaplan's LSAT courses and when Kaplan launched its LSAT Advanced course for top scorers, it turned to Glen to head the curriculum development team. A 95th percentile LSAT scorer, Glen is a *cum laude* graduate of the Sandra Day O'Connor School of Law at Arizona State University, where a background in anthropology led him to specialize in Federal Indian Law. Glen draws on his academic background and his experience in both private and public interest law practice to make his LSAT instruction relevant, engaging, and inspirational.

Introduction to the LSAT

The Law School Admissions Test (LSAT) is probably unlike any other test you've taken in your academic career. Most tests you've encountered in high school and college have been content based—that is, they have required you to recall facts, formulas, theorems, or other acquired knowledge.

The LSAT, however, is a skills-based test. It doesn't ask you to repeat memorized facts or to apply learned formulas to specific problems. In fact, all you'll be asked to do on the LSAT is think—thoroughly, quickly, and strategically. There's no required content to study.

But the lack of specific content to memorize is one of things that makes preparing for the LSAT so challenging. Before you get the idea that you can skate into the most important test of your life without preparing, remember that learning skills and improving performance take practice. You can't cram for the test.

ABOUT THE LSAT

The LSAT is a standardized test written by the Law School Admissions Council (LSAC) and administered four times each year. The test is a required component of your application to all American Bar Association–approved law schools as well as some others.

The LSAT is designed to measure the skills necessary (according to the governing bodies of law schools) for success in your first year of law school, such as strategic reading, analyzing arguments, understanding formal logic, and making deductions. Because these skills will serve you well throughout law school and your professional life, consider your LSAT preparation an investment in your career.

You may already possess some level of proficiency with LSAT-tested skills. However, you probably haven't yet mastered how to use those skills to your advantage in the context of a standardized, skills-based test that requires careful time management.

The LSAT is also a test of endurance—five 35-minute blocks of multiple-choice testing plus a 35-minute writing sample. Add in the administrative tasks at both ends of the test and a 10- to 15-minute break midway through, and you can count on being in the test room for at least four and a half hours. It's a grueling experience, but it's not as bad if you are familiar with the test and ready to handle every section. You want to approach the test with confidence so that you can maintain your focus, limit your stress, and get your highest score on test day. That's why it's so important to take control of the test, just as you will take control of the rest of the application process.

Our material is as up-to-date as possible at the time of this printing, but test specifications may change at any time. Please visit our website at http://kaptest.com/LSAT for the latest news and updates.

How Do I Register for the LSAT?

The LSAT is administered by the Law School Admissions Council (LSAC). Be sure to register as soon as possible, as your preferred test site can fill up quickly. You can register for the LSAT in three ways:

- Online: Sign up at http://lsac.org.
- Telephone: Call LSAC at (215) 968-1001.
- Email: Contact LSAC for a registration packet at lsacinfo@lsac.org.

If you have additional questions about registration, contact the LSAC by phone or by email.

The LSAT Sections

The LSAT consists of five multiple-choice sections: two Logical Reasoning sections, one Logic Games section, one Reading Comprehension section, and one unscored "experimental" section that looks exactly like one of the other multiple-choice sections. At the end of the test, there is a Writing Sample section during which you'll write a short essay. Here's how the sections break down:

Section	Number of Questions	Minutes
Logical Reasoning	24–26	35
Logical Reasoning	24–26	35
Logic Games	22–24	35
Reading Comprehension	26–28	35
"Experimental"	23–28	35
Writing Sample	n/a	35

The five multiple-choice sections can appear in any order, but the Writing Sample is always last. You will also get a 10- or 15-minute break between the third and fourth sections of the test.

You'll be answering roughly 125 multiple-choice questions (101 of which are scored) over the course of three intense hours. Taking control of the LSAT means increasing your test speed only to the extent that you can do so without sacrificing accuracy.

First, just familiarize yourself with the sections and the kinds of questions asked in each one.

Logical Reasoning

WHAT IT IS: The Logical Reasoning sections consist of 24–26 each questions that reward your ability to analyze a "stimulus" (a paragraph or a dialogue between two speakers) and make judgments accordingly. You will evaluate the logic and structure of arguments and make inferences from the statements as well as find underlying assumptions, strengthen and weaken arguments, determine logical flaws, and identify parallel argument structures.

WHY IT'S ON THE TEST: Law schools want to see whether you can understand, analyze, evaluate, and manipulate arguments, and draw reliable conclusions—as every law student and attorney must. This question type makes up half of your LSAT score, which means this is a valuable skill to master.

Logic Games

WHAT IT IS: In the Logic Games (a.k.a. Analytical Reasoning) section, you'll find four games (critical-thinking puzzles) with five to seven questions each for a total of 22–24 questions. They reward your ability to make valid deductions from a set of rules or restrictions in order to determine what can, must, or cannot be true in various circumstances.

WHY IT'S ON THE TEST: In law school, your professors will have you read dozens of cases, extract their rules, and apply them to or distinguish them from hypothetical cases. The Logic Games section rewards the same skill set: attention to detail, rigorous deductive reasoning, an understanding of how rules limit and order behavior (the very definition of law), and the ability to discern the conditions under which those rules do and do not apply.

Reading Comprehension

WHAT IT IS: The Reading Comprehension section consists of three passages, each 450–550 words, and a set of two short passages that total 450–550 words. Each passage is followed by five to eight questions. The topics may range from areas of social science, humanities, natural science, and law. Because content isn't tested, you won't need any outside knowledge.

WHY IT'S ON THE TEST: The Reading Comprehension section tests your ability to quickly understand the gist and structure of long, difficult prose—just as you'll have to do in law school and throughout your career.

The Writing Sample

WHAT IT IS: During the Writing Sample section, you will read a paragraph that presents a problem and lists two possible solutions. Each solution will have strengths and weaknesses; you must argue in favor of one based on the given criteria. There is no right or wrong answer, and the writing sample is unscored. However, law schools will receive a copy of your essay along with your LSAT score.

WHY IT'S ON THE TEST: The Writing Sample shows law schools your ability to argue for a position while attacking an opposing argument under timed conditions. In addition, it may be used to verify that your writing style is similar to that in your personal statement.

How the LSAT Is Scored

You'll receive one score for the LSAT ranging between 120 and 180 (no separate scores for Logical Reasoning, Logic Games, and Reading Comprehension). There are roughly 101 scored multiple-choice questions on each exam:

- About 52 from the two Logical Reasoning sections
- About 22 from the Logic Games section
- About 27 from the Reading Comprehension section

Your **raw score,** the number of questions that you answer correctly, will be multiplied by a complicated scoring formula (different for each test, to accommodate differences in difficulty level) to yield the **scaled score**—the one that will fall somewhere in that 120–180 range—which is reported to the schools.

Because the test is graded on a largely preset curve, the scaled score will always correspond to a certain percentile, also indicated on your score report. A score of 160, for instance, corresponds roughly to the 80th percentile, meaning that 80 percent of test takers scored at or below your level. The percentile figure is important because it allows law schools to see where you fall in the pool of applicants.

All scored questions are worth the same amount—one raw point—and there's no penalty for guessing. That means that you should always fill in an answer for every question, whether you get to that question or not.

What's a "Good" LSAT Score?

What you consider a "good" LSAT score depends on your own expectations and goals, but here are a few interesting statistics.

If you got about half of all of the scored questions right (a raw score of roughly 50), you would earn a scaled score of roughly 147, putting you in about the 30th percentile—not a great performance. But on the LSAT, a little improvement goes a long way. In fact, getting only one

additional question right every 10 minutes would give you a raw score of about 64, pushing you into the 60th percentile—a huge improvement.

Sample Percentiles Approx. Scaled Score		
Percentile	**(Range 120–180)**	**Approx. Raw Score**
99th percentile	174	~94 correct out of 101
95th percentile	168	~88 correct out of 101
90th percentile	164	~82 correct out of 101
80th percentile	160	~76 correct out of 101
75th percentile	157	~71 correct out of 101
50th percentile	152	~61 correct out of 101

Note: Exact percentile-to-scaled-score relationships vary from test to test.

As you can see, you don't have to be perfect to do well. On most LSATs, you can get as many as 28 questions wrong and still remain in the 80th percentile or as many as 20 wrong and still be in the 90th percentile. Most students who score 180 get a handful of questions wrong.

Although many factors play a role in admissions decisions, the LSAT score is usually one of the most important. And—generally speaking—being average won't cut it. The median LSAT score is somewhere around 152. If you're aiming for the top, you've got to do even better.

By using the strategies in this book, you'll learn how to approach—and master—the test in a general way. As you'll see, knowing specific strategies for each type of question is only part of your task. To do your best, you have to approach the entire test with the proactive, take-control kind of thinking it inspires—the LSAT mindset.

For more information on the LSAT experience, see Part IV of this book.

GO ONLINE

For extra strategies and detailed question breakdowns to supplement the text of this book, you can register for your *LSAT Logic Games: Strategies and Practice* online companion at kaptest. com/booksonline. You'll be asked for a specific password derived from the text in this book, so have your book handy when you log in.

Good luck!

PART I

HOW LOGIC GAMES WORK

CHAPTER 1

EVERY QUESTION HAS AN ANSWER

If you've tried an LSAT logic game, you know that it can seem like a bizarre, abstract exercise. For many test takers, the first reaction to the Logic Games section is "I'm not even sure what they're asking for," or "How am I supposed to do all of this in 35 minutes?" If that sounds like you, don't be alarmed. But resolve from this point forward to remember (and follow) one simple principle: Every logic games question on the LSAT has one correct answer. The test always gives you enough information to determine the correct answer (and the four wrong ones). Logic games are unusual, unlike any academic task you've likely faced before, but they're fair and they're designed to reward skills that will be essential to your success as a law student. By adopting the approach laid out in this book, you'll learn how logic games are put together and how you can take them apart efficiently, effectively, and routinely. If you practice the methods and strategies introduced here, your logic games performance, and your LSAT score, will improve.

A SAMPLE LOGIC GAMES QUESTION

Here's a logic games question. See whether you can answer it in 30 seconds.

If the storm passes over Oceana at some time before it passes over Lofton, then which one of the following must be true?

(A) The third town the storm passes over receives only rain.
(B) The fourth town the storm passes over receives only rain.
(C) The fourth town the storm passes over receives hail and rain.
(D) The fifth town the storm passes over receives only rain.
(E) The fifth town the storm passes over receives hail and rain.[1]

I hope your immediate reaction was, "That's not fair. I can't answer this; I don't even know the setup or the rules." And that's the point. The test makers will always supply the preliminary information you need to determine the right answer. They want to reward your critical thinking and your ability to make deductions from the relevant restrictions they provide. In this case, all of the information you need in order to answer this question is in the following paragraph, the game's setup. After reading the setup, try again to answer the question in 30 seconds.

One afternoon, a single thunderstorm passes over exactly five towns—Jackson, Lofton, Nordique, Oceana, and Plattesville—dropping some form of precipitation on each. The storm is the only source of precipitation in the towns that afternoon. On some towns, it drops both hail and rain; on the remaining towns, it drops only rain. It passes over each town exactly once and does not pass over any two towns at the same time. The following must obtain:
 The third town the storm passes over is Plattesville.
 The storm drops hail and rain over the second town it passes over.
 The storm drops only rain on both Lofton and Oceana.
 The storm passes over Jackson at some time after it passes over Lofton and at some time after it passes over Nordique.[2]

If the storm passes over Oceana at some time before it passes over Lofton, then which one of the following must be true?

(A) The third town the storm passes over receives only rain.
(B) The fourth town the storm passes over receives only rain.
(C) The fourth town the storm passes over receives rain and hail.
(D) The fifth town the storm passes over receives only rain.
(E) The fifth town the storm passes over receives rain and hail.[3]

[1] PrepTest 46, Sec. 4, Q 16
[2] PrepTest 46, Sec. 4, Game 3
[3] PrepTest 46, Sec. 4, Q 16

If you're thinking, "Well great, how am I supposed to deal with all of that?" or "I'm sure all of the information is there, but it will take me forever to comb through all of that," don't panic. Logic games are designed to feel overwhelming. So is the first year of law school. By the end of this book, you'll see this game as a standard variation, amenable to the Kaplan Method and its strategies. In fact, when you approach the question above, you'll organize the rules and restrictions into a sketch that looks something like this:

If the storm passes over Oceana at some time before it passes over Lofton, then which one of the following must be true?

(A)   The third town the storm passes over receives only rain.

(B)   The fourth town the storm passes over receives only rain.

(C)   The fourth town the storm passes over receives rain and hail.

(D)   The fifth town the storm passes over receives only rain.

(E)   The fifth town the storm passes over receives rain and hail.[4]

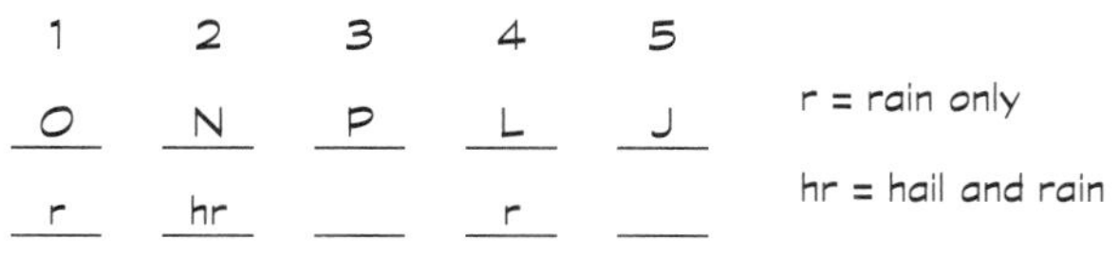

```
     1     2     3     4     5
     O     N     P     L     J       r = rain only
     r     hr          r             hr = hail and rain
```

Figure 1.1

If you try the question now, you'll likely spot the one correct answer in far less than 30 seconds.

The right answer, the one that increases your LSAT score, is (B). A glance at Figure 1.1 confirms that the fourth town receives only rain. Just as importantly, that same glance reveals why each of the wrong answers is wrong. Choice (C) contradicts the sketch. And choices (A), (D), and (E) all deal with spaces that the sketch leaves undetermined, so they don't have to be as true as the question stem calls for.

The Road Ahead

Unfortunately, logic games don't come with pre-drawn sketches like that one. It's the test makers' job to challenge you to demonstrate the reasoning skills you'll need for law school. That's where this book comes in. In the following pages and chapters, you'll learn everything you need to make every logic game, every question, and every correct answer as clear and direct as the one above. You'll discover how to interpret the game's task, turn it into a simple, useful sketch, apply the rules and restrictions, and draw the additional deductions that make the correct answers unequivocal. In short, you'll learn the Kaplan Method for Logic Games.

What you learn about logic games counts for nothing if it doesn't turn into correct answers, quickly and consistently, on test day. A lot of LSAT books and courses set out to show you how much their authors and teachers know about logic games. They sometimes have elaborate, impressive systems for categorizing game types or even fancy names for the rules you'll see. Guess what? You don't get any points on the LSAT for giving a game the right name. You have

---

4 PrepTest 46, Sec. 4, Q 16

no opportunity to show off your mastery of a new nomenclature. You have four games, 22 to 24 questions, and only 35 minutes to get them all right. Recognizing certain patterns that recur in logic games can be very helpful (and Part II of this book will break down the various game types in detail). Beginning from an understanding of the skills that all logic games are designed to reward, you'll find that a simple, concrete method will earn you more points on logic games time and again, whether the game you're tackling seems as familiar as an old T-shirt or as unexpected as an avant-garde film. So keep your focus on getting the right answers, and the rest of what you need to know will follow.

Job one is to clarify what you're being asked for. Using the Thunderstorm game and a couple of others, I'll illustrate how to identify each task the test makers set out for you.

A SAMPLE LOGIC GAMES TASK
"But What Kind of Game Is This?"

Over the years, I've heard countless students ask this question about a countless number of games. What they're really saying is, "I don't know how to begin unless I recognize the game as one of the predetermined game types, one that I've memorized a sketch for." My answer is always the same: Read the opening paragraph and see what your task is. Imagine you went to work for a lawyer who came in one day and said, "I'm meeting our client in a half hour. Would you please whip up a quick chart showing the order that the defense witnesses are likely to appear in and what each is going to testify about?" I trust that you wouldn't say, "I don't know how to begin that unless you provide me with the defense witness testimony template." You'd simply get the case file, pull the relevant information, and put it into a simple chart or document that would be easy for your boss to read and share with the client. Don't let logic games stymie you. They all involve relatively simple tasks, and you don't get bonus style points for having the "right" diagram.

Take another look at the setup for the game you've already seen:

One afternoon, a single thunderstorm passes over exactly five towns—Jackson, Lofton, Nordique, Oceana, and Plattesville—dropping some form of precipitation on each. The storm is the only source of precipitation in the towns that afternoon. On some towns, it drops both hail and rain; on the remaining towns, it drops only rain. It passes over each town exactly once and does not pass over any two towns at the same time. The following must obtain:

The third town the storm passes over is Plattesville.
The storm drops hail and rain over the second town it passes over.

The storm drops only rain on both Lofton and
Oceana.
The storm passes over Jackson at some time after it
passes over Lofton and at some time after it passes
over Nordique.[5]

Your starting point for understanding any logic game on the LSAT is the real-world scenario,
or Situation (as you'll come to call it), described in the opening paragraph. Use the Situation
to visualize the task; then use that image to begin a simple sketch or chart that will help you
organize all of the information in the game's rules and restrictions. In the Thunderstorm game,
there are two things you'll need to account for: the order of the towns the storm passes over
and the type of precipitation it drops on them.

There are many ways you could logically organize these tasks. The one that will work best is the
one that fits the information as it's presented in the game's setup. The key question to ask is
"What here is concrete and what's still up in the air?" If the test supplied you with some kind of
map or told you the directions among the towns, you might come up with something like this:

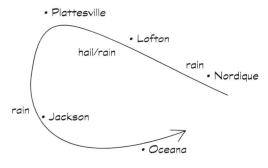

Figure 1.2

That's great for the storm tracker on the news channel, but it's not going to be of any use to
you. The towns' locations are completely up in the air. What is certain is that the storm travels
in one direction; it passes over each town only once, one at a time. So get ready to organize
the information about the order of the towns like this:

J	L	N	O	P
1	2	3	4	5
—	—	—	—	—

Figure 1.3

That chart will allow you to handle the first task—the order in which the storm passes over
the towns—just fine. But there was a second task to deal with, too: determining the type of
precipitation dropped on each town. For a lot of test takers, the instinctual response is to create a separate chart for this information, something like this:

---

[5] PrepTest 46, Sec. 4, Game 3

Figure 1.4

That's okay, but it's not as useful as it could be. When the test makers present you with two tasks in a logic game (and they usually do so once or twice per test), they'll ask questions that combine the tasks. In fact, you already saw this in the question examined earlier. It asked you about the type of precipitation dropped on the third, or fourth, or fifth town the storm passed over.

> If the storm passes over Oceana at some time before it passes over Lofton, then which one of the following must be true?
>
> (A)   The third town the storm passes over receives only rain.
> (B)   The fourth town the storm passes over receives only rain.
> (C)   The fourth town the storm passes over receives rain and hail.
> (D)   The fifth town the storm passes over receives only rain.
> (E)   The fifth town the storm passes over receives rain and hail.[6]

Just as important, notice how the rules of the game combine information about the two tasks. The three highlighted rules illustrate this point: the first tells you about the order of towns the storm passes over, the second about the order of the precipitation dropped, and the third about the type of precipitation dropped on certain towns.

> One afternoon, a single thunderstorm passes over exactly five towns—Jackson, Lofton, Nordique, Oceana, and Plattesville—dropping some form of precipitation on each. The storm is the only source of precipitation in the towns that afternoon. On some towns, it drops both hail and rain; on the remaining towns, it drops only rain. It passes over each town exactly once and does not pass over any two towns at the same time. The following must obtain:
> The third town the storm passes over is Plattesville.
> The storm drops hail and rain over the second town it passes over.
> The storm drops only rain on both Lofton and Oceana.
> The storm passes over Jackson at some time after it passes over Lofton and at some time after it passes over Nordique.[7]

---

[6] PrepTest 46, Sec. 4, Q 16
[7] PrepTest 46, Sec. 4, Game 3

With practice, you'll spot connections like this almost automatically. For now, take to heart that with a good strategic reading of the setup, you can always build a useful sketch for any logic game. Just as it's unlikely that you'd hand your boss, the lawyer, two separate charts—one for the order in which the witnesses appear and another for their likely testimony—it's not really intuitive to separate out the game's tasks either.

For the Thunderstorm game, your sketch or framework should look like this:

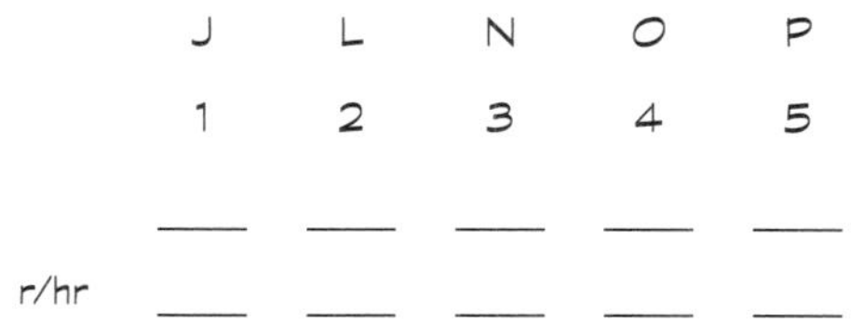

$$
\begin{array}{ccccc}
J & L & N & O & P \\
1 & 2 & 3 & 4 & 5
\end{array}
$$

r/hr ___ ___ ___ ___ ___

Figure 1.5

In later chapters, you'll come to recognize this as a typical Sequencing-Matching Hybrid game. You'll see other sketches that look a lot like this one because they fit the task so well. But, and this underlines a point I made earlier, you didn't need to know the game's name or have a particular sketch in mind in order to draw an entirely effective diagram. To tell you the truth, I've seen an over-reliance on memorizing game types backfire on many, many test takers. These include students who learn a couple of standard diagrams, get really excited about how well they worked in some games, and then try to fit any and every logic game into one of them, even when the task doesn't fit the sketch. They also include those students who freeze the moment that a game's task doesn't obviously fit something they've previously learned to manage. That's why it's important for you to realize that you can handle any game by carefully reading the Situation, visualizing your task, and creating a sketch that fits the information.

Before moving on to some other typical game tasks, let me make two more points. First, everyone's sketches look a little bit different. That's fine. It's no problem if you saw the Thunderstorm game fitting into a grid, or with the numbers ordering the towns at the bottom, or even arranged vertically instead of horizontally. These variations might look different, but each would organize the game's key information in exactly the same way as the master example, and all would get you the LSAT points you need on test day (which is what matters, right?).

1 2 3 4 5
JLNOP
r/hr
J L N O P
r/hr
1 2 3 4 5
JLNOP
1
2
3
4
5
r/hr

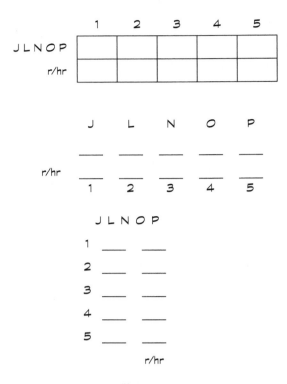

Figure 1.6

You should find the way that's easiest for you to draw accurate, repeatable sketches in the small space that you have in the test booklet. Adopt the best principles for sketching and diagramming given here, and pay attention to the essential notations (I'll always tell you when something is non-negotiable), but don't worry if your sketches aren't carbon copies of what's in this book.

The second point, before I have you look at some other games with different tasks, relates to the rules and deductions that you'll need to add into the diagrams and frameworks you create. Remember the sketch that helped you answer the LSAT question?

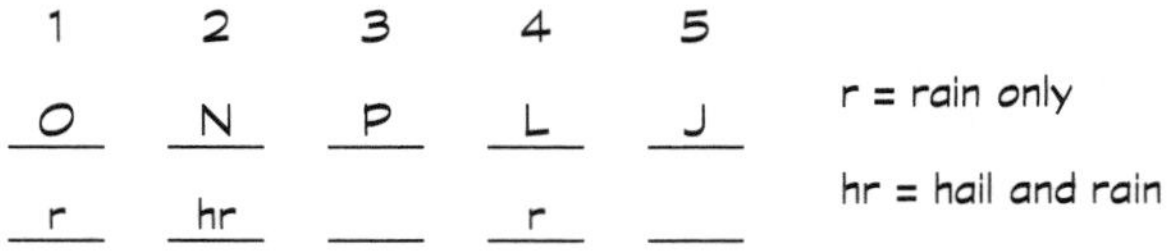

1 2 3 4 5
O N P L J
r hr r
r = rain only
hr = hail and rain

Figure 1.7

This sketch was created specifically for that question. It took all of the rules and deductions from the game setup and added in the restriction from the question's "if" clause.

> If the storm passes over Oceana at some time before it passes over Lofton, then which one of the following must be true?[8]

[8] PrepTest 46, Sec. 4, Q 16

You'll learn to build the rules and deductions into your Master Sketch in the remainder of this chapter and perfect your technique over the course of the next three chapters. In the chapter dealing with question types, you'll see how valuable it is to draw new "mini-sketches" for questions containing hypothetical "if" clauses. For now, I just want you to note that it's imperative that you keep your sketches clear, accurate, and simple so they can be just as useful as the mini-sketch for the earlier question was.

DEFINE THE TASK

Although your sketch simplified the tasks in the Thunderstorm game and made them quite manageable, that game—because it contains two actions—is actually among the more complex games found on the LSAT. I hope that's comforting. Before challenging you to identify and begin setting up games on your own, I'll walk you through a few more games' Situations to give you a feel for the variety of tasks you're likely to see on test day.

"Abel, You're Third in Line. Baker, up Front. Space 1."

Here's an example of the task most commonly used on the LSAT. Take a few seconds and look it over. Then go ahead and try to draw the initial framework for this game.

> Exactly six guideposts, numbered 1 through 6, mark a
> mountain trail. Each guidepost pictures a different one of
> six animals—fox, grizzly, hare, lynx, moose, or porcupine.
> The following conditions must apply:
>   The grizzly is pictured on either guidepost 3 or
>   guidepost 4.
>   The moose guidepost is numbered lower than the
>   hare guidepost.
>   The lynx guidepost is numbered lower than the
>   moose guidepost but higher than the fox guidepost.[9]

There are many things you could be asked to do with guideposts. You could be asked to assign each of them a different color. Or you could be asked to determine which of two different artists creates the image for each guidepost. Neither of those tasks would be unusual on the LSAT, but neither of them is your task here. The key phrase in the setup is "numbered 1 through 6." The test makers will ask you questions related to the order of the guideposts. A quick check of the rules confirms this. Each one either restricts a particular guidepost's possible positions or tells you something about certain guideposts' order relative to each other. Your sketch should look like this:

---

[9] PrepTest 46, Sec. 4, Game 1

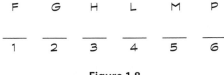

Figure 1.8

Notice that this game, although it has six signs instead of five towns, tasks you with just the Sequencing half of the Thunderstorm game's setup. That's why I said that the Thunderstorm game is more complex. Complex games aren't necessarily harder or easier than their simpler counterparts (as you'll see in the next chapter, game difficulty is, more than anything, a function of how concrete the rules and restrictions are), but it is essential that you grasp the task or tasks that the questions ask about.

That last point provides the opportunity for an important digression. A lot of test takers go astray by focusing on a game's subject matter. When asked for the game's Situation, they'll say "a thunderstorm" or "trail markers." That tells you nothing. Remember, the test makers could ask you what color each sign is, or which artist painted which signs, or any number of other possible tasks. In logic games, subject matter is irrelevant. Instead, you should look for a clear and descriptive presentation of the Situation that helps you see how the game works. Saying "the Situation is the order of six trail markers" is better. But what I really want you to shoot for is a mental picture of the task. There's a trail in front of you. Under one arm, you have the six signs. In the other hand, you have a mallet to pound them into place. If you put the Grizzly sign in the third space, it's no longer in your hand and no other sign is going in the third space. Now, you can abstract that task into a simple, helpful diagram *and* you can anticipate the kinds of rules, restrictions, and even questions you're going to see. Try that on the next setup.

"Abel, After Charlie. Baker, After Abel."

Take about 30 seconds, compose a picture of the task in your mind, and decide how you'd begin to set this one up. It's similar to the Trail Markers game, but it has a couple of important differences that I'll point out in a moment.

A courier delivers exactly eight parcels—G, H, J, K, L, M, N, and O. No two parcels are delivered at the same time, nor is any parcel delivered more than once. The following conditions must apply:

L is delivered later than H.
K is delivered earlier than O.
H is delivered earlier than M.
O is delivered later than G.
M is delivered earlier than G.
Both N and J are delivered earlier than M.[10]

---

[10] PrepTest 51, Sec. 4, Game 4

Sure enough, your task is to determine the order of the deliveries. You may have seen that when you read "No two parcels are delivered at the same time, nor is any parcel delivered more than once" in the short opening paragraph. But your mental picture is really fleshed out by the indented rules that follow. Notice that they all restrict the parcels relative to one another. There are no rules here similar to the previous game's restriction of the Grizzly guidepost to spaces 3 or 4. Note, too, that several of the parcels are each mentioned in more than one of the rules. For example, consider the appearance of parcel G in both the fourth and fifth rules:

> A courier delivers exactly eight parcels—G, H, J, K, L, M, N, and O. No two parcels are delivered at the same time, nor is any parcel delivered more than once. The following conditions must apply:
> L is delivered later than H.
> K is delivered earlier than O.
> H is delivered earlier than M.
> O is delivered later than G.
> M is delivered earlier than G.
> Both N and J are delivered earlier than M.[11]

When you have a game like this one—in which all of the rules are relative—you need not create a framework with specific spaces at all. Decide which direction is earlier and which is later, and simply use lines to connect the entities (parcels, in this game) as described by the rules. Without trying to set up the complete game (you'll be doing that soon), here's what the fourth and fifth rules would look like:

Figure 1.9

In this case, earlier deliveries are at the top of the diagram and later ones at the bottom.

Perhaps you pictured yourself as the delivery person arranging the parcels in the back of your truck before you set out on your route. You can't determine the order entirely (there'd be no game if you could), but from the hints in the rules, you can see that some of the packages are going to be dropped off before certain other ones. If this were your real-life job and your route took you to Maple Street before Oak Avenue, you would want to load the Maple deliveries closer to the door of your truck so you wouldn't have to climb over the Oak deliveries to get them.

---

[11] PrepTest 51, Sec. 4, Game 4

By the way, there's a side benefit to doing a quick assessment of the Situation and game tasks: it will reduce your anxiety. With a mental picture of the task, you can arrange your entities logically. You're on your way to law school, so of course you can handle arranging some parcels in a delivery van.

"Abel, You're on Team X. Baker, You're on Team Y."

This next game is quite different from those you've seen thus far, but I'll still challenge you to assess the Situation and task before I explain them in any detail. Take a minute to visualize the Situation, and try to start setting up this game.

> On a field trip to the Museum of Natural History, each of six children—Juana, Kyle, Lucita, Salim, Thanh, and Veronica—is accompanied by one of three adults—Ms. Margoles, Mr. O'Connell, and Ms. Podorski. Each adult accompanies exactly two of the children, consistent with the following conditions:
>
> If Ms. Margoles accompanies Juana, then Ms. Podorski accompanies Lucita.
>
> If Kyle is not accompanied by Ms. Margoles, then Veronica is accompanied by Mr. O'Connell.
>
> Either Ms. Margoles or Mr. O'Connell accompanies Thanh.
>
> Juana is not accompanied by the same adult as Kyle; nor is Lucita accompanied by the same adult as Salim; nor is Thanh accompanied by the same adult as Veronica.[12]

The task here is entirely unrelated to the order in which the children go to the museum. But if you picture the Situation, everything becomes clear. There's a classroom, and six kids are standing in alphabetical order. You introduce the three adult chaperones at the front of the room and explain that each grown-up will be responsible for two of the children. Now, just turn that Situation into a simple diagram.

Figure 1.10

It's really beside the point whether you use dashes or boxes or circles to represent each chaperone's assignments, but it's absolutely non-negotiable that you account for exactly two children with each adult. Any of these diagrams would give you what you need:

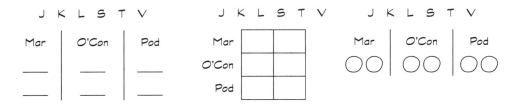

Figure 1.11

You'll come to call this game's action Distribution, dividing a set of entities up into teams. The important thing to notice with this type of game is how clearly the numbers are defined. In the end, it's unimportant that the entities are students and chaperones. What will make this game manageable is that you're splitting six entities into three teams of exactly two players each.

"Abel, You're in This Scene. Baker, You're Not."

Here's one more scenario for you to examine. The sketch will turn out to be remarkably simple (although this game turns out to be pretty challenging for reasons you'll come to appreciate in the chapter on formal logic). Take a few seconds to figure out what you're being asked to do here.

> An album contains photographs picturing seven friends: Raimundo, Selma, Ty, Umiko, Wendy, Yakira, Zack. The friends appear either alone or in groups with one another, in accordance with the following:
>
> Wendy appears in every photograph that Selma appears in.
> Selma appears in every photograph that Umiko appears in.
> Raimundo appears in every photograph that Yakira does not appear in.
> Neither Ty nor Raimundo appears in any photograph that Wendy appears in.[13]

This is another game that involves making groups. But this time, there are no chaperones (or coaches, or teams, or whatever) with which the seven friends are being paired. Instead, you're a photographer. You've got the camera set up and you're telling people, "Selma, I want you in this one. Wendy, you too." You could create two lists for any given photo—an "in" group and an "out" group—like so:

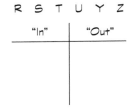

Figure 1.12

---

[13] PrepTest 45, Sec. 3, Game 3

An even simpler way to diagram this, and one that would use less of the blank space available on the page (no scratch paper is allowed on test day), is to jot down a list of all seven friends and then circle those who are "in" and strike through those who are "out."

R S T U W Y Z

Figure 1.13

Thus, if you find out that S is in a picture, you know from the rules that W is as well. Since W's appearance knocks out T and R, you'd have a sketch that looks like this:

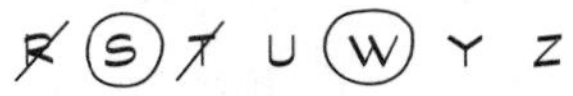

R̶ Ⓢ T̶ U Ⓦ Y Z

Figure 1.14

This, I'll refer to as a Selection game. This task is almost always straightforward—choose her, reject him. The challenge, as I hinted at above, comes in understanding all of the conditional restrictions the test makers apply to these Situations—"If you include *x*, you have to include *y* but reject *z*," and so on. Fortunately, there are standard ways to interpret and diagram all of the formal logic you'll encounter on the LSAT. But one thing at a time.

Right now, I want you to try your hand at a short drill to test your ability to assess Situations and tasks.

DRILL: DEFINING GAME TASKS

Here are five logic game setups. Take less than one minute with each. Assess the Situation, visualize your task, and use the space next to each one to draw the initial framework or diagram. Don't worry about sketching all of the rules or trying to make additional deductions at this point. You'll be doing all of that soon. Explanations of the game tasks follow the Drill.

1.

In the course of one month Garibaldi has exactly seven different meetings. Each of her meetings is with exactly one of five foreign dignitaries: Fuentes, Matsuba, Rhee, Soleimani, or Tbahi. The following constraints govern Garibaldi's meetings:

> She has exactly three meetings with Fuentes, and exactly one with each of the other dignitaries.
> She does not have any meetings in a row with Fuentes.
> Her meeting with Soleimani is the very next one after her meeting with Tbahi.
> Neither the first nor last of her meetings is with Matsuba.[14]

2.

The three highest-placing teams in a high school debate tournament are the teams from Fairview, Gillom, and Hilltop high schools. Each team has exactly two members. The individuals on these three teams are Mei, Navarro, O'Rourke, Pavlovich, Sethna, and Tsudama. The following is the case:

> Sethna is on the team from Gillom High.
> Tsudama is on the second-place team.
> Mei and Pavlovich are not on the same team.
> Pavlovich's team places higher than Navarro's team.
> The team from Gillom High places higher than the team from Hilltop High.[15]

3.

Three folk groups—Glenside, Hilltopper, Levon—and three rock groups—Peasant, Query, Tinhead—each perform on one of two stages, north or south. Each stage has three two-hour performances: north at 6, 8, and 10; south at 8, 10, and 12. Each group performs individually and exactly once, consistent with the following conditions:

> Peasant performs at 6 or 12.
> Glenside performs at some time before Hilltopper.
> If any rock group performs at 10, no folk group does.
> Levon and Tinhead perform on different stages.
> Query performs immediately after a folk group, though not necessarily on the same stage.[16]

4.

Workers at a water treatment plant open eight valves—G, H, I, K, L, N, O, and P—to flush out a system of pipes that needs emergency repairs. To maximize safety and efficiency, each valve is opened exactly once, and no two valves are opened at the same time. The valves are opened in accordance with the following conditions:

> Both K and P are opened before H.
> O is opened before L but after H.
> L is opened after G.
> N is opened before H.
> I is opened after K.[17]

5.

In a repair facility there are exactly six technicians: Stacy, Urma, Wim, Xena, Yolanda, and Zane. Each technician repairs machines of at least one of the following three types— radios, televisions, and VCRs—and no other types. The following conditions apply:

> Xena and exactly three other technicians repair radios.
> Yolanda repairs both televisions and VCRs.
> Stacy does not repair any type of machine that Yolanda repairs.
> Zane repairs more types of machines than Yolanda repairs.
> Wim does not repair any type of machine that Stacy repairs.
> Urma repairs exactly two types of machines.[18]

[14] PrepTest 44, Sec. 3, Game 1

[15] PrepTest 53, Sec. 2, Game 4

[16] PrepTest 48, Sec. 2, Game 4

[17] PrepTest 52, Sec. 2, Game 1

[18] PrepTest 48, Sec. 2, Game 3

Explanations

Now, compare your work to the suggested visualizations and sketches below.

1.

In the course of one month Garibaldi has exactly seven different meetings. Each of her meetings is with exactly one of five foreign dignitaries: Fuentes, Matsuba, Rhee, Soleimani, or Tbahi. The following constraints govern Garibaldi's meetings:

> She has exactly three meetings with Fuentes, and exactly one with each of the other dignitaries.
> She does not have any meetings in a row with Fuentes.
> Her meeting with Soleimani is the very next one after her meeting with Tbahi.
> Neither the first nor last of her meetings is with Matsuba.[19]

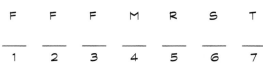

Figure 1.15

Your task is only hinted at in the opening paragraph by the phrases "in the course of one month" and "each of her meetings is with exactly one of five foreign dignitaries." You may already have a mental picture of an appointment calendar in mind. A quick scan of the rules confirms your suspicion: The test makers want you to determine the order of the seven meetings, and you can set up a sketch much like the one you used for the Trail Markers game. There is one unusual feature that I hope you caught. Garibaldi has seven meetings with just five people, but each meeting is with only one dignitary. Rule 1 clears it all up. She'll meet with Fuentes three times. As a result, it's very helpful to list F three times in your roster of the entities: "F F F M R S T." Along the way, a question may give you enough information to determine the position of one or two of the meetings with F, so you could cross those off your roster. This way, you'll still have a visual reminder of all meetings that remain undetermined.

2.

The three highest-placing teams in a high school debate tournament are the teams from Fairview, Gillom, and Hilltop high schools. Each team has exactly two members. The individuals on these three teams are Mei, Navarro, O'Rourke, Pavlovich, Sethna, and Tsudama. The following is the case:

> Sethna is on the team from Gillom High.
> Tsudama is on the second-place team.
> Mei and Pavlovich are not on the same team.
> Pavlovich's team places higher than Navarro's team.
> The team from Gillom High places higher than the team from Hilltop High.[20]

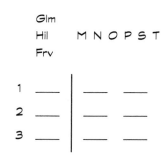

Figure 1.16

Here's another complex game. Your tasks are thoroughly intertwined. You'll need to determine the final ranking of the top three teams and figure out which two debaters competed for each school. Your mental picture may be something like the awards stands at the Olympics, with the

---

[19] PrepTest 44, Sec. 3, Game 1
[20] PrepTest 53, Sec. 2, Game 4

gold, silver, and bronze medalists facing the crowd. When you have two different categories of entities, it's a good idea to abbreviate them in visually distinct ways. In the sample sketch, three-letter abbreviations were used for the schools, one-letter abbreviations for the debaters. Kudos if you noticed a similarity between this game and the Thunderstorm game that kicked off this chapter. In each, your task is to determine an order and make some assignments to each position within the order. There are two key differences, though. In the Thunderstorm game, you could assign "rain" or "hail and rain" multiple times, but once a debater competes for a team in this game, he or she can't be re-used. Of course, in the Thunderstorm game, you matched only one feature—the type of precipitation—with each town or numbered space. Here, you must match two debaters to each school or position. Still, the similarities outweigh the differences, and the rules in this game should seem quite familiar already. One final note: While the order in the Thunderstorm game was arranged horizontally, the rank of the schools here is vertical. That's a matter of taste and not at all crucial to the diagram. For many, the idea of arranging rank vertically from top to bottom will just seem intuitive. Go with it if that's the case.

3.

Three folk groups—Glenside, Hilltopper, Levon—and three rock groups—Peasant, Query, Tinhead—each perform on one of two stages, north or south. Each stage has three two-hour performances: north at 6, 8, and 10; south at 8, 10, and 12. Each group performs individually and exactly once, consistent with the following conditions:

 Peasant performs at 6 or 12.
 Glenside performs at some time before Hilltopper.
 If any rock group performs at 10, no folk group does.
 Levon and Tinhead perform on different stages.
 Query performs immediately after a folk group, though not necessarily on the same stage.[21]

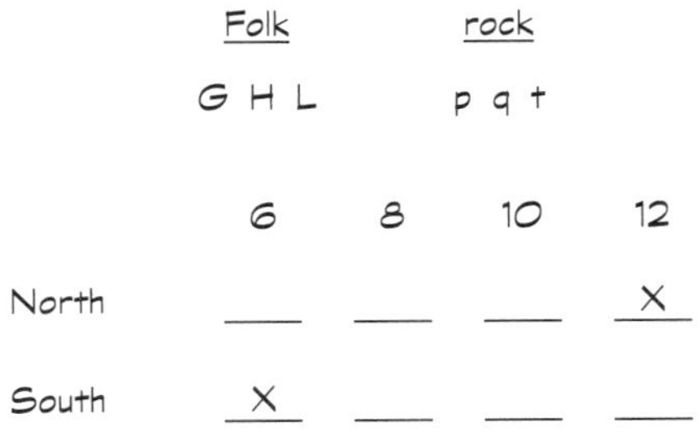

Figure 1.17

Have you ever been to a music festival? It's not hard to picture the two stages or a handbill that announces who'll be on which stage at what time. It's a little subtler than in the Debate Teams game, but you have two tasks here, too. You're going to be asked about the order in which the bands appear *and* about which stage each one's on. That makes it very helpful to

---

[21] PrepTest 48, Sec. 2, Game 4

integrate the sketch so that you can see both the time of the performance and the stage in the same glance. I'm sure you've seen schedules for events that are laid out like this:

<u>North Stage</u>
6 pm   Peasant — rock
8 pm   Tinhead — rock
10 pm   Hilltopper — folk

<u>South Stage</u>
8 pm   Glenside — folk
10 pm   Levon — folk
midnight   Query — rock

Figure 1.18

That makes it a lot harder to manage the information. Note, too, that the sample sketch abbreviates the folk bands in capital letters and the rock bands in lowercase. A clear visual distinction like that is much easier to use on test day than having a separate label next to each entity every time you have draw it into the sketch.

4.

Workers at a water treatment plant open eight valves—G, H, I, K, L, N, O, and P—to flush out a system of pipes that needs emergency repairs. To maximize safety and efficiency, each valve is opened exactly once, and no two valves are opened at the same time. The valves are opened in accordance with the following conditions:

  Both K and P are opened before H.
  O is opened before L but after H.
  L is opened after G.
  N is opened before H.
  I is opened after K.[22]

["Loose Sequencing": No framework needed.]

Figure 1.19

Here's another of those so-called "Loose Sequencing" games (like the Parcel Delivery example). These games task you with determining the order of a set of actions, but they give you rules that restrict the entities only with respect to one another. No framework is required or even very helpful. You'll just link all of the entities with lines showing their relationships. If you see a game like this and automatically draw out eight slots (and, trust me, a lot of us LSAT experts have done that over the years), no problem. You'll just wind up ignoring them. In anticipation of the chapters on rules and deductions, your final sketch here will look like this:

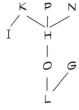

Figure 1.20

Don't worry if you don't see how all of that came together yet. In no time, you'll be making full Master Sketches and attacking the questions with ease.

5.
In a repair facility there are exactly six technicians: Stacy, Urma, Wim, Xena, Yolanda, and Zane. Each technician repairs machines of at least one of the following three types— radios, televisions, and VCRs—and no other types. The following conditions apply:

   Xena and exactly three other technicians repair radios.
   Yolanda repairs both televisions and VCRs.
   Stacy does not repair any type of machine that Yolanda repairs.
   Zane repairs more types of machines than Yolanda repairs.
   Wim does not repair any type of machine that Stacy repairs.
   Urma repairs exactly two types of machines.[23]

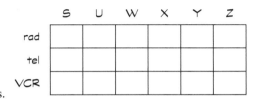

Figure 1.21

Games like this one can give students fits. "How do I know whether to assign the technicians to the gadgets or vice versa?" has been the cry of many a frustrated test taker. Fortunately, the answer is that it doesn't really matter. Probably the most instinctive mental picture is to see the six technicians at a line of work stations and then imagine that some of them are working on only one type of machine while others have two or three different kinds. If you make a chart showing the types of machines and listing who works on each, all you're really doing is flipping the orientation of the same picture.

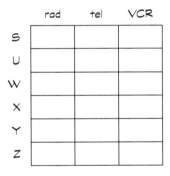

Figure 1.22

Another matter of preference is whether to use a grid (like those shown above) or simply to list the gadgets under each of the technicians. Make your decision based on which is easiest for you to construct and to copy as you handle the various questions. Here's an example of the list approach with the first four rules included:

---

[23] PrepTest 48, Sec. 2, Game 3

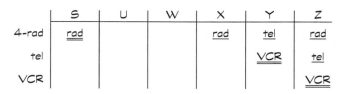

Figure 1.23

The double lines indicate that the technician's assignments have been completely determined. They "close off" the column, so to speak. When we encounter Matching games like this one later in the book, I'll illustrate both approaches to sketching. Practice them and see which variation works best for you. Remember, you don't get style points. Use what works (provided that you capture all of the information accurately).

By the way, if you're getting the impression that a lot of these games are quite similar, that's because they are. The games selected in this chapter and throughout the book are designed to be representative of what you're most likely to see on test day. While there are trends (see chapter 14 for a breakdown of what's appeared on the most recent exams), the core game actions are remarkably consistent. Test-prep books that are more interested in showing off the author's exhaustive store of LSAT logic games esoterica than in helping your prepare for the test often make rare, outdated games seem just as important as those that recent tests have featured most often. By the time you're in Part II of this book, you'll have internalized this knowledge and you'll be handling many logic games without having to stop and think. By test day, they'll be second nature. Nothing will improve your efficiency more than that.

Before wrapping up this chapter and moving on to an in-depth look at logic games rules, I want to respond to a couple of other common complaints that I've heard from hundreds of test takers over the years. I'll also introduce you to the five-step Kaplan Method for Logic Games, which will make your work in this section routine and effective.

RIGHT THINKING, WRONG ANSWERS
"I Think I Just Got The Question Backward."

Almost as common as students saying, "I didn't know how to set this game up," is the comment, "I had everything set up right, but I still got this question wrong. How did that happen?" My answer is always the same. I begin by asking the test taker to read the question back to me and explain what it's asking for. This nearly always reveals that the student misinterpreted the question stem and wound up picking the right answer *for the wrong question*.

In chapter 5, I'll break down all of the question types that the LSAT test makers use in the Logic Games section, and I'll show you how to handle each one correctly. For now, take a look at a handful of questions that illustrate the most common ways in which students waste time and choose the wrong answer even when they've correctly interpreted the game's task, setup, and rules.

Sometimes (more often than students care to admit, actually), it's just a matter of sloppy reading. Here's a question from the Parcel Delivery game:

> If K is the seventh parcel delivered, then each of the following could be true EXCEPT:
>
> (A) G is the fifth parcel delivered.
> (B) M is the fifth parcel delivered.
> (C) H is the fourth parcel delivered.
> (D) L is the fourth parcel delivered.
> (E) J is the third parcel delivered.[24]

Four of the answers—the wrong ones—*could be true.* I can't tell you the number of students who I've seen read choice (A) in a question like this one and say, "Yeah, that works." They bubble the answer into their answer grid and move on to the next question. You can see the problem already. Our minds are wired to look for what's okay, what works, what *could be true.* The test makers know this, and they design questions to punish those who aren't reading strategically. In this question, the correct answer is choice (C). It's the only one that *must be false*, which is the characteristic you're actually looking for in the correct choice.

In chapter 5, I'll take you through guided practice and a Drill on characterizing answer choices. For now, just remember that every LSAT question has one correct, credited answer and four unequivocally, demonstrably incorrect ones. There's never a "better" answer, only a right one. It is always worth a few seconds to carefully read each question stem and characterize what the correct answer must contain. Any time you spend producing a wrong answer is wasted time.

Another way in which students who do good work setting up a game wind up choosing a wrong answer is by confusing "must" and "could." Take this example, from the Folk/Rock Festival game.

> Which of the following groups must perform earlier than 10?
>
> (A) Glenside
> (B) Hilltopper
> (C) Levon
> (D) Peasant
> (E) Tinhead[25]

---

24 PrepTest 51, Sec. 4, Q 21
25 PrepTest 48, Sec. 2, Q 19

Remember this question when we revisit this game in later chapters. You'll find that each of the five bands listed in the answer choices could perform earlier than 10. A test taker who makes one sketch that *could* work and sees Hilltopper performing at 8, let's say, might choose (B) and move on. That test taker might not make any mistakes interpreting the game's action or applying its rules, but would nevertheless choose a wrong answer because the question isn't asking which band *could* perform before 10. It's asking which band *must* perform before 10. A more strategic approach to this type of question would be to look for sketches in which bands could perform at 10 or 12 and eliminate the answer choices that include those bands. The correct answer—which happens to be choice (A), by the way—names the only band that can *never* perform at 10 or 12.

As you proceed through this book, look for opportunities to practice *thinking on both sides* of statements and questions like these. The test makers are very fond of checking whether you can interpret both the affirmative and negative ways of saying the same thing. When a rule tells you that one entity *must* be placed on a different team than another, it means that they *cannot* be placed together. If a correct answer *must be false*, all four wrong answers *could be true.* You never know whether the LSAT will use affirmative or negative language in its rules, question stems, and answer choices. You will be rewarded, however, for being able to discern whether statements are equivalent in meaning despite being phrased in different ways.

THE KAPLAN METHOD
"I could have gotten them all right if I'd just had more time."

Of all the gripes students have with the LSAT, this is the most common and the one most likely to lead to poor test-taking decisions. Fortunately, it's also the most preventable. The key is to avoid confusing speed with efficiency. By trying to speed up and going too fast, students get sloppy. They misunderstand game tasks, construct poor sketches, miss deductions, and make the kinds of mistakes with the questions that you just saw. All of that might take less time than would a more patient approach, but it winds up being wasted time because it produces wrong answers (or produces a few right answers only after the student realizes how badly things are going and slows down to redo the game from the start).

Efficiency is found in the optimal mix of speed and correct answers. More than anything else, it's your efficiency that will improve as you follow the principles and strategies laid out in this book. At the top of the list is the 5 Step Kaplan Method for Logic Games. Use this method on every logic game, from the simplest to the most challenging. Use it until it becomes automatic. This method will underlie everything you do in this book from here on out, and it provides the basis for the organization of the rest of Part I.

THE KAPLAN METHOD FOR LOGIC GAMES

STEP 1 Overview
Assess the game's Situation and determine your task(s).

STEP 2 Sketch
Draw a simple, useful framework to organize the game's information and restrictions.

STEP 3 Rules
Add the Rules into the Sketch in clear notation.

STEP 4 Deductions
Combine the Rules and restrictions to determine what must be true and false.

STEP 5 Questions
Answer the questions efficiently using the information from your Master Sketch.

It often surprises students that, for any given game, Steps 1 through 4 may take as long as or longer than Step 5. Given that you have 35 minutes to tackle four games, you should plan on averaging around eight to eight and a half minutes per game. That's eight minutes to read the game, set it up, make your deductions, and answer five to seven questions. Test takers who rush through the earlier parts of a game are those who most often run out of time. That's because they're treating each question as a novel task. If you take a minute or two to answer each question, you'll soon be over the eight minutes allotted for a game.

Following the Kaplan Method, you'll find that spending three, four, or sometimes even five minutes creating a complete and accurate Master Sketch increases your efficiency. Because a complete Master Sketch depicts all of the rules and deductions in a user-friendly chart or diagram, you can often answer most, if not all, of the questions in a matter of seconds each. Think of times when you struggled to understand some complex scientific or historical details in a lecture until the professor put up that one slide that made it all so clear. You could *see* it. That's what the first four steps of the Kaplan Method help you accomplish with logic games. It will take some more explanation (and a lot of practice), but commit now to learning this proven method. It has helped literally hundreds of thousands of test takers improve their logic games performance. It will do the same for you.

The Kaplan Method in Action

To show you how the Kaplan Method works, I'll apply it to the Thunderstorm game. This time, I'll take on the whole thing, from start to finish. Keep in mind that this is just one game, and you'll be seeing all the restrictions, rules, deductions, and questions addressed in subsequent chapters. Here's the Thunderstorm game as it appeared in the June 2005 LSAT:

Questions 12–16

One afternoon a single thunderstorm passes over exactly five towns—Jackson, Lofton, Nordique, Oceana, and Plattesville—dropping some form of precipitation on each. The storm is the only source of precipitation in the towns that afternoon. On some towns, it drops both hail and rain; on the remaining towns, it drops only rain. It passes over each town exactly once and does not pass over any two towns at the same time. The following must obtain:

The third town the storm passes over is Plattesville.
The storm drops hail and rain on the second town it passes over.
The storm drops only rain on both Lofton and Oceana.
The storm passes over Jackson at some time after it passes over Lofton and at some time after it passes over Nordique.

12. Which one of the following could be the order, from first to fifth, in which the storm passes over the towns?

   (A) Lofton, Nordique, Plattesville, Oceana, Jackson
   (B) Lofton, Oceana, Plattesville, Nordique, Jackson
   (C) Nordique, Jackson, Plattesville, Oceana, Lofton
   (D) Nordique, Lofton, Plattesville, Jackson, Oceana
   (E) Nordique, Plattesville, Lofton, Oceana, Jackson

13. If the storm passes over Oceana at some time before it passes over Jackson, then each of the following could be true EXCEPT:

   (A) The first town the storm passes over is Oceana.
   (B) The fourth town the storm passes over is Lofton.
   (C) The fourth town the storm passes over receives hail and rain.
   (D) The fifth town the storm passes over is Jackson.
   (E) The fifth town the storm passes over receives only rain.

14. If the storm drops only rain on each town it passes over after passing over Lofton, then which one of the following could be false?

   (A) The first town the storm passes over is Oceana.
   (B) The fourth town the storm passes over receives only rain.
   (C) The fifth town the storm passes over is Jackson.
   (D) Jackson receives only rain.
   (E) Plattesville receives only rain.

15. If the storm passes over Jackson at some time before it passes over Oceana, then which one of the following could be false?

   (A) The storm passes over Lofton at some time before it passes over Jackson.
   (B) The storm passes over Lofton at some time before it passes over Oceana.
   (C) The storm passes over Nordique at some time before it passes over Oceana.
   (D) The fourth town the storm passes over receives only rain.
   (E) The fifth town the storm passes over receives only rain.

16. If the storm passes over Oceana at some time before it passes over Lofton, then which one of the following must be true?

   (A) The third town the storm passes over receives only rain.
   (B) The fourth town the storm passes over receives only rain.
   (C) The fourth town the storm passes over receives hail and rain.
   (D) The fifth town the storm passes over receives only rain.
   (E) The fifth town the storm passes over receives hail and rain.[26]

STEPS 1 AND 2: **Overview and Sketch**

Believe it or not, you've already got a great head start on Steps 1 and 2 of the Kaplan Method from the work you did determining game tasks earlier in this chapter. There, I encouraged you to look at the game's Situation, the real-life scenario described in the setup. As I said, it's not enough to simply say, "It's about a thunderstorm." The test could involve any of many tasks related to thunderstorms. To get better at conducting the Overview, you can actually divide your assessment of the setup into four questions (a lot of Kaplan teachers call them the SEAL questions, creating an acronym out of their keywords):

> *What is the **S**ituation?*
>
> *Who or what are the **E**ntities?*
>
> *What's the **A**ction?*
>
> *What are the **L**imitations?*

Answering these four questions will yield a thorough understanding of the scenario that allows you to create a mental picture of your task. Take a few seconds now to refresh your memory of this game's setup. Ask the SEAL questions and develop a mental picture of what the game entails.

One afternoon, a single thunderstorm passes over exactly five towns—Jackson, Lofton, Nordique, Oceana, and Plattesville—dropping some form of precipitation on each. The storm is the only source of precipitation in the towns that afternoon. On some towns, it drops both hail and rain; on the remaining towns, it drops only rain. It passes over each town exactly once and does not pass over any two towns at the same time. The following must obtain:

> The third town the storm passes over is Plattesville.
> The storm drops hail and rain over the second town it passes over.
> The storm drops only rain on both Lofton and Oceana.
> The storm passes over Jackson at some time after it passes over Lofton and at some time after it passes over Nordique.[27]

The *situation* involves a storm passing over five towns, of course. The towns are the first set of *entities* described in the setup. The *limitations*—the storm passes over each town only once, one town at a time—reveal that the *action* involves Sequencing. You're also told that the storm will drop one of two kinds of precipitation—this is your second set of entities—on each town. So Matching either hail and rain or just rain to each town or position is the second *action* you're asked to perform. Seeing all of that (in your mind, at least) leads to starting a sketch like this one:

---

[27] PrepTest 46, Sec. 4, Game 3

J L N O P
1 2 3 4 5
r/hr

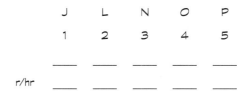

Figure 1.24

Go ahead and copy that down on the page displaying the complete game. This particular game left a lot of space at the bottom of the page (remember, you don't get any scratch paper for the LSAT), so I'd encourage you to write it in small, neat writing an inch or so below question 13.

STEP 3: Rules

Now, you're ready to add the rules into the sketch. Notice that I said *into*. Whenever possible, you'll want to leverage the full power of your visual description of the game. Just reading the rules or jotting them down off to the side isn't nearly as powerful as using them to show the restrictions that are occurring within the game's framework. The rules are your greatest allies in handling games. They restrict the possible arrangements that will work. At the outset of this game, there are 3,840 possible arrangements of the towns and the types of precipitation. By the time you're done with the rules and deductions, there will be only 10. That's powerful. Here's how it works.

Rule 1 deals with the order of the towns.

> The third town that the storm passes over is Plattesville.[28]

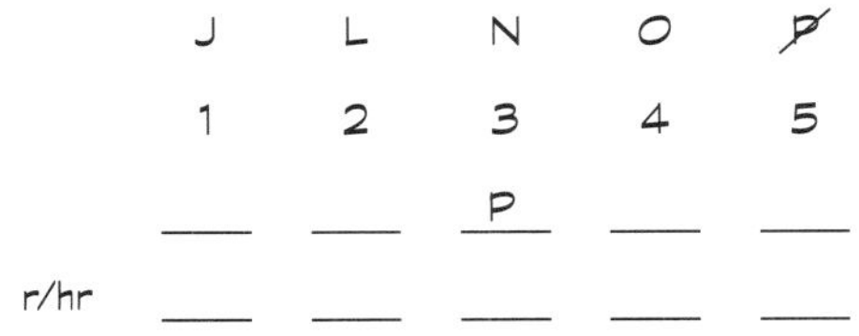

J L N O P
1 2 3 4 5
P
r/hr

Figure 1.25

That goes directly into the sketch in an obvious way. It makes P what you'll come to call an Established Entity.

Rule 2 does the same thing on the line representing precipitation.

---

[28] PrepTest 46, Sec. 4, Game 3

The storm drops hail and rain on the second town it passes over.[29]

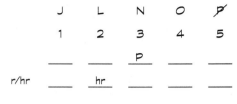

Figure 1.26

Rule 3 determines the type of precipitation that two of the towns receive. Since you don't yet know which position those towns will take in the storm's path, show the connection within your roster of entities.

The storm drops only rain on both Lofton and Oceana.[30]

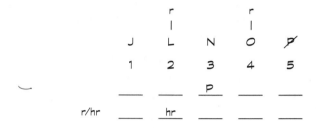

Figure 1.27

Rule 4 gives the relationship between Jackson and Lofton and between Jackson and Nordique. (Don't make more of a rule than what's actually there. This rule doesn't tell you anything about the relationship between Lofton and Nordique.)

The storm passes over Jackson at some point after it passes over Lofton and at some point after it passes over Nordique.[31]

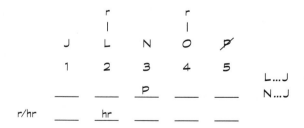

Figure 1.28

This is a rule that you have to jot down in shorthand beneath or beside the framework. There's just no way, at this point, to build it into the framework. When you get this kind of rule, don't be haphazard. Depict the rule in the same "visual vocabulary" that you've used for the Sketch. Make the letters depicting the entities about the same size as the spaces you've created for them, and make sure the orientation is the same as what you've used in the framework diagram.

If you haven't done so already, add these illustrations of the rules to the Master Sketch you constructed in Step 2. You're just about ready to make deductions. That's where the magic will happen.

STEP 4: Deductions

The sketch as you currently have it, with the rules represented as simple graphics, is about as far as the average LSAT test taker is likely to go. It's not far enough to maximize your efficiency when it comes to the questions. You could muddle through the questions (try it if you want to), but you'd soon find that the more complex questions are costing you an inordinate amount of time. After you complete the Deductions step, you'll find that you're able to answer any of the questions here in 30 seconds or less.

Deductions are valid inferences (facts that *must be true* or *must be false*) that you can make by combining the game's individual rules and restrictions. As you identify them, build them right into the Master Sketch so that you have them visually represented. In chapter 4, you'll learn that there are five types of rules that combine to create logic games deductions. For now, follow this principle: Start with the most concrete information and work your way down until you've exhausted all that you can know with certainty. This principle is extremely important, and following it will make your logic games experience much more pleasant. But more on that later. Back to the game at hand.

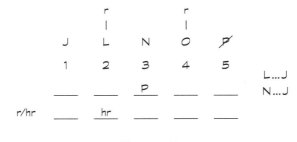

Figure 1.29

Look first at the line representing the order of towns that the storm passes over. Established Entity P sits in space 3. Which other rule restricts the order of towns? It's Rule 4, the one that says L and N must both come before J. Consider what must be true when you combine that rule with the one placing P in space 3.

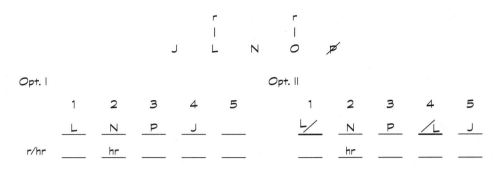

Figure 1.30

J comes after at least two towns—L and N—and P already occupies space 3. That means J has to be in either space 4 or space 5. Throughout the book, we'll refer to deductions like this one, in which every acceptable arrangement conforms to one of two patterns, as Limited Options. Whenever you find Limited Options, draw both acceptable arrangements in your Master Sketch.

By the way, do you see why town N must take space 2 in either option? You know from the second rule that the second town receives hail and rain. That was already in your Master Sketch from Rule 2. You also knew that L and O (the only remaining towns) receive only rain. That's Rule 3. In fact, go ahead and add that to your deductions.

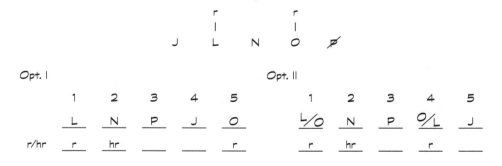

Figure 1.31

In Option I, O has to take space 5. In Option II, you don't know which of L and O takes space 1 and which takes space 4, but you know either way that spaces 1 and 4 will receive only rain.

Put the completed Master Sketch (with both options) at the bottom of the page with the full game on it. With this Sketch, you're ready to tackle the questions. This game doesn't include all of the question types you'll see on test day (it's very rare that any one game does), but it provides a great example of the power of the Kaplan Method, the rules, and the deductions.

STEP 5: **Questions**

I'll answer the questions for this game in the order in which they appear. At times, it's advantageous to tackle the questions out of order (you'll see this discussed in Part III of the book, when I talk about managing the games and sections), but going straight through is the most efficient approach in this case. If you'd like to try any of the questions on your own now that you have the Master Sketch, feel free. But pay very close attention to the explanations below, because the takeaway message at this point in the book is to see how to tackle the questions with maximum effectiveness.

12. **(A)**

> Which one of the following could be the order, from
> first to fifth, in which the storm passes over the
> towns?
>
> (A) Lofton, Nordique, Plattesville, Oceana, Jackson
> (B) Lofton, Oceana, Plattesville, Nordique, Jackson
> (C) Nordique, Jackson, Plattesville, Oceana, Lofton
> (D) Nordique, Lofton, Plattesville, Jackson, Oceana
> (E) Nordique, Plattesville, Lofton, Oceana, Jackson[32]

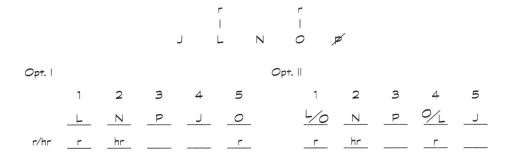

Figure 1.32

This is called an Acceptability question. The correct answer is simply the one that works, that violates no rules. Use the rules (or in this case, your Master Sketch) to eliminate answers that violate the rules. You can see that in either Option, the only acceptable town for space 1 is L or O. That gets rid of choices (C), (D), and (E). Cross out those answers completely; you have no reason to look at them again.

---

[32] PrepTest 46, Sec. 4, Q 12

Which one of the following could be the order, from first to fifth, in which the storm passes over the towns?

(A)   Lofton, Nordique, Plattesville, Oceana, Jackson
(B)   Lofton, Oceana, Plattesville, Nordique, Jackson
(C)   ~~Nordique, Jackson, Plattesville, Oceana, Lofton~~
(D)   ~~Nordique, Lofton, Plattesville, Jackson, Oceana~~
(E)   ~~Nordique, Plattesville, Lofton, Oceana, Jackson~~[33]

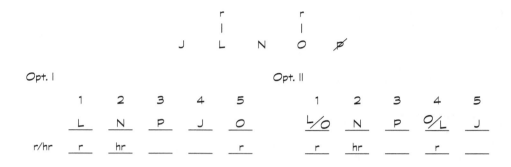

Figure 1.33

Now check space 2. N is acceptable. O is not. Choice (A) is correct. That would take you all of 10 seconds on test day. Your investment in the initial Sketch, Rules, and Deductions steps pays dividends immediately.

13. **(C)**

If the storm passes over Oceana at some time before it passes over Jackson, then each of the following could be true EXCEPT:

(A)   The first town the storm passes over is Oceana.
(B)   The fourth town the storm passes over is Lofton.
(C)   The fourth town the storm passes over receives hail and rain.
(D)   The fifth town the storm passes over is Jackson.
(E)   The fifth town the storm passes over receives only rain.[34]

Figure 1.34

All of the remaining questions are "If" questions. That is, they begin with an additional, hypothetical restriction. Such restrictions apply only to the individual question in which they appear. They don't carry over to restrict other questions that follow. In this game, the "if" questions demonstrate the power of your Limited Options deduction. Here, for example, the "if" says that O precedes J. That can only happen in Option II. So you know which part of your Master Sketch to refer to.

---

[33] PrepTest 46, Sec. 4, Q 12
[34] PrepTest 46, Sec. 4, Q 13

Now, characterize the answer choices. The four wrong answers *could be true*. They're all things that *could* happen in Option II. But the "EXCEPT" tells you that the correct answer *must be false*. The answer you're looking for will violate Option II. Go through the choices one at a time:

Choice (A) says that O is the first town. That's okay in Option II. Cross out the answer completely and move on.

Choice (B) puts L in space 4. That's acceptable in Option II. Cross it out.

Choice (C) has town 4 getting hail and rain. That's impossible in Option II. This is the correct answer. Circle it. You're done.

You may wonder whether you need to check answer choices (D) and (E). The answer is "no." But it's "no" because you had a complete Master Sketch with all of the deductions, because you used the "if" to narrow your search to Option II, *and* because you characterized the answer choices before evaluating them. Without those essential steps in the Kaplan Method, you'd still be floundering around with this question.

14. **(E)**

> If the storm drops only rain on each town it passes over after passing over Lofton, then which one of the following could be false?
>
> (A)   The first town the storm passes over is Oceana.
> (B)   The fourth town the storm passes over receives only rain.
> (C)   The fifth town the storm passes over is Jackson.
> (D)   Jackson receives only rain.
> (E)   Plattesville receives only rain.[35]

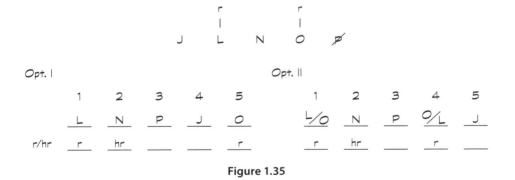

Figure 1.35

This is another "If" question. This time, the "if" restricts all towns after L to receiving only rain. Checking the options, that clearly cannot happen in Option I, where the very next town after L receives hail and rain. In Option II, it can only happen when L is the fourth town the storm passes over. And if every town after L receives only rain, you know that's what J receives. If it's helpful, you can draw this as a mini-sketch next to the question.

1	2	3	4	5
O	N	P	L	J
r	hr	___	r	r

Figure 1.36

If you're already looking at the answer choices, wait. Did you characterize what you're looking for? The correct answer here *could be false*. It's something that doesn't have to be true in the mini-sketch from Option II. That means that all four wrong answers *must be true*. When you see an answer that *must be true* in the mini-sketch, cross it out.

Choice (A) must be true. O is right there in space 1. Cross this one out.

Choice (B) must also be true. In Option II, town 4 always gets only rain. Cross it out.

Choice (C) must be true. J is last in Option II. Gone.

Choice (D) must be true in this case. The "if" restricts towns following L to receiving only rain. J follows L. Ergo, cross it out.

That means choice (E) is the winner. The only town for which you cannot determine the type of precipitation is P, in space 3. Since you can't determine its precipitation, it *could be false* that it receives only rain.

Learning when to draw a new mini-sketch to help you with an individual question takes some experience and practice. I'll always point out when and where a new sketch is beneficial.

15. **(D)**

If the storm passes over Jackson at some time before it passes over Oceana, then which one of the following could be false?

(A) The storm passes over Lofton at some time before it passes over Jackson.
(B) The storm passes over Lofton at some time before it passes over Oceana.
(C) The storm passes over Nordique at some time before it passes over Oceana.
(D) The fourth town the storm passes over receives only rain.
(E) The fifth town the storm passes over receives only rain.[36]

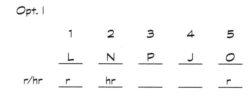

Opt. I

	1	2	3	4	5
	L	N	P	J	O
r/hr	r	hr	___	___	r

Figure 1.37

Same singer, different tune. In this question, the "if" puts J earlier than O in the storm's path. How can that happen? Only in Option I. Again, the question asks what *could be false*. That means that the wrong answers *must be true*. Be bold. Check each answer against Option I and eliminate those that have to be true there.

Choice (A) actually must be true in every instance. Rule 4 told you that L comes earlier than J. Eliminate.

Choice (B) is definitely true in Option I. Get rid of it, too.

Choice (C) must be true in Option I. N is in space 2. O is in space 5. Strike through this one.

Choice (D) could be false in Option I. The type of precipitation that falls on J in space 4 is undetermined here. Circle choice (D) and move on.

The more you work with the Kaplan Method, the more confident you will be in tackling all types of questions. Early in this book (and early in your practice), don't be afraid to slow down and learn to master all of the strategies and techniques. Your speed (and more importantly, your efficiency) will increase naturally as you get more and more comfortable thinking along with the test.

16. **(B)**

If the storm passes over Oceana at some time before it passes over Lofton, then which one of the following must be true?

(A)   The third town the storm passes over receives only rain.
(B)   The fourth town the storm passes over receives only rain.
(C)   The fourth town the storm passes over receives hail and rain.
(D)   The fifth town the storm passes over receives only rain.
(E)   The fifth town the storm passes over receives hail and rain.[37]

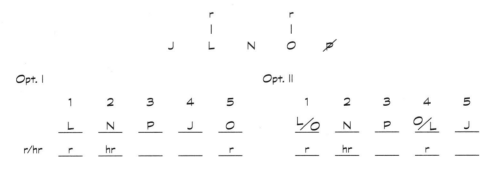

Figure 1.38

You already know the answer to this one from the opening of the chapter, but I'll review it in the context of the Kaplan Method in order to close the loop. I hope you'll see how far you've already come in understanding what makes logic games tick.

---

[37] PrepTest 46, Sec. 4, Q 16

The "if" in this question—O positioned earlier than L—puts you squarely in Option II and, in fact, limits you to the following mini-sketch (the one you saw earlier, though you didn't know how it was derived at that point).

1	2	3	4	5
O	N	P	L	J
r	hr	___	r	___

Figure 1.39

You're asked for the answer that *must be true*. Each of the wrong answers, therefore, *could be false*. Evaluate them one at a time, just for practice.

Choice (A) could be false. The mini-sketch shows that the type of precipitation in space 3 is undetermined. So it need not be true that it's only rain. Cross out choice (A).

Choice (B) must be true. Indeed, the town in space 4 always gets only rain in Option II. Circle choice (B). You've gotten all the points from this game.

That's the Kaplan Method in a nutshell. In the following chapters, I'll elaborate on Steps 3, 4, and 5 in detail. By the time you've worked through those chapters, you'll have seen the variety of rules and restrictions used by the test makers, the types of deductions you're consistently rewarded for making, and every type of question that appears in the logic games section of the LSAT. You're well on your way to logic games mastery. I'll make just one more comment about efficiency before closing the chapter.

Don't Let Perfect Be the Enemy of Good (and Vice Versa)

On one hand, the desire to be perfect can be frustrating. You'll have a tendency to get hung up on one difficult game, or even one tough question, and have the sinking feeling that you'll never get this stuff. (That's compounded by the fact that it's much easier to see later, in hindsight, how each logic games question should have been done.) The test can use that tendency against you, if you let it, by placing difficult games and questions at exactly the points where you'll grind to a halt. If you take the bait, you can wind up spending five precious minutes to get one point, only to miss out on five or six eminently "gettable" points because you ran out of time.

On the other hand, the desire to see quick gains leads some students to compromise when they don't need to. I've had hundreds of students over the years who, after a little practice, find themselves still struggling to finish a section. They come to me with questions like "Should I just try to do three games as well as I can and give up on the last one?" That question is almost always premature. Students want to see more points *now*. But as with anything that rewards skill, there are growing pains during your LSAT practice. Don't give up on what you know to be the best approach because it's difficult at first. By the time test day rolls around, you want to get as many points as possible from all of the games. Don't abandon the methods and strategies that will get you there in order to make practice feel easier or more immediately gratifying.

The only real solution to this dilemma is patience, both with yourself and with the test. Spend the time now to thoroughly understand and internalize all of the information in Part I of this book. As the right approach—the strategic one—becomes second nature, you'll see the gains in efficiency (and, therefore, LSAT points) that are the reason you bought this book in the first place. Mastering the LSAT isn't easy; it's not supposed to be. You're going to law school, after all. But it's going to be worth it.

CHAPTER 2

RULES AND SKETCHES

LEARN TO "THINK WITH RULES"

As a future law student, you probably have a good intuitive understanding of rules, and you're probably quite comfortable in a world where the rule of law helps keep things running smoothly and helps ensure a level playing field. So there's no reason to have an adverse reaction to the rules in logic games. In fact, there's every reason to embrace the rules as your greatest allies. In this chapter, you'll see how the rules can turn directly into points. You'll also see how the set of rules always allows you to answer one particular question type—Acceptability questions—quickly and accurately. Finally, I'll show you how to assess the power of rules, a skill that allows you to take control of the entire game by spotting its most restricted entities.

Rules Reduce Uncertainty

It's the rules and limitations that reduce the task from an unmanageable riot of possible arrangements down to fewer than a couple dozen. Recall that the rules (and their concomitant deductions) allowed you to take the Thunderstorm game from 3,840 possible arrangements down to just 10. Take a closer look at how the rules enable you to take control of all logic games.

To appreciate how much help rules are giving you, first take a look at just how many arrangements a typical game task permits. In every LSAT course I teach, I ask my students a math question. I'll ask you the same thing. (Now, there's no math on the LSAT and this certainly isn't something you'll need to do on test day, but indulge me for a moment.) Imagine a straightforward Sequencing game; let's say seven students are to be assigned to seven different desks, with one student per desk. How many possible acceptable arrangements does that task permit? It's not unusual for students to answer, "Umm . . . 49?" Some guess a little higher. Some have no idea at all. The correct answer is that there are 7-factorial possible arrangements. That's $7 \times 6 \times 5 \times 4 \times 3 \times 2 \times 1$, or 5,040 acceptable arrangements. No wonder logic games are challenging.

But now consider what happens when I add just one rule. Let's call the students A, B, C, D, E, F, and G and number the desks 1 through 7. If I tell you "D always sits in desk 3," the number of possible arrangements falls from 7-factorial to 6-factorial.

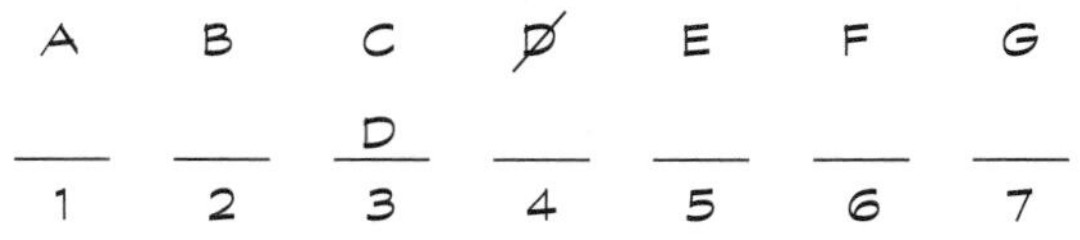

Figure 2.1

You're down to 720 acceptable arrangements. If I add another rule—"C sits in a lower-numbered desk than B"—then you're down to 330 acceptable permutations.

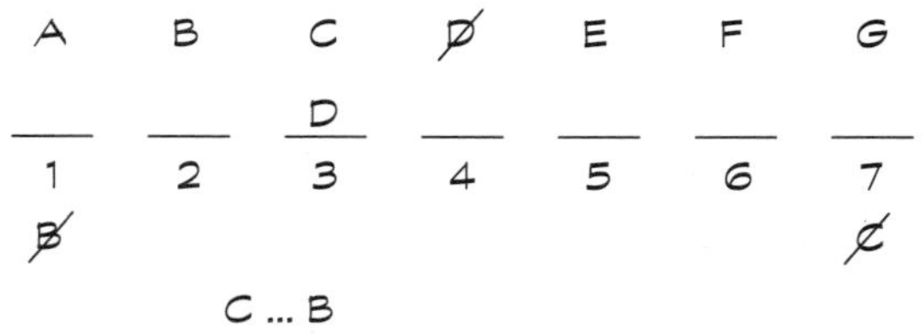

Figure 2.2

That rule restricts two entities, but it's nowhere near as concrete as the first rule, which established D's position exactly. Keeping D in seat 3, but making the second rule stronger by telling you that "C sits in a desk numbered exactly one number lower than the desk B sits in" reduces the number of acceptable arrangements to just 56.

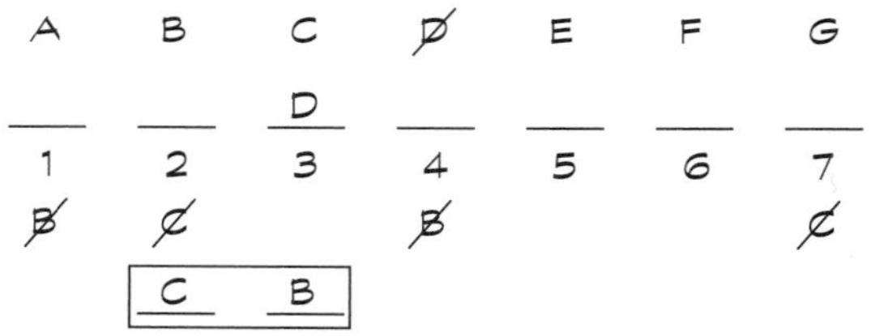

Figure 2.3

Given that most logic games on the LSAT have between three and six rules, it's no surprise that they typically wind up with fewer than a couple dozen acceptable arrangements, sometimes far fewer. I'll bring you back to this example and show you how the rules have the same helpful impact on some released games later in this chapter, but first I want to show you how you can sometimes turn the rules directly into LSAT points.

RULES TURN (DIRECTLY) INTO POINTS

It's rare that a legal case (at least one that goes to trial) turns on just one rule. On the LSAT, though, it does happen that a single rule can get you a right answer. Learning to *think with rules*, to see what they forbid and what they allow, is a first, small step in your legal education, but a giant leap on the test. Recall the game from PrepTest 52 with the students and their chaperones going on a field trip to the natural history museum.

On a field trip to the Museum of Natural History, each of six children—Juana, Kyle, Lucita, Salim, Thanh, and Veronica—is accompanied by one of three adults—Ms. Margoles, Mr. O'Connell, and Ms. Podorski. Each adult accompanies exactly two of the children, consistent with the following conditions:

If Ms. Margoles accompanies Juana, then Ms. Podorski accompanies Lucita.

If Kyle is not accompanied by Ms. Margoles, then Veronica is accompanied by Mr. O'Connell.

Either Ms. Margoles or Mr. O'Connell accompanies Thanh.

Juana is not accompanied by the same adult as Kyle; nor is Lucita accompanied by the same adult as Salim; nor is Thanh accompanied by the same adult as Veronica.[1]

Figure 2.4

Now, take a look at two of the five questions that accompanied that game. Take less than one minute to consider each and try to zero in on the rule(s) that would allow you to answer it.

11. Ms. Podorski CANNOT accompany which one of the following pairs of children?

    (A) Juana and Lucita
    (B) Juana and Salim
    (C) Kyle and Salim
    (D) Salim and Thanh
    (E) Salim and Veronica[2]

12. Mr. O'Connell CANNOT accompany which one of the following pairs of children?

    (A) Juana and Lucita
    (B) Juana and Veronica
    (C) Kyle and Thanh
    (D) Lucita and Thanh
    (E) Salim and Veronica[3]

How did you do? Did you see that the questions could be answered with reference to just one rule each?

---

[1] PrepTest 52, Sec. 2, Game 2

[2] PrepTest 52, Sec. 2, Q 11

[3] PrepTest 52, Sec. 2, Q 12

The correct answer to question 11 came from Rule 3. Since T has to go with either Ms. Margoles or Mr. O'Connell, Ms. Podorski cannot accompany T regardless of who the other student is. That makes choice (D) correct.

Question 12 needed only Rule 2, which makes clear that when K is not with Ms. Margoles, V must be with Mr. O'Connell. Thus, choice (C) is a pair that cannot go together with Mr. O'Connell. It takes K away from Ms. Margoles without placing V with Mr. O'Connell.

More often, of course, the test rewards you for synthesizing multiple rules. That's why the Deductions step in the Kaplan Method for Logic Games is so important. You'll see its full payoff in chapter 4. Still, it's worth noting that even without a fully rendered sketch or the comprehensive deductions you'll soon learn to make, you need not be daunted by the prospect of combining rules to get a correct answer.

In fact, the most common way to get points using nothing but the rules comes from Acceptability questions. You can always get these points in a matter of seconds using nothing but the rules. The next section will show you how.

ACCEPTABILITY QUESTIONS
Each Wrong Answer Breaks a Rule

Most LSAT Logic Games sections feature three or four Acceptability questions; most often, there's one per game (though, of course, there are exceptions). When they include Acceptability questions, the test makers usually make them the first question after the game's setup and rules. Here are a couple of representative question stems. You may recognize the games from which these questions were pulled; you saw them in chapter 1.

> Which one of the following could be an accurate list of the animals pictured on the guideposts, listed in order from guidepost 1 to guidepost 6?[4]
> Which one of the following could be the order of deliveries from first to last?[5]

Occasionally, the test makers will even use the phrase "acceptable arrangement."

Regardless of how they word the question stem, the correct answer to an Acceptability question is simply the one that violates no rules. Each and every one of the four wrong answers breaks one or more of the rules in the game. This simple fact allows you to answer Acceptability questions accurately in a matter of seconds.

Consider again the Museum Field Trip game. Take a look at the setup, rules, and first question—the Acceptability question—from that game.

---

[4] PrepTest 46, Sec. 4, Q 1
[5] PrepTest 51, Sec. 4, Q 16

On a field trip to the Museum of Natural History, each of six children—Juana, Kyle, Lucita, Salim, Thanh, and Veronica—is accompanied by one of three adults—Ms. Margoles, Mr. O'Connell, and Ms. Podorski. Each adult accompanies exactly two of the children, consistent with the following conditions:

If Ms. Margoles accompanies Juana, then Ms. Podorski accompanies Lucita.

If Kyle is not accompanied by Ms. Margoles, then Veronica is accompanied by Mr. O'Connell.

Either Ms. Margoles or Mr. O'Connell accompanies Thanh.

Juana is not accompanied by the same adult as Kyle; nor is Lucita accompanied by the same adult as Salim; nor is Thanh accompanied by the same adult as Veronica.[6]

8. Which one of the following could be an accurate matching of the adults to the children they accompany?

(A) Ms. Margoles: Juana, Thanh; Mr. O'Connell: Lucita, Veronica; Ms. Podorski: Kyle, Salim

(B) Ms. Margoles: Kyle, Thanh; Mr. O'Connell: Juana, Salim; Ms. Podorski: Lucita, Veronica

(C) Ms. Margoles: Lucita, Thanh; Mr. O'Connell: Juana, Salim; Ms. Podorski: Kyle, Veronica

(D) Ms. Margoles: Kyle, Veronica; Mr. O'Connell: Juana, Thanh; Ms. Podorski: Lucita, Salim

(E) Ms. Margoles: Salim, Veronica; Mr. O'Connell: Kyle, Lucita; Ms. Podorski: Juana, Thanh[7]

The mistake that most test takers make is searching through the answer choices to find one that works. That can take an inordinate amount of time because you have no idea which (if any) rule a given answer choice violates. I suggest a far more efficient approach. Simply take the rules, one at a time, and eliminate any answer choice that breaks the rule. Do that along with me here.

Look for one or more answers that break Rule 1. That is, find every answer in which J is with Ms. Margoles, but L isn't with Ms. Podorski.

That eliminates choice (A). Strike it through and look for a choice that violates Rule 2.

---

[6] PrepTest 52, Sec. 2, Game 2

[7] PrepTest 52, Sec. 2, Q 8

8. Which one of the following could be an accurate matching of the adults to the children they accompany?

   (A) ~~Ms. Margoles: Juana, Thanh; Mr. O'Connell: Lucita, Veronica; Ms. Podorski: Kyle, Salim~~
   (B) Ms. Margoles: Kyle, Thanh; Mr. O'Connell: Juana, Salim; Ms. Podorski: Lucita, Veronica
   (C) Ms. Margoles: Lucita, Thanh; Mr. O'Connell: Juana, Salim; Ms. Podorski: Kyle, Veronica
   (D) Ms. Margoles: Kyle, Veronica; Mr. O'Connell: Juana, Thanh; Ms. Podorski: Lucita, Salim
   (E) Ms. Margoles: Salim, Veronica; Mr. O'Connell: Kyle, Lucita; Ms. Podorski: Juana, Thanh[8]

To violate Rule 2, an answer must place K with either Mr. O'Connell or Ms. Podorski (in other words, "not accompanied by Ms. Margoles") *and* place V with an adult other than Mr. O'Connell (in other words, with Ms. Margoles or Ms. Podorski). Do you see any such answers?

Choice (C) has both K and V with Ms. Podorski, and choice (E) has K with Mr. O'Connell and V with Ms. Margoles. Get rid of both.

8. Which one of the following could be an accurate matching of the adults to the children they accompany?

   (A) ~~Ms. Margoles: Juana, Thanh; Mr. O'Connell: Lucita, Veronica; Ms. Podorski: Kyle, Salim~~
   (B) Ms. Margoles: Kyle, Thanh; Mr. O'Connell: Juana, Salim; Ms. Podorski: Lucita, Veronica
   (C) ~~Ms. Margoles: Lucita, Thanh; Mr. O'Connell: Juana, Salim; Ms. Podorski: Kyle, Veronica~~
   (D) Ms. Margoles: Kyle, Veronica; Mr. O'Connell: Juana, Thanh; Ms. Podorski: Lucita, Salim
   (E) ~~Ms. Margoles: Salim, Veronica; Mr. O'Connell: Kyle, Lucita; Ms. Podorski: Juana, Thanh~~[9]

Rule 3 is easy to look for. It's unacceptable to find T with Ms. Podorski. Do any of the remaining choices have that problem?

No. Neither choice (B) nor choice (D) has T with Ms. Podorski. Move on to the fourth rule. You know exactly what to do. Either choice (B) or choice (D) must include one of the forbidden pairs listed in Rule 4: J and K, L and S, or T and V. Find the violator.

It's choice (D), which has L and S both accompanied by Ms. Podorski. So choice (B) is the correct answer.

[8] PrepTest 52, Sec. 2, Q 8
[9] PrepTest 52, Sec. 2, Q 8

8. Which one of the following could be an accurate matching of the adults to the children they accompany?

(A) ~~Ms. Margoles: Juana, Thanh; Mr. O'Connell: Lucita, Veronica; Ms. Podorski: Kyle, Salim~~

(B) Ms. Margoles: Kyle, Thanh; Mr. O'Connell: Juana, Salim; Ms. Podorski: Lucita, Veronica

(C) ~~Ms. Margoles: Lucita, Thanh; Mr. O'Connell: Juana, Salim; Ms. Podorski: Kyle, Veronica~~

(D) ~~Ms. Margoles: Kyle, Veronica; Mr. O'Connell: Juana, Thanh; Ms. Podorski: Lucita, Salim~~

(E) ~~Ms. Margoles: Salim, Veronica; Mr. O'Connell: Kyle, Lucita; Ms. Podorski: Juana, Thanh~~ [10]

That's it. Once you're comfortable with this approach, you'll never need more than 15 to 30 seconds to answer an Acceptability question.

Before I have you look at another example, let me be explicit about a couple of things you saw in the previous question. First, once you found that an answer violated one of the rules, I had you cross it out completely. That's a practice you should adopt because it prevents you from wasting time figuring out whether the answer violated any other rules. Once you determine that an answer is wrong, don't look it again. Second, this question happened to have two answer choices that violated one rule. That won't always happen. In fact, it's more common to find that a single rule is violated by only one wrong answer. Check for any and all violators of the rule you're evaluating, but don't expect to find multiple wrong answers from a given rule.

Try another example. Here are the setup and rules from the Water Treatment Plant game you saw in chapter 1. This time, it's accompanied by its Acceptability question. (As usual, the Acceptability question was the first one in the question set.)

Workers at a water treatment plant open eight valves—G, H, I, K, L, N, O, and P—to flush out a system of pipes that needs emergency repairs. To maximize safety and efficiency, each valve is opened exactly once, and no two valves are opened at the same time. The valves are opened in accordance with the following conditions:

Both K and P are opened before H.
O is opened before L but after H.
L is opened after G.
N is opened before H.
I is opened after K. [11]

---

[10] PrepTest 52, Sec. 2, Q 8

[11] PrepTest 52, Sec. 2, Game 1

1. Which one of the following could be the order, from first
   to last, in which the valves are opened?

   (A)   P, I, K, G, N, H, O, L
   (B)   P, G, K, N, L, H, O, I
   (C)   G, K, I, P, H, O, N, L
   (D)   N, K, P, H, O, I, L, G
   (E)   K, I, N, G, P, H, O, L[12]

Use the same approach. The challenge in this Loose Sequencing example will be to keep straight whether you're looking for a given letter before or after another. If L is required to be after G, an answer that has L before G will be the violator.

Assess Rule 1. The violator will be a choice in which either K or P comes after H in the list.

It turns out that none of the answer choices violates this rule. Don't despair. The same approach will work. The test makers just didn't happen to use this rule to distinguish a wrong answer.

Approach Rule 2 carefully. It has O before L but after H. In other words, it requires this sequence: H-O-L. If an answer violates any aspect of the order, eliminate it.

That rule gets rid of choice (B), where L precedes both H and O.

Which one of the following could be the order, from
first to last, in which the valves are opened?

   (A)   P, I, K, G, N, H, O, L
   (B)   ~~P, G, K, N, L, H, O, I~~
   (C)   G, K, I, P, H, O, N, L
   (D)   N, K, P, H, O, I, L, G
   (E)   K, I, N, G, P, H, O, L[13]

On to Rule 3: L must come after G. Look for an answer or answers in which L comes before G.

Choice (D) should jump out, not least because G is in last place and you know from Rule 3 that L must come after it in an acceptable sequence.

1. Which one of the following could be the order, from first
   to last, in which the valves are opened?

   (A)   P, I, K, G, N, H, O, L
   (B)   ~~P, G, K, N, L, H, O, I~~
   (C)   G, K, I, P, H, O, N, L
   (D)   ~~N, K, P, H, O, I, L, G~~
   (E)   K, I, N, G, P, H, O, L[14]

---

[12] PrepTest 52, Sec. 2, Q 1

[13] PrepTest 52, Sec. 2, Q 1

[14] PrepTest 52, Sec. 2, Q 1

You've got two answers left to eliminate and two rules left to check. You can see just what's going to happen. Check Rule 4 next. Any answer choice that places N after H violates this one.

That gets rid of choice (C).

> Which one of the following could be the order, from first to last, in which the valves are opened?
>
> (A)   P, I, K, G, N, H, O, L
> (B)   ~~P, G, K, N, L, H, O, I~~
> (C)   ~~G, K, I, P, H, O, N, L~~
> (D)   ~~N, K, P, H, O, I, L, G~~
> (E)   K, I, N, G, P, H, O, L[15]

And so, either choice (A) or choice (E) is going to place I before K, breaking Rule 5.

Choice (A) incorrectly orders I and K. Eliminate it. Choice (E) is the correct answer.

> Which one of the following could be the order, from first to last, in which the valves are opened?
>
> (A)   ~~P, I, K, G, N, H, O, L~~
> (B)   ~~P, G, K, N, L, H, O, I~~
> (C)   ~~G, K, I, P, H, O, N, L~~
> (D)   ~~N, K, P, H, O, I, L, G~~
> (E)   K, I, N, G, P, H, O, L[16]

Now try your hand at a few more Acceptability questions on your own.

---

[15] PrepTest 52, Sec. 2, Q 1

[16] PrepTest 52, Sec. 2, Q 1

DRILL: ANSWERING ACCEPTABILITY QUESTIONS

Each game setup is followed by that game's Acceptability question. Take about a minute to acquaint (or reacquaint) yourself with the game. Then use the Kaplan Method to answer each Acceptability question in no more than 30 seconds by systematically assessing each rule and eliminating any answer choices that violate it. The correct answers and explanations follow the Drill.

1.

In the course of one month Garibaldi has exactly seven different meetings. Each of her meetings is with exactly one of five foreign dignitaries: Fuentes, Matsuba, Rhee, Soleimani, or Tbahi. The following constraints govern Garibaldi's meetings:

  She has exactly three meetings with Fuentes, and exactly one with each of the other dignitaries.
  She does not have any meetings in a row with Fuentes.
  Her meeting with Soleimani is the very next one after her meeting with Tbahi.
  Neither the first nor last of her meetings is with Matsuba.

Which one of the following could be the sequence of the meetings Garibaldi has with the dignitaries?

  (A) Fuentes, Rhee, Tbahi, Soleimani, Fuentes, Matsuba, Rhee
  (B) Fuentes, Tbahi, Soleimani, Matsuba, Fuentes, Fuentes, Rhee
  (C) Fuentes, Rhee, Fuentes, Matsuba, Fuentes, Tbahi, Soleimani
  (D) Fuentes, Tbahi, Matsuba, Fuentes, Soleimani, Rhee, Fuentes
  (E) Fuentes, Tbahi, Soleimani, Fuentes, Rhee, Fuentes, Matsuba[17]

2.

Three short seminars—Goals, Objections, and Persuasion—and three long seminars—Humor, Negotiating, and Telemarketing—will be scheduled for a three-day sales training conference. On each day, two of the seminars will be given consecutively. Each seminar will be given exactly once. The schedule must conform to the following conditions:

  Exactly one short seminar and exactly one long seminar will be given each day.
  Telemarketing will not be given until both Goals and Objections have been given.
  Negotiating will not be given until Persuasion has been given.

Which one of the following could be an accurate schedule for the sales training conference?

  (A) first day: Persuasion followed by Negotiating
       second day: Objections followed by Telemarketing
       third day: Goals followed by Humor
  (B) first day: Objections followed by Humor
       second day: Goals followed by Telemarketing
       third day: Persuasion followed by Negotiating
  (C) first day: Objections followed by Negotiating
       second day: Persuasion followed by Humor
       third day: Goals followed by Telemarketing
  (D) first day: Objections followed by Goals
       second day: Telemarketing followed by Persuasion
       third day: Negotiating followed by Humor
  (E) first day: Goals followed by Humor
       second day: Persuasion followed by Telemarketing
       third day: Objections followed by Negotiating[18]

3.

A summer program offers at least one of the following seven courses: geography, history, literature, mathematics, psychology, sociology, zoology. The following restrictions on the programs must apply:

If mathematics is offered, then either literature or sociology (but not both) is offered.

If literature is offered, then geography is also offered but psychology is not.

If sociology is offered, then psychology is also offered but zoology is not.

If geography is offered, then both history and zoology are also offered.

Which one of the following could be a complete and accurate list of the courses offered by the summer program?

(A)   history, psychology
(B)   geography, history, literature
(C)   history, mathematics, psychology
(D)   literature, mathematics, psychology
(E)   history, literature, mathematics, sociology[19]

---

[19] PrepTest 49, Sec. 1, Game 3, Q 13

Intentionally left blank.

Explanations

1. **(C)**

In the course of one month, Garibaldi has exactly seven different meetings. Each of her meetings is with exactly one of five foreign dignitaries: Fuentes, Matsuba, Rhee, Soleimani, or Tbahi. The following constraints govern Garibaldi's meetings:

> She has exactly three meetings with Fuentes and exactly one with each of the other dignitaries.
> She does not have any meetings in a row with Fuentes.
> Her meeting with Soleimani is the very next one after her meeting with Tbahi.
> Neither the first nor last of her meetings is with Matsuba.

Which one of the following could be the sequence of the meetings Garibaldi has with the dignitaries?

(A)	~~Fuentes, Rhee, Tbahi, Soleimani, Fuentes, Matsuba, Rhee~~	Rule 1
(B)	~~Fuentes, Tbahi, Soleimani, Matsuba, Fuentes, Fuentes, Rhee~~	Rule 2
(C)	Fuentes, Rhee, Fuentes, Matsuba, Fuentes, Tbahi, Soleimani	
(D)	~~Fuentes, Tbahi, Matsuba, Fuentes, Soleimani, Rhee, Fuentes~~	Rule 3
(E)	~~Fuentes, Tbahi, Soleimani, Fuentes, Rhee, Fuentes, Matsuba~~[20]	Rule 4

You're familiar with this Sequencing game from the first chapter. Here, each of the rules eliminated one wrong answer. Rule 1 requires three meetings with F. That eliminates choice (A), in which she has only two. Rule 2 forbids consecutive meetings with F. That gets rid of choice (B). Rule 3 places the meeting with S immediately after the one with T. Choice (D) violates this rule. Finally, Rule 4 proscribes the M meeting from being first or last. The M meeting is last in choice (E), making that answer incorrect. You're left with choice (C), the correct response.

2. **(B)**

Three short seminars—Goals, Objections, and Persuasion— and three long seminars—Humor, Negotiating, and Telemarketing—will be scheduled for a three-day sales training conference. On each day, two of the seminars will be given consecutively. Each seminar will be given exactly once. The schedule must conform to the following conditions:

> Exactly one short seminar and exactly one long seminar will be given each day.
> Telemarketing will not be given until both Goals and Objections have been given.
> Negotiating will not be given until Persuasion has been given.

---

[20] PrepTest 44, Sec. 3, Game 1, Q 1

Which one of the following could be an accurate
schedule for the sales training conference?

(A) ~~first day: Persuasion followed by Negotiating~~
~~second day: Objections followed by~~
~~Telemarketing~~   Rule 2
~~third day: Goals followed by Humor~~

(B)   first day: Objections followed by Humor
      second day: Goals followed by Telemarketing
      third day: Persuasion followed by Negotiating

(C) ~~first day: Objections followed by Negotiating~~
~~second day: Persuasion followed by Humor~~   Rule 3
~~third day: Goals followed by Telemarketing~~

(D) ~~first day: Objections followed by Goals~~
~~second day: Telemarketing followed by~~
~~Persuasion~~   Rule 1
~~third day: Negotiating followed by Humor~~

(E) ~~first day: Goals followed by Humor~~
~~second day: Persuasion followed by~~
~~Telemarketing~~   Rule 2
~~third day: Objections followed by Negotiating~~[21]

In this Sequencing-Matching Hybrid game, you're tasked with deciding the order and the pairing of six seminars over three days. The answer choices in the Acceptability question actually give you a great idea of the sketch you'll use for the complete game. You may have noticed that this game is quite similar to the one from PrepTest 53 that asked you to pair the debaters and rank their schools' teams. The biggest difference is that, in this game, the order of presentation within each pairing also matters.

Here, you were given only three rules, so you know that at least one of them eliminates two or more answer choices. Rule 1 restricts each day to a pair with one long (H, N, or T) and one short (g, o, or p) seminar. (Remember to make a visual distinction, such as upper- and lowercase letters, between different categories of entities.) Any answer that includes a day with two long or two short seminars would be a violator. Answer choice (D) breaks this rule on both the first day and the third day. Rule 2 requires T to come after both g and o. Choice (A) has T on the second day and g on the third. Choice (E) has T on the second day and o on the third. Eliminate choices (A) and (E). So one of the two remaining choices must violate the third rule. Rule 3 dictates that N come after p. The rule-breaker is choice (C), where N is on the first day and p is on the second. That leaves correct answer choice (B) as the only acceptable arrangement.

3. (A)

A summer program offers at least one of the following
seven courses: geography, history, literature, mathematics,
psychology, sociology, zoology. The following restrictions
on the programs must apply:

 If mathematics is offered, then either literature or
  sociology (but not both) is offered.

 If literature is offered, then geography is also offered
  but psychology is not.

 If sociology is offered, then psychology is also offered
  but zoology is not.

 If geography is offered, then both history and
  zoology are also offered.

Which one of the following could be a complete
and accurate list of the courses offered by the
summer program?

 (A)   history, psychology
 (B)   geography, history, literature   Rule 4
 (C)   history, mathematics, psychology   Rule 1
 (D)   literature, mathematics, psychology   Rule 2
 (E)   history, literature, mathematics, sociology[22]   Rule 1

Here's a game in which the rules are all conditional ("if/then") formal logic, but that shouldn't
affect your approach to the Acceptability question. You can still eliminate violators one by one.
The first rule is the most complicated. It states that anytime M is offered, you have to have
just one of L or S. So an answer with M and neither L nor S, or one with M and both L and S,
will be a violator. Choice (C) makes the first mistake, having M but neither L nor S. Choice (E)
violates the second provision, having M with both L and S. Eliminate both choices. To test Rule
2, look for L in the remaining choices. If an answer has L but doesn't have G *or* has L and has P,
it violates Rule 2. Choice (D) makes both mistakes. Neither of the remaining choices—(A) and
(B)—has S, so there's no way either could violate Rule 3. Move on to Rule 4, which requires
that both H and Z accompany G. Choice (B) is the rule-breaker this time. It has G and H but
lacks Z. Only choice (A) remains, and you've got another LSAT point.

---

[22] PrepTest 49, Sec. 1, Game 3, Q 13

THE POWER OF RULES AND LIMITATIONS

Now, think back to the discussion of the power of rules—of how they allow you to take control of games—that opened this chapter. In this section, you'll see how being able to think with rules and to assess the restrictions they place on games allows you to identify easier games and to get all of their points.

You can take control of logic games. In fact, the test makers provide you with exactly what you need to do so. You don't need an in-depth mathematical analysis of the games on your test to see a couple of important takeaways here: First, games with fewer possible arrangements are easier; second, games with more concrete restrictions are the ones with fewer possible arrangements. With a little practice, you can get a feel for spotting easier games. The easiest of all have only a few entities, a strict task, and concrete restrictions. In fact, concreteness and simplicity are more important factors in assessing a game's difficulty than is the game type.

Not All Rules Are Created Equal

On LSAT logic games, all rules are helpful, but some are more helpful than others. The most helpful, of course, are those that contribute the greatest restriction. It takes practice to spot, at a glance, the strongest rules, but three guidelines will go a long way toward making you better at this.

THE STRONGEST RULES . . .

RULE 1 **Create Established Entities**
Established Entities wind up affecting all others because they take up one slot, match, or position, keeping others out.

RULE 2 **Control More Than One Entity**
A rule restricting three entities is generally stronger than a rule restricting two; a rule restricting two entities is generally stronger than a rule restricting just one.

RULE 3 **Contain Concrete Language**
Look for words such as "exactly," "cannot," or "must"; relative or conditional rules provide less certainty.

To see these guidelines in action, recall our hypothetical game with the seven students—A, B, C, D, E, F, and G—and seven desks, numbered 1 through 7. Allow for the typical one-student-per-desk limitation to apply (as it likely would in any similar game on the test). As I noted earlier, this setup allows for 5,040 acceptable arrangements. There isn't space to show all of those possibilities here, but seeing how to get that number will be helpful in understanding the impact of the possible rules. Take desk 1. There are seven possibilities for who could sit there.

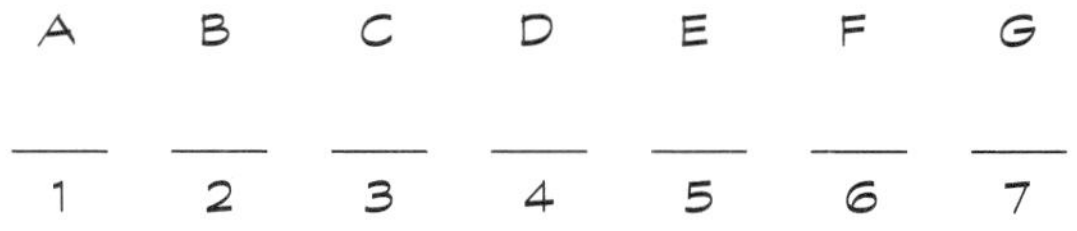

```
A    B    C    D    E    F    G

___  ___  ___  ___  ___  ___  ___
 1    2    3    4    5    6    7
```

Figure 2.7

Once you determine who is in that desk, there are six possibilities left for desk 2.

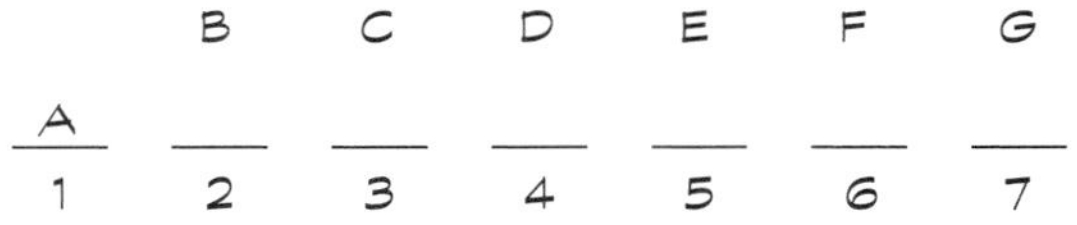

```
     B    C    D    E    F    G
 A
___  ___  ___  ___  ___  ___  ___
 1    2    3    4    5    6    7
```

Figure 2.8

Determining who is in desk 2 leaves five potential occupants for desk 3. And so on.

```
     B    C         E    F    G
 A   D
___  ___  ___  ___  ___  ___  ___
 1    2    3    4    5    6    7
```

Figure 2.9

Remember, you have all of those possible permutations when A is in desk 1, when B is in desk 1, when C is in desk 1, and on and on. But the good news is that every time you determine or restrict a possible placement, you dramatically reduce the overall number of possible assignments.

Consider the following rules as they apply to the students and desks. Using the "strong rule" guidelines, see which ones provide more restriction (and, thus, most help you to solve the game). Don't worry about combining the rules at this point; that's for the chapter on deductions. (All of the following rules are identical in meaning to rules that have appeared on actual released LSATs, just not all at the same time.)

Seven students—A, B, C, D, E, F, and G—are assigned to seven desks, numbered 1 through 7. Each student occupies exactly one desk. The following restrictions apply:

    D occupies desk 4.

    G sits in a lower-numbered desk than the desk C sits in.

    At least one desk separates the desks in which E and F sit.

    B sits in a desk numbered exactly one higher than the desk C sits in.

    G sits in either desk 1 or desk 7.

    There are exactly two desks between the desks in which A and B sit.

    A's desk is numbered lower than E's desk but higher than C's.

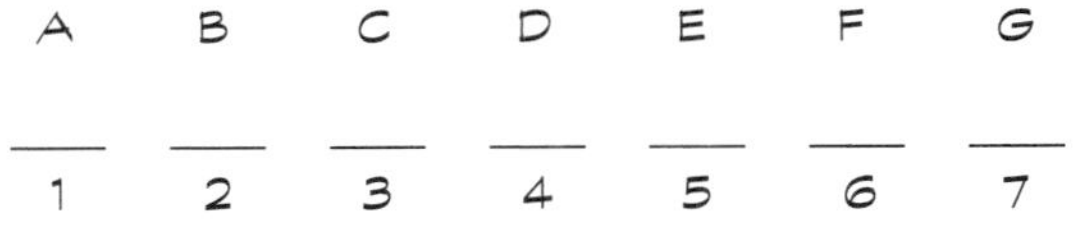

```
 A    B    C    D    E    F    G

___  ___  ___  ___  ___  ___  ___
 1    2    3    4    5    6    7
```

Figure 2.10

As I have you review each of the rules, I'll go over your considerations for how to depict the rule visually. Making rules concrete—being able to literally *see* them in action—is vital to your ability to use them when answering questions. Pay attention to the suggested sketches and depictions of the rules throughout Part I of this book. When drawing rules, follow this plan:

TO ADD RULES TO A SKETCH

RULE 1 **Consider what the rule does (and does not) tell you.**

RULE 2 **Whenever possible, draw the rule directly into the framework.**

RULE 3 **Failing that, add the rule beneath or beside your framework using the same visual vocabulary.**

By "visual vocabulary," I mean: Make the rule look just like the framework you've used in the sketch. For example, if your sequencing spaces are dashes on which you picture the entities sitting, use dashes with the entities sitting on them in your depiction of the rules as well. Have the dashes and letters you use for the entities be the same size as those in your framework. That way, you can mentally picture where the entities in the rule will and won't fit within the framework. Keeping everything visually consistent will help you enormously when it comes to using the rules to answer the questions.

Here are the rules in action:

D occupies desk 4.

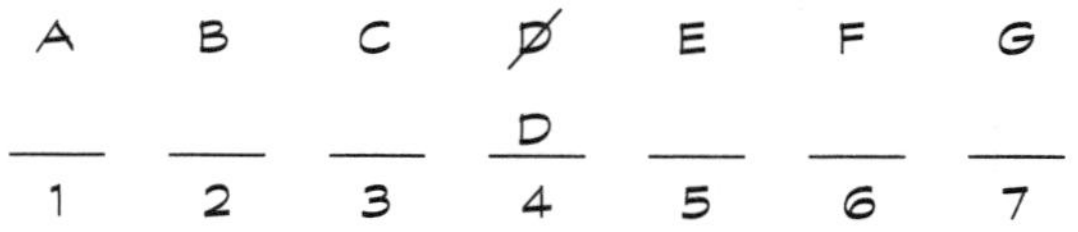

Figure 2.11

This rule is quite powerful. It makes D an Established Entity and, as such, you can draw the rule directly into the framework of your sketch. D will never take another position, and no other student will ever occupy desk 4. By itself, this rule reduces the number of possible arrangements from 5,040 to just 720. D is locked in place, while the other six entities can move wherever they like (besides desk 4, of course).

G sits in a lower-numbered desk than the desk C sits in.

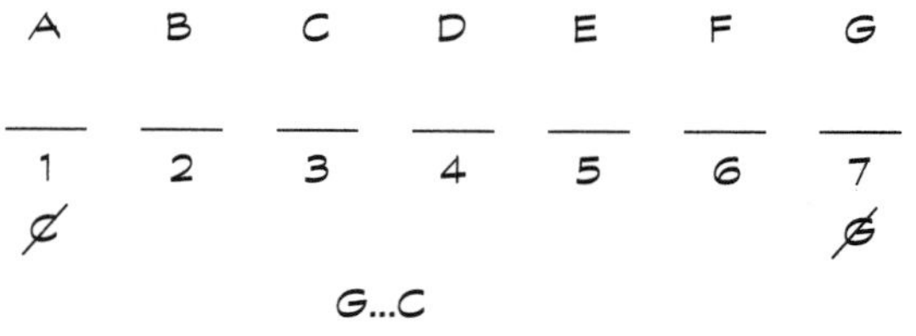

Figure 2.12

This rule affects two entities, but it gives only their relative positions. Thus, the sample scratch work uses an ellipsis to indicate that the order of the entities is known, but the number of spaces between them isn't. You can, however, enter two concrete, negative pieces of information into your sketch. C can never sit in desk 1 and G can never sit in desk 7. This rule by itself reduces the number of acceptable arrangements from 5,040 to 2,520. It leaves 21 acceptable arrangements for G and C (six when G is in desk 1, five when G is in desk 2, 4 when G is in desk 3, etc.), while the other five entities move wherever they like.

At least one desk separates the desks in which E and F sit.

A	B	C	D	E	F	G
1	2	3	4	5	6	7

E/F ___ ... F/E

Figure 2.13

Be very careful with a rule like this one. It tells you something about the relative distance between E and F, but nothing about their order. Notice that there is a blank slot *and* an ellipsis between the two occupied positions in the drawing of the rule. The entities could be farther apart, but no closer, since the rule states that "[a]t least one desk" separates them. This rule by itself is less powerful than the previous one, allowing for 3,600 acceptable arrangements. The reason that it's less restrictive is that either E or F could be the entity taking the lower-numbered seat.

B sits in a desk numbered exactly one higher than the desk C sits in.

Figure 2.14

While it's impossible to place this block exactly within the framework, the certainty of the relationship between B and C makes this a very powerful rule. Make sure your drawing indicates that no spaces separate the two entities and that they are consecutive. You can also indicate that B will never appear in the first slot and that C will never appear in the final slot. Since it limits the C-B block to just six possible placements (1 and 2, 2 and 3, 3 and 4, 4 and 5, 5 and 6, or 6 and 7), this rule allows for only 720 possible arrangements. The word "exactly" always indicates strong, helpful restrictions in logic games. Not to get too far ahead, but if you combined the C-B block with the first rule establishing D in desk 4, you'd have only 96 possible arrangements. In the chapter devoted to deductions, you'll learn to always look for the interaction of Established Entities and blocks of entities in Sequencing games.

G sits in either desk 1 or desk 7.

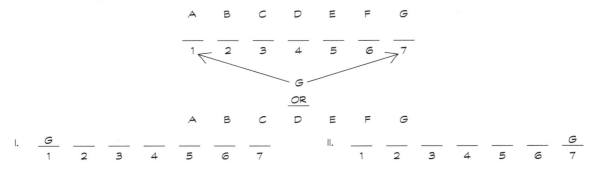

Figure 2.15

While not making G an Established Entity, this rule is still quite strong. You may choose to depict this rule with arrows indicating the two possible positions for G. But if G is duplicated in any other rules or if its placement affects other entities directly, it creates Limited Options (the scenario—like that in the Thunderstorm game—in which only two arrangements are possible), and you should make two separate frameworks, one for each possible position for G. Then you would fill in the other rules as acceptable in each option. The rule by itself limits the game to 1,440 possible arrangements (720 for each possible placement of G).

There are exactly two desks between the desks in which A and B sit.

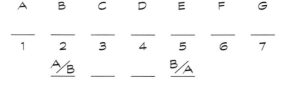

Figure 2.16

Here's another rule that defines the distance between two entities without telling you their order. Make sure to depict the slots separating A and B concretely. There are only eight ways to arrange A and B without violating the rules. You must place one entity each in either seats 1 and 4, 2 and 5, 3 and 6, or 4 and 7, remembering that either one could be placed earlier or later. With the other five entities still able to move around at will, this rule on its own leaves 960 acceptable arrangements.

A's desk is numbered lower than E's desk but higher than C's.

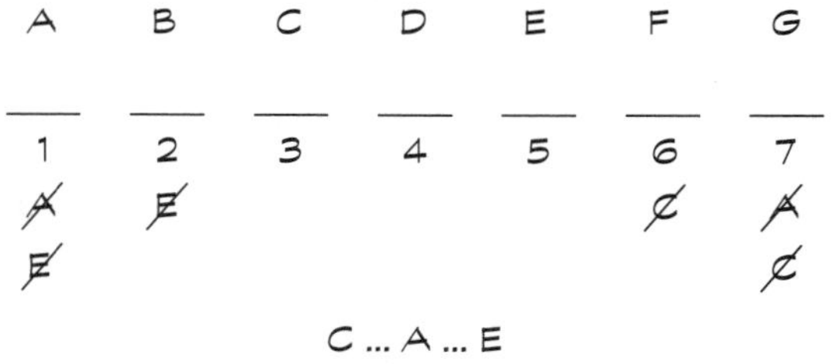

A	B	C	D	E	F	G
1	2	3	4	5	6	7
A̶	E̶				C̶	A̶
E̶						C̶

C ... A ... E

Figure 2.17

This rule's strength derives from its restriction of three entities relative to one another. Despite the fact that it doesn't determine the exact number of spaces between the entities, it leaves only 850 acceptable arrangements. Moreover, you can confidently eliminate A from seats 1 and 7, E from seats 1 and 2, and C from seats 6 and 7.

The test makers would never use all of these rules in the same game because, by the time they are combined, there are only two acceptable solutions left for the entire sequence. But as examples, they illustrate the power that rules have to make games manageable. On test day, you'll never need to calculate the number of arrangements that would be acceptable after applying any given rule. You will, however, be rewarded for spotting the easiest and most restricted games and doing them first, as well as for identifying the most powerful and concrete rules and using those as the basis for making deductions and answering questions.

Now, put those skills to work on a couple of real LSAT games.

Rules Determine What You Know and What You Don't: Practice

Here, again, is the setup for the Trail Markers game, which you saw in chapter 1. Start by thinking through the setup and reconstructing the framework of your sketch. This time, I want you to assess the rules, too. Try to add each to your sketch. Remember the strategy for depicting rules: Think clearly about what the rules tell you and what they don't. Add the rules directly into the sketch framework whenever possible. When you need to depict the rule beneath the sketch, use the same visual vocabulary you used in drawing the framework. Make your sketch and rules look consistent so that you can easily see where the entities restricted by the rule(s) will and won't be acceptable within the game.

As you try that here, consider which rules provide the most restriction. Hint: There's one entity that escapes restriction altogether. After you finish your scratch work, review the setup and rules. Then I'll have you try the questions from this game. And, as a word to the wise, don't worry about being fast just yet. Efficiency comes with practice. Right now, just get your feet wet and see how your newfound appreciation for the rules can turn into points.

Exactly six guideposts, numbered 1 through 6, mark a mountain trail. Each guidepost pictures a different one of six animals—fox, grizzly, hare, lynx, moose, or porcupine. The following conditions must apply:

The grizzly is pictured on either guidepost 3 or guidepost 4.

The moose guidepost is numbered lower than the hare guidepost.

The lynx guidepost is numbered lower than the moose guidepost but higher than the fox guidepost.[23]

I'll review the setup and sketch by taking you through the steps in the Kaplan Method.

---

[23] PrepTest 46, Sec. 4, Game 1

STEPS 1 AND 2: **Overview and Sketch**

By now, you're getting used to seeing Sequencing tasks, so whether you remembered the sketch from chapter 1 or not, I imagine you came up with something much like this:

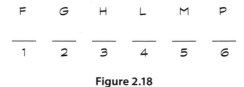

Figure 2.18

The setup states that "[e]ach guidepost pictures a different one of six animals," so you know that you'll be sequencing the entities one per slot. In case you're interested, this setup—six pictures on six signs, one per sign—allows for 720 possible arrangements (before the rules, that is).

STEP 3: **Rules**

There were just three rules here, but two of them—the first and the third—were very restrictive. Before reviewing the questions, check your sketch and see whether you interpreted each of the rules correctly. Compare your diagrams to those that follow.

The grizzly is pictured on either guidepost 3 or guidepost 4.[24]

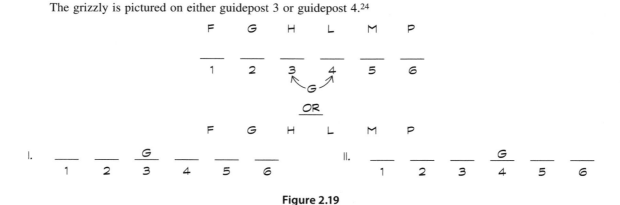

Figure 2.19

Either of these depictions of this rule about G would work. G is not quite an Established Entity, but its wiggle room has been reduced to just one of two spots. This rule reduces the number of acceptable arrangements to just 240. Well over half of your work disappeared with just one rule.

The moose guidepost is numbered lower than the hare guidepost.[25]

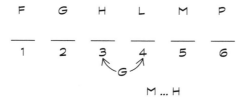

Figure 2.20

24 PrepTest 46, Sec. 4, Game 1
25 PrepTest 46, Sec. 4, Game 1

On its own, this rule is pretty loose. It establishes the order, but not the relative distance of M and H. Note, however, that you can absolutely rule out M in space 6 and H in space 1. Adding this rule to the sketch along with Rule 1 reduces the number of acceptable arrangements to 120.

The lynx guidepost is numbered lower than the moose guidepost but higher than the fox guidepost.[26]

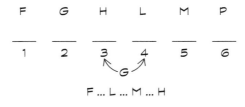

Figure 2.21

This rule, which restricts three entities, really locks things down. Make sure that you depicted it accurately in your scratch work. The best way to approach it is to realize that you already have "M . . . H" diagrammed. So when the first part of Rule 3 says L is on a lower-numbered guidepost than M, you can just supplement the picture you made for Rule 2: "L . . . M . . . H." Then the second half of Rule 3 connects F to this string, restricting it to a space before L's: "F . . . L . . . M . . . H." This scratch work allows you to see that F can never appear in spaces 4, 5, or 6, since three other entities must follow it. But did you notice that it cannot be in space 3, either? That's because G has to take either space 3 or space 4. If the three entities that follow F as a result of Rules 2 and 3 are placed in spaces 4, 5, and 6, G will have to take space 3. (There's a question coming that rewards this observation.) Likewise, L cannot be in spaces 1, 5, or 6; M cannot be in spaces 1, 2, or 6; and H cannot be in spaces 1, 2, 3, or 4. You can draw all of those negative implications into your sketch if you like, but by test day, you'll be so adept at thinking with the rules and reading your scratch work that I imagine it will seem unnecessary.

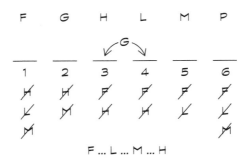

Figure 2.22   Optional sketch with negative implications included

Before moving on, there's just one more thing you should do: Figure out what you *don't* know. Remember my hint? One entity is entirely unrestricted. It's P. Put a little star or asterisk above P in the list of entities to remind yourself that it can be placed anywhere within the sequence. One question rewards you directly for making that observation.

---

[26] PrepTest 46, Sec. 4, Game 1

STEP 4: Deductions

There really aren't any deductions to add to this game. Rules 2 and 3 combined via the shared entity M, but you were able to accommodate that as you drew out the two rules. Games like this, with no (or very few) deductions, will pop up from time to time. When they do, rest assured that you have all you need to answer the questions. Here, then, is your completed Master Sketch:

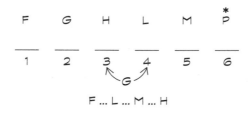

Figure 2.23

STEP 5: Questions

Compare your scratch work to what's here. On the next page, you'll see the game laid out in its entirety, questions and all, just as it was in PrepTest 46. Copy your sketch and rules onto that page, then try the questions. You'll find that you can answer some directly from your depiction of the rules. Others may require a new mini-sketch that incorporates the "if" clause from the question stem. Again, don't worry at this point about speed. Just practice implementing what you've learned so far. If you get stuck on a question, don't let it stress you. Just take your best shot and, after you finish, review the explanations for each question to see whether you applied the rules accurately.

Questions 1–6

Exactly six guideposts, numbered 1 through 6, mark a mountain trail. Each guidepost pictures a different one of six animals—fox, grizzly, hare, lynx, moose, or porcupine. The following conditions must apply:

The grizzly is pictured on either guidepost 3 or guidepost 4.

The moose guidepost is numbered lower than the hare guidepost.

The lynx guidepost is numbered lower than the moose guidepost but higher than the fox guidepost.

1. Which one of the following could be an accurate list of the animals pictured on the guideposts, listed in order from guidepost 1 through guidepost 6?

   (A)   fox, lynx, grizzly, porcupine, moose, hare
   (B)   fox, lynx, moose, hare, grizzly, porcupine
   (C)   fox, moose, grizzly, lynx, hare, porcupine
   (D)   lynx, fox, moose, grizzly, hare, porcupine
   (E)   porcupine, fox, hare, grizzly, lynx, moose

2. Which one of the following animals CANNOT be the one pictured on guidepost 3?

   (A)   fox
   (B)   grizzly
   (C)   lynx
   (D)   moose
   (E)   porcupine

3. If the moose is pictured on guidepost 3, then which one of the following is the lowest numbered guidepost that could picture the porcupine?

   (A)   guidepost 1
   (B)   guidepost 2
   (C)   guidepost 4
   (D)   guidepost 5
   (E)   guidepost 6

4. If guidepost 5 does not picture the moose, then which one of the following must be true?

   (A)   The lynx is pictured on guidepost 2.
   (B)   The moose is pictured on guidepost 3.
   (C)   The grizzly is pictured on guidepost 4.
   (D)   The porcupine is pictured on guidepost 5.
   (E)   The hare is pictured on guidepost 6.

5. Which one of the following animals could be pictured on any one of the six guideposts?

   (A)   fox
   (B)   hare
   (C)   lynx
   (D)   moose
   (E)   porcupine

6. If the moose guidepost is numbered exactly one higher than the lynx guidepost, then which one of the following could be true?

   (A)   Guidepost 5 pictures the hare.
   (B)   Guidepost 4 pictures the moose.
   (C)   Guidepost 4 pictures the porcupine.
   (D)   Guidepost 3 pictures the lynx.
   (E)   Guidepost 3 pictures the porcupine.[27]

---

[27] PrepTest 46, Sec. 4, Game 1, Qs 1–6

Explanations

Review your work to see how the rules revealed each of the correct answers unequivocally.

1. **(A)**

> Which one of the following could be an accurate list of the animals pictured on the guideposts, listed in order from guidepost 1 through guidepost 6?
>
> (A)   fox, lynx, grizzly, porcupine, moose, hare
> (B)   fox, lynx, moose, hare, grizzly, porcupine
> (C)   fox, moose, grizzly, lynx, hare, porcupine
> (D)   lynx, fox, moose, grizzly, hare, porcupine
> (E)   porcupine, fox, hare, grizzly, lynx, moose[28]

This is a run-of-the-mill Acceptability question. Did you use the rules to eliminate violators? Here's the best way to handle this question.

Rule 1 said that G must be in either space 3 or space 4. That eliminated answer (B), where G is found in space 5.

> Which one of the following could be an accurate list of the animals pictured on the guideposts, listed in order from guidepost 1 through guidepost 6?
>
> (A)   fox, lynx, grizzly, porcupine, moose, hare
> (B)   ~~fox, lynx, moose, hare, grizzly, porcupine~~
> (C)   fox, moose, grizzly, lynx, hare, porcupine
> (D)   lynx, fox, moose, grizzly, hare, porcupine
> (E)   porcupine, fox, hare, grizzly, lynx, moose[29]

Rule 2 had you check to make sure that M always preceded H. Choice (E) broke this rule.

> Which one of the following could be an accurate list of the animals pictured on the guideposts, listed in order from guidepost 1 through guidepost 6?
>
> (A)   fox, lynx, grizzly, porcupine, moose, hare
> (B)   ~~fox, lynx, moose, hare, grizzly, porcupine~~
> (C)   fox, moose, grizzly, lynx, hare, porcupine
> (D)   lynx, fox, moose, grizzly, hare, porcupine
> (E)   ~~porcupine, fox, hare, grizzly, lynx, moose~~[30]

Finally, Rule 3 gave you the "F . . . L . . . M" lineup. Choice (C), where the order went F-M-L, and choice (D), where it went L-F-M, both violated this one. Choice (A) is the correct answer.

---

[28] PrepTest 46, Sec. 4, Game 1, Q 1

[29] PrepTest 46, Sec. 4, Game 1, Q 1

[30] PrepTest 46, Sec. 4, Game 1, Q 1

Which one of the following could be an accurate list of the animals pictured on the guideposts, listed in order from guidepost 1 through guidepost 6?

(A)   fox, lynx, grizzly, porcupine, moose, hare
(B)   ~~fox, lynx, moose, hare, grizzly, porcupine~~
(C)   ~~fox, moose, grizzly, lynx, hare, porcupine~~
(D)   ~~lynx, fox, moose, grizzly, hare, porcupine~~
(E)   ~~porcupine, fox, hare, grizzly, lynx, moose~~[31]

2. (A)

Which one of the following animals CANNOT be the one pictured on guidepost 3?

(A)   fox
(B)   grizzly
(C)   lynx
(D)   moose
(E)   porcupine[32]

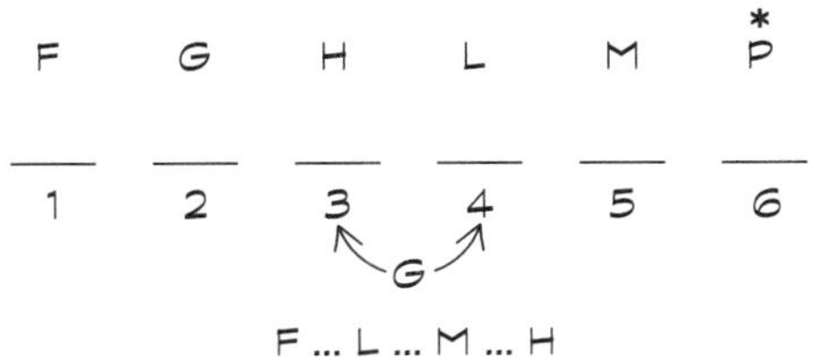

Figure 2.24

This question rewarded you for seeing something that the rules made impossible. I went over why F can never appear in spaces 3, 4, 5, or 6 in the review of the rules. According to Rules 2 and 3, L, M, and H must all follow F. Even if you squeezed those three into spaces 4, 5, and 6, Rule 1 told you that G needed to take one of spaces 3 and 4. So F is never going to get into space 3, making choice (A) the correct answer. As for the wrong answers, there are five acceptable arrangements with G in space 3. Any one of them allows you to eliminate choice (B).

Figure 2.25

For each of the remaining answers, G would take space 4. Here are the acceptable arrangements illustrating how choices (C), (D), and (E) are all possible.

---

[31] PrepTest 46, Sec. 4, Game 1, Q 1
[32] PrepTest 46, Sec. 4, Game 1, Q 2

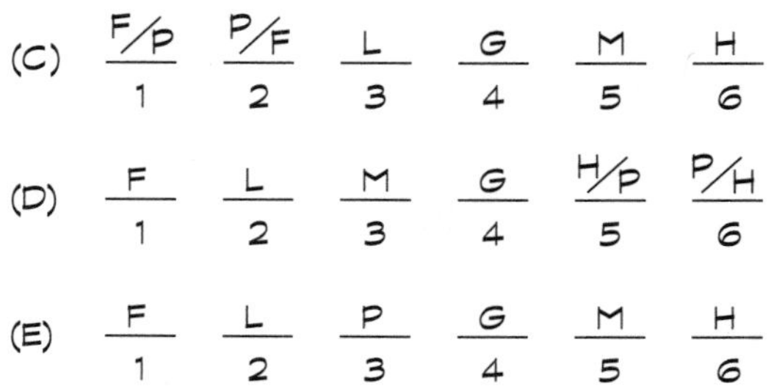

(C)

F/P	P/F	L	G	M	H
1	2	3	4	5	6

(D)

F	L	M	G	H/P	P/H
1	2	3	4	5	6

(E)

F	L	P	G	M	H
1	2	3	4	5	6

Figure 2.26

3. (D)

If the moose is pictured on guidepost 3, then which one of the following is the lowest numbered guidepost that could picture the porcupine?

(A) guidepost 1
(B) guidepost 2
(C) guidepost 4
(D) guidepost 5
(E) guidepost 6[33]

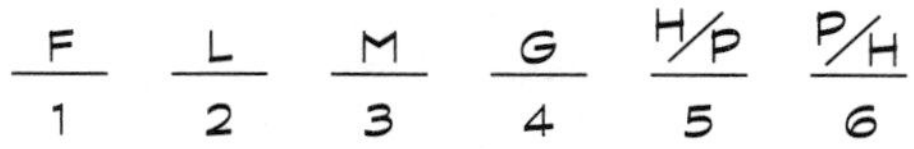

F	L	M	G	H/P	P/H
1	2	3	4	5	6

Figure 2.27

This question—with its "if" clause—is one that benefitted from a mini-sketch based on the new restriction in the question stem. It's pictured above. Here's how you should have created it. Start with the "if" clause. Place M in space 3.

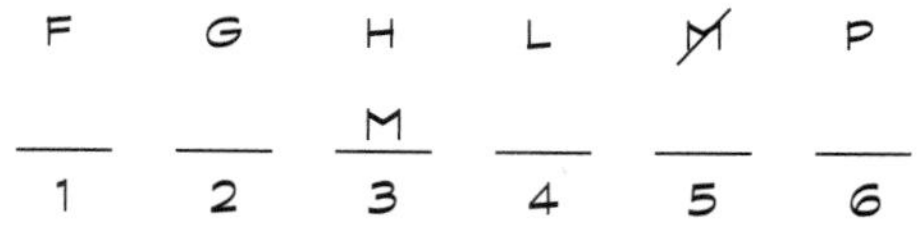

F   G   H   L   M̸   P

		M			
1	2	3	4	5	6

Figure 2.27A

With M taking space 3, Rule 1 requires G to take space 4.

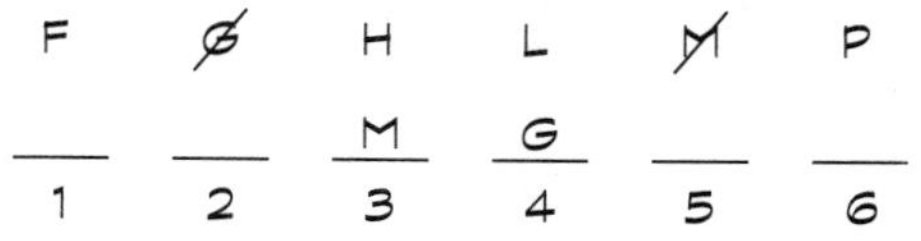

F   G̸   H   L   M̸   P

		M	G		
1	2	3	4	5	6

Figure 2.28

Likewise, Rules 2 and 3 require F and L to take spaces numbered lower than M's. In this case, those are spaces 1 and 2, respectively.

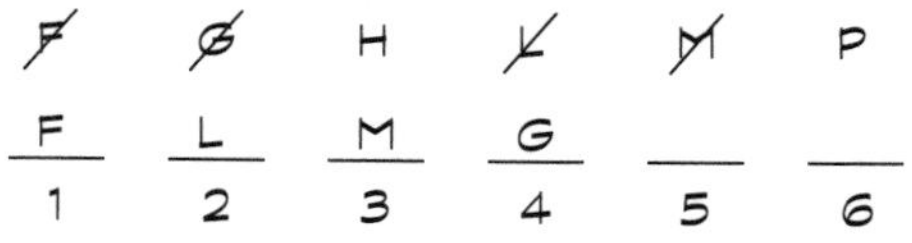

F̸   G̸   H   L̸   M̸   P

F	L	M	G		
1	2	3	4	5	6

Figure 2.29

---

[33] PrepTest 46, Sec. 4, Game 1, Q 3

The only two remaining entities are H, which just has to take a spot following M's, and P, which can go anywhere.

$$\underset{1}{\underline{\text{F}}} \quad \underset{2}{\underline{\text{L}}} \quad \underset{3}{\underline{\text{M}}} \quad \underset{4}{\underline{\text{G}}} \quad \underset{5}{\underline{\text{H/P}}} \quad \underset{6}{\underline{\text{P/H}}}$$

Figure 2.30

In this case, P can take space 5 or space 6, so the correct answer to the question—which is "the lowest numbered" spot P can take—is choice (D).

Students often hesitate to create new mini-sketches for "If" questions, fearing that it will take them too long to draw the new scratch work. But with your framework and rules in order as you have them, the new sketch takes a matter of seconds. Moreover, just look at how quickly and clearly the correct answer shows itself. Do the same thing with the "if" in the next question.

4. **(A)**

If guidepost 5 does not picture the moose, then which one of the following must be true?

(A) The lynx is pictured on guidepost 2.
(B) The moose is pictured on guidepost 3.
(C) The grizzly is pictured on guidepost 4.
(D) The porcupine is pictured on guidepost 5.
(E) The hare is pictured on guidepost 6.[34]

$$\underset{1}{\underline{\text{F}}} \quad \underset{2}{\underline{\text{L}}} \quad \underset{3}{\underline{\text{M/G}}} \quad \underset{4}{\underline{\text{G/M}}} \quad \underset{5}{\underline{\text{H/P}}} \quad \underset{6}{\underline{\text{P/H}}}$$

Figure 2.31

Another "if" clause means another mini-sketch. Here's how you get to this one.

Start with the question stem. If M isn't in space 5, where could it be? Check your original Master Sketch. M can't be in space 6, since H must follow it. It also can't be in spaces 1 or 2, since both F and L must precede it. That leaves only spaces 3 and 4. Whichever one M doesn't take will be taken by G.

$$\underset{1}{\underline{}} \quad \underset{2}{\underline{}} \quad \underset{3}{\underline{\text{M/G}}} \quad \underset{4}{\underline{\text{G/M}}} \quad \underset{5}{\underline{}} \quad \underset{6}{\underline{}}$$

Figure 2.32

The scratch work for Rules 2 and 3 makes it clear that F and L must take spaces 1 and 2, respectively.

---

[34] PrepTest 46, Sec. 4, Game 1, Q 4

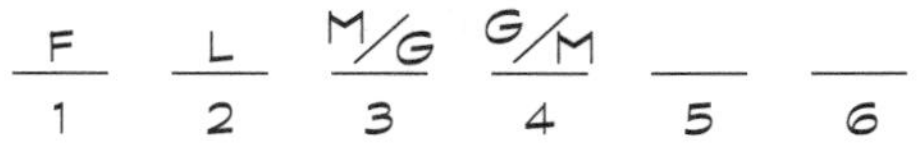

$$\frac{F}{1} \quad \frac{L}{2} \quad \frac{M/G}{3} \quad \frac{G/M}{4} \quad \frac{}{5} \quad \frac{}{6}$$

Figure 2.33

The remaining entities are H and P. Spaces 5 and 6 are open to them, and nothing restricts either H or P from taking either of those positions.

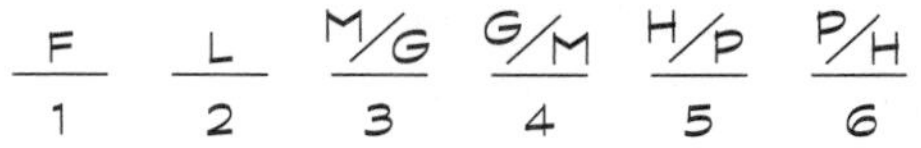

$$\frac{F}{1} \quad \frac{L}{2} \quad \frac{M/G}{3} \quad \frac{G/M}{4} \quad \frac{H/P}{5} \quad \frac{P/H}{6}$$

Figure 2.34

Now that you've got your ticket to a quick, definite answer, get on the train. The question stem asks for what *must be true*. Notice that your mini-sketch established the positions of two of the entities absolutely: F in space 1 and L in space 2. One of those has to be the correct answer, since those are the two things that must be true in this case. Choice (A) turns out to have L in space 2 and is the correct answer. Notice that all of the wrong answers deal with entities that still have wiggle room—M, G, P, and H. Because of that wiggle room, none of these could be the correct answer to a *must be true* question.

5. **(E)**

Which one of the following animals could be pictured on any one of the six guideposts?

(A) fox
(B) hare
(C) lynx
(D) moose
(E) porcupine[35]

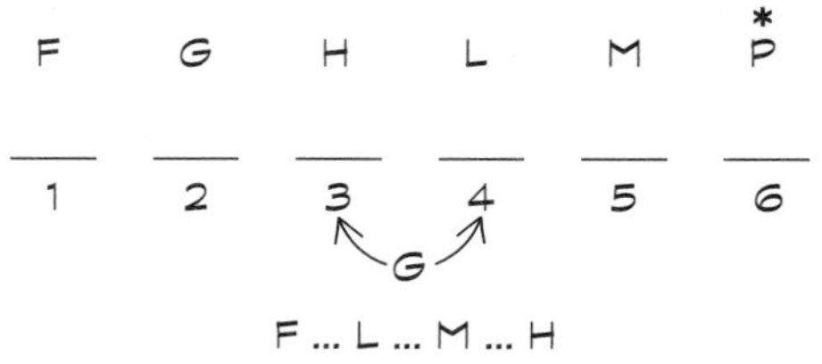

F   G   H   L   M   *P

$$\frac{}{1} \quad \frac{}{2} \quad \frac{}{3} \quad \frac{}{4} \quad \frac{}{5} \quad \frac{}{6}$$

G

F ... L ... M ... H

Figure 2.35

As a savvy test taker—one trained by Kaplan, that is—you can get this point in five seconds. Look at your Master Sketch. Who had the asterisk? P, the entity unrestricted by any rule. Of course, that's the one that can take any position. Choose (E) and you're done, just that fast.

6. **(A)**

If the moose guidepost is numbered exactly one higher than the lynx guidepost, then which one of the following could be true?

(A) Guidepost 5 pictures the hare.
(B) Guidepost 4 pictures the moose.
(C) Guidepost 4 pictures the porcupine.
(D) Guidepost 3 pictures the lynx.
(E) Guidepost 3 pictures the porcupine.[36]

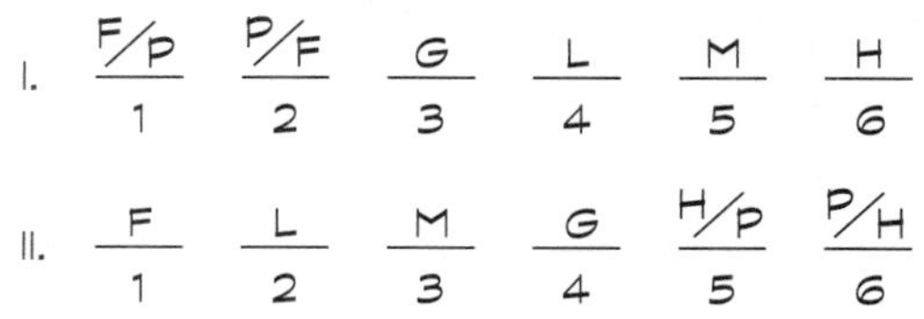

I.
$$\frac{F/P}{1} \quad \frac{P/F}{2} \quad \frac{G}{3} \quad \frac{L}{4} \quad \frac{M}{5} \quad \frac{H}{6}$$

II.
$$\frac{F}{1} \quad \frac{L}{2} \quad \frac{M}{3} \quad \frac{G}{4} \quad \frac{H/P}{5} \quad \frac{P/H}{6}$$

Figure 2.36

---

[35] PrepTest 46, Sec. 4, Game 1, Q 5

[36] PrepTest 46, Sec. 4, Game 1, Q 6

This was the toughest question in the set, the toughest even to draw a mini-sketch for. The "if" clause told you to make L and M a solid block; they must be consecutive entities. That part is easily depicted as a variation on your picture of Rules 2 and 3.

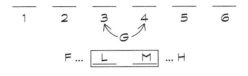

Figure 2.37

What's tougher is seeing how that relates to Rule 1. To take control of the question, simply make two frameworks. Put G in space 3 in one of them, space 4 in the other.

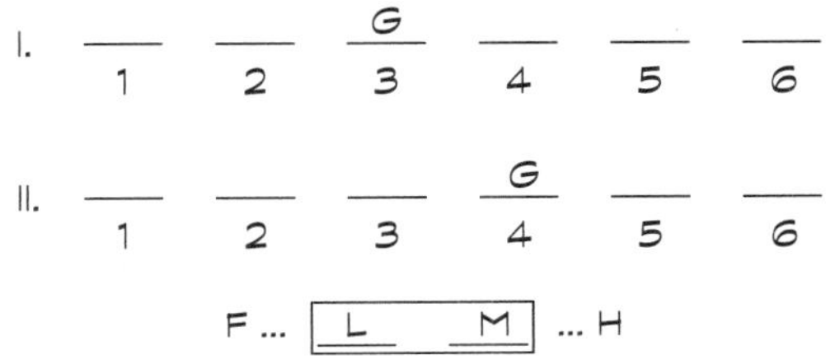

Figure 2.38

Now consider how the revised Rule 2/3 block of entities could fit in. The solid L-M block must follow G when G is in space 3. It must precede G when G is in space 4. There's not enough room to accommodate the block any other way.

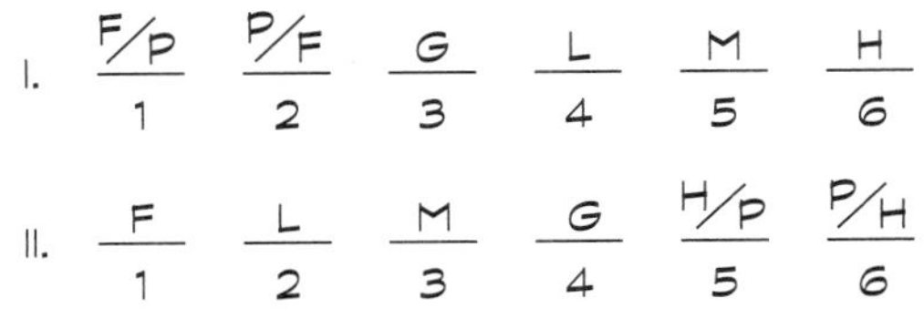

Figure 2.39

Now that you have a perfect pair of mini-sketches, make sure you've understood the question. The correct answer will be the only one that's acceptable in one of these mini-sketches. The wrong answers will all be impossible in both. Choice (A) does the trick. H could appear in space 5 in the second option, the one with G in space 4. Check them if you want to, but all of the remaining choices have to violate both mini-sketches.

Rules Create Key Entities

Another way in which the rules allow you to take control of a game is by creating key entities, players that restrict several of the other entities or limit much of the action. In the preceding game, G was limited to just one of two spaces, and P was important because it was completely unrestricted. Still, the real heavy lifting in that game was done by the string of four entities that kept pushing each other to the front or the back.

In this next game, the opposite is true. It's a game you haven't seen before, so take some time and review the setup and rules. Try your hand at sketching them out and then use the review to see how you did. Above all, see if your assessment of the rules helps you find two key entities, those that will be involved in every question.

> Henri has exactly five electrical appliances in his dormitory room: a hairdryer, a microwave oven, a razor, a television, and a vacuum. As a consequence of fire department regulations, Henri can use these appliances only in accordance with the following conditions:
> > Henri cannot use both the hairdryer and the razor simultaneously.
> > Henri cannot use both the hairdryer and the television simultaneously.
> > When Henri uses the vacuum, he cannot at the same time use any of the following: the hairdryer, the razor, and the television.[37]

How'd you do? I'll take you through the Kaplan Method as it applies to this game. As you see the setup, sketch, and rules come together, take note of the two entities that will drive the action.

STEPS 1 AND 2: Overview and Sketch

Your job here is to determine which appliances Henri can use simultaneously and which ones he needs to keep turned off to avoid blowing a fuse. That makes this a Selection game. Each entity is either "off" or "on" at any given time. You needn't draw a framework or chart. Just list the entities. You can circle those that are "on" and cross out those that are "off" as the questions require it.

STEP 3: Rules

Each of the three rules creates one or more "impossible pairs."

> Henri cannot use both the hairdryer and the razor simultaneously.[38]

Figure 2.40

---

[37] PrepTest 48, Sec. 2, Game 1

[38] PrepTest 48, Sec. 2, Game 1

You might choose to depict this rule in any of the ways pictured. I'll stick with the first one as I proceed, though some test takers find that striking through impossible pairs makes it harder to read their scratch work. Choose the way that works best for you, but be consistent within any particular game to avoid confusion about what the rules mean.

Henri cannot use both the hairdryer and the television simultaneously.[39]

Figure 2.41

There's the hairdryer again. That thing must really use a lot of juice. At any rate, it's starting to look pretty important to account for the hairdryer in any given scenario, isn't it?

When Henri uses the vacuum, he cannot at the same time use any of the following: the hairdryer, the razor, and the television.[40]

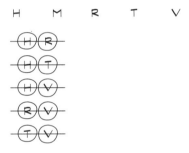

Figure 2.42

This rule introduces three more impossible pairs. All of them involve the vacuum. It, too, has become a key entity in this game. Notice that this rule also creates a third impossible pair for the hairdryer. In fact, if Henri wants to use another appliance along with either the hairdryer or the vacuum, his only option is the microwave. The television and razor, on the other hand, have only two exclusions each. Those two exclusions are, of course, the hairdryer and the vacuum.

Did you also account for what you don't know? Like P in the previous game, the microwave here is a "floater," an entity completely unrestricted by any of the rules. It's the one entity that can accompany any of the others. Put a star or asterisk above it. Here's your final sketch:

---

[39] PrepTest 48, Sec. 2, Game 1
[40] PrepTest 48, Sec. 2, Game 1

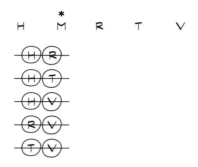

Figure 2.43

STEP 4: **Deductions**

This is another game with very little to do in the Deductions step. The one thing to consider is what you've uncovered about the maximum number of appliances Henri could use at the same time. To do so, Henri will need to avoid using the hairdryer or the vacuum, each of which knock out three other entities. So the maximum that he can use together is three: the razor, the television, and the unrestricted entity, the microwave.

STEP 5: **Questions**

With your rules sketched out and considered, you should be able to nail down all of the questions associated with this game. Copy your diagrams of the rules over onto the page with the full game. Then take your time with the questions. Be systematic as you apply the rules, and jot out a list of your entities when there is a new "if" clause at the beginning of a question stem.

Questions 1–3

Henri has exactly five electrical appliances in his dormitory room: a hairdryer, a microwave oven, a razor, a television, and a vacuum. As a consequence of fire department regulations, Henri can use these appliances only in accordance with the following conditions:

Henri cannot use both the hairdryer and the razor simultaneously.

Henri cannot use both the hairdryer and the television simultaneously.

When Henri uses the vacuum, he cannot at the same time use any of the following: the hairdryer, the razor, and the television.

1. Which one of the following is a pair of appliances Henri could be using simultaneously?

    (A)   the hairdryer and the razor
    (B)   the hairdryer and the television
    (C)   the razor and the television
    (D)   the razor and the vacuum
    (E)   the television and the vacuum

2. Assume that Henri is using exactly two appliances and is not using the microwave oven. Which one of the following is a list of all the appliances, other than the microwave oven, that Henri CANNOT be using?

    (A)   hairdryer
    (B)   razor
    (C)   vacuum
    (D)   hairdryer, razor
    (E)   hairdryer, vacuum

3. Which one of the following CANNOT be true?

    (A)   Henri uses the hairdryer while using the microwave oven.
    (B)   Henri uses the microwave oven while using the razor.
    (C)   Henri uses the microwave oven while using two other appliances.
    (D)   Henri uses the television while using two other appliances.
    (E)   Henri uses the vacuum while using two other appliances.[41]

---

[41] PrepTest 48, Sec. 2, Game 1, Qs 1-6

Explanations

Only question 2 had new "if" clauses (although it used the word "assume" instead of "if"). All of the other questions could be answered with nothing more than your expertly sketched set of the rules. Take a look.

1. **(C)**

Which one of the following is a pair of appliances Henri could be using simultaneously?

(A) the hairdryer and the razor
(B) the hairdryer and the television
(C) the razor and the television
(D) the razor and the vacuum
(E) the television and the vacuum[42]

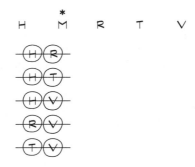

Figure 2.44

Your scratch work made short work of this one. The wrong answers all list forbidden pairs. In fact, they list the first two and the last two from your sketch. The correct answer, choice (C), is the only one that lists a pair not forbidden by the rules.

2. **(E)**

Assume that Henri is using exactly two appliances and is not using the microwave oven. Which one of the following is a list of all the appliances, other than the microwave oven, that Henri CANNOT be using?

(A) hairdryer
(B) razor
(C) vacuum
(D) hairdryer, razor
(E) hairdryer, vacuum[43]

Figure 2.45

For this question, it was efficient to create a new mini-sketch based on the "if" clause in the question stem. Don't let the word change—"assume" instead of "if"—throw you. The hypothetical situation introduced at the beginning of the question is just the same here as it is in any other new "if" question.

The condition you need to account for states that Henri is using two appliances, neither of which is the microwave. Start your mini-sketch like this:

Figure 2.46

---

[42] PrepTest 48, Sec. 2, Q 1
[43] PrepTest 48, Sec. 2, Q 2

Now, consider the rules. With the microwave (remember, it's the only appliance with no restrictions) out of the picture, the only pair that is not forbidden is the razor and television. The rules had already identified the hairdryer and vacuum as the most difficult appliances to find matches for. So cross the hairdryer and the vacuum off of the list in your mini-sketch, too.

Figure 2.47

The question stem is long, but your mini-sketch helps you interpret it. The correct answer is simply the one that includes everything you crossed off your list besides the microwave. That's choice (E).

3. **(E)**

Which one of the following CANNOT be true?

(A)   Henri uses the hairdryer while using the microwave oven.

(B)   Henri uses the microwave oven while using the razor.

(C)   Henri uses the microwave oven while using two other appliances.

(D)   Henri uses the television while using two other appliances.

(E)   Henri uses the vacuum while using two other appliances.[44]

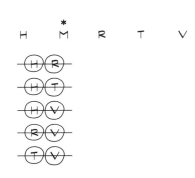

Figure 2.48

The correct answer here is the one that is impossible given the rules. That means that all four wrong answers are acceptable. If you approached this question by eliminating wrong answers, you should have noticed that both choices (A) and (B) mention exactly two appliances including the microwave, the unrestricted entity. It can be used with anything, so both (A) and (B) give possible scenarios and are therefore wrong answers. Choices (C) and (D) both assign Henri three appliances. You knew, from considering the rules, that Henri could use the razor, television, and microwave simultaneously. So both (C) and (D) give acceptable selections. By process of elimination, you know that choice (E) is the correct answer. It has Henri using the vacuum with two other appliances. Impossible. The vacuum can only be used with the microwave.

It's exciting to see how much you can accomplish with a strategic understanding of the rules. Not all games can be handled as easily as the previous two were with just the rules. That's why there's a chapter on Deductions in this book. Still, it should boost your confidence to realize that even when there aren't a lot of additional inferences to pull from the rules, the game will always give you enough information to answer every question. That's true no matter how complicated the action is.

---

[44] PrepTest 48, Sec. 2, Q 3

Rules Remove Complications

Of course, the test makers won't announce the difficulty of each game in the section on test day. Sometimes students see what appears to be a complicated task and assume that they've encountered a difficult game. But if the rules are sufficiently concrete, your task will ultimately be quite manageable. As a case in point, revisit the Debate Teams game you saw in the Game Tasks Drill in chapter 1.

> The three highest-placing teams in a high school debate tournament are the teams from Fairview, Gillom, and Hilltop high schools. Each team has exactly two members. The individuals on these three teams are Mei, Navarro, O'Rourke, Pavlovich, Sethna, and Tsudama. The following is the case:
>   Sethna is on the team from Gillom High.
>   Tsudama is on the second-place team.
>   Mei and Pavlovich are not on the same team.
>   Pavlovich's team places higher than Navarro's team.
>   The team from Gillom High places higher than the team from Hilltop High.[45]

For a test taker who is trained only to see the "game type," this is a dreaded Hybrid game: You have to Sequence the order of the schools, Distribute the students into teams of two, and Match the student pairs to the schools. Described that way, the game sounds daunting. But now consider this game from the perspective of its restrictions. It's going to seem much easier in a moment. First, there are just six possible ways to Sequence the schools:

1	Frv	Frv	Gil	Gil	Hil	Hil
2	Gil	Hil	Frv	Hil	Frv	Gil
3	Hil	Gil	Hil	Frv	Gil	Frv

Figure 2.49

One of the three high schools is in first place, and then there are just two ways to arrange the remaining schools. (Remember, the math is just here to help you see the restrictions more clearly; by test day, you'll be able to assess game difficulties by feel and experience.)

There are actually only 90 ways to combine and match the students. (Feel free to roll your eyes at the idea of *only* 90, but remember that the "simple" seven students, seven desks game had 5,040 permutations.) The simplicity comes from the fact that once you have one combination, say M and N, there are only four debaters remaining, so they can combine in only three ways: OP, ST; OS, PT; or OT, PS. So once you assign any given pair to a rank—first, second, or third place—there are only six ways to complete the picture. Here are the possibilities when you rank the MN pair first:

---

[45] PrepTest 53, Sec. 2, Game 4

1	2	3	4	5	6
M N	M N	M N	M N	M N	M N
O P	O S	O T	P S	P T	S T
S T	P T	P S	O T	O S	O P

Figure 2.50

Since there are 15 possible first-place pairings, there are 90 possible ways to pair and match the debaters. With six ways to sequence the teams and 90 ways to combine and match the students, this game has 540 acceptable arrangements, already much simpler than our hypothetical seven students, seven desks game.

But you haven't considered the impact of the rules yet, and it's a big impact. Take a moment and think about how each of the rules limits the acceptable "solutions" to this game. Start sketching the rules. It will help.

> The three highest-placing teams in a high school debate tournament are the teams from Fairview, Gillom, and Hilltop high schools. Each team has exactly two members. The individuals on these three teams are Mei, Navarro, O'Rourke, Pavlovich, Sethna, and Tsudama. The following is the case:
> Sethna is on the team from Gillom High.
> Tsudama is on the second-place team.
> Mei and Pavlovich are not on the same team.
> Pavlovich's team places higher than Navarro's team.
> The team from Gillom High places higher than the team from Hilltop High.[46]

The most restrictive of the rules is actually the fifth. It cuts the number of solutions in half. By eliminating any sequence in which Hilltop finishes higher than Gillom, there are only three ways to rank the teams:

I.		II.		III.	
Gil	_ _	Gil	_ _	Frv	_ _
Hil	_ _	Frv	_ _	Gil	_ _
Frv	_ _	Hil	_ _	Hil	_ _

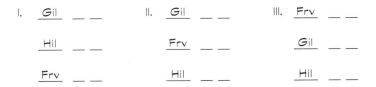

Figure 2.51

46 PrepTest 53, Sec. 2, Game 4

You can use this as the framework for your Master Sketch. You're limited to just three options.

The remaining rules all eliminate a number of the possible pairings and matches. Since Rule 5 means that Gillom High will place first or second, Rule 1 gets rid of all cases in which S could be matched to the third-place team. You've just eliminated 30 more possible solutions.

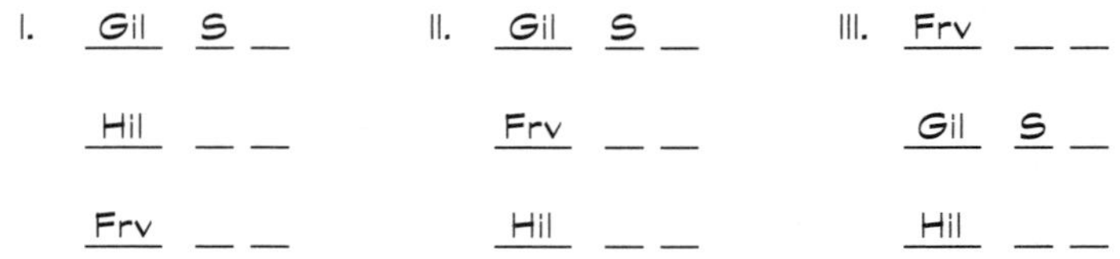

I.   Gil S __   II. Gil S __   III. Frv __ __

     Hil __ __   Frv __ __   Gil S __

     Frv __ __   Hil __ __   Hil __ __

Figure 2.52

The second rule is stronger, since it gets rid of all arrangements in which T could be on the first-place or third-place teams. So it removes 60 possible solutions.

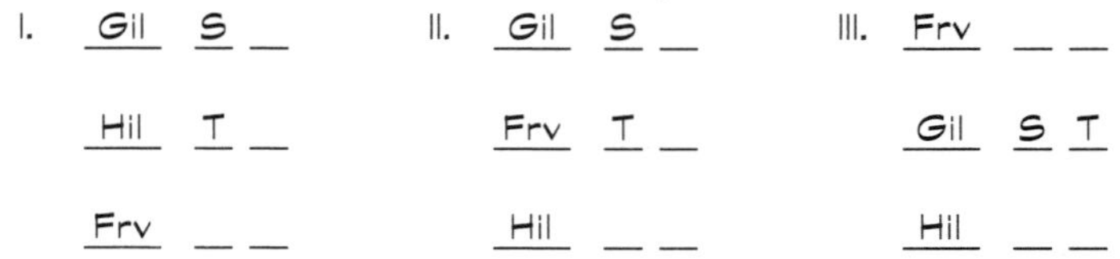

I.   Gil S __   II. Gil S __   III. Frv __ __

     Hil T __   Frv T __   Gil S T

     Frv __ __   Hil __ __   Hil __ __

Figure 2.53

Rules 3 and 4 ensure that the MP and NP pairs are never permitted. Moreover, Rule 4 tells you that you'll never find P on the third-place team and you'll never find N on the first-place team.

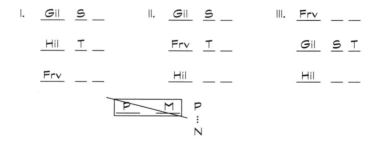

Figure 2.54

To find out just how limited the possible solutions are, consider the three ranking options in light of the rules restricting potential pairs and matches.

There are five ways to complete the picture in Option I. P must be on a higher-ranking team than N. That can happen in three ways:

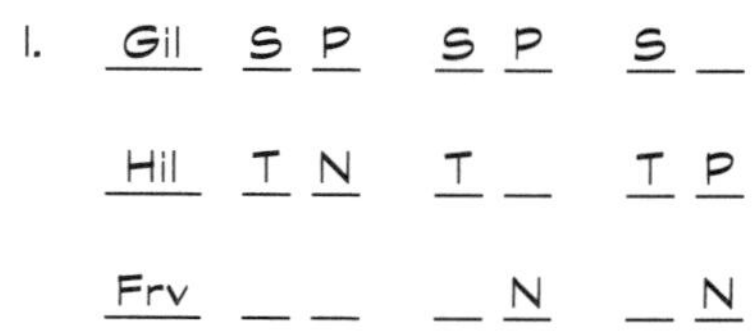

I.   Gil S P   S P   S __

     Hil T N   T __   T P

     Frv __ __   __ N   __ N

Figure 2.55

Those arrangements make it easy to see where M and O could fit in:

I.
Gil	S	P	S	P	S	O/M
Hil	T	N	T	O/M	T	P
Frv	M	O	M/O	N	M/O	N

Figure 2.56

Since M and O could swap places in the second and third of these possible solutions, there are five ways to finish Option I.

Option II, where Fairview finishes second and Hilltop third, has the same five possible pairings and matches:

II.
Gil	S	P	S	P	S	O/M
Frv	T	N	T	O/M	T	P
Hil	M	O	M/O	N	M/O	N

Figure 2.57

In Option III, where the TS pair is assigned to second-place Gillom High, there's only one way to complete the sketch. P must go in first place and N in third place. Since the MP pair is forbidden, this is the only solution:

III.
Frv	P	O
Gil	T	S
Hil	N	M

Figure 2.58

Those in the business of trying to scare you about the LSAT rather than to help you master it would characterize this as a daunting, complex triple-hybrid. But with the rules and restrictions fully considered, this game in fact has only 11 possible solutions. Period. Of course, I would never encourage a student to sketch out all 11 possible solutions. The Master Sketch I'd recommend would stop here:

The three highest-placing teams in a high school debate tournament are the teams from Fairview, Gillom, and Hilltop high schools. Each team has exactly two members. The individuals on these three teams are Mei, Navarro, O'Rourke, Pavlovich, Sethna, and Tsudama. The following is the case:

Sethna is on the team from Gillom High.

Tsudama is on the second-place team.

Mei and Pavlovich are not on the same team.

Pavlovich's team places higher than Navarro's team.

The team from Gillom High places higher than the team from Hilltop High.[47]

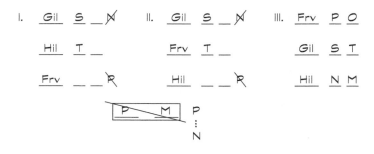

Figure 2.59

But this exercise has given you a much greater appreciation of just how many possible arrangements are taken off the table because of the rules that forbid the MP pair and place P on a higher-ranked team than N. Not surprisingly, one of the questions associated with this game directly rewards students for being able to count acceptable arrangements. Take a look (and get the right answer while you're at it).

21. If Pavlovich and Tsudama are teammates, then for how many of the individuals can it be exactly determined where his or her team placed?

(A) two
(B) three
(C) four
(D) five
(E) six[48]

The "if" clause here means that you can only be in Options I or II. Once you place P on the second-place team with T, you know that N has to be on the third-place team. That leaves only M and O to swap places.

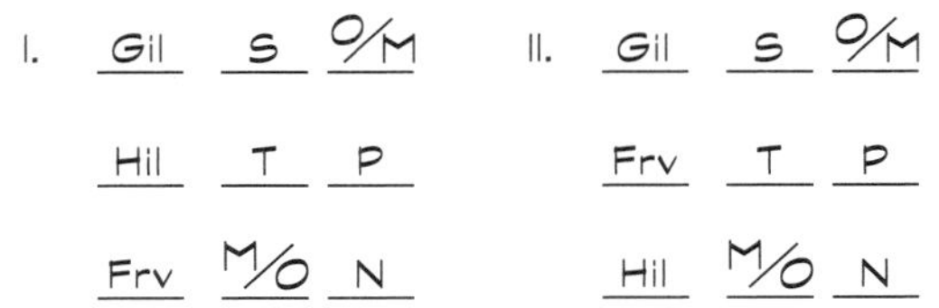

I. Gil   S   O/M   II.   Gil   S   O/M

    Hil   T   P   Frv   T   P

    Frv   M/O   N   Hil   M/O   N

Figure 2.60

Four of the students' rankings are determined for sure, making choice (C) the correct answer.

Rules Help You Score Points

In games of any complexity level, rules are your best friends. They reduce a galaxy of options down to just a few acceptable arrangements. In the next chapter, you'll see how to combine the rules and restrictions to makes games even more definite. It's something that untrained test takers are rarely able to do accurately or efficiently (if at all), and it will provide you with the greatest possible advantage over your competition.

In Part II of this book, by the way, you'll find lists and descriptions of all the rules most commonly associated with each game type. For now, keep your attention on the Kaplan Method and the steps you need to take in all games. Doing so will make Part II's exhaustive discussion of game types and variations even more valuable.

CHAPTER 3

FORMAL LOGIC

USING FORMAL LOGIC ON THE LSAT

Over the years, I've found that one type of logic games rule seems to intimidate students more than all the others: formal logic. Formal logic in the Logic Games section consists of the conditional, or "if-then" rules that dictate what must follow from a certain situation and what's necessary for that situation to occur. I understand why students get anxious about formal logic. Philosophers and other academics refer to it with daunting terms like "first-order predicate calculus," "predicate logic," and "quantification theory." Look it up on the Internet and you'll encounter a dizzying array of terms and symbol systems. But take a deep breath. You don't get any LSAT points for knowing *about* formal logic, just for being able to use it to answer LSAT questions. If you follow what's laid out for you in this book, there's no need for you to take a formal logic class unless you have a personal interest in it. A philosophy- or math-department logic course provides excellent thinking practice, but it won't do much to change your LSAT score.

How to Use Formal Logic on the LSAT

My main goal for this chapter is to help you overcome your trepidation about formal logic and learn to *use* it. To do that, you'll need to be able to do four things. I'll outline them here and then elaborate on each in its own subsection.

1. Recognize formal logic statements.

Look at this rule:

> If literature is offered, then geography is also offered
> but psychology is not.[1]

Its "if-then" grammar is a dead giveaway that it is standard, conditional formal logic. Once you've practiced the techniques in this section, you'll be able to handle the rule flawlessly and rake in the associated LSAT points. But what if the test makers had written it like this?

> Literature is offered only if geography is also offered
> and only if psychology is not offered.

The two rules are actually identical in meaning and have precisely the same impact on the logic game. But if you fail to recognize that the second version represents the same conditional rule, if you fail to see that it dictates a "sufficient-necessary" relationship among its terms, then you won't be able to use it to score points on the LSAT.

2. Translate formal logic statements.

This skill has two elements. The first is directly related to recognizing formal logic. You must be able to turn any English sentence that expresses a conditional rule into its "if-then" equivalent. For example, the sentence "Bobby won't go to the dance unless Jane goes to the dance" has the same meaning as "If Bobby goes to the dance, then so does Jane." I'll have you spend some time learning to assess the implications of these sentences, however they're written, so that you can use them effectively as logic games rules.

The second element involves translating the "if-then" proposition into simple, consistent symbols. The rule about Bobby and Jane can thus be written as:

$$\text{If } B_d \rightarrow J_d$$

Figure 3.1

Don't try to run before you walk, though. Translating formal logic rules into symbolic notation doesn't get you any LSAT points unless you understand what the symbols, and the rules they depict, actually mean. Symbolism is a great way to organize information once you've understood it.

3. Determine the statement's contrapositive.

Here's one of those fancy-sounding terms that sometimes confuses students. A statement's "contrapositive" is simply another way of saying the same thing. It's the logical equivalent of

---

[1] PrepTest 49, Sec. 1, Game 3

the original statement, constructed using negated terms. For the rule that says "If Bobby goes to the dance, then so does Jane," the contrapositive is "If Jane does not go to the dance, then neither will Bobby." In symbols, it looks like this:

$$\text{If } J\!\!\!/ \rightarrow B\!\!\!/$$

Figure 3.2

The reason why finding the contrapositive is so valuable to you in logic games is that it essentially doubles the restrictions on the game's action (or at least doubles your ability to spot them). As you saw in chapter 2, restrictions are what make games easier and more manageable. Additionally, the test makers often relate the questions directly to the contrapositive expression of a rule. In the case of Bobby and Jane, the question might ask, "If Jane does not go to the dance, which one of the following must be true?" Because you've already considered the contrapositive, it's easy to see at least one fact that must follow from the seemingly new "if" clause: Bobby will not go to the dance.

4. Combine formal logic rules.

When the test makers include formal logic rules, they most often provide additional rules with which you can combine them. For example, in the imaginary game with Bobby and Jane, they might give you a rule that says, "If Bobby does not go to the dance, then Martha will not go to the football game." Translating this, you get:

$$\text{If } B\!\!\!/ \rightarrow M\!\!\!/$$

Figure 3.3

Notice that this allows for a deduction. By combining the contrapositive of the rule about Bobby and Jane with the rule about Bobby and Martha, you can see the connection between Jane and Martha.

$$\text{If } J\!\!\!/ \rightarrow B\!\!\!/$$
$$\text{If } B\!\!\!/ \rightarrow M\!\!\!/$$
$$\text{Thus, if } J\!\!\!/ \rightarrow M\!\!\!/$$

Figure 3.4

If Jane avoids the dance, then so does Bobby. And when Bobby avoids the dance, Martha avoids the football game. Thus, if Jane doesn't go to the dance, Martha won't go to the football game. As your skill with contrapositives grows, you'll see that the statement "If Martha goes to the football game, then Jane goes to the dance" also follows from this combination of rules. (A great number of LSAT Logical Reasoning questions reward the same skill, by the way. The practice you're doing here will help you on other sections of the test.)

The test makers consistently reward your ability to spot these types of connections. In games with multiple formal logic rules, every question may turn on your ability to make the correct combinations.

"But I don't get the whole 'if-then' thing."

I've lost count of the hours that I've spent thinking about how best to present formal logic material to future test takers. I know that dozens (if not hundreds) of other Kaplan teachers have pondered this, too. In this chapter, you'll reap the fruits of that thinking: the discussion of necessity and sufficiency, suggested symbols, "translations," and a foolproof system for determining statements' contrapositives. These tools will allow you to manage the formal logic that you encounter in the logic games section. But those students who've made greatest breakthroughs with formal logic are the ones who have put it in perspective. They've seen that formal logic is itself a tool, one that helps them get correct answers. For them, formal logic transformed from obstacle to opportunity. I'll help you learn from their experiences.

To help reduce your anxiety, here are a few reasons why you should learn to love formal logic on the LSAT:

You use formal logic every day.

Formal logic, or at least the small part of it that appears on the LSAT, is actually something that you use consistently without even realizing it. Every time you make a statement such as "The TV has to be plugged in if you want it to work" or "You can't travel to China without a visa," you're using exactly the same conditional logic that is used on the test. You can draw on that nearly intuitive understanding of conditional rules as you learn to master the test.

Formal logic is a small part of logic games.

Understanding formal logic is one of the Core 4 LSAT Skills. That being said, it's actually a bigger part of Logical Reasoning than it is of Logic Games on most administrations of the exam. On some recent exams (PrepTests 50, 52, and 53, for example, from which many of the games in this book are drawn), you won't find more than one or two formal logic statements in the Logic Games section. Arguably, there are tests (such as PrepTest 46) where you find none at all. Every once in a while, of course, you'll find a game that turns entirely on formal logic rules. You'll deal with a couple of those at the end of this chapter. By then, you'll have everything you need to master such games (and to do so much more easily than your competition).

Formal logic brings certainty.

Some test takers love learning how to diagram formal logic statements and their contrapositives. There's a feeling of mathlike precision that can be very comforting. Others find the algebraic approach overwhelming and deal with the statements as regular sentences providing rules for the game. Use the approach that fits your learning style. Regardless, learn to appreciate the fact that formal logic rules lead you to absolutely certainty about the right answer.

When formal logic is involved, you can determine without doubt what must, cannot, or could be true or false in a given case.

Formal logic is often just a complicated way to say simple things.

Consider the following rule:

> Neither Ty nor Raimundo appears in any photograph that
> Wendy appears in.[2]

You could diagram it, in all its formal logic glory, like this:

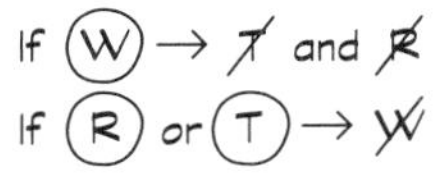

Figure 3.5

As you'll see shortly, that's an accurate depiction of the rule. But think about what the rule means, the restrictions that it places on the game. It's just telling you to keep Wendy apart from Ty and from Raimundo. So if it's clearer to you, just jot the rule like this:

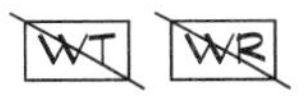

Figure 3.6

Keep formal logic rules simple and represent them in helpful ways. In logic games, your goals should always be to seek clarity and to avoid confusion. You'll find that when you think through what formal logic rules mean to the game, they're often quite easy to visualize, and thus to represent symbolically without a lot of fancy (and unnecessary) gibberish.

IDENTIFY FORMAL LOGIC: DISTINGUISH BETWEEN *SUFFICIENT* AND *NECESSARY*

The Sufficient-Necessary Relationship

At the heart of all formal logic statements on the LSAT are the twin concepts of sufficiency and necessity. Don't let the terms intimidate you; just use their ordinary meanings. "Sufficient" means "enough by itself" and "Necessary" means "required." Don't confuse the two. Plenty of things are necessary for a given result without being sufficient for it, or vice versa. If your car has an internal combustion engine, gasoline is necessary for it to run, but gasoline by itself isn't enough. The car might have plenty of gas, but if it doesn't have spark plugs, or if the battery is dead, it's not going to work. Having gasoline is necessary, but not sufficient, for your car to run. On the flip side, winning the lottery is sufficient to make you rich, but it's not necessary.

---

[2] PrepTest 45, Sec. 3, Game 3

You could also get rich by working hard, investing well, discovering a sunken treasure, or inheriting a large sum of money. The takeaway message is that you already understand these concepts, almost intuitively.

To make sure you get the idea, consider the following example. Say there's a watch you'd like to buy. It costs $100. Each of the following statements tells you something that is *sufficient but not necessary*, *necessary but not sufficient*, or *both sufficient and necessary* in order for you to purchase the watch. Consider each statement and label it accordingly.

You have at least $50. _____

You have exactly $100. _____

You have $400. _____

You have at least $100. _____

Here are the answers:

You have at least $50: *Necessary, but not sufficient.* If you don't have at least $50, there's no way you can have the $100 you would need to buy the watch. But, $50 is not enough, by itself, for you to buy the watch. So, it's not sufficient.

You have exactly $100: *Sufficient, but not necessary.* With $100, you can definitely buy the watch. But, it's not necessary for you to have exactly $100. You could buy the watch if you had $101 or $105 or $5,000. Always pay attention to the wording of LSAT rules, questions, and answer choices. The test makers' word choice is always intentional.

You have $400: *Sufficient, but not necessary.* You could buy the watch and plenty more. So, it's sufficient (and nice) for you to have $400, but it's not necessary that you have so much in order to get the watch.

You have at least $100: *Both sufficient and necessary.* Knowing that you have at least $100 guarantees that you can buy the watch. It's also necessary. If you don't have at least $100, you can't buy the watch.

You can write conditional statements in the same language the test makers use for formal logic rules on the LSAT. Think back to the first example, the one identifying gasoline as necessary (but not sufficient) for your car to run.

If the car runs, then it has gasoline.

If the car does not have gasoline, then it will not run.

The car runs only if it has gasoline.

Only when the car has gasoline will it run.

The car will not run unless it has gasoline.

All of those statements mean exactly the same thing. Moreover, switching the places of the key terms—the car's running and its having gas—would create nonsense. Make sure you see why.

If the car has gasoline, then it will run: Not necessarily; it might have a dead battery or lack spark plugs.

The car has gasoline only if it runs: Same problem; you could have a full tank in a nonfunctioning car.

The car does not have gasoline unless it runs: yet another variation on the same faulty logic.

Why don't any of the latter three statements work? Because they've mistaken the sufficient term for the necessary one. The test makers test your understanding of necessity and sufficiency throughout the test, and they design wrong answers to catch those who mistake one for the other.

Interpreting a Formal Logic Rule

In chapter 2, I said that logic games rules are like laws. Nowhere is this truer than in formal logic rules. To see this, and to see how important it will be to use formal logic in logic games, consider this legal rule:

> To legally vote in Country X, you must be at least 18 years of age and you must be properly registered.

First, determine the sufficient-necessary relationship. Which of the terms is enough, by itself, to establish the truth of other term(s)? Which are needed in order to have another condition? If you're confused, try fitting the terms—there are three this time: "vote legally," "at least 18," and "properly registered"—into the following sentences:

If _____, then _____.

You cannot _____ unless you are _____.

If not _____, then not _____.

You can _____ only if you are _____.

The sufficient term is "vote legally." Someone who has voted legally in Country X must be both 18 or older *and* properly registered. The necessary terms are "at least 18" and "properly registered." You cannot legally vote in Country X unless you are both at least 18 *and* properly registered. So a potential voter who fails to satisfy either of the necessary conditions cannot vote legally. Thus, if you are not at least 18 *or* are not properly registered, then you cannot vote legally. Remember that "only" and "only if" signify necessity. Here's how each sentence might be properly completed:

If *legally voting*, then *at least 18* and *properly registered*.
You *cannot legally vote* unless you are at least 18 and properly registered.
If *not at least 18* or *not properly registered*, then *not voting legally*.
You can *vote legally* only if you are *at least 18* and *properly registered*.

The LSAT is always interested in what must, cannot, or could be true given a particular set of circumstances or rules, especially in the Logic Games section. That is, the test wants to know what you can validly infer. Imagine a citizen of Country X named John. Try to complete the following conditional sentences based on the voting rule above. Here's a hint: The correct inference may be something that must be true, something that must be false, or it may be "I don't know; there's not enough information to draw a conclusion from the rule."

If John is 15 years old, then _____.

If John is 35 years old, but not registered to vote, then _____.

If John is 20 years old and he is properly registered to vote, then _____.

If John can vote legally in Country X, then _____.

Check and see how you did.

The first sentence should read: "If John is 15 years old, then *he cannot legally vote in Country X.*" It doesn't matter whether he's registered. When you lack either of two necessary conditions, whatever is in the sufficient term cannot be true.

The second sentence should read: "If John is 35 years old, but not registered to vote, then *he cannot legally vote in Country X.*" Again, failure to meet either of the necessary terms is enough to know that John cannot cast his ballot legally.

The third sentence is the trickiest (and one that the test makers love to use). It should read: "If John is 20 years old and he is properly registered to vote, then *I don't know whether John can vote legally in Country X or not.*" Being above the minimum age and being properly registered to vote are requirements for legal voting, but they are not assurances of it. That is, they are necessary but not sufficient. Perhaps a past criminal conviction makes him ineligible to vote. Maybe he's been found mentally unfit to vote. Maybe in order to vote in Country X, you have to be registered with the military draft board and John isn't. Remember, there could be necessary conditions that haven't been stated in the rule. The test makers include many wrong answers that catch test takers who confuse necessity and sufficiency. The best you can do with the third sentence is to say that John fulfills two of the requirements for legal voting in Country X. He may be able to vote legally, but he also may not.

The fourth sentence should read: "If John can vote legally in Country X, then *he is at least 18 years old* and *he is legally registered to vote.*" This sentence begins by affirming the sufficient condition. Given that, you know unequivocally that both the necessary conditions must be true.

Now, try your hand at recognizing the sufficient and necessary terms in some actual LSAT rules.

DRILL: IDENTIFYING SUFFICIENT AND NECESSARY TERMS

For each of the following rules, determine which of the terms is sufficient and which necessary. Then complete the sentences that follow by jotting down what must be true or must be false, or by saying, "I don't know." (NOTE: All of these rules are taken from official, recently released LSAT exams. However, you should *not* combine rules in this exercise. Even if you notice that some of the rules come from the same game as each other, contain your analysis to one rule at a time.)

1.
If the keeshond is placed on Monday, the greyhound is placed on Tuesday.[3]
Sufficient: _____
Necessary: _____
    (a) If the greyhound is placed on Tuesday,
        then _____.
    (b) If the greyhound is placed on Wednesday, then
        _____.
    (c) If the keeshond is placed on Tuesday, then
        _____.
    (d) If the keeshond is placed on Monday, then
        _____.

2.
Selma appears in every photograph that Umiko appears in.[4]
Sufficient: _____
Necessary: _____
    (a) If Umiko appears in the photograph, then
        _____.
    (b) If Selma appears in the photograph, then
        _____.
    (c) If Umiko does not appear in the photograph, then _____.
    (d) If Selma does not appear in the photograph, then _____.

3.
Raimundo appears in every photograph that Yakira does not appear in.[5]
Sufficient: _____
Necessary: _____
    (a) If Raimundo does not appear in the photograph,
        then _____.
    (b) If Yakira appears in the photograph, then _____.
    (c) If Raimundo appears in the photograph, then
        _____.
    (d) If Yakira does not appear in the photograph, then _____.

4.
If Figueroa's delivery is earlier than Malpighi's, then Leacock's delivery is earlier than Harris's.[6]
Sufficient: _____
Necessary: _____
    (a) If Figueroa's delivery is earlier than Malpighi's, then _____.
    (b) If Figueroa's delivery is later than Malpighi's, then _____.
    (c) If Leacock's delivery is earlier than Harris's, then _____.
    (d) If Leacock's delivery is later than Harris's, then _____.

---

[3] PrepTest 44, Sec. 3, Game 2
[4] PrepTest 45, Sec. 3, Game 3
[5] PrepTest 45, Sec. 3, Game 3

[6] PrepTest 52, Sec. 2, Game 4

Intentionally left blank.

Explanations

1.

If the keeshond is placed on Monday, the greyhound is
placed on Tuesday.[7]
Sufficient: *The keeshond is placed on Monday.*
Necessary: *The greyhound is placed on Tuesday.*

(a) If the greyhound is placed on Tuesday, then *I don't know.*

The greyhound being placed on Tuesday is necessary, but not sufficient, for the keeshond to be placed on Monday. The best you can say here is that the keeshond *could* go on Monday, but you don't know that it will.

(b) If the greyhound is placed on Wednesday, then *the keeshond cannot be placed on Monday.*

The greyhound being placed on Tuesday is necessary for the keeshond to be placed on Monday. Once you know that the greyhound goes anywhere other than Tuesday, you can conclude that the keeshond goes on a day other than Monday.

(c) If the keeshond is placed on Tuesday, then *I don't know.*

When the keeshond is placed on Monday, you know that the greyhound is placed on Tuesday. When the keeshond goes on any other day, you cannot make any determination about the greyhound. The greyhound could be placed on any day, as far as this rule is concerned.

(d) If the keeshond is placed on Monday, then *the greyhound must be placed on Tuesday.*

This is just a restatement of the rule. The keeshond's being placed on Monday is sufficient to conclude that the greyhound is placed on Tuesday. The greyhound cannot be placed on any other day.

2.

Selma appears in every photograph that Umiko appears in.[8]
Sufficient: *Umiko appears in the photograph.*
Necessary: *Selma is in the photograph.*

(a) If Umiko appears in the photograph, then *Selma appears in the photograph.*

This rule wasn't written in "if-then" form, but the sufficient-necessary relationship is the same. Selma is required (necessary) to be in any photograph that Umiko appears in. In this sentence, Umiko is in the picture, so Selma must be, too.

(b) If Selma appears in the photograph, then *I don't know.*

The rule requires Selma to be included whenever Umiko is, but it doesn't preclude her from appearing solo. Knowing that Selma is in the photo tells you nothing about whether Umiko is in it. The best you can say is that Umiko *might* be in the photo, but she also might not.

(c) If Umiko does not appear in the photograph, then *I don't know.*

The rule requires Selma's appearance when Umiko *appears* in a photo. When Umiko *does not appear*, you can't make any deductions about Selma. The best you can say here is that Selma *might* appear in the photo.

(d) If Selma is not in the photograph, then *Umiko does not appear in the photograph.*

Since the rule requires Selma's appearance in any photo featuring Umiko, you know that Umiko cannot appear without Selma. Take away what's necessary, and you can't have the sufficient condition occur.

---

[7] PrepTest 44, Sec. 3, Game 2
[8] PrepTest 45, Sec. 3, Game 3

3.

Raimundo appears in every photograph that Yakira does
not appear in.[9]
Sufficient: *Either Yakira or Raimundo not appearing in the photograph*
Necessary: *The other person appearing in the photograph*
At first glance, it may seem that only Yakira's not appearing is a sufficient term, but think about it for a
moment. If Raimundo is in *every* photo in which Yakira doesn't appear, it must be true that Yakira is in *every*
photo in which Raimundo does not appear. If she weren't there, he'd have to be. You can simplify this rule
like so: "At least one of Yakira and Raimundo appears in every photograph."

   (a) If Raimundo does not appear in the photograph, then *Yakira appears in the photograph.*
      Since the rule tells you that Raimundo is always included when Yakira is not, it's impossible for both
      of them to be missing from the same photo. Since this sentence begins by excluding Raimundo from
      the photo, you can conclude that Yakira is included.

   (b) If Yakira appears in a photograph, then *I don't know.*
      The rule tells you that Raimundo must be included when Yakira *does not* appear, but it says nothing
      about what happens when Yakira *does* appear. A rule like this one tells you that *at least one* of the
      two is in every picture; it does not preclude any photo from featuring both of them.

   (c) If Raimundo appears in a photograph, then *I don't know.*
      Just as you saw in the previous sentence, *including* one of the two friends tells you nothing about the
      other. If Raimundo were left out of the picture, you'd know that Yakira must be in. Since this sentence
      begins by including Raimundo, you can only say that Yakira may or may not be in the picture.

   (d) If Yakira does not appear in a photograph, then *Raimundo appears in the photograph.*
      This is really just a restatement of the original rule. Since Raimundo appears whenever Yakira doesn't,
      and this sentence begins by telling you that Yakira is left out of the photo, you can conclude that
      Raimundo is in the photo.

4.

If Figueroa's delivery is earlier than Malpighi's, then
Leacock's delivery is earlier than Harris's.[10]
Sufficient: *Figueroa's delivery is before Malpighi's* (or *Malpighi's delivery is after Figueroa's*).
Necessary: *Leacock's delivery is before Harris's* (or *Harris's delivery is after Leacock's*).

   (a) If Figueroa's delivery is earlier than Malpighi's, then *Leacock's delivery is earlier than Harris's.*
      This is just a restatement of the rule. Knowing that Figueroa gets a delivery before Malpighi is
      sufficient to ensure that Leacock gets a delivery before Harris.

   (b) If Figueroa's delivery is later than Malpighi's, then *I don't know.*
      According to the rule, you know what happens when Figueroa receives a delivery before Malpighi,
      but not what happens when Malpighi gets a delivery earlier than Figueroa. In this case, Leacock's
      delivery might still come before Harris's, but Harris's might come before Leacock's. That wouldn't
      violate the rule, since the rule is only triggered when Figueroa gets a delivery earlier than Malpighi.

   (c) If Leacock's delivery is earlier than Harris's, then *I don't know.*
      Leacock getting a delivery before Harris is necessary for Figueroa to get one before Malpighi, but it is
      not sufficient to know that Figueroa gets a delivery before Malpighi. All you can safely say here is that
      Figueroa *might* get a delivery before Malpighi. Whether that happens or not, the rule is satisfied.

   (d) If Leacock's delivery is later than Harris's, then *Malpighi's delivery is earlier than Figueroa's.*
      According to the rule, *whenever* Figueroa gets delivery before Malpighi, Leacock gets one before
      Harris. Since this sentence begins by telling you that Harris gets a delivery prior to Leacock, you know
      that this cannot be a case in which Figueroa gets a delivery before Malpighi. Malpighi must, in this
      case, get a delivery prior to Figueroa and not the other way around.

(NOTE: The explanations for questions 5–8 are in your Online Companion.)

---

[9] PrepTest 45, Sec. 3, Game 3
[10] PrepTest 52, Sec. 2, Game 4

Sufficient and Necessary Terms Help Unlock Formal Logic

You can see from that drill that the test makers present conditional "if-then" rules in a variety of ways. Learning to recognize the sufficient-necessary relationship whenever it appears and however it's worded is actually the heavy-lifting part of dealing with formal logic. What follows will help you organize and keep track of these rules on the pages of your test booklet. It provides a very useful shorthand notation system and shows you how to spot all of the additional deductions that come from combining formal logic rules. But remember, this work will be for naught if you've mistaken the sufficient and necessary terms or failed to appreciate what they tell you must, can, and cannot be true within the logic game.

TRANSLATE FORMAL LOGIC: SYMBOLIZE AND ABBREVIATE

As you've seen already, formal logic statements can be wordy. That's why translating them into a simple "if-then" shorthand is so helpful on test day. This is one place in which the test makers are quite helpful. Since they always create lists of entities that can be shortened into one- or two-letter abbreviations, your symbolic representations of formal logic rules can be clear and compact.

Common Examples

The most straightforward examples occur when the rule is written in "if-then" terms from the start.

> If the stand carries kiwis, then it does not carry pears.[11]

You don't need to "translate" the language of this rule in order to identify the sufficient-necessary relationship. The sufficient term—"carries kiwis"—is in the "if" clause, and the necessary term—"not carry pears"—follows "then." To write this in symbols, simply jot it down like this:

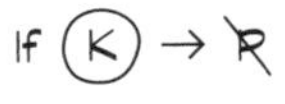

$$\text{If } \textcircled{K} \rightarrow \cancel{R}$$

Figure 3.7

The arrow stands in place of "then," indicating that what precedes it is sufficient and what follows it is necessary. The strike-through indicates negation; the stand does *not* carry pears. As always, I'll encourage you to use the symbols that are clearest and easiest for you. So if you prefer to use a tilde (~) or the word "NOT" to indicate negation, feel free.

---

11 PrepTest 36, Sec. 4, Game 1

$$\text{If } (\text{K}) \rightarrow \sim\text{P}$$
$$\text{If } (\text{K}) \rightarrow \text{NOT P}$$

Figure 3.8

Just make sure that by test day you've settled on a single, consistent symbol set that makes every rule crystal clear for you.

Students sometimes hesitate to symbolize formal logic rules as they become more complex or when they move away from the standard "if-then" grammar. Don't fall into that trap. When the test makers choose to phrase formal logic differently, simply apply what you've already learned in this section. Once you've identified the statement as formal logic, distinguish the sufficient term(s) from the necessary term(s). Then symbolize the logic as you would with a straightforward "if-then." Take this rule from the Friends' Photographs game, for instance:

Selma appears in every photograph that Umiko appears in.[12]

Since Selma is required (necessary) in every photo that has Umiko, Selma's appearance is the necessary term and Umiko's the sufficient term. The rule is thus symbolized as:

$$\text{If } (\text{U}) \rightarrow (\text{S})$$

Figure 3.9

Twists on Common Examples

Here are a few more common twists that you should learn to symbolize.

When the rule involves both an entity and a particular location or characteristic, use a subscript for the secondary characteristic. For example, you can depict this rule

If the keeshond is placed on Monday, the greyhound is placed on Tuesday.[13]

neatly like this:

$$\text{If } K_{Mon} \rightarrow G_{Tue}$$

Figure 3.10

The subscript Mon and Tue are clear. If you want to reflect the layout of your framework, something along these lines works just as well:

---

[12] PrepTest 45, Sec. 3, Game 3
[13] PrepTest 44, Sec. 3, Game 2

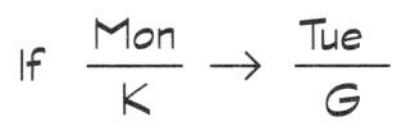

$$\text{If} \quad \frac{\text{Mon}}{\text{K}} \rightarrow \frac{\text{Tue}}{\text{G}}$$

Figure 3.11

When a formal logic rule contains two terms in either the sufficient clause or the necessary clause, determine whether the rule is requiring both terms (X *and* Y) or at least one of the terms (X *or* Y) and use the appropriate conjunction—"and" or "or"—between the two terms in your symbolism of the rule. Look at this rule:

> If sociology is offered, then psychology is also offered
> but zoology is not.[14]

The inclusion of sociology requires both the inclusion of psychology and the exclusion of zoology. Thus, your scratch work would look like this:

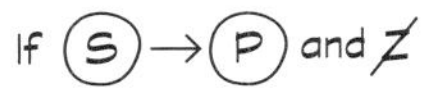

$$\text{If} \; \textcircled{S} \rightarrow \textcircled{P} \; \text{and} \; \cancel{Z}$$

Figure 3.12

Occasionally, a rule will call on you to translate the language and to use creative symbolism. This is especially true in Sequencing games where you need to represent the entities' relative positions. Consider this rule:

> A film in Greek is not shown unless a film in Italian
> is going to be shown the next day.[15]

Now, identify the sufficient and necessary terms, and use your Sequencing scratch work to illustrate the relevant restriction within the game.

$$\text{If} \; G \rightarrow \boxed{\begin{array}{cc} G & I \end{array}}$$

Figure 3.13

There are no right or wrong ways for formal logic symbolism to *look*, although there are, of course, right and wrong arrangements for the sufficient and necessary terms. And there are helpful and unhelpful depictions of all rules on the test. Use the following Drill to jump-start your practice with symbolizing formal logic. Use the explanations that follow to check your work. If you misplace or make mistakes with any of the sufficient or necessary terms, go back and review the rule to avoid making similar mistakes in the future.

---

[14] PrepTest 49, Sec. 1, Game 3
[15] PrepTest 49, Sec. 1, Game 1

DRILL: SYMBOLIZING RULES

For each of the following rules, first identify the sufficient and necessary terms. Then, symbolize the rule using the previously outlined principles.

1.
If Traugott signs with Star Agency, West also signs with Star Agency.[16]
Sufficient: _____
Necessary: _____
Symbolism: _____

2.
None of the nations exports both wheat and oranges.[17]
Sufficient: _____
Necessary: _____
Symbolism: _____

3.
If the stand carries watermelons, then it carries figs or tangerines or both.[18]
Sufficient: _____
Necessary: _____
Symbolism: _____

4.
If geography is offered, then both history and zoology are also offered.[19]
Sufficient: _____
Necessary: _____
Symbolism: _____

5.
If a site dates from the eighth century, it was discovered by Oliphant.[20]
Sufficient: _____
Necessary: _____
Symbolism: _____

---

[16] PrepTest 53, Sec. 2, Game 1

[17] PrepTest 45, Sec. 3, Game 4

[18] PrepTest 36, Sec. 4, Game 1

[19] PrepTest 49, Sec. 1, Game 3

[20] PrepTest 44, Sec. 3, Game 3

Answer Explanations follow on the next page.

Explanations

1.

If Traugott signs with Star Agency, West also signs with
Star Agency.[21]
  Sufficient: *Traugott signs with Star.*
  Necessary: *West signs with Star.*
  Symbolism:

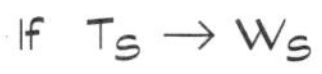

$$\text{If} \quad T_S \rightarrow W_S$$

Figure 3.14

The rule is in standard "if-then" format. Use subscript to designate the specific agency (Star)
that triggers this rule. Make sure not to misinterpret this rule; it does not mean that Traugott
and West must always sign with the same agency as each other.

2.

None of the nations exports both wheat and oranges.[22]
  Sufficient: *A nation exporting either wheat or oranges*
  Necessary: *The nation not exporting the other crop*
  Symbolism:

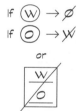

Figure 3.15

It doesn't matter which of the crops you use as your trigger. In fact, in the next section you'll
learn that the two "if-then" statements are one another's contrapositives. Of course, the simplest
visual depiction of the rule is just to strike through or negate the WO pair.

3.

If the stand carries watermelons, then it carries figs or
tangerines or both.[23]
  Sufficient: *Carries watermelons*
  Necessary: *Carries figs or tangerines*
  Symbolism:

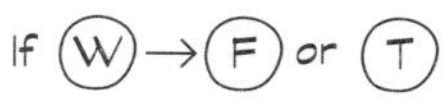

If (W) → (F) or (T)

Figure 3.16

---

[21] PrepTest 53, Sec. 2, Game 1
[22] PrepTest 45, Sec. 3, Game 4
[23] PrepTest 36, Sec. 4, Game 1

There are two terms in the necessary statement this time. The rule requires only one of them to happen, however. You need to use the word "or" between the terms in the "then" clause. It's worth noting that the "or both" on the end is superfluous. In order to carry watermelons, the stand must carry either figs or tangerines. If it has both, then it has clearly met the requirement. So there's no need to add that to your symbolism.

4.

If geography is offered, then both history and zoology are also offered.[24]

    Sufficient: *Geography is offered.*
    Necessary: *History is offered* and *zoology is offered.*
    Symbolism:

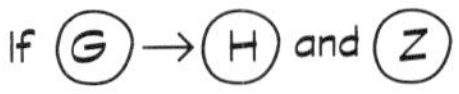

$$\text{If } (G) \rightarrow (H) \text{ and } (Z)$$

Figure 3.17

This time, both of the terms in the "then" clause are necessary for the sufficient condition. Therefore, use "and" to link H and Z in your symbolism. Knowing that geography is offered is sufficient to show that both history and zoology are also on the schedule.

5.

If a site dates from the eighth century, it was discovered by Oliphant.[25]

    Sufficient: *The site dates from the eighth century.*
    Necessary: *The site was discovered by Oliphant.*
    Symbolism:

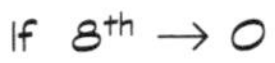

$$\text{If } 8^{th} \rightarrow O$$

Figure 3.18

This rule is in the standard "if-then" formal logic format. The only thing that might have given you pause is that it restricts a match rather than a selection or sequence. Don't let that concern you. The sufficient-necessary relationship is still the same. If you've organized the Matching action in your sketch with slots for the age of the site and its discoverer, you could also symbolize the rule like so:

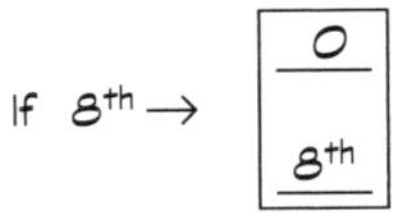

$$\text{If } 8^{th} \rightarrow \boxed{\begin{array}{c} O \\ \hline 8^{th} \end{array}}$$

Figure 3.19

---

24 PrepTest 49, Sec. 1, Game 3
25 PrepTest 44, Sec. 3, Game 3

Translate and Symbolize for Success on Test Day

Once you've mastered these first two techniques—identifying sufficiency and necessity and translating formal logic rules into symbols—you'll be ready to use any formal logic rule that you encounter on the test. Next, you'll see how to double your advantage by determining the contrapositives of formal logic rules and adding them to your scratch work.

DETERMINE THE CONTRAPOSITIVE: REVERSE AND NEGATE
Simple "If-Thens"

The contrapositive is one of those confusing-sounding aspects of formal logic that's actually quite straightforward. In fact, you've been using contrapositives already in this section. A contrapositive is the logical equivalent of any conditional formal logic statement, with the key (sufficient and necessary) terms reversed and negated. Here's how it works.

Say you want to go to a club to see a concert. At the door of the concert hall, a bouncer greets you with a rule in formal logic: "You cannot enter the club unless I see your ID." Since you're an LSAT test taker, you identify the statement as formal logic and distinguish the sufficient condition—"enter the club"—from the necessary one—"show ID." Knowing that the necessary condition follows the arrow, you translate the statement into symbols.

$$\text{If enter club} \quad \rightarrow \quad \text{Show ID}$$

Figure 3.20

Maybe the bouncer grows impatient with you as you're working this out and says, "Do you know what happens if you don't show me your ID?" Of course you do. Failure to show your ID negates the necessity clause of the rule, which means that you cannot have the sufficient condition. You answer, "If I do not show my ID, I cannot enter the club," and show the bouncer your new scratch work.

$$\text{If NOT show ID} \quad \rightarrow \quad \text{NOT enter club}$$

Figure 3.21

That's the contrapositive of the original rule. Actually, it is better to say that the two statements are contrapositives of one another. It doesn't matter whether you start with the terms expressed affirmatively or negatively. For any formal logic statement, reversing and negating the key terms forms the contrapositive. Both ways of expressing the rule are valid restrictions within the logic game.

Try it with another example from earlier in the chapter. Identify the sufficient and necessary terms in the following statement. Translate it into symbols. Then reverse and negate the terms to form the contrapositive.

The car will run only if it has gasoline.
>   Sufficient: _____
>   Necessary: _____
>   Translation: _____
>   Contrapositive: _____

What did you come up with? Check your work against the following:
The car will run only if it has gasoline.
>   Sufficient: *Car runs*
>   Necessary: *Car has gasoline*
>   Translation:

$$\text{If} \quad C_{runs} \quad \rightarrow \quad C_{gas}$$

Figure 3.22

>   Contrapositive:

$$\text{If} \quad \cancel{C_{gas}} \quad \rightarrow \quad \cancel{C_{runs}}$$

Figure 3.22A

If you translated the rule into negative terms first and then wrote the contrapositive in the affirmative, no problem. Remember, both expressions are just different ways of writing the same rule.

Before I go on, here's an important warning: Never ever reverse without negating or negate without reversing. Doing so confuses the sufficient and necessary terms in the rule and will lead straight to wrong answers. Showing your ID may not be enough to get you into the concert. A car can have gasoline and still not run. The logic is just as flawed when you make these mistakes with logic game's rules. Try it out with this one. Translate it and then reverse and negate to form the contrapositive.

If Traugott signs with Star Agency, West also signs with
Star Agency.[26]
>   Translation: _____
>   Contrapositive: _____
>   Translation:

$$\text{If} \quad T_S \quad \rightarrow \quad W_S$$

Figure 3.23

Contrapositive:

$$\text{If} \quad \cancel{W_S} \quad \rightarrow \quad \cancel{T_S}$$

Figure 3.24

Notice what the rule, expressed in contrapositives, tells you and what it doesn't. Whenever Traugott signs with Star, West must also sign with Star. When West does not sign with Star,

---

[26] PrepTest 53, Sec. 2, Game 1

neither does Traugott. But be careful. Knowing that Traugott signs with an agency other than Star tells you nothing about West. Likewise, learning that West signs with Star doesn't allow for any valid inferences about Traugott. The first of these incorrect translations negates without reversing. The second reverses without negating. Rest assured that the test makers will design wrong answers to catch students who cannot correctly interpret and contrapose the rule.

Complex "If-Thens": Change "And" to "Or"

When either of the clauses in a formal logic rule has more than one term linked with either "and" or "or," you must complete one more step in making the contrapositive. To see how it works, consider the following example.

> If a painting is by Monet, then it is by a famous artist *and* it is by a French artist.

If you like, you can symbolize that statement this way:

$$\text{If Monet} \rightarrow A_{famous} \text{ and } A_{French}$$

Figure 3.25

Now, imagine that your friend shows you a painting. You ask, "Who painted it?" Your friend answers, "I don't know the artist's name, but I know that he was relatively unknown." What can you infer? Right. The painting isn't by Monet.

$$\text{If } \cancel{A}_{famous} \rightarrow \cancel{Monet}$$

Figure 3.26

Rewind. This time, when you ask your friend who painted the picture, she says, "I don't know the artist's name, but I know he was Italian." Again, you can safely conclude that you're not looking at a Monet.

$$\text{If } \cancel{A}_{French} \rightarrow \cancel{Monet}$$

Figure 3.27

Now, put those two inferences together and compare them to the original statement.

$$\text{If } \cancel{A}_{famous} \text{ or } \cancel{A}_{French} \rightarrow \cancel{Monet}$$

Figure 3.28

Here, the contrapositives are formed by reversing and negating the terms and by changing "and" to "or." It works just as well the other way around. Here's a rule in which the sufficient clause has two terms:

If you're male and you have children, then you are a father.
Take a moment to write the rule and its contrapositive in formal logic symbols.

    Translations: _____
    Contrapositive: _____
    Here's how it should look:

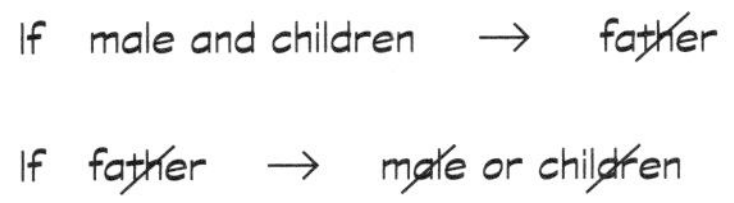

If   male and children   →   father

If   father   →   male or children

Figure 3.29

Notice that the "and" must change to "or" in order to make the contrapositive valid. You could have children, but if you're female, you're not a father. Likewise, you may be male, but if you have no children, you're not a father. In short, if you're not a father, at least one of the terms in the sufficient clause of the original rule must be negated.

Now, apply this procedure to a rule from an LSAT logic game. Translate the rule into symbols and form its contrapositive.

If geography is offered, then both history and
zoology are also offered.[27]
    Translations: _____
    Contrapositive: _____

How did you do? Compare your work to the correct contrapositives.

If (G)   →   (H)   and   (Z)

If H or Z   →   G

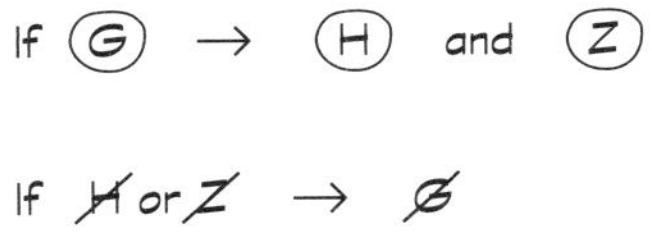

Figure 3.30

Having the "or" in a contrapositive is important because a question might read, "If zoology is not offered, which one of the following must be true?" The "or" tells you that excluding zoology is enough, by itself, to infer that you must exclude geography.

Form the Contrapositive in Two Steps

That's the sum total of what you need to know to form the correct contrapositives of any formal logic rule you will encounter on the LSAT.

TO FORM THE CONTRAPOSITIVE . . .

1. Reverse and negate the sufficient and necessary terms.

2. If needed, change "and" to "or," or vice versa.

---

[27] PrepTest 49, Sec. 1, Game 3

Contrapositives in Sequencing Rules

Most formal logic rules in Selection, Distribution, and Matching games are pretty straightforward once you get the hang of translating and forming contrapositives. Even the complex rules in these games use all of the familiar terms.

> If the stand carries oranges, then it carries both pears and watermelons.[28]

Your symbolization of the translation and contrapositive follows exactly the steps you've just seen.

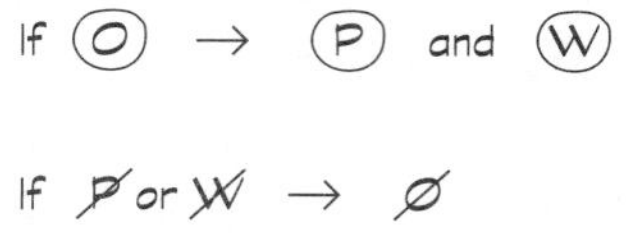

$$\text{If } \textcircled{O} \rightarrow \textcircled{P} \text{ and } \textcircled{W}$$

$$\text{If } \not{P} \text{ or } \not{W} \rightarrow \not{O}$$

Figure 3.31

Everything in these statements is *by the numbers*: reverse, negate, change "and" to "or."

Formal logic Sequencing rules can throw students for a loop at first because they often have multiple terms but lack the standard "and/or" conjunctions. Instead, the sufficient and necessary terms show the relative order of two entities. Here's an example:

> If Figueroa's delivery is earlier than Malpighi's, then Leacock's delivery is earlier than Harris's.[29]

(For the purposes of this rule, assume that none of the deliveries occur at the same time.)

You should symbolize the rule this way:

$$\text{If } \begin{matrix} F \\ | \\ M \end{matrix} \rightarrow \begin{matrix} L \\ | \\ H \end{matrix} \quad \text{or} \quad \text{If } F \ldots m \rightarrow L \ldots H$$

Figure 3.32

To form the contrapositive, do what you would with any formal logic statement: reverse and negate the terms. Here, since no two deliveries occur simultaneously, the negation of "Leacock's delivery is earlier than Harris's" is "Harris's delivery is earlier than Leacock's." Likewise, the negation of "Figueroa's delivery is earlier than Malpighi's" is "Malpighi's delivery is earlier than Figueroa's." Thus, you can symbolize the contrapositive like this:

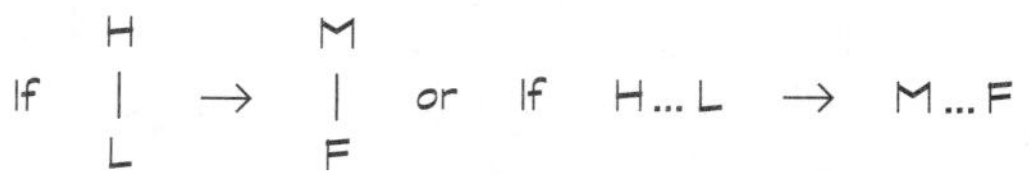

$$\text{If } \begin{matrix} H \\ | \\ L \end{matrix} \rightarrow \begin{matrix} M \\ | \\ F \end{matrix} \quad \text{or} \quad \text{If } H \ldots L \rightarrow M \ldots F$$

Figure 3.33

---

[28] PrepTest 36, Sec. 4, Game 1
[29] PrepTest 52, Sec. 2, Game 4

When you depict the game's action or framework within your scratch work for the rule, use it in forming the contrapositive as well. As always, the most important thing is for your symbols to be clear and helpful to you. No one else will see your test-day scratch work; they'll only see how many correct answers you produce.

"If, but Only If": A Special Case

One variant that has appeared very rarely on the LSAT is the so-called "bi-conditional" statement, in which two terms are linked by "if, and only if" or "if, but only if." Here's a recent example:

Nation X exports soybeans if, but only if, Nation Y
does also.[30]

This rule contains not just one, but two conditional, formal logic statements. The phrase "if, but only if" designates Nation Y's exporting soybeans as both sufficient ("if") and necessary ("only if") for Nation X to export them. There are two ways you can add this rule into your scratch work. You could write out the two formal logic rules and their contrapositives:

$$
\begin{aligned}
\text{If } \quad Y_S &\rightarrow X_S \\
\text{If } \quad X_{\cancel{S}} &\rightarrow Y_{\cancel{S}} \\
\text{If } \quad X_S &\rightarrow Y_S \\
\text{If } \quad Y_{\cancel{S}} &\rightarrow X_{\cancel{S}}
\end{aligned}
$$

Figure 3.34

Or you could summarize the impact of the rule:

$$
\boxed{Y_S \; X_S} \quad or \quad \boxed{Y_{\cancel{S}} \; X_{\cancel{S}}}
$$

Figure 3.35

In every acceptable arrangement in this game, either both X and Y will export soybeans or neither of them will. In the unlikely event that you encounter a biconditional statement on test day, keep in mind that "if" signals sufficiency while "only if" signals necessity, and you'll interpret the rule correctly. Regardless of the context, the rule you see will function exactly as the one you've just seen.

Continue your practice with translating formal logic and forming the contrapositives of each of the rules in the following Drill.

---

[30] PrepTest 45, Sec. 3, Game 4

DRILL: WRITING CONTRAPOSITIVES

First, translate each of the following rules into formal logic symbols. Then, determine and write the rule's contrapositive.

1.
If the stand carries kiwis, then it does not carry pears.[31]
    Translation: _____
    Contrapositive: _____

2.
Onawa is at Souderton if Juarez is at Randsborough.[32]
    Translation: _____
    Contrapositive: _____

3.
A film in Italian is not shown unless a film in
Norwegian is going to be shown the next day.[33]
    Translation: _____
    Contrapositive: _____

4.
If the schnauzer is placed on Wednesday, the husky is
placed on Tuesday.[34]
    Translation: _____
    Contrapositive: _____

5.
If Nation Y exports rice, then Nations X and Z both
export tea.[35]
    Translation: _____
    Contrapositive: _____

---

[31] PrepTest 36, Sec. 4, Game 1

[32] PrepTest 34, Sec. 4, Game 4

[33] PrepTest 49, Sec. 1, Game 1

[34] PrepTest 44, Sec. 3, Game 2

[35] PrepTest 45, Sec. 3, Game 4

Answer Explanations follow on the next page.

Explanations

As you review these explanations, don't worry if your "translation" matches the given contrapositive, and vice versa. As long as the two statements you've written match the two suggested symbolizations, you've done the right work. Remember, the two statements are simply contrapositives of one another.

1.

If the stand carries kiwis, then it does not carry pears.[36]
    Translation:

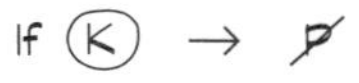

$$\text{If } Ⓚ \rightarrow \cancel{P}$$

Figure 3.36

Contrapositive:

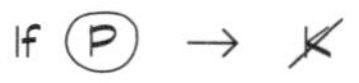

$$\text{If } Ⓟ \rightarrow \cancel{K}$$

Figure 3.37

This is a common rule to see in Selection, Distribution, and Matching games. Essentially, it just tells you that the two entities must be kept apart. While it's important to understand the translation and its contrapositive, on test day, you'll likely want to symbolize this rule more simply:

Figure 3.38

2.

Onawa is at Souderton if Juarez is at Randsborough.[37]
    Translation:

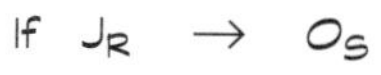

$$\text{If } J_R \rightarrow O_S$$

Figure 3.39

Contrapositive:

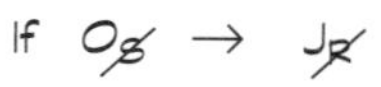

$$\text{If } O_{\cancel{S}} \rightarrow J_{\cancel{R}}$$

Figure 3.40

This is another fairly straightforward "if-then." One thing to be careful of here is the fact that the "if" clause (the sufficient condition) follows the "then" (necessary) clause in the sentence. Also note that if there are only two groups into which you can place the entities (in this game, everyone has to be assigned to only one clinic, either Souderton or Randsborough), you can also symbolize the rule this way:

---

[36] PrepTest 36, Sec. 4, Game 1
[37] PrepTest 34, Sec. 4, Game 4

$$\text{If } \quad O_R \quad \rightarrow \quad J_S$$

Figure 3.41

This is possible because, with only two possible placements, *not* being placed in Souderton is the same thing as being placed at Randsborough, and vice versa. Use discretion, though, because this would not work in a case where more than two placements are possible or where not every entity had to be used.

3.

A film in Italian is not shown unless a film in Norwegian is going to be shown the next day.[38]

    Translation:

Figure 3.42

Contrapositive:

Figure 3.43

This rule provides a golden opportunity to exploit the framework of your sketch. The more that your scratch work allows you to "see" which arrangements follow the rules and which ones break them, the faster you'll be able to eliminate wrong answers and zero in on the correct choice.

4.

If the schnauzer is placed on Wednesday, the husky is placed on Tuesday.[39]

    Translation:

$$\text{If } \quad S_{Wed} \quad \rightarrow \quad H_{Tue}$$

Figure 3.44

Contrapositive:

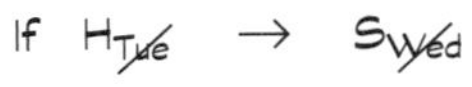

$$\text{If } \quad \cancel{H_{Tue}} \quad \rightarrow \quad \cancel{S_{Wed}}$$

Figure 3.45

This is a rule that requires you to account not only for the entity, but also for the day. In this game, by the way, there were more than two days on which each dog could be placed, so the alternative symbolism suggested for the previous rule would not work here.

---

[38] PrepTest 49, Sec. 1, Game 1
[39] PrepTest 44, Sec. 3, Game 2

5.

If Nation Y exports rice, then Nations X and Z both export tea.[40]

Translation:

$$\text{If } Y_r \rightarrow X_+ \text{ and } Z_+$$

Figure 3.46

Contrapositive:

$$\text{If } X_{\cancel{+}} \text{ or } Z_{\cancel{+}} \rightarrow Y_{\cancel{r}}$$

Figure 3.47

This is your run-of-the-mill, complex "if-then," meaning simply that it restricts three entities. Provided that you correctly swap the "and" in the necessary clause for an "or" in the sufficient clause of the contrapositive, this one should pose no special problems.

COMBINE FORMAL LOGIC RULES: IF A ➜ B + IF B ➜ C = IF A ➜ C

There's just one more thing that you need to learn to do with formal logic to have complete mastery of the topic on test day. In this section, I'll teach you how to combine formal logic rules in order to achieve even greater certainty about the acceptable arrangements or selections. This will be your first foray into the Deductions step of the Kaplan Method, and it makes a perfect springboard for the next chapter. As you'll soon see, for some LSAT logic games, combinations of the formal logic rules are the only deductions you need to make in order to get all of the questions right.

Create Strings of Logic

Somewhere along the line, you've probably seen someone reason by means of a syllogism. They used two (or more) premises that shared a common term to reach a valid deduction. Here are a couple of examples:

> Socrates is human.
> All humans are mortal.
> Therefore, Socrates is mortal.

> All dogs are mammals.
> All mammals are warm-blooded.
> Therefore, dogs are warm-blooded.

---

[40] PrepTest 45, Sec. 3, Game 4

Those logical deductions probably sound familiar (at least in the form they take). What you may not have realized is that they're created by linking two conditional "if-then" formal logic statements in order to draw a valid inference. Look at the two syllogisms again, this time symbolized as formal logic.

$$\text{If } S \rightarrow h$$
$$\text{If } h \rightarrow M$$
$$\text{Thus, If } S \rightarrow M$$

$$\text{If } d \rightarrow M$$
$$\text{If } M \rightarrow Wb$$
$$\text{Thus, If } d \rightarrow Wb$$

Figure 3.48

Notice that, in each case, the two premises can be combined because the necessary ("then") clause of the first contains precisely the same term as the sufficient ("if") clause of the second.

This is another reason why your ability to correctly form the contrapositive of formal logic rules is so valuable. Imagine that you have two rules for assigning students to various Physical Education activities:

1. If Dave plays soccer, then Carl must play soccer.
2. If Evelyn plays basketball, then Carl cannot play soccer.

Carl is duplicated in both rules, but it may not be immediately apparent how the rules can be combined. One of them has a condition sufficient to demonstrate that Carl plays soccer, while the other has a condition sufficient to prevent his playing soccer. But take a moment to translate the rules and form their contrapositives, and it will become clear.

$$1.\ \text{If } D_s \rightarrow C_s$$
$$\text{If } C_{\cancel{s}} \rightarrow D_{\cancel{s}}$$
$$2.\ \text{If } E_b \rightarrow C_{\cancel{s}}$$
$$\text{If } C_s \rightarrow E_{\cancel{b}}$$

Figure 3.49

The translation of Rule 1 combines perfectly with the contrapositive of Rule 2. By combining the two, you can infer that whenever Dave plays soccer, Evelyn does not play basketball. Moreover, the translation of Rule 2 combines with the contrapositive of Rule 1. When Evelyn plays basketball, Carl cannot play soccer. And when Carl doesn't play soccer, Dave can't either. Thus, you have an additional, valid restriction available to limit the acceptable assignments of students to teams: Whenever Evelyn plays basketball, Dave cannot play soccer.

Students often ask whether they should take the time to write out all of the combinations and connections they spot among formal logic rules before they tackle the questions on test day. I'd recommend against it, provided that you make a clear, easy-to-reference list of the formal logic rules and their contrapositives as I have done. With a list like that one, you can quickly spot any "then" results that trigger other "if" clauses. From there, you'll be able to assemble the strings of logic: "When A is chosen, so is B. And if B is chosen, D is ruled out. If no D, then no F," and so on.

Look for "Thens" that Trigger "Ifs"

Now, take a look at how the LSAT test makers design logic games to reward you for recognizing these strings of logic.

Below, I've reproduced the setup and rules from a Selection game. You've seen a couple of the rules already in your translation and contrapositive practice. As you see the setup in its entirety, notice that every one of the rules is a conditional, formal logic "if-then." Take a couple of minutes to symbolize each of the rules and form their contrapositives. Try to follow the suggestion above and line them up neatly, so that you'll be able spot the connections among the rules. When you're done, check your scratch work for each of the individual rules against the sample symbolizations I've provided. Then I'll quiz you on your ability to spot the connections and combine the rules to make additional deductions.

A fruit stand carries one of the following kinds of fruit: figs, kiwis, oranges, pears, tangerines, and watermelons. The stand does not carry any other kind of fruit. The selection of fruits the stand carries is consistent with the following conditions:

> If the stand carries kiwis, then it does not carry pears.
> If the stand does not carry tangerines, then it carries kiwis.
> If the stand carries oranges, then it carries both pears and watermelons.
> If the stand carries watermelons, then it carries figs or tangerines or both.[41]

---

[41] PrepTest 36, Sec. 4, Game 1

Explanations

How did you do?

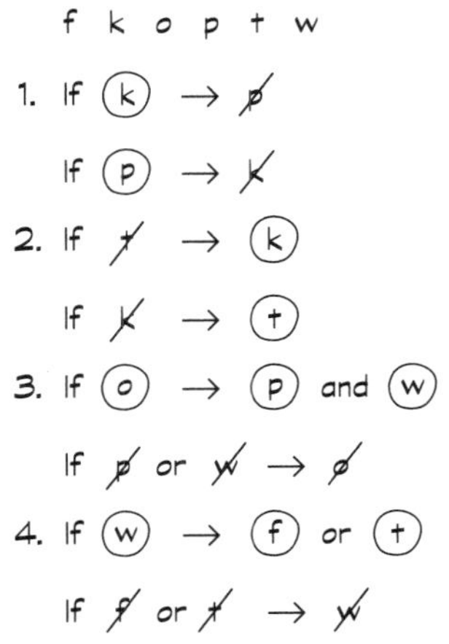

```
        f  k  o  p  t  w
1. If (k) → p̸
   If (p) → k̸
2. If k̸ → (k)
   If k̸ → (t)
3. If (o) → (p) and (w)
   If p̸ or w̸ → o̸
4. If (w) → (f) or (t)
   If f̸ or t̸ → w̸
```

Figure 3.50

If your scratch work matches what's here, you've absorbed the earlier portions of this chapter expertly already. If you missed (or messed up) any of the translations or contrapositives, make sure you review the rule to see where you went off course. For now, you can consult the sample scratch work provided in order to see how the rules combine to yield additional deductions. I've numbered the rules here to make this discussion easier to follow. You won't need to number them on test day.

Here's an example of what I'll be asking you to do.

If the stand carries kiwis, what else can you determine? _____

The correct answer here would be: "The stand does not carry pears and does not carry oranges."

Make sure you see how you get to that answer. The sufficient condition in the question is that the stand carries kiwis. "If k" appears in Rule 1. It's sufficient to rule out pears. That result (no pears) appears in the "if" clause of Rule 3's contrapositive: If pears *or* watermelons are out, then so are oranges. You know nothing about watermelons in this case, but since you've ruled out pears, you can rule out oranges as well. Scan down the list of "ifs." "No oranges" doesn't appear in any of them. So you know that you've exhausted the available deductions.

Try another one.

If the stand carries figs, what else can you determine? _____

The correct answer this time is: "Nothing."

Scan down the list of statements. Choosing figs never appears as the sufficient ("if") condition in any of the rules or contrapositives. Only *not* carrying figs has additional implications (as seen in the contrapositive of Rule 4).

DRILL: COMBINING FORMAL LOGIC RULES

Use the same game setup and scratch work to answer the questions below. For each, push the "string of logic" deductions as far as they can go with certainty, but no farther. Remember, some of the questions may produce no further deductions. In such cases, answer "Nothing."

A fruit stand carries one of the following kinds of fruit: figs, kiwis, oranges, pears, tangerines, and watermelons. The stand does not carry any other kind of fruit. The selection of fruits the stand carries is consistent with the following conditions:

   If the stand carries kiwis, then it does not carry pears.
   If the stand does not carry tangerines, then it carries kiwis.
   If the stand carries oranges, then it carries both pears and
     watermelons.
   If the stand carries watermelons, then it carries figs or
     tangerines or both.[42]

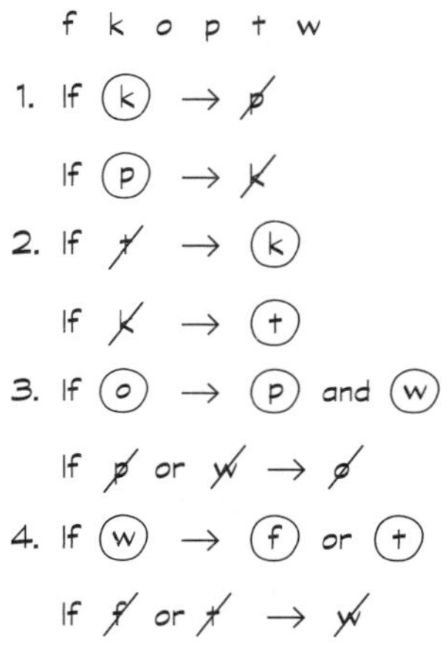

f k o p t w

1. If ⓚ → p̸

   If ⓟ → k̸

2. If k̸ → ⓚ

   If k̸ → ⓣ

3. If ⓞ → ⓟ and ⓦ

   If p̸ or w̸ → o̸

4. If ⓦ → ⓕ or ⓣ

   If f̸ or t̸ → w̸

Figure 3.51

1. If the stand does not carry figs, what else can you determine?

   _____

2. If the stand does not carry kiwis, what else can you determine?

   _____

3. If the stand carries oranges, what else can you determine?

   _____

4. If the stand does not carry oranges, what else can you determine?

   _____

---

[42] PrepTest 36, Sec. 4, Game 1

Answer Explanations follow on the next page.

Explanations

1. If the stand does not carry figs, what else can you determine?

Nothing. "No figs *and* no tangerines" is a trigger in the contrapositive of Rule 4. So if you also knew that tangerines were forbidden, learning that figs are out would allow you to make additional deductions. But knowing only that figs are out doesn't trigger any of the rules' "if" clauses.

2. If the stand does not carry kiwis, what else can you determine?

The stand carries tangerines. "No kiwis" is the sufficient condition in the contrapositive of Rule 2, resulting in "carries tangerines." The stand carrying tangerines doesn't trigger any other rules, so no additional deductions are available.

3. If the stand carries oranges, what else can you determine?

The stand carries pears, watermelons, and tangerines; the stand does not carry kiwis. This one has huge implications for the game. "Carries oranges" is the sufficient trigger in Rule 3, resulting in "carries pears *and* carries watermelons." Pursue each of those results separately. "Carries pears" is the sufficient condition in the contrapositive of Rule 1, resulting in "no kiwis." "No kiwis" is the sufficient condition in the contrapositive of Rule 2, resulting in "carries tangerines." That exhausts one string of logic, but you still need to find out what's triggered by "carries watermelons." That's the trigger in Rule 4, resulting in "carries at least one of figs or tangerines." Since tangerines are already definitely in, the best you can say is that the stand *could* carry figs. It's not certain that the stand will carry figs, however.

4. If the stand does not carry oranges, what else can you determine?

Nothing. "No oranges" isn't found in any "if" clause. So knowing that it's true doesn't lead to any additional combinations or deductions.

5. If the stand carries pears, what else can you determine?

The stand does not carry kiwis; the stand carries tangerines. "Carries pears" is the trigger in the contrapositive of Rule 1. It results in "no kiwis." "No kiwis" is then the trigger in the contrapositive of Rule 2, resulting in "carries tangerines." That result is not found in the "if" clause of any further rules, so your string of logic runs out here.

Notice how some of the hypothetical situations posed in the questions led to long strings of deductions, while others yielded nothing at all. That's the way it will always be in games that feature formal logic. Don't feel that you've failed when you find out that some rules or conditions don't lead to additional deductions. In fact, you've succeeded anytime you can say, with certainty, "Nothing else can be determined here." Remember, the test makers ask for what must, cannot, and could be true. Sometimes you can infer, "The stand will not carry oranges in this case." Other times, you wind up saying, "The stand might carry oranges, but it doesn't have to." Depending on the question, either of those could be the right answer.

Speaking of question and answers, it's time to apply all that you've learned about formal logic to some complete logic games. In the section that follows, I'll have you translate all of the rules, form their contrapositives, and look for the strings of logic that are likely to be most limiting and helpful. Finally, I'll show that you can answer all of the questions associated with the games using nothing more than what you've learned in this chapter.

COMPLETE GAME PRACTICE

From time to time, the test makers will present you with games that turn entirely on formal logic rules. You may or may not get a game like this one on your official LSAT, but if you do, think back to this chapter and put all of the skills and techniques discussed here into practice. You've already seen the following game setup, but now you can look at it knowing that you've been exposed to everything you'll need in order to handle it flawlessly.

Start by taking around four minutes to set it up. Sketch it out. List out all of the rules and their contrapositives, and look for rules that can be combined for additional deductions. Then I'll review the correct step-by-step application of the Kaplan Method.

> An album contains photographs picturing seven friends:
> Raimundo, Selma, Ty, Umiko, Wendy, Yakira, Zack. The
> friends appear either alone or in groups with one another, in
> accordance with the following:
> > Wendy appears in every photograph that Selma appears in.
> > Selma appears in every photograph that Umiko appears in.
> > Raimundo appears in every photograph that Yakira does
> > not appear in.
> > Neither Ty nor Raimundo appears in any photograph that
> > Wendy appears in.[43]

STEPS 1 AND 2: Overview and Sketch

It's not hard to get a picture (pun intended) of your task here. You're a photographer, and you have to ensure that the correct groups are together in the shots. Sometimes that will mean calling for someone else to get in the shot; sometimes you'll have to ask someone to step out of the frame. "Choose her; reject him"—this is a Selection game. As such, there's no need for you to create any framework within your sketch. Just maintain a list of the entities. You'll circle those who are included and strike through those who are excluded in any given question.

---

[43] PrepTest 45, Sec. 3, Game 3

STEP 3: Rules

All of the rules are formal logic, albeit in language that requires some careful translation to be sure that you've correctly identified the sufficient and necessary terms. Compare your list of translations and contrapositives with the scratch work below. Again, I've numbered the rules for convenience in referencing them in the discussion and explanations.

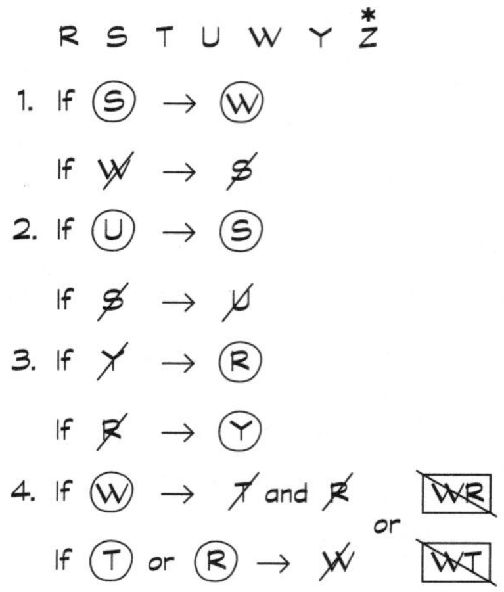

Figure 3.52

Here are a few key questions to ask as you're reviewing your setup work:

- Did you get the correct terms in the "if" and "then" positions in Rules 1 and 2?
- Did you remember that Rule 3 means "At least one of Y or R is included every time"?
- Did you recognize that Rule 3 allows Y and R to be together in a photograph?
- Did you translate the "Neither . . . nor . . ." construction in Rule 4 correctly?
- Did you remember to swap the "and" for "or" in the contrapositive of Rule 4?
- Did you indicate that Z is the floater, unrestricted by any of the rules?

If you got the rules and contrapositives sketched correctly, you're ready for the Deductions step..

STEP 4: Deductions

While the next chapter will cover all of the various types of deductions you'll be rewarded for making on test day, you have learned enough about formal logic in this chapter to cover all the deductions in this game. If you haven't done so already, take a moment to note which rules can be combined.

Here's the list:

- Rules 1 and 2 combine because they share Selma. Together, they allow you to deduce that whenever Umiko is chosen, Wendy will be, too. Combining their contrapositives, you can see that whenever Wendy is not in the photo, Umiko will not be, either.

- Rules 1 and 4 combine because they share Wendy. Together, they allow you to deduce that whenever Selma appears in the photo, Ty and Raimundo must stay out of the picture. Likewise, the contrapositives of the two rules tell you that if either Ty or Raimundo is included in the picture, Selma must stay out.
- Finally, Rules 3 and 4 combine because they share Raimundo. Thus, whenever Yakira does not appear, Wendy must not appear. Conversely—link the two contrapositives—when Wendy is in the picture, Raimundo is out, so Yakira must be in.

Because of all these shared entities, the combinations can actually allow you to link all four rules into one long string of logic, depending on your starting point. For example, if Umiko appears, Rule 2 tells you that Selma must also appear. Rule 1 is triggered, and Wendy must also get into the photo. That puts Rule 4 into play; both Ty and Raimundo are excluded. Raimundo's exclusion triggers Rule 3, and Yakira must step into the shot. Only floater Zack remains untouched in this string of valid inferences.

On test day, I encourage you *not* to try to determine (or write out) all of the various possible linkages. Rather, make your list of rules and contrapositives clear and easy to consult. You can note the "likely suspects," but the various "if" questions will trigger your strings of logic, which will lead you straight to the right answers.

STEP 5: Questions

Go ahead and try the question set now. You've seen a couple of these questions before, but doing them again with a complete sketch will be good practice.

An album contains photographs picturing seven friends: Raimundo, Selma, Ty, Umiko, Wendy, Yakira, Zack. The friends appear either alone or in groups with one another, in accordance with the following:

Wendy appears in every photograph that Selma appears in.
Selma appears in every photograph that Umiko appears in.
Raimundo appears in every photograph that Yakira does not appear in.
Neither Ty nor Raimundo appears in any photograph that Wendy appears in.

13. Which one of the following could be a complete and accurate list of the friends who appear together in a photograph?

(A) Raimundo, Selma, Ty, Wendy
(B) Raimundo, Ty, Yakira, Zack
(C) Raimundo, Wendy, Yakira, Zack
(D) Selma, Ty, Umiko, Yakira
(E) Selma, Ty, Umiko, Zack

14. If Ty and Zack appear together in a photograph, then which one of the following must be true?

(A) Selma also appears in the photograph.
(B) Yakira also appears in the photograph.
(C) Wendy also appears in the photograph.
(D) Raimundo does not appear in the photograph.
(E) Umiko does not appear in the photograph.

15. What is the maximum number of friends who could appear in a photograph that Yakira does not appear in?

(A) six
(B) five
(C) four
(D) three
(E) two

16. If Umiko and Zack appear together in a photograph, then exactly how many of the other friends must also appear in that photograph?

(A) four
(B) three
(C) two
(D) one
(E) zero

17. If exactly three friends appear together in a photograph, then each of the following could be true EXCEPT:

(A) Selma and Zack both appear in the photograph.
(B) Ty and Yakira both appear in the photograph.
(C) Wendy and Selma both appear in the photograph.
(D) Yakira and Zack both appear in the photograph.
(E) Zack and Raimundo both appear in the photograph.[44]

---

[44] PrepTest 45, Sec. 3, Game 3, Qs 13–17

Answer Explanations follow on the next page.

Explanations

13. **(B)**

Which one of the following could be a complete and
accurate list of the friends who appear together in a photograph?

(A)   Raimundo, Selma, Ty, Wendy
(B)   Raimundo, Ty, Yakira, Zack
(C)   Raimundo, Wendy, Yakira, Zack
(D)   Selma, Ty, Umiko, Yakira
(E)   Selma, Ty, Umiko, Zack[45]

You've seen this Acceptability question in chapter 2. Did you remember to eliminate answers rule-by-rule as you spotted violations? Rule 1 got rid of choices (D) and (E), both of which have Selma but not Wendy. Rule 4 eliminated choices (A) and (C), both of which have Wendy and Raimundo appearing together in the photograph. That left (B) as the correct answer, the only one to violate none of the rules.

14. **(E)**

If Ty and Zack appear together in a photograph, then
which one of the following must be true?

(A)   Selma also appears in the photograph.
(B)   Yakira also appears in the photograph.
(C)   Wendy also appears in the photograph.
(D)   Raimundo does not appear in the photograph.
(E)   Umiko does not appear in the photograph.[46]

Here's the first question that put your formal logic deductions to the test. The "if" clause at the beginning of the question prompts you to create a mini-sketch consisting of your list of entities. Circle T and Z as prescribed by the question stem.

R S Ⓣ U W Y Ⓩ

Figure 3.53

Zack is the floater, so his inclusion won't trigger any additional deductions. But the inclusion of Ty in the photo calls for the contrapositive of Rule 4. Since T is in, cross W off the list.

R S Ⓣ U W̸ Y Ⓩ

Figure 3.54

"No Wendy" triggers the contrapositive of Rule 1. Thus, cross S off the list, too.

R S̸ Ⓣ U W̸ Y Ⓩ

Figure 3.55

---

[45] PrepTest 45, Sec. 3, Q 13

[46] PrepTest 45, Sec. 3, Q 14

"No Selma" puts the contrapositive of Rule 2 into play. Exclude U from the photo.

$$R \;\not{S}\; \textcircled{T} \;\not{U}\; \not{W} \; Y \; \textcircled{Z}$$

Figure 3.56

You can't make any further deductions, so you're ready for the answer choices. The only one that must be true according to your mini-sketch is choice (E). Choices (A) and (C) must be false, while choices (B) and (D) could be either true or false in this case.

15. **(D)**

What is the maximum number of friends who could appear in a photograph that Yakira does not appear in?

(A) six
(B) five
(C) four
(D) three
(E) two[47]

This question stem doesn't begin with an "if" clause, but it still presents you with a hypothetical condition: "a photograph that Yakira does not appear in." Begin your work with a list of the entities with Y struck out.

$$R \; S \; T \; U \; W \; \not{Y} \; Z$$

Figure 3.57

Y's exclusion triggers Rule 3, of course, and that means that Raimundo must be in the photograph. Circle R in your list.

$$\textcircled{R} \; S \; T \; U \; W \; \not{Y} \; Z$$

Figure 3.58

Including R in the photo means excluding W, according to Rule 4's contrapositive. So cross out W.

$$\textcircled{R} \; S \; T \; U \; \not{W} \; \not{Y} \; Z$$

Figure 3.59

"No Wendy" triggers the contrapositive of Rule 1. That means that you must cross S off the list.

$$\textcircled{R} \;\not{S}\; T \; U \; \not{W} \; \not{Y} \; Z$$

Figure 3.60

---

[47] PrepTest 45, Sec. 3, Q 15

Finally, eliminating S is the sufficient condition in the contrapositive of Rule 2. Eliminate U from your mini-sketch list.

$$\text{(R)} \;\; \cancel{S} \;\; T \;\; \cancel{U} \;\; \cancel{W} \;\; \cancel{Y} \;\; Z$$

Figure 3.60A

You've exhausted all four rules here, so evaluate the answer choices. According to your list Raimundo is definitely in the picture, while Ty and floater Zack could be. The maximum number of friends who could appear is three, making (D) the correct answer.

16. **(B)**

If Umiko and Zack appear together in a photograph, then exactly how many of the other friends must also appear in that photograph?

(A) four
(B) three
(C) two
(D) one
(E) zero[48]

Here's yet another question that calls for a mini-sketch and a string of logic. This will be no surprise to you by test day. Begin your work this time with a list of entities with U and Z circled as per the question stem.

$$\text{R} \;\; \text{S} \;\; \text{T} \;\; \text{(U)} \;\; \text{W} \;\; \text{Y} \;\; \text{(Z)}$$

Figure 3.61

Floater Zack doesn't impact any other entities, so the deductions will come as a result of including Umiko. Do you remember the long string of inferences that her appearance triggers? Here it is again.

Rule 2: Including Umiko means including Selma.

$$\text{R} \;\; \text{(S)} \;\; \text{T} \;\; \text{(U)} \;\; \text{W} \;\; \text{Y} \;\; \text{(Z)}$$

Figure 3.62

Rule 1: Including Selma means including Wendy.

$$\text{R} \;\; \text{(S)} \;\; \text{T} \;\; \text{(U)} \;\; \text{(W)} \;\; \text{Y} \;\; \text{(Z)}$$

Figure 3.63

---

[48] PrepTest 45, Sec. 3, Q 16

Rule 4: Including Wendy means excluding Ty and Raimundo.

R̸ (S) T̸ (U) (W) Y (Z)

Figure 3.64

Finally, Rule 3's contrapositive: Excluding Raimundo means including Yakira.

R̸ (S) T̸ (U) (W) (Y) (Z)

Figure 3.65

Your entire list is determined. Everyone is either in or out. There are a total of five friends in the picture, which means that there are three in addition to Umiko and Zack. Choice (B) is the correct answer.

17. **(A)**

> If exactly three friends appear together in a photograph, then each of the following could be true EXCEPT:
>
> (A)   Selma and Zack both appear in the photograph.
> (B)   Ty and Yakira both appear in the photograph.
> (C)   Wendy and Selma both appear in the photograph.
> (D)   Yakira and Zack both appear in the photograph.
> (E)   Zack and Raimundo both appear in the photograph.[49]

This question doesn't provide a hypothetical "if" that you can easily write out as a mini-sketch. Rather, it provides a number-based restriction: Exactly three friends are in the photograph. Moreover, the correct answer will be the one that *cannot* have exactly three friends in it. Still, you can apply what you've learned from this chapter and get the correct answer straightaway. Simply turn each answer into a mini-sketch and make the deductions that follow. One, and only one, of the answers will not allow you to have exactly three friends in the picture.

Starting with choice (A), write out the list of entities and circle S and Z.

R (S) T U W Y (Z)

Figure 3.66

According to Rule 1, including Selma means including Wendy.

R (S) T U (W) Y (Z)

Figure 3.67

49 PrepTest 45, Sec. 3, Q 17

Wendy's appearance triggers Rule 4, meaning that you can cross off R and T.

$$\cancel{R} \; \textcircled{S} \; \cancel{T} \; \cup \; \textcircled{W} \; Y \; \textcircled{Z}$$

Figure 3.68

Removing Raimundo from the photograph triggers the contrapositive of Rule 3 and requires Yakira to get into the picture.

$$\cancel{R} \; \textcircled{S} \; \cancel{T} \; \cup \; \textcircled{W}\textcircled{Y}\textcircled{Z}$$

Figure 3.69

Voilà! Choice (A) requires at least four friends to be in the photograph. That means it cannot be true under the conditions of the question. You've got the right answer.

All four of the other choices would allow you to stop with exactly three friends in the photo. Try sketching them out for practice. But on test day, stop right here. You have the right answer and you can move on to the next game.

COMPLETE GAME PRACTICE

Speaking of the next game, there's one more formal logic-intensive game that I'd like you to try before moving on to the next chapter. Again, it's a Selection game and again, all of the rules are conditional, formal logic statements. The challenge in the Friends' Photograph game was in translating the rules. In the game that follows, all of the rules are presented in the standard "if-then" format. But be careful. They are quite complex. Take your time and make sure you've gotten your symbolism for the rules and contrapositives clear and correct. If you want to double-check your setup work before tackling the questions, turn to the Explanations and review Steps 1 through 4 of the Kaplan Method. Then come back and try the questions. I'm confident that with the rules and their contrapositives sketched correctly, you can get all of the points available here.

Complete this game and all of its questions. Do not time yourself. Your goal, at this point, should be to interpret each of the rules correctly, determine their contrapositives, and make all of the deductions as called for by the questions. Your speed and efficiency will improve with additional practice.

Questions 13–17

A summer program offers at least one of the following seven courses: geography, history, literature, mathematics, psychology, sociology, zoology. The following restrictions on the program must apply:

If mathematics is offered, then either literature or sociology (but not both) is offered.

If literature is offered, then geography is also offered but psychology is not.

If sociology is offered, then psychology is also offered but zoology is not.

If geography is offered, then both history and zoology are also offered.

13. Which one of the following could be a complete and accurate list of the courses offered by the summer program?

    (A) history, psychology
    (B) geography, history, literature
    (C) history, mathematics, psychology
    (D) literature, mathematics, psychology
    (E) history, literature, mathematics, sociology

14. If the summer program offers literature, then which one of the following could be true?

    (A) Sociology is offered.
    (B) History is not offered.
    (C) Mathematics is not offered.
    (D) A total of two courses are offered.
    (E) Zoology is not offered.

15. If history is not offered by the summer program, then which one of the following is another course that CANNOT be offered?

    (A) literature
    (B) mathematics
    (C) psychology
    (D) sociology
    (E) zoology

16. If the summer program offers mathematics, then which one of the following must be true?

    (A) Literature is offered.
    (B) Psychology is offered.
    (C) Sociology is offered.
    (D) At least three courses are offered.
    (E) At most four courses are offered.

17. Which one of the following must be false of the summer program?

    (A) Both geography and psychology are offered.
    (B) Both geography and mathematics are offered.
    (C) Both psychology and mathematics are offered.
    (D) Both history and mathematics are offered.
    (E) Both geography and sociology are offered.[50]

(Don't Fear) Formal Logic

If you were a test taker who came to this book intimidated by formal logic with its jargon and symbols, I hope this chapter has given you some confidence. There's no way to know whether formal logic will feature prominently in the logic games section on your LSAT, but by learning (and, more importantly, by practicing) the principles and techniques presented here, you'll be able to turn any formal logic you encounter into certain LSAT points.

The strings of logic you can create by combining formal logic statements are just one type of deduction that will put you in control of logic games. In the next chapter, I'll outline the others, five types of deductions that will make it possible for you to answer any logic games question that the test makers can devise.

CHAPTER 4

DEDUCTIONS

WHY YOU MAKE DEDUCTIONS

You're standing on the edge of logic games mastery. Step 4 of the Kaplan Method—Deductions—is so important that I want to pause for a moment to put it in context. Remember back to chapter 1, where I gave you an example of a real-world task that you might have working in a law office. Your boss, the attorney, asks you for a document showing the order of witnesses for an upcoming trial and what each witness will testify about. In chapter 1, you were just concerned with understanding your task and with picturing how you'd lay out such a document so that it would be easy to use in a meeting with the client. As you get ready for the meeting, you're going to consult the case files and start pulling the information together. It will have notes that resemble logic games rules: Jones cannot testify about payroll; we don't want Martin to be the first witness; if we have Norris testify about investments, we'll have O'Brien cover payroll; etc.

You don't want to head into the meeting with the client with a bunch of scattered papers and sticky notes. So you start entering what you know into your document. And you anticipate what your boss and the client will ask. They'll want to know what's determined and what still needs to be decided. You'll go in ready to say, "Jones has to be the first witness," or, "Either Norris or Paulino will testify about the investments." That same work, figuring out from your notes what must, can't, or could be the case, is what you're doing when you make deductions in logic games. At work, it will impress your boss that you're so organized and ready for the meeting. On the LSAT, it will get you the right answers and add points to your score.

Start with What's Most Certain

Learning to make deductions quickly and accurately takes some time. Almost all test takers realize the need to make games visual, even when they aren't yet very adept at doing so. They realize the need to account for the game's rules, even when they haven't learned to analyze them or add them into the sketch. But it is only the best test takers who develop the patience and rigor that it takes to make deductions.

The shortest path from the scramble of rules and restrictions to the clarity of deductions is to move from the most concrete restrictions in a game to the least. Fortunately, you've got a great head start on that from the work you did analyzing rules in chapter 2. To see how helpful deductions can be and to see what I mean by moving from the most to the least concrete restrictions, take a look at a fairly challenging game from PrepTest 53. Apply Steps 1 through 3 of the Kaplan Method—that is, conduct your overview to get a handle on the task, draw out your initial sketch, and analyze the rules. Afterward, I'll review the rules and show you how making the available deductions will allow you to answer the questions flawlessly in a matter of a few seconds each.

Questions 12–17

Detectives investigating a citywide increase in burglaries questioned exactly seven suspects—S, T, V, W, X, Y, and Z—each on a different one of seven consecutive days. Each suspect was questioned exactly once. Any suspect who confessed did so while being questioned. The investigation conformed to the following:

T was questioned on day three.
The suspect questioned on day four did not confess.
S was questioned after W was questioned.
Both X and V were questioned after Z was questioned.
No suspects confessed after W was questioned.
Exactly two suspects confessed after T was questioned.

12. Which one of the following could be true?

   (A) X was questioned on day one.
   (B) V was questioned on day two.
   (C) Z was questioned on day four.
   (D) W was questioned on day five.
   (E) S was questioned on day six.

13. If Z was the second suspect to confess, then each of the following statements could be true EXCEPT:

   (A) T confessed.
   (B) T did not confess.
   (C) V did not confess.
   (D) X confessed.
   (E) Y did not confess.

14. If Y was questioned after V but before X, then which one of the following could be true?

   (A) V did not confess.
   (B) Y confessed.
   (C) X did not confess.
   (D) X was questioned on day four.
   (E) Z was questioned on day two.

15. Which one of the following suspects must have been questioned before T was questioned?

   (A) V
   (B) W
   (C) X
   (D) Y
   (E) Z

16. If X and Y both confessed, then each of the following could be true EXCEPT:

   (A) V confessed.
   (B) X was questioned on day five.
   (C) Y was questioned on day one.
   (D) Z was questioned on day one.
   (E) Z did not confess.

17. If neither X nor V confessed, then which one of the following must be true?

   (A) T confessed.
   (B) V was questioned on day two.
   (C) X was questioned on day four.
   (D) Y confessed.
   (E) Z did not confess.[1]

Hopefully, you were able to apply Steps 1 through 3 of the Kaplan Method on this game without too much trouble.

STEPS 1 AND 2: Overview and Sketch

Your task is to set out a schedule of seven interrogations that happen, one per day, over the course of seven days. Along with the schedule, you'll need to keep track of who did and did not confess during questioning. Just like the Thunderstorm game from chapter 1, this is a hybrid of Sequencing and Matching. It's a little harder on the Sequencing side than the Thunderstorm game was (seven suspects versus five towns), but the sketch should look almost identical.

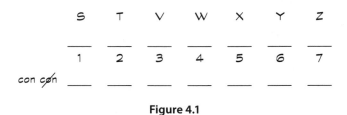

Figure 4.1

STEP 3: Rules

Seeing six rules should be a comfort; there simply has to be a great deal of restriction on the action. Make sure you jotted them down accurately.

Rule 1 was easy. T goes right into the sketch.

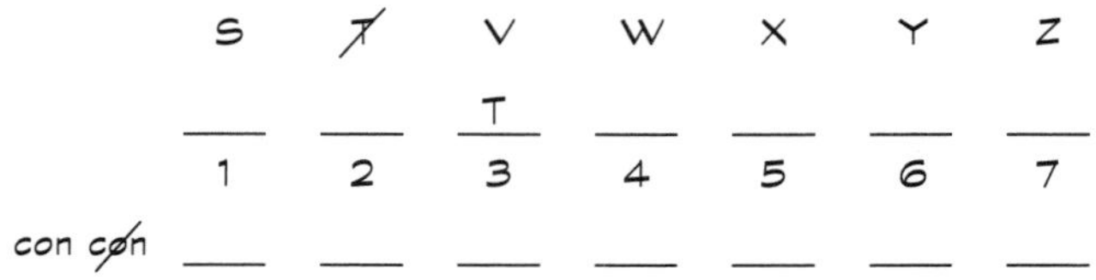

Figure 4.2

Rule 2 goes right in, too.

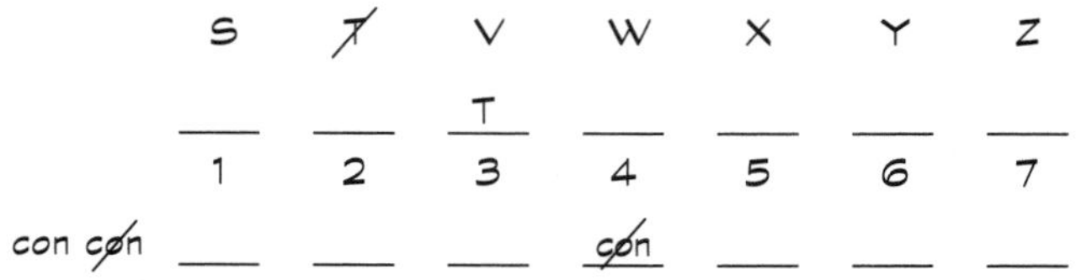

Figure 4.3

Rules 3 and 4 both restrict entities relative to each other. Make sure you recognize that Rule 4 does not give you any information about V and X relative to one another, only relative to Z.

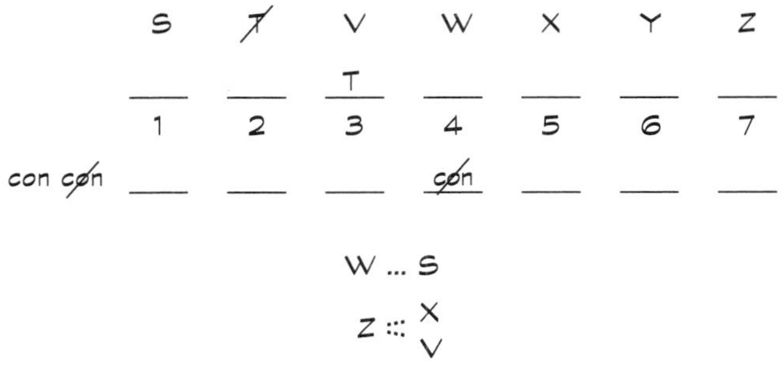

Figure 4.4

Rule 5 tells you that no one confessed after W's questioning, although it doesn't tell you whether W confessed.

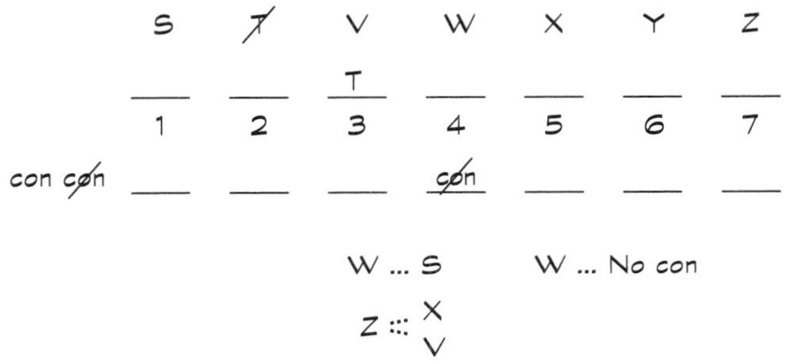

Figure 4.5

Finally, Rule 6 restricts three positions. There will be two cons on the bottom row after T's space on the top row.

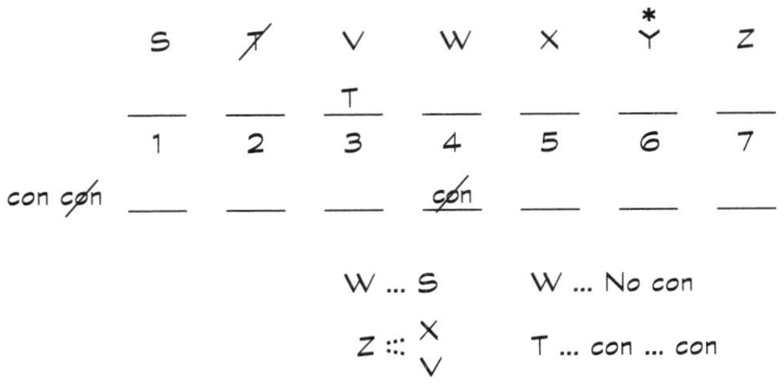

Figure 4.6

Notice, too, that Y is starred in that last sketch. It's the floater, unaffected by any rule.

This is about as far as most students ever learn to go. While it's always a good thing to get more rules in logic games, without deductions all of those rules can feel like the jumble of sticky notes in the case file. That's not how you wanted to go into the client meeting, and it's not how you want to go into the LSAT question set, either. If you have to deal with all six rules individually for every question, you can feel overwhelmed, make sloppy mistakes, and run out of time. If you're feeling ambitious, go back and try the questions. But don't spend too long. If you feel that you're getting bogged down or confused, I'll show you how making the deductions sorts all of this information and puts you in control of the questions.

STEP 4: Deductions

All of the information that you need is, in fact, contained in the setup and the rules, but it will still take you a long time to work through the questions if you don't pause to synthesize that information. The solution is Step 4 of the Kaplan Method: Deductions. There, you'll take a couple of minutes to organize the rules within your sketch. Before tackling the question set, you'll know precisely what is and isn't determined within the game.

The key to effective deductions is to work from what's concrete to what's less defined. Ask, "Who is the most restricted entity in this game?" and "Who presents the greatest restriction for the other entities and spaces?" Try that here.

In this game, the most restricted entity is T. Rule 1 establishes its position once and for all in space 3. Moreover, because of Rule 6, T imposes restrictions on two of the four positions that follow it. By combining those two rules, you can deduce that there will be two confessions and two non-confessions among interrogations 4 through 7.

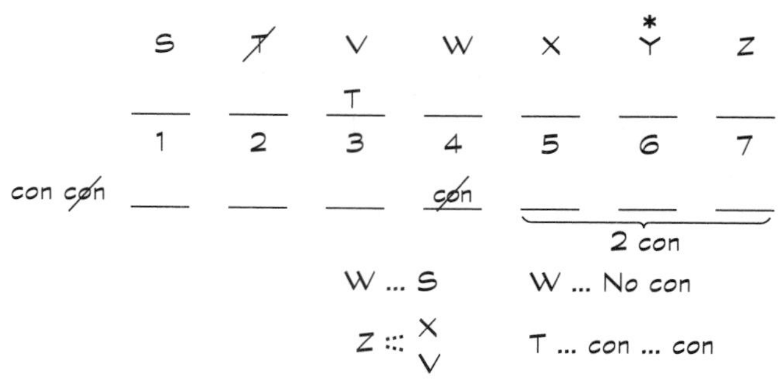

Figure 4.7

That deduction, in turn, implicates Rule 2. Since the fourth interrogation does not produce a confession, the two confessions following T must be from interrogations 5 and 6, 5 and 7, or 6 and 7. Who's affected by that? The answer is W, the other entity that shows up in two of the rules.

From Rules 3 and 5, you can conclude that S does not confess. Now that you've made the deductions regarding T and the interrogations that must produce confessions, you can add W and S right into the sketch. Since two people confess after T and no one confesses after W, W has to follow T. And according to Rule 3, S follows W.

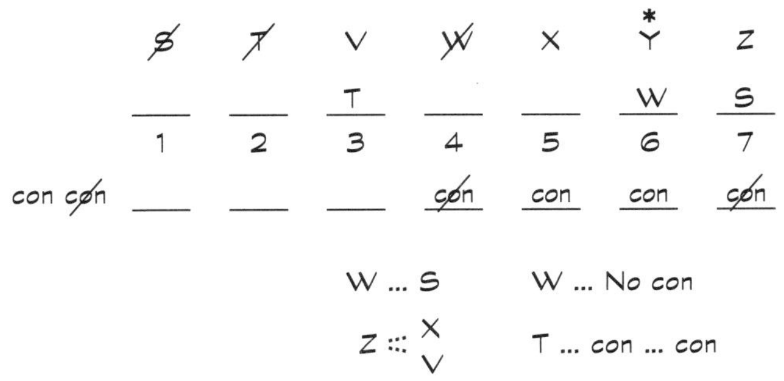

Figure 4.8

Since S must follow W (Rule 3), W cannot be the seventh suspect questioned. Since no one can confess after W is questioned (Rule 5), W must to be the sixth suspect interrogated. That makes S seventh, and it locks down interrogations 5 and 6 as the two that produce confessions following T's questioning.

Now you can see that Z, X, and V, all of whom are restricted in Rule 4, and floater Y, are the only entities left for interrogations 1, 2, 4, and 5. Of those entities, Z, which we know must precede both X and V is the most restricted. Z will wind up in either space 1 or space 2. You can write out the implications of those two Options:

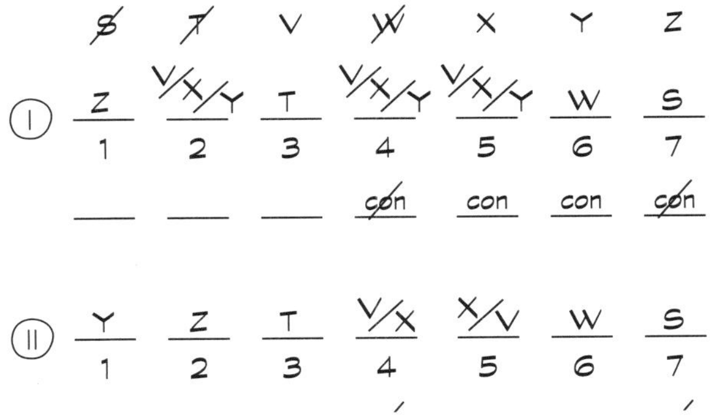

Figure 4.9

When Z is first, V, X, and Y can be arranged in any order among spaces 2, 4, and 5. When Z is second, Y will be the first suspect interrogated and V and X will take positions 4 and 5 in either order. At this point, the only thing you have no idea about is whether spaces 1 through 3 will produce any confessions.

You were able to add an enormous amount of additional certainty to this game. Reflect on how you did it. You started from the most restricted entity—T—and asked, "Which entities or spaces does its placement limit?" Adding your answer to that question into the sketch, you asked, "And what does *that* restrict?" and so on. Throughout this chapter, you'll get better at taking those steps, but that's essentially what making deductions always entails. When you get to the point at which you're just speculating—"I guess space 1 could confess, but it doesn't have to," for example—you're ready for the questions. You know all that can be known.

STEP 5: Questions

Using the final Master Sketch, go back and try to answer the question set. With a complete Master Sketch, I predict that you'll be able to answer all of the questions far more accurately (and much faster) than you could have before.

Explanations

I've reproduced the setup and Master Sketch here, for your reference. But, really, the sketch is all that you'll need. Take a look.

Detectives investigating a citywide increase in burglaries questioned exactly seven suspects—S, T, V, W, X, Y, and Z—each on a different one of seven consecutive days. Each suspect was questioned exactly once. Any suspect who confessed did so while being questioned. The investigation conformed to the following:

T was questioned on day three.
The suspect questioned on day four did not confess.
S was questioned after W was questioned.
Both X and V were questioned after Z was questioned.
No suspects confessed after W was questioned.
Exactly two suspects confessed after T was questioned.[2]

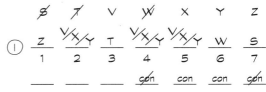

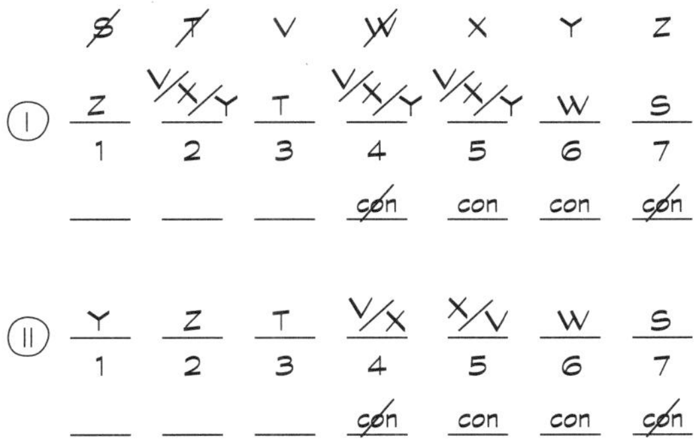

Figure 4.10

12. (B)

Which one of the following could be true?

(A) X was questioned on day one.
(B) V was questioned on day two.
(C) Z was questioned on day four.
(D) W was questioned on day five.
(E) S was questioned on day six.[3]

This question can be answered with nothing but a glance at your Master Sketch. Only choice (B) is possible (see Option I).

13. (E)

If Z was the second suspect to confess, then each of the following statements could be true EXCEPT:

(A) T confessed.
(B) T did not confess.
(C) V did not confess.
(D) X confessed.
(E) Y did not confess.[4]

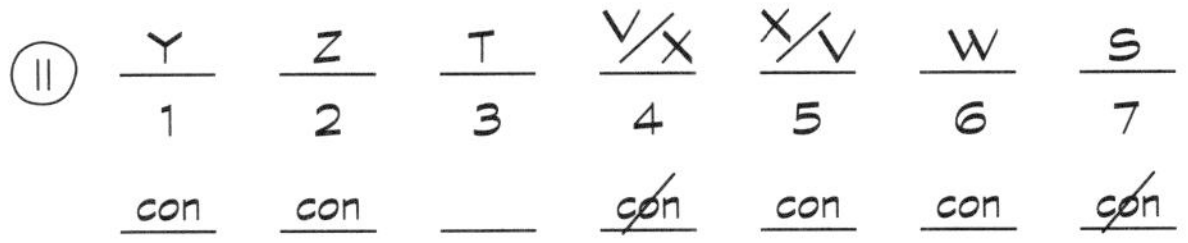

	Y	Z	T	V/X	X/V	W	S
(II)	1	2	3	4	5	6	7
	con	con		c~~on~~	con	con	c~~on~~

Figure 4.11

This question begins with a new "if" clause. If Z produces the second confession, you must consult Option II (after all, Z is in space 1 in Option I, so that won't work). Moreover, you now know that the first two interrogations produced confessions. That gives you the mini-sketch to use as you evaluate the answers for this question.

---

[2] PrepTest 53, Sec. 2, Game 3
[3] PrepTest 53, Sec. 2, Q 12
[4] PrepTest 53, Sec. 2, Q 13

The correct answer is the one that *must be false,* because the question stem says that the four wrong answers *could be true.* Only choice (E) *must be false.* Y must confess in this scenario, since it takes space 1 and Z produces the second confession in space 2.

14. **(A)**

If Y was questioned after V but before X, then which one of the following could be true?

(A) V did not confess.
(B) Y confessed.
(C) X did not confess.
(D) X was questioned on day four.
(E) Z was questioned on day two.[5]

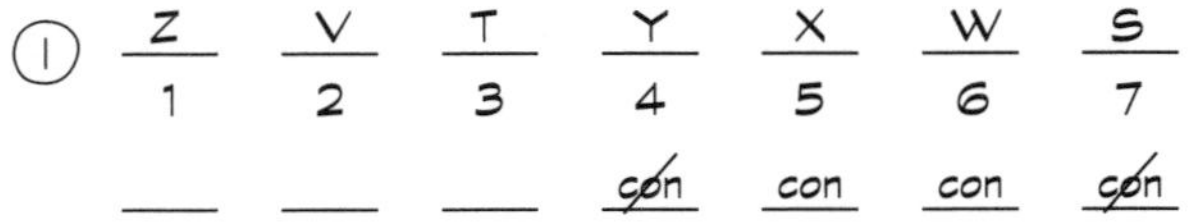

Figure 4.12

Here, the new "if" results in a completely determined sequence of interrogations. The only way to produce the order "V . . . Y . . . X" called for in the question stem is to use Option I. (In Option II, Y has to be in space 1.) Complete your mini-sketch with V in space 2, Y in space 4, and X in space 5. The only wiggle room left is whether spaces 1 through 3 did or didn't produce confessions.

The correct answer *could be true.* Choice (A) gives you such a statement. Since V is space 2 and you don't know whether the second interrogation produced a confession, it might be the case that V didn't confess. Consult your mini-sketch to see that all four wrong answers *must be false.* Y is in space 4 and did not confess. Choice (B) is out. X is in space 5 and did confess. That knocks out choices (C) and (D). In this scenario, Z must be the first interrogation. Choice (E) is impossible, too.

15. **(E)**

Which one of the following suspects must have been questioned before T was questioned?

(A) V
(B) W
(C) X
(D) Y
(E) Z[6]

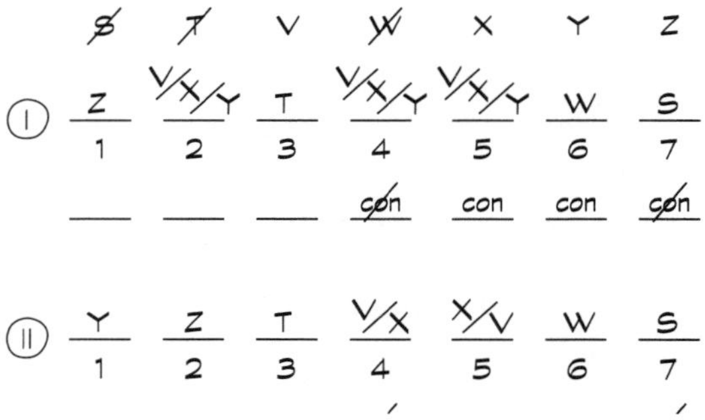

Figure 4.13

There's no new "if" restriction here, so as you did with question 12, answer this one directly from your Master Sketch. Which of the five entities in the answer choices comes prior to T in either Option? It's Z, of course, which must take either space 1 or space 2. That's choice (E), and you're done.

---

[5] PrepTest 53, Sec. 2, Q 14

[6] PrepTest 53, Sec. 2, Q 15

This question is a perfect illustration of the value of Step 4. If you try to forgo the time and effort of making a complete Master Sketch that includes your deductions, getting this answer could take you minutes as you work through the permutations of the six rules to be sure that V, W, X, and Y can each be acceptably placed after T. With the Deductions step behind you, this question takes all of five to ten seconds to answer correctly.

16. **(A)**

If X and Y both confessed, then each of the following could be true EXCEPT:

(A) V confessed.
(B) X was questioned on day five.
(C) Y was questioned on day one.
(D) Z was questioned on day one.
(E) Z did not confess.[7]

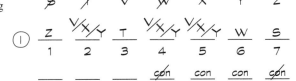

Figure 4.14

The "if" in this question can be accommodated in either Option I or Option II. What's important is to keep both X and Y out of space 4, where you know that the suspect does *not* confess.

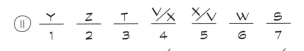

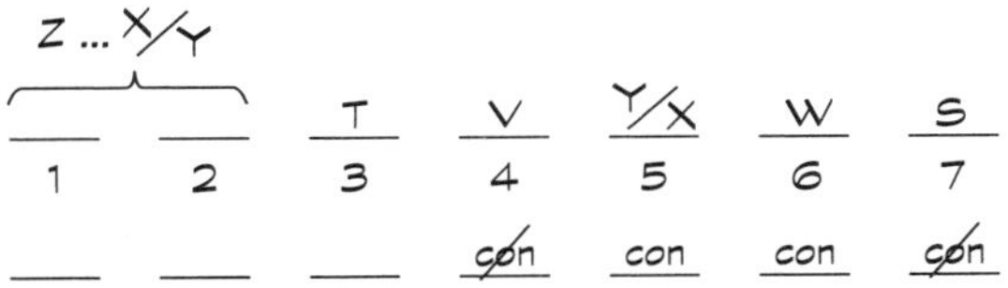

Figure 4.15

In either option, this forces V into the fourth slot. Thus, it cannot be true that V confessed. Choice (A) is the correct answer.

17. **(D)**

If neither X nor V confessed, then which one of the following must be true?

(A) T confessed.
(B) V was questioned on day two.
(C) X was questioned on day four.
(D) Y confessed.
(E) Z did not confess.[8]

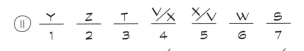

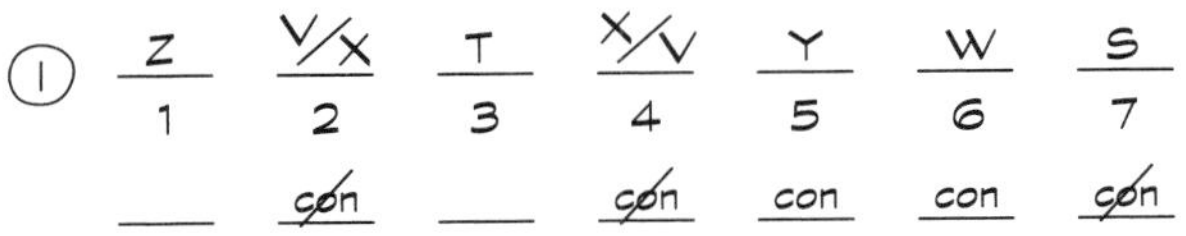

Figure 4.16

---

[7] PrepTest 53, Sec. 2, Q 16
[8] PrepTest 53, Sec. 2, Q 17

This time, the "if" can occur only in Option I. (In Option II, one of V or X must take the fifth slot and confess.) To keep V and X from confessing in Option I, you have to put them in spaces 2 and 4, forcing Y into the fifth spot (see the mini-sketch). The fifth suspect questioned always confesses, so choice (D) *must be true*. That's the correct answer.

Step Four Scores You Points

Step 4 of the Kaplan Method is what separates logic games amateurs from logic games masters. I've heard hundreds of students proclaim how easy the questions are once they have a "complete sketch." Those who really took their own words to heart and learned to make the available deductions every time are the ones who transformed their logic games performance. Take a closer look at the Deductions step as I outline the five types of rules that will lead to deductions game after game.

A DEDUCTIONS CHECKLIST
"How do I know if I've made all the deductions?"

When you're first practicing Step 4, the hardest thing to get a feel for is when you've made all of the available deductions. This is a double-edged sword. On the one hand, you may miss a crucial deduction and head into the questions without much more than what you got from the rules. That experience leaves some impatient test takers with a "why bother" attitude, and they don't practice making deductions enough to use the skill effectively. On the other hand, perfectionists will sit and stare at the game setup thinking, "There must be more that I can figure out." As a result, they wind up spending far too long before they move on to the questions and concluding that they just can't afford the time that the Deductions step takes.

Fortunately, there is a way to avoid both aspects of that dilemma, a checklist of the kinds of rules that lead to deductions. Learning it will ensure that you quickly find all available deductions *and* that you know when you've found them all so that you can move on to the questions with confidence.

RULES AND LIMITATIONS THAT LEAD TO DEDUCTIONS

Blocks of Entities
  Rules that join two or more entities such that when one is placed, the other must follow or move in response; e.g., "A and B occupy consecutive seats," "D and E play on the same team."

Limited Options
  Rules or restrictions that force all acceptable arrangements to follow one of two patterns; e.g., "F is either in position 1 or position 6," "Either three or four of the seven bills are paid on Wednesday and the rest on Thursday."

Established Entities
> Rules that place an entity in one position or within one group once and for all; e.g., "T is assigned to boat 3," "Y is the fourth client interviewed."

Number Restrictions
> Rules or restrictions that limit the numerical dimensions of the game; e.g., "Each committee has three members," "No more than two clients are interviewed per day."

Duplications
> Two or more rules that restrict a common entity or space; e.g., "M is assigned to boat 1" and "M and N are assigned to different boats;" "If T is chosen, then U is not chosen" and "If S is chosen, then U is chosen."

Not all LSAT logic games have all five of these types of rules and restrictions. As you've seen, games featuring formal logic may include nothing but a string of duplications. Sequencing actions are likely to have blocks of entities—"K and L are separated by exactly one space"—but rarely allow for numerical deductions, since they usually provide for one entity per space. As you're setting up a game and analyzing the rules, simply catalogue the potential deductions and look for the points of greatest restriction (i.e., the most restrictive or restricted entities).

The first letters of these five types of rules create the acronym BLEND. That's helpful for remembering what to look for while you're learning how to make deductions, but don't confuse it for an ordered series of steps. You don't look for blocks of entities first, Limited Options second, and so on. Remember, work from what's most concrete down to what's least concrete. In order to give you a better handle on the BLEND rule types, I'll point them out next in a handful of games, some of which you've seen in earlier chapters.

GUIDED PRACTICE: BLEND IN ACTION
Duplications and Number Restrictions

Here's another game with a lot of rules. That's good, of course, because it will provide a lot of restriction to where the entities can be placed. But it puts a high premium on your ability to make deductions. Go through Steps 1 through 3 of the Kaplan Method on your own. I'll review the setup and analysis of the rules before moving on to Step 4.

In a repair facility there are exactly six technicians: Stacy, Urma, Wim, Xena, Yolanda, and Zane. Each technician repairs machines of at least one of the following three types—radios, televisions, and VCRs—and no other types. The following conditions apply:

Xena and exactly three other technicians repair radios.

Yolanda repairs both televisions and VCRs.

Stacy does not repair any type of machine that Yolanda repairs.

Zane repairs more types of machines than Yolanda repairs.

Wim does not repair any type of machine that Stacy repairs.

Urma repairs exactly two types of machines.[9]

STEPS 1 AND 2: Overview and Sketch

You might remember this game from the discussion of game tasks. Likely, you pictured the six technicians at their work stations. Walking by, you could see that so-and-so has only radios at her station or that what's-his-name has televisions and VCRs. So your initial framework sketch looks like this:

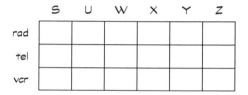

Figure 4.17

You can put a check mark to indicate a match and an X when you've ruled out a match. When you're unsure whether a given technician repairs a given machine, just leave the box blank.

STEP 3: Rules

As always, your goal should have been to build the rule inside the framework if possible. You can do that with the first rule. Put a check mark in Xena's radio box. Don't forget to also account for the number restriction given by this rule: You'll need a total of four of the radio boxes checked.

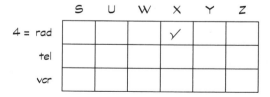

Figure 4.18

---

9 PrepTest 48, Sec. 2, Game 3

Rule 2 can also go into the sketch. Don't make more of the rule than is there, though. You don't know whether Yolanda repairs radios.

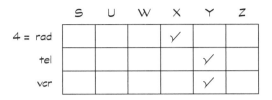

Figure 4.19

You can jot down the third rule in shorthand underneath the sketch. Because Rules 2 and 3 share Yolanda, you've now got duplications. You'll be coming back to them to make an important deduction.

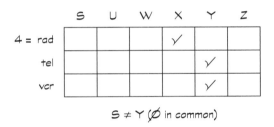

Figure 4.20

Rule 4 goes beneath the sketch as well.

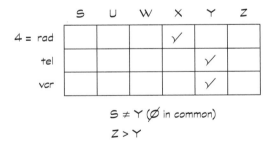

Figure 4.21

Rule 5 is just like Rule 3. Notice that Stacy is mentioned in both. She's on her way to becoming very important in the Deductions step.

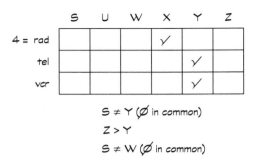

Figure 4.22

Finally, you can note Rule 6 above or below Urma's column within the framework.

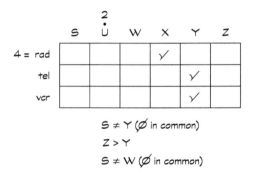

Figure 4.23

This is, at a minimum, what you should have on the page at the end of Step 3.

You may have noticed one or more deductions already. Students sometimes ask, "If I see some deductions while I'm diagramming the rules, should I put them in the sketch right then or should I wait until after I've written out all of the rules?" The answer is that, as you first begin to practice, you should probably wait until you have all of the rules down. That way, you'll learn to be more systematic and thorough. The truth of the matter, however, is that as you get more and more adept at this Step, you'll likely start making some deductions as you go. There's nothing wrong with that, as long as you've learned to catch all available deductions and you don't allow yourself to be sloppy.

STEP 4: Deductions

Here's what you're looking at as you begin Step 4:

In a repair facility there are exactly six technicians: Stacy, Urma, Wim, Xena, Yolanda, and Zane. Each technician repairs machines of at least one of the following three types—radios, televisions, and VCRs—and no other types. The following conditions apply:

Xena and exactly three other technicians repair radios.
Yolanda repairs both televisions and VCRs.
Stacy does not repair any type of machine that Yolanda repairs.
Zane repairs more types of machines than Yolanda repairs.
Wim does not repair any type of machine that Stacy repairs.
Urma repairs exactly two types of machines.[10]

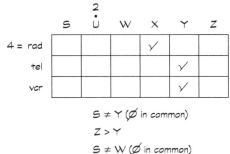

Figure 4.24

To get yourself started, determine the most restricted (or restrict*ive*) entity. No technician's column is completely established, but Xena and Yolanda each have at least some of their cells checked. Of the two, notice that Yolanda is a "duplicator"—she's present in two more rules. Without a doubt, Yolanda is your starting point for deductions.

Start with Rule 4, which shares Yolanda with Rule 2 and adds a number restriction. Since Yolanda already repairs two types of machines, Zane must repair all three types in order to obey the rule. Moreover, you now know that Yolanda does not repair radios. (If she did, Zane couldn't repair more types of machines than she does.)

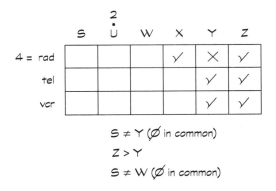

Figure 4.25

Just like that, two columns—Y's and Z's—are completely established.

Now, consider Yolanda's role in Rule 3, the other rule in which she is a duplicator. Since Yolanda and Stacy can have nothing in common, you now know that Stacy repairs only radios. A third column is locked down.

---

[10] PrepTest 48, Sec. 2, Game 3

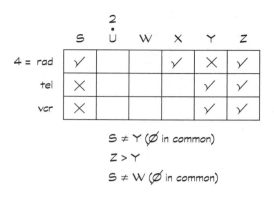

Figure 4.26

Stacy, whose column you just determined, is also a duplicator, present in Rules 3 and 5. Since you now know that she will repair radios, you know that Wim won't repair them.

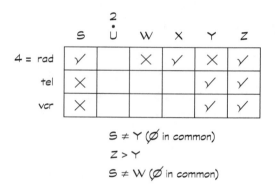

Figure 4.27

Don't push this further than what you can validly deduce, though. You cannot determine, at this point, whether Wim repairs televisions, VCRs, or both.

You've wrung everything you can from Rules 2, 3, 4, and 5. But there's still more that you can determine. Remember that Rule 1 contained a number restriction: Four of the technicians will repair radios. You noted that next to the "radio" row. What you've now added to your sketch allows you to see that Urma must also repair radios. And one of your rows is now completely determined, too.

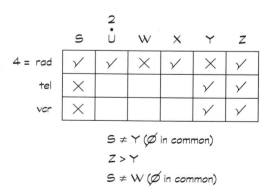

Figure 4.28

Urma is the subject of Rule 6. You can't make any concrete deductions from this rule, but you can now see that she'll repair either radios and televisions *or* radios and VCRs.

You were able to add a lot of certainty to this game. Consider how you did it. The bulk of the restrictions—and this is typical of Matching games—came from duplications and number restrictions. You started with the most restricted and restrictive entity, Yolanda, who appeared in three rules. She allowed you to determine Zane's column and set off a string of deductions that ran through Stacy, Wim, and Urma. By the end of the Deductions step, you are able to see precisely which cells are determined and which are still in play. I'll have you come back to this game in the next chapter, where you'll focus on the questions. For now, take a look at a game in which the most important deductions come from different elements in the BLEND checklist.

Established Entities and Blocks of Entities

Here's a game that you haven't seen before, but I'm sure that its action and arrangement will seem familiar once you conduct your overview and visualize the task. Take a couple of minutes and complete Steps 1 through 3 of the Kaplan Method. Once you're done, review your analysis of the rules. Then, I'll take you through this game's all-important Deductions step.

> In a single day, exactly seven trucks—S, T, U, W, X, Y, and Z—are the only arrivals at a warehouse. No truck arrives at the same time as any other truck, and no truck arrives more than once that day. Each truck is either green or red (but not both). The following conditions apply:
> > No two consecutive arrivals are red.
> > Y arrives at some time before both T and W.
> > Exactly two of the trucks that arrive before Y are red.
> > S is the sixth arrival.
> > Z arrives at some time before U.[11]

STEPS 1 AND 2: Overview and Sketch

It's not hard to imagine the scene. You'll need to lay out a series of seven numbered slots in which you'll keep track of the trucks' arrival order. Beneath each numbered slot (or beside it, if you arrange your sketch vertically), you'll put another slot to account for the color of each truck, either red or green.

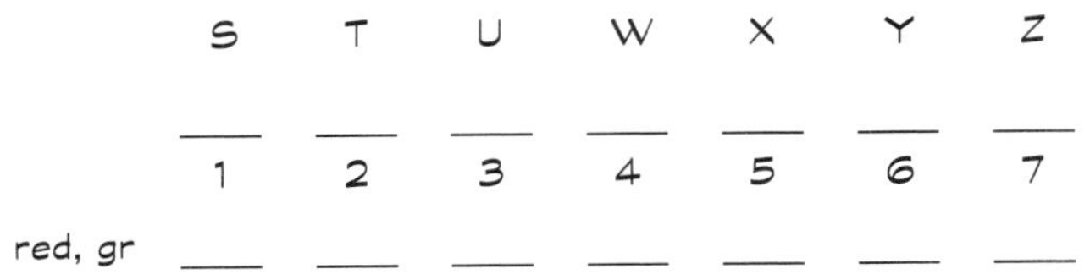

	S	T	U	W	X	Y	Z
	—	—	—	—	—	—	—
	1	2	3	4	5	6	7
red, gr	—	—	—	—	—	—	—

Figure 4.29

11 PrepTest 37, Sec. 3, Game 2

STEP 3: Rules

The rules that accompany this game are succinct and, at first, may appear to restrict the entities loosely. Only one of them can be placed immediately within the framework.

Rule 1 creates an "anti-block." It tells you that you can never see red trucks next to each other.

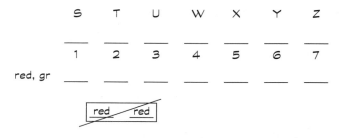

Figure 4.30

Notice that the rule is phrased negatively: Red trucks *cannot* arrive consecutively. Think about its affirmative implications, though. It tells you that any red truck must have a green truck in the space right before or right after it. Don't confuse this with a rule that says that red and green must alternate throughout the order, though; green trucks *can* arrive consecutively.

Rule 2 creates a loose block, but it restricts three entities. Y precedes both T and W. Remember, this rule doesn't tell you anything about the relationship between T and W.

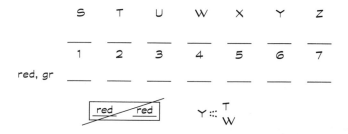

Figure 4.31

Rule 3 creates another loose block, and again, three spaces are restricted. Rule 2 restricts truck Y with regard to two other named trucks. This time, Y is restricted with regard to the number of red trucks that precede its arrival.

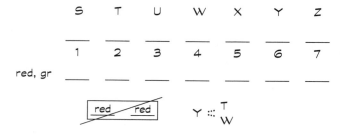

Figure 4.31A

Finally, Rule 4 gives you something concrete. S can go right into the framework.

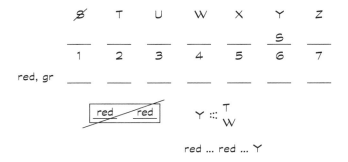

Figure 4.32

Rule 5 creates another loose block, giving the relative order of two trucks that hadn't been mentioned before. You'll just have to write this down below the framework, too.

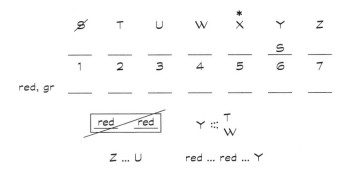

Figure 4.32A

Finally, notice that truck X is the floater, the unrestricted entity, as shown with the asterisk.

So far, so good. Your current understanding of the rules would allow you to trudge through the questions. But as you'll see, making the available deductions puts you in a far better position to breeze through the question set.

STEP 4: Deductions

Here's the state of the game at the outset of Step 4:

In a single day, exactly seven trucks—S, T, U, W, X, Y, and Z—are the only arrivals at a warehouse. No truck arrives at the same time as any other truck, and no truck arrives more than once that day. Each truck is either green or red (but not both). The following conditions apply:

No two consecutive arrivals are red.
Y arrives at some time before both T and W.
Exactly two of the trucks that arrive before Y are red.
S is the sixth arrival.
Z arrives at some time before U.[12]

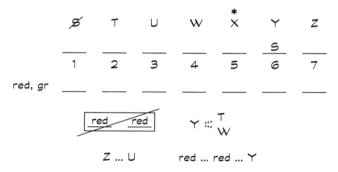

Figure 4.33

This game presents a great example of the importance of identifying the greatest point of restriction within a game. There's no doubt that S is the most restrict*ed* entity. It's established in space 6, after all. But beyond occupying a space in the order, S is not at all restrict*ive*—it doesn't appear explicitly in any other rule. There is, however, an entity that restricts (and, thus, is restricted by) a great number of other entities and/or spaces. Do you spot which one it is?

Truck Y is the entity that will initiate your deductions here. It's a duplicator, appearing in both Rule 2 and Rule 3, each of which makes Y part of a block of entities. Consider the effect of these two blocks as they work in concert to establish Y's position in the game. The latest Y can appear is in space 4. Both T and W must follow Y in the order of arrival. Because space 6 is already occupied by Established Entity S, a minimum of three other entities must follow Y in the sequence. So you can push Y no farther toward the back of the list than space 4.

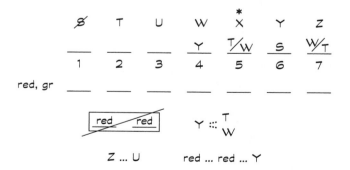

Figure 4.34

In fact, you can't push Y any closer to the front of the list than space 4, either. Because of Rule 3, Y must be preceded by two red trucks. And because of Rule 1, those red trucks must be separated by at least one green truck. Thus, the combination of the two loose blocks (along with the presence of the established entity in space 6) locks Y firmly in space 4.

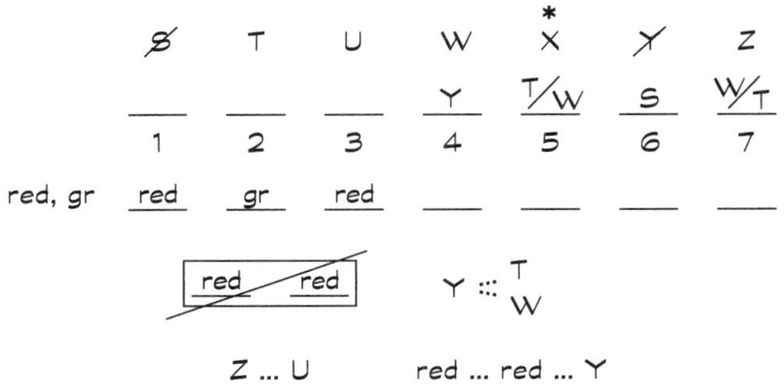

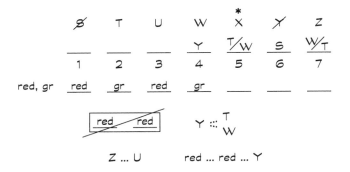

Figure 4.35

Note that with Y in space 4, you know that one of T and W will take space 5 and the other will take space 7. Likewise, you now know that the first and third trucks are red (they're the two red trucks that must precede Y's arrival) and that the second truck is green.

In fact, there's another truck whose color you can determine: You know with certainty that the fourth truck—truck Y—is green. Were it red, Rule 1 would be violated.

Figure 4.36

The remaining trucks are Z and U (in that order, according to Rule 5) and floater X. They'll take the only open spaces—spaces 1 through 3—in one of the following orders:

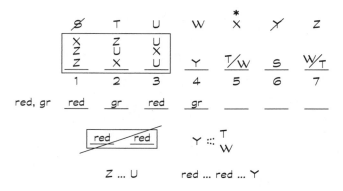

Figure 4.37

On test day, you may choose to forgo writing in those three possibilities for X, Z, and U, depending on the space you have for your sketch. Just make sure that you've seen how restricted even these loosely related entities and the floater are by the time you've completed your deductions.

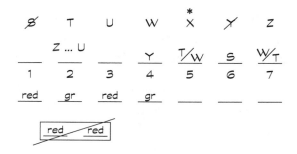

Figure 4.38

With this as your final Master Sketch, there's nothing the test makers can throw at you in the question set that you won't be able to handle quickly.

Limited Options

Limited Options, the scenario in which the entire game breaks down into one of two possibilities, is often the most helpful type of deduction you can make. Think of Limited Options as the test maker's way of saying "either . . . or . . ." Indeed, at times the rules giving rise to Limited Options are that literal. When a game offers you Limited Options, make two complementary sketches, one for each option. Once you've created the dual sketches and filled in the additional deductions that arise within each, you're usually left with only a handful of acceptable arrangements. You'll be close to being able to see all of the ways that the game can be completed.

Limited Options stem from one of three conditions. It's worth remembering what they are.

LIMITED OPTIONS COME FROM . . .

1. A "Key Player"
When a particular entity can take exactly two positions or placements, either of which give rise to additional restrictions among the remaining entities

2. Number Restrictions
When exactly two numerical arrangements are acceptable; for example, Committee A has three members and Committee B has four, or vice versa

3. Blocks of Entities
When a block can occupy exactly two different positions or be placed on exactly two different teams, either of which gives rise to additional restrictions among the remaining entities

You've seen Limited Options games already in this book, and you'll see several more. They're often the subtlest of all deductions to spot, and it will take practice before you're an expert. But whenever they're available, they're invaluable. Keep a keen eye out for the possibility of Limited Options in Parts II and III of this book, where I'll discuss game types and have you do full section practice. Here are a couple of tips: Occasionally, Limited Options will be announced by a single rule. This is especially true of key players—"G is either in seat 1 or else in seat 6." More often, you'll need to combine rules to derive the Limited Options. In fact, the very first game I had you look at in chapter 1—the Thunderstorm game—is a great example. In that game, the rules combined to limit the town Jackson to the two spaces at the end of the sequence. Review that game after this discussion and see how you'd now be able to deduce the Limited Options scenario yourself.

First, take a look at a game that you haven't seen before. Start by performing Steps 1 through 3 of the Kaplan Method: Conduct an overview, create the basic sketch, and fill in the rules. When you've finished those Steps, pause for a moment and see if you can spot the rule or rules that lead to a valuable Limited Options deduction.

Exactly six people—Lulu, Nam, Ofelia, Pachai, Santiago, and Tyrone—are the only contestants in a chess tournament. The tournament consists of four games, played one after the other. Exactly two people play in each game, and each person plays in at least one game. The following conditions must apply:

Tyrone does not play in the first or third game.

Lulu plays in the last game.

Nam plays in only one game and it is not against Pachai.

Santiago plays in exactly two games, one just before and one just after the only game that Ofelia plays in.[13]

STEPS 1 AND 2: Overview and Sketch

In this game, you're being asked to set up a schedule of four games in a chess tournament. The order of the games is important; you're told that they're "played one after the other." Naturally, you'll need to match the two contestants in each game as well. You could arrange this game horizontally or vertically. Either way, you'll have four numbered positions with spaces for two players each.

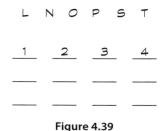

Figure 4.39

It's worth noting that you have six players for eight game positions. Since "each person plays in at least one game," either one player will have to participate in three games or two of them will have to participate in two games each. The others will play only once each.

STEP 3: Rules

You can depict Rule 1 within the framework of the sketch, but only negatively.

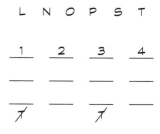

Figure 4.40

Without knowing whether Tyrone plays in one game or two, you can't place him affirmatively in game 2, game 4, or both.

---

[13] PrepTest 45, Sec. 3, Game 2

Rule 2 is also amenable to placement within the framework.

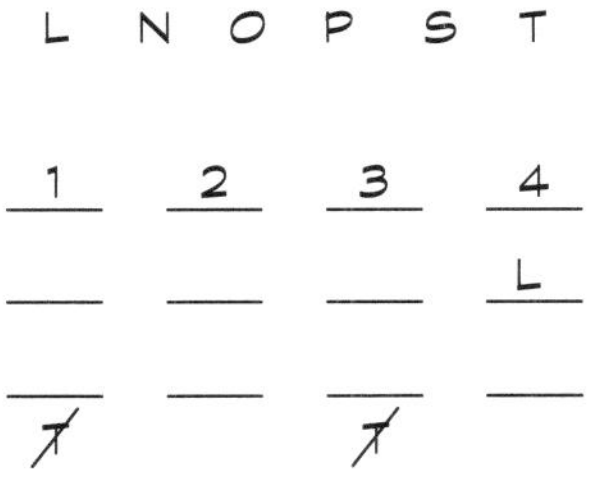

Figure 4.41

Here again, exercise restraint. You don't know that game 4 is Lulu's only appearance in the tournament.

Rule 3 has two elements, but you can't draw either of them in the sketch at this point. Make a note above N in the roster of entities to indicate that Nam makes only one appearance in the tournament. Beside your framework, diagram the "anti-block" that prevents N and P from being opponents.

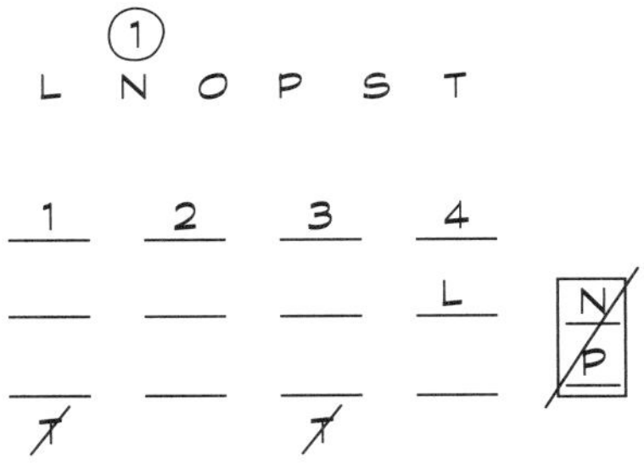

Figure 4.42

The final rule is huge. It restricts two entities and determines a block of three consecutive spaces. Make note of what you learn about the numbers: O appears only once, and S appears exactly twice. More importantly, draw out this order of game assignments in a way that reflects your framework.

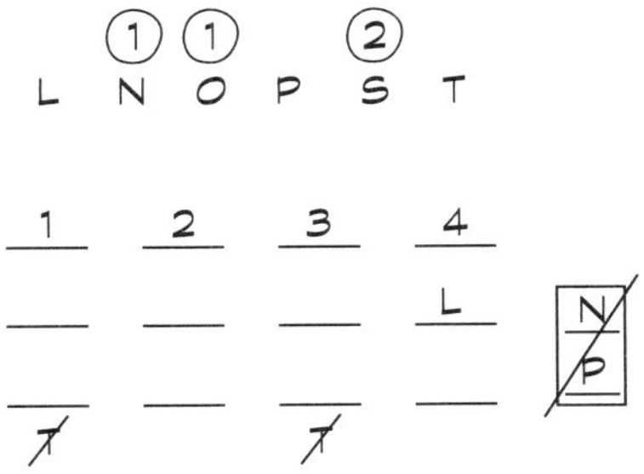

Figure 4.43

If you tried the questions from this game with nothing more than what you have here, you'd be in for a fairly tiring slog. But with just a little more effort, this game's acceptable arrangements begin to take fairly clear shape.

STEP 4: Deductions

Looking at the game as you have it after diagramming the rules, can you see an "either/or" scenario that will allow you to determine a chunk of the possible arrangements here? Think about which of the rules creates the greatest restriction within the game.

Exactly six people—Lulu, Nam, Ofelia, Pachai, Santiago, and Tyrone—are the only contestants in a chess tournament. The tournament consists of four games, played one after the other. Exactly two people play in each game, and each person plays in at least one game. The following conditions must apply:

Tyrone does not play in the first or third game.
Lulu plays in the last game.
Nam plays in only one game and it is not against Pachai.
Santiago plays in exactly two games, one just before and one just after the only game that Ofelia plays in.[14]

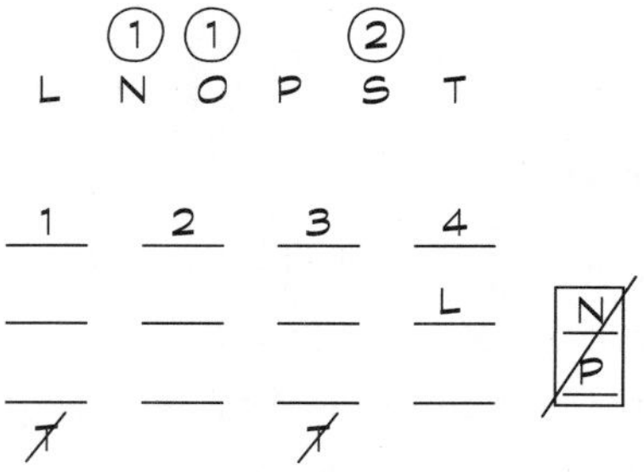

Figure 4.44

Rule 4 creates a block of entities that extends over three of the four games played in the tournament. That means that there are exactly two ways that it can be placed into the framework of the game: *Either* the S-O-S block appears in games 1 through 3, *or* it appears in games 2 through 4. Represent those two Limited Options in complementary sketches.

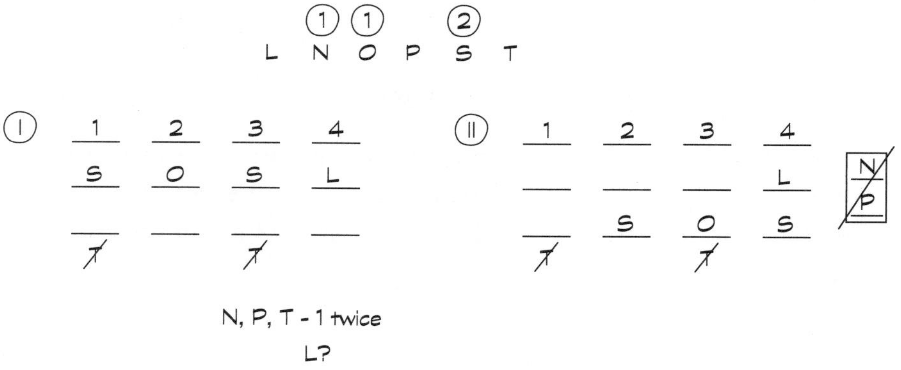

Figure 4.45

Drawing out the two options gives the game much more coherence. Consider what else you're able to deduce in each option.

In Option I, you still need to place N, P, and T. In the fourth open spot, you'll place L, P, or T a second time. Make note of that beneath the Option I diagram. There's no risk of N and P being opponents in this scenario, so no more can made of Rule 3. Nor does Rule 1 apply any

---

[14] PrepTest 45, Sec. 3, Game 2

additional restriction. It's possible for T to appear in game 2, game 4, or both. You've learned as much as possible from Option I.

Option II is another story. There's only one position open to Tyrone, so you can safely place T in game 2, competing against S.

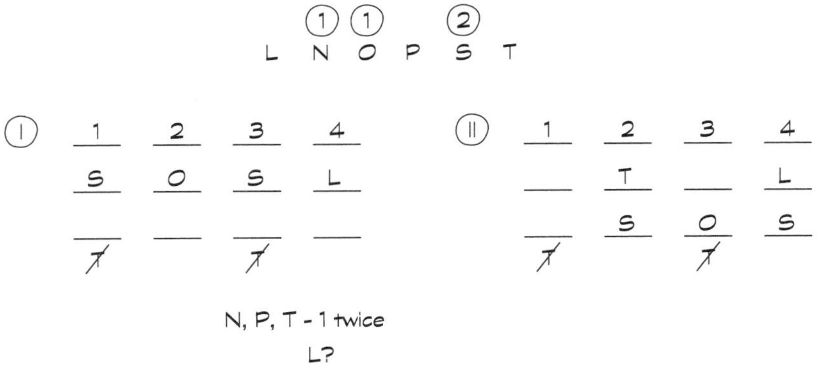

Figure 4.46

Rule 3 prevents N and P from being opponents. One must be assigned to game 1 and the other to game 3. Represent those alternatives as follows:

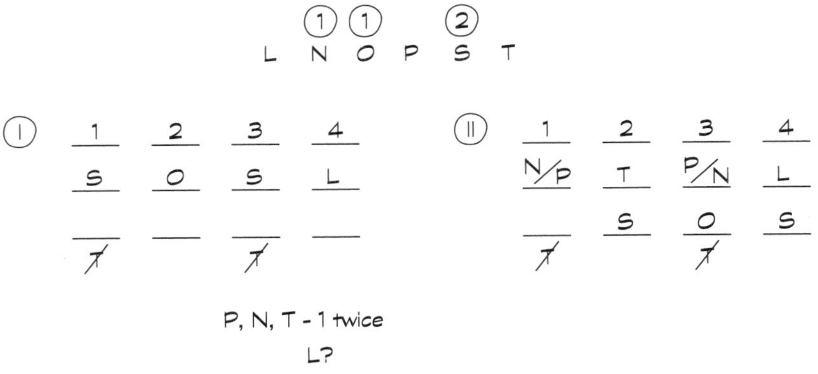

Figure 4.47

There's only one entity that can take the final open space in game 1. Since either N or P is playing in the game already, Rule 3 prevents the other one from taking the open seat. O and S are already placed within the game (and Rule 4, remember, dictates that S plays exactly twice and O exactly once). T can never play in the first game by virtue of Rule 1. So in Option II, L will play twice, once in game 4 and once in game 1.

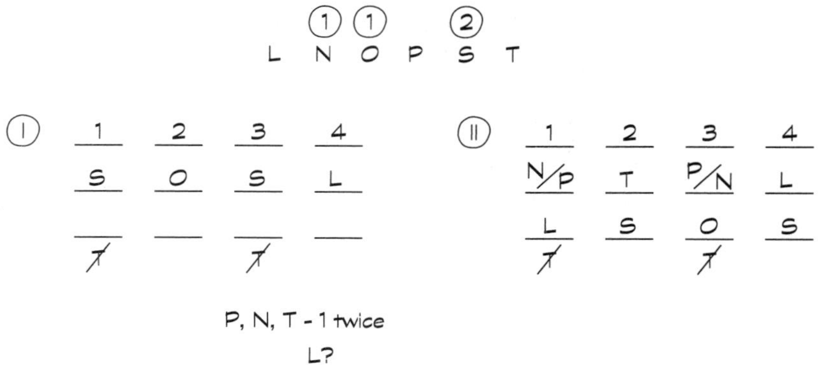

```
            ①  ①      ②
         L   N   O   P   S   T

①   1    2    3    4        ②   1    2    3    4
    S    O    S    L            N/P  T   P/N   L
    ___  ___  ___  ___          ___  ___  ___  ___
     ✗        ✗                  L    S    O    S
                                 ✗         ✗

         P, N, T - 1 twice
              L?
```

Figure 4.48

Your Master Sketch, and this is always the case with Limited Options, consists of both options, presented side by side or one under the other.

It's quite common in Limited Options games to have one option that is almost completely determined while the other has much more wiggle room. In the Chess Tournament game, Option II was the more determined. Savvy test takers will anticipate a couple of questions that call attention to one of the options, a couple more that require considering the other option, and a couple that take both into account.

As profoundly helpful as the Deductions step can be, most Logic Games sections also include a game with few, if any, deductions beyond the original rules. It's very important to know when you've made all of the available deductions and be confident that it's time to move on to the question set. Take a look at how the BLEND checklist can help you in such games.

Don't Struggle to Find Deductions That Aren't There

Here's a game you haven't seen before. Its task should seem quite familiar by now. Take a few minutes to assess what you're being asked to do. Try to design the framework for the sketch and add the rules as best you can. Then I'll show you how the Deductions step will work on a game like this one.

> There are exactly six groups in this year's Civic Parade: firefighters, gymnasts, jugglers, musicians, puppeteers, and veterans. Each group marches as a unit; the groups are ordered from first, at the front of the parade, to sixth, at the back. The following conditions apply:
>   At least two groups march behind the puppeteers but ahead of the musicians.
>   Exactly one group marches behind the firefighters but ahead of the veterans.
>   The gymnasts are the first, third, or fifth group.[15]

---

[15] PrepTest 43, Sec. 4, Game 1

STEPS 1 AND 2: Overview and Sketch

The setup of this game provides a pretty clear mental picture. You can see the six groups marching one at a time. This is a typical Sequencing action. What's more, the inclusion in the rules of specific numbers of spaces between groups tells you to draw this with a Strict Sequencing framework. At this point, your sketch looks something like this:

Figure 4.49

STEP 3: Rules

The rules in this game provide fairly strong restrictions, but they require you to read carefully and analyze their impact before writing them down. A sloppy mistake with one of the rules in this game could wind up costing you four or five points, so make sure you pay close attention.

The first rule is the most complicated. It tells you the relative order and distance between the puppeteers and the musicians. The puppeteers are earlier in the parade order, and *at least* two groups march between them and the musicians' group. Diagram the rule with something along these lines:

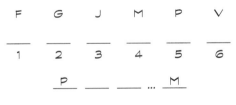

Figure 4.50

Note that despite the specificity of this rule, you can't place the groups precisely within the framework. The puppeteers will be limited to spaces 1 through 3 and the musicians to spaces 4 through 6. Beyond that, it's impossible to nail down their positions.

Rule 2 presents a similar restriction on the firefighters and the veterans, but this rule's distance restriction is more precise: *Exactly* one space intervenes here. Here's the rule added to the sketch:

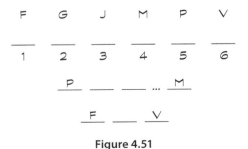

Figure 4.51

Again, there's no way to place the block of entities precisely within the framework. It might take spaces 1 and 3, 2 and 4, 3 and 5, or 4 and 6.

The final rule controls just one of the entities, the gymnasts. It restricts them to one of the odd-numbered spaces within the parade order. Enter that rule into your diagram like this, at least initially:

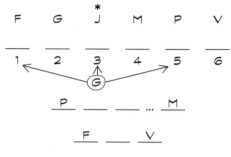

Figure 4.52

Note, too, that the jugglers are unrestricted. Entity J is your floater, acceptable in any open space. That's where you are at the end of the Rules step. Your job in the Deductions step is to see how the restrictions interact to reveal further limitations on the game.

STEP 4: Deductions

Right away, you get a big clue that there will be few, if any, deductions: It's difficult to spot a particular entity that qualifies as the most restricted. The puppeteers, musicians, and gymnasts are restricted to three possible spaces each and the firefighters and veterans to four each. Even worse, it's not immediately apparent how any of the rules interact, though they must at some level. None of them share a common entity and none mentions a common position or slot in the order.

For many test takers, especially those who are very diligent about finding all possible restrictions, the temptation is to forgo making deductions and give in to random speculation. Going about things this way will leave you breathless: "If the gymnasts are third, then the puppeteers could be first and the musicians could be last. Of course, the puppeteers could also be second and the musicians fifth. Then the firefighters and veterans could take spaces four and six. That means…" If you get caught up in trying to reason through every possible permutation, you'll have no time left to actually answer the questions and get the LSAT points.

Instead, turn to the BLEND checklist and reason through Step 4 like so:

Blocks of Entities: There are two blocks here, one each from Rules 1 and 2. Do they allow for any further certainty? In this game, they don't. Your initial diagram for each rule allows the blocks to shift up and down the order. There are no deductions here.

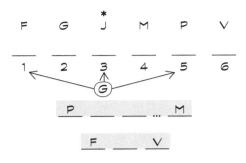

Figure 4.53

Limited Options: Arguably, Rule 3 provides a three-way Limited Options set for the gymnasts. LSAT experts can argue pretty heatedly about whether it's beneficial to draw out three alternate sketches for Limited Options (although we all agree that two-sketch Limited Options are of enormous value). The real takeaway from Rule 3 in this game is that, even if you did draw out three framework lines in order to show where G could be placed, you wouldn't give the game any further clarity.

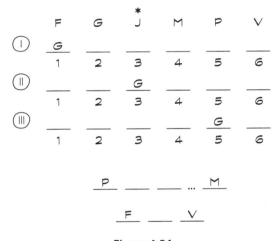

Figure 4.54

The gymnasts don't restrict any other entities directly, and both blocks still have wiggle room within any of the three potential options.

Established Entities: There are none here.

Number Restrictions: The entities are limited to one space each—the setup said, "Each group marches as a unit"—but that distribution is as simple as possible already. Numbers won't give you any additional deductions here.

Duplications: No rules share common entities or restrict common spaces.

In this game, there just aren't any deductions to make beyond understanding the restrictions that the rules provide. That will happen in some games. In situations like this, rather than doubt yourself, just run down the BLEND checklist. If none of the elements lead to additional certainties, you're ready for the questions. You could, I suppose, write out the negative implications of the two sequence rules like so:

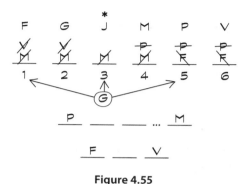

Figure 4.55

Some LSAT prep books make a big deal out these negative inferences. But really, those crossed-out letters are implied by the rules as you originally wrote them. Jot them down if doing so is helpful to you, but realize that they fall short of true deductions in the sense of combining rules to reveal additional restrictions.

STEP 5: Questions

Don't allow a lack of earth-shattering deductions to shake your confidence. When there are no additional restrictions to build into your sketch, simply turn directly to the questions. One thing you'll likely notice is that games with few up-front deductions usually have a high number of "If" questions. Each of these "ifs" supplies an additional restriction that will lead to additional deductions within that question. Start by drawing a mini-sketch containing the new "if," and work out from there. In a sense, it's as if these questions defer the Deductions step until you're already in the question set. The upside is that they always provide a starting point for your work.

Here's the Civic Parade game, complete with its Master Sketch and question set. Take about four or five minutes to try the questions. You'll see that you can answer them all with nothing more than the information you already have. Make sure to draw a mini-sketch and use it for a "mini-Deductions step" on each of the three "If" questions.

Questions 1–3

There are exactly six groups in this year's Civic Parade: firefighters, gymnasts, jugglers, musicians, puppeteers, and veterans. Each group marches as a unit; the groups are ordered from first, at the front of the parade, to sixth, at the back. The following conditions apply:

> At least two groups march behind the puppeteers but ahead of the musicians.
> Exactly one group marches behind the firefighters but ahead of the veterans.
> The gymnasts are the first, third, or fifth group.

1. Which one of the following could be an accurate list of the groups in the Civic Parade in order from first to last?

    (A)   firefighters, puppeteers, veterans, musicians, gymnasts, jugglers
    (B)   gymnasts, puppeteers, jugglers, musicians, firefighters, veterans
    (C)   veterans, puppeteers, firefighters, gymnasts, jugglers, musicians
    (D)   jugglers, puppeteers, gymnasts, firefighters, musicians, veterans
    (E)   musicians, veterans, jugglers, firefighters, gymnasts, puppeteers

2. If the gymnasts march immediately ahead of the veterans, then which one of the following could be the fourth group?

    (A)   gymnasts
    (B)   jugglers
    (C)   musicians
    (D)   puppeteers
    (E)   veterans

3. If the veterans march immediately behind the puppeteers, then which one of the following could be the second group?

    (A)   firefighters
    (B)   gymnasts
    (C)   jugglers
    (D)   musicians
    (E)   veterans[16]

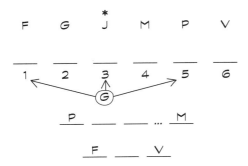

Figure 4.56

---

[16] PrepTest 43, Sec. 4, Game 1, Qs 1–5

Explanations

1. (D)

Which one of the following could be an accurate list of
the groups in the Civic Parade in order from first to last?

(A) firefighters, puppeteers, veterans, musicians,
     gymnasts, jugglers
(B) gymnasts, puppeteers, jugglers, musicians,
     firefighters, veterans
(C) veterans, puppeteers, firefighters, gymnasts,
     jugglers, musicians
(D) jugglers, puppeteers, gymnasts, firefighters,
     musicians, veterans
(E) musicians, veterans, jugglers, firefighters,
     gymnasts, puppeteers[17]

This is a run-of-the-mill Acceptability question. You know how to approach these efficiently:
Go rule-by-rule and eliminate the answers that break them.

Rule 1 takes care of choices (A) and (B), each of which has only one space between the puppeteers and the musicians, and choice (E), which has the musicians earlier in the parade than the
puppeteers. Rule 2 knocks out the remaining violator, choice (C), where the veterans precede
the firefighters. That leaves choice (D), the correct answer.

Acceptability questions rarely reward the Deductions step. They turn on your understanding
of what each rule individually allows and prohibits. Your approach to Acceptability questions
should not change, regardless of how many deductions you were able to find.

2. (E)

If the gymnasts march immediately ahead of the
veterans, then which one of the following could be the fourth group?

(A) gymnasts
(B) jugglers
(C) musicians
(D) puppeteers
(E) veterans[18]

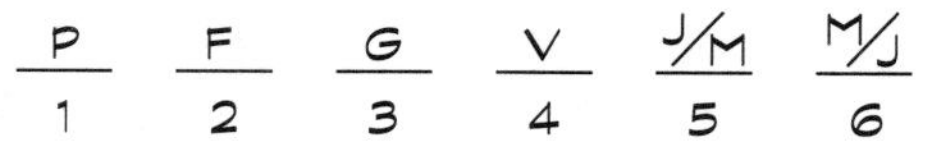

$$\begin{array}{cccccc} P & F & G & V & J/M & M/J \\ \hline 1 & 2 & 3 & 4 & 5 & 6 \end{array}$$

Figure 4.57

Take note how the "if" in this question stem triggers additional deductions. The stem tells you
to place the gymnasts right before the veterans. Thus, G goes in the middle of the F-V block.

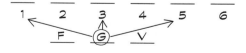

Figure 4.58

Now, the restriction from Rule 3 kicks in. G cannot go in space 1 in this case because there would be no room for F at the beginning of the parade. Likewise, if you tried to put G in space 5, F would occupy space 4 and V space 6, leaving no room for the P-M block in your game. Thus, G must take space 3, with F in 2 and V in 4.

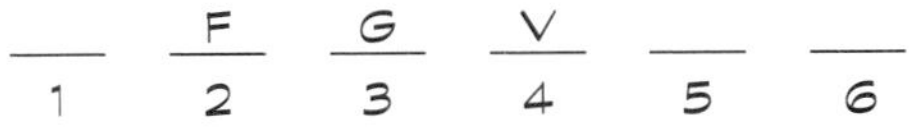

$$\frac{\quad}{1} \quad \frac{F}{2} \quad \frac{G}{3} \quad \frac{V}{4} \quad \frac{\quad}{5} \quad \frac{\quad}{6}$$

Figure 4.59

Now you can see that Rule 1 requires P to take space 1 and M to take either space 5 or space 6. Whichever space isn't occupied by M will go to floater J.

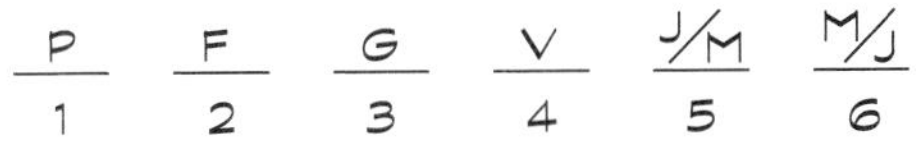

$$\frac{P}{1} \quad \frac{F}{2} \quad \frac{G}{3} \quad \frac{V}{4} \quad \frac{J/M}{5} \quad \frac{M/J}{6}$$

Figure 4.60

With that mini-sketch to consult, choice (E) is clearly correct. In fact, the veterans *must* be the fourth group in the parade under these conditions.

3. **(A)**

If the veterans march immediately behind the puppeteers, then which one of the following could be the second group?

(A)   firefighters
(B)   gymnasts
(C)   jugglers
(D)   musicians
(E)   veterans[19]

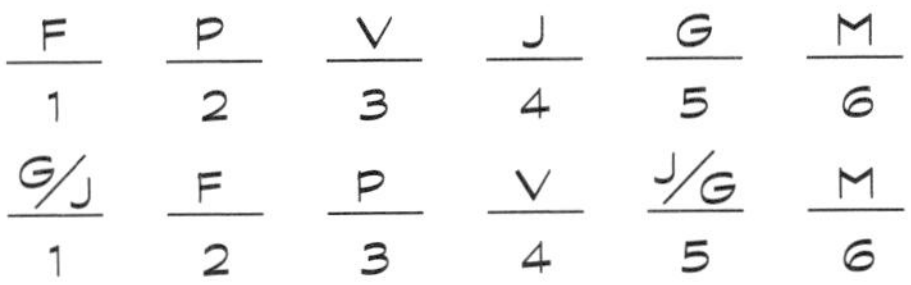

$$\frac{F}{1} \quad \frac{P}{2} \quad \frac{V}{3} \quad \frac{J}{4} \quad \frac{G}{5} \quad \frac{M}{6}$$

$$\frac{G/J}{1} \quad \frac{F}{2} \quad \frac{P}{3} \quad \frac{V}{4} \quad \frac{J/G}{5} \quad \frac{M}{6}$$

Figure 4.61

This time, the new "if" combines Rules 1 and 2. By placing the puppeteers right before the veterans (and thus in the middle of the F-V block), you can see a string of five spaces.

$$\frac{F}{\quad} \quad \frac{P}{\quad} \quad \frac{V}{\quad} \quad \frac{\quad}{\quad} \quad \cdots \quad \frac{M}{\quad}$$

Figure 4.62

There are only six spaces available in the parade, so the firefighters must march either first or second. In any other position, they'd push M right off the other end of the framework.

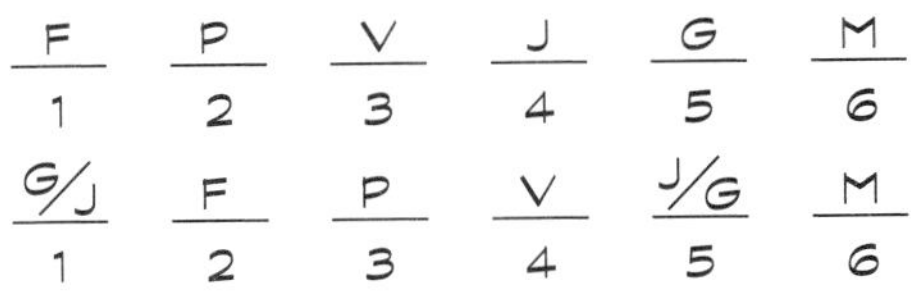

$$\frac{F}{1} \quad \frac{P}{2} \quad \frac{V}{3} \quad \frac{J}{4} \quad \frac{G}{5} \quad \frac{M}{6}$$

$$\frac{G/J}{1} \quad \frac{F}{2} \quad \frac{P}{3} \quad \frac{V}{4} \quad \frac{J/G}{5} \quad \frac{M}{6}$$

Figure 4.63

---

[19] PrepTest 43, Sec. 4, Q 3

So there are only two groups who could march second, the firefighters or the puppeteers. Of the two, only one is mentioned in an answer choice, of course. That's the firefighters, in choice (A).

LSAT logic games always reward the Deductions step. Sometimes they shift the burden up front and design questions that can be answered quickly from the deductions you make from the rules. Other times, as you saw here with the Civic Parade game, they offer almost nothing in the way of initial deductions but reward your ability to combine the rules triggered by the new "if" conditions in the question stems. Learn to make all of the deductions that you can in Step 4, but don't be stymied or shell-shocked when they don't appear. Go through the BLEND checklist systematically. When you've gotten all that's available, even when that's nothing, head into the question set with complete confidence that you'll have the information necessary to get all of the points.

The Power of Deductions

When you finish Step 4 of the Kaplan Method, you will be ready to handle the set of questions associated with any logic game. As you've seen in this chapter, Step 4 may involve stringing together several deductions that leave you with near-certainty about the acceptable arrangements of the entities in the game. At other times, you'll find few deductions available from the rules themselves and anticipate "If" questions that will precipitate further deductions within the questions. Either way, use the BLEND checklist to find all of the available deductions. Make them and account for them within your Master Sketch. Being able to conduct this step efficiently and effectively may be the most powerful tool in your LSAT toolkit. With it now available to you, turn to the final step in the Kaplan Method: answering the questions.

CHAPTER 5

THE QUESTIONS (AND WHAT THEY'RE ASKING FOR)

THE ANATOMY OF LOGIC GAMES QUESTIONS

It all comes down to Step 5 of the Kaplan Method, answering the questions. The four preceding steps are for naught if they don't turn into points. As you've seen, creating a complete setup and making all of the available deductions gives you all of the information you need to answer every logic games question. At times, the right answers can seem nearly inevitable once your Master Sketch is in place. Indeed, you've been answering logic games questions since chapter 1. But as I discussed there, the most common mistake that test takers make is to answer the wrong question. They choose an answer that *must be true* when the question calls for what *could be false*, for example.

So if it's just a matter of paying attention to the call of the question stem, why have a separate chapter for the Questions step? Because even here, and even with all of your setup work done perfectly, you have a chance to improve your logic games speed and accuracy. Once you learn how the test makers put together their various question types, you'll be able to approach each in the most strategic way.

"If" or Not "If": That Is the Question Stem

The first thing to notice about any LSAT logic games question is whether it has an "if" clause, a conditional clause that adds a further restriction applicable to that particular question. You've seen questions without the "if" clause in now-familiar Acceptability questions:

Which one of the following could be an accurate list
of the animals pictured on the guideposts, listed in
order from guidepost 1 through guidepost 6?[1]

"Non-If" questions might also ask simply what must, can, or cannot be true within a game:

Which one of the following must be true?[2]
Which one of the following must be false?[3]
Each of the following could be true EXCEPT:[4]

Or "Non-If" questions might ask complex questions specific to the action and restrictions of a particular game:

Which one of the following is a pair of songs that must
occupy consecutive tracks on the CD?[5]
Which one of the following statements, if true,
guarantees that Henri is using no more than one of the
following: the hairdryer, the razor, the television?[6]

There are even a couple of rarer "Non-If" question types that I'll address later in this chapter. What all "Non-If" questions have in common is that they can be answered from the information in your completed Master Sketch, or in the case of Acceptability questions, from the rules themselves.

"If" questions, of course, are defined by the additional restrictions they add to the game. They offer, if you like, hypothetical situations within which you apply the game setup and deductions. By definition, those additional constraints mean that "If" questions are testing fewer possible arrangements than their "Non-If" counterparts. But to leverage that advantage, you need to be able to visualize the new restriction. That's why making a new mini-sketch based on the hypothetical is so important.

In the clause that follows the hypothetical, the test makers ask the same range of questions that they do in "Non-If" stems. They may simply follow the "If" with a question about what must, can, or cannot be true:

If K is the fourth valve opened, then which one of the
following could be true?[7]
If there are exactly two colors in the costume, then
which one of the following must be false?[8]

---

[1] PrepTest 46, Sec. 4, Q 1

[2] PrepTest 48, Sec. 2, Q 14

[3] PrepTest 51, Sec. 4, Q 4

[4] PrepTest 51, Sec. 4, Q 20

[5] PrepTest 51, Sec. 4, Q 12

[6] PrepTest 48, Sec. 2, Q 5

[7] PrepTest 52, Sec. 2, Q 5

[8] PrepTest 51, Sec. 4, Q 2

Or the call of the question—the part of the stem following the "if"—may be more complex and game-specific:

> If Henri were to use exactly three appliances, then what is the total number of different groups of three appliances any one of which could be the group of appliances he is using?[9]
> If two films in French are going to be shown, one on day 3 and one on day 5, which one of the following is a pair of films that could be shown on day 1 and day 6, respectively?[10]

In short, "If" questions can and will mimic all of the same tasks found in "Non-If" questions, just with the added restriction in the stem. You may even see "If" questions that call for an "acceptable arrangement" under the hypothetical situation. In that case, the "If" clause becomes one more rule. You can eliminate any answer choice that violates it.

Characterize the Right Choice and the Wrong Ones

You'll learn to distinguish between "If" and "Non-If" questions and to handle each appropriately, in short order. It's mostly a matter of familiarity and practice. The second aspect of handling logic games questions efficiently requires a bit more discipline.

Before evaluating the answer choices, you need to characterize what the stem is asking for. To do this properly—to be completely prepared to evaluate the answer choices—you need to articulate (to yourself, of course) the characteristics that distinguish the one right answer *and* the four wrong ones. Take this question from the Water Treatment Plant game as an example; I've included the Master Sketch for your reference:

> Workers at a water treatment plant open eight valves—G, H, I, K, L, N, O, and P—to flush out a system of pipes that needs emergency repairs. To maximize safety and efficiency, each valve is opened exactly once, and no two valves are opened at the same time. The valves are opened in accordance with the following conditions:
> Both K and P are opened before H.
> O is opened before L but after H.
> L is opened after G.
> N is opened before H.
> I is opened after K.[11]

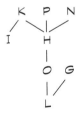

Figure 5.1

2. Each of the following could be the fifth valve opened EXCEPT:

(A) H
(B) I
(C) K
(D) N
(E) O[12]

---

9 PrepTest 48, Sec. 2, Q 4

10 PrepTest 49, Sec. 1, Q 5

11 PrepTest 52, Sec. 2, Game 1

12 PrepTest 52, Sec. 2, Q 2

Here, each of the four wrong answers *could* be the fifth valve opened. So the correct answer is the one with the entity that *cannot* be fifth. Now, you're ready for the answer choices. Looking at choice (A), you ask, "Can H ever be fifth?" Consult your Master Sketch or your work from other questions. Your answer will be, "Yes, it *can*." In this question, that's the characteristic of a *wrong* answer. Cross out choice (A) and move on. When you get to the right answer—it happens to be choice (C) in this case—your answer will be, "No, it can't be opened fifth." Characterizing the answer choices allows you to get to the correct answer efficiently and confidently.

Characterizing the answer choices means mentally preparing the question that you will ask as you read each one. Never read answer choices passively. Be ready to distinguish the *relevant* aspect of the choice. Think of it as knowing the chief characteristic of a "likely suspect." If I showed you a lineup of five people and told you "The culprit was over six feet tall," you'd be wasting time if you studied their eye colors or tattoos.

For *could be true* or *must be false* question stems, the question you'll ask to distinguish the likely suspect is straightforward. "Is choice (A) acceptable?" "How about choice (B)?" And so on. For a handful of questions, though, you'll need to tailor your query to the wording of the question stem. Consider an example that you'll recognize from the preceding chapter:

A locally known guitarist's demo CD contains exactly seven different songs—S, T, V, W, X, Y, and Z. Each song occupies exactly one of the CD's seven tracks. Some of the songs are rock classics; the others are new compositions. The following conditions must hold:

    S occupies the fourth track of the CD.
    Both W and Y precede S on the CD.
    T precedes W on the CD.
    A rock classic occupies the sixth track of the CD.
    Each rock classic is immediately preceded on the CD by a
     new composition.
    Z is a rock classic.[13]

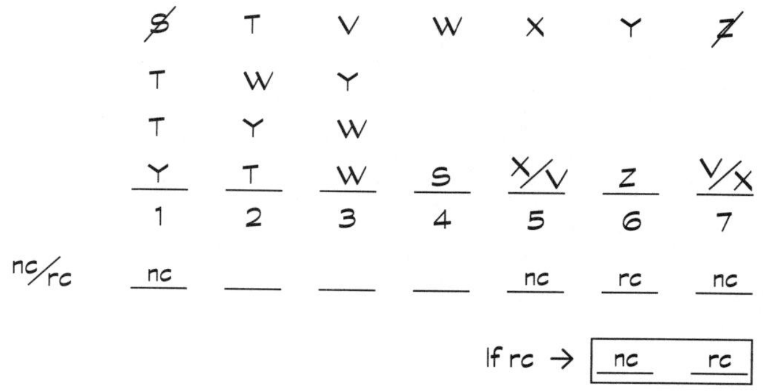

Figure 5.2

12. Which one of the following is a pair of songs that must occupy consecutive tracks on the CD?

   (A) S and V
   (B) S and W
   (C) T and Z
   (D) T and Y
   (E) V and Z[14]

In this case, you can't ask, "Does this choice have to be true?" The right approach here is to ask instead, "Can I separate these two entities?" The answer to this question will be "yes" for every wrong answer and "no" for the correct answer. So you'd approach choice (A) by asking, "Can I separate S and V?" A glance at your Master Sketch shows that S is in space 4 and V can be in either space 5 or space 7. So you answer, "Yes, they can be separated." That's the characteristic of a wrong answer. Cross out choice (A) and ask the same question about the pair of entities in choice (B).

I'll have you practice characterizing right and wrong answers for each of the question types that you'll see on the test. It's something that will soon become second nature and won't cost you any time as you're taking the section. But, it is a non-negotiable part of your overall strategic approach to logic games questions.

Question Sets Are Clues

In a typical Logic Games *section*, about half of the questions will have new "Ifs" and about half will be of the "Non-If" variety. But that won't be case with individual games. In fact, seeing a concentration of "if" or of "Non-If" questions often reveals the extent to which you can deduce the game's acceptable arrangements before you reach the Questions step.

In the Electronics Technician game, for instance, you were able to establish 12 of the 18 possible matches before attacking the questions. You completely determined Stacy's, Yolanda's, and Zane's columns and knew exactly who did and did not repair radios.

In a repair facility there are exactly six technicians: Stacy, Urma, Wim, Xena, Yolanda, and Zane. Each technician repairs machines of at least one of the following three types—radios, televisions, and VCRs—and no other types. The following conditions apply:

    Xena and exactly three other technicians repair radios.
    Yolanda repairs both televisions and VCRs.
    Stacy does not repair any type of machine that Yolanda repairs.
    Zane repairs more types of machines than Yolanda repairs.
    Wim does not repair any type of machine that Stacy repairs.
    Urma repairs exactly two types of machines.[15]

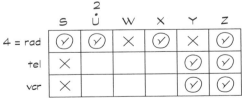

	S	U	W	X	Y	Z
4 = rad	✓	✓	✗	✓	✗	✓
tel	✗				✓	✓
vcr	✗				✓	✓

Figure 5.3

---

14 PrepTest 51, Sec. 4, Q 12
15 PrepTest 48, Sec. 2, Game 3

With two-thirds of the possible matches predetermined, the test makers don't have a lot of room for new "ifs", so they'll design the questions to reward you for front-loading your work. Take a look at the question stems that accompanied this game:

13. For exactly how many of the six technicians is it possible to determine exactly which of the three types of machines each repairs?

14. Which one of the following must be true?

15. Which one of the following must be false?

16. Which one of the following pairs of technicians could repair all and only the same types of machines as each other?

17. Which one of the following must be true?[16]

There's not an "If" question in the bunch. That's not by accident. Each of the questions associated with this game rewards you for making all of the available deductions. When you see this kind of question set, you can rest assured that there is a good deal of certainty involved in the initial setup even before you've completed Steps 1 through 4 of the Kaplan Method.

In contrast, take a look at the following game setup. You first saw it in chapter 1, where you determined that its task involves creating the schedule of Garibaldi's meetings. Take three to four minutes to sketch it, add in the rules, and make any possible deductions.

In the course of one month, Garibaldi has exactly seven different meetings. Each of her meetings is with exactly one of five foreign dignitaries: Fuentes, Matsuba, Rhee, Soleimani, or Tbahi. The following constraints govern Garibaldi's meetings:

She has exactly three meetings with Fuentes, and exactly one with each of the other dignitaries.
She does not have any meetings in a row with Fuentes.
Her meeting with Soleimani is the very next one after her meeting with Tbahi.
Neither the first nor last of her meetings is with Matsuba.[17]

Here's what your Master Sketch should look like:

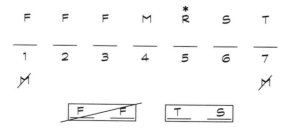

Figure 5.4

---

[16] PrepTest 48, Sec. 2, Qs 13–17
[17] PrepTest 44, Sec. 3, Game 1

The standard Sequencing task is reflected in the seven numbered slots. Rule 1 is shown in the list of entities, which has F repeated three times. Rules 2 and 4 are negative restrictions limiting the acceptable arrangements within the game but not leading to any further deductions immediately. Rule 3 creates a block of entities out of T and S but isn't connected to any other rules or any specific spaces. A run through the BLEND checklist doesn't produce any further deductions. An untrained test taker might be alarmed at the lack of specificity and spend precious minutes fruitlessly speculating about the possible arrangements here. But a look at the question set shows that you should expect little concreteness from this setup.

1. Which one of the following could be the sequence of the meetings Garibaldi has with the dignitaries?

2. If Garibaldi's last meeting is with Rhee, then which one of the following could be true?

3. If Garibaldi's second meeting is with Fuentes, then which one of the following is a complete and accurate list of the dignitaries with any one of whom Garibaldi's fourth meeting could be?

4. If Garibaldi's meeting with Rhee is the very next one after Garibaldi's meeting with Soleimani, then which one of the following must be true?

5. If Garibaldi's first meeting is with Tbahi, then Garibaldi's meeting with Rhee could be the

6. If Garibaldi's meeting with Matsuba is the very next meeting after Garibaldi's meeting with Rhee, then with which one of the following dignitaries must Garibaldi's fourth meeting be?[18]

This question set signals a game in which it's unlikely that you'll be able to make many (if any) big deductions. The first question is a standard Acceptability question, and then it's all "ifs" the rest of the way. Seeing all of those "If" questions tells you that the test makers know that there are many acceptable permutations remaining to be explored. A quick scan of this question set should tell you not to spend extra time trying to chase a phantom "big deduction." You'll get all of the additional restrictions you need to answer the questions once you add each "if" to the rules.

Those two examples are, of course, at the extreme ends of the spectrum. Most games have a mix of "If" questions and their various "Non-If" counterparts. And not surprisingly, most games fall somewhere in between these two in terms of how much can be deduced up front. It's impossible to predict whether you'll see games like these on test day, but it's worth your time to take a quick glance over the question set for each game you face, especially if you're hesitant about whether you've made all of the available deductions.

---

[18] PrepTest 44, Sec. 3, Qs 1–6

Next, turn your attention to the various question types you'll see on the LSAT. For each, I'll point out the language in the question stem that identifies the type, go through a few representative examples, and explain the most strategic approach for you to take.

ACCEPTABILITY QUESTIONS

You're already thoroughly familiar with Acceptability questions. I covered this question type in chapter 2 because of its close association with the rules. Typically, Acceptability question stems ask for the answer that could be an "accurate" or "acceptable" arrangement, list, or order of the entities or groups in the game.

> Which one of the following could be an accurate list of the contestants who play in each of the four games?[19]

> Which one of the following is an acceptable order of the films for the retrospective, listed by their language, from day 1 through day 6?[20]

As I mentioned in chapter 2, the most common pattern is to have one Acceptability question per game and for it to be the first question in the set. Every once in a while, you'll find a game with no Acceptability question and, very rarely, you may find an Acceptability question later in the set. But you won't go wrong to expect the "one-and-first" pattern most of the time.

It's worth commenting briefly here on question stems that ask for a "complete and accurate list" of entities within a game. These are usually, but not always, Acceptability questions. Consider two examples:

> Which one of the following could be a complete and accurate list of the performers who sign with each agency?[21]

> Which one of the following is a complete and accurate list of the days, any one of which is a day on which a film in Italian could be shown?[22]

The first of these stems indicates an Acceptability question. The wording—"list of the performers who sign with each agency"—tells you that the answer choices will cover all of the entities and groups within the game. You should treat this question exactly as you would any other Acceptability question.

---

[19] PrepTest 45, Sec. 3, Q 7

[20] PrepTest 49, Sec. 1, Q 1

[21] PrepTest 53, Sec. 2, Q 1

[22] PrepTest 49, Sec. 1, Q 4

The second stem limits your focus to just one of the entities. It's asking for the answer choice that has *any and all* acceptable placements for Italian films. We'll cover this type shortly under the heading "Complete and Accurate List Questions." You'll deal with it in a different way.

The takeaway from these examples is to always read question stems thoroughly and strategically. It should also come as no surprise that the first of those two stems belonged to the first question in its set (the position in which Acceptability questions are nearly always found), while the second belonged to the fourth question in the set for its game.

Eliminate Answers Rule by Rule

As you'll recall, the best strategy for Acceptability questions is to eliminate wrong answers rule by rule. Trying to evaluate choice by choice is a fool's errand. Take a look at this example:

Workers at a water treatment plant open eight valves—G, H, I, K, L, N, O, and P—to flush out a system of pipes that needs emergency repairs. To maximize safety and efficiency, each valve is opened exactly once, and no two valves are opened at the same time. The valves are opened in accordance with the following conditions:

  Both K and P are opened before H.
  O is opened before L but after H.
  L is opened after G.
  N is opened before H.
  I is opened after K.

1. Which one of the following could be the order, from first to last, in which the valves are opened?

  (A) P, I, K, G, N, H, O, L
  (B) P, G, K, N, L, H, O, I
  (C) G, K, I, P, H, O, N, L
  (D) N, K, P, H, O, I, L, G
  (E) K, I, N, G, P, H, O, L[23]

If you took the approach of saying, "Is choice (A) acceptable? Let me check," you'd wind up checking all five rules before determining that, in fact, choice (A) is a violator. Then you'd start the process all over again for choice (B). That inefficiency is compounded by the fact that the correct answer is the one that won't violate any of the rules. What winds up happening to many test takers is that they find the right answer but still question whether they missed something. They wind up going over the list of rules two or three times before they're confident enough to circle the correct choice and move on.

---

[23] PrepTest 52, Sec. 2, Q 1

As you know from chapter 2, the efficient approach is to work rule by rule, systematically eliminating the violators. In the example from the Water Treatment Plant, Rule 1 is never broken. Choice (B) breaks Rule 2. Choice (D) breaks Rule 3. Choice (C) breaks Rule 4. Finally, choice (A) breaks Rule 5. Your efficiency is increased by the fact that once you've eliminated a choice, you need not consider it again. Once you've eliminated an answer choice, strike through it completely in your test booklet. It doesn't matter if it breaks any other rules; you've already determined that it's unacceptable.

Using this approach, no Acceptability question should take you more than a few seconds on test day. Moreover, you'll be able to get the Acceptability points even in games that you struggle to set up completely.

Partial Acceptability: A Partial Exception

Partial Acceptability questions are cousins of Acceptability questions, which you will handle *almost* identically. The answer choices in Partial Acceptability questions have the same characteristics as those in Acceptability questions. That is, the four wrong answers each break one or more of the rules, while the correct answer breaks none of them. The difference is that Partial Acceptability answer choices don't contain the entire arrangement of entities in the game. Here's an example:

> Three folk groups—Glenside, Hilltopper, Levon—and three rock groups—Peasant, Query, Tinhead—each perform on one of two stages, north or south. Each stage has three two-hour performances: north at 6, 8, and 10; south at 8, 10, and 12. Each group performs individually and exactly once, consistent with the following conditions:
>> Peasant performs at 6 or 12.
>> Glenside performs at some time before Hilltopper.
>> If any rock group performs at 10, no folk group does.
>> Levon and Tinhead perform on different stages.
>> Query performs immediately after a folk group, though not necessarily on the same stage.

18. Which one of the following could be a complete and accurate ordering of performances on the north stage, from first to last?

(A) Glenside, Levon, Query
(B) Glenside, Query, Hilltopper
(C) Hilltopper, Query, Peasant
(D) Peasant, Levon, Tinhead
(E) Peasant, Query, Levon[24]

---

[24] PrepTest 48, Sec. 2, Game 4, Q 18

The question is looking for an acceptable arrangement, but the answer choices display the bands on the north stage only. In order for the north-stage arrangement to be acceptable, it will have to allow for an acceptable south-stage program as well. You have to keep that in mind as you assess the choices. It would help to be able to see the south stage, too. That's why it's more important to wait until you have your sketch, rules, and deductions all diagrammed before evaluating the answers. Go through the process here, and you'll see what I mean.

Rule 1 provides that Peasant must perform at 6 or 12, that is, first or last on the program. If you merely glance at the answers, the violator might not jump out at you. But remember that in this game, the north stage has bands only at 6, 8, and 10.

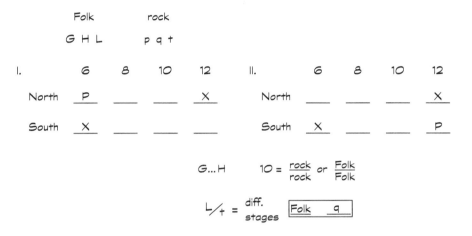

Figure 5.5

So answer (C) violates Rule 1 by having Peasant perform at 10.

18. Which one of the following could be a complete and accurate ordering of performances on the north stage, from first to last?

(A)   Glenside, Levon, Query
(B)   Glenside, Query, Hilltopper
(C)   Hilltopper, Query, Peasant
(D)   Peasant, Levon, Tinhead
(E)   Peasant, Query, Levon[25]

Rule 2 requires Glenside to perform before Hilltopper. You see Glenside in choices (A) and (B), and they perform first in both cases. So there's no problem there. In choices (D) and (E), Glenside and Hilltopper perform on the south stage (you can't see them). Still, there's nothing to suggest that Glenside couldn't perform earlier than Hilltopper on the south stage, so it doesn't appear that Rule 2 is broken.

---

[25] PrepTest 48, Sec. 2, Q 18

Rule 3 is another one that is impossible to assess with only the north stage visible. Rock bands perform at 10 in choices (A) and (E), but since you can't see who's on the south stage at that time, this doesn't give you any way to spot violations. Press on.

Rule 4 eliminates two wrong answers. See if you can determine which ones are the rule-breakers. Saying that Levon and Tinhead must perform on different stages is just another way of saying you must have exactly one of them on the north stage and exactly one on the south stage. Choice (D) is a clear violator, since you can see both bands on the north stage. But this rule also eliminates choice (B), where you see neither. Thinking with rules in Partial Acceptability questions can involve taking stock of what *doesn't* show up in the answer choices as well as what does.

18. Which one of the following could be a complete and
     accurate ordering of performances on the north stage,
     from first to last?

     (A)   Glenside, Levon, Query
     (B)   ~~Glenside, Query, Hilltopper~~   Neither L nor T
     (C)   ~~Hilltopper, Query, Peasant~~
     (D)   ~~Peasant, Levon, Tinhead~~
     (E)   Peasant, Query, Levon[26]

Rule 5 is another that's more easily assessed when you can refer to the initial sketch.

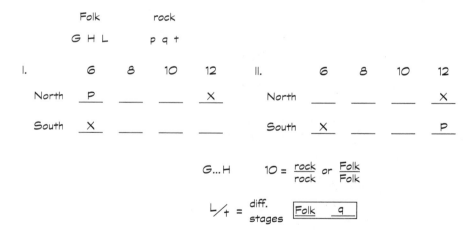

Figure 5.6

Recognizing that there is only one performance at 6 reveals that choice (E) violates Rule 4. In that choice, Query performs at 8 and there is no way a folk group can perform at 6, since Peasant is on the north stage and the south stage is empty at that time.

[26] PrepTest 48, Sec. 2, Game 4, Q 18

18. Which one of the following could be a complete and accurate ordering of performances on the north stage, from first to last?

    (A) Glenside, Levon, Query
    (B) ~~Glenside, Query, Hilltopper~~
    (C) ~~Hilltopper, Query, Peasant~~
    (D) ~~Peasant, Levon, Tinhead~~
    (E) ~~Peasant, Query, Levon~~[27]

Thus, choice (A) is the correct answer.

Partial Acceptability questions are not as common as their standard Acceptability cousins. It's unlikely that you'll see more than one in the entire Logic Games section, and many tests feature none at all. Unlike standard Acceptability questions, they may appear anywhere in the question set.

Often, when they appear in the middle or at the end of a question set, Partial Acceptability questions will contain language that clearly identifies them.

> Which one of the following could be an accurate partial list of the architects, each matched with his or her design's place in the order in which the designs are presented?[28]

That's all you need to know in order to handle Acceptability questions and Partial Acceptability questions with minimum effort and maximum efficiency. They won't constitute the bulk of your points, but they're fast and they're certain. Treat them as the starting blocks for the race, and use the strategic approach outlined here to get a jump on the section and on your competition.

MUST BE/COULD BE TRUE/FALSE QUESTIONS

Recognizing these questions is a no-brainer. Most often, the question stems are simple and short.

> Which one of the following could be true?[29]
> Which one of the following must be false?[30]

From time to time, you'll see game-specific variants, like this twist on a *must be true* question:

> Which one of the following suspects must have been questioned before T was questioned?[31]

---

[27] PrepTest 48, Sec. 2, Game 4, Q 18

[28] PrepTest 53, Sec. 2, Q 11

[29] PrepTest 53, Sec. 2, Q 2

[30] PrepTest 52, Sec. 2, Q 23

[31] PrepTest 53, Sec. 2, Q 15

Or this slightly more complex variation on a *must be false* question stem:

> Sethna's teammate could be any one of the following
> EXCEPT:[32]

Do you see why I categorized that as a *must be false* question? The "EXCEPT" at the end means that the correct answer is an entity who *cannot* be Sethna's teammate. That analysis anticipates the most important step you'll need to take when tackling this question type: how to correctly characterize the answer choices.

Characterize the Answer Choices

You can always derive the correct answer to Must/Could be True/False question types from your Master Sketch. But as I emphasized earlier in this chapter, you have to know what you're looking for. To analyze these questions' answer choices, you need to picture two columns. The first represents the level of certainty, and the second represents the affirmative or negative "charge" of the question stem.

Level of Certainty	"Charge"
Must	True
Could	False

The correct answer combines one of the levels of certainty with one of the charges. The four wrong answers combine the other two terms. Here's a straightforward example:

> Which one of the following must be true?[33]

Since the correct answer clearly combines "must" and "true" in this question, you know beyond a shadow of a doubt that the four wrong answers all *could be false*. I'll put the question in context to show you how that analysis plays out.

> Five performers—Traugott, West, Xavier, Young, and Zinser—are recruited by three talent agencies—Fame Agency, Premier Agency, and Star Agency. Each performer signs with exactly one of the agencies and each agency signs at least one of the performers. The performers' signing with the agencies is in accord with the following:
>
> Xavier signs with Fame Agency.
> Xavier and Young do not sign with the same agency as each other.
> Zinser signs with the same agency as Young.
> If Traugott signs with Star Agency, West also signs with Star Agency.

---

[32] PrepTest 53, Sec. 2, Q 23
[33] PrepTest 53, Sec. 2, Q 3

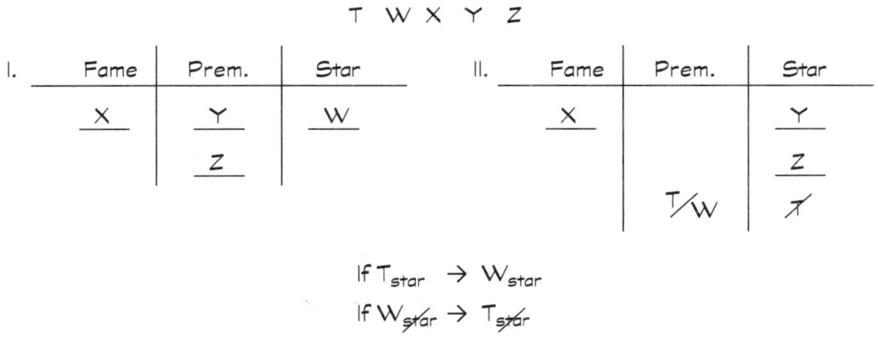

T W X Y Z

I.	Fame	Prem.	Star		II.	Fame	Prem.	Star
	X	Y	W			X		Y
		Z						Z
							T/W	X̶

If T$_{star}$ → W$_{star}$

If W̶$_{star}$ → T̶$_{star}$

Figure 5.7

3. Which one of the following must be true?

    (A) West and Zinser do not sign with the same agency as each other.
    (B) Fame Agency signs at most two of the performers.
    (C) Fame Agency signs the same number of the performers as Star Agency.
    (D) Traugott signs with the same agency as West.
    (E) West does not sign with Fame Agency.[34]

This is the Talent Agency game that you set up in the Deductions chapter. You can see the Limited Options Master Sketch next to the game's setup. Knowing that the correct answer *must be true*, you can evaluate the answer choices without hesitation.

Look at answer choice (A). Must West and Zinser sign with different agencies? Not in Option II. There, both West and Zinser could sign with Star, provided that Traugott signs with Premier. So the statement in choice (A) *could be false.*

Turn to choice (B). Must it be true that Fame signs a maximum of two artists? Yes. In Option I, Fame could sign Xavier and Traugott, but everyone else is already assigned. In Option II, either Traugott or West could join Xavier, but the other has to sign with Premier. So it *must be true* that Fame signs at most two of the performers. Choice (B) is the correct answer. On test day, you could stop right here. For practice, evaluate the remaining choices to identify how they *could be false.*

Examine choice (C). Must it be true that Fame and Star sign the same number of performers? No. In Option I, one of the two agencies will sign two performers, while the other signs only one. You may notice that in Option II, it is possible for both Fame and Star to sign two performers, but that's not enough to make this a correct answer to a *must be true* question. Remember, if a statement does not have to be true, it *could be false.*

---

34 PrepTest 53, Sec. 2, Game 1

The statement in choice (D) could be true in either option. Traugott and West could both sign with Star Agency in Option I, and both could sign with Premier in Option II. But the statement *could be false* in either option, too. Nothing prevents Traugott from signing with Fame or Premier, in Option I. In Option II, Traugott could sign with Fame while West signs with Premier, or Traugott could sign with Premier while West signs with Fame or Star. Since the statement could be false, choice (D) is a wrong answer.

Negative language can be confusing, and the test makers most assuredly know it. Make sure you understand what it would mean to say that choice (E) must be true. Evaluate the answer choice by asking, "Must it be true that West does *not* sign with Fame?" If West can sign with Fame, then this choice's statement could be false. West can, of course, sign with Fame in Option II. Choice (E) does not have to be true, so it's a wrong answer.

Take a look at one more question from that game. Characterize the one correct and the four wrong answers, and then use the Master Sketch to identify the correct answer.

2. Which one of the following could be true?

   (A) West is the only performer who signs with Star Agency.
   (B) West, Young, and Zinser all sign with Premier Agency.
   (C) Xavier signs with the same agency as Zinser.
   (D) Zinser is the only performer who signs with Star Agency.
   (E) Three of the performers sign with Fame Agency.[35]

Since the correct answer takes "could" as its level of certainty and "true" as its charge, the four wrong answers *must be false*. Were you able to stop as soon as you saw choice (A)? On test day, you'll be able to. You know that the one, correct choice *could be true*. West could be Star Agency's only client in Option I. Choice (A) must be correct.

For the record, all four of the wrong choices offer statements that are impossible within the restrictions of the game. Take choice (B). West, Young, and Zinser can never be together at Premier Agency. They could all join Star Agency in Option II, but that's not what the answer choice states. Move on to choice (C). Xavier joins Fame Agency in both options, while Zinser is a client of either Premier or Star, so choice (C) must be false. Likewise for choice (D): A glance at the Master Sketch reminds you that Young accompanies Zinser (Rule 3) no matter where the latter signs.

Choice (E) deserves a more in-depth look. It *must be false*, of course. In Option I, Fame Agency could sign Xavier and Traugott, but not anyone else. In Option II, either Traugott or West could join Fame, but the other would have to sign with Premier. So there's no way Fame Agency could ever sign three performers. What I want you to notice, though, is the relationship between this wrong answer and the correct answer to question 3 from this game.

[35] PrepTest 53, Sec. 2, Q 2

2. Which one of the following could be true?

…

(E)   Three of the performers sign with Fame Agency.

3. Which one of the following must be true?

…

(B)   Fame Agency signs at most two of the
         performers.[36]

Although the two mean exactly the same thing, choice (E) in question 2 is a wrong answer and choice (B) in question 3 is the correct answer. If it *must be true* that Fame signs at most two performers, it *must be false* that the agency signs three performers.

This illustrates what it means to *evaluate* the answer choices. Understanding what the choice *says* is necessary but not sufficient to know whether it's a right or wrong answer. You must know whether the characteristics of the statement in each answer choice fit those of the correct answer or the incorrect answers in a given question. The test makers are acutely aware of a statement's charge, but they'll flip the language around again and again: If Bob is scheduled before Dave, Bob is not scheduled after Dave; and Dave is scheduled after Bob; and Dave is *not* scheduled before Bob. Characterize the answer choices' meaning, but be ready for the statements in the choices to be phrased in any of those ways.

Now, try characterizing the choices in a slightly more complex question stem.

Each of the following could be true EXCEPT:[37]

In this case, the correct answer *must be false*. Each of the four wrong answers could be true. Don't let "EXCEPT" confuse you. It's simply telling you that the correct answer takes the two attributes *not* assigned to the wrong answers. Since the wrong answers have "could" as their level of certainty and "true" as their charge, the correct answer will take "must" and "false." Learn to recognize what you do *and* what you don't know for certain about the arrangement within a game. The test makers reward you for being able to pop back and forth between certainty and possibility, or between truth and falsity, in almost every question in the section.

Variations on the Must/Could Theme

Occasionally, the test makers will reward the same analysis that you've been using on the preceding questions but apply it to question stems that are more game-specific. Don't let that rattle you. Identify the level of certainty ("must" or "could") called for in the question stem, and then characterize the correct answer. The four wrong answers will take the opposite attributes and will negate the rest of the stem. Here's an example.

---

[36] PrepTest 53, Sec. 2, Qs 2–3

[37] PrepTest 51, Sec. 4, Q 20

> Which one of the following suspects must have been
> questioned before T was questioned?[38]

Since the correct answer here lists a suspect who *must* have been questioned *before* T, the four wrong answers will contain entities that *could* have been questioned *after* T. This question is simply a variation on questions in which the right answer *must be true* and the wrong answers *could be false*. If you want to see the question in context again, flip back to the beginning of chapter 4, where I explained it in association with the game's deductions.

Here's a question stem from another game that you've already seen. Characterize its right and wrong answers.

> Which one of the following animals could be
> pictured on any one of the guideposts?[39]

This time, you have a variation on the *could be true* question stem. Since the correct choice will contain an animal that *could* go on any of the signposts, the four wrong answers will list animals that *must* avoid certain signposts. Put even more simply, the animal in the correct answer can go anywhere. The animals in the wrong answers can't. This one is worth seeing in its original context. Take a couple of moments to get reacquainted with the game's task, rules, and deductions. Then see whether you can zero in on the correct answer.

> Exactly six guideposts, numbered 1 through 6, mark a
> mountain trail. Each guidepost pictures a different one of
> six animals—fox, grizzly, hare, lynx, moose, or porcupine.
> The following conditions must apply:
>   The grizzly is pictured on either guidepost 3 or
>   guidepost 4.
>   The moose guidepost is numbered lower than the hare
>   guidepost.
>   The lynx guidepost is numbered lower than the moose
>   guidepost but higher than the fox guidepost.

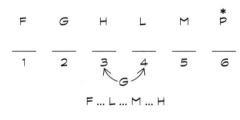

5. Which one of the following animals could be
    pictured on any one of the six guideposts?

    (A) fox
    (B) hare
    (C) lynx
    (D) moose
    (E) porcupine[40]

Remember, the correct answer lists an animal that *could* be pictured anywhere, without restriction. That's choice (E), the porcupine. Unsurprisingly, a glance at your Master Sketch shows

---

[38] PrepTest 53, Sec. 2, Q 15

[39] PrepTest 46, Sec. 4, Q 5

[40] PrepTest 46, Sec. 4, Q 5

that P is the floater, the entity unrestricted by any rules. The wrong answers each contain an animal that is restricted within the rules, as reflected in the Master Sketch. Fox, hare, lynx, and moose are all part of the big, loose block of entities created by Rules 2 and 3, and thus *cannot* be featured on some of the guideposts; they each have a restriction. Let this question stand as a reminder of just how integrated the Kaplan Method and the Logic Games section really are.

Before I move on, try your hand at characterizing the answer choices for a few more questions. This practice will benefit you with the "If" questions that follow, too, since most of them append similar questions to the hypothetical restrictions in their opening clauses.

DRILL: CHARACTERIZING ANSWER CHOICES

For each of the following question stems, jot down the characteristics of the correct answer and those of four wrong answers. Where appropriate, consider the level of certainty and the charge of both the right and the wrong answers.

Level of Certainty	"Charge"
Must	True
Could	False

1. Which one of the following must be true?[41]

   Correct answer characteristics: _____
   Incorrect answer characteristics: _____

2. Each of the following could be the fifth valve opened EXCEPT:[42]

   Correct answer characteristics: _____
   Incorrect answer characteristics: _____

3. Mr. O'Connell CANNOT accompany which one of the following pairs of children?[43]

   Correct answer characteristics: _____
   Incorrect answer characteristics: _____

4. Which one of the following could be true?[44]

   Correct answer characteristics: _____
   Incorrect answer characteristics: _____

5. Which one of the following is a pair of songs that must occupy consecutive tracks on the CD?[45]

   Correct answer characteristics: _____
   Incorrect answer characteristics: _____

6. Each of the following could be true EXCEPT:[46]

   Correct answer characteristics: _____
   Incorrect answer characteristics: _____

7. Which one of the following must be false of the summer program?[47]

   Correct answer characteristics: _____
   Incorrect answer characteristics: _____

8. Which one of the following CANNOT be true?[48]

   Correct answer characteristics: _____
   Incorrect answer characteristics: _____

9. Which one of the following pairs of technicians could repair all and only the same types of machines as each other?[49]

   Correct answer characteristics: _____
   Incorrect answer characteristics: _____

10. Which one of the following groups could perform at 6?[50]

    Correct answer characteristics: _____
    Incorrect answer characteristics: _____

---

[41] PrepTest 52, Sec. 2, Q 5
[42] PrepTest 52, Sec. 2, Q 2
[43] PrepTest 52, Sec. 2, Q 12
[44] PrepTest 46, Sec. 4, Q 20
[45] PrepTest 51, Sec. 4, Q 12

[46] PrepTest 51, Sec. 4, Q 20
[47] PrepTest 49, Sec. 1, Q 17
[48] PrepTest 48, Sec. 2, Q 3
[49] PrepTest 48, Sec. 2, Q 16
[50] PrepTest 48, Sec. 2, Q 20

Explanations

1. Which one of the following must be true?[51]

   Correct answer characteristics: Must be true.

   Incorrect answer characteristics: Could be false.

This is a straightforward question stem. The correct answer takes "must" as its level of certainty and "true" as its charge. The wrong answers will simply take the counterparts in each column.

2. Each of the following could be the fifth valve opened
   EXCEPT:[52]

   Correct answer characteristics: Could be the fifth valve opened.

   Incorrect answer characteristics: Must *not* be the fifth valve opened. Alternately, must be a valve other than the fifth one opened.

3. Mr. O'Connell CANNOT accompany which one of
   the following pairs of children?[53]

   Correct answer characteristics: Must be a pair that cannot go with Mr. O'Connell. Alternately, must be a pair that goes with Ms. Margoles or Ms. Podorski.

   Incorrect answer characteristics: Could be pair that goes with Mr. O'Connell. Alternately, a pair that is not limited to Ms. Margoles or Ms. Podorski.

4. Which one of the following could be true?[54]

   Correct answer characteristics: Could be true.

   Incorrect answer characteristics: Must be false.

5. Which one of the following is a pair of songs that must
   occupy consecutive tracks on the CD?[55]

   Correct answer characteristics: Must be a contiguous pair.

   Incorrect answer characteristics: Could be separated by intervening tracks.

6. Each of the following could be true EXCEPT:[56]

   Correct answer characteristics: Must be false.

   Incorrect answer characteristics: Could be true.

7. Which one of the following must be false of the summer program?[57]

   Correct answer characteristics: Must be false.

   Incorrect answer characteristics: Could be true.

---

[51] PrepTest 52, Sec. 2, Q 5

[52] PrepTest 52, Sec. 2, Q 2

[53] PrepTest 52, Sec. 2, Q 12

[54] PrepTest 46, Sec. 4, Q 20

[55] PrepTest 51, Sec. 4, Q 12

[56] PrepTest 51, Sec. 4, Q 20

[57] PrepTest 49, Sec. 1, Q 17

8. Which one of the following CANNOT be true?[58]

   Correct answer characteristics: Must be false.

   Incorrect answer characteristics: Could be true.

Note that examples 6, 7, and 8 are all exactly the same kind of question. Don't lose sight of how much the test makers like to play with positive and negative language while saying the same thing.

9. Which one of the following pairs of technicians could repair all and only the same types of machines as each other?[59]

   Correct answer characteristics: Could have exactly the same matches in their respective columns. Alternately, could repair exactly the same machines as one another.

   Incorrect answer characteristics: Must have some difference between their columns.

Note the phrase "all and only." The wrong answers contain pairs of technicians who must repair different types of machines *or* must repair a different number of machines. The correct answer gives a pair of technicians who could repair *exactly* the same machines as one another.

10. Which one of the following groups could perform at 6?[60]

    Correct answer characteristics: Could perform at 6.

    Incorrect answer characteristics: Must not perform at 6. Alternately, must perform at 8, 10, or 12.

Get Familiar with Must/Could Be True/False Questions

Along with the new "If" questions, which you'll explore next, Must/Could be True/False questions are your bread and butter in the Logic Games section. Their question stems can be either deceptively simple or deceptively hard. The fact of the matter is that, beneath the veneer of "must" and "could" and "EXCEPT," this is just one more way in which the test makers are rewarding you for honing the core LSAT skills of making deductions and understanding formal logic. Indeed, saying that something *must* occur is equivalent to saying that it's necessary. With these questions, rather than having you wrestle with "if-then" statements, the test makers want you to show that you've already determined what must or must not happen in the course of the game.

NEW "IF" QUESTIONS

I'll stay on the theme of understanding formal logic as I lead you through the "If" question type. Recall from chapter 3 that every conditional "if-then" rule defines a sufficient-necessary relationship. Whatever is stated in the "if" clause is sufficient to make what's stated in the

---

[58] PrepTest 48, Sec. 2, Q 3

[59] PrepTest 48, Sec. 2, Q 16

[60] PrepTest 48, Sec. 2, Q 20

"then" clause happen. Whatever's in the "then" clause is necessary for what's in the "if" clause to occur. Here's an example to help refresh your memory:

If Ms. Margoles accompanies Juana, then Ms. Podorski accompanies Lucita.[61]

If $J_{mar} \rightarrow L_{pod}$

If $L_{p\not od} \rightarrow J_{m\not ar}$

Figure 5.9

In this game, any time that Juana's chaperone is Ms. Margoles, Lucita's must be Ms. Podorski. Likewise, if Lucita goes with anyone other than Ms. Podorski—if Ms. Podorski is *not* Lucita's chaperone—Juana must go with someone other than Ms. Margoles. To use the precise terminology, Ms. Margoles accompanying Juana is *sufficient* to establish that Ms. Podorski accompanies Lucita. Ms. Podorski's accompanying Lucita is *necessary* for Ms. Margoles to be able to accompany Juana.

That same relationship is mirrored in "if" questions, except that instead of a complete conditional statement, the test makers are giving you just the "if" clause and then asking you to supply the result, the "then" that follows. In other words, the beginning of the question stem is sufficient to tell you that something must, can't, or could occur. Here's an example from the Water Treatment Plant game. I've included the Master Sketch for your reference.

Workers at a water treatment plant open eight valves—G, H, I, K, L, N, O, and P—to flush out a system of pipes that needs emergency repairs. To maximize safety and efficiency, each valve is opened exactly once, and no two valves are opened at the same time. The valves are opened in accordance with the following conditions:
  Both K and P are opened before H.
  O is opened before L but after H.
  L is opened after G.
  N is opened before H.
  I is opened after K.

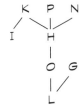

Figure 5.10

4. If L is the seventh valve opened, then each of the following could be the second valve opened EXCEPT:

  (A) G
  (B) I
  (C) K
  (D) N
  (E) P[62]

The new condition imposed here is that L is opened seventh. Checking the Master Sketch, you see that, in order for that to happen, I will have to be opened eighth. I is, in fact, the only valve that can be opened after L. Jot down a new mini-sketch (more on these in a minute) that contains the condition imposed by the "if" clause.

---

[61] PrepTest 52, Sec. 2, Game 2
[62] PrepTest 52, Sec. 2, Q 4

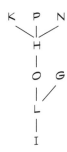

Figure 5.11

Now, consider the question in the "then" clause of the stem and then characterize the right and wrong answers. The wrong answers have entities that *could* be opened second. Thus, the correct answer contains an entity that *must not* be opened second. That's choice (B). The "if" clause, which said that L is opened seventh, is sufficient to establish that I is the eighth valve in the sequence. I can't be opened second, making choice (B) the right answer.

Notice that you didn't consider the question in the stem until after you'd dealt with the deductions triggered by the new "if." That's how you should always approach these questions. Read the "if." Determine its implications, what it's sufficient to establish. Then, and only then, proceed to the question itself. You're not ready for the question until you've played out the results of the "if."

In rare cases, the Master Sketch was so complete that there is no need for a new mini-sketch to deal with the "if" restriction. For the most part, however, train yourself to make a quick, accurate copy of the Master Sketch in which to work out the new deductions that follow from the "if" restriction. This must become a part of your logic games training.

New "Ifs" Call for New Sketches and New Deductions

You've seen this many times already in the first few chapters of this book. A new "If" question imposes a new restriction on the game. In order to see its effect, you need to combine the new "if" information with what's in your Master Sketch and add in the resulting implications. The problem is that you don't want to mess with your actual Master Sketch. The new "If" is applicable only to its one, particular question. If you wrote it and its deductions into the Master Sketch, you'd have to erase them back out before the next question. That costs you time and effort, and it dramatically increases the possibility of introducing an error into your Master Sketch. That last risk is one you can't afford to take.

The solution is the mini-sketch, a small, abbreviated copy of the Master Sketch that you draw right next to the question. There, you can put in the new "if" information and play out all of the available deductions. It should only take you 10 or 15 seconds to create a mini-sketch, but your reward is enormous. It will reveal precisely what can, can't, and must happen in the situation that results from the new "if." You'll be able to see the correct answer directly.

Students who try to save time by skipping the mini-sketch process are chasing a false efficiency. Logic games are simply too complex to keep all of their moving parts straight in your head. Without a concrete diagram, you'll wind up taking longer on the question as well as risking sloppy mistakes. Making mini-sketches and their resulting deductions is essential to your overall efficiency in the section.

Here are a few examples. Sometimes the new "if" produces a single deduction and leads directly to the right answer. Other times, it will produce a string of consequences, all of which you'll need to capture on the page. Don't rush through these examples. Take the time to re-familiarize yourself with the game's task, its rules, and its Master Sketch. Then try each of the questions in turn. Learning the mini-sketch process will make you faster and more accurate in the long run.

> In a single day, exactly seven trucks—S, T, U, W, X, Y, and Z—are the only arrivals at a warehouse. No truck arrives at the same time as any other truck, and no truck arrives more than once that day. Each truck is either green or red (but not both). The following conditions apply:
>
>   No two consecutive arrivals are red.
>   Y arrives at some time before both T and W.
>   Exactly two of the trucks that arrive before Y are red.
>   S is the sixth arrival.
>   Z arrives at some time before U.

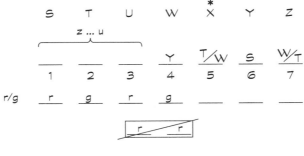

Figure 5.12

9. If exactly three of the trucks are green, then which one of the following trucks must be green?

    (A) S
    (B) T
    (C) U
    (D) W
    (E) Z[63]

This is a game you'll remember from the chapter on deductions. By combining the two rules involving Y with the established entity S, you were able to lock Y into space four. As a result, you determined the colors of the first four trucks to arrive and learned that T and W were limited to spaces 4 and 6.

The new "if" in this question draws your attention back to the color line. It tells you that exactly three of the trucks will be green. Combine the "if" with the rule that forbids red trucks from arriving consecutively. Since you already have two green trucks in spaces 2 and 4 in your Master Sketch, you can complete the color line by including the new restriction.

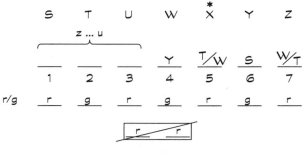

Figure 5.13

The third green truck has to arrive in the sixth spot. That's the only way to avoid consecutive red arrivals. That's just what you need to figure out which truck *must* be green.

Choice (A) is the correct answer. The new "if" allowed you to deduce that the sixth arrival is green, and Rule 4 has had truck S locked into space 6 all along. In this situation, trucks T and W will definitely be red, and there's no way to tell about trucks U and Z. All four of the trucks in the wrong answers most certainly *could* be red.

The next question is going to require you to make a longer string of deductions. The game— Garibaldi's Meetings—was featured earlier in this chapter. You'll recall that its setup and rules allowed for no additional restrictions. Because of that, I had you note that, with the exception of the Acceptability question, each question in the question set began with an "if." The one you'll try here is particularly illustrative.

In the course of one month Garibaldi has exactly seven different meetings. Each of her meetings is with exactly one of five foreign dignitaries: Fuentes, Matsuba, Rhee, Soleimani, or Tbahi. The following constraints govern Garibaldi's meetings:

  She has exactly three meetings with Fuentes, and exactly one with each of the other dignitaries.
  She does not have any meetings in a row with Fuentes.
  Her meeting with Soleimani is the very next one after her meeting with Tbahi.
  Neither the first nor last of her meetings is with Matsuba.

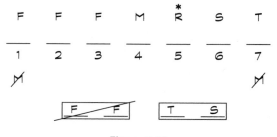

Figure 5.14

5. If Garibaldi's first meeting is with Tbahi, then
   Garibaldi's meeting with Rhee could be the

   (A) second meeting
   (B) third meeting
   (C) fifth meeting
   (D) sixth meeting
   (E) seventh meeting[64]

As soon as you see the "if," you can copy the framework slots from your Master Sketch and plug in the new restriction. Here, that means putting T in space 1:

$$\underset{1}{\underline{\text{T}}} \quad \underset{2}{\underline{}} \quad \underset{3}{\underline{}} \quad \underset{4}{\underline{}} \quad \underset{5}{\underline{}} \quad \underset{6}{\underline{}} \quad \underset{7}{\underline{}}$$

Figure 5.15

Checking the rules as they're depicted in the Master Sketch, you see that S always follows immediately after T.

$$\underset{1}{\underline{\text{T}}} \quad \underset{2}{\underline{\text{S}}} \quad \underset{3}{\underline{}} \quad \underset{4}{\underline{}} \quad \underset{5}{\underline{}} \quad \underset{6}{\underline{}} \quad \underset{7}{\underline{}}$$

Figure 5.16

Now, you have five open spaces. Three of them must belong to F and the other two to M and R. Which rule allows you to make some of those spaces concrete? It's Rule 2, the one forbidding consecutive meetings with F. There's only one way to fit in three noncontiguous meetings with F:

$$\underset{1}{\underline{\text{T}}} \quad \underset{2}{\underline{\text{S}}} \quad \underset{3}{\underline{\text{F}}} \quad \underset{4}{\underline{}} \quad \underset{5}{\underline{\text{F}}} \quad \underset{6}{\underline{}} \quad \underset{7}{\underline{\text{F}}}$$

Figure 5.17

Looking at your Master Sketch, you can see that there's nothing more to determine concretely. R is the floater. His meeting can go anywhere. M is restricted from meetings 1 and 7, but you're at no risk of running afoul of that rule in this case. You can't say for sure which of M or R takes space 4 or space 6, so just write them in as alternatives.

$$\underset{1}{\underline{\text{T}}} \quad \underset{2}{\underline{\text{S}}} \quad \underset{3}{\underline{\text{F}}} \quad \underset{4}{\underline{\text{M/R}}} \quad \underset{5}{\underline{\text{F}}} \quad \underset{6}{\underline{\text{R/M}}} \quad \underset{7}{\underline{\text{F}}}$$

Figure 5.18

Now, examine the question in the stem. It asks for a space in which R *could* go. You know that the right answer will say either "fourth" or "sixth." Choice (D) is the one that has an acceptable placement for R. Voilà. Choice (D) is the right answer.

---

[64] PrepTest 44, Sec. 3, Q 5

That took a little patience, but imagine trying to test the answer choices in your head. You'd still be trying them out, and you'd likely wind up sketching them anyway to see which one worked.

Learn to deal with all "if" questions in the two-phase process I've just described. Combine the "if" information with what's in the Master Sketch, and derive all of the available deductions. Then turn to the question itself and characterize the choices. Most of the time, a mini-sketch will be invaluable to you as you go through those steps.

There is one exception, though. When a game breaks down into Limited Option sketches, new "ifs" often simply point you to the appropriate option. Take a look at how this works.

New "Ifs" in Limited Options Games

You'll recall Limited Options (the L in the BLEND checklist) as the Deductions triggered by "either . . . or" rules and restrictions. Because they limit the acceptable arrangements of games into one of two possible solutions, I taught you to make *twin* sketches in these cases. Those dual sketches are incredibly powerful ways to organize logic games that break down into just two alternative arrangements. The time you spend making the two sketches really pays you back when the game has "if" questions associated with it. Because you've determined so much of what must be true in the game, the new "ifs" here usually don't require a mini-sketch at all. Take a look at the following examples and take note of how the "if" question(s) in each tell you which option to examine in order to derive the correct answer.

Five performers—Traugott, West, Xavier, Young, and Zinser—are recruited by three talent agencies—Fame Agency, Premier Agency, and Star Agency. Each performer signs with exactly one of the agencies and each agency signs at least one of the performers. The performers' signing with the agencies is in accord with the following:

    Xavier signs with Fame Agency.
    Xavier and Young do not sign with the same agency as each other.
    Zinser signs with the same agency as Young.
    If Traugott signs with Star Agency, West also signs with Star Agency.

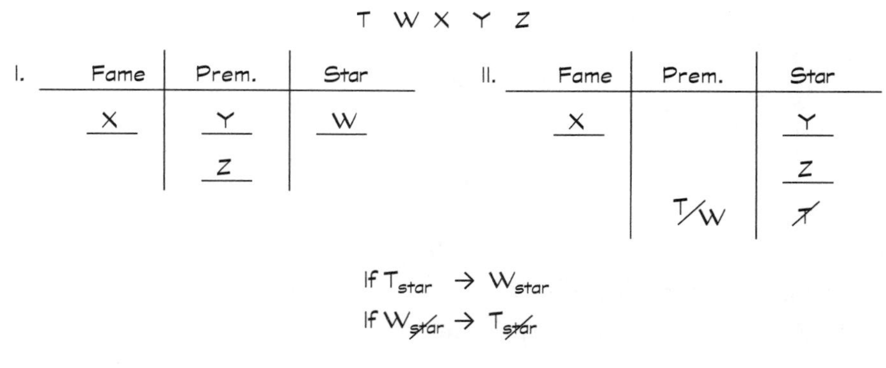

Figure 5.19

5. If Zinser signs with Star Agency, which one of the
following must be false?

(A) Premier Agency signs exactly one performer.
(B) Star Agency signs exactly three of the performers.
(C) Traugott signs with Star Agency.
(D) West signs with Star Agency.
(E) None of the other performers signs with the same
agency as Xavier.[65]

The basis for the Limited Options sketches in this game is the placement of the Young-Zinser block. You knew from Rules 2 and 3 that Young had to accompany Zinser and avoid Xavier. And from Rule 1, you knew that Xavier was a Fame Agency client. Thus, the Young-Zinser block was signing with either Premier Agency (Option I) or Star Agency (Option II).

The "if" in this question places you solidly in Option II. Check that option, and you can see that Traugott is forbidden from signing with Star.

It's no coincidence that the question asks for what *must be false*. You know that Traugott cannot sign with Star Agency, and that's exactly what choice (C) says. It's your right answer, just that quickly.

In that example, the "if" language echoed the very language you used in setting up the Limited Option scenario. Occasionally, a game's Limited Options are so clear that all of the "ifs" relate directly to criteria you used to create the two sketches. In these games, you may be able to handle the question set in a matter of a minute or two. Try it out in the game about the Clown Costume that you first saw in chapter 4. I've included all three "If" questions from its question set. By test day, you'll be handling all three more quickly than you would have handled just one of them when you first cracked open this book.

A clown will select a costume consisting of two pieces and no others: a jacket and overalls. One piece of the costume will be entirely one color, and the other piece will be plaid. Selection is subject to the following restrictions:

If the jacket is plaid, then there must be exactly three colors in it.

If the overalls are plaid, then there must be exactly two colors in them.

The jacket and overalls must have exactly one color in common.

Green, red, and violet are the only colors that can be in the jacket.

Red, violet, and yellow are the only colors that can be in the overalls.

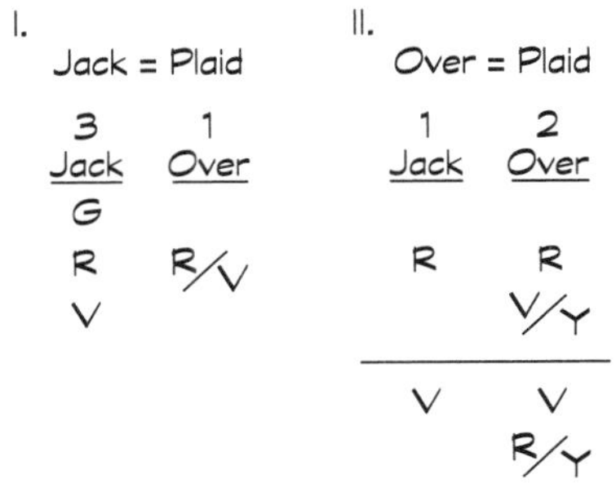

Figure 5.29

2. If there are exactly two colors in the costume, then
   which one of the following must be false?

   (A)   At least part of the jacket is green.
   (B)   At least part of the jacket is red.
   (C)   The overalls are red and violet.
   (D)   The overalls are red and yellow.
   (E)   The overalls are violet and yellow.

3. If at least part of the jacket is green, then which one of
   the following could be true?

   (A)   The overalls are plaid.
   (B)   No part of the jacket is red.
   (C)   No part of the jacket is violet.
   (D)   At least part of the overalls are yellow.
   (E)   At least part of the overalls are violet.

5. If there are exactly three colors in the costume, the
   overalls must be

   (A)   entirely red or else red and violet plaid
   (B)   entirely yellow or else violet and yellow plaid
   (C)   entirely violet or else red and violet plaid
   (D)   entirely red or else entirely yellow
   (E)   entirely red or else entirely violet[66]

You'll recall that the Limited Options in this game derived from the fact that either the jacket or the overalls were plaid and the other item plain. When the jacket is the plaid piece (Option I), it has three colors—green, red, and violet—and the plain overalls are either entirely red or entirely violet. When it's the overalls that are plaid (Option II), they have two colors from among red, violet, and yellow. The jacket in that case is one color, either red or violet, matching one of the colors in the overalls.

Now, look back at the three question stems. Question 2 put you in Option II (in Option I, there are three colors in the costume) and asked you what *must be false*. Question 3 put you in Option I (the jacket cannot have green in Option II) and asked you what *could be true*. Finally, question 5 again referred to Option I (that's where the costume has three colors) but, this time, asked what *must be true*.

You'd probably like to know the correct answers. For question 2, the right answer was choice (A). It *must be false* that the jacket has any green in Option II. For question 3, the right choice was (E). The overalls *could* be violet in Option I. For number 5, the correct choice was again (E). In Option I, the overalls *must be* entirely one color, either red or violet. Review the wrong answer choices on your own. Remember that all four must take the characteristics opposite those of the correct answer. In question 2, the four wrong answers could be true; in question 3, they must be false; and in question 5, they could be false.

---

[66] PrepTest 51, Sec. 4, Qs 2, 3, and 5

Those three questions serve as a nice microcosm illustrating what you need to remember about "If" questions in the Limited Options context. Use the "if" to identify which of the options to refer to. Then characterize the right and wrong answers and evaluate the choices. You're coming to the point where you've learned the Kaplan Method from top to bottom. Your ability to pull out these various tools and strategies and use them in harmony to get points quickly and confidently is almost complete.

In the remainder of this chapter, I'll have you look at the handful of other question types you may see on test day. These are much rarer than those you've practiced so far, but each comes with its own little twist.

MINIMUM/MAXIMUM QUESTIONS

Of the remaining logic games question types, those asking for the minimum or maximum number of entities or spaces that can be acceptably selected, grouped, or matched are the most common. Even so, you're unlikely to see more than two or three in a section; depending on the types of games represented in the section, you may see none at all. Minimum/maximum questions are most likely to accompany a Selection task ("What's the greatest/smallest number you can choose?"), but as you'll see, the test makers find subtle ways to ask about numbers in all types of logic games.

> What is the maximum number of friends who could appear in a photograph that Yakira does not appear in?[67]
> The tour group could visit at most how many sites that were discovered by Ferrara?[68]

The first thing to recognize is that, regardless of the game's task, the test makers cannot ask this kind of question unless the number restrictions within the game are in play. They can't, for example, ask you for the maximum number of candidates you can select if the game setup says, "Exactly four of the seven candidates will be selected." They can't ask you for the minimum number of entities recruited to the red team if the game setup or a rule states, "Each team recruits exactly three players." So you have a good heads-up that a question like this may be coming when, at the end of the Deductions step, you still don't have a definitive answer to some issue involving the game's numbers.

That was the case in the Friends Photograph game I presented as an illustration of the Selection task and of formal logic rules. Refresh your memory of the game's setup and rules. Take note of which rules can be combined into further deductions. Then I'll discuss the Maximum/Minimum question that follows.

---

[67] PrepTest 45, Sec. 3, Q 15
[68] PrepTest 44, Sec. 3, Q 17

An album contains photographs picturing seven friends: Raimundo, Selma, Ty, Umiko, Wendy, Yakira, Zack. The friends appear either alone or in groups with one another, in accordance with the following:

Wendy appears in every photograph that Selma appears in.
Selma appears in every photograph that Umiko appears in.
Raimundo appears in every photograph that Yakira does not appear in.

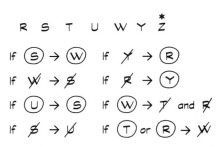

Figure 5.30

15. What is the maximum number of friends who could appear in a photograph that Yakira does not appear in?

(A) six
(B) five
(C) four
(D) three
(E) two[69]

In this game, all of the rules involve conditional, formal logic statements. Depending on who appears in the photograph, other friends must be included or excluded. Nothing in the setup or rules gives you a set number of entities that must be in a given photo, so this game is a likely candidate to have a minimum/maximum question. The particular question asks for a maximum number, but it places a condition on the question. It asks for the maximum number of friends who could appear *when Yakira does not appear*. That's like a hidden "if." A question asking for the maximum number who could appear *in any case* would be a different question and have a different answer.

So start with the condition that Yakira is excluded from the list.

R S T U W Y̶ Z̶*

Figure 5.31

Checking the rules, you see that when Yakira is out, Raimundo is in.

Ⓡ S T U W Y̶ Z̶*

Figure 5.32

Raimundo's presence knocks out Wendy, pursuant to Rule 4.

Ⓡ S T U W̶ Y̶ Z̶*

Figure 5.33

_____

[69] PrepTest 45, Sec. 3, Q 15

The loss of Wendy triggers Rule 1, which says that without Wendy, you can't have Selma.

$$\text{\textcircled{R}} \quad \cancel{S} \quad T \quad U \quad \cancel{W} \quad \cancel{X} \quad \overset{*}{Z}$$

Figure 5.34

And finally, that triggers Rule 2, which tells you that if you get rid of Selma, you must also get rid of Umiko.

$$\text{\textcircled{R}} \quad \cancel{S} \quad T \quad \cancel{U} \quad \cancel{W} \quad \cancel{X} \quad \overset{*}{Z}$$

Figure 5.35

Now, you can see the correct answer unequivocally. The maximum number of friends available for the photograph is three: Raimundo, Ty, and Zack. Don't be surprised when elements of more than one question type appear together. You probably wouldn't have categorized this as an "If" question right off the bat, but once you see that there is a limiting condition in the question stem, you know to deal with it by way of a mini-sketch before evaluating the answer choices.

The next example lacks any conditional, "if"-type language.

A tour group plans to visit exactly five archaeological sites. Each site was discovered by exactly one of the following archaeologists—Ferrara, Gallagher, Oliphant—and each dates from the eighth, ninth, or tenth century (A.D.). The tour must satisfy the following conditions:

  The site visited second dates from the ninth century.
  Neither the site visited fourth nor the site visited fifth was discovered by Oliphant.
  Exactly one of the sites was discovered by Gallagher, and it dates from the tenth century.
  If a site dates from the eighth century, it was discovered by Oliphant.
  The site visited third dates from a more recent century than does either the site visited first or that visited fourth.

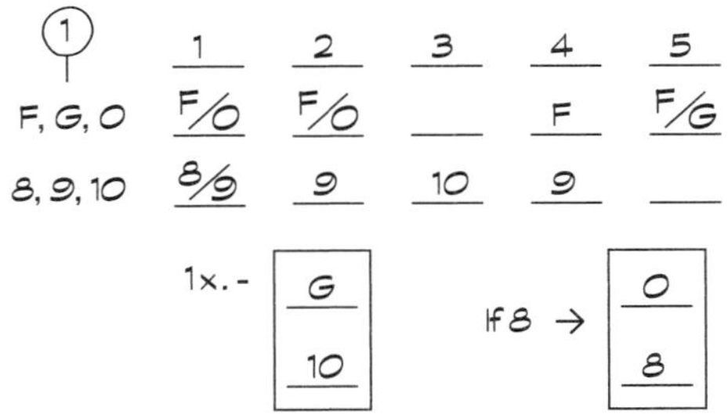

Figure 5.36

17. The tour group could visit at most how many sites that were discovered by Ferrara?

  (A) one
  (B) two
  (C) three
  (D) four
  (E) five[70]

---

[70] PrepTest 44, Sec. 3, Q 17

This time, all you have to do is check the Master Sketch to see how many of the sites could have been discovered by Ferrara. You can see that nothing prevents Ferrara from discovering any given one of the five sites. The third rule, though, tells you that Gallagher must have discovered exactly one site, so Ferrara cannot have discovered *all* of the sites. Oliphant *may* have discovered a site, but you don't know that for sure. The maximum number Ferrara could have found is thus four. With this kind of minimum/maximum question, you can predict the correct answer before evaluating the choice. In this case, it's choice (D).

COMPLETE AND ACCURATE LIST QUESTIONS

Most of the time, when you see "complete and accurate list" in a question stem, it is part of a regular Acceptability question. But as I mentioned in the section on Acceptability questions, you will occasionally see Complete and Accurate List questions that focus on a narrower part of the game, such as a single entity or a specific space.

> Which one of the following could be a complete and accurate list of the lunch trucks, each of which serves all three of the office buildings?[71]

> Which one of the following is a complete and accurate list of the sites each of which CANNOT be the site discovered by Gallagher?[72]

These questions are less common than the other question types covered so far in this chapter. It's very rare to find more than one or two of these in the Logic Games section, and many tests include none at all. That said, take a look at a couple of examples in context to learn the best ways to approach them should you encounter one on test day or later in your practice with this book.

The first example comes from the Archaeological Site Tour game you saw earlier in this chapter. Take a few moments to refresh your memory of the game and review the deductions that led to the Master Sketch.

A tour group plans to visit exactly five archaeological sites. Each site was discovered by exactly one of the following archaeologists—Ferrara, Gallagher, Oliphant—and each dates from the eighth, ninth, or tenth century (A.D.). The tour must satisfy the following conditions:

The site visited second dates from the ninth century.
Neither the site visited fourth nor the site visited fifth was discovered by Oliphant.
Exactly one of the sites was discovered by Gallagher, and it dates from the tenth century.
If a site dates from the eighth century, it was discovered by Oliphant.
The site visited third dates from a more recent century than does either the site visited first or that visited fourth.

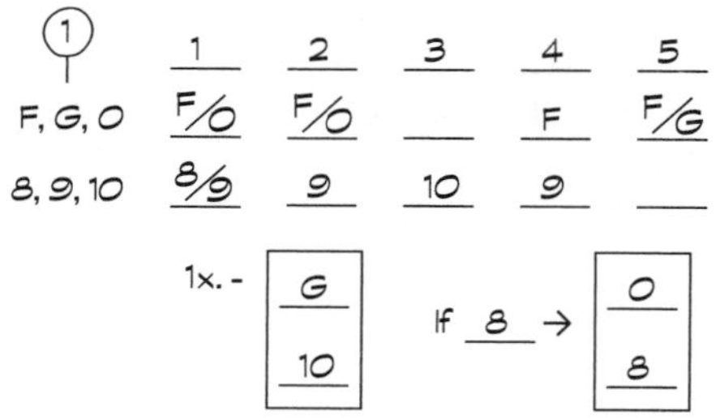

Figure 5.37

[71] PrepTest 43, Sec. 4, Q 21
[72] PrepTest 44, Sec. 3, Q 16

16. Which one of the following is a complete and accurate
     list of the sites each of which CANNOT be the site
     discovered by Gallagher?

     (A) third, fourth, fifth
     (B) second, third, fourth
     (C) first, fourth, fifth
     (D) first, second, fifth
     (E) first, second, fourth[73]

In a case like this one, you can predict the correct answer with precision before you evaluate the choices. Looking at the Master Sketch, you see that Gallagher is ruled out of the first, second, and fourth sites and no others. That's your complete and accurate list, and it fits answer choice (E) exactly.

It's great when your answer is as clear-cut as that one, but it won't always happen. In the next example, I'll go over a Complete and Accurate List question where you're better off eliminating the wrong choices than you are trying to figure out the correct response before evaluating the answer choices.

> Exactly six people—Lulu, Nam, Ofelia, Pachai, Santiago, and
> Tyrone—are the only contestants in a chess tournament. The
> tournament consists of four games, played one after the other.
> Exactly two people play in each game, and each person plays
> in at least one game. The following conditions must apply:
>   Tyrone does not play in the first or third game.
>   Lulu plays in the last game.
>   Nam plays in only one game and it is not against Pachai.
>   Santiago plays in exactly two games, one just before and
>   one just after the only game that Ofelia plays in.

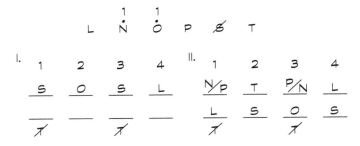

Figure 5.38

11. Which one of the following is a complete and accurate
     list of the contestants who CANNOT play against Tyrone in any game?

     (A) Lulu, Pachai
     (B) Nam, Ofelia
     (C) Nam, Pachai
     (D) Nam, Santiago
     (E) Ofelia, Pachai[74]

---

[73] PrepTest 44, Sec. 3, Q 16

[74] PrepTest 45, Sec. 3, Q 11

This time, there's no way to simply look at the Master Sketch and say, "Oh, those are the players who can't compete against Tyrone." Instead, you'll need to first examine the options and eliminate answers containing players who *can* be matched against Tyrone in the tournament. Cross out wrong answers completely. Option II is quite clear. There, Tyrone is scheduled to face off against Santiago in Game 2. That eliminates choice (D). In Option I, Tyrone could face Ofelia in Game 2. That gets rid of choices (B) and (E). Tyrone could also face Lulu in Option I, Game 4. So strike out choice (A). That leaves only choice (C), the correct answer.

Whenever you encounter Complete and Accurate List questions, you'll work through them in one of those two ways, either determining the content of the correct answer from the Master Sketch *or* using the restrictions shown in the Master Sketch to eliminate wrong answers. Remember that the correct answer to a Complete and Accurate List question must include *any and all* entities, groups, or spaces that fit the call of the question. That means that an answer can be incorrect not only for being inaccurate (including the wrong entities or spaces) but also for being incomplete (not including all of the right entities or spaces).

Complete and Accurate List questions are never going to make or break your Logic Games section performance. There simply aren't enough of them to have that kind of impact. Just make sure you know how to approach them and keep your focus on the Rules and Deductions steps of the Kaplan Method. If you do, Complete and Accurate List questions should become just one more small element of the Logic Games section that you can handle flawlessly.

COMPLETE SOLUTION QUESTIONS

Very occasionally, the test makers will pose a question that asks you what additional restriction would allow you to completely determine the arrangement of all entities in the game.

> Which one of the following, if known, would allow one to determine the entire lecture schedule and identify for each week the philosopher who is lectured on that week?[75]

> It can be determined in which department each of the seven applicants is hired if which one of the following statements is true?[76]

Questions like these can be associated with any task, but the game must be close enough to completion that the addition of one restriction will lock all of the entities into place. That tells you to look for one of two alternatives as you evaluate the answer choices. Either a floater or loosely restricted entity will be established into position, or an entity that restricts several others will be further limited. Take a look at this example from the Talent Agency game:

---

[75] PrepTest 34, Sec. 4, Q 10
[76] PrepTest 38, Sec. 2, Q 16

Five performers—Traugott, West, Xavier, Young, and Zinser—are recruited by three talent agencies—Fame Agency, Premier Agency, and Star Agency. Each performer signs with exactly one of the agencies and each agency signs at least one of the performers. The performers' signing with the agencies is in accord with the following:

Xavier signs with Fame Agency.

Xavier and Young do not sign with the same agency as each other.

Zinser signs with the same agency as Young.

If Traugott signs with Star Agency, West also signs with Star Agency.

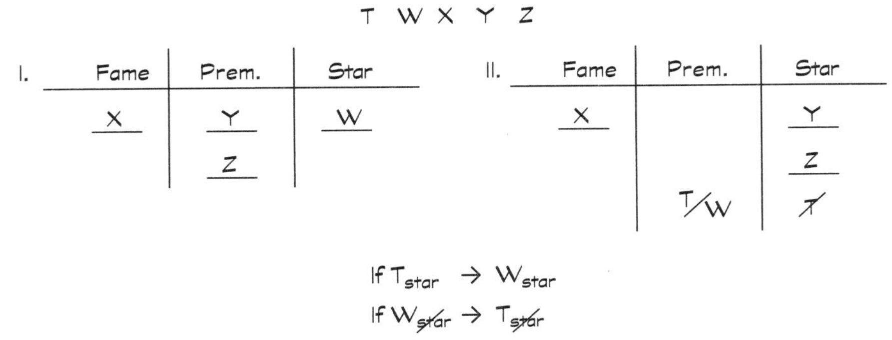

T W X Y Z

I.	Fame	Prem.	Star
	X	Y	W
		Z	

II.	Fame	Prem.	Star
	X		Y
			Z
		T/W	~~T~~

If $T_{star} \rightarrow W_{star}$

If $W_{\cancel{star}} \rightarrow T_{\cancel{star}}$

Figure 5.39

4. The agency with which each of the performers signs is completely determined if which one of the following is true?

(A) Traugott signs with Fame Agency.
(B) Traugott signs with Star Agency.
(C) West signs with Premier Agency.
(D) Xavier signs with Fame Agency.
(E) Zinser signs with Premier Agency.[77]

One of the answers will provide the last puzzle piece, so to speak. Think about each of the entities mentioned in the choices. Who would it be most helpful to know more about?

Start with choice (D). Xavier is already established in Fame Agency. That much you've known since you first read Rule 1. And yet there's some ambiguity left in the game. Eliminate choice (D).

Choice (E) focuses on Zinser. Along with Young, Zinser provided the trigger for your Limited Options deduction. Zinser can sign with either Premier or Star, but in neither case does knowing about Zinser finish the picture. Eliminate choice (E).

The remaining answers focus on West and Traugott, both of whom are restricted by the formal logic in Rule 4. That makes choices (A), (B), and (C) all more likely than choices (D) and (E) were, but choice (B) should stand out. The statement in choice (B) exactly matches the "if" clause of Rule 4. Traugott can be placed in Star's column only in Option I. In fact, Traugott is the only

---

[77] PrepTest 53, Sec. 2, Q 4

entity yet to be placed in Option I. So knowing that Traugott signs with Star Agency is, indeed, enough to determine every performer's placement in the game.

For the record, Traugott could sign with Fame Agency in either option, so choice (A) doesn't determine everyone's placement. And while placing West under the Premier heading definitely puts you in Option II, it doesn't tell you whether Traugott signs with Fame or Premier. So choice (C) doesn't quite get the job done either.

It shouldn't surprise you that this question type accompanied a Limited Options game, where a restricted set of potential arrangements could be predetermined. And, once you see the answer choices in action, it shouldn't surprise you to find that the correct answer involved a statement that could only be true in Option I, the more limited of the two options. Perhaps most telling of all, though, is the fact that the correct answer provided a fact *sufficient* to trigger additional restrictions. The correct answer to a Complete Solution question doesn't have to trigger formal logic per se, but it must lead to additional concrete restrictions within the game.

Every once in a great while, the test makers will pose a variation on the Complete Solution question that asks for a fact that would lead to more specific additional restrictions. You saw one of these in the Dorm Room Appliances game in chapter 2.

> 5. Which one of the following statements, if true, guarantees that Henri is using no more than one of the following: the hairdryer, the razor, the television?[78]

These questions are rare indeed. In the five years' worth of LSATs released from PrepTest 39 through PrepTest 53, there were only these two examples. If you should chance upon one on test day or in your further practice, remember to keep your eyes peeled for the answer choice that triggers additional restrictions. You'll know, coming out of Step 4, where ambiguity and wiggle room remain within the setup. The correct answer to one of these Complete Solution questions will focus exactly there. It will hit the target so precisely that only one position is available to each of the entities.

"RULE-CHANGERS"

Nearly as rare as Complete Solution questions (there were, again, two of these among all of the logic games from PrepTest 39 through PrepTest 53), "Rule-Changers" are questions that ask you to replace one of the original rules with a new restriction applicable only to this question.

> Suppose the restriction that Miller rows closer to the front than Singh is replaced by the restriction that Singh rows closer to the front than Miller. If the other two restrictions remain in effect, then each of the following could be an accurate matching of athletes to seats EXCEPT:[79]

---

[78] PrepTest 48, Sec.2, Q 5
[79] PrepTest 43, Sec. 4, Q 12

> Assume that the original condition that the linen
> dress hangs immediately to the right of the silk dress
> is replaced by the condition that the wool dress hangs
> immediately to the right of the silk dress. If all the
> other initial conditions remain in effect, which one of
> the following must be false?[80]

These question stems are long, but they look more intimidating than they are. In effect, they're super-"Ifs", because they force you to alter your original Master Sketch. But as with a regular "If" question, you can take control of them through a new mini-sketch. Notice, too, that the questions they ask after instructing you to swap positions are exactly the same ones you practiced earlier in this chapter: What must/could be true/false? What is or is not an acceptable arrangement? Moreover, they're always explicit—not only about the rule that is changing, but also that the other original restrictions are not.

"Rule-Changers" Always Appear Last

Something that many test takers fail to realize is that these questions, when they do occur, are always the last of the questions in the set for that game. The test makers bank on "Rule-Changers" being time-consuming, and at least part of the reason for their inclusion is almost certainly to slow down test takers who aren't being strategic with their time. Don't fall into that trap. If you find a "Rule-Changer" too time-consuming, skip it and leave yourself ample time to get all of the remaining points in the Logic Games section. It's far better to sacrifice that one question than to find yourself unable to complete one of the remaining games. I'll talk more about strategic time management in Part III of this book. For now, just remember that your goal must be to get as many right answers as you can overall. Don't overinvest your time in one complex question.

The placement of these questions at the end of the question set has one other consequence. Assuming you've finished all of the other questions, this is the one exceptional circumstance in which I'd tell you that it's okay to mess with your Master Sketch if doing so is easier or more efficient than making a new mini-sketch. Since the question stem is changing or replacing one of the original restrictions, you'll need to see the ripple effect that the rule change has on the other deductions you made in Step 4.

"Rule-Changer" Practice

Here's an example from a game that you've already seen. I've included the game's setup, its original Master Sketch, and the question. Give it a try, and then I'll go over it. Make sure that you take the time to consider which parts of the Master Sketch the "Rule-Changer" does and doesn't alter.

---

[80] PrepTest 41, Sec. 2, Q 7

A fruit stand carries at least one kind of the following kinds of fruit: figs, kiwis, oranges, pears, tangerines, and watermelons. The stand does not carry any other kind of fruit. The selection of fruits the stand carries is consistent with the following conditions:

    If the stand carries kiwis, then it does not carry pears.
    If the stand does not carry tangerines, then it carries kiwis.
    If the stand carries oranges, then it carries both pears and watermelons.
    If the stand carries watermelons, then it carries figs or tangerines or both.

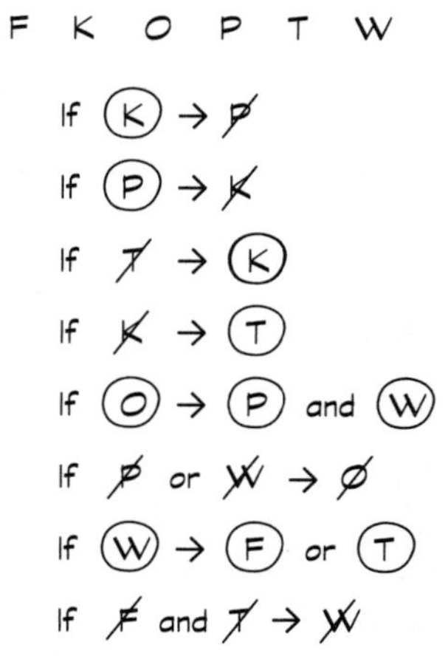

F K O P T W

If (K) → P̷
If (P) → K̷
If T̷ → (K)
If K̷ → (T)
If (O) → (P) and (W)
If P̷ or W̷ → Ø
If (W) → (F) or (T)
If F̷ and T̷ → W̷

Figure 5.40

6. If the condition that if the fruit stand does not carry tangerines then it does carry kiwis is suspended, and all other conditions remain in effect, then which one of the following CANNOT be a complete and accurate list of the kinds of fruit the stand carries?

(A) pears
(B) figs, pears
(C) oranges, pears, watermelons
(D) figs, pears, watermelons
(E) figs, oranges, pears, watermelons[81]

In this example, one of the original rules—Rule 2—is suspended. The presence of Rule 2 in the original Master Sketch told you that you had to have at least one of kiwis or tangerines. Now, that restriction is lifted and an arrangement with neither kiwis nor tangerines is fine, provided that it meets the game's other requirements. You needn't do more than cross Rule 2 off the list and you're ready to evaluate the answer choices.

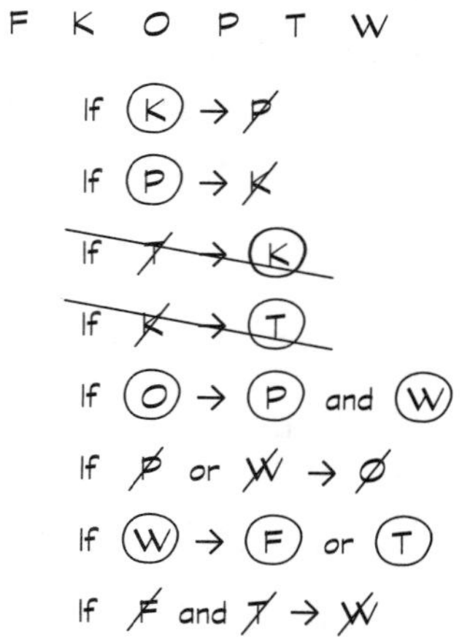

F K O P T W

If (K) → P̷
If (P) → K̷
~~If T̷ → (K)~~
~~If K̷ → (T)~~
If (O) → (P) and (W)
If P̷ or W̷ → Ø
If (W) → (F) or (T)
If F̷ and T̷ → W̷

Figure 5.41

[81] PrepTest 36, Sec. 4, Q 6

The question calls for the one *un*acceptable arrangement. This is the opposite of an Acceptability question stem: The right answer will violate a rule, but the wrong answers will not.

Choice (A) is acceptable. The only thing that including pears triggers is the exclusion of kiwis. Notice that under the original rules, this would have necessitated the inclusion of tangerines. Now that Rule 2 has been suspended, that second requirement is gone. Since choice (A) is acceptable, it's a wrong answer.

Choice (B), too, offers an acceptable arrangement and is, therefore, a wrong answer. Including figs doesn't trigger any additional rules, so figs and pears is a fine combination for the fruit stand's offerings.

Choice (C), though, runs afoul of Rule 4, which is still in effect under this question stem's terms. Including watermelons requires including either figs or tangerines, neither of which is included in the answer choice. As a rule-violator, choice (C) is the correct answer.

Choices (D) and (E) offer acceptable arrangements, of course. There are always one correct and four demonstrably incorrect answer choices. That point really encapsulates the final takeaway message of both this chapter and Part I of this book.

TAKEAWAY: ANSWER THE QUESTION THE TEST IS ASKING

I'll say it one more time: One right, four rotten. Unlike some tests you may have encountered in school, there is no "best" answer on the LSAT. There is always one unequivocally correct choice and four unequivocally wrong ones. And remember the very first point I made in chapter 1: Every question has an answer. The test always provides you with enough information to determine the correct answer.

The LSAT is tough but fair. If you encounter any question that seems to have more than one right answer (or one that seems to have no right answer), you can rest assured that you've made one of two mistakes: Either you missed a rule or deduction in the game's setup, or you misread the question stem. Avoiding the first of those mistakes is a matter of practicing with Steps 1 through 4 of the Kaplan Method, something you've already made great strides with. To avoid the latter mistake—to ensure that you're answering the right question—you must remain diligent. Characterize the choices before you evaluate them. Discipline yourself to do that on every question, because it's tempting to let the easiest questions make you sloppy. Avoid those two pitfalls and you're on the road to a great Logic Games section and a great LSAT score.

In the next chapter, I'll have you work through a few games from top to bottom, putting all five steps of the Kaplan Method into action.

CHAPTER 6

COMPLETE GAME PRACTICE

PUT IT ALL TOGETHER

You're ready to try your hand at some full games, top to bottom, start to finish. I won't be interrupting you with hints or analyses this time. You've learned how to manage any logic game effectively using the Kaplan Method. Now, use it systematically to practice the five steps in order, exactly as you'll use them on test day.

THE 5-STEP KAPLAN METHOD FOR LOGIC GAMES

STEP 1 Overview
Assess the game's Situation and determine your task(s).

STEP 2 Sketch
Draw a simple, useful framework to organize the game's information and restrictions.

STEP 3 Rules
Add the Rules into the Sketch in clear notation.

STEP 4 Deductions
Combine the Rules and restrictions to determine what must be true and false.

STEP 5 Questions
Answer the question efficiently using the information from your Master Sketch.

Take the games one at a time. They're laid out just as they will be on the real exam, so practice using the space on the page to manage your scratch work and mini-sketches. You won't get any scratch paper for your official LSAT, so get used to working in the test booklet now.

After you've completed each one, review it thoroughly using the explanations that follow it. That will help you see where you've mastered the concepts and strategies and where your approach still needs some polishing. More importantly, don't limit yourself to reviewing only the questions you got wrong. Even when you wound up with the correct answer, you need to be sure that you did so as efficiently as possible.

Those are your Dos. Now, for a couple of Don'ts. First, don't try to go too fast. You'll have the chance to practice timing and efficiency in Part III of this book. Use this chapter as a chance to practice being methodical, accurate, and effective; after all, you must be able to do logic games properly before you can do them fast. That's another reason why, at this point in your practice, it's so important to study the explanations to those questions you got right as well as those you got wrong.

Second, don't worry too much about categorizing each game. Part II of this book will outline and teach you to recognize the game types. For now, assess each game as you read it. Try to understand your task and to create a helpful, logical sketch. I want you to be confident that you can handle every game you see on test day, even if you can't give it a special name.

The four games in this chapter constitute a fairly representative sample of the games you're most likely to see on test day. You may recognize bits and pieces of some of them, but you haven't worked through the complete set of rules or deductions for any of them at this point. Challenge yourself to employ the relevant strategies from chapters 1–5. You may be surprised at how routine much of this is beginning to feel.

GAME 1

Questions 1–7

A closet contains exactly six hangers—1, 2, 3, 4, 5, and 6—hanging, in that order, from left to right. It also contains exactly six dresses—one gauze, one linen, one polyester, one rayon, one silk, and one wool—a different dress on each of the hangers, in an order satisfying the following conditions:

The gauze dress is on a lower-numbered hanger than the polyester dress.

The rayon dress is on hanger 1 or hanger 6.

Either the wool dress or the silk dress is on hanger 3.

The linen dress hangs immediately to the right of the silk dress.

1. Which one of the following could be an accurate matching of the hangers to the fabrics of the dresses that hang on them?

   (A) 1: wool; 2: gauze; 3: silk; 4: linen; 5: polyester; 6: rayon
   (B) 1: rayon; 2: wool; 3: gauze; 4: silk; 5: linen; 6: polyester
   (C) 1: polyester; 2: gauze; 3: wool; 4: silk; 5: linen; 6: rayon
   (D) 1: linen; 2: silk; 3: wool; 4: gauze; 5: polyester; 6: rayon
   (E) 1: gauze; 2: rayon; 3: silk; 4: linen; 5: wool; 6: polyester

2. If both the silk dress and the gauze dress are on odd-numbered hangers, then which one of the following could be true?

   (A) The polyester dress is on hanger 1.
   (B) The wool dress is on hanger 2.
   (C) The polyester dress is on hanger 4.
   (D) The linen dress is on hanger 5.
   (E) The wool dress is on hanger 6.

3. If the silk dress is on an even-numbered hanger, which one of the following could be on the hanger immediately to its left?

   (A) the gauze dress
   (B) the linen dress
   (C) the polyester dress
   (D) the rayon dress
   (E) the wool dress

4. If the polyester dress is on hanger 2, then which one of the following must be true?

   (A) The silk dress is on hanger 1.
   (B) The wool dress is on hanger 3.
   (C) The linen dress is on hanger 4.
   (D) The linen dress is on hanger 5.
   (E) The rayon dress is on hanger 6.

5. Which one of the following CANNOT be true?

   (A) The linen dress hangs immediately next to the gauze dress.
   (B) The polyester dress hangs immediately to the right of the rayon dress.
   (C) The rayon dress hangs immediately to the left of the wool dress.
   (D) The silk dress is on a lower-numbered hanger than the gauze dress.
   (E) The wool dress is on a higher-numbered hanger than the rayon dress.

6. Which one of the following CANNOT hang immediately next to the rayon dress?

   (A) the gauze dress
   (B) the linen dress
   (C) the polyester dress
   (D) the silk dress
   (E) the wool dress

7. Assume that the original condition that the linen dress hangs immediately to the right of the silk dress is replaced by the condition that the wool dress hangs immediately to the right of the silk dress. If all the other initial conditions remain in effect, which one of the following must be false?

   (A) The linen dress is on hanger 1.
   (B) The gauze dress is on hanger 2.
   (C) The wool dress is on hanger 4.
   (D) The silk dress is on hanger 5.
   (E) The polyester dress is on hanger 6.[1]

---

[1] PrepTest 41, Sec. 2, Game 1, Qs 1–7

Explanations—Game 1

STEPS 1 AND 2: Overview and Sketch

This is an easy game to visualize: a closet with six hangers, numbered 1 through 6. That easily turns into a standard Sequencing framework.

1 2 3 4 5 6
G L P R S W
1 2 3 4 5 6

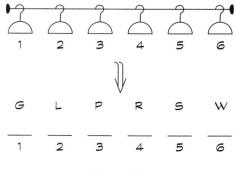

Figure 6.1

Make sure that you notice when games establish a direction for the numbering of slots. Here, the numbers increase as you go from left to right. Just a glance at the rules shows you that some of them pinpoint specific spaces. Anticipate being able to draw some of the restrictions right into the picture.

STEP 3: Rules

Rule 1 is relative, or "loose."

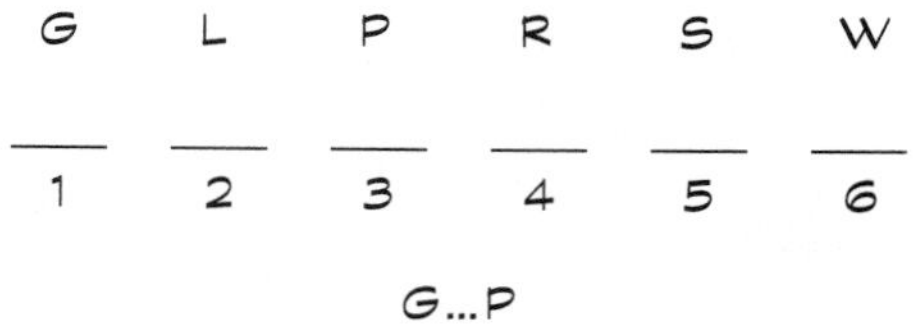

G L P R S W
1 2 3 4 5 6
G...P

Figure 6.2

Rule 2 presents an "either/or" situation, but since the rayon dress isn't implicated in any other rule, it's probably overkill to make dual Limited Options sketches here. Simply depict it like this:

G L P R S W
R
1 2 3 4 5 6
G...P

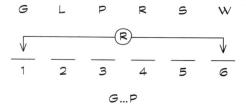

Figure 6.3

Rule 3 provides for another "either/or," this time involving a space rather than an entity.

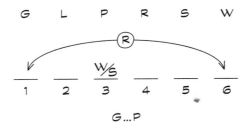

Figure 6.4

Rule 4 makes a strong block of entities S and L. You know both their order and their proximity.

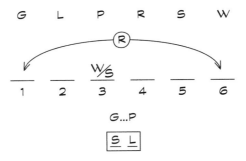

Figure 6.5

Not one of those rules should seem unfamiliar at this point. You haven't seen precisely this combination, but you've seen several examples of how similar rules work together. There are no floaters in this game. Every entity is restricted by at least one rule.

STEP 4: Deductions

You can combine only two of the four rules in this game, Rules 3 and 4. They share entity S, the silk dress. So place the result of that duplicated entity into your framework and you have your Master Sketch.

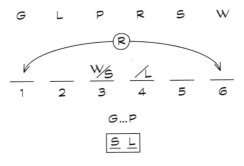

Figure 6.6

One of the key questions to ask yourself is whether you spent time unnecessarily looking for additional deductions that weren't there to find. Did you consult the BLEND checklist? If so, you knew that only the block created by Rule 4 and the duplicated entity S would help you. That meant getting to the questions faster.

STEP 5: Questions

The question set here is fairly balanced: one Acceptability question, three "If" questions, two Must Be False questions, and one "Rule-Changer." The fact that there are seven questions means that this game is especially important to your performance on the section. This one game represented close to 30 percent of the logic games points available on PrepTest 41. If you handled the questions here efficiently, you had the foundation for an outstanding section performance. See how you did.

1. **(A)**
2. **(B)**
3. **(E)**
4. **(E)**
5. **(B)**
6. **(D)**
7. **(D)**

Sequencing games like this one have been the most common games to appear on the LSAT over the past two decades. This example is almost stereotypical. The level of restriction here is standard, neither overly constrained nor overly vague. Even the question set is balanced, with just enough new "If" questions to allow you to work out several acceptable permutations that you can then leverage against the more opened-ended Must Be False questions. Consider this game to be the archetype of Strict Sequencing. That will give proper context to the variations on this game type that you'll see in Part II.

GAME 2

Questions 6–10

Six hotel suites—F, G, H, J, K, L—are ranked from most expensive (first) to least expensive (sixth). There are no ties. The ranking must be consistent with the following conditions:

H is more expensive than L.

If G is more expensive than H, then neither K nor L is more expensive than J.

If H is more expensive than G, then neither J nor L is more expensive than K.

F is more expensive than G, or else F is more expensive than H, but not both.

6. Which one of the following could be the ranking of the suites, from most expensive to least expensive?

    (A)   G, F, H, L, J, K
    (B)   H, K, F, J, G, L
    (C)   J, H, F, K, G, L
    (D)   J, K, G, H, L, F
    (E)   K, J, L, H, F, G

7. If G is the second most expensive suite, then which one of the following could be true?

    (A)   H is more expensive than F.
    (B)   H is more expensive than G.
    (C)   K is more expensive than F.
    (D)   K is more expensive than J.
    (E)   L is more expensive than F.

8. Which one of the following CANNOT be the most expensive suite?

    (A)   F
    (B)   G
    (C)   H
    (D)   J
    (E)   K

9. If L is more expensive than F, then which one of the following could be true?

    (A)   F is more expensive than H.
    (B)   F is more expensive than K.
    (C)   G is more expensive than H.
    (D)   G is more expensive than J.
    (E)   G is more expensive than L.

10. If H is more expensive than J and less expensive than K, then which one of the following could be true?

    (A)   F is more expensive than H.
    (B)   G is more expensive than F.
    (C)   G is more expensive than H.
    (D)   J is more expensive than L.
    (E)   L is more expensive than K.[2]

Explanations—Game 2

STEPS 1 AND 2: Overview and Sketch

The notion of ranking should put you on immediate notice that you're dealing with a Sequencing action. It's also likely that your instinctive reaction is to arrange this game vertically. The very words *higher* and *lower* ranked imply this orientation. If you started to scratch out six slots, that's fine. But there's really no need for a framework here at all. All of the rules are "loose"; they give only the relative positions of the entities they restrict.

STEP 3: Rules

Sometimes, Loose Sequencing rules are so integrated that you can simply start with Rule 1 and then add on the remaining rules to the sketch one at a time. Here, however, the formal logic in Rules 2 and 3 makes that direct approach too difficult. So jot down all four rules and then combine them in Step 4: Deductions.

Rule 1 is the only one that's truly straightforward: H is ranked above L.

H
|
L

Figure 6.7

Rules 2 and 3 create two incompatible alternative scenarios. Don't worry if you didn't see that as you sketched Rule 2. Once you saw that the conditional clauses of the two rules are contradictions of one another, you'd know that you have to consider two arrangements.

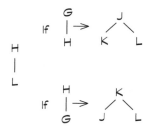

Figure 6.8

Rule 4 also gives you alternative arrangements. It's easy to depict F as either more expensive than G or more expensive than H, but the "but not both" at the end is what gives this rule its true power. When F is more expensive than G, F must be less expensive than H. When F is more expensive than H, F must be less expensive than G.

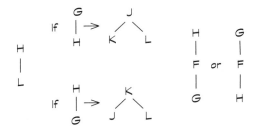

Figure 6.9

Creating a complete picture of Rule 4 is the springboard to the additional deductions that give this game its full concreteness.

STEP **4: Deductions**

If you struggled with the questions in this game, it's likely that Step 4 is actually where you went off course. Review this step carefully and make sure you wound up with the recommended Master Sketch.

Your starting point—the point of greatest restriction in this game—is Rule 4. It creates the fundamental Limited Options sketches you'll build off of. Every acceptable ranking contains either the order H–F–G or the order G–F–H among the entities.

Figure 6.10

Next, add Rule 1 to each of the options.

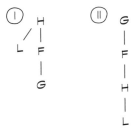

Figure 6.11

In Option I, you don't know anything about the relationship between L and the F-G portion of the string. In Option II, you can see that the order G–F–H–L is required.

Now, consider Rules 2 and 3 in light of the Limited Options. The alternate orderings of G and H relative to F in Rule 4 match the two sufficient clauses of the formal logic rules. Rule 2 is triggered by Option II, while Rule 3 is triggered by Option I. So add J and K into each option accordingly.

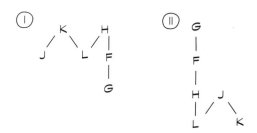

Figure 6.12

This Master Sketch puts you fully in control of the game. You can already anticipate "If" questions that will indicate which of the two options you need to use.

STEP 5: Questions

There are only five questions this time. The key to handling them lies in using the Limited Options sketches effectively. As you review, check not only whether you got the correct answer, but also if you got it as quickly *and confidently* as possible. Review your work.

6. **(B)**
7. **(C)**
8. **(A)**
9. **(D)**
10. **(D)**

This game, like the first game in this chapter, tasked you with determining the entities' order or sequence. The big difference is that, in the Hotel Suites game, all of the rules were relative, or "loose." None of the rules lock an entity into a particular space or dictate a specific distance that separates any of the entities. In the past, Loose Sequencing games were typically very simple, and you were able to link all of the entities within a single "tree" framework. More recently—and I'll go into more detail about this in Part II of the book—the test makers have been more creative, and Loose Sequencing games have become more complex. This example is somewhere in between the simplest and most complex of these games. The inclusion of formal logic rules and the presence of the Limited Options deduction are reminders that what you've learned about Steps 3 and 4 of the Kaplan Method applies to all logic games.

GAME 3

Questions 18–22

Each of exactly six lunch trucks sells a different one of six kinds of food: falafel, hot dogs, ice cream, pitas, salad, or tacos. Each truck serves one or more of exactly three office buildings: X, Y, or Z. The following conditions apply:

> The falafel truck, the hot dog truck, and exactly one other truck each serve Y.
> The falafel truck serves exactly two of the office buildings.
> The ice cream truck serves more of the office buildings than the salad truck.
> The taco truck does not serve Y.
> The falafel truck does not serve any office building that the pita truck serves.
> The taco truck serves two office buildings that are also served by the ice cream truck.

18. Which one of the following could be a complete and accurate list of each of the office buildings that the falafel truck serves?

   (A) X
   (B) X, Z
   (C) X, Y, Z
   (D) Y, Z
   (E) Z

19. For which one of the following pairs of trucks must it be the case that at least one of the office buildings is served by both of the trucks?

   (A) the hot dog truck and the pita truck
   (B) the hot dog truck and the taco truck
   (C) the ice cream truck and the pita truck
   (D) the ice cream truck and the salad truck
   (E) the salad truck and the taco truck

20. If the ice cream truck serves fewer of the office buildings than the hot dog truck, then which one of the following is a pair of lunch trucks that must serve exactly the same buildings as each other?

   (A) the falafel truck and the hot dog truck
   (B) the falafel truck and the salad truck
   (C) the ice cream truck and the pita truck
   (D) the ice cream truck and the salad truck
   (E) the ice cream truck and the taco truck

21. Which one of the following could be a complete and accurate list of the lunch trucks, each of which serves all three of the office buildings?

   (A) the hot dog truck, the ice cream truck
   (B) the hot dog truck, the salad truck
   (C) the ice cream truck, the taco truck
   (D) the hot dog truck, the ice cream truck, the pita truck
   (E) the ice cream truck, the pita truck, the salad truck

22. Which one of the following lunch trucks CANNOT serve both X and Z?

   (A) the hot dog truck
   (B) the ice cream truck
   (C) the pita truck
   (D) the salad truck
   (E) the taco truck[3]

---

[3] PrepTest 43, Sec. 4, Game 4, Qs 18–22

Explanations—Game 3

STEPS 1 AND 2: Overview and Sketch

The most important language in this game's setup text is that "[e]ach truck serves *one or more*" of the office buildings. This game would play out differently (and be much easier) if the trucks were assigned to only one building each. At any rate, you can see your task: Construct a list or chart showing the trucks that serve (and those that don't serve) each of the buildings. The buildings don't move, of course, but the trucks might. So you'll set up your framework in one of these ways:

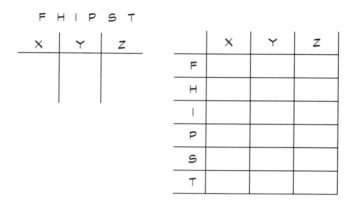

Figure 6.13

It's pretty much a matter of taste whether you want to jot down lists of the trucks under each building's column or make a grid with checks and *X*s. I'll illustrate both here so that you can check your handling of the rules and deductions either way.

STEP 3: Rules

Rule 1 is very restrictive. You can affirmatively indicate F's and H's inclusion in building Y's column. You also need to note that Y's column will have exactly three matches.

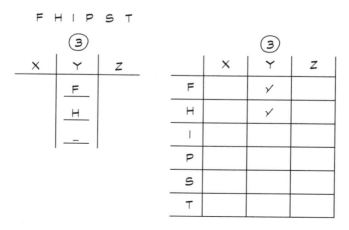

Figure 6.14

Rule 2 gives you the precise number of buildings that F will serve. Since one of F's matches has already been indicated by Rule 1, you can see that further deductions for F are forthcoming.

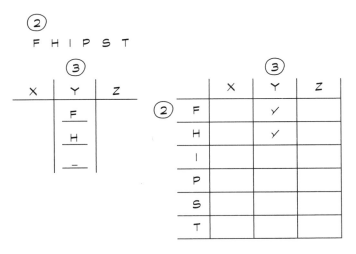

Figure 6.15

Rule 3 cannot be drawn into the framework yet, but as the game becomes clearer, expect all of these numerical restrictions to start acting in concert during the Deduction step.

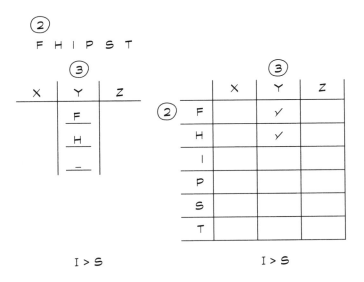

Figure 6.16

Rule 4 is negative but absolute. Diagram it right into the framework, regardless of whether you used a list or a grid.

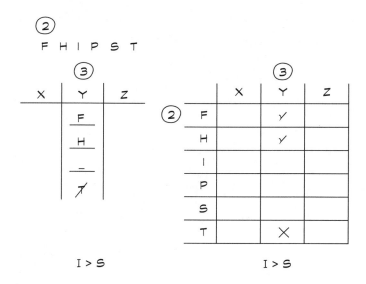

Figure 6.17

Rule 5 is yet another that touches on F. You can anticipate that the relationship between F and P will be central to how the game plays out.

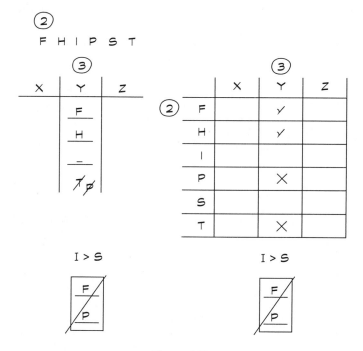

Figure 6.18

Rule 6 might seem tricky to diagram. But since T is excluded from building Y already, you can actually put this rule right into the framework. Make sure you don't read too much into this rule, though. Truck T can't serve building Y, but truck I still might.

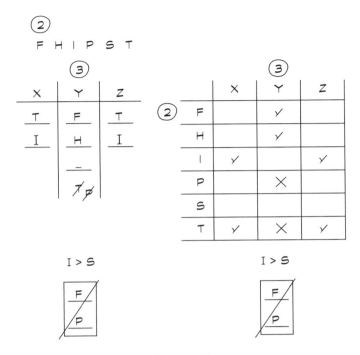

Figure 6.19

There are several rules that duplicate entities in this game and several that impose numerical limitations on the rows and columns. Their interactions should be your focus in the Deduction step.

STEP 4: Deductions

Three entities are each duplicated in two or more rules: F (Rules 1, 2, and 5), I (Rules 3 and 6), and T (Rules 4 and 6). Truck T is the most restricted, but it's so restricted that you've already learned all you can about it. T will serve buildings X and Z and won't serve building Y. T's row is closed.

Truck F will serve exactly two buildings, one of which is building Y. So F yields Limited Options, serving either buildings X and Y or buildings Y and Z. In a grid-type framework, you may choose to depict the two options without two separate sketches. Draw whichever is clearest. It's the information (not the style) that gets you LSAT points.

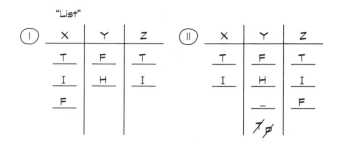

"List"

(I)	X	Y	Z		(II)	X	Y	Z
	T	F	T			T	F	T
	I	H	I			I	H	I
	F						—	F
							~T ∅	

"Grid"   ③

②		X	Y	Z
	F	X̸/y	y	X̸/y
	H		y	
	I	y		y
	P		X	
	S			
	T	y	X	y

Figure 6.20

When you add in Rule 5, truck P becomes part of the Limited Options as well. It will serve *only* the one building *not* served by F.

"List"

(I)	X	Y	Z		(II)	X	Y	Z
	T	F	T			T	F	T
	I	H	I			I	H	I
	F	—					—	F
	∅	~T ∅	P̸			F̸	~T ∅	∅

"Grid"   ③

②		X	Y	Z
	F	y/X	y	X/y
	H		y	
	I	y		y
	P	X/y	X	y/X
	S			
	T	y	X	y

Figure 6.21

So no matter what, you know the acceptable arrangements for trucks F, P, and T. Now, consider I and S. One of them (but not both) will serve building Y, which must have three trucks serving it (Rule 1). Notice that if S serves building Y, that's the only building it can serve. Rule 3 requires that I serve more buildings than S. If I serves building Y, then S could serve either or both of buildings X and Z. I recommend against drawing out even more options to depict these permutations. Rather, just highlight the numerical restrictions between I and S and keep an eye on how they play out.

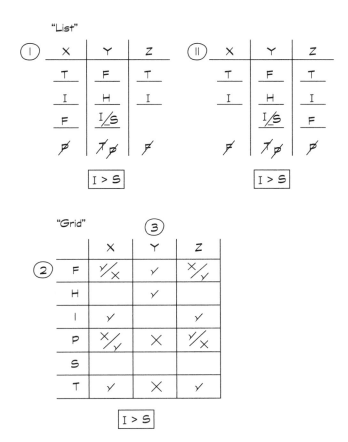

Figure 6.22

That leaves only truck H. You know from Rule 1 that it will serve building Y. Since it's otherwise unrestricted and unrestrictive, it can serve either or both of the other two buildings, but it need not do so. It's the closest thing you have to a floater in this game.

STEP 5: Questions

Of the five questions in this set, only one has a new "if." Seeing that should prompt you to be extra patient in the Rules and Deductions steps, since you'll need to have a big chunk of this game worked out before you answer the questions. Review your answers.

18. **(D)**

19. **(C)**

20. **(E)**

21. **(A)**

22. **(C)**

That is by no means an easy game, but it is a perfect example of how far you've come already. By accomplishing Steps 1–4 of the Kaplan Method, you were able to remove the largest part of the game's ambiguity before diving into the question set.

GAME 4

Questions 19–23

An airline has four flights from New York to Sarasota—
flights 1, 2, 3, and 4. On each flight there is exactly one pilot
and exactly one co-pilot. The pilots are Fazio, Germond, Kyle,
and Lopez; the co-pilots are Reich, Simon, Taylor, and Umlas.
Each pilot and co-pilot is assigned to exactly one flight.

  The flights take off in numerical order.

  Fazio's flight takes off before Germond's, and at least one
  other flight takes off between their flights.

  Kyle is assigned to flight 2.

  Lopez is assigned to the same flight as Umlas.

19. Which one of the following pilot and co-pilot teams
    could be assigned to flight 1?

    (A) Fazio and Reich
    (B) Fazio and Umlas
    (C) Germond and Reich
    (D) Germond and Umlas
    (E) Lopez and Taylor

20. If Reich's flight is later than Umlas's, which one of the
    following statements cannot be true?

    (A) Fazio's flight is earlier than Simon's.
    (B) Kyle's flight is earlier than Reich's.
    (C) Kyle's flight is earlier than Taylor's.
    (D) Simon's flight is earlier than Reich's.
    (E) Taylor's flight is earlier than Kyle's.

21. If Lopez's flight is earlier than Germond's, which one of
    the following statements could be false?

    (A) Fazio's flight is earlier than Umlas's.
    (B) Germond is assigned to flight 4.
    (C) Either Reich's or Taylor's flight is earlier than Umlas's.
    (D) Simon's flight is earlier than Umlas's.
    (E) Umlas is assigned to flight 3.

22. What is the maximum possible number of different pilot
    and co-pilot teams, any one of which could be assigned
    to flight 4?

    (A) 2
    (B) 3
    (C) 4
    (D) 5
    (E) 6

23. If Simon's flight is later than Lopez's, then which one of
    the following statements could be false?

    (A) Germond's flight is later than Reich's.
    (B) Germond's flight is later than Taylor's.
    (C) Lopez's flight is later than Taylor's.
    (D) Taylor's flight is later than Reich's.
    (E) Umlas's flight is later than Reich's. [4]

---

[4] PrepTest 36, Sec. 4, Game 4, Qs 19–23

Explanations—Game 4

STEPS 1 AND 2: Overview and Sketch

Your mental picture of this game probably begins with the four numbered airplanes. More specifically, you likely picture the cockpits, with seats for the pilots and co-pilots, respectively. It's not tough to turn that into a useful framework for the game.

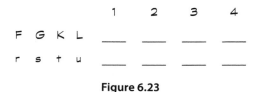

Figure 6.23

The numbers of the game work out simply and evenly: four planes, four pilots, four co-pilots, with one of each type of operator per plane. The number of acceptable arrangements will decrease dramatically with each of the pilots or co-pilots that you place.

STEP 3: Rules

Rule 1 is a little deceptive. You already knew that the flights were numbered 1 through 4, but it's not until this rule that you know that those are more than names. The numbers are connected to the action as well. This doesn't change or add to your sketch, but you can now anticipate other rules and questions that reward you for keeping track of who flies earlier or later than someone else.

Rule 2 delivers immediately on the promise of Rule 1; it defines the relative order and minimum proximity of two pilots' flights.

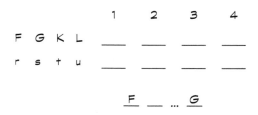

Figure 6.24

Rule 3 establishes the position of yet another pilot.

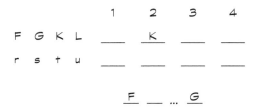

Figure 6.25

Rule 4 gives one of the pairings.

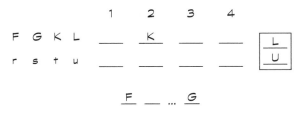

Figure 6.26

By this point, the game should be reminiscent of at least a couple of the games you saw earlier in the book. It shares the same Sequencing-Matching combination of tasks as the Thunderstorm and Suspects' Confessions games. The chief distinction is that, in this game, you have just as many entities to order on the second line as you do on the first. Still, you can anticipate the questions that the test makers will ask: What are the acceptable orders and pairings of pilots and co-pilots? See what additional information you can obtain in the Deductions step.

STEP **4**: Deductions

As always, work with the most concrete restrictions first. Three of the four rules restrict the pilots, while only one deals with a co-pilot. On the pilots' line, you know that K is established in flight 2. Given that restriction, the F-G sequence from Rule 2 creates a Limited Options scenario.

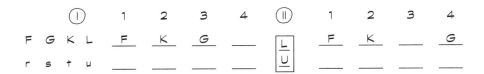

Figure 6.27

Given the requirement that at least one flight takes off after F's and before G's, F can only take flight 1. That leaves either flight 3 or flight 4 for G.

With three of the four pilots placed in each option, fitting in pilot L is a snap. And per Rule 4, U goes wherever L does.

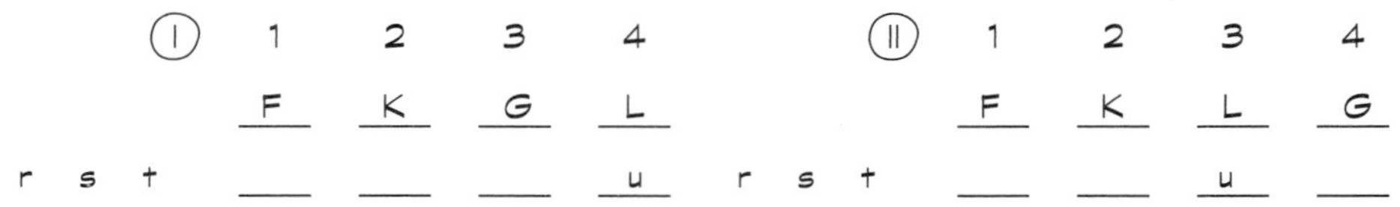

Figure 6.28

The remaining three spaces, all on the co-pilot line, belong to R, S, and T in any order. It's certainly not worth the time to try to draw out the six different arrangements available to those three entities in each of the options. But expect at least one or two of the "If" questions to impose restrictions involving the remaining undefined co-pilots.

STEP 5: Questions

There are five questions in the set, three of which start with an "if." Expect to be rewarded for having made the Limited Options deduction and for paying attention to what can or cannot be true among the yet-unplaced co-pilots. Review your answers.

19. **(A)**

20. **(C)**

21. **(D)**

22. **(C)**

23. **(D)**

What you see in this game is representative of what you've seen throughout this chapter and, indeed, what you'll see on test day. The games you'll encounter from this point on won't be identical to games you've already done, but they'll be similar enough to seem familiar. The actions, the rules, even the deductions will follow patterns that you've seen and worked with. In the next part of this book, I'll show you how to make the most of that familiarity to maximize your efficiency without becoming so pigeonholed that you lose the ability to look at new games holistically. First, I want to break down a few of the ways in which the test makers make game setups and questions harder. As I introduce you to game types and variations, I want you be able to distinguish games that are simply *different* than usual from those that are truly more *difficult* than usual.

CHAPTER 7

How the LSAT Makes Games Harder

I hope I've shown you by now that the Kaplan Method will allow you to get through any logic game with maximum efficiency and accuracy. Still, as you've already seen, some games are harder than others. By studying test takers' responses and noting which games consistently produce a lower percentage of correct answers, Kaplan has been able to determine four factors that make games more difficult.

WHAT MAKES LOGIC GAMES HARDER

Easier	Harder
Concrete	Ambiguous
Simple	Complex
Brief	Long
Familiar	Strange

As you can see, some of these factors are purely objective; a complex game, for example, is complex for all test takers, though some test takers will handle that complexity better than others will. On the other hand, a factor like familiarity with the game is at least somewhat subjective; it's within your control to become familiar with as many game patterns and tasks as you can. By studying this book, you're making yourself familiar with games, rules, and strategies that at least some of your competition simply won't know.

In this chapter, I'll show you how to recognize and respond to the higher-difficulty games you encounter. In Part III of the book, I'll come back to these factors when I teach you to "triage" the Logic Games section and prioritize the easiest games to maximize your score in the 35 minutes you're given on test day.

REDUCING AMBIGUITY

As you know from the chapter on rules, restrictions make games easier. They reduce the enormous number of acceptable permutations to a manageable handful. So it stands to reason that games with fewer restrictions—less concreteness, if you will—are harder than games that lock entities into place. Be careful, though: A failure to interpret the rules or make the available deductions in the setup should not be confused with true ambiguity.

Actual versus Perceived Ambiguity

Any logic game can appear ambiguous and incomplete prior to the Deductions step. The game that tasked you with sequencing the red and green trucks' arrivals is a good example of one in which untrained students fail to make all of the available deductions. As a result, they struggle with the questions, either missing them entirely or spending far too long to get what should be a straightforward answer.

> In a single day, exactly seven trucks—S, T, U, W, X, Y, and Z—are the only arrivals at a warehouse. No truck arrives at the same time as any other truck, and no truck arrives more than once that day. Each truck is either green or red (but not both). The following conditions apply:
>
> No two consecutive arrivals are red.
> Y arrives at some time before both T and W.
> Exactly two of the trucks that arrive before Y are red.
> S is the sixth arrival.
> Z arrives at some time before U.[1]

If you record all of the rules correctly, you'd have this to work with:

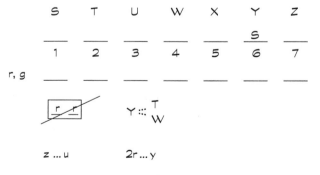

Figure 7.1

---

[1] PrepTest 37, Sec. 3, Game 2

That's a far cry from the Master Sketch you learned to create in chapter 4. As a Kaplan-trained test taker, you're already aware of how much certainty the game's setup and rules signal here. This game's rules use words like "exactly" and "no." None of the rules is conditional; there's not even an "either/or" type of restriction. Using the BLEND checklist and starting with the most restricted entity (you'll recall that it's truck Y), you were able to produce a Master Sketch that determined or severely limited most of the slots in the game.

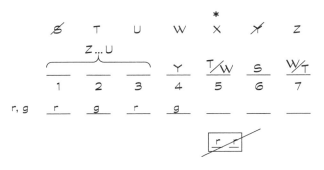

Figure 7.2

The result was a set of questions you could answer in a matter of seconds each.

So your greatest ally in combating ambiguity is Step 4 of the Kaplan Method. That's true even when there aren't many deductions to make. Recall the Civic Parade game in chapter 4? There, you had almost nothing to add to your Master Sketch beyond the original rules. Indeed, the key to your efficiency on that game was to recognize that you had all the information available to handle the question set.

The Kaplan Method is not only for games with lots of deductions and intricate diagrams. Following the method—sketching the rules and using the BLEND checklist to determine how much additional certainty Step 4 can add—puts you in the driver's seat every time. While you'll always prefer concreteness to ambiguity, what's most important is that you create a Master Sketch that shows exactly what can and what cannot be determined. That's what LSAT logic games questions always reward.

Recognizing Ambiguous Setups

What are the signs that a game is less concrete, or more ambiguous, than most? You already know that words like "exactly," "must," and "not" or "never" are good indicators of certainty. On the other hand, seeing a plethora of conditional rules or either/or restrictions stated in the alternative (e.g., "H ranks higher than P or else H ranks lower than L, but not both") is a sign that you'll find less concreteness.

But your assessment of a game's ambiguity actually begins as soon as you identify the task. If asked to schedule appointments, you'd prefer to schedule six appointments over six days, one per day, than, say, to schedule those same six appointments over the course of four days with no more than two appointments per day. The latter scenario means that you might have two days with two appointments each and two days with one each. Or you might have three days with two appointments each and one with zero.

Other tasks contain their own built-in signals of ambiguity. Would you rather be asked to select *exactly* four new hires from a pool of six applicants or to select *at least* one new hire? Emphatically, you'd prefer the former. Indeed, as you've already seen in multiple examples, a little extra complexity in a game's task can easily be offset by extra concreteness in its restrictions.

Review the following game's setup and rules to determine whether you find it concrete or ambiguous and to what extent. Here's a hint: As you consider the task, think about what kind of information would help you nail down the answers and whether that information is present.

> Each of exactly six doctors—Juarez, Kudrow, Longtree, Nance, Onawa, and Palermo—is at exactly one of two clinics: Souderton or Randsborough. The following conditions must be satisfied:
>> Kudrow is at Randsborough if Juarez is at Souderton.
>> Onawa is at Souderton if Juarez is at Randsborough.
>> If Longtree is at Souderton, then both Nance and Palermo are at Randsborough.
>> If Nance is at Randsborough, then so is Onawa.
>> If Palermo is at Randsborough, then both Kudrow and Onawa are at Souderton.[2]

The task here is straightforward: You need to make a simple chart showing which doctors are assigned to each clinic. That should be easy, but this game turns out to be quite challenging. The reason is its lack of concreteness.

Remember my hint suggesting that you think about what you'd like to know in order to make your job easier? First on your list should have been, "Tell me how many doctors are assigned to each clinic." Numerical restrictions are enormously helpful in a Distribution game like this one. But here, you get none. For all you know, it's possible to have all six doctors at one of the clinics and none at the other, five doctors at one and one at the other, four and two, three and three, two and four, etc. The rules will serve to keep some of the doctors apart, but even there you get little of what you hoped for. You'd prefer rules that create Established Entities ("Doctor so-and-so is at Randsborough") or, at the very least, rules that tell you who had to be placed together or who had to be kept apart. Unfortunately, you get none of that. Every rule here is conditional. Take Rule 1, for instance. When Doctor Juarez is at Souderton, Doctor Kudrow is not. When Juarez is at Randsborough, though, you can't reach any conclusions about Kudrow's location. There's nothing unfamiliar or even very complex about this game, but its lack of concreteness makes it a formidable exercise.

---

[2] PrepTest 34, Sec. 4, Game 4

A quick read of this game's setup and rules is enough to tell you that it's not the easiest game you'll encounter in the section; indeed, it may well be the toughest. In fact, I'll have you come back to this game in Part II as an example of a challenging Distribution action. There, you'll see how to manage it as efficiently as possible, though I doubt that it will ever be one of your favorites.

Being able to spot games that lack concreteness is valuable for two reasons. As I'll discuss further in Part III of this book, you'll want to be able to locate the easiest games in the section on test day. Prioritizing the easiest games will help you manage your time effectively to get the greatest number of points. Deferring an ambiguous, and therefore challenging, setup like this one is a good idea. The other benefit is psychological. When you know that the game in front of you is challenging (and even more so when you know *why* it's so challenging), it helps you avoid panic and frustration that could derail your performance throughout the entire section. "Forewarned is forearmed," as they say, and that's certainly true when it comes to recognizing ambiguous logic games.

PEELING BACK THE LAYERS OF COMPLEXITY
"Hybrid" Doesn't Have to Mean "Hard"

The number-one way in which the test makers increase games' complexity is to "hybridize" them, or blend two or more tasks together. This can be especially perplexing for students who become over-reliant on giving each task a specific name: "This is Sequencing" or "This is Matching." The fact is, most LSATs include at least one Hybrid game, made up of a combination of common game actions. It's important not to think that all Hybrid games are "hard" games. Each of the following is a Hybrid game that you've already handled successfully in the earlier chapters of this book. You can see that they cover a range of difficulty levels. Consider what makes each of these games easier or harder and how you were able to take control of each one.

In a single day, exactly seven trucks—S, T, U, W, X, Y, and Z—are the only arrivals at a warehouse. No truck arrives at the same time as any other truck, and no truck arrives more than once that day. Each truck is either green or red (but not both). The following conditions apply:

　No two consecutive arrivals are red.
　Y arrives at some time before both T and W.
　Exactly two of the trucks that arrive before Y are red.
　S is the sixth arrival.
　Z arrives at some time before U.[3]

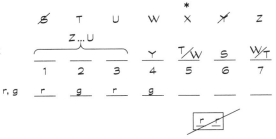

Figure 7.3

This game is a hybrid of Sequencing (determining the order in which the trucks arrive) and Matching (assigning each truck a color). As you'll learn in Part II, Sequencing-Matching is the most common Hybrid variant on the LSAT. The Thunderstorm game, the Pilots and Co-pilots

---

[3] PrepTest 37, Sec. 3, Game 2

game, and the Guitarist's CD game are all examples of this combination of actions. Typically, the Sequencing action dominates the game and serves as the anchor for your sketch. By drawing the sketch in a way that allows you to see the interaction between the two actions—the color assignments limit the possible order and vice versa, for instance—you are able to boil this game down to two lines: one for the trucks and one for their colors. Depicting both actions within the same sketch is the key to handling almost all Hybrid games. And here, the Sketch and Deductions steps make this Hybrid much easier than several of the single-action games you've already encountered.

> Exactly six people—Lulu, Nam, Ofelia, Pachai, Santiago, and Tyrone—are the only contestants in a chess tournament. The tournament consists of four games, played one after the other. Exactly two people play in each game, and each person plays in at least one game. The following conditions must apply:
> Tyrone does not play in the first or third game.
> Lulu plays in the last game.
> Nam plays in only one game and it is not against Pachai.
> Santiago plays in exactly two games, one just before and one just after the only game that Ofelia plays in.[4]

Figure 7.4

This is another game in which the test makers have blended Sequencing and Matching elements. This time, though, the complexity stems from the fact that you must decide how the chess players pair up against one another rather than being asked to assign each player an attribute. The other thing that makes this game intimidating is that you must determine the number of games in which each person plays. As you remember from chapter 4—and as you can see in the sketch above—you were able to turn the tables on the test maker by employing a Limited Options sketch. It's always worth remembering that with additional complexity comes additional restriction. The concreteness of the S-O-S block more than makes up for the complexity of the action.

---

[4] PrepTest 45, Sec. 3, Game 2

The three highest-placing teams in a high school debate tournament are the teams from Fairview, Gillom, and Hilltop high schools. Each team has exactly two members. The individuals on these three teams are Mei, Navarro, O'Rourke, Pavlovich, Sethna, and Tsudama. The following is the case:

Sethna is on the team from Gillom High.

Tsudama is on the second-place team.

Mei and Pavlovich are not on the same team.

Pavlovich's team places higher than Navarro's team.

The team from Gillom High places higher than the team from Hilltop High.[5]

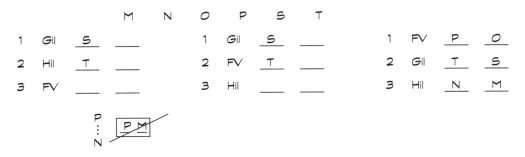

Figure 7.5

This game's task is the most complex you've yet seen in this book. Here, you must sequence the schools by rank, match team members in pairs, and distribute the members among the three schools' teams. That's a Hybrid game combining three tasks. But look again and refresh your memory of the Master Sketch. By the time you've made the available deductions, only three patterns are possible and, in one of them, every entity's place is determined. Let this game stand as a reminder of rules' power to make your job easier. With three schools to rank, there are six acceptable arrangements. But adding just Rule 5—Gillom places higher than Hilltop—cuts that number in half.

This game illustrates a second consideration as well. Whenever the test makers combine tasks, they will also simplify each one. In a typical Sequencing game, you must order six or seven entities; here, only three schools. Likewise, most Distribution games don't specify the exact number of entities in each group. Here, the six students form three teams of two members each, a very concrete and simple pattern. Even the Matching element—one team per school—is too easy to stand on its own as a logic game.

Now, you can conceive of all types of enormous and difficult games. The test makers could come up with something in which you're asked to sequence six entities and then match between one and three attributes to each. To picture this, imagine that the following game asked you to place the technicians at Workstations 1 through 6 as well as determining which kinds of devices each repairs.

---

[5] PrepTest 53, Sec. 2, Game 4

> In a repair facility there are exactly six technicians: Stacy, Urma, Wim, Xena, Yolanda, and Zane. Each technician repairs machines of at least one of the following three types—radios, televisions, and VCRs—and no other types. The following conditions apply:[6]

Nothing makes a game like that impossible *in theory*, but it would simply be too time-consuming to include on the test. Even the very best test takers would be unable to finish such a game and still have time left for the other three games in the section. Remember, the test maker's objective is to make a test that distinguishes levels of ability with the Core 4 LSAT Skills. They'll use complexity to make some games more challenging than others, but they still set out to design a section in which the top scorers can get to every question. Indeed, the section is designed so that a small handful of test takers will even get every question right. I'd like to see you among that select group.

Thinking Exercises: Complex Tasks

There's one more consideration that will help you master complex games: When a game includes multiple tasks, one of the tasks may logically precede or restrict the other(s). Take a look at how recognizing this makes your job easier.

Jewelry Display Case

Imagine you work in a jewelry store that has a display case containing four pedestals, numbered 1 through 4 from left to right. The store's inventory includes seven necklaces, one each of coral, garnet, jade, onyx, pearl, ruby, sapphire, and turquoise. Your manager tells you to put exactly one of those necklaces on each of the four display pedestals. Think about the decisions you must make and the order in which they must be made: Before you can sequence necklaces on pedestals 1 through 4, you must first determine which four of the seven necklaces will be displayed. In a Selection-Sequencing Hybrid, the Selection element logically precedes the Sequencing element.

Now, indeed, in real life, just as in a logic game, your boss could give you restrictions on either the selection of necklaces or on their positions in the display case. Think about their effects on your job. He might say, "Put the onyx necklace just to the right of the sapphire one." In that case, you have some guidance about the sequence. The sapphire and onyx necklaces will go on pedestals 1 and 2, 2 and 3, or 3 and 4, respectively. But more importantly, you know that the onyx and sapphire necklaces will be among those displayed. Two of your four selected entities are now determined. Think about how much more powerful that would be, as a logic game rule, than if your boss had said, "*If* you put the onyx necklace on display, I want it to be just to the right of the sapphire one." Now, your boss's instruction is conditional. Selecting the sapphire necklace requires selecting the onyx and determines their relative order. But if you

---

[6] PrepTest 48, Sec. 2, Game 3

leave the sapphire necklace out of the display case, you know nothing. That, in turn, is more powerful than if your boss said, "Should you choose to put both the sapphire and the onyx necklaces on display, I want the sapphire necklace to be just to the right of the onyx one." This rule gives you no guidance about which necklaces to select, only about the sequence of onyx and sapphire *if* you put both on display. The LSAT rewards your ability to identify the most powerful and restrictive rules in all games; in games with complex tasks, rules that impose concrete restrictions on multiple elements of your task will, of necessity, be more powerful.

Basketball Scrimmage

Here's another complex task—far larger and more unwieldy than any you'd see on test day—to get you thinking about how the test makers design Hybrid games and their rules.

Imagine you're a basketball coach. You have a team with 12 players on the roster: Anna, Betty, Carolyn, Danielle, Evelyn, Francis, Gwendolyn, Helen, Iris, Jane, Karla, and Lorraine. At today's practice, you'll have them scrimmage on two teams—the gold team and the purple team—of five players each. Each team will have one center, one power forward, one small forward, one shooting guard, and one point guard. If this were a logic game, which tasks would it include? Which of those tasks logically precedes or follows the other(s)? What types of rules or restrictions would the test makers be likely to include? Which of those would be most helpful to you? Take a few minutes and brainstorm your answers to those questions. Sketch out the framework you'd use to organize the information. Then review your thinking with the discussion that follows. See how complete a picture you had of the tasks and potential rules.

Basketball Scrimmage: Discussion

If the basketball scrimmage scenario were a logic game, you'd identify it as a three-part Hybrid. First, you'd have to choose which 10 of your 12 team members would play in the game. That's Selection. Then, you'd need to divide the 10 selected players into two teams of 5 players each. That's Distribution. Finally, you'd need to assign each player to a position. Consider that a Matching task (or if you number the positions—point guard is 1, shooting guard is 2, etc.—you could think of it as Sequencing). Your framework for such a game would look like this:

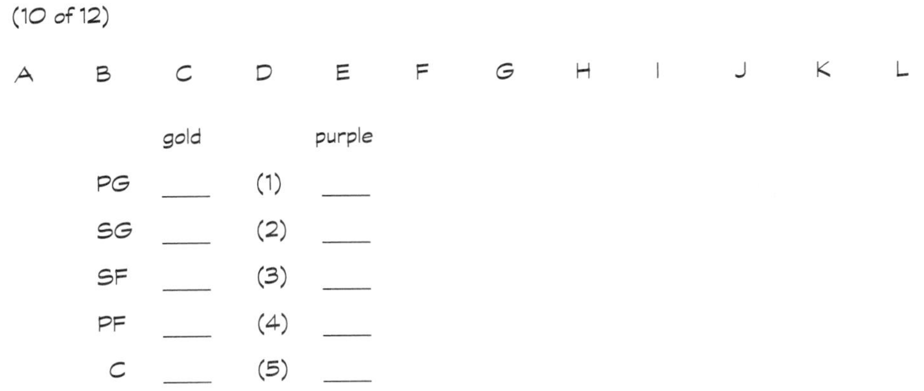

(*10 of 12*)

A   B   C   D   E   F   G   H   I   J   K   L

	gold		purple
PG	____	(1)	____
SG	____	(2)	____
SF	____	(3)	____
PF	____	(4)	____
C	____	(5)	____

Figure 7.6

In making this into a logic game, the test makers could give you rules that covered any of the three tasks. But the farther up the logical chain the rule is, the more restrictive (and helpful) it will be. For example:

"Karla plays power forward for the gold team." This tells you that Karla is selected and gives you the team and position she's assigned to. Karla is a completely established entity in this case.

(10 of 12)
A B C D E F G H I J K L
gold
purple
PG
SG
SF
PF
C
K

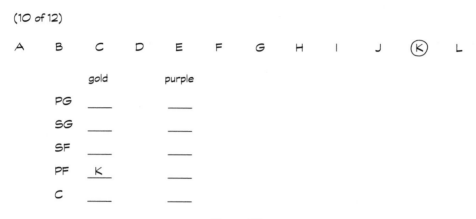

Figure 7.7

"Karla plays for the gold team." This is slightly less helpful. Karla is selected and assigned to a team, but her position is still up in the air.

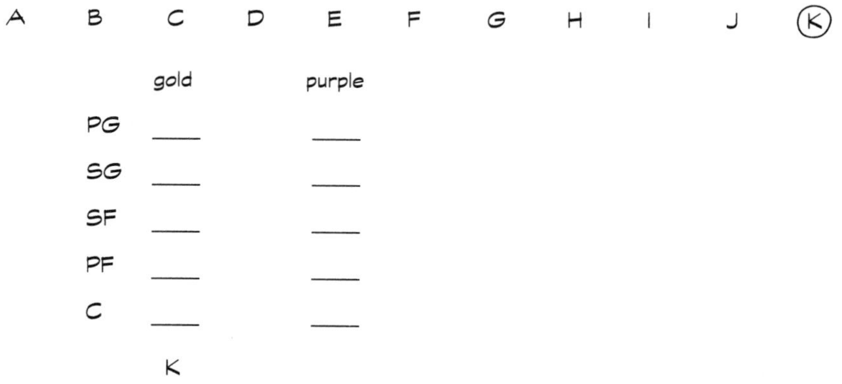

A B C D E F G H I J K L
gold
purple
PG
SG
SF
PF
C
K

Figure 7.8

"If Betty plays in the game, then Danielle plays in the game." This rule affects only the Selection element of the game. Moreover, it's conditional. It restricts the game only if Betty plays or if Danielle doesn't.

Figure 7.9

"If Betty plays in the game, then Danielle is the point guard on the purple team." This rule is also conditional, but its necessary term—"Danielle plays point guard on the purple team"—is much more specific. If you determine that Betty is selected, you can place Danielle precisely. And if Danielle does not play, does not play on the purple team, or does not play point guard, then Betty won't be selected at all.

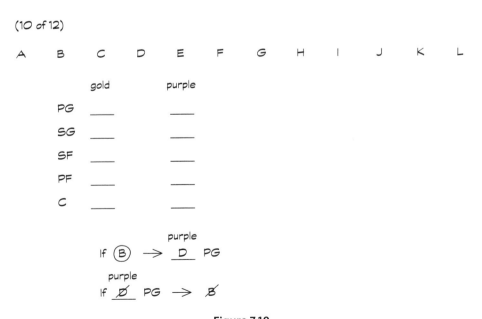

Figure 7.10

"Gwendolyn and Anna cannot play together on a team." Be careful with a rule like this one. If you know that Gwendolyn is playing on the gold team, then either Anna plays on the purple team *or* she doesn't play at all. Since being selected to play in the scrimmage logically precedes assignment to a team, a rule like this presents more than one alternative.

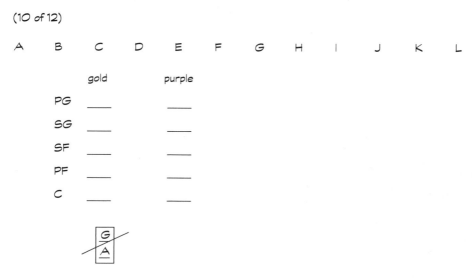

Figure 7.11

You could—and maybe you did—go on and on designing rules for a hypothetical game like this one. It's good mental practice for you, and exercises like this one give you a much clearer understanding of what goes into creating a logic game. Your takeaway here should be that the internal logic of all complex games requires that some decisions precede others. In the end, your mastery of any logic game starts with Step 1 of the Kaplan Method, where you conduct your overview and get a clear picture of your task or tasks. With that, you'll be able to see the restrictions that the rules impose, allowing you to take control of the game all the way through answering the questions.

Very rarely, the test makers may "complexify" a single task. They might, for example, ask you to determine the order of six patients' appointments with each of two health professionals, a dietician and a physician. Something like this:

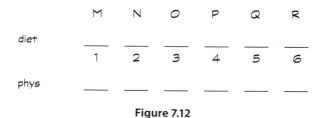

Figure 7.12

I'll go over a few of the recent variations on single-action games in Part II of this book, so it's very unlikely you'll encounter some wholly novel twist on logic games when you take your test.

Remember that no matter how many tasks the test makers put into a game, there will always be a trade-off between complexity and concreteness. By sticking to the Kaplan Method and using the Rules and Deductions steps to their fullest capacities, you will have all of the information you need to answer every question. When the test makers don't give you enough information to determine where an entity *must* be placed, they can ask you where it *could* be placed, but they never leave you hanging.

GETTING TO THE HEART OF LONG GAMES

For the most part, you should be happy when the text of a game's setup is long and detailed. Why? Because the extra text will usually mean additional rules and restrictions, providing more certainty and making your job easier. So don't fear a long setup just because it's long. For sure, there are times when the test makers are unnecessarily descriptive. Remember the Water Treatment Plant game?

> Workers at a water treatment plant open eight valves—G, H, I, K, L, N, O, and P—to flush out a system of pipes that needs emergency repairs. To maximize safety and efficiency, each valve is opened exactly once, and no two valves are opened at the same time. The valves are opened in accordance with the following conditions:[7]

Knowing that there's "a system of pipes that needs emergency repairs" or that the reason for opening the pipes one at a time is to "maximize safety and efficiency" adds nothing to your understanding of the game. You might prefer it if the test makers just cut to the chase like so:

> Workers at a water treatment plant open eight valves—G, H, I, K, L, N, O, and P. Each valve is opened exactly once, and no two valves are opened at the same time. The valves are opened in accordance with the following conditions:

But the extra information doesn't really make the game any harder to understand, either. In minor cases like this, just tune out the redundant or background language and jump right into your task using the Kaplan Method.

The real problem comes when the test makers use unnecessarily convoluted phraseology. This could happen in a rule, a question stem, or even an answer choice. In such cases, untangle the language and find the straightest line of reasoning from the restrictions to the right answer.

---

[7] PrepTest 52, Sec. 2, Game 1

Paraphrase Convoluted Language

Paraphrasing is a skill rewarded throughout the LSAT (and in law school, too). Your ability to transform dense, confusing prose into clear statements is vital to your success in understanding logical reasoning arguments and reading comprehension passages. Many of the correct answers in those sections are simply accurate rewordings of what the author of the passage or argument said. Naturally, on a test as integrated and skills-based as the LSAT, the test makers find a way to reward paraphrasing in the Logic Games section, too.

Take this question stem from the Red and Green Trucks game:

> For exactly how many of the seven trucks can one
> determine exactly how many trucks arrived before it?[8]

Any test taker would prefer it if the test makers simply asked, "How many of the trucks are locked into one certain arrival space?" But since that's what the question means, it's within your power (and it's to your advantage) to paraphrase the question stem for yourself before you evaluate the choices. Knowing exactly how many trucks arrive before a given truck means nothing more than knowing exactly when that truck arrives. Use that certainty to gain the advantage over your competition on test day.

The most important thing to remember is that *LSAT language is never imprecise*. However wordy the test makers get, however much they use double negatives or say, "each of the following could be true EXCEPT," instead of, "which one of the following must be false," they never leave instructions or limitations open to interpretation. You can rest absolutely assured that the rule or question means just what the test makers want it to.

One area in which you've already made great strides at taking control of complex language is in dealing with formal logic rules. If you think about it, you're paraphrasing every time you translate a formal logic rule. The following rule, as an English-language sentence, is pretty unruly:

> F is more expensive than G, or else F is more expensive
> than H, but not both.[9]

But dealing with the following diagram is fairly straightforward.

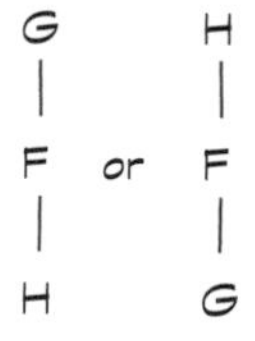

Figure 7.13

---

[8] PrepTest 37, Sec. 3, Q 10
[9] PrepTest 51, Sec. 4, Game 2

The LSAT Always Defines "Special" Terms

There is one other way in which the test makers can use language to make games longer or trickier. It's by using or defining a term in a special way to impose additional restrictions within the game. They don't do this very often, but it can catch the untrained test taker off guard when they do. Here's an example:

> Exactly seven professors—Madison, Nilsson, Orozco, Paton, Robinson, Sarkis, and Togo—were hired in the years 1989 through 1995. Each professor has one or more specialties, and any two professors hired in the same year or in consecutive years do not have a specialty in common. The professors were hired according to the following conditions:
> Madison was hired in 1993, Robinson in 1991.
> There is at least one specialty that Madison, Orozco, and Togo have in common.
> Nilsson shares a specialty with Robinson.
> Paton and Sarkis were each hired at least one year before Madison and at least one year after Nilsson.
> Orozco, who shares a specialty with Sarkis, was hired in 1990.[10]

This game's setup is long and dense, but the task is simple: Sequence the professors by hiring year.

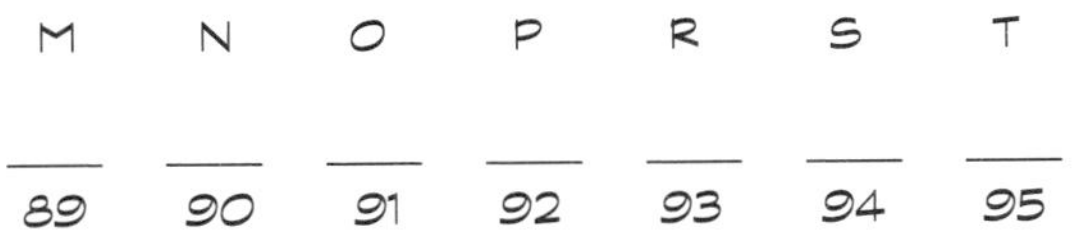

M	N	O	P	R	S	T
89	90	91	92	93	94	95

Figure 7.14

The unusual term (or more precisely, the term used in an unusual way) is "specialty." It's clearly important, as it shows up in three of the rules. But what does it mean? And why aren't you told what the specialties are? Don't let a term like this throw you. Simply look for the definition that must be present in the game's setup. The test makers will never introduce a term or use a word in a special way without defining it. The importance of a professor's specialty is given in the setup text: "[A]ny two professors hired in the same year or in consecutive years do not have a specialty in common." (Notice that the test makers could have called a "specialty" anything they wanted to: "Each professor hired has one or more *frim frams*, and any two professors hired in the same year or in consecutive years do not have a *frim fram* in common" would have served the same purpose.) Now, use that definition and create a Master Sketch for this game. Draw out the rules and make all available deductions. You'll be surprised by how much certainty the shared "specialties" add to the game.

---

[10] PrepTest 35, Sec. 3, Game 4

I gave you the basic framework for this game earlier. So consider Steps 1 and 2 complete; you start out with a clear idea of your task. But there's one thing I wonder if you caught. It's actually something that the setup *didn't* say. In this game, there's no requirement that one professor was hired each year. Never take restrictions for granted. When the test is silent on something, it's silent intentionally. To solve this game correctly, in fact, one year must see no professors hired while another sees two hired. If you didn't catch that, take a look at the rules and deductions to see why it must be true.

Rules

The first rule establishes two of the professors' hiring years; Madison and Robinson can go right into the framework.

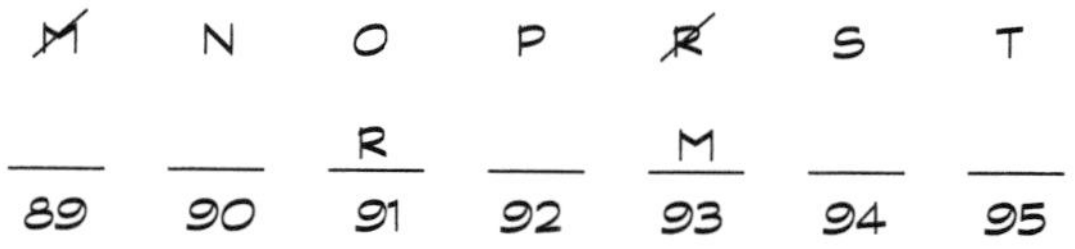

Figure 7.15

Rule 2 tells you that three of the professors share a specialty. Make note of that to the side.

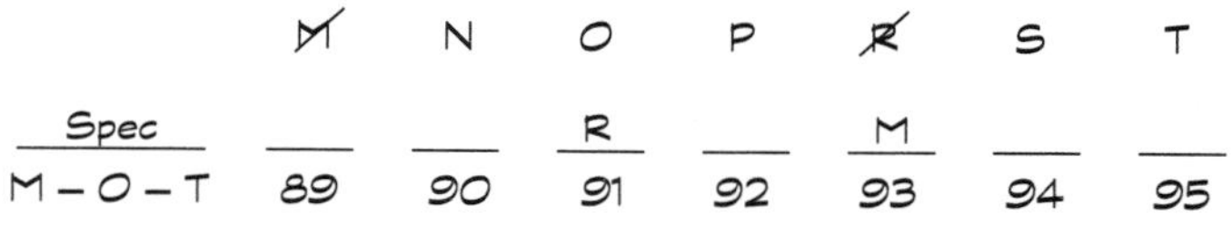

Figure 7.16

Rule 3 gives you another pair who share a specialty. Add them to the list.

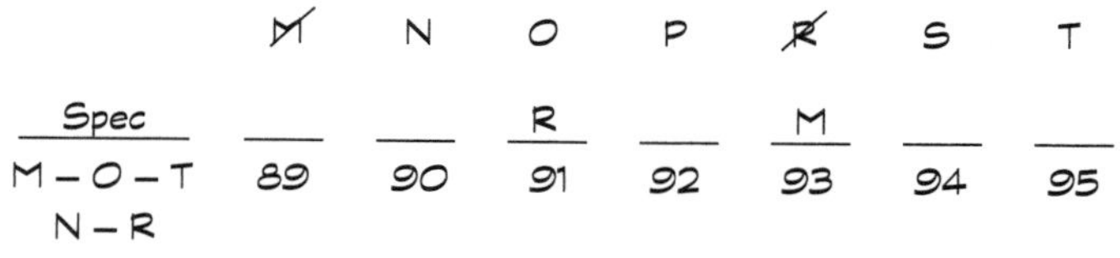

Figure 7.17

Rule 4 makes two loose blocks of three professors each. Record that beneath the framework for easy reference.

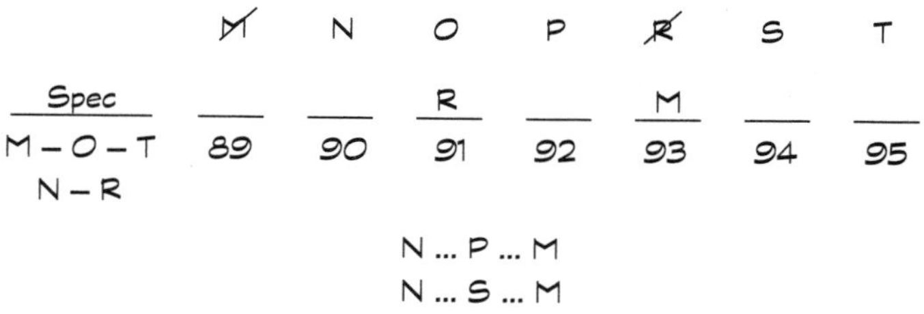

Figure 7.18

Read Rule 5 carefully. It allows you to place Orozco into the framework directly, but it also tells you to add Orozco-Sarkis under the shared-specialty list.

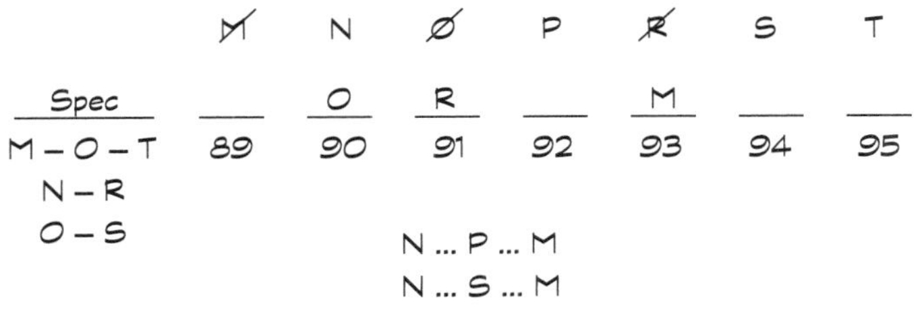

	M̶	N	Ø	P	R̶	S	T
Spec		O	R		M		
M – O – T	89	90	91	92	93	94	95
N – R							
O – S			N … P … M				
			N … S … M				

Figure 7.19

With the rules recorded effectively, turn to the Deductions step. All of these rules combine in one way or another to add additional certainty to the game.

Deductions

Start, as always, with what's most clearly established. Rule 1 put Madison in 1993. Think about whom Madison affects. In Rule 2, you are told that Madison, Orozco, and Togo all share a specialty. Orozco's hiring year is already established (by Rule 5) as 1990, but what about Togo? Since professors sharing a specialty can't be hired in the same year or in consecutive years, Rule 2 means that Togo cannot have been hired in '89, '90, or '91 (because of Orozco) or in '92, '93, or '94 (because of Madison). Togo must have been hired in 1995, and you now have four of the seven professors locked into place.

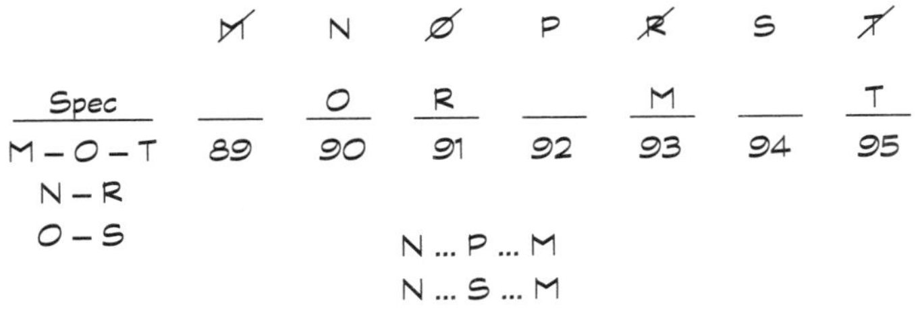

	M̶	N	Ø	P	R̶	S	T̶
Spec		O	R		M		T
M – O – T	89	90	91	92	93	94	95
N – R							
O – S			N … P … M				
			N … S … M				

Figure 7.20

Madison's influence isn't exhausted in Rule 2. In Rule 4, you see that Nilsson, Paton, and Sarkis were all hired prior to Madison. Of those three, consider Nilsson first. Since Rule 3 tells you that Nilsson shares a specialty with Robinson, Nilsson's blocked out of '90, '91, and '92. The only way for Nilsson to obey both Rule 4 and Rule 3 is to take 1989. Yet another professor's hiring has been precisely determined.

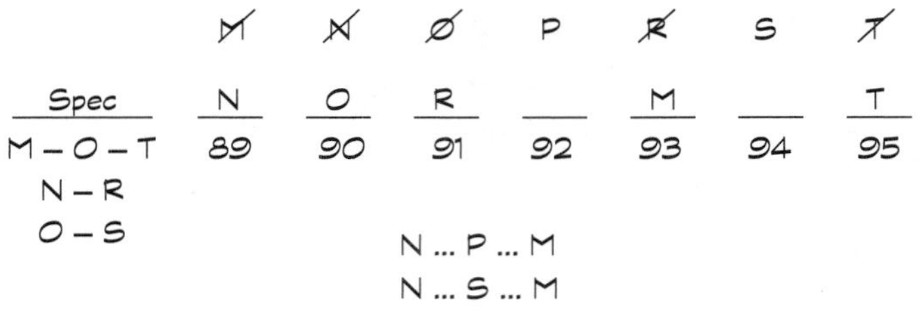

Figure 7.21

Now, go back to Rule 4 for Paton and Sarkis. Sarkis, who shares a specialty with Orozco according to Rule 5, is blocked out of '89, '90, and '91. In order for Sarkis's hiring year to fall between those of Nilsson and Madison, Sarkis must have been hired in 1992. Add that to the sketch.

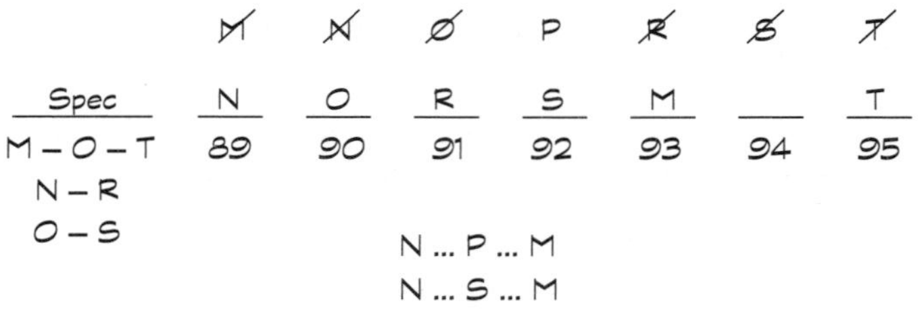

Figure 7.22

The only professor you haven't completely locked down is Paton. He must have been hired after Nilsson and before Madison (Rule 4), but otherwise has no restrictions. He shares no specialties with any other professor. So indicate that Paton could have been hired in '90, '91, or '92, and you're done.

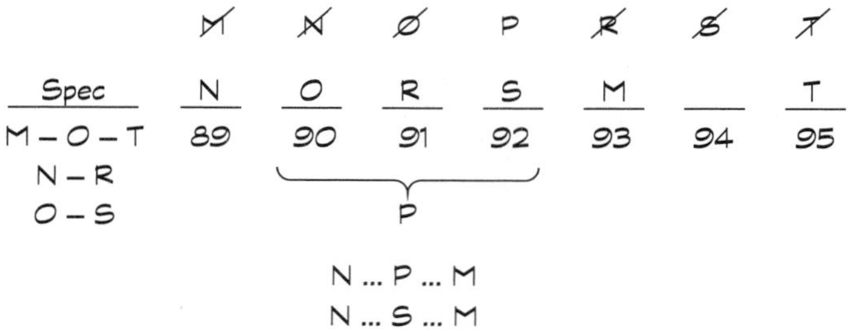

Figure 7.23

Far from being a problem, the special definition of "specialty" turned out to provide some of the strongest restrictions in the game. I'll have you come back to this game (and try its questions) in Part II when I discuss variations on Sequencing. For now, just appreciate how you turned a tricky term into a powerful restriction.

So in short, don't fear long or convoluted language in LSAT logic games. The guidelines and questions are always precise; a simple, accurate paraphrase just makes them more useful.

CONFRONTING UNFAMILIARITY

I won't say a lot at this point about what to do when you encounter an unfamiliar game. After all, the goal of Part II of this book is to ensure that it simply won't happen to you. It's within your power to encounter all of the game types that the test makers have used. From test to test, the game types change very little, and it's likely that all of the games on your test will seem familiar from this book. You may be flipping switches on an electrical grid instead of opening valves in a water treatment plant, but the task won't be much (if any) different.

I will caution now—and I'll repeat this caution throughout Part II—that you don't become over-reliant on being able to name or categorize a game. The Kaplan Method will allow you to handle anything that the test makers can design. It's done so for hundreds of thousands of test takers over the years. By conducting an overview of the game—defining your task, the entities you're manipulating, and the broad limitations on the action—you'll be able to draw an initial sketch with which to manage all of the rules and deductions that give you the information you need. When you first saw the Debate Teams game, it's nearly certain you'd never encountered a logic game like it before, nor would you have known to call it a Sequencing-Matching-Distribution Hybrid game.

> The three highest-placing teams in a high school debate tournament are the teams from Fairview, Gillom, and Hilltop high schools. Each team has exactly two members. The individuals on these three teams are Mei, Navarro, O'Rourke, Pavlovich, Sethna, and Tsudama. The following is the case:
> Sethna is on the team from Gillom High.
> Tsudama is on the second-place team.
> Mei and Pavlovich are not on the same team.
> Pavlovich's team places higher than Navarro's team.
> The team from Gillom High places higher than the team from Hilltop High.[11]

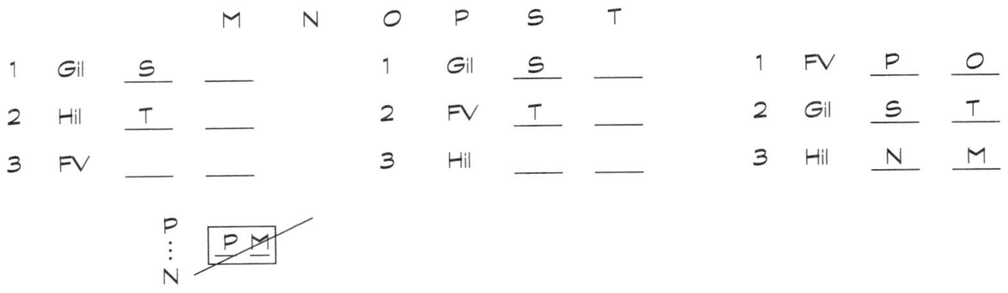

Figure 7.24

[11] PrepTest 53, Sec. 2, Game 4

Nor would it matter if you called it an Ordering-Pairing-Association game, for that matter. By getting a handle on the task and understanding the inherent restrictions within the rules, you're able to turn this into a short, manageable puzzle with a handful of acceptable solutions. Do that on test day, and you'll be rocking the Logic Games section ... and your competition.

Given the time you're devoting to practice and the resources available in this book and through all of Kaplan's other materials and services, encountering an unfamiliar game on your test should be way, way down on your list of concerns.

HOW THE LSAT MAKES GAMES HARDER . . . AND WHAT YOU CAN DO ABOUT IT

On any given LSAT, there is almost always one easy game, two of medium difficulty, and one harder one. The criteria in this chapter can help you identify which is which. The easiest game is usually quite concrete, simple, short, and familiar. The medium-difficulty games typically add one or two complicating factors. The hardest game throws in everything. (But remember, your diligent practice deprives the test maker of using unfamiliarity as a way to make games harder for you.)

As I'll discuss at greater length in Part III of this book, it's in your best interest to manage the Logic Games section strategically and tackle the easiest games first. That will allow you to rack up the quickest points and, perhaps, even bank some extra time for the toughest game. When you do dive into the hardest game, remember the strategies from this chapter to help you deal with any lack of concreteness, complex tasks, or difficult language you encounter.

Above all, remember the very first point that I made in chapter 1: Every question has an answer. The test makers set out to create a challenging, but fair, test. They always provide the information you need to distinguish the one correct answer from the four wrong ones. In that sense, you should approach the hardest logic games exactly as you approach the easiest ones. Adhering to the Kaplan Method is the best way to ensure that you glean that information clearly, accurately, and completely in every logic game you do.

PART II

GAME TYPES

CHAPTER 8

THE LOGIC GAMES TASKS

In Part II, I'll take you through each of the standard logic game types you'll see on the LSAT. I'll show you the routine versions of each game type, as well as examples of the variations and twists that have appeared on recent tests. I'll also go through the best ways to set up the sketches for each game type, cover the most common rules associated with them, and even show you how real-world versions of these puzzles can help you manage the process. There's no cognitive task tested by logic games that you haven't managed successfully in your personal, professional, or academic life. But the connections aren't always obvious, to say the least. Taking the mystery out of logic games is a valuable step.

While the test makers will offer variations on the standard game setups, the basic tasks that underlie the game types have remained remarkably consistent. Your chances of seeing familiar games on test day are far greater than those of seeing something novel or surprising. You're better off mastering the most common game types than you would be scouring old tests for variations you're unlikely to see on test day. Use what you learn in this section to make your work more efficient. By recognizing familiar game patterns, you can make better sketches faster and tackle the rules and deductions with greater confidence—and add points to your score.

IDENTIFYING GAME TYPES

If you've completed Part I of this book, you've already seen examples of every common logic games task. There, I deliberately mixed in various game types in order to keep the focus on the steps in the Kaplan Method and to illustrate how you can use them to master all LSAT logic games. In Part II, I'll break the games down by type to show you how recognizing certain patterns can make you even more efficient. Once you see the games arranged by type, you'll notice that the test makers consistently employ the same types of tasks but incorporate different rules, limitations, and number restrictions to make each game unique. Students who learn logic games' underlying similarities and use their common features to create the most useful sketches are those who become the most effective test takers. I'll now give you a brief overview of the common tasks posed by logic games. I'll then elaborate each with its own chapter.

The Standard Tasks

The LSAT test makers reuse the standard games tasks test after test. With maybe a dozen exceptions since 1991 (and *none* since 2003), every logic game that's appeared on the 60-plus released LSATs falls into one of the five main categories listed below. Even those games that fall into the Hybrid category are devised by combining two or three of the tasks listed in the first four main groupings. Logic games aren't identical from test to test, but they have far more commonalities than they do distinctions—a fact you can use to your advantage.

Sequencing Games

Far and away the most common game task (and the one most often combined into Hybrid games), Sequencing games task you with determining schedules, rankings, or numerical orderings of entities. As you already know from Part I, the test may give you a Strict Sequencing task, in which entities are limited to specific days or numbered slots within the order, or in which the exact number of spaces separating entities is given. Alternatively, the test might serve up Loose Sequencing, providing only relative restrictions among the entities, such as "M ranks higher than P" or "L is visited later than both C and D." It's not uncommon for a test to include each type of Sequencing game. Over the years, the test makers have very occasionally used other twists on the task; these include Circular Sequencing, in which entities are ordered around a table, and Double Sequencing, in which the same set of players must be ordered twice. I'll show you recent variations like these, but your main goal should be to master the basics of Sequencing games. Even in the most unusual examples, the fundamental questions—Which entities are before, after, or beside others? And how far are these two entities separated?—will give you the insights you need to answer the questions.

Matching Games

Matching games—the second most popular category, albeit a distant second—are defined by having two sets of entities. One of the entity sets is static, and your job is to assign the attributes or players that make up the second set to particular entities from the first group. In Part I, you saw the Electronics Technicians game, in which various types of machine were assigned to each of six technicians, and the Lunch Trucks game, in which three buildings were served by a fleet of lunch trucks that each sold a different kind of food. It's important to remember that in Matching games you may assign each of the "moveable" entities more than once. Four of the technicians, for example, repaired radios. The ice cream truck served at least two of the buildings. You'll come to see that this provides a huge clue for how to attack these games.

Determining how many matches a given entity can have or how many times a certain attribute can be assigned is always important to the limitations that make Matching games manageable.

Selection Games

Selection games are the type most closely associated with formal logic. Your job is always to take a list of entities and distinguish those that are chosen, or included, from those rejected, or excluded. So rules that designate entities whose inclusion is sufficient or necessary for the inclusion of others are particularly well suited to this action. In some of the Selection examples you saw in Part I—think of the Friends' Photographs game—all of the rules were in the form of conditional formal logic statements. Beyond handling the formal logic tasks, your main concern in Selection games is to determine the numerical possibilities. The test makers are fond of asking Minimum/Maximum questions that reward you for being able to count how many or how few entities could constitute an acceptable selection. Pay close attention to whether the test makers have determined up front the number of entities to be chosen—have they said, "Exactly five of the seven applicants will be hired"?—or whether they've left the numbers open-ended—for example, "The company will hire at least one of the applicants." That distinction provides the basis for the two basic subtypes within the Selection family.

Distribution Games

Cousins of Matching games, Distribution games ask you to divide a group of entities into two, three, or sometimes four groups. The primary distinction between Matching and Distribution is that in the latter, each entity can be placed only one time. Think of choosing sports teams at recess as a good model for Distribution: Once you place Bobby on the red team, you can't place him anywhere else. Numbers are just as important to Distribution games as they are to Selection. Once you recognize a game a presenting a Distribution task, your first question should be, "How many entities go into each group or team?" The more definite that aspect of the game is—for example, "Nine players will be divided among three teams, three players per team"—the easier the game is likely to be. But when the test makers don't specify how many entities go on each team—"Seven doctors will each serve at one of two hospitals, with at least one doctor at each hospital"—your task will be more challenging. Knowing how to quickly assess a game's difficulty is one of the major benefits of learning the game types and their characteristics.

Hybrid Games

I talked a little about Hybrid games in Part I. There's no doubt that combining two or three tasks can make a game more difficult, but in the chapter on Hybrid games that follows, I'll show you how identifying a Hybrid game's constituent tasks allows you to avoid many potential complications. Make sure you recognize the four preceding tasks, and know what makes each one easier or harder before you turn to the chapter on Hybrids. What you'll come to realize is that, while Hybrid games combine two or more of these other tasks, the individual tasks that comprise them are, on their own, quite simple. For example, a game might ask you to divide a group of six entities into two teams and rank each team's members from first through third. Dividing six entities into two teams of exactly three each is about as simple as Distribution tasks get. Similarly, ranking three entities would never stand on its own as a Sequencing task; it simply presents too few permutations to be challenging. As your familiarity with the patterns in Hybrid games increases, their ability to intimidate you will decrease. When you learn how to represent compound tasks with simple sketches, you'll find that Hybrids are susceptible to precisely the same limitations and deductions as are single-action games.

Rare Games

There's no special chapter of the book for the Mapping and Process games, the only game types that have appeared on the LSAT that don't fit easily into one of the above categories. That's because, with the exception of one Mapping game from PrepTest 40 (June 2003), none of the rare games has appeared on a released test since 1997. It's very unlikely that one of these will appear on a new exam. Once you're comfortable and confident with the more common games, you may want to consult my e-book *LSAT Logic Games: Rare and Difficult* in order to read and practice the Rare Games chapter. Just being familiar with their construction and seeing the selected setups and questions will put you miles ahead of your competition in the unlikely event that the test makers ever decide to revisit these largely forgotten games.

THE LIMITS OF TAXONOMY
You Don't Get Any Points for Knowing the Game Type

"What kind of game is this one?" I've heard this a thousand times. But the fact is that it means different things depending on the context in which it's asked. Sometimes the student is saying, "I messed up this game somehow, and I don't have the information I need to answer the questions." Knowing the game type *might* set the student on the right track, but what's more important here is trusting in the Overview step of the Kaplan Method to reveal the task and goal of each game so that the rules and deductions have meaning. At other times, the student is really saying, "I was torn about how to sketch this game; show me what you'd do." Certain game types are definitely associated with certain sketch structures, but the sketch should ultimately flow organically from the game's task. No one, including the law school admissions committee, will ever see the scratch work you put in the test booklet. There's no "right" sketch, just one that's best for you in the context of the game. Worst of all is when the student asking the question is saying, "I'm stuck; I need this to be like a game I've already done," implying that there's no way forward unless the game matches something completely familiar.

That's the problem with prioritizing taxonomy and memorization ahead of the principles and fundamentals that allow you to answer the questions to any logic game. You're far better off learning the fundamentals of how to recognize and complete the types of games the test makers use most often. That way, the test won't throw you off by changing one tiny thing and making you think you've never seen a similar game before.

You don't get any points for giving the game the right name. You get points for answering the questions. That's the great advantage of studying and practicing for the test the way you did in Part I of this book. You're prepared to tackle any game of any type using the Kaplan Method. You're not dependent on recognizing certain buzzwords, and you won't be hamstrung if the test makers decide to throw in an unusual rule or scenario. You're in a position to use a taxonomy of game types in the right way, by engaging your knowledge of the characteristics of the standard game types to help you make good strategic choices about how best to manage all of the games in your section. If you're on an outing in the desert, it's great to have memorized exactly which snakes you might encounter. What's more important, though, is that you know the characteristics of those that are poisonous and those that are harmless and can identify them at a moment's notice. Approaching this portion of the book with a similar goal will help you avoid getting bitten by logic games on test day.

Keeping the Taxonomy Up-to-Date

If you take the time to catalogue the games covered in this book (although, to be honest, I don't know why you would), you'll find that all of them appeared on tests administered within the last decade or so.

Now, there's nothing wrong *per se* with practicing games from earlier PrepTests. Many of those games are just additional examples of the standard game types that continue to appear on the LSAT. But I will caution you against two things. Don't comb those old tests just to find one more variation or oddity and then spend time analyzing that one old twist at the expense of learning the fundamentals of the games that the test makers use most often *now*. That leads to the second caution: Don't set your study priorities according to the frequency of game types found in those older tests. Loose Sequencing games are just one example of games that have appeared more frequently than they used to and have gotten much tougher than they used to be. In the chapter on Recent Trends at the end of Part II, I'll go over what has been on the latest tests released by the LSAC so that you can assess what you're most likely to see on test day.

CHAPTER 9

SEQUENCING GAMES

As I indicated in the previous chapter, Sequencing games are far and away the most common game type found on the LSAT. Many recent exams feature two, or even three, Sequencing games or Hybrid games in which Sequencing is one of the actions. Perhaps as a result of how often they're employed by the test makers, Sequencing tasks also show the broadest range of variations. Some variations—like the Circular Sequencing game covered near the end of this chapter—are so unusual that there's no way you'll miss them. Other variations—such as omitting the require-ment that you schedule one entity per space (you saw this in the Professors' Hiring Year game in chapter 7)—are more subtle, and as such, potentially more dangerous. Taking a few minutes to think about the real-world tasks that require you to arrange, sequence, and schedule items in your life and work will help you visualize this range of Sequencing variations more clearly.

REAL-LIFE SEQUENCING

If you think about it, you'll realize that there's probably not a day in your adult life in which you don't sequence something. Every time you alphabetize, schedule, rank, or decide the order of steps in a process, you're sequencing. The most common scenario—the *default*, if you will—is that things in the sequence happen one at a time or that items are ranked without ties, one per space. If I asked you to rank your 10 favorite songs, I doubt you'd ask, "Are 3 songs supposed to be tied at number two?" or "Should I avoid repeating the same song twice in my list?" You might have difficulty ranking your favorites, but you'd *assume* that I intended the list to have 10 songs and 10 slots with one song per slot.

Never assume anything on LSAT logic games. While it's true that most (it's fair to say the *vast majority of*) Sequencing games contain one-at-a-time, one-per-space restrictions, the test makers must be, and will be, explicit about all restrictions that are to apply. Make sure you always pay attention to the overall limitations that affect a game's action and account for them in your sketch.

If your analysis of the setup reveals the expected one-at-a-time, one-per-space format, great. But, don't let variations throw you off or undermine your confidence. After all, you deal with different sequencing scenarios just fine in everyday life. If I asked you to list the order of people you met with at work last week, it might well be the case that you had a single meeting with each of four coworkers but met with another person three times. So your final list of meetings would look something like this:

Mon	Tue	Wed	Thurs	Fri
Tom	Ed	Jane	Tom	
Hiromi	Tom		Paul	

Figure 9.1

Don't let the test makers throw you by saying, "Thomas will schedule seven meetings with five potential investors. He'll have one meeting with each of investors A, B, C, and D and three meetings with investor E."

A class schedule presents another understandable variation. It might be that a law student has some classes only on Tuesdays and Thursdays, others only on Mondays, Wednesdays, and Fridays. For good measure, throw one of those long, once-per-week classes into the mix. You have no problem interpreting this student's schedule at a glance.

	Mon	Tues	Wed	Thurs	Fri
9 – 10 am	Tort		Tort		Tort
10:30 – noon		Civ Pro		Civ Pro	
1 – 2:30 pm		Prop		Prop	
2 – 3 pm	Crim		Crim		Crim
6 – 9 pm		Leg writing			

Figure 9.2

So even if a game asks you to use some entities multiple times or to leave a slot open, it's nothing you haven't done before.

Another trap that the test makers employ is revealed by considering your real-world assumptions. If I ask you to create a sequence of eight departments in a certain company, your default would almost certainly be to start with a sketch like one of these:

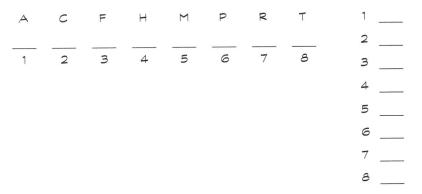

Figure 9.3

Our default orientations are generally top to bottom and left to right. But now imagine if I said that the eight departments occupy one floor each in an eight-story building. If I include a rule like "Human Resources occupies a higher floor than Marketing," your sketch needs to be numbered from the bottom up.

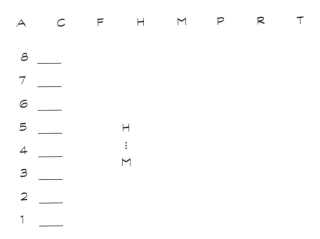

Figure 9.4

The same confusion can be avoided by paying attention to the differences between games in which entities are ranked and those in which they're assigned to numbered positions. Consider two examples: If I tell you that seven salespeople will be ranked on their performance over the past quarter, a rule such as "Baker was ranked lower than Carty" should be depicted like this:

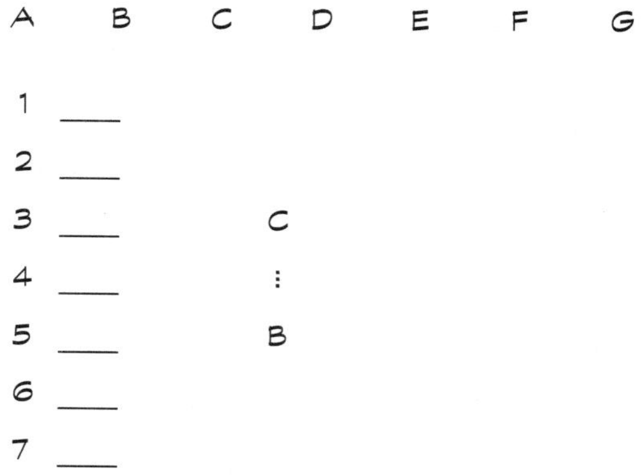

```
      A    B    C    D    E    F    G

  1  ____

  2  ____

  3  ____           C

  4  ____           ⋮

  5  ____           B

  6  ____

  7  ____
```

Figure 9.5

Being ranked lower means taking a position closer to number seven. On the other hand, if the game assigns seven salespeople to seven offices, numbered 1 through 7, the rule "Baker is assigned a lower-numbered office than Carty" should be written like this:

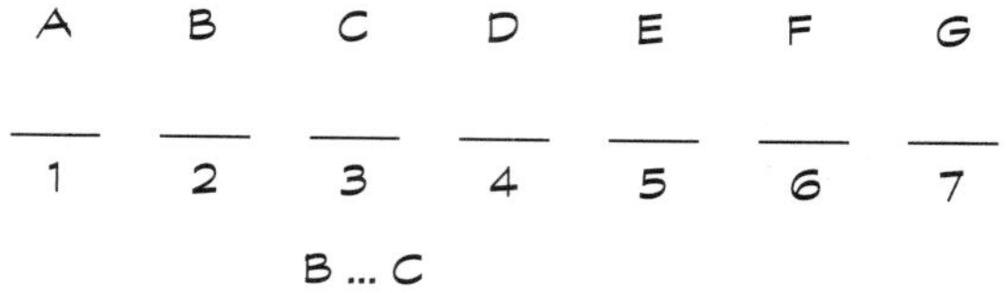

```
    A    B    C    D    E    F    G

   ___  ___  ___  ___  ___  ___  ___
    1    2    3    4    5    6    7

            B ... C
```

Figure 9.6

Here, having a *lower-numbered* office means taking an office *closer to number 1.*

The test makers can even reward you for paying attention to the criterion on which items are ranked. Imagine a game show host telling you, "Put these five products in order by price" or a gym teacher who says, "Line up by height. You'd make sure to know whether you are supposed to arrange the products from cheapest to most expensive or vice versa, whether the students were supposed to go from tallest to shortest or the other way around. The test makers will always be explicit about the order you're supposed to use. There have been many examples over the years of relatively simple Sequencing games that test takers missed or struggled with because they failed to catch these distinctions. In fact, you'll be given the opportunity to make this very mistake in the Hotel Suites game later in this chapter, so stay alert.

When you're conducting your overview in Step 1 of the Kaplan Method, use the real-world scenario that's described to your advantage. Ask the logical questions about your task and make sure you reflect all of the restrictions or definitions in your sketch framework. It's better to jot down "Cheapest" at the top of your sketch and "Most Expensive" at the bottom than to set up the whole game incorrectly and have to start over from scratch.

STANDARD SEQUENCING GAMES

You've already seen the two basic subcategories of Sequencing games: strict and loose. Strict Sequencing games contain rules and restrictions that associate certain entities with specific slots, or rules that tell you precisely how many spaces separate two or more entities. The framework for such games should always be numbered slots or spaces, and entities should be placed as definitely as possible within them.

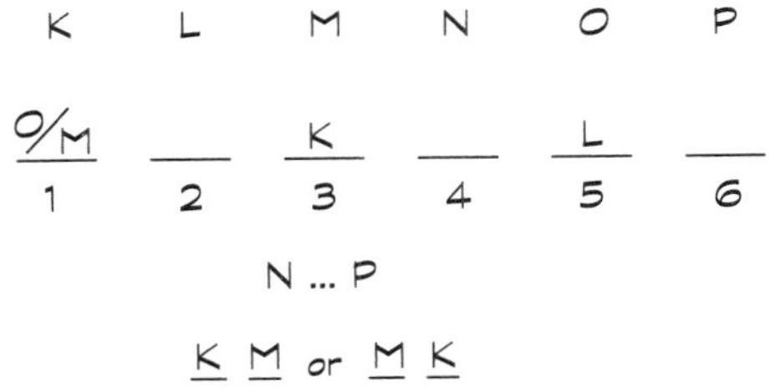

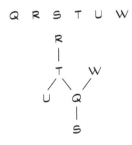

Figure 9.7

Even when you're unable to place many of the entities within the framework initially, the strict framework will enhance your understanding of the rules and acceptable arrangements.

In Loose Sequencing games, on the other hand, all of the rules are "relative." That is, they tell you only the relative order of two or more entities, with no restrictions as to the specific slots that the entities must take or avoid and no information about how close to or far from each other the entities must be placed. In these games, you will use the "tree" model for your framework. Numbered slots do nothing to give you further concreteness in the sketch.

Figure 9.8

Strict Sequencing

In the most routine Strict Sequencing games, the number of slots and entities will be the same and the setup will be unequivocal in telling you to arrange the entities one per slot. The Trail Markers game is representative of this pattern.

Exactly six guideposts, numbered 1 through 6, mark a mountain trail. Each guidepost pictures a different one of six animals—fox, grizzly, hare, lynx, moose, or porcupine. The following conditions must apply:

The grizzly is pictured on either guidepost 3 or guidepost 4.

The moose guidepost is numbered lower than the hare guidepost.

The lynx guidepost is numbered lower than the moose guidepost but higher than the fox guidepost.[1]

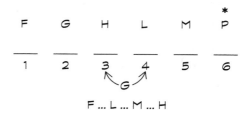

Figure 9.9

In this case, it's Rule 1 that signals the usefulness of the strict framework. You need to be able to *see* the impact of placing G in either space 3 or space 4. Note, too, that the orientation of the sketch is irrelevant. The relative restrictions in Rules 2 and 3 refer to lower- or higher-*numbered* guideposts. Guidepost 1 is the lowest-numbered and guidepost 6 the highest-numbered, no matter how you draw it. So the presumptive left-to-right slot numbering is fine. But top-to-bottom or bottom-to-top would be just as good, so long as it's logical and clear to you.

Here's another standard Strict Sequencing setup. Take a few moments to look it over and determine which rule(s) make it clear that a numbered-slot framework is called for.

Exactly eight computer processor chips—F, G, H, J, K, L, M, and O—are ranked according to their speed from first (fastest) to eighth (slowest). The ranking must be consistent with the following:

There are no ties.

Either F or G is ranked first.

M is not the slowest.

H is faster than J, with exactly one chip intermediate in speed between them.

K is faster than L, with exactly two chips intermediate in speed between them.

O is slower than both J and L.[2]

F   G   H   J   K   L   M   O

$$\frac{F}{G} \quad \underline{} \quad \underline{} \quad \underline{} \quad \underline{} \quad \underline{} \quad \underline{} \quad \underline{}$$

1   2   3   4   5   6   7   8

H___J
K_____L...O

Figure 9.10

This time, Rule 1 explicitly mentions the first position. Moreover, Rules 3 and 4 both designate the specific number of spaces that separate pairs of entities. Even though you weren't able to put a lot of these entities into the framework at the outset, it would be nearly impossible

---

[1] PrepTest 46, Sec. 4, Game 1
[2] PrepTest 49, Sec. 1, Game 4

to assess the impact without the accompanying framework. Being able to quickly see that placing K in space 2 means placing L in space 5 is vital, and this sketch allows you to do that.

The two preceding games also stand as good reminders of what leads to most deductions within Strict Sequencing games: Established Entities and Blocks of Entities. In the Trail Markers game, no entity is completely determined, but the G comes very close. Combining G's restriction to either space 3 or 4 with the long F-L-M-H block leaves only 10 acceptable arrangements for the game. Likewise, in the Processor Chip game, no entity is entirely established, but you know for certain that space 1 is occupied by either F or G. That means that the K-L block, which has to be followed by O, can only fit in spaces 2 and 5, 3 and 6, or 4 and 7, severely limiting the number of acceptable solutions. At times, the position taken by an Established Entity leaves a Block of Entities only two acceptable positions. That's relatively rare, but when it happens, you can create a Limited Options sketch. What's more common, and is seen in both of the previous examples, is the presence of Duplications. In the Trail Markers game, the moose allows you to combine Rules 2 and 3. In the Processor Chip game, J appears in Rules 4 and 6 and L in Rules 5 and 6, allowing the three rules to be combined into a long string. The one element of the BLEND checklist that's unlikely to be of help in most Strict Sequencing games is Number Restrictions. That's because the numbers—one entity per space—are as simple as they can be. You can see a couple of exceptions under the "Uneven Numbers" heading below. But for the most part, once you've confirmed that you're working with a standard one-per-space format, you can take the numbers out of consideration. There's just no way to make them any clearer than they are.

Loose Sequencing

For many years, Loose Sequencing games were (rightly) considered easier than their strict counterparts. If you're prepping with outdated materials, you will (wrongly) get the impression that it's still the case. In the easiest of these games (the majority of them prior to PrepTest 33), all of the rules were relatively straightforward—"X ranks lower than Y," and "W ranks higher than Y"—and all of the rules combined. So you wound up with a single "tree" diagram that, while not completely determining the exact lineup, gave the relative position of every entity. A few of the more recent examples preserve that format. The Water Treatment Plant game is a perfect illustration.

Workers at a water treatment plant open eight valves—G, H, I, K, L, N, O, and P—to flush out a system of pipes that needs emergency repairs. To maximize safety and efficiency, each valve is opened exactly once, and no two valves are opened at the same time. The valves are opened in accordance with the following conditions:

Both K and P are opened before H.
O is opened before L but after H.
L is opened after G.
N is opened before H.
I is opened after K.[3]

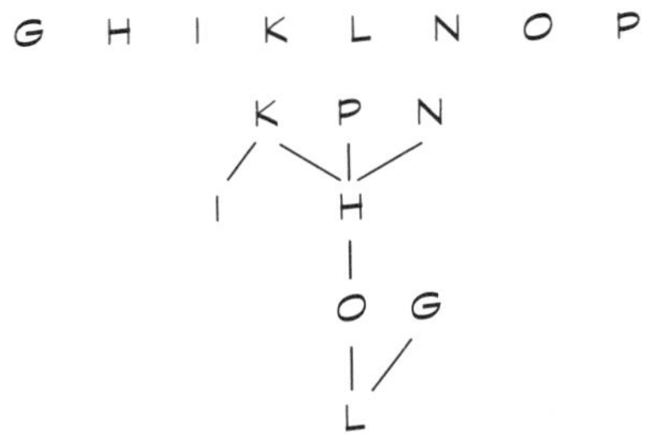

Figure 9.11

---

[3] PrepTest 52, Sec. 2, Game 1

Take note of how you knew to draw this one with a loose sketch. None of the rules mentions a specific slot, and none gives you any idea of how distant two entities are from one another. All of the rules give you the relative positions of two or more entities. There would be nothing to place into slots even if you drew them. But there's a lot to learn by combining the relative restrictions. That puts a huge premium on Duplications, the most important of the BLEND elements in Loose Sequencing deductions. As is typical in Loose Sequencing games, every entity in this game relates to at least one other.

Once you've created your Loose Sequencing sketch, you can figure out the acceptable positions for any of the entities. In the Water Treatment Plant game, for example, H could only be opened fourth, fifth, or sixth. There are eight entities in total, and H must come after K, P, and N and before O and L. H is pretty heavily restricted here. G, on the other hand, has only one restriction: It must be opened before L. So G could be opened in any position first through seventh. Be very careful not to make unwarranted assumptions based on the drawing. In the previous sketch, G may be lower on the page than K, P, N, or H, but it isn't restricted by any entity except L.

Don't misinterpret the name Loose Sequencing to indicate a lack of concreteness. Although there are no Established Entities in the Water Treatment Plant game, notice that all of the rules are direct and restrictive. There are no conditional rules and none that offer restrictions in the alternative (e.g., "Either K is opened before P but after I, or else K is opened after P but before I"). The absence of those types of rules is a good sign that this is one of the easier Loose Sequencing games you'll encounter, and it makes the Water Treatment Plant game reminiscent of the stereotypical older Loose Sequencing games.

PrepTest 52, the test that featured the Water Treatment Plant game, had another Loose Sequencing game as well. In fact, this second game from PrepTest 52 is much more representative of Loose Sequencing as it has appeared recently. Take a couple of minutes and review the setup and rules. Note what makes the Bread Truck game more challenging to set up and how it rewards deductions beyond the string of Duplications that allowed you to stitch together all of the entities in the Water Treatment Plant game.

A bread truck makes exactly one bread delivery to each of six restaurants in succession—Figueroa's, Ginsberg's, Harris's, Kanzaki's, Leacock's, and Malpighi's—though not necessarily in that order. The following conditions must apply:

> Ginsberg's delivery is earlier than Kanzaki's but later than Figueroa's.
> Harris's delivery is earlier than Ginsberg's.
> If Figueroa's delivery is earlier than Malpighi's, then Leacock's delivery is earlier than Harris's.
> Either Malpighi's delivery is earlier than Harris's or it is later than Kanzaki's, but not both.[4]

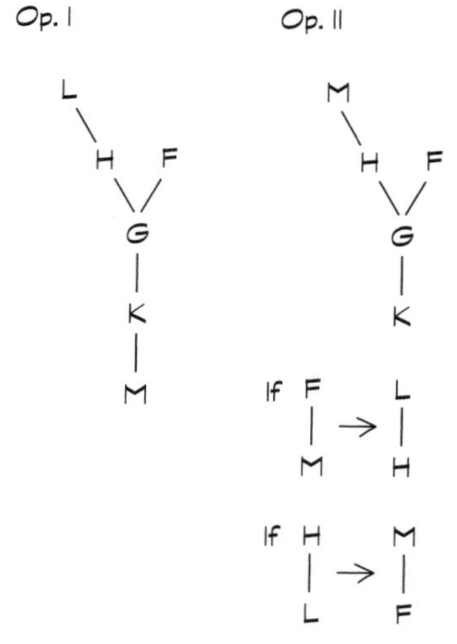

---

[4] PrepTest 52, Sec. 2, Game 4

Figure 9.12

The scenario and the first two rules could come from any Loose Sequencing game. They're direct and, unsurprisingly, they share a duplicated entity, G. Combined, Rules 1 and 2 start a sketch that might appear in any Loose Sequencing game.

Figure 9.13

It's the third and fourth rules that set this game apart from the Water Treatment Plant and from most of the older Loose Sequencing games. Because they are conditional and present alternative possibilities respectively, Rules 3 and 4 cannot simply be snapped onto the block created by Rules 1 and 2 in order to create a single Master Sketch. A lot of the newer Loose Sequencing games reward a Limited Options approach. Here's how it works in this game.

Rule 4 creates the Limited Options. Either M is earlier than both H and K, or it is later than both H and K.

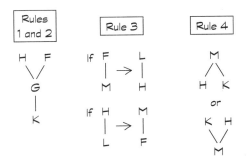

Figure 9.14

Since H and K are included in the block created by Rules 1 and 2, you can simply add M after K to create Option I or before H to create Option II.

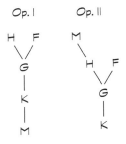

Figure 9.15

Now, consider the applicability of the conditional rule, Rule 3.

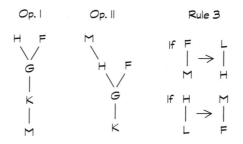

Figure 9.16

In Option I, F must come before M. Therefore, L must come before H. In this option, all six entities are related and you're done.

Figure 9.17

In Option II, however, three possibilities remain. On test day, you probably wouldn't write out all three, provided that you can see how they work. I'll illustrate the three possibilities now, so that you can be sure you've got them straight. (By the way, take another look at the sample Master Sketch above; now you can see why I wrote Rule 3 below Option II, where its conditions are still applicable.) It could be the case that F comes before M. That's the sufficient trigger in Rule 3's formal logic, meaning that L would have to come before H.

Figure 9.18

Likewise, it could be that H comes before L. That's the sufficient trigger in Rule 3's contrapositive, meaning that F would come after M.

Op. II (b)

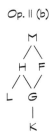

Figure 9.19

Finally, it could be that neither of the sufficient triggers in Rule 3 is present. F could come after M and H could come after L.

Op. II (c)

Figure 9.20

That's a lot to keep track of and, indeed, this is one of the toughest Loose Sequencing games you're likely to see. But it's a good reminder not to take Loose Sequencing for granted and to practice using recent materials. A lot of test takers could be caught off guard if they ran into something like the Bread Delivery game. Fortunately, knowing how to deal with alternative possibilities by using a Limited Options sketch means that you'll be far more likely to take control of this game than will someone who hasn't trained with the Kaplan Method. Chances are that if you have a Loose Sequencing game on your test, it will fall somewhere in between the difficulty levels presented by these two examples. I'll have you take another crack at Loose Sequencing with Limited Options shortly. For now, take a look at how the test makers throw some more variety into their favorite game type.

SEQUENCING TWISTS
Uneven Numbers

As I discussed above, when asked to put things in an order—to rank, schedule, or arrange them in a row—your default is to assume that there are no ties. Most of the time, the test makers want you to adhere to one-at-a-time, one-per-space limitations. But when they do, they'll be explicit about it. Taking one-entity-per-space for granted is a good way to go off track on games in which the test makers don't include that restriction.

You saw the setup for this next game in chapter 7. Refresh your memory of the overview, sketch, rules, and deductions, keeping in mind that while there are seven professors hired over seven years, nothing in the setup text says that one professor must be hired each year. If you're fuzzy on how you were able to deduce so much about the arrangement of professors to hiring years, revisit chapter 7, where I took you through Steps 1–4 of the Kaplan Method on this game.

Exactly seven professors—Madison, Nilsson, Orozco, Paton, Robinson, Sarkis, and Togo—were hired in the years 1989 through 1995. Each professor has one or more specialties, and any two professors hired in the same year or in consecutive years do not have a specialty in common. The professors were hired according to the following conditions:

Madison was hired in 1993, Robinson in 1991.

There is at least one specialty that Madison, Orozco, and Togo have in common.

Nilsson shares a specialty with Robinson.

Paton and Sarkis were each hired at least one year before Madison and at least one year after Nilsson.

Orozco, who shares a specialty with Sarkis, was hired in 1990.[5]

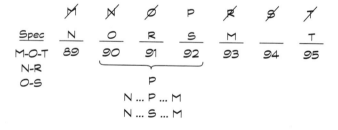

Figure 9.21

There are two big takeaways from this game. First, you must pay attention to the restrictions that are and *are not* included in the setup. Test takers who struggle with this game make unwarranted assumptions and then fail to be patient and methodical enough in the Deductions step to demonstrate that Paton will have to be hired in the same year as one of the other professors. Second, variations don't necessarily make games harder. It's certainly the exception to have a Sequencing game in which you don't place one entity per slot. The test makers count on unfamiliar twists to throw off a certain percentage of test takers. But remember that familiarity is entirely within your control. Your practice with this book and other Kaplan resources immunizes you against the very difficulties the test makers will present to throw off much of your competition. Here, your expert use of the Kaplan Method has allowed you to establish the hiring years of six of the seven professors. Now, tackling the question set has to be pretty

---

[5] PrepTest 35, Sec. 3, Game 4

easy; there's just not much left to account for. Try it out. Give yourself five minutes for the six questions. Pay special attention to Paton, the only professor whose hiring year isn't locked down in the Master Sketch. Remember, too, what it means to "share a specialty." Professors who share a specialty cannot be hired in the same year as each other or in consecutive years.

18. Which one of the following is a complete and accurate list of the professors who could have been hired in the years 1989 through 1991?

    (A) Nilsson, Orozco, Robinson
    (B) Orozco, Robinson, Sarkis
    (C) Nilsson, Orozco, Paton, Robinson
    (D) Nilsson, Orozco, Paton, Sarkis
    (E) Orozco, Paton, Robinson, Sarkis

19. If exactly one professor was hired in 1991, then which one of the following could be true?

    (A) Madison and Paton share a specialty.
    (B) Robinson and Sarkis share a specialty.
    (C) Paton was hired exactly one year after Orozco.
    (D) Exactly one professor was hired in 1994.
    (E) Exactly two professors were hired in 1993.

20. Which one of the following must be false?

    (A) Nilsson was hired in 1989.
    (B) Paton was hired in 1990.
    (C) Paton was hired in 1991.
    (D) Sarkis was hired in 1992.
    (E) Togo was hired in 1994.

21. Which one of the following must be true?

    (A) Orozco was hired before Paton.
    (B) Paton was hired before Sarkis.
    (C) Sarkis was hired before Robinson.
    (D) Robinson was hired before Sarkis.
    (E) Madison was hired before Sarkis.

22. If exactly two professors were hired in 1992, then which one of the following could be true?

    (A) Orozco, Paton, and Togo share a specialty.
    (B) Madison, Paton, and Togo share a specialty.
    (C) Exactly two professors were hired in 1991.
    (D) Exactly two professors were hired in 1993.
    (E) Paton was hired in 1991.

23. If Paton and Madison have a specialty in common, then which one of the following must be true?

    (A) Nilsson does not share a specialty with Paton.
    (B) Exactly one professor was hired in 1990.
    (C) Exactly one professor was hired in 1991.
    (D) Exactly two professors were hired in each of two years.
    (E) Paton was hired at least one year before Sarkis.[6]

_____

[6] PrepTest 35, Sec. 3, Qs 18–23

Explanations

In this question set, the question types are equally divided: three of them have a new "if" and three don't. Reviewing them in two groups will point out a valuable pattern. For the "if" questions, Paton (the one professor whose hiring year is not completely determined) will have to be involved. Let's begin with those that lack a new "if"; these are questions you can answer with just a glance at your Master Sketch.

18. **(C)**

Which one of the following is a complete and accurate list of the professors who could have been hired in the years 1989 through 1991?

(A) Nilsson, Orozco, Robinson
(B) Orozco, Robinson, Sarkis
(C) Nilsson, Orozco, Paton, Robinson
(D) Nilsson, Orozco, Paton, Sarkis
(E) Orozco, Paton, Robinson, Sarkis[7]

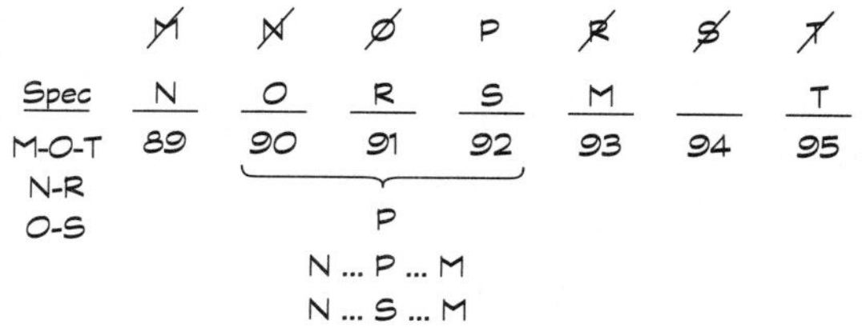

Figure 9.22

This question asks for a "complete and accurate list," in other words *any and all* of the professors who could have been hired between '89 and '91. As the Master Sketch illustrates, the correct answer must include N, O, R, and P and cannot include S, M, or T, who were all hired in '92 or later. That makes choice (C) the correct answer. Choice (A) misses Paton, while choices (B), (D), and (E) all incorrectly include Sarkis and miss one or more of the professors who should be included. Notice the role that Paton, the one entity who can still move, plays here. Paton *could* have been hired within the years in question, and so must be included in the correct answer.

20. **(E)**

Which one of the following must be false?

(A) Nilsson was hired in 1989.
(B) Paton was hired in 1990.
(C) Paton was hired in 1991.
(D) Sarkis was hired in 1992.
(E) Togo was hired in 1994.[8]

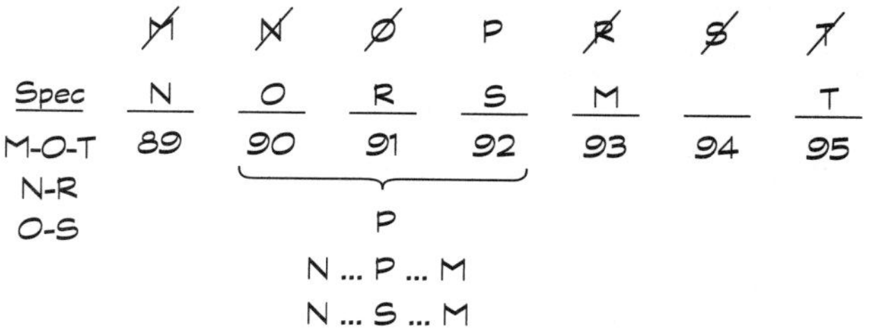

Figure 9.23

Here, the correct answer *must be false*. Togo, you can see from the Master Sketch, must be hired in 1995, making choice (E) the correct answer. Note that here, Paton, who could have been hired in '90, '91, or '92, is included in two of the wrong answers, both of which *could be true*.

---

[7] PrepTest 35, Sec. 3, Q 18
[8] PrepTest 35, Sec. 3, Q 20

21. **(D)**

Which one of the following must be true?

(A) Orozco was hired before Paton.
(B) Paton was hired before Sarkis.
(C) Sarkis was hired before Robinson.
(D) Robinson was hired before Sarkis.
(E) Madison was hired before Sarkis.[9]

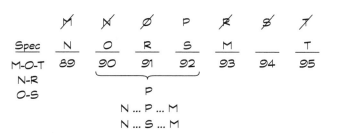

Figure 9.24

This time, the correct answer *must be true*. Since R was hired in '91 and S in '92, choice (D) fits the bill. As with question 20, it's no surprise to find Paton in two of the wrong answers here. P could have been hired before S, but P could also have been hired the same year as S. So choice (B) *could be false*. And P could have been hired the same year as or later than O. Therefore, choice (A) could also be false.

P's status as the one professor that can be hired the same year as another played a role in those "Non-If" questions, but it will become even more central in the "If" questions. As the only entity who can move, Paton must be involved in any conditional statements.

19. **(A)**

If exactly one professor was hired in 1991, then which one of the following could be true?

(A) Madison and Paton share a specialty.
(B) Robinson and Sarkis share a specialty.
(C) Paton was hired exactly one year after Orozco.
(D) Exactly one professor was hired in 1994.
(E)   Exactly two professors were hired in 1993.[10]

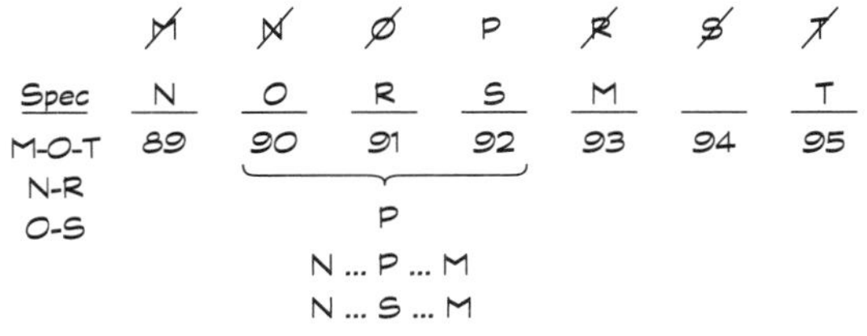

Spec	N	O	R	P	S	M		T
M-O-T	89	90	91		92	93	94	95
N-R				P				
O-S								

N ... P ... M
N ... S ... M

Figure 9.25

Usually, a new "if" calls for a mini-sketch. There's no harm in making one here. If only one professor is hired in '91, you know that P was hired in either '90 or '92.

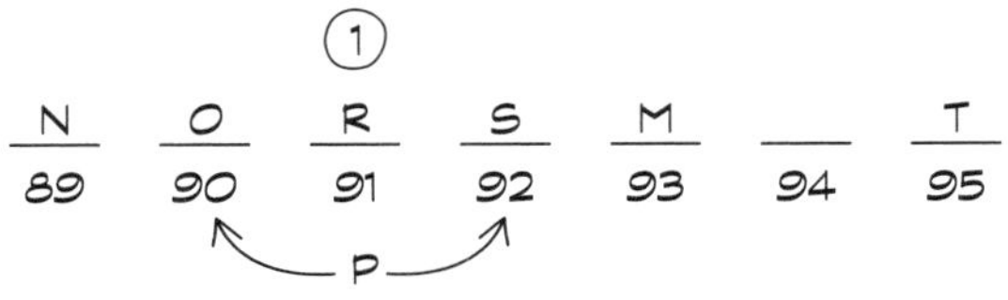

①

N	O	R	S	M		T
89	90	91	92	93	94	95

P

Figure 9.26

[9] PrepTest 35, Sec. 3, Q 21
[10] PrepTest 35, Sec. 3, Q 19

With so much certainty in this game, though, you may just have elected to answer this one from your Master Sketch, telling yourself "P can't be in '91." Either way, you can tell that P is the focus of this question. The correct answer is one that *could be true*, after all. If hired in '90, P could share a specialty with M, which would require that they not be hired in the same or consecutive years. Choice (A) is the correct answer. The only other choice involving P is ruled out by the "if" condition in the question stem. Since P can't be hired in '91, choice (C) *must be false*. The other three choices must be false because they contradict the Master Sketch.

22. **(A)**

If exactly two professors were hired in 1992, then which one of the following could be true?

(A) Orozco, Paton, and Togo share a specialty.
(B) Madison, Paton, and Togo share a specialty.
(C) Exactly two professors were hired in 1991.
(D) Exactly two professors were hired in 1993.
(E) Paton was hired in 1991.[11]

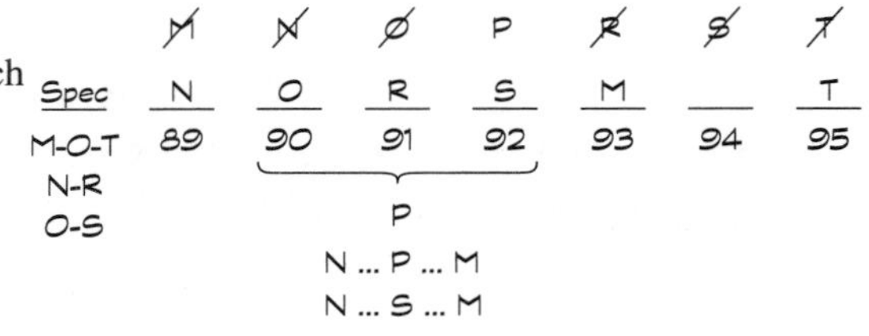

Figure 9.27

Again, with so much certainty, a mini-sketch is optional. The new "if" simply means that P was hired in '92, something you can likely keep clear in your head.

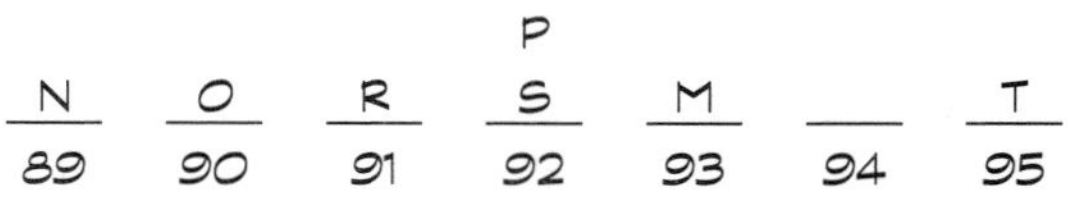

Figure 9.28

The correct answer *could be true*. That's choice (A). With P in '92, O, P, and T are all kept apart by more than a year, meaning that they can share a specialty. The four wrong answers *must be false*. The "if" condition puts P and M in consecutive years, meaning that they cannot share a specialty. That eliminates choice (B). Moreover, with P hired in '92, choices (C), (D), and (E) are all impossible.

---

[11] PrepTest 35, Sec. 3, Q 22

23. **(E)**

If Paton and Madison have a specialty in common, then which one of the following must be true?

(A) Nilsson does not share a specialty with Paton.
(B) Exactly one professor was hired in 1990.
(C) Exactly one professor was hired in 1991.
(D) Exactly two professors were hired in each of two years.
(E) Paton was hired at least one year before Sarkis.[12]

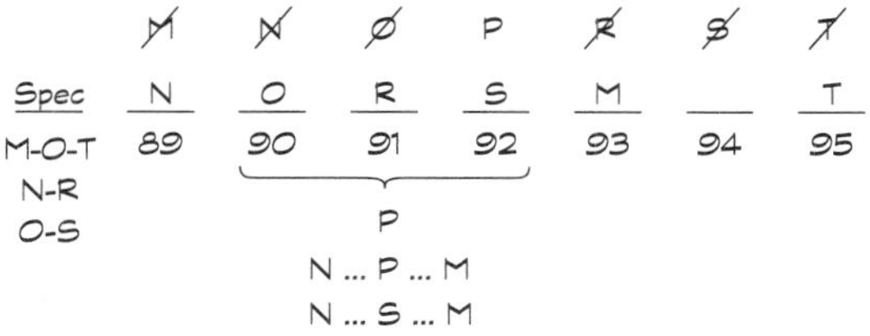

Spec	N̶	N̶	Ø	P	M̶	S̶	T̶
	N	O	R	S	M		T
M-O-T	89	90	91	92	93	94	95
N-R							
O-S			P				

N ... P ... M
N ... S ... M

Figure 9.29

This is the toughest of the "if" conditions. It requires applying the restriction that comes from having a specialty in common. If P and M share a specialty, they cannot have been hired in the same or consecutive years. That means that, for this question, P was hired in either '90 or '91.

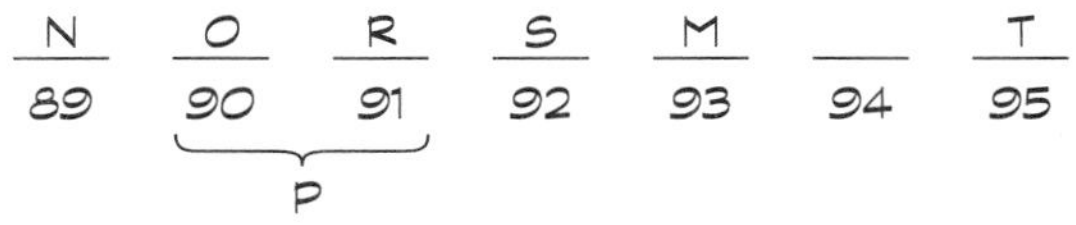

N	O	R	S	M		T
89	90	91	92	93	94	95

P

Figure 9.30

The correct answer *must be true*, leading you to choice (E). If P was hired in '90 or '91, S was hired later. Note that choices (B) and (C) could be false. P could be hired in either '90 or '91. Likewise with choice (A): If hired in '91, P could share a specialty with N, who was hired in '89. Choice (D) makes a statement that is always false in this game, regardless of when P was hired.

That game has derailed many test takers over the years. Students who try to impose a one-entity-per-space requirement where none exists get confused and frustrated and never make the deductions that wind up precisely determining six of the seven entities' positions. By training yourself to recognize when the test makers have departed from their usual modus operandi, you'll be at a double advantage. First, by not insisting on a restriction that doesn't exist, you'll manage the Deductions step effectively. Second, you'll realize that the exceptional situation (here, the fact that P must be the second professor hired during one of the years) must be the focus of at least some of the questions. The test makers have no reason to create unusual situations unless they want to reward the test takers who can notice and correctly analyze them.

Another way the test makers present Sequencing actions with uneven numbers is through Selection-Sequencing Hybrid games. There, they ask you to select some number of entities and then arrange those that you've selected in order. This has a different effect on the game than what you saw in the Professor Hiring scenario. Once you've selected your entities, the test makers will likely have you sequence them in routine one-per-space fashion. Instead of having the possibility of having an empty slot or a slot with multiple entities, you'll have to consider the impact of certain entities being included or excluded in the selection process. I'll take you through an example of such a game in the chapter on Hybrids.

---

[12] PrepTest 35, Sec. 3, Q 23

Strict Sequencing with Conditional Rules

You've already seen how the test can use conditional formal logic rules in Loose Sequencing games (the Bread Truck Deliveries setup featured them). In recent years, formal logic has appeared more often in Loose Sequencing games than it has in their Strict Sequencing counterparts. Still, it's worth taking the time to see how the test makers use conditional rules in Strict Sequencing games. The following game, which first appeared on the June 2003 exam, is a great example.

I'll let you try the game on your own and then review it in its entirety after you're done. Give yourself eight and a half minutes to try the game and all of its questions. If you find that you're struggling, stop and review Steps 1–4 of the Kaplan Method. Once you're sure that you've got a good Master Sketch and an understanding of the how the game works, go back and try the question set again.

Charlie makes a soup by adding exactly six kinds of foods—kale, lentils, mushrooms, onions, tomatoes, and zucchini—to a broth, one food at a time. No food is added more than once. The order in which Charlie adds the foods to the broth must be consistent with the following:

  If the mushrooms are added third, then the lentils are added last.

  If the zucchini is added first, then the lentils are added at some time before the onions.

  Neither the tomatoes nor the kale is added fifth.

  The mushrooms are added at some time before the tomatoes or the kale, but not before both.

1. Which one of the following could be the order in which the foods are added to the broth?

   (A) kale, mushrooms, onions, lentils, tomatoes, zucchini
   (B) kale, zucchini, mushrooms, tomatoes, lentils, onions
   (C) lentils, mushrooms, zucchini, kale, onions, tomatoes
   (D) zucchini, lentils, kale, mushrooms, onions, tomatoes
   (E) zucchini, tomatoes, onions, mushrooms, lentils, kale

2. Which one of the following foods CANNOT be added first?

   (A) kale
   (B) lentils
   (C) mushrooms
   (D) onions
   (E) tomatoes

3. If the lentils are added last, then which one of the following must be true?

    (A)   At least one of the foods is added at some time before the zucchini.

    (B)   At least two of the foods are added at some time before the kale.

    (C)   The mushrooms are added third.

    (D)   The zucchini is added third.

    (E)   The tomatoes are added fourth.

4. Which one of the following could be an accurate partial ordering of the foods added to the broth?

    (A)   lentils: second; mushrooms: third

    (B)   mushrooms: fourth; lentils: last

    (C)   onions: second; mushrooms: fifth

    (D)   zucchini: first; lentils: last

    (E)   zucchini: first; mushrooms: second

5. If the zucchini is added first, then which one of the following CANNOT be true?

    (A)   The kale is added second.

    (B)   The tomatoes are added second.

    (C)   The lentils are added third.

    (D)   The lentils are added fourth.

    (E)   The onions are added fourth.[13]

---

[13] PrepTest 40, Sec. 2, Game 1, Qs 1–5

Explanations

STEPS 1 AND 2: Overview and Sketch

You're able to identify this as a Sequencing game right from the start. The entities—the six kinds of foods—will be added to the broth one at a time, with restrictions on the order in which they're added. It's an easy task to picture. There's a big pot of water on the stove, and six kinds of food are being prepared and arrayed in bowls in front of you. The task is clear: What goes into the pot first, second, third, and so on?

Up to this point, the game could be either Strict or Loose Sequencing. But a quick check of the rules tells you that they definitely implicate specific slots in the order. The first, third, fifth, and last spots are all mentioned explicitly. So a Strict Sequencing framework is in order.

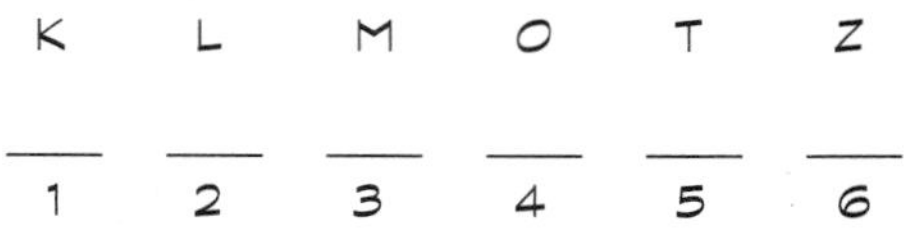

$$K \quad L \quad M \quad O \quad T \quad Z$$

$$\overline{\;\;1\;\;} \quad \overline{\;\;2\;\;} \quad \overline{\;\;3\;\;} \quad \overline{\;\;4\;\;} \quad \overline{\;\;5\;\;} \quad \overline{\;\;6\;\;}$$

Figure 9.31

STEP 3: Rules

Here's where things start to seem a little out of the ordinary. The rules themselves aren't strange. It's just that, with the exception of Rule 3, you don't normally associate them with Strict Sequencing.

Rules 1 and 2 are formal logic statements. You know that their conditional nature won't allow you to build them directly into the sketch, so record each, along with its contrapositive, below the framework slots.

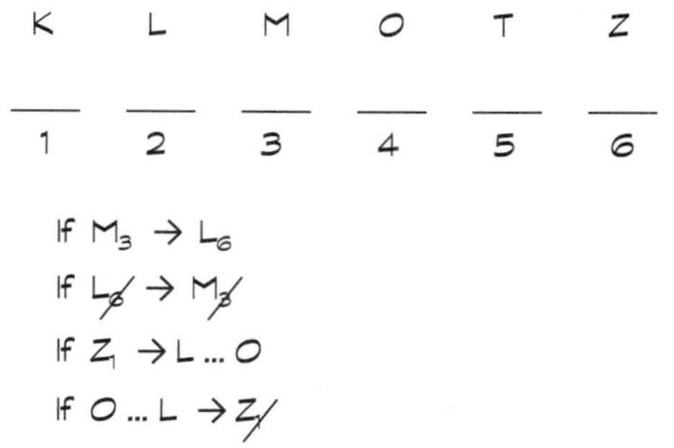

$$K \quad L \quad M \quad O \quad T \quad Z$$

$$\overline{\;\;1\;\;} \quad \overline{\;\;2\;\;} \quad \overline{\;\;3\;\;} \quad \overline{\;\;4\;\;} \quad \overline{\;\;5\;\;} \quad \overline{\;\;6\;\;}$$

If $M_3 \rightarrow L_6$

If $\cancel{L_6} \rightarrow \cancel{M_3}$

If $Z_1 \rightarrow L \ldots O$

If $O \ldots L \rightarrow \cancel{Z_1}$

Figure 9.32

Make sure you got the negation correct for Rule 2. In a game where each item goes into the pot "one food at a time," negating "the lentils are added at some time before the onions" means that the onions would have to be added at some time before the lentils.

Rule 3 is a standard negative restriction. Record it beneath space 5 in the framework.

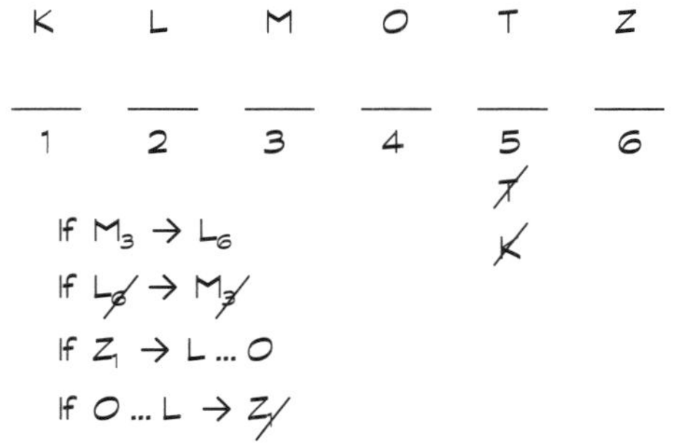

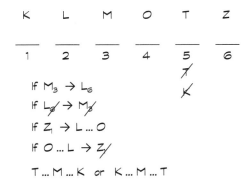

K   L   M   O   T   Z

___ ___ ___ ___ ___ ___
1   2   3   4   5   6
                     T̷
If M₃ → L₆   K̷
If L̷ → M̷
If Z₁ → L ... O
If O ... L → Z̷

Figure 9.32A

Rule 4 presents two alternatives. The mushrooms must be added either after the tomatoes and before the kale, or after the kale and before the tomatoes. Again, there's no way to put this firmly into the sketch (there are just too many open slots), so record the options beneath the framework. You can add notes below the framework indicating that the mushrooms can never be first or sixth, but you can't determine affirmatively where they will go.

K   L   M   O   T   Z

___ ___ ___ ___ ___ ___
1   2   3   4   5   6
                     T̷
If M₃ → L₆   K̷
If L̷ → M̷
If Z₁ → L ... O
If O ... L → Z̷
T ... M ... K or K ... M ... T

Figure 9.33

You may have been tempted to create dual Limited Options sketches based on Rule 4. But ask yourself what you'd be able to do with such sketches. Rule 4 doesn't trigger any of the other restrictions here (at least until you have more certainty about the mushrooms' placement), so the "or" in the diagram will serve to remind you that one of these two patterns must apply.

STEP 4: Deductions

In Strict Sequencing, the strongest deductions derive from Established Entities and Blocks of Entities. You have no Established Entities in this game, and the only blocks you're given are too loose to allow for any additional headway in the sketch. Sometimes when you have multiple conditional statements, they combine, with the result of one triggering the other. But not here.

Rules 1 and 2 cover entirely different entities. Your Master Sketch is just the framework with the rules diagrammed below.

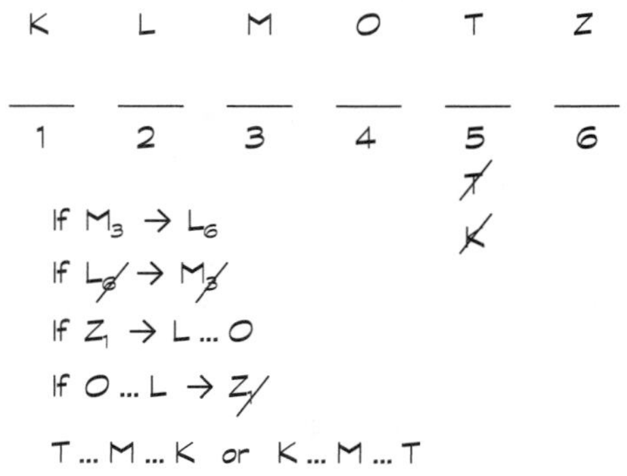

$$K \quad L \quad M \quad O \quad T \quad Z$$

$$\underline{} \quad \underline{} \quad \underline{} \quad \underline{} \quad \underline{} \quad \underline{}$$
$$1 \quad\;\; 2 \quad\;\; 3 \quad\;\; 4 \quad\;\; 5 \quad\;\; 6$$

If $M_3 \rightarrow L_6$

If $\cancel{L_6} \rightarrow \cancel{M_3}$

If $Z_1 \rightarrow L \ldots O$

If $O \ldots L \rightarrow \cancel{Z_1}$

$T \ldots M \ldots K$ or $K \ldots M \ldots T$

Figure 9.34

STEP 5: Questions

What can you expect from the questions in this game? The question set is a routine collection: an Acceptability question, a Partial Acceptability question, two "If" questions, and one "Non-If" question. But you should expect that the "If" questions will trigger one of the two conditional rules. So will at least some of the answer choices in the Acceptability-based questions. The "Non-"If" question, on the other hand, you should be able to answer using Rules 3 or 4.

1. **(D)**

   Which one of the following could be the order in which the foods are added to the broth?

   (A)   kale, mushrooms, onions, lentils, tomatoes, zucchini
   (B)   kale, zucchini, mushrooms, tomatoes, lentils, onions
   (C)   lentils, mushrooms, zucchini, kale, onions, tomatoes
   (D)   zucchini, lentils, kale, mushrooms, onions, tomatoes
   (E)   zucchini, tomatoes, onions, mushrooms, lentils, kale[14]

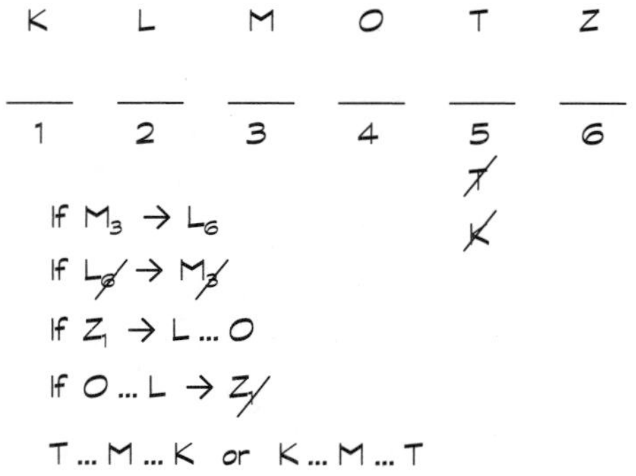

$$K \quad L \quad M \quad O \quad T \quad Z$$

$$\underline{} \quad \underline{} \quad \underline{} \quad \underline{} \quad \underline{} \quad \underline{}$$
$$1 \quad\;\; 2 \quad\;\; 3 \quad\;\; 4 \quad\;\; 5 \quad\;\; 6$$

If $M_3 \rightarrow L_6$

If $\cancel{L_6} \rightarrow \cancel{M_3}$

If $Z_1 \rightarrow L \ldots O$

If $O \ldots L \rightarrow \cancel{Z_1}$

$T \ldots M \ldots K$ or $K \ldots M \ldots T$

Figure 9.35

Approach this Acceptability question as you would any other, by using the rules to eliminate violators. Given that Rules 1 and 2 will only apply in certain conditions, though, it will be easier to start with Rules 3 and 4. Rule 3 eliminates choice (A), which has tomatoes added fifth. Rule 4 knocks out choice (C), where mushrooms are found before both tomatoes and kale. With those two choices out of the way, it's easier to check the conditional rules. To check Rule 1, look for an answer in which mushrooms are added third. That's only true in choice (B). Since choice (B)

---

[14] PrepTest 40, Sec. 2, Q 1

doesn't have lentils in the sixth spot, it breaks Rule 1. Get rid of it. Both of choices (D) and (E) have zucchini in the first spot. That implicates Rule 2 and requires that lentils precede onions into the broth. Choice (E) reverses the order of lentils and onion and breaks the rule. Choice (D) complies with the rule and is correct.

When a game offers you a mix of concrete and conditional rules, attack Acceptability questions using the more definite rules first. This makes it easier to spot the choices containing the conditions that trigger the formal logic.

2. **(C)**

Which one of the following foods CANNOT be added first?

(A) kale
(B) lentils
(C) mushrooms
(D) onions
(E) tomatoes[15]

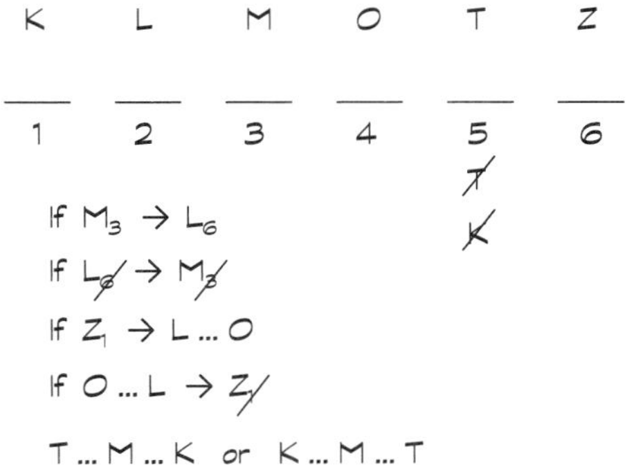

K   L   M   O   T   Z

—   —   —   —   —   —
1   2   3   4   5   6
                5̸
                K̸

If M₃ → L₆

If L̸ → M̸

If Z₁ → L ... O

If O ... L → Z̸

T ... M ... K   or   K ... M ... T

Figure 9.36

Since this question lacks an "if" condition, it's unlikely to involve either of the conditional rules. Since it involves the first space, there's no way it can involve Rule 3. Go directly to Rule 4 and get your answer. The food that can never be added first is mushrooms, which always follow either tomatoes or kale into the broth. Choice (C) is correct.

3. **(A)**

If the lentils are added last, then which one of the following must be true?

(A) At least one of the foods is added at some time before the zucchini.
(B) At least two of the foods are added at some time before the kale.
(C) The mushrooms are added third.
(D) The zucchini is added third.
(E) The tomatoes are added fourth.[16]

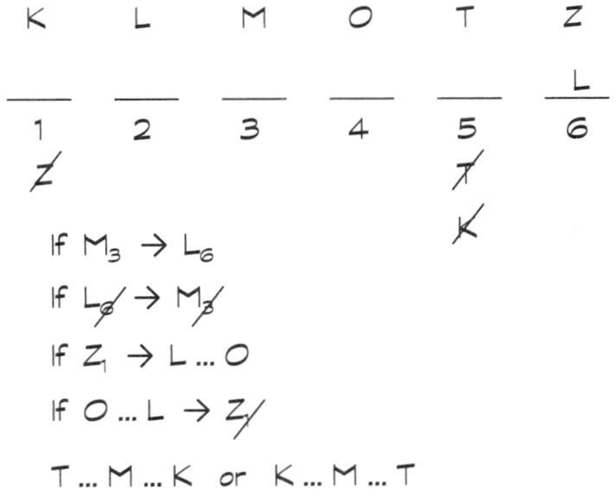

K   L   M   O   T   Z

—   —   —   —   —   L
1   2   3   4   5   6
Z̸   5̸
                K̸

If M₃ → L₆

If L̸ → M̸

If Z₁ → L ... O

If O ... L → Z̸

T ... M ... K   or   K ... M ... T

Figure 9.37

Seeing the "if" in the question stem, your instinct at this point should be to draw a mini-sketch like the one next to the question. You won't get far, though, before you realize that the "if"

---

[15] PrepTest 40, Sec. 2, Q 2
[16] PrepTest 40, Sec. 2, Q 3

condition here is simply meant to trigger Rule 2. As soon as you make L the final ingredient in the soup, you know that O must precede it. That's the sufficient condition in Rule 2's contrapositive.

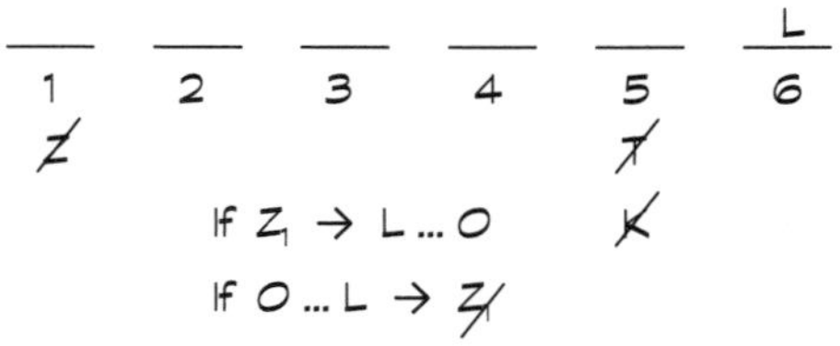

Figure 9.38

The result is that zucchini cannot be the first ingredient. That means that choice (A) *must be true*, which makes it the correct answer. Since there's nothing else that you can conclude from the "if" condition, none of the four remaining choices must be true.

4. **(C)**

Which one of the following could be an accurate partial ordering of the foods added to the broth?

(A) lentils: second; mushrooms: third
(B) mushrooms: fourth; lentils: last
(C) onions: second; mushrooms: fifth
(D) zucchini: first; lentils: last
(E) zucchini: first; mushrooms: second[17]

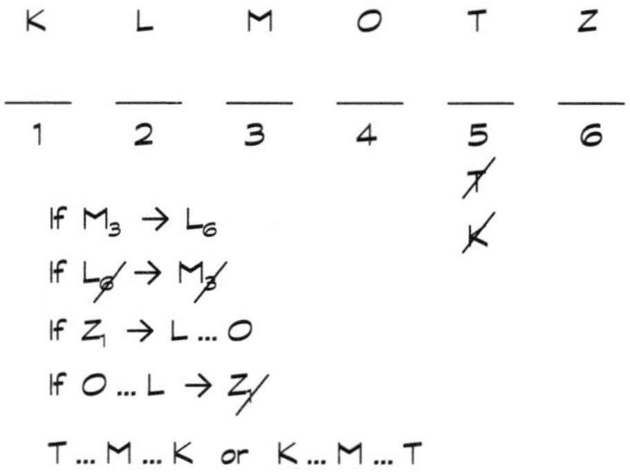

Figure 9.39

You can tackle this Partial Acceptability question just as you would a regular Acceptability question, indeed, just as you tackled question 1. Use the rules and eliminate the violators, remembering that you can only see two of the spaces in any of the answer choices this time. Start with the most concrete rule, Rule 3. Only one of the answers—choice (C)—mentions the fifth spot, and it doesn't have kale or tomatoes there. So Rule 3's not a problem for any of the answers. Rule 4 is, though. Choice (E) has mushrooms second. That's okay, provided that either tomatoes or kale is first. But choice (E) has lentils being added first. It violates Rule 4's placement of mushrooms between tomatoes and kale. So does choice (B), albeit in a subtler way. With mushrooms added fourth, either tomatoes or kale must come afterwards. Unfortunately, you know from Rule 3 that tomatoes and kale are excluded from space 5 and choice (B) blocks them out of space 6, too, by placing lentils there. That leaves choices (A), (C), and (D). Two of them must violate the conditional rules. Look no further than choice (A) to find the choice that violates Rule 1; it has mushrooms third and lentils first, instead of sixth. It's choice (D)

[17] PrepTest 40, Sec. 2, Q 4

that violates Rule 2; it has zucchini as the first vegetable but places lentils in sixth place, when the rule requires onions to follow lentils. Only choice (C) remains. It's the correct answer.

5. **(D)**

If the zucchini is added first, then which one of the following CANNOT be true?

(A)   The kale is added second.
(B)   The tomatoes are added second.
(C)   The lentils are added third.
(D)   The lentils are added fourth.
(E)   The onions are added fourth.[18]

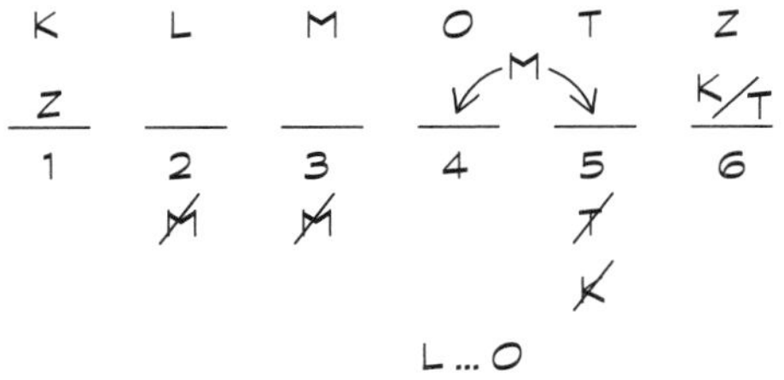

Figure 9.40

At this point, you could have expected it. The final question's "if" condition will, naturally, trigger one of the conditional rules. As soon as you see zucchini being added first, you know you're dealing with Rule 2.

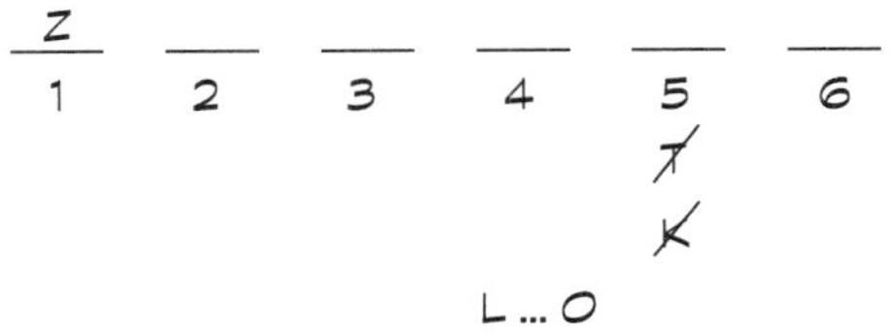

Figure 9.41

Did that make you realize that you were, by extension, dealing with Rule 1, as well? Since lentils must precede onions pursuant to Rule 2, lentils can't be in space 6. That triggers the contrapositive of Rule 1. With lentils not in space 6, mushrooms can't take space 3.

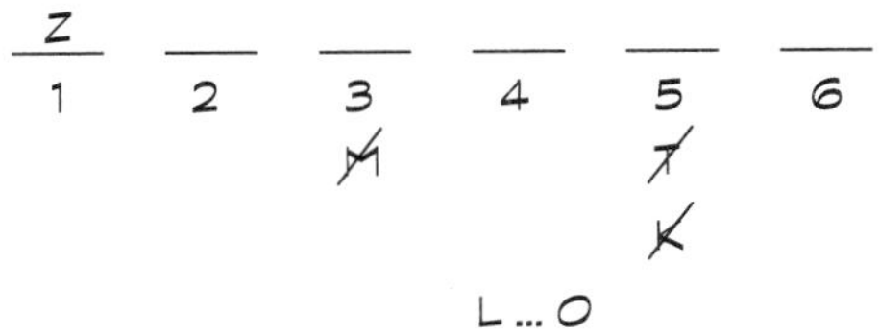

Figure 9.42

Nor can mushrooms take space 2. Rule 4 requires that the mushrooms be added in between the tomatoes and kale. With zucchini in space 1, there's no way to abide by Rule 4 with the mushrooms in space 2.

---

[18] PrepTest 40, Sec. 2, Q 5

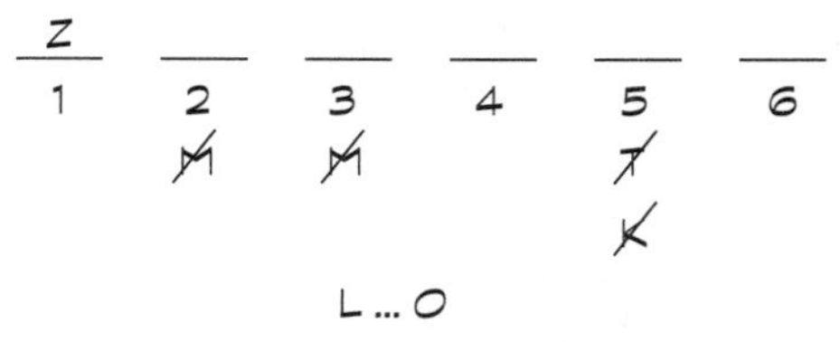

Figure 9.43

So the mushrooms will take either space 4 or space 5, and either tomatoes or kale—one of which must follow the mushrooms—will take space 6. Those two foods are excluded from space 5 by Rule 3.

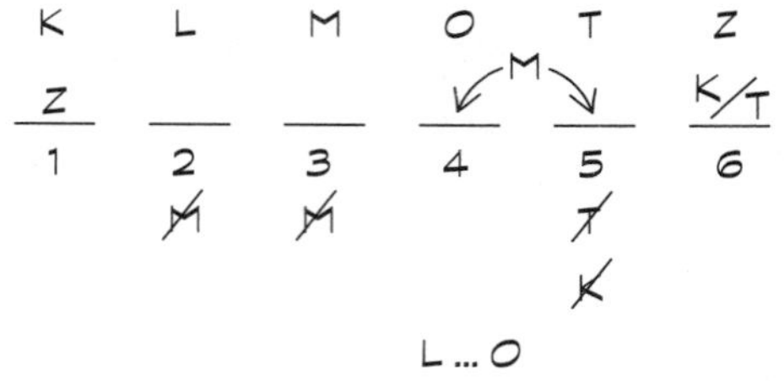

Figure 9.44

There's a little wiggle room left for lentils, onions, and whichever of tomatoes and kale isn't in space 6, but this is enough information to answer the question. Remember: When you've pushed your deductions as far as they'll go, you *always* have enough information to answer the question.

The correct answer *must be false*. Nothing prevents either tomatoes or kale from being added second. So both choice (A) and choice (B) are possible. Eliminate them. In fact, eliminate choice (C) as well, because with either tomatoes or kale added second, lentils would be added third. But slow down on choice (D). In this scenario, adding lentils fourth would mean adding mushrooms fifth. But if tomatoes or kale must follow mushrooms in space 6, then there's no space left for onions to follow lentils, as it must in this question. Choice (D) must be false and is, therefore, the right answer. For the record, onions could be fourth with mushrooms fifth. Nothing is violated by that arrangement, so choice (E) could be true.

That's not a hard game. Indeed, that's the point. Variations aren't difficult just because they're variations. You're less likely to see a Strict Sequencing game that prominently features formal logic rules than to see one without them. If you happen to have one on your test, remember a few takeaways from this game. First, you know how to diagram formal logic and to form the contrapositives of conditional statements. Many of your competitors on test day won't. That's one advantage for you right from the outset. Second, since conditional formal logic rules are only triggered by the presence of their sufficient conditions, use the more concrete, universal rules to eliminate violators first. Then turn to the conditional rules and see which remaining answer choices they apply to. Finally, expect the "If" questions—at least some of them—to trigger the conditional rules. Here, both of them did.

See how it's all coming together? Knowing the standard form that game types take allows you to spot the exceptions. Spotting the exceptions allows you to focus on what the test makers intend to reward or punish by using the unusual rules or limitations. As you progress through the rest of this chapter and the remainder of Part II, keep in mind that you're eliminating any possibility of being thrown off your game by anything out of the ordinary.

I'll show you a couple of extremely rare variations on the Strict Sequencing game type shortly. First, though, I want you to tackle a couple of the hardest Sequencing games out there; one is strict and one loose. They'll show you that if you've taken Part I of this book and the Kaplan Method to heart, you're ready for just about anything.

DIFFICULT SEQUENCING GAMES

On any given administration of the LSAT, the test makers are likely to include one easy game, two of medium difficulty, and one that they intend to be the hardest for all test takers. There's no way to anticipate which types of game they'll use for the various difficulty levels. There have even been tests on which the easiest and hardest games were both Sequencing games. As you try the toughest examples of each game type here and in the remaining chapters of this section, take note of what they all have in common: a lack of concreteness, complexity in the task, and long and tricky wording in either the rules or the questions.

While it's a fact that you're going to see a hard game on test day, your best chance of conquering it will be in recognizing the game type and seeing what makes this particular game more challenging. Including the toughest games in your preparation gives you a psychological edge, too. You'll go in to the test confident that you've seen the worst it can offer and knowing that the same method and strategies allowed you to handle it effectively.

Difficult Strict Sequencing

In chapter 2, you learned to assess the power of rules, distinguishing those that provided a great deal of certainty from those that offered only relative or conditional restrictions. Harder games will nearly always include fewer concrete rules. To compound that inherent difficulty, the test makers can give you more open-ended tasks, leaving more ambiguity in the framework of your sketch. The following game does both, making it a truly challenging Strict Sequencing example. Take your time with this game. I'd rather you spend the time to explore its intricacies than try to rush through it and miss what makes it tough. You'll have the opportunity to do more difficult games under timed conditions in Part III of this book. By the way, this was the third game in the Logic Games section on this test. That's the most common place to find the toughest game, though the test makers have placed the toughest game second or fourth in the section on occasion. Give this one a try. If you are really confused by the setup, check the explanations for Steps 1–4 of the Kaplan Method as they apply here. Then go back and try the questions.

A bakery makes exactly three kinds of cookie—oatmeal, peanut butter, and sugar. Exactly three batches of each kind of cookie are made each week (Monday through Friday) and each batch is made, from start to finish, on a single day. The following conditions apply:

No two batches of the same kind of cookie are made on the same day.

At least one batch of cookies is made on Monday.

The second batch of oatmeal cookies is made on the same day as the first batch of peanut butter cookies.

The second batch of sugar cookies is made on Thursday.

13. Which one of the following could be a complete and accurate list of the days on which the batches of each kind of cookie are made?

   (A)   oatmeal: Monday, Wednesday, Thursday
         peanut butter: Wednesday, Thursday, Friday
         sugar: Monday, Thursday, Friday
   (B)   oatmeal: Monday, Tuesday, Thursday
         peanut butter: Tuesday, Wednesday, Thursday
         sugar: Monday, Wednesday, Thursday
   (C)   oatmeal: Tuesday, Wednesday, Thursday
         peanut butter: Wednesday, Thursday, Friday
         sugar: Tuesday, Thursday, Friday
   (D)   oatmeal: Monday, Tuesday, Thursday
         peanut butter: Monday, Wednesday, Thursday
         sugar: Monday, Thursday, Friday
   (E)   oatmeal: Monday, Thursday, Friday
         peanut butter: Tuesday, Wednesday, Thursday
         sugar: Monday, Thursday, Friday

14. How many of the days, Monday through Friday, are such that at most two batches of cookies could be made on that day?

   (A)   one
   (B)   two
   (C)   three
   (D)   four
   (E)   five

15. If the first batch of peanut butter cookies is made on Tuesday, then each of the following could be true EXCEPT:

   (A)   Two different kinds of cookie have their first batch made on Monday.
   (B)   Two different kinds of cookie have their first batch made on Tuesday.
   (C)   Two different kinds of cookie have their second batch made on Wednesday.
   (D)   Two different kinds of cookie have their second batch made on Thursday.
   (E)   Two different kinds of cookie have their third batch made on Friday.

16. If no batch of cookies is made on Wednesday, then which one of the following must be true?

   (A)   Exactly three batches of cookies are made on Tuesday.
   (B)   Exactly three batches of cookies are made on Friday.
   (C)   At least two batches of cookies are made on Monday.
   (D)   At least two batches of cookies are made on Thursday.
   (E)   Fewer batches of cookies are made on Monday than on Tuesday.

17. If the number of batches made on Friday is exactly one, then which one of the following could be true?

   (A)   The first batch of sugar cookies is made on Monday.
   (B)   The first batch of oatmeal cookies is made on Tuesday.
   (C)   The third batch of oatmeal cookies is made on Friday.
   (D)   The first batch of peanut butter cookies is made on Wednesday.
   (E)   The second batch of peanut butter cookies is made on Tuesday.

18. If one kind of cookie's first batch is made on the same day as another kind of cookie's third batch, then which one of the following could be false?

   (A)   At least one batch of cookies is made on each of the five days.
   (B)   At least two batches of cookies are made on Wednesday.
   (C)   Exactly one batch of cookies is made on Monday.
   (D)   Exactly two batches of cookies are made on Tuesday.
   (E)   Exactly one batch of cookies is made on Friday.[19]

---

[19] PrepTest 42, Sec. 1, Game 3, Qs 13–18

Explanations

STEPS 1 AND 2: Overview and Sketch

Your task is to lay out the weekly baking schedule for cookies made at a bakery. The framework, then, is familiar from the real world and any number of other Strict Sequencing games.

$$\underline{\quad M \quad} \underline{\quad Tu \quad} \underline{\quad W \quad} \underline{\quad Th \quad} \underline{\quad F \quad}$$

Figure 9.45

The first complicating factor you encounter in this game is in the setup's description of the entities. Instead of nine different kinds of cookies, you're asked to schedule three batches each of three kinds of cookies. You can start to take control of the task by writing the entities out like this:

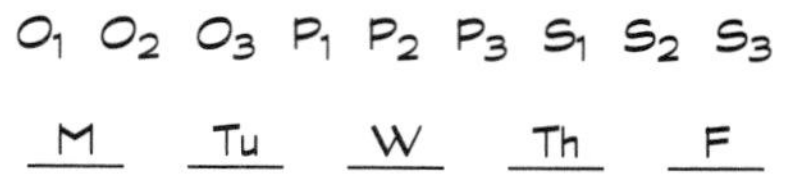

$$O_1 \; O_2 \; O_3 \; P_1 \; P_2 \; P_3 \; S_1 \; S_2 \; S_3$$

$$\underline{\quad M \quad} \underline{\quad Tu \quad} \underline{\quad W \quad} \underline{\quad Th \quad} \underline{\quad F \quad}$$

Figure 9.46

Looking at the beginnings of your sketch reveals the second complicating factor. Like the Professor Hiring game you saw earlier in this chapter, you're going to have some spaces in your sequence with more than one entity. More importantly, there's nothing requiring you to schedule a batch every day. The bakery may have days off. Don't impose limitations where none exist.

STEP 3: Rules

Rule 1 tells you that you can't bake two batches of the same kind of cookie on the same day. Just note that next to your entity list.

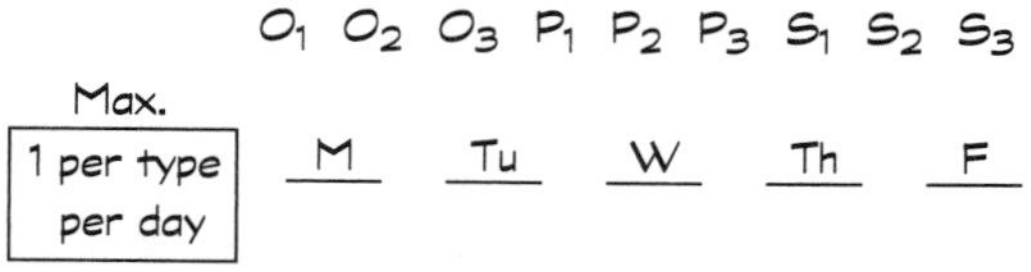

$$O_1 \; O_2 \; O_3 \; P_1 \; P_2 \; P_3 \; S_1 \; S_2 \; S_3$$

Max.
| 1 per type per day |

$$\underline{\quad M \quad} \underline{\quad Tu \quad} \underline{\quad W \quad} \underline{\quad Th \quad} \underline{\quad F \quad}$$

Figure 9.47

Rule 2 tells you to include at least one batch of cookies on Monday. If you hadn't caught the fact that there could be days without any batches scheduled, this rule should have put you on alert.

O1 O2 O3 P1 P2 P3 S1 S2 S3
Max.
1 per type per day
≥ 1
M
Tu
W
Th
F

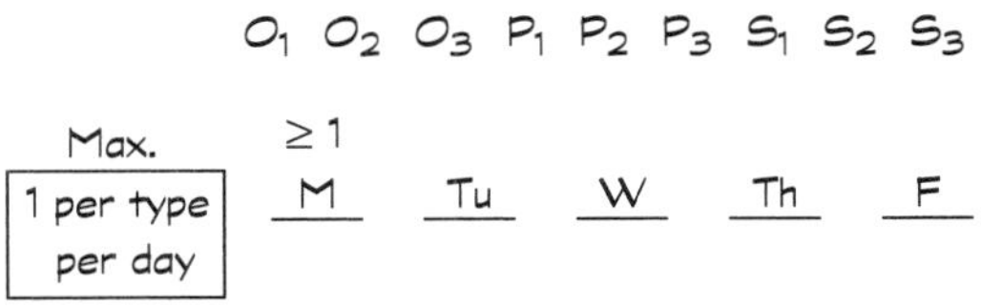

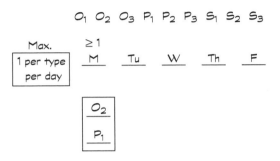

Figure 9.48

Rule 3 creates a Block of Entities. O_2 and P_1 will be scheduled for the same day. I'll have you come back in Step 4 to think about how this rule interacts with Rule 1.

O1 O2 O3 P1 P2 P3 S1 S2 S3
Max.
1 per type per day
≥ 1
M
Tu
W
Th
F
O2
P1

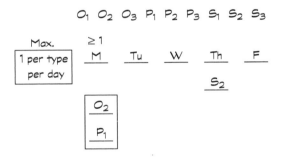

Figure 9.49

Rule 4, thankfully, gives you an Established Entity. Put this restriction right in the framework.

O1 O2 O3 P1 P2 P3 S1 S2 S3
Max.
1 per type per day
≥ 1
M
Tu
W
Th
F
S2
O2
P1

Figure 9.50

At this point, it may seem as if you have six floaters, since only three of the batches have been cited in the rules. But that's not quite true. Because Rule 1 limits all batches of the same kind of cookie, you actually have some guidance here about all of the cookie batches you need to schedule. That will become even clearer in the Deductions step.

STEP 4: Deductions

Starting, as always with the most concrete restriction, you can add one more Established Entity into your sketch. Since S_2 is on Thursday, S_3 has to be on Friday.

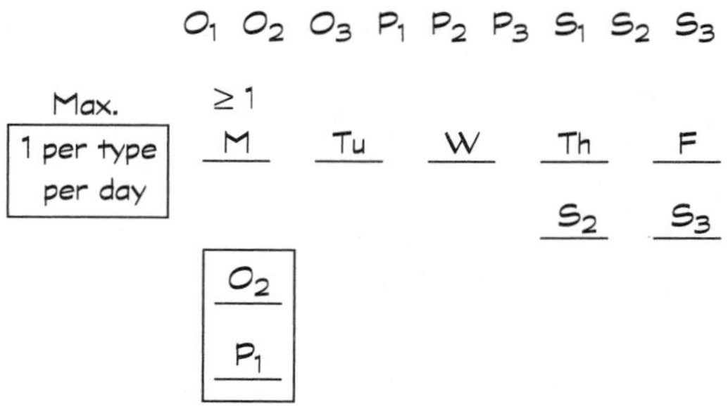

O_1 O_2 O_3 P_1 P_2 P_3 S_1 S_2 S_3

Max.
1 per type
per day

≥ 1
M   Tu   W   Th   F
              S_2 S_3

O_2
P_1

Figure 9.51

As I hinted, Rules 1 and 3 also combine to provide a powerful deduction. Since you cannot bake two batches of the same kind of cookie on a given day, the P_1–O_2 block can only be placed on Tuesday or Wednesday. The first batch of oatmeal must be baked before the second, of course, and the second and third batches of peanut butter have to follow the first. This leads to a Limited Options scenario:

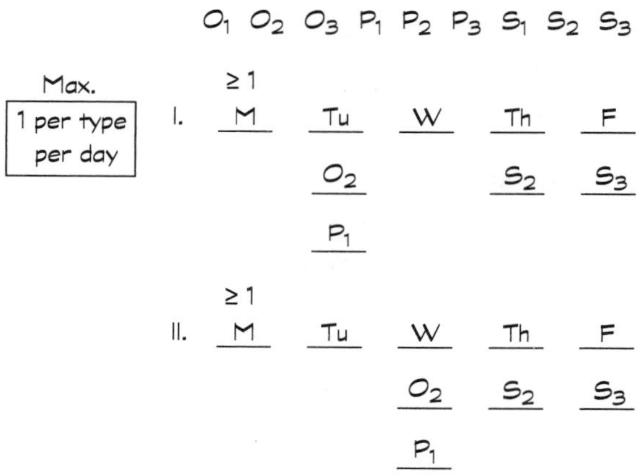

O_1 O_2 O_3 P_1 P_2 P_3 S_1 S_2 S_3

Max.
1 per type
per day

I.
≥ 1
M   Tu   W   Th   F
     O_2 S_2 S_3
     P_1

II.
≥ 1
M   Tu   W   Th   F
          O_2 S_2 S_3
          P_1

Figure 9.52

With a game this open and complex, you can be sure it's worth your time to explore the deductions thoroughly. In Option I, you know for sure that the bakery will make O_1 on Monday, while P_2 and P_3 will be baked sometime between Wednesday and Friday.

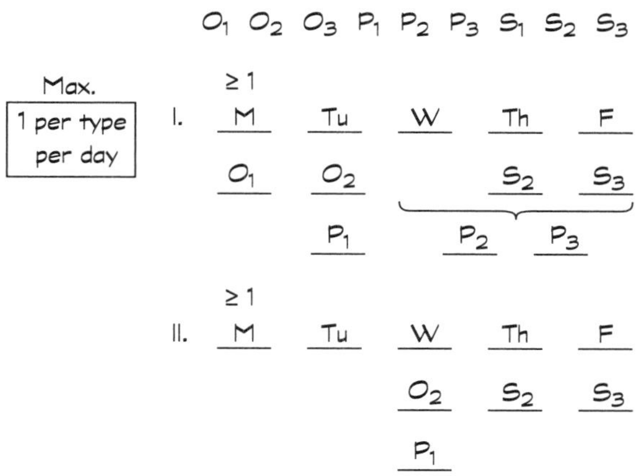

Figure 9.53

Option II, on the other hand, locks down all three peanut butter batches. Since you know that the bakery makes at least one batch of cookies on Monday, you can be sure that S_1, O_1, or both occur that day. The bakery will make O_3 on either Thursday or Friday.

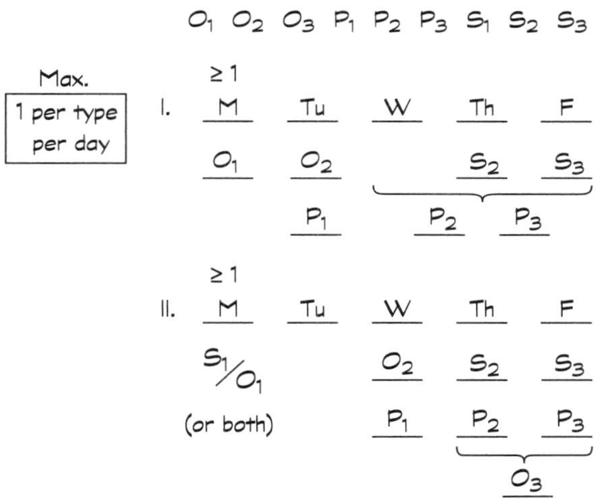

Figure 9.54

So it turns out that you have at least some information about all nine cookie batches that you need to schedule. In fact, with the Limited Options sketches in place and all of your deductions accurately reflected in them, the question set turns out not to be too bad after all.

STEP 5: Questions

The question set here contains an Acceptability question (that will be no problem for you at this point), a Minimum/Maximum-type question, and four "if" questions. Remember our discussion of "If" questions in Limited option games from chapter 5. The new "if" conditions will almost certainly put you into one option or the other. Use that to take on these questions more efficiently.

13. **(A)**

Which one of the following could be a complete and accurate list of the days on which the batches of each kind of cookie are made?

(A) oatmeal: Monday, Wednesday, Thursday
peanut butter: Wednesday, Thursday, Friday
sugar: Monday, Thursday, Friday

(B) oatmeal: Monday, Tuesday, Thursday
peanut butter: Tuesday, Wednesday, Thursday
sugar: Monday, Wednesday, Thursday

(C) oatmeal: Tuesday, Wednesday, Thursday
peanut butter: Wednesday, Thursday, Friday
sugar: Tuesday, Thursday, Friday

(D) oatmeal: Monday, Tuesday, Thursday
peanut butter: Monday, Wednesday, Thursday
sugar: Monday, Thursday, Friday

(E) oatmeal: Monday, Thursday, Friday
peanut butter: Tuesday, Wednesday, Thursday
sugar: Monday, Thursday, Friday[20]

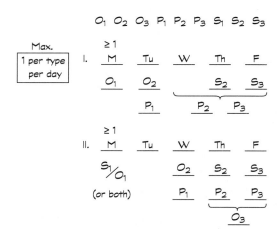

Figure 9.55

This is a routine Acceptability question. As always, use the rules to eliminate those answers that contain violations. The correct answer will be the last one standing.

Rule 1 isn't broken in any of the choices. Scanning horizontally across each line, you never see the same day mentioned twice for any kind of cookie.

Rule 2 gets rid of choice (C). None of the batches is baked on Monday in this answer.

Rule 3 knocks out both choice (D) and choice (E). Both of those choices have P_1 and O_2 on different days.

Finally, Rule 4 takes care of choice (B), where S_2 is improperly baked on Wednesday.

That leaves choice (A), the correct answer. Did you notice that choice (A) matches Option II of your Master Sketch? That's a good confirmation that you're on the right track with this tricky game.

14. **(A)**

How many of the days, Monday through Friday, are such that at most two batches of cookies could be made on that day?

(A) one
(B) two
(C) three
(D) four
(E) five[21]

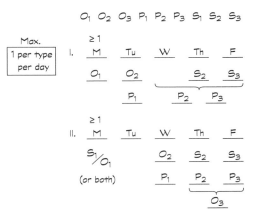

Figure 9.56

Make sure you understand what any question stem is calling for. Here, the correct answer is the number of days on which it's *impossible* to bake three batches of cookies. The answer choices, of course, range from one through five, since there are five days in the bakery schedule. Take a look at Option II. There, you can see that Thursday and Friday are days on which all three kinds of cookies can be made. Eliminate choices (D) and (E). In fact, eliminate choice (C) as well. If you have the bakery make S_1 on Wednesday, there's another day on which it can bake three batches. Now, the only question is whether Tuesday is a day that can have all three kinds of cookies. Option I shows that it is. You can have the bakery make S_1 on Tuesday in that option. Eliminate choice (B). Monday turns out to be the only day on which you must bake at most two batches of cookies, making choice (A) correct. The earliest you can bake P_1 is on Tuesday, although that's moot at this point, since the test makers did not include "zero" among the answer choices.

15. **(C)**

If the first batch of peanut butter cookies is made on Tuesday, then each of the following could be true EXCEPT:

(A) Two different kinds of cookie have their first batch made on Monday.
(B) Two different kinds of cookie have their first batch made on Tuesday.
(C) Two different kinds of cookie have their second batch made on Wednesday.
(D) Two different kinds of cookie have their second batch made on Thursday.
(E) Two different kinds of cookie have their third batch made on Friday.[22]

I.

M	Tu	W	Th	F
O_1	O_2		S_2	S_3
	P_1		P_2	P_3

Figure 9.57

[21] PrepTest 42, Sec. 1, Q 14
[22] PrepTest 42, Sec. 1, Q 15

The "if" for this question lands you squarely in Option I. There's no need to redraw or add anything. Remember, though, to characterize the answer choices before you evaluate them. The four wrong answers here *could be true*. That means that the correct answer *must be false*.

There's no problem with choice (A). S_1 could be baked on Monday along with O_1. Eliminate it.

Choice (B) is acceptable as well. It just means that S_1 is baked on Tuesday. This choice could be true so it's wrong.

Choice (C), however, is impossible. In Option I, O_2 is on Tuesday and S_2 is on Thursday. Only P_2 could go on Wednesday. Choice (C) is the correct answer.

Choices (D) and (E) *could*, of course, *be true*. In Option I, both P_2 and S_2 could be baked on Thursday, and any of the third cookie batches could be baked on Friday.

16. **(D)**

    If no batch of cookies is made on Wednesday, then which one of the following must be true?

    (A)   Exactly three batches of cookies are made on Tuesday.
    (B)   Exactly three batches of cookies are made on Friday.
    (C)   At least two batches of cookies are made on Monday.
    (D)   At least two batches of cookies are made on Thursday.
    (E)   Fewer batches of cookies are made on Monday than on Tuesday.[23]

I.

M	Tu	W	Th	F
O_1	O_2		S_2	S_3
	P_1		P_2	P_3

Figure 9.58

This question stem's "if" condition puts you in Option I. (In Option II, remember, cookies have to be baked on Wednesday.) The correct answer here *must be true*. In Option I, the bakery has to make P_1 and O_2 on Tuesday, so choice (D) fits the bill. All four of the wrong answers offer statements that *could be false* in Option I.

17. **(A)**

    If the number of batches made on Friday is exactly one, then which one of the following could be true?

    (A)   The first batch of sugar cookies is made on Monday.
    (B)   The first batch of oatmeal cookies is made on Tuesday.
    (C)   The third batch of oatmeal cookies is made on Friday.
    (D)   The first batch of peanut butter cookies is made on Wednesday.
    (E)   The second batch of peanut butter cookies is made on Tuesday.[24]

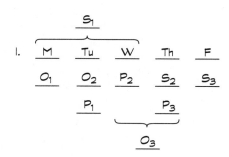

Figure 9.59

Here again, the question stem gives you an "if" that's only possible in Option I. Since the "if" allows only one batch of cookies on Friday, your mini-sketch (see above) should adapt Option I to reflect that P_2 and P_3 will be on Wednesday and Thursday, respectively, and that O_3 will be on either Wednesday or Thursday, although which one isn't important. That leaves only S_1 unaccounted for. The bakery could bake it on Monday, Tuesday, or Wednesday under these conditions.

The correct answer *could be true*. All four wrong answers *must be false*. As soon as you check choice (A), you see that it could be true. If you anticipated that S_1 would be involved in the correct answer, you are becoming an expert LSAT test taker. As the least restricted entity, it's the least likely to be included in a statement that must be false.

On test day, there would be no need for you to check the four remaining answer choices. The test maker will always include one demonstrably correct and four demonstrably incorrect answers. Go through choices (B) through (E) and confirm with the mini-sketch that they *must be false* if you want the practice. On test day, though, take the point and move on.

18. **(E)**

If one kind of cookie's first batch is made on the same day as another kind of cookie's third batch, then which one of the following could be false?

(A) At least one batch of cookies is made on each of the five days.
(B) At least two batches of cookies are made on Wednesday.
(C) Exactly one batch of cookies is made on Monday.
(D) Exactly two batches of cookies are made on Tuesday.
(E) Exactly one batch of cookies is made on Friday.[25]

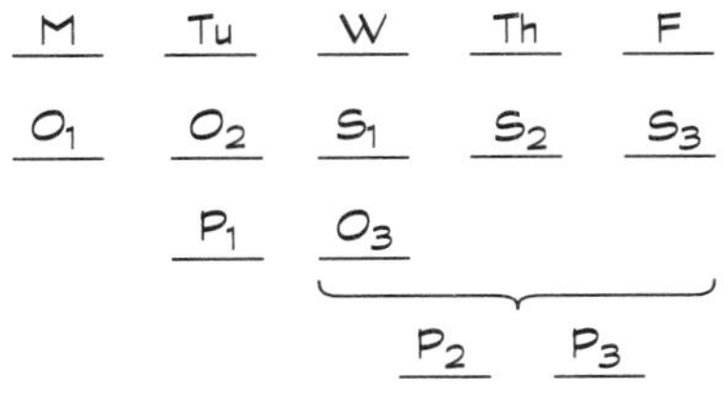

M	Tu	W	Th	F
O_1	O_2	S_1	S_2	S_3
		P_1	O_3	

P_2 P_3

Figure 9.60

This "if" is tricky, but with a little thought, you'll see that it leads to a fantastically clear and conclusive deduction. There is only one day on which you bake one kind of cookie's first batch and another kind's third batch: Wednesday. That's the only day that can be followed *and* preceded by two other batches. Now, look at the Master Sketch and figure out how and where this "if" could be accommodated.

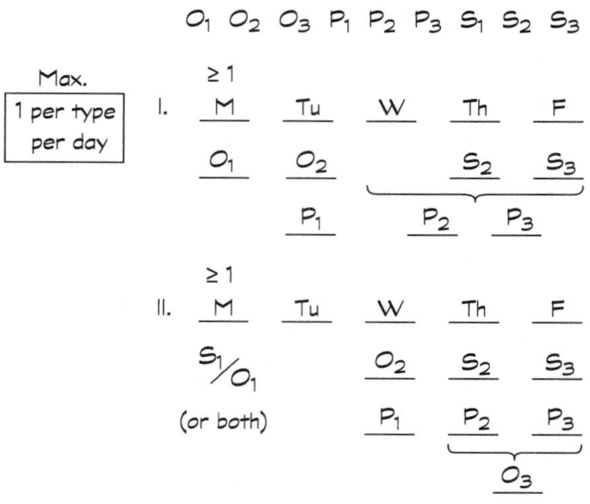

$$O_1 \quad O_2 \quad O_3 \quad P_1 \quad P_2 \quad P_3 \quad S_1 \quad S_2 \quad S_3$$

Figure 9.61

It has to happen in Option I, for sure. In Option II, all of the third batches are restricted to Thursday or Friday. But in Option I, S_1 and O_3 could be baked on Wednesday.

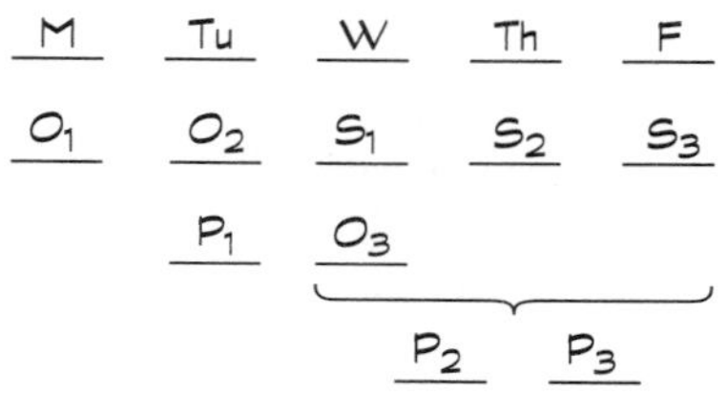

Figure 9.62

Now, evaluate the choices. The correct answer *could be false*, so all four wrong answers *must be true*. Remembering that P_2 and P_3 will be baked between Wednesday and Friday, choices (A) through (D) all *must be true*. Only choice (E) could be falsified, by having P_3 and S_3 both baked on Friday. Choice (E) is the correct answer, and you've conquered one of the most challenging Strict Sequencing games you're likely to encounter.

I wish I could say that you were unlikely to encounter a game this tough on test day, but that wouldn't be true. You will see one hard game and it might be a Strict Sequencing variant. What I can say, though, is that if you see such a game, it's going to share at least some of this game's elements—an unusual entity set, an uneven correspondence among entities and spaces, and broad or ambiguous rules. So you might ask, what do we do differently on these hardest examples? The answer, politely, is "Nothing." You used the Kaplan Method as you normally would, just with a little extra attention and little more patience. In most of the hardest games you'll encounter, the heavy lifting is done during Steps 1–4. By getting the Limited Options sketches and all of their deductions up front, you made the question set on this tough game no more difficult that it would be on any other.

Difficult Loose Sequencing

You've handled a tough Loose Sequencing game already, even in this chapter. The setup for the Bread Delivery game was as difficult as the one in the game featured next. But given the high number of these games in recent years (and the fact that the test makers have upped the ante in Loose Sequencing generally), it's worth your while to work through one more, questions and all. Without giving away too much, I'll remind you of the features common to difficult Loose Sequencing games. You'll see either conditional rules or rules that apply in one of two alternate ways, maybe both. Keep your eyes open for the opportunity to use Limited Options sketches to take control of the alternatives. Don't time yourself on this game. Be patient and thorough. It's important that you gain experience with how games like this one work. Speed and efficiency will come with your continued practice. If you find yourself struggling mightily with the questions, stop and compare your Master Sketch to the one developed in Steps 1–4 in the explanations. Once you're sure you've got the right starting point, return to the questions.

A competition is being held to select a design for Yancy College's new student union building. Each of six architects—Green, Jackson, Liu, Mertz, Peete, and Valdez—has submitted exactly one design. There are exactly six designs, and they are presented one at a time to the panel of judges, each design being presented exactly once, consistent with the following conditions:

Mertz's design is presented at some time before Liu's and after Peete's.

Green's design is presented either at some time before Jackson's or at some time after Liu's, but not both.

Valdez's design is presented either at some time before Green's or at some time after Peete's, but not both.

6. Which one of the following could be the order in which the designs are presented, from first to last?

(A) Jackson's, Peete's, Mertz's, Green's, Valdez's, Liu's
(B) Peete's, Jackson's, Liu's, Mertz's, Green's, Valdez's
(C) Peete's, Mertz's, Jackson's, Liu's, Green's, Valdez's
(D) Peete's, Mertz's, Valdez's, Green's, Liu's, Jackson's
(E) Valdez's, Liu's, Jackson's, Peete's, Mertz's, Green's

7. Mertz's design CANNOT be presented

(A) sixth
(B) fifth
(C) fourth
(D) third
(E) second

8. If Liu's design is presented sixth, then which one of the following must be true?

(A) Green's design is presented at some time before Jackson's.
(B) Jackson's design is presented at some time before Mertz's.
(C) Peete's design is presented at some time before Green's.
(D) Peete's design is presented at some time before Valdez's.
(E) Valdez's design is presented at some time before Green's.

9. If Jackson's design is presented at some time before Mertz's, then each of the following could be true EXCEPT:

(A) Jackson's design is presented second.
(B) Peete's design is presented third.
(C) Peete's design is presented fourth.
(D) Jackson's design is presented fifth.
(E) Liu's design is presented fifth.

10. Which one of the following designs CANNOT be the design presented first?

(A) Green's
(B) Jackson's
(C) Liu's
(D) Peete's
(E) Valdez's

11. Which one of the following could be an accurate partial list of the architects, each matched with his or her design's place in the order in which the designs are presented?

(A) first: Mertz; fourth: Liu; fifth: Green
(B) second: Green; third: Peete; fourth: Jackson
(C) second: Mertz; fifth: Green; sixth: Jackson
(D) fourth: Peete; fifth: Liu; sixth: Jackson
(E) fourth: Valdez; fifth: Green; sixth: Liu[26]

Explanations

STEPS 1 AND 2: Overview and Sketch

There's nothing unusual about the task here. Six designs are presented, and you're asked to determine the order. They even come in one at a time, as you'd expect. At this point, you'll want to steal a glance at the rules to see whether you'll be using a strict or loose sketch. Since none of the rules mentions a specific space or gives you the specific distance between any two entities, you'll be making a Loose Sequencing "tree." There's no framework to draw, so just list the entities and move into the rules.

STEP 3: Rules

At this point, the complexity of this game becomes clear. You have three rules, each of which mentions three entities. Moreover, two of the rules present alternative possibilities. Jot down all three before you think about how to combine them.

Rule 1 is fairly straightforward, at least compared to the other two. It creates the following definite order:

Figure 9.63

Rule 2 gives you two possibilities. Either G comes before J and L, or G comes after J and L.

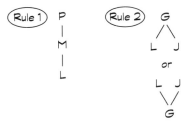

Figure 9.64

Rule 3 works the same way as Rule 2. Either V comes before G and P, or V comes after G and P.

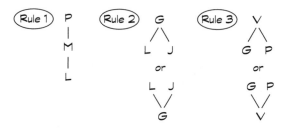

Figure 9.65

You can see that there are Duplications here: L appears in Rules 1 and 2, G appears in Rules 2 and 3, and P appears in Rules 1 and 3. But all those alternatives are making this game complicated.

STEP 4: Deductions

The alternate possibilities presented by Rules 2 and 3 suggest that you should make Limited Options sketches. But how do you decide which of the two alternatives to use as the basis for your dual sketches? The answer comes from recognizing that in order to use V in Rule 3, you need to know where P and G are. That will come from combining Rules 1 and 2 first. Copy the P-M-L chain from Rule 1, and attach one of the alternatives presented by Rule 2 to each.

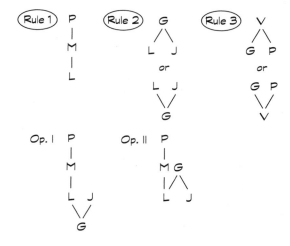

Figure 9.66

Now you can see that Rule 3 adds only one entity—V—to those you've already sketched. You might be tempted to create another set of dual sketches to show the possibilities for V, a sort of Option IA and IB, IIA and IIB format.

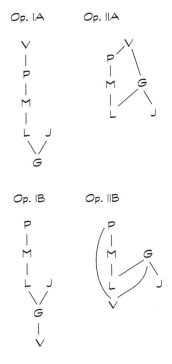

Figure 9.67

If you did that (and got everyone into the right orders), that's fine. But given the limited amount of space in the test booklet, I'd suggest something a little simpler. Just show that V can go in one of two places in either option, like so:

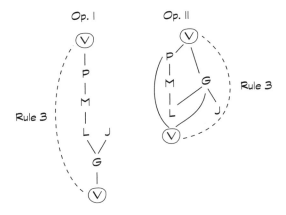

Figure 9.68

This is Loose Sequencing, so there are no floaters. And while there are still several ways that the presentations can be ordered, you've got about as clear a picture of basic options as possible. What you can know with confidence is that you have enough information to answer all of the questions.

STEP 5: **Questions**

If you're daunted by a tough game, one thing you can do to help yourself get a handle on the situation is to attack the clearest questions first. Here, that would be questions 6 (a standard Acceptability question), 7, and 10. The choices in those latter two are short, and you should be able to pick up the points quickly while gaining a little more familiarity with your complex sketch at the same time.

6. **(C)**

Which one of the following could be the order in which the designs are presented, from first to last?

(A) Jackson's, Peete's, Mertz's, Green's, Valdez's, Liu's

(B) Peete's, Jackson's, Liu's, Mertz's, Green's, Valdez's

(C) Peete's, Mertz's, Jackson's, Liu's, Green's, Valdez's

(D) Peete's, Mertz's, Valdez's, Green's, Liu's, Jackson's

(E) Valdez's, Liu's, Jackson's, Peete's, Mertz's, Green's[27]

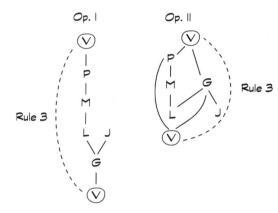

Figure 9.69

It's comforting to know that even the hardest games almost always give you the chance to get one point in such a routine way. As you would with any Acceptability question, use the rules one at a time and eliminate the answer choices that violate them.

Rule 1 created the P-M-L chain. That eliminates choices (B) and (E).

Rule 2 requires G to be before L and J or after L and J, but forbids him to be between them. He's between them in choice (A). Eliminate it.

Rule 3 requires V to be before G and P or after G and P. V will be between them in the one remaining wrong answer. That's choice (D), and you're all set. The correct answer is (C).

7. **(A)**

Mertz's design CANNOT be presented

(A) sixth
(B) fifth
(C) fourth
(D) third
(E) second[28]

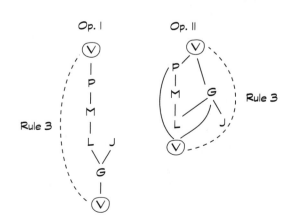

Figure 9.70

---

[27] PrepTest 53, Sec. 2, Q 6
[28] PrepTest 53, Sec. 2, Q 7

You can actually answer this question with nothing more than Rule 1. There are six designs presented in the game. M is always behind P and always ahead of L, so M cannot be first or sixth. That makes answer choice (A) impossible and thus correct.

Again, the test has given you an easy point within the context of a hard game. On test day, don't abandon an entire game; you're almost always able to get a least a couple of right answers to add to your score.

10. **(C)**

Which one of the following designs CANNOT be the design presented first?

(A) Green's
(B) Jackson's
(C) Liu's
(D) Peete's
(E) Valdez's[29]

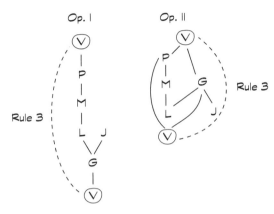

Figure 9.71

You can get the right answer to this question either by eliminating answers with entities who can be in first place (P, J, or V in Option I; P, G, or V in Option II) or by recognizing that Rule 1 makes it impossible for either M or L to ever be first. Either way, the correct answer—choice (C)—is unequivocal. Liu's design is never going to be the first presented.

That's now three points in your coffers in a matter of a few seconds each. The next two questions we'll cover—the "If" questions, numbers 8 and 9—will put your Limited Options sketches to the test.

8. **(A)**

If Liu's design is presented sixth, then which one of the following must be true?

(A) Green's design is presented at some time before Jackson's.
(B) Jackson's design is presented at some time before Mertz's.
(C) Peete's design is presented at some time before Green's.
(D) Peete's design is presented at some time before Valdez's.
(E) Valdez's design is presented at some time before Green's.[30]

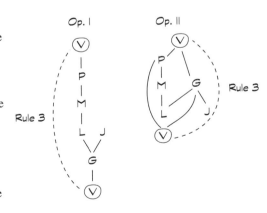

Figure 9.72

Whenever you approach an "If" question in a Limited Options scenario, ask, "Which option does this 'if' push me into?" Here, you can only consider Option II. That's because G has to follow L in Option I. Option II was created to account for the situations in which G is presented earlier than L and J. Thus, choice (A) *must be true*. If G comes before L, then it comes before J, too, according to Rule 2. All of the other answers could be either true or false in Option II.

9.   **(D)**

If Jackson's design is presented at some time before Mertz's, then each of the following could be true EXCEPT:

(A)   Jackson's design is presented second.
(B)   Peete's design is presented third.
(C)   Peete's design is presented fourth.
(D)   Jackson's design is presented fifth.
(E)   Liu's design is presented fifth.[31]

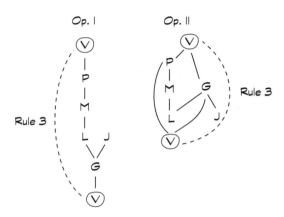

Figure 9.73

This question is alarming at first glance because it doesn't clearly put you into one of the two options. J could precede M in either case. But hold on for a moment. Do you remember what you learned about M's position in question 7? Right, it can never be sixth. So if J is to precede M, J's position cannot be fifth. That makes choice (D) correct in this "could be true EXCEPT" question. There's an irony to this question stem that leads to a strategic insight: Once you realize that either option is in play *and* notice that the four wrong answers all could be true (heck, lots of things could be true between the two options, right?), you should be telling yourself that the exact limitation described in the "if" must be the trigger to what makes the correct answer false. Students that aren't trained in the Kaplan Method are likely to use a time-consuming, confusing hunt-and-peck method and test all of the answer choices. Learning to appreciate the specific call of each question stem is one of the final pieces in true logic games mastery.

11.   **(B)**

Which one of the following could be an accurate partial list of the architects, each matched with his or her design's place in the order in which the designs are presented?

(A)   first: Mertz; fourth: Liu; fifth: Green
(B)   second: Green; third: Peete; fourth: Jackson
(C)   second: Mertz; fifth: Green; sixth: Jackson
(D)   fourth: Peete; fifth: Liu; sixth: Jackson
(E)   fourth: Valdez; fifth: Green; sixth: Liu[32]

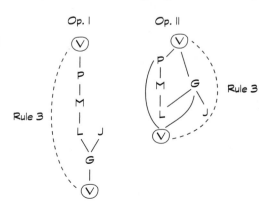

Figure 9.74

Although this is a Partial Acceptability question, it's probably the most difficult question in the set. That's true for a couple of reasons. First, Partial Acceptability questions are always tough in Loose Sequencing games, where you're used to assessing the entire pattern. Second, and specific to this question, the test makers have associated the entities with numbered spaces in the answer choices, something that the setup of this game doesn't easily lend itself to. Still, there's no better way to attack than to look for rule violators. Here's how you'd do it. Rule 1 eliminates choice (A): You know that M must follow P, so it can't be first. Rule 1 also takes care of choice (D): M has to follow P, and there's no room for it to do so here. Rule 2 states that G cannot be in between L and J, but G would have to be in between them in choices (C) and (E). Cross out those two, and you're left with only choice (B), the correct answer.

That game was complex, for sure, and somewhat time-consuming to set up. But like the Cookie Batches game, once you had a complete picture (or complete pictures, if you like), the question set was manageable. Probably the most important takeaway from this section on Difficult Sequencing is not to panic: The same approach you take on less complex games will get you through. In fact, it will have you outpacing your competition dramatically. Having learned the fundamentals first, you can confidently respond to quirky twists and variations.

In the final part of this chapter, I'll have you take a look at two extremely rare variations on Sequencing games. I don't expect that you'll see either of them on your test, but practicing them here will help you be ready for anything and give you another chance to see how the Kaplan Method and strategies unlock any task that the test makers can think up.

UNUSUAL SEQUENCING VARIATIONS

The games in this section are truly weird. These varieties have appeared only a few times over the past 20 years. Statistically, test takers have encountered such a game less than 2 percent of the time. So please don't give more than 2 percent of your practice or concern to them. Test takers who spend their time hunting down the strangest of games but who fail to master the fundamental logic games skills are at a great disadvantage. Those who master the Kaplan Method and its associated strategies are able to handle unusual, and unusually difficult, games by using what's familiar in them to create logical, useful sketches and recognizing the rules and deductions that provide the most restriction.

Circular Sequencing

Of the more than 260 games released by the LSAC at the time this book was written, just three fall under the category of Circular Sequencing. The first appeared in 1991, the second in 1998, and the third (the one you'll try here) in October of 2003. As the name implies, these games ask you to arrange entities in a circular pattern. In the example you're about to try, the scenario involves people eating around a circular picnic table. Getting a clear mental picture of your task is essential to making a useful framework for your sketch. Once you have that, it's pretty easy to anticipate what the rules and questions will be about. What are we always concerned about when choosing a seat? We want to know who's sitting next to us or across from us. The rules for these games, of course, work just the same way.

Give yourself eight and half minutes to set up the game and attempt the questions. If you find that you're struggling, check the explanations for Steps 1–4 of the Kaplan Method. Once you're sure you've got a useful sketch and have made the available deductions, go back and try the questions again. This game originally had seven questions associated with it. I'll only have you do five; that's more than enough to get a thorough understanding of how Circular Sequencing works.

Eight people—Fiona, George, Harriet, Ingrid, Karl, Manuel, Olivia, and Peter—are sitting, evenly spaced, around a circular picnic table. Any two of them are said to be sitting directly across from one another if and only if there are exactly three other people sitting between them, counting in either direction around the table. The following conditions apply:

Fiona sits directly across from George.
Harriet sits immediately next to neither Fiona nor Karl.
Ingrid sits immediately next to, and immediately clockwise from, Olivia.

18. Which one of the following could be the order in which four of the people are seated, with no one else seated between them, counting clockwise around the table?

(A) George, Peter, Karl, Fiona
(B) Harriet, Olivia, Ingrid, Karl
(C) Ingrid, Fiona, Peter, Manuel
(D) Olivia, Manuel, Karl, George
(E) Peter, Harriet, Karl, Fiona

19. If Harriet and Olivia each sits immediately next to George, then which one of the following could be the two people each of whom sits immediately next to Peter?

(A) Fiona and Karl
(B) Fiona and Olivia
(C) Harriet and Ingrid
(D) Harriet and Karl
(E) Karl and Manuel

21. If Manuel sits immediately next to Olivia, then which one of the following people must sit immediately next to Fiona?

(A) Harriet
(B) Ingrid
(C) Karl
(D) Manuel
(E) Peter

22. What is the minimum possible number of people sitting between Ingrid and Manuel, counting clockwise from Ingrid around the table?

(A) zero
(B) one
(C) two
(D) three
(E) four

23. If Karl sits directly across from Ingrid, then each of the following people could sit immediately next to Olivia EXCEPT:

(A) Fiona
(B) George
(C) Harriet
(D) Manuel
(E) Peter[33]

Explanations

STEPS 1 AND 2: Overview and Sketch

As I said in the introduction to this game, getting a clear mental picture of the task is essential. Fortunately, it's also pretty easy. The real-world situation described is familiar and simple. Probably the easiest way to picture it is to draw four lines, the end points of each representing the eight seats arrayed "evenly spaced" around the table.

Figure 9.75

The chairs aren't numbered or labeled with any other directional information (such as "north," "south," etc.), so you know that the restrictions will all involve who is or isn't next to or across from whom.

STEP 3: Rules

Rule 1 puts F and G at opposite ends of one of the lines.

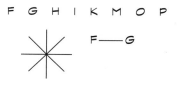

Figure 9.76

Rule 2 is the negative restriction you anticipated. H won't sit next to F or K. Make sure you show that F and K will not be adjacent to H on either side.

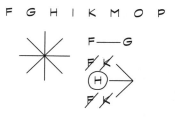

Figure 9.77

Rule 3 has the pair that wants to be together. I and O take consecutive seats, with I clockwise from O. Depict that in a way that allows you to see I's position relative to O no matter where around the circle you need to place them.

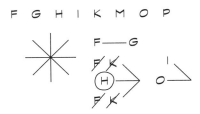

Figure 9.78

Make sure you recognize the familiar restrictions provided by Rules 1 and 3. Both create Blocks of Entities. Rule 1 could have been written in standard Sequencing language as "Exactly three seats will be between the seats in which F and G sit." Rule 3 could have been written "I sits in the seat immediately after the seat in which O sits" (provided that you substitute "after" for "clockwise," of course). Just as they would in a regular, linear Sequencing game, these rules will provide the basis for the greatest restrictions within the arrangement.

The floaters here are P and M. It's very important to make note of that in your Master Sketch.

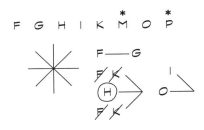

Figure 9.79

Those two will be able to sit anywhere, filling in any gaps around the table.

step 4: Deductions

There aren't really any deductions to add to this setup. That's less alarming when you note that the majority of questions contain "ifs" that are going to give you specific scenarios in which to test the rules. In the original appearance of this game, five of the seven questions had new "ifs." The only rules that share an entity are Rules 1 and 2. I suppose you could add the restriction on H and F to the F-G line, like so:

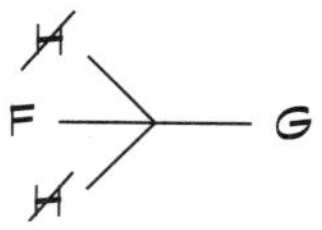

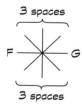

Figure 9.80

Even that's not much of a breakthrough, since the same information is visible in your depiction of Rule 2. At any rate, you've just learned a valuable lesson: Unusual games are just like normal ones in the sense that some have lots of deductions and some very few. With fewer deductions, you know to anticipate more "if" questions, and that's precisely what you get here.

STEP 5: Questions

This game had a Partial Acceptability question, a Minimum/Maximum type question, and as we noted already, five "If" questions, three of which I included for you to work on. You'll be drawing a lot of mini-sketches, no doubt.

18. **(C)**

Which one of the following could be the order in which four of the people are seated, with no one else seated between them, counting clockwise around the table?

(A) George, Peter, Karl, Fiona
(B) Harriet, Olivia, Ingrid, Karl
(C) Ingrid, Fiona, Peter, Manuel
(D) Olivia, Manuel, Karl, George
(E) Peter, Harriet, Karl, Fiona[34]

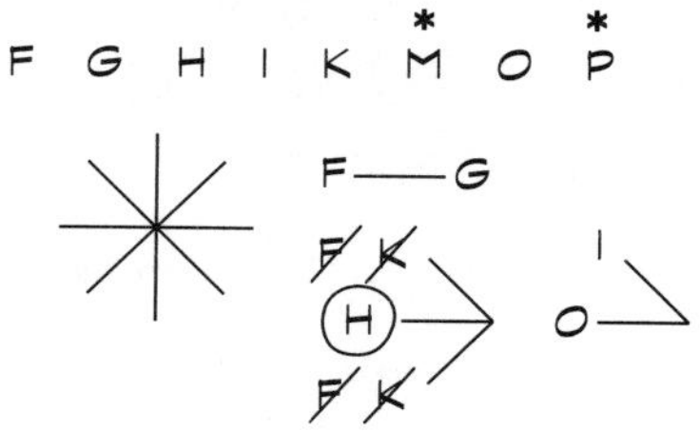

Figure 9.81

This is a Partial Acceptability question. Each answer shows four of the seats around the table in clockwise order. Use the rules to eliminate violators just as you would in any Partial Acceptability question. How do you check Rule 1 here? Since F and G must face one another, they will always have three seats between them on both sides.

Figure 9.82

No matter how you slice it, any four consecutive seats you extract from the sequence will have one of F and G and will not have the other. That allows you to eliminate choice (A), where both F and G appear, and choice (B), where neither appears.

---

[34] PrepTest 41, Sec. 2, Q 18

Choice (E) violates Rule 2 by having H and K sit next to one another. And choice (D) violates Rule 3 by having M, instead of I, clockwise from O.

Choice (C) remains. It's the correct answer.

19. **(D)**

If Harriet and Olivia each sits immediately next to George, then which one of the following could be the two people each of whom sits immediately next to Peter?

(A) Fiona and Karl
(B) Fiona and Olivia
(C) Harriet and Ingrid
(D) Harriet and Karl
(E) Karl and Manuel[35]

Figure 9.83

Here's the first of the "If" questions. Start your mini-sketch with the condition imposed by the question stem. For O to obey Rule 3, he'll have to sit clockwise from G. That puts H counter-clockwise from G.

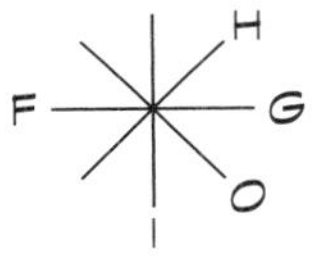

Figure 9.84

Of the remaining picnickers, only P and M (the floaters) can sit next to H.

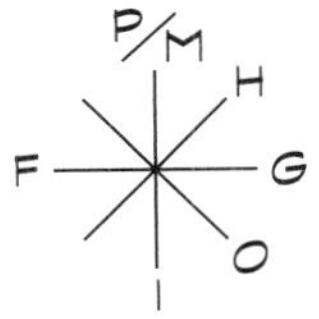

Figure 9.85

The question asks for two people who could sit next to P. Two of the answer choices include H, who you can see is one of P's possible neighbors. Choice (C) has H and I, but I would be across the table from P in this scenario. Eliminate that answer. Choice (D) has H and K. That would be possible, with K between F and P and M between I and F. Choice (D) is the correct answer here.

For the record, for choice (A) to work, K would have to sit next to H in violation of Rule 2. Choice (B) is impossible, since O is already between G and I. Choice (E) just cannot fit into the

---

[35] PrepTest 41, Sec. 2, Q 19

spaces provided by this question's "if"; K and M could be on either side of F here, but not on either side of P.

21. **(C)**

If Manuel sits immediately next to Olivia, then which one of the following people must sit immediately next to Fiona?

(A) Harriet
(B) Ingrid
(C) Karl
(D) Manuel
(E) Peter[36]

Figure 9.86

Here's another "if" question calling for a new mini-sketch. In order for M to sit next to O, M needs to be counterclockwise from O so that I can sit clockwise from O in accordance with Rule 3.

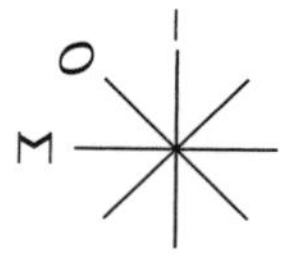

Figure 9.87

Now, you can add the F-G line. It doesn't matter which of those two sits next to M and which next to I.

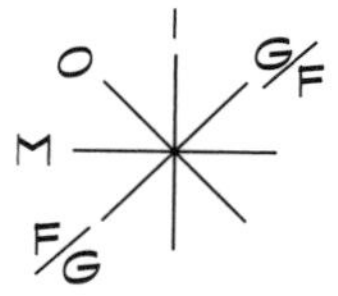

Figure 9.88

The remaining picnickers are H, K, and P. In order to keep K and H apart, P will have to sit directly across from O.

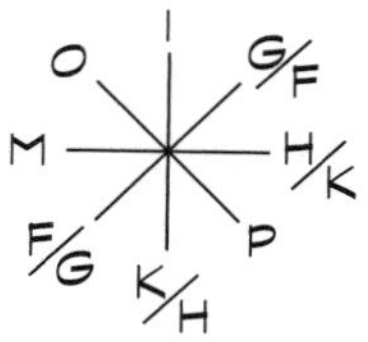

Figure 9.89

---

36 PrepTest 41, Sec. 2, Q 21

Remember that H has to avoid being next to F, too, according to Rule 2. Therefore, K will have to take the seat next to F. That makes choice (C) the right answer.

While F *could* sit next to I (choice (B)) or M (choice (D)), the question stem asks for who F *must* sit next to. Regardless of which side of the table F sits on, K will be her neighbor there.

22. **(A)**

What is the minimum possible number of people sitting between Ingrid and Manuel, counting clockwise from Ingrid around the table?

(A) zero
(B) one
(C) two
(D) three
(E) four[37]

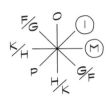

Figure 9.90

With a question like this one, make sure you understand the question stem. You need to see how close you can get I and M, with M to the clockwise side of I. The other way to make a simple, but fatal, error here is to miss the word "between." If M can be immediately next to I, there will be zero seats *between* them. Don't confuse that with M being *one seat away from* I; that's not what the question is asking.

If you're being very strategic here, you can answer this question in a few seconds. Remember the mini-sketch you made for question 19?

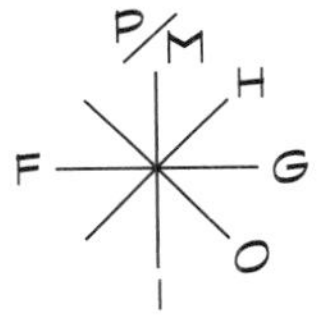

Figure 9.91

There, it was acceptable to place M between I and F. So M can sit immediately next to I, with zero seats *between* them. Choice (A) is the correct answer. No matter how bizarre the game, the Kaplan strategies work every time.

23. **(B)**

If Karl sits directly across from Ingrid, then each of the following people could sit immediately next to Olivia EXCEPT:

(A) Fiona
(B) George
(C) Harriet
(D) Manuel
(E) Peter

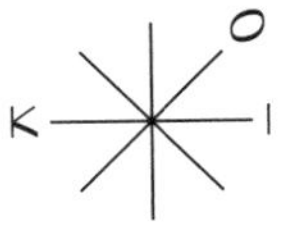

Figure 9.92

---

[37] PrepTest 41, Sec. 2, Q 22

Here's one more "If" question. Start your mini-sketch with the restriction in the stem.

Figure 9.93

Once you know I's position, Rule 3 dictates O's.

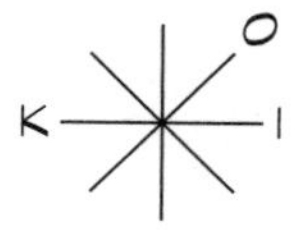

Figure 9.94

Now, think strategically about who could sit next to O on her counterclockwise side. The correct answer will be someone who *cannot* sit there. The floaters won't present a problem, so you can eliminate choices (D) and (E). Now, you can just test the three remaining choices. Placing F next to O presents no problems. G would be opposite F, and H could sit between I and G.

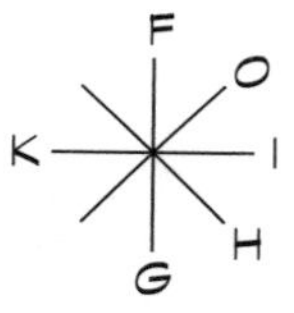

Figure 9.95

Eliminate choice (A).

When you try to put G next to O, you see the trouble. With F opposite G, there's nowhere for H that isn't next to either K or F, the two entities she's forbidden from sitting next to in Rule 2. G *cannot* sit next to O, and choice (B) is the correct answer.

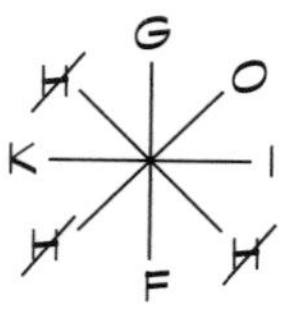

Figure 9.96

If you test choice (C), you'll of course find an acceptable arrangement. With H next to O on O's counterclockwise side, you can place G next to H, putting F across the table clockwise from I. The only remaining entities are the floaters—P and M—who can sit anywhere.

Chances are very slim that you'll encounter Circular Sequencing on your test. If you do see such a game, remember how much more prepared for it you are than someone who hasn't learned the Kaplan Method and the crucial skills and strategies that you have. Remember to base your sketch on the task described, which will allow you to anticipate the restrictions rewarded by the game. In a Circular scenario, that must involve who is or isn't next to someone else and how close or far apart they can be seated. Remember Circular Sequencing the next time you have to make seating arrangements for a wedding reception or social event. It might turn out to have real-life consequences.

There's just one more variation on Sequencing that the test makers have employed. It's almost as rare as Circular Sequencing, but its underlying task is actually closer to regular Strict Sequencing. Give it a look for the sake of completeness, but don't exaggerate its importance. Chances are, you won't see Circular Sequencing or Double Sequencing on your test.

Double Sequencing

Over the years, the LSAT has featured a couple of varieties of what I'll call Double Sequencing games. In one older example, two editors had to review the same six books, although they were restricted from reviewing the same book simultaneously. You'll see another later in this book, so I won't spoil the big "reveal" on that one. None of the four Double Sequencing games that have appeared on the LSAT are exactly identical, but they all ask you to sequence the entities twice or, in the game you're about to see, to schedule the entities once, but according to either of two criteria.

In the example that follows, you're asked to create a schedule for five pieces of music that will be performed at a concert. The "doubling" in this game derives from the fact that each of the pieces of music are performed on a specific pair of instruments. As you'll see, the rules restrict the acceptable sequences based on the instruments as well as the pieces being performed. I won't give too much away until you've had a chance to try the game on your own, but here's a hint: Pay attention to your main task—sequencing the pieces—and ask how knowing about the instruments helps you do that. The game ranks very hard based on test takers' responses, but a strategic test taker finds a lot of restrictions to guide her through the questions. Give yourself eight and half minutes and try to complete this game. If you get stuck, review the explanations for Steps 1–4 of the Kaplan Method. Then return to the question set.

Musicians perform each of exactly five pieces—Nexus, Onyx, Synchrony, Tailwind, and Virtual—once, and one at a time; the pieces are performed successively (though not necessarily in that order). Each piece is performed with exactly two instruments: Nexus with fiddle and lute, Onyx with harp and mandolin, Synchrony with guitar and harp, Tailwind with fiddle and guitar, and Virtual with lute and mandolin. The following conditions must apply:

    Each piece shares one instrument with the piece performed immediately before it or after it (or both).
    Either Nexus or Tailwind is performed second.

20. Which one of the following could be the order, from first to last, in which the pieces are performed?

    (A)   Nexus, Synchrony, Onyx, Virtual, Tailwind
    (B)   Synchrony, Tailwind, Onyx, Nexus, Virtual
    (C)   Tailwind, Nexus, Onyx, Virtual, Synchrony
    (D)   Tailwind, Nexus, Synchrony, Onyx, Virtual
    (E)   Virtual, Nexus, Synchrony, Onyx, Tailwind

21. Which one of the following instruments CANNOT be shared by the third and fourth pieces performed?

    (A)   fiddle
    (B)   guitar
    (C)   harp
    (D)   lute
    (E)   mandolin

22. If each piece (except the fifth) shares one instrument with the piece performed immediately after it, then which one of the following could be true?

    (A)   Virtual is performed first.
    (B)   Synchrony is performed second.
    (C)   Onyx is performed third.
    (D)   Nexus is performed fourth.
    (E)   Tailwind is performed fifth.

23. Each of the following could be the piece performed first EXCEPT:

    (A)   Nexus
    (B)   Onyx
    (C)   Synchrony
    (D)   Tailwind
    (E)   Virtual

24. If Synchrony is performed fifth, then which one of the following could be true?

    (A)   Nexus is performed third.
    (B)   Onyx is performed third.
    (C)   Tailwind is performed fourth.
    (D)   Virtual is performed first.
    (E)   Virtual is performed second.[38]

---

[38] PrepTest 38, Sec. 2, Qs 20–24

Explanations

STEPS 1 AND 2: Overview and Sketch

The opening paragraph that describes this game is quite long. That's a good sign that it will contain some helpful restrictions. The nature of your task is introduced at the beginning: Pieces of music "are performed successively." Up to that point, this is a very straightforward Sequencing task. You're creating the program for a performance.

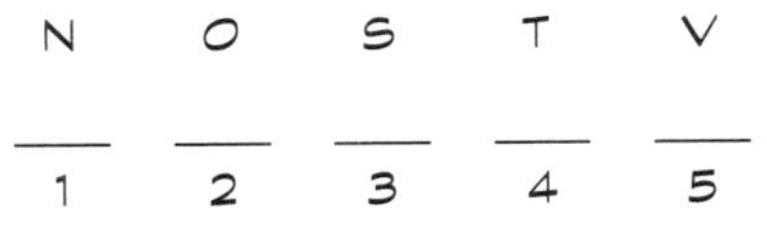

```
    N    O    S    T    V
   ___  ___  ___  ___  ___
    1    2    3    4    5
```

Figure 9.97

The twist comes in when the paragraph starts describing the instruments that each piece is performed on. Although what restrictions the instruments provide isn't made clear until the rules, you can rest assured that you should record the instruments associated with each piece as you list the entities. We've all been at some kind of performance in which the featured artists are listed along with the pieces; in this case, it's the featured instruments that will be listed there.

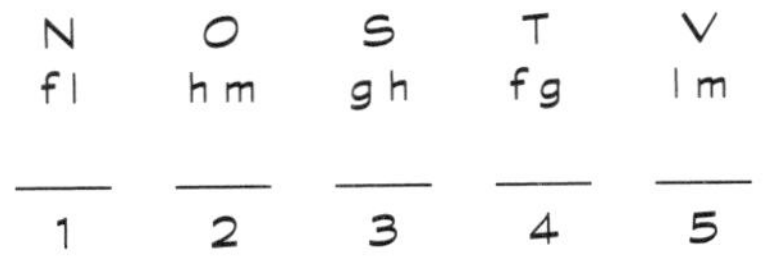

```
    N    O    S    T    V
    fl   hm   gh   fg   lm
   ___  ___  ___  ___  ___
    1    2    3    4    5
```

Figure 9.98

A glance at Rule 2 indicates that at least one specific space in the order is restricted, so a Strict Sequencing sketch is likely to be useful as you proceed.

STEP 3: Rules

There are only two rules, but each is very powerful.

Rule 1 tells you that each piece must share an instrument with the piece either before or after it in the schedule. There's no better way to diagram this rule than to note it in shorthand beside your sketch framework.

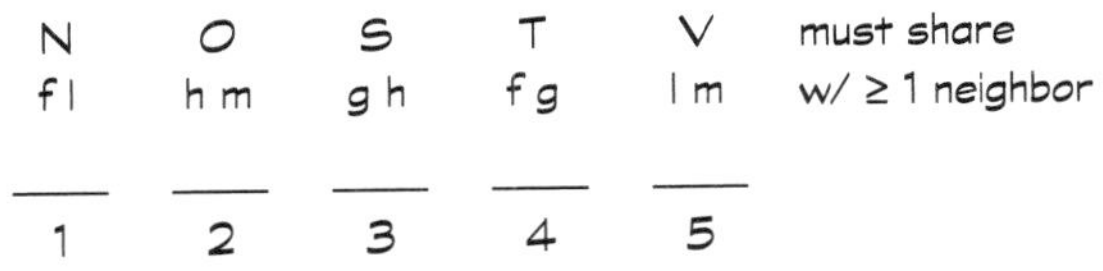

```
    N    O    S    T    V    must share
    fl   hm   gh   fg   lm   w/ ≥ 1 neighbor
   ___  ___  ___  ___  ___
    1    2    3    4    5
```

Figure 9.99

Did you take a moment to appreciate the impact of that rule on the game? Each piece is played on exactly two instruments. And each instrument is mentioned exactly two times. Thus, Synchrony, let's say, which is performed on guitar and harp, cannot be sandwiched in between Virtual and Nexus, neither of which feature guitar or harp. What's more, Synchrony couldn't be stuck at either end of the list if the only adjacent piece were Virtual or Nexus, either. In fact, the way the instruments are distributed, every piece has two other pieces with which it shares an instrument and two pieces with which it shares none. You can visualize that nicely by displaying the pieces in a ring so that each is joined to one with which it shares an instrument. It's a little reminiscent of a daisy chain:

N O S T V
fl hm gh fg lm
must share
w/ ≥ 1 neighbor
1 2 3 4 5
T
f g
N S
l h
m m
V O

Figure 9.100

This shows neatly that Nexus must be next to at least one of Tailwind or Virtual, Tailwind next to at least one of Virtual or Synchrony, and so on. Don't worry if you didn't come up with a fancy diagram, but take to heart just how much this rule actually gives you. Remember my hint? I told you to stay focused on your main job—sequencing the pieces—and to ask how the associated instruments would help you. From this one rule, you'll be able to eliminate literally dozens of unacceptable arrangements.

Rule 2 is much simpler, but no less important. It uses space 2 to create a Limited Options scenario.

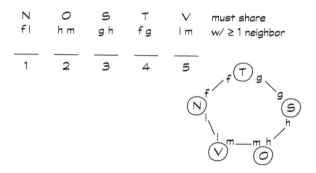

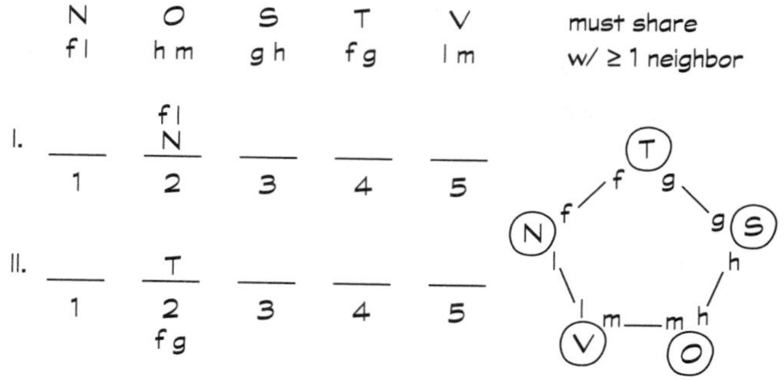

N O S T V
fl hm gh fg lm
must share
w/ ≥ 1 neighbor
I.
fl
N
1 2 3 4 5
II.
T
1 2 3 4 5
fg
T
f g
N S
l h
m m
V O

Figure 9.101

STEP 4: Deductions

There's really only one thing to add to your sketch under Step 4, but this one additional deduction will turn directly into points. Did you notice that there's a Duplication involved in the two rules? It comes from the fact that restricting space 2 to either Nexus or Tailwind also means restricting it to fiddle and lute (Nexus) or fiddle and guitar (Tailwind). Since the piece that is played first must share an instrument with the piece played second, you can see that in Option I, only Tailwind or Virtual could be the first piece, and in Option II, only Synchrony or Nexus.

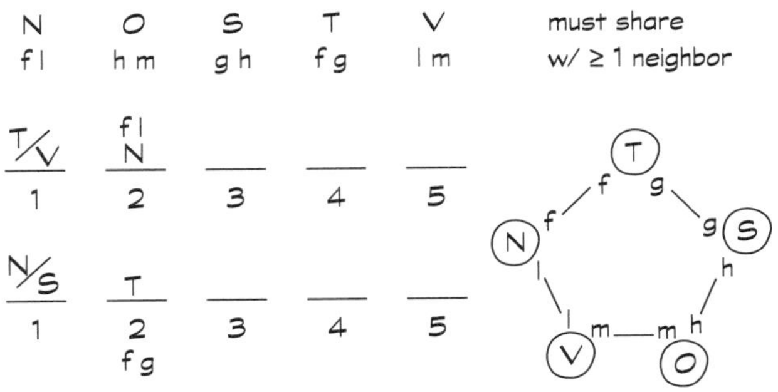

Figure 9.102

With that, you have everything you need to be able to answer the questions. The restrictions that come from Rule 1's requirement that every piece share an instrument with one of its neighbors will allow you to determine everything that can happen in either of the options.

STEP 5: Questions

One of the things that can cost test takers points and time is rushing to get to the questions. In this game, there are only five questions, and none of them are very long. When I teach students this game in class, I force them to spend four minutes on the setup, rules, and deductions to ensure that they get as complete a picture of their task and restrictions as possible. They often chafe a little at this. "What else are we supposed to do here?" But then they see the payoff. With a complete sketch and a thorough understanding of how the instruments limit the arrangement of pieces, they find that they can complete the question set easily in four minutes, sometimes far less. You can actually beat the timing average of eight and half minutes per game on a legendarily tough game like this one by being patient enough to extract all of the implications of the setup and rules before turning to the questions.

20. **(D)**

Which one of the following could be the order, from first to last, in which the pieces are performed?

(A) Nexus, Synchrony, Onyx, Virtual, Tailwind
(B) Synchrony, Tailwind, Onyx, Nexus, Virtual
(C) Tailwind, Nexus, Onyx, Virtual, Synchrony
(D) Tailwind, Nexus, Synchrony, Onyx, Virtual
(E) Virtual, Nexus, Synchrony, Onyx, Tailwind[39]

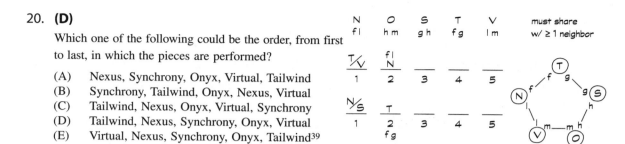

Figure 9.103

This is a run-of-the-mill Acceptability question in a decidedly *not* run-of-the-mill game. With only two rules, you know that at least one of them will eliminate multiple answer choices. Given that Rule 1 affects all of the entities, it's a good bet that it will do most of the heavy lifting. Since Rule 2 is so easy to check—just look for answer choices that have a piece other than N or T in the second spot—use it to clear out any clear violators first. Rule 2 knocks out only choice (A), which has S in the second space. Now, back to Rule 1. You'll need to find three choices in which an entity has no instrument shared with its neighbor(s). Even so, don't hunt blindly. Start with the easiest places to check, at either end of the program. In the remaining choices, the pieces in spaces 1 and 2 all share an instrument. Those you could check with just a glance at your Limited Options. The end of the program, however, reveals two violations. In choice (C), S shares nothing with V (glance at the ring of associated instruments if you need confirmation). In choice (E), T shares nothing with O. You're now left with choices (B) and (D). Look to the middle to make your final cut. In choice (B), O is sandwiched between T and N. Since neither of those pieces shares an instrument with O, choice (B) violates Rule 1, too. Only choice (D) is acceptable and, therefore, is the correct answer.

21. **(A)**

Which one of the following instruments CANNOT be shared by the third and fourth pieces performed?

(A) fiddle
(B) guitar
(C) harp
(D) lute
(E) mandolin[40]

N	O	S	T	V	must share
f l	h m	g h	f g	l m	w/ ≥ 1 neighbor

T/V   f l/N   ___   ___   ___
1   2   3   4   5

N/S   T   ___   ___   ___
1   2   3   4   5
    f g

Figure 9.104

[39] PrepTest 38, Sec. 2, Q 20
[40] PrepTest 38, Sec. 2, Q 21

With your Limited Options sketch illustrating the instruments locked into space 2 with N or T, this is an easy point. Regardless of which option is in use, one of the two fiddles is dedicated to space 2. There's no way a fiddle could be shared between spaces 3 and 4. Choice (A) is correct, and you've got one more point in the bag.

22. **(A)**

If each piece (except the fifth) shares one instrument with the piece performed immediately after it, then which one of the following could be true?

(A) Virtual is performed first.
(B) Synchrony is performed second.
(C) Onyx is performed third.
(D) Nexus is performed fourth.
(E) Tailwind is performed fifth.[41]

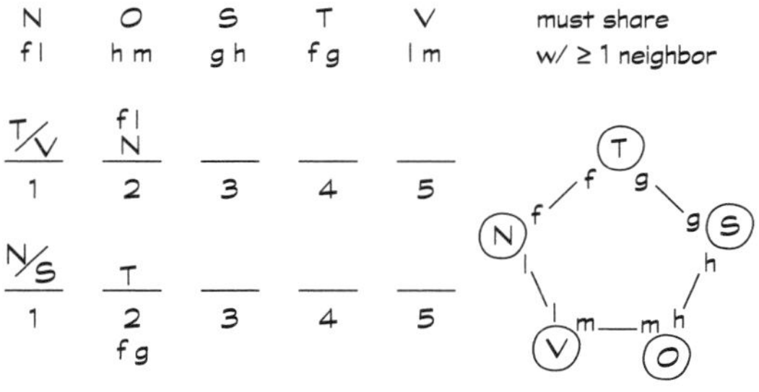

N	O	S	T	V	must share
f l	h m	g h	f g	l m	w/ ≥ 1 neighbor

Figure 9.105

This is a rare "If" question that doesn't call for a mini-sketch. That's because instead of imposing a condition that places an entity within the arrangement, this "if" imposes an additional universal restriction on the game. In effect, the "if" here changes the original restriction that each entity share an instrument with at least one of its neighbors to require them to share an instrument specifically with the piece that follows. In other words, these arrangements simply proceed in order around the "daisy chain," as they must in order for every piece to share an instrument with the following piece. Looking at the Limited Options sketches, you see that there are four ways this can happen, one for each of the four possible first pieces. For Option I, the arrangements could go T-N-V-O-S or V-N-T-S-O. For Option II, they could be S-T-N-V-O or N-T-S-O-V. That observation is enough to prove that choice (A) is acceptable. The other four choices never occur within the four arrangements acceptable under this stem's "if."

23. **(B)**

Each of the following could be the piece performed first EXCEPT:

(A) Nexus
(B) Onyx
(C) Synchrony
(D) Tailwind
(E) Virtual[42]

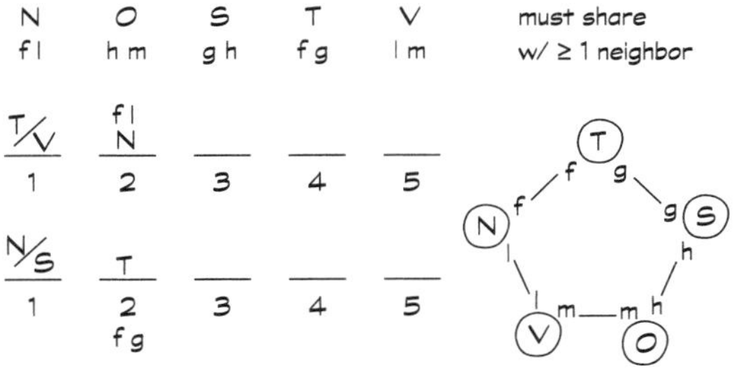

N	O	S	T	V	must share
f l	h m	g h	f g	l m	w/ ≥ 1 neighbor

Figure 9.106

---

[41] PrepTest 38, Sec. 2, Q 22
[42] PrepTest 38, Sec. 2, Q 23

With the Limited Options diagrams, this question takes all of 10 seconds to answer. O is the one piece that cannot be first. That's choice (B).

24. **(D)**

If Synchrony is performed fifth, then which one of the following could be true?

(A) Nexus is performed third.
(B) Onyx is performed third.
(C) Tailwind is performed fourth.
(D) Virtual is performed first.
(E) Virtual is performed second.[43]

$$\underset{V}{\overset{l\,m}{\underline{\quad}}} \quad \underset{N}{\overset{l\,f}{\underline{\quad}}} \quad \underset{T}{\overset{f\,g}{\underline{\quad}}} \quad \underset{O}{\overset{h\,m}{\underline{\quad}}} \quad \underset{S}{\overset{g\,h}{\underline{\quad}}}$$

Figure 9.107

Here, finally, is an "if" question that benefits from a mini-sketch. The "if" in the stem tells you to place S in the final position.

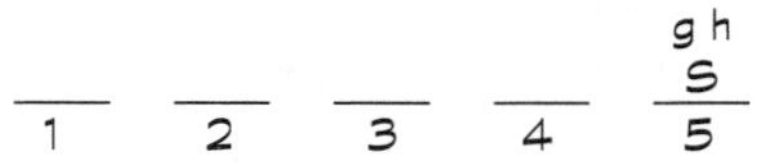

$$\underline{\quad}_{1} \quad \underline{\quad}_{2} \quad \underline{\quad}_{3} \quad \underline{\quad}_{4} \quad \underset{5}{\overset{g\,h}{\underset{S}{\underline{\quad}}}}$$

Figure 9.108

S shares instruments with T and O, so you might as well make dual mini-sketches, one for each possibility.

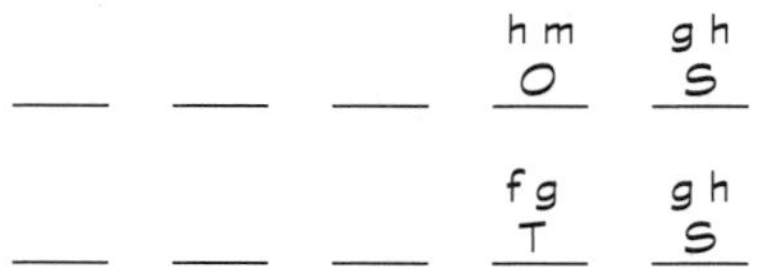

$$\underline{\quad} \quad \underline{\quad} \quad \underline{\quad} \quad \overset{h\,m}{\underset{O}{\underline{\quad}}} \quad \overset{g\,h}{\underset{S}{\underline{\quad}}}$$

$$\underline{\quad} \quad \underline{\quad} \quad \underline{\quad} \quad \overset{f\,g}{\underset{T}{\underline{\quad}}} \quad \overset{g\,h}{\underset{S}{\underline{\quad}}}$$

Figure 9.109

It doesn't take long to eliminate the second possibility from consideration. With T in space 4, N must take space 2. This puts you in Option I of the Master Sketch.

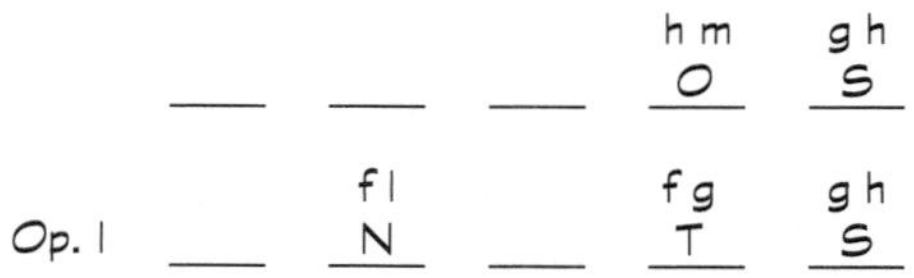

$$Op.\,I \quad \underline{\quad} \quad \overset{f\,l}{\underset{N}{\underline{\quad}}} \quad \underline{\quad} \quad \overset{f\,g}{\underset{T}{\underline{\quad}}} \quad \overset{g\,h}{\underset{S}{\underline{\quad}}}$$

(with h m / O and g h / S above spaces 4 and 5)

Figure 9.110

Since T is in space 4, V must take space 1. That leaves O for space 3.

---
[43] PrepTest 38, Sec. 2, Q 24

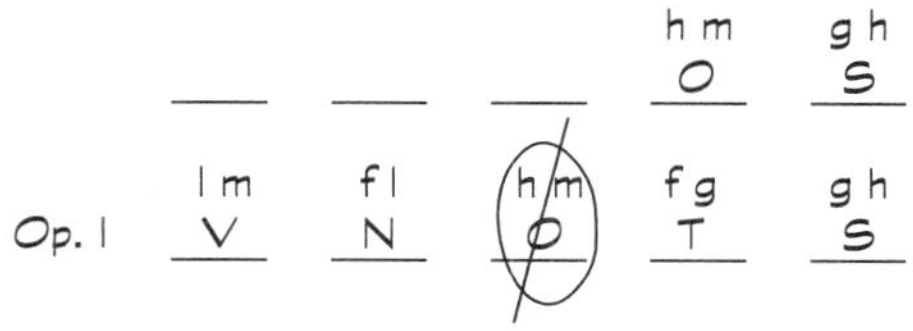

Figure 9.111

But O cannot take a position between N and T. It shares an instrument with neither. That alternative, with T in space 4, is impossible and you can eliminate choices (B) and (C).

While you're at it, eliminate choice (E), too. It violates Rule 2. V can never be second, "if" or no "if."

That leaves only choices (A) and (D) to consider. Test either one. If you find the acceptable choice, circle it and you're done. If you find the unacceptable one, cross it out and you're done.

Testing choice (A), you find that it doesn't work.

Figure 9.112

With N in space 3, T must take space 2. But that would require either S or N to take space 1, and here only V is left for space 1. Since choice (A) won't work, you know that choice (D) is correct. Test it if you need confirmation; you'll find that V can take the first position here when N takes the second position and T the third.

Figure 9.113

That is, indeed, a rare variation on Sequencing. You may never see one like it again. And yet, by starting from the familiar task—schedule these five pieces of music—you were able to turn the bizarre aspect of the game (the secondary attributes of the entities, the instruments) into a helpful set of restrictions. By adapting that game using the familiar Limited Options sketches, you were able to get a couple of the questions in a few seconds each. That's the underlying message of this chapter (of Part II, generally): Look for the familiar tasks, and leverage the familiar sketches and deductions. Then ask how the unfamiliar part of the game (if there is one) helps you determine the acceptable arrangements or eliminate the unacceptable ones.

YOU CAN HANDLE UNUSUAL GAMES

Don't let the unusual games in this part intimidate you. The chances are much greater that the Sequencing game or games you'll see on your test will be more like the Trail Signs game or the Water Treatment Plant game than that they'll be like one of the variations you've just seen. Keep in mind that you handled all of the games featured here—from the garden-variety examples to those with the strangest twists—using the Kaplan Method. In all of them, you see the importance of understanding your task, using the assistance of the rules, and having the patience to make all of the available deductions. Stick to those fundamental skills and you'll always have what you need to answer the questions. It comes back to the first statement in this book: Every question has an answer.

CHAPTER 10

DISTRIBUTION GAMES

Far less common than Sequencing, Distribution games are defined by tasks in which you will divide a set of entities into two or more groups. As you'll see clearly when we discuss real-life Distribution tasks, the salient question is always, "How many entities go into each group?" Sometimes the test makers will simply tell you; they might, for example, give you a game in which nine students are divided into three study groups of three students each. You'll appreciate it when that's the case, but it's more common for the test makers to leave the numbers initially ambiguous. When they do, use the rules and restrictions to determine as much as you can about the number of entities per group. At times, the numbers will reveal Limited Options scenarios such as, "Four employees serve on the charities committee and three on the travel committee, or vice versa." When you see that the numbers break down into only two possible arrangements in a Distribution game, make dual sketches and explore their implications.

REAL-LIFE DISTRIBUTION

You engage in Distribution tasks whenever you choose teams for a game, decide which piece of clothing goes in which closet, assign people to certain tasks or committees at work or school, or even when you deal out cards from a deck. The key thing to notice is that, in Distribution tasks, once you assign someone or something to a team or a place, you can't simultaneously assign it somewhere else; the grey suit can't hang in the hall closet and the bedroom closet at the same time; Joe can't play for the Blue team and for the Red team concurrently. Think of the entities in Distribution games as individual, physical beings or objects. You might move the green chair from the living room to the den, but it can't be in both places at once. This, by the way, is the main distinction between Distribution games and Matching games. In Matching tasks, you can use one set of entities multiple times. Serving coffee to Anne, for example, doesn't prevent you from serving it to Betty as well. I'll discuss the distinctions and overlap between these two tasks in the chapter on Matching games. For now, just keep the task of choosing teams as your model for Distribution.

Because real-world models for Distribution so often spring from activities like games and sports, your default assumption will often be that the teams or groups must be made up of equal numbers of players or entities. In most real-world games, each player gets the same number of cards or playing pieces to start. As I've said (and will again), check your assumptions at the door when you approach logic games. The test makers must be explicit about numbers restrictions in Distribution games. If they aren't, don't impose your own limitations.

While there are examples of Distribution tasks that follow an "equal groups" model, they're the exception. A better real-world model for most Distribution games is to picture something like a work assignment in which your boss tells you to assign eight employees to three different projects.

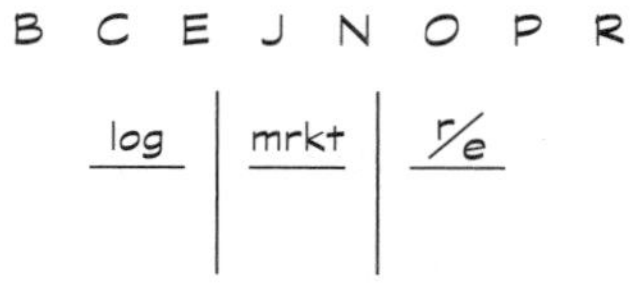

B C E J N O P R

$$\underline{\text{log}} \quad | \quad \underline{\text{mrkt}} \quad | \quad \underline{r\!/\!e}$$

Figure 10.1

Your first question might be, "How many people do you want on each task?" But your boss responds, "You tell me. I want those projects finished ASAP. If the marketing initiative needs more bodies than the real estate plan, so be it." Like a Distribution setup on the test, your boss might impose some limits without giving you exact numbers: for example, "Just don't put more than four people on the real estate plan."

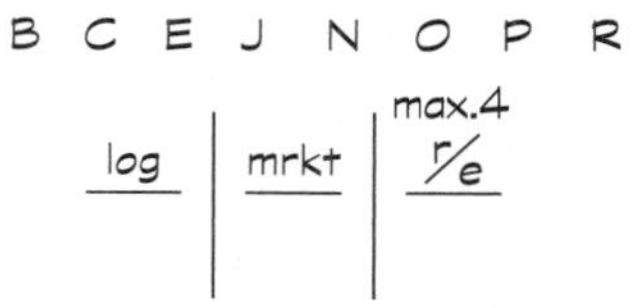

B C E J N O P R

$$\underline{\text{log}} \quad | \quad \underline{\text{mrkt}} \quad | \quad \overset{\text{max.4}}{\underline{r\!/\!e}}$$

Figure 10.2

You might wish that your boss would be more definite, but you wouldn't let this response stop you from making the proposed assignments. Don't let the lack of numbers stop you from attacking a Distribution game, either.

What's definite in almost any real-world Distribution task is that there are certain people or items you'll want to keep together and certain ones you'll want to keep apart. In choosing basketball teams, you might say, "Tom and Dave are team captains," in order to keep the two tallest guys from being on the same team. Arranging your furniture, you might think, "The chair could go in the living room or the den, but either way, the ottoman has to go with it." Even your boss might tell you, "I don't care which project you put Peggy on, but don't assign Chuck to the same one," or, "Just make sure Evelyn and Nancy are working together; they're a good team."

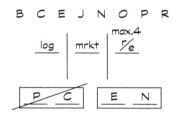

Figure 10.3

Thinking about how common such restrictions are in real life should take a lot of the sting out of formal logic rules in Distribution games. I doubt you'd wring your hands or get confused if you boss said, "Look, if you assign Evelyn to the marketing campaign, then put Rosa on the real estate planning team."

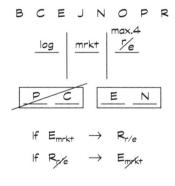

Figure 10.4

Don't let the test makers undermine your confidence when they use formal conditions, either.

STANDARD DISTRIBUTION

Up to this point in the book, you've seen a couple of Distribution games. Not surprisingly, they represent examples of the two standard Distribution subtypes: One had definite numbers for the assignments, and one had indefinite numbers. I'll refresh your memory of both and show you a couple of new examples for practice.

Distribution with Definite Numbers

Over the years, the LSAT has used Distribution games with definite numbers slightly less often than their more open-ended counterparts. In recent years, those with indefinite numbers have become the norm. Still, Distribution with definite numbers is the right place to start; these games provide the less complicated version of the task while using many of the same kinds of rules and restrictions to limit the placement of the entities. Here's an example that you worked with in Part I of the book:

On a field trip to the Museum of Natural History, each of six children—Juana, Kyle, Lucita, Salim, Thanh, and Veronica— is accompanied by one of three adults—Ms. Margoles, Mr. O'Connell, and Ms. Podorski. Each adult accompanies exactly two of the children, consistent with the following conditions:

If Ms. Margoles accompanies Juana, then Ms. Podorski accompanies Lucita.
If Kyle is not accompanied by Ms. Margoles, then Veronica is accompanied by Mr. O'Connell.
Either Ms. Margoles or Mr. O'Connell accompanies Thanh. Juana is not accompanied by the same adult as Kyle; nor is Lucita accompanied by the same adult as Salim; nor is Thanh accompanied by the same adult as Veronica.[1]

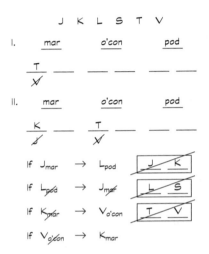

Figure 10.5

The key to the sketch is showing the number restrictions clearly. Each adult accompanies exactly two children. Even though you can't place many of the children into your initial Master Sketch, draw the individual slots beneath each chaperone. Do this whenever the test makers tell you how many entities are in each group.

The rules in this game are typical of Distribution games. The only one that's a little unusual is Rule 3, which creates the Limited Options based on the two possible placements for Thanh. The others you would expect to find in any game with a Distribution task. Rules 1 and 2 offer conditional formal logic restrictions, and Rule 4—which is really three rules in one—creates "impossible pairs," designating pairs of entities that cannot be assigned to the same adult as each other. Beyond noting that Veronica cannot share a chaperone with Thanh, there were no additional deductions here, so you can head in to the question set expecting to see "if" questions and questions that reward you for eliminating answers that violate the catalogue of rules. Try a couple of "if" questions from this game to practice applying Deduction game restrictions.

---

[1] PrepTest 52, Sec. 2, Game 2

9. If Ms. Margoles accompanies Lucita and Thanh, then which one of the following must be true?
   (A) Juana is accompanied by the same adult as Veronica.
   (B) Kyle is accompanied by the same adult as Salim.
   (C) Juana is accompanied by Mr. O'Connell.
   (D) Kyle is accompanied by Ms. Podorski.
   (E) Salim is accompanied by Ms. Podorski.[2]

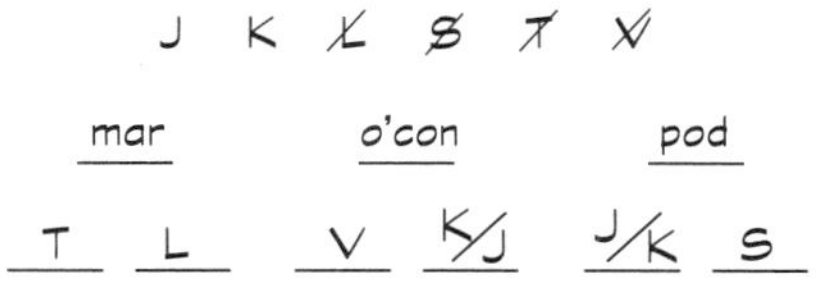
J K L S T V
mar
o'con
pod
T L V K/J J/K S

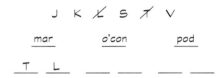

Figure 10.5A

The "if" condition tells you to use Option I, adding L under Margoles's heading. That leaves J, K, S, and V to be placed.

J K L S T V
mar
o'con
pod
T L

Figure 10.6

Since K isn't with Margoles in this question, Rule 2 requires V to go with O'Connell.

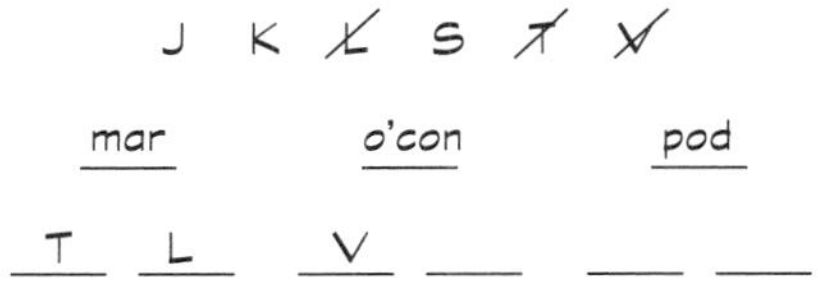
J K L S T V
mar
o'con
pod
T L V

Figure 10.7

Rule 4 requires you to keep J and K separate, though there's no way to know which of those students will go with O'Connell and which with Podorski. Either way, it's clear that S must go with Podorski and your picture is complete.

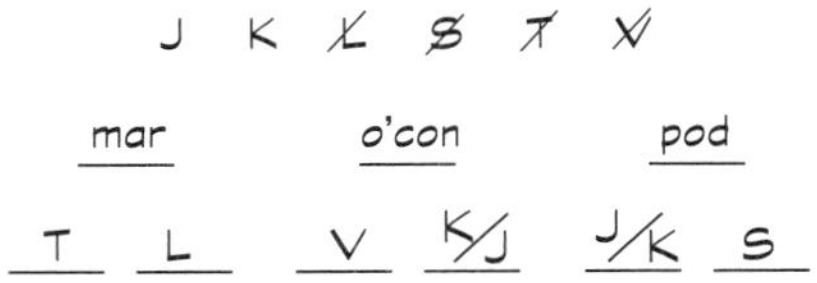
J K L S T V
mar
o'con
pod
T L V K/J J/K S

Figure 10.8

---

[2] PrepTest 52, Sec. 2, Q 9

The question stem calls for what must be true as a result of the new "if" condition. Unsurprisingly, choice (E) rewards you for deducing that S is chaperoned by Podorski. That's your correct answer. (It's also no surprise that all four wrong answers mention either J or K, the two entities whose placement *cannot* be completely determined here.)

That question is a good illustration of how the test makers write Distribution game rules so that they can be combined to lead to greater certainty. The next question works the same way, though its "if" will lead you to a different assignment of students to chaperones. Give it a try.

10. If Ms. Podorski accompanies Juana and Veronica, then Ms. Margoles could accompany which one of the following pairs of children?

    (A) Kyle and Salim
    (B) Kyle and Thanh
    (C) Lucita and Salim
    (D) Lucita and Thanh
    (E) Salim and Thanh[3]

Figure 10.9

This time, you can begin your mini-sketch by assigning Podorski her charges based on the question stem.

Figure 10.10

You may think that leaves either option available, but consider the implications of Rule 2. Since V is not with O'Connell in this situation, the contrapositive of Rule 2 tells you that K must be assigned to Margoles.

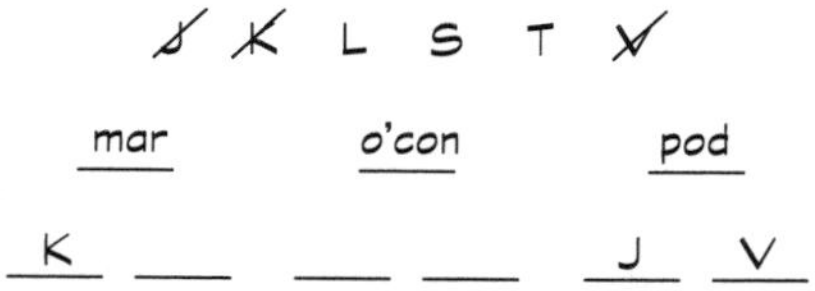

Figure 10.11

---

[3] PrepTest 52, Sec. 2, Q 10

In Option I, that would mean that L and S are stuck together with O'Connell, but Rule 4 prevents you from placing L and S together. So you have to use Option II in order to accommodate this question's "if" condition and its resultant deductions.

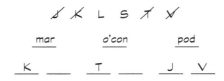

Figure 10.12

Now, it doesn't matter which of L and S goes with Margoles or O'Connell. Either way, you're ready to answer the question.

Figure 10.13

The question asks for a pair of entities who *could* go with Margoles. You can see from your mini-sketch that the correct answer will say either "Kyle and Lucita" or "Kyle and Salim." Choice (A) has the second of those two possibilities and is correct. None of the other answers is a possible pair for Margoles here.

Distribution Practice

The next game is one that you haven't seen before. But like the Museum Chaperones game, it asks you to distribute entities in pairs. I'll let you try it out on your own and then go through the explanations with you. Here's one hint before you begin: The fact that the groups are days of the week gives some test takers the impression that this is a kind of Sequencing-Distribution Hybrid game. In fact, the days of the week work just like the three chaperones in the previous game. There are no rules or restrictions based on the ordering of the entities, nothing saying, for example, that K must come *earlier* or *later* in the week than P.

Give yourself eight and a half minutes for the game and its questions. If you feel stuck, review the explanations for Steps 1–4 of the Kaplan Method. Once you're sure you have a strong Master Sketch and understand the deductions, go back to the questions and complete your work.

During a certain week, an animal shelter places exactly six dogs—a greyhound, a husky, a keeshond, a Labrador retriever, a poodle, and a schnauzer—with new owners. Two are placed on Monday, two on Tuesday, and the remaining two on Wednesday, consistent with the following conditions:

The Labrador retriever is placed on the same day as the poodle.

The greyhound is not placed on the same day as the husky.

If the keeshond is placed on Monday, the greyhound is placed on Tuesday.

If the schnauzer is placed on Wednesday, the husky is placed on Tuesday.

7. Which one of the following could be a complete and accurate matching of dogs to the days on which they are placed?

   (A) Monday: greyhound, Labrador retriever
       Tuesday: husky, poodle
       Wednesday: keeshond, schnauzer
   (B) Monday: greyhound, keeshond
       Tuesday: Labrador retriever, poodle
       Wednesday: husky, schnauzer
   (C) Monday: keeshond, schnauzer
       Tuesday: greyhound, husky
       Wednesday: Labrador retriever, poodle
   (D) Monday: Labrador retriever, poodle
       Tuesday: greyhound, keeshond
       Wednesday: husky, schnauzer
   (E) Monday: Labrador retriever, poodle
       Tuesday: husky, keeshond
       Wednesday: greyhound, schnauzer

8. Which one of the following must be true?

   (A) The keeshond is not placed on the same day as the greyhound.
   (B) The keeshond is not placed on the same day as the schnauzer.
   (C) The schnauzer is not placed on the same day as the husky.
   (D) The greyhound is placed on the same day as the schnauzer.
   (E) The husky is placed on the same day as the keeshond.

9. If the poodle is placed on Tuesday, then which one of the following could be true?

   (A) The greyhound is placed on Monday.
   (B) The keeshond is placed on Monday.
   (C) The Labrador retriever is placed on Monday.
   (D) The husky is placed on Tuesday.
   (E) The schnauzer is placed on Wednesday.

10. If the greyhound is placed on the same day as the keeshond, then which one of the following must be true?

    (A) The husky is placed on Monday.
    (B) The Labrador retriever is placed on Monday.
    (C) The keeshond is placed on Tuesday.
    (D) The poodle is not placed on Wednesday.
    (E) The schnauzer is not placed on Wednesday.

11. If the husky is placed the day before the schnauzer, then which one of the following CANNOT be true?

    (A) The husky is placed on Monday.
    (B) The keeshond is placed on Monday.
    (C) The greyhound is placed on Tuesday.
    (D) The poodle is placed on Tuesday.
    (E) The poodle is placed on Wednesday.

12. If the greyhound is placed the day before the poodle, then which one of the following CANNOT be placed on Tuesday?

    (A) the husky
    (B) the keeshond
    (C) the Labrador retriever
    (D) the poodle
    (E) the schnauzer[4]

Answer Explanations follow on the next page.

Explanations

STEPS 1 and 2: Overview and Sketch

The similarities between this game and Museum Field Trip game are overwhelming. In both cases, six entities are grouped into three pairs and each pair assigned under a designated heading. It makes no difference at all that the headings were people in the prior game but days of the week in this one. If you called Margoles "Ms. Monday" or O'Connell "Mr. Tuesday," you'd wind up with exactly the same initial framework.

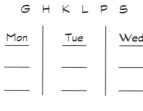

Figure 10.14

The more practice you do, the more these common patterns will show themselves and the greater your efficiency and confidence in setting up games will be.

STEP 3: Rules

The four rules from this game are about as typical a set of Distribution restrictions as you'll find. One establishes a pair of entities that must be together, one keeps a pair of entities apart, and two impose conditional restrictions on the distribution of pairs among the days of the week.

Rule 1 creates the established pairing.

Figure 10.15

Rule 2 designates the "impossible pair."

Figure 10.16

Rules 3 and 4 both involve formal logic. As you learned to do in Part I, translate each into "if then" notation and record its contrapositive as well.

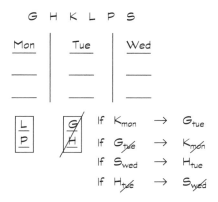

Figure 10.17

Those last two rules are the only ones that associate the entities—the dogs—with particular days of the week. Since they're conditional, you can anticipate a number of "if" questions here, each of which will designate the placement of certain dogs on certain days and reward you for being able to determine the implications of those designations.

STEP 4: Deductions

Each acceptable solution to this game's task will include three pairs. One of those pairs is established by Rule 1. Think about that in conjunction with Rule 2, and you'll realize that there are only two ways in which the remaining four dogs can be paired up. Since G and H must be kept apart, each will be paired with either K or S. There you have it.

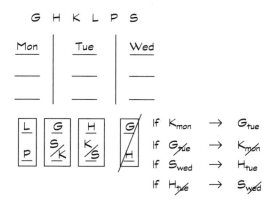

Figure 10.18

From here on out, everything in the game will focus on either those two possible pairings or on which days the various pairs are placed. "If" question stems will trigger the conditions in Rules 3 and 4, and you'll be able to figure out any and all of the acceptable arrangements easily.

STEP 5: Questions

Given that it's the formal logic rules that remain in play, it's no surprise to see that four of six questions here involve new "if" conditions. Knock out the Acceptability question and the one *must be true* example first, and then get ready to make several mini-sketches.

7. **(E)**

    Which one of the following could be a complete and accurate matching of dogs to the days on which they are placed?

    (A) Monday: greyhound, Labrador retriever
         Tuesday: husky, poodle
         Wednesday: keeshond, schnauzer
    (B) Monday: greyhound, keeshond
         Tuesday: Labrador retriever, poodle
         Wednesday: husky, schnauzer
    (C) Monday: keeshond, schnauzer
         Tuesday: greyhound, husky
         Wednesday: Labrador retriever, poodle
    (D) Monday: Labrador retriever, poodle
         Tuesday: greyhound, keeshond
         Wednesday: husky, schnauzer
    (E) Monday: Labrador retriever, poodle
         Tuesday: husky, keeshond
         Wednesday: greyhound, schnauzer[5]

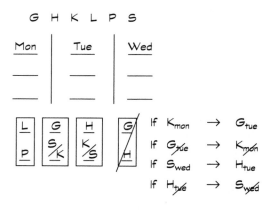

Figure 10.19

With four rules and four wrong answers, you should know what to anticipate from this Acceptability question: Look to knock out one violator with each rule. Rule 1 gets rid of choice (A); L and P aren't together there. Rule 2 gets rid of choice (C); G and H cannot be together. Rule

---

[5] PrepTest 44, Sec. 3, Q 7

3 eliminates choice (B), which has K on Monday but doesn't have G on Tuesday. And Rule 4 knocks out choice (D), where S is on Wednesday but H isn't on Tuesday. That leaves the correct answer, choice (E).

8. **(B)**

Which one of the following must be true?

(A)   The keeshond is not placed on the same day as the greyhound.
(B)   The keeshond is not placed on the same day as the schnauzer.
(C)   The schnauzer is not placed on the same day as the husky.
(D)   The greyhound is placed on the same day as the schnauzer.
(E)   The husky is placed on the same day as the keeshond.[6]

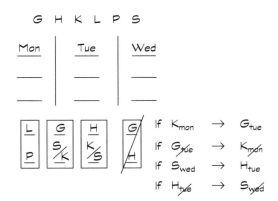

Figure 10.20

This question directly rewards the one big deduction you were able to make in Step 4 of the Kaplan Method. Just look at your diagram of the possible pairings, and you'll see that K and S must be placed on separate days. That's choice (B), the correct answer to this *must be true* question. You should even have been able to predict the four wrong answers here, one for each of the acceptable pairs: G is able to be placed on the same day as either K, choice (A), or S, choice (D); likewise, H can be placed on the same day as either K, choice (E), or as S, choice (C).

9. **(A)**

If the poodle is placed on Tuesday, then which one of the following could be true?

(A)   The greyhound is placed on Monday.
(B)   The keeshond is placed on Monday.
(C)   The Labrador retriever is placed on Monday.
(D)   The husky is placed on Tuesday.
(E)   The schnauzer is placed on Wednesday.[7]

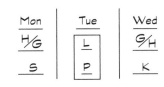

Figure 10.21

From here on out, it's all "If" questions. Begin your mini-sketch for this one with the information from the question stem.

6 PrepTest 44, Sec. 3, Q 8
7 PrepTest 44, Sec. 3, Q 9

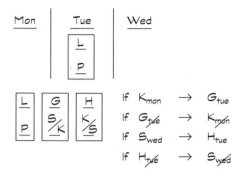

Figure 10.22

With P and, of course, L placed on Tuesday, Tuesday is full. That triggers the contrapositive of Rule 3. When G isn't placed on Tuesday, K can't be placed on Monday. Therefore, K (along with either G or H, to keep those two apart) is placed on Wednesday.

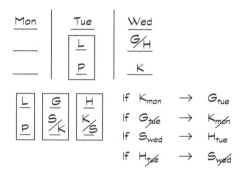

Figure 10.23

That means that S will go on Monday, along with either G or H.

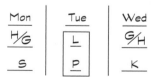

Figure 10.24

Since this is a *could be true* question, you should expect the correct answer to involve either G or H, the two dogs whose placement hasn't been established. Choice (A) is the right answer. G could be placed on Monday as the mini-sketch shows. The other four answers all *must be false*. Choice (D) mentions H but tries to place it on Tuesday, which is already occupied by L and P.

10. **(E)**

If the greyhound is placed on the same day as the keeshond, then which one of the following must be true?

(A) The husky is placed on Monday.
(B) The Labrador retriever is placed on Monday.
(C) The keeshond is placed on Tuesday.
(D) The poodle is not placed on Wednesday.
(E) The schnauzer is not placed on Wednesday.[8]

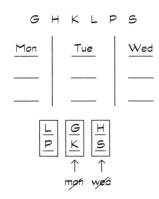

Figure 10.25

This time, the "if" establishes another pairing of dogs. If G and K are together, then so are H and S. Your three pairs are certain.

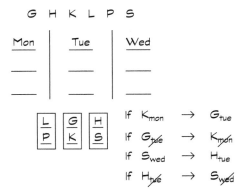

Figure 10.26

You can't know exactly the precise days on which any of the pairs are placed, but there are a couple of possibilities you can rule out. Rule 3 prevents the K-G pair from going on Monday, since placing K on Monday would mean placing G on Tuesday. Likewise, Rule 4 prevents the H-S pair from going on Wednesday, since placing S on Wednesday means placing H on Tuesday.

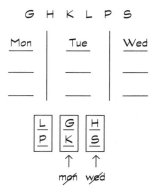

Figure 10.27

That's plenty of information to answer the question. The correct answer *must be true*. You know from the mini-sketch that S cannot be placed on Wednesday, and that's exactly what choice (E) says. All of the remaining choices could be true or false under the conditions established by this question stem.

11. **(D)**

If the husky is placed the day before the schnauzer, then which one of the following CANNOT be true?

(A) The husky is placed on Monday.
(B) The keeshond is placed on Monday.
(C) The greyhound is placed on Tuesday.
(D) The poodle is placed on Tuesday.
(E) The poodle is placed on Wednesday.[9]

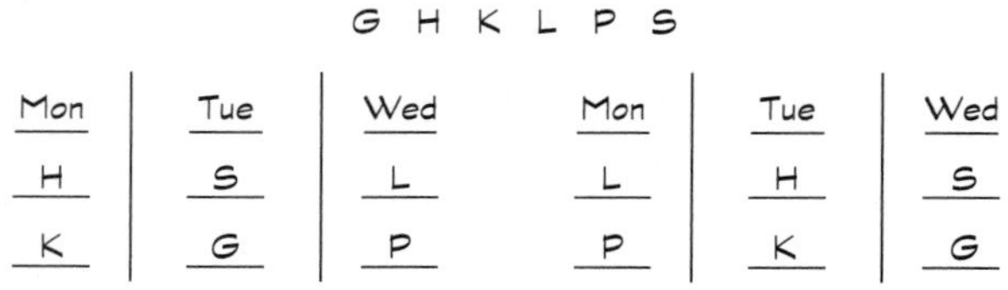

Figure 10.28

There are two ways to accommodate this "if": H on Monday and S on Tuesday or H on Tuesday and S on Wednesday. Jot down both.

G H K L P S

Mon	Tue	Wed	Mon	Tue	Wed
H	S	___	___	H	S
___	___	___	___	___	___

Figure 10.29

Since S isn't with H in either case, it has to be with G, and K has to be with H.

GHKLPS

Mon	Tue	Wed	Mon	Tue	Wed
H	S	___	___	H	S
K	G	___	___	K	G

Figure 10.30

The remaining day—Wednesday in the first scenario, Monday in the second—belongs to the L-P pairing.

GHKLPS

Mon	Tue	Wed	Mon	Tue	Wed
H	S	L	L	H	S
K	G	P	P	K	G

Figure 10.31

That's a perfect picture of the two acceptable arrangements allowed by this question stem. Now, characterize the answer choices. The correct answer *must be false*. That fits choice (D), which cannot happen under either alternative. The other four choices are all possible in one of the two options acceptable here.

12. **(A)**

If the greyhound is placed the day before the poodle, then which one of the following CANNOT be placed on Tuesday?

(A)   the husky
(B)   the keeshond
(C)   the Labrador retriever
(D)   the poodle
(E)   the schnauzer[10]

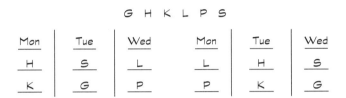

Figure 10.32

The "if" for this question works the same way as the one in question 11 did. G and P are either on Monday and Tuesday or on Tuesday and Wednesday, respectively.

Mon	Tue	Wed	Mon	Tue	Wed
G	P	___	___	G	P
___	___	___	___	___	___

Figure 10.33

---

[10] PrepTest 44, Sec. 3, Q 12

You know from the Master Sketch that either K or S accompanies G and that L always accompanies P.

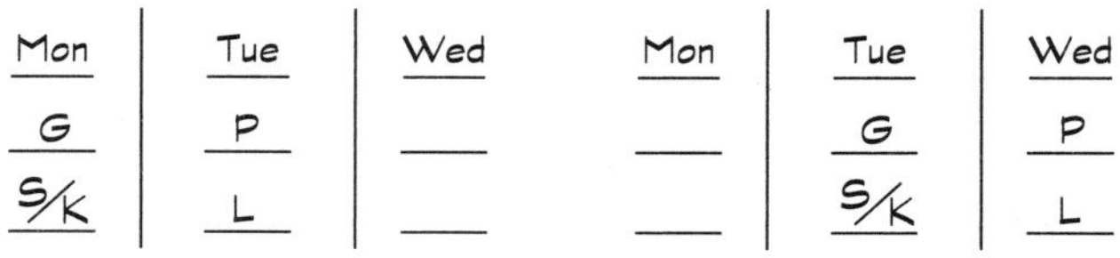

Mon	Tue	Wed	Mon	Tue	Wed
G	P	___	___	G	P
S/K	L	___	___	S/K	L

Figure 10.34

Now, H (along with either K or S) will take Monday or Wednesday, depending on which alternative you're considering.

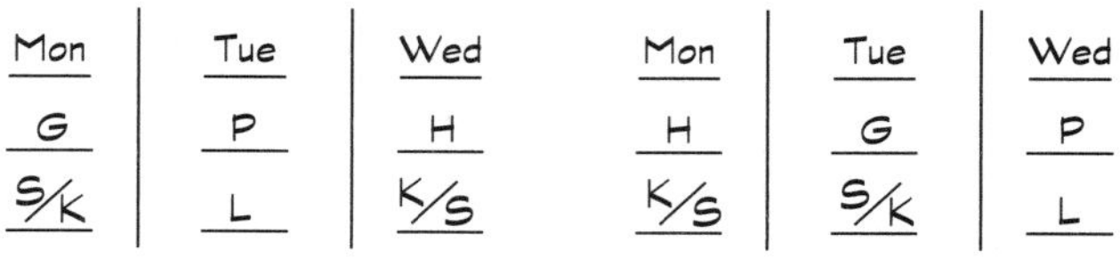

Mon	Tue	Wed	Mon	Tue	Wed
G	P	H	H	G	P
S/K	L	K/S	K/S	S/K	L

Figure 10.35

This time, the question asks for a dog that can *never* be placed on Tuesday. The only one ruled out is H, and that's the correct answer, choice (A). Every other dog can find its way to a Tuesday placement here. The four wrong answers *could be true.*

The two games you just saw began from almost exactly the same premise: Six entities will be distributed among three groups. The certainty with which the numbers were determined—two entities per group—allowed you to focus on two factors: the group to which an entity was assigned or the other entity it was paired with. Not every Distribution game with definite numbers will place pairs of entities—it could be trios of entities, or it could be two entities in two groups and three entities in another, or whatever. In any case, it is always helpful to have definite numbers in Distribution games. You can always take advantage of that clear restriction by drawing the slots that the entities will occupy into your Master Sketch. You'll know, too, to expect rules that affect the relationships between or among entities, as well as rules that require or forbid certain group assignments.

Now, turn your attention to the more common Distribution variation, in which the numbers aren't so definite at the outset. As you'll see, your Deductions step will be aimed at giving as much certainty as possible to numbers in each group.

Distribution with Ambiguous Numbers

Just as your boss left it up to you to determine how many employees should be assigned to each task in the "real-life" example near the beginning of this chapter, most Distribution games leave it up to you to determine how many entities can go in each group. But while the test makers don't tell you explicitly how many entities to assign per group, the rules always ensure that some restrictions within the numbers exist. Think about it like this: Any rule that tells you to keep two entities apart from one another is, at the same time, telling you that two of the groups get at least one entity each. To see this in action, look back at the Talent Agency game you learned to set up in Part I.

> Five performers—Traugott, West, Xavier, Young, and Zinser—are recruited by three talent agencies—Fame Agency, Premier Agency, and Star Agency. Each performer signs with exactly one of the agencies and each agency signs at least one of the performers. The performers' signing with the agencies is in accord with the following:
>> Xavier signs with Fame Agency.
>> Xavier and Young do not sign with the same agency as each other.
>> Zinser signs with the same agency as Young.
>> If Traugott signs with Star Agency, West also signs with Star Agency.[11]

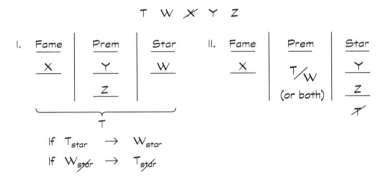

Figure 10.36

Here, the first three rules allow you to create Limited Options sketches. X has to be placed with Fame, while Y must avoid X. That leaves only Premier or Star available for Y. Since Z accompanies Y, you have two options that account for three of the entities, for sure. Since the opening description of this game tells you that "each agency signs at least one of the performers," the number arrangements here are nearly set. In Option I, W has to sign with Star. To follow Rule 3, W will sign with Star if T does, and to ensure that Star represents at least one performer, W will have to sign there if T doesn't. Depending on where T is assigned in Option I, the number of performers per agency will be 2-2-1, 1-3-1, or 1-2-2 for Fame, Premier, and Star, respectively.

In Option II, placing T with Star is impossible (since Rule 3 would require W to be placed with Star as well, leaving Premier with no performers). So in this option, the possible number arrangements are 2-1-2, 1-2-2, or 1-1-3 for Fame, Premier, and Star, respectively, depending on where T and W wind up.

---

[11] PrepTest 53, Sec. 2, Game 1

The constant interplay between acceptable pairings of entities and the minimum and maximum number of entities per group is the feature that allows you to take full control of the acceptable and unacceptable arrangements within the game. The test directly rewards your understanding of that interplay, as these two problems illustrate. Take a minute to get familiar with the questions and then read the explanations that follow.

2. Which one of the following could be true?

    (A)   West is the only performer who signs with Star Agency.
    (B)   West, Young, and Zinser all sign with Premier Agency.
    (C)   Xavier signs with the same agency as Zinser.
    (D)   Zinser is the only performer who signs with Star Agency.
    (E)   Three of the performers sign with Fame Agency.

3. Which one of the following must be true?

    (A)   West and Zinser do not sign with the same agency as each other.
    (B)   Fame Agency signs at most two of the performers.
    (C)   Fame Agency signs the same number of the performers as Star Agency.
    (D)   Traugott signs with the same agency as West.
    (E)   West does not sign with Fame Agency.[12]

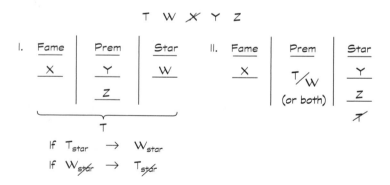

Figure 10.37

Choice (A) is the correct answer to question 2. W could be the one performer assigned to Star in Option I. Choice (B) is the correct answer to question 3. In either option, Fame cannot sign more than two of the performers. After all, in Option I, only T remains to be placed. In Option II, if Fame takes both T and W, no one is left to sign with Premier. Those questions illustrate just how central the issue of numbers is for all Distribution games. Whenever the test makers leave the numbers open, they'll design questions to reward you for determining any and all restrictions on the possible number of entities per group.

[12] PrepTest 53, Sec. 2, Qs 2–3

Distribution with Ambiguous Numbers Practice

The following game echoes the task of the Talent Agency game almost exactly. There are five entities (pieces of mail now, instead of performers) to distribute among three groups (housemates this time, instead of agencies). You can start with an identical framework. The rules are different, of course, because the test makers don't copy games exactly from one test to another. But one restriction (the most important one) remains the same: Each group (housemate, agency) is assigned at least one entity (piece of mail, performer). Use that as the starting point for your assessment of the acceptable number arrangements.

Give yourself eight and a half minutes to try this game (on the next page) and its question set. If you find that you're getting stuck, stop and review the explanations for Steps 1–4 of the Kaplan Method. Then return to the question set and see if you can finish it once you're clear on the deductions and Master Sketch.

There are exactly five pieces of mail in a mailbox: a flyer, a letter, a magazine, a postcard, and a survey. Each piece of mail is addressed to exactly one of three housemates: Georgette, Jana, or Rini. Each housemate has at least one of the pieces of mail addressed to her. The following conditions must apply:

> Neither the letter nor the magazine is addressed to Georgette.
> If the letter is addressed to Rini, then the postcard is addressed to Jana.
> The housemate to whom the flyer is addressed has at least one of the other pieces of mail addressed to her as well.

8. Which one of the following could be a complete and accurate matching of the pieces of mail to the housemates to whom they are addressed?

   (A)   Georgette: the flyer, the survey
         Jana: the letter
         Rini: the magazine
   (B)   Georgette: the flyer, the postcard
         Jana: the letter, the magazine
         Rini: the survey
   (C)   Georgette: the magazine, the survey
         Jana: the flyer, the letter
         Rini: the postcard
   (D)   Georgette: the survey
         Jana: the flyer, the magazine
         Rini: the letter, the postcard
   (E)   Georgette: the survey
         Jana: the letter, the magazine, the postcard
         Rini: the flyer

9. Which one of the following is a complete and accurate list of the pieces of mail, any one of which could be the only piece of mail addressed to Jana?

   (A)   the postcard
   (B)   the letter, the postcard
   (C)   the letter, the survey
   (D)   the magazine, the survey
   (E)   the letter, the magazine, the postcard

10. Which one of the following CANNOT be a complete and accurate list of the pieces of mail addressed to Jana?

    (A)   the flyer, the letter, the magazine
    (B)   the flyer, the letter, the postcard
    (C)   the flyer, the letter, the survey
    (D)   the flyer, the magazine, the postcard
    (E)   the flyer, the magazine, the survey

11. Which one of the following CANNOT be a complete and accurate list of the pieces of mail addressed to Rini?

    (A)   the magazine, the postcard
    (B)   the letter, the survey
    (C)   the letter, the magazine
    (D)   the flyer, the magazine
    (E)   the flyer, the letter

12. If the magazine and the survey are both addressed to the same housemate, then which one of the following could be true?

    (A)   The survey is addressed to Georgette.
    (B)   The postcard is addressed to Rini.
    (C)   The magazine is addressed to Jana.
    (D)   The letter is addressed to Rini.
    (E)   The flyer is addressed to Jana.[13]

Answer Explanations follow on the next page.

Explanations

STEPS 1 and 2: Overview and Sketch

The situation described here is almost certainly something you've done in real life. You go to the mailbox to find five pieces of mail. You check who each one is addressed to and place them on that person's desk or dresser. As you start to draw a framework for this information, you'll see a picture that looks almost exactly like that described in the Talent Agency game.

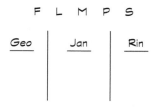

Figure 10.38

Beyond telling you that each piece of mail is addressed to one of the housemates and that each housemate gets at least one piece of mail, the setup gives you no guidance on the number limitations. So there's no way to add more than one slot under each housemate's name. You can anticipate learning more about the number possibilities from the rules and deductions, though.

STEP 3: Rules

Draw out each of the rules one at a time.

The first rule gives you two negative restrictions. You won't deliver L or M to Georgette.

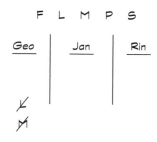

Figure 10.39

Rule 2 is conditional. Translate it into formal logic notation, and determine its contrapositive at the same time.

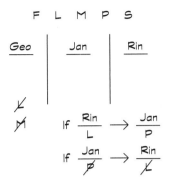

Figure 10.40

Rule 3 is verbose, but you can paraphrase it into a very simple restriction. F is delivered with at least one other piece of mail. No housemate will receive only F.

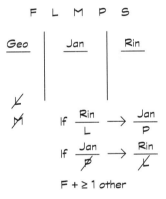

Figure 10.41

STEP 4: Deductions

Three of the five elements of the BLEND checklist are of little or no help to you here. The only block is created by Rule 3, and it tells you only that F is delivered as a block with one of the other pieces of mail; it doesn't tell you which one. There are no rules here that lead to a Limited Options scenario or that give you an Established Entity. So you won't have as complete-looking a Master Sketch as you did in the Talent Agency game. One area in which you can gain some traction is in the Number Restrictions. Because of Rule 3 and the limitation that requires each housemate to receive at least one piece of mail, you can be sure that the numbers will play out in one of two ways: Either two housemates will receive one piece of mail each and one will receive three, or one housemate will receive one piece of mail and the other two housemates will receive two pieces each. It's also worth noting that L is duplicated in Rules 1 and 2. L will be delivered to either Jana or Rini. And when Rini receives L, Jana has to get P.

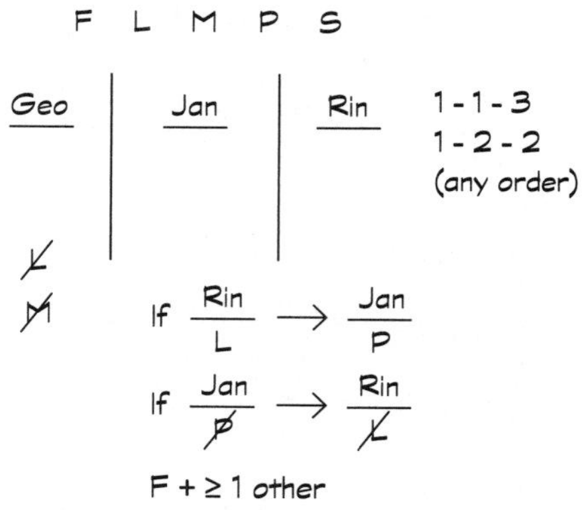

Figure 10.42

Make note of those two possible patterns within the numbers and move on to the questions.

STEP 5: Questions

The questions in this game are a little unusual. You might well have anticipated seeing three or four "if" stems in a game with this few deductions. Instead, the test makers give you three variations on the Complete and Accurate List question type. With a set of questions like this one, you'll be more efficient if you take on the Acceptability question and the "if" question first and then move on to the rarer Complete and Accurate List items.

8. **(B)**

Which one of the following could be a complete and accurate matching of the pieces of mail to the housemates to whom they are addressed?

(A) Georgette: the flyer, the survey
Jana: the letter
Rini: the magazine
(B) Georgette: the flyer, the postcard
Jana: the letter, the magazine
Rini: the survey
(C) Georgette: the magazine, the survey
Jana: the flyer, the letter
Rini: the postcard
(D) Georgette: the survey
Jana: the flyer, the magazine
Rini: the letter, the postcard
(E) Georgette: the survey
Jana: the letter, the magazine, the postcard
Rini: the flyer[14]

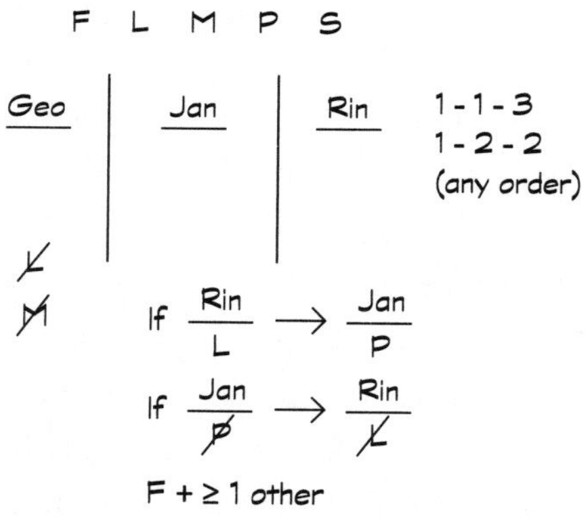

Figure 10.43

In any Acceptability question, use the rules to eliminate answer choices that violate them. Here, Rule 1 knocks out choice (C), where Georgette receives M. Rule 2 eliminates choice (D), where Rini receives L but Jana doesn't get P. Rule 3 knocks out choice (E), where F is delivered alone. How can it be that you have gone through the rules but still have two choices left? Well, remember that the game's opening paragraph contains two more restrictions: Each housemate gets a piece of mail and all five pieces of mail need to be distributed. That helps you see that choice (A) is also impossible. It overlooks P and has only four pieces of mail delivered. Cross out choice (A), and you see that choice (B) is the correct answer here.

12. **(E)**

If the magazine and the survey are both addressed to the same housemate, then which one of the following could be true?

(A) The survey is addressed to Georgette.
(B) The postcard is addressed to Rini.
(C) The magazine is addressed to Jana.
(D) The letter is addressed to Rini.
(E) The flyer is addressed to Jana.[15]

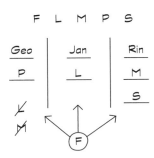

Figure 10.44

The "if" in this stem doesn't seem to assign any pieces of mail to a particular housemate, but don't be too hasty. Work through the deductions that follow from this "if," and you'll actually get quite a bit of certainty. Start by adding the "If" condition as a new rule.

Figure 10.45

Since Georgette is forbidden from receiving M, the newly formed M-S block must be delivered to either Jana or Rini.

---

[15] PrepTest 49, Sec. 1, Q 12

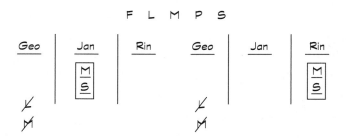

Figure 10.46

It only takes a moment to see that the first of these alternatives is impossible under the rules. F will have to be delivered along with L, P, or the M-S block. If you give P to Rini, there's nothing left that Georgette can receive. If you give L to Rini, on the other hand, P must go to Jana under the terms of Rule 2. Again, Georgette would be shut out.

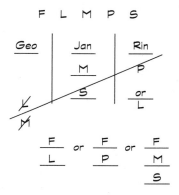

Figure 10.47

With only the second possibility in play, you can nearly complete the sketch. Georgette can't receive L, so she must get either F and P or just P as her mail.

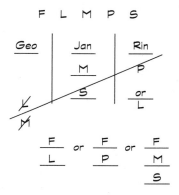

Figure 10.48

That leaves either F and L or just L as Jana's mail.

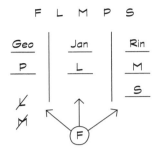

Figure 10.49

Now, characterize the answers and evaluate the choices. The correct answer here *could be true*. The four wrong answers *must be false*. Given that the right answer could be true, you should suspect that F is involved. After all, it's the only entity that isn't locked down. Indeed, choice (E), the only answer that includes F, is correct. Check the other four answers against the mini-sketch if you like; all four are impossible there.

Now, back up to the three Complete and Accurate List questions from this game.

9. **(B)**

    Which one of the following is a complete and accurate list of the pieces of mail, any one of which could be the only piece of mail addressed to Jana?

    (A) the postcard
    (B) the letter, the postcard
    (C) the letter, the survey
    (D) the magazine, the survey
    (E) the letter, the magazine, the postcard[16]

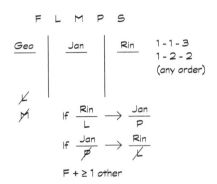

Figure 10.50

With any question of this kind, make sure you read the question stem carefully so that you know what will distinguish the one right answer from the four wrong ones. In question 9, the correct answer contains any and all pieces of mail that could be the *only* one Jana receives. You know from your mini-sketch for question 12 that it would be acceptable for her to receive only L.

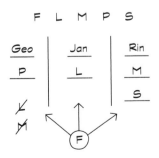

Figure 10.51

---

[16] PrepTest 49, Sec. 1, Q 9

That allows you to eliminate choices (A) and (D), both of which exclude L from the list.

Next, test P, which appears in both choice (B) and choice (E). If she can receive only P, you can eliminate choice (D). If she cannot receive only P, choice (D) is the correct answer. Giving only P to Jana leaves F, L, M, and S to be delivered. Georgette can't receive either L or M, so she'll have to get F and S. Rini would receive L and M in this situation.

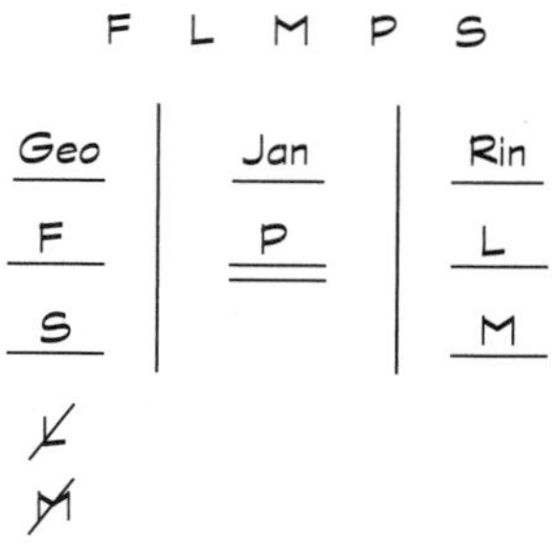

Figure 10.52

That arrangement abides by all of the rules, so P must be included in your complete and accurate list. Eliminate choice (D).

The only thing that distinguishes choices (B) and (E) is the presence of M in choice (E). It doesn't take long to see why M cannot be on the list. Try making M the only piece of mail Jana receives. In that case, you'd have to give L to Rini (L can never go to Georgette because of Rule 1). But Rule 2 says that when Rini receives L, Jana gets P. So M cannot be the *only* piece of mail Jana receives. Eliminate choice (E).

Choice (B), with L and P, is the correct answer. Only those two pieces of mail could be Jana's only deliveries.

10. **(E)**

Which one of the following CANNOT be a complete and accurate list of the pieces of mail addressed to Jana?

(A) the flyer, the letter, the magazine
(B) the flyer, the letter, the postcard
(C) the flyer, the letter, the survey
(D) the flyer, the magazine, the postcard
(E) the flyer, the magazine, the survey[17]

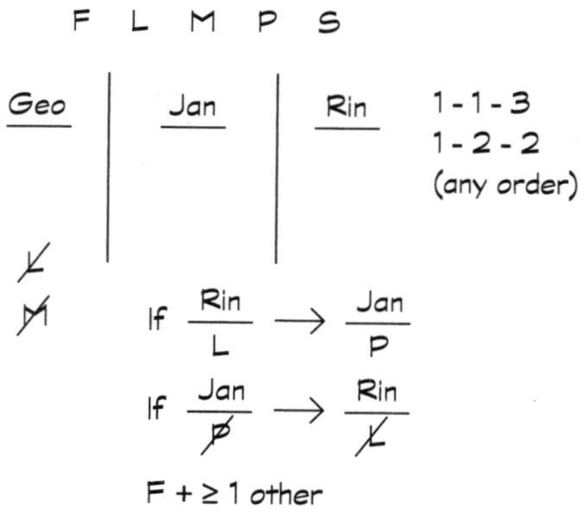

Figure 10.53

[17] PrepTest 49, Sec. 1, Q 10

For the untrained test taker (or for the test taker who isn't trained in the Kaplan Method and strategies), this question is a nightmare. The correct answer is the one that *cannot* be Jana's mail. Most test takers will have no choice but to start testing the answers. But you, realizing how important the numbers are, can be much more efficient. Each of these answer choices contains three entities, leaving only two to distribute. Take a moment to jot down which pieces of mail are left over next to each of the answer choices.

The answer that should now pop out to you is choice (E). With L and P left to distribute to Georgette and Rini, you've got a problem. Georgette can't get L, and when Rini gets L, Jana has to receive P (Rule 2), leaving Georgette with no mail. There's simply no way you can acceptably deliver F, M, and S to Jana, so choice (E) is the correct answer.

11. **(B)**

Which one of the following CANNOT be a complete and accurate list of the pieces of mail addressed to Rini?

(A)   the magazine, the postcard
(B)   the letter, the survey
(C)   the letter, the magazine
(D)   the flyer, the magazine
(E)   the flyer, the letter[18]

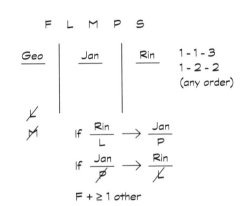

Figure 10.54

Here again, the correct choice is a list that cannot be acceptable. And again, the only option available to most test takers is a random, hunt-and-peck approach that will have them testing answers in the hope of finding the one that won't work out. You can be much more strategic. Consider who is mentioned in the question stem: Rini, who triggers Rule 2 when she receives L. Take a moment to think about the implications of L being delivered to Rini. In that case, Jana gets P.

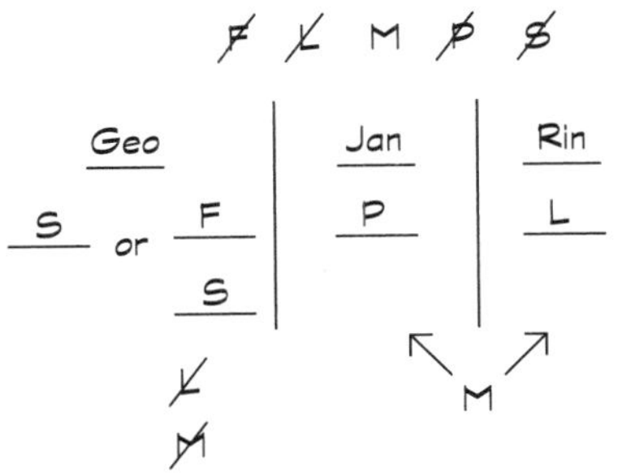

Figure 10.55

That leaves F, M, and S to be delivered. Georgette needs to get mail, but she cannot be the recipient of M. That means she needs to get just S or F and S (since F cannot be delivered alone, according to Rule 3). Either way, Rini cannot get L and S at the same time. Choice (B) is the correct answer.

Comparing the Housemates' Mail game with the Talent Agencies game is a good exercise in seeing how the test makers can re-use a game format, and yet make one of the two games harder than the other. Housemates' Mail is harder, in part, because of its tough question set. But it also lacks some of the helpful rules (a definite Block of Entities, a key entity that leads to Limited Options) that gave the Talent Agencies game a clearer Master Sketch. What I hope is clear is that when the test makers do not define the number of entities per group, you should turn your attention to determining the number restrictions as best you can. Once you can see the minimum and maximum number of entities that a given group can take, you're able to eliminate many potential arrangements.

In recent years, the test makers have been much more likely to offer Distribution games that lack definite numbers. These games vary in difficulty, but for the most part, they're harder than those that set out a set number of entities per group. In the next section, I'll have you go back a ways to try your hand with one of the toughest Distribution games the test makers have ever devised.

DIFFICULT DISTRIBUTION

Unlike Sequencing games, the test makers don't seem to go out of their way to find many obscure twists on Distribution games. When they want to make them more challenging, they simply take one of the standard variations—with or without definite numbers—and make the game less concrete. In the one you're about to try, for example, you get no help from number restrictions in the setup text, and all five of the rules are conditional formal logic statements. Brace yourself for a challenge, but don't feel overwhelmed. You mastered the formal logic element back in chapter 3. Now, apply that expertise. See how the rules interact to give you more certainty, especially as regards the number restrictions.

Don't time yourself as you try this tough example. Approach it strategically and put each step of the Kaplan Method to work for you. Once you have a strong Master Sketch, you'll find that the questions are actually fairly straightforward. There's no trickery involved on the part of the test makers, just a challenging version of a standard game type. If you find yourself struggling with the questions, check through the explanations for Steps 1–4 of the Kaplan Method. Once you're sure you've got the ideal Master Sketch, return to the question set and get the points.

Each of exactly six doctors—Juarez, Kudrow, Longtree, Nance, Onawa, and Palermo—is at exactly one of two clinics: Souderton or Randsborough. The following conditions must be satisfied:

> Kudrow is at Randsborough if Juarez is at Souderton.
> Onawa is at Souderton if Juarez is at Randsborough.
> If Longtree is at Souderton, then both Nance and Palermo are at Randsborough.
> If Nance is at Randsborough, then so is Onawa.
> If Palermo is at Randsborough, then both Kudrow and Onawa are at Souderton.

19. Which one of the following could be a complete and accurate list of the doctors that are at Souderton?

    (A) Juarez, Kudrow, Onawa
    (B) Juarez, Nance, Onawa, Palermo
    (C) Kudrow, Longtree, Onawa
    (D) Nance, Onawa
    (E) Nance, Palermo

20. If Palermo is at Randsborough, then which one of the following must be true?

    (A) Juarez is at Randsborough.
    (B) Kudrow is at Randsborough.
    (C) Longtree is at Souderton.
    (D) Nance is at Randsborough.
    (E) Onawa is at Randsborough.

21. What is the minimum number of doctors that could be at Souderton?

    (A) zero
    (B) one
    (C) two
    (D) three
    (E) four

22. If Nance and Onawa are at different clinics, which one of the following must be true?

    (A) Juarez is at Souderton.
    (B) Kudrow is at Souderton.
    (C) Palermo is at Randsborough.
    (D) Four doctors are at Souderton.
    (E) Four doctors are at Randsborough.

23. Which one of the following CANNOT be a pair of the doctors at Randsborough?

    (A) Juarez and Kudrow
    (B) Juarez and Palermo
    (C) Kudrow and Onawa
    (D) Nance and Onawa
    (E) Nance and Palermo

24. If Kudrow is at Souderton, then which one of the following must be true?

    (A) Juarez is at Souderton.
    (B) Nance is at Souderton.
    (C) Onawa is at Randsborough.
    (D) Palermo is at Souderton.
    (E) Palermo is at Randsborough.[19]

Explanations

STEPS 1 AND 2: Overview and Sketch

You can't ask for a shorter setup or a clearer task from an LSAT logic game. There are two clinics and your job is to assign each of six doctors to one or the other. That task, no more complicated than separating whites and colors for the laundry or dividing friends into two teams for a board game, is easy to depict.

Figure 10.56

You'll just jot down each doctor under the headings for Souderton or Randsborough as you determine his or her placement. The one thing that's sorely missing, though, is any ability to determine how many of the doctors will be assigned to each clinic. From what you're given in the opening paragraph of this game, you could have 0 and 6, 1 and 5, 2 and 4, 3 and 3, 4 and 2, 5 and 1, or 6 and 0 of the doctors at Souderton and Randsborough, respectively. Steps 2 and 3 will have to reduce that daunting number of possibilities.

STEP 3: Rules

It doesn't take more than a glance to see that all of the rules here are conditional formal logic statements, although Rules 1 and 2 try to disguise this a little by placing the "if" clauses in the second half of the sentences.

You know what to do. Translate each of the rules and determine its contrapositive. Try as best you can to keep all of the "ifs" in a neat line so that you can see when the result of one rule triggers the "if" in another. Here's how you should depict the translations and contrapositives:

Rule 1:

$$\text{If } J_{sou} \rightarrow K_{ran}$$
$$\text{If } K_{sou} \rightarrow J_{ran}$$

Figure 10.57

Because there are only two possible placements for each doctor, and because all of the doctors will be placed, the negation of "K is at Randsborough" is, simply, "K is at Souderton." The negation of "J is at Souderton" is "J is at Randsborough." Keeping all of the formal logic in the affirmative makes it a lot easier to see the impact of each condition on the entities in the game. You'll notice that I will translate and contrapose the rules this way throughout the game.

Rule 2:

$$\text{If } J_{ran} \quad \rightarrow \quad O_{sou}$$
$$\text{If } O_{ran} \quad \rightarrow \quad J_{sou}$$

Figure 10.58

Rule 3:

$$\text{If } L_{sou} \quad \rightarrow \quad N_{ran} \text{ and } P_{ran}$$
$$\text{If } N_{sou} \text{ or } P_{sou} \quad \rightarrow \quad L_{ran}$$

Figure 10.59

Don't forget to change "and" to "or" when you contrapose clauses that contain more than one entity. Either N being placed at Souderton *or* P being placed there is sufficient to know that L must be placed at Randsborough. You don't need both of the triggers in the contrapositive to be true; just one is enough to trigger the result. The same is true of Rule 5, of course.

Rule 4:

$$\text{If } N_{ran} \quad \rightarrow \quad O_{ran}$$
$$\text{If } O_{sou} \quad \rightarrow \quad N_{sou}$$

Figure 10.60

Rule 5:

$$\text{If } P_{ran} \quad \rightarrow \quad K_{sou} \text{ and } O_{sou}$$
$$\text{If } K_{ran} \text{ or } O_{ran} \quad \rightarrow \quad P_{sou}$$

Figure 10.61

Most test takers, of course, cannot even get this far. But with your training, you can gain an even clearer picture of how this game will work out. Learning to front-load your work in Steps 1–4 of the Kaplan Method is probably the single most valuable lesson of this book when it comes to the most difficult games.

STEP 4: Deductions
Several of the rules in this game combine, and you could spend an inordinate amount of time working out all of the various possibilities. But the first two rules suggest an easy solution. The

trigger for Rule 1 is "J is at Souderton," and the trigger for Rule 2 is "J is at Randsborough." That makes an easy starting point for Limited Options sketches. Try them out. You're sure to gain some important insights into the arrangements acceptable in this game.

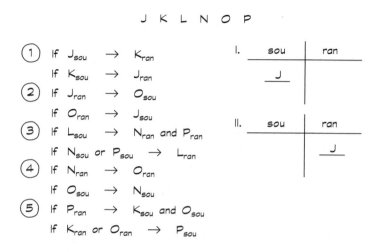

Figure 10.62

With J at Souderton, you know from Rule 1 that K is at Randsborough.

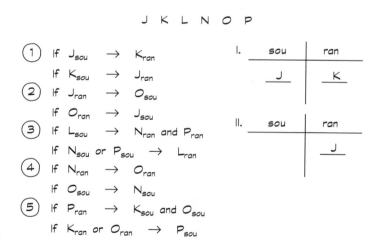

Figure 10.63

That, in turn, triggers the contrapositive of Rule 5. You can place P at Souderton, too. Notice how important it was to change that "and" into an "or" in the contrapositive of Rule 5.

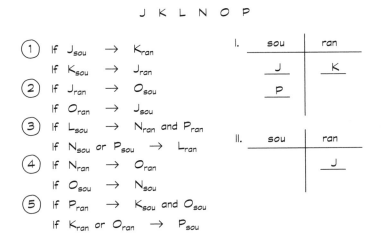

Figure 10.64

Placing P at Souderton means placing L at Randsborough. That's the contrapositive of Rule 3.

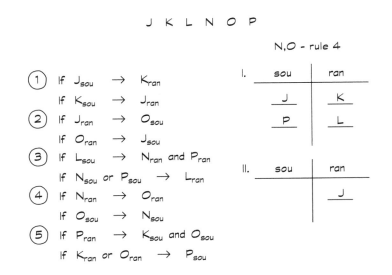

Figure 10.65

L's placement doesn't trigger any additional deductions. So Option I is complete, although it's worth noticing that the two entities that remain—N and O—restrict one another in Rule 4. Either they're together at one of the clinics, or N is at Souderton and O at Randsborough.

Go to work on Option II. With J at Randsborough, Rule 2 tells you to place O at Souderton.

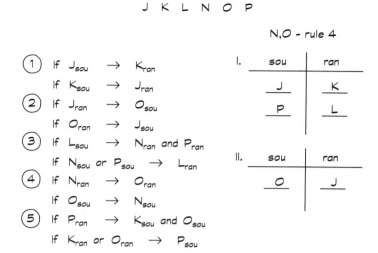

Figure 10.66

That requires N to be at Souderton as well, according to Rule 4.

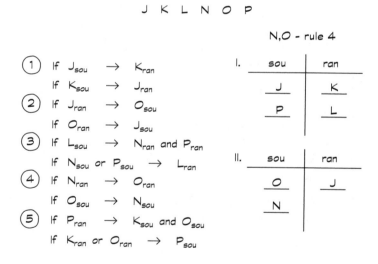

Figure 10.67

Placing N at Souderton triggers the contrapositive of Rule 3. L must take a place at Randsborough in this option.

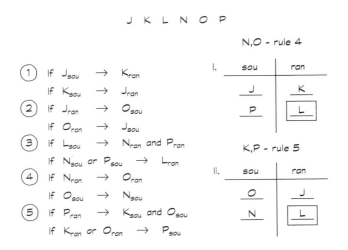

Figure 10.68

This is one of your breakthrough moments in this game. L, you now know, is always going to be placed at Randsborough because that must happen in both of your Limited Options. You've created an Established Entity in a game where you thought none existed.

You can't push Option II any farther, but here again, the two entities that remain—K and P—limit one another, this time in Rule 5: P is at Randsborough with K at Souderton, K is at Randsborough with P at Souderton, or P and K are together at Souderton.

When all is said and done (and deduced!), this game has only six acceptable arrangements. You could even list them out:

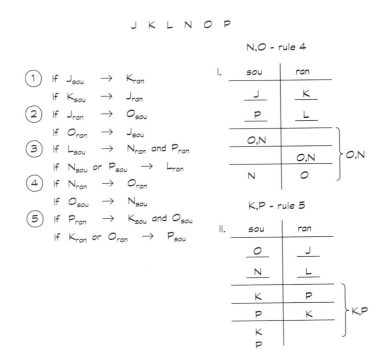

Figure 10.69

Whether you go to that extent or not, you'd do well to note that the possible number restrictions are down to 2 and 4, 3 and 3, or 4 and 2 of the doctors at Souderton and Randsborough, respectively.

STEP 5: Questions

This is a balanced question set: One Partial Acceptability, three "Ifs," one Minimum/Maximum, and one Must Be False question. There's no reason to take the questions out of order here. Given the Limited Options sketches you spent time making during Step 4, you should be prepared to tackle them all without hesitation. This is the payoff for your patience in Steps 1–4, and it's where you'll outshine your competition come test day on a game like this one.

19. **(B)**

Which one of the following could be a complete and accurate list of the doctors that are at Souderton?

(A) Juarez, Kudrow, Onawa
(B) Juarez, Nance, Onawa, Palermo
(C) Kudrow, Longtree, Onawa
(D) Nance, Onawa
(E) Nance, Palermo[20]

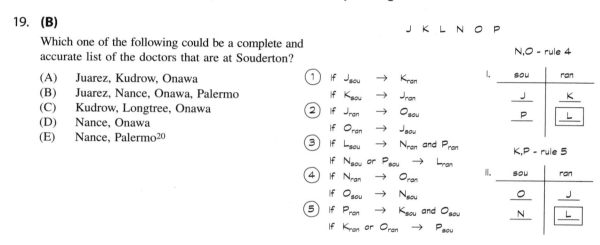

Figure 10.70

This is a Partial Acceptability question. In this case, use your Master Sketch to eliminate the violators. It's tough to apply the rules when only one side of the Distribution is visible in the answer choices, but in your sketch, you can zero in on Souderton and easily spot the unacceptable groupings there. First, L can never appear at Souderton, so cross out choice (C). Next, notice that when J is at Souderton (that's Option I, of course), P must be there, too. Eliminate choice (A), which has J but lacks P. The three remaining choices all contain N. You may notice that choice (B) is acceptable under Option I. Or you may eliminate choices (D) and (E) because neither N and O nor N and P can ever be the *only* entities at Souderton. Either way, choice (B) is the correct answer. Your Limited Options deductions will continue to pay dividends right down the line.

---

[20] PrepTest 34, Sec. 4, Q 19

20. **(A)**

If Palermo is at Randsborough, then which one of the following must be true?

(A) Juarez is at Randsborough.
(B) Kudrow is at Randsborough.
(C) Longtree is at Souderton.
(D) Nance is at Randsborough.
(E) Onawa is at Randsborough.[21]

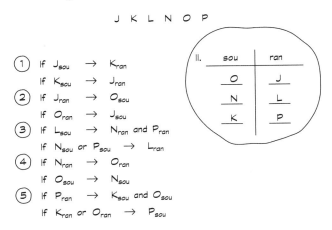

Figure 10.71

A quick check of the Master Sketch shows that P can only be assigned to Randsborough in Option II. When P is at Randsborough, Rule 5 requires that K be at Souderton. Now, you have the complete mini-sketch above. Choice (A), which is the very definition of Option II, *must be true*, making it the correct answer. All of the remaining choices *must be false* in this situation.

21. **(C)**

What is the minimum number of doctors that could be at Souderton?

(A) zero
(B) one
(C) two
(D) three
(E) four[22]

J K L N O P

N,O - rule 4

① If J$_{sou}$ → K$_{ran}$
   If K$_{sou}$ → J$_{ran}$
② If J$_{ran}$ → O$_{sou}$
   If O$_{ran}$ → J$_{sou}$
③ If L$_{sou}$ → N$_{ran}$ and P$_{ran}$
   If N$_{sou}$ or P$_{sou}$ → L$_{ran}$
④ If N$_{ran}$ → O$_{ran}$
   If O$_{sou}$ → N$_{sou}$
⑤ If P$_{ran}$ → K$_{sou}$ and O$_{sou}$
   If K$_{ran}$ or O$_{ran}$ → P$_{sou}$

I.	sou	ran
	J	K
	P	[L]

K,P - rule 5

II.	sou	ran
	O	J
	N	[L]

Figure 10.72

Here's a question you've known the answer to since you made your Limited Options sketches. The minimum number of doctors at either facility is two. Choice (C) is correct, and you're half-way home in this question set.

21 PrepTest 34, Sec. 4, Q 20
22 PrepTest 34, Sec. 4, Q 21

22. **(A)**

If Nance and Onawa are at different clinics, which one of the following must be true?

(A)   Juarez is at Souderton.
(B)   Kudrow is at Souderton.
(C)   Palermo is at Randsborough.
(D)   Four doctors are at Souderton.
(E)   Four doctors are at Randsborough.[23]

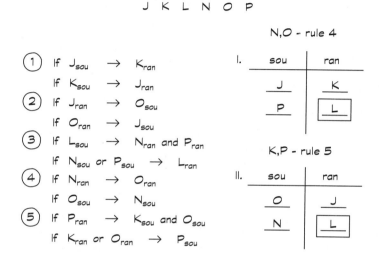

Figure 10.73

The "if" from this question stem can only happen in Option I. Choice (A), the very definition of Option I, *must be true* and is, therefore, the correct answer. Notice that the stem for question 20 put you in Option II and rewarded you for knowing that J must be at Randsborough, while the stem for question 22 put you in Option I and rewarded you for knowing that J was at Souderton. There's not much doubt that the test makers were aware of what they were doing with the complementary conditions in Rules 1 and 2.

23. **(E)**

Which one of the following CANNOT be a pair of the doctors at Randsborough?

(A)   Juarez and Kudrow
(B)   Juarez and Palermo
(C)   Kudrow and Onawa
(D)   Nance and Onawa
(E)   Nance and Palermo[24]

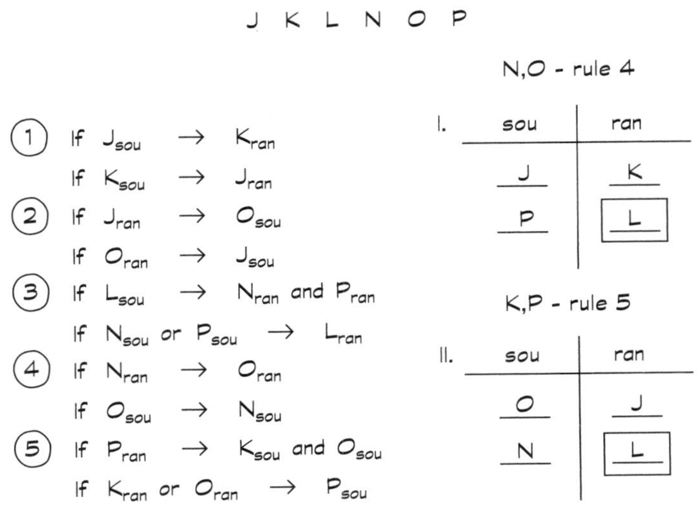

J K L N O P

N,O - rule 4

(1) If J$_{sou}$ → K$_{ran}$

If K$_{sou}$ → J$_{ran}$

(2) If J$_{ran}$ → O$_{sou}$

If O$_{ran}$ → J$_{sou}$

(3) If L$_{sou}$ → N$_{ran}$ and P$_{ran}$

If N$_{sou}$ or P$_{sou}$ → L$_{ran}$

(4) If N$_{ran}$ → O$_{ran}$

If O$_{sou}$ → N$_{sou}$

(5) If P$_{ran}$ → K$_{sou}$ and O$_{sou}$

If K$_{ran}$ or O$_{ran}$ → P$_{sou}$

I.

sou	ran
J	K
P	L

K,P - rule 5

II.

sou	ran
O	J
N	L

Figure 10.74

With no new "if" condition, you know that this question can be answered from your Master Sketch (provided that you have an adequate one). The correct answer here *must be false*. So eliminate anything that could be true. Choices (A) and (B) are both possible in Option II. Choices (C) and (D) are both possible in Option I. N and P can never be together at Randsborough (a fact you could also derive by combining Rule 5 and the contrapositive of Rule 4). Thus, choice (E) is correct. In fact, if you check the Limited Options Master Sketch, you can see that either N or P is always assigned to Souderton. That's enough to make this correct answer apparent.

24. **(B)**

If Kudrow is at Souderton, then which one of the following must be true?

(A)   Juarez is at Souderton.
(B)   Nance is at Souderton.
(C)   Onawa is at Randsborough.
(D)   Palermo is at Souderton.
(E)   Palermo is at Randsborough.[25]

---

25 PrepTest 34, Sec. 4, Q 24

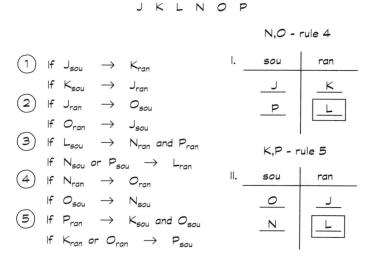

Figure 10.75

Here's one final "If" question. Its stem puts you into Option II, the only one that allows K to be at Souderton. The correct answer *must be true*. N must be at Souderton in Option II. Choice (B) is correct and you're done. For the record, choices (A) and (C) *must be false* in Option II, while choices (D) and (E) *could be* either true or false there.

That's a remarkable game. It's strained the brains of a lot of test takers. But it's also an example of a game in which the solution is hiding in plain sight. In fact, when you look at the set of rules now, you'll see that it's almost as if the test makers were trying to give you a clue.

> Kudrow is at Randsborough if Juarez is at Souderton.
> Onawa is at Souderton if Juarez is at Randsborough.
> If Longtree is at Souderton, then both Nance and Palermo
>   are at Randsborough.
> If Nance is at Randsborough, then so is Onawa.
> If Palermo is at Randsborough, then both Kudrow and
>   Onawa are at Souderton.[26]

Not only are those two rules written in a way that creates the Limited Options that unlock the game, but they're the only two in which the "if" clause is put at the end of the sentence. I don't want to encourage you to look for "secret messages" on the LSAT or to suggest that the test makers always leave obscure clues for you to discern. I do, however, want you to recognize that the information you need is always there, and it's always explicit.

As you've seen (and will continue to see throughout this section), the toughest examples of any game type always reward a little extra time in the Deductions step. Most test takers suffer through tough question sets because they haven't adequately interpreted and synthesized the rules and restrictions. All of the formal logic work you did on the Clinic Assignments game will help you again in the next chapter on Selection games.

---

[26] PrepTest 34, Sec. 4, Game 4

CHAPTER 11

SELECTION GAMES

Before you dive in to this chapter on Selection games, make sure you're fully familiar with formal logic, which is covered in chapter 3. Conditional statements are at the heart of every Selection game. That's because Selection tasks are all about choosing a smaller group out of a larger one. The situations described in these games' setups vary wildly, but you can always safely anticipate seeing rules that tell you, "If A is chosen, then B is not chosen," "If C is chosen, then D is chosen," or "If E is not chosen, then F is chosen," or some variation on those. It's a safe bet that you can combine some of the rules to make additional deductions, too. The most basic example would be a case in which the test makers include two rules such as, "If X is chosen, then Y is chosen" and "If Y is chosen, then Z is chosen." That means that choosing X entails choosing Y *and* Z. It also indicates that not choosing Z means not choosing Y *and* not choosing X. If it's not immediately apparent to you why that's the case, revisit chapter 3 of this book and shore up your formal logic skills.

REAL-LIFE SELECTION

You make selections all the time in your day-to-day life. You might be deciding which guests to invite to a wedding or a dinner. At work, you might need to choose which of six employees to send to a conference or meeting. Preparing to go to the conference, you might need to choose which of your clothes to pack for the trip. Often, the toughest part of real-life selection lies in figuring out what *not* to include. That's true on the LSAT as well. Always remember that coming up with a complete and accurate list of which ones are *not* chosen is just as valuable as the list of which ones *are*. In real life, these tasks involve wildly different numbers of choices, professional considerations, and even personal feelings. Fortunately, the LSAT always limits you to choosing from among a limited set of options, typically from among five to nine entities.

Thinking about a real-life selection task will reveal the variations that the test makers use when designing these games. Here's a typical case: Imagine that you and a roommate are going to throw a party; maybe you have friends coming over to watch a big football game. One of you asks, "What snacks should we have?" In real life, that question is open-ended. You could have as many or as few snacks as you like. As you try to make your decision, it's likely that your first question (much as it is in Distribution games) will be, "How many snacks will we serve?" You know enough about how LSAT logic games are constructed to anticipate that, for the most part, the test makers aren't going to answer that question directly. That's been true especially on more recent tests. All of the Selection games you've seen up to this point in the book put the burden on you to determine the minimum or maximum number of entities that could be chosen.

In the real-life version of the task, you could buy all of the snacks, make all of them at home, or decide on some combination of the two. You and your roommate might say, "We're too busy to make anything; let's just buy the snacks." Or you might decide, "Let's make two snacks and buy two others." It will always be important to note whether the test makers have designated subdivisions within the entities. They could, for example, say simply, "The roommates will choose from among eight snacks: almonds, cupcakes, garlic bread, licorice, meatballs, pretzels, tortilla chips, and wings." Or they could put the snacks into two categories, like so: "The roommates will choose from among four homemade snacks—cupcakes, garlic bread, meatballs, and wings—and four store-bought snacks—almonds, licorice, pretzels, and tortilla chips." When the test makers use one of the latter scenarios, look for restrictions based on the subcategories, with rules like "At least two homemade snacks and at least two store-bought snacks must be served," for example.

However the entity set is constructed, you can anticipate the types of rules that will be used. They're the same kinds of "rules" that guide your real-world decision. You might say, "If we serve pretzels, let's not have tortilla chips," or "If we have wings, then we have to have garlic bread." That leads to one of the friendliest features of Selection games: your sketch is basically no different than what you'd do in real life. "Okay, let's list out our potential snacks. We'll circle the ones we're going to serve and cross out the ones we're not."

Figure 11.1

You know that I'm a big fan of understanding logic games in a real-world context. Re-contextualizing a seemingly difficult LSAT task into a simple, real-life scenario will help you earn points confidently and quickly on test day.

STANDARD SELECTION GAMES

You've already seen a handful of the most representative logic games that appeared between PrepTest 33 and PrepTest 53. I'll reprint two of the games' setups and Master Sketches here to refresh your memory. If you can review these games and think, "Yeah, I've got it," then you're ready for the Selection game(s) you're most likely to see on test day.

An album contains photographs picturing seven friends: Raimundo, Selma, Ty, Umiko, Wendy, Yakira, Zack. The friends appear either alone or in groups with one another, in accordance with the following:

Wendy appears in every photograph that Selma appears in.
Selma appears in every photograph that Umiko appears in.
Raimundo appears in every photograph that Yakira does not appear in.
Neither Ty nor Raimundo appears in any photograph that Wendy appears in.[1]

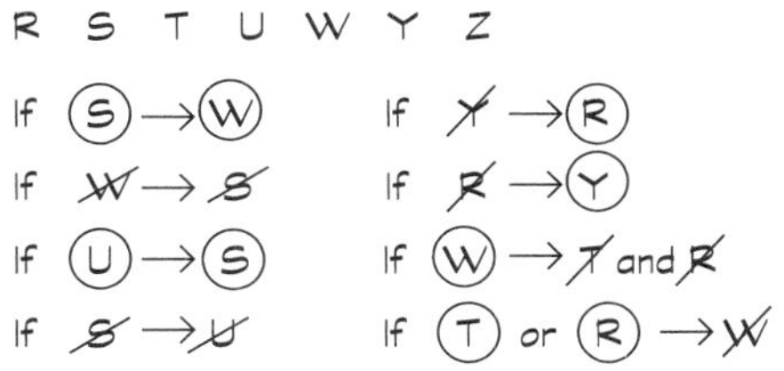

R S T U W Y Z

If (S)→(W)   If Y̶→(R)
If W̶→S̶   If R̶→(Y)
If (U)→(S)   If (W)→Y̶ and R̶
If S̶→U̶   If (T) or (R) →W̶

Figure 11.2

A summer program offers at least one of the following seven courses: geography, history, literature, mathematics, psychology, sociology, zoology. The following restrictions on the program must apply:

If mathematics is offered, then either literature or sociology (but not both) is offered.
If literature is offered, then geography is also offered but psychology is not.
If sociology is offered, then psychology is also offered but zoology is not.
If geography is offered, then both history and zoology are also offered.[2]

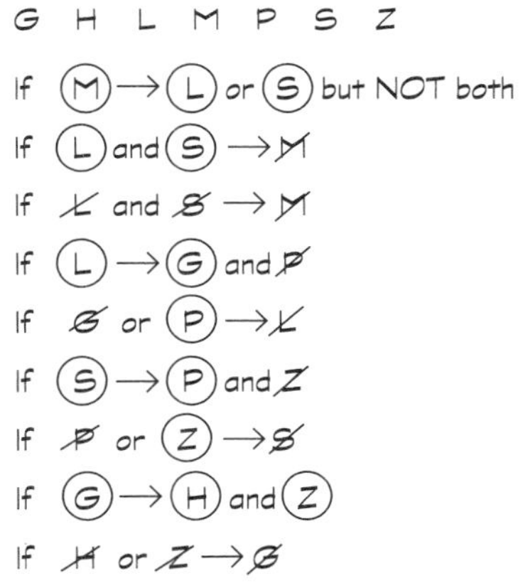

G H L M P S Z

If (M)→(L) or (S) but NOT both
If (L) and (S) →M̶
If L̶ and S̶ →M̶
If (L)→(G) and P̶
If S̶ or (P) →L̶
If (S)→(P) and Z̶
If P̶ or (Z) →S̶
If (G)→(H) and (Z)
If H̶ or Z̶ →G̶

Figure 11.3

Those two games, especially the Summer School Courses game, are among the most difficult Selection games offered in the last decade. (The Dorm Room Appliances game from chapter 2 is one of the easier examples.) But notice that all of the Selection games you've seen have exactly the same task: Choose some of the entities and reject others. Each friend is either in the photograph or out of it; the courses are either offered or not offered during the summer. The games don't specify up front how many of the entities will be "in" or "out." They are anchored by formal logic, "if-then" rules. The big insight this reveals is that the test makers don't need to use weird twists or variations in order to make Selection games harder.

---

[1] PrepTest 45, Sec. 3, Game 3
[2] PrepTest 49, Sec. 1, Game 3

So what is it that makes these two games so much harder? One key consideration is simply the number of entities. It's inherently harder to choose from among seven items than it is to choose from among five. Notice, too, that in the Friends Photographs and Summer School Courses games, the test makers made the rules hard to translate. In Friends Photographs, they did this by making the sufficient and necessary terms harder to distinguish. The rule "Selma appears in every photograph that Umiko appears in" makes Umiko's inclusion sufficient to establish Selma's and Selma's inclusion necessary for Umiko's. It translates as follows, with the contrapositive included for good measure:

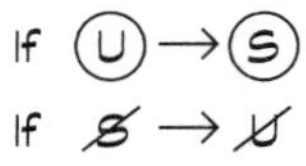

If $(U) \rightarrow (S)$
If $\cancel{S} \rightarrow \cancel{U}$

Figure 11.4

In the Summer School Courses game, there's no attempt to hide the sufficient and necessary terms. Each rule is a plain vanilla "if-then" statement. What they've done this time is include an additional term in the necessary clause and, in some cases, mix included and excluded entities into the same clause. Take this rule, for example:

If literature is offered, then geography is also offered but psychology is not.[3]

It translates:

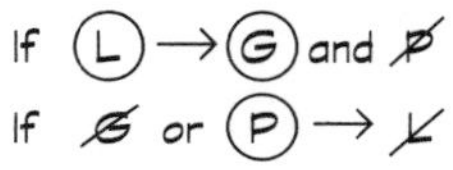

If $(L) \rightarrow (G)$ and $\cancel{P}$
If $\cancel{G}$ or $(P) \rightarrow \cancel{L}$

Figure 11.5

A mastery of formal logic rules, translations, and contrapositives is non-negotiable for the test taker who wants the points from a Selection game. While some test administrations have little or no formal logic in the Logic Games section, other (quite recent) tests have featured two Selection games, each packed with formal logic rules.

There's one more feature, also related to formal logic, common to all Selection games. In every case, some of the rules can be combined. In the Friends Photographs game, for example, there is a string of deductions triggered by the inclusion of Umiko.

---

[3] PrepTest 49, Sec. 1, Game 3

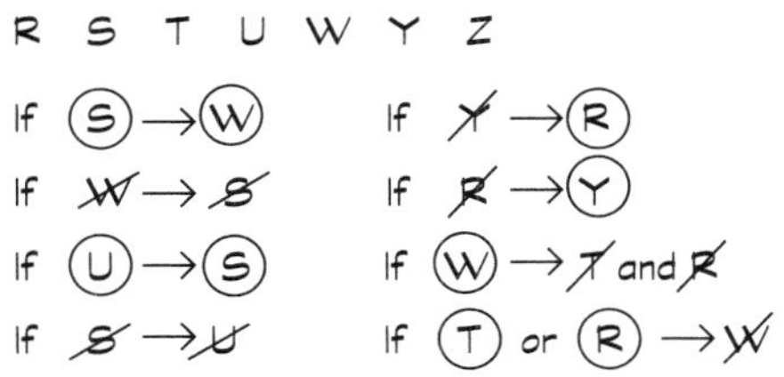

R S T U W Y Z

If (S)→(W)   If X̶→(R)

If W̶→S̶   If R̶→(Y)

If (U)→(S)   If (W)→X̶ and R̶

If S̶→U̶   If (T) or (R)→W̶

Figure 11.6

Having Umiko in the picture requires having Selma (Rule 2). Selma's inclusion entails Wendy's inclusion (Rule 1). Once Wendy is in, Raimundo is out (Rule 4). And Raimundo's exclusion means that Yakira must be in the photo (Rule 3).

In the Dorm Room Appliances game, turning on the hairdryer means turning off the razor, the television, and the vacuum.

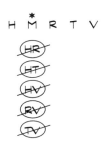

Figure 11.7

In the Summer School Course game, there are several strings of deductions triggered when one of the courses either is or is not offered. One example occurs when literature is offered.

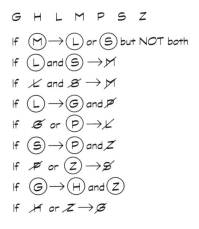

Figure 11.8

Including literature among the courses offered means that geography must be offered, too (Rule 2). Including geography, in turn, means offering history and zoology (Rule 4). But including zoology means cutting sociology from the summer schedule (Rule 3, contrapositive).

Many of my students have asked me whether they should take the time to sketch out the implications of every possible rule combination, and I've told them not to. Adding all of those results to your scratch work runs the risk of simply filling the page with so much information that you can no longer see it clearly or use it effectively. Moreover, if you miss a combination, you could go into the questions thinking you've got every possible arrangement figured out when you don't. A better approach is to write out all of formal logic neatly in a line, as you see in the sample sketches. That way, you can scan all of the triggers quickly to see whether a given result triggers another statement. Combine all of the statements that you can. When you get to a result that doesn't trigger another statement, you have the information you need to answer the question at hand. Caution: You must be familiar and handy with formal logic to do this. Keep practicing what you learned in chapter 3 until forming contrapositives and combining statements is second nature.

Standard Selection Practice

There's one more standard Selection game that you saw in Part I. There, I had you do an exercise based on the game's rules in chapter 3 and you saw a couple of the questions in chapter 5, but you haven't had a chance to try the game all the way through. I'll reprint the game here, this time in its entirety. Take eight and half minutes to tackle this game and its question set. If you find that you're getting bogged down in the questions, stop and review the explanations for Steps 1–4 of the Kaplan Method. When you're sure you've got a complete and accurate picture of the game's rules and deductions, go back to the questions. Here's a hint: Pay special attention to rules that reduce the maximum number or increase the minimum number of entities that you can select.

A fruit stand carries at least one kind of the following kinds of fruit: figs, kiwis, oranges, pears, tangerines, and watermelons. The stand does not carry any other kind of fruit. The selection of fruits the stand carries is consistent with the following conditions:

> If the stand carries kiwis, then it does not carry pears.
> If the stand does not carry tangerines, then it carries kiwis.
> If the stand carries oranges, then it carries both pears and watermelons.
> If the stand carries watermelons, then it carries figs or tangerines or both.

1. Which one of the following could be a complete and accurate list of the kinds of fruit the stand carries?

    (A) oranges, pears
    (B) pears, tangerines
    (C) oranges, pears, watermelons
    (D) oranges, tangerines, watermelons
    (E) kiwis, oranges, pears, watermelons

2. Which one of the following could be the only kind of fruit the stand carries?

    (A) figs
    (B) oranges
    (C) pears
    (D) tangerines
    (E) watermelons

3. Which one of the following CANNOT be a complete and accurate list of the kinds of fruit the stand carries?

    (A) kiwis, tangerines
    (B) tangerines, watermelons
    (C) figs, kiwis, watermelons
    (D) oranges, pears, tangerines, watermelons
    (E) figs, kiwis, oranges, pears, watermelons

4. If the stand carries no watermelons, then which one of the following must be true?

    (A) The stand carries kiwis.
    (B) The stand carries at least two kinds of fruit.
    (C) The stand carries at most three kinds of fruit.
    (D) The stand carries neither oranges nor pears.
    (E) The stand carries neither oranges nor kiwis.

5. If the stand carries watermelons, then which one of the following must be false?

    (A) The stand does not carry figs.
    (B) The stand does not carry tangerines.
    (C) The stand does not carry pears.
    (D) The stand carries pears but not oranges.
    (E) The stand carries pears but not tangerines.

6. If the condition that if the fruit stand does not carry tangerines then it does carry kiwis is suspended, and all other conditions remain in effect, then which one of the following CANNOT be a complete and accurate list of the kinds of fruit the stand carries?

    (A) pears
    (B) figs, pears
    (C) oranges, pears, watermelons
    (D) figs, pears, watermelons
    (E) figs, oranges, pears, watermelons[4]

---

[4] PrepTest 36, Sec. 4, Qs 1–6

Explanations

STEPS 1 and 2: Overview and Sketch

Your task is pretty easy to picture. You have a warehouse with six kinds of fruits in it. Your job is to man the stand at which you sell the fruit, and it's your responsibility to pick which fruits will be displayed at any given time. You'll choose which fruits to display and which to leave in storage.

As a typical Selection task, this doesn't call for a special framework. Just list the entities in a line. Circle those that are included for display and cross out those that are rejected.

F   K   O   P   T   W

Figure 11.9

STEP 3: Rules

As usual in Selection games, all four of the rules are conditional formal logic statements. Take them one at a time. Translate and diagram the statements and their contrapositives as you go.

Rule 1 is a standard "if-then."

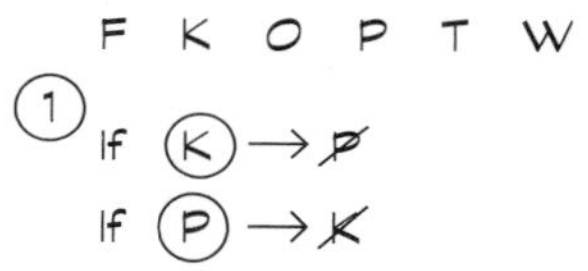

F   K   O   P   T   W
① If Ⓚ → P̶
If Ⓟ → K̶

Figure 11.10

Rule 1 reduces the maximum number of fruits that you can have on display at any given time. Either kiwis or pears must stay in the warehouse, since displaying either one would prevent you from displaying the other. It's fine if you display neither kiwis nor pears, but not if you display both.

Rule 2 is another standard "if-then," but this time the sufficient "trigger" is negative.

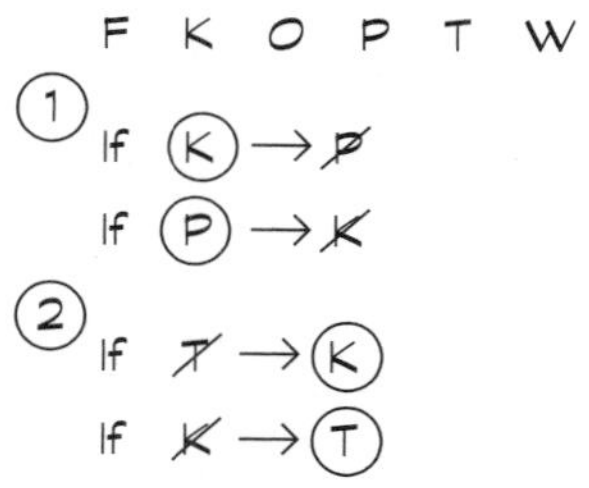

F   K   O   P   T   W
① If Ⓚ → P̶
If Ⓟ → K̶
② If T̶ → Ⓚ
If K̶ → Ⓣ

Figure 11.11

This rule increases the minimum number of fruits that you can have on display at any given time: Either tangerines or kiwis must be chosen. Note that nothing in this rule prevents you from having both, but you must at least have one or the other.

Rules 3 and 4 are formal logic statements that restrict three entities each. Rule 3 translates like this:

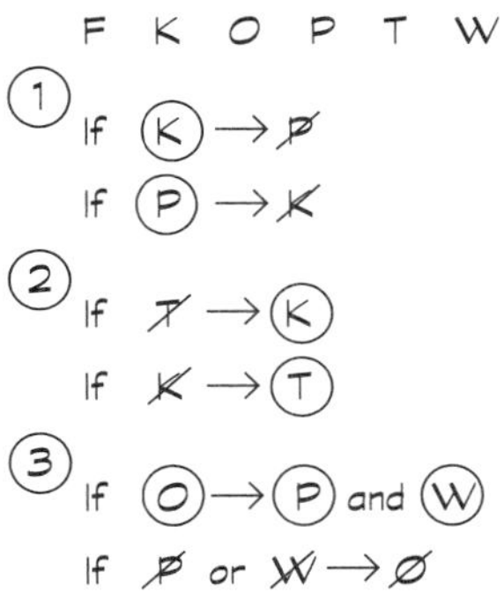

Figure 11.12

Remember that when you negate "and," it becomes "or." Excluding either pears or watermelons forces you to exclude oranges.

Rule 4 looks weirder than it is.

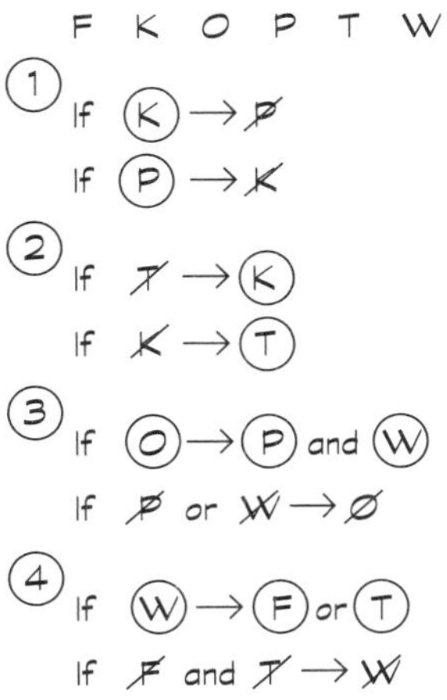

Figure 11.13

The "or both" at the end of the rule is actually redundant to the logic. If you display watermelons, you need to display at least one of figs or tangerines. If you display both figs and tangerines, you have, by definition, displayed at least one of them.

With a pure formal logic game like this (and this is like nearly all Selection games), keep your string of formal logic translations in a neat line. That will help you immensely when you need to see which of the rules combine.

STEP 4: Deductions

It's tempting to try to put all of the various combinations of formal logic together before moving on to the questions. But as I discussed above, this is usually more trouble than it's worth. For now, just scan the list of rules quickly and take note of which ones may potentially be combined. In the contrapositive of Rule 1, for example, choosing pears means excluding kiwis. That, in turn, triggers the contrapositive of Rule 2: Excluding kiwis means including tangerines. You could go on like this through all of the rules, but don't. The questions will signal which of the rules are at issue in a given situation. As long as you're able to see the implications of the rule(s) triggered, you'll handle the questions just fine.

STEP 5: Questions

This is a balanced question set for a balanced game. The first three questions can be answered without any new scratch work. The next three have new "ifs" (as you'll see, question 6 is actually a Rule-Changer) and will benefit from mini-sketches.

1. **(B)**

    Which one of the following could be a complete and accurate list of the kinds of fruit the stand carries?

    (A)   oranges, pears
    (B)   pears, tangerines
    (C)   oranges, pears, watermelons
    (D)   oranges, tangerines, watermelons
    (E)   kiwis, oranges, pears, watermelons[5]

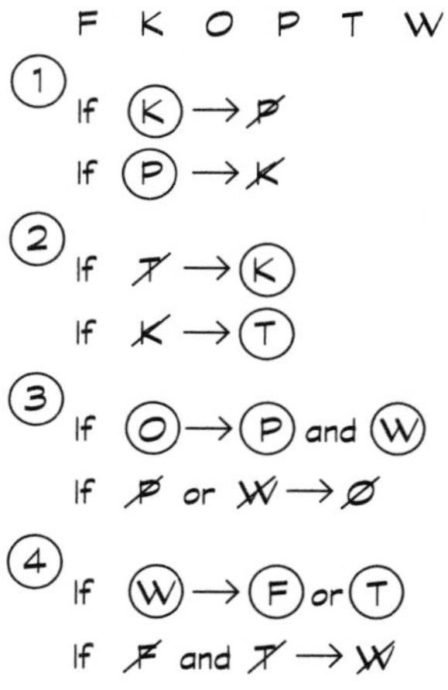

Figure 11.14

This is a standard Acceptability question. As you've done so often before, use the rules to eliminate answer choices that violate them. Rule 1 knocks out choice (E), where K and P are found together. Rule 2 eliminates choices (A) and (C), both of which lack both K and T. Rule 3 knocks out choice (D), which has O and W, but lacks P. That leaves choice (B), the correct answer.

---

[5] PrepTest 36, Sec. 4, Q 1

2. **(D)**

Which one of the following could be the only kind of fruit the stand carries?

(A) figs
(B) oranges
(C) pears
(D) tangerines
(E) watermelons[6]

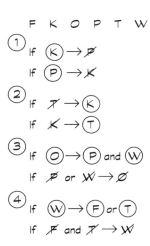

Figure 11.15

This is a funny little question that drives students crazy. That's because they dive in and try to test choices before they've taken time to think about the stem. What's the most important word there? It's "only." The correct answer is a fruit that could be on display without any other fruits being selected. This has to implicate Rule 2, which requires that, in every case, you must display either K or T. One of those two fruits must be the right answer. No matter what other fruit you put on display, you'd have to choose either K or T, too. So the right answer has either K or T. It turns out to be choice (D), with T. All four of the wrong answers have fruits that would have to be accompanied by either T or K and so cannot be the *only* fruit selected.

3. **(E)**

Which one of the following CANNOT be a complete and accurate list of the kinds of fruit the stand carries?

(A) kiwis, tangerines
(B) tangerines, watermelons
(C) figs, kiwis, watermelons
(D) oranges, pears, tangerines, watermelons
(E) figs, kiwis, oranges, pears, watermelons[7]

```
     F  K  O  P  T  W
 ①  If  Ⓚ → P̸
     If  Ⓟ → K̸
 ②  If  T̸ → Ⓚ
     If  K̸ → Ⓣ
 ③  If  Ⓞ → Ⓟ and Ⓦ
     If  P̸ or W̸ → Ø
 ④  If  Ⓦ → Ⓕ or Ⓣ
     If  F̸ and T̸ → W̸
```

Figure 11.16

This is a *must be false* question. It functions like an anti-Acceptability question, where the one rule violator is the correct answer. Fortunately, you need only test Rule 1 in order to find the correct choice. Answer choice (E) includes both K and P. That means it cannot be an accurate list of the fruits on display, and it is therefore the correct answer.

---

[6] PrepTest 36, Sec. 4, Q 2
[7] PrepTest 36, Sec. 4, Q 3

4. **(C)**

    If the stand carries no watermelons, then which one of the following must be true?

    (A)   The stand carries kiwis.
    (B)   The stand carries at least two kinds of fruit.
    (C)   The stand carries at most three kinds of fruit.
    (D)   The stand carries neither oranges nor pears.
    (E)   The stand carries neither oranges nor kiwis.[8]

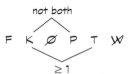

Figure 11.17

This is the first "If" question in the set. Copy your list of entities and cross off W in accordance with the question stem.

F   K   O   P   T   W̶

Figure 11.18

Crossing off W means crossing off O according to the contrapositive of Rule 3.

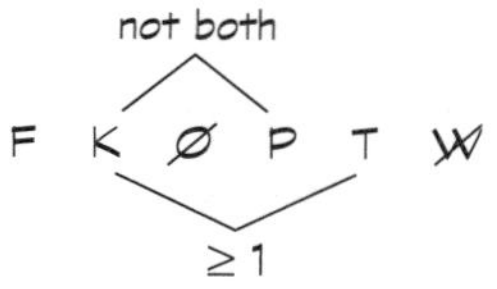

F   K   Ø   P   T   W̶
≥ 1
not both

Figure 11.19

Crossing off O doesn't trigger any of the other rules, so you're done with the mini-sketch. But take a moment to notice which of the fruits remain undetermined in your list: F, K, P, and T. At least one of K and P has to be excluded, according to Rule 1. At least one of K and T has to be included, according to Rule 2. F can stay or go; it's not restricted by anything here.

Now, characterize the choices. The correct answer *must be true*. The four wrong answers *could be false*. Evaluate them until you find the *must be true* choice.

Choice (A) *could be false*. You are required to have either K or T. So here, you might have T and leave K off display. Eliminate it.

Choice (B) *could be false*. You know from question 2 that K or T could be the only fruit displayed on a given day. Get rid of this answer, too.

Choice (C) *must be true*. At this point in the mini-sketch, four fruits remain possible for display. But two of them are K and P, which cannot be displayed together under Rule 1. So three fruits (either F, K, T or F, P, T) is the maximum that can go on display in this scenario. Choice (C) is correct.

---

[8] PrepTest 36, Sec. 4, Q 4

For the record, both of choices (D) and (E) could be false. The stand could display either P or K, respectively.

5. **(E)**

If the stand carries watermelons, then which one of the following must be false?

(A) The stand does not carry figs.
(B) The stand does not carry tangerines.
(C) The stand does not carry pears.
(D) The stand carries pears but not oranges.
(E) The stand carries pears but not tangerines.[9]

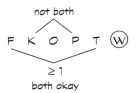

Figure 11.20

You saw this question in chapter 5, where I introduced the mini-sketch approach for "If" questions. Here's another "If," so start another mini-sketch. Copy the list of entities. This time, circle W, as the question stem instructs.

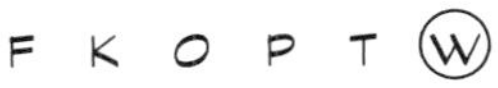

F K O P T (W)

Figure 11.21

Circling W triggers Rule 4. Carrying watermelons means carrying figs, tangerines, or both. Those three possible results make this a little tricky to sketch, but something like this should suffice.

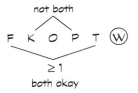

Figure 11.22

Neither the inclusion of F nor that of T triggers any other results. (The *exclusion* of T is sufficient in Rule 2, but don't confuse that with its inclusion here.) You've exhausted the deductions, so evaluate the answer choices. The correct answer *must be false*. Each of the wrong answers *could be true*.

Choice (E) is the correct answer. Take a moment to see why choice (E) *must be false*. If you include P, Rule 1 says you must exclude K. But Rule 2 requires that you have either K or T in every case. You simply can't include P but exclude T. You don't even need the "if" from the question stem to know that this choice *must be false* in every instance.

Choices (A) through (D) all could be true. See chapter 5 for a fuller discussion if you are confused by any of them.

---

[9] PrepTest 36, Sec. 4, Q 5

6. **(C)**

If the condition that if the fruit stand does not carry tangerines then it does carry kiwis is suspended, and all other conditions remain in effect, then which one of the following CANNOT be a complete and accurate list of the kinds of fruit the stand carries?

(A) pears
(B) figs, pears
(C) oranges, pears, watermelons
(D) figs, pears, watermelons
(E) figs, oranges, pears, watermelons[10]

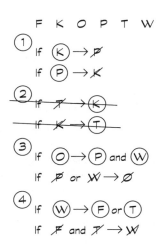

Figure 11.23

This question was also explained in chapter 5. It's a Rule-Changer, a rare question type, but one you should know how to handle. Here, Rule 2 is suspended. The presence of Rule 2 in the original Master Sketch told you that you had to have at least one of K or T. With that restriction lifted, an arrangement with neither K nor T is fine, provided that it meets the game's other requirements. You needn't do more than cross Rule 2 off the list and you're ready to evaluate the answer choices.

Even without Rule 2, choice (C) cannot be an acceptable selection. It violates Rule 4, which is still in effect under this question stem's terms. Including W requires including F or T, neither of which is included in the answer choice. As a rule violator, choice (C) is the correct answer.

The wrong answers all represent acceptable arrangements under the altered circumstances presented by the question stem. A full discussion of the wrong answers appears in chapter 5.

If you have a Selection game on your test, it's likely to remind you of the Fruit Stand game or one of the others you've reviewed in this section. In recent years, the test makers haven't often employed the twists and variations you'll see in the remainder of the chapter. However, you might see something like the tasks that follow mixed into a Hybrid game. So practice the games that follow to learn the basics of Selection involving definite numbers. Doing so will give you additional formal logic practice, too.

SELECTION TWISTS

The main variation on Selection that you could see on test day involves telling you how many entities to choose. Instead of saying, "There are seven people applying for jobs with your firm; you'll hire some of them," these games say, "You will hire exactly four of the seven applicants." You should welcome such specificity with the numbers. It both makes your task clearer and removes any possibility that you'll be tested on the minimum or maximum number of

---

[10] PrepTest 36, Sec. 4, Q 6

selections. Take a look at a couple of examples to see how the test makers construct games like this and how they try to make them more challenging.

Selection with Definite Numbers

Perhaps in order to compensate for the additional certainty that comes from giving you a definite number of entities to choose, the test makers almost always complicate the set of entities. I gave you an example of this above when I subdivided the snacks at your imaginary football party into subgroups: homemade and store-bought. This can seem confusing at first, but for the Kaplan-trained test taker, it's just one more way in which the test makers may restrict the acceptable solutions. Take a look at an example of a Selection game with definite numbers.

> A panel of five scientists will be formed. The panelists will be
> selected from among three botanists—F, G, and H—three
> chemists—K, L, and M—and three zoologists—P, Q, and R.
> Selection is governed by the following conditions:
>   The panel must include at least one scientist of each of the
>   three types.
>   If more than one botanist is selected, then at most one
>   zoologist is selected.
>   F and K cannot both be selected.
>   K and M cannot both be selected.
>   If M is selected, both P and R must be selected.[11]

Unlike any of the games in the first section of this chapter, this game tells you to choose exactly five of the nine scientists. It also subdivides the scientists into three categories: botanists, chemists, and zoologists. Look for ways in which those subdivisions can help you get a handle on the game's setup. In fact, the first two rules introduce further number restrictions based on the subgroups. Without those rules, you could make any of the following 12 arrangements.

Bot	Chem	Zoo
3	2	0
3	1	1
3	0	2
2	3	0
2	2	1
2	1	2
2	0	3
1	3	1
1	2	2
1	1	3
0	3	2
0	2	3

---

[11] PrepTest 42, Sec. 1, Game 1

Rule 1 tells you that you must have at least one of each category of scientist. That, by itself, knocks out half of the possible patterns.

Bot	Chem	Zoo
~~3~~	~~2~~	~~0~~
3	1	1
~~3~~	~~0~~	~~2~~
~~2~~	~~3~~	~~0~~
2	2	1
2	1	2
~~2~~	~~0~~	~~3~~
1	3	1
1	2	2
1	1	3
~~0~~	~~3~~	~~2~~
~~0~~	~~2~~	~~3~~

Rule 2 tells you that any time you have two or three botanists, you can have only one zoologist. That removes another possible arrangement within the selection.

Bot	Chem	Zoo
~~3~~	~~2~~	~~0~~
3	1	1
~~3~~	~~0~~	~~2~~
~~2~~	~~3~~	~~0~~
2	2	1
~~2~~	~~1~~	~~2~~
~~2~~	~~0~~	~~3~~
1	3	1
1	2	2
1	1	3
~~0~~	~~3~~	~~2~~
~~0~~	~~2~~	~~3~~

Rule 4 provides even more clarity. Since both K and M are chemists, you know that there's no way to select all three chemists. That knocks out one more arrangement, leaving you only four ways in which the numbers can work out in this game.

Bot	Chem	Zoo
3	2	0
3	**1**	**1**
3	0	2
2	3	0
2	2	1
2	1	2
2	0	3
1	3	1
1	**2**	**2**
1	**1**	**3**
0	3	2
0	2	3

Accounting for the possible number of entities that you can select from each subgroup makes your life much simpler when you need to identify acceptable and unacceptable arrangements in the questions.

Contrast that game with the following. Take a look and see why the subgroups are of less help than they were in the preceding example.

For a behavioral study, a researcher will select exactly six individual animals from among three monkeys—F, G, and H—three pandas—K, L, and N—and three raccoons—T, V, and Z. The selection of animals for the study must meet the following conditions:

F and H are not both selected.
N and T are not both selected.
If H is selected, K is also selected.
If K is selected, N is also selected.[12]

Here again, you're asked to select a definite number: six out of nine, in this case. And just as they were in the Science Panel game, the nine entities are subdivided into three groups of three each. Did you notice, though, that there are no rules specifying the numbers that must be chosen for any of the subgroups? That's going to make this game a little more challenging. Rule 1 makes it impossible to have all three of the monkeys, but the numbers from each subcategory are otherwise up in the air.

---

[12] PrepTest 40, Sec. 2, Game 4

Selection with Definite Numbers Practice

Try this game out for practice. Give yourself eight and half minutes to complete the setup, make the deductions, and try the questions. As always, if you find yourself struggling, consult the explanations for Steps 1–4 of the Kaplan Method. Then go back and try to finish the question set, knowing that you have all of the rules and deductions clearly represented on the page. I'll give you one hint: Remember that excluding three of the nine entities is the same as including six of them. You may make as much headway on some of the questions by noting what *cannot* be included as you will by figuring out what can.

For a behavioral study, a researcher will select exactly six individual animals from among three monkeys—F, G, and H—three pandas—K, L, and N—and three raccoons—T, V, and Z. The selection of animals for the study must meet the following conditions:

F and H are not both selected.

N and T are not both selected.

If H is selected, K is also selected.

If K is selected, N is also selected.

18. Which one of the following is an acceptable selection of animals for the study?

(A) F, G, K, N, T, V
(B) F, H, K, N, V, Z
(C) G, H, K, L, V, Z
(D) G, H, K, N, V, Z
(E) G, H, L, N, V, Z

19. If H and L are among the animals selected, which one of

the following could be true?

(A) F is selected.
(B) T is selected.
(C) Z is selected.
(D) Exactly one panda is selected.
(E) Exactly two pandas are selected.

20. Each of the following is a pair of animals that could be selected together EXCEPT:

(A) F and G
(B) H and K
(C) K and T
(D) L and N
(E) T and V

21. If all three of the raccoons are selected, which one of the following must be true?

(A) K is selected.
(B) L is selected.
(C) Exactly one monkey is selected.
(D) Exactly two pandas are selected.
(E) All three of the monkeys are selected.

22. If T is selected, which one of the following is a pair of animals that must be among the animals selected?

(A) F and G
(B) G and H
(C) K and L
(D) K and Z
(E) L and N

23. The selection of animals must include:

(A) at most two of each kind of animal
(B) at least one of each kind of animal
(C) at least two pandas
(D) exactly two monkeys
(E) exactly two raccoons[13]

Explanations

STEPS 1 AND 2: Overview and Sketch

Your task is straightforward. You have a list of nine animals, and you have to choose six of them. You don't need a special sketch. Just list the animals, noting their subcategories. You'll circle those that are selected for research and cross out those that aren't.

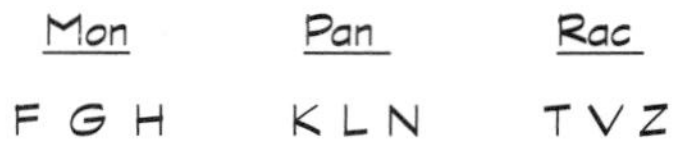

Mon
Pan
Rac
F G H
K L N
T V Z

Figure 11.24

STEP 3: Rules

All four rules, in typical Selection game fashion, involve formal logic. Rules 1 and 2 create "impossible pairs." They're very easy to diagram.

Mon
Pan
Rac
F G H
K L N
T V Z
FH
NT

Figure 11.25

Rules 3 and 4 are straightforward "if-then" statements. Translate each and add its contrapositive.

Mon
Pan
Rac
F G H
K L N
T V Z
FH
NT
If H → K
If K → H
If K → N
If N → K

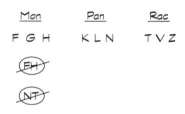

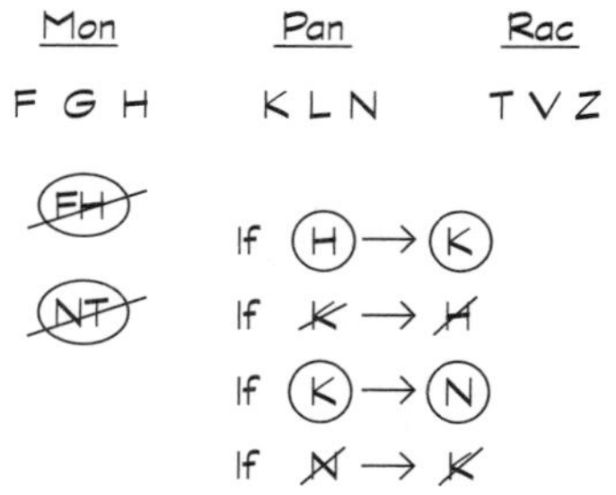

Figure 11.26

The contrapositives of those two rules tell you that when you reject either K or N, you'll have to reject additional animals as well. That could get dicey, given that you can only reject three of the nine animals.

It's worth noting, before you move on, that L, V, and Z are floaters. None of them are restricted by any of the rules.

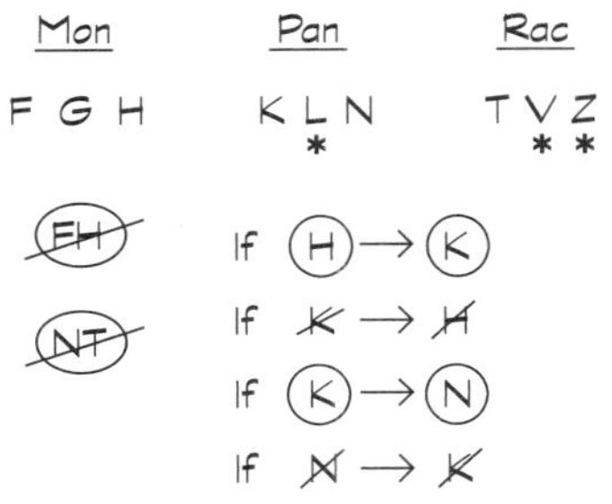

Mon	Pan	Rac
F G H	K L N	T V Z
	*	* *

Figure 11.27

STEP 4: Deductions

There aren't many deductions to make in this game. Rules 3 and 4 share K and can thus be combined. If you choose H, you'll need to choose K and N. If you eliminate N, you'll have to eliminate K and H. But that much is clear at a glance.

The one place you get a little traction on the number restrictions is in Rule 1. Since F and H cannot both be selected, you'll have to choose either one or two of the monkeys. You may be thinking, "Wait, why can't I just have all six animals from the panda and raccoon subgroups and choose no monkeys at all?" The answer lies in Rule 2. Since N and T are an impossible pair, the sum of pandas and raccoons can never be more than five. You'll have to choose at least one animal from each subgroup in order to select six animals altogether.

You could, I suppose, try to figure out all of the possible selections from the monkey subgroup, where you could choose F-G, G-H, or just one of the monkeys F, G, or H. But that's five arrangements to work out, and there are only six questions. You're better off heading into the question set, aware of the restrictions as they are. The Acceptability question will help you gain some additional clarity, and there are three "If" questions that will be driven by mini-sketches anyway.

STEP 5: Questions

This is a balanced question set, featuring three questions with new "ifs" and three without. If you struggle with questions 20 or 23, complete the "If" questions first and use your work from them to help eliminate wrong answers in the Must/Could questions.

18. **(D)**

Which one of the following is an acceptable selection of animals for the study?

(A)   F, G, K, N, T, V
(B)   F, H, K, N, V, Z
(C)   G, H, K, L, V, Z
(D)   G, H, K, N, V, Z
(E)   G, H, L, N, V, Z[14]

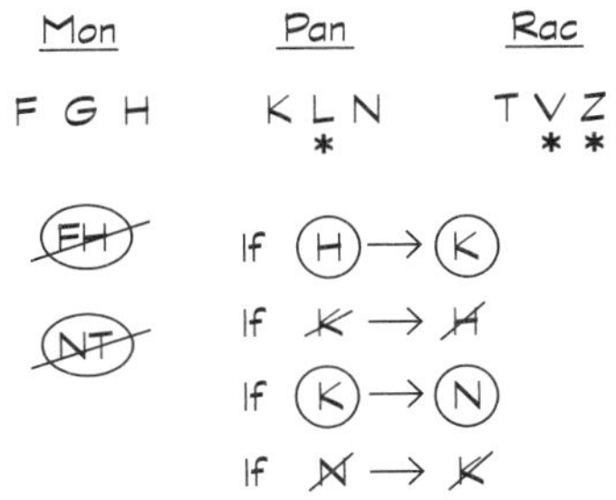

Mon	Pan	Rac
F G H	K L N	T V Z
	*	* *

Figure 11.28

---

[14] PrepTest 40, Sec. 2, Q 18

Four rules, four wrong answers—this is as clear an Acceptability question as you could ask for. Choice (B) breaks Rule 1; you can't select both F and H. Choice (A) breaks Rule 2; you can't select both N and T. Choice (E) breaks Rule 3; when you choose H, you must choose K as well. Choice (C) breaks Rule 4; when you choose K, you must choose N as well. That leaves only choice (D), the correct answer.

19. **(C)**
    If H and L are among the animals selected, which one of the following could be true?

    (A) F is selected.
    (B) T is selected.
    (C) Z is selected.
    (D) Exactly one panda is selected.
    (E) Exactly two pandas are selected.[15]

Mon   Pan   Rac

F̶ G (H)   (K)(L)(N)   T̶ V Z

Figure 11.29

"If" questions are always welcome in Selection games; mini-sketches are easy to make by copying the entity list, and the "if" restriction will almost always set off a chain of deductions within the formal logic rules. Here, the question stem tells you to circle H and L in the list of animals.

Mon   Pan   Rac

F G (H)   K (L) N   T V Z

Figure 11.30

The inclusion of H triggers Rules 1 and 3. From Rule 1, you know to cross out F.

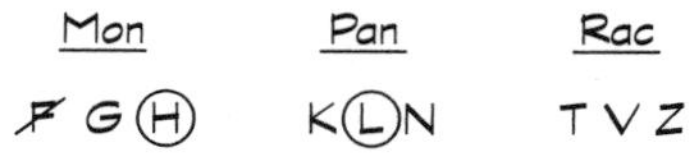

Mon   Pan   Rac

F̶ G (H)   K (L) N   T V Z

Figure 11.31

From Rule 3, you know to circle K.

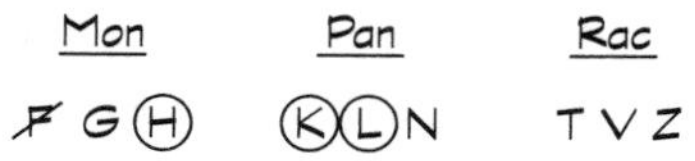

Mon   Pan   Rac

F̶ G (H)   (K)(L) N   T V Z

Figure 11.32

Including K sets off Rule 4 and then Rule 2. You need to circle N and cross out T.

---

[15] PrepTest 40, Sec. 2, Q 19

Mon   Pan   Rac

F̶ G (H)   (K)(L)(N)   T̶ V Z

Figure 11.33

Four of your selections—H, K, L, and N—are certain. The remaining two will come from among G, V, and Z. Assess the answer choices. The correct answer *could be true*; the four wrong answers all *must be false*.

Choice (C) is correct. Z is among the remaining possible selections. You can see that F and T have already been crossed off the list, making choices (A) and (B) incorrect. You can also see that you'll have to choose all three pandas, making choices (D) and (E) wrong answers, too.

20. **(C)**

Each of the following is a pair of animals that could be selected together EXCEPT:

(A) F and G
(B) H and K
(C) K and T
(D) L and N
(E) T and V[16]

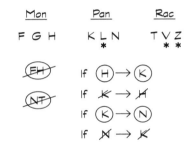

Figure 11.34

This question rewards you for being able to combine the rules. The correct answer is a pair of entities that cannot be selected together. The wrong answers all feature pairs that are acceptable together.

Choice (A) is incorrect. Nothing prevents F and G from being the two monkeys you select.

Choice (B) is also wrong. In fact, when H is selected, K must be.

Choice (C) is correct. Choosing K necessitates choosing N (Rule 4), and N and T are incompatible (Rule 2). Thus, K and T are incompatible as well.

Choices (D) and (E) both include floaters, N and V, respectively. Neither of those entities directly affects any other, so you know these choices are acceptable.

---

[16] PrepTest 40, Sec. 2, Q 20

21. **(B)**

If all three of the raccoons are selected, which one of the following must be true?

(A) K is selected.
(B) L is selected.
(C) Exactly one monkey is selected.
(D) Exactly two pandas are selected.
(E) All three of the monkeys are selected.[17]

<u>Mon</u>   <u>Pan</u>   <u>Rac</u>

F G H̸   K̸ L N̸   Ⓣ Ⓥ Ⓩ

Figure 11.35

This question is one in which you'll derive the three animals that are *not* selected before you get to the six that are. Start your mini-sketch with the restriction from the stem. Circle all three raccoons—T, V, and Z.

<u>Mon</u>   <u>Pan</u>   <u>Rac</u>

F G H   K L N   Ⓣ Ⓥ Ⓩ

Figure 11.36

Of those three animals, only T entails additional restrictions. According to Rule 2, choosing T means rejecting N.

<u>Mon</u>   <u>Pan</u>   <u>Rac</u>

F G H   K L N̸   Ⓣ Ⓥ Ⓩ

Figure 11.37

Kicking N off your list means kicking K and H off, as well (Rules 3 and 4, contrapositives).

<u>Mon</u>   <u>Pan</u>   <u>Rac</u>

F G H̸   K̸ L N̸   Ⓣ Ⓥ Ⓩ

Figure 11.38

That's it. Once you've rejected three animals, the six that remain must be your final selection. F, G, and L must be selected along with the raccoons in this situation. That makes choice (B) the correct answer; it *must be true*. Your mini-sketch proves that all four wrong answers are false here.

---

[17] PrepTest 40, Sec. 2, Q 21

22. **(A)**

If T is selected, which one of the following is a pair of animals that must be among the animals selected?

(A) F and G
(B) G and H
(C) K and L
(D) K and Z
(E) L and N[18]

Mon	Pan	Rac
F G H̶	K̶ L N̶	(T) (V) (Z)

Figure 11.39

The "if" to this question produces precisely the same mini-sketch as the one used for question 21. Since T's inclusion precipitates the exclusion of N (Rule 2), K (Rule 4), and H (Rule 3), exactly the same six animals chosen in question 21 must be selected again. Thus, choice (A), with F and G, represents a pair that must be chosen. Each of the four wrong answers includes at least one of the rejected entities—H, K, or L.

23. **(B)**

The selection of animals must include:

(A) at most two of each kind of animal
(B) at least one of each kind of animal
(C) at least two pandas
(D) exactly two monkeys
(E) exactly two raccoons[19]

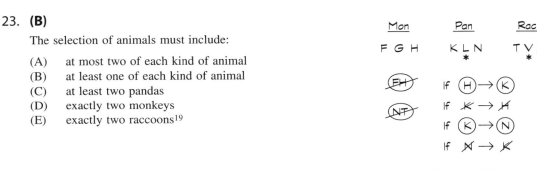

Figure 11.40

You've known the answer to this question since you first added the rules to your sketch. Since Rule 1 allows you to take at most two of the monkeys and Rule 2 means that you can't have all six of the pandas and raccoons together, you must choose at least one animal from each of the subgroups. Choice (B) *must be true*, so it is correct.

When all is said and done, that game isn't so different from a standard Selection game. Moreover, the two big differences—the requirements that you select exactly six of the nine entities and at least one from each of the three subgroupings—played to your advantage. Although the test makers didn't include explicit limits on the number of animals from each subgroup, the questions wound up rewarding you for being able to see how many of the animals from a subgroup could or could not be chosen.

Selection with Entities Belonging to Multiple Subcategories

There's one more, very rare, twist on Selection that I want to make sure you have a chance to practice. The test makers haven't used anything exactly like this since PrepTest 35, originally administered in October of 2001. What makes the following game unique is that the entities

---

[18] PrepTest 40, Sec. 2, Q 22
[19] PrepTest 40, Sec. 2, Q 23

are subcategorized twice, with each entity belonging to one of two groups within each sub-category. Take a minute to read the game's setup text and you'll see what I mean.

> From among eight candidates, four astronauts will be selected
> for a space flight. Four of the candidates—F, J, K, and L—are
> experienced astronauts and four—M, N, P, and T—are
> inexperienced astronauts. F, M, P, and T are geologists
> whereas J, K, L, and N are radiobiologists. The astronauts
> must be selected according to the following conditions:[20]

The eight astronauts are each either experienced or inexperienced ("Ex" or "InEx"), and each does one of two jobs (G or R). Thus, each astronaut could receive one of four designations: "ExG," "InExG," "ExR," or "InExR." In the long run, all of this categorization will help you, since it provides additional restrictions along two dimensions. Initially, though, it puts the burden on you to categorize and mark the entities clearly and effectively.

Using what I've talked about so far, give this game a try. Take eight and half minutes to tackle the game from top to bottom. If you find yourself struggling with the questions, stop and review Steps 1–4 of the Kaplan Method in the explanations. Once you're sure you have a strong Master Sketch, go back and complete the question set.

---

[20] PrepTest 35, Sec. 3, Game 1

From among eight candidates, four astronauts will be selected for a space flight. Four of the candidates—F, J, K, and L—are experienced astronauts and four—M, N, P, and T—are inexperienced astronauts. F, M, P, and T are geologists whereas J, K, L, and N are radiobiologists. The astronauts must be selected according to the following conditions:

Exactly two experienced astronauts and two inexperienced astronauts are selected.

Exactly two geologists and two radiobiologists are selected.

Either P or L or both are selected.

1. Which one of the following is an acceptable selection of astronauts for the space flight?

   (A)   F, J, N, and T
   (B)   F, L, M, and P
   (C)   F, M, N, and P
   (D)   J, L, M, and T
   (E)   K, L, N, and T

2. If F and P are selected for the space flight, the other two astronauts selected must be:

   (A)   a radiobiologist who is an experienced astronaut and a radiobiologist who is an inexperienced astronaut
   (B)   a radiobiologist who is an experienced astronaut and a geologist who is an inexperienced astronaut
   (C)   a radiobiologist and a geologist, both of whom are experienced astronauts
   (D)   two radiobiologists, both of whom are experienced astronauts
   (E)   two radiobiologists, both of whom are inexperienced astronauts

3. If F and J are selected for the space flight, which one of the following must also be selected?

   (A)   K
   (B)   L
   (C)   M
   (D)   N
   (E)   T

4. If M and T are selected for the space flight, which one of the following could be, but need not be, selected for the flight?

   (A)   F
   (B)   J
   (C)   L
   (D)   N
   (E)   P

5. If N is selected for the space flight, which one of the following must also be selected?

   (A)   F
   (B)   J
   (C)   L
   (D)   M
   (E)   T[21]

---

[21] PrepTest 35, Sec. 3, Qs 1–5

Explanations

STEPS 1 AND 2: Overview and Sketch

In this game, Steps 1 and 2 are probably your biggest challenge; even so, the task isn't an unusual one in everyday life. Imagine you're staging a play that calls for a cast of four actors: one older woman, one older man, one young woman, and one young man. You might well have a list of actors who have auditioned, divided into groups for males and females and categorized by age group. Your task here is identical.

Start by listing the astronauts by experience level.

Figure 11.41

Now, under each one, list his or her job.

Figure 11.42

Right away, you notice something interesting. Only one of the experienced astronauts is a geologist, and only one of the inexperienced astronauts is a radiobiologist. Keep that in mind as you add the rules and deductions to this game. Astronauts F and N are sure to be central to at least some of the questions.

STEP 3: Rules

Rules 1 and 2 are similar, but focus on different subgroupings. Just make note of these two rules off to the side. They don't allow you to circle or cross out any entities yet.

```
            Exp            Inexp
          F  J K L       m  n  p  t
          |  | | |       |  |  |  |
          g  r r r       g  r  g  g

        2 Exp, 2 Inexp
        2 g, 2 r
```

Figure 11.43

Rule 3 tells you that all acceptable selections in this game will follow one of three patterns. Probably the clearest way to depict this rule is by making a three-way Limited Options sketch.

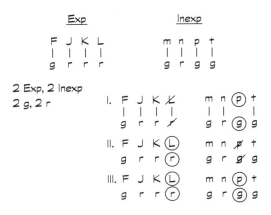

Figure 11.44

It's not always worth your while to make separate sketches when you have more than two options, but it is of paramount importance in this game that you maintain a clear picture of who's in and out, what their experience level is, and what job they do. So, the triple-sketch is probably worthwhile, especially with four "If" questions that are each likely to plop you into one of the options.

STEP 4: Deductions

Running through your BLEND checklist, there's simply nothing to add to your Master Sketch. Now you know why the test makers used so many "If" questions for this game.

STEP 5: Questions

As I had you note, the question set is dominated by "If" questions. You'll probably wind up making four mini-sketches here. Fortunately, with this being a Selection game, all that means is copying the list of entities and starting to circle them or cross them out.

1. **(D)**

Which one of the following is an acceptable selection of astronauts for the space flight?

(A) F, J, N, and T
(B) F, L, M, and P
(C) F, M, N, and P
(D) J, L, M, and T
(E) K, L, N, and T[22]

```
                                Exp              Inexp

                            F  J  K  L        m  n  p  t
                            |  |  |  |        |  |  |  |
                            g  r  r  r        g  r  g  g

       2 Exp, 2 Inexp
       2 g, 2 r                  I.  F  J  K  L̸     m  n (p) t
                                    |  |  |  |     |  |     |
                                    g  r  r  r̸     g  r (g) g

                                 II.  F  J  K (L)     m  n  p̸  t
                                     g  r  r (r)     g  r  g̸  g

                                III.  F  J  K (L)     m  n (p) t
                                      g  r  r (r)     g  r (g) g
```

Figure 11.45

No surprises here; the one "Non-If" question is a plain old Acceptability question. You know the drill. Use the rules to eliminate wrong answers. Rule 1 gets rid of choice (C), which has only one experienced astronaut along with three inexperienced ones. Rule 2 knocks out choice (B), which has too many geologists, and choice (E), which has too many radiobiologists. Rule 3 takes care of the final violator, choice (A), which has a list with neither L nor P. The last answer standing, choice (D), is acceptable and correct.

2. **(A)**

If F and P are selected for the space flight, the other two astronauts selected must be:

(A)   a radiobiologist who is an experienced astronaut and a radiobiologist who is an inexperienced astronaut

(B)   a radiobiologist who is an experienced astronaut and a geologist who is an inexperienced astronaut

(C)   a radiobiologist and a geologist, both of whom are experienced astronauts

(D)   two radiobiologists, both of whom are experienced astronauts

(E)   two radiobiologists, both of whom are inexperienced astronauts[23]

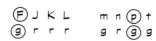

Figure 11.46

Start a mini-sketch with the condition from the question stem. Circle F and P (see figure above). The first thing to notice is that you now have both your geologists, including one experienced and one inexperienced. You'll need an "ExR" and an "InExR" to complete your selection. That's exactly what the correct answer, choice (A), says. All four wrong answers would produce the wrong mix of experience levels and jobs.

3. **(D)**

If F and J are selected for the space flight, which one of the following must also be selected?

(A)   K
(B)   L
(C)   M
(D)   N
(E)   T[24]

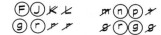

Figure 11.47

Use the "if" from the question stem to start your mini-sketch. Circle F and J in the list.

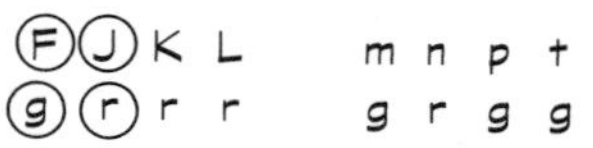

F J K L   m n p t
g r r r   g r g g

Figure 11.48

---

[23] PrepTest 35, Sec. 3, Q 2
[24] PrepTest 35, Sec. 3, Q 3

That tells you a lot. You have all of the experienced astronauts that you can take. Cross off K and L.

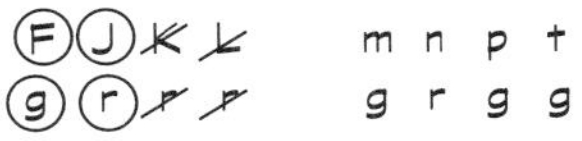

Figure 11.49

Once L is gone from the roster, you know from Rule 3 that you must include P.

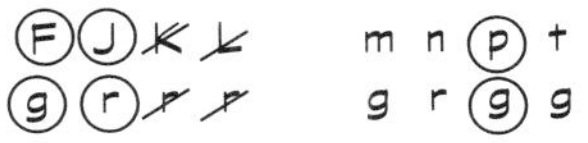

Figure 11.50

You need one more inexperienced astronaut who must also be a radiobiologist. The only acceptable entity is N.

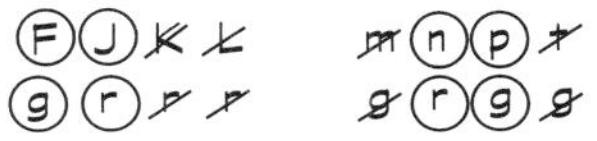

Figure 11.51

You now have the entire crew for your space flight. The correct answer to this question has an entity that must be included. That's choice (D), with N, your final deduction. Each of the wrong answers lists an astronaut who cannot go on the flight in this scenario.

4.   **(B)**

If M and T are selected for the space flight, which one of the following could be, but need not be, selected for the flight?

(A)   F
(B)   J
(C)   L
(D)   N
(E)   P[25]

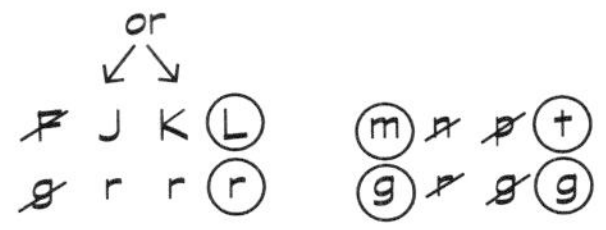

Figure 11.52

This question starts you off with two inexperienced astronauts. Create a mini-sketch and circle M and T, pursuant to the "if." Choosing M and T means you can't choose any more inexperienced astronauts or any more geologists, so N, P, and F are all out.

Figure 11.53

25 PrepTest 35, Sec. 3, Q 4

With P no longer on your flight crew, Rule 3 requires that you have L; circle it.

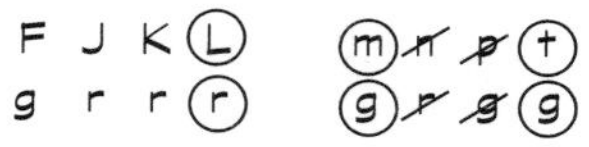

F J K Ⓛ   ⓜ ⌿ ⌿ Ⓣ
g r r Ⓡ   Ⓖ ⌿ ⌿ Ⓖ

Figure 11.54

Now you need one more crew member: an experienced radiobiologist. Your options are J and K.

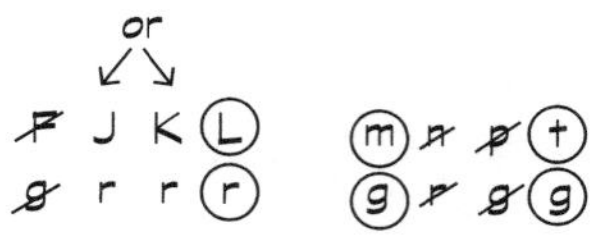

or
↙ ↘
Ⅎ J K Ⓛ   ⓜ ⌿ ⌿ Ⓣ
g̶ r r Ⓡ   Ⓖ ⌿ g̶ Ⓖ

Figure 11.55

So what does the test maker ask you? Who could, but doesn't have to, be on the flight crew? You know that the correct answer will say either "J" or "K." Choice (B), which lists J, is the correct answer. A sloppy reader might fall for choice (C). But because L *must* go on the flight, choice (C) doesn't contain an astronaut who "could be, but need not be, selected for the flight." The other wrong answers simply list astronauts who cannot go on the flight in this case.

5.   **(A)**

   If N is selected for the space flight, which one of the
   following must also be selected?

   (A)   F
   (B)   J
   (C)   L
   (D)   M
   (E)   T[26]

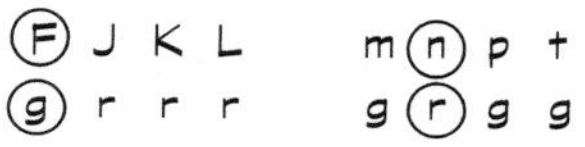

Ⓕ J K L   m Ⓝ p t
Ⓖ r r r   g Ⓡ g g

Figure 11.56

This is the hardest question from this game (and it's still not that hard, given the clear setup you have). Start your mini-sketch with the "if" condition—N is on the flight—and see what it reveals.

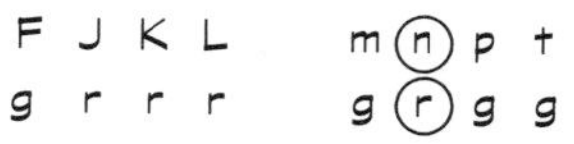

F J K L   m Ⓝ p t
g r r r   g Ⓡ g g

Figure 11.57

Do you remember why N is important? Because choosing N gives you the only inexperienced radiobiologist, the other inexperienced astronaut selected must be a geologist. That means that your two experienced astronauts need to be one geologist and one radiobiologist in order

---

[26] PrepTest 35, Sec. 3, Q 5

for you to get the right mix of experience levels and jobs. The only experienced astronaut who is a geologist is F, so F must be on the flight.

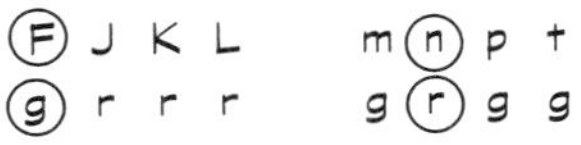

$$\begin{array}{cccccc}
\text{Ⓕ} & \text{J} & \text{K} & \text{L} & \text{m} & \text{ⓝ} & \text{p} & \text{t} \\
\text{ⓖ} & \text{r} & \text{r} & \text{r} & \text{g} & \text{ⓡ} & \text{g} & \text{g}
\end{array}$$

Figure 11.58

You can't determine for sure who the experienced radiobiologist or the inexperienced geologist is, but you don't need to. The question asks for an astronaut who *must* be selected. Choice (A), with F, is correct.

That game illustrates a unique twist on the Selection task, one that the test maker hasn't used much in the past and may not use again. But in a way, it's the exception that proves the rule. Ultimately, what makes this game manageable is what makes any game easier: the restrictions. By having two entities that each belong to two of four subgroups, the test makers severely restricted the possible choices in this game. Any time the test throws you an unusual variation or twist on a familiar action, look for what you know is true of how all games work. You'll wind up spotting the most important restrictions and letting the rest of the deductions work out from there.

DIFFICULT SELECTION

Believe it or not, you've already completed the most challenging examples of Selection representative of anything you're likely to see on test day. Unless there's a big reversal in the trend, the test makers seem unlikely to include Selection games with definite numbers. In the past decade, they've moved more and more to what I've called the "standard" Selection game type, with the numbers open-ended and questions that test your ability to determine minimums and maximums. Of the standard Selection games you've seen, Friends' Photographs, Summer School Courses, and Fruit Stand all rank about equal in difficulty and were all challenging for test takers. The main thing that makes those games tough is the inclusion of so much formal logic. But for you, conditional statements, translations, and contrapositives have been familiar since chapter 3. Provided that you continue your practice and keep your formal logic skills sharp, you've got little to worry about from this game type.

In the next chapter, we'll cover the last of the four common game tasks: Matching games. You've already managed a handful of these, so concentrate on their shared features and on what makes them recognizable. Once you know you're working with a Matching task, I don't expect you to have too much trouble recognizing the relevant restrictions.

CHAPTER 12

MATCHING GAMES

Matching games are the fourth and last of the standard game tasks that I'll cover. The games based on this task are distinguished by the fact that there are always two sets of entities. Your job is to assign the items or attributes in one set to the members of the other. You might, for example, have hikers who carry various types of equipment, or mannequins that receive different colors of clothing. Many test takers find the distinction between Matching and Distribution confusing. In fact, the two game types are very similar and use, at times, comparable sketches. The main difference is that, in Distribution, you may assign each entity only once. If you place Anna on the Blue Team, she can't play for the Red Team at the same time. Matching tasks, on the other hand, allow you to re-use the items or attributes on more than one of the other group's entities. Mannequins A and B can both wear blue shirts while mannequins B and C both have red pants. I'll point out this feature as I take you through the standard Matching examples below. In the end, it's less important that you give a game the "right" name than that you properly assess the task and restrictions.

REAL-LIFE MATCHING

Like all logic game tasks, Matching games correspond to real-life situations that you deal with regularly. Making decisions about what each of several guests will have for dinner provides a perfect illustration. Imagine you have five friends or family members coming over for a meal;

call them A, B, C, D, and E. You've prepared plenty of food for everyone. You have two kinds of soup: split pea and minestrone. You have three different entrées: ham, pasta, and roast beef. You've even made a dessert. In real life, absent any artificial rules, your guests could say, "Oh, I want to try both soups," or, "I'll have a little ham and a little of the pasta." Some of your guests will have dessert, and some might be too full. Your main concern—and this is what corresponds with the Matching task in a logic game—is that there's plenty for everyone. You can give B ham and still have some left to serve to D and E if they'd like to have it, too. Nothing (except running out) prevents you from serving everyone the roast beef, or anything else, for that matter.

Now, you can see how the LSAT imposes restrictions on this kind of game. The test makers can limit the number of entrées each guest has. (The simplest games would simply say, "Each guest will have exactly one kind of soup and exactly one entrée.") They could set restrictions among the guests, e.g., "C will not have any kind of food that A has," or, "B and D will have the same kind of soup." Likewise, they can impose restrictions based on the foods, e.g., "Any guest who has the split pea soup will have ham for an entrée," or, "No guest will have both the minestrone soup and the pasta." Number restrictions are just as important in Matching games as they are in Distribution or Selection games, but because the items to be matched can be re-used, the numbers will play out along two dimensions of the game. In our dinner example, you'll need to pay attention to how many kinds of food you serve to individual guests and how many servings of each kind of food you serve. It's always valuable in Matching to have a clear orientation (an *x*-axis and *y*-axis, if you will) for each part of your task.

	A	B	C	D	E
min					
s/p					
ham					
Pas					
r/b					
des					

Figure 12.1

Record the number restrictions along the appropriate rows and columns. That diagram isn't tough to understand, although this fictional menu is more complicated than any Matching game that has actually appeared on the LSAT over the last 10–12 years.

STANDARD MATCHING

In Part I, you saw a couple of games that exemplify the standard tasks you're likely to encounter if you should have a Matching game on your test. Review the following two setups to refresh your memory of what the test makers were asking you to do. Take special note of the fact that in each game, one set of entities is "stationary" (on the *x*-axis), and your job is to match one or more of the entities from the other set (on the *y*-axis) to members of the first group. There are more entities along the *x*-axis in the first game and more along the *y*-axis in the second, although the two games turn out to have exactly the same number of "cells" in their Master Sketches.

In a repair facility there are exactly six technicians: Stacy, Urma, Wim, Xena, Yolanda, and Zane. Each technician repairs machines of at least one of the following three types—radios, televisions, and VCRs—and no other types. The following conditions apply:

Xena and exactly three other technicians repair radios.
Yolanda repairs both televisions and VCRs.
Stacy does not repair any type of machine that Yolanda repairs.
Zane repairs more types of machines than Yolanda repairs.
Wim does not repair any type of machine that Stacy repairs.
Urma repairs exactly two types of machines.[1]

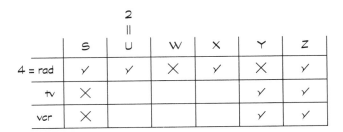

Figure 12.2

---

[1] PrepTest 48, Sec. 2, Game 3

Each of exactly six lunch trucks sells a different one of six kinds of food: falafel, hot dogs, ice cream, pitas, salad, or tacos. Each truck serves one or more of exactly three office buildings: X, Y, or Z. The following conditions apply:

The falafel truck, the hot dog truck, and exactly one other truck each serve Y.

The falafel truck serves exactly two of the office buildings.

The ice cream truck serves more of the office buildings than the salad truck.

The taco truck does not serve Y.

The falafel truck does not serve any office building that the pita truck serves.

The taco truck serves two office buildings that are also served by the ice cream truck.[2]

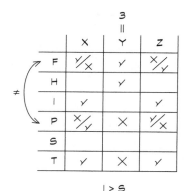

Figure 12.3

Test takers often ask, "How do I know which set of entities to put along the top and which to put along the side?" The answer is that it doesn't really matter. As long as the task is clear, you can orient the game in whichever way fits best in the space on the test booklet page. Most test takers simply acquire a habit of putting the "stationary" entities along one axis or the other (my personal tendency is to put them horizontally across the top of the sketch), but the orientation makes no difference in the logic or restrictions of the game.

As you reviewed those two games, did you notice what set them apart from a standard Distribution game? In the first game, several of the technicians repaired radios, several repaired TVs, and several repaired VCRs. In the second game, the trucks could serve multiple buildings. In both games, the number restrictions served to limit the number of matched items each "stationary" entity could receive *and* the number of times that the "movable" entities could be re-used.

In both games, the most important deductions came from those number restrictions (N in the BLEND checklist) and from the rules that had entities in common, the duplications (D in the BLEND checklist). This will almost always be the case in Matching games. In the Appliance Technician game, for example, Rule 2 affirmatively designated two matches that Yolanda would receive, while Rule 3 prevented Stacy from receiving any matches in common with Yolanda. That allowed you to figure out the exact matches that Stacy and Yolanda would receive and the ones they wouldn't. Rule 4 also duplicated Yolanda, relating her to Zane based on the number of matches each could receive. Again, the result was a precise deduction of exactly which appliances Zane would repair.

[2] PrepTest 43, Sec. 4, Game 4

Standard Matching Practice

Here's one more typical Matching game for you to try. It's different from those above in one significant way: As you conduct your Overview of the game, you'll see that each of the "stationary" entities (the nations) will export *exactly* two crops. Thus, you're likely to do better with a sketch that, beneath each nation, has two slots in which you can record the matches for that nation.

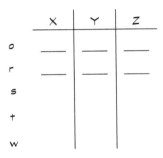

Figure 12.4

Use that as a template for your sketch and give the game a try. Take eight and half minutes to cover the setup, rules, deductions, and questions. Then review the game with the explanations that follow. If you're struggling with the questions, stop and review Steps 1–4 in the explanations to make sure you have a complete Master Sketch. Then return to the question set and give it another try.

The Export Alliance consists of exactly three nations: Nation X, Nation Y, and Nation Z. Each nation in the Alliance exports exactly two of the following five crops: oranges, rice, soybeans, tea, and wheat. Each of these crops is exported by at
least one of the nations in the Alliance. The following conditions hold:

> None of the nations exports both wheat and oranges.
> Nation X exports soybeans if, but only if, Nation Y does also.
> If Nation Y exports rice, then Nations X and Z both export tea.
> Nation Y does not export any crop that Nation Z exports.

18. Which one of the following could be an accurate list, for each of the nations, of the crops it exports?

    (A) Nation X: oranges, rice; Nation Y: oranges, tea; Nation Z: soybeans, wheat
    (B) Nation X: oranges, tea; Nation Y: oranges, rice; Nation Z: soybeans, wheat
    (C) Nation X: oranges, wheat; Nation Y: oranges, tea; Nation Z: rice, soybeans
    (D) Nation X: rice, wheat; Nation Y: oranges, tea; Nation Z: oranges, soybeans
    (E) Nation X: soybeans, rice; Nation Y: oranges, tea; Nation Z: soybeans, wheat

19. If Nation X exports soybeans and tea, then which one of the following could be true?

    (A) Nation Y exports oranges.
    (B) Nation Y exports rice.
    (C) Nation Y exports tea.
    (D) Nation Z exports soybeans.
    (E) Nation Z exports tea.

20. If Nation Z exports tea and wheat, then which one of the following must be true?

    (A) Nation X exports oranges.
    (B) Nation X exports tea.
    (C) Nation X exports wheat.
    (D) Nation Y exports rice.
    (E) Nation Y exports soybeans.

21. It CANNOT be the case that both Nation X and Nation Z export which one of the following crops?

    (A) oranges
    (B) rice
    (C) soybeans
    (D) tea
    (E) wheat

22. Which one of the following pairs CANNOT be the two crops that Nation Y exports?

    (A) oranges and rice
    (B) oranges and soybeans
    (C) rice and tea
    (D) rice and wheat
    (E) soybeans and wheat[3]

---

[3] PrepTest 45, Sec. 3, Game 4, Qs 18–22

Explanations

STEPS 1 AND 2: Overview and Sketch

It's understandable if this game reminded you of a Distribution game. The only thing that sets it apart is the fact that you'll have to use one of the crops twice. There are six spaces to fill in the Sketch, but only five different crops are exported.

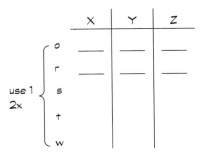

Figure 12.5

In fact, determining which of the crops is repeated is central to the Deduction step.

STEP 3: Rules

As expected, the rules cut across both dimensions of this game. Some restrict the crops that can be exported together, while others present restrictions among the nations.

Rule 1 provides that wheat and oranges cannot be exported by the same nation.

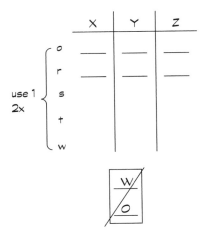

Figure 12.6

Rule 2 is a rare formal logic construction, the "if, and only if" statement. I actually showed you this rule back in chapter 3. As you'll recall, "if, and only if" (or as it is stated here, "if, *but* only if") makes the second term in the statement both necessary and sufficient for the first term. You can depict the rule like this:

$$\text{If } X_s \rightarrow Y_s \quad \text{If } Y_s \rightarrow X_s$$
$$\text{If } Y_{\cancel{s}} \rightarrow X_{\cancel{s}} \quad \text{If } X_{\cancel{s}} \rightarrow Y_{\cancel{s}}$$

Figure 12.6A

Or like this:

$$X_s \leftrightarrow Y_s$$

Figure 12.7

Either way, the important thing to take away from this rule is that either both Nations X and Y export soybeans, or neither does. That provides a Limited Options scenario that you can add to your Sketch.

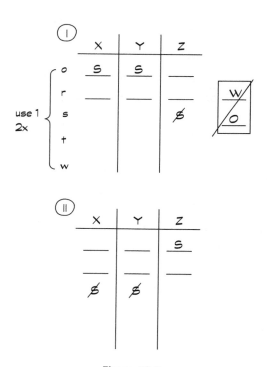

Figure 12.8

Rule 3 is another conditional formal logic statement, albeit of a more routine kind than Rule 2. Jot it down along with its contrapositive.

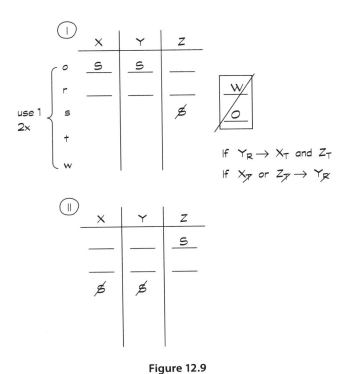

Figure 12.9

Rule 4 creates a restriction between two of the nations: Y and Z cannot have any exports in common.

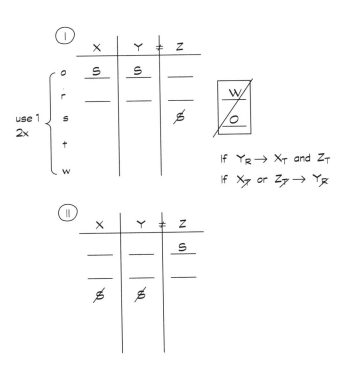

Figure 12.10

There are no floaters in this game. All of the nations and all of the crops have at least one restriction pertinent to them.

STEP 4: Deductions

If you didn't create a Limited Options sketch based on Rule 2, you'd need to do that now. Nothing creates more restriction within the game than that.

The next area to investigate is the number restrictions within the game. Since each nation exports exactly two crops, and since the opening paragraph of the game's setup tells you that all of the crops must be exported, you know that you'll use exactly one crop two times in any acceptable arrangement.

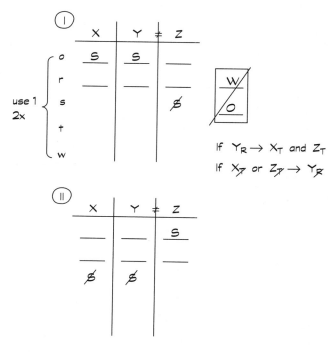

Figure 12.11

In Option I, where X and Y both export soybeans, the four other crops will be used only one time each. That implicates Rule 3. You can deduce that, in Option I, Nation Y cannot export rice. If it did, both Nation X and Nation Z would have to export tea. There wouldn't be any space left at that point to export both wheat and oranges. Add that deduction to the sketch for Option I.

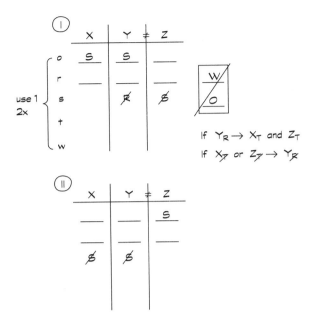

Figure 12.12

Nation Y can, but does not have to, export rice in Option II. You can note that Y may not export both rice and tea in Option II, however. Once Nation Y exports rice, both X and Z will export tea. Since you must use only one of the crops exactly two times and each of the others one time, you can safely conclude that Y won't be allowed to export both rice and tea.

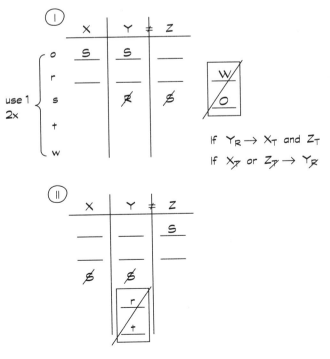

Figure 12.13

None of the remaining rules combine to lead to further deductions. So you're ready to tackle the questions.

STEP 5: **Questions**

There are five questions for this game, and they're arranged in the perfect order. The Acceptability question is first (as it nearly always is). Then you have two "If" questions. Finally, two Must Be False questions finish the set.

18. **(A)**

Which one of the following could be an accurate list, for each of the nations, of the crops it exports?

(A)   Nation X: oranges, rice; Nation Y: oranges, tea;
      Nation Z: soybeans, wheat
(B)   Nation X: oranges, tea; Nation Y: oranges, rice;
      Nation Z: soybeans, wheat
(C)   Nation X: oranges, wheat; Nation Y: oranges, tea;
      Nation Z: rice, soybeans
(D)   Nation X: rice, wheat; Nation Y: oranges, tea;
      Nation Z: oranges, soybeans
(E)   Nation X: soybeans, rice; Nation Y: oranges, tea;
      Nation Z: soybeans, wheat[4]

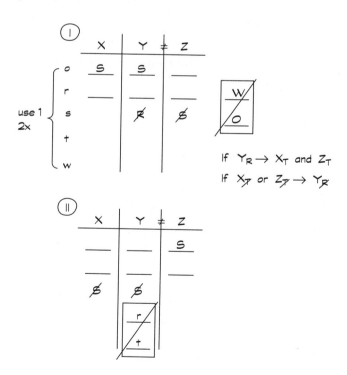

Figure 12.14

As always, attack this Acceptability question by using the rules to eliminate answer choices that break them.

Choice (C) breaks Rule 1 because it has Nation X exporting oranges *and* wheat.

Choice (E) breaks Rule 2; this answer has Nation X exporting soybeans, but not Nation Y.

Choice (B) breaks Rule 3; Nation Y is exporting rice, but Nation Z is not exporting tea.

Choice (D) breaks Rule 4; Nations Y and Z are both exporting oranges.

That leaves choice (A), the correct answer.

19. **(A)**

If Nation X exports soybeans and tea, then which one of the following could be true?

(A)   Nation Y exports oranges.
(B)   Nation Y exports rice.
(C)   Nation Y exports tea.
(D)   Nation Z exports soybeans.
(E)   Nation Z exports tea.[5]

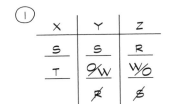

Figure 12.15

The "if" in this question stem places you in Option I (because Nation X is exporting soybeans) and adds some extra information as well. To start your mini-sketch, copy over Option I and add T under Nation X's column.

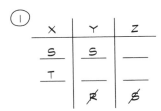

Figure 12.16

Now, consider the remaining crops—oranges, rice, and wheat—each of which must be exported. Oranges and wheat cannot be exported by the same country (Rule 1). So Nation Y will export one of them and Nation Z the other.

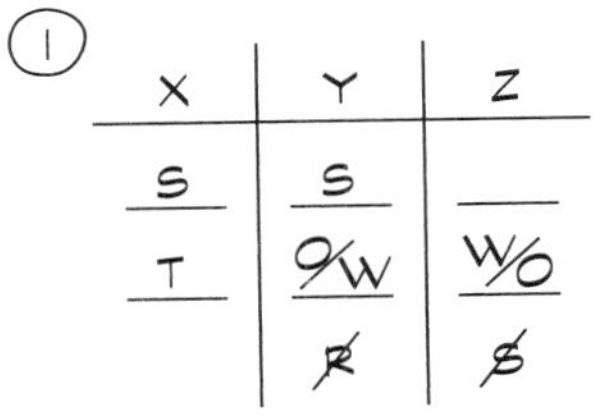

Figure 12.17

---

5 PrepTest 45, Sec. 3, Q 19

That leaves only rice to be exported and only one open space within the framework. Nation Z must export rice.

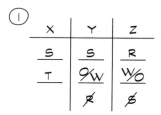

Figure 12.18

Now, characterize the answer choices. The correct answer *could be true* (you can already guess that it concerns oranges or wheat, the only two crops that aren't strictly determined), while the four wrong answers *must be false*. Choice (A) is the correct answer; Nation Y *could*, but does not have to, export oranges. A quick glance confirms that all four remaining answers are impossible in the mini-sketch for this question.

20. **(E)**

   If Nation Z exports tea and wheat, then which one of the following must be true?

   (A) Nation X exports oranges.
   (B) Nation X exports tea.
   (C) Nation X exports wheat.
   (D) Nation Y exports rice.
   (E) Nation Y exports soybeans.[6]

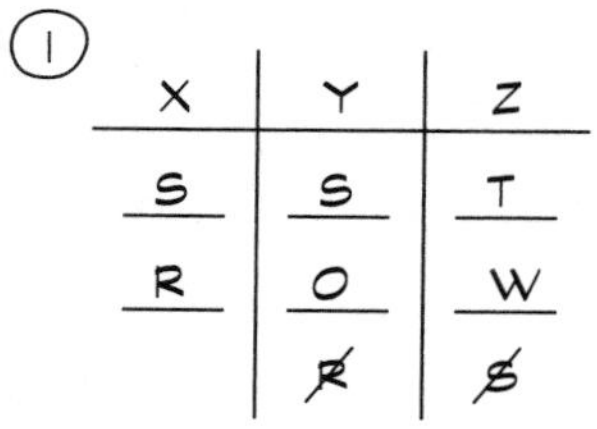

Figure 12.19

This question's "if" allows you to determine all six spaces within the framework. Since the "if" requires Nation Z to export tea and wheat, you know that you're in Option I (as Nation Z must export soybeans in Option II). Start a mini-sketch by using Option I and adding T and W in Nation Z's column.

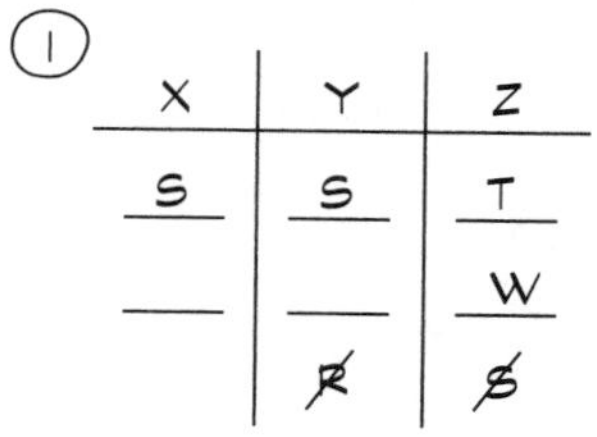

Figure 12.20

That leaves only rice and oranges to be placed. Nation Y cannot export rice in Option I. So Nation X will export rice and Nation Y, oranges.

---

[6] PrepTest 45, Sec. 3, Q 20

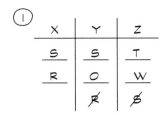

Figure 12.21

Naturally, with a completed sketch for this question, the stem calls for a *must be true* answer. That's choice (E); Nation Y will export soybeans here. As your mini-sketch illustrates, all four wrong answers are false under this question's conditions.

21. **(C)**

It CANNOT be the case that both Nation X and Nation Z export which one of the following crops?

(A) oranges
(B) rice
(C) soybeans
(D) tea
(E) wheat[7]

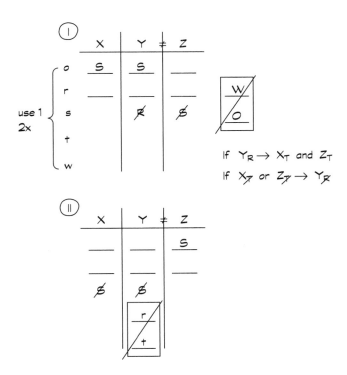

Figure 12.22

_____

[7] PrepTest 45, Sec. 3, Q 21

This question goes straight to the heart of your Limited Options sketch. The crop that Nations X and Z cannot both export is soybeans, of course. Choice (C) gets it right. You've had it right since you analyzed Rule 2 in light of the overall number restrictions in this game.

22. **(C)**

Which one of the following pairs CANNOT be the two crops that Nation Y exports?

(A) oranges and rice
(B) oranges and soybeans
(C) rice and tea
(D) rice and wheat
(E) soybeans and wheat[8]

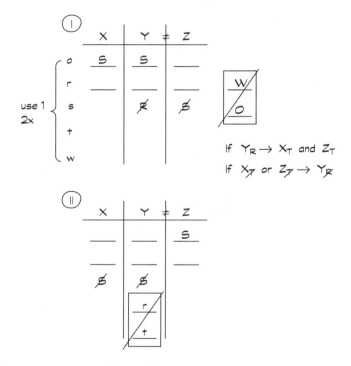

Figure 12.23

Like question 21, this question grants you a point simply for making deductions. Looking at your Master Sketch, you see two potential answers to this question. Nation Y may export neither soybeans and rice nor rice and tea. Choice (C) seizes on the second of those two forbidden pairs and is thus the correct answer. Recall how you deduced that Nation Y could not export both rice and tea: The overall number restrictions in the game provided that exactly one crop would be exported by two nations, and the other four crops by one nation each. When Nation Y exports rice, Rule 2 kicks in, and Nations X and Z export tea. So if you were to have Nation

Y export tea in this case, there would be three nations exporting tea and at least one crop would not be exported.

While the Sketch for this game looked a little different than those for the Appliance Technician and Lunch Trucks games, this game should still be considered a standard Matching task. There were "stationary" entities (the nations) and "movable" ones (the crops). The rules provided restrictions among both the "stationary" and the "movable" entities. Most importantly, one of the "movable" entities had to be re-used in order to complete the game. Be willing to modify your Sketch when doing so better fits a game's task and restrictions. Use that as your rule of thumb in the next section of this chapter, and the minor twists and variations that you encounter won't present more than a speed bump along your road to success with Matching games.

MATCHING TWISTS

Apart from Sequencing, Matching is probably the game type that has seen the greatest variety of minor departures from the norm over the years. Unlike Sequencing, where the variations themselves fall into categories (Loose Sequencing, Double Sequencing, Circular Sequencing, and the like), Matching variations tend to come along as one-time twists on the expected theme. This is probably because Matching isn't as common a task as Sequencing (which appears on nearly every LSAT). In this section, I'll show you three relatively recent Matching variants. What I want you to see is that, in each case, conducting a careful overview of the game allows you to create a useful, strategic sketch. Once that's in place, you can manage the game with no more difficulty (and sometimes considerably less) than in any of the standard Matching games you'll see in this book (or on your official test day).

The first Matching variant is a game that you saw in Part I of this book. Take a few moments to refresh your memory of the game and its restrictions. I'll give it a brief review below.

> A clown will select a costume consisting of two pieces and
> no others: a jacket and overalls. One piece of the costume
> will be entirely one color, and the other piece will be plaid.
> Selection is subject to the following restrictions:
>> If the jacket is plaid, then there must be exactly three
>> colors in it.
>> If the overalls are plaid, then there must be exactly two
>> colors in them.
>> The jacket and overalls must have exactly one color in
>> common.
>> Green, red, and violet are the only colors that can be in
>> the jacket.
>> Red, violet, and yellow are the only colors that can be in
>> the overalls.[9]

---

[9] PrepTest 51, Sec. 4, Game 1

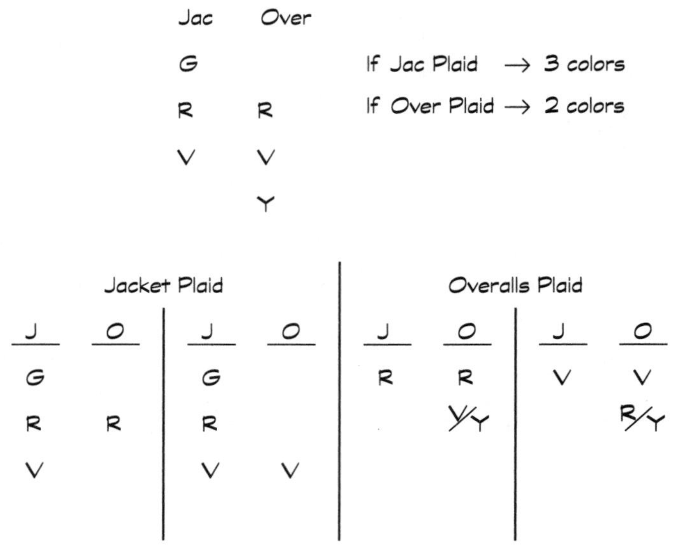

```
        Jac      Over

         G                      If  Jac Plaid   →  3 colors

         R        R             If  Over Plaid  →  2 colors

         V        V

                  Y


      Jacket Plaid                    Overalls Plaid

   J    O  │  J    O    │    J    O  │  J    O

     G     │    G       │      R    R │    V    V

     R    R │    R      │       Y̶/Y   │     R̶/Y

     V     │    V    V
```

Figure 12.24

In this game, the "stationary" entities are the jacket and overalls. The "movable" entities are the colors. The test makers' use of "plain" and "plaid" at first appears to be a third consideration, but notice that it's actually just a clever way of introducing number restrictions. When the jacket is plaid, you match three colors to it; when the overalls are plaid, they get two matching colors. Once you use Rules 1 and 2 to set up dual Limited Options sketches, the further restrictions imposed by Rules 4 and 5 leave you only six ways in which this Matching puzzle can be solved. Test takers who spend the time to make a complete, thoughtful Master Sketch find the questions associated with this game to be a snap.

Matching with a Limited Pool of Entities

The next game is new to you, so take a few minutes to complete Steps 1–4 of the Kaplan Method and produce a Master Sketch reflecting all of the available deductions. As you set this one up, think about which of the "stationary" entities (the weeks) are the most restricted. Starting from the two most limited weeks, you can set off a string of deductions that leaves you with only a handful of acceptable arrangements. Take four minutes and see how much certainty you can derive.

> A five-week adult education course consists of exactly five lectures with a different lecture given each week. No lecture is given more than once. Each lecture is delivered by a different speaker. The following conditions are true about the speakers and their lectures:
>
> Each speaker lectures on a philosopher in whom he or she specializes.
>
> No two speakers lecture on the same philosopher.
>
> The first week's speaker specializes in Kant, Locke, and Mill, and no other philosophers.
>
> The second week's speaker specializes in Kant, Locke, Mill, and Nietzsche, and no other philosophers.
>
> The third week's and fourth week's speakers each specialize in Mill and Nietzsche, and no other philosophers.
>
> The fifth week's speaker specializes in Nietzsche, Ockham, and Plato, and no other philosophers.[10]

By changing a couple of the rules, the test makers could easily turn this game into a Sequencing action. But notice why I don't categorize it that way. None of the rules here impose any restriction based on one entity being earlier or later than another. Nor do any of them require that any of the lectures be separated by a certain number of spaces. Thus, the five weeks of the philosophy program act as "stationary" entities. Your task is to match an acceptable lecture to each one.

Your overview should have noted that the primary restrictions pertain to the numbers. Each week sees one lecture, and the lectures are never repeated (an unusually tight limitation for a Matching action, but one that makes this game much easier in the long run).

1 per wk.	1	2	3	4	5
No repeats					

Figure 12.25

Four of the six rules fill in the possible matches for each week.

1 per wk.	1	2	3	4	5
	K	K	M	M	N
No repeats	L	L	N	N	O
	M	M			P
		N			

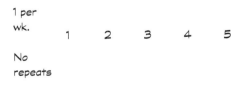

Figure 12.26

---

[10] PrepTest 34, Sec. 4, Game 2

Remember that I told you to look for the two most restricted weeks. With this sketch, it's clear that they are weeks 3 and 4. What must happen during those two weeks? The M and N lectures, and only those lectures, must be delivered. There simply are no other alternatives. That means that you can cross M and N off of the list under any other weeks. That leaves:

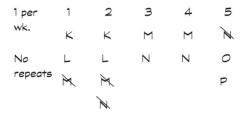

Figure 12.27

Weeks 1 and 2 will have lectures K-L or L-K; weeks 3 and 4 will have lectures M-N or N-M; week 5 will have either lecture O or lecture P. There are only eight acceptable arrangements for this game.

Take a look at how the test makers rewarded you for making those important deductions.

8. Which one of the following statements could be true?

    (A) The first speaker lectures on Mill.
    (B) The second speaker lectures on Mill.
    (C) The second speaker lectures on Nietzsche.
    (D) The fifth speaker lectures on Nietzsche.
    (E) The fifth speaker lectures on Ockham.[11]

The first four answer choices all deal with lectures M or N. You know that those can only occur in weeks 3 and 4. Your Master Sketch reveals that choices (A)–(D) *must be false*. The correct *could be true* answer is choice (E); lecture O is possible in week 5.

The next one is little bit harder. Use your Master Sketch to determine which answer would lock down the lecture schedule for all five weeks. Eliminate the choices that leave one or more of the weeks up in the air.

10. Which one of the following, if known, would allow one to determine the entire lecture schedule and identify for each week the philosopher who is lectured on that week?

    (A) the weeks that Kant, Locke, and Mill are lectured on
    (B) the weeks that Kant, Mill, and Nietzsche are lectured on
    (C) the weeks that Kant, Mill, and Ockham are lectured on
    (D) the weeks that Mill, Nietzsche, and Ockham are lectured on
    (E) the weeks that Mill, Nietzsche, and Plato are lectured on[12]

---

[11] PrepTest 34, Sec. 4, Q 8

[12] PrepTest 34, Sec. 4, Q 10

In order to determine all five of the weeks' lectures, you'll need to know three things: the lecture for either week 1 or week 2, the lecture for either week 3 or week 4, and the lecture for week 5. Choice (C) is the one that provides all three. Thus, it's the correct answer. Notice that choices (A) and (B) both fail to clear up the lecture in week 5, while choices (D) and (E) both leave weeks 1 and 2 undetermined.

Matching with Spatial Restrictions

In the next game, you're asked to match one of three decorative light colors to each of 10 stores. If 10 stores sounds like a lot of entities for an LSAT logic game, it is. But pay attention to how those 10 "stationary" entities are arranged. With a strong overview, you can get a very clear picture of the task and lay out your sketch in a way that will allow you to anticipate most of the restrictions in this game. Take four minutes to go through Steps 1–4 of the Kaplan Method and produce your Master Sketch for this game.

There are exactly ten stores and no other buildings on Oak Street. On the north side of the street, from west to east, are stores 1, 3, 5, 7, and 9; on the south side of the street, also from west to east, are stores 2, 4, 6, 8, and 10. The stores on the north side are located directly across the street from those on the south side, facing each other in pairs, as follows: 1 and 2; 3 and 4; 5 and 6; 7 and 8; 9 and 10. Each store is decorated with lights in exactly one of the following colors: green, red, and yellow. The stores have been decorated with lights according to the following conditions:

   No store is decorated with lights of the same color as those
    of any store adjacent to it.
   No store is decorated with lights of the same color as those
    of the store directly across the street from it.
   Yellow lights decorate exactly one store on each side of
    the street.
   Red lights decorate store 4.
   Yellow lights decorate store 5.[13]

Did you use the description in the game setup to take control of this game's task? Although the opening paragraph is one of the longest you'll see, it conveys a very clear picture of the "stationary" entities' arrangement.

Figure 12.28

Compare your sketch to that picture, and make sure you were rigorous in following the instructions laid out in the setup text.

13 PrepTest 33, Sec. 4, Game 4

Once you saw how the shops were arranged, you should have anticipated the kinds of restrictions introduced in Rules 1 and 2. The game was so specific about which shops were next to or directly across from one another that the test makers must have had in mind that adjacent or facing shops would be subject to restrictions on their colors of lights.

G, R, Y

Facing diff.	1	3	5	7	9
Adjacent diff.	2	4	6	8	10

Figure 12.29

Rule 3 further restricted the possible arrangements. In fact, the north side of the street will have one shop with yellow lights and four with either red or green.

G, R, Y

Facing diff.	1	3	5	7	9 ← 1Y
Adjacent diff.	2	4	6	8	10 ← 1Y

Figure 12.30

Rules 4 and 5 imposed strict assignments for two of the stores.

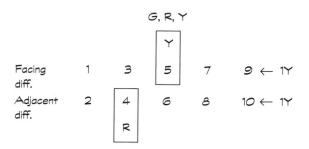

Figure 12.31

Did you use those last two rules to make further deductions about the shops adjacent to and across from stores 4 and 5? Since store 3 is next to a store with yellow lights and across from one with red, its lights must be green.

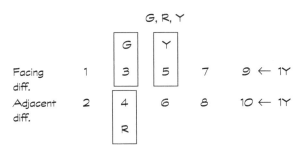

Figure 12.32

That, in turn, told you that store 1's lights must be red (remember, only one store per side of the street can have yellow lights according to Rule 3).

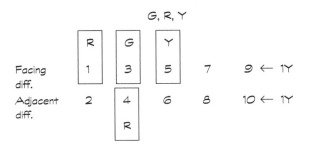

Figure 12.33

Like store 3, store 6 is also restricted from having yellow lights and from having red lights. Its lights must be green.

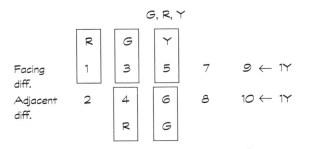

Figure 12.34

From what you have at this point, you can determine that stores 2, 8, 7, and 9 are limited to two options.

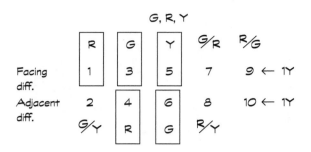

Figure 12.35

Only store 10 remains entirely unrestricted at the end of the Deductions step. Even it, of course, will be restricted by any further information about store 8 or store 9.

Take a look at a couple of the questions associated with this game, and you'll see how your use of Steps 1–4 of the Kaplan Method turn directly into points on the test.

20. If green lights decorate store 7, then each of the following statements could be false EXCEPT:

   (A)   Green lights decorate store 2.
   (B)   Green lights decorate store 10.
   (C)   Red lights decorate store 8.
   (D)   Red lights decorate store 9.
   (E)   Yellow lights decorate store 2.[14]

For this one, create a mini-sketch based on the new "if" condition introduced in the question stem.

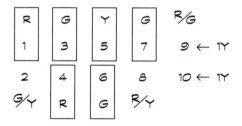

Figure 12.36

With store 7 assigned green lights, you know that store 9 must have red lights.

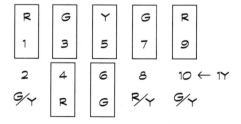

Figure 12.37

---

[14] PrepTest 33, Sec. 4, Q 20

At this point, you cannot determine precisely which lights will decorate stores 2, 8, and 10. And that's the point. The four wrong answers in this question *could be false*, and all four of them— choices (A), (B), (C), and (E)—involve stores 2, 8, or 10. The correct answer *must be true* and goes directly to the deduction that follows from the question's new "if" clause. You determined that store 9 must have red lights, and that's exactly what the correct answer, choice (D), says.

21. Which one of the following statements must be true?

    (A)   Green lights decorate store 10.
    (B)   Red lights decorate store 1.
    (C)   Red lights decorate store 8.
    (D)   Yellow lights decorate store 8.
    (E)   Yellow lights decorate store 10.[15]

For this question, you needn't do more than characterize the correct answer—it *must be true*—and consult your Master Sketch. Store 1 must have red lights, just as the correct answer, choice (B), states. Notice that, here again, the wrong answers all involve stores whose color of lights can't be determined.

Those unusual Matching games are good examples of why, in the end, you shouldn't agonize over categorizing game types and subtypes and variations. In all three cases, you were able to manage the game by using the Overview step to assess the situation that the test makers described and what they were asking you to do with it. By attending to the task described in the setup, you were able to construct an effective sketch. You can see from those games that having a sketch that organizes the game's information in a clear, strategic way—a way that's *applicable to the game*—is more valuable than memorizing a limited number of set sketches and trying to make them accommodate every game action, regardless of how unusual or specific the test makers have designed it to be. Take what's familiar in a game and base your approach on that, but be open to what you need to do a little differently when the tasks described by the test makers don't fit the stereotype. The test makers always provide the information and restrictions needed to answer every question. Some test takers cut themselves off from the most helpful part of a game because it doesn't fit their preconceived notion of how a specific game type is "supposed to" work.

DIFFICULT MATCHING

The most difficult examples of Matching games are often built out of standard Matching game tasks. Rather than rely on unusual twists and turns to make these games harder, the test makers simply present the typical combination of "stationary" and "movable" entities, but provide fewer or less powerful restrictions.

---

[15] PrepTest 33, Sec. 4, Q 21

Difficult Matching Practice

Give the following game a try. Don't time yourself on this challenging example. Instead, go through it carefully, applying each step of the Kaplan Method appropriately. When you're finished, or if you find yourself struggling with the setup, check your work against the explanations. Here's a hint: Pay as much attention to which matches you *cannot* determine as you do to those you can.

For the school paper, five students—Jiang, Kramer, Lopez, Megregian, and O'Neill—each review one or more of exactly three plays: *Sunset*, *Tamerlane*, and *Undulation*, but do not review any other plays. The following conditions must apply:

Kramer and Lopez each review fewer of the plays than Megregian.

Neither Lopez nor Megregian reviews any play Jiang reviews.

Kramer and O'Neill both review *Tamerlane*.

Exactly two of the students review exactly the same play or plays as each other.

19. Which one of the following could be an accurate and complete list of the students who review only *Sunset*?

   (A)   Lopez
   (B)   O'Neill
   (C)   Jiang, Lopez
   (D)   Kramer, O'Neill
   (E)   Lopez, Megregian

20. Which one of the following must be true?

   (A)   Jiang reviews more of the plays than Lopez does.
   (B)   Megregian reviews more of the plays than Jiang does.
   (C)   Megregian reviews more of the plays than O'Neill does.
   (D)   O'Neill reviews more of the plays than Jiang does.
   (E)   O'Neill reviews more of the plays than Kramer does.

21. If exactly three of the students review *Undulation*, which one of the following could be true?

   (A)   Megregian does not review *Undulation*.
   (B)   O'Neill does not review *Undulation*.
   (C)   Jiang reviews *Undulation*.
   (D)   Lopez reviews *Tamerlane*.
   (E)   O'Neill reviews *Sunset*.

22. Which one of the following could be an accurate and complete list of the students who review *Tamerlane*?

   (A)   Jiang, Kramer
   (B)   Kramer, O'Neill
   (C)   Kramer, Lopez, O'Neill
   (D)   Kramer, Megregian, O'Neill
   (E)   Lopez, Megregian, O'Neill

23. If Jiang does not review *Tamerlane*, then which one of the following must be true?

   (A)   Jiang reviews *Sunset*.
   (B)   Lopez reviews *Undulation*.
   (C)   Megregian reviews *Sunset*.
   (D)   Megregian reviews *Tamerlane*.
   (E)   O'Neill reviews *Undulation*.[16]

Explanations

STEPS 1 AND 2: **Overview and Sketch**

The difficulty of this game is roughly equal to that of the first two games you reviewed in this chapter, the Appliance Technicians game and the one with the Lunch Trucks. So you've handled games of this caliber already. Here, the scenario described involves five student reporters who will each review one or more of three plays. The plays aren't going anywhere, so use them as your "stationary" entities.

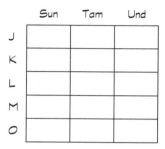

Figure 12.38

According to the opening paragraph of the game, each of the students reviews between one and three of the plays. The more clearly you understand the number restrictions in this game, the easier it will be.

STEP 3: **Rules**

The rules in this game impose limits either on the number of plays each student can review or on which students can review the same play(s) as one another.

Rule 1 tells you that K and L each review fewer plays than M. Just jot that down beneath the framework for the time being.

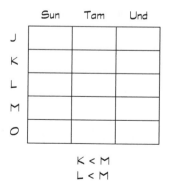

Figure 12.39

Rule 2 restricts L and M from reviewing any play that J reviews. You can depict that as formal logic or with a descriptive note.

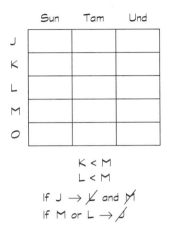

Figure 12.40

Rule 3 you can add into the framework. This concreteness is most welcome.

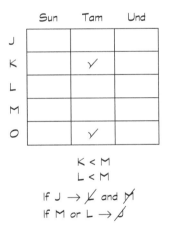

Figure 12.41

The last rule is worded in a tricky way. Make sure you capture its meaning with a quick paraphrase: Exactly two of the students (not three, not four) will review exactly the same roster of plays as one another. If a particular arrangement threatens to create three students with the same list of reviews, that arrangement is unacceptable.

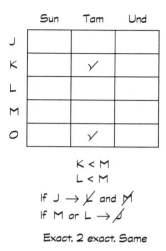

Figure 12.42

There are no floaters here. All of the students are restricted to some extent. But it's well worth noting that while O will definitely review *Tamerlane*, O has no restrictions with respect to any of the other students and thus may, or may not, review any of the other plays.

STEP 4: Deductions

You can learn a lot about this game by considering the number restrictions. Start with M, the most restricted entity in the game. M must review at least two plays (Rule 1), but can't review any play that J reviews (Rule 2). Thus, M cannot review all three plays. Add notation to your sketch signifying that M will review exactly two plays.

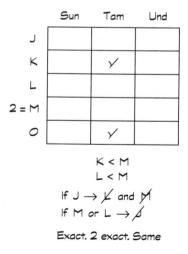

Figure 12.43

Since M reviews only two plays and reviews more plays than K or L (Rule 1), you can conclude that K and L review one play each.

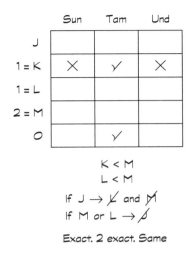

Figure 12.44

Notice that, thanks to Rule 3, K's row is now closed off. K reviews only *Tamerlane*.

Similarly, since M is reviewing two plays but cannot review any play that J reviews (Rule 2), you know that J reviews only one play as well.

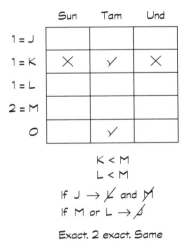

Figure 12.45

It's worth noting that J must review the one play M does not review, and M must review the two plays J does not. Between the two of them, they'll cover all three plays every time.

STEP 5: Questions

Expect the test makers to reward you for your deductions about the numbers. Expect, too, that they'll involve Rule 4—the one requiring exactly two students to review exactly the same play(s)—in at least one or two questions about acceptable arrangements.

19. **(A)**

Which one of the following could be an accurate and complete list of the students who review only *Sunset*?

(A) Lopez
(B) O'Neill
(C) Jiang, Lopez
(D) Kramer, O'Neill
(E) Lopez, Megregian[17]

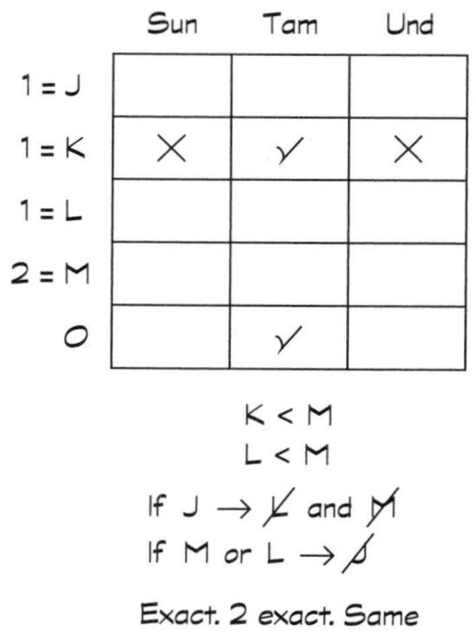

	Sun	Tam	Und
1 = J			
1 = K	✗	✓	✗
1 = L			
2 = M			
O		✓	

K < M
L < M
If J → L̸ and M̸
If M or L → J̸

Exact. 2 exact. Same

Figure 12.46

Make sure you read this question stem carefully. The correct answer is an acceptable list of those who review *only Sunset*. That allows you to get rid of choices (B) and (D) immediately. You know that K and O review *Tamerlane* (Rule 3). You can also eliminate choice (E), since M must review two plays. *Sunset* cannot be M's only review. That leaves choices (A) and (C). A check of the rules in your sketch reminds you that L and J may not review the same play(s) as one another. Eliminate choice (C). The correct answer is choice (A); L could be the only student who reviews only *Sunset*.

20. **(B)**

Which one of the following must be true?

(A) Jiang reviews more of the plays than Lopez does.
(B) Megregian reviews more of the plays than Jiang does.
(C) Megregian reviews more of the plays than O'Neill does.
(D) O'Neill reviews more of the plays than Jiang does.
(E) O'Neill reviews more of the plays than Kramer does.[18]

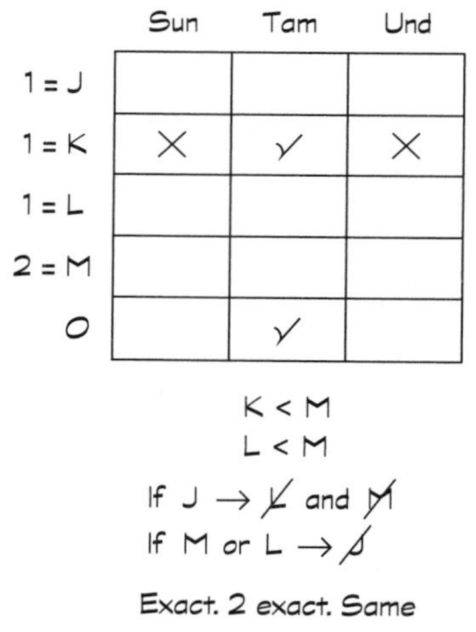

	Sun	Tam	Und
1 = J			
1 = K	✗	✓	✗
1 = L			
2 = M			
O		✓	

K < M
L < M
If J → L̸ and M̸
If M or L → J̸

Exact. 2 exact. Same

Figure 12.47

There's nothing fancy about this question. Characterize the answer choices and evaluate them based on your Master Sketch. The correct answer *must be true*. So each of the four wrong answers *could be false*.

---

[17] PrepTest 42, Sec. 1, Q 19
[18] PrepTest 42, Sec. 1, Q 20

Choice (A) is definitely false. J and L each review one play. Eliminate this choice.

Choice (B) must be true. You deduced that M reviews two plays and J one. This choice is correct and is the first point produced directly by your number-based deductions.

All three of the remaining choices—choices (C), (D), and (E)—include O, who you'll remember is the "almost floater" here. Since O can review one, two, or all three of the plays, there's no way to determine that O must review more or fewer plays than anyone else.

21. **(E)**

If exactly three of the students review *Undulation*, which one of the following could be true?

(A) Megregian does not review *Undulation*.
(B) O'Neill does not review *Undulation*.
(C) Jiang reviews *Undulation*.
(D) Lopez reviews *Tamerlane*.
(E) O'Neill reviews *Sunset*.[19]

	Sun	Tam	Und
1 = J			✗
1 = K	✗	✓	✗
1 = L	✗	✗	✓
2 = M			✓
O		✓	✓

Figure 12.48

This is the first "If" question in the set. Create a mini-sketch by copying over your Master Sketch framework and adding the new condition.

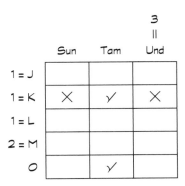

3
||

	Sun	Tam	Und
1 = J			
1 = K	✗	✓	✗
1 = L			
2 = M			
O		✓	

Figure 12.49

Consider how you could get three reviewers for *Undulation*. K is already out. Adding J would make it impossible to have L or M (Rule 2), leaving only two possible reviewers. Thus, you cannot have J review *Undulation*. The three student reviewers there will have to be L, M, and O.

19 PrepTest 42, Sec. 1, Q 21

	Sun	Tam	Und
1 = J			X
1 = K	X	✓	X
1 = L	X	X	✓
2 = M			✓
O		✓	✓

Figure 12.50

Since L can review only one play, L's row is closed off.

At this point, you know that either J reviews *Sunset* and M reviews *Tamerlane,* or vice versa. But there's no way to determine which. You also have no way of knowing whether O reviews *Sunset.*

Since the question stem calls for a statement that *could be true,* one of the open possibilities just mentioned will be in the correct answer. The wrong answers, which *must be false,* will be ruled out in the mini-sketch.

Choices (A) through (D) all *must be false.* Check the mini-sketch and you'll see each of them contradicted there. The correct answer is choice (E). O could review *Sunset* under this question's conditions.

22. **(D)**

Which one of the following could be an accurate and complete list of the students who review *Tamerlane?*

(A) Jiang, Kramer
(B) Kramer, O'Neill
(C) Kramer, Lopez, O'Neill
(D) Kramer, Megregian, O'Neill
(E) Lopez, Megregian, O'Neill[20]

	Sun	Tam	Und
1 = J			
1 = K	X	✓	X
1 = L			
2 = M			
O		✓	

K < M
L < M
If J → K̸ and M̸
If M or L → J̸

Exact. 2 exact. Same

Figure 12.51

From Rule 3, you know that a list of students reviewing *Tamerlane* must include K and O. That allows you to eliminate choice (A), which lacks O, and choice (E), which lacks K. The three remaining choices all have K and O, but choices (B) and (C) lack both J and M. Remember that you deduced that between them, J and M would review all three plays. So one of J or M must be in a list of the students reviewing *Tamerlane.* Only choice (D) is acceptable and, therefore, the correct answer.

---

[20] PrepTest 42, Sec. 1, Q 22

23. **(D)**

If Jiang does not review *Tamerlane*, then which one of the following must be true?

(A) Jiang reviews *Sunset*.
(B) Lopez reviews *Undulation*.
(C) Megregian reviews *Sunset*.
(D) Megregian reviews *Tamerlane*.
(E) O'Neill reviews *Undulation*.[21]

	Sun	Tam	Und
1 = J	X	✓	X
1 = K	X	✓	X
1 = L		X	
2 = M	✓	X	✓
O		✓	

Figure 12.52

Here's one more "If" question. Copy over the Master Sketch framework, and add in the new condition.

	Sun	Tam	Und
1 = J	X	✓	X
1 = K	X	✓	X
1 = L			
2 = M			
O		✓	

Figure 12.53

As soon as you know that J does not review *Tamerlane*, you can be certain that M does.

	Sun	Tam	Und
1 = J	X	✓	X
1 = K	X	✓	X
1 = L		X	
2 = M	✓	X	✓
O		✓	

Figure 12.54

That's as far as you need to go. The correct answer *must be true*. It's choice (D), which says that M reviews *Tamerlane*.

Congratulations. That was among the toughest Matching games to appear in the last ten years. Most test takers—those that haven't trained with the Kaplan Method, anyway—don't consider the impact that rules have on the number restrictions within the game. Because you've learned to look for the limitations that will allow you to reduce the number of acceptable arrangements down to a manageable handful, you're able to find the key deductions that the questions reward. The test makers may use unfamiliar patterns, odd scenarios, or obscure-sounding rules in their attempt to make some games harder. Your work with the Kaplan Method neutralizes all of those tactics.

In the next chapter, you'll see Matching tasks again, but they'll be mixed with Sequencing or Selection tasks. Hybrid games intimidate test takers who haven't trained in the fundamentals. For you, they're just one more way the test makers reward you for useful sketches, well-analyzed rules, and thorough deductions.

CHAPTER 13

HYBRID GAMES

Taken as a whole, Hybrid games are the second most common type of game on the LSAT, behind Sequencing games. While that statement is true, it's a bit misleading. Here's why. First, Hybrid games are created out of combinations of the four common logic games tasks. Test takers often handle Hybrids just fine without even realizing that they're dealing with Hybrids. In the midst of a Logic Games section, it's more important to clearly articulate your task than to define a game type. Being able to say, "I need to determine the order in which the seven trucks arrive and whether each one is green or red," is far more important than saying, "Aha, I have a Sequencing-Matching Hybrid here." Keep your focus in the overview on understanding what you're being asked for and designing a sketch that reflects the setup and restrictions. Second, the term Hybrid is a catch all phrase for games with multiple or multi-part tasks. So while Sequencing-Matching tasks are very common, Matching-Selection tasks have appeared all of two times in the past 20 years.

In this chapter, I'll have you review some of the Hybrid games you've already seen and solved in this book and introduce you to a couple of new examples of the most common Hybrid games. I'll finish up with a look at a couple of unusual Hybrid games to give you the flavor of just how diverse this category can be.

If you haven't done so already, review the portion of chapter 7 on handling complex games. There, I laid out two basic goals that you should try to accomplish any time you encounter a multi-part, multi-task game. First, determine the logical order of the tasks. If you have to schedule interviews for four out of six job candidates, you can't really schedule the interviews until you know who's being considered for the position. Thus, in a Selection-Sequencing Hybrid, the Selection task is logically prior to the Sequencing task. Second, always seek to integrate both tasks into your sketch. The Red and Green Trucks game is particularly illustrative. There, the rules sometimes created restrictions based purely on the Sequencing task ("Z arrives at some time before H"), purely on the Matching task ("No two consecutive arrivals are red"), or on a mixture of the two ("Exactly two of the trucks that arrive before Y are red"). You need a sketch that allows you to see how a restriction on one of the actions affects entities from the other action. In the examples that follow, pay attention to how the tasks are consistently integrated.

REAL-LIFE HYBRIDS

I suppose, if you think about it, almost everything we do in real life is a Hybrid task. I have a Kaplan colleague who likes to compare logic games to planning a wedding. You have to decide who you'll invite. That's Selection. You have to plan who'll sit together at dinner, like a huge Distribution game. You even have to decide the order in which the wedding party members will walk down the aisle, a kind of Matching-Sequencing task. As you plan that last task, you and your spouse-to-be will have some Rules that dictate who must walk earlier or later and others that determine who will walk with whom, exactly what the test makers would outline in a comparable logic game.

The one thing you can count on is that the tasks that are blended into an LSAT Hybrid game will, individually, be quite simple. The LSAT will never ask you to Sequence the six appliance technicians and assign each of them between one and three of the electronics categories to repair. They don't expect even the most expert test takers to able to complete a game like that in eight and half minutes. As you review and try the games below, take note of how the test makers limit the scope of one or both of the tasks. Usually, one of the two tasks is more complicated than the other. In both of the first two Sequencing-Matching games you'll review, the Sequencing task dominates your sketch. The Matching aspect of the game serves, as much as anything, simply to restrict some of the acceptable Sequencing arrangements. Take a look to see what I mean.

SEQUENCING-MATCHING HYBRIDS

In Part I, you saw several Sequencing-Matching Hybrid games. That's no surprise, given their prominence on recent tests. Between PrepTests 43 and 53, there were more Sequencing-Matching Hybrids than there were Selection or Distribution games. The most common pattern used by the test makers in these games is to ask you to sequence six or seven entities and to assign one of two conditions or attributes to each. The two examples that follow illustrate this "default" pattern that you first saw in Part I.

> Detectives investigating a citywide increase in burglaries questioned exactly seven suspects—S, T, V, W, X, Y, and Z—each on a different one of seven consecutive days. Each suspect was questioned exactly once. Any suspect who confessed did so while being questioned. The investigation conformed to the following:
>
> T was questioned on day three.
> The suspect questioned on day four did not confess.
> S was questioned after W was questioned.
> Both X and V were questioned after Z was questioned.
> No suspects confessed after W was questioned.
> Exactly two suspects confessed after T was questioned.[1]

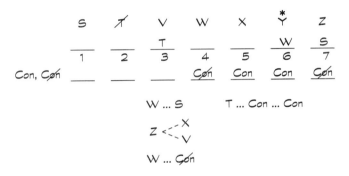

Figure 13.1

> A locally known guitarist's demo CD contains exactly seven different songs—S, T, V, W, X, Y, and Z. Each song occupies exactly one of the CD's seven tracks. Some of the songs are rock classics; the others are new compositions. The following conditions must hold:
>
> S occupies the fourth track of the CD.
> Both W and Y precede S on the CD.
> T precedes W on the CD.
> A rock classic occupies the sixth track of the CD.
> Each rock classic is immediately preceded on the CD by a
> new composition.
> Z is a rock classic.[2]

---

[1] PrepTest 53, Sec. 2, Game 3
[2] PrepTest 51, Sec. 4, Game 3

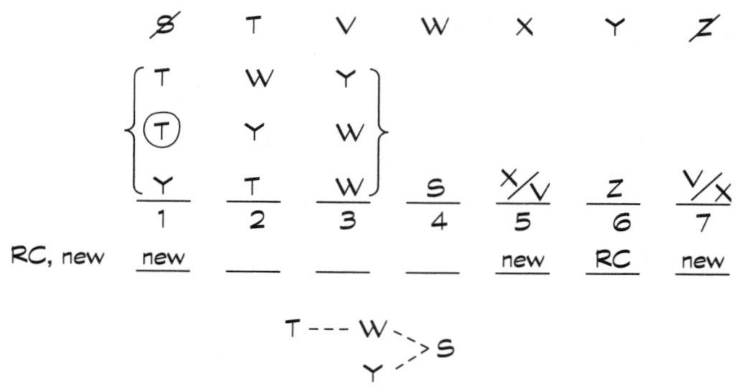

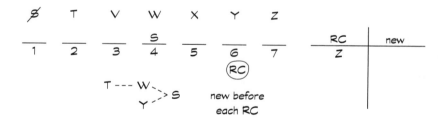

Figure 13.2

I could just as easily have displayed the Thunderstorm game from chapter 1 or the Red and Green Trucks game from chapter 5 here. They're comprised of the same tasks and produce nearly identical sketches.

Notice that in both of the games, you were able to make some deductions along the "Sequencing line" where you arrange the suspects or songs, while you could make others along the "Matching line" where you assign the attributes (confess or not confess; new composition or rock classic). Indeed, learning that track 6 on the guitarist's CD is designated a rock classic allows you to deduce that song Z is the sixth track. Untrained test takers often try to deal with the two tasks in a Hybrid game in two different sketches.

Figure 13.3

Trying to handle the tasks in that way risks missing important interactions between the two tasks. Integrated sketches, like those beside the games above, are always preferable.

The next game is another Sequencing-Matching Hybrid that you saw in Part I, and it's a game that illustrates the power of Limited Options sketches, a strategy I hope you now use without hesitation. Look at the game again, this time paying attention to the way in which the test makers blended Sequencing and Matching rules.

Exactly six people—Lulu, Nam, Ofelia, Pachai, Santiago, and Tyrone—are the only contestants in a chess tournament. The tournament consists of four games, played one after the other. Exactly two people play in each game, and each person plays in at least one game. The following conditions must apply:

Tyrone does not play in the first or third game.

Lulu plays in the last game.

Nam plays in only one game and it is not against Pachai.

Santiago plays in exactly two games, one just before and one just after the only game that Ofelia plays in.[3]

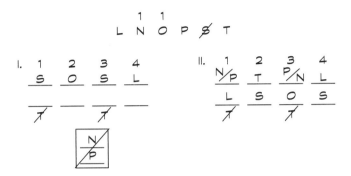

Figure 13.4

In this game, the test makers put a greater emphasis on the Matching aspect of the Hybrid by having you determine the possible "matchups" in the tournament as well as the order in which the games were played. Although three of the rules (Rules 1, 2, and 4) deal with the order in which participants appear, the final Master Sketch leaves open a number of questions about who faces whom in various games. As a result, the questions in this game rewarded you for determining the possible pairings of opponents.

You'll notice that in this game, two of the players play in two games each, while the other four play in only one game apiece. The test makers told you the number of games for three of the players (Nam, Ofelia, and Santiago), but left it up to you to determine the number of games for the other players. That added a little difficulty to the game, although you were able to clear up some of that uncertainty through your use of the Limited Options sketches.

In the next game, the test makers left the number restrictions even more wide open. While they limited the Sequencing task to just three entities—the eighth, ninth, and tenth centuries AD—they didn't specify that all three times had to be used. They pulled a similar stunt with the Matching task. Each site is found by one of the three archaeologists, but nothing requires all three archaeologists to have found sites. At this point in your practice, I'm not telling you anything new when I say, "Never assume restrictions that aren't explicit in the setup or rules." Many test takers have gone way off track with this game by assuming that all three times or all three archaeologists had to be used. Even if they eventually sorted out that not all of the entities had to be placed, they wasted a lot of time making unwarranted deductions.

A tour group plans to visit exactly five archaeological sites. Each site was discovered by exactly one of the following archaeologists—Ferrara, Gallagher, Oliphant—and each dates from the eighth, ninth, or tenth century (A.D.). The tour must satisfy the following conditions:

The site visited second dates from the ninth century.

Neither the site visited fourth nor the site visited fifth was discovered by Oliphant.

Exactly one of the sites was discovered by Gallagher, and it dates from the tenth century.

If a site dates from the eighth century, it was discovered by Oliphant.

The site visited third dates from a more recent century than does either the site visited first or that visited fourth.[4]

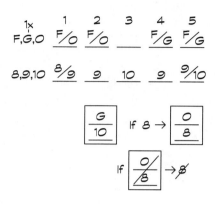

Figure 13.5

Notice one more interesting, and telling, feature of the Archaeological Sites game. While Rule 5 is, by definition, a Sequencing rule (it relates two entities chronologically, after all), the sketch is best integrated by assigning dates to the entities rather than the other way around. Imagine trying to set up the game with a sketch like this:

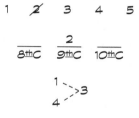

Figure 13.6

You'd be hard-pressed to find a way to relate the sites to their discoverers without creating a separate, and thus confusing, second framework. Always let the sketch evolve naturally from a game's task. Test takers who memorize misleading "rules" (like, "Always write out the dates first and then put the entities underneath them") miss the opportunity to use the most helpful and strategic scratch work in their test booklets. Such test takers classify all Hybrids as "hard games" simply because they don't fit a familiar framework. In fact, Hybrid games have a range of difficulties. Make sure you're not allowing games to intimidate you for no good reason.

SEQUENCING-DISTRIBUTION HYBRIDS

The second most common Hybrid task is Sequencing-Distribution. The main distinction between this variation and Sequencing-Matching games is that, in Sequencing-Distribution games, each entity is used only once. These games call for the entities to be placed in an order,

---

[4] PrepTest 44, Sec. 3, Game 3

either chronological or hierarchical, and then grouped. Most often, some of the entities are paired with others in the groups while others take their positions alone in the sequence. The Concert Stages game provides an example that you worked with in Part I of the book.

Three folk groups—Glenside, Hilltopper, Levon—and three rock groups—Peasant, Query, Tinhead—each perform on one of two stages, north or south. Each stage has three two-hour performances: north at 6, 8, and 10; south at 8, 10, and 12. Each group performs individually and exactly once, consistent with the following conditions:

Peasant performs at 6 or 12.
Glenside performs at some time before Hilltopper.
If any rock group performs at 10, no folk group does.
Levon and Tinhead perform on different stages.
Query performs immediately after a folk group, though not necessarily on the same stage.[5]

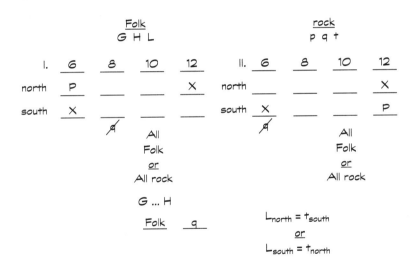

Figure 13.7

It's very important, in a game like this one, that you create a sketch that reflects the situation described in the setup. Offsetting the slots on the two stages so that you can see which groups are performing at the same time is essential.

Take note of which rules restrict which action within the Hybrid task. Rules 1, 2, and 5 refer exclusively to the Sequencing aspect of the game. Rule 4 limits only the Distribution of the two entities it names. Rule 3 refers explicitly to a time slot, but it affects both the order of the groups and their pairings.

The Concert Stages game is also a good reminder that all of the strategies you've learned thus far can be applied in Hybrid games. Rule 1 presents an "either/or" situation, calling for Limited

---

5 PrepTest 48, Sec. 2, Game 4

Options sketches. While you can't fill in many of the slots initially, seeing that every acceptable arrangement must fit one of those two patterns proves very helpful as you attack the questions.

Sequencing-Distribution Hybrid Practice

Try one more Sequencing-Distribution game, one that you haven't seen before. Here, six paintings will be divided into two groups of three and then sequenced (early-, middle-, and late-period) within those groups. As you set up the game, take note of which rules and restrictions govern the Distribution task and which limit the Sequencing. Note, too, how the test makers can use rules from one of the tasks to affect the other. Here's a hint: If the first group already has a middle-period painting, it can't take another one.

Give yourself eight and a half minutes to try this game and all of its questions. Use the Kaplan Method to assess the game's task, create your sketch, add the rules, and make all of the available deductions. Then try the question set. If you find that you're struggling with one or more of the questions, check the explanations for Steps 1–4 of the Kaplan Method. Once you're sure you have a complete, accurate Master Sketch, return to the questions and give them another shot.

Questions 13–17

Exactly six of an artist's paintings, entitled *Quarterion, Redemption, Sipapu, Tesseract, Vale,* and *Zelkova,* are sold at auction. Three of the paintings are sold to a museum, and three are sold to a private collector. Two of the paintings are from the artist's first (earliest) period, two are from her second period, and two are from her third (most recent) period. The private collector and the museum each buy one painting from each period. The following conditions hold:

> *Sipapu,* which is sold to the private collector, is from an earlier period than *Zelkova,* which is sold to the museum.
> *Quarterion* is not from an earlier period than *Tesseract.*
> *Vale* is from the artist's second period.

13. Which one of the following could be an accurate list of the paintings bought by the museum and the private collector, listed in order of the paintings' periods, from first to third?

    (A)   museum: *Quarterion, Vale, Zelkova*
          private collector: *Redemption, Sipapu, Tesseract*
    (B)   museum: *Redemption, Zelkova, Quarterion*
          private collector: *Sipapu, Vale, Tesseract*
    (C)   museum: *Sipapu, Zelkova, Quarterion*
          private collector: *Tesseract, Vale, Redemption*
    (D)   museum: *Tesseract, Quarterion, Zelkova*
          private collector: *Sipapu, Redemption, Vale*
    (E)   museum: *Zelkova, Tesseract, Redemption*
          private collector: *Sipapu, Vale, Quarterion*

14. If *Sipapu* is from the artist's second period, which one of the following could be two of the three paintings bought by the private collector?

    (A)   *Quarterion* and *Zelkova*
    (B)   *Redemption* and *Tesseract*
    (C)   *Redemption* and *Vale*
    (D)   *Redemption* and *Zelkova*
    (E)   *Tesseract* and *Zelkova*

15. Which one of the following is a complete and accurate list of the paintings, any one of which could be the painting from the artist's first period that is sold to the private collector?

    (A)   *Quarterion, Redemption*
    (B)   *Redemption, Sipapu*
    (C)   *Quarterion, Sipapu, Tesseract*
    (D)   *Quarterion, Redemption, Sipapu, Tesseract*
    (E)   *Redemption, Sipapu, Tesseract, Zelkova*

16. If *Sipapu* is from the artist's second period, then which one of the following paintings could be from the period immediately preceding *Quarterion's* period and be sold to the same buyer as *Quarterion*?

    (A)   *Redemption*
    (B)   *Sipapu*
    (C)   *Tesseract*
    (D)   *Vale*
    (E)   *Zelkova*

17. If *Zelkova* is sold to the same buyer as *Tesseract* and is from the period immediately preceding *Tesseract's* period, then which one of the following must be true?

    (A)   *Quarterion* is sold to the museum.
    (B)   *Quarterion* is from the artist's third period.
    (C)   *Redemption* is sold to the private collector.
    (D)   *Redemption* is from the artist's third period.
    (E)   *Redemption* is sold to the same buyer as *Vale.*[6]

Explanations

STEPS 1 AND 2: Overview and Sketch

The opening paragraph of this game is lengthy, but it explains the game's premise in a way that allows you to draw a perfect sketch. You need to keep track of who (museum or private collector) bought each of the six paintings. At the same time, you need to record which of the artist's three periods each painting represents. The final limitation ("The private collector and the museum each buy one painting from each period") clarifies your sketch even more.

Figure 13.8

Now you can see that there will be a one-to-one matchup; in any acceptable arrangement, there will be one painting per slot.

STEP 3: Rules

The first rule affects both parts of the Hybrid action. You learn which buyers purchased S and Z, and you also learn their relative order.

Figure 13.9

The second rule gives only a Sequencing relationship. Be careful: The rule says that Q cannot be earlier than T; that doesn't rule out their being from the same period.

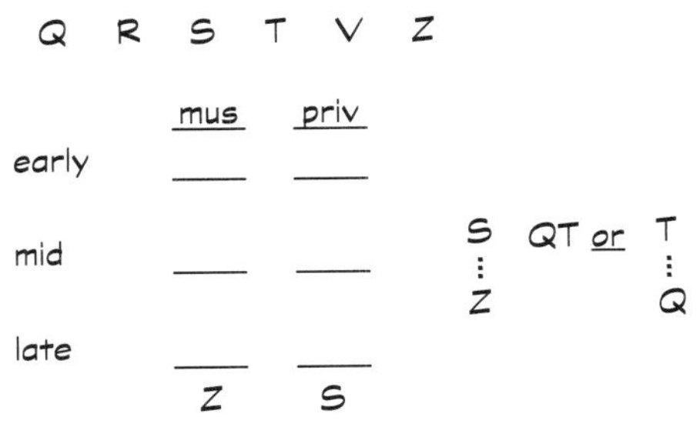

Q R S T V Z
mus
priv
early
mid
late
Z
S
S ⋮ Z
QT or T ⋮ Q

Figure 13.10

The final rule establishes V's period but not its buyer.

Q R* S T V Z
mus
priv
early
mid
V
late
Z
S
S ⋮ Z
QT or T ⋮ Q

Figure 13.11

Make sure you noted that R is a floater in this game, able to take either buyer and any of the three periods.

STEP 4: Deductions

The first rule in this game allows for a quasi–Limited Options approach. Since S must come from an earlier period than Z, you can set twin sketches like this:

Q R* S T V Z
I. mus
priv
II. mus
priv
early
S
mid
Z/
V
S
late
/Z
Z
QT or T ⋮ Q

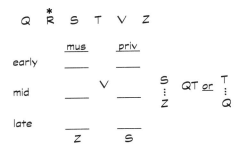

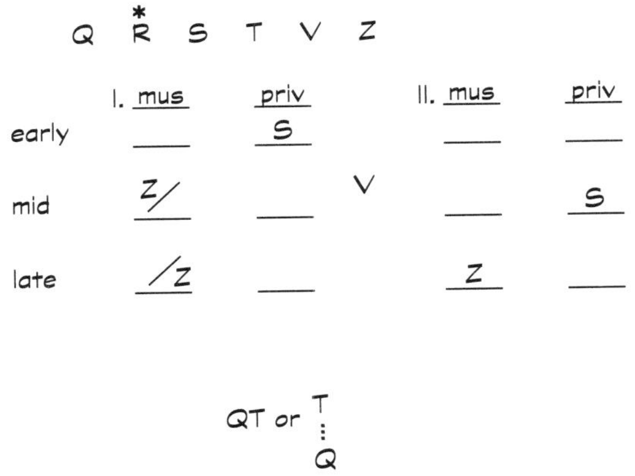

Figure 13.12

In Option I, you can't lock Z into a specific space unless you want to draw a sort of Option I(a) with Z in the middle period and an Option I(b) with Z in the late period. That's fine, provided that it doesn't take you too long, but frankly, it's probably overkill. The previous sketches are more than sufficient to get the questions right.

In either option, you know that V will be from the middle period (Rule 2). That means that the museum purchased V in Option II.

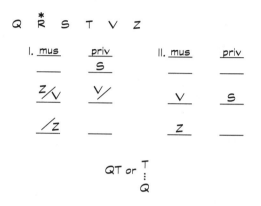

Figure 13.13

In Option I, you can't do more with Rule 2 than to note it to the side. In Option II, however, it's clear that T must be from the early period, while either Q or R is the private collector's purchase in the late period.

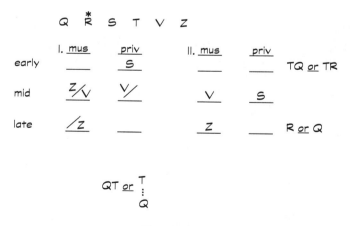

Figure 13.14

Like most Limited Options scenarios, one of the two arrangements leads to more certainty and one remains more open. Still, you have plenty to go on and the question set will add further clarity in its three "If" questions.

STEP 5: Questions

The questions from this game appear long and complex. Don't be thrown off, though. This is mostly just the effect of the entities' long, italicized names. In fact, the question set is pretty standard: One Acceptability question, one Complete and Accurate List question, and three "If" questions. Jump in and get the points.

13. **(B)**

Which one of the following could be an accurate list of the paintings bought by the museum and the private collector, listed in order of the paintings' periods, from first to third?

(A)   museum: *Quarterion, Vale, Zelkova*
        private collector: *Redemption, Sipapu, Tesseract*
(B)   museum: *Redemption, Zelkova, Quarterion*
        private collector: *Sipapu, Vale, Tesseract*
(C)   museum: *Sipapu, Zelkova, Quarterion*
        private collector: *Tesseract, Vale, Redemption*
(D)   museum: *Tesseract, Quarterion, Zelkova*
        private collector: *Sipapu, Redemption, Vale*
(E)   museum: *Zelkova, Tesseract, Redemption*
        private collector: *Sipapu, Vale, Quarterion*[7]

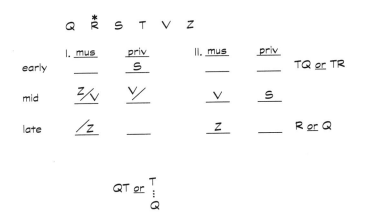

Figure 13.15

Approach this Acceptability question as you would any other. The fact that this is a Hybrid game is irrelevant to how you handle the questions.

Rule 1 knocks out choice (C), where S is sold to the museum, and choice (E), where Z is from the same period as S.

Rule 2 eliminates choice (D), where V is not found in the middle period.

Rule 3 gets rid of choice (A), where Q's period precedes T's.

That leaves only the correct answer, choice (B).

---

[7] PrepTest 43, Sec. 4, Q 13

14. **(B)**

If *Sipapu* is from the artist's second period, which one of the following could be two of the three paintings bought by the private collector?

(A) *Quarterion* and *Zelkova*
(B) *Redemption* and *Tesseract*
(C) *Redemption* and *Vale*
(D) *Redemption* and *Zelkova*
(E) *Tesseract* and *Zelkova*[8]

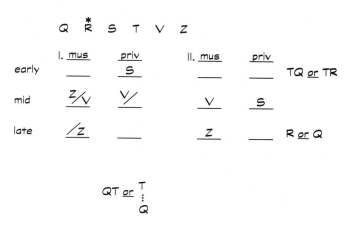

Figure 13.16

This question stem's new "if" condition places you squarely in Option II. The question asks for a pair of paintings that could have been sold to the private collector. In Option II, the museum buys V and Z. Eliminate all of the answers featuring either V or Z and you're left with only one choice, the correct answer, choice (B).

15. **(D)**

Which one of the following is a complete and accurate list of the paintings, any one of which could be the painting from the artist's first period that is sold to the private collector?

(A) *Quarterion, Redemption*
(B) *Redemption, Sipapu*
(C) *Quarterion, Sipapu, Tesseract*
(D) *Quarterion, Redemption, Sipapu, Tesseract*
(E) *Redemption, Sipapu, Tesseract, Zelkova*[9]

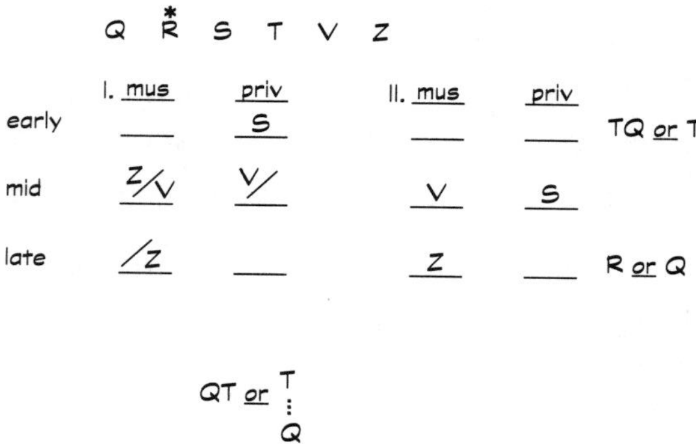

Figure 13.17

[8] PrepTest 43, Sec. 4, Q 14
[9] PrepTest 43, Sec. 4, Q 15

This question calls for any and all early-period paintings that could have been sold to the private collector. Glancing at the options, you can see that S is certainly a possibility. Eliminate choice (A), which lacks S in its list. At the same time, the options clearly reveal that Z cannot have been sold to the private collector. So cross out choice (E), which has Z in its list. The remaining possibilities from the list must come from Option II. There, the early-period paintings could be Q, R, or T. There's nothing restricting any of those paintings to the museum, so the correct answer must have those three paintings and painting S. That's choice (D), the correct answer.

16. **(B)**

If *Sipapu* is from the artist's second period, then which one of the following paintings could be from the period immediately preceding *Quarterion's* period and be sold to the same buyer as *Quarterion*?

(A) *Redemption*
(B) *Sipapu*
(C) *Tesseract*
(D) *Vale*
(E) *Zelkova*[10]

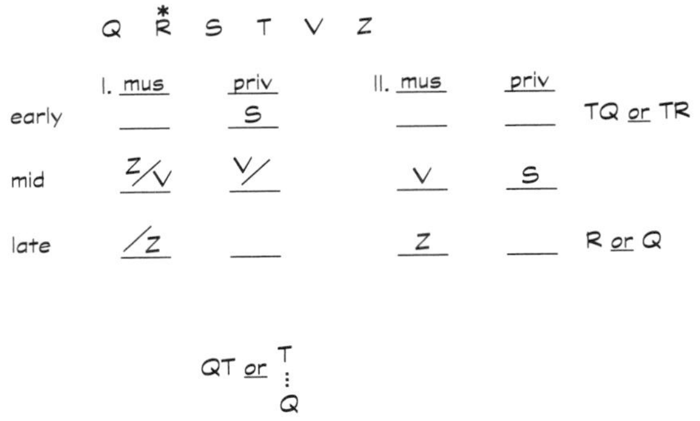

Figure 13.18

Did you notice that the "if" in this question is precisely the same as the one in question 14? So, here again, just consult Option II. The question asks for an entity that could immediately precede Q and be sold to the same collector. In Option II, the only way for Q to accommodate the question's "if" is to be the late-period painting sold to the private collector. That would be S from the immediately preceding period in the private collector's column. That's choice (B), the right answer to this question.

17. **(B)**

If *Zelkova* is sold to the same buyer as *Tesseract* and is from the period immediately preceding *Tesseract's* period, then which one of the following must be true?

(A) *Quarterion* is sold to the museum.
(B) *Quarterion* is from the artist's third period.
(C) *Redemption* is sold to the private collector.
(D) *Redemption* is from the artist's third period.
(E) *Redemption* is sold to the same buyer as *Vale*.[11]

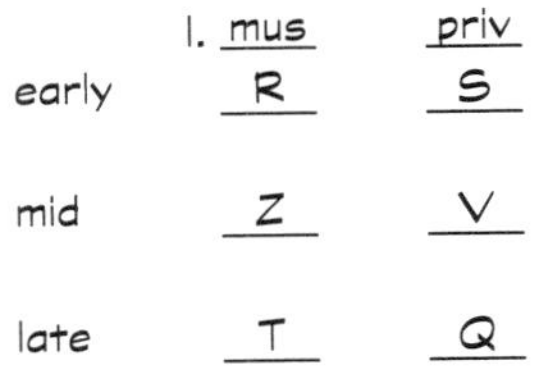

Figure 13.19

---

10 PrepTest 43, Sec. 4, Q 16
11 PrepTest 43, Sec. 4, Q 17

Here, at last, is an "if" question that will reward you for building a mini-sketch based on the "if" condition in the stem. The premise of the question, that Z comes from an earlier period than T, means you'll have to use Option I to begin your diagram. With Z immediately before T and both paintings sold to the same buyer, you have this:

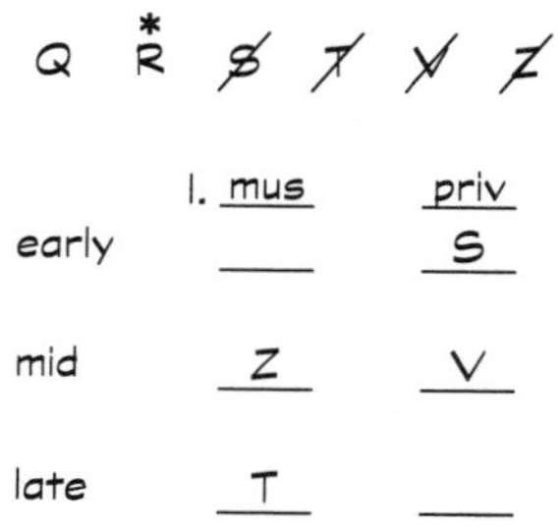

Q R̶* S̶ T̶ V̶ Z̶

	I. mus	priv
early		S
mid	Z	V
late	T	

Figure 13.20

To accommodate Rule 2 in this mini-sketch, Q will have to be from the artist's late period and must be sold to the private collector.

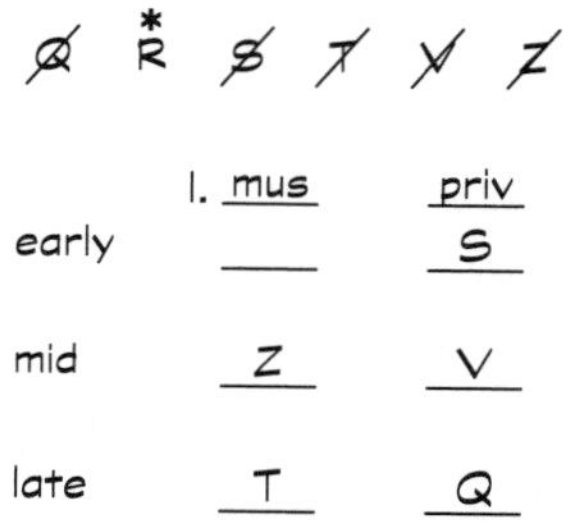

Q̶ R̶* S̶ T̶ V̶ Z̶

	I. mus	priv
early		S
mid	Z	V
late	T	Q

Figure 13.21

The only painting left to account for is the floater, R, which must be from the artist's early period and must be sold to the museum.

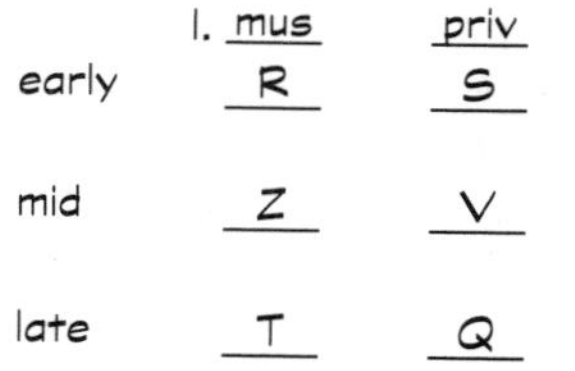

	I. mus	priv
early	R	S
mid	Z	V
late	T	Q

Figure 13.22

You have placed all six paintings precisely. The question calls for a *must be true* answer. Scan the choices and find the one answer that matches something in the mini-sketch. That's choice (B), and you're done with another game.

Sequencing-Distribution is much less common than Sequencing-Matching. When you encounter it, look for a way to design the sketch so that it reflects the grouping of the entities along one dimension and the order of the entities along the other. If you compare the sketch for the Concert Stages game with that for the Artist's Paintings game, you'll see that the Sequencing task ran horizontally in the first and vertically in the second. Either sketch could be rotated 90° without altering the basic information. The key is that both diagrams allow you to see how the Sequencing part of the Hybrid affects the Distribution, and vice versa. Don't sweat the small stuff. Get the fundamental tasks right and the game will fall into place.

SEQUENCING-SELECTION HYBRIDS

There's one more combination of tasks common enough to warrant its own section in this chapter, the Sequencing-Selection Hybrid. In these games, you'll always have more entities in the original list than you're allowed to place within the order required by the Sequencing action. The selection may be small (choose 5 of 6 entities) or, as in the game that follows, fairly large (choose 6 of 12 entities). Either way, the Selection part of the game is logically prior to the Sequencing element; you can't put the entities in order until you know who they are. Because of the Selection aspect present in the game, expect to see formal logic statements among the rules. Keep in mind that a condition sufficient to bring about a particular sequence of entities is, therefore, sufficient to bring about the selection of those entities. For example, in the following game, you find this rule: "A film in Italian is not shown unless a film in Norwegian is going to be shown the next day." Thus, showing an Italian film means selecting a Norwegian film *and* sequencing it for the next day after the Italian film, creating an I-N block, if you will.

Sequencing-Selection Hybrid Practice

Give this game a try. Take eight and a half minutes for the entire game and its question set. If you find yourself struggling with the questions, stop and review Steps 1–4 of the Kaplan Method in the explanations. Once you're satisfied that you have a complete Master Sketch, go back and finish the questions.

Questions 1–7

During an international film retrospective lasting six consecutive days—day 1 through day 6—exactly six different films will be shown, one each day. Twelve films will be available for presentation, two each in French, Greek, Hungarian, Italian, Norwegian, and Turkish. The presentation of the films must conform to the following conditions:

Neither day 2 nor day 4 is a day on which a film in Norwegian is shown.

A film in Italian is not shown unless a film in Norwegian is going to be shown the next day.

A film in Greek is not shown unless a film in Italian is going to be shown the next day.

1. Which one of the following is an acceptable order of films for the retrospective, listed by their language, from day 1 through day 6?

   (A) French, Greek, Italian, Turkish, Norwegian, Hungarian
   (B) French, Hungarian, Italian, Norwegian, French, Hungarian
   (C) Hungarian, French, Norwegian, Greek, Norwegian, Italian
   (D) Norwegian, Turkish, Hungarian, Italian, French, Turkish
   (E) Turkish, French, Norwegian, Hungarian, French, Turkish

2. If two films in Italian are going to be shown, one on day 2 and one on day 5, then the film shown on day 1 could be in any one of the following languages EXCEPT:

   (A) French
   (B) Greek
   (C) Hungarian
   (D) Norwegian
   (E) Turkish

3. If two films in Italian are shown during the retrospective, which one of the following must be false?

   (A) A film in French is shown on day 3.
   (B) A film in Greek is shown on day 1.
   (C) A film in Hungarian is shown on day 6.
   (D) A film in Norwegian is shown on day 5.
   (E) A film in Turkish is shown on day 4.

4. Which one of the following is a complete and accurate list of the days, any one of which is a day on which a film in Italian could be shown?

   (A) day 1, day 3, day 5
   (B) day 2, day 4, day 5
   (C) day 2, day 5, day 6
   (D) day 1, day 3
   (E) day 2, day 4

5. If two films in French are going to be shown, one on day 3 and one on day 5, which one of the following is a pair of films that could be shown on day 1 and day 6, respectively?

   (A) a film in French, a film in Turkish
   (B) a film in Greek, a film in Hungarian
   (C) a film in Italian, a film in Norwegian
   (D) a film in Norwegian, a film in Turkish
   (E) a film in Turkish, a film in Greek

6. If neither a film in French nor a film in Italian is shown during the retrospective, which one of the following must be true?

   (A) A film in Norwegian is shown on day 1.
   (B) A film in Norwegian is shown on day 5.
   (C) A film in Turkish is shown on day 4.
   (D) A film in Hungarian or else a film in Norwegian is shown on day 3.
   (E) A film in Hungarian or else a film in Turkish is shown on day 2.

7. If a film in Greek is going to be shown at some time after a film in Norwegian, then a film in Norwegian must be shown on

   (A) day 1
   (B) day 3
   (C) day 5
   (D) day 1 or else day 3
   (E) day 3 or else day 5[12]

---

[12] PrepTest 49, Sec. 1, Game 1, Qs 1-7

Answer Explanations follow on the next page.

Explanations

STEPS 1 AND 2: Overview and Sketch

The first sentence of this game's setup is familiar. It implies a typical Sequencing game with six spaces. The second sentence is the one that may cause a moment of hesitation. Twelve entities? That seems inordinately high. It's a relief, then, to discover that the 12 films come from just six countries and they're evenly distributed, with 2 films from each. Did you reflect the entity list in a way that was easy to understand?

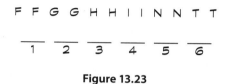

Figure 13.23

While it's clear from the game's description that you'll only be using half of the available films, nothing at the outset suggests that you need to take films from a minimum or maximum number of countries. You may be showing two films each from three countries, one film from each of the six different countries, or any other combination that gives you a total of six films for the festival.

STEP 3: Rules

There are only three rules, and none of them are very strict. You'll discover more about what can't happen than about what must.

Rule 1 tells you to rule out N for days 2 and 4.

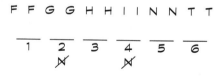

Figure 13.24

Rules 2 and 3 are conditional formal logic statements. Translate each into formal logic shorthand and formulate their contrapositives as well.

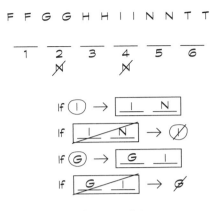

Figure 13.25

As I had you note earlier, both of these rules tell you something about the films that are chosen and about their order. You won't be able to show an Italian film without a Norwegian one being shown the next day, nor a Greek film without an Italian one immediately following. These rules will lead to big deductions when combined with the first rule.

STEP 4: Deductions

None of the rules give you anything positive that you can place into the sketch framework, but at least Rule 1 specifically ruled out a couple of film placements. Now, consider Rule 2 in light of what you know from Rule 1. Italian films cannot be shown on day 1 or day 3.

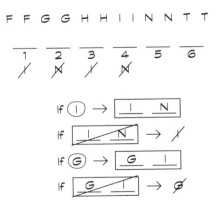

Figure 13.26

Did you notice that Italian films cannot be shown on day 6, either? Since that's the last day of the retrospective, there's no way an Italian film shown on day 6 could be followed by a Norwegian film the next day.

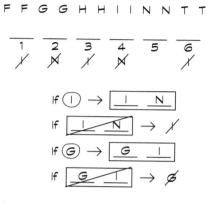

Figure 13.27

Make the comparable deductions stemming from Rule 3.

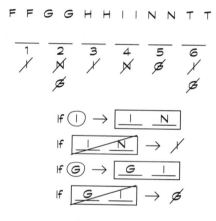

Figure 13.28

Since you can't show Italian films on days 3 and 6, you can't show Greek films on days 2 and 5. Nor can you show a Greek film on day 6, since there's no way it could be followed by an Italian film.

Now, realize there's every possibility that no Greek, Italian, or Norwegian films will be shown at all. Both French films, both Hungarian films, and both Turkish films act as floaters in this game. It's perfectly acceptable to schedule the retrospective with only those films. But it wouldn't make for a very fun logic game. Expect the test makers to reward your Deduction step with several questions that get at the intricate relationship among Greek, Italian, and Norwegian films.

STEP 5: Questions

Five of the seven questions associated with this game were "If"s. That shouldn't surprise you, given the dearth of affirmative deductions. Learning to trust that there's adequate information to answer every question—realizing that when you can't determine what must be true, the test makers will ask you for what *could be true*—is a key step in becoming a logic games expert. For your work here, I've selected five illustrative questions from the set.

1. **(E)**

   Which one of the following is an acceptable order of films for the retrospective, listed by their language, from day 1 through day 6?

   (A) French, Greek, Italian, Turkish, Norwegian, Hungarian

   (B) French, Hungarian, Italian, Norwegian, French, Hungarian

   (C) Hungarian, French, Norwegian, Greek, Norwegian, Italian

   (D) Norwegian, Turkish, Hungarian, Italian, French, Turkish

   (E) Turkish, French, Norwegian, Hungarian, French, Turkish[13]

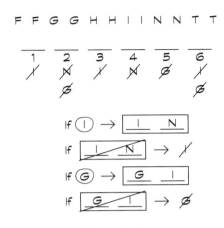

Figure 13.29

This is a straightforward Acceptability question. Each of the wrong answers will violate one of the rules. Testing each answer choice would cost you an inordinate amount of time. As always, use the rules to eliminate incorrect answer choices.

Rule 1 takes out choice (B), which has a Norwegian film on day 4.

Rule 2 gets rid of all the other wrong answers. Choice (A) is impossible because it has an Italian film (day 3) followed immediately by a Turkish film (day 4). Choice (C) violates the rule by scheduling an Italian film for day 6. Choice (C) breaks Rule 3 as well, by having a Greek film followed by a Norwegian one, but you needn't ever get that far. Choice (D) violates Rule 2 by having an Italian film (day 4) followed immediately by a French film (day 5).

The one answer choice that breaks none of the rules is correct; that's choice (E).

2. **(D)**

   If two films in Italian are going to be shown, one on day 2 and one on day 5, then the film shown on day 1 could be in any one of the following languages EXCEPT:

   (A) French
   (B) Greek
   (C) Hungarian
   (D) Norwegian
   (E) Turkish[14]

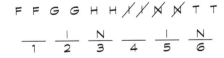

Figure 13.30

Use the "if" condition to start a mini-sketch for this question.

13 PrepTest 49, Sec. 1, Q 1
14 PrepTest 49, Sec. 1, Q 2

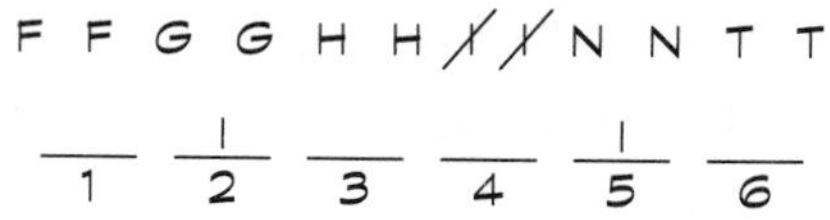

F F G G H H X X N N T T

$$\frac{}{1} \quad \frac{|}{2} \quad \frac{}{3} \quad \frac{}{4} \quad \frac{|}{5} \quad \frac{}{6}$$

Figure 13.31

With Italian films on days 2 and 5, you know you must have Norwegian films on days 3 and 6.

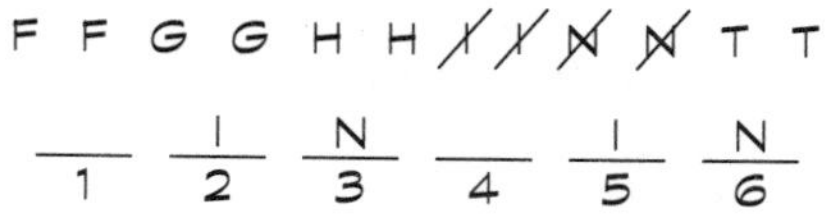

F F G G H H X X X X T T

$$\frac{}{1} \quad \frac{|}{2} \quad \frac{N}{3} \quad \frac{}{4} \quad \frac{|}{5} \quad \frac{N}{6}$$

Figure 13.32

That uses up both Norwegian films in the roster, so the film on day 1 cannot be in Norwegian. That's choice (D). Test takers who forget the Selection element in this game or those who fail to list their entities in a way that reminds them that there are only two films in each language are stymied by this deceptively simple question.

3. **(A)**

If two films in Italian are shown during the retrospective, which one of the following must be false?

(A) A film in French is shown on day 3.
(B) A film in Greek is shown on day 1.
(C) A film in Hungarian is shown on day 6.
(D) A film in Norwegian is shown on day 5.
(E) A film in Turkish is shown on day 4.[15]

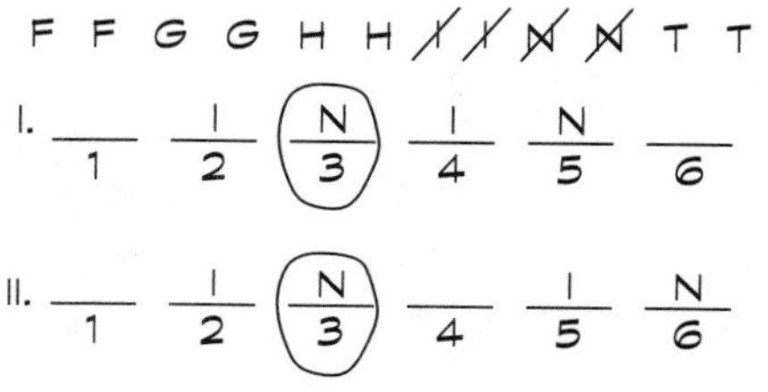

F F G G H H X X X X T T

I. $$\frac{}{1} \quad \frac{|}{2} \quad \left(\frac{N}{3}\right) \quad \frac{|}{4} \quad \frac{N}{5} \quad \frac{}{6}$$

II. $$\frac{}{1} \quad \frac{|}{2} \quad \left(\frac{N}{3}\right) \quad \frac{}{4} \quad \frac{|}{5} \quad \frac{N}{6}$$

Figure 13.33

Start a mini-sketch for this question based on the "if" condition in the stem. There are two ways to show two Italian films in the retrospective.

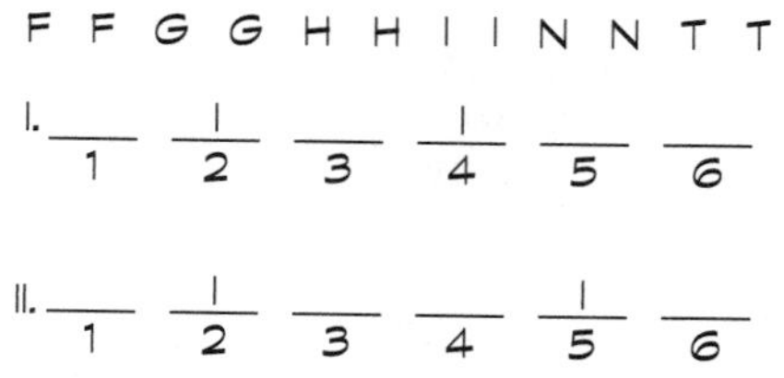

F F G G H H I I N N T T

I. $$\frac{}{1} \quad \frac{|}{2} \quad \frac{}{3} \quad \frac{|}{4} \quad \frac{}{5} \quad \frac{}{6}$$

II. $$\frac{}{1} \quad \frac{|}{2} \quad \frac{}{3} \quad \frac{}{4} \quad \frac{|}{5} \quad \frac{}{6}$$

Figure 13.34

In either case, Norwegian films must follow both Italian films. No matter what, an Italian film must be shown on day 2, so a Norwegian film must be shown on day 3.

---

[15] PrepTest 49, Sec. 1, Q 3

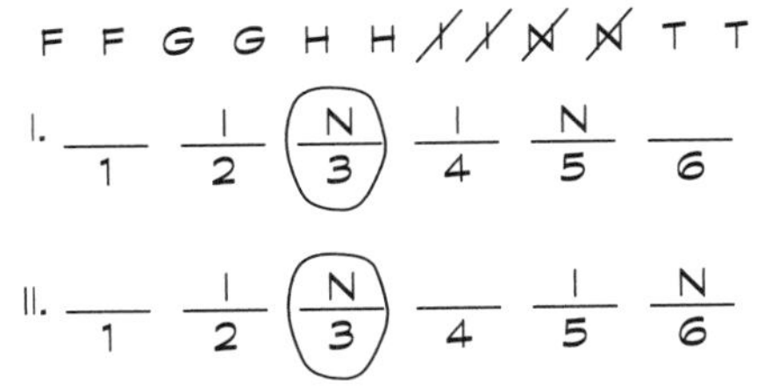

F F G G H H X̸ X̸ X̸ X̸ T T

I. ___ _I_ (N) _I_ _N_ ___
    1   2   3   4   5   6

II. ___ _I_ (N) ___ _I_ _N_
     1   2   3   4   5   6

Figure 13.35

That means that choice (A) *must be false* and is the correct answer. All of the remaining choices could be true in one or both of the arrangements provided for in the mini-sketch.

4. **(B)**

Which one of the following is a complete and accurate list of the days, any one of which is a day on which a film in Italian could be shown?

(A) day 1, day 3, day 5
(B) day 2, day 4, day 5
(C) day 2, day 5, day 6
(D) day 1, day 3
(E) day 2, day 4[16]

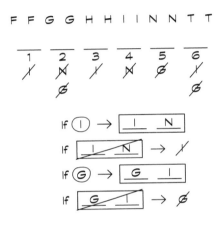

Figure 13.36

You can get the answer to this question from your Master Sketch or from the mini-sketch you just drew for question 3. Italian films may be shown on any of days 2, 4, and 5. That's choice (B).

5. **(D)**

If two films in French are going to be shown, one on day 3 and one on day 5, which one of the following is a pair of films that could be shown on day 1 and day 6, respectively?

(A) a film in French, a film in Turkish
(B) a film in Greek, a film in Hungarian
(C) a film in Italian, a film in Norwegian
(D) a film in Norwegian, a film in Turkish
(E) a film in Turkish, a film in Greek[17]

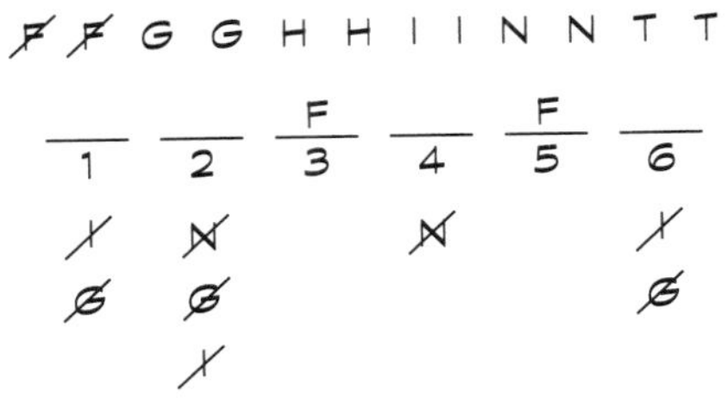

F̸ F̸ G G H H I I N N T T

___ ___ _F_ ___ _F_ ___
  1   2   3   4   5   6
 X̸   X̸   X̸   X̸
 ø   ø   ø
      X̸

Figure 13.37

The "if" in this question allows you to place the two French films with certainty.

16 PrepTest 49, Sec. 1, Q 4
17 PrepTest 49, Sec. 1, Q 5

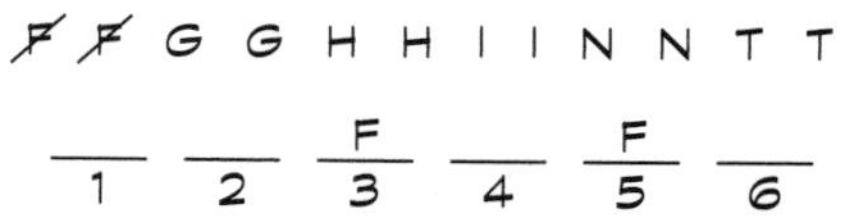
F F G G H H I I N N T T
F
F
1
2
3
4
5
6

Figure 13.38

Since this precludes a film in Norwegian from being shown on day 3, you can add Italian to your list of films that cannot be shown on day 2.

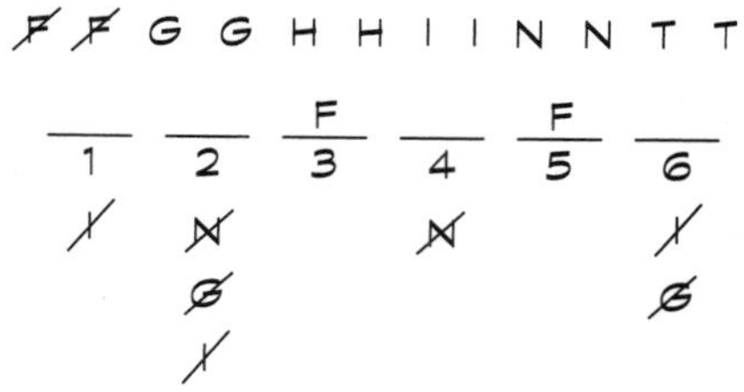
F F G G H H I I N N T T
F
F
1
2
3
4
5
6

Figure 13.39

If no Italian film can be shown on day 2, no Greek film may be shown on day 1.

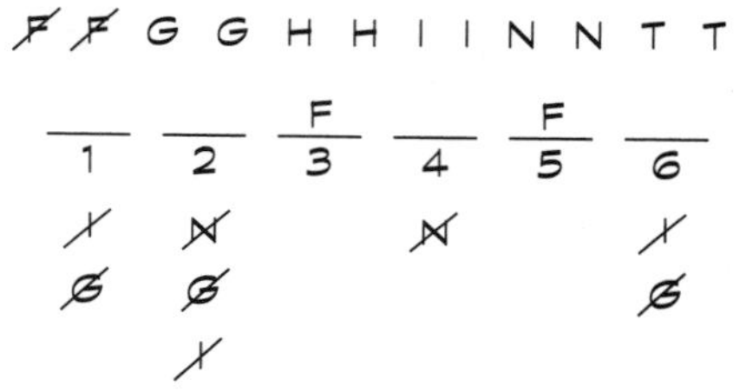
F F G G H H I I N N T T
F
F
1
2
3
4
5
6

Figure 13.40

Now, characterize the answer choices. The correct answer is the one with acceptable films for days 1 and 6 under this question's "if" condition. Eliminate choices in which either day's film assignment is impossible in the mini-sketch.

Choice (A) is out; both French films are accounted for in days 3 and 5, so there can't be one shown on day 1. Choice (B) tries to show a Greek film on day 1. That won't work under these conditions, as you deduced while completing the mini-sketch. Get rid of choice (B), too. Choice (C) can't work; you can never show an Italian film on day 1 under any circumstances in this game. Choice (D) is fine. There are no restrictions on Norwegian films for day 1, and there are no restrictions at all for Turkish films. This answer's films are acceptable for days 1 and 6, and thus it's correct. Choice (E) goes wrong by trying to put a Greek film on day 6, something that's never acceptable in this game.

6. **(E)**

If neither a film in French nor a film in Italian is shown during the retrospective, which one of the following must be true?

(A)   A film in Norwegian is shown on day 1.
(B)   A film in Norwegian is shown on day 5.
(C)   A film in Turkish is shown on day 4.
(D)   A film in Hungarian or else a film in Norwegian is shown on day 3.
(E)   A film in Hungarian or else a film in Turkish is shown on day 2.[18]

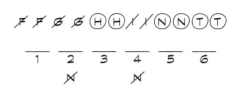

Figure 13.41

Question 6 strikes at the heart of the Selection component of this Hybrid game. Copy your Selection roster and cross off all the French and Italian films.

Figure 13.42

If you cannot show any Italian films, you cannot show any Greek films either. Strike the Greek films off the list, too.

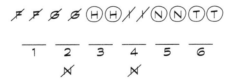

Figure 13.43

You can see the six films that will be shown in the retrospective. The only relevant restrictions involve the films in Norwegian. Rule 1 forbids them being shown on days 2 or 4.

The only answer that must be true here is choice (E); one of the two acceptable non-Norwegian films must be shown that day. All of the other choices could be false. The Norwegian films could be shown on days 3 and 6, so choices (A) and (B) need not be true. A film in Hungarian could be shown on day 4, so choice (C) doesn't have to be true. A Turkish film could be scheduled for day 3, so choice (D) need not be true, either.

---

[18] PrepTest 49, Sec. 1, Q 6

7. **(D)**

If a film in Greek is going to be shown at some time after a film in Norwegian, then a film in Norwegian must be shown on:

(A)   day 1
(B)   day 3
(C)   day 5
(D)   day 1 or else day 3
(E)   day 3 or else day 5[19]

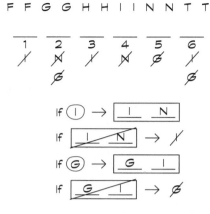

Figure 13.44

You can find the answer to this question by consulting your Master Sketch. Greek films may only be shown on days 1, 3, and 4. You can't have a Norwegian film on day 2. Thus, for a Greek film to follow one in Norwegian, the Norwegian film must be scheduled for day 1 or day 3. That's choice (D). There you have it. Yet another game falls to your strategic approach.

Sequencing-Selection Hybrids aren't common, and chances are fairly slim that you'll see one on test day. If you do, remember what you know about the two game types that combine to form this Hybrid task. Most test takers who go off track with a game like this one lose sight of one of the actions involved or simply lack the strategic approach to tackle a somewhat complex game.

OTHER HYBRIDS

Over the years, the test makers have combined any and all of the standard tasks to come up with what were, at the time, new Hybrid game types. Don't worry about trying to track them all down or come up with predetermined sketches. It's unlikely that you'll see anything exactly like any of them. Instead, concentrate your efforts on being rigorous and perceptive in the Overview step. When the test makers describe an apparently novel situation or combination of tasks, pay attention to what they're asking you to produce. That's just what you did with the Debate Teams game, a Hybrid in which you had to distribute six students into three two-person teams, match the resulting teams with three schools, and then sequence the schools into first, second, and third places. If you're dependent on knowing what a Sequencing-Distribution-Matching sketch is supposed to look like, you'll go nowhere with a game like that. But if you read the setup text strategically and think logically about how to organize the information, you'll come up with a serviceable framework in which you build a helpful Master Sketch.

---

[19] PrepTest 49, Sec. 1, Q 7

The three highest-placing teams in a high school debate
tournament are the teams from Fairview, Gillom, and Hilltop
high schools. Each team has exactly two members. The
individuals on these three teams are Mei, Navarro, O'Rourke,
Pavlovich, Sethna, and Tsudama. The following is the case:

    Sethna is on the team from Gillom High.
    Tsudama is on the second-place team.
    Mei and Pavlovich are not on the same team.
    Pavlovich's team places higher than Navarro's team.
    The team from Gillom High places higher than the team
     from Hilltop High.[20]

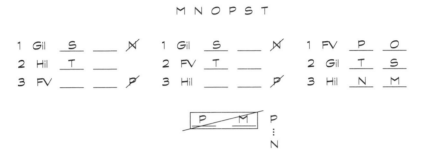

Figure 13.45

By determining what the questions would ask you for, you were able to create a clear orientation
for the order of the schools and for each school's team members. By the time you completed
the deductions, you had a very small number of acceptable arrangements laid out for use in
evaluating the questions. The key was "seeing" what you were being asked for and finding a
simple, logical way to depict it. It's unlikely that particular sketch will ever be useful again, but
the principles that led you to create it are helpful every time.

I'll have you try one more game in this chapter. Not to scare you, but it's almost legendary
for being one of the toughest games ever to appear on a released LSAT test. I won't go into
detail about the game until after you've had a chance to try it out. I will, however, give you
one hint: Try your best to get a picture in your mind of the situation described, and then turn
that into a simplified diagram in which you can record the given information. Do your best,
too, to make your depiction of each rule look like the framework. That way, you'll be able to
see how each rule potentially fits (or doesn't fit) into the framework under various conditions.

Don't time yourself on this game. And don't let it overwhelm you. As I said, it's a very hard
game. Take it methodically and strategically, getting as much as you can from each step in the
Kaplan Method. When you're done, I'll go through the game, break down the tasks that make
up its Hybrid action, and show you a model sketch that will help you untangle its questions.

---

[20] PrepTest 53, Sec. 2, Game 4

Questions 14–18

Gutierrez, Hoffman, Imamura, Kelly, Lapas, and Moore ride a bus together. Each sits facing forward in a different one of the six seats on the left side of the bus. The seats are in consecutive rows that are numbered 1, 2, and 3 from front to back. Each row has exactly two seats: a window seat and an isle seat. The following conditions must apply:

Hoffman occupies the aisle seat immediately behind Gutierrez's aisle seat.
If Moore occupies an aisle seat, Hoffman sits in the same row as Lapas.
If Gutierrez sits in the same row as Kelly, Moore occupies the seat immediately and directly behind Imamura's seat.
If Kelly occupies a window seat, Moore sits in row 3.
If Kelly sits in row 3, Imamura sits in row 1.

14. Which one of the following could be true?

   (A)   Imamura sits in row 2, whereas Kelly sits in row 3.
   (B)   Gutierrez sits in the same row as Kelly, immediately and directly behind Moore.
   (C)   Gutierrez occupies a window seat in the same row as Lapas.
   (D)   Moore occupies an aisle seat in the same row as Lapas.
   (E)   Kelly and Moore both sit in row 3.

15. If Lapas and Kelly each occupy a window seat, then which one of the following could be true?

   (A)   Moore occupies the aisle seat in row 3.
   (B)   Imamura occupies the window seat in row 3.
   (C)   Gutierrez sits in the same row as Kelly.
   (D)   Gutierrez sits in the same row as Moore.
   (E)   Moore sits in the same row as Lapas.

16. If Moore sits in row 1, then which one of the following must be true?

   (A)   Hoffman sits in row 2.
   (B)   Imamura sits in row 2.
   (C)   Imamura sits in row 3.
   (D)   Kelly sits in row 1.
   (E)   Lapas sits in row 3.

17. If Kelly occupies the aisle seat in row 3, then each of the following must be true EXCEPT:

   (A)   Gutierrez sits in the same row as Imamura.
   (B)   Hoffman sits in the same row as Lapas.
   (C)   Lapas occupies a window seat.
   (D)   Moore occupies a window seat.
   (E)   Gutierrez sits in row 1.

18. If neither Gutierrez nor Imamura sits in row 1, then which one of the following could be true?

   (A)   Hoffman sits in row 2.
   (B)   Kelly sits in row 2.
   (C)   Moore sits in row 2.
   (D)   Imamura occupies an aisle seat.
   (E)   Moore occupies an aisle seat.[21]

Answer Explanations follow on the next page.

Explanations

STEPS 1 AND 2: Overview and Sketch

To visualize this game, picture a typical bus. On each side of the aisle are two seats, one by the window and one by the aisle. This game deals with three such rows. It even tells you that the seats in question are on the left side of the bus. You should have no trouble turning that into a clear framework.

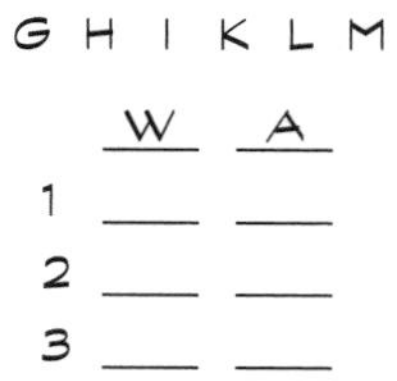

Figure 13.46

The test makers go easy on you here in one respect. They provide six passengers and ask you to arrange them as you would expect to, one per seat.

So this game has a Sequencing element: The rows are numbered 1–3, and the rules restrict entities by placing them closer to the front or back relative to one another. There's also a Matching element: Some of the passengers may or may not sit with others. Finally, there's an aspect of Distribution: Certain rules are predicated on pairs of entities sitting in certain rows. When all is said and done, this game looks and feels an awful lot like the Debate Tournament, doesn't it?

STEP 3: Rules

There are five rules here, although four of them are conditional. It's the formal logic, more than anything, that makes this game tougher than the Debate Tournament game, despite their similar tasks.

Rule 1 creates a block of H and G and places the block in the aisle seats. With only three rows, this allows for a Limited Options approach to the game.

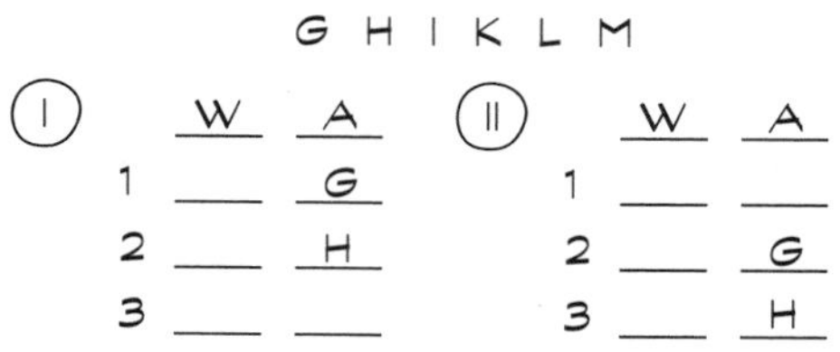

Figure 13.47

You'll revisit those options several times as you work through the questions.

Rule 2 is triggered by M taking an aisle seat. When that happens, H and L occupy the same row. Thus, L will have to take the window seat, since Rule 1 already placed H and G in the aisle seats.

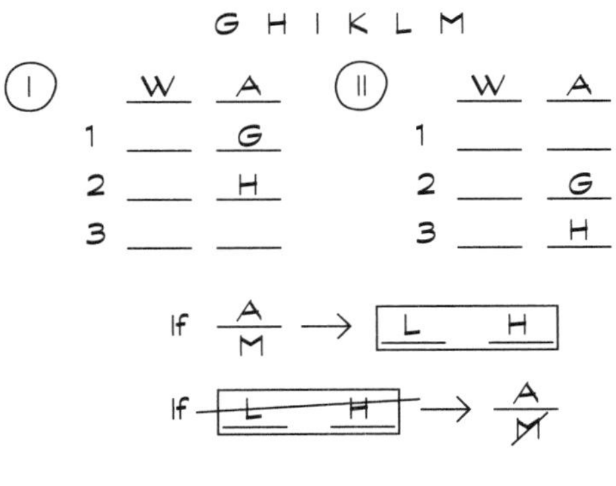

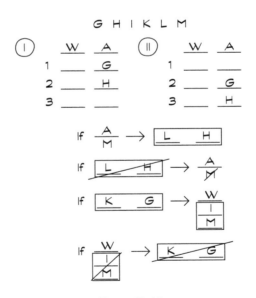

Figure 13.48

Rule 3 is triggered when K takes the window seat next to G. When that happens, I and M become a block, with M's seat directly behind I's. Did you notice that the I-M block can only take consecutive window seats? Remember, G and H will always be in two of the three aisle seats (Rule 1), so there's no room for another block of entities in the aisle column.

Figure 13.49

Rule 4 is relatively benign formal logic for this game. Translate it and diagram its contrapositive like so:

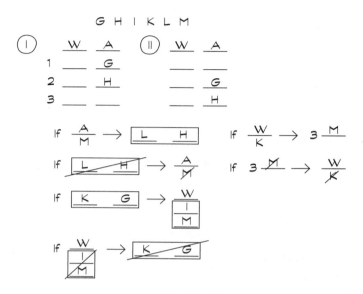

Figure 13.50

Rule 5 is another fairly straightforward formal logic rule. Here are the translation and contrapositive:

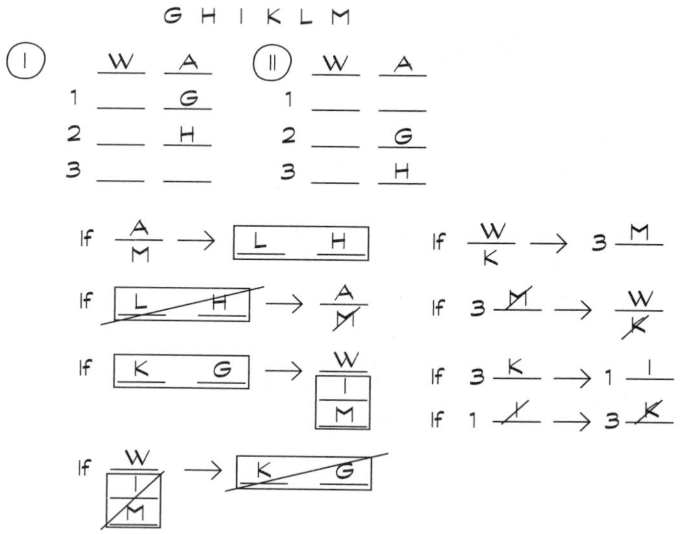

Figure 13.51

Nothing is more important to this game than getting the formal logic right. A close second is sketching each rule so that you can see clearly how it can or can't fit into the framework.

STEP 4: **Deductions**

Because Rules 2–5 are conditional, there's no way to make further affirmative deductions in this game. You'll have to wait until an "If" question triggers a sufficient statement in one of the rules or its contrapositive. That's all right. Four of the five questions here have new "if" conditions, so you can be sure you'll have a chance to work out the implications of the rules there.

STEP 5: **Questions**

As I just noted, four of the five questions here are "If" questions. Expect to use the options from Rule 1 along with whichever of the other rules might be put into play.

14. **(E)**

Which one of the following could be true?

(A)   Imamura sits in row 2, whereas Kelly sits in
        row 3.
(B)   Gutierrez sits in the same row as Kelly,
        immediately and directly behind Moore.
(C)   Gutierrez occupies a window seat in the same row
        as Lapas.
(D)   Moore occupies an aisle seat in the same row as
        Lapas.
(E)   Kelly and Moore both sit in row 3.[22]

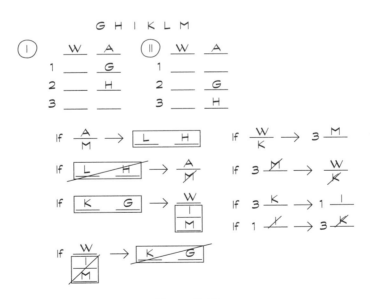

Figure 13.52

The correct answer to this question *could be true*. That means that each of the wrong answers *must be false*. Test the choices one at a time. Eliminate those that are impossible. The correct answer is the only one that will contain an acceptable statement.

---

[22] PrepTest 36, Sec. 4, Q 14

Choice (A) is impossible and can be eliminated. It directly violates Rule 5.

Choice (B) violates Rule 3. When G and K sit in the same row, M must sit behind I. There's not enough room in the aisle seats for I, M, G, and H. You can eliminate this one, too.

Choice (C) simply puts G in the wrong kind of seat. According to Rule 1, G is always on the aisle. Cross out choice (C).

Choice (D) violates Rule 2. When M sits in an aisle seat, L shares a row with H. Eliminate this choice and all that's left is the correct answer, choice (E).

15. **(A)**

If Lapas and Kelly each occupy a window seat, then which one of the following could be true?

(A) Moore occupies the aisle seat in row 3.
(B) Imamura occupies the window seat in row 3.
(C) Gutierrez sits in the same row as Kelly.
(D) Gutierrez sits in the same row as Moore.
(E) Moore sits in the same row as Lapas.[23]

Figure 13.53

Start a mini-sketch with the information from this question's "if" condition. There's no way to tell which of the options this triggers initially, so hold off on placing G and H for a moment.

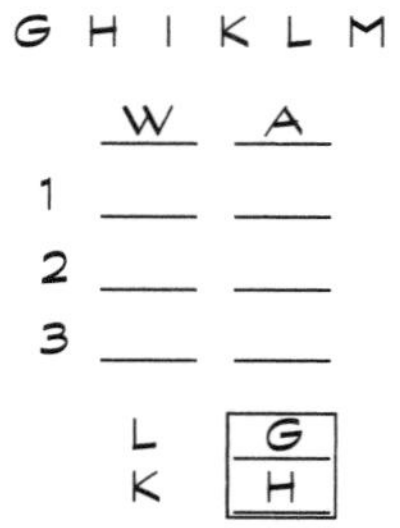

G H I K L M

```
        W    A
1     ___  ___
2     ___  ___
3     ___  ___

      L   | G |
      K   | H |
```

Figure 13.54

By placing K in a window seat, the "if" here triggers Rule 4. You know that M sits in row 3, although not whether the seat will be window or aisle.

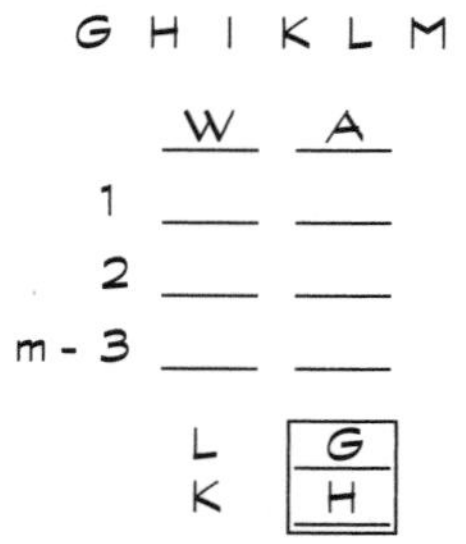

G H I K L M

```
         W    A
   1   ___  ___
   2   ___  ___
m-3   ___  ___

      L   | G |
      K   | H |
```

Figure 13.55

---

23 PrepTest 36, Sec. 4, Q 15

Now, you can test the options. With Option I, try M in the aisle seat of row 3, behind H.

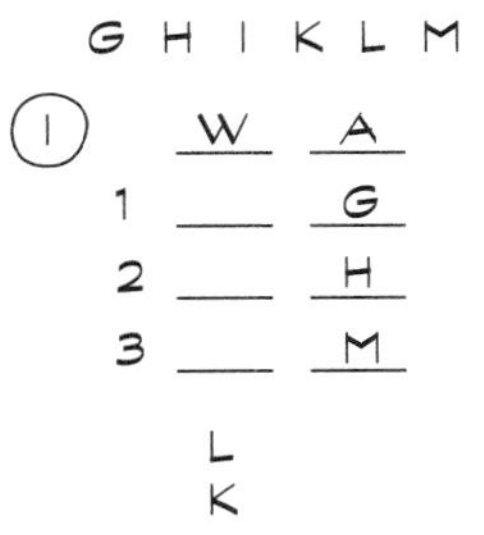

Figure 13.56

When M takes an aisle seat, Rule 2 is triggered. Place L in the window next to H in row 2.

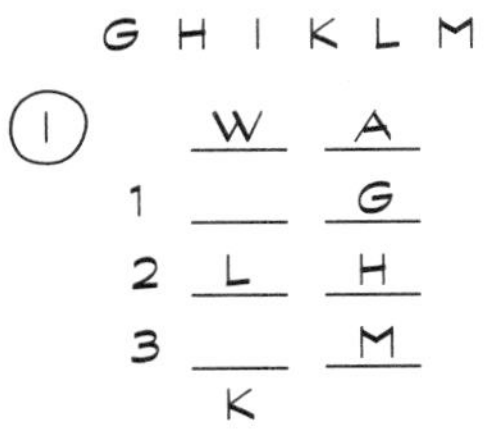

Figure 13.57

Now, you must place I and K. If you tried to put K in the window seat of row 1, you'd trigger Rule 3. But since there's no way for M to sit directly behind I in that case, you know K can't sit in the front row here. If you place K in row 3, however, everything's fine. Giving K a seat in row 3 triggers Rule 5. I can take the window seat in row 1 in this situation, so you've produced one acceptable option.

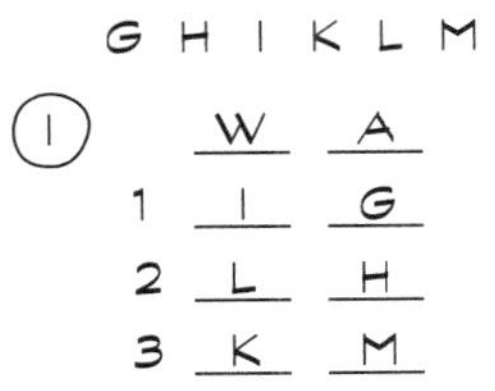

Figure 13.58

That's actually enough to get you the right answer. This is a *could be true* question, and you've just shown that the statement in choice (A) is possible.

The remaining choices *must be false*, of course. Take a moment to consider why. The same sketch you just made rules out choice (B). Since M must take row 3 in this question, the only way for I to take the window seat in row 3 is for M to take the aisle. But you've just seen that when M takes the aisle, I winds up in row 1.

Choice (C) is impossible here because G and H are already occupying two of the aisle seats and this question's "if" has L and K occupying two of the window seats. Thus, one of I and M will be in a window seat and one in an aisle. Since Rule 3 says that I and M will both take window seats anytime G and K share a row, you know choice (C) is impossible here.

Choice (D) is out because this question requires M to take row 3, and G always takes either row 1 or row 2 as a result of Rule 1.

Choice (E) can't work under this question's conditions. Rule 2 makes clear that when M is in an aisle seat, L must sit in the same row as H. Since the question's "if" condition is that L is in a window seat, M's taking an aisle seat ensures that they won't be in the same row.

16. **(D)**

If Moore sits in row 1, then which one of the following must be true?

(A) Hoffman sits in row 2.
(B) Imamura sits in row 2.
(C) Imamura sits in row 3.
(D) Kelly sits in row 1.
(E) Lapas sits in row 3.[24]

G H I K L M
11
W A
1 M K
2 I/L G
3 L/I H

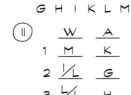

Figure 13.59

Start by sketching this question's "if" condition.

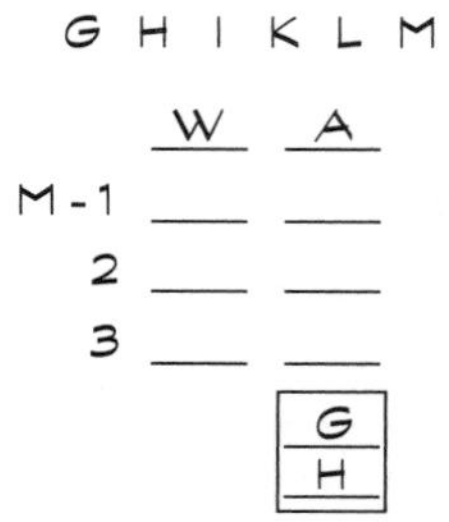
G H I K L M
W A
M - 1
2
3
G
H

Figure 13.60

Placing M in row 1 triggers the contrapositive of Rule 4. If M is in row 1, then he certainly isn't in row 3. Whenever M is not in row 3, K takes an aisle seat.

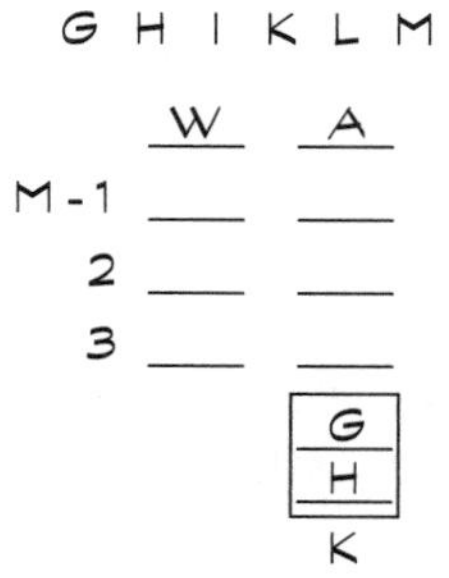
G H I K L M
W A
M - 1
2
3
G
H
K

Figure 13.61

[24] PrepTest 36, Sec. 4, Q 16

There are now two possibilities for the aisle seats, corresponding to the two options in Rule 1: G-H-K or K-G-H in rows 1–3, respectively.

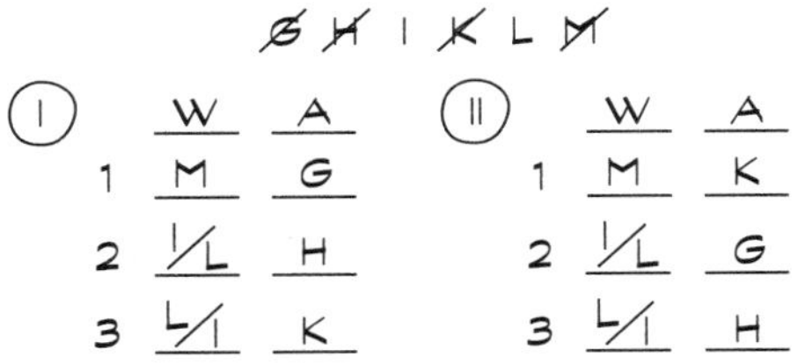

Figure 13.62

The first of those options is impossible. Placing K in row 3 triggers Rule 5, which requires that I take row 1. But there's no room in row 1 now. So only the second option is possible here.

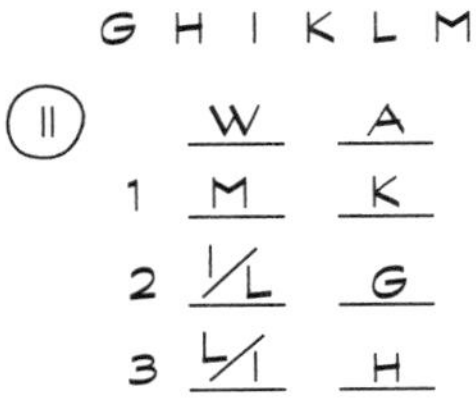

Figure 13.63

It doesn't matter which of the remaining seats I and L occupy; you've already got enough to answer this *must be true* question. Choice (D) says that K is in row 1, and that *must be true* under these conditions.

17. **(B)**

If Kelly occupies the aisle seat in row 3, then each of the following must be true EXCEPT:

(A) Gutierrez sits in the same row as Imamura.
(B) Hoffman sits in the same row as Lapas.
(C) Lapas occupies a window seat.
(D) Moore occupies a window seat.
(E) Gutierrez sits in row 1.[25]

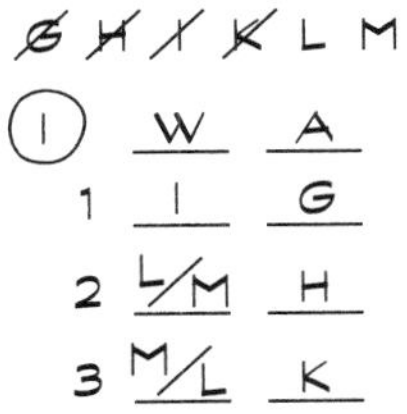

Figure 13.64

In this question, the "if" is very specific. Start by copying the framework and placing K in the aisle seat of row 3. That only works in Option I, of course.

---

[25] PrepTest 36, Sec. 4, Q 17

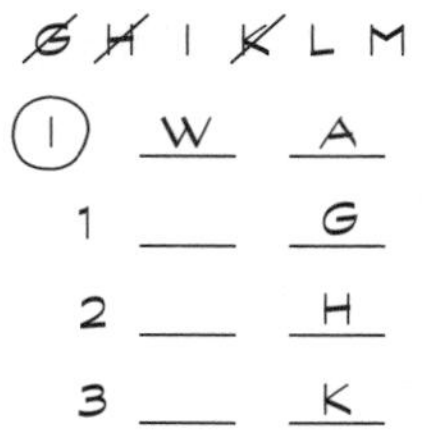

G̶ H̶ I K̶ L M

1̶ W̲ A̲
1 __ G̲
2 __ H̲
3 __ K̲

Figure 13.65

Placing K in row 3 triggers Rule 5. I will take a seat in row 1. The only open seat there is by the window.

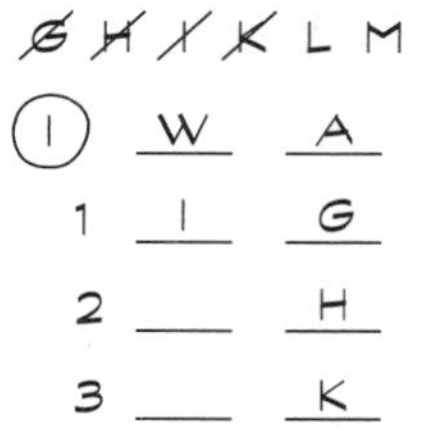

G̶ H̶ I̶ K̶ L M

1̶ W̲ A̲
1 I̲ G̲
2 __ H̲
3 __ K̲

Figure 13.66

Nothing in this arrangement limits the acceptability of either remaining seat for L or M, so just list them as the alternatives for the window seats in rows 2 and 3.

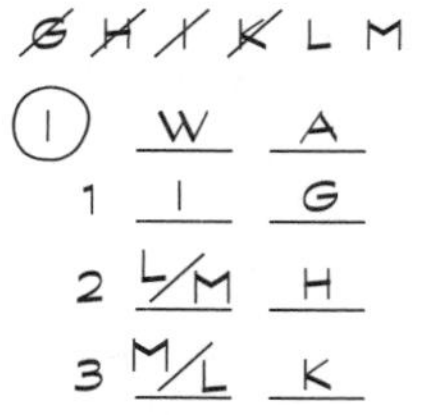

G̶ H̶ I̶ K̶ L M

1̶ W̲ A̲
1 I̲ G̲
2 L̶/M H̲
3 M̶/L K̲

Figure 13.67

The question asks for the *could be false* answer. That's choice (B). Since L may sit in either row 2 or 3, it's possible that H doesn't sit next to L. The other four answers must be true, as your mini-sketch shows unequivocally.

18. **(C)**

If neither Gutierrez nor Imamura sits in row 1, then which one of the following could be true?

(A) Hoffman sits in row 2.
(B) Kelly sits in row 2.
(C) Moore sits in row 2.
(D) Imamura occupies an aisle seat.
(E) Moore occupies an aisle seat.[26]

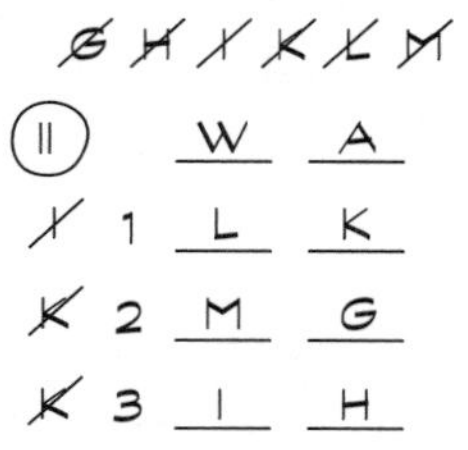

G̶ H̶ I̶ K̶ L̶ M̶

II W̲ A̲
I̶ 1 L̲ K̲
K̶ 2 M̲ G̲
K̶ 3 I̲ H̲

Figure 13.68

---
26 PrepTest 36, Sec. 4, Q 18

The condition in the question stem is only possible in Option II. Start there, indicating that I cannot take a seat in row 1 either. That means that I will sit in a window seat.

Figure 13.69

Denying I a seat in row 1 triggers the contrapositive of Rule 5. K cannot take a seat in row 3 in this question.

Figure 13.70

K cannot sit in row 2 next to G, either. That would trigger Rule 3, and I and M would have to sit in consecutive window seats. That's impossible here. So you've narrowed K's seat down to row 1.

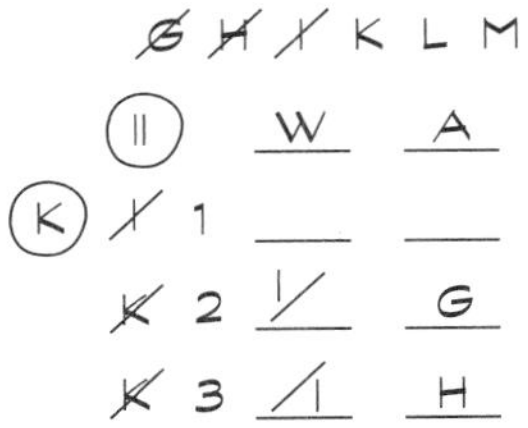

Figure 13.71

That's enough to eliminate three of the answer choices. The correct answer to this question *could be true*. Your mini-sketch already shows that choices (A), (B), and (D) must be false.

The two remaining choices both involve M. Test either one. If it produces an acceptable arrangement, it's the correct answer. If not, the other choice is correct.

Testing choice (C) produces an acceptable arrangement. If you place M in the window seat in row 2, you must place I in the window seat of row 3.

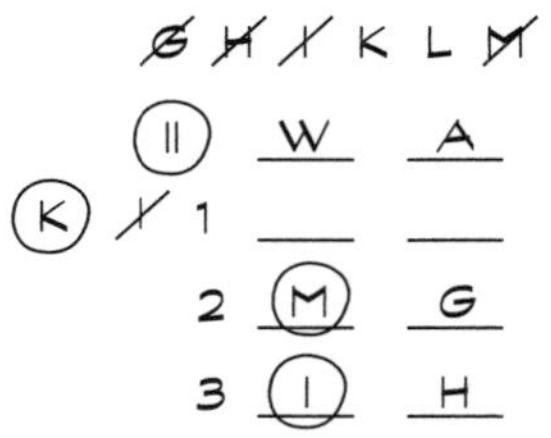

Figure 13.72

Since M isn't in row 3, you know from the contrapositive of Rule 4 that K will take the aisle seat in row 1.

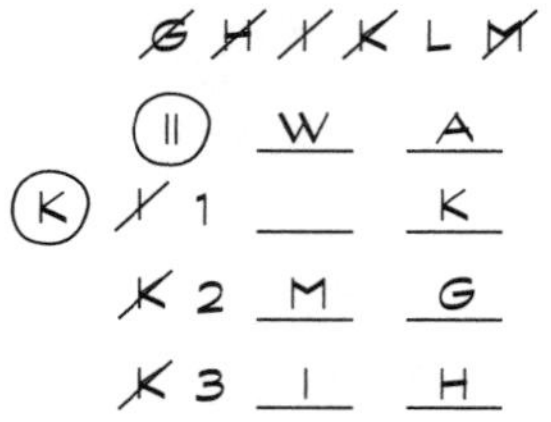

Figure 13.73

That leaves the window seat in row 1 for L.

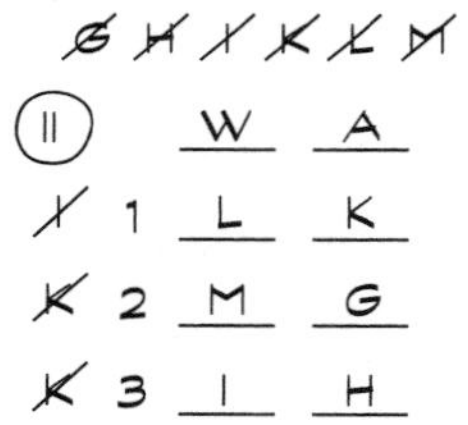

Figure 13.74

There's no violation of the rules in this arrangement, so choice (C) is correct.

Were you to try choice (E), on the other hand, you'd be unable to complete the mini-sketch. The only aisle seat open for M is in row 1, which would put K in the adjacent window seat.

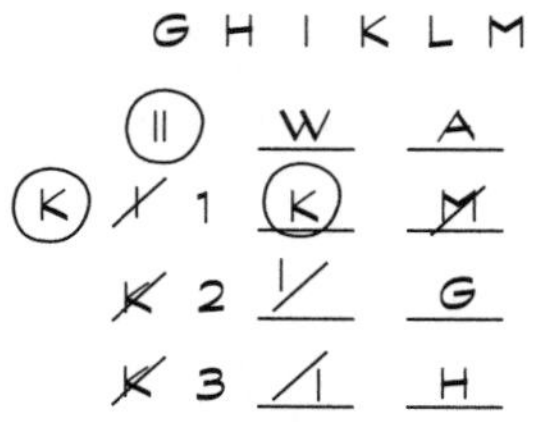

Figure 13.75

But that contradicts Rule 4. When K takes a window seat, M has to be in row 3. Choice (E), therefore, must be false.

I know that I won't make any friends by introducing you to that game. The truth is, there have been few (if any) games more difficult than that in the past 20 years or so. All of those conditional rules make for quite a slog.

But step back for a minute and realize one thing: All of the questions did have one correct answer and four that were demonstrably incorrect. The test makers lived up to their end of the bargain by giving you all of the information you needed to distinguish the right answers from the wrong ones. If a game even close to this difficulty level appears on your test, it's going to be challenging for everyone taking the test. In fact, it will be much more challenging for those who haven't trained as effectively as you have. On every LSAT, you're scored against the other test takers for that administration. If you get two points out of a game like this and they only get one, you'll have the higher score.

Don't take the test personally. When it comes to the LSAT, the rain falls on everyone. By taking the time to assess the game's setup and task and turn that into a descriptive and useful sketch, at least you'll have the best umbrella in the room.

KEEP HYBRIDS IN A FAMILIAR CONTEXT

Hybrid games are important parts of your logic games practice. Taking all Hybrids as a group, they're second only to Sequencing games as the most common games to appear on the exam. But remember that Hybrids are always made up of familiar game tasks. Consider the tasks, combine them into a single, interrelated sketch, and pay attention to which of the rules affect which of the tasks, and you're right back on familiar ground.

CHAPTER 14

RECENT TRENDS

With all of the effort you're putting into your LSAT preparation, it's always important to stay on top of the latest trends and patterns appearing in the types of games and questions that the test makers are using. In this brief chapter, I'll outline the game types that have appeared on the exams released most recently at the time of this writing. While there's no guarantee that the test makers will use a particular assortment of games on your official test, the LSAT tends to change rather slowly, and patterns of game and question distribution are pretty similar from year to year.

The following chart shows the eight most recent exams released prior to this book's publication.

RECENT LSATs: LOGIC GAMES SECTIONS

PrepTest 54 (June '08) Game 1—Selection Game 2—Strict Sequencing Game 3—Strict Sequencing Game 4—Strict Sequencing	**PrepTest 55 (Oct '08)** Game 1—Hybrid Distribution/Matching Game 2—Strict Sequencing Game 3—Loose Sequencing Game 4—Hybrid Matching/Sequencing
PrepTest 56 (Dec '08) Game 1—Strict Sequencing Game 2—Matching Game 3—Selection Game 4—Hybrid Sequencing/Distribution	**PrepTest 57 (June '09)** Game 1—Strict Sequencing Game 2—Hybrid Matching/Sequencing Game 3—Hybrid Selection/Matching Game 4—Hybrid Matching/Sequencing
PrepTest 58 (Oct '10) Game 1—Strict Sequencing Game 2—Selection Game 3—Hybrid Matching/Sequencing Game 4—Selection	**PrepTest 59 (Dec '10)** Game 1—Strict Sequencing Game 2—Strict Sequencing Game 3—Selection Game 4—Strict Sequencing
PrepTest 60 (June '10) Game 1—Strict Sequencing Game 2—Loose Sequencing Game 3—Strict Sequencing Game 4—Hybrid Distribution/Matching	**PrepTest 61 (Oct '10)** Game 1—Distribution Game 2—Loose Sequencing Game 3—Hybrid Selection/Sequencing Game 4—Strict Sequencing

NOTE: The LSAC does not routinely release February exams to the public. Thus, the eight most recently released exams cover just over two years' worth of LSAT administrations.

Strict Sequencing Is Still the Favorite

The first takeaway from this chart is that Strict Sequencing, the old warhorse, remains by far the test makers' favorite game type. No fewer than 13 of the 32 games represented on these tests are single-task Strict Sequencing games. When you add in the Strict Sequencing tasks that are blended into Hybrid games, Strict Sequencing is involved in well over half of the test's most recent offerings.

It's also important to note that on two of the tests—PrepTests 54 and 59—three of the four games had Strict Sequencing tasks. There is no other game type that the test makers use in such a heavy concentration.

A handful of the recent Strict Sequencing games had twists like those you saw in chapter 9. In a couple of them, the setup described a situation—e.g., floors of a building or layers of a cake—in which you need to count from the bottom up. Another had a situation in which more than one of the entities could occupy the same position in the order; in this case, you were to rank six entities in four levels, so you knew that there would be some overlap. A couple of the games had a Double Sequencing feel to them. In one, for example, you had to schedule six entities over the course of three days, using one morning and one evening appointment each day.

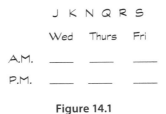

Figure 14.1

The rules played off the scenario, with some limiting certain entities to a time of day regardless of day and others limiting entities to certain days regardless of time. Still, this isn't true Double Sequencing. Each entity is assigned to only one position. Saying, "R takes an afternoon position," in this game is really no different than saying, "R is placed second, fourth, or sixth," in a run-of-the-mill Sequencing setup. Don't let seeming novelties throw you; look for the familiar core tasks of LSAT logic games that you've learned in this book, and you'll seldom run into anything unmanageable.

No New Game Types

The second takeaway from this chart should be that the test has introduced no new game types. The second and third most common games during this period were Selection and Sequencing-Matching Hybrids. If you've completed the work in this book up to this point, you've had ample practice with both of those game types. The recent games in both of these categories worked much like examples in this book, with the test makers adding little if anything in the way of twists or additions. Selection, as always, rewards formal logic skills above all. Sequencing-Matching Hybrids, as you've come to see, most often use the Matching restrictions to limit the possible Sequencing arrangements. That remains true in these recent examples. It's also worth noting that these two game types are the only ones apart from Strict Sequencing to appear more than once on the same test.

The rarest find among these recent games is the Selection-Matching Hybrid on PrepTest 57. While this game was made up of two common tasks, this particular blend has only been used a couple of times by the test makers. In this particular game, you were asked to choose five of seven toys and assign each of them one of four colors. For test takers who can only perform if they've memorized standardized sketches, this game was intimidating. For those who were able to conduct a helpful overview and say, "The acceptable arrangements will have five toys circled and two crossed out, and they'll use the colors to limit which ones I can choose," this game, though an unusual Hybrid, was eminently manageable.

A New Question Type

For LSAT watchers, the biggest innovation in the past couple of years was the introduction of a new question type. Really, the question type is a variation on the Rule-Changer. I'll refer to it as a Rule Substitution question. Here's what it looks like:

> Which one of the following, if substituted for the condition that Hibiscus must be hung somewhere before Katydid but cannot be the first photograph, would have the same effect in determining the arrangement of the photographs?[1]

> Which one of the following, if substituted for the restriction that if music is taken, then neither physics nor theater can be taken, would have the same effect in determining which courses the student can take?[2]

As you can see, these questions reward you for being able to assess the strength and effect of a particular rule. The standard Rule-Changer question got at this same ability by asking you to rethink the Master Sketch with one of the rules removed or altered. This newer variation poses the same puzzle by telling you, in effect, to remove a rule and then substitute the correct answer to wind up with exactly the same Master Sketch. When you think about it, this question type is really just asking you to paraphrase the original rule accurately. In fact, that's the strategy you should use as you approach these problems. Remove the rule from the Master Sketch and consider its effect. Then substitute the answer choices and choose the one that restores the Master Sketch to its original state. By rewarding your ability to paraphrase the rules, this question type is just one more way in which the test makers reward the core skill of Strategic Reading.

Indeed, remember that the test makers always reward the Core 4 LSAT Skills—Strategic Reading, Understanding Formal Logic, Analyzing Arguments, and Making Deductions—that you first encountered at the beginning of this book. With those key skills in mind, you're unlikely

---

[1] PrepTest 59, Sec. 1, Q 10
[2] PrepTest 58, Sec. 3, Q 23

to encounter anything on test day (in any of the test's sections) that seems truly novel. If, at first glance, you seem to be face-to-face with a game or question you haven't seen before,

stop and get a handle on what you're being asked for. Then remember that the test makers always provide you with everything you need in order to determine the question's one correct answer. Approaching the LSAT from that perspective, all that you just learned about typical LSAT patterns is just icing on the cake.

PART III

FULL-SECTION PRACTICE

CHAPTER 15

TIMING AND SECTION MANAGEMENT IN A NUTSHELL

You're ready to put it all together. Timed, section-length practice is the final step in your preparation for LSAT logic games. You've been building up to this stage since the opening of chapter 1. Step-by-step, you've mastered the Kaplan Method, adopted the strategies associated with the various tasks and question types, and then learned to recognize the standard game types and variations that the test makers use. In Part II, you even did most of your practice on individual games under timed conditions. All of that was training and conditioning for taking the full Logic Games section—four games in 35 minutes—as you will on test day.

Here, in Part III, I'll introduce you to a handful of principles that will help you manage your time and maximize your score. Then you'll have the chance to take two complete Logic Games sections. Take them one at a time and review each of them thoroughly, studying the explanations for the game setups and all of the questions (even those you got right). Before you go any farther, though, I want to issue a strong CAUTION: **Don't take a timed section until you've completed Parts I and II of this book.** Taking a timed section without adequate preparation is likely to be a frustrating experience that won't contribute to your test day readiness. So if you're exploring this part of the book before you've completed the earlier chapters, go back and get yourself ready. If you have completed the earlier parts, please proceed.

EFFICIENCY VS. SPEED

"I could have gotten all of the questions right if I'd just had more time. How do I get faster?" I told you right at the beginning of the book that I've heard this question from my LSAT students hundreds of times, if not thousands. My response is always the same: You're much more likely to improve your score with improved efficiency than you are by blindly trying to speed up. Timing is a part of the test. The test makers are rewarding you for making smart, strategic decisions about how to spend your limited time. You'll face similar challenges in law school. There's simply too much to read and too much work to complete to take a plodding, bulldozer approach to the material. Just as you do on the LSAT, you'll learn to distinguish the relevant from the irrelevant and target the parts of the material that lead to points on your exams.

Ironically, one key to efficiency on the LSAT is patience. This is especially true in the Logic Games section. You've seen plenty of games in this book in which spending three or even four minutes creating a complete Master Sketch made it possible for you to answer all of the questions in a matter of a few seconds each. On the other hand, rushing the setup and making a mistake with one of the rules or missing a deduction can lead to disaster. Think about it like this: The test rewards only correct answers, so any time you spend producing a wrong answer is wasted time. Nobody will proudly proclaim, "Yeah, I missed all of the questions from that game, but I did it very fast." Even if you did the entire game in four minutes, you simply threw those four minutes away if they didn't produce correct answers.

OPTIMAL TIMING

Here's what you should be shooting for. With 35 minutes to complete four games, you need to average about eight minutes and 30 seconds per game. I'll talk about what to do with that leftover minute shortly. Within the eight and a half minutes you have for a given game don't hesitate to spend three to four minutes on Steps 1–4 of the Kaplan Method. (A few games may even reward you for spending longer. Think back to the Professors' Hiring game or the Music Program game in which each piece was performed on two instruments. Once you'd made all of the deductions in those games, the question sets wouldn't take you more than three minutes to complete.)

LSAT Logic Games Timing Guidelines	
Section—Four Games	35 minutes
Game—Setup and Questions	8 minutes 30 seconds
Setup (Kaplan Method Steps 1–4)	3–4 minutes
Questions (Kaplan Method Step 5)	4½ to 5½ minutes

Spending three to four minutes setting up the game leaves four and a half to five and a half minutes for the questions, which should be enough time, even if the set has several "If" questions.

Strategic Guessing

One important thing to remember is that, unlike the SAT, the LSAT has no wrong-answer penalty. You should enter an answer, even if it's a random guess, for every question. In fact, becoming a good strategic guesser can increase your score. If you come to a question that would take you two minutes to answer, ask yourself whether that time would be better spent setting up the next game, where you might be able to get five to seven more points.

Getting into an "ego battle" with the test is almost always detrimental. Our psychological tendency is to say, "I couldn't get it, so I had to give up and guess." I want you to change that message to yourself. From here on, say, "I made a smart decision to guess because battling it out with that one question wasn't in *my* best interest." Take the LSAT; don't let it take you.

It's tough to let go of a very difficult or time-consuming question once you have your teeth in it. But the best scorers do. They realize that the only glory on the LSAT comes from getting more points overall and that no one, not even the law school admissions officers, will ever see which questions you solved correctly and which you guessed on. Too many LSAT students try to be perfect and wind up costing themselves several points down the road. Learn not to over-invest in a single point.

SECTION MANAGEMENT: YOU'RE IN CONTROL
Section Triage: Ordering the Games

If you stick to an average of eight and a half minutes per game, you'll spend 34 minutes setting up games and answering questions. So what do you do with that one leftover minute in your section? The answer is that you spend it up front, deciding the order in which you want to tackle the games. The test makers do not necessarily arrange the games in the optimal order for you. Indeed, they often place the most time-consuming or difficult game second or third in the section. Nothing about the rules or structure of the LSAT obligates you to complete the games in order. You must work on only the announced *section* at any given time on test day, but you can move back and forth within that section in the way that's best for your performance.

So spend the first minute of the section (not more) assessing the difficulty of the four games. You'll want to tackle the easiest game first and leave the toughest game for last. In many aspects of life, it's good to get the hardest part out of way and delay the easiest, most pleasurable part of your task. Not on the LSAT. This is an "eat dessert first" test. Taking on the easiest game first accomplishes three things: (1) It builds your confidence, (2) it offers the immediate reward of several points, and (3) it allows you to bank some additional time for the hardest game if you can complete the easiest one in less than eight and a half minutes.

Here's a chart showing student performance on a representative Logic Games section. Note that the bars indicate the percentage of students who gave *wrong* answers to each question.

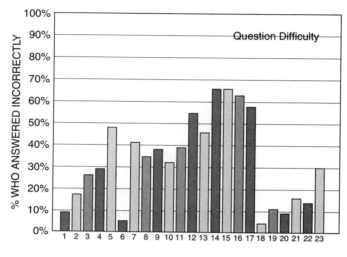

Figure 15.1

The hardest game on this exam was the third one. Many, maybe even most, of the students who took the section in order, just following the test maker's design, missed the opportunity for easier points in Game 4 or found themselves so rushed in the final game that they weren't able to take advantage of how much easier it was than Game 3.

How do you learn to identify the easiest and hardest games in just one minute? Kaplan calls this *triage*, after the procedure that doctors use to prioritize patients in emergency situations. The LSAT isn't as literally life-or-death, but you can still learn some good practices by following the doctors' example. When a big accident, for example, brings many patients into the hospital simultaneously, the doctor or triage nurse in charge assesses all of the patients and determines the order in which they'll be treated on the basis of several factors: how severely they're injured, how long it would take or how many staff members it would take to treat them, and the chances that they can be saved. The goal is to save as many of the patients as possible. To do that—and this is the real lesson for you as a test taker—the triage doctor may have to make the extremely difficult choice to postpone the treatment of the most severely injured patient. In order to help as many people as possible, the doctor says, "This person would require several hours and several doctors or nurses; we have to let his procedure wait." That's the kind of difficult but strategic decision you must make in order to get as many points on the test as possible.

In order for triage to work in the ER, doctors must be fast and confident in their assessments. They have guidelines that they follow in order to make their decisions quickly and accurately. You have one minute to assess your "patients," so you'll need the same thing. Fortunately, you're already familiar with the criteria you should use as you triage the section. Remember the four criteria you used to assess game difficulty in chapter 7?

WHAT MAKES LOGIC GAMES HARDER

Easier	Harder
Concrete	Ambiguous
Simple	Complex
Brief	Long
Familiar	Strange

Those are the same factors you should use to decide the order in which you'll handle the games. As you know from all of the work you've done up to this point, nothing is more salient to a game's difficulty than whether it's concrete or ambiguous. Simplicity and brevity can help make a game more manageable, but they won't compensate for rules and restrictions that are too open-ended. Familiarity is the wild card. If you simply don't know how to approach a certain game, you should put it off for later. The equivalent situation in the hospital would be a patient with an injury or condition that no one on duty knows how to treat. Of course, a well-run hospital will schedule its staff so that there's a wide range of expertise available at all times. Likewise, your practice should include all of the basic game types so that you're unlikely to run into a game you find utterly baffling.

In addition to the factors listed above, you may consider the number and types of questions associated with each game as you assess the section. If you find two games of equal difficulty, one of which has seven questions and the other only five, you should prioritize the former. Without a clear-cut case like that, though, you should base your priorities on the difficulty of the games' setups and rules.

Learning to triage effectively takes a little practice, something you can begin on the sections that follow. In order to be valuable, triage cannot take you several minutes to complete. Even if your assessment of the section is perfect, you can't afford more than about a minute to prioritize the games. (Imagine a doctor who correctly assessed each patient's prospects but ran out of time to treat them.) When you triage, be clear and decisive in your choices. In the end, I'd rather have you say, "If I had it to do over, I think I would have done Game 3 before Game 2," than to spend several minutes deciding between the two.

I'll review section triage in the explanations for each of the full-length sections that follow.

Question Triage: Ordering the Questions

Your ability to optimize your performance through strategic decision making doesn't end when you decide the order of the games. Within a given game, too, you can approach the questions in any order. Once you've completed Steps 1–4 and you have a strong, useful Master Sketch, take a moment to consider the questions. Are most of them "If" questions calling for new mini-sketches? Are they mostly Must/Could questions that you can answer from the deductions in your Master Sketch? Does the set have a balance of question types? You'll likely have an impression of what to expect from the questions based on the game type and how thoroughly you were able to fill in the framework in your Master Sketch. There's nothing wrong with taking the questions in the order presented and, most of the time, you probably will. But there are a handful of considerations that can help you better manage your time within a question set:

- Do Acceptability questions first. They're fast. Your approach—using the rules to eliminate the violators—is consistent. And the correct answer provides an acceptable arrangement you can use when evaluating answers to later questions.

- Your scratch work from "If" questions can help you answer Must/Could questions. For example, since the wrong answers to a *must be false* question all *could be true*, you can eliminate any choice that you've seen as acceptable in another question.

- Questions in which each answer choice is conditional are usually time-consuming. If a question's answer choices start with the word "if," consider skipping the question or guessing if time is tight. Remember that when the given conditions match the mini-sketches from any other question you've done, you can use your prior work to evaluate that answer.

- Always characterize the answer choices (e.g., the correct answer *could be true*, so the wrong answers *must be false*) before you evaluate them, regardless of the order in which you answer the questions. Answering the "wrong question" is always a waste of time and points.

The same caution that I issued with regard to section triage also applies when you assess the question set. Don't spend an inordinate amount of time (more than a few seconds, in this case) trying to come up with the perfect order. For the most part, take the questions in order, but be willing to skip a question as soon as you realize that it's not going anywhere. As you work through the rest of the questions for that game, you may get help with the question you skipped. If not, you can either guess strategically or come back to spend time with the question before you move on to the next game. What you *must* avoid is throwing off the timing for an entire game or section because you insist on getting the answer to a single question. The cost to you in time (and the emotional toll you pay for your frustration) simply isn't worth it.

That last statement, in many ways, summarizes the takeaway message of this chapter. The best test takers are those that get the most points. They don't let the perfect become the enemy of the good. Learn from them. They know that the test taker is in control of the section, and they'll take the games in whatever order is best for their overall performance. They're also willing to skip or guess on a question, when trying to complete it would be too time-consuming or is likely to end in frustration. The LSAT would be a different test if it reported to law schools which test takers had solved the toughest questions. It doesn't. It reports, quite simply, who answered *more* questions correctly. Use the test's design to your benefit. Learn to manage the section for maximum efficiency.

CHAPTER 16

FULL-LENGTH SECTION PRACTICE

In the following two chapters, you'll have the opportunity to take two full Logic Games sections, just as they appeared on the original exams. When you take them, make sure that you'll have 35 uninterrupted minutes in a quiet place. You'll want to time yourself strictly and follow the test instructions to the letter.

WHEN AND HOW TO USE SECTION PRACTICE

As I cautioned earlier, don't take a full-length section before you've completed the first two parts of this book. Section practice is about "putting it all together." Don't use section practice to learn game types or methods (although you'll certainly review your performance with the explanations that follow each section). Use section practice to improve your timing and performance with skills and strategies you've already mastered. Trying to practice timing before you've achieved a level of proficiency with the games will lead to mistakes and frustrations, and it will turn your review of the section into an exercise in learning the basics, when it should be an assessment of your efficiency in applying best practices to each game.

On your official test day, you will get credit only for the answers on your bubble sheet. No one will look in your test booklet to see what you've circled or indicated there.

Depending on how much time you have before your official exam, you may want to wait a few days between practice sections. Use what you learn from reviewing the first section to go back and refresh your understanding of the Kaplan Method, strategies, and game types as appropriate. One thing is for sure—if you take the sections back-to-back, you'll likely have almost exactly the same performance on the second that you did on the first.

HOW TO CALCULATE YOUR SCORE

With timed, section-length practice, your goal must be to get as many points as possible. Distinguish that from the goal of handling each game perfectly. Skip and guess as you need to in order to maximize your efficiency in the section and the overall number of correct answers you can produce.

Once you've completed the section, score your responses against the provided answer key. Mark each of the answers you got right or wrong, but review the entire game, Steps 1–5, using the explanations following the section. Test scores are calculated based on the overall number of correct answers you produced in all of the scored sections on a test, so there's no way to determine your overall LSAT score based on any single section. Here are a couple of score conversion tables from recently released LSATs. There are almost always 101 scored questions per LSAT, of which 22–24 come from the Logic Games section.

CONVERSION CHART

For converting Raw Score to the 120–180 LSAT Scaled Score
LSAT Prep Test 47

REPORTED SCORE	LOWEST RAW SCORE	HIGHEST RAW SCORE
180	99	100
179	98	98
178	97	97
177	96	96
176	--*	--*
175	95	95
174	94	94
173	93	93
172	92	92
171	91	91
170	90	90
169	89	89
168	88	88
167	87	87
166	85	86
165	84	84
164	83	83
163	81	82
162	80	80
161	78	79
160	77	77
159	75	76
158	73	74
157	72	72
156	70	71
155	68	69
154	66	67
153	65	65
152	63	64
151	61	63
150	59	60
149	57	58
148	55	56
147	54	54
146	52	53
145	50	51
144	48	49
143	46	47
142	45	45
141	43	44
140	41	42
139	40	40
138	38	39
137	36	37
136	35	35
135	33	34
134	32	32
133	30	31
132	29	29
131	27	28
130	26	26
129	25	25
128	24	24
127	22	23
126	21	21
125	20	20
124	19	19
123	18	18
122	17	17
121	16	16
120	0	15

*There is no raw score that will produce this scaled score for the test.

CONVERSION CHART

For converting Raw Score to the 120–180 LSAT Scaled Score
LSAT Prep Test 50

REPORTED SCORE	LOWEST RAW SCORE	HIGHEST RAW SCORE
180	98	100
179	97	97
178	--*	--*
177	96	96
176	95	95
175	94	94
174	--*	--*
173	93	93
172	92	92
171	91	91
170	90	90
169	89	89
168	88	88
167	86	87
166	85	85
165	84	84
164	83	83
163	81	82
162	80	80
161	78	79
160	77	77
159	75	76
158	73	74
157	72	72
156	70	71
155	68	69
154	66	67
153	64	65
152	63	63
151	61	62
150	59	60
149	57	58
148	55	56
147	53	54
146	52	52
145	50	51
144	48	49
143	46	47
142	45	45
141	43	44
140	41	42
139	40	40
138	38	39
137	36	37
136	35	35
135	33	34
134	32	32
133	30	31
132	29	29
131	27	28
130	26	26
129	25	25
128	23	24
127	22	22
126	21	21
125	20	20
124	18	19
123	17	17
122	16	16
121	15	15
120	0	14

*There is no raw score that will produce this scaled score for the test.

Figure 16.1

```
                    SCORING WORKSHEET

  1. Enter the number of questions you answered
     correctly in each section

                              NUMBER
                              CORRECT

        SECTION I . . . . . . . . . .  _____

        SECTION II . . . . . . . .  _____

        SECTION III. . . . . . . .  _____

        SECTION IV . . . . . . . .  _____


  2. Enter the sum here:    _____   THIS IS YOUR
                                      RAW SCORE.
```

Figure 16.2

By estimating the number of correct responses you'd generate from the remaining sections of the test, you can gain an idea of the impact your logic games performance will have on your score. To improve your performance on the other sections of the test, study this book's companion volumes, *LSAT Reading Comprehension: Strategies and Tactics* and *LSAT Logical Reasoning: Strategies and Tactics*.

If you haven't done so already, register for the Kaplan LSAT Experience test by calling 1-800-KAPTEST or visiting www.kaplanlsat.com for more information. This provides you with the chance to take the most recently released full-length LSAT under all of the proctoring conditions and rules that will apply on test day. You'll also receive your score, explanations for all of the questions, and a video review of the test delivered by some of Kaplan's most experienced LSAT teachers.

Remember that there is no "guessing penalty," so fill in an answer for every question, just as you would on test day. If you're able to eliminate two or three of the wrong answers, guess from among the remaining choices. When you review the section, you can look to see how you would be able to answer the question quickly and effectively, but don't let that deter you from guessing and skipping when it's in your interest to do so.

Good luck on the sections. Do your best.

CHAPTER 17

FULL-LENGTH SECTION I[1]

Time—35 minutes

22 Questions

Directions: Each group of questions in this section is based on a set of conditions. In answering some of the questions, it may be useful to draw a rough diagram. Choose the response that most accurately and completely answers each question, and blacken the corresponding space on your answer sheet.

---

[1] PrepTest 47, Sec. 4

Questions 1–5

Exactly seven products—P, Q, R, S, T, W, and X—are each to be advertised exactly once in a section of a catalog. The order in which they will be displayed is governed by the following conditions:

Q must be displayed in some position before W.
R must be displayed immediately before X.
T cannot be displayed immediately before or immediately after W.
S must be displayed either first or seventh.
Either Q or T must be displayed fourth.

1. Which one of the following CANNOT be the product that is displayed first?

    (A)   P
    (B)   Q
    (C)   R
    (D)   T
    (E)   X

2. If X is displayed immediately before Q, then which one of the following could be true?

    (A)   T is displayed first.
    (B)   R is displayed fifth.
    (C)   Q is displayed last.
    (D)   Q is displayed second.
    (E)   P is displayed second.

3. If P is displayed second, then which one of the following could be displayed third?

    (A)   R
    (B)   S
    (C)   T
    (D)   W
    (E)   X

4. Which one of the following could be true?

    (A)   Q is displayed fifth.
    (B)   Q is displayed seventh.
    (C)   R is displayed third.
    (D)   W is displayed third.
    (E)   X is displayed fifth.

5. If R is displayed sixth, then which one of the following must be displayed fifth?

    (A)   P
    (B)   Q
    (C)   T
    (D)   W
    (E)   X

Questions 6–11

A lighting control panel has exactly seven switches, numbered from 1 to 7. Each switch is either in the on position or in the off position. The circuit load of the panel is the total number of its switches that are on. The control panel must be configured in accordance with the following conditions:

> If switch 1 is on, then switch 3 and switch 5 are off.
> If switch 4 is on, then switch 2 and switch 5 are off.
> The switch whose number corresponds to the circuit load of the panel is itself on.

6. Which one of the following could be a complete and accurate list of the switches that are on?

(A)   switch 2, switch 3, switch 4, switch 7
(B)   switch 3, switch 6, switch 7
(C)   switch 2, switch 5, switch 6
(D)   switch 1, switch 3, switch 4
(E)   switch 1, switch 5

7. If switch 1 and switch 3 are both off, then which one of the following could be two switches that are both on?

(A)   switch 2 and switch 7
(B)   switch 4 and switch 6
(C)   switch 4 and switch 7
(D)   switch 5 and switch 6
(E)   switch 6 and switch 7

8. If exactly two of the switches are on, then which one of the following switches must be off?

(A)   switch 3
(B)   switch 4
(C)   switch 5
(D)   switch 6
(E)   switch 7

9. If switch 6 and switch 7 are both off, then what is the maximum circuit load of the panel?

(A)   one
(B)   two
(C)   three
(D)   four
(E)   five

10. If switch 5 and switch 6 are both on, then which one of the following switches must be on?

(A)   switch 1
(B)   switch 2
(C)   switch 3
(D)   switch 4
(E)   switch 7

11. What is the maximum circuit load of the panel?

(A)   three
(B)   four
(C)   five
(D)   six
(E)   seven

Questions 12–17

In Crescentville there are exactly five record stores, whose names are abbreviated S, T, V, X, and Z. Each of the five stores carries at least one of four distinct types of music: folk, jazz, opera, and rock. None of the stores carries any other type of music. The following conditions must hold:

Exactly two of the five stores carry jazz.
T carries rock and opera but no other type of music.
S carries more types of music than T carries.
X carries more types of music than any other store in Crescentville carries.
Jazz is among the types of music S carries.
V does not carry any type of music that Z carries.

12. Which one of the following could be true?

    (A)   S carries folk and rock but neither jazz nor opera.
    (B)   T carries jazz but neither opera nor rock.
    (C)   V carries folk, rock, and opera, but not jazz.
    (D)   X carries folk, rock, and jazz, but not opera.
    (E)   Z carries folk and opera but neither rock nor jazz.

13. Which one of the following could be true?

    (A)   S, V, and Z all carry folk.
    (B)   S, X, and Z all carry jazz.
    (C)   Of the five stores, only S and V carry jazz.
    (D)   Of the five stores, only T and X carry rock.
    (E)   Of the five stores, only S, T, and V carry opera.

14. If exactly one of the stores carries folk, then which one of the following could be true?

    (A)   S and V carry exactly two types of music in common.
    (B)   T and S carry exactly two types of music in common.
    (C)   T and V carry exactly two types of music in common.
    (D)   V and X carry exactly two types of music in common.
    (E)   X and Z carry exactly two types of music in common.

15. Which one of the following must be true?

    (A)   T carries exactly the same number of types of music as V carries.
    (B)   V carries exactly the same number of types of music as Z carries.
    (C)   S carries at least one more type of music than Z carries.
    (D)   Z carries at least one more type of music than T carries.
    (E)   X carries exactly two more types of music than S carries.

16. If V is one of exactly three stores that carry rock, then which one of the following must be true?

    (A)   S and Z carry no types of music in common.
    (B)   S and V carry at least one type of music in common.
    (C)   S and Z carry at least one type of music in common.
    (D)   T and Z carry at least one type of music in common.
    (E)   T and V carry at least two types of music in common.

17. If S and V both carry folk, then which one of the following could be true?

    (A)   S and T carry no types of music in common.
    (B)   S and Z carry no types of music in common.
    (C)   T and Z carry no types of music in common.
    (D)   S and Z carry two types of music in common.
    (E)   T and V carry two types of music in common.

Questions 18–22

Maggie's Deli is open exactly five days every week: Monday through Friday. Its staff, each of whom works on at least one day each week, consists of exactly six people—Janice, Kevin, Nan, Ophelia, Paul, and Seymour. Exactly three of them—Janice, Nan, and Paul—are supervisors. The deli's staffing is consistent with the following:

Each day's staff consists of exactly two people, at least one of whom is a supervisor.

Tuesday's and Wednesday's staffs both include Ophelia.

Of the days Nan works each week, at least two are consecutive.

Seymour does not work on any day before the first day Paul works that week.

Any day on which Kevin works is the first day during the week that some other staff member works.

18. Which one of the following could be an accurate staffing schedule?

   (A)   Monday: Janice, Kevin
         Tuesday: Nan, Ophelia
         Wednesday: Nan, Paul
         Thursday: Kevin, Paul
         Friday: Janice, Seymour
   (B)   Monday: Paul, Seymour
         Tuesday: Ophelia, Paul
         Wednesday: Nan, Ophelia
         Thursday: Kevin, Nan
         Friday: Janice, Seymour
   (C)   Monday: Janice, Kevin
         Tuesday: Nan, Ophelia
         Wednesday: Nan, Ophelia
         Thursday: Kevin, Paul
         Friday: Paul, Seymour
   (D)   Monday: Janice, Kevin
         Tuesday: Janice, Ophelia
         Wednesday: Nan, Ophelia
         Thursday: Nan, Seymour
         Friday: Kevin, Paul
   (E)   Monday: Paul, Seymour
         Tuesday: Ophelia, Paul
         Wednesday: Nan, Ophelia
         Thursday: Janice, Kevin
         Friday: Nan, Paul

19. If Kevin and Paul work Thursday, who must work Friday?

   (A)   Janice
   (B)   Kevin
   (C)   Nan
   (D)   Paul
   (E)   Seymour

20. Each of the following could be true EXCEPT:

   (A)   Janice works Monday and Tuesday.
   (B)   Kevin and Paul work Friday.
   (C)   Seymour works Monday and Friday.
   (D)   Janice and Kevin work Thursday.
   (E)   Paul works Monday and Friday.

21. Which one of the following CANNOT be the pair of staff that works Monday?

   (A)   Janice and Seymour
   (B)   Kevin and Paul
   (C)   Paul and Seymour
   (D)   Nan and Ophelia
   (E)   Janice and Nan

22. Which one of the following could be true?

   (A)   Nan works Wednesday and Friday only.
   (B)   Seymour works Monday and Paul works Tuesday.
   (C)   Kevin works Monday, Wednesday, and Friday.
   (D)   Nan works Wednesday with Ophelia and Thursday with Kevin.
   (E)   Ophelia and Kevin work Tuesday.

ANSWER KEY

1. E	9. C	17. B
2. A	10. C	18. C
3. C	11. C	19. E
4. A	12. E	20. B
5. D	13. D	21. A
6. B	14. B	22. B
7. A	15. C	
8. B	16. C	

TRIAGE REVIEW

This is a Logic Games section that can be taken in order. The easiest game for most students is the first, which is a standard Strict Sequencing game. Although it doesn't have a great many deductions up front, it has five rules that limit the possible arrangements down to a manageable number.

The second and third games are the two that you might have taken in either order. They are basically equal in difficulty for the majority of test takers. The second is a standard Selection game with one unusual feature—a special term that's defined in the game's setup and which you must understand in order to use one of the rules. The third game is a fairly complex Matching game, but one on which you can do most of the work up front. It has six rules that, if combined, solve more than half the game before you ever tackle a question. Your decision about which of those two games to do first should be guided, frankly, by personal preference. If you are comfortable with formal logic and you like Selection, take on game two first. If you've tended to do well with the Matching games you've seen thus far, prioritize game three.

The final game was the hardest for most students and not just because it came last. It's a Strict Sequencing game, but one in which you have to re-use some of the entities. Moreover, you have to schedule two entities on each of five days, so there's a Double Sequencing feel to the task. With only five questions, it's an easy one to leave for last. But given that it has an Acceptability question and three short "Non-If" questions, it's definitely in your interest to try to leave adequate time to get to this game. You're likely to add at least a few more right answers to your score.

EXPLANATIONS

Game 1—Product Advertisements

Questions 1–5

Exactly seven products—P, Q, R, S, T, W, and X—are each
to be advertised exactly once in a section of a catalog. The
order in which they will be displayed is governed by the
following conditions:

Q must be displayed in some position before W.
R must be displayed immediately before X.
T cannot be displayed immediately before or
  immediately after W.
S must be displayed either first or seventh.
Either Q or T must be displayed fourth.[2]

STEPS 1 AND 2: Overview and Sketch

There's nothing out of the ordinary in this standard Sequencing game. You have seven products to arrange in order, one at a time. A quick glance at the rules shows that they mention definite spaces in the order, and one gives the precise number of spaces between two of the entities. These rules call for a Strict Sequencing framework.

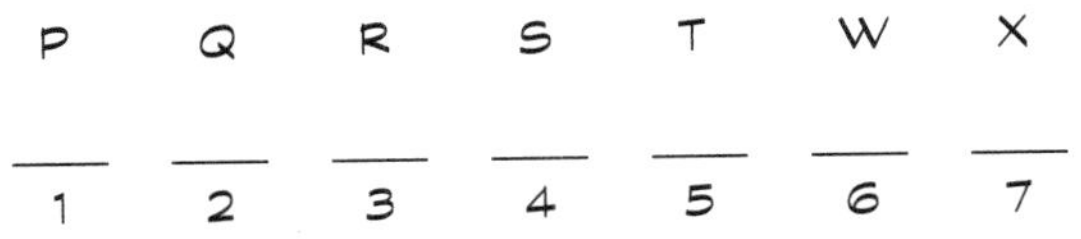

P   Q   R   S   T   W   X

___   ___   ___   ___   ___   ___   ___
1   2   3   4   5   6   7

Figure 17.1

STEP 3: Rules

There are five rules here, but only a couple that can be built directly into the framework.

Rule 1 gives the relative order of (but not the distance between) Q and W.

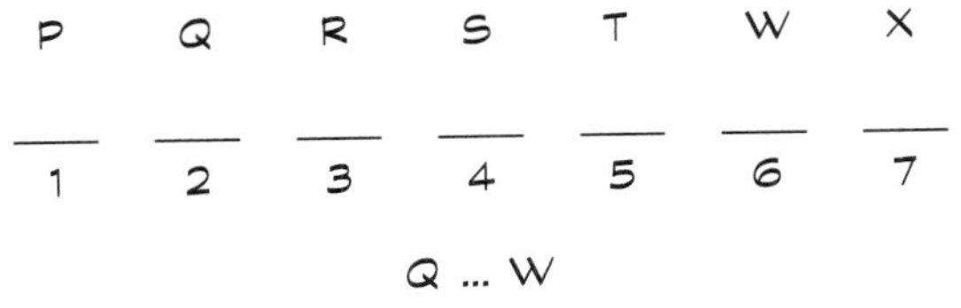

P   Q   R   S   T   W   X

___   ___   ___   ___   ___   ___   ___
1   2   3   4   5   6   7

Q ... W

Figure 17.2

Rule 2 creates a block of entities.

2 PrepTest 47, Sec. 4, Game 1

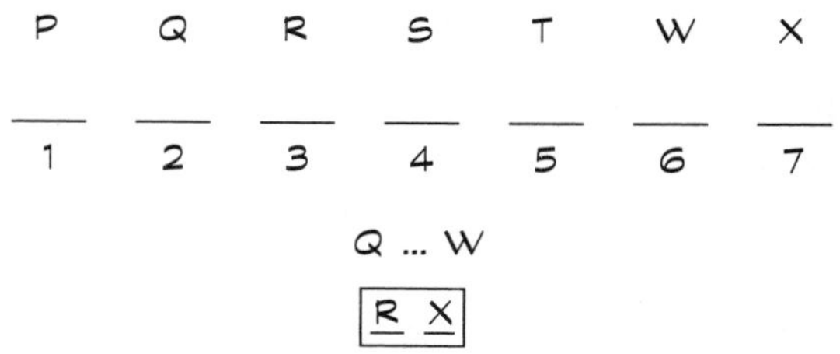

P   Q   R   S   T   W   X

___ ___ ___ ___ ___ ___ ___
1   2   3   4   5   6   7

Q ... W

⬚ R X ⬚

Figure 17.3

Rule 3 restricts two entities from being next to each other, regardless of their order.

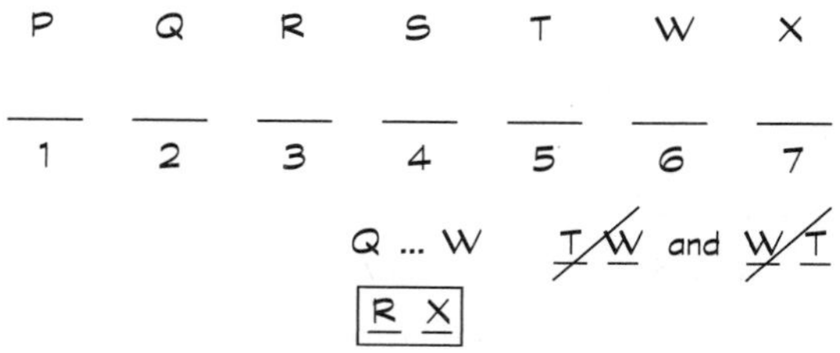

P   Q   R   S   T   W   X

___ ___ ___ ___ ___ ___ ___
1   2   3   4   5   6   7

Q ... W   T̶W̶ and W̶T̶

⬚ R X ⬚

Figure 17.4

Rule 4 gives S only two options. Given that S's position doesn't affect any of the other entities, however, you need not make two separate sketches. Depicting Rule 4 like this works just fine:

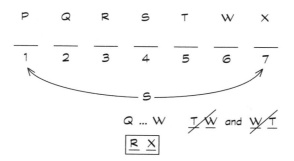

Figure 17.5

Rule 5 gives you two options for a specific space within the order.

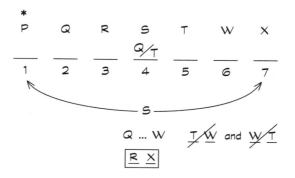

Figure 17.6

Note, too, that P is marked as the floater. That's the one product not mentioned in any of the rules.

STEP 4: Deductions

The only firm deduction available here is relatively minor. You know that R cannot take space 3, since X cannot take space 4. Likewise, you know that X can't take space 5, since R cannot take space 4.

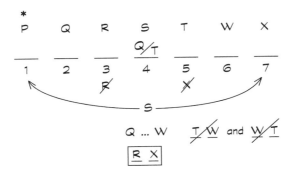

Figure 17.7

There are no additional deductions to be made in this game. The rules that share entities—W appears in Rules 1 and 3, T in Rules 3 and 5, and Q in Rules 1 and 5—are suggestive, but not strong enough to allow you to add any specifics into the framework. Rather than spend time speculating ("What if T is in space 4?" or, "What if Q is there?"), move into the questions. The three "If" questions will definitely give you the additional specificity you need to build mini-sketches.

STEP 5: Questions

This is a fairly standard question set, with three "If" questions and two Must/Could questions. If you struggle with either of the Must/Could questions, work through the "If" questions first to see if their mini-sketches help you evaluate the Must/Could answer choices.

1. **(E)**
   Which one of the following CANNOT be the product that is displayed first?
   (A) P
   (B) Q
   (C) R
   (D) T
   (E) X[3]

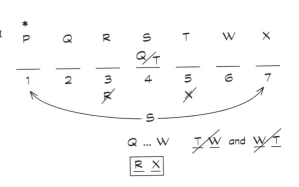

Figure 17.8

---

[3] PrepTest 47, Sec. 4, Q 1

Looking through the rules, only two entities are prevented from being first: W (Rule 1) and X (Rule 2). One of those two entities must be in the correct answer. It turns out to be X, in choice (E).

2. **(A)**

    If X is displayed immediately before Q, then which one of the following could be true?
    (A)   T is displayed first.
    (B)   R is displayed fifth.
    (C)   Q is displayed last.
    (D)   Q is displayed second.
    (E)   P is displayed second.[4]

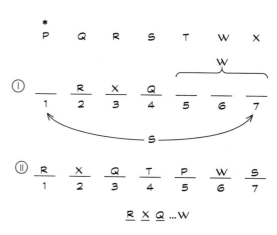

Figure 17.9

The "if" condition in the question stem calls for a mini-sketch. Start your mini-sketch with the "if" from the stem.

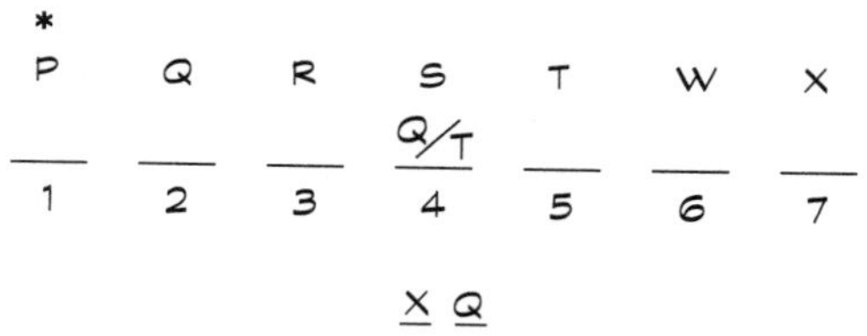

Figure 17.10

Rule 2 places R immediately before X in every case.

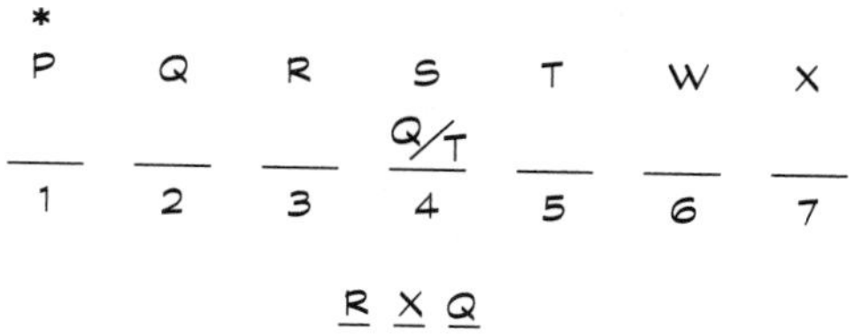

Figure 17.11

Rule 1 tells you that W must follow Q.

---

[4] PrepTest 47, Sec. 4, Q 2

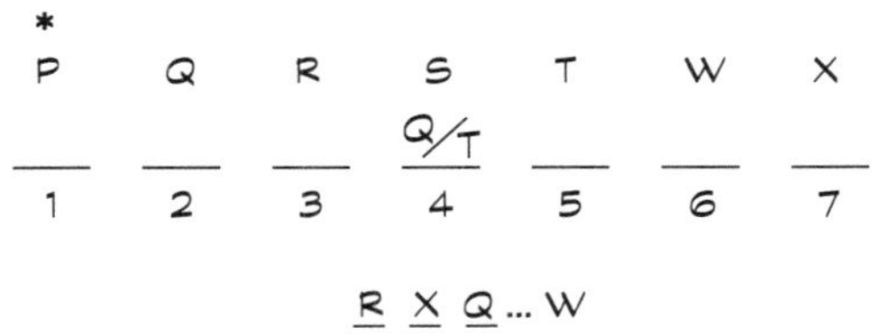

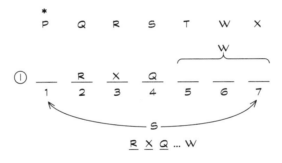

Figure 17.12

That's enough to eliminate three of the wrong answers. The correct answer *could be true*, so each of the four wrong answers *must be false*. Choice (B) is impossible since R is followed by three entities. Choices (C) and (D) are impossible since Q is followed by W and preceded by two entities. Now, you need to check whether T can be first (choice (A)) or whether P can be second (choice (E)).

Consider where the list you've created can fit in light of Rule 5. When Q is in space 4, R and X take spaces 2 and 3, respectively, and W takes a space between 5 and 7.

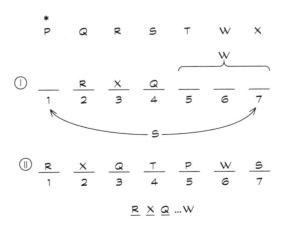

Figure 17.13

When T takes space 4, R-X-Q must take spaces 1–3, and W must take space 6 in order to avoid being adjacent to T and thus violating Rule 3. S will have to take space 7 in this scenario, since space 1 is occupied by R. That leaves space 5 for the floater, P.

Figure 17.14

Either way, there's no possibility of P being in space 2. Choice (E) is impossible and, therefore, choice (A) is correct. If you need confirmation, test T in the first option (where Q takes space 4). In that case, S would take space 7 and P and W would takes spaces 5 and 6 in either order. No problem. You may not have needed to push the mini-sketch to this level of completeness. Once you were able to confidently pick choice (A) or eliminate choice (D), you were done.

3. **(C)**

If P is displayed second, then which one of the following could be displayed third?
(A) R
(B) S
(C) T
(D) W
(E) X[5]

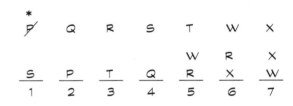

Figure 17.15

Adding the one entity from the "if" in the question stem tells you an enormous amount about the sketch. That's because the entity you're adding is the floater, P.

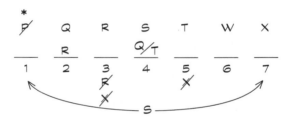

Figure 17.16

The question calls for an entity that can take space 3. S can never take space 3 (Rule 4), so you can get rid of choice (B). R can never take space 3, since X must follow immediately after it (Rule 2), so eliminate choice (A). And with P in space 2, you know that X cannot take space 3 either, since X must follow immediately after R (Rule 2). Eliminate choice (E), too.

Now, all you need to do is check T or W for space 3, and you'll have the answer. If you try W in space 3, Q would have to take space 1 to comply with Rule 1. That would put T in space 4.

```
    *
    P̸   Q   R   S   T   W   X
    Q   P   W̸  T̸  __  __  S
    1   2   3   4   5   6   7
```

Figure 17.17

Rule 3 forbids T and W from being in adjacent spaces. So choice (D) is incorrect.

That means choice (C) must be acceptable, and indeed, placing T in space 3 works out fine. S would take space 1 in this situation, and W and the R-X block would bring up the rear (their precise order is irrelevant).

Figure 17.18

4. **(A)**

Which one of the following could be true?
(A)   Q is displayed fifth.
(B)   Q is displayed seventh.
(C)   R is displayed third.
(D)   W is displayed third.
(E)   X is displayed fifth.[6]

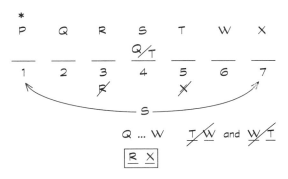

Figure 17.19

The correct answer to this short question *could be true*. That means that each of the wrong answers *must be false*. The quickest route to the right answer is to eliminate each of the impossible choices.

Choice (B) won't work because of Rule 1; if Q was in the final position, there'd be no room for W in the sequence.

Choice (C) is out because of Rule 2; X is unable to take space 4.

Choice (D) cannot happen. You discovered why this is true as you tested choice (D) in question 3. If W takes space 3, Q must take space 1 or space 2 and leave space 4 for T. If W and T are contiguous, Rule 3 is violated.

Choice (E) breaks Rule 2. X can never take space 5 since R can never take space 4.

Voilà. Choice (A) is correct. It's the only answer with an acceptable placement.

---

[6] PrepTest 47, Sec. 4, Q 4

5. **(D)**

If R is displayed sixth, then which one of the following must be displayed fifth?
(A) P
(B) Q
(C) T
(D) W
(E) X[7]

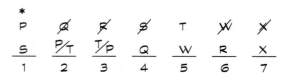

Figure 17.20

Push the implications of the "if" condition from this stem until space 5's occupant is clear. Start with R in space 6.

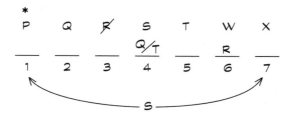

Figure 17.21

R must, of course, be followed by X (Rule 2).

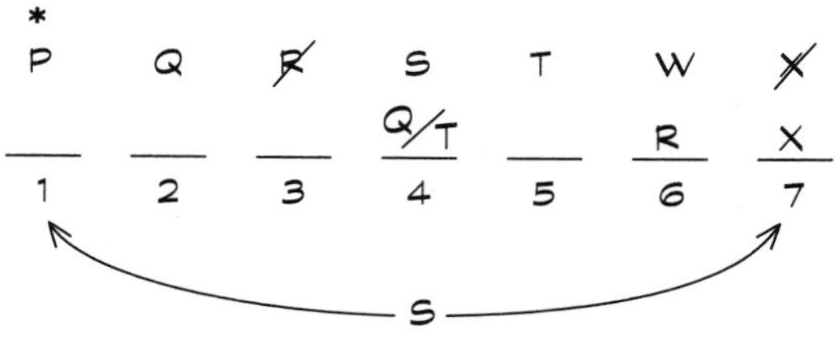

Figure 17.22

With X in the final spot, S needs to take space 1.

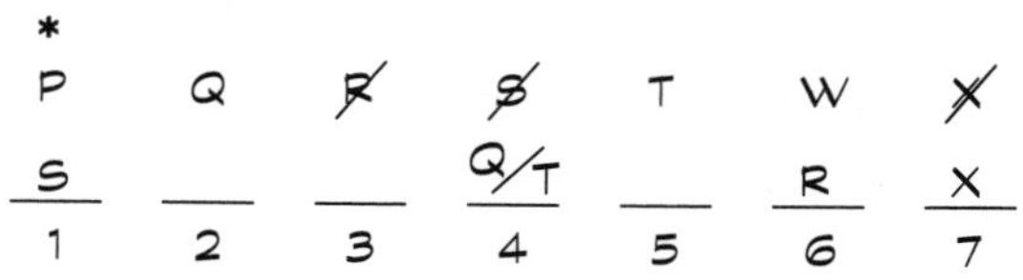

Figure 17.23

At this point, you can see that W may not take space 2 (there's no room for Q to be in front of W). Nor can W take space 3 (that would put Q in space 2 and T in space 4, and Rule 3 would be violated). So W will have to take space 5.

---

[7] PrepTest 47, Sec. 4, Q 5

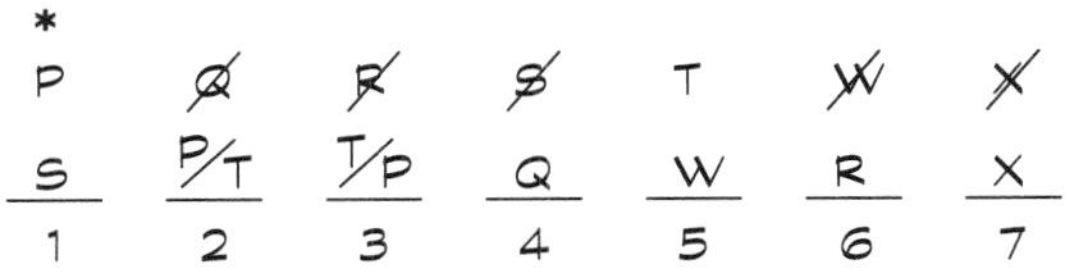

Figure 17.24

That makes choice (D) the correct answer.

This game was a standard Strict Sequencing game. The lack of strong deductions up front meant that you had to be patient in making mini-sketches and applying the rules to eliminate wrong answers. Provided that you did those things, this game likely proved manageable.

Game 2—Light Switches

Questions 6–11

A lighting control panel has exactly seven switches, numbered from 1 to 7. Each switch is either in the on position or in the off position. The circuit load of the panel is the total number of its switches that are on. The control panel must be configured in accordance with the following conditions:

If switch 1 is on, then switch 3 and switch 5 are off.
If switch 4 is on, then switch 2 and switch 5 are off.
The switch whose number corresponds to the circuit load of the panel is itself on.[8]

STEPS 1 AND 2: Overview and Sketch

Picture the task that's being described, and the game type will be revealed. You have a panel of seven numbered switches.

Figure 17.25

Each switch is either *on* or *off*.

Figure 17.26

You've seen this pattern many times. This is a standard Selection game. There's no need for any other sketch or framework; a roster of the entities that you can circle or strike through is perfect.

The one oddity here is the specially defined term "circuit load." When the test offers a made-up term like this, it will always give you a definition. For this game, "circuit load" means the

---

[8] PrepTest 47, Sec. 4, Game 2

total number of switches that are turned on. If three switches are on, the circuit load is three. If four switches are on, the circuit load is four. Just follow the definition and you'll be fine.

STEP 3: **Rules**

The first two rules, as you should expect with Selection, are conditional formal logic statements. Translate each and jot down its contrapositive, too. Remember to change "and" to "or" as you form the contrapositive.

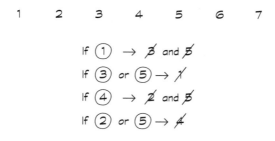

Figure 17.27

The third rule requires you to read carefully. The rule tells you that the switch with the number corresponding to the circuit load must be on. So if three switches are on, switch 3 must be on. If four switches are on, switch 4 must be on. Just note that rule in a shorthand paraphrase you'll be sure to understand.

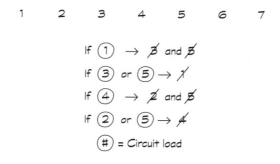

Figure 17.28

STEP 4: **Deductions**

There's just one big deduction to make, and it comes from the number restrictions. With any standard Selection game, it's valuable to consider the minimum and maximum numbers. In this game, the minimum number of switches that must be on is zero. No rule or restriction requires that you turn on any switch. The maximum is a little trickier. That's because of Rule 3, which states that the maximum number of switches that can be on must include the switch with that number. By combining Rules 1 and 2, you can see that it's impossible to have more than five switches on; turning on switch 1, switch 4, or switch 5 requires you to turn two other switches off. So the relevant question is: Can you have a maximum number (a circuit load, if you will) of five switches on? To abide by Rule 3, switch 5 has to be one of the five switches turned on. Turning on switch 5 entails turning off switches 1 and 4.

Figure 17.29

But once those two are off, nothing prevents the remaining five from being on simultaneously. Your maximum circuit load (the maximum number of switches that can be on) is five.

STEP 5: Questions

The question set is perfectly suited to a standard Selection game. It has one Acceptability question, four "If" questions, and (lo and behold) a Minimum/Maximum question, one that you've already figured out. Start off with the two quickest points—questions 6 and 11—and then work your way through the "Ifs," using mini-sketches to make your work concrete.

6. **(B)**

Which one of the following could be a complete and accurate list of the switches that are on?
(A) switch 2, switch 3, switch 4, switch 7
(B) switch 3, switch 6, switch 7
(C) switch 2, switch 5, switch 6
(D) switch 1, switch 3, switch 4
(E) switch 1, switch 5[9]

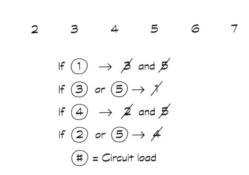

Figure 17.30

The correct answer here is an acceptable selection of switches that are turned on. Use the rules to eliminate the unacceptable choices. Rule 1 eliminates choice (D) and choice (E); if switch 1 is on, switches 3 and 5 must both be off. Rule 2 gets rid of choice (A); switches 2 and 4 cannot be on simultaneously. Rule 3 knocks out choice (C); the circuit load here is three, yet switch 3 is off. (Notice that Rule 3 would eliminate choice (E) as well; there, the circuit load is two, but switch 2 is not on.) The correct answer is choice (B), the only answer that doesn't break any of the rules.

7. **(A)**

If switch 1 and switch 3 are both off, then which one of the following could be two switches that are both on?
(A) switch 2 and switch 7
(B) switch 4 and switch 6
(C) switch 4 and switch 7
(D) switch 5 and switch 6
(E) switch 6 and switch 7[10]

Figure 17.31

---

[9] PrepTest 47, Sec. 4, Q 6
[10] PrepTest 47, Sec. 4, Q 7

For each of the "If" questions in this game, create mini-sketches based on the conditions laid out in the question stems. Here, begin by listing the switches and crossing out switches 1 and 3.

1 2 3 4 5 6 7

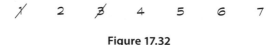

Figure 17.32

That leaves five switches. The most important are switches 2 and 4, which are in conflict due to Rule 2. Thinking about the implications of that rule, you soon realize that switch 4 must be off. Turning it on would mean turning off switches 2 and 5. That would leave you with three switches, but without switches 1, 2, and 3. So you'd have no way of turning on the switch with the number matching the circuit load.

1 2 3 4 5 6 7

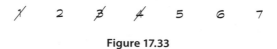

Figure 17.33

Now, you have four switches, but switches 1, 3, and 4 are off, so the maximum circuit load possible is two. switch 2 must be turned on along with one other switch.

1 2 3 4 5 6 7
1 of these

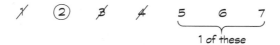

Figure 17.34

The only answer that matches this arrangement is choice (A), the correct answer.

8. **(B)**

If exactly two of the switches are on, then which one of the following switches must be off?

(A) switch 3
(B) switch 4
(C) switch 5
(D) switch 6
(E) switch 7[11]

(2 on/5 off)
1 2 3 4 5 6 7

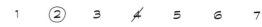

Figure 17.35

The "if" in this stem tells you more than you might realize at first. If exactly two switches are on, the circuit load is two. According to Rule 3, then, switch 2 must be turned on in this situation.

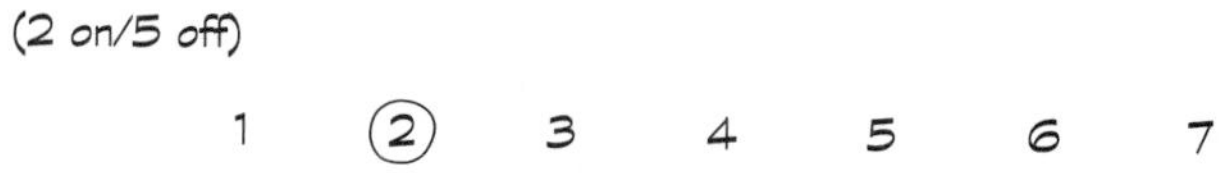
(2 on/5 off)
1 2 3 4 5 6 7

Figure 17.36

[11] PrepTest 47, Sec. 4, Q 8

Turning on switch 2 triggers Rule 2. Switch 4 must be turned off.

(2 on/5 off)

1   ②   3   4̸   5   6   7

Figure 17.37

That makes choice (B) the correct answer. Switch 4 must be off.

9. **(C)**

1   2   3   4   5   6̸   7̸

If switch 6 and switch 7 are both off, then what is the maximum circuit load of the panel?

(A)   one
(B)   two
(C)   three
(D)   four
(E)   five[12]

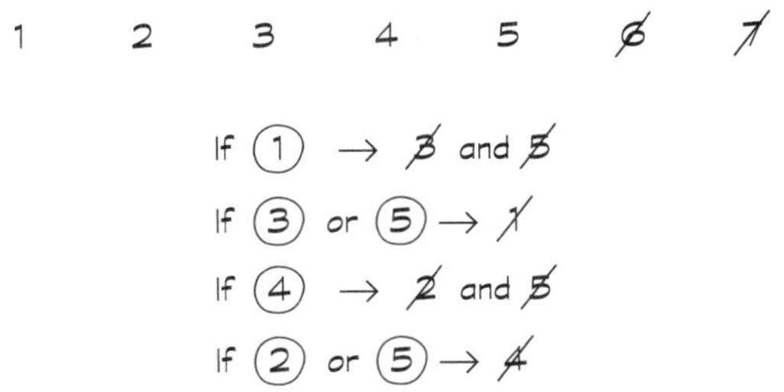

If ① → 2̸ and 5̸

If ③ or ⑤ → 1̸

If ④ → 2̸ and 5̸

If ② or ⑤ → 4̸

Figure 17.37A

Once you cross off switches 6 and 7 in accordance with the "if" in the question stem, you can deduce the answer to this question. Rules 1 and 2 make it impossible to have more than three of the remaining switches turned on. You can achieve a circuit load of three by having switches 2, 3, and 5 turned on. Choice (C) is correct.

10. **(C)**

If switch 5 and switch 6 are both on, then which one of the following switches must be on?

(A)   switch 1
(B)   switch 2
(C)   switch 3
(D)   switch 4
(E)   switch 7[13]

Cir. load   1̸   2̸   ③   4̸   ⑤   ⑥   7̸
3

Cir. load   1̸   ②   ③   4̸   ⑤   ⑥   ⑦
5

Figure 17.38

Start your mini-sketch by circling switches 5 and 6 as instructed by the question stem.

1   2   3   4   ⑤   ⑥   7

Figure 17.39

---

[12] PrepTest 47, Sec. 4, Q 9

[13] PrepTest 47, Sec. 4, Q 10

Turning on switch 5 requires you to turn off switches 1 and 4 (see Rules 1 and 2).

Figure 17.40

The remaining switches are all compatible under the rules, provided that the switch with the circuit load number is on (Rule 3). To follow that requirement, you have two possibilities. The circuit load might be three:

Figure 17.41

Or it might be five:

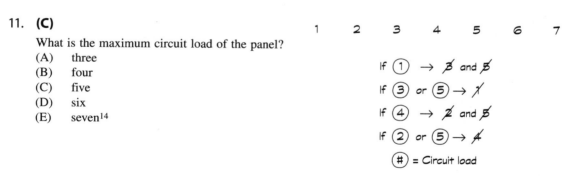

Figure 17.42

In either case, switch 3 *must be* turned *on*, making choice (C) the correct answer. The switches in choices (A) and (D) *must be off* in this scenario, while those in choices (B) and (E) *could* but don't *have to be on*.

11. **(C)**

What is the maximum circuit load of the panel?
(A) three
(B) four
(C) five
(D) six
(E) seven[14]

You've known the answer to this question since Step 4. The maximum number of switches that can be on (that's the definition of "circuit load") is five: switches 2, 3, 5, 6, and 7. Rule 3 requires that you turn on the switch with the number corresponding to the circuit load. Since the circuit load is five and switch 5 is on, you're fine here. Choice (C) is the correct answer.

The one aspect of that game that most students complain about is the unusual definition of "circuit load." Instead of calmly remembering that the test makers will always define an unusual

---

[14] PrepTest 47, Sec. 4, Q 11

term, they panic and say, "I don't know what that means." But those specially defined terms always result in important restrictions within the game. (Remember the professors who "shared a specialty" in the Professors' Hiring game from chapter 7?) Make sure you understand how the test makers are defining the special term, and make note of it next to or beneath your sketch. Do that, and you'll be at an enormous advantage over other test takers who aren't patient enough to take full advantage of the game setup and restrictions.

Game 3—Crescentville's Record Stores
Questions 12–17

> In Crescentville there are exactly five record stores, whose names are abbreviated S, T, V, X, and Z. Each of the five stores carries at least one of four distinct types of music: folk, jazz, opera, and rock. None of the stores carries any other type of music. The following conditions must hold:
>
> Exactly two of the five stores carry jazz.
> T carries rock and opera but no other type of music.
> S carries more types of music than T carries.
> X carries more types of music than any other store in Crescentville carries.
> Jazz is among the types of music S carries.
> V does not carry any type of music that Z carries.[15]

STEPS 1 AND 2: Overview and Sketch

While record stores aren't as common as they were a few years ago, you can still picture this task pretty easily. You arrive in a new town and you want to see where you can shop for different kinds of music. According to the game's setup, there are five record stores to check and four types of music you're interested in. Since you're a fastidious LSAT test taker, you can keep track of your findings in a brief chart.

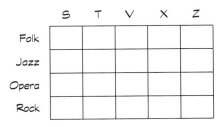

Figure 17.44

When you find out that a certain record store carries a type of music, put a check mark in the corresponding box. When you find out it doesn't, record that with an X. Once you see this framework, you know you're working with a Matching game. In fact, this game should remind you a lot of the Appliance Repair Shop game with radios, TVs, and VCRs.

---

[15] PrepTest 47, Sec. 4, Game 3

STEPS 3 AND 4: Rules and Deductions

There are six rules. Provided that you are patient and record them one by one, you'll wind up with a lot of restriction here. This game provides an example of a fairly rare phenomenon; it's a game in which you can actually make the deductions as you're listing the rules. That's because the rules are listed in a logical order, such that each new rule builds off of something you've already put into the sketch framework. It doesn't happen often, so don't expect to see it on test day. But if you encounter a game built like this, take advantage of the opportunity to take the two steps together.

Rule 1 establishes the number of stores that carry jazz records.

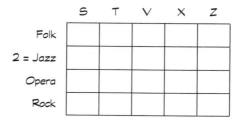

Figure 17.45

Rule 2 establishes T's column precisely.

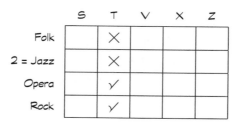

Figure 17.46

Rule 3 allows you to determine that store S carries either three or four types of music.

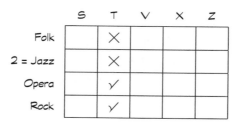

Figure 17.47

Rule 4 gives even more clarity to the numbers. Since store X carries the most types of music, you can now determine that store S carries exactly three types and that store X carries all four types.

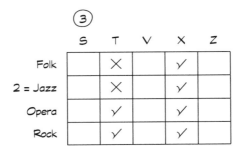

Figure 17.48

Rule 5 tells you to check the jazz box in store S's column. Notice that you now know exactly which stores carry jazz—S and X. You can close off the jazz row.

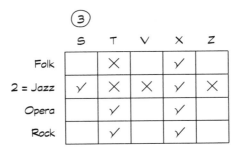

Figure 17.49

Finally, Rule 6 is one that you'll just have to list under the framework. You'll use it when the questions give you additional information about store V or store Z.

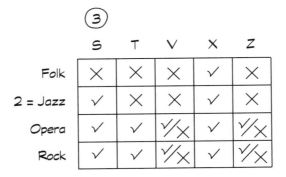

Figure 17.50

That's your Master Sketch. Eleven of the 20 boxes are determined. Some restrictions apply to each of those that remain open: Store S will carry a total of three types of music, and stores

V and Z have to avoid having any overlap. You should be amply prepared to breeze through this question set.

STEP 5: Questions

Just over half of the potential matches in this game have been established or ruled out. It's no surprise then that half of the questions here—questions 12, 13, and 15—reward you for your Master Sketch, while half—questions 14, 15, and 17—are "If" questions that will add information for those open boxes.

12. **(E)**

Which one of the following could be true?
(A) S carries folk and rock but neither jazz nor opera.
(B) T carries jazz but neither opera nor rock.
(C) V carries folk, rock, and opera, but not jazz.
(D) X carries folk, rock, and jazz, but not opera.
(E) Z carries folk and opera but neither rock nor jazz.[16]

③

	S	T	V	X	Z
Folk	X	X	X	✓	X
2 = Jazz	✓	X	X	✓	X
Opera	✓	✓	✓/X	✓	✓/X
Rock	✓	✓	✓/X	✓	✓/X

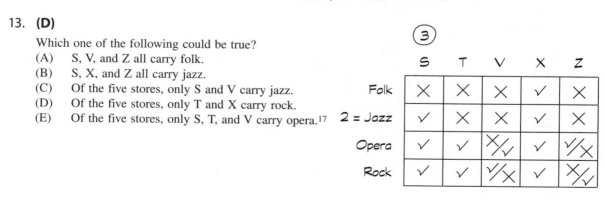

Figure 17.51

Just use your Master Sketch to answer this Could Be True question. The correct answer is acceptable within the sketch, while each of the wrong answers *must be false.*

Choice (A) must be false. You know that store S carries jazz.

Choice (B) must be false. Store T carries opera and rock but not jazz.

Choice (C) must be false. V cannot carry all three of folk, rock, and opera. That would leave nothing for store Z to carry and would thus violate Rule 6.

Choice (D) must be false. Store X carries all four types of music.

That leaves choice (E) as the correct answer. If store Z carries folk and opera, store V can carry rock. There's no violation of Rule 6 with this answer, so it *could be true.*

13. **(D)**

Which one of the following could be true?
(A) S, V, and Z all carry folk.
(B) S, X, and Z all carry jazz.
(C) Of the five stores, only S and V carry jazz.
(D) Of the five stores, only T and X carry rock.
(E) Of the five stores, only S, T, and V carry opera.[17]

③

	S	T	V	X	Z
Folk	X	X	X	✓	X
2 = Jazz	✓	X	X	✓	X
Opera	✓	✓	X/✓	✓	✓/X
Rock	✓	✓	✓/X	✓	X/✓

Figure 17.52

[16] PrepTest 47, Sec. 4, Q 12
[17] PrepTest 47, Sec. 4, Q 13

This question works exactly like question 12 did. Use your Master Sketch to eliminate the four *must be false* answers.

Choice (A) must be false. Rule 6 prevents V and Z from having any types of music in common.

Choice (B) must be false. Rule 1 allows for exactly two stores to carry jazz music.

Choice (C) must be false. You know from your Master Sketch that stores S and X are the ones that carry jazz.

Choice (D), however, *could be true*. Stores T and X definitely carry rock according to your Master Sketch. There's no rule that requires stores S, V, or Z to carry rock. Store S could carry folk, jazz, and opera as its three types of music. Of stores V and Z, one could carry opera and the other folk. This is the correct answer.

You already know that choice (E) is definitely false and therefore wrong. Store X always carries opera.

14. **(B)**

If exactly one of the stores carries folk, then which one of the following could be true?
(A) S and V carry exactly two types of music in common.
(B) T and S carry exactly two types of music in common.
(C) T and V carry exactly two types of music in common.
(D) V and X carry exactly two types of music in common.
(E) X and Z carry exactly two types of music in common.[18]

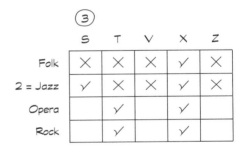

Figure 17.53

This question benefits from a mini-sketch. Some students avoid making mini-sketches in Matching games (or other games with somewhat complex frameworks) for fear that it will take them too long to copy the Master Sketch. With a little practice, though, it should take you only 10–15 seconds to copy your Master Sketch. The time you save (and the wrong answers you avoid) by doing so is well worth this small time investment. Trying to alter your Master Sketch and then erase when another new "if" is introduced is no faster and will, in short order, lead you to a messy sketch and confusion over what was in the original sketch and what you added for a particular question. Watch how well it works. Start your mini-sketch by copying over your Master Sketch and crossing out all boxes in the "folk" row except for Xs.

[18] PrepTest 47, Sec. 4, Q 14

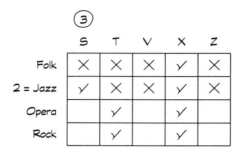

Figure 17.54

Now, you can see that store S will carry jazz, opera, and rock as its requisite three types of music. Moreover, between stores V and Z, one will carry rock and the other opera, although which carries which doesn't matter.

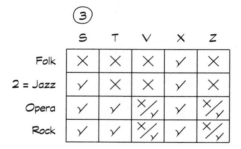

Figure 17.55

You have almost every box in the framework filled in. Evaluating the choices should be a snap. The correct answer *could be true*. The four wrong answers, therefore, *must be false*.

Choice (A) must be false under these conditions. After all, store V will carry only one type of music.

Choice (B) is the correct answer. It must, in fact, be true. In this case, stores S and T will both carry opera and rock.

Choices (C), (D), and (E) must all be false. Each answer includes either store V or store Z, which you know will carry only one type of music each under the conditions of this question.

15. **(C)**

Which one of the following must be true?
(A)   T carries exactly the same number of types of music as V carries.
(B)   V carries exactly the same number of types of music as Z carries.
(C)   S carries at least one more type of music than Z carries.
(D)   Z carries at least one more type of music than T carries.
(E)   X carries exactly two more types of music than S carries.[19]

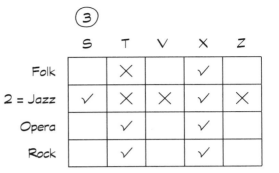

Figure 17.55

To answer this question, simply refer to your Master Sketch. The correct answer *must be true*, so you can eliminate any choice that *could be false*.

Choice (A) could be false. Store T always carries two types of music, but store V may carry only one.

Choice (B) could be false as well. Stores V and Z might carry one type of music each, but nothing prevents one of them from carrying two types as long as it doesn't duplicate the type of music that the other carries.

Choice (C), on the other hand, must be true. It's the correct answer. Store S will always carry three types of music. Store Z can carry, at most, two types of music. If it carried three types, it would share a type of music carried by store V in violation of Rule 6.

You know that choices (D) and (E) are wrong answers. In fact, both *must be false*. For review, make sure you can articulate why that's the case. Choice (D) is false because store T carries two types of music, and store Z can carry either one or two types. Choice (E) is false because store X carries exactly *one* more type of music than store S carries.

16. **(C)**

If V is one of exactly three stores that carry rock, then which one of the following must be true?
(A)   S and Z carry no types of music in common.
(B)   S and V carry at least one type of music in common.
(C)   S and Z carry at least one type of music in common.
(D)   T and Z carry at least one type of music in common.
(E)   T and V carry at least two types of music in common.[20]

③

	S	T	V	X	Z
Folk	✓	✗		✓	
2 = Jazz	✓	✗	✗	✓	✗
Opera	✓	✓		✓	
3 = Rock	✗	✓	✓	✓	✗

Figure 17.56

---

[19] PrepTest 47, Sec. 4, Q 15
[20] PrepTest 47, Sec. 4, Q 16

Here again, the new "if" in the question stem calls for a mini-sketch. Quickly copy over the Master Sketch information and add a check mark in the rock box under store V's column. Because the "if" says that exactly three stores carry rock, you can close off the rock row at this point.

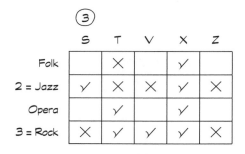

Figure 17.57

With store S unable to carry rock, its three types of music must be folk, jazz, and opera.

③

	S	T	V	X	Z
Folk	✓	✗		✓	
2 = Jazz	✓	✗	✗	✓	✗
Opera	✓	✓		✓	
3 = Rock	✗	✓	✓	✓	✗

Figure 17.58

The only boxes left undetermined are those for folk and opera in store V's and store Z's columns. You know that store Z will have to carry at least one of those types of music and, of course, that stores V and Z can have no types of music in common (Rule 6).

Take the time to characterize the answers before you evaluate the choices. The correct answer *must be true*. That means that each of the wrong answers *could be false*.

Eliminate choice (A). Store S carries two types of music—folk and opera—that store Z might carry, too.

Get rid of choice (B) as well. Store V may carry only rock and have no types of music in common with store S.

Choice (C) is the correct answer. It *must be true* that store S, which carries folk, jazz, and opera in this case, shares at least one type of music with store Z, which will have to carry folk, opera, or both.

In the scenario created by this question's "if" condition, choice (D) could be false. Store T carries rock and opera and no other types of music; store Z might carry only folk music here.

The same is true of choice (E). In this situation, store V may or may not carry opera. There's no way to know for sure.

17. **(B)**

If S and V both carry folk, then which one of the following could be true?

(A) S and T carry no types of music in common.
(B) S and Z carry no types of music in common.
(C) T and Z carry no types of music in common.
(D) S and Z carry two types of music in common.
(E) T and V carry two types of music in common.[21]

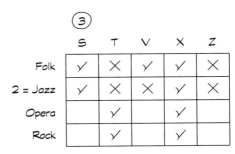

Figure 17.59

The "if" in this question stem isn't as restrictive as some you've seen in this game. Still, basing a mini-sketch on it will allow you to make all of the available deductions and ensure you have the information you need to answer the question. Start by copying the Master Sketch information and adding to it that stores S and V carry folk.

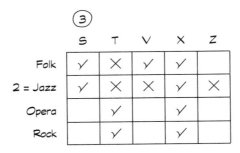

Figure 17.60

Knowing that store V carries a type of music tells you that store Z won't carry it. Indicate that store Z cannot carry folk in this case.

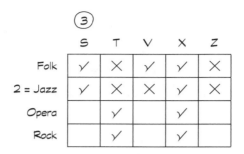

Figure 17.61

You can't push the implications of the "if" any further than that. At this point, you know that store S will carry either opera or rock but not both. As for stores V and Z, each will carry opera or rock or both, but that's as certain as it gets here.

So characterize the answer choices and dive in. The correct answer *could be true*. That means that all four wrong answers *must be false*. It should be relatively easy to spot the impossible answer choices and eliminate them.

Choice (A) must be false. Store T always carries opera and rock, and store S will have to carry one of those here.

Choice (B) *could be true*. This is the correct answer. It's possible that store S will carry rock and store Z will carry opera, or vice versa. While it's possible that they carry a type of music in common, they aren't required to by anything in this scenario.

At this point, you know that choices (C), (D), and (E) must be false. For the purposes of review, make sure you see why. Choice (C) is out because store Z will carry either opera or rock or both, giving it some overlap with store T. Choice (D) goes wrong because, no matter what, store S can carry only one of opera and rock, store Z's two options. Choice (E) is false because store V, which carries folk under the "if" of this question, can carry only one of opera and rock. It has to leave the other for store Z. Thus, stores T and V can have, at most, one type of music in common.

This is a game that puts a high premium on your initial sketch and deductions. That's often true of Matching tasks. The payoff comes when you use your thorough Master Sketch to make short work of the questions.

Game 4—Maggie's Deli Schedule

Questions 18–22

Maggie's Deli is open exactly five days every week: Monday through Friday. Its staff, each of whom works on at least one day each week, consists of exactly six people— Janice, Kevin, Nan, Ophelia, Paul, and Seymour. Exactly three of them—Janice, Nan, and Paul—are supervisors. The deli's staffing is consistent with the following:

Each day's staff consists of exactly two people, at least one of whom is a supervisor.

Tuesday's and Wednesday's staffs both include Ophelia.

Of the days Nan works each week, at least two are consecutive.

Seymour does not work on any day before the first day Paul works that week.

Any day on which Kevin works is the first day during the week that some other staff member works.[22]

STEPS 1 AND 2: Overview and Sketch

It's very important that you're patient with the Overview step in this game. You've probably worked at a job that had a weekly schedule for who's on duty each day. It may even have designated a "shift leader" or manager on duty, as this game does. At Maggie's Deli, the fictional business in this game, every member of the staff works on at least one day of the week. Rule 1 tells you that exactly two people work each day, Monday through Friday, and that at least one is a supervisor (but notice that doesn't preclude two supervisors working together). Form a mental picture of the weekly schedule as it might be posted on the office door, and translate it into a framework for the game:

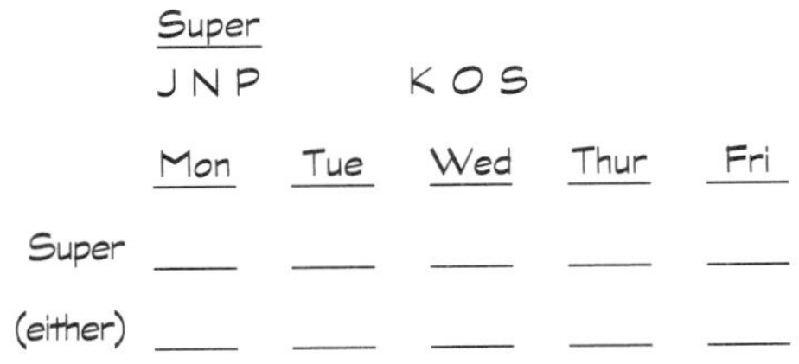

Figure 17.62

Make sure your initial sketch clearly distinguishes the supervisors, and include a note that reminds you that each day needs at least one supervisor but may have two.

STEP 3: Rules

The game has five long rules. They'll provide helpful restrictions but only if you take the time to make sure you know what each says (and what it doesn't) and find a clear way to add it into or underneath the sketch framework.

22 PrepTest 47, Sec. 4, Game 4

The first rule you've already worked into the overall framework. It's more of a global limitation than a specific rule.

Rule 2 allows you to place O on two days. O is not a supervisor, so make sure to enter her on the bottom row in your sketch.

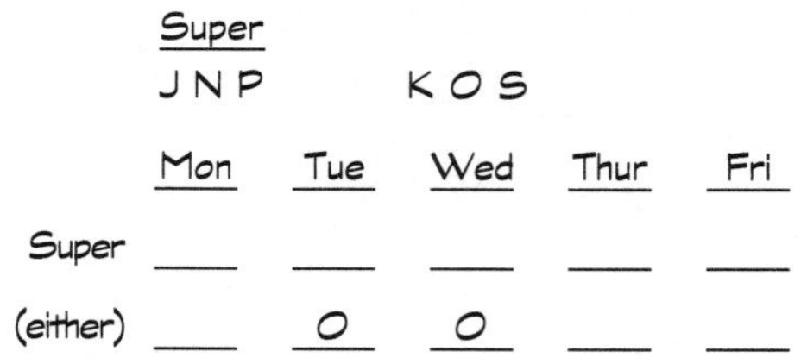

Figure 17.63

Make sure you didn't over-interpret the rule. It doesn't tell you that Tuesday and Wednesday are necessarily O's only days.

Rule 3 tells you that you'll need to have two days in a row with N scheduled. Again, note that she may or may not work more than that.

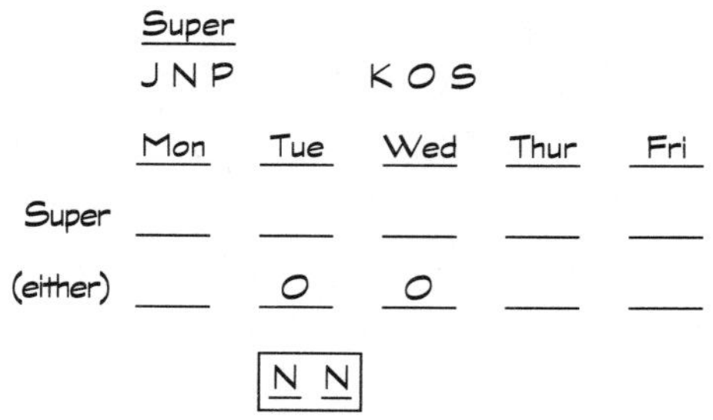

Figure 17.64

Rule 4 restricts S from being scheduled *earlier* in the week than P. Make sure you appreciate that S and P may have the same first day in the week, however.

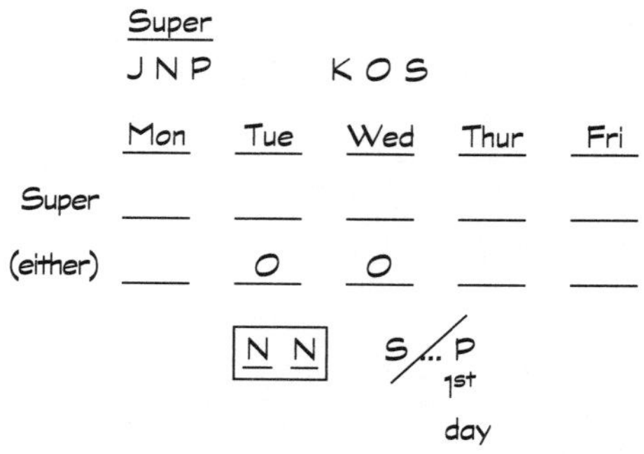

Figure 17.65

Rule 5 sounds a little bizarre, but it actually provides a very clear restriction. Any time K works, it's the shift's other worker's first day that week.

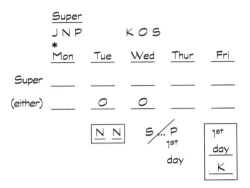

Figure 17.66

As you depict that rule, keep in mind that K is not a supervisor. Show him always on the bottom row in the framework. Note, too, that J is the floater, with no rules or restrictions limiting her placement.

STEP 4: Deductions

There aren't any solid deductions that you can add to your Sketch for this game. It is not a good use of your time, especially on the final game in the set, to start speculating about all the possibilities. Go quickly through the BLEND list of potential deductions. When you discover there aren't any, trust that the rules as they are will give you everything you need to determine the right and wrong answers.

STEP 5: Questions

With the exception of the Acceptability question, where the answers must display the entire five-day schedule, the questions here are short. There is only one "If" question, so you can tell that you'll be asked to assess the acceptability or unacceptability of arrangements based on the original rules and the small amount of information you've been able to put in your Master Sketch.

18. **(C)**

Which one of the following could be an accurate staffing schedule?

(A)   Monday: Janice, Kevin
       Tuesday: Nan, Ophelia
       Wednesday: Nan, Paul
       Thursday: Kevin, Paul
       Friday: Janice, Seymour

(B)   Monday: Paul, Seymour
       Tuesday: Ophelia, Paul
       Wednesday: Nan, Ophelia
       Thursday: Kevin, Nan
       Friday: Janice, Seymour

(C)   Monday: Janice, Kevin
       Tuesday: Nan, Ophelia
       Wednesday: Nan, Ophelia
       Thursday: Kevin, Paul
       Friday: Paul, Seymour

(D)   Monday: Janice, Kevin
       Tuesday: Janice, Ophelia
       Wednesday: Nan, Ophelia
       Thursday: Nan, Seymour
       Friday: Kevin, Paul

(E)   Monday: Paul, Seymour
       Tuesday: Ophelia, Paul
       Wednesday: Nan, Ophelia
       Thursday: Janice, Kevin
       Friday: Nan, Paul[23]

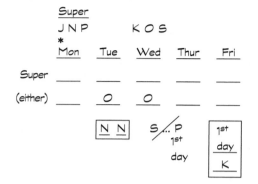

Figure 17.67

There's a lot of information to look through, but each answer choice is organized in the same way, so be methodical. One thing that the test makers did not do for you is to distinguish the supervisors from the other employees. It will be helpful that you've distinguished the supervisors in your Master Sketch.

Rule 1 says that each day must have at least one supervisor. If you find a day without J, N, or P, eliminate the entire answer choice. Scanning the answers, you never find this rule violated. Move on to the next one.

Rule 2 requires O on Tuesday and Wednesday. That rule is broken in choice (A). One down.

Rule 3 says that, during the week, you need to have N on consecutive days at some point. Be careful, N may work on other days, too. The rule simply requires that, at least once, she works back-to-back days. Choice (E) violates that rule. Eliminate it.

Rule 4 says that you may not find S scheduled prior to P's first day during the week. Again, be careful. S can be scheduled *on* P's first day, just not before it. That rule knocks out choice (D), where P's first day is Friday, but you find S scheduled on Thursday.

---

[23] PrepTest 47, Sec. 4, Q 18

Finally, Rule 5 tells you that any day on which K is scheduled is the other employee's first day of work for the week. In other words, if K is working alongside someone who has previously worked during the week, you can cross out that answer choice. The answer that violates this rule is choice (B). Thursday in choice (B) is both N's second day and a day on which K is scheduled.

That leaves only the correct answer, choice (C), the one answer that's violation-free.

19. **(E)**

If Kevin and Paul work Thursday, who must work Friday?

(A) Janice
(B) Kevin
(C) Nan
(D) Paul
(E) Seymour[24]

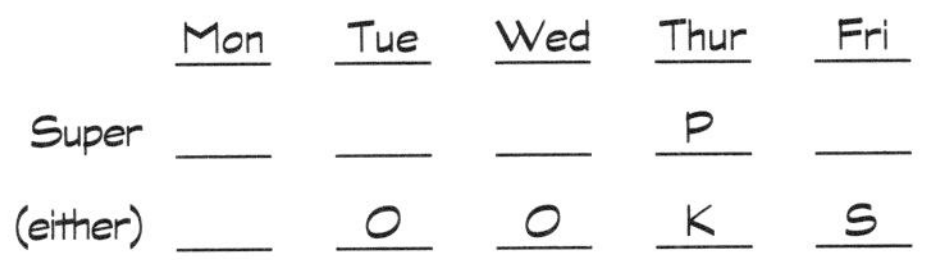

	Mon	Tue	Wed	Thur	Fri
Super	___	___	___	P	___
(either)	___	O	O	K	S

Figure 17.68

This question rewards you for understanding Rules 4 and 5. The relationship of the "if" in the question stem to those rules is made absolutely clear once you start your mini-sketch. Copy the framework, and put P and K in the Thursday column.

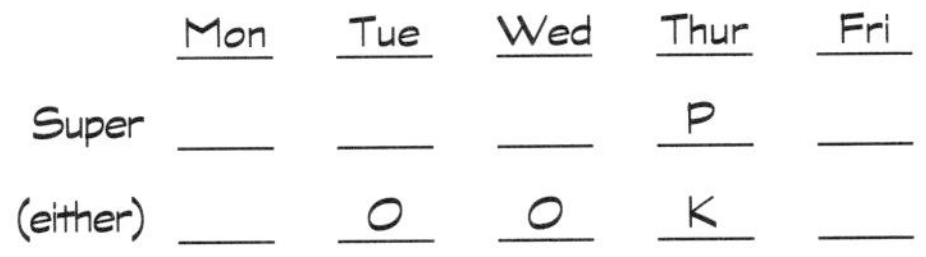

	Mon	Tue	Wed	Thur	Fri
Super	___	___	___	P	___
(either)	___	O	O	K	___

Figure 17.69

You know from Rule 5 that Thursday must be P's first day for the week. That, in turn, triggers Rule 4. S cannot work prior to P's first day. Since S cannot work with P on Thursday in this question, he must work on Friday.

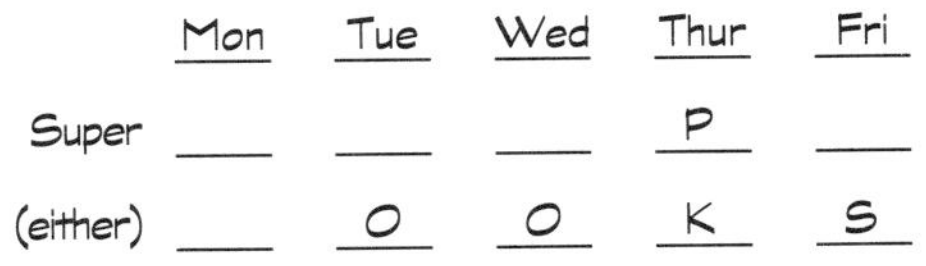

	Mon	Tue	Wed	Thur	Fri
Super	___	___	___	P	___
(either)	___	O	O	K	S

Figure 17.70

That matches the correct answer, choice (E).

---

24 PrepTest 47, Sec. 4, Q 19

20. **(B)**

Each of the following could be true EXCEPT:
(A) Janice works Monday and Tuesday.
(B) Kevin and Paul work Friday.
(C) Seymour works Monday and Friday.
(D) Janice and Kevin work Thursday.
(E) Paul works Monday and Friday.[25]

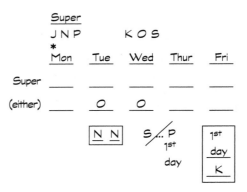

Figure 17.71

For this question, characterize the answer choices and then evaluate each against the rules and the Master Sketch. The correct answer here *must be false*. Each of the wrong answers *could be true*.

Choice (A) *could be true*. In fact, J is the floater, with no restrictions at all in the setup or rules.

Choice (B) *must be false*, so it's the correct answer. If K and P work together on Friday, there's no room in the schedule for S. This answer works just like the "if" from question 19, except that K and P are moved one day later in the week. But just like the preceding question, you're rewarded for understanding how Rules 4 and 5 work together.

You can check the remaining choices if you like, but you know that each will produce an acceptable result. On test day, you should stop once you find choice (B), the *must be false* answer.

21. **(A)**

Which one of the following CANNOT be the pair of staff that works Monday?
(A) Janice and Seymour
(B) Kevin and Paul
(C) Paul and Seymour
(D) Nan and Ophelia
(E) Janice and Nan[26]

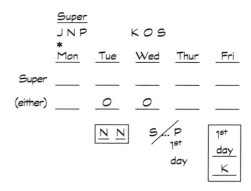

Figure 17.72

The last two questions had you looking at the end of the week. This one puts the focus on the beginning of the week. The correct answer is an unacceptable pair of employees for Monday. As soon as you see choice (A), you're done. Rule 4 tells you that S may not work prior to P's first day. Since choice (A) schedules S on Monday with someone other than P, this answer is unacceptable.

---

[25] PrepTest 47, Sec. 4, Q 20
[26] PrepTest 47, Sec. 4, Q 21

The pairs in the remaining choices are all fine for Monday assignments. You'll notice that choice (C) also schedules S, but this time, the other employee is P, so there's no violation of Rule 4.

22. **(B)**

Which one of the following could be true?
- (A)   Nan works Wednesday and Friday only.
- (B)   Seymour works Monday and Paul works Tuesday.
- (C)   Kevin works Monday, Wednesday, and Friday.
- (D)   Nan works Wednesday with Ophelia and Thursday with Kevin.
- (E)   Ophelia and Kevin work Tuesday.[27]

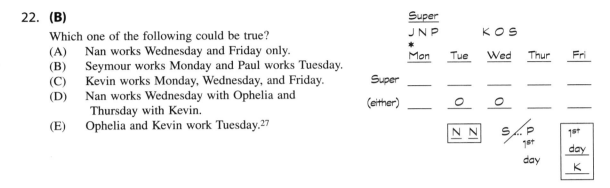

Figure 17.73

The stem for this final question is simple, but as you'll see, the correct answer has a trick up its sleeve. The correct answer here *could be true*. That means the four wrong answers *must be false*.

Choice (A) must be false. Rule 3 requires that N be scheduled on consecutive days at some point in the week, but here, her two days are non consecutive.

Choice (B) could be true. This is the correct answer. Rule 4 requires that if S works on Monday, then so does P. That rule doesn't forbid P from working on other days, too. Most test takers who miss this answer do so because they *misread* this answer. It does not say that Tuesday is P's first or only day.

For the record:

Choice (C) must be false. Any day on which K works must be the other employee's first day of the week (Rule 5). Wednesday is, at least, O's second day. Also, if K and O are the employees scheduled for a given day, there's no room for a supervisor on that day.

Choice (D) must be false. This answer, too, violates Rule 5 by having Kevin work alongside N on her second day.

Choice (E) must be false. Neither K nor O is a supervisor, and Rule 1 requires that a supervisor be scheduled each day.

[27] PrepTest 47, Sec. 4, Q 22

CHAPTER 18

FULL-LENGTH SECTION II[1]

Time—35 minutes
22 Questions

Directions: Each group of questions in this section is based on a set of conditions. In answering some of the questions, it may be useful to draw a rough diagram. Choose the response that most accurately and completely answers each question and blacken the corresponding space on your answer sheet.

---

[1] PrepTest 50, Sec. 3

Questions 1–5

At each of six consecutive stops—1, 2, 3, 4, 5, and 6—that a traveler must make in that order as part of a trip, she can choose one from among exactly four airlines—L, M, N, and O—on which to continue. Her choices must conform to the following constraints:

Whichever airline she chooses at a stop, she chooses one of the other airlines at the next stop.

She chooses the same airline at stop 1 as she does at stop 6.

She chooses the same airline at stop 2 as she does at stop 4.

Whenever she chooses either L or M at a stop, she does not choose N at the next stop.

At stop 5, she chooses N or O.

1. Which one of the following could be an accurate list of the airlines the traveler chooses at each stop, in order from 1 through 6?

   (A)   L, M, M, L, O, L
   (B)   M, L, O, M, O, M
   (C)   M, N, O, N, O, M
   (D)   M, O, N, O, N, M
   (E)   O, M, L, M, O, N

2. If the traveler chooses N at stop 5, which one of the following could be an accurate list of the airlines she chooses at stops 1, 2, and 3, respectively?

   (A)   L, M, N
   (B)   L, O, N
   (C)   M, L, N
   (D)   M, L, O
   (E)   N, O, N

3. If the only airlines the traveler chooses for the trip are M, N, and O, and she chooses O at stop 5, then the airlines she chooses at stops 1, 2, and 3, must be, respectively,

   (A)   M, O, and N
   (B)   M, N, and O
   (C)   N, M, and O
   (D)   N, O, and M
   (E)   O, M, and N

4. Which one of the following CANNOT be an accurate list of the airlines the traveler chooses at stops 1 and 2, respectively?

   (A)   L, M
   (B)   L, O
   (C)   M, L
   (D)   M, O
   (E)   O, N

5. If the traveler chooses O at stop 2, which one of the following could be an accurate list of the airlines she chooses at stops 5 and 6, respectively?

   (A)   M, N
   (B)   N, L
   (C)   N, O
   (D)   O, L
   (E)   O, N

Questions 6–11

The members of a five-person committee will be selected from among three parents—F, G, and H—three students—K, L, and M—and four teachers—U, W, X, and Z. The selection of committee members will meet the following conditions:

The committee must include exactly one student.
F and H cannot both be selected.
M and Z cannot both be selected.
U and W cannot both be selected.
F cannot be selected unless Z is also selected.
W cannot be selected unless H is also selected.

6. Which one of the following is an acceptable selection of committee members?

   (A) F, G, K, L, Z
   (B) F, G, K, U, X
   (C) G, K, W, X, Z
   (D) H, K, U, W, X
   (E) H, L, W, X, Z

7. If W and Z are selected, which one of the following is a pair of people who could also be selected?

   (A) U and X
   (B) K and L
   (C) G and M
   (D) G and K
   (E) F and G

8. Which one of the following is a pair of people who CANNOT both be selected?

   (A) F and G
   (B) F and M
   (C) G and K
   (D) H and L
   (E) M and U

9. If W is selected, then any one of the following could also be selected EXCEPT:

   (A) F
   (B) G
   (C) L
   (D) M
   (E) Z

10. If the committee is to include exactly one parent, which one of the following is a person who must also be selected?

    (A) K
    (B) L
    (C) M
    (D) U
    (E) X

11. If M is selected, then the committee must also include both

    (A) F and G
    (B) G and H
    (C) H and K
    (D) K and U
    (E) U and X

Questions 12–17

Within a five-year period from 1991 to 1995, each of three friends—Ramon, Sue, and Taylor—graduated. In that period, each bought his or her first car. The graduations and car purchases must be consistent with the following:

Ramon graduated in some year before the year in which Taylor graduated.

Taylor graduated in some year before the year in which he bought his first car.

Sue bought her first car in some year before the year in which she graduated.

Ramon and Sue graduated in the same year as each other.

At least one of the friends graduated in 1993.

12. Which one of the following could be an accurate matching of each friend and the year in which she or he graduated?

    (A) Ramon: 1991; Sue: 1991; Taylor: 1993
    (B) Ramon: 1992; Sue: 1992; Taylor: 1993
    (C) Ramon: 1992; Sue: 1993; Taylor: 1994
    (D) Ramon: 1993; Sue: 1993; Taylor: 1992
    (E) Ramon: 1993; Sue: 1993; Taylor: 1995

13. Which one of the following could have taken place in 1995?

    (A) Ramon graduated.
    (B) Ramon bought his first car.
    (C) Sue graduated.
    (D) Sue bought her first car.
    (E) Taylor graduated.

14. Which one of the following must be false?

    (A) Two of the friends each bought his or her first car in 1991.
    (B) Two of the friends each bought his or her first car in 1992.
    (C) Two of the friends each bought his or her first car in 1993.
    (D) Two of the friends each bought his or her first car in 1994.
    (E) Two of the friends each bought his or her first car in 1995.

15. Which one of the following must be true?

    (A) None of the three friends graduated in 1991.
    (B) None of the three friends graduated in 1992.
    (C) None of the three friends bought his or her first car in 1993.
    (D) None of the three friends graduated in 1994.
    (E) None of the three friends bought his or her first car in 1995.

16. If Taylor graduated in the same year that Ramon bought his first car, then each of the following could be true EXCEPT:

    (A) Sue bought her first car in 1991.
    (B) Ramon graduated in 1992.
    (C) Taylor graduated in 1993.
    (D) Taylor bought his first car in 1994.
    (E) Ramon bought his first car in 1995.

17. If Sue graduated in 1993, then which one of the following must be true?

    (A) Sue bought her first car in 1991.
    (B) Ramon bought his first car in 1992.
    (C) Ramon bought his first car in 1993.
    (D) Taylor bought his first car in 1994.
    (E) Taylor bought his first car in 1995.

Questions 18–22

A child eating alphabet soup notices that the only letters left in her bowl are one each of these six letters: T, U, W, X, Y, and Z. She plays a game with the remaining letters, eating them in the next three spoonfuls in accord with certain rules. Each of the six letters must be in exactly one of the next three spoonfuls, and each of the spoonfuls must have at least one and at most three of the letters. In addition, she obeys the following restrictions:

The U is in a later spoonful than the T.

The U is not in a later spoonful than the X.

The Y is in a later spoonful than the W.

The U is in the same spoonful as either the Y or the Z, but not both.

18. Which one of the following could be an accurate list of the spoonfuls and the letters in each of them?

(A)   first: Y
       second: T, W
       third: U, X, Z
(B)   first: T, W
       second: U, X, Y
       third: Z
(C)   first: T
       second: U, Z
       third: W, X, Y
(D)   first: T, U, Z
       second: W
       third: X, Y
(E)   first: W
       second: T, X, Z
       third: U, Y

19. If the Y is the only letter in one of the spoonfuls, then which one of the following could be true?

(A)   The Y is in the first spoonful.
(B)   The Z is in the first spoonful.
(C)   The T is in the second spoonful.
(D)   The X is in the second spoonful.
(E)   The W is in the third spoonful.

20. If the Z is in the first spoonful, then which one of the following must be true?

(A)   The T is in the second spoonful.
(B)   The U is in the third spoonful.
(C)   The W is in the first spoonful.
(D)   The W is in the second spoonful.
(E)   The X is in the third spoonful.

21. Which one of the following is a complete list of letters, any one of which could be the only letter in the first spoonful?

(A)   T
(B)   T, W
(C)   T, X
(D)   T, W, Z
(E)   T, X, W, Z

22. If the T is in the second spoonful, then which one of the following could be true?

(A)   Exactly two letters are in the first spoonful.
(B)   Exactly three letters are in the first spoonful.
(C)   Exactly three letters are in the second spoonful.
(D)   Exactly one letter is in the third spoonful.
(E)   Exactly two letters are in the third spoonful.

ANSWER KEY

1.	D	9.	A	17.	E
2.	B	10.	E	18.	B
3.	C	11.	B	19.	D
4.	E	12.	B	20.	E
5.	B	13.	B	21.	D
6.	E	14.	C	22.	A
7.	D	15.	A		
8.	B	16.	E		

TRIAGE REVIEW

This section mixes in some variations on the standard game types. Remember not to assume that twists necessarily make games harder. Concreteness (above all), along with simplicity and brevity, is what indicates the easier games.

Game 1 is a Strict Sequencing game, but you have only four entities to fill six spaces. You know you'll re-use at least one of the entities as you schedule the traveler's flights. Still, with five rules and a fairly balanced question set, you should be able to make some headway on the acceptable arrangements in the Rules and Deductions steps.

Game 2 is a Selection game with definite numbers. You're tasked with choosing five committee members from among nine people who are divided into three subcategories. While Selection with definite numbers and subgroups is less common than a simple "choose some of the entities" Selection task, the restrictions involved here indicate a game that won't be inordinately challenging.

Game 3 is Double Sequencing. You must decide the order in which certain people graduated and the order in which they got their first cars. This game isn't likely to be the easiest in the set, but with five rules, it won't be unmanageable either.

Game 4 is a Hybrid of Distribution and Sequencing. The setup looks long and complicated, so you'll need to make sure that you understand and sketch the task appropriately. Look for help from the number restrictions. There are only a handful of ways to split six entities up into three groups.

You will likely be best served taking the two Sequencing games—Game 1 and Game 3—first. Then you could take Game 2 and finish up with Game 4. If you know that Selection is your weakest area, you may reasonably decide to take Game 4 before Game 2. Otherwise, 1-3-2-4 is probably your optimal order.

EXPLANATIONS
Game 1—Flights and Airlines
<u>Questions 1–5</u>

> At each of six consecutive stops—1, 2, 3, 4, 5, and 6—that a traveler must make in that order as part of a trip, she can choose one from among exactly four airlines—L, M, N, and O—on which to continue. Her choices must conform to the following constraints:
>> Whichever airline she chooses at a stop, she chooses one of the other airlines at the next stop.
>> She chooses the same airline at stop 1 as she does at stop 6.
>> She chooses the same airline at stop 2 as she does at stop 4.
>> Whenever she chooses either L or M at a stop, she does not choose N at the next stop.
>> At stop 5, she chooses N or O.[2]

STEPS 1 AND 2: **Overview and Sketch**

It's not hard to picture your task. Just imagine yourself planning out a business trip with six destinations. For each, you have to decide which airline to fly to the next stop. There is nothing special about the departure points; they're just called stops 1–6. Several of the rules mention specific stops, so a standard Strict Sequencing framework is called for.

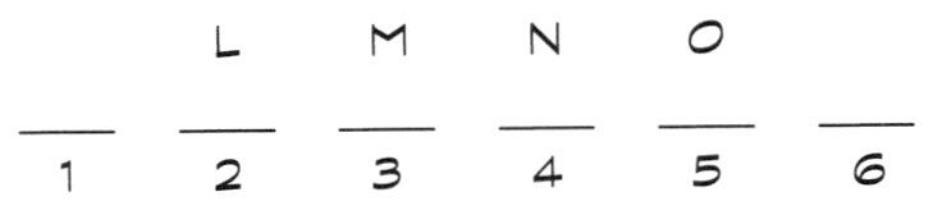

Figure 18.1

The twist comes from the fact that there are only four airlines to choose from. So one or more of the entities (the airlines) will appear more than once in the list of flights. It is essential that you notice that there is no requirement that all four airlines be used. Remember never to impose restrictions that aren't explicit in the game's setup and rules.

STEP 3: **Rules**

Rule 1 is simple but important: You can't use the same airline at consecutive stops.

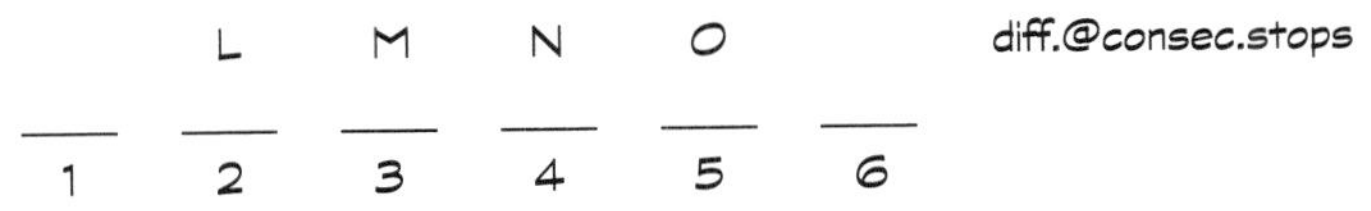

Figure 18.2

Rule 2 tells you to use the same airline at stops 1 and 6.

---

[2] PrepTest 50, Sec. 3, Game 1

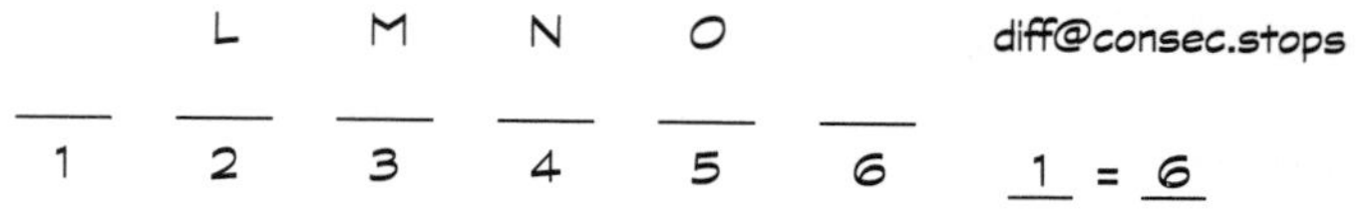

Figure 18.3

Rule 3 offers the same restriction as Rule 2, this time for stops 2 and 4.

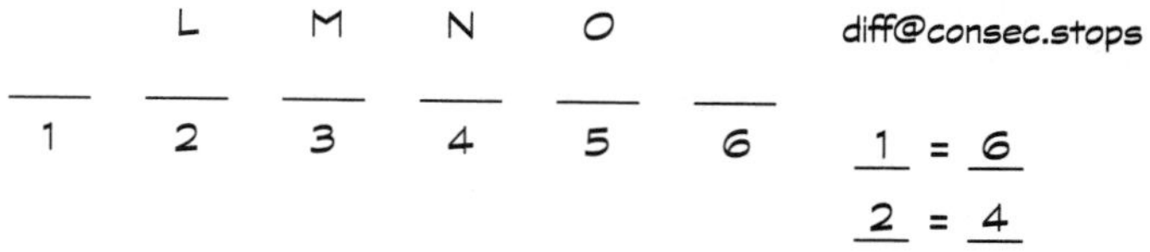

Figure 18.4

Rule 4 creates two "anti-blocks." Airline N can't be at the next stop after either airline L or airline M is used.

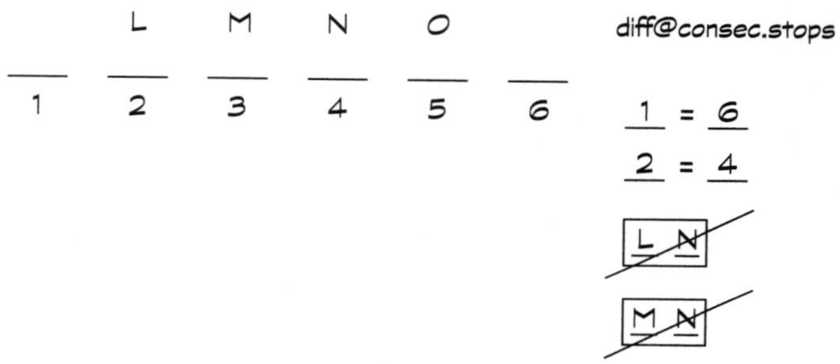

Figure 18.5

Rule 5 creates a Limited Options scenario based on the airline used for stop 5.

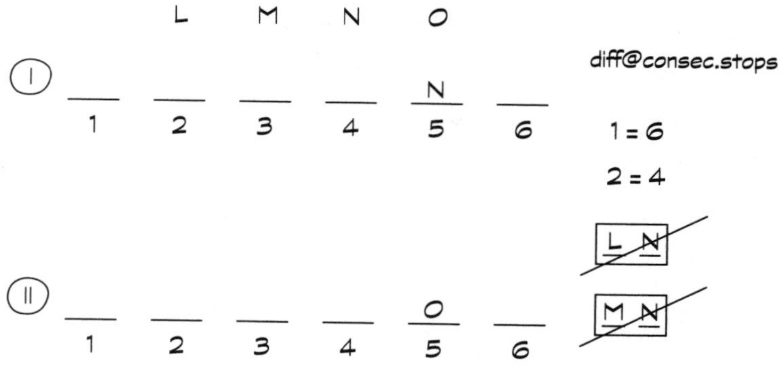

Figure 18.6

There are no floaters in the game. So move on to deductions. It's pretty clear that the Limited Options will provide the starting point for additional exploration of this game's restrictions.

STEP 4: **Deductions**

Start with Option I, where N is the airline at stop 5. Rule 4 makes it clear that neither L nor M can be the airline at stop 4, while Rule 1 excludes the possibility of having N at consecutive stops, so you must use O there.

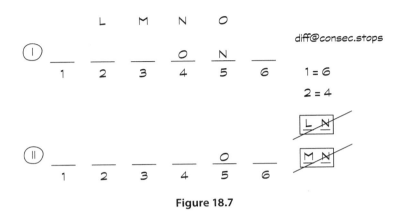

Figure 18.7

Placing O in stop 4 triggers Rule 3. O must be the airline at stop 2 as well.

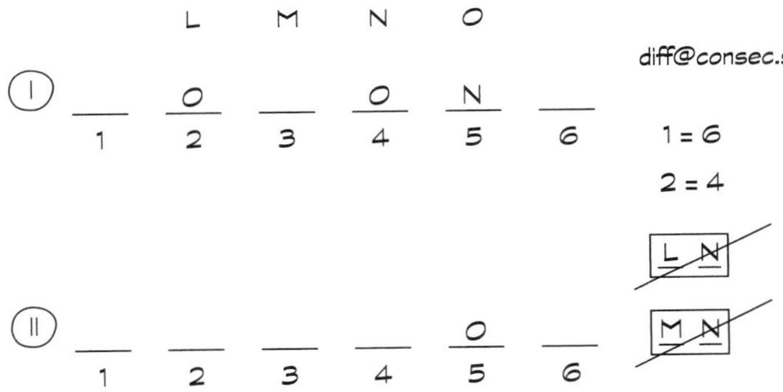

Figure 18.8

Don't forget the implications of Rule 1 for this option. Since N is at stop 5, it cannot be used again at stop 6. Likewise, since O is at stop 2, it can't be used again at stops 1 or 3.

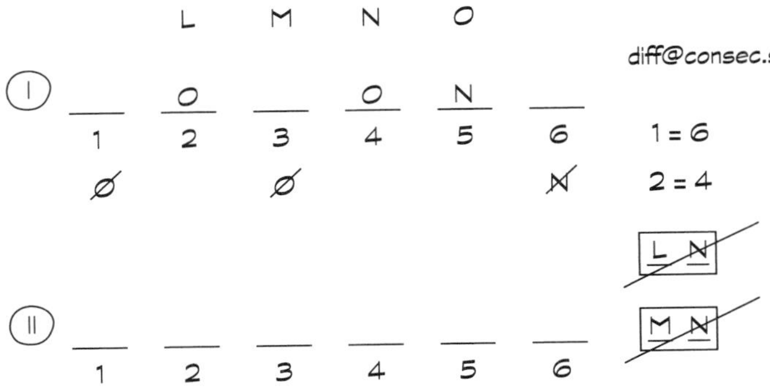

Figure 18.9

Since Rule 2 requires the same airline for stops 1 and 6, you now know that those two stops will use either airline L or airline M.

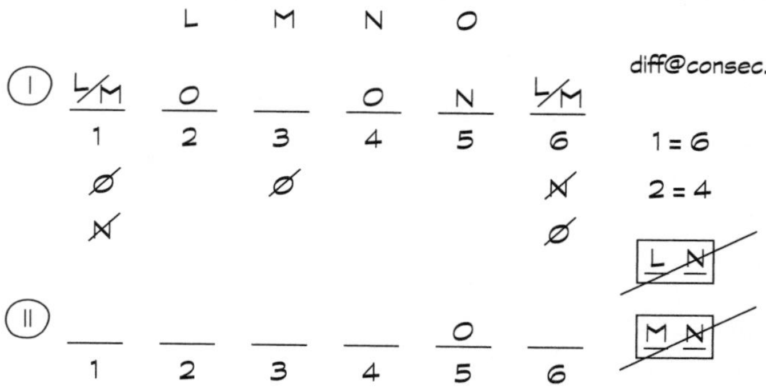

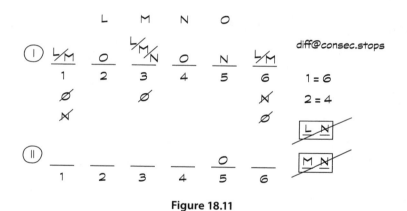

Figure 18.10

Only stop 3 has more than two possibilities in this option.

Figure 18.11

In Option II, you can't make nearly as much headway. With O used at stop 5, you know it will not be used at either stop 4 or stop 6.

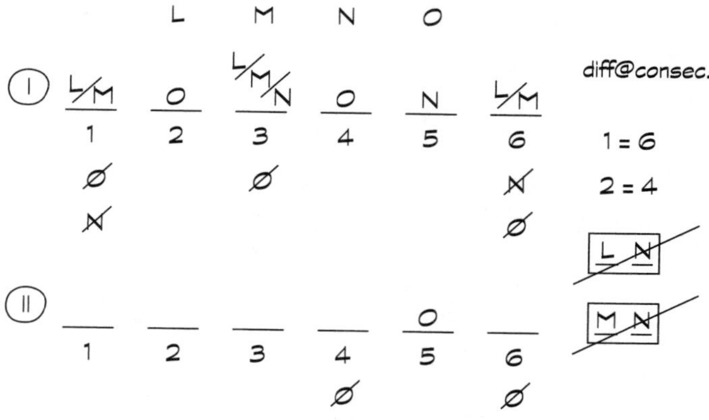

Figure 18.12

By extension, Rules 2 and 3 mean that O cannot be the airline for stops 1 or 2 either.

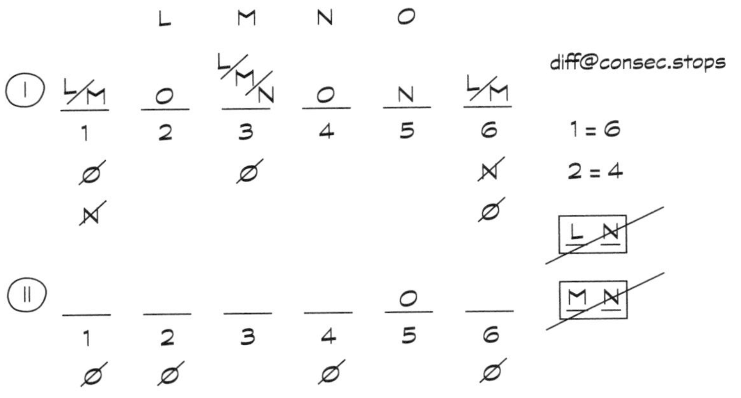

Figure 18.13

Since airline O is the only one that can be used at a stop immediately preceding a stop of N's, you can conclude that airline N will not be used at stops 2 or 3. And of course, if N isn't the airline at stop 2, it cannot be the airline for stop 4 (Rule 3).

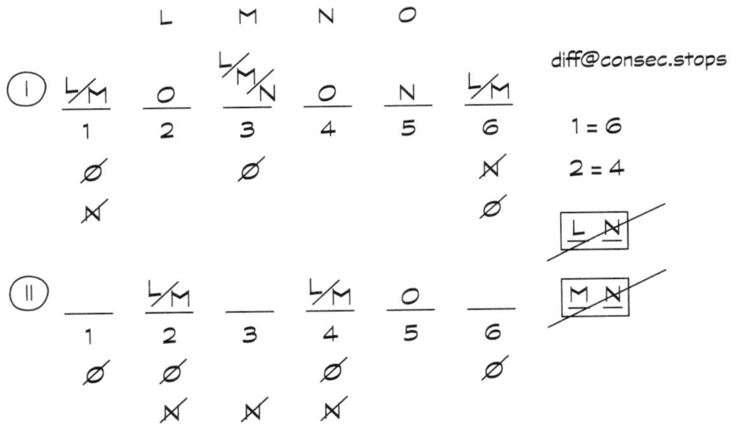

Figure 18.14

That last deduction brings home the value of always asking about both the positive and the negative implications of any restriction found in a logic game. Once you're aware that one arrangement cannot happen, ask, "Well, then, what can?" Once you find an affirmative requirement, ask, "And what does that rule out?"

Even with fewer affirmative deductions in Option II, you have a lot of certainty in this game. This Master Sketch should make the questions a snap.

STEP 5: **Questions**

There are three "If" question in this set, but each of them should put you into one or the other of the options, dramatically reducing the amount of resketching you'll need.

1. **(D)**

    Which one of the following could be an accurate list of the airlines the traveler chooses at each stop, in order from 1 through 6?

    (A) L, M, M, L, O, L
    (B) M, L, O, M, O, M
    (C) M, N, O, N, O, M
    (D) M, O, N, O, N, M
    (E) O, M, L, M, O, N[3]

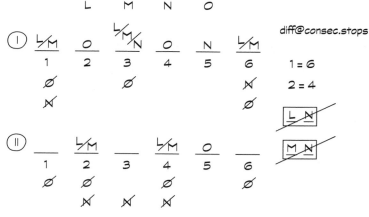

Figure 18.15

This is a straightforward Acceptability question. The easiest rule to check for violations is Rule 5. But a quick scan shows that all five answer choices have either N or O at stop 5. With four rules left to check and four wrong answers to eliminate, you pretty much know what to expect.

Rule 1 eliminates choice (A); M appears at consecutive stops.

Rule 2 eliminates choice (E); O flies from stop 1, but N from stop 6.

Rule 3 gets rid of choice (B); L flies from stop 2 and M from stop 4.

Rule 4 knocks out the final violator, choice (C); airline M immediately precedes airline N at stops 1 and 2, respectively.

That leaves only the correct answer, choice (D).

---

[3] PrepTest 50, Sec. 3, Q 1

2. **(B)**

If the traveler chooses N at stop 5, which one of the following could be an accurate list of the airlines she chooses at stops 1, 2, and 3, respectively?

(A)   L, M, N
(B)   L, O, N
(C)   M, L, N
(D)   M, L, O
(E)   N, O, N[4]

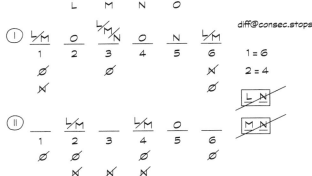

Figure 18.16

This question's new "if" condition simply tells you, "Consult Option I." Do so, and choose the one answer that would be acceptable for stops 1–3 there. Glancing at your Master Sketch, you see that airline O must fly from stop 2 in Option I. That allows you to strike through choices (A), (C), and (D). Since either airline L or airline M must fly from stop 1 in Option I, you can eliminate choice (E), too. The correct answer is choice (B), just that fast.

3. **(C)**

If the only airlines the traveler chooses for the trip are M, N, and O, and she chooses O at stop 5, then the airlines she chooses at stops 1, 2, and 3, must be, respectively,

(A)   M, O, and N
(B)   M, N, and O
(C)   N, M, and O
(D)   N, O, and M
(E)   O, M, and N[5]

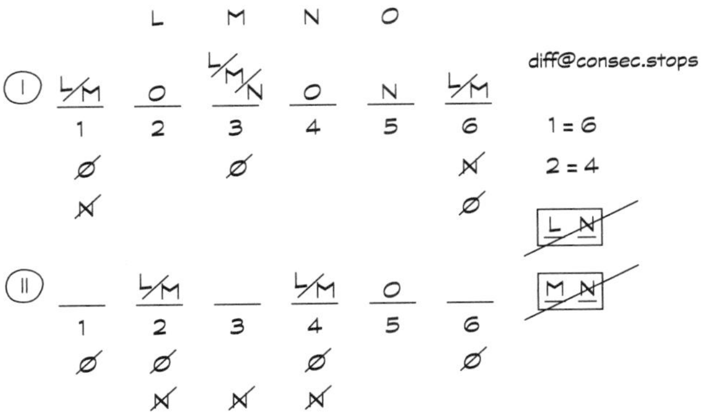

Figure 18.17

There are two parts to the "if" in this question. Take the second clause of the stem—"she chooses O at stop 5"—first. That puts you in Option II. Now, consider the first clause in light of Option II. If you use only airlines M, N, and O in this option, the first two airlines you use

---

[4] PrepTest 50, Sec. 3, Q 2
[5] PrepTest 50, Sec. 3, Q 3

must be N and M, respectively. The only choice that begins "N, M" is choice (C). That's the right answer and you can move on.

4. **(E)**

Which one of the following CANNOT be an accurate list of the airlines the traveler chooses at stops 1 and 2, respectively?

(A) L, M
(B) L, O
(C) M, L
(D) M, O
(E) O, N[6]

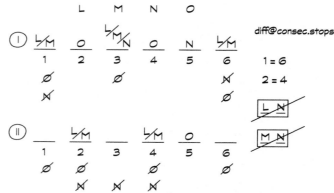

Figure 18.18

This question does not have an "if" clause. You need to consider both options here. The correct answer is the one with an unacceptable pair of airlines for stops 1 and 2. Stop 2 is the easier one to check. It can have only airline O in Option I and only airlines L or M in Option II. In other words, airline N can never be used at stop 2. That, by itself, is enough to show that choice (E) is impossible and, therefore, the correct answer.

5. **(B)**

If the traveler chooses O at stop 2, which one of the following could be an accurate list of the airlines she chooses at stops 5 and 6, respectively?

(A) M, N
(B) N, L
(C) N, O
(D) O, L
(E) O, N[7]

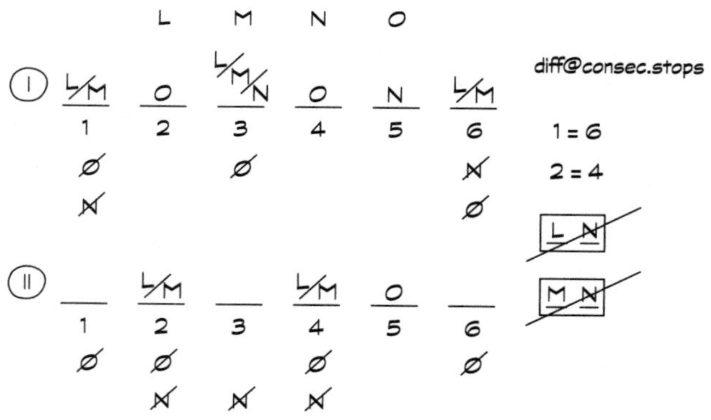

Figure 18.19

[6] PrepTest 50, Sec. 3, Q 4

[7] PrepTest 50, Sec. 3, Q 5

Once again, the "if" condition makes it clear which option you may use. Choosing airline O at stop 2 is tantamount to saying, "Use Option I." Now that you know which option to employ, consider the rest of the question stem. It calls for airlines acceptable at stops 5 and 6, respectively. In Option I, airline N must be used at stop 5. Eliminate choices (A), (D), and (E). Airlines L and M are the only acceptable choices for stop 6 in Option I. Choice (C) is thus unacceptable, but choice (B) works just fine. It's the correct answer.

That game looked a little unusual at first with just four entities for six spaces. Once you made your way through the rules, however, the possibility of Limited Options sketches emerged and the result was an extremely helpful set of deductions. If you were patient enough to create a complete Master Sketch, you may even have been able to complete the question set quickly enough to bank some time for the tougher games later in the section.

Game 2—Student-Parent-Teacher Committee

Questions 6–11

The members of a five-person committee will be selected from among three parents—F, G, and H—three students—K, L, and M—and four teachers—U, W, X, and Z. The selection of committee members will meet the following conditions:

The committee must include exactly one student.
F and H cannot both be selected.
M and Z cannot both be selected.
U and W cannot both be selected.
F cannot be selected unless Z is also selected.
W cannot be selected unless H is also selected.[8]

STEPS 1 AND 2: Overview and Sketch

Here, your task is to select the members of a 5-person committee from among 10 people. The people are designated as parents, students, or teachers. So you can anticipate that the game will impose restrictions on how many of the committee's members can come from one or more of the subgroups. Make sure your roster of entities reflects the subgroups.

5 of 10

Par	Stu	Teach
FGH	KLM	UWXZ

Figure 18.20

You'll circle the chosen entities and strike through the rejected ones, just as you would in any Selection game. It's a good idea to write "5 of 10" near the roster so that you remember the specific number restriction in this game.

STEP 3: Rules

With the entities divided into subgroups, you can anticipate that one or more of the rules will limit the number of entities you can select from each subgroup. Indeed, that's exactly what Rule 1 tells you.

5 of 10

(1)

Par	Stu	Teach
FGH	KLM	UWXZ

Figure 18.21

---

[8] PrepTest 50, Sec. 3, Game 2

That rule will prove to be the most important in the Deductions step, but get the other restrictions down first. Then circle back and consider them in light of the number restrictions.

Rules 2, 3, and 4 each create "impossible pairs."

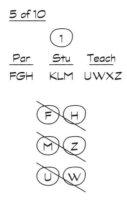

Figure 18.22

The last two rules are routine formal logic statements. Translate them and diagram the contrapositives as you learned to do in chapter 3.

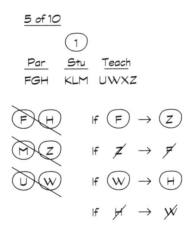

Figure 18.23

With your sketch at this point, you would be able to work your way through all of the questions, albeit somewhat slowly. With a little attention to the number restrictions, you'll be able to breeze through this question set.

STEP 4: Deductions

Rule 1 provides a clear limit; just one student must serve on the committee. That leaves four committee members to account for.

Par	Stu	Teach
	Max.	
	1	

Figure 18.24

Rule 2 limits you to using just one or two parents on the committee. Since F and H cannot serve together, there is no way you can use all three parents.

Par	Stu	Teach
Max.	Max.	
2	1	

Figure 18.25

Rule 4 has a comparable effect on the teacher subgroup. Since U and W cannot serve together, you can have at most three teachers on the committee.

Par	Stu	Teach
Max.	Max.	Max.
2	1	3

Figure 18.25A

Thus, you have only two options: one parent, one student, and three teachers; or two parents, one student, and two teachers. It's worth it to sketch out the implications of each option.

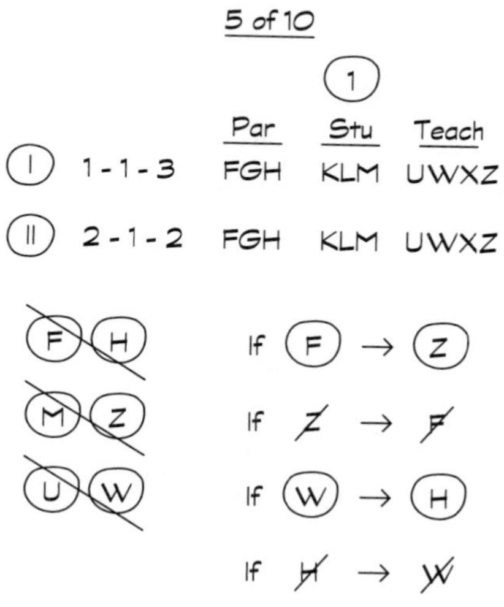

5 of 10

①

		Par	Stu	Teach
Ⓘ	1-1-3	FGH	KLM	UWXZ
Ⓘⓘ	2-1-2	FGH	KLM	UWXZ

F̶H̶   If F → Z

M̶Z̶   If Z̶ → F̶

U̶W̶   If W → H

            If H̶ → W̶

Figure 18.26

In Option I, the teachers will have to be X, Z, and one of U or W.

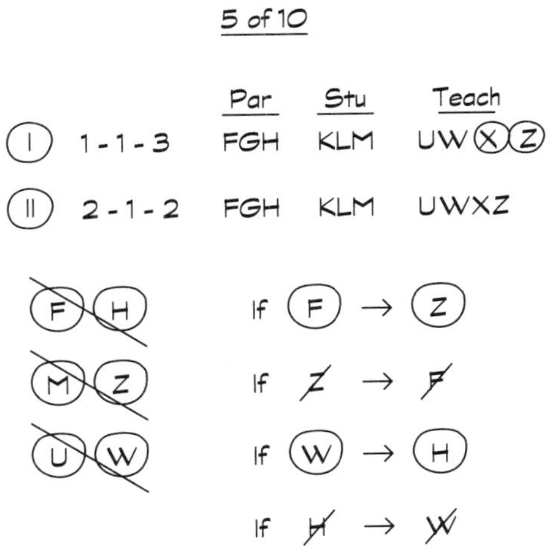

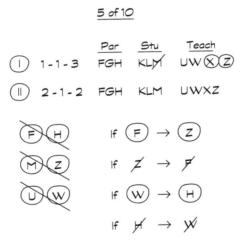

Figure 18.27

Because Z is included among the teachers on the committee, M cannot be the student (Rule 3).

5 of 10

Figure 18.28

Any one of the three parents can serve on the committee in Option I, though if the parent is not H, the third teacher will have to be U, not W (Rule 6).

In Option II, you can't make as many additions to the sketch. Using Rule 2, you know that the parents will be G and either F or H.

5 of 10
Par
Stu
Teach
I 1-1-3 FGH KLM UWXZ
II 2-1-2 FGH KLM UWXZ
FH
MZ
UW
If F → Z
If Z → F
If W → H
If H → W

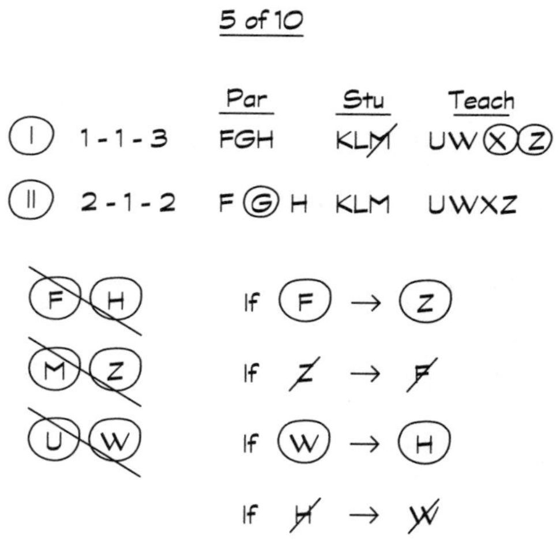

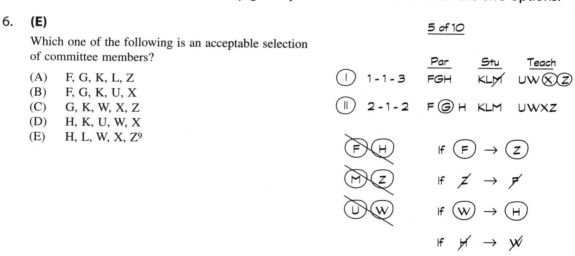

Figure 18.29

The remaining selections in Option II will depend on the "impossible pairs" restricted by Rules 3 and 4 and on the formal logic in Rules 5 and 6. That's too speculative to pursue without some additional information. Move on to the questions.

STEP 5: Questions

This question set contains a standard Acceptability question, a Must Be False question, and four "If" questions, some of which may guide you to one or the other of the two options.

6. **(E)**

Which one of the following is an acceptable selection of committee members?

(A) F, G, K, L, Z
(B) F, G, K, U, X
(C) G, K, W, X, Z
(D) H, K, U, W, X
(E) H, L, W, X, Z[9]

5 of 10
Par
Stu
Teach
I 1-1-3 FGH KLM UWXZ
II 2-1-2 FGH KLM UWXZ
FH
MZ
UW
If F → Z
If Z → F
If W → H
If H → W

Figure 18.30

This is a typical Acceptability question. Test the rules one at a time, and cross off any answer that breaks a rule.

Rule 1 eliminates choice (A), which includes two students, K and L.

[9] PrepTest 50, Sec. 3, Q 6

Rule 2 isn't broken in any of the choices.

Nor is Rule 3 violated anywhere.

Rule 4, though, eliminates choice (D), which has both U and W.

Rule 5 eliminates choice (B), where F is included without Z.

Finally, Rule 6 takes out choice (C); there, W is included without H.

That leaves the correct answer, choice (E).

7. **(D)**

If W and Z are selected, which one of the following is a pair of people who could also be selected?

(A) U and X
(B) K and L
(C) G and M
(D) G and K
(E) F and G[10]

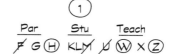

Figure 18.31

The "if" from this question's stem doesn't automatically limit you to one of the options, so build a mini-sketch to see the implications of the new condition. Start with the entity list and circle W and Z.

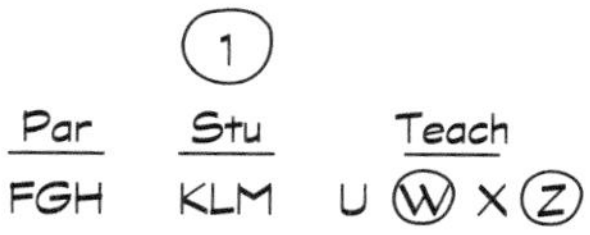

Figure 18.32

Including Z triggers Rule 3. Cross M off the list.

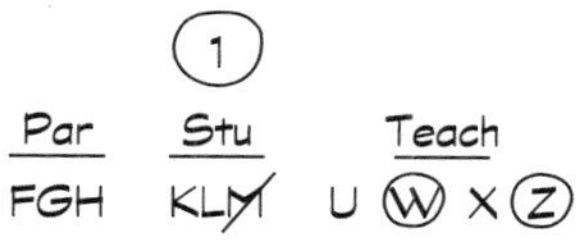

Figure 18.33

Including W triggers Rule 4. Get rid of U.

[10] PrepTest 50, Sec. 3, Q 7

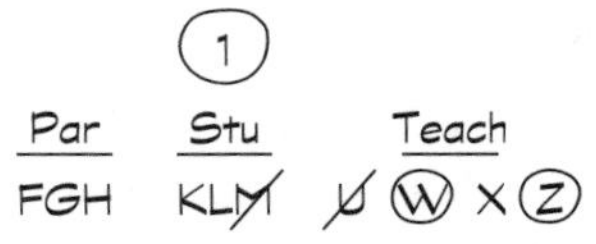

Par   Stu   Teach
FGH   KLM̶   U̶ Ⓦ X Ⓩ

Figure 18.34

W's inclusion also triggers the formal logic in Rule 6. You must select H in this question.

Par   Stu   Teach
F G Ⓗ KLM̶   U̶ Ⓦ X Ⓩ

Figure 18.35

H is incompatible with F according to Rule 1. So strike F off the list here.

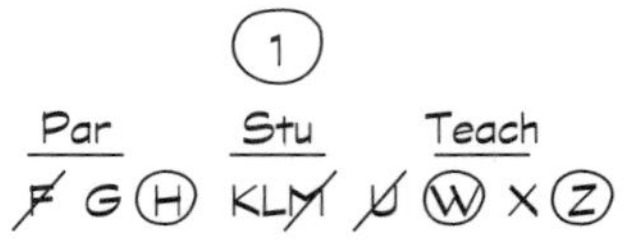

F̶ G Ⓗ KLM̶ U̶ Ⓦ X Ⓩ

Figure 18.36

It's still impossible to tell which option you're in, but you can't push the deductions any further. Go ahead and characterize the answer choices. The correct answer is a pair of entities that can both be selected. That means each wrong answer will include at least one entity that cannot be selected or will be a pair that cannot be selected together.

Get rid of any answer that includes an entity you've already crossed off the list. That eliminates choice (A), which includes U, choice (C), which includes M, and choice (E), which includes F.

Which of the remaining choices is impossible? That's choice (B), which has two students. You know from Rule 1 that only one student will serve on the committee. Cross out choice (B), leaving only the correct answer, choice (D). G and K can both serve on the committee under the conditions given in this question stem.

8. **(B)**

Which one of the following is a pair of people who CANNOT both be selected?

(A)   F and G
(B)   F and M
(C)   G and K
(D)   H and L
(E)   M and U[11]

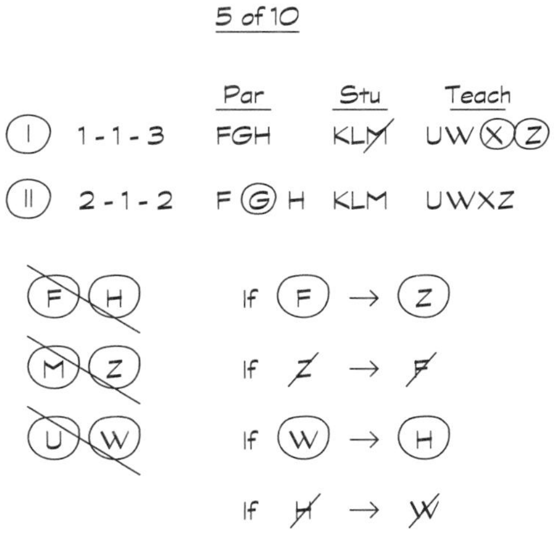

		Par	Stu	Teach
I	1-1-3	FGH	KLM̸	UW⊗Ⓩ
II	2-1-2	F Ⓖ H	KLM	UWXZ

Ⓕ⊗Ⓗ   If Ⓕ → Ⓩ

Ⓜ⊗Ⓩ   If Z̸ → F̸

Ⓤ⊗Ⓦ   If Ⓦ → Ⓗ

          If H̸ → W̸

Figure 18.37

If you find yourself struggling with this question or tempted to just start writing out mini-sketches in an attempt to test each answer, slow down and take a more strategic approach. The correct answer is an "impossible pair"—two entities who cannot serve together on the committee. That means each of the four wrong answers contains an acceptable pair. You can eliminate any answer choices that contain pairs you've already seen in acceptable arrangements. Thus, you can get rid of choice (D). After all, H and L both appear in the correct answer to question 6; that choice is, by definition, an acceptable arrangement. You can also get rid of choice (C); G and K were acceptable as a pair in the correct answer to question 7.

From here, you can either wait until you finish the remaining "If" questions to see if they help you eliminate other acceptable pairs or you can test the remaining answer choices. Either way, you'll find that the correct answer—with the "impossible pair"—is choice (B). When F is selected, Z must be as well (Rule 5); and Z cannot serve with M (Rule 3). Thus, F and M cannot serve together on the committee.

9. **(A)**

If W is selected, then any one of the following could also be selected EXCEPT:

(A)   F
(B)   G
(C)   L
(D)   M
(E)   Z[12]

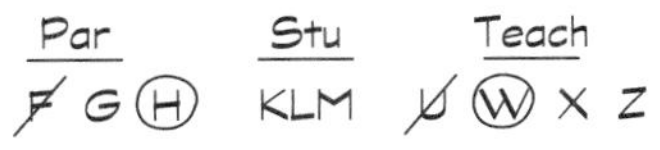

Par	Stu	Teach
F̸ G Ⓗ	KLM	U̸ Ⓦ X Z

Figure 18.38

Selecting W does not, by itself, place you in either of the Limited Options. So copy out the list of entities and circle W.

---

[11] PrepTest 50, Sec. 3, Q 8

[12] PrepTest 50, Sec. 3, Q 9

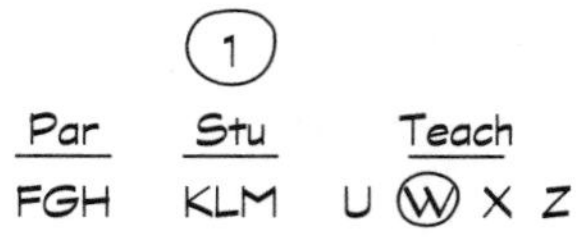

①

Par	Stu	Teach
FGH	KLM	U (W) X Z

Figure 18.39

Selecting W has two direct consequences: You must eliminate U (Rule 4), and you must include H (Rule 6).

Par	Stu	Teach
F G (H)	KLM	U̸ (W) X Z

Figure 18.40

Selecting H triggers Rule 2. You must reject F in this case.

Par	Stu	Teach
F̸ G (H)	KLM	U̸ (W) X Z

Figure 18.41

That's as far as you can push the deductions, but it's (of course) enough to answer the question easily. The correct answer is an entity that cannot be selected under these conditions. That's F, choice (A).

10. **(E)**

If the committee is to include exactly one parent, which one of the following is a person who must also be selected?

(A) K
(B) L
(C) M
(D) U
(E) X[13]

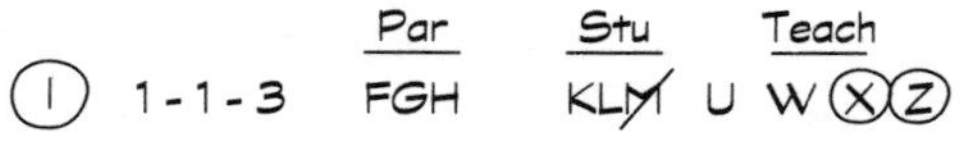

① 1-1-3

Par	Stu	Teach
FGH	KLM̸	U W (X)(Z)

Figure 18.42

The "if" for this question steers you straight to Option I. Checking that option, you see that both X and Z must be selected for the committee. X is in choice (E), making it the correct answer.

11. **(B)**

If M is selected, then the committee must also include both:

(A) F and G
(B) G and H
(C) H and K
(D) K and U
(E) U and X[14]

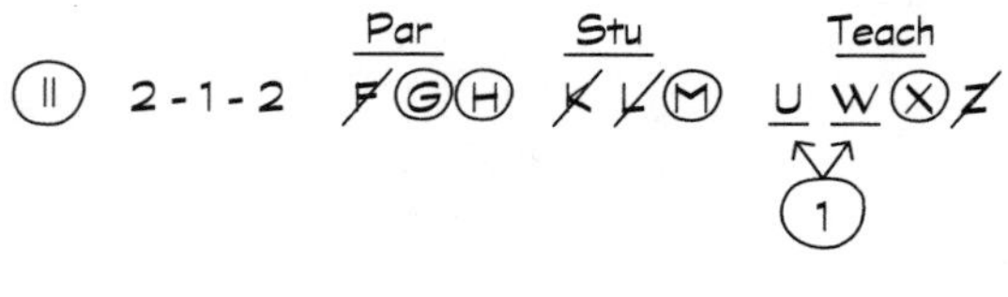

② 2-1-2

Par	Stu	Teach
F̸ (G)(H)	K̸ L̸ (M)	U W (X) Z̸

①

Figure 18.43

---

[13] PrepTest 50, Sec. 3, Q 10

[14] PrepTest 50, Sec. 3, Q 11

This question's "if" restricts you to Option II. That's because M cannot be used in Option I. Create a mini-sketch based on Option II with M as the student on the committee.

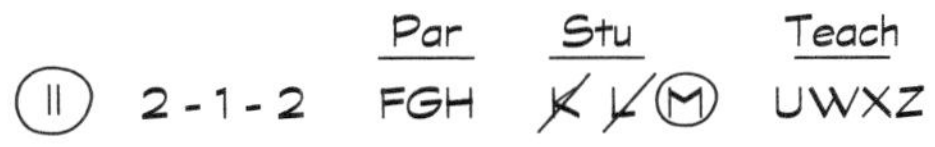

Figure 18.44

Selecting M means rejecting Z (Rule 3). Thus, the teachers on the committee must be X and one of U and W (you cannot select both U and W because of Rule 4, remember).

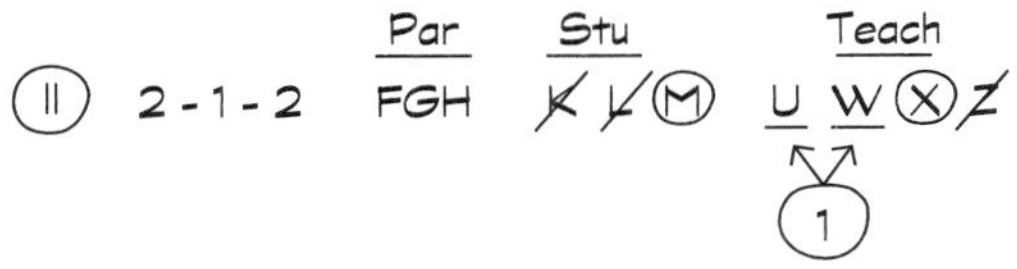

Figure 18.45

Finally, without Z on the committee, you aren't permitted to select F (Rule 5).

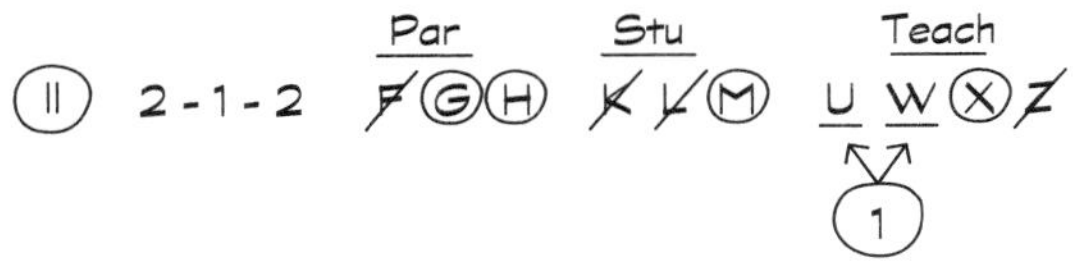

Figure 18.46

Thus, the parents for this arrangement must be G and H. Those are the entities listed in choice (B). Since the question stem calls for a pair of entities that *must be selected*, choice (B) is the correct answer.

Choices (A), (C), and (D) all include entities that cannot be selected in this situation (F and K), while choice (E) includes U, which doesn't have to be selected here.

Game 3—Graduation and First Car

Questions 12–17

> Within a five-year period from 1991 to 1995, each of three
> friends—Ramon, Sue, and Taylor—graduated. In that period,
> each bought his or her first car. The graduations and car
> purchases must be consistent with the following:
>> Ramon graduated in some year before the year in which
>> Taylor graduated.
>> Taylor graduated in some year before the year in which he
>> bought his first car.
>> Sue bought her first car in some year before the year in
>> which she graduated.
>> Ramon and Sue graduated in the same year as each other.
>> At least one of the friends graduated in 1993.[15]

STEPS 1 AND 2: Overview and Sketch

This game sounds like a conversation you may have had with people you met in college,
although it's pretty unlikely that you would have made a chart to keep track of everyone. You
will here, although it will just be a standard Strict Sequencing line with five slots for the five
years covered by the game's setup.

$$\underline{\hspace{1cm}} \quad \underline{\hspace{1cm}} \quad \underline{\hspace{1cm}} \quad \underline{\hspace{1cm}} \quad \underline{\hspace{1cm}}$$
$$91 \qquad 92 \qquad 93 \qquad 94 \qquad 95$$

Figure 18.47

Some test takers try to make this game much more complicated than it needs to be by making
one line for graduations and one for cars. In fact, you should just treat each friend's graduation and car as two separate entities. Use "G" and "C" after the letter representing the friend
to distinguish his or her graduation from his or her getting a car.

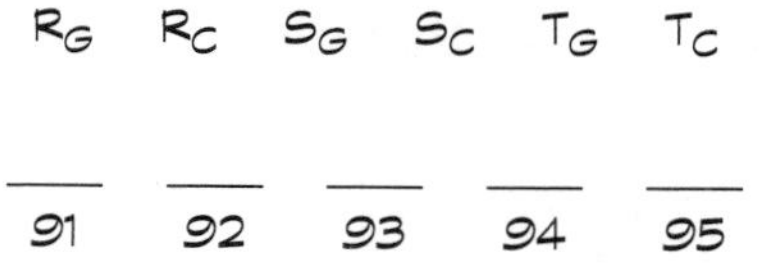

$$R_G \quad R_C \quad S_G \quad S_C \quad T_G \quad T_C$$

$$\underline{\hspace{1cm}} \quad \underline{\hspace{1cm}} \quad \underline{\hspace{1cm}} \quad \underline{\hspace{1cm}} \quad \underline{\hspace{1cm}}$$
$$91 \qquad 92 \qquad 93 \qquad 94 \qquad 95$$

Figure 18.48

Now, you have six events to fit into five years, so you know that at least one year saw two of
the events occur. That's all right, there's no restriction saying that one event has to happen
each year. There may even be years in which three or four of these events or none of these
events happened. The rules will give you more clarity on that.

---

[15] PrepTest 50, Sec. 3, Game 3

STEP **3: Rules**

The first rule relates Ramon's graduation (R_G) to Taylor's graduation (T_G). You can't place that into the framework yet.

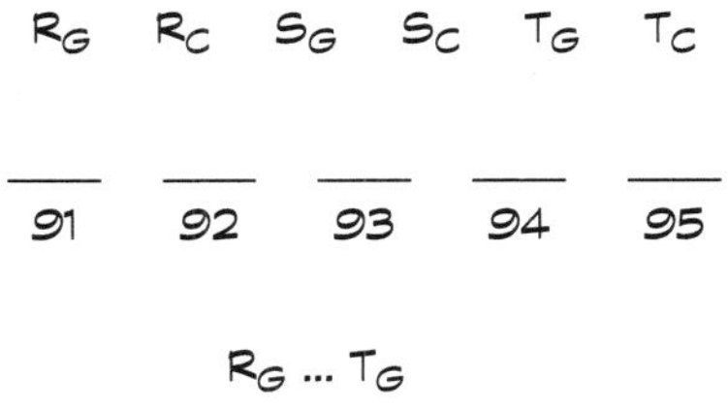

$$R_G \quad R_C \quad S_G \quad S_C \quad T_G \quad T_C$$

$$\underline{\quad}_{91} \quad \underline{\quad}_{92} \quad \underline{\quad}_{93} \quad \underline{\quad}_{94} \quad \underline{\quad}_{95}$$

$$R_G \ldots T_G$$

Figure 18.49

The second rule can simply be appended to the first. Taylor's first car (T_C) followed his graduation (T_G).

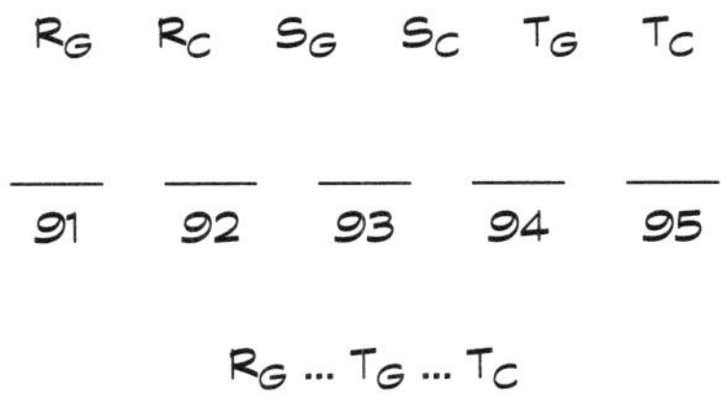

$$R_G \quad R_C \quad S_G \quad S_C \quad T_G \quad T_C$$

$$\underline{\quad}_{91} \quad \underline{\quad}_{92} \quad \underline{\quad}_{93} \quad \underline{\quad}_{94} \quad \underline{\quad}_{95}$$

$$R_G \ldots T_G \ldots T_C$$

Figure 18.50

The third rule gives the order of S's two events.

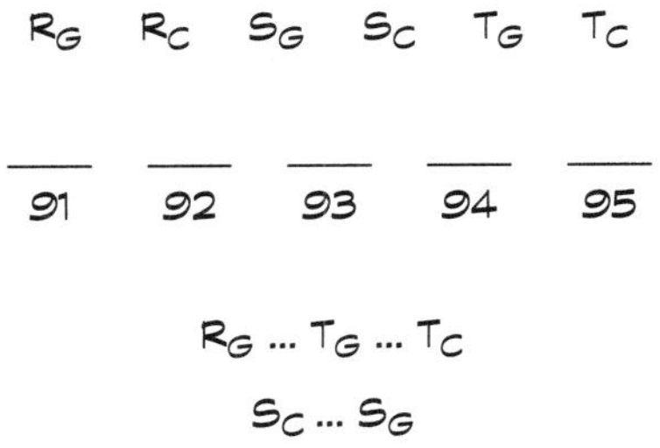

$$R_G \quad R_C \quad S_G \quad S_C \quad T_G \quad T_C$$

$$\underline{\quad}_{91} \quad \underline{\quad}_{92} \quad \underline{\quad}_{93} \quad \underline{\quad}_{94} \quad \underline{\quad}_{95}$$

$$R_G \ldots T_G \ldots T_C$$
$$S_C \ldots S_G$$

Figure 18.51

The fourth rule tells you that Ramon and Sue graduated the same year ($R_G = S_G$).

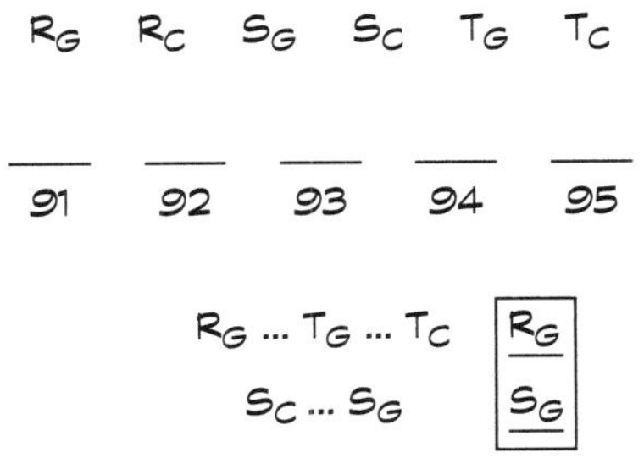

$$R_G \quad R_C \quad S_G \quad S_C \quad T_G \quad T_C$$

$$\underline{\quad}_{91} \quad \underline{\quad}_{92} \quad \underline{\quad}_{93} \quad \underline{\quad}_{94} \quad \underline{\quad}_{95}$$

$$R_G \ldots T_G \ldots T_C \quad \boxed{\begin{array}{c} R_G \\ \underline{S_G} \end{array}}$$
$$S_C \ldots S_G$$

Figure 18.52

Did you note that Rule 4 allows you to join the S_C-S_G block to the R_G-T_G-T_C string you already diagrammed? If so, that's great. If not, you would have gotten it as you considered the duplications (the rules sharing the same entity) under Step 4.

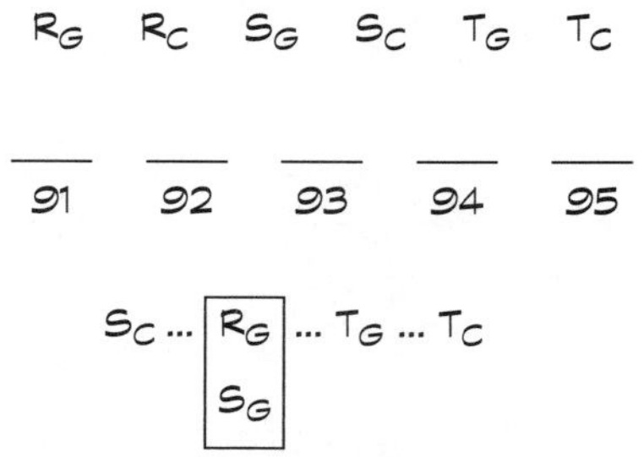

Figure 18.53

The final rule tells you that at least one of the graduations happened in '93. Just make a note of this rule beneath the framework.

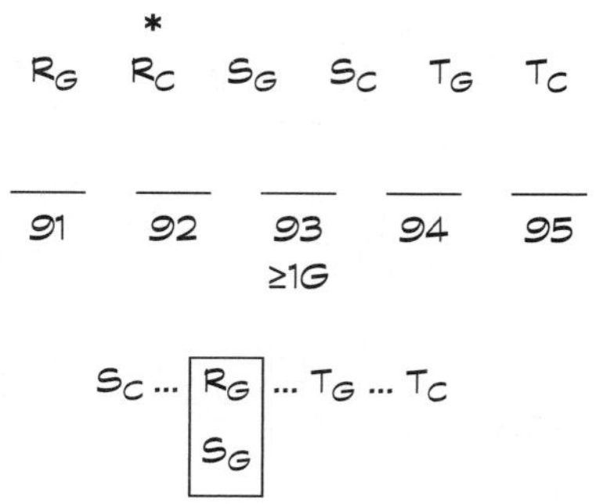

Figure 18.54

It's about to become very important. Notice, too, the asterisk above RC, reminding you that it is the floater.

STEP 4: Deductions

As I pointed out when discussing Rule 4, the first four rules all connect to form a string of relationships among five of the six entities.

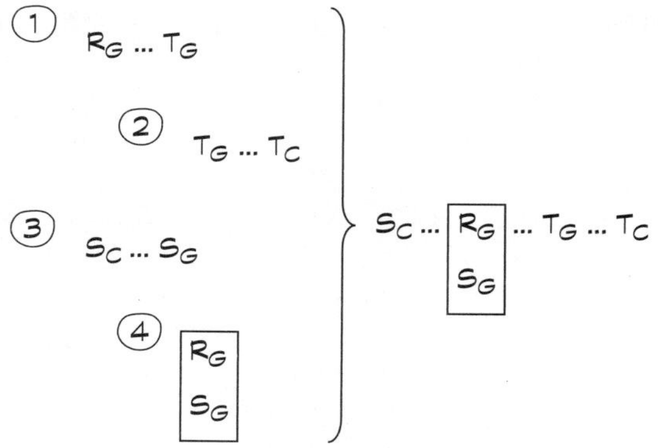

Figure 18.55

Consider how that string can fit into the framework in light of Rule 5, which says that at least one graduation took place in 1993. You quickly see that either '93 was the year of Sue's and Ramon's graduations, or it was the year of Taylor's. That allows you to set up dual Limited Options sketches.

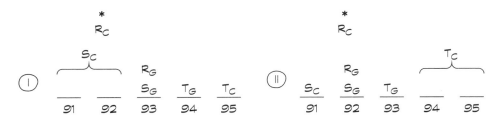

Figure 18.56

When Sue and Ramon are the '93 grads, Taylor's graduation must take place in '94 and the purchase of his first car in '95. In Option I, Sue gets her car in either '91 or '92. When Taylor is the '93 grad, Sue's car gets pushed back to '91, and Sue's and Ramon's graduation occurs in '92. Taylor gets his car after his graduation, so in Option II, he'll get it in either '94 or '95. Remember that the one unknown in either option is when Ramon got his car.

STEP 5: Questions

Since so much of this game could be determined in the Deduction step, it's not surprising to see only two "If" questions. Keep the fact that R_C is a floater in mind when you're asked what *could be true*.

12. **(B)**

Which one of the following could be an accurate matching of each friend and the year in which she or he graduated?

(A) Ramon: 1991; Sue: 1991; Taylor: 1993
(B) Ramon: 1992; Sue: 1992; Taylor: 1993
(C) Ramon: 1992; Sue: 1993; Taylor: 1994
(D) Ramon: 1993; Sue: 1993; Taylor: 1992
(E) Ramon: 1993; Sue: 1993; Taylor: 1995[16]

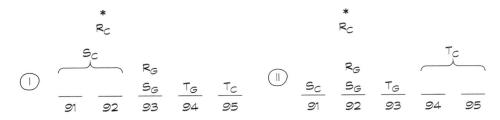

Figure 18.57

---

[16] PrepTest 50, Sec. 3, Q 12

This is a Partial Acceptability question, asking only for the possible graduation dates. With the Master Sketch you have, you can see that there are only two possible solutions: either R_G/S_G in '92 and T_G in '93, or else R_G/S_G in '93 and T_G in '94. Choice (B) matches the first of those two arrangements and is the correct answer.

13. **(B)**

Which one of the following could have taken place in 1995?

(A)   Ramon graduated.
(B)   Ramon bought his first car.
(C)   Sue graduated.
(D)   Sue bought her first car.
(E)   Taylor graduated.[17]

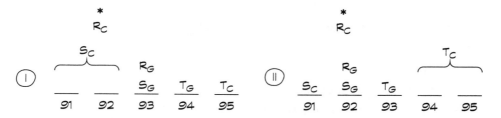

Figure 18.58

Checking the Master Sketch, you can tell that only two events could have taken place in '95, TC or RC (the floater, as you recall, which can go anywhere). The only choice that matches one of these possibilities is (B), so it's the correct answer.

14. **(C)**

Which one of the following must be false?

(A)   Two of the friends each bought his or her first car in 1991.
(B)   Two of the friends each bought his or her first car in 1992.
(C)   Two of the friends each bought his or her first car in 1993.
(D)   Two of the friends each bought his or her first car in 1994.
(E)   Two of the friends each bought his or her first car in 1995.[18]

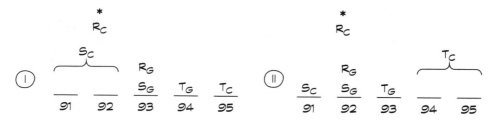

Figure 18.59

[17] PrepTest 50, Sec. 3, Q 13
[18] PrepTest 50, Sec. 3, Q 14

Here is yet another question that can be answered straight from the Master Sketch. The correct answer *must be false*, meaning that the four wrong answers *could be true*. If you find a choice acceptable in either option, eliminate that answer.

Choice (A) is acceptable in either option; Sue and Ramon could both have gotten their cars in '91. Cross out this answer.

Choice (B) is acceptable in Option I; there, Sue and Ramon could both have gotten their cars in '92. Get rid of choice (B), too.

Choice (C) is impossible, and thus, the right answer. Only Ramon could have gotten his car in '93.

For the record, choices (D) and (E) are both possible in Option II, where the two friends to have gotten their cars would be Taylor and Ramon.

15. **(A)**

Which one of the following must be true?

(A)   None of the three friends graduated in 1991.
(B)   None of the three friends graduated in 1992.
(C)   None of the three friends bought his or her first car in 1993.
(D)   None of the three friends graduated in 1994.
(E)   None of the three friends bought his or her first car in 1995.[19]

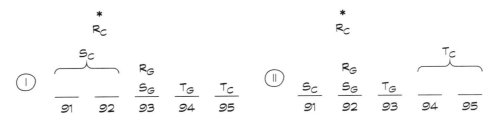

Figure 18.60

One last "Non-If" question: this one asks for what *must be true*. That means that each of the wrong answers *could be false* in one or both of the options. You don't have to look far to find the right answer. Choice (A) *must be true*; all three graduations take place in '93 and '94 (Option I) or '92 and '93 (Option II). Each of the wrong answers, choices (B)–(E), could be false in at least one of the two options.

19 PrepTest 50, Sec. 3, Q 15

16. **(E)**

If Taylor graduated in the same year that Ramon bought his first car, then each of the following could be true EXCEPT:

(A) Sue bought her first car in 1991.
(B) Ramon graduated in 1992.
(C) Taylor graduated in 1993.
(D) Taylor bought his first car in 1994.
(E) Ramon bought his first car in 1995.[20]

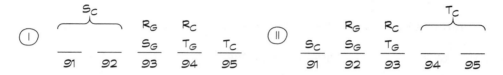

Figure 18.61

The "if" condition described in this question stem could happen in either of the two options. In Option I, R_C would occur in '94. In Option II, R_C would happen in '93. If it's helpful, you can add that to a quick mini-sketch like the one you see above.

Make sure you characterize the answer choices on an "EXCEPT" question like this one. The correct answer *must be false*. Since R_C can happen only in '93 or '94, choice (E) cannot be true and is, therefore, the correct choice. You'll notice that all of the remaining choices are possible in one or both of the options.

17. **(E)**

If Sue graduated in 1993, then which one of the following must be true?

(A) Sue bought her first car in 1991.
(B) Ramon bought his first car in 1992.
(C) Ramon bought his first car in 1993.
(D) Taylor bought his first car in 1994.
(E) Taylor bought his first car in 1995.[21]

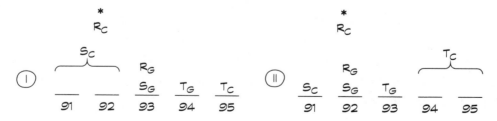

Figure 18.62

This question's "if" puts you squarely in Option I. Simply consult that option and determine which answer *must be true*. It's unclear in Option I whether Sue got her car in '91 or '92, so choice (A) could be false. Eliminate it. Ramon could have gotten his first car in any one of the five years in either option; RC is this game's floater. That allows you to eliminate choices (B) and (C). Taylor gets his car in '95 in Option I. That makes choice (D) false and wrong. But the same fact means that choice (E) *must be true.*

This game stands as one more example illustrating that somewhat oddball variations on game types needn't make games more difficult. By sticking to the fundamental and strategic approach guaranteed by the Kaplan Method, you were able to make a Master Sketch with which you could just mow down the question set. In the end, the complexity involved in sequencing each entity in two distinct ways was neutralized by treating them as six distinct events.

Game 4—Alphabet Soup Game

Questions 18–22

> A child eating alphabet soup notices that the only letters left in her bowl are one each of these six letters: T, U, W, X, Y, and Z. She plays a game with the remaining letters, eating them in the next three spoonfuls in accord with certain rules. Each of the six letters must be in exactly one of the next three spoonfuls, and each of the spoonfuls must have at least one and at most three of the letters. In addition, she obeys the following restrictions:
>
> The U is in a later spoonful than the T.
> The U is not in a later spoonful than the X.
> The Y is in a later spoonful than the W.
> The U is in the same spoonful as either the Y or the Z, but not both.[22]

STEPS 1 AND 2: Overview and Sketch

Admittedly, this is one of the odder situations described in an LSAT logic game. But haven't we all done something like this, trying to get only the red cereal in our spoon or eating the monkeys before the lions from our animal crackers? Whether or not you can imagine playing this game yourself, it's not hard to picture this situation. The child will take three more spoonfuls of soup. Each spoonful will have between one and three pasta letters in it. This is a Distribution-Sequencing task.

Figure 18.63

You can anticipate at least some rules about which letters can or cannot be together in a spoonful and others about the relative order of the letters, which ones she eats in earlier or later bites.

---

[22] PrepTest 50, Sec. 3, Game 4

STEP 3: Rules

None of the rules is concrete. None says, "T is in spoonful 1," or, "T and Z are in the same spoonful." So at least initially, there's nothing to draw inside the framework. Record each of the rules beside or beneath the framework and assess their relationships in step 4.

Rule 1 gives you the relative order of T and U.

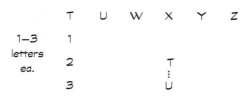

Figure 18.64

Read Rule 2 carefully. U can be in an earlier spoonful than X or in the same spoonful as X, just *not* in a later one.

Figure 18.65

Rule 3 tells you that Y follows W.

Figure 18.66

The final rule tells you that U has at least one partner, either Y or Z. The "but not both" language at the end is important. Without it, U could share a spoonful with Y and Z. But in this game, that possibility is ruled out. Make note of that.

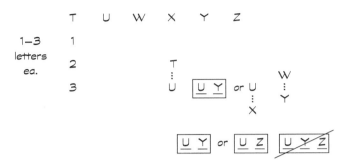

Figure 18.67

You can tell that U, which appears in three of the five rules, will be the lynchpin of what can happen in any acceptable arrangement.

STEP 4: Deductions

The biggest drawback to this game is the impossibility of any concrete deductions. Don't waste your time chasing down every speculative arrangement. Start with the most restricted (and restrictive) entity and see what you can learn, but once you're just stabbing at possibilities, draw the line and move on to the questions.

As you noted above, U is most restricted entity in the set. According to Rule 4, U must share a spoonful with either Y or Z, but not both.

Figure 18.68

In either case, T must be an earlier spoonful than U.

Figure 18.69

U's other rule is Rule 2. X may share U's spoonful or come later. Note that like this:

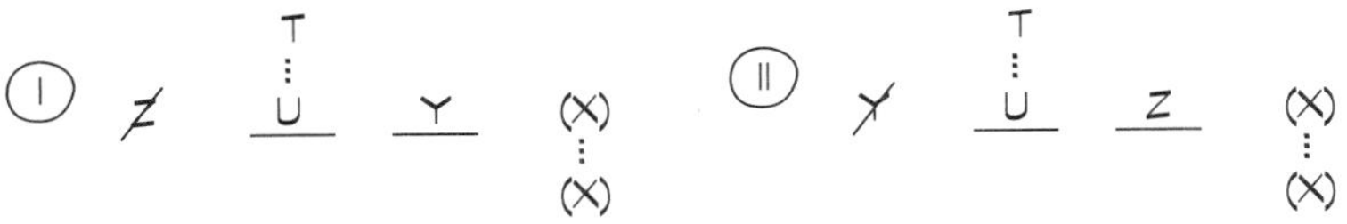

Figure 18.70

In the first option, you can add Rule 3, which requires that W be in an earlier spoonful than Y. In Option II, you'll just have to note that relationship off to the side.

Figure 18.71

W could partner with U and Z in the second option, but only if X and Y are found in the third spoonful.

There's nothing more that you can add with certainty. Trust that the test makers have given you everything you'll need to answer the questions, and move on.

STEP 5: Questions

Of the five questions in this set, three have new "if"s—not surprising, given the number of possible arrangements that remain open. Question 21 is a Complete and Accurate List question. You may be able to use what you've learned from the "If" questions to help you answer it.

18. **(B)**

Which one of the following could be an accurate list of the spoonfuls and the letters in each of them?

(A)   first: Y
      second: T, W
      third: U, X, Z

(B)   first: T, W
      second: U, X, Y
      third: Z

(C)   first: T
      second: U, Z
      third: W, X, Y

(D)   first: T, U, Z
      second: W
      third: X, Y

(E)   first: W
      second: T, X, Z
      third: U, Y[23]

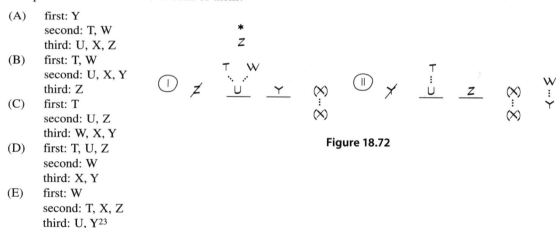

Figure 18.72

The concreteness (or lack thereof) in a game doesn't change your approach to Acceptability questions. Just use the rules to spot and remove violating answer choices. Here, Rule 1 takes out choice (D); U must be in a *later* spoonful than T. Rule 2 gets rid of choice (E); U must *not* be in a later spoonful than X. Rule 3 eliminates choices (A) and (C); Y must be in a *later* spoonful than W. That leaves only the correct answer, choice (B).

---

[23] PrepTest 50, Sec. 3, Q 18

19. **(D)**

If the Y is the only letter in one of the spoonfuls, then which one of the following could be true?

(A) The Y is in the first spoonful.
(B) The Z is in the first spoonful.
(C) The T is in the second spoonful.
(D) The X is in the second spoonful.
(E) The W is in the third spoonful.[24]

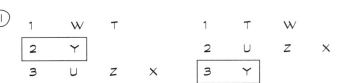

Figure 18.73

If Y is alone in one of the spoonfuls, then Option II is the only option in play. Since Y must follow W (Rule 3), Y can only be in spoonful 2 or spoonful 3, with W in an earlier spoonful.

Figure 18.74

Since the question stem requires Y to be alone, you know Z must accompany U (Rule 4). U, of course, must always follow T (Rule 1).

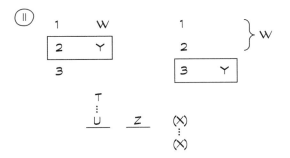

Figure 18.75

Think for a moment about where T and U-Z can go in each option.

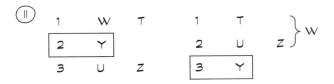

Figure 18.76

Now, add X to each side of the mini-sketch, pursuant to Rule 2. Remember that Y must stay alone according to this question's stem.

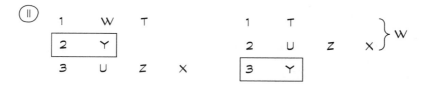

Figure 18.77

This makes it clear that W must be in the first spoonful in either possible arrangement, since the maximum number of letters that can appear in a spoonful is three.

Figure 18.78

With this mini-sketch, you can evaluate the choices in a few seconds. Only choice (D) could be true (in the second arrangement), so it's the right answer.

20. **(E)**

   If the Z is in the first spoonful, then which one of the following must be true?

   (A) The T is in the second spoonful.
   (B) The U is in the third spoonful.
   (C) The W is in the first spoonful.
   (D) The W is in the second spoonful.
   (E) The X is in the third spoonful.[25]

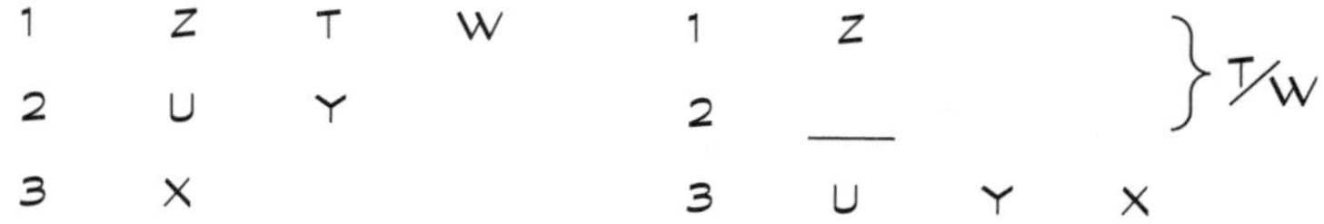

```
   1     Z    T    W        1     Z
   2     U    Y             2     ____        } T/W
   3     X                  3     U    Y    X
```

Figure 18.79

The "if" in this stem produces another two-option mini-sketch. Start by placing Z in the first spoonful.

```
   1     Z
   2
   3
```

Figure 18.80

[25] PrepTest 50, Sec. 3, Q 20

Since U cannot be in the first spoonful (U must follow T because of Rule 1), you know that Y will share U's spoonful (Rule 4). They'll be either in spoonful 2 or spoonful 3.

Figure 18.81

In the first option, W must take spoonful 1 in order to appear earlier than Y (Rule 3). That leaves only X to appear in spoonful 3.

Figure 18.82

In the second option, X must take spoonful 3 in order not to break Rule 2. At least one of T and W must be in the second spoonful, although it's fine if both are.

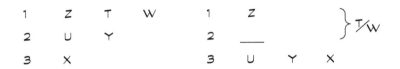

Figure 18.83

Now, characterize the answer choices. The correct answer *must be true*. That means that the four wrong answers *could be false*. Only choice (E) *must be true* in either option. The other four choices include entities that can move into either of two possible spoonfuls under this question's conditions.

21. **(D)**

Which one of the following is a complete list of letters, any one of which could be the only letter in the first spoonful?

(A) T
(B) T, W
(C) T, X
(D) T, W, Z
(E) T, X, W, Z[26]

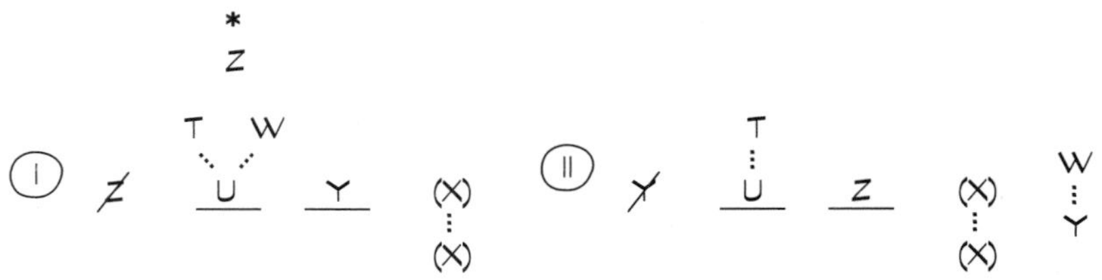

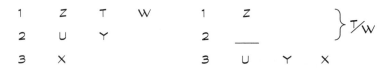

Figure 18.84

The answer to question 20 helps you answer this question in a matter of seconds. You saw in the preceding question that Z could be alone in spoonful 1.

Figure 18.85

Since the correct answer to this question must include Z, eliminate choices (A), (B), and (C). The only difference between choices (D) and (E) is that choice (E) includes X. Since Rule 2 tells you that X cannot be in an earlier spoonful than U, you know X cannot be in spoonful 1 alone. Eliminate choice (E) and you're left with the correct answer, choice (D). There's another point for you, and it took you all of 10 seconds to get it.

22. **(A)**

If the T is in the second spoonful, then which one of the following could be true?

(A) Exactly two letters are in the first spoonful.
(B) Exactly three letters are in the first spoonful.
(C) Exactly three letters are in the second spoonful.
(D) Exactly one letter is in the third spoonful.
(E) Exactly two letters are in the third spoonful.[27]

Figure 18.86

---

[26] PrepTest 50, Sec. 3, Q 21
[27] PrepTest 50, Sec. 3, Q 22

Here's another "If" question and, again, a mini-sketch will reveal the limitations that result from the new condition. Start with T in spoonful 2.

```
1
2      T
3
```

Figure 18.87

Placing T triggers Rule 1. U will have to take spoonful 3.

```
1
2      T
3      U
```

Figure 18.88

Because of Rule 2, X must also be in spoonful 3 in this case. And because of Rule 4, either Y or Z will be there, too.

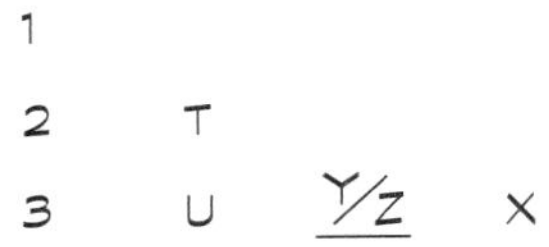

```
1
2      T
3      U      Y/Z    X
```

Figure 18.89

That leaves either W and Z or W and Y still to be determined. When Z takes spoonful 3, every letter's spoonful can be established.

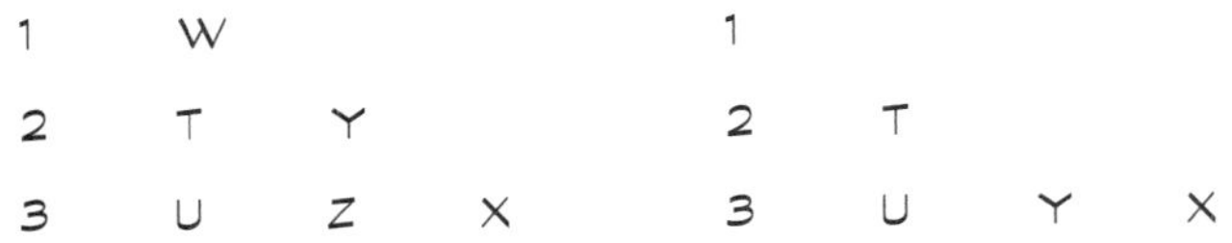

```
1      W                1
2      T      Y         2      T
3      U      Z    X    3      U      Y      X
```

Figure 18.90

When Y is in the third spoonful, however, W and Z can be in spoonful 1 or 2, alone or together, as long as at least one of them is in spoonful 1.

```
1      W                1      ___
2      T      Y         2      T           } W/Z
3      U      Z    X    3      U      Y      X
```

Figure 18.91

The question stem calls for the answer that *could be true*. The four wrong answers in this question *must be false*. Choice (A) could be true; W and Z could be together in spoonful 1. That's the correct answer, and you're done with this game. Note that choices (B)–(E) all contain impossible placements under the terms of this question.

This game stands as a great example of a game in which you may be tempted to spend far too long on the Deductions step. You could spend minutes figuring out all of the possible permutations, but it wouldn't be a good investment of your time. Since the most restricted entity in the game—letter U—didn't lead to any concrete deductions, you know you can (and should) move on to the questions. The test maker always gives you the information you need to answer every question. Sometimes you're allowed to figure out almost all of the possible arrangements up front; other times, you have to wait until the questions give you more guidance. Learning to assess when it's time to move from Step 4 to Step 5 is one of the final stages in complete logic games mastery.

PART IV

THE TEST DAY EXPERIENCE

CHAPTER 19

GET READY FOR TEST DAY

Congratulations. Your work with the Kaplan Method and strategies gives you the knowledge and practice you need for LSAT success. Now, it's time for you to schedule a test date, register for the exam (if you haven't done so already), and put yourself in the right frame of mind to take the next step on the road to law school.

The details of registering for the test are covered in "An Introduction to the LSAT" at the beginning of the book. Follow the steps and recommendations mentioned there to ensure that you have a spot at the next test administration or on the test date that's best for you. In the remainder of this chapter, I'll cover what you need to do to have yourself mentally and emotionally ready for the rigors and rewards of test day.

YOU ARE PREPARED

First, remember (and remind yourself) that you are prepared. By learning the lessons and doing the work from this book, you can know, with confidence, that there is nothing else you need to *know* about LSAT logic games. The Kaplan Method, the specific strategies, and the analysis of the games that I've presented in this book are the result not only of my own 15-year tenure as an LSAT instructor; they're the summation of five decades of Kaplan expertise and research. Hundreds of great LSAT minds—including those of perfect scorers, legal scholars, and psychometricians—have contributed to the development, testing, and refinement of Kaplan's LSAT pedagogy. If we know it, you now know it. So strike from your mind any concern that there's one more secret to uncover or a mysterious LSAT Rosetta Stone to search for. You have the most complete, proven system for LSAT Logic Games success available. If you've already studied and practiced from this book's companion volumes—*Kaplan LSAT Reading Comprehension: Strategies and Tactics* and *Kaplan LSAT Logical Reasoning: Strategies and Tactics*—you can say the same thing about the entire exam.

Now, saying that you *know* everything you need to about the Logic Games section doesn't mean you're ready to *do* everything you need to do to achieve your goal score. You need to continue to practice and review. Indeed, I'll cover that in the next section of this chapter. But first, I want to make sure you're translating your comprehensive knowledge of logic games into confidence on test day. From now until the day you sit for your official administration of the LSAT, you need to exhibit the confidence your preparation has earned you.

There are some very practical steps you can take to reinforce your test day confidence. Once you're registered for the test, visit your test site. You may even want to take a logic game to practice in the very room where you'll be sitting for the real test. At a minimum, know where you're going to be, how you'll get there, and where you'll park or where public transportation will drop you off. You want no surprises on the morning of your official LSAT.

The day before your test, relax. There's no way to cram for a skills-based exam. While your competition is scrambling and fretting, go to the gym, watch your favorite movie, or have a nice dinner. Gather what you need for the next day, and keep yourself one step ahead of everything you need to do. It sounds a little corny, but acting confident will actually make you feel more confident. Get to bed relatively early, have a good night's sleep, and wake ready to have the best day of your (test-taking) life.

The following is a list of what you'll need to have with you on test day:

LSAT SURVIVAL KIT

You MUST have the following:

- Admissions ticket
- Photo ID
- Several sharpened #2 pencils
- 1-gallon transparent zip-top bag

You SHOULD also have:

- Pencil sharpener
- Eraser
- Analog wristwatch
- Aspirin
- Snack and drink for the break

You CANNOT have:

- Cell phone
- MP3 player
- Computer or electronic reader
- Electronic or digital timers
- Weapons
- Papers other than your admission ticket

That list conforms to the rules for the test site as they stand at the time of this writing. You should check www.lsac.org periodically before your test date to make sure there haven't been any changes or amendments to the Law School Administration Council's (LSAC) policies.

Of course, the "MUSTs" are non-negotiable. You need those to be allowed entry to the testing room. Some of the "SHOULDs," on the other hand, you may not need at all. But if you begin to feel a little headache coming on, or if you find your stomach grumbling midway through Section 3 of the test, you'll be awfully glad you took along those "just in case" items. As for the "CANNOTs," do yourself a favor and avoid any conflict with the proctors or test administrators. Just leave your phone or electronics in the car or at home.

One other very practical thing you can do is to dress in layers. The LSAT is usually administered during the weekend and almost always in a large, institutional building. It's really tough to predict whether the room will be too hot or too cold or whether it will fluctuate throughout the day. Take the Goldilocks approach and make sure the temperature is always "just right" for you by wearing or taking the kind of sweater or light jacket that's easy (and quiet) to slip on or off.

The stress levels of test takers around you will be high. But if you demonstrate nothing but preparation and confidence on the morning of the test, you'll feel calmer, more clear-headed, and ready for the real challenges of the test itself.

CHAMPIONS PRACTICE. VIRTUOSOS PRACTICE. YOU PRACTICE.

To put my earlier point about practice into formal logic terms, knowledge of the test is necessary, but not sufficient, for test day success. Mistaking this relationship is something that leads a lot of test takers off track. They haven't achieved the score they want, so they say, "There must be something I don't know yet," or, "What am I missing?" The fact is that many of these test takers know all about the test, but they haven't practiced taking the test. Ask almost any great performer, musician, public speaker, or athlete and they'll tell you that the key to their success is practice. A great violinist may study a composer's compositional theory, historical context, or even personal life in order to better understand a piece before performing it. But all of that will mean little if the performer hasn't practiced. The audience would be pretty disappointed if the violinist showed up to give a lecture about the composer instead of playing a concert. It's the same with the LSAT. Your audience, law school admissions officers, won't care what you know about the exam, just how well you perform on it.

So how can you best practice? First, lay out a study and practice schedule for yourself that runs from now until test day—one that's ambitious but practical. Fill in as much as you can about which sections or question types you'll be practicing each day or week. If you're working on different parts of the test, vary the sections you're practicing and the materials you're using.

If you haven't completed and reviewed the full-section practice in this book, make sure you do so. Leave time for review of your work. Remember that you're not just checking to see whether you produced the correct answer, you're asking whether you did so as efficiently and effectively as you could have. That means that you should always be reviewing the questions you got right as well as those you got wrong. Look for what features in a game or question you're likely to see again on test day. You won't see the games from this book on your test, but every game on your test will have similarities—in the setup, the entities, the rules and deductions, and the questions—to those you've practiced here.

If you're looking for additional practice, consider the following additional resources:

OTHER KAPLAN LSAT RESOURCES

Logic Games On Demand
Logical Reasoning On Demand
Reading Comprehension On Demand
Comprehensive, section-specific courses for in-depth instruction and targeted practice.

LSAT Advantage—On Site, Anywhere or On Demand
Our most popular option—complete, targeted, and focused prep designed for busy students.

LSAT Advanced—On Site or Anywhere
Fast-paced for high-scorers focusing on the most advanced content. (158+ required to enroll.)

LSAT Extreme—On Site or Anywhere
Maximum in-class instruction plus tutoring for students who want extra time, review, and more practice.

LSAT One on One—On Site or Anywhere
An expert tutor designs a one-on-one, custom program around your individual needs, goals, and schedule.

LSAT Summer Intensive
Six weeks of total LSAT immersion in a residential academic program at Boston University

Check out *www.kaplanlsat.com* for courses and free events live, online, and in your area.

All of those additional resources will provide the outstanding instruction, coaching, and practice you expect from Kaplan test prep. Consider which ones work best for your schedule, learning style, and admissions timeline. Kaplan is committed to helping you achieve your educational and career goals.

THE PSYCHOLOGICAL DIMENSIONS OF TEST DAY

There's no doubt that taking your official LSAT is one of the most important steps (maybe *the* most important) you'll take on the road to law school. That's a lot of pressure. It's natural to have a little excitement and some extra adrenaline for such a big event. Those are actually healthy things to feel, provided that you channel your emotions into energy and concentration, rather than anxiety and confusion. I'd be pretty disappointed if, after weeks or months of practice and preparation, one of my students said, "Eh, I don't really care what happens on the test." Of course you care. That's why you're reading this book and working so hard. So embrace the big day.

I've already talked about how you can begin to foster an attitude of confidence and act in ways that support and sustain it. Here are a couple of practical steps you can take to carry your confidence right into the testing room.

Know What to Expect

It is easy to lay out the order of events on test day. Here's a chart that shows you what will happen from the time you arrive at the test site.

Event	What Happens	Time
Check-In	Show admissions ticket, ID, fingerprints, room and seat assignment	10–30 minutes
Rules and Procedures	Test booklets distributed, proctor reads the rules, test takers fill out grid information	30 minutes
LSAT Administration		
Section 1	Logic Games, Logical Reasoning, or Reading Comprehension Section	35 minutes
Section 2	Logic Games, Logical Reasoning, or Reading Comprehension Section	35 minutes
Section 3	Logic Games, Logical Reasoning, or Reading Comprehension Section	35 minutes

Break	Test booklets and grids collected, test takers have break, return to seats, booklets and grids redistributed	12–20 minutes (10 minute break with additional time for administrative tasks)
Section 4	Logic Games, Logical Reasoning, or Reading Comprehension Section	35 minutes
Section 5	Logic Games, Logical Reasoning, or Reading Comprehension Section	35 minutes
Prepare for Writing Sample	Test booklets and grids collected, test takers given a chance to cancel scores, Writing Sample booklets distributed	5–10 minutes
Writing Sample	Test takers produce Writing Samples	35 minutes

You can see that even if everything goes as smoothly as possible, you're in for around five hours from start to finish. This is another reason that it's so important to be rested, comfortable, and nourished. Students who are too groggy to be at their best in Section 1 or too exhausted and hungry to keep up their performance in Section 5 will have trouble competing with someone like you, who's prepared for the entire testing day, from start to finish.

One thing that star performers do—I don't care if you're thinking of singers, actors, athletes, or even great trial lawyers—is to warm up before they "go on." You can do the same on the morning of your test by reviewing a Logic Game, Logical Reasoning question, or Reading Comprehension passage that you've done before. As you revisit the game or question, go over the steps in the Kaplan Method that allowed you to be successful with the item before. This will get your brain warmed up just as a quarterback would loosen his arm or a singer would warm up her vocal cords. Don't try new material, and certainly don't try a full section. Just start reading and thinking—calmly and confidently—in the LSAT way. You'll be miles ahead of the unprepared test taker who looks shell-shocked for most of Section 1.

In order to maintain a high level of performance, it's important to stay hydrated and nourished. Mental work makes most people hungry. So drink water at the break and have a small, healthy snack. Don't, however, eat a sleep-inducing turkey sandwich or gobble sugar that will have you crashing out during Section 5.

Knowing what to expect also helps you manage your mental preparation for test day in other small, but important, ways. A lot of test takers don't know that the proctors will ask whether

anyone in the room wants to cancel his or her score right after Section 5 is completed and the test booklets are collected. If you're not expecting that question, it can throw you into a moment of self-doubt. It's human nature to underestimate your performance on the test. You will remember the handful of questions that gave you trouble while ignoring the dozens of questions you answered routinely with no problem. I've personally known students who canceled their scores when they shouldn't have. The LSAC allows you a number of days after the test to cancel your score, so don't worry about it during the exam. Complete the Writing Sample to the best of your ability. You can always consider things that might have caused you to underperform—illness, a personal crisis—after you've completed the test.

You Will Panic, but Don't Panic

Over the course of four to five hours of rigorous, detailed, strictly timed test taking, you're going to reach a point at which you lose focus, feel overwhelmed, or just downright panic for a moment. It's normal. So first thing, don't feed the panic by blaming yourself or saying, "Oh, I knew this would happen." There's nothing wrong with you for having those feelings. In fact, panic is a physical response to high-pressure situations. It's related to the autonomic nervous system, the "flight or fight" response we've adapted to survive danger. Your heart beats faster; blood leaves your brain to go to your extremities; your breathing gets rapid and shallow. That's all very important when the danger you face is a predator or enemy. It's just not very helpful when you're facing a standardized test.

If—when—you face a point of doubt, confusion, or panic on test day, take a moment. Collect yourself physically first. Take a deep breath; sit up in a straight, comfortable posture; put both feet flat on the floor and lower your shoulders; even close your eyes for a second while you breathe. Then open your eyes and remind yourself that whatever you're looking at, it's just an LSAT question. The fact is that you've seen one like it and done one like it before. You know that's the case because of your preparation. Get your concentration back by reciting the Kaplan Method as your work through the problem. You know that will provide a strategic, purposeful approach every time.

Worry Only about What's in Your Control

When I have students in LSAT prep courses, they often ask a lot of questions about what to do if things go wrong on test day. "What if the proctor doesn't give us a verbal five minute warning?" "What if someone is being noisy right behind me?" "What if the school marching band is rehearsing in the courtyard under the window?" All of those and a few weirder, more distracting things have happened to test takers. But my students' concern about such occurrences before test day is misplaced. They should be taking care of the things that are within their control—learning the Kaplan Method, practicing logic game setups and deductions—not worrying about the things that aren't. The vast majority of LSAT administrations go off without more than a minor hitch. Your job is to be ready to have a peak performance on a routine test day.

When the unexpected happens, stay calm. If there is something that you notice before the test begins—a window is open, letting in cold air or street noise; the lights in the back of the room aren't turned on, making it dark where you're sitting—just let the proctor know (politely) and ask if it can be remedied. If something happens during a section—another test taker is unconsciously tapping his pencil; the proctor forgets the five-minute announcement—keep working. Raise your hand and get a proctor's attention. When they come to your seat, quickly and quietly explain the situation. Most of the time, they'll take action to remedy the situation. But don't let those things throw you off your game. If something truly bizarre happens that seriously impedes your performance—a fire alarm goes off, a wrecking crew starts to jackhammer the building—follow the proctor's instructions, keep a record of what happened, and follow up with the LSAC by telephone or in writing after the test concludes. You are welcome to contact 1-800-KAPTEST and ask for advice from one of our LSAT experts, too. A word to the wise: The LSAC will not add points to a score as a remedy for a distracting test administration, but they have found other ways to accommodate test takers who, through no fault of their own, have been unable to complete the test or who encountered unmanageable distractions.

GET READY FOR TEST DAY

This chapter really boils down to one message: Prepare yourself for the perfect test day. Display confidence and preparation in all that you do. Get ready for consistent, focused performance from start to finish. When that's the attitude you take into the test, you're more likely to outperform your competition and have your best day regardless of what else does or doesn't happen.

CHAPTER 20

SECRETS OF THE LSAT

The "secrets" of the LSAT aren't really secrets at all. They're well-known facts that many test takers fail to take full advantage of. The best test takers use the structure and format of the test to their advantage. Just as a great football or basketball coach adjusts the team's strategy when time is running out on the clock, or just as a great conductor rearranges an orchestra to take advantage of the acoustics in a new venue, you can learn to adjust your approach to the test you're taking. We might well laud the insightful coach or conductor by saying, "Wow, he really knows the 'secrets' of this game (or stadium or theater)." But in fact, he's simply taking account of all the circumstances and making the right strategic decisions for that time and place. Consider a handful of facts that make the LSAT a unique testing experience, and see how you can use them to your advantage.

EVERY QUESTION IS WORTH THE SAME AMOUNT TO YOUR SCORE

Many tests you've taken (even some standardized tests) rewarded you more for certain questions or sections than for others. In school, it's common for a professor to say, "The essay counts for half of your score," or to make a section of harder questions worth five points each while easier ones are worth less. With such exams, you may simply be unable to get a top score without performing well on a given question or topic. It makes sense, then, to target the areas the professor will reward most highly.

As you well know, that's not the case on the LSAT. Every question—easy or hard, short or long, common or rare—is worth exactly the same amount as every other question. That means that you should seek out the questions, games, and passages that are the easiest for you to handle. Far too many test takers get their teeth into a tough question and won't let go. That hurts them

in two ways. First, they spend too much time—sometimes three or four minutes—on such a question, sacrificing their chances with other, easier questions. Second, since questions like these are tough or confusing, they're less likely to produce a right answer no matter how much time you spend. Learn to skip questions when it's in your interest to do so. Mark questions that you skip by circling the entire question in your test booklet. That way, those questions will be easy to spot if you have time left after you complete the other questions in the section. If you've eliminated one or two obviously incorrect answer choicess, strike them through completely so that you don't spend time rethinking them when you come back to the question.

When schools receive your score report, the only thing they see is your score. They don't know—and they don't care—whether you've answered the easiest or the toughest questions on the LSAT. They only care that you answered more questions correctly than the other applicants. Becoming a good manager of the test sections is invaluable. You'll do that, in part, by triaging the games or passages and choosing to put off the toughest for last. Even more often, you'll manage the section by skipping and guessing strategically. Don't slug it out with a tough question for minutes and then grudgingly move on. Boldly seek out questions on which you can exert your strengths, and be clearheaded and decisive in your decisions to move past questions you know are targeted at your weaknesses. Take the test; don't let it take you.

ONE RIGHT, FOUR ROTTEN

I'm sure you've had the experience, on a multiple-choice test in school, of having a teacher tell you, "More than one answer may be correct, but pick the best answer for each question." Given that you're a future law student, I wouldn't be surprised to learn that you may even have debated with your instructor, making a case for why a certain answer should receive credit. As a result, you're used to comparing answer choices to one another. On the LSAT, however, that's a recipe for wasted time and effort. The test makers design the correct answer to be unequivocally correct; it will respond to the call of the question stem precisely. Likewise, the four wrong answers are demonstrably wrong, not just "less good."

For the well-trained test taker—for you, that is—this leads to an important, practical adjustment in strategy. Throughout the test, you should seek to predict the correct answer before assessing the answer choices. In Logical Reasoning, you will, on most questions, be able to anticipate the content of the correct answer, sometimes almost word for word. In Reading Comprehension and Logic Games, you should spend the time up front to have a clear passage road map or game sketch. At a minimum, you must characterize the correct and incorrect answers (if the correct answer *must be true*, for example, each of the wrong answers *could be false*). Then seek out the one answer that matches your prediction or characterization.

The bottom line is that, on the LSAT, you are always comparing the answers against what you know must be correct, not against one another. When locating the correct choice is difficult or time-consuming, you can always turn the tables on the test maker and eliminate the wrong ones.

In Logic Games, Acceptability questions provide the perfect example. Testing answer choices to find the passable arrangement can take minutes, but using the rules to eliminate the choices that violate them takes only a few seconds. Because you know that there will always be one correct choice and that you can always identify the characteristics that make wrong answers wrong, you can always take the most direct route to the LSAT point.

THERE'S NO WRONG-ANSWER PENALTY

This point is easy to understand, but sometimes hard to remember when you're working quickly through an LSAT section. The LSAT is scored only by counting the number of correct responses you bubble in. Unlike some standardized tests—the SAT is the most notorious example—you're not penalized for marking incorrect responses. Simply put, there's nothing to lose, so mark a response, even if it's a blind guess, for every answer.

Of course, strategic guessing is better than just taking a wild stab at the correct answer. Even if a question gives you a lot of trouble, see if you can eliminate one or more answer choices as clearly wrong. When you can, take your guess from the remaining choices. Removing even one clearly incorrect choice improves your chances of hitting on the right one from 20 percent to 25 percent; getting rid of two wrong answers, of course, gives you a one-in-three chance of guessing correctly. Provided that you do it quickly (not taking time away from questions you can handle with little trouble), strategic guessing can improve your score.

Students ask another question related to this point about the answer choices. They want to know if a particular answer choice—(A), (B), (C), (D), or (E)—shows up more often than others, or whether it's better, when guessing, to pick a particular choice for all guesses. The answer to both questions is no. Over the course of a full LSAT, all five answer choices show up just about equally. There's no pattern associated with particular question types. You're no more likely to see any particular answer early or late in a section. Thus, when you're blind guessing, you have a one-in-five chance of hitting the correct answer whatever you choose. And there's no benefit from guessing choice (C) or choice (D) over and over. It's far more valuable to spend your limited time trying to eliminate one or more wrong answers than it is to fret over any illusory patterns within the choices.

THE LSAT IS A MARATHON . . . MADE UP OF SPRINTS

At this point in your academic career, you've had long tests and you've had tests that put time pressure on you. But chances are, you've never encountered as intense a combination of the two as you will on the LSAT. In the last chapter, I already talked about the importance of stamina. Including the administrative tasks at the beginning, the breaks, and the collection and distribution of your testing materials, you're in for around a five-hour test day. It's important to remember that, over the course of that marathon, the first and fifth sections are just as valuable as those in the middle. Unsurprisingly, Kaplan's research has shown that, for the untrained test taker, those sections are likely to produce the poorest performance. You can counteract the inherent difficulties in the schedule by doing a little warm-up so that you're ready to hit the ground running at the start of Section 1, and by staying relaxed and having a healthy snack at the break so that you're still going strong at the end of Section 5. Just taking these simple steps could add several points to your score.

At the same time that you're striving to maintain focus and sustain your performance, you're trying to manage a very fast 35 minutes in each section. I've talked already about how you can triage a section to maximize your opportunity to attack the easiest games, passages, and questions. Combine that with confident, strategic guessing and you'll be outperforming many test takers who succumb to the "ego battle" with tough or time-consuming questions. But there's one more thing that you have to add to your repertoire of test day tactics: You have to learn to not look back. Over the years, I've talked to many students who could tell me how they thought they performed on each of the test's sections. To be honest with you, I find that a little disappointing. Sure, you may remember that the game with the Cowboys and Horses or the passage on Nanotechnology was really challenging, but it's a waste of time and mental capacity to try and assess your performance as you're taking the test. Once you've answered a question, leave it behind. Give your full concentration to what you're working on. This is even more important when it comes to sections. Once time is called, you may no longer work on the section, not even to bubble in the answers to questions you completed in your test booklet. If a proctor sees you continuing to work on a section for which the time has expired, he or she can issue you a misconduct slip, and the violation will be reported to all of the schools to which you apply. More importantly, you're harming your work on the current section.

There's no rearview mirror on the LSAT. Work diligently, mark the correct answers, and move on to the next question. Keep this in mind: Even if you could accurately assess your performance as you worked (you can't, but imagine it for a moment), it wouldn't change anything. You'd still need to get the remaining questions right. So learn this lesson—and the other "secrets" of the LSAT—now. Be like those seemingly brilliant coaches and performers. By knowing how the LSAT test day works, you can gain an edge over test takers who treat this just as they have every other exam in their academic careers.

CHAPTER 21

LSAT STRATEGIES AND TACTICS

At last, I'll bring you full circle back to the premise at the start of this book. The LSAT may be unlike any other test you've studied or prepared for, but it need not be mysterious or overwhelming. The underlying principle that has informed this book is that **every question has an answer**. The twist is that you're not expected to know the answers. How could you? This is a test that rewards what you can do, not what you've learned. In that sense, you can't *study* for the test. And you certainly can't cram for it. What you can do, indeed what you've been doing throughout this book, is to *practice* for the test. Instead of thinking of the LSAT as a test, think of it as your law school audition or tryout. A play's director or a team's coach doesn't ask you what you know; she wants to see what you can do. And just as the director or coach will give you everything you need to demonstrate your skill, the test makers always give you everything you need to produce the correct answers on the LSAT.

THE LSAT REWARDS THE CORE 4 SKILLS

Law schools don't expect incoming students to know the law. Indeed, much as the LSAT does, your professors may try to use your outside knowledge and assumptions against you. What the schools are looking for is incoming students who have the skills they'll need to succeed through the coming three years of rigorous legal training. That, at least in part, is what they're looking for your LSAT score to indicate. That's why the LSAT is a skills-based, rather than a knowledge-based, exam. Back near the beginning of this book, you learned the central skills rewarded on the test.

THE CORE 4 LSAT SKILLS
1. **Strategic Reading**
2. **Analyzing Arguments**
3. **Understanding Formal Logic**
4. **Making Deductions**

USE WHAT YOU'VE LEARNED THROUGHOUT THE TEST

One nice thing to realize is that much of the work you've done here, preparing for the Logic Games section specifically, will translate to exceptional performance throughout the test. Your understanding of the sufficient-necessary relationship highlighted by formal logic rules will be rewarded by several questions in each of the Logical Reasoning sections. Your discipline in setting up a complete Master Sketch mirrors the process of mapping passages in the Reading Comprehension section. To be successful on the LSAT, you must make deductions and draw valid inferences from related rules and statements dozens of times in every scored section.

So let me leave you with this: The LSAT is designed to reward the skills that will make you a successful law student. You know that you have those skills. You are, after all, seeking this path with passion and focus. The work you've done in this book is all about honing your skills and preparing you for a successful test day. Take the insights you've gathered about LSAT logic games and apply them throughout the exam. Take what you've learned about yourself as a test taker, and use it not only for a stronger, more confident performance on test day, but also throughout your law school endeavor, during your bar exam, and into your legal career. Best of luck to you. Now, go out and accomplish great things.

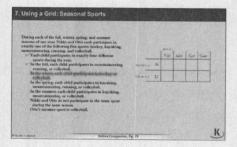
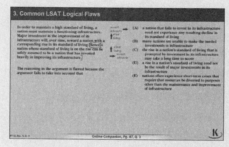
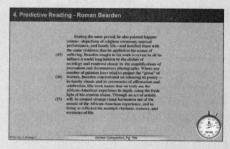

Kaplan's Most Sought After LSAT Instructors Break-It-Down

Practice with More Official LSAT Questions